W9-BRC-152

THE ROUGH GUIDE TO

Thailand

written and researched by

Paul Gray and Lucy Ridout

with additional contributions from

Steve Vickers

ROUGH GUIDES

roughguides.com

Contents

Introduction to
Thailand

With sixteen million foreigners flying into the country each year, Thailand is Asia's primary holiday destination. Yet despite this vast influx of visitors, Thailand's cultural integrity remains largely undamaged – a country that adroitly avoided colonization has been able to absorb Western influences while maintaining its own rich heritage. Though the high-rises and neon lights occupy the foreground of the tourist picture, the typical Thai community is still the farming village, and you need not venture far to encounter a more traditional scene of fishing communities, rubber plantations and Buddhist temples. Around forty percent of Thais earn their living from the land, based around the staple rice, which forms the foundation of the country's unique and famously sophisticated cuisine.

Tourism has been just one factor in the country's development which, since the deep-seated uncertainties surrounding the Vietnam War faded, has been free, for the most part, to proceed at death-defying pace – for a time in the 1980s and early 1990s, Thailand boasted the fastest-expanding economy in the world. Politics in Thailand, however, has not been able to keep pace. Since World War II, coups d'état have been as common a method of changing government as general elections; the malnourished democratic system – when the armed forces allow it to operate – is characterized by corruption and cronyism.

Through all the changes of the last sixty years, the much-revered constitutional monarch, King Bhumibol, who sits at the pinnacle of an elaborate hierarchical system of deference covering the whole of Thai society, has lent a measure of stability. Furthermore, some 85 percent of the population are still practising Theravada Buddhists, a unifying faith that colours all aspects of daily life – from the tiered temple rooftops that dominate every skyline, to the omnipresent saffron-robed monks and the packed calendar of festivals.

ABOVE AKHA WOMAN; RED AND GREEN CHILLIES

Where to go

The clash of tradition and modernity is most intense in **Bangkok**, the first stop on almost any itinerary. Within its historic core you'll find resplendent temples, canalside markets and the opulent indulgence of the eighteenth-century **Grand Palace**, while downtown's forest of skyscrapers shelters cutting-edge fashion and decor boutiques and some achingly hip bars and clubs. After touchdown in Bangkok, much of the package-holiday traffic flows east to **Pattaya**, the country's seediest resort, but for prettier beaches you're better off venturing just a little further, to the islands of **Ko Samet** and the **Ko Chang archipelago**, with their squeaky white sand and shorefront bungalows.

Few tourists visit **Isaan**, the poorest and in some ways the most traditionally Thai region. Here, a trip through the gently modulating landscapes of the **Mekong River** valley, which defines Thailand's northeastern extremities, takes in archetypal agricultural villages and a fascinating array of religious sites, while the southern reaches of Isaan hold some of Thailand's best-kept secrets – the magnificent stone temple complexes of **Phimai**, **Phanom Rung** and **Khao Phra Viharn**, all built by the Khmers of Cambodia almost ten centuries ago. Closer to the capital, **Khao Yai National Park** encapsulates the phenomenal diversity of Thailand's flora and fauna, which here range from wild orchids to strangling figs, elephants to hornbills.

At the heart of the northern uplands, **Chiang Mai** is both an attractive historic city and a vibrant cultural centre, with a strong tradition of arts, crafts and festivals. It does a burgeoning line in self-improvement courses – from ascetic meditation to the more earthly pleasures of Thai cookery classes – while the overriding enticement of the surrounding region is the prospect of **trekking** through villages inhabited by a richly mixed population of tribal peoples. Plenty of outdoor activities and courses, as well as hot springs and massages, can be enjoyed at **Pai**, a surprisingly cosmopolitan hill station for travellers, four hours northwest of Chiang Mai.

FACT FILE

- Divided into 77 provinces or *changwat*, Thailand was known as **Siam** until 1939 (and again from 1945 to 1949); some academics suggest changing the name back again, to better reflect the country's Thai and non-Thai diversity.

- The **population** of 63 million is made up of ethnic Thais (75 percent) and Chinese (14 percent), with the rest comprising mainly immigrants from neighbouring countries as well as hill-tribespeople.

- Buddhism is the national **religion**, Islam the largest minority religion, but nearly all Thais also practise some form of animism (spirit worship).

- Since 1932 the country has been a **constitutional** monarchy. King Bhumibol, also known as Rama IX (being the ninth ruler of the Chakri dynasty), is the world's longest-ruling head of state, having been on the throne since 1946; the current prime minister, Yingluck Shinawatra, entered politics only six weeks before winning the general election in 2011 with an absolute majority.

- Thailand fell to 153rd out of 178 countries on Reporters without Borders' index on **press freedom** in 2010, because of a surge in the use of the lese-majesty laws.

- The world record for **nonstop kissing** was set by two Thai men in Pattaya on Valentine's Day, 2012, at a gobsmacking 50 hours, 25 minutes and 1 second.

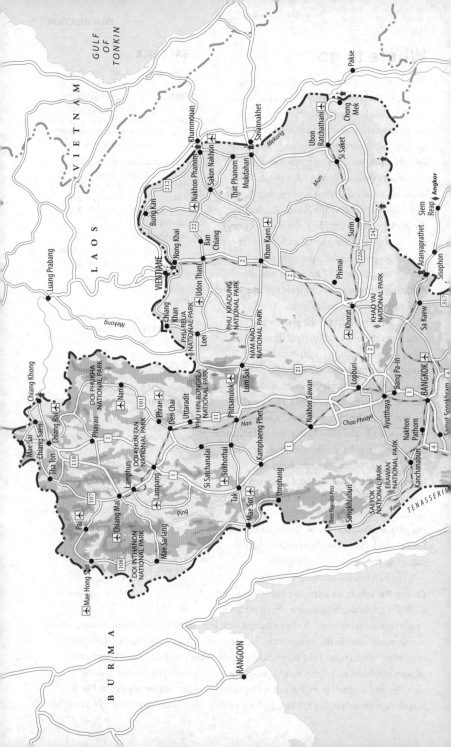

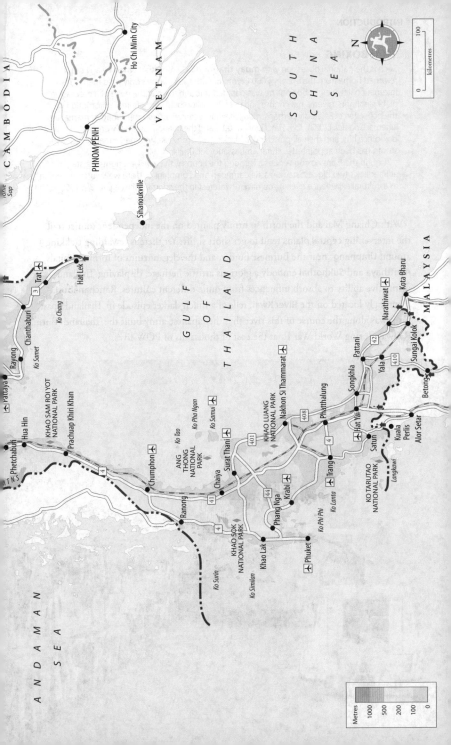

THAI BOXING

Such is the national obsession with **muay thai**, or Thai boxing, that when Wijan Ponlid returned home from the Sydney 2000 Olympics with the country's only gold medal (for international flyweight boxing), he was paraded through town at the head of a procession of 49 elephants, given a new house and over 20 million baht, and offered a promotion in the police force. Belatedly perhaps, *muay thai* has recently entered the canon of martial-arts cinema: *Ong Bak* (2003), *Tom Yum Goong* (2005) and their various sequels were global box-office hits, and their all-punching, all-kicking star, Tony Jaa, who performed all his own stunts, has been appointed Cultural Ambassador for Thailand.

Though there are boxing venues all around the country, the very best fights are staged at Bangkok's two biggest stadiums, Rajdamnoen and Lumphini, and are well worth attending as a cultural experience even if you have no interest in the sport itself (see p.45 & p.165).

With Chiang Mai and the north so firmly planted on the independent tourist trail, the intervening **central plains** tend to get short shrift. Yet there is rewarding trekking around **Umphang**, near the Burmese border, and the elegant ruins of former capitals **Ayutthaya** and **Sukhothai** embody a glorious artistic heritage, displaying Thailand's distinctive ability to absorb influences from quite different cultures. **Kanchanaburi**, stunningly located on the **River Kwai**, tells of a much darker episode in Thailand's past, for it was along the course of this river that the Japanese army built the Thailand–Burma Railway during World War II, at the cost of thousands of POW lives.

Author Picks

Having finally settled down in Thailand after twenty years of toing and froing, our author, Paul, has plenty to write home about. Here are some of his personal favourites.

Kneads must A good pummelling at the massage pavilions amid the historic, kaleidoscopic architecture of Wat Pho is one of Bangkok's unbeatable experiences. p.92

Road trips You'll get to know the mighty Mekong River up close and personal along the Chiang Khan–Nong Khai road in Isaan (p.492), while the three thousand bends of the Mae Hong Son loop reveal the pick of Thailand's upland scenery. p.330

Islands ahoy Messing about in boats is a big part of island life, and it's hard to beat a short, richly diverse circuit of Ko Tao and the causeway beaches of Ko Nang Yuan. p.571

Aaaaaah-roy "Deliciousness" is never far away in Thailand, be it fluffy deep-fried catfish with a tangy mango salad, toothsome beef green curry, or mango with sticky rice and coconut milk. p.38

Let yourself go Mad, bad and bawdy carousing at Yasothon's Rocket Festival (p.472) and Phi Ta Khon in Dan Sai. p.485

Simply celadon Among dozens of highly skilled, good-value handicrafts in Thailand, one that's especially appealing is celadon, elegant stoneware subtly glazed in green. p.302

Khon It's hard to catch these days, but if you come across a performance, sit down and soak up the haunting music, beautiful costumes and exquisite gestures of Thailand's highest dramatic art. p.47

Best view? You decide: a godlike panorama of the concrete jungle from Bangkok's *Sky Bar* (p.162), wave after wave of forested mountains from Doi Chang Moob (p.368), or the implausible limestone turrets in Phang Nga bay (p.654)?

> Our author recommendations don't end here. We've flagged up our favourite places – a perfectly sited hotel, an atmospheric bar, a special restaurant – throughout the guide, highlighted with the ★ symbol.

LEFT TRAVELLERS ARRIVING ON KO SAMUI
FROM TOP JAMES BOND ISLAND; BANANA LEAF PARCELS

Sand and sea are what most Thai holidays are about, though, and the pick of the coasts are in southern Thailand, where the Samui archipelago off the **Gulf coast** is one of the highlights. **Ko Samui** itself has the most sweeping white-sand beaches, and the greatest variety of accommodation and facilities to go with them. **Ko Pha Ngan** next door is still largely backpacker territory, where you have a stark choice between desolate coves and **Hat Rin**, Thailand's party capital. The remotest island, rocky **Ko Tao**, is acquiring increasing sophistication as Southeast Asia's largest dive-training centre.

Across on the other side of the peninsula, the **Andaman coast** boasts even more exhilarating scenery and the finest coral reefs in the country, in particular around the **Ko Similan** island chain, which ranks among the best dive sites in the world. The largest Andaman coast island, **Phuket**, is one of Thailand's top tourist destinations and graced with a dozen fine beaches, though several have been overdeveloped with a glut of high-rises and tacky nightlife. Beautiful little **Ko Phi Phi** is a major party hub, surrounded by the turquoise seas and dramatic limestone cliffs that characterize the coastline throughout **Krabi province**. Large, forested **Ko Lanta** is, for the moment at least, a calmer alternative for families, but for genuine jungle you'll need to head inland, to the rainforests of **Khao Sok National Park**.

Further down the Thai peninsula, in the provinces of the **deep south**, the teeming sea life and unfrequented sands of the **Trang islands** and **Ko Tarutao National Marine Park** are the main draws. There's now the intriguing possibility of **island-hopping** your way down through them – in fact, all the way from Phuket to Penang in Malaysia – without setting foot on the mainland.

When to go

The **climate** of most of Thailand is governed by three seasons: rainy (roughly May–Oct), caused by the southwest monsoon dumping moisture gathered from the Andaman Sea and the Gulf of Thailand; cool (Nov–Feb); and hot (March–May). The **rainy season** is the least predictable of the three, varying in length and intensity from year to year, but it's never a case of the heavens opening in May and not closing again till October: there'll be rain most days, but often only for a few hours in the afternoon or at night. The rains usually gather force

SPIRIT HOUSES

Although the vast majority of Thais are Buddhist, nearly everyone also believes that the physical world is inhabited by **spirits** (see p.750). These spirits can cause trouble if not given enough care and attention, and are apt to wreak havoc when made homeless. Therefore, whenever a new building is constructed – be it a traditional village house or a multistorey office block – the owners will also construct a home for the spirits who previously occupied that land. Crucially, these spirit houses must be given the best spot on the site – which in Bangkok often means on the roof – and must also reflect the status of the building in question, so their architecture can range from the simplest wooden structure to an elaborate scale model of a particularly ornate temple or even a sleek little icon of modernism. Daily **offerings** of flowers, incense and candles are set inside the spirit house, sometimes with morsels of food.

RAT OR RAJA?

There's no standard system of **transliterating** Thai script into Roman, so you're sure to find that the Thai words in this book don't always match the versions you'll see elsewhere. Maps and street signs are the biggest sources of confusion, so we've generally gone for the transliteration that's most common on the spot; where it's a toss-up between two equally popular versions, we've used the one that helps best with pronunciation. However, sometimes you'll need to do a bit of lateral thinking, bearing in mind that a classic variant for the town of Ayutthaya is Ayudhia, while among street names, Thanon Rajavithi could come out as Thanon Ratwithi – and it's not unheard of to find one spelling posted at one end of a road, with another at the opposite end.

---

between June and August, coming to a peak in September and October, when unpaved roads are reduced to mud troughs. The **cool season** is the pleasantest time to visit, although temperatures can still reach a broiling 30°C in the middle of the day. In the **hot season**, when temperatures often rise to 35°C in Bangkok, the best thing to do is to hit the beach.

Within this scheme, slight variations are found from region to region (see p.59). The upland, less humid **north** experiences the greatest range of temperatures: at night in the cool season the thermometer dips markedly, occasionally approaching zero on the higher slopes, and this region is often hotter than the central plains between March and May. It's the **northeast** that gets the very worst of the hot season, with clouds of dust gathering above the parched fields, and humid air too. In **southern Thailand**, temperatures are more consistent throughout the year, with less variation the closer you get to the equator. The rainy season hits the **Andaman coast** of the southern peninsula harder than anywhere else in the country: rainfall can start in April and usually persists until November.

One area of the country, the **Gulf coast** of the southern peninsula, lies outside this general pattern. With the sea immediately to the east, this coast and its offshore islands feel the effects of the northeast monsoon, which brings rain between October and January, especially in November, but suffers less than the Andaman coast from the southwest monsoon.

Overall, the cool season is the **best time** to come to Thailand: as well as having more manageable temperatures and less rain, it offers waterfalls in full spate and the best of the upland flowers in bloom. Bear in mind, however, that it's also the busiest season, so forward planning is essential.

RIGHT BANGKOK SKYLINE

30

things not to miss

It's not possible to see everything that Thailand has to offer in one trip – and we don't suggest you try. What follows, in no particular order, is a selective taste of the country's highlights: beautiful beaches, outstanding national parks, magnificent temples and thrilling activities. All entries have a page reference to take you straight into the guide, where you can find out more.

4 KHMER RUINS
Pages 451, 453 & 463

The Khmers of neighbouring Angkor left a chain of magnificent temple complexes across the northeast, including this one at Phimai.

5 KHAO SOK NATIONAL PARK
Page 610

Mist-clad outcrops, jungle trails serenaded by whooping gibbons, and the vast Cheow Lan Lake all make Khao Sok a rewarding place to explore.

6 CHATUCHAK WEEKEND MARKET
Page 129

Thailand's top shopping experience features over eight thousand stalls selling everything from cooking pots to designer lamps.

7 JIM THOMPSON'S HOUSE
Page 120

The house of the legendary American adventurer, entrepreneur and art collector is a small, personal museum of Thai crafts and architecture.

8 LOY KRATHONG
Page 244

At this festival in honour of the water spirits, Thais float baskets of flowers and lighted candles on rivers, candles, ponds and seashores.

9 WAT PHO
Page 90

A lively and lavish temple, encompassing the awesome Reclining Buddha.

10 NAKHON SI THAMMARAT
Page 580

Home to superb food and the chief religious and cultural riches of the south.

11 SONGKHRAN
Page 286
Thai New Year is the excuse for a national waterfight.

12 KHAO YAI NATIONAL PARK
Page 440
Easy trails and tours, night safaris and a healthy cast of hornbills and gibbons.

13 WAT PHRA THAT DOI SUTHEP, CHIANG MAI
Page 305
One of the most harmonious ensembles of temple architecture in the country.

14 FOLKLORE MUSEUM, PHITSANULOK
Page 236
One of Thailand's best ethnology museums, complete with a reconstructed village home.

15 THE MAE HONG SON LOOP
Page 330
A spectacular 600km trip, winding over steep forested mountains.

16 NIGHT MARKETS
Page 38
Evening gatherings of pushcart kitchens, which are usually the best-value places to eat.

17 THE GRAND PALACE
Page 84

No visitor should miss this huge complex, which encompasses the country's holiest and most beautiful temple, Wat Phra Kaeo.

18 THAI COOKERY CLASSES IN CHIANG MAI
Page 283

Of the many courses on offer in the town, cookery classes are the most instantly gratifying and popular.

19 NAN
Page 324

Set in rich mountain scenery, with a strong handicraft tradition and some intriguing temples.

20 TRADITIONAL MASSAGE
Page 49

Combining elements of acupressure and yoga, a pleasantly brutal way to end the day.

21 AO PHANG NGA
Page 654

Boat or kayak your way through the bizarre and beautiful rock formations rising out of the Andaman Sea.

22 FULL MOON PARTY AT HAT RIN, KO PHA NGAN
Page 564

Apocalypse Now without the war.

23 KO LANTA
Page 688

A popular choice for families, with its many long beaches and plentiful but low-key resort facilities.

21

22

23

24 TREKKING
Page 54

Walking through the beautiful, rainforested scenery of northern Thailand's mountains comes with the bonus of getting to know the fascinating hill tribes.

25 WAT PHU TOK
Page 501

A uniquely atmospheric meditation temple on a steep, wooded outcrop.

26 SILK
Page 462

Weavers from the northeast produce the country's most exquisite silk.

27 RIDING THE DEATH RAILWAY, RIVER KWAI
Page 204

Thailand's most scenic train journey is also its most historic, using the track constructed by World War II POWs.

28 ROCK-CLIMBING
Page 652, 672 & 676

Even novice climbers can scale the cliffs at Ko Yao Noi, Phi Phi or the Railay peninsula for an unbeatable perspective on the Andaman seascape.

29 SUKHOTHAI
Page 240

Hire a bicycle to explore the elegant ruins of Thailand's thirteenth-century capital.

30 THE NATIONAL MUSEUM, BANGKOK
Page 95

A colossal hoard of Thailand's artistic treasures.

24

25

26

27

28

29

30

Itineraries

The following itineraries cover Thailand in all its diversity, from running the rapids in the northern mountains to beach-bumming your way through the Andaman archipelagos. Whether you want to feel the buzz of adventure in the great outdoors, feast on the never-ending variety of Thai cuisine, or find the nearest thing to a desert island paradise, these will point the way.

THE GREAT OUTDOORS

Thailand now offers an astonishing range of good-value active pursuits, both on land and in the teeming tropical seas.

❶ **Khao Yai National Park** One of the very few national parks to maintain a network of hiking trails that visitors can explore by themselves, passing dramatic waterfalls, orchids and an abundance of wildlife. **See p.440**

❷ **Chiang Mai** The best single base for outdoor activities, offering cycling day-trips and multi-day tours, mountain biking, trekking, rafting, rock-climbing and many others. **See p.280**

❸ **Pai rafting** A good place for trekking, but the real highlight here is the two-day whitewater rafting trip down the Pai River, taking in waterfalls, hot springs and a night in a jungle camp. **See p.349**

❹ **Umphang trekking** The best way to reach the 200m-high Tee Lor Su Falls is by rafting and hiking your way through the jungle on a three-day trip. **See p.267**

❺ **Diving and snorkelling off Ko Similan** The underwater scenery at this remote chain of national park islands is world-class and can be explored on appealing, small-scale live-aboards. **See p.620**

❻ **Sea-canoeing in Ao Phang Nga** Low-impact paddling on day, night or multi-day trips is the best way to explore the secret caves and mangrove swamps of this extraordinary bay. **See p.656**

❼ **Ko Yao Noi** This relaxing island on the edge of Phang Nga bay is a low-key hub for active visitors, who kayak, snorkel, dive and climb rocks. **See p.649**

❽ **Rock-climbing on the Railay peninsula** Offering courses for beginners, as well as equipment rental and guides, this is Thailand's premier site for climbers, with over seven hundred bolted routes amid awesome scenery. **See p.672**

THE FOODIE TRAIL

We're not daring to claim that the restaurants mentioned below are the very best in Thailand, but they're all locally famous places serving regional specialities where you can eat extremely well.

❶ **Chiang Rai** Not a town renowned for its gastronomy, but *Salungkham* always stops the traffic and delivers the goods – and you might well want to take away some of its home-smoked pork. **See p.363**

❷ **Chiang Mai** The nearest thing to nirvana for foodies: loads of Thai cooking classes, culinary walking tours and a choice between central Thai and Burmese-influenced northern Thai food at restaurants such as *Huen Phen*. **See p.283, p.295 & p.296**

ABOVE SNORKELLERS, KO SIMILAN; DELICIOUS THAI FOOD; HAEW SUWAT FALLS, KHAO YAI NATIONAL PARK

❸ Bangkok Among fifty thousand places to eat in the capital, a couple of restaurants can be singled out for special mention: *Taling Pling*, with a long list of dishes from the four corners of the country praised by Thai food critics; and *Bolan*, for its meticulous commitment to traditional recipes and the "Slow Food" philosophy. **See p.158 & p.159**

❹ Hua Hin Long the favourite seaside retreat of Bangkok's food-loving middle classes, Hua Hin has built up a thriving culinary scene – *Baan Itsara's* creative seafood dishes stand out. **See p.524**

❺ Phuket Among Phuket's swanky, big-name restaurants, *The Seacret* may seem an unlikely choice, but it delivers fantastic local dishes such as dried and smoked shrimp relish (*nam prik kung siap*) and stewed pork belly with cinnamon. **See p.644**

❻ Krabi You may have to queue for a table at *Ko Tung*, but it's worth the wait for the fresh, southern-style seafood such as delicious sweet mussels and baked crab. **See p.664**

❼ Ko Samui The island now has some great hotel restaurants, but our favourite spot is still *Ban Hua Thanon Seafood*, a wooden shophouse with waterfront tables and superb shredded prawns with mango salad. **See p.557**

❽ Nakhon Si Thammarat *Krua Thale* is almost reason in itself to go to Nakhon – don't miss the chunky mussels in herb soup. **See p.586**

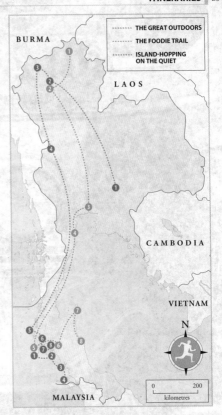

ISLAND-HOPPING ON THE QUIET

Ferries now join up the karst islands of the southern Andaman coast, so it's possible to get from Phuket to Penang in Malaysia without setting foot on the mainland. You can avoid the crowds, and save yourself money and hassle, by bypassing the kiss-me-quick honeypots of Phuket, Ko Phi Phi and Ko Lipe in favour of these island beauties.

❶ Phuket Town Base yourself among the Sino-Portuguese architecture of the island capital, which has better-value and more interesting places to stay and eat than the big-name beaches, and much better transport links. **See p.627**

❷ With around 20km of west-facing sands and a laidback, family-friendly atmosphere, **Ko Lanta** offers a wide range of affordable accommodation and an almost endless choice of beach bars for sundowners. **See p.688**

A short detour from Lanta brings you to **Ko Jum**'s half a dozen wild and lonely beaches facing the sunset, with boat trips to enjoy and a small mountain to climb. **See p.684**

❸ There's a variety of good resorts for all budgets on **Ko Hai** and a gorgeous panorama of jagged limestone islands. **See p.710**

A quick hop from Ko Hai, **Ko Mook**'s main draw is the stunning Emerald Cave, with its inland beach of fine sand at the base of a spectacular natural chimney. **See p.713**

Just southwest of Ko Mook, **Ko Kradan** is a remote island that's uninhabited apart from its half-dozen resorts, with a long, powdery, east-facing strand, crystal-clear waters and a reef for snorkellers to explore. **See p.714**

❹ Ko Tarutao Huge national park island with mangroves and jungle tracks to explore, and the most unspoilt beaches in the area. **See p.718**

TUK-TUK

Basics

Getting there

Thailand currently has six international airports, in Bangkok, Chiang Mai, Hat Yai, Krabi, Phuket and Ko Samui. The vast majority of travellers fly into Bangkok's Suvarnabhumi Airport (see p.133).

Air fares to Thailand generally depend on the **season**, with the highest being approximately mid-November to mid-February, when the weather is best (with premium rates charged for flights between mid-Dec and New Year), and in July and August to coincide with school holidays. You will need to book several months in advance to get reasonably priced tickets during these peak periods.

The cheapest way of getting to most **regional Thai airports** is usually to buy a flight to Bangkok and then a separate domestic ticket (see p.31). However, there are dozens of potentially useful, mostly seasonal, international routes into **Phuket**, including direct flights with several airlines from Australia. For **Ko Samui**, there are flights from Singapore, Hong Kong (both Bangkok Airways) and Kuala Lumpur (Berjaya Airlines and Firefly); for **Krabi** you can fly from KL with Air Asia, from Singapore with Tiger Airways or nonstop on seasonal, mostly charter flights from Scandinavia; and for **Chiang Mai**, Silk Air fly from Singapore, Air Asia from KL and Macau, while Korean Airlines from Seoul is a popular route for North American visitors.

Flights from the UK and Ireland

The fastest and most comfortable way of reaching Thailand **from the UK** is to fly nonstop from London to Bangkok with Qantas (Ⓦqantas.com.au), British Airways (Ⓦba.com), Thai Airways (Ⓦthaiair .com) or Eva Airways (Ⓦevaair.com), a journey of about eleven and a half hours. These airlines sometimes have special promotions, but a typical fare in high season might come in at around £900. Fares on indirect scheduled flights to Bangkok are always cheaper than nonstop flights – about £600 in high season if booked well in advance with Qatar Airways (Ⓦqatarairways.com), for example – though these journeys can take anything from two to twelve hours longer.

There are no nonstop flights from any **regional airports** in Britain or from any **Irish airports**, and rather than routing via London, you may find it convenient to fly to another hub such as Frankfurt (with Lufthansa; Ⓦlufthansa.com), Zurich (with Swiss; Ⓦswiss.com), Abu Dhabi (with Etihad; Ⓦetihadairways.com) or Dubai (with Emirates;

Ⓦemirates.com), and take a connecting flight from there. Return flights from Newcastle upon Tyne with Emirates, for example, currently start at around £675 in high season, from Dublin via Copenhagen with SAS (Ⓦflysas.com), at around €800.

Flights from the US and Canada

Thai Airways (Ⓦthaiair.com) offers convenient flights from LA to Bangkok, with a one-hour stop in Seoul, charging around US$1600 in high season. Plenty of other airlines run to Bangkok from East and West Coast cities with one stop en route; it's generally easier to find a reasonable fare on flights via Asia than via Europe, even if you're departing from the East Coast. From New York, expect to pay upwards of US$1375 return in high season, including taxes, US$1250 from LA. Air Canada (Ⓦaircanada.com) has the most convenient service to Bangkok from the largest number of Canadian cities; from Vancouver, expect to pay from around Can$1450 in high season; from Toronto, Can$1675. Cheaper rates are often available if you're prepared to make two or three stops and take more time.

Minimum **flying times** are twenty hours from New York or Toronto (westbound or eastbound), including stopovers, seventeen hours (nonstop) or nineteen and a half hours (with one stop) from LA, and eighteen hours from Vancouver.

Flights from Australia and New Zealand

There's no shortage of **scheduled flights** to Bangkok **from Australia**, with direct services from major cities operated by Thai Airways (Ⓦthaiair .com), Qantas (Ⓦqantas.com.au) and half a dozen others (around nine hours from Sydney and Perth), and plenty of indirect flights via Asian hubs, which take at least eleven and a half hours. You can also fly nonstop to Phuket from Sydney (with Jetstar; Ⓦjetstar.com), Melbourne, Brisbane (both Air Australia; Ⓦairaustralia.com) and Perth (on Thai and Virgin Australia; Ⓦvirginaustralia.com). There's often not much difference between the fares on nonstop and indirect flights with the major carriers, nor between the fares with the major eastern cities. From Sydney, if you book far in advance, you should be able to get a ticket to Bangkok in high season for around Aus$900, on a low-cost carrier such as Jetstar or through a special promotion with one of the major airlines; nonstop flights with the major airlines more typically cost around Aus$1200. Fares from Perth and Darwin are up to Aus$200 cheaper.

A BETTER KIND OF TRAVEL

At Rough Guides we are passionately committed to travel. We believe it helps us understand the world we live in and the people we share it with – and of course tourism is vital to many developing economies. But the scale of modern tourism has also damaged some places irreparably, and climate change is accelerated by most forms of transport, especially flying. All Rough Guides' flights are carbon-offset, and every year we donate money to a variety of environmental charities.

From **New Zealand**, Thai Airways runs nonstop twelve-hour flights between Auckland and Bangkok, costing from around NZ$1700 (including taxes) in high season. British Airways/Qantas flights from Auckland make brief stops in Sydney, adding about three hours to the trip, and other major Asian airlines offer indirect flights via their hubs (from 13hr, but more typically 17hr): fares for indirect flights can start as low as NZ$1500 in high season.

Flights from South Africa

From **South Africa**, Thai Airways (Wthaiair.com), code-sharing with South African Airways (Wflysaa.com), currently operate three nonstop flights a week from Johannesburg to Bangkok, taking eleven and a half hours and costing from around ZAR9,500 return for an advance booking in high season, including taxes. Otherwise, you'll be making a stop either in the Middle East or in Hong Kong or Southeast Asia, with fares starting at around ZAR8000 in high season.

AGENTS AND OPERATORS

Adventure Center US ☎ 1-800/228-8747, Wadventurecenter.com. Hiking and "soft adventure" specialist agent, offering dozens of packages to Thailand with well-regarded tour operators from all over the world.

All Points East UK ☎ 023/9225 8859, Thailand ☎ 081 885 9490; Wallpointseast.com. Southeast Asia specialist operating small-group adventure holidays with off-the-beaten-track itineraries.

Andaman Discoveries Thailand Wandamandiscoveries.com. Village-based homestay community tourism programmes around Khuraburi on the north Andaman coast, lasting from one to five days, which allow visitors to experience daily activities such as soap making, cashew-nut farming and roof thatching. Other tours include four-day trips to Ko Surin National Park to learn about Moken life.

Asian Trails Thailand Wasiantrails.net. Well-regarded company that offers self-drive tours, cycling adventures, homestay programmes, river and sea cruises, plus more typical package tours.

Creative Events Asia Thailand Wcreativeeventsasia.com. Wedding specialists for everything from paperwork to the ceremony and guest accommodation.

Crooked Trails US ☎ 206/383-9828, Wcrookedtrails.com. Not-for-profit community-based tourism organization offering homestays along the Andaman coast, featuring volunteer work as well as cultural tours.

Eastern & Oriental Express UK ☎ 0845 077 2222, US ☎ 1-800/524 2420; Worient-express.com. Tours by luxury train between Bangkok and Singapore, as well as to northern and northeastern Thailand.

ETC (Educational Travel Centre) Thailand Wetc.co.th. Unusual tour programmes including Thai cooking holidays, rice-barge cruises to Ayutthaya, and community-based programmes and homestays that might include trekking and teaching.

Flight Centre Australia ☎ 13 31 33, Canada ☎ 1-877/967 5302, New Zealand ☎ 0800/243 544, South Africa ☎ 0860 400 727, UK ☎ 0870/499 0040, US ☎ 1-877/992 4732; Wflightcentre.com. Guarantees to offer the lowest international air fares.

Grasshopper Adventures Australia ☎ 03/9016 3172, Thailand ☎ 02 280 0832, UK ☎ 020/8123 8144, US ☎ 818/921-7101; Wgrasshopperadventures.com. Cycling day-tours around Bangkok, longer rides to Kanchanaburi and Ko Samui, and around Chiang Mai.

Intrepid Travel Australia ☎ 1300/018 871, Canada ☎ 1-866/360-1151, Ireland ☎ 01/524 0071, New Zealand ☎ 0800/600 610, South Africa ☎ 087 985 2798, UK ☎ 0800 781 1660, US ☎ 1-800/970 7299; Wintrepidtravel.com. Well-regarded, small-group, off-the-beaten-track tour operator that offers over sixty trips to Thailand.

North South Travel UK ☎ 01245/608 291, Wnorthsouthtravel .co.uk. Friendly, competitive travel agency, offering discounted fares worldwide. Profits are used to support projects in the developing world, especially the promotion of sustainable tourism.

Origin Asia Thailand Walex-kerr.com. Cultural programmes that teach and explain living Thai arts such as dance, music, martial arts, textiles, flower offerings and cooking. Courses last from one day to a week and are held in Bangkok and Chiang Mai.

Responsible Travel UK ☎ 01273/600030, Wresponsibletravel .com. One-stop shop for scores of fair-trade, ethically inclined holidays in Thailand, including trips that focus on wildlife, meditation, family activities and village life.

Spice Roads Thailand Wspiceroads.com. Escorted bike tours through north, central and southern Thailand.

STA Travel Australia ☎ 134 782, New Zealand ☎ 0800/474 400, South Africa ☎ 0861/781 781, Thailand ☎ 02 236 0262, UK ☎ 0871/230/0040, US ☎ 1-800/781-4040; Wstatravel.com. Worldwide specialists in independent travel. Good discounts for students and under-26s.

Symbiosis UK ☎ 0845/123 2844, Wsymbiosis-travel.com. Upmarket, off-the-beaten-track tours with an environmentally sensitive, fair-trade focus, including visiting hill tribes by mountain bike, and kayaking at Khao Sok and Ko Tarutao.

Telltale Travel UK ☎ 0800/011 2571, ⓦ telltaletravel.co.uk.
Tailor-made, upscale company that offers off-the-beaten-track wildlife, cultural, family, cooking and well-being tours, as well as group trips for solo travellers.

Thailand Birdwatching Thailand ⓦ thailandbirdwatching.com.
Specialist birdwatching tours in national parks and nature reserves.

Trailfinders UK ☎ 0845 058 5858, Ireland ☎ 01 677 7888; ⓦ trailfinders.com. One of the best-informed and most efficient agents for independent travellers, with 24 branches in Britain and Ireland.

Travel Cuts Canada ☎ 1-800/667 2887, US ☎ 1-800/592-2887; ⓦ travelcuts.com. Popular, long-established specialists in budget travel, including student and youth discount offers.

USIT Australia ☎ 1800 092499, Ireland ☎ 01/602 1906; ⓦ usit.ie. Ireland's main outlet for discounted, youth and student fares, with a branch in Sydney.

Travel via neighbouring countries

Sharing land borders with Burma, Laos, Cambodia and Malaysia, Thailand works well as part of many overland itineraries, both across Asia and between Europe and Australia. Bangkok is also one of the major regional flight hubs for Southeast Asia.

The main restrictions on overland routes in and out of Thailand are determined by where the permitted land crossings lie and by **visas**. Details of visa requirements for travel to Thailand's immediate neighbours are outlined below, but should be double-checked before you travel. All **Asian embassies** are located in Bangkok (see p.171), but waiting times can be shorter at visa-issuing consulates outside the capital: China and India run consulates in Chiang Mai (see p.303), and Laos and Vietnam have consulates in Khon Kaen (see p.479). In Bangkok, many Khao San tour agents offer to get your visa for you, but beware: some are reportedly **faking the stamps**, which could get you into pretty serious trouble, so it's safer to go to the embassy yourself.

The right paperwork is also crucial if you're planning to **drive your own car or motorbike** into Thailand; see the Golden Triangle Rider website (ⓦ gt-rider.com) for advice.

Burma

There is no overland access from **Burma (Myanmar)** into Thailand and access in the opposite direction is restricted. Western tourists are only allowed to make limited-distance trips into Burma, usually just for the day, at Thachileik opposite Mae Sai, at Myawaddy near Mae Sot, and at Kaw Thaung (Victoria Point) near Ranong. The crossing at Three Pagodas Pass near Kanchanaburi is currently open only to Thai tourists. At these borders you generally enter Burma on a temporary US$10 (or B500) **visa** and then get a new fifteen-day visa when returning to Thailand; see relevant accounts for details.

Cambodia

At the time of writing, six overland crossings on the **Thai–Cambodia border** are open to non-Thais. See the relevant town accounts for specific details on all the border crossings; for travellers' up-to-the-minute experiences, plus an account of the common **scam** on through-transport from Bangkok to Siem Reap, consult ⓦ talesofasia.com/cambodia-overland.htm.

Most travellers use either the crossing at Poipet, which has transport connections to Sisophon, Siem Reap and Phnom Penh and lies just across the border from the Thai town of Aranyaprathet (see p.383), with its transport to Bangkok and, with a change in Sa Kaew, to Chanthaburi; or they follow the route from Sihanoukville in Cambodia via Koh Kong and Hat Lek to Trat (see p.408), which is near Ko Chang on Thailand's east coast.

The crossings in northeast Thailand include the Chong Chom–O'Smach border pass, near Kap Choeng in Thailand's Surin province (see p.461), and the Sa Ngam–Choam border in Si Saket province (see p.464); from both these borders there's transport to Anlong Veng and Siem Reap. There are also two crossings in Chanthaburi province (see p.405), with transport to and from Pailin in Cambodia.

Thirty-day tourist **visas** for Cambodia are issued to travellers on arrival at Phnom Penh and Siem Reap airports, and at all the above-listed land borders; you need US$20 and one photo for this. If you want to buy an advance thirty-day visa, you can do so online at ⓦ mfaic.gov.kh/evisa which takes three working days and costs US$25; these "e-visas" can only be used at the international airports and at Poipet and Ko Kong land borders, but might help you to avoid the more excessive scams at the land borders.

Laos and Vietnam

There are five main points along the **Lao border** where tourists can cross into Thailand: Houayxai (for Chiang Khong; see p.376); Vientiane (for Nong Khai;

see p.497); Khammouan (aka Thakhek, for Nakhon Phanom; see p.503); Savannakhet (for Mukdahan; see p.505); and Pakse (for Chong Mek; see p.472). All these borders can also be used as exits into Laos; see relevant town account for transport details.

Visas are required for all non-Thai visitors to Laos. A thirty-day **visa on arrival** can be bought for US$30–42 (depending on your nationality), plus one photo, at Vientiane, Luang Prabang and Pakse airports, and all the above-listed land borders. Or you can buy one in advance from either the Lao Embassy in Bangkok or the Lao Consulate in Khon Kaen for about the same fee.

It's possible to travel **from Vietnam** to Thailand via Savannakhet on the Lao–Thai border in a matter of hours; you'll need to use Vietnam's Lao Bao border crossing, west of Dong Ha, where you can catch a bus to Savannakhet and then another bus across the Mekong bridge to Mukdahan. All travellers into Vietnam need to buy a visa in advance. Thirty-day visas can take up to four working days to process at the embassy in Bangkok and cost from around B1000, depending on nationality (much more for same- or next-day processing); processing is usually quicker at the Vietnamese consulate in Khon Kaen.

Malaysia and Singapore

Travelling between Thailand and **Malaysia and Singapore** has in the past been a straightforward and very commonly used overland route, with plentiful connections by bus, minibus, share-taxi and train, most of them routed through the southern Thai city and transport hub of Hat Yai. However, because of the ongoing **violence in Thailand's deep south** (see p.705), all major Western governments are currently advising people not to travel to or through Songkhla, Pattani, Yala and Narathiwat provinces, unless essential (and consequently most insurance companies are not covering travel there). This encompasses Hat Yai and the following border crossings to and from Malaysia: at Padang Besar, on the main rail line connecting Butterworth in Malaysia (and, ultimately, Kuala Lumpur and Singapore) with Hat Yai and Bangkok; at Sungai Kolok, terminus of a railway line from Hat Yai and Bangkok, and at adjacent Ban Taba, both of which are connected by road to nearby Kota Bharu in Malaysia; and at the road crossings at Sadao, south of Hat Yai, and at Betong, south of Yala. (The routes towards Kota Bharu and Betong pass through particularly volatile territory, with martial law declared in Pattani, Yala and Narathiwat provinces; however, martial law is not in effect in Hat Yai itself.)

Nevertheless, the provinces of Trang and Satun on the west coast are not affected, and it's still perfectly possible to travel **overland via Satun**: by ferry between Satun's Thammalang pier and Kuala Perlis or the island of Langkawi, or overland between Ban Khuan and Kangar (see p.724); or by boat between Ko Lipe and Langkawi (see p.721). For up-to-the-minute advice, consult your government travel advisory (see p.62).

Most Western tourists can spend thirty days in Malaysia and fourteen days in Singapore without having bought a visa beforehand, and there are useful Thai embassies or consulates in Kuala Lumpur, Kota Bharu, Penang and Singapore (see p.64).

Getting around

Travel in Thailand is inexpensive and efficient, if not always speedy. Unless you travel by plane, long-distance journeys in Thailand can be arduous, especially if a shoestring budget restricts you to hard seats and no air conditioning.

Nonetheless, the wide range of transport options makes travelling around Thailand easier than elsewhere in Southeast Asia. **Buses** are fast, cheap and frequent, and can be quite luxurious; **trains** are slower but safer and offer more chance of sleeping during overnight trips; moreover, if travelling by day you're likely to follow a more scenic route by rail than by road. Inter-town **songthaews**, air-cond**itioned minibuses** and **share-taxis** are handy, and **ferries** provide easy access to all major islands. Local transport comes in all sorts of permutations, both public and chartered.

Inter-town buses

Buses, overall the most convenient way of getting around the country, come in four main categories. In ascending order of comfort, speed and cost, they are **ordinary** buses (*rot thammadaa*; not air-conditioned, usually orange-coloured) and three types of **air-con** bus (*rot air* or *rot thua*; usually blue): second-class, first-class and VIP. Ordinary and many air-con buses are run by Baw Khaw Saw (BKS), the government-controlled transport company, while privately owned, licensed air-con buses (*rot ruam*, usually translated as "join buses"), some of which operate from Baw Khaw Saw terminals, also ply the most popular long-distance routes. Be warned that long-distance overnight buses, on which some drivers are rumoured to take amphetamines to stay awake, seem to be involved in more than their fair share of accidents; because of this, some travellers prefer to do the overnight journeys by train and then make a shorter bus connection to their destination.

Ordinary and second-class

On most routes, including nearly all services out of Bangkok, **second-class** (*baw sawng*; look for the "2" on the side of the vehicle) air-con buses have now replaced **ordinary buses** as the main workhorses of the Thai bus system, though you'll still see plenty of the latter on shorter routes in more remote parts of the country. Whether air-con or not, these basic buses are incredibly inexpensive, generally run frequently during daylight hours, pack as many people in as possible and stop often, which slows them down considerably.

It's best to ask locally where to catch your bus. Failing that, designated **bus stops** are often marked by **sala**, small, open-sided wooden structures with bench seats, located at intervals along the main long-distance bus route through town or on the fringes of any decent-sized settlement, for example on the main highway that skirts the edge of town. Where there is only a bus shelter on the "wrong" side of the road, you can be sure that buses travelling in both directions will stop there for any waiting passengers; simply leave your bag on the right side of the road to alert the bus driver and wait in the shade. But if you're in the middle of nowhere with no *sala* in sight, any ordinary or second-class bus should stop for you if you flag it down.

First-class and VIP

Express services, with fewer stops, are mostly operated by **first-class** (*baw neung*; look for the "1" on the side of the vehicle) and **VIP** (usually written in English on the side) buses. These are your best option for long-distance journeys: you'll generally be allotted specific seats, there'll be a toilet, and on the longest journeys you may get blankets, snacks and nonstop DVDs. The first-class services have fewer seats than second-class and more leg room for reclining, VIP services fewer seats again. Other nomenclature for the top-of-the-range services is also used, especially by the **private "join" companies**: "999", "super VIP" (with even fewer seats), "Gold Class" and, confusingly, sometimes even "First Class" (in imitation of airlines, with just eighteen huge, well-equipped seats).

On a lot of long-distance routes private "join" buses are indistinguishable from government ones and operate out of the same Baw Khaw Saw bus terminals. The major private companies, such as Nakhon Chai Air (☎02 936 0009), Sombat Tour (☎02 792 1444) and, operating out of Chiang Mai, Green Bus (☎053 266480), have roughly similar fares, though naturally with more scope for price variation, and offer comparable facilities and standards of service. The opposite is unfortunately true of a number of the smaller, private, unlicensed companies, which have a poor reputation for service and comfort, but gear themselves towards foreign travellers with bargain fares and convenient timetables. The long-distance tour buses that run **from Thanon Khao San** in Banglamphu to Chiang Mai and Surat Thani are a case in point; though promised VIP buses, travellers on these routes frequently complain about shabby furnishings, ineffective air conditioning, unhelpful (even aggressive) drivers, lateness and a frightening lack of safety awareness – and there are frequent reports of theft from luggage on these routes, too, and even the spraying of "sleeping gas" so that hand luggage can be rifled without interruption. Generally it's best to travel with the government or licensed private bus companies from the main bus terminals (who have a reputation with their regular Thai customers to maintain) or to go by train instead – the extra comfort and peace of mind are well worth the extra baht.

Tickets and timetables

Tickets for all buses can be bought from the departure terminals, but for ordinary and second-class air-con buses it's normal to buy them on board. First-class and VIP buses may operate from a separate station or office, and tickets for the more popular routes should be booked a day in advance. As a rough indication of **fares**, a trip from Bangkok to Chiang Mai, a distance of 700km, costs B600–800 for VIP, around B500 for first-class air-con and B400 for second-class air-con.

Long-distance buses often depart in clusters around the same time (early morning or late at night, for example), leaving a gap of five or more hours during the day with no services at all. Local TAT offices occasionally keep up-to-date bus **timetables**, but the best source of information, apart from the bus stations themselves, is ⓦthai ticketmajor.com, which carries timetables in English for 360 routes as well as useful information on how to **buy tickets** in advance. Options include buying them online through the site; by phone on ☎02 262 3456 (making your payment within five hours at, for example, any branch of 7–Eleven); and buying them at 83 major post offices (as listed on the site), including the GPO in Bangkok, the Ratchadamnoen post office in Banglamphu and the Thanon Na Phra Lan post office opposite the entrance to the Grand Palace in Ratanakosin.

Songthaews, share-taxis and air-conditioned minibuses

In rural areas, the bus network is often supplemented by **songthaews** (literally "two rows"), which are open-ended vans (or occasionally cattle-trucks) onto which the drivers squash as many passengers as possible on two facing benches, leaving latecomers to swing off the running board at the back. As well as their essential role within towns (see p.32), songthaews ply set routes from larger towns out to their surrounding suburbs and villages, and, where there's no call for a regular bus service, between small towns: some have destinations written on in Thai, but few are numbered. In most towns you'll find the songthaew "terminal" near the market; to pick one up between destinations just flag it down. To indicate to the driver that you want to get out, the normal practice is to rap hard with a coin on the metal railings as you approach the spot (or press the bell if there is one).

In the deep south (see p.704) they do things with a little more style – **share-taxis** connect many of the major towns, though they are inexorably being replaced by more comfortable **air-conditioned minibuses** (*rot tuu*, meaning "cupboard cars"). Scores of similar private air-conditioned minibus services are now cropping up all over the country, generally operating out of small offices or pavement desks in town centres – or from the roads around Bangkok's Victory Monument. Some of these services have a timetable, but many just aim to leave when they have a full complement of passengers; then again, some companies publish a timetable but depart when they're full – whether before or after the published time. They cover the distance faster than buses, but often at breakneck speed and they can be uncomfortably cramped when full – they're not ideal for travellers with huge rucksacks, who may be required to pay extra. These services are usually licensed and need to keep up their reputation with their regular Thai passengers but, as with full-sized buses (see p.29), you should be wary of unlicensed private companies that offer minibuses solely for farangs from Bangkok's Thanon Khao San.

In many cases, long-distance songthaews and air-conditioned minibuses will drop you at an exact address (for example a particular guesthouse) if you warn them far enough in advance. As a rule, the **cost** of inter-town songthaews is comparable to that of air-con buses, that of air-conditioned minibuses perhaps a shade more.

Trains

Managed by the State Railway of Thailand (SRT), the **rail** network consists of four main lines and a few branch lines. The **Northern Line** connects Bangkok with Chiang Mai via Ayutthaya, Lopburi, Phitsanulok and Lampang. The **Northeastern Line** splits into two just beyond Ayutthaya, the lower branch running eastwards to Ubon Ratchathani via Khorat and Surin, the more northerly branch linking the capital with Nong Khai (with a short extension over the Mekong into Laos; see p.497) via Khon Kaen and Udon Thani. The **Eastern Line** also has two branches, one of which runs from Bangkok to Aranyaprathet on the Cambodian border, the other of which connects Bangkok with Si Racha and Pattaya. The **Southern Line** extends via Hua Hin, Chumphon and Surat Thani, with spurs off to Trang and Nakhon Si Thammarat, to Hat Yai (see p.705), where it branches: one line continues down the west coast of Malaysia, via Butterworth, where you usually change trains for Kuala Lumpur and Singapore; the other heads down the eastern side of the peninsula to Sungai Kolok on the Thailand–Malaysia border (20km from Pasir Mas on Malaysia's interior railway). At Nakhon Pathom a branch of this line veers off to Nam Tok via Kanchanaburi – this is all that's left of the Death Railway, of *Bridge on the River Kwai* notoriety (see p.204).

Fares depend on the class of seat, whether or not you want air conditioning, and on the speed of the train; those quoted here exclude the "speed" supplements (see opposite). Hard, wooden or thinly padded third-class seats are much cheaper than buses (Bangkok–Chiang Mai B121, or B221 with air-conditioner), and are fine for about three hours, after which numbness sets in. For longer journeys you'd be wise to opt for the padded and often reclining seats in second class (Bangkok–Chiang Mai B281, or B391 with air-conditioner). On long-distance trains, you also usually have the option of second-class berths (Bangkok–Chiang Mai B381–431, or B491–631 with air-conditioner), with day seats that convert into comfortable curtained-off bunks in the evening; lower bunks, which are more expensive than upper, have a few cubic centimetres more of space, a little more shade from the lights in the carriage, and a window. Female passengers can sometimes request a berth in an all-female section of a carriage. Travelling first class (Bangkok–Surat B1063–1263 per person) generally means a two-person air-con sleeping compartment, complete with washbasin.

There are several different **types of train**: slowest of all is the third-class-only Ordinary service, which is generally (but not always) available only on short and medium-length journeys and has no speed supplement. Next comes the misleadingly named Rapid train (B20–110 supplement), a trip on which from Bangkok to Chiang Mai, for example, takes fifteen hours; the Express (B150 supplement), which does the Chiang Mai route in about the same time; and the Special Express (B170–190 supplement) which covers the ground in around fourteen hours. Among the last-mentioned, fastest of all are the mostly daytime Special Express Diesel Railcars, which can usually be relied on to run roughly on time (most other services pay only lip service to their timetables). Nearly all long-distance trains have **dining cars**, and rail staff will also bring meals to your seat.

Booking at least one day in advance is strongly recommended for second- and first-class seats on all lengthy journeys, and sleepers should be booked as far in advance as possible (reservations open sixty days before departure). You can make bookings for any journey in Thailand at the train station in any major town, and it's now also possible to book online, at least two days in advance, at SRT's Ⓦthairailticket.com. The website is allocated only a limited number of seats, but it allows you to pay by credit card and simply print off your ticket. Otherwise, you can arrange advance bookings over the internet with reputable Thai travel agencies such as Thai Focus (Ⓦthaifocus .com) or Thailand Train Ticket (Ⓦthailandtrainticket .com). Trains out of Bangkok can be booked **in person** at Hualamphong Station (see p.134).

Ferries

Regular **ferries** connect all major islands with the mainland, and for the vast majority of crossings you simply buy your ticket on board. Safety standards are generally just about adequate but there have been a small number of sinkings in recent years – avoid travelling on boats that are clearly overloaded or in poor condition. In tourist areas competition ensures that prices are kept low, and fares tend to vary with the speed of the crossing: thus Chumphon–Ko Tao costs between B200 (6hr) and B600 (1hr 45min).

On the east coast and the Andaman coast boats generally operate a reduced service during the monsoon season (May–Oct), when the more remote spots become inaccessible. Ferries in the Samui archipelago are fairly constant year-round. Details on island connections are given in the relevant chapters.

Flights

Thai Airways (Ⓦthaiair.com) and Bangkok Airways (Ⓦbangkokair.com) are the major full-service airlines on the internal **flight** network, which extends to all parts of the country, using some two-dozen airports. Air Asia (Ⓦairasia.com), Nok Air (Ⓦnokair.com), which is part-owned by Thai Airways, and Orient Thai (formerly One-Two-Go; Ⓦflyorientthai.com) provide the main, "low-cost" competition; Thai Airways are also about to set up a new low-cost arm, Thai Smile. In a recently deregulated but ever-expanding market, other smaller airlines come and go with surprising frequency – and while they are operating, schedules tend to be erratic and flights are sometimes cancelled.

In some instances a flight can save you days of travelling: a flight from Chiang Mai to Phuket with Thai Airways or Air Asia, for example, takes two hours, as against a couple of days by meandering train and/or bus. Book early if possible – you can reserve online with all companies – as fares fluctuate wildly. For a fully flexible economy ticket, Bangkok to Chiang Mai costs around B4000 with Thai Airways, but you'll find flights on the same route with the "low-cost" carriers for under B1000 (with restrictions on changes), if you book online far enough in advance.

If you're planning to make lots of domestic flights, you might want to consider the **airpasses** offered by Thai or Bangkok Airways – their complex conditions and prices are posted on their websites.

Local transport

Most sizeable towns have some kind of **local transport system**, comprising a network of buses, songthaews or even longtail boats, with set fares and routes but not rigid timetabling – in many cases vehicles wait until they're full before they leave.

Buses and songthaews

A few larger cities such as Bangkok, Khorat, Ubon Ratchathani and Phitsanulok have a **local bus** network that usually extends to the suburbs and operates from dawn till dusk (through the night in Bangkok). Most vehicles display route numbers in Western numerals – see the relevant accounts for further details.

Within medium-sized and large towns, the main transport role is often played by **songthaews**. The size and shape of vehicle used varies from town to town – and in some places they're known as "tuk-tuks" from the noise they make, not to be confused with the smaller tuk-tuks, described below, that operate as private taxis – but all have the tell-tale two facing benches in the back. In some towns, especially in the northeast, songthaews follow fixed routes; in others such as Chiang Mai, they act as communal taxis, picking up a number of people who are going in roughly the same direction and taking each of them right to their destination. To hail a songthaew just flag it down, and to indicate that you want to get out, either rap hard with a coin on the metal railings, or ring the bell if there is one. Fares within towns are around B10–20, depending on distance.

Longtail boats

Wherever there's a decent public waterway, there'll be a **longtail boat** ready to ferry you along it. Another great Thai trademark, these elegant, streamlined boats are powered by deafening diesel engines – sometimes custom-built, more often adapted from cars or trucks – which drive a propeller mounted on a long shaft that is swivelled for steering. Longtails carry between eight and twenty passengers: generally you'll have to charter the whole boat, but on popular fixed routes, for example between small, inshore islands and the mainland, it's cheaper to wait until the boatman gets his quorum.

Taxi services

Taxis also come in many guises, and in bigger towns you can often choose between taking a tuk-tuk, a samlor and a motorbike taxi. The one thing common to all modes of chartered transport, bar metered taxis in Bangkok and one or two cities in the northeast, is that you must establish the **fare** beforehand: although drivers nearly always pitch their first offers too high, they do calculate with traffic and time of day in mind, as well as according to distance – if successive drivers scoff at your price, you know you've got it wrong.

Tuk-tuks

Named after the noise of its excruciatingly unsilenced engine, the three-wheeled, open-sided **tuk-tuk** is the classic Thai vehicle. Painted in primary colours, tuk-tuks blast their way round towns and cities on two-stroke engines, zipping around faster than any car and taking corners on two wheels. They aren't as dangerous as they look though, and can be an exhilarating way to get around, as long as you're not too fussy about exhaust fumes. Fares come in at around B60 for a medium-length journey (over B100 in Bangkok) regardless of the number of passengers – three is the safe maximum, though six is not uncommon. It's worth paying attention to advice on how to avoid getting ripped off by Bangkok tuk-tuk drivers (see p.141).

Samlors

Tuk-tuks are also sometimes known as samlors (literally "three wheels"), but the original **samlors** are tricycle rickshaws propelled by pedal power alone. Slower and a great deal more stately than tuk-tuks, samlors still operate in one or two towns around the country.

A further permutation are the motorized samlors (often called "skylabs" in northeastern Thailand), where the driver relies on a motorbike rather than a bicycle to propel passengers to their destination. They look much the same as cycle samlors, but often sound as noisy as tuk-tuks.

Motorbike taxis

Even faster and more precarious than tuk-tuks, **motorbike taxis** feature both in towns and in out-of-the-way places. In towns – where the drivers are identified by coloured, numbered vests – they have the advantage of being able to dodge traffic jams, but are obviously only really suitable for the single traveller, and motorbike taxis aren't the easiest mode of transport if you're carrying luggage. In remote spots, on the other hand, they're often the only alternative to hitching or walking, and are especially useful for getting between bus stops on main roads, around car-free islands and to national parks or ancient ruins.

Within towns motorbike-taxi fares can start at B10 for very short journeys, but for trips to the outskirts the cost rises steeply – reckon on at least B200 for a 20km round trip.

Vehicle rental

Despite first impressions, a high accident rate and the obvious mayhem that characterizes Bangkok's roads, **driving** yourself around Thailand can be fairly straightforward. Many roads, particularly in the northeast and the south, are remarkably uncongested. Major routes are clearly signed in English, though this only applies to some minor roads; unfortunately there is no perfect English-language map to compensate (see p.70).

Outside the capital, the eastern seaboard and the major tourist resorts of Ko Samui and Phuket, local drivers are generally considerate and unaggressive; they very rarely use their horns for example, and will often indicate and even swerve away when it's safe for you to overtake. The most inconsiderate and dangerous road-users in Thailand are bus drivers and lorry drivers, many of whom drive ludicrously fast, hog the road, race round bends on the wrong side of the road and use their horns remorselessly; worse still, many of them are tanked up on amphetamines, which makes them quite literally fearless.

Bus and lorry drivers are at their worst after dark (many of them only drive then), so it's best **not to drive at night** – a further hazard being the inevitable stream of unlit bicycles and mopeds in and around built-up areas, as well as poorly signed roadworks, which are often not made safe or blocked off from unsuspecting traffic. Orange signs, or sometimes just a couple of tree branches or a pile of stones on the road, warn of hazards ahead.

As for local **rules of the road**, Thais drive on the left, and the speed limit is 60kph within built-up areas and 90kph outside them. Beyond that, there are few rules that are generally followed – you'll need to keep your concentration up and expect the unexpected from fellow road-users. Watch out especially for vehicles pulling straight out of minor roads, when you might expect them to give way. An oncoming vehicle flashing its lights means it's coming through no matter what; a right indicator signal from the car in front usually means it's not safe for you to overtake, while a left indicator signal usually means that it is safe to do so.

Theoretically, foreigners need an international **driver's licence** to rent any kind of vehicle, but most car-rental companies accept national licences, and the smaller operations have been known not to ask for any kind of proof whatsoever; motorbike renters very rarely bother. A popular rip-off on islands such as Ko Pha Ngan is for small agents to charge renters exorbitant amounts for any minor damage to a jeep or motorbike, even paint chips, that they find on return – they'll claim that it's very expensive to get a new part shipped over from the mainland. Be sure to check out any vehicle carefully before renting.

Petrol (*nam man*, which can also mean oil) currently costs around B38 a litre, gasohol, which can be used in most rental cars (though it's worth checking), B36 a litre. The big fuel stations are the least costly places to fill up (*hai tem*), and many of these also have toilets, mini-marts and restaurants, though some of the more decrepit-looking fuel stations on the main highways only sell diesel. Most small villages have easy-to-spot roadside huts where the fuel is pumped out of a large barrel.

Renting a car

If you decide to **rent a car**, go to a reputable dealer, such as Avis, Budget or National (see p.34), or a rental company recommended by TAT, and make sure you get insurance from them. There are international car-rental places at many airports, including Bangkok's Suvarnabhumi, which is not a bad place to kick off, as you're on the edge of the city and within fairly easy, signposted reach of the major regional highways.

Car-rental places in provincial capitals and resorts are listed in the relevant accounts in this book. The price of a small car at a reputable company can start as low as B900 per day if booked online. In some parts of the country, including Chiang Mai, you'll still be able to rent a car or air-conditioned minibus with driver, which will cost from around B1000 for a local day-trip, more for a longer day-trip, up to about B3000 per day for a multi-day trip, including the driver's keep and petrol.

Jeeps or basic four-wheel drives are a lot more popular with farangs, especially on beach resorts and islands like Pattaya, Phuket and Ko Samui, but they're notoriously dangerous; a huge number of tourists manage to roll their jeeps on steep hillsides and sharp bends. Jeep rental usually works out somewhere around B1000–1200 per day.

International companies will accept your credit-card details as surety, but smaller agents will usually want to hold on to your passport.

CAR RENTAL AGENCIES

Avis Ⓦ avisthailand.com
Budget Ⓦ budget.co.th
Master Ⓦ mastercarrental.com
National Ⓦ nationalcarthailand.com
Thai Rentacar Ⓦ thairentacar.com

Renting a motorbike

One of the best ways of exploring the countryside is to **rent a motorbike**, an especially popular option in the north of the country. You'll never be asked for a driving licence, but take it easy out there – Thailand's roads are not really the place to learn to ride a motorbike from scratch. Bikes of around 100cc, either fully automatic or with step-through gears, are best for inexperienced riders, but aren't really suited for long slogs. If you're going to hit the dirt roads you'll certainly need something more powerful, like a 125–250cc trail bike. These have the edge in gear choice and are the best bikes for steep slopes, though an inexperienced rider may find these machines a handful; the less widely available 125–250cc road bikes are easier to control and much cheaper on fuel.

Rental **prices** for the day usually work out at somewhere around B150–200 for a small bike and B500 for a good trail bike, though you can bargain for a discount on a long rental. Renters will often ask for a deposit and your passport or credit-card details; insurance is not often available, so it's a good idea to make sure your travel insurance covers you for possible mishaps.

Before signing anything, **check the bike** thoroughly – test the brakes, look for oil leaks, check the treads and the odometer, and make sure the chain isn't stretched too tight (a tight chain is more likely to break) – and preferably take it for a test run. As you will have to pay an inflated price for any damage when you get back, make a note on the contract of any defects such as broken mirrors, indicators and so on. Make sure you know what kind of fuel the bike takes as well.

As far as **equipment** goes, a helmet is essential – most rental places provide poorly made ones, but they're better than nothing. Helmets are obligatory on all motorbike journeys, and the law is often rigidly enforced with on-the-spot fines in major tourist resorts. You'll need sunglasses if your helmet doesn't have a visor. Long trousers, a long-sleeved top and decent shoes will provide a second skin if you go over, which most people do at some stage. Pillions should wear long trousers to avoid getting nasty burns from the exhaust. For the sake of stability, leave most of your luggage in baggage storage and pack as small a bag as possible, strapping it tightly to the bike with bungy cords – these can usually be provided. Once on the road, oil the chain at least every other day, keep the radiator topped up and fill up with oil every 300km or so.

For expert **advice** on motorbike travel in Thailand, check out David Unkovich's website (Ⓦ gt-rider .com).

Cycling

The options for **cycling** in Thailand are numerous, whether you choose to ride the length of the country from the Malaysian border to Chiang Rai, or opt for a dirt-road adventure in the mountains around Chiang Mai. Most Thai roads are in good condition and clearly signposted; although the western and northern borders are mountainous, the rest of the country is surprisingly flat. The secondary **roads** (distinguished by their three-digit numbers) are paved but carry far less traffic than the main arteries and are the preferred cycling option. Traffic is reasonably well behaved and personal safety is not a major concern as long as you "ride to survive"; dogs, however, can be a nuisance on minor roads so it's probably worth having rabies shots before your trip. There are bike shops in nearly every town, and basic equipment and repairs are cheap. Unless you head into the remotest regions around the Burmese border you are rarely more than 25km from food, water and accommodation. Overall, the best time to cycle is during the cool, dry season from November to February and the least good from April to July (see p.10).

The traffic into and out of Bangkok is dense so it's worth hopping on a bus or train for the first 50–100km to your starting point. Intercity buses, taxis and most Thai domestic planes will **carry your bike** free of charge. Intercity trains will only transport your bike (for a cargo fare – about the price of a person) if there is a luggage carriage attached, unless you dismantle it and carry it as luggage in the compartment with you. Songthaews will carry your bike on the roof for a fare (about the price of a person).

Local one-day cycle tours and **bike-rental outlets** (B30–100 per day) are listed throughout this book. There are also a number of organized **cycle tours**, both nationwide (see p.26) and in northern Thailand (see p.280). A very useful English-language resource is Ⓦ bicyclethailand.com, while Biking Asia with Mr Pumpy (Ⓦ mrpumpy.net) gives detailed but dated accounts of some cycling routes in Thailand.

Cycling practicalities

Strong, light, quality **mountain bikes** are the most versatile choice. 26-inch wheels are standard throughout Thailand and are strongly recommended; dual-use (combined road and off-road) tyres are best for touring. As regards panniers and **equipment**, the most important thing is to travel light. Carry a few spare spokes, but don't overdo it with too many tools and spares; parts are cheap in Thailand and most problems can be fixed quickly at any bike shop.

Bringing your bike from home is the best option as you are riding a known quantity. **Importing** it by plane should be straightforward, but check with the airlines for details. Most Asian airlines do not charge extra.

Buying in Thailand is also a possibility: the range is reasonable and prices tend to be cheaper than in the West or Australia. In Bangkok, the best outlet is Probike at 237/2 Thanon Rajdamri (actually off Soi Sarasin next to Lumphini Park; ☎02 253 3384, ⓦprobike.co.th); Velo Thailand (see p.138) also sell international-brand aluminium-frame bikes, as well as renting mountain bikes for B300 per day. You can also rent good mountain bikes through the Bangkok cycle-tour operator Spice Roads (☎02 712 5305, ⓦspiceroads.com) for B280–400 per day. There are a few good outlets in Chiang Mai, too (see also ⓦchiangmaicycling.org): Cacti (see p.290), who also **rent** all manner of mountain and city bikes; Chaitawat, on Thanon Phra Pokklao, south off Thanon Ratchamankha, on the right (☎053 279890); and Canadian-owned Top Gear, 173 Thanon Chang Moi (☎053 233450).

Hitching

Public transport being so inexpensive, you should only have to resort to **hitching** in the most remote areas, in which case you'll probably get a lift to the nearest bus or songthaew stop quite quickly. On routes served by buses and trains, hitching is not standard practice, but in other places locals do rely on regular passers-by (such as national park officials), and you can make use of this "service" too. As with hitching anywhere in the world, think twice about hitching solo or at night, especially if you're female. Like bus drivers, truck drivers are notorious users of amphetamines, so you may want to wait for a safer offer.

Accommodation

For the simplest double room, prices start at a bargain B150 in the outlying regions, B200 in Bangkok, and B400 in the pricier resorts. Tourist centres invariably offer a tempting range of more upmarket choices but in these areas rates fluctuate according to demand, plummeting during the off-season, peaking over the Christmas fortnight and, in some places, rising at weekends throughout the year.

Guesthouses, bungalows and hostels

Most of Thailand's **budget accommodation** is in **guesthouses** and **bungalows**. These are small, traveller-friendly hotels whose services nearly always include an inexpensive restaurant and safe storage for valuables and left luggage, and often also run to internet access (sometimes even in-room wi-fi) and a tour desk. The difference between guesthouses and bungalows is mostly in their design, with "bungalows" – which are generally found on the beach and in rural areas – mostly comprising detached or semi-detached rooms in huts, villas, chalets or indeed bungalows, and "guesthouses" being either a purpose-built mini-hotel or a

---

ACCOMMODATION PRICES

Throughout this guide, the prices given for guesthouses, bungalows and hotels represent the **minimum** you can expect to pay in each establishment in the **high season** (roughly July, Aug and Nov–Feb) for a typical **double room**, booked via the hotel website where available; there may however be an extra "peak" supplement for the Christmas–New Year period. If travelling on your own, expect to pay between sixty and one hundred percent of the rates quoted for a double room. Where a hostel or guesthouse also offers **dormitory beds**, the minimum price per bed is also given; where a place has rooms in distinct categories (eg fan/air-con, shared bathroom/en suite), we've given the minimum price for a double in each category. Top-end hotels will add **seven percent tax** and **ten percent service charge** to your bill; the prices given in the guide are net rates after taxes have been added.

BATHROOM ETIQUETTE

Although modern, Western-style bathrooms are commonplace throughout Thailand, it's as well to be forewarned about local bathroom etiquette.

Sit-down **toilets** are the norm but public amenities, especially at bus and train stations, and in some homes and old-style guesthouses and hotels, tend to be squat toilets. Thais traditionally don't use **paper** but wash rather than wipe themselves after going to the toilet. Modern bathrooms are fitted with a special hose for this purpose, while more primitive bathrooms just provide a **bucket of water and a dipper**. Thais always use their left hand for washing – and their right hand for eating (see p.40). As Thai plumbing is notoriously sluggish, where toilet paper is provided, it's normal to throw it in the waste basket and not down the U-bend. If a toilet is not plumbed in, you flush it yourself with water from the bucket. In really basic hotel bathrooms with no **shower** facilities, you also use the bucket and dipper for scoop-and-slosh bathing.

converted home. En-suite showers and flush toilets are common in both, but at the cheapest places you might be showering with a bowl dipped into a large water jar, and using squat toilets.

Many guesthouses and bungalows offer a spread of options to cater for all budgets: their **cheapest rooms** will often be furnished with nothing more than a double bed, a blanket and a fan (window optional, private bathroom extra) and might cost anything from B150–300 for two people, depending on the location and the competition. A similar room with **en-suite** bathroom, and possibly more stylish furnishings, generally comes in at B200–600, while for a room with **air-conditioner**, and perhaps a TV and fridge as well, you're looking at B350–1500. In the north of Thailand in the cool season, air conditioning is more or less redundant, but you might want to check that your room has a hot shower.

In the most popular tourist centres at the busiest times of year, the best-known guesthouses are often full night after night. Some will take **bookings** and advance payment via their websites, but for those that don't it's usually a question of turning up and waiting for a vacancy. At most guesthouses **checkout time** is either 11am or noon.

Generally you should be wary of taking accommodation advice from a **tout** or tuk-tuk driver, as they demand commission from guesthouse owners, which, if not passed directly on to you via a higher room price, can have a crippling effect on the smaller guesthouses. If a tout claims your intended accommodation is "full" or "no good" or has "burnt down", it's always worth phoning to check yourself. Touts can come into their own, however, on islands such as Ko Lanta where it can be a long and expensive ride to your chosen beach, and frustrating if you then discover your bungalow is full; island touts usually sweet-talk you on the

boat and then transport you for free to view their accommodation, ideally with no obligation to stay.

With only a dozen or so registered **youth hostels** in the country, bookable via ⓦtyha.org, it's not worth becoming a Hostelling International member just for your trip to Thailand, especially as card-holders get only a small discount and room rates work out the same as or more expensive than guest-house equivalents. In addition, there are a small but growing number of smart, modern, non-affiliated **hostels**, especially in Bangkok. They usually work out more expensive than budget guesthouses but are good places to meet other travellers.

Budget hotels

Thai sales reps and other people travelling for business rather than pleasure rarely use guesthouses, opting instead for **budget hotels**, which offer rooms for around B150–600. Usually run by Chinese-Thais, these functional three- or four-storey places are found in every sizeable town, often near the bus station or central market. Beds are large enough for a couple, so it's quite acceptable for two people to ask and pay for a "single" room (*hawng thiang diaw*, literally a "one-bedded room"). Though the rooms are generally clean, en suite and furnished with either a fan or air-con, there's rarely an on-site restaurant and the atmosphere is generally less convivial than at guesthouses. A number of budget hotels also double as brothels, though as a farang you're unlikely to be offered this sideline, and you might not even notice the goings-on.

Advance reservations are accepted over the phone, but this is rarely necessary, as such hotels rarely fill up. The only time you may have difficulty finding a budget hotel room is during Chinese New Year (a moveable three-day period in late Jan or Feb), when many Chinese-run hotels close and others get booked up fast.

Tourist hotels

The rest of the accommodation picture is all about **tourist hotels** which, like anywhere in the world, come in all sizes and qualities and are often best booked via online discount accommodation booking services such as Ⓦsawadee.com. One way or another, it's a good idea to **reserve ahead** in popular tourist areas during peak season.

Rates for **middle-ranking hotels** fall between B600 and B2000. For this you can expect many of the trimmings of a top-end hotel – air-con, TV and mini-bar in the room, plus an on-site pool, restaurant and perhaps nightclub – but with dated and possibly faded furnishings and little of the style of the famous big names; they're often the kind of places that once stood at the top of the range, but were outclassed when the multinational luxury hotels muscled in.

Many of Thailand's **expensive hotels** belong to the big international chains: Sheraton, Marriott and Sofitel all have a strong presence in the country and are closely followed by upmarket home-grown groups such as Amari, Dusit and Centara. Between them they maintain premium standards in Bangkok and major resorts at prices of B3000 (£60/US$100) and upward for a double – far less than you'd pay for equivalent accommodation in the West.

Thailand also boasts an increasing number of deliciously stylish **luxury hotels**, many of them designed as intimate, small-scale **boutique** hotels, with chic, minimalist decor, exceptional service and excellent facilities that often include private plunge pools and a spa. A night in one of these places will rarely cost you less than B6000 (£120/US$200), and may set you back more than twice as much, though they're still often outstanding value for the honeymoon-style indulgence that they offer; see accommodation listings for Bangkok, Chiang Mai, Ko Samui, Khao Lak and Phuket for some suggestions. As in the West, however, the term "boutique" is overused, and a "boutique" guesthouse or hotel may in practice be little more than "small". Some luxury hotels quote rates in US dollars, though you can always pay in baht.

Homestays

As guesthouses have become increasingly hotel-like and commercial in their facilities and approach, many tourists looking for old-style local hospitality are choosing **homestay accommodation** instead. Homestay facilities are nearly always simple, and cheap at around B150 per person per night, with guests staying in a shared spare room and eating with the family. Homestays give an unparalleled insight into typical Thai (usually rural) life and can often be incorporated into a programme that includes experiencing village activities such as rice farming, squid fishing, rubber tapping or silk weaving. They are also a positive way of supporting small communities, as all your money will feed right back into the village. As well as listed homestays in Amphawa (see p.186), Doi Inthanon (see p.333), Mae Sariang (see p.337), Mae Hong Son (see p.341 & p.347), Chiang Rai (see p.358), Ban Prasat (see p.449), Mukdahan (see p.501), Ban Khiriwong (see p.587), Khuraburi (see p.606) and Krabi (see p.660), there are many others bookable through tour operators (see p.26) or via, for example, Ⓦhomestaybooking.com /homestay-thailand.

National parks and camping

Nearly all the **national parks** have accommodation facilities, usually comprising a series of simple concrete bungalows that cost at least B600 for two or more beds plus a basic bathroom. Because most of their custom comes from Thai families and student groups, park officials are sometimes loath to discount them for lone travellers, though a few parks do offer dorm-style accommodation at around B100 a bed. In most parks, advance booking is unnecessary except at weekends and national holidays.

If you do want to pre-book, you can do so up to sixty days ahead of your stay at Ⓦdnp.go.th. As credit-card payment is not possible on this website, you need to pay in cash or via bank draft within two days of booking, most conveniently at any branch of Krung Thai bank, at designated international banks, or at the National Park headquarters in question; see the website given above for comprehensive details. Affiliated with the National Parks department, a new website, Ⓦthaiforest booking.com, in theory allows booking with a credit card (up to 65 days in advance), though it doesn't work very well. If you turn up without booking, check in at the park headquarters, which is usually adjacent to the visitor centre.

In a few parks, private operators have set up low-cost guesthouses on the outskirts, and these generally make more attractive and economical places to stay.

Camping

You can usually **camp** in a national park for a nominal fee of B60 per two-person tent, and some national parks also rent out fully equipped tents from B150 (bookable through a separate section on Ⓦ dnp.go.th). Unless you're planning an extensive tour of national parks, though, there's little point in lugging a tent around Thailand: accommodation everywhere else is very inexpensive, and there are no campsites inside town perimeters, though camping is allowed on nearly all islands and beaches, many of which are national parks in their own right.

Food and drink

Bangkok and Chiang Mai are the country's big culinary centres, boasting the cream of gourmet Thai restaurants and the best international cuisines. The rest of the country is by no means a gastronomic wasteland, however, and you can eat well and cheaply in even the smallest provincial towns, many of which offer the additional attraction of regional specialities. In fact you could eat more than adequately without ever entering a restaurant, as itinerant food vendors hawking hot and cold snacks materialize in even the most remote spots, as well as on trains and buses – and night markets often serve customers from dusk until dawn.

Hygiene is a consideration when eating anywhere in Thailand, but being too cautious means you'll end up spending a lot of money and missing out on some real local treats. Wean your stomach gently by avoiding excessive amounts of chillies and too much fresh fruit in the first few days.

You can be pretty sure that any noodle stall or curry shop that's permanently packed with customers is a safe bet. Furthermore, because most Thai dishes can be cooked in under five minutes, you'll rarely have to contend with stuff that's been left to smoulder and stew. Foods that are generally considered high risk include salads, ice cream, shellfish and raw or undercooked meat, fish or eggs. If you're really concerned about health standards you could stick to restaurants and food stalls displaying a "**Clean Food Good Taste**" sign, part of a food sanitation project set up by the Ministry of Public Health, TAT and the Ministry of the Interior.

Most restaurants in Thailand are open every day for lunch and dinner; we've given full opening hours throughout the Guide. In a few of the country's most expensive restaurants, mostly in Bangkok, a ten percent service charge and possibly even seven percent VAT may be added to your bill.

For those interested in **learning Thai cookery**, short courses designed for visitors are held in Bangkok (see p.153), Chiang Mai (see p.283) and dozens of other tourist centres around the country.

Where to eat

A lot of tourists eschew the huge range of Thai **places to eat**, despite their obvious attractions, and opt instead for the much "safer" restaurants in guesthouses and hotels. Almost all tourist accommodation has a kitchen, and while some are excellent, the vast majority serve up bland imitations of Western fare alongside equally pale versions of common Thai dishes. Having said that, it can be a relief to get your teeth into a processed-cheese sandwich after five days' trekking in the jungle, and guesthouses do serve comfortingly familiar Western breakfasts.

Throughout the country most **inexpensive Thai restaurants** and cafés specialize in one general food type or preparation method, charging around B40–50 a dish – a "noodle shop", for example, will do fried noodles and/or noodle soups, plus maybe a basic fried rice, but they won't have curries or meat or fish dishes. Similarly, a restaurant displaying whole roast chickens and ducks in its window will offer these sliced, usually with chillies and sauces and served over rice, but their menu probably won't extend to noodles or fish, while in "curry shops" your options are limited to the vats of curries stewing away in the hot cabinet.

To get a wider array of low-cost food, it's sometimes best to head for the local **night market** (*talaat yen*), a term for the gatherings of open-air night-time kitchens found in every town. Sometimes operating from 6pm to 6am, they are typically to be found on permanent patches close to the fruit and vegetable market or the bus station, and as often as not they're the best and most entertaining places to eat, not to mention the least expensive – after a lip-smacking feast of savoury dishes, a fruit drink and a dessert you'll come away no more than B150 poorer.

A typical night market has maybe thirty-odd "specialist" pushcart kitchens (*rot khen*) jumbled together, each fronted by several sets of tables and stools. Noodle and fried-rice vendors always feature prominently, as do sweets stalls, heaped high with sticky rice cakes wrapped in banana leaves or thick with bags of tiny sweetcorn pancakes hot from the

FRUITS OF THAILAND

You'll find **fruit** (*phonlamai*) offered everywhere in Thailand – neatly sliced in glass boxes on hawker carts, blended into delicious shakes and served as a dessert in restaurants. The fruits described below can be found in all parts of Thailand, though some are seasonal. The country's more familiar fruits include forty varieties of **banana** (*kluay*), dozens of different **mangoes** (*mamuang*), three types of **pineapple** (*sapparot*), **coconuts** (*maprao*), **oranges** (*som*), **limes** (*manao*) and **watermelons** (*taeng moh*). Thailand's most prized and expensive fruit is the **durian** (*thurian*; see p.131).

To avoid stomach trouble, **peel all fruit** before eating it, and use common sense if you're tempted to buy it pre-peeled on the street, avoiding anything that looks fly-blown or seems to have been sitting in the sun for hours.

Custard apple (soursop; *noina*; July–Sept). Inside the knobbly, muddy green skin is a creamy, almond-coloured blancmange-like flesh, with a strong flavour of strawberries and pears, and a hint of cinnamon, and many seeds.

Guava (*farang*; year-round). The apple of the tropics has green textured skin and sweet, crisp pink or white flesh, studded with tiny edible seeds. Has five times the vitamin C content of an orange and is sometimes eaten cut into strips and sprinkled with sugar and chilli.

Jackfruit (*khanun*; year-round). This large, pear-shaped fruit can weigh up to 20kg and has a thick, bobbly, greeny-yellow shell protecting sweet yellow flesh. Green, unripe jackfruit is sometimes cooked as a vegetable in curries.

Longan (*lamyai*; July–Oct). A close relative of the lychee, with succulent white flesh covered in thin, brittle skin.

Lychee (*linjii*; April–May). Under rough, reddish-brown skin, the lychee has sweet, richly flavoured white flesh, rose scented and with plenty of vitamin C.

Mangosteen (*mangkut*; April–Sept). The size of a small apple, with smooth, purple skin and a fleshy inside that divides into succulent white segments that are sweet though slightly acidic.

Papaya (paw-paw; *malakaw*; year-round). Looks like an elongated watermelon, with smooth green skin and yellowy-orange flesh that's a rich source of vitamins A and C. It's a favourite in fruit salads and shakes, and sometimes appears in its green, unripe form in salads, notably *som tam*.

Pomelo (*som oh*; Oct–Dec). The largest of all the citrus fruits, it looks rather like a grapefruit, though it is slightly drier and has less flavour.

Rambutan (*ngaw*; May–Sept). The bright red rambutan's soft, spiny exterior has given it its name – *rambut* means "hair" in Malay. Usually about the size of a golf ball, it has a white, opaque flesh of delicate flavour, similar to a lychee.

Rose apple (*chomphuu*; year-round). Linked in myth with the golden fruit of immortality; small and egg-shaped, with white, rose-scented flesh.

Sapodilla (sapota; *lamut*; Sept–Dec). These small, brown, rough-skinned ovals look a bit like kiwi fruit and conceal a grainy, yellowish pulp that tastes almost honey-sweet.

Tamarind (*makhaam*; Dec–Jan). A Thai favourite and a pricey delicacy – carrying the seeds is said to make you safe from wounding by knives or bullets. Comes in rough, brown pods containing up to ten seeds, each surrounded by a sticky, dry pulp which has a sour, lemony taste.

griddle – and no night market is complete without its fruit-drink stall, offering banana shakes and freshly squeezed orange, lemon and tomato juices. In the best setups you'll find a lot more besides: curries, barbecued sweetcorn, satay sticks of pork and chicken, deep-fried insects, fresh pineapple, watermelon and mango and – if the town's by a river or near the sea – heaps of fresh fish. Having decided what you want, you order from the cook (or the cook's dogsbody) and sit down at the nearest table; there is no territorialism about night markets, so it's normal to eat several dishes from separate stalls and rely on the nearest cook to sort out the bill.

Some large markets, particularly in Bangkok, have separate **food court** areas where you buy coupons first and select food and drink to their value at the stalls of your choice. This is also usually the modus operandi in the food courts found in department stores and shopping centres across the country.

For a more relaxing ambience, Bangkok and the larger towns have a range of **upmarket restaurants**, some specializing in **"royal" Thai cuisine**, which is differentiated mainly by the quality of the ingredients, the complexity of preparation and the way the food is presented. Great care is taken over how individual dishes look: they are served in small portions and decorated with carved fruit and vegetables in a way that used to be the prerogative of royal cooks, but has now filtered down to the common folk. The cost of such delights is not prohibitive, either – a meal in one of these places is unlikely to cost more than B500 per person.

How to eat

Thai food is eaten with a **fork** (left hand) and a **spoon** (right hand); there is no need for a knife as food is served in bite-sized chunks, which are forked onto the spoon and fed into the mouth. Cutlery is often delivered to the table wrapped in a perplexingly tiny pink napkin: Thais use this, not for their lap, but to give their fork, spoon and plate an extra wipe-down before they eat. Steamed **rice** (*khao*) is served with most meals, and indeed the most commonly heard phrase for "to eat" is *kin khao* (literally, "eat rice"). **Chopsticks** are provided only for noodle dishes, and northeastern sticky-rice dishes are always eaten with the **fingers of your right hand**. Never eat with the fingers of your left hand, which is used for washing after going to the toilet.

So that complementary taste combinations can be enjoyed, the dishes in a Thai meal are served all at once, even the soup, and shared communally. The more people, the more taste and texture sensations;

if there are only two of you, it's normal to order three dishes, plus your own individual plates of steamed rice, while three diners would order four dishes, and so on. Only put a serving of one dish on your rice plate each time, and then only one or two spoonfuls.

Bland food is anathema to Thais, and restaurant tables everywhere come decked out with **condiment sets** featuring the four basic flavours (salty, sour, sweet and spicy): usually fish sauce with chopped chillies; vinegar with chopped chillies; sugar; and dried chillies – and often extra bowls of ground peanuts and a bottle of chilli ketchup as well. Similarly, many individual Thai dishes are served with their own specific, usually spicy, condiment dip (*nam jim*). If you do bite into a **chilli**, the way to combat the searing heat is to take a mouthful of plain rice and/or beer: swigging water just exacerbates the sensation.

What to eat

Five fundamental tastes are identified in Thai cuisine – spiciness, sourness, bitterness, saltiness and sweetness – and diners aim to share a variety of dishes that impart a balance of these flavours, along with complementary textures. Lemon grass, basil, coriander, galangal, chilli, garlic, lime juice, coconut milk and fermented fish sauce are just some of the distinctive components that bring these tastes to life. A detailed food and drink glossary can be found at the end of "Contexts" (see p.794).

VEGETARIANS AND VEGANS

Very few Thais are **vegetarian** (*mangsawirat*) but, if you can make yourself understood, you can often get a non-meat or fish alternative to what's on the menu; simply ask the cook to exclude meat and fish: *mai sai neua, mai sai plaa*. You may end up eating a lot of unexciting vegetable fried rice and *phat thai* minus the shrimps, but in better restaurants you should be able to get veggie versions of most curries; the mushroom version of chicken and coconut soup is also a good standby: ask for *tom kha hed*. Browsing food stalls also expands your options, with barbecued sweetcorn, nuts, fruit and other non-meaty goodies all common. The two ingredients that you will have to consider compromising on are the fermented **fish sauce** and **shrimp paste** that are fundamental to most Thai dishes; only in the vegan Thai restaurants described below, and in tourist spots serving specially concocted Thai and Western veggie dishes, can you be sure of avoiding them.

If you're **vegan** (*jay*, sometimes spelt "*jeh*") you'll need to stress when you order that you don't want egg, as they get used a lot; cheese and other dairy produce, however, don't feature at all in Thai cuisine. Many towns will have one or more **vegan restaurants** (*raan ahaan jay*), which are usually run by members of a temple or Buddhist sect and operate from unadorned premises off the main streets; because strict Buddhists prefer not to eat late in the day, most of the restaurants open early, at around 6 or 7am, and close by 2pm. Most of these places have a yellow and red sign, though few display an English-language name. Nor is there ever a menu: customers simply choose from the trays of veggie stir-fries and curries, nearly all of them made with soya products, that are laid out canteen-style. Most places charge around B40 for a couple of helpings served over a plate of brown rice.

Curries and soups

Thai **curries** (*kaeng*) have a variety of curry pastes as their foundation: elaborate blends of herbs, spices, garlic, shallots and chilli peppers ground together with pestle and mortar. The use of some of these spices, as well as coconut cream, was imported from India long ago; curries that don't use coconut cream are naturally less sweet and thinner, with the consistency of soups. While some curries, such as *kaeng karii* (mild and yellow) and *kaeng matsaman* ("Muslim curry", with potatoes, peanuts and usually beef), still show their roots, others have been adapted into quintessentially Thai dishes, notably *kaeng khiaw wan* (sweet and green), *kaeng phet* (red and hot) and *kaeng phanaeng* (thick and savoury, with peanuts). *Kaeng som* generally contains fish and takes its distinctive sourness from the addition of tamarind or, in the northeast, okra leaves. Traditionally eaten during the cool season, *kaeng liang* uses up bland vegetables, but is made aromatic with hot peppercorns.

Eaten simultaneously with other dishes, not as a starter, Thai **soups** often have the tang of lemon grass, kaffir lime leaves and galangal, and are sometimes made extremely spicy with chillies. Two favourites are *tom kha kai*, a creamy coconut chicken soup; and *tom yam kung*, a hot and sour prawn soup without coconut milk. *Khao tom*, a starchy rice soup that's generally eaten for breakfast, meets the approval of few Westerners, except as a traditional hangover cure.

Salads

One of the lesser-known delights of Thai cuisine is the *yam* or **salad**, which imparts most of the fundamental flavours in an unusual and refreshing harmony. *Yam* come in many permutations – with noodles, meat, seafood or vegetables – but at the heart of every variety is a liberal squirt of lime juice and a fiery sprinkling of chillies. Salads to look out for include *yam som oh* (pomelo), *yam hua plee* (banana flowers) and *yam plaa duk foo* (fluffy deep-fried catfish).

Noodle and rice dishes

Sold on street stalls everywhere, **noodles** come in assorted varieties – including *kway tiaw* (made with rice flour) and *ba mii* (egg noodles) – and get boiled up as soups (*nam*), doused in gravy (*rat na*) or stir-fried (*haeng*, "dry", or *phat*, "fried"). Most famous of all is *phat thai* ("Thai fry-up"), a delicious combination of noodles (usually *kway tiaw*), egg, tofu and spring onions, sprinkled with ground peanuts and lime, and often spiked with tiny dried shrimps.

Other faithful standbys include fried rice (*khao phat*) and cheap, one-dish meals served on a bed of steamed rice, notably *khao kaeng* (with curry).

Regional dishes

Many of the specialities of **northern Thailand** originated in Burma, including *khao soi*, featuring both boiled and crispy egg noodles plus beef, chicken or pork in a curried coconut soup; and *kaeng hang lay*, a pork curry with ginger, turmeric and tamarind. Also look out for spicy dipping sauces such as *nam phrik ong*, made with minced pork, roast tomatoes and lemon grass, and served with crisp cucumber slices.

The crop most suited to the infertile lands of **Isaan** is sticky rice (*khao niaw*), which replaces the standard grain as the staple for northeasterners. Served in a rattan basket, it's usually eaten with the fingers, rolled up into small balls and dipped into chilli sauces. It's perfect with such spicy local delicacies as *som tam*, a green-papaya salad with raw chillies, green beans, tomatoes, peanuts and dried shrimps (or fresh crab). Although you'll find basted barbecued chicken on a stick (*kai yaang*) all over Thailand, it originated in Isaan and is especially tasty in its home region. Raw minced pork, beef or chicken is the basis of another popular Isaan and northern dish, *laap*, a salad that's subtly flavoured with mint and lime. A similar northeastern salad is *nam tok*, featuring grilled beef or pork and roasted rice powder, which takes its name, "waterfall", from its refreshing blend of complex tastes.

Aside from putting a greater emphasis on seafood, **southern Thai** cuisine displays a marked Malaysian and Muslim aspect as you near the border, notably in *khao mok kai*, the local version of a biryani: chicken and rice cooked with turmeric and other Indian spices, and served with chicken soup. Southern markets often serve *khao yam* for breakfast or lunch, a delicious salad of dried cooked rice, dried shrimp and grated coconut served with a sweet sauce. You'll also find many types of *roti*, a flatbread sold from pushcart griddles and, in its plain form, rolled with condensed milk. Other versions include savoury *mataba*, with minced chicken or beef, and *roti kaeng*, served with curry sauce for breakfast. A huge variety of curries are also dished up in the south, many substituting shrimp paste for fish sauce. Two of the most distinctive are *kaeng luang*, "yellow curry", featuring fish, turmeric, pineapple, squash, beans and green papaya; and *kaeng tai plaa*, a powerful combination of fish stomach with potatoes, beans, pickled bamboo shoots and turmeric.

Desserts

Desserts (*khanom*) don't really figure on most restaurant menus, but a few places offer bowls of *luk taan cheum*, a jellied concoction of lotus or palm seeds floating in a syrup scented with jasmine or other aromatic flowers. Coconut milk is a feature of most other desserts, notably delicious coconut ice cream, *khao niaw mamuang* (sticky rice with mango), and a royal Thai cuisine special of coconut custard (*sangkhayaa*) cooked inside a small pumpkin, whose flesh you can also eat.

Drinks

Thais don't drink water straight from the tap, and nor should you; plastic bottles of drinking **water** (*nam plao*) are sold countrywide, in even the smallest villages, for around B10 and should be used even when brushing your teeth. Cheap restaurants and hotels generally serve free jugs of boiled water, which should be fine to drink, though they are not as foolproof as the bottles. In some large towns, notably Chiang Mai, you'll come across blue-and-white roadside machines that dispense purified water for B1 for 1–2 litres (bring your own bottle).

Night markets, guesthouses and restaurants do a good line in freshly squeezed **fruit juices** such as lime (*nam manao*) and orange (*nam som*), which often come with salt and sugar already added, particularly upcountry. The same places will usually do **fruit shakes** as well, blending bananas (*nam kluay*), papayas (*nam malakaw*), pineapples (*nam sapparot*) and others with liquid sugar or condensed milk (or yoghurt, to make lassi). Fresh **coconut water** (*nam maprao*) is another great thirst-quencher – you buy the whole fruit dehusked, decapitated and chilled – as is **pandanus-leaf juice** (*bai toey*); Thais are also very partial to freshly squeezed **sugar-cane juice** (*nam awy*), which is sickeningly sweet.

Bottled and canned brand-name **soft drinks** are sold all over the place, with a particularly wide range in the ubiquitous 7-Eleven chain stores. Glass soft-drink bottles are returnable, so some shops and drink stalls have a system of pouring the contents into a small plastic bag (fastened with an elastic band and with a straw inserted) rather than charging you the extra for taking away the bottle. The larger restaurants keep their soft drinks refrigerated, but smaller cafés and shops add **ice** (*nam khaeng*) to glasses and bags. Most ice is produced commercially under hygienic conditions, but it might become less pure in transit so be wary (ice cubes are generally a better bet than shaved ice) –

and don't take ice if you have diarrhoea. For those travelling with children, or just partial themselves to **dairy products**, UHT-preserved milk and chilled yoghurt drinks are widely available (especially at 7-Eleven stores), as are a variety of soya drinks.

Weak Chinese **tea** (*narn chaa*) makes a refreshing alternative to water and often gets served in Chinese restaurants and roadside cafés, while posher restaurants keep stronger Chinese and Western-style teas. Instant Nescafé is usually the **coffee** (*kaafae*) offered to farangs, even if freshly ground Thai-grown coffee – notably several excellent kinds of coffee from the mountains of the north – is available. If you would like to try traditional Thai coffee, most commonly found at Chinese-style cafés in the south of the country or at outdoor markets, and prepared through filtering the grounds through a cloth, ask for *kaafae thung* (literally, "bag coffee"; sometimes known as *kaafae boran* – "traditional coffee" – or *kopii*), normally served very bitter with sugar as well as sweetened condensed milk alongside a glass of black or Chinese tea to wash it down with. Fresh Western-style coffee (*kaafae sot*) in the form of Italian espresso, cappuccino and other derivatives has recently become popular among Thais, so you'll now come across espresso machines in large towns all over the country (though some of these new coffee bars, frustratingly, don't open for breakfast, as locals tend to get their fix later in the day).

Alcoholic drinks

The two most famous local **beers** (*bia*) are Singha (ask for "bia sing") and Chang, though many travellers find Singha's weaker brew, Leo, more palatable than either. In shops you can expect to pay around B30 for a 330ml bottle of these beers, B50 for a 660ml bottle. All manner of slightly pricier foreign beers are now brewed in Thailand, including Heineken and Asahi, and in the most touristy areas you'll find expensive imported bottles from all over the world.

Wine is now found on plenty of upmarket and tourist-oriented restaurant menus, but expect to be disappointed by both quality and price, which is jacked up by heavy taxation. Thai wine is now produced at several vineyards, including at Château de Loei near Phu Reua National Park in the northeast, which produces quite tasty reds, whites including a dessert wine, a rosé and brandy (see p.488).

At about B80 for a hip-flask-sized 375ml bottle, the local **whisky** is a lot better value, and Thais think nothing of consuming a bottle a night, heavily diluted with ice and soda or Coke. The most palatable and widely available of these is Mekong, which is very pleasant once you've stopped expecting it to taste like Scotch; distilled from rice, Mekong is 35 percent proof, deep gold in colour and tastes slightly sweet. If that's not to your taste, a pricier Thai **rum** is also available, Sang Som, made from sugar cane, and even stronger than the whisky at forty percent proof. Check the menu carefully when ordering a bottle of Mekong from a bar in a tourist area, as they often ask up to five times more than you'd pay in a guesthouse or shop. A hugely popular way to enjoy whisky or rum at beach resorts is to pick up a bucket, containing a quarter-bottle of spirit, a mixer, Red Bull, ice and several straws, for around B200: that way you get to share with your friends and build a sandcastle afterwards.

You can **buy** beer and whisky in food stores, guesthouses and most restaurants; **bars** aren't strictly an indigenous feature as Thais traditionally don't drink out without eating, but you'll find plenty of Western-style drinking holes in Bangkok and larger centres elsewhere in the country, ranging from ultra-hip haunts in the capital to basic, open-to-the-elements "**bar-beers**".

Culture and etiquette

Tourist literature has marketed Thailand as the "Land of Smiles" so successfully that a lot of farangs arrive in the country expecting to be forgiven any outrageous behaviour. This is just not the case: there are some things so universally sacred in Thailand that even a hint of disrespect will cause deep offence.

The monarchy

It is both socially unacceptable and a criminal offence to make critical or defamatory remarks about the **royal family**. Thailand's monarchy might be a constitutional one, but almost every household displays a picture of King Bhumibol and Queen Sirikit in a prominent position, and respectful crowds mass whenever either of them makes a public appearance. The second of their four children, Crown Prince Vajiralongkorn, is the heir to the throne; his younger sister, Princess Royal Maha Chakri Sirindhorn, is often on TV and in the English-language newspapers as she is involved in many charitable projects. When addressing or speaking

about royalty, Thais use a special language full of deference, called *rajasap* (literally "royal language").

Thailand's **lese-majesty laws** are among the most strictly applied in the world, increasingly invoked as the Thai establishment becomes ever more uneasy over the erosion of traditional monarchist sentiments and the rise of critical voices, particularly on the internet (though these are generally quickly censored). Accusations of *lese-majesty* can be levelled by and against anyone, Thai national or farang, and must be investigated by the police. As a few high-profile cases involving foreigners have demonstrated, they can be raised for seemingly minor infractions, such as defacing a poster or being less than respectful in a work of fiction. Transgressions are met with jail sentences of up to 15 years.

Aside from keeping any anti-monarchy sentiments to yourself, you should be prepared to stand when the **king's anthem** is played at the beginning of every cinema programme, and to stop in your tracks if the town you're in plays the **national anthem** over its public address system – many small towns do this twice a day at 8am and again at 6pm, as do some train stations and airports. A less obvious point: as the king's head features on all Thai currency, you should never step on a coin or banknote, which is tantamount to kicking the king in the face.

Religion

Almost equally insensitive would be to disregard certain **religious** precepts. **Buddhism** plays a fundamental role in Thai culture, and Buddhist monuments should be treated with respect – which basically means wearing long trousers or knee-length skirts, covering your arms and removing your shoes whenever you visit one.

All **Buddha images** are sacred, however small, tacky or ruined, and should never be used as a backdrop for a portrait photo, clambered over, placed in a position of inferiority or treated in any manner that could be construed as disrespectful. In an attempt to prevent foreigners from committing any kind of transgression the government requires a special licence for all Buddha statues exported from the country (see p.63).

Monks come only just beneath the monarchy in the social hierarchy, and they too are addressed and discussed in a special language. If there's a monk around, he'll always get a seat on the bus, usually right at the back. Theoretically, monks are forbidden to have any close contact with women, which means, as a female, you mustn't sit or stand next to a monk, or even brush against his robes; if it's essential to pass him something, put the object down so that he can then pick it up – never hand it over directly. Nuns, however, get treated like ordinary women.

See "Contexts" for more on religious practices in Thailand (see p.746).

The body

The Western liberalism embraced by the Thai sex industry is very unrepresentative of the majority Thai attitude to the body. **Clothing** – or the lack of it – is what bothers Thais most about tourist behaviour. You need to dress modestly when entering temples (see p.85), but the same also applies to other important buildings and all public places. Stuffy and sweaty as it sounds, you should keep short shorts and vests for the real tourist resorts, and be especially diligent about covering up and, for women, wearing bras in rural areas. Baring your flesh on beaches is very much a Western practice: when Thais go swimming they often do so fully clothed, and they find topless and nude bathing offensive.

According to ancient Hindu belief, the **head** is the most sacred part of the body and the **feet** are the most unclean. This belief, imported into Thailand, means that it's very rude to touch another person's head or to point your feet either at a human being or at a sacred image – when sitting on a temple floor, for example, you should **tuck your legs beneath you** rather than stretch them out towards the Buddha. These hierarchies also forbid people from wearing **shoes** (which are even more unclean than feet) inside temples and most private homes, and – by extension – Thais take offence when they see someone sitting on the "head", or prow, of a boat. **Putting your feet up** on a table, a chair or a pillow is also considered very uncouth, and Thais will always take their shoes off if they need to stand on a train or bus seat to get to the luggage rack, for example. On a more practical note, the **left hand** is used for washing after going to the toilet (see p.40), so Thais never use it to put food in their mouth, pass things or shake hands – as a farang though, you'll be assumed to have different customs, so left-handers shouldn't worry unduly.

Social conventions

Thais rarely shake hands, instead using the **wai** to greet and say goodbye and to acknowledge respect, gratitude or apology. A prayer-like gesture made with raised hands, the *wai* changes according to the relative status of the two people involved: Thais can instantaneously assess which *wai* to use, but as a farang your safest bet is to raise your hands close to your chest, bow your head and place your fingertips just below your nose. If someone makes a *wai* at you, you should generally *wai* back, but it's safer not to initiate.

Public displays of **physical affection** in Thailand are more common between friends of the same sex than between lovers, whether hetero- or homosexual. Holding hands and hugging is as common among male friends as with females, so if you're caressed by a Thai acquaintance of the same sex, don't assume you're being propositioned.

Finally, there are three specifically Thai **concepts** you're bound to come across, which may help you comprehend a sometimes laissez-faire attitude to delayed buses and other inconveniences. The first, **jai yen**, translates literally as "cool heart" and is something everyone tries to maintain: most Thais hate raised voices, visible irritation and confrontations of any kind, so losing one's cool can have a much more inflammatory effect than in more combative cultures. Related to this is the oft-quoted response to a difficulty, **mai pen rai** – "never mind", "no problem" or "it can't be helped" – the verbal equivalent of an open-handed shoulder shrug, which has its basis in the Buddhist notion of karma (see p.747). And then there's **sanuk**, the wide-reaching philosophy of "fun", which, crass as it sounds, Thais do their best to inject into any situation, even work. Hence the crowds of inebriated Thais who congregate at waterfalls and other beauty spots on public holidays (travelling solo is definitely not *sanuk*), the reluctance to do almost anything without high-volume musical accompaniment, and the national waterfight which takes place during Songkhran every April on streets right across Thailand.

Thai names

Although all Thais have a first **name** and a family name, everyone is addressed by their first name – even when meeting strangers – prefixed by the title "**Khun**" (Mr/Ms); no one is ever addressed as Khun Surname, and even the phone book lists people by their given name. In Thailand you will often be addressed in an anglicized version of this convention, as "Mr Paul" or "Miss Lucy" for example. Bear in mind, though, that when a man is introduced to you as Khun Pirom, his wife will definitely not be Khun Pirom as well (that would be like calling them, for instance, "Mr and Mrs Paul"). Among friends and relatives, **Phii** ("older brother/sister") is often used instead of Khun when addressing older familiars (though as a tourist you're on surer ground with Khun), and **Nong** ("younger brother/sister") is used for younger ones.

Many Thai **first names** come from ancient Sanskrit and have an auspicious meaning; for example, Boon means good deeds, Porn means blessings, Siri means glory and Thawee means to increase. However, Thais of all ages are commonly known by the **nickname** given them soon after birth rather than by their official first name. This tradition arises out of a deep-rooted superstition that once a child has been officially named the spirits will begin to take an unhealthy interest in them, so a nickname is used instead to confuse the spirits. Common nicknames – which often bear no resemblance to the adult's personality or physique – include Yai (Big), Oun (Fat) and Muu (Pig); Lek or Noi (Little), Nok (Bird), Noo (Mouse) and Kung (Shrimp); and English nicknames like Apple, Joy or even Pepsi.

Family names were only introduced in 1913 (by Rama VI, who invented many of the aristocracy's surnames himself), and are used only in very formal situations, always in conjunction with the first name. It's quite usual for good friends never to know each other's surname. Ethnic Thais generally have short surnames like Somboon or Srisai, while the long, convoluted family names – such as Sonthanasumpun – usually indicate Chinese origin, not because they are phonetically Chinese but because many Chinese immigrants have chosen to adopt new Thai surnames and Thai law states that every newly created surname must be unique. Thus anyone who wants to change their surname must submit a shortlist of five unique Thai names – each to a maximum length of ten Thai characters – to be checked against a database of existing names. As more and more names are taken, Chinese family names get increasingly unwieldy, and more easily distinguishable from the pithy old Thai names.

The media

To keep you abreast of world affairs, there are several English-language newspapers in Thailand, though relatively mild forms of censorship (and self-censorship) affect all newspapers and the predominantly state-controlled media.

Newspapers and magazines

Of the hundreds of **Thai-language newspapers and magazines** published every week, the sensationalist daily tabloid *Thai Rath* attracts the widest readership, with circulation of around a million, while the moderately progressive *Matichon* is the leading quality daily, with an estimated circulation of 600,000.

Alongside these, two daily **English-language papers** – the *Bangkok Post* (Ⓦbangkokpost.com) and the *Nation* (Ⓦnationmultimedia.com) – are capable of adopting a fairly critical attitude to political goings-on and cover major domestic and international stories as well as tourist-related issues. The *Nation*, however, has recently adopted a split personality (and a more overt anti-red shirt stance) and now covers mostly business news. The *Post*'s *Spectrum* supplement, which comes inside the Sunday edition, carries investigative journalism. Both the *Post* and *Nation* are sold at most newsstands in the capital as well as in major provincial towns and tourist resorts; the more isolated places receive their few copies one day late. Details of local English-language publications are given in the relevant Guide accounts.

You can also pick up **foreign** magazines such as *Newsweek* and *Time* in Bangkok, Chiang Mai and the major resorts. English-language bookshops such as Bookazine and some expensive hotels carry air-freighted, or sometimes locally printed and stapled, copies of foreign national newspapers for at least B50 a copy; the latter are also sold in tourist-oriented minimarkets in the big resorts.

Television

There are six government-controlled, terrestrial **TV channels** in Thailand: channels 3, 5 (owned and operated by the army), 7 and 9 transmit a blend of news, documentaries, soaps, sports, talk and quiz shows, while the more serious-minded PBS (formerly Thaksin Shinawatra's ITV) and NBT are public-service channels, owned and operated by the government's public relations department. **Cable** networks – available in many mid-range and most upmarket hotel rooms – carry channels from all around the world, including CNN from the US, BBC World from the UK and sometimes ABC from Australia, as well as English-language movie channels, MTV and various sports and documentary channels. Both the *Bangkok Post* and the *Nation* print the daily TV and cable **schedule**.

Radio

Thailand boasts over five hundred **radio stations**, mostly music-oriented, ranging from Virgin Radio's Eazy (105.5 FM), which serves up Western pop, through *luk thung* (see p.772) on 95FM, to Fat Radio, which plays Thai indie sounds (104.5 FM). Chulalongkorn University Radio (101.5 FM) plays classical music from 9.30pm to midnight every night. Net 107 on 107 FM is one of several stations that include English-language news bulletins.

With a **shortwave radio** – or by going **online** – you can pick up the BBC World Service (W bbc .co.uk/worldservice), Radio Australia (W radio australia.net.au), Voice of America (W voanews .com), Radio Canada (W rcinet.ca) and other international stations right across Thailand. Times and wavelengths change regularly, so get hold of a recent schedule just before you travel or consult the websites for frequency and programme guides.

Festivals

Nearly all Thai festivals have a religious aspect. The most theatrical are generally Brahmin (Hindu) in origin, honouring elemental spirits and deities with ancient rites and ceremonial costumed parades. Buddhist celebrations usually revolve round the local temple, and while merit-making is a significant feature, a light-hearted atmosphere prevails, as the wat grounds are swamped with food and trinket vendors and makeshift stages are set up to show *likay* folk theatre, singing stars and beauty contests.

Many of the **secular festivals** (like the elephant roundups and the Bridge over the River Kwai spectacle) are outdoor local culture shows, geared specifically towards Thai and farang tourists. Others are thinly veiled but lively trade fairs held in provincial capitals to show off the local speciality, be it exquisite silk weaving or especially tasty rambutans.

Few of the **dates** for religious festivals are fixed, so check with TAT for specifics (W tourismthailand.org). The names of the most touristy celebrations are given here in English; the more low-key festivals are more usually known by their Thai name (*ngan* means "festival"). Some of the festivals below are designated as national holidays (see p.71).

A festival calendar

JANUARY–MARCH

Chinese New Year Nakhon Sawan (three days between mid-Jan and late Feb). In Nakhon Sawan, the new Chinese year is welcomed in with particularly exuberant parades of dragons and lion dancers, Chinese opera performances, an international lion-dance competition and a fireworks display. Also celebrated in Chinatowns across the country, especially in Bangkok and Phuket.

Flower Festival Chiang Mai (usually first weekend in Feb). Enormous floral sculptures are paraded through the streets.

Makha Puja Nationwide (particularly Wat Benjamabophit in Bangkok, Wat Phra That Doi Suthep in Chiang Mai and Wat Mahathat in Nakhon Si Thammarat; Feb full-moon day). A day of merit-making marks the occasion when 1250 disciples gathered spontaneously to hear the Buddha preach, and culminates with a candlelit procession round the local temple's bot.

Ngan Phrabat Phra Phutthabat, near Lopburi (early Feb and early March). Pilgrimages to the Holy Footprint attract food and handicraft vendors and travelling players. See p.230.

King Narai Reign Fair Lopburi (Feb). Costumed processions and a *son et lumière* show at Narai's palace.

Ngan Phra That Phanom That Phanom (Feb). Thousands come to pay homage at the holiest shrine in Isaan, which houses relics of the Buddha.

Kite fights and flying contests Nationwide (particularly Sanam Luang, Bangkok; late Feb to mid-April).

APRIL AND MAY

Poy Sang Long Mae Hong Son and Chiang Mai (early April). Young Thai Yai boys precede their ordination into monkhood by parading the streets in floral headdresses and festive garb. See p.340 and p.286.

Songkhran Nationwide (particularly Chiang Mai, and Bangkok's Thanon Khao San; usually April 13–15). The most exuberant of the national festivals welcomes the Thai New Year with massive waterfights, sandcastle building in temple compounds and the inevitable parades and "Miss Songkhran" beauty contests. See p.286.

Ngan Phanom Rung Prasat Hin Khao Phanom Rung (usually April). The three-day period when the sunrise is perfectly aligned through fifteen doorways at these magnificent eleventh-century Khmer ruins is celebrated with daytime processions and nightly *son et lumière*. See p.453.

Visakha Puja Nationwide (particularly Bangkok's Wat Benjamabophit, Wat Phra That Doi Suthep in Chiang Mai and Nakhon Si Thammarat's Wat Mahathat; May full-moon day). The holiest day of the Buddhist year, commemorating the birth, enlightenment and death of the Buddha all in one go; the most public and photogenic part is the candlelit evening procession around the wat.

Raek Na Sanam Luang, Bangkok (early May). The royal ploughing ceremony to mark the beginning of the rice-planting season; ceremonially clad Brahmin leaders parade sacred oxen and the royal plough, and interpret omens to forecast the year's rice yield. See p.94.

Rocket Festival Yasothon (Bun Bang Fai; weekend in mid-May). Beautifully crafted, painted wooden rockets are paraded and fired to ensure plentiful rains; celebrated all over Isaan, but especially lively in Yasothon. See p.472.

JUNE–SEPTEMBER

Phi Ta Khon Dan Sai, near Loei (end June or beginning July). Masked re-enactment of the Buddha's penultimate incarnation. See p.485.

Candle Festival Ubon Ratchathani (Asanha Puja; July, three days around the full moon). This nationwide festival marking the Buddha's first sermon and the subsequent beginning of the annual Buddhist retreat period (Khao Pansa) is celebrated across the northeast with parades of enormous wax sculptures, most spectacularly in Ubon Ratchathani. See p.465.

Tamboon Deuan Sip Nakhon Si Thammarat (Sept or Oct). Merit-making ceremonies to honour dead relatives accompanied by a ten-day fair. See p.581.

OCTOBER–DECEMBER

Vegetarian Festival Phuket and Trang (Ngan Kin Jeh; Oct or Nov). Chinese devotees become vegetarian for a nine-day period and then parade through town performing acts of self-mortification such as pushing skewers through their cheeks. Celebrated in Bangkok's Chinatown, with most food vendors and restaurants turning vegetarian for about a fortnight. See p.629 and p.706.

Bang Fai Phaya Nak Nong Khai and around (usually Oct). The strange appearance of pink balls of fire above the Mekong River draws sightseers from all over Thailand. See p.496.

Tak Bat Devo and Awk Pansa Nationwide (especially Ubon Ratchathani and Nakhon Phanom; Oct full-moon day). Offerings to monks and general merrymaking to celebrate the Buddha's descent to earth from Tavatimsa heaven and the end of the Khao Pansa retreat. Celebrated in Ubon with a procession of illuminated boats along the rivers, and in Nakhon Phanom with another illuminated boat procession and Thailand–Laos dragon-boat races along the Mekong.

Chak Phra Surat Thani (mid-Oct). The town's chief Buddha images are paraded on floats down the streets and on barges along the river. See p.538.

Boat Races Nan, Nong Khai, Phimai and elsewhere (Oct to mid-Nov). Longboat races and barge parades along town rivers.

Thawt Kathin Nationwide (the month between Awk Pansa and Loy Krathong, generally Oct–Nov). During the month following the end of the monks' rainy-season retreat, it's traditional for the laity to donate new robes to the monkhood and this is celebrated in most towns with parades and a festival, and occasionally, when it coincides with a kingly anniversary, with a spectacular Royal Barge Procession down the Chao Phraya River in Bangkok.

Loy Krathong Nationwide (particularly Sukhothai and Chiang Mai; full moon in Nov). Baskets (*krathong*) of flowers and lighted candles are floated on any available body of water (such as ponds, rivers, lakes, canals and seashores) to honour water spirits and celebrate the end of the rainy season. Nearly every town puts on a big show, with bazaars, public entertainments, fireworks, and in Chiang Mai, the release of paper hot-air balloons; in Sukhothai it is the climax of a *son et lumière* festival that's held over several nights. See p.244 and p.286.

Ngan Wat Saket Wat Saket, Bangkok (first week of Nov). Probably Thailand's biggest temple fair, held around the Golden Mount, with all the usual festival trappings.

Elephant Roundup Surin (third weekend of Nov). Two hundred elephants play team games, perform complex tasks and parade in battle dress. See p.457.

River Kwai Bridge Festival Kanchanaburi (ten nights from the last week of Nov into the first week of Dec). Spectacular *son et lumière* at the infamous bridge.

Silk and Phuk Siao Festival Khon Kaen (Nov 29–Dec 10). Weavers from around the province come to town to sell their lengths of silk. See p.475.

World Heritage Site Festival Ayutthaya (mid-Dec). Week-long celebration, including a nightly historical *son et lumière* romp, to commemorate the town's UNESCO designation. See p.216.

New Year's Eve Countdown Nationwide (Dec 31). Most cities and tourist destinations welcome in the new year with fireworks, often backed up by food festivals, beauty contests and outdoor performances.

Entertainment and sport

Bangkok is the best place to catch authentic performances of classical Thai dance, though more easily digestible tourist-oriented shows are staged in some of the big tourist centres as well as in Bangkok. The country's two main Thai boxing stadia are also in the capital, but you'll come across local matches in the provinces too.

Drama and dance

Drama pretty much equals **dance** in classical Thai theatre, and many of the traditional dance-dramas are based on the *Ramakien*, the Thai version of the Hindu epic *Ramayana*, an adventure tale of good versus evil that is taught in all schools. Not understanding the plots can be a major disadvantage, so try reading an abridged version beforehand (see p.788 and p.88) and check out the wonderfully imaginative murals at Wat Phra Kaeo in Bangkok. There are three broad categories of traditional Thai dance-drama – khon, lakhon and likay – described below in descending order of refinement.

Khon

The most spectacular form of traditional Thai theatre is **khon**, a stylized drama performed in masks and elaborate costumes by a troupe of highly trained classical dancers. There's little room for individual interpretation in these dances, as all the movements follow a strict choreography that's been passed down through generations: each graceful, angular gesture depicts a precise event, action or emotion which will be familiar to educated *khon* audiences. The dancers don't speak, and the story is chanted and sung by a chorus who stand at the side of the stage, accompanied by a classical *phipat* orchestra.

A typical *khon* performance features several of the best-known **Ramakien** episodes, in which the main characters are recognized by their masks, headdresses and heavily brocaded costumes. Gods and humans don't wear masks, but the hero Rama and heroine Sita always wear tall gilded headdresses and often appear as a trio with Rama's brother Lakshaman. Monkey **masks** are wide-mouthed: monkey army chief Hanuman always wears white, and his two right-hand men – Nilanol, the god of fire, and Nilapat, the god of death – wear red and black respectively. In contrast, the demons have grim mouths, clamped shut or snarling; Totsagan, king of the demons, wears a green face in battle and a gold one during peace, but always sports a two-tier headdress carved with two rows of faces.

Khon is performed with English subtitles at Bangkok's Sala Chalermkrung (see p.164) and is also featured within the various cultural **shows** staged by tourist restaurants in Bangkok, Phuket and Pattaya. Even if you don't see a show, you're bound to come across finely crafted real and replica *khon* masks both in museums and in souvenir shops all over the country.

Lakhon

Serious and refined, **lakhon** is derived from *khon* but is used to dramatize a greater range of stories, including Buddhist *Jataka* tales, local folk dramas and of course the *Ramakien*.

The form you're most likely to come across is *lakhon chatri*, which is performed at shrines like Bangkok's Erawan and at a city's *lak muang* as entertainment for the spirits and a token of gratitude from worshippers. Usually female, the *lakhon chatri* dancers perform as an ensemble, executing sequences that, like *khon* movements, all have minute and particular symbolism. They also wear ornate costumes, but no masks, and dance to the music of a *phipat* orchestra. Unfortunately, as resident shrine troupes tend to repeat the same dances a dozen times a day, it's rarely the sublime display it's cracked up to be. Bangkok's National Theatre stages the more elegantly executed *lakhon nai*, a dance form that used to be performed at the Thai court and often re-tells the *Ramakien*.

Likay

Likay is a much more popular and dynamic derivative of *khon* – more light-hearted, with lots of comic interludes, bawdy jokes and panto-style over-the-top acting and singing. Some *likay* troupes perform *Ramakien* excerpts, but a lot of them adapt pot-boiler romances or write their own and most will ham things up with improvisations and up-to-the-minute topical satire. Costumes might be traditional as in *khon* and *lakhon*, modern and Western as in films, or a mixture of both.

Likay troupes travel around the country doing shows on makeshift outdoor stages wherever they think they'll get an audience, most commonly at temple fairs. Performances are often free and generally last for about five hours, with the audience strolling in and out of the show, cheering and joking with the cast throughout. Televised *likay* dramas get huge audiences and always follow romantic soap-opera-style plot-lines. Short *likay* dramas are also a staple of Bangkok's National Theatre, but for more radical and internationally minded *likay*, look out for performances by **Makhampom** (ⓦ makhampom .net), a famous, long-established troupe with bases in Bangkok and Chiang Dao that pushes *likay* in new directions to promote social causes and involve minority communities.

Nang

Nang, or shadow plays (see p.584), are said to have been the earliest dramas performed in Thailand, but now are rarely seen except in the far south, where the Malaysian influence ensures an appreciative audience for *nang thalung*. Crafted from buffalo hide, the two-dimensional *nang thalung* puppets play out scenes from popular dramas against a backlit screen, while the storyline is told through songs, chants and musical interludes. An even rarer *nang* form is the *nang yai*, which uses enormous cut-outs of whole scenes rather than just individual characters, so the play becomes something like an animated film.

Film

All sizeable towns have a **cinema** or two – Bangkok has over fifty (see p.165) – and tickets generally start at around B80. The website ⓦ movieseer.com lists the weekly schedule for many cinemas around the country. In some rural areas, villagers still have to make do with the travelling cinema, or *nang klarng plaeng*, which sets up a mobile screen in wat compounds or other public spaces, and often entertains the whole village in one sitting. However makeshift the cinema, the **king's anthem** is always played before every screening, during which the audience is expected to stand up.

Fast-paced Chinese blockbusters have long dominated the programmes at Thai cinemas, serving up a low-grade cocktail of sex, spooks, violence and comedy. Not understanding the dialogue is rarely a drawback, as the storylines tend to be simple and the visuals more entertaining than the words. In the cities, **Western films** are also popular, and new releases often get subtitled rather than dubbed. They are also quickly available as pirated DVDs sold at street stalls in the main cities and resorts.

In recent years Thailand's own film industry (see p.782) has been enjoying a boom, and in the larger cities and resorts you may be lucky enough to come across one of the bigger Thai hits showing with English subtitles.

Thai boxing

Thai boxing (*muay thai*) enjoys a following similar to football or baseball in the West: every province has a stadium and whenever the sport is shown on TV you can be sure that large noisy crowds will gather round the sets in streetside restaurants. The best place to see Thai boxing is at one of Bangkok's two main stadia, which between them hold bouts every night of the week (see p.165), but many tourist resorts also stage regular matches.

There's a strong spiritual and **ritualistic** dimension to *muay thai*, adding grace to an otherwise brutal sport. Each boxer enters the ring to the wailing music of a three-piece *phipat* orchestra, wearing the statutory red or blue shorts and, on his head, a sacred rope headband or *mongkhon*. Tied around his biceps are *phra jiat*, pieces of cloth that are often decorated with cabalistic symbols and may contain Buddhist tablets. The fighter then bows, first in the direction of his birthplace and then to the north, south, east and west, honouring both his teachers and the spirit of the ring. Next he performs a slow dance, claiming the audience's attention and demonstrating his prowess as a performer.

Any part of the body except the head may be used as an **offensive weapon** in *muay thai*, and all parts except the groin are fair targets. Kicks to the head are the blows that cause most knockouts. As the action hots up, so the orchestra speeds up its tempo and the betting in the audience becomes more frenetic. It can be a gruesome business, but it was far bloodier before modern boxing gloves were made compulsory in the 1930s, when the Queensbury Rules were adapted for *muay* – combatants used to wrap their fists with hemp impregnated with a face-lacerating dosage of ground glass.

A number of *muay thai* gyms and camps offer training **courses** for foreigners, including several in Bangkok, as well as Chiang Mai, Hua Hin, Ko Pha Ngan and Ko Yao Noi – see the relevant accounts for details.

Takraw

Whether in Bangkok or upcountry, you're quite likely to come across some form of **takraw** game being played in a public park, a school, a wat compound or just in a backstreet alley. Played with a very light rattan ball (or one made of plastic to look like rattan), the basic aim of the game is to keep the ball off the ground. To do this you can use any part of your body except your hands, so a well-played *takraw* game looks extremely balletic, with players leaping and arching to get a good strike.

There are at least five versions of **competitive takraw**, based on the same principles. The version featured in the Southeast Asian Games and most frequently in school tournaments is played over a volleyball net and involves two teams of three; the other most popular competitive version has a team ranged round a basketball-type hoop trying to score as many goals as possible within a limited time period before the next team replaces them and tries to outscore them.

Other *takraw* games introduce more complex rules (like kicking the ball backwards with your heels through a ring made with your arms behind your back) and many assign points according to the skill displayed by individual players rather than per goal or dropped ball.

Spas and traditional massage

With their focus on indulgent self-pampering, spas are usually associated with high-spending tourists, but the treatments on offer at Thailand's five-star hotels are often little different from those used by traditional medical practitioners, who have long held that massage and herbs are the best way to restore physical and mental well-being.

Thai massage (*nuad boran*) is based on the principle that many physical and emotional problems are caused by the blocking of vital energy channels within the body. The masseur uses his or her feet, heels, knees and elbows, as well as hands, to exert pressure on these channels, supplementing this acupressure-style technique by pulling and pushing the limbs into yogic stretches. This distinguishes Thai massage from most other massage styles, which are more concerned with tissue manipulation. One is supposed to emerge from a Thai massage feeling both relaxed and energized, and it is said that regular massages produce long-term benefits in muscles as well as stimulating the circulation and aiding natural detoxification.

Thais will visit a masseur for many conditions, including fevers, colds and muscle strain, but bodies that are not sick are also considered to benefit from the restorative powers of a massage, and nearly every hotel and guesthouse will be able to put you in touch with a **masseur**. On the more popular beaches, it can be hard to walk a few hundred metres without being offered a massage – something Thai tourists are just as enthusiastic about as foreigners. Thai masseurs do not traditionally use oils or lotions and the client is treated on a mat or mattress; you'll often be given a pair of loose-fitting trousers and perhaps a loose top to change into. English-speaking masseurs will often ask if there are any areas of your body that you would like them to concentrate on, or if you have any problem areas that you want them to avoid; if your masseur doesn't speak English, the simplest way to signal the latter is to point at the offending area while saying *mai sabai* ("not well"). If you're in pain during a massage, wincing usually does the trick, perhaps adding *jep* ("it hurts"); if your masseur is pressing too hard for your liking, say *bao bao na khrap/kha* ("gently please").

The best places for a basic massage are usually the government-accredited clinics and hospitals that are found in large towns all over the country. A session should ideally last at least one and a half hours and will cost from around B250. If you're a bit wary of submitting to the full works, try a **foot massage** first, which will apply the same techniques of acupressure and stretching to just your feet and lower legs. Most places also offer **herbal massages**, in which the masseur will knead you with a ball of herbs (*phrakop*) wrapped in a cloth and steam-heated; they're said to be particularly good for stiffness of the neck, shoulders and back.

The **science** behind Thai massage has its roots in Indian Ayurvedic medicine, which classifies each component of the body according to one of the four elements (earth, water, fire and air), and holds that balancing these elements within the body is crucial to good health. Many of the stretches and manipulations fundamental to Thai massage are thought to have derived from yogic practices introduced to Thailand from India by Buddhist missionaries in about the second century BC; Chinese acupuncture and reflexology have also had a strong influence. In the nineteenth century, King Rama III ordered a series of murals illustrating the principles of Thai massage to be painted around the courtyard of Bangkok's Wat Pho, and they are still in place today, along with statues of ascetics depicted in typical massage poses.

Wat Pho has been the leading school of Thai massage for hundreds of years, and it is possible to take courses there as well as to receive a massage (see p.92); it also runs a residential massage school and clinic in Nakhon Pathom province (Wwatpo massage.com). Masseurs who trained at Wat Pho are considered to be the best in the country and masseurs all across Thailand advertise this as a credential, whether or not it is true. Many Thais consider blind masseurs to be especially sensitive practitioners.

While Wat Pho is the most famous place to take a **course** in Thai massage, many foreigners interested in learning this ancient science head for Chiang Mai, which offers the biggest concentration of massage schools (including another satellite branch of the Wat Pho school), though you will find others all over Thailand, including in Bangkok and at southern beach resorts.

All **spas** in Thailand feature traditional Thai massage and herbal therapies in their programmes, but most also offer dozens of other international treatments, including facials, aromatherapy, Swedish massage and various body wraps. Spa centres in upmarket hotels and resorts are usually open to non-guests but generally need to be booked in advance. Day-spas that are not attached to hotels are generally cheaper and are found in some of the bigger cities and resorts – some of these may not require reservations.

Meditation centres and retreats

Of the hundreds of meditation temples in Thailand, a few cater specifically for foreigners by holding meditation

sessions and retreats in English. Novices as well as practised meditators are generally welcome at these wats, but absolute beginners might like to consider the regular retreats at Wat Suan Mokkh and Wat Khao Tham, which are conducted by supportive and experienced Thai and Western teachers and include talks and interviews on Buddhist teachings and practice. The meditation taught is mostly Vipassana, or "insight", which emphasizes the minute observation of internal sensations; the other main technique you'll come across is Samatha, which aims to calm the mind and develop concentration (these two techniques are not entirely separate, since you cannot have insight without some degree of concentration).

Longer **retreats** are for the serious-minded only. All the temples listed below welcome both male and female English-speakers, but strict segregation of the sexes is enforced and many places observe a vow of silence. Reading and writing are also discouraged, and you'll generally not be allowed to leave the retreat complex unless absolutely necessary, so try to bring whatever you'll need in with you. All retreats expect you to wear modest clothing, and some require you to wear white – check ahead whether there is a shop at the retreat complex or whether you are expected to bring this with you.

An average day at any one of these monasteries starts with a **wake-up call** at around 4am and includes several hours of **group meditation** and chanting, as well as time put aside for chores and personal reflection. However long their stay, visitors are usually expected to keep the eight main Buddhist precepts, the most restrictive of these being the abstention from food after midday and from alcohol, tobacco, drugs and sex at all times. Most wats ask for a minimal daily **donation** (around B200) to cover the costs of the simple accommodation and food.

Further details about many of the temples listed below – including how to get there – are given in the relevant sections in the Guide chapters. A useful **resource** is Ⓦdhammathai.org, which provides lots of general background, practical advice and details of meditation temples and centres around Thailand. In addition, Ⓦwanderingdhamma.org is a very interesting blog written by an American Ph.D. student, with some fascinating articles, information

on English-speaking retreats in Thailand and lots of good links. Meanwhile, Little Bangkok Sangha (Ⓦlittlebang.org) is a handy blog maintained by a British-born monk, Phra Pandit, which gives details of talks in Bangkok and retreats. Also in Bangkok, keep an eye out for developments at the Buddhadasa Indapanno Archives in Chatuchak Park in the north of the city, a recently built centre in honour of the founder of Wat Suan Mokkh (see p.536), which may well host more events for English-speakers in the future.

MEDITATION CENTRES AND RETREAT TEMPLES

In addition to those listed below, additional meditation centres and retreat temples are listed in the Guide chapters, including **Wat Khao Tham** on Ko Pha Ngan (see p.562), **Wat Mahathat** in Bangkok (see p.95), several retreats and sessions in **Chiang Mai** (see p.288), and **Wat Suan Mokkh** in Chaiya (see p.536) and on Ko Samui (see p.541).

House of Dhamma Insight Meditation Centre 26/9 Soi Lardprao 15, Chatuchak, Bangkok ☎ 02 511 0439, Ⓦhouseof dhamma.com. Regular two-day courses in Vipassana, as well as day workshops in Metta (Loving Kindness) meditation. Courses in reiki and other subjects available.

Thailand Vipassana Centres Ⓦdhamma.org. Frequent courses in a Burmese Vipassana tradition for beginners (10 days) and practised meditators (1–45 days), in Khon Kaen, Lamphun, Phitsanulok (see p.238), Prachinburi (near Bangkok) and Sangkhlaburi. Foreign students must pre-register by email (application form available on the website).

Wat Pah Nanachat Ban Bung Wai, Amphoe Warinchamrab, Ubon Ratchathani 34310 Ⓦwatpahnanachat.org. The famous monk, Ajahn Chah, established this forest monastery, 17km west of Ubon Ratchathani, in 1975 specifically to provide monastic training for non-Thais, with English the primary language. Visitors who want to practise with the resident community are welcome, but the atmosphere is serious and intense and not for beginners or curious sightseers, and accommodation for students is limited, so you should write to the monastery before visiting, allowing several weeks to receive a written response.

Wat Phra Si Chom Thong Insight Meditation Centre ☎ 053 826869, ✉ watchomtong@sirimangalo.org. Located in Chom Thong (see p.331), 58km south of Chiang Mai, this is the centre of the Northern Insight Meditation School developed by the well-known Phra Ajarn Tong Sirimangalo (the meditation teachers at Chiang Mai's Wat Ram Poeng and Wat Doi Suthep are all students of Phra Tong). Offers 4- to 21-day Vipassana meditation courses taught in English and Thai and some European languages as well. By donation.

World Fellowship of Buddhists (WFB) 616 Benjasiri Park, Soi Medhinivet off Soi 24, Thanon Sukhumvit, Bangkok ☎ 02 661 1284–7, Ⓦwfbhq.org. Headquarters of an influential worldwide organization of (mostly Theravada) Buddhists, founded in Sri Lanka in 1950, this is the main information centre for advice on English-speaking retreats in Thailand.

Outdoor activities

Many travellers' itineraries take in a few days' trekking in the hills and a stint snorkelling or diving off the beaches of the south. Trekking is concentrated in the north, but there are smaller, less touristy trekking operations in Kanchanaburi, Sangkhlaburi and Umphang. There are also plenty of national parks to explore and opportunities for rock climbing and kayaking.

Diving and snorkelling

Clear, warm waters (averaging 28°C), prolific marine life and affordable prices make Thailand a very rewarding place for **diving** and **snorkelling**. Most islands and beach resorts have at least one dive centre that organizes trips to outlying islands, teaches novice divers and rents out equipment, and in the bigger resorts there are dozens to choose from.

Thailand's three coasts are subject to different monsoon **seasons**, so you can dive all year round; the seasons run from November to April along the Andaman coast (though there is sometimes good diving here up until late Aug), and all year round on the Gulf and east coasts. Though every diver has their favourite reef, Thailand's **premier diving destinations** are generally considered to be Ko Similan, Ko Surin, Richelieu Rock and Hin Muang and Hin Daeng – all of them off the Andaman coast (see p.642). As an accessible base for diving, Ko Tao off the Gulf coast is hard to beat, with deep, clear inshore water and a wide variety of dive sites in very close proximity.

Whether you're snorkelling or diving, try to minimize your impact on the fragile reef structures by **not touching the reefs** and by asking your boatman not to anchor in the middle of one; **don't buy coral souvenirs**, as tourist demand only encourages local entrepreneurs to dynamite reefs.

Should you scrape your skin on coral, wash the wound thoroughly with boiled water, apply antiseptic and keep protected until healed. Wearing a T-shirt is a good idea when snorkelling to stop your back from getting sunburnt.

Diving

It's usually worth having a look at several **dive centres** before committing yourself to a trip or a course. Always verify the dive instructors' PADI (Professional Association of Diving Instructors) or

---

THAILAND'S MAIN DIVE RESORTS

THE EAST COAST
Ko Chang (see p.416)
Pattaya (see p.389)

THE GULF COAST
Ko Pha Ngan (see p.560)
Ko Samui (see p.541)
Ko Tao (see p.574)

THE ANDAMAN COAST
Ao Nang (see p.665)
Khao Lak (see p.618)
Ko Lanta (see p.691)
Ko Phi Phi (see p.676)
Phuket (see p.642)

THE DEEP SOUTH
Ko Lipe (see p.720)

---

equivalent accreditation and check to see if the dive shop is a member of PADI's International Resorts and Retailers Association (IRRA) as this guarantees a certain level of professionalism. You can view a list of IRRAs in Thailand at ⓦ padi.com.

We've highlighted IRRA dive shops that are accredited Five-Star centres, as these are considered by Padi to offer very high standards, but you should always consult other divers first if possible. Some dive operators do fake their PADI credentials. Avoid booking ahead over the internet without knowing anything else about the dive centre, and be wary of any operation offering extremely cheap courses: maintaining diving equipment is an expensive business in Thailand so any place offering unusually good rates will probably be cutting corners and compromising your safety. Ask to **meet your instructor** or dive leader, find out how many people there'll be in your group, check out the kind of instruction given (some courses are over-reliant on videos) and look over the equipment, checking the quality of the air in the tanks yourself and also ensuring there's an oxygen cylinder on board. Most divers prefer to travel to the dive site in a decent-sized **boat** equipped with a radio and emergency medical equipment rather than in a longtail. If this concerns you, ask the dive company about their boat before you sign up; firms that use longtails generally charge less.

Insurance should be included in the price of courses and introductory dives; for qualified divers, you're better off checking that your general travel insurance covers diving, though some diving shops can organize cover for you. There are **recompression chambers** in Pattaya, on Ko Samui and on Phuket and it's a good idea to check whether your dive centre is a member of one of these outfits, as recompression services are extremely expensive for anyone who's not.

There are a number of useful books available on diving in Thailand (see p.788).

Trips and courses

All dive centres run programmes of one-day **dive trips** (featuring two dives) and **night dives** for B1500–4500 (with reductions if you bring your own gear), and many of the Andaman-coast dive centres also do three- to seven-day **live-aboards** to the exceptional reefs off the remote Similan and Surin islands (from B11,900). Most dive centres can rent **underwater cameras** for about B1500 per day.

All dive centres offer a range of **courses** from beginner to advanced level, with equipment rental usually included in the cost; Ko Tao is now the largest, and most competitive, dive-training centre in Southeast Asia, with around fifty dive companies including plenty of PADI Five-Star centres. The most popular courses are the one-day **introductory** or resort dive (a pep talk and escorted shallow dive, open to anyone aged 10 or over), which costs anything from B2000 for a very local dive to B7000 for an all-inclusive day-trip to the Similan Islands; and the four-day **open-water course**, which entitles you to dive without an instructor (from B9800 on Ko Tao in high season). Kids' Bubblemaker courses, for children aged 8–9, cost around B2000.

Snorkelling

Boatmen and tour agents on most beaches offer **snorkelling** trips to nearby reefs and many dive operators welcome snorkellers to tag along for discounts of thirty percent or more; not all diving destinations are rewarding for snorkellers though, so check the relevant account in this book first. As far as snorkelling **equipment** goes, the most important thing is that you buy or rent a mask that fits. To check the fit, hold the mask against your face, then breathe in and remove your hands – if it falls off, it'll leak water. If you're buying equipment, you should be able to kit yourself out with a mask, snorkel and fins for about B1000, available from most dive centres. Few places rent fins, but a mask and snorkel set usually costs about B150 a day to rent, and if you're going on a snorkelling day-trip they are often included in the price.

National parks and wildlife observation

Thailand's hundred-plus **national parks** (see box, p.54), which are administered by the National Park, Wildlife and Plant Conservation Department (𝕎dnp.go.th), are generally the best places to **observe wildlife**. Though you're highly unlikely to encounter tigers or sun bears, you have a good chance of spotting gibbons, civets, mouse deer and hornbills and may even get to see a wild elephant. A number of wetlands also host a rewarding variety of birdlife. All parks charge an **entrance fee**, which for foreigners is usually B200 (B100 for children), though some charge B100 and a few charge B400.

Waymarked hiking **trails** in most parks are generally limited and rarely very challenging and decent park maps are hard to come by, so for serious national-park treks you'll need to hire a guide and venture beyond the public routes. Nearly all parks provide **accommodation** and/or campsites (see p.37). Some national parks **close** for several weeks or months every year for conservation, safety or environmental reasons; dates are listed on the National Parks' website.

A detailed guide to Thailand's wildlife and their habitats, a look at the environmental issues, and a list of Thai wildlife charities and volunteer projects are provided in "Contexts" (see p.767).

Rock climbing

The limestone karsts that pepper southern Thailand's Andaman coast make ideal playgrounds for **rock-climbers**, and the sport has really taken off here in the past fifteen years. Most climbing is centred round **East Railay** and **Ton Sai** beaches on Laem Phra Nang in Krabi province (see p.672), where there are dozens of routes within easy walking distance of tourist bungalows, restaurants and beaches. **Offshore Deep Water Soloing** – climbing a rock face out at sea, with no ropes, partner or bolts and just the water to break your fall – is also huge round here. Several **climbing schools** at East Railay and Ton Sai provide instruction (from B1000 per half-day), as well as guides and equipment rental (about B1300 per day for two people). Ko Phi Phi (see p.676) also offers a few routes and a couple of climbing schools, as does the quieter and potentially more interesting Ko Yao Noi (see p.652) and Ko Lao Liang (see p.716). Climbing is also popular near Chiang Mai (see p.280), and there are less developed climbing areas on Ko Tao (see p.577) and in Lopburi province (see p.232). For an introduction to climbing

TOP NATIONAL PARKS

Ang Thong (p.557). Spectacular archipelago in the Gulf of Thailand, generally visited on a day-trip from Ko Samui or Ko Pha Ngan.

Doi Inthanon (p.331). Waterfalls, hill tribes, orchids, around four hundred bird species and the country's highest peak.

Erawan (p.199). An exceptionally pretty, seven-tiered waterfall that extends deep into the forest. Hugely popular as a day-trip from Kanchanaburi.

Khao Sam Roi Yot (p.527). Coastal flats on the Gulf coast known for their rich birdlife plus an extensive stalactite-filled cave system.

Khao Sok (p.610). Southern Thailand's most visited park has rainforest trails and caves plus a flooded river system with eerie outcrops and raft-house accommodation.

Khao Yai (p.440). Thailand's most popular national park, three hours from Bangkok,

features half a dozen upland trails plus organized treks and night safaris.

Ko Similan (p.620). Remote group of Andaman Sea islands with famously fabulous reefs and fine above-water scenery. Mostly visited by dive boat but limited national park accommodation is provided.

Ko Surin (p.607). National marine park archipelago of beautiful coastal waters in the Andaman Sea, though much of its coral became severely bleached in 2010. Good snorkelling and national park campsites.

Ko Tarutao (p.717). Beautiful and wildly varied land- and seascapes on the main 26km-long island and fifty other smaller islands on its western side.

Phu Kradung (p.486). Dramatic and strange 1300m-high plateau, probably best avoided at weekends.

on Railay and elsewhere in south Thailand, see ⓦ railay.com, while *Rock Climbing in Thailand* and *King Climbers: Thailand Route Guide Book* are regularly updated guidebooks that concentrate on Railay, Ton Sai and the islands.

Sea kayaking and whitewater rafting

Sea kayaking is also centred around Thailand's Andaman coast, where the limestone outcrops, sea caves, *hongs* (hidden lagoons), mangrove swamps and picturesque shorelines of Ao Phang Nga in particular (see p.656) make for rewarding paddling. Kayaking day-trips around Ao Phang Nga can be arranged from any resort in Phuket, at Khao Lak, at all Krabi beaches and islands, and on Ko Yao Noi; multi-day kayaking expeditions are also possible. Over on Ko Samui, Blue Stars (see p.558) organize kayaking trips around the picturesque islands of the Ang Thong National Marine Park, while Kayak Chang (see p.414) offers half- to seven-day trips around Ko Chang. Many bungalows at other beach resorts have free kayaks or rent them out (from B100/hr) for casual, independent coastal exploration.

You can go **river kayaking** and **whitewater rafting** on several rivers in north, west and south Thailand. Some stretches of these rivers can run quite fast, particularly during the rainy season from July to November, but there are plenty of options for novices too. The best time is from October

through February; during the hot season (March–June), many rivers run too low. The most popular whitewater-rafting rivers include the Umphang and Mae Khlong rivers near Umphang (see p.267) and the Pai River near Pai (see p.349). Gentler rafting excursions take place as part of organized treks in the north, as well as on the River Kwai and its tributaries near Kanchanaburi (see p.198), on the Kok River from Tha Ton (see p.355), and at Mae Hong Son (see p.342) and Pai (see p.349). Southwest of Chiang Mai, rafts can be rented from the adjacent national park headquarters for trips in Ob Luang Gorge (see p.334).

Trekking

Trekking in the mountains of north Thailand differs from trekking in most other parts of the world in that the emphasis is not primarily on the scenery but on the region's inhabitants. Northern Thailand's **hill tribes**, now numbering over 800,000 people living in around 3500 villages, have preserved their subsistence-oriented way of life with comparatively little change over thousands of years (see p.777). In recent years, the term **mountain people** (a translation of the Thai *chao khao*) is increasingly used as a less condescending way to describe them; since these groups have no chief, they are technically not tribes. While some of the villages are near enough to a main road to be reached on a day-trip from a major town, to get to the other, more traditional villages usually entails joining a guided party for a few days, roughing it in a different place each night. For most visitors, however, these hardships are far outweighed by the experience of encountering peoples of so different a culture, travelling through beautiful tropical countryside and tasting the excitement of elephant riding and river rafting.

On any trek you are necessarily confronted by the **ethics** of your role. About a hundred thousand travellers now go trekking in Thailand each year, the majority heading to certain well-trodden areas such as the Mae Taeng valley, 40km northwest of Chiang Mai, and the hills around the Kok River west of Chiang Rai. Beyond the basic level of disturbance caused by any tourism, this steady flow of trekkers creates pressures for the traditionally insular hill tribes. Foreigners unfamiliar with hill-tribe customs can easily cause grave offence, especially those who go looking for drugs. Though tourism acts as a distraction from their traditional way of life, most tribespeople are genuinely welcoming and hospitable to foreigners, appreciating the contact with Westerners and the minimal material benefits which

trekking brings them. Nonetheless, to minimize disruption, it's important to take a responsible attitude when trekking. While it's possible to trek independently from one or two spots such as *Cave Lodge* near Soppong (see p.346), the lone trekker will learn very little without a guide as intermediary, and is far more likely to commit an unwitting offence against the local customs; it's best to go with a sensitive and knowledgeable **guide** who has the welfare of the local people in mind, and follow the basic guidelines on etiquette outlined below. If you don't fancy an organized trek in a group, it's possible to hire a personal guide from an agent, at a cost of about B1000–1500 per day.

The hill tribes are big business in northern Thailand: in **Chiang Mai** there are hundreds of agencies, which between them cover just about all the trekkable areas in the north. **Chiang Rai** is the second-biggest trekking centre, and agencies can also be found in Nan, Mae Sariang, Mae Hong Son, Pai, Chiang Dao, Tha Ton and Mae Salong, which usually arrange treks only to the villages in

HILL-TRIBE TREKKING ETIQUETTE

As the guests, it's up to farangs to adapt to the customs of the hill tribes and not to make a nuisance of themselves. Apart from keeping an open mind and not demanding too much of your hosts, a few **simple rules** should be observed.

- **Dress modestly**, in long trousers or skirt (or at least knee-length shorts if you must) and a T-shirt or shirt. Getting dressed or changing your clothes in front of villagers is also offensive.

- Loud voices and **boisterous behaviour** are out of place. Smiling and nodding establishes good intent. A few hill-tribe phrasebooks and dictionaries are available from local bookshops and you'll be a big hit if you learn some words of the relevant language.

- If travelling with a loved one, avoid **displays of public affection** such as kissing, which are extremely distasteful, and disrespectful, to local people.

- Look out for **taboo signs** (*ta-laew*), woven bamboo strips, on the ground outside the entrance to a village, on the roof above a house entrance or on a fresh tree branch; these mean a special ceremony is taking place and that you should not enter. Be careful about what you touch; in Akha villages, keep your hands off cult structures like the entrance gates and the giant swing. Ask first before entering a house, and do not step or sit on the doorsill, which is often considered the domain of the house spirits. If the house has a raised floor on stilts, take off your shoes. Most hill-tribe houses contain a religious shrine: do not touch or photograph this shrine, or sit underneath it. If you are permitted to watch a ceremony, this is not an invitation to participate unless asked. Like the villagers themselves, you'll be expected to pay a fine for any violation of local customs.

- Some villagers like to be photographed, most do not. Point at your **camera** and nod if you want to take a photograph. Never insist if the answer is an obvious "no". Be particularly careful with the sick and the old, and with pregnant women and babies – most tribes believe cameras affect the soul of the foetus or newborn.

- Taking **gifts** can be dubious practice. If you want to take something, writing materials for children and clothing are welcome, as well as sewing tools (like needles) for women – ask your guide to pass any gifts to the village headman for fair distribution. However, money, sweets and cigarettes may encourage begging and create unhealthy tastes.

- Do not ask for **opium**, as this will offend your hosts.

their immediate area. Guided trekking on a smaller scale than in the north is available in Umphang, Kanchanaburi and Sangkhlaburi.

The basics

The cool, dry season from November to February is the best time for treks, which can be as short as two days or as long as ten, but are typically of three or four days' duration. The standard size of a group is between five and twelve people; being part of a small group is preferable, enabling you to strike a more informative relationship with your guides and with the villagers. Everybody in the group usually sleeps on a mattress in the village's guest hut, with a guide cooking communal meals, for which some ingredients are brought from outside and others are found locally.

Each trek usually follows a regular **itinerary** established by the agency, although they can sometimes be customized, especially for smaller groups and with agencies in the smaller towns. Some itineraries are geared towards serious hikers while others go at a much gentler pace, but on all treks much of the walking will be up and down steep forested hills, often under a burning sun, so a reasonable level of fitness is required. Many treks now include a ride on an elephant and a trip on a bamboo raft – exciting to the point of being dangerous if the river is running fast. The typical three-day, two-night trek **costs** about B1600–3000 in Chiang Mai (including transport, accommodation, food and guide), sometimes less in other towns, much less without rafting and elephant-riding.

Choosing a trek

There are several features to look out for when **choosing a trek**. If you want to trek with a small group, get an assurance from your agency that you won't be tagged onto a larger group. Make sure the trek has at least two guides – a leader and a back-marker; some trekkers have been known to get lost for days after becoming separated from the rest of the group. Check exactly when the trek starts and ends and ask about transport to and from base; most treks begin with a pick-up ride out of town, but on rare occasions the trip can entail a long public bus ride. If at all possible, meet and chat with the other trekkers in advance, as well as the guides, who should speak reasonable English and know about hill-tribe culture, especially the details of etiquette in each village. Finally, ask what meals will be included, check how much walking is involved per day and get a copy of the route map to gauge the terrain.

While everybody and their grandmother act as **agents**, only a few know their guides personally, so choose a reputable agent or guesthouse. When picking an agent, you should check whether they and their guides have licences and certificates from the Tourist Authority of Thailand, which they should be able to show you: this ensures at least a minimum level of training, and provides some comeback in case of problems. Word of mouth is often the best recommendation, so if you hear of a good outfit, try it. Each trek should be **registered** with the tourist police, stating the itinerary, the duration and the participants, in case the party encounters any trouble – it's worth checking with the agency that the trek has been registered with the tourist police before departure.

What to take

The right **clothing** is the first essential on any trek. Strong boots with ankle protection are the best footwear, although in the dry season training shoes are adequate. Wear thin, loose clothes – long trousers should be worn to protect against thorns and, in the wet season, leeches – and a hat, and cover your arms if you're prone to sunburn. Antiseptic, antihistamine cream, anti-diarrhoea **medicine** and insect repellent are essential, as is a mosquito net – check if one will be provided where you're staying. At least two changes of clothing are needed, plus a sarong or towel (women in particular should bring a sarong to wash or change underneath).

If you're going on an organized trek, **water** is usually provided by the guide, as well as a small backpack. **Blankets** or, preferably, a **sleeping bag** are also supplied, but might not be warm enough in the cool season, when night-time temperatures can dip to freezing; you should bring at least a sweater, and perhaps buy a cheap, locally made balaclava to be sure of keeping the chill off.

It's wise not to take anything valuable with you; most guesthouses in trekking-oriented places like Chiang Mai have safes and left-luggage rooms.

Travelling with children

Despite the relative lack of child-centred attractions in Thailand, there's plenty to appeal to families, both on the beach and inland, and Thais are famously welcoming to young visitors.

Of all the **beach resorts** in the country, two of the most family friendly are the islands of Ko Samui and Ko Lanta. Both have plenty of on-the-beach accommodation for mid- and upper-range budgets, and lots of easy-going open-air shorefront restaurants so that adults can eat in relative peace while kids play within view. Both islands also offer many day-tripping activities, from elephant riding to snorkelling. Phuket is another family favourite, though shorefront accommodation here is at a premium; there are also scores of less mainstream alternatives. In many beach resorts older kids will be able to go kayaking or learn rock climbing, and many dive centres will teach the PADI children's scuba courses on request: the Bubblemaker programme is open to 8- and 9-year-olds and the Discover Scuba Diving day is designed for anyone 10 and over.

Inland, the many **national parks** and their waterfalls and caves are good for days out, and there are lots of opportunities to go **rafting** and **elephant riding**. Kanchanaburi is a rewarding centre for all these, with the added plus that many of the town's guesthouses are set round decent-sized lawns. Chiang Mai is another great hub for all the above and also offers boat trips, an attractive, modern zoo and aquarium, the chance to watch umbrella-makers and other craftspeople at work, and, in the Mae Sa valley, many family-oriented attractions, such as the botanical gardens and **butterfly farms**. Bangkok has several child-friendly **theme parks** and activity centres (see p.122).

Should you be in Thailand in January, your kids will be able to join in the free entertainments and activities staged all over the country on **National Children's Day** (Wan Dek), which is held on the second Saturday of January. They also get free entry to zoos that day, and free rides on public buses.

Hotels and transport

Many of the expensive **hotels** listed in this guide allow one or two under-12s to share their parents' room for free, as long as no extra bedding is required. It's often possible to cram two adults and two children into the double rooms in budget and mid-range hotels (as opposed to guesthouses), as beds in these places are usually big enough for two. An increasing number of guesthouses now offer three-person rooms, and may even provide special family accommodation. Decent cots are available free in the bigger hotels, and in some smaller ones (though cots in these places can be a bit grotty), and top and mid-range rooms often come with a small fridge. Many hotels can also provide a **babysitting** service.

Few museums or transport companies offer student reductions, but in some cases children get **discounts**. One of the more bizarre provisos is the State Railway's regulation that a child aged 3 to 12 qualifies for half-fare only if under 150cm tall; some stations have a measuring scale painted onto the ticket-hall wall. Most domestic airlines charge ten percent of the full fare for under-2s, and fifty percent for under-12s.

Other practicalities

Although most Thai babies don't wear them, **disposable nappies** (diapers) are sold at convenience stores, pharmacies and supermarkets in big resorts and sizeable towns; for stays on lonely islands, consider bringing some washable ones as back-up. A **changing mat** is another necessity as there are few public toilets in Thailand, let alone ones with baby facilities (though posh hotels are always a useful option). International brands of powdered milk are available throughout the country, and brand-name baby food is sold in big towns and resorts, though some parents find restaurant-cooked rice and bananas go down just as well. Thai women do not **breastfeed** in public.

For touring, child-carrier backpacks are ideal. Opinions are divided on whether or not it's worth bringing a **buggy** or three-wheeled **stroller**. Where they exist, Thailand's pavements are bumpy at best, and there's an almost total absence of ramps; sand is especially difficult for buggies, though less so for three-wheelers. Buggies and strollers do, however, come in handy for feeding and even bedding small children, as highchairs and cots are only provided in more upmarket restaurants and hotels. You can buy buggies fairly cheaply in most towns, but if you bring your own and then wish you hadn't, most hotels and guesthouses will keep it for you until you leave. Bring an appropriately sized **mosquito net** if necessary (see p.66) or buy one locally in any department store; a mini **sun tent** for the beach is also useful. Taxis and car-rental companies almost never provide baby **car seats**, and even if you bring your own you'll often find there are no seatbelts to strap them in with. Most department stores have dedicated kids' sections selling everything from bottles to dummies. There are even several Mothercare outlets in Bangkok.

Hazards

Even more than their parents, children need protecting from the sun, unsafe drinking water, heat and unfamiliar **food**. Consider packing a jar of a favourite spread so that you can always rely on toast if all else fails to please. As with adults, you should be careful about unwashed fruit and salads and about dishes that have been left uncovered for a long time. As diarrhoea could be dangerous for a child, rehydration solutions (see p.68) are vital if your child goes down with it. Other significant **hazards** include thundering traffic; huge waves, strong currents and jellyfish; and the **sun** – not least because many beaches offer only limited shade, if at all. Sunhats, sunblock and waterproof suntan lotions are essential, and can be bought in the major resorts. You should also make sure, if possible, that your child is aware of the dangers of **rabies**; keep children away from **animals**, especially dogs and monkeys, and ask your medical advisor about rabies jabs.

INFORMATION AND ADVICE

Nancy Chandler's Family Travel ⓦ nancychandler.net /travelwkids.asp. Plenty of unusual ideas on Thai-style entertainment for kids, plus tips, links and Thailand-themed kids' books.
Thailand 4 Kids ⓦ thailand4kids.com. Lots of advice on the practicalities of family holidays in Thailand.

Travel essentials

Charities and volunteer projects

Reassured by the plethora of well-stocked shopping plazas, efficient services and apparent abundance in the rice fields, it is easy to forget that life is extremely hard for many people in Thailand. Countless **charities** work with Thailand's many poor and disadvantaged communities: listed below are a few that would welcome help in some way from visitors. The website of the *Bangkok Post* also carries an extensive list of charitable foundations and projects in Thailand at ⓦ bangkokpost.com /outlookwecare. Longer-term placements, volunteer jobs on charitable wildlife projects and organized holidays that feature community-based programmes are also available (see p.69, p.767 and p.26 respectively).

Baan Unrak, Home of Joy Sangkhlaburi ⓦ baanunrak.org. Works with ethnic-minority refugee women and children from Burma. Visitors and volunteers welcome. See p.210.

Foundation to Encourage the Potential of Disabled Persons Chiang Mai ⓦ assistdisabled.org. This foundation provides, among other things, free wheelchairs, home visits and residential care for disabled people. Volunteers, donations and sponsorships for wheelchairs and severely disabled children are sought.

Children's World Academy Kapong, near Khao Lak ☎ 087 271 2552, ⓦ yaowawit.com. Set in quiet countryside on the Takua Pa–Phang Nga road, Yaowawit School was set up for tsunami orphans and socially disadvantaged children. It accepts donations, volunteer teachers and guests who wish to stay at its lodge, a hospitality training centre.

Hill Area and Community Development Foundation Chiang Rai ⓦ naturalfocus-cbt.com. Aiming to help hill tribes in dealing with problems such as environmental management, HIV/AIDS, child and drug abuse, the foundation has set up a community-based tourism company, Natural Focus (see p.358), to offer mountain-life tours, volunteer opportunities and study and work programmes.

Human Development Foundation 100/11 Kae Ha Klong Toey 4, Thanon Damrongratthaphipat, Klong Toey, Bangkok ☎ 02 671 5313, ⓦ mercycentre.org. Founded in 1973, Father Joe Maier's organization provides education and support for Bangkok's street kids and slum-dwellers, as well as for sea gypsies in the south. It now runs two dozen kindergartens in the slums, among many other projects. Contact the centre for information about donations, sponsoring and volunteering. *The Slaughterhouse: Stories from Bangkok's Klong Toey Slum* (see p.786) gives an eye-opening insight into this often invisible side of Thai life.

Koh Yao Children's Community Center Ko Yao Noi ⓦ koyao-ccc .com. Aims to improve the English-language and lifelong learning skills

---

ADDRESSES IN THAILAND

Thai **addresses** can be immensely confusing, mainly because property is often numbered twice, first to show which real-estate lot it stands in, and then to distinguish where it is on that lot. Thus 154/7–10 Thanon Rajdamnoen means the building is on lot 154 and occupies numbers 7–10. However, neither of these numbers will necessarily help you to find a particular building on a long street; when asking for directions or talking to taxi drivers, it's best to be able to quote a nearby temple, big hotel or other landmark. There's an additional idiosyncrasy in the way Thai roads are sometimes named: in large cities a minor road running off a major road is often numbered as a soi ("lane" or "alley", though it may be a sizeable thoroughfare), rather than given its own street name. Thanon Sukhumvit for example – Bangkok's longest – has minor roads numbered Soi 1 to Soi 103, with odd numbers on one side of the road and even on the other; so a Thanon Sukhumvit address could read something like 27/9–11 Soi 15, Thanon Sukhumvit, which would mean the property occupies numbers 9–11 on lot 27 on minor road number 15 running off Thanon Sukhumvit.

AVERAGE MAXIMUM DAILY TEMPERATURES AND MONTHLY RAINFALL

	Jan	Feb	Mar	Apr	May	Jun	Jul	Aug	Sep	Oct	Nov	Dec
BANGKOK												
Max temp (°C)	26	28	29	30	30	29	29	28	28	28	27	26
Rainfall (mm)	11	28	31	72	190	152	158	187	320	231	57	9
CHIANG MAI												
Max temp (°C)	21	23	26	29	29	28	27	27	27	26	24	22
Rainfall (mm)	8	6	15	45	153	136	167	227	251	132	44	15
PATTAYA												
Max temp (°C)	26	28	29	30	30	29	29	28	28	28	27	26
Rainfall (mm)	12	23	41	79	165	120	166	166	302	229	66	10
KO SAMUI												
Max temp (°C)	26	26	28	29	29	28	28	28	28	27	26	25
Rainfall (mm)	38	8	12	63	186	113	143	123	209	260	302	98
PHUKET												
Max temp (°C)	27	28	29	28	28	28	28	28	27	27	27	27
Rainfall (mm)	35	31	39	163	348	213	263	263	419	305	207	52

of islanders on Ko Yao Noi. Visitors, volunteers and donations welcome. See p.651.

Lifelong Learning Foundation (Thailand) ☎ 081 894 6936, ⓦ trangsea.com & ⓦ lifelong-learning.org. Promoting nature conservation and the personal development of sea gypsies and other local people in Trang province, this nonprofit organization seeks donations, encourages partnerships with sympathetic overseas organizations, and especially welcomes the custom of tourists at its resorts at Ban Chao Mai (see p.709) and on Ko Mook (see p.713) and Ko Libong (see p.715), and on its award-winning tours.

Mae Tao Clinic Mae Sot ⓦ maetaoclinic.org. Award-winning health centre providing free care to Burmese refugees. Visitors, donations and volunteers welcome. See p.260.

The Mirror Foundation 106 Moo 1, Ban Huay Khom, Tambon Mae Yao, Chiang Rai ☎ 053 737412, ⓦ themirrorfoundation.org. NGO working with the hill tribes in Chiang Rai province to help combat such issues as drug abuse, erosion of culture and trafficking of women and children; it offers trekking and homestays, as well as a guesthouse in Chiang Rai (see p.358). Volunteers, interns and donations sought.

The Students' Education Trust (SET) ⓦ thaistudentcharity.org. High-school and further education in Thailand is a luxury that the poorest kids cannot afford so many are sent to live in temples instead. The SET helps such kids pursue their education and escape from the poverty trap. Some of their stories are told in *Little Angels: The Real-Life Stories of Twelve Thai Novice Monks* (see p.786). SET welcomes donations.

Thai Child Development Foundation Pha To ⓦ thaichild development.org. This small Thai-Dutch-run village project in Chumphon province helps educate, feed and look after needy local children. The foundation welcomes donations of materials and money, takes on volunteers, and has an ecotourism arm (see p.396).

Climate

There are three main **seasons** in most of Thailand: rainy, caused by the southwest monsoon (the least predictable, but roughly May–Oct); cool (Nov–Feb; felt most distinctly in the far north, but hardly at all in the south); and hot (March–May). The Gulf coast's climate is slightly different: it suffers less from the southwest monsoon, but is then hit by the northeast monsoon, making November its rainiest month.

Costs

Thailand can be a very cheap place to travel. At the bottom of the scale, you can manage on a **budget** of about B650 (£13/US$20) per day if you're willing to opt for basic accommodation, eat, drink and travel as the locals do, and stay away from the more expensive resorts like Phuket, Ko Samui and Ko Phi Phi – and you'd have to work hard to stick to this daily allowance in Bangkok. On this budget, you'll be spending around B200 for a dorm or shared room (more for a single room), around B200 on three meals (eating mainly at night markets and simple noodle shops, and eschewing beer), and the rest on travel (sticking to the cheaper buses and third-class trains where possible) and incidentals. With extras like air conditioning in rooms, taking the various forms of taxi rather than buses or shared songthaews for cross-town journeys, and a meal and beer in a more touristy restaurant, a day's outlay would look more like B1000 (£20/US$30). Staying in well-equipped, mid-range hotels and eating in the more exclusive restaurants, you should be able to live very comfortably for around B2000 a day (£40/US$60).

Travellers soon get so used to the low cost of living in Thailand that they start **bargaining** at every available opportunity, much as Thai people do. Although it's expected practice for a lot of commercial transactions, particularly at markets and when hiring tuk-tuks and unmetered taxis (though not in supermarkets or department stores), bargaining is a delicate art that requires humour, tact and patience. If your price is way out of line, the vendor's vehement refusal should be enough to make you increase your offer: never forget that the few pennies or cents you're making such a fuss over will go a lot further in a Thai person's hands than in your own.

It's rare that foreigners can bargain a price down as low as a Thai could, anyway, while **two-tier pricing** has been made official at government-run sights, as a kind of informal tourist tax: at national parks, for example, foreigners pay up to B400 entry while Thais generally pay just B20. A number of privately owned tourist attractions follow a similar two-tier system, posting an inflated price in English for foreigners and a lower price in Thai for locals.

Big-spending shoppers who are departing via Suvarnabhumi, Chiang Mai, Hat Yai, Ko Samui, Krabi, Pattaya or Phuket airports can save some money by claiming a **Value Added Tax refund** (Ⓦrd.go.th /vrt), though it's a bit of a palaver for seven percent (the current rate of VAT). The total amount of your purchases (gems are excluded) from participating shops needs to be at least B5000 per person, with a minimum of B2000 per shop per day. You'll need to show your passport and fill in an application form (to which original tax invoices need to be attached) at the shop. At the relevant airport, you'll need to show your form and purchases to customs officers before checking in, then make your claim from VAT refund officers – from which fees of at least B100 are deducted.

Crime and personal safety

As long as you keep your wits about you, you shouldn't encounter much trouble in Thailand. **Pickpocketing** and **bag-snatching** are two of the main problems – not surprising considering that a huge percentage of the local population scrape by on under US$5 per day – but the most common cause for concern is the number of con-artists who dupe gullible tourists into parting with their cash. There are various Thai laws that tourists need to be aware of, particularly regarding passports, the age of consent and smoking in public.

Theft

To **prevent theft**, most travellers prefer to carry their valuables with them at all times, but it's often possible to use a locker in a hotel or guesthouse – the safest are those that require your own padlock, as there are occasional reports of valuables being stolen by hotel staff. **Padlock your luggage** when leaving it in hotel or guesthouse rooms, as well as when consigning it to storage or taking it on public transport. Padlocks also come in handy as extra security on your room, particularly on the doors of beachfront bamboo huts.

Theft from some long-distance **buses** is also a problem, with the majority of reported incidents taking place on the temptingly cheap overnight buses run by private companies direct from Bangkok's Thanon Khao San (as opposed to those that depart from the government bus stations) to destinations such as Chiang Mai and southern beach resorts. The best solution is to go direct from the bus stations (see p.29).

Personal safety

On any bus, private or government, and on any train journey, never keep anything of value in luggage that is stored out of your sight and be wary of accepting food and drink from fellow passengers as it may be drugged. This might sound paranoid, but there have been enough **drug-muggings** for TAT to publish a specific warning about the problem. Drinks can also be spiked in bars and clubs; at full moon parties on Ko Pha Ngan this has led to sexual assaults against farang women, while prostitutes sometimes spike drinks so they can steal from their victim's room.

Violent crime against tourists is not common, but it does occur, and there have been several serious attacks on women travellers in recent years. However, bearing in mind that fourteen million foreigners visit Thailand every year, the statistical likelihood of becoming a victim is extremely small. **Obvious precautions** for travellers of either sex include locking accessible windows and doors at night – preferably with your own padlock (doors in many of the simpler guesthouses and beach bungalows are designed for this) – and not travelling alone at night in a taxi or tuk-tuk. Nor should

REPORTING A CRIME OR EMERGENCY

In emergencies, contact the English-speaking **tourist police**, who maintain a 24-hour toll-free nationwide line (☎1155) and have offices in the main tourist centres; getting in touch with the tourist police first is invariably more efficient than directly contacting the local police, ambulance or fire service. The tourist police's job is to offer advice and tell you what to do next, but they do not file crime reports, which must be done at the nearest police station.

The British Embassy in Bangkok provides **advice** for British victims of crime in Thailand and also posts practical tips and a list of useful contacts on its website (☎02 305 8333, ⊛ukinthailand.fco.gov.uk/en/help-for-british-nationals).

you risk jumping into an unlicensed taxi at the airport in Bangkok at any time of day: there have been some very violent robberies in these, so take the well-marked licensed, metered taxis instead.

Among hazards to watch out for in the natural world, **riptides** claim a number of tourist lives every year, particularly off Phuket, Ko Chang (Trat), Hua Hin, Cha-am, Rayong, Pattaya and the Ko Samui archipelago during stormy periods of the monsoon season, so always pay attention to warning signs and red flags, and always ask locally if unsure. **Jellyfish** can be a problem on any coast, especially just after a storm (see p.67).

Unfortunately, it is also necessary for female tourists to think twice about spending time alone with a **monk**, as not all men of the cloth uphold the Buddhist precepts and there have been rapes and murders committed by men wearing the saffron robes of the monkhood.

Though unpalatable and distressing, Thailand's high-profile **sex industry** is relatively unthreatening for Western women, with its energy focused exclusively on farang men; it's also quite easily avoided, being contained within certain pockets of the capital and a couple of beach resorts.

As for **harassment** from men, it's hard to generalize, but most Western women find it less of a problem in Thailand than they do back home. Outside the main tourist spots, you're more likely to be of interest as a foreigner rather than a woman and, if travelling alone, as an object of concern rather than of sexual aggression.

Regional issues

It's advisable to travel with a guide if you're going off the main roads in certain **border areas** or, at the very least, to take advice before setting off. As these regions are generally covered in dense unmapped jungle, you shouldn't find yourself alone in the area anyway, but the main stretches to watch are the immediate vicinity of the Burmese border, where fighting on the other side of the border now and again spills over and where there are occasional clashes between Thai security forces and illegal traffickers; and the border between Cambodia and southern Isaan, which is littered with unexploded mines and which has seen recent clashes between the Thai and Cambodian armies over the disputed line of the border, especially at Khao Phra Viharn (Preah Vihear).

Because of the **violence in the deep south**, all Western governments are currently advising against travel to or through the border provinces of Songkhla, Yala, Pattani and Narathiwat, unless essential (see p.705). For up-to-the-minute advice on current political trouble-spots, consult your government's travel advisory (see box, p.62).

Scams

Despite the best efforts of guidebook writers, TAT and the Thai tourist police, countless travellers to Thailand get scammed every year. Nearly all **scams** are easily avoided if you're on your guard against anyone who makes an unnatural effort to befriend you. We have outlined the main scams in the relevant sections of this guide, but con-artists are nothing if not creative, so if in doubt walk away at the earliest opportunity. The worst areas for scammers are the busy tourist centres, including many parts of Bangkok and the main beach resorts.

Many **tuk-tuk drivers** earn most of their living through securing **commissions** from tourist-oriented shops; this is especially true in Bangkok, where they will do their damnedest to get you to go to a gem shop (see p.170). The most common tactic is for drivers to pretend that the Grand Palace or other major sight you intended to visit is closed for the day (see p.85), and to then offer to take you on a round-city tour instead, perhaps even for free. The tour will invariably include a visit to a gem shop. The easiest way to avoid all this is to take a **metered taxi**; if you're fixed on taking a tuk-tuk, ignore any tuk-tuk that is parked up or loitering and be firm about where you want to go.

Self-styled **tourist guides**, **touts** and anyone else who might introduce themselves as **students** or

business people and offer to take you somewhere of interest, or invite you to meet their family, are often the first piece of bait in a well-honed chain of con-artists. If you bite, chances are you'll end up either at a gem shop or in a gambling den, or, at best, at a tour operator or hotel that you had not planned to patronize. This is not to say that you should never accept an invitation from a local person, but be extremely wary of doing so following a street encounter in Bangkok or the resorts. Tourist guides' ID cards are easily faked.

For many of these characters, the goal is to get you inside a dodgy **gem shop**, nearly all of which are located in Bangkok (see box, p.170), but the bottom line is that if you are not experienced at buying and trading in valuable gems you will definitely be ripped off, possibly even to the tune of several thousand dollars. Check the 2Bangkok website's account of a typical gem scam (@ 2bangkok.com/2bangkok-scams-sapphire.html) before you shell out any cash at all.

A less common but potentially more frightening scam involves a similar cast of warm-up artists leading tourists into a **gambling** game. The scammers invite their victim home on an innocent-sounding pretext, get out a pack of cards, and then set about fleecing the incomer in any number of subtle ways. Often this can be especially scary as the venue is likely to be far from hotels or recognizable landmarks. You're unlikely to get any sympathy from police, as gambling is **illegal** in Thailand.

An increasing number of travel agents in tourist centres all over the country are trying to pass themselves off as official government tourist information offices, displaying nothing but "**TOURIST INFORMATION**" on their shop signs or calling themselves names like "T&T" (note that the actual

TAT, the Tourism Authority of Thailand, does not book hotels or sell any kind of travel ticket). Fakers like this are more likely to sell you tickets for services that turn out to be sub-standard or even not to exist. A word of warning also about **jet skis**: operators, who usually ask for a passport as guarantee, will often try to charge renters exorbitant amounts of money for any minor damage they claim to find on return.

Age restrictions and other laws

Thai law requires that tourists **carry their original passports** at all times, though sometimes it's more practical to carry a photocopy and keep the original locked in a safety deposit. The **age of consent** is 15, but the law allows anyone under the age of 18, or their parents, to file charges in retrospect even if they consented to sex at the time. It is against the law to have sex with a prostitute who is under 18. It is illegal for **under-18s** to buy cigarettes or to drive and you must be 20 or over to **buy alcohol** or be allowed into a **bar or club** (ID checks are sometimes enforced in Bangkok). It is illegal for anyone to **gamble** in Thailand (though many do).

Smoking in public is widely prohibited. The ban covers all air-conditioned public buildings (including restaurants, bars and clubs) and air-conditioned trains, buses and planes and even extends to parks and the street; violators may be subject to a B2000 fine. Dropping cigarette butts, **littering** and spitting in public places can also earn you a B2000 fine. There are fines for **overstaying your visa** (see p.64), **working without a permit**, **not wearing a motor-cycle helmet** and violating other **traffic laws**.

Drugs

Drug-smuggling carries a maximum penalty in Thailand of death and **dealing drugs** will get you anything from four years to life in a Thai prison; penalties depend on the drug and the amount involved. Travellers caught with even the smallest amount of drugs at airports and international borders are prosecuted for trafficking, and no one charged with trafficking offences gets bail. Heroin, amphetamines, LSD and ecstasy are classed as Category 1 drugs and carry the most severe penalties: even **possession** of Category 1 drugs for personal use can result in a **life sentence**. Away from international borders, most foreigners arrested in possession of small amounts of cannabis are released on bail, then fined and deported, but the law is complex and prison sentences are possible.

Despite occasional royal pardons, don't expect special treatment as a farang: you only need to read

GOVERNMENTAL TRAVEL ADVISORIES

Australian Department of Foreign Affairs @ dfat.gov.au.

British Foreign & Commonwealth Office @ fco.gov.uk.

Canadian Department of Foreign Affairs @ international.gc.ca.

Irish Department of Foreign Affairs @ foreignaffairs.gov.ie.

New Zealand Ministry of Foreign Affairs @ mfat.govt.nz.

South African Department of Foreign Affairs @ dfa.gov.za.

US State Department @ state.gov.

one of the first-hand accounts by foreign former prisoners (see p.786) or read the blogs at ⓦthai prisonlife.com to get the picture. The **police** actively look for tourists doing drugs, reportedly searching people regularly and randomly on Thanon Khao San, for example. They have the power to order a urine test if they have reasonable grounds for suspicion, and even a positive result for marijuana consumption could lead to a year's imprisonment. Be wary also of **being shopped** by a farang or local dealer keen to earn a financial reward for a successful bust (there are setups at the Ko Pha Ngan full moon parties, for example), or having substances slipped into your luggage (simple enough to perpetrate unless all fastenings are secured with padlocks).

If you are arrested, ask for your embassy to be contacted immediately (see p.171), which is your right under Thai law, and embassy staff will talk you through procedures; the website of the British Embassy in Thailand also posts useful information, including a list of English-speaking lawyers, at ⓦukinthailand.fco.gov.uk/en/help-for -british-nationals. The British charity Prisoners Abroad (ⓦprisonersabroad.org.uk) carries a detailed survival guide on its website, which outlines what to expect if arrested in Thailand, from the point of apprehension through trial and conviction to life in a Thai jail; if contacted, the charity may also be able to offer direct support to a British citizen facing imprisonment in a Thai jail.

Customs regulations

The **duty-free** allowance on entry to Thailand is 200 cigarettes (or 250g of tobacco) and a litre of spirits or wine.

To **export antiques** or newly cast **Buddha images** from Thailand, you need to have a licence granted by the Fine Arts Department (the export of antique Buddhas is forbidden). Licences can be obtained for example through the Office of Archeology and National Museums, 81/1 Thanon Si Ayutthaya (near the National Library), Bangkok (☏02 628 5032), or through the national museums in Chiang Mai or Phuket. Applications take at least three working days in Bangkok, generally more in the provinces, and need to be accompanied by the object itself, some evidence of its rightful possession, two postcard-sized colour photos of it, taken face-on and against a white background, and photocopies of the applicant's passport; further-more, if the object is a Buddha image, the passport photocopies need to be certified by your embassy in Bangkok. Some antiques shops can organize all this for you.

Departure taxes

International and domestic **departure taxes** are included in the price of all tickets.

Electricity

Mains **electricity** is supplied at 220 volts AC and is available at all but the most remote villages and basic beach huts. Where electricity is supplied by generators and/or solar power, for example on the smaller, less populated islands, it is often rationed to evenings only. If you're packing phone and camera chargers, a hair dryer, laptop or other appliance, you'll need to take a set of travel-plug adapters with you as several plug types are commonly in use, most usually with two round pins, but also with two flat-blade pins, and sometimes with both options.

Entry requirements

There are three main entry categories for visitors to Thailand; for all of them, under International Air Travel Association rules, your passport should be valid for at least six months. As visa requirements are subject to frequent change, you should always consult before departure a Thai embassy or consulate, a reliable travel agent, or the Thai Ministry of Foreign Affairs' website at ⓦmfa.go.th/web/2637 .php. For further, unofficial but usually reliable, details on all visa matters, go to ⓦthaivisa.com and especially their various moderated forums.

Most Western passport holders (that includes citizens of the UK, Ireland, the US, Canada, Australia, New Zealand and South Africa) are allowed to enter the country for short **stays** without having to apply for a visa – officially termed the **tourist visa exemption**. You'll be granted a thirty-day stay at an international airport but only fifteen days at an overland border; the period of stay will be stamped into your passport by immigration officials upon entry. You're supposed to be able to somehow show proof of means of living while in the country (B10,000 per person, B20,000 per family), and in theory you may be put back on the next plane without it or sent back to get a sixty-day tourist visa from the nearest Thai embassy, but this is unheard of. You are also required to show proof of tickets to leave Thailand again within the allotted time. This is rarely checked by Thai immigration authorities, though there have been a few cases recently, mostly at the Cambodian border. However, if you have a one-way air ticket to Thailand and no evidence of onward travel arrangements, it's best to buy a tourist visa in advance: some airlines will stop you boarding the plane without one, as they would be liable for flying you back to your point of origin if you did happen to be stopped.

If you're fairly certain you may want to stay longer than fifteen/thirty days, then from the outset you should apply for a **sixty-day tourist visa** from a Thai embassy or consulate, accompanying your application – which generally takes several days to process – with your passport and one or two photos. The sixty-day visa currently costs, for example, £25 in the UK; multiple-entry versions are available, costing £25 per entry, which may be handy if you're going to be leaving and re-entering Thailand. Ordinary tourist visas are valid for three months, ie you must enter Thailand within three months of the visa being issued by the Thai embassy or consulate, while multiple-entry versions are valid for six months. Visa application forms can be downloaded from, for example, the Thai Ministry of Foreign Affairs' website.

Thai embassies also consider applications for **ninety-day non-immigrant visas** (£50, in the UK for example, for single entry, £125 multiple-entry) as long as you can offer a reason for your visit, such as study, business or visiting family/friends (there are different categories of non-immigrant visa for which different levels of proof are needed). As it can be a hassle to organize a ninety-day visa, it's generally easier to apply for a thirty-day extension to your sixty-day visa once inside Thai borders.

It's not a good idea to **overstay** your visa limits. Once you're at the airport or the border, you'll have to pay a fine of B500 per day before you can leave Thailand. More importantly, however, if you're in the country with an expired visa and you get involved with police or immigration officials for any reason, however trivial, they are obliged to take you to court, possibly imprison you, and deport you.

Border runs, extensions and re-entry permits

Setting aside the caveats about proof of funds and onward tickets (see p.63), it's generally easy to get a new fifteen-day tourist visa exemption by hopping **across the border** into a neighbouring country and back. Such tourist visa exemptions can be **extended** within Thailand for a further seven days, sixty-day tourist visas for a further thirty days, at the discretion of immigration officials; extensions

cost B1900 and are issued over the counter at immigration offices (*kaan khao muang*; ☎1111 for 24hr information in English, ⓦimmigration.go.th) in nearly every provincial capital – most offices ask for one or two photos as well, plus one or two photocopies of the main pages of your passport including your Thai departure card, arrival stamp and visa. Many Khao San tour agents offer to get your visa extension for you, but beware: some are reportedly faking the stamps, which could get you into serious trouble. Immigration offices also issue **re-entry permits** (B1000 single re-entry, B3800 multiple) if you want to leave the country and come back again while maintaining the validity of your existing visa.

THAI EMBASSIES AND CONSULATES ABROAD

For a full listing of Thai diplomatic missions abroad, consult the Thai Ministry of Foreign Affairs' website at ⓦmfa.go.th/web/2712.php; their other site, ⓦthaiembassy.org, has links to the websites of most of the offices below.

Australia 111 Empire Circuit, Yarralumla, Canberra ACT 2600 ☎02/6206 0100; plus consulate at 131 Macquarrie St, Sydney, NSW 2000 ☎02/9241 2542–3.

Burma 94 Pyay Rd, Dagon Township, Rangoon ☎01/226721.

Cambodia 196 Preah Norodom Blvd, Sangkat Tonle Bassac, Khan Chamcar Mon, Phnom Penh ☎023/726306–10.

Canada 180 Island Park Drive, Ottawa, ON, K1Y 0A2 ☎613/722-4444; plus consulate at 1040 Burrard St, Vancouver, BC, V6Z 2R9 ☎604/687-1143.

Laos Vientiane: embassy at Avenue Kaysone Phomvihane, Saysettha District ☎021/214581–2, consular section at Unit 15 Bourichane Rd, Ban Phone Si Nuan, Muang Si Sattanak ☎021/453916; plus consulate at Khanthabouly District, Savannakhet Province, PO Box 513 ☎041/212373.

Malaysia 206 Jalan Ampang, 50450 Kuala Lumpur ☎03/2148 8222; plus consulates at 4426 Jalan Pengkalan Chepa, 15400 Kota Bharu ☎09/748 2545; and 1 Jalan Tunku Abdul Rahman, 10350 Penang ☎04/226 9484.

New Zealand 110 Molesworth St, Thorndon, Wellington ☎04/476 8616.

Singapore 370 Orchard Rd, Singapore 238870 ☎6737 2158.

South Africa 428 Pretorius/Hill St, Arcadia, Pretoria 0083 ☎012/342 5470.

UK & Ireland 29–30 Queens Gate, London SW7 5JB ☎020/7589 2944. Visa applications by post are not accepted here, but can be sent to various honorary consulates, including those in Hull (ⓦthaiconsul-uk .com) and Dublin (ⓦthaiconsulateireland.com).

US 1024 Wisconsin Ave NW, Suite 401, Washington, DC 20007 ☎202/944-3600; plus consulates at 700 North Rush St, Chicago, IL 60611 ☎312/664-3129; 611 North Larchmont Blvd, 2nd Floor, Los Angeles, CA 90004 ☎323/962-9574; and 351 E 52nd St, New York, NY 10022 ☎212/754-1770.

Vietnam 63–65 Hoang Dieu St, Hanoi ☎ 04/3823-5092–4; plus consulate at 77 Tran Quoc Thao St, District 3, Ho Chi Minh City ☎ 08/3932-7637–8.

Gay and lesbian Thailand

Buddhist tolerance and a national abhorrence of confrontation and victimization combine to make Thai society relatively tolerant of **homosexuality**, if not exactly positive about same-sex relationships. Most Thais are extremely private and discreet about being gay, generally pursuing a "don't ask, don't tell" understanding with their family. The majority of people are horrified by the idea of gay-bashing and generally regard it as unthinkable to spurn a child or relative for being gay.

Hardly any Thai celebrities are out, yet the predilections of several respected social, political and entertainment figures are widely known and accepted. There is no mention of homosexuality at all in Thai law, which means that the **age of consent** for gay sex is fifteen, the same as for heterosexuals. However, this also means that gay rights are not protected under Thai law.

Although excessively physical displays of affection are frowned upon for both heterosexuals and homosexuals, Western gay couples should get no hassle about being seen together in public – it's much more acceptable, and common, in fact, for friends of the same sex (gay or not) to walk hand-in-hand, than for heterosexual couples to do so.

Transvestites (known as *katoey* or "ladyboys") and **transsexuals** are also a lot more visible in Thailand than in the West. You'll find cross-dressers doing ordinary jobs, even in small upcountry towns, and there are a number of transvestites and transsexuals in the public eye too – including national volleyball stars and champion *muay thai* boxers. The government tourist office vigorously promotes the transvestite cabarets in Pattaya, Phuket and Bangkok, all of which are advertised as family entertainment. *Katoey* also regularly appear as characters in soap operas, TV comedies and films, where they are depicted as stereotyped but harmless figures of fun. Richard Totman's *The Third Sex* (see p.787) offers an interesting insight into Thai *katoey*, their experiences in society and public attitudes towards them.

The scene

Thailand's gay scene is mainly focused on **mainstream venues** like karaoke bars, restaurants, massage parlours, gyms, saunas and escort agencies. For the sake of discretion, gay venues are usually intermingled with straight ones. Bangkok, Phuket and Pattaya have the biggest concentrations of farang-friendly gay bars and clubs; and Chiang Mai has an established bar scene. For a detailed guide to the gay and lesbian scene throughout the country, see the *Utopia Guide to Thailand* by John Goss, which can be ordered or downloaded as an e-book via ⓦ utopia-asia.com.

Thai **lesbians** generally eschew the word lesbian, which in Thailand is associated with male fantasies, instead referring to themselves as either *tom* (for tomboy) or *dee* (for lady). There are hardly any dedicated *tom-dee* venues in Thailand, but we've listed established ones where possible; unless otherwise specified, gay means male throughout this guide.

The farang-oriented gay **sex industry** is a tiny but highly visible part of Thailand's gay scene. With its tawdry floor shows and host services, it bears a dispiriting resemblance to the straight sex trade, and is similarly most active in Bangkok, Pattaya, Patong (on Phuket) and Chiang Mai. Like their female counterparts in the heterosexual fleshpots, many of the boys working in the gay sex bars that dominate these districts are underage; note that anyone caught having sex with a prostitute below the age of 18 faces imprisonment. A significant number of gay prostitutes are gay by economic necessity rather than by inclination. As with the straight sex scene, we do not list commercial gay sex bars in the guide.

INFORMATION AND CONTACTS FOR GAY TRAVELLERS

Bangkok Lesbian ⓦ bangkoklesbian.com. Organized by foreign lesbians living in Thailand, Bangkok Lesbian hosts regular parties and posts general info and listings of the capital's lesbian-friendly hangouts on its website.

Dreaded Ned's ⓦ dreadedned.com. Guide to the scene in Thailand that's most useful for its what's-on listings.

Gay People in Thailand ⓦ thaivisa.com /forum/Gay-People -Thailand-f27.html. Popular forum for gay expats.

Utopia ⓦ utopia-asia.com and ⓦ utopia-asia.com/womthai.htm. Asia's best gay and lesbian website lists clubs, events, accommodation, tour operators and organizations for gays and lesbians and has useful links to other sites in Asia and the rest of the world.

Health

Although Thailand's climate, wildlife and cuisine present Western travellers with fewer health worries than in many Asian destinations, it's as well to know in advance what the risks might be, and what preventive or curative measures you should take.

For a start, there's no need to bring huge supplies of non-prescription medicines with you, as Thai **pharmacies** (raan khai yaa; typically open daily 8.30am–8pm) are well stocked with local and international branded medicaments, and of course they are generally much less expensive than at home. Nearly all pharmacies are run by trained English-speaking pharmacists, who are usually the best people to talk to if your symptoms aren't acute enough to warrant seeing a doctor. The British pharmacy chain, Boots, now has branches in many big cities (see ⓦth.boots.com for locations). These are the best place to stock up on some Western products such as **tampons** (which Thai women do not use).

Hospital (rong phayabaan) cleanliness and efficiency vary, but generally hygiene and health-care standards are good and the ratio of medical staff to patients is considerably higher than in most parts of the West. As with head pharmacists, doctors speak English. Several Bangkok hospitals are highly regarded (see p.172), and all provincial capitals have at least one hospital: if you need to get to one, ask at your accommodation for advice on, and possibly transport to, the nearest or most suitable. In the event of a major health crisis, get someone to contact your embassy (see p.171) and insurance company – it may be best to get yourself transported to Bangkok or even home.

There have been outbreaks of **Avian Influenza** (**bird flu**) in domestic poultry and wild birds in Thailand (most recently in 2008) which have led to a small number of human fatalities, believed to have arisen through close contact with infected poultry. There has been no evidence of human-to-human transmission in Thailand, and the risk to humans is believed to be very low. However, as a precaution, you should avoid visiting live-animal markets and other places where you may come into close contact with birds, and ensure that poultry and egg dishes are thoroughly cooked.

Inoculations

There are no compulsory **inoculation** requirements for people travelling to Thailand from the West, but you should consult a doctor or other health professional, preferably at least four weeks in advance of your trip, for the latest information on recommended immunizations. In addition to making sure that your recommended immunizations for life in your home country are up to date, most doctors strongly advise vaccinations or boosters against tetanus, diphtheria, hepatitis A and, in many cases, typhoid, and in some cases they might also recommend protecting yourself against Japanese encephalitis, rabies and hepatitis B. There is currently no vaccine against malaria (see below). If you forget to have all your inoculations before leaving home, or don't leave yourself sufficient time, you can get them in Bangkok at, for example, the Thai Red Cross Society's Queen Saovabha Institute or Global Doctor (see p.172).

Mosquito-borne diseases

Mosquitoes in Thailand spread not only malaria, but also diseases such as dengue fever and the very similar chikungunya fever, especially during the rainy season. The main message, therefore, is to **avoid being bitten** by mosquitoes. You should smother yourself and your clothes in **mosquito repellent** containing the chemical compound DEET, reapplying regularly (shops, guesthouses and department stores all over Thailand stock it, but if you want the highest-strength repellent, or convenient roll-ons or sprays, do your shopping before you leave home). DEET is strong stuff, and if you have sensitive skin, a natural alternative is citronella (available in the UK as Mosi-guard), made from a blend of eucalyptus oils; the Thai version is made with lemon grass.

At night you should sleep either under a **mosquito net** sprayed with DEET or in a bedroom with **mosquito screens** across the windows (or in an enclosed air-con room). Accommodation in tourist spots nearly always provides screens or a net (check both for holes), but if you're planning to go way off the beaten track or want the security of having your own mosquito net just in case, wait until you get to Bangkok to buy one, where department stores sell them for much less than you'd pay in the West. Plug-in insecticide vaporizers, insect room sprays and mosquito coils – also widely available in Thailand – help keep the insects at bay; electronic "buzzers" are useless.

Malaria

Thailand is **malarial**, with the disease being carried by mosquitoes that bite from dusk to dawn, but the risks involved vary across the country.

There is a significant risk of malaria, mainly in rural and forested areas, in a narrow strip along the **borders with Cambodia** (excluding Ko Chang), **Laos** and **Burma** (the highest-risk area, including the countryside around Mae Hong Son, but excluding, for example, Chiang Mai, Chiang Rai and Kanchanaburi towns, and resorts and road and rail routes along the Gulf coast). Discuss with your travel health adviser which anti-malarial drugs are currently likely to be effective in these areas, as prophylaxis advice can change from year to year.

Elsewhere in Thailand the risk of malaria is considered to be so low that anti-malarial tablets are not advised.

The **signs of malaria** are often similar to flu, but are very variable. The incubation period for malignant malaria, which can be fatal, is usually 7–28 days, but it can take up to a year for symptoms of the benign form to occur. The most important symptom is a raised temperature of at least 38°C beginning a week or more after the first potential exposure to malaria: if you suspect anything, go to a hospital or clinic immediately.

Dengue fever

Dengue fever, a debilitating and occasionally fatal viral disease that is particularly prevalent during and just after the rainy season, is on the increase throughout tropical Asia, and is endemic to many areas of Thailand, with over 115,000 reported cases in 2010. Unlike malaria, dengue fever is spread by mosquitoes that can bite during daylight hours, so you should also use mosquito repellent during the day. Symptoms include fever, headaches, fierce joint and muscle pain ("breakbone fever" is another name for dengue), and possibly a rash, and usually develop between five and eight days after being bitten.

There is no vaccine against dengue fever; the only treatment is lots of rest, liquids and paracetamol (or any other acetaminophen painkiller, not aspirin), though more serious cases may require hospitalization.

Rabies

Rabies is widespread in Thailand, mainly carried by dogs (between four and seven percent of stray dogs in Bangkok are reported to be rabid), but also cats and monkeys. It is transmitted by bites, scratches or even occasionally licks. Dogs are everywhere in Thailand and even if kept as pets they're often not very well cared for; hopefully their mangy appearance will discourage the urge to pat them, as you should steer well clear of them. Rabies is invariably fatal if the patient waits until symptoms begin, though modern vaccines and treatments are very effective and deaths are rare. The important thing is, if you are bitten, licked or scratched by an animal, to vigorously clean the wound with soap and disinfect it, preferably with something containing iodine, and to seek medical advice regarding treatment right away.

Other bites and stings

Thailand's seas are home to a few dangerous creatures that you should look out for, notably **jellyfish**, which tend to be washed towards the beach by rough seas during the monsoon season but can appear at any time of year. All manner of stinging and non-stinging jellyfish can be found in Thailand – as a general rule, those with the longest tentacles tend to have the worst stings – but reports of serious incidents are rare; ask around at your resort or at a local dive shop to see if there have been any sightings of venomous varieties. You also need to be wary of venomous **sea snakes**, **sea urchins** and a couple of less conspicuous species – **stingrays**, which often lie buried in the sand, and **stonefish**, whose potentially lethal venomous spikes are easily stepped on because the fish look like stones and lie motionless on the sea bed.

If **stung or bitten** you should always seek medical advice as soon as possible, but there are a few ways of alleviating the pain or administering your own first-aid in the meantime. If you're stung by a jellyfish, wash the affected area with salt water (not fresh water) and, if possible, with vinegar (failing that, ammonia, citrus fruit juice or even urine may do the trick), and try to remove the fragments of tentacles from the skin with a gloved hand, forceps, thick cloth or credit card. The best way to minimize the risk of stepping on the toxic spines of sea urchins, stingrays and stonefish is to wear thick-soled shoes, though these cannot provide total protection; sea urchin spikes should be removed after softening the skin with ointment, though some people recommend applying urine to help dissolve the spines; for stingray and stonefish stings, alleviate the pain by immersing the wound in hot water while awaiting help.

In the case of a **venomous snake bite**, don't try sucking out the venom or applying a tourniquet: wrap up and immobilize the bitten limb and try to stay still and calm until medical help arrives; all provincial hospitals in Thailand carry supplies of antivenins.

Some of Thailand's wilder, less developed beaches are plagued by **sandflies**, tiny, barely visible midges whose bites can trigger an allergic response, leaving big red weals and an unbearable itch, and possible infection if scratched too vigorously. Many islanders say that slathering yourself in (widely available) coconut oil is the best deterrent as sandflies apparently don't like the smell. Applying locally made camphor-based yellow oil (see p.406) quells the itch, but you may need to resort to antihistamines for the inflammation. **Leeches** aren't dangerous but can be a bother when walking in forested areas, especially during and just after the rainy season. The most effective way to get leeches off your skin is to burn them with a lighted cigarette, or douse them in salt; oily suntan lotion or insect repellent sometimes makes them lose their grip and fall off.

Worms and flukes

Worms can be picked up through the soles of your feet, so avoid going barefoot. They can also be ingested by eating undercooked meat, and liver **flukes** by eating raw or undercooked freshwater fish. Worms which cause schistosomiasis (bilharziasis) by attaching themselves to your bladder or intestines can be found in freshwater rivers and lakes. The risk of contracting this disease is low, but you should avoid swimming in the southern reaches of the Mekong River and in most freshwater lakes.

Digestive problems

By far the most common travellers' complaint in Thailand, **digestive troubles** are often caused by contaminated food and water, or sometimes just by an overdose of unfamiliar foodstuffs (see p.38 and p.42).

Stomach trouble usually manifests itself as simple **diarrhoea**, which should clear up without medical treatment within three to seven days and is best combated by drinking lots of fluids. If this doesn't work, you're in danger of getting **dehydrated** and should take some kind of rehydration solution, either a commercial sachet of ORS (oral rehydration solution), sold in all Thai pharmacies, or a do-it-yourself version, which can be made by adding a handful of sugar and a pinch of salt to every litre of boiled or bottled water (soft drinks are not a viable alternative). If you can eat, avoid fatty foods.

Anti-diarrhoeal agents such as Imodium are useful for blocking you up on long bus journeys, but only attack the symptoms and may prolong infections; an antibiotic such as ciprofloxacin, however, can often reduce a typical attack of traveller's diarrhoea to one day. If the diarrhoea persists for a week or more, or if you have blood or mucus in your stools, or an accompanying fever, go to a doctor or hospital.

HIV and AIDS

HIV infection is widespread in Thailand, primarily because of the sex trade (see p.127). **Condoms** (*meechai*) are sold in pharmacies, convenience stores, department stores, hairdressers and even street markets. Due to rigorous screening methods, Thailand's medical blood supply is now considered safe from HIV/AIDS infection.

MEDICAL RESOURCES

Canadian Society for International Health ☎ 613/241-5785, ⓦ csih.org. Extensive list of travel health centres.

CDC ☎ 1-800/232 4636, ⓦ cdc.gov/travel. Official US government travel health site.

Hospital for Tropical Diseases Travel Clinic UK ⓦ thehtd.org.

International Society for Travel Medicine US ☎ 1-404/373-8282, ⓦ istm.org. Has a full list of travel health clinics.

MASTA (Medical Advisory Service for Travellers Abroad) UK ⓦ masta.org.

NHS Travel Health Website UK ⓦ fitfortravel.scot.nhs.uk.

The Travel Doctor – TMVC ☎ 1300/658 844, ⓦ tmvc.com.au. Lists travel clinics in Australia, New Zealand and South Africa.

Tropical Medical Bureau Ireland ☎ 1850/487 674, ⓦ tmb.ie.

Insurance

Most visitors to Thailand will need to take out **specialist travel insurance**, though you should check exactly what's covered. Insurers will generally not cover travel in Songkhla, Yala, Pattani and Narathiwat provinces in the deep south, as Western governments are currently advising against going to these areas unless it's essential (see p.705). Policies generally also exclude so-called **dangerous sports** unless an extra premium is paid: in Thailand this can mean such things as scuba diving, whitewater rafting and trekking.

ROUGH GUIDES TRAVEL INSURANCE

Rough Guides has teamed up with WorldNomads.com to offer great travel insurance deals. Policies are available to residents of over 150 countries, with cover for a wide range of adventure sports, 24hr emergency assistance, high levels of medical and evacuation cover and a stream of travel safety information. Roughguides.com users can take advantage of their policies online 24/7, from anywhere in the world – even if you're already travelling. And since plans often change when you're on the road, you can extend your policy and even claim online. Roughguides.com users who buy travel insurance with WorldNomads.com can also leave a positive footprint and donate to a community development project. For more information go to ⓦ roughguides.com/shop.

Internet

Internet access is very widespread and very cheap in Thailand. You'll find traveller-oriented **internet cafés** in every touristed town and resort in the country – there are at least twenty in the Banglamphu district of Bangkok, for example. In untouristed neighbourhoods throughout the country you can always check your email at the ubiquitous online games centres, favourite after-school haunts that are easily spotted from the piles of schoolboy pumps outside the door. Competition keeps prices low: upcountry you could expect to pay as little as B20 per hour, while rates in tourist centres average B1 per minute.

Increasing numbers of budget guesthouses and cheap hotels, especially in Bangkok, offer **wi-fi** in all or parts of their establishment; all upmarket hotels have it, though rates are sometimes astronomical. Plenty of cafés, restaurants, bars and other locations across the country provide wi-fi, which is usually free to customers. For a list of hot spots nationwide, try Ⓦ jiwire.com; for free locations, go to Ⓦ stickman weekly.com.

Laundry

Guesthouses and cheap hotels all over the country run low-cost, same-day **laundry** services, though in luxury hotels, it'll cost an arm and a leg. In some places you pay per item, in others you're charged by the kilo (generally around B30–50 per kg); ironing is often included in the price.

Left luggage

Most major train stations have **left luggage** facilities, where bags can be stored for up to twenty days (around B30–80 per item per day); at bus stations you can usually persuade someone official to look after your stuff for a few hours. Many guesthouses and basic hotels also offer an inexpensive and reliable service, while upmarket hotels should be able to look after your luggage for free. There's also left luggage at Bangkok, Chiang Mai and Phuket international airports (B80–140 per day).

Living in Thailand

The most common source of **employment** in Thailand is **teaching English**, and Bangkok and Chiang Mai are the most fruitful places to look for jobs. You can search for openings at schools all over Thailand on Ⓦ ajarn.com, which also features extensive general advice on teaching and living in Thailand. Another useful resource is the excellent Ⓦ thaivisa.com, whose scores of well-used forums focus on specific topics that range from employment in Thailand to legal issues and cultural and practical topics.

If you're a qualified **dive instructor**, you might be able to get seasonal work at one of the major resorts – in Phuket, Khao Lak and Ao Nang and on Ko Chang, Ko Phi Phi, Ko Lanta, Ko Samui and Ko Tao, for example. Guesthouse noticeboards occasionally carry adverts for more unusual jobs, such as playing extras in Thai movies. A tourist visa does not entitle you to work in Thailand, so, legally, you'll need to apply for a **work permit**.

STUDY, WORK AND VOLUNTEER PROGRAMMES

In addition to the programmes listed below, voluntary opportunities with smaller grassroots projects (see p.58) and wildlife charity projects (see p.767) are available.

AFS Intercultural Programs Australia ☎ 02/9215 0077, Canada ☎ 1-800/361-7248, NZ ☎ 0800/600 300, South Africa ☎ 11/447 2673, US ☎ 1-800/AFS-INFO; Ⓦ afs.org. Intercultural exchange organization with programmes in over fifty countries.

Council on International Educational Exchange (CIEE) US ☎ 1-207/553-4000, Ⓦ ciee.org. Leading NGO that organizes paid year-long placements as English teachers in schools in Thailand.

Phuket English teachers Ⓦ phukethasbeengoodtous.org. Welcomes short- and longer-term volunteers to teach and assist on its Practical English Language programme at schools on Phuket. The aim of the foundation is to improve kids' standards of English so that they can get the better-paid jobs in Phuket's tourist industry.

Starfish Ventures Ⓦ starfishvolunteers.com. Paying volunteer and gap-year placements in Thailand in the areas of health, childcare, wildlife conservation, community development and teaching.

Volunteer Teaching in Thailand Ⓦ volunteerteacherthailand .org. Continuing the good work begun by the thousands of volunteers who came to Khao Lak to help rebuild lives and homes following the 2004 tsunami, this organization teaches English to Khao Lak kids and adults to enhance their future prospects in the local tourist industry. Teaching experience is appreciated but not essential.

Volunthai Ⓦ volunthai.com. Invites young volunteers to teach English in rural schools mostly in northeast Thailand. The minimal fees cover homestay accommodation.

Thai language classes

The most popular places to **study Thai** are Chiang Mai and Bangkok, where there's plenty of choice, including private and group lessons for both tourists and expats; note, however, that some schools' main reason for existence is to provide educational visas for long-staying foreigners. The longest-running and best-regarded courses and private lessons are provided by AUA (American University Alumni; ⓦauathailand.org), which has outlets in Bangkok, Pattaya, Rayong and Chiang Mai (see p.304).

Mail

Overseas airmail usually takes around seven days from Bangkok, a little longer from the more isolated areas (it's worth asking at the post office about their express EMS services, which can cut this down to three days and aren't prohibitively expensive). **Post offices** in Thailand have recently been quite successfully privatized, and many now offer money-wiring facilities (in association with Western Union), parcel packing, long-distance bus tickets, amulets, whitening cream, you name it. They're generally open Monday to Friday 8.30am to 4.30pm, Saturday 9am to noon; some close Monday to Friday noon to 1pm and may stay open until 6pm, and a few open 9am to noon on Sundays and public holidays. Almost all main post offices across the country operate a **poste restante** service and will hold letters for one to three months. Mail should be addressed: *Name* (family name underlined or capitalized), Poste Restante, GPO, *Town or City*, Thailand. It will be filed by surname, though it's always wise to check under your first initial as well. The smaller post offices pay scant attention to who takes what, but in the busier GPOs you need to show your passport, pay B1 per letter or B2 per parcel received, and sign for them.

Post offices are the best places to buy **stamps**, though hotels and guesthouses often sell them too, usually charging an extra B1 per stamp. An airmail letter of under 10g costs B17 to send to Europe or Australia and B19 to North America; postcards and aerogrammes cost B15, regardless of where they're going. The **surface** rate for parcels to the UK is B950 for the first kg, then B175 per kg; to the US B550 for the first kg, then B140 per kg; and to Australia B650 for the first kg, then B110 per kg; the package should reach its destination in three months. The **airmail** rate for parcels to the UK is B900 for the first kg, then B380 per kg; to the US B950 for the first kg, then B500 per kg; and to Australia B750 for the first kg, then B350 per kg; the package should reach its destination in one or two weeks.

Maps

For most major destinations, the **maps** in this book should be all you need, though you may want to supplement them with larger-scale maps

of Bangkok and the whole country. Bangkok bookshops are the best source of these; where appropriate, detailed local maps and their stockists are recommended throughout the Guide. If you want to buy a map before you get there, Rough Guides' 1:1,200,000 map of Thailand is a good option – and, since it's printed on special rip-proof paper, it won't tear. Reasonable alternatives include the 1:1,500,000 maps produced by Nelles and Bartholomew.

For **drivers**, the best atlas is *Thailand Deluxe Atlas* published by thinknet (ⓦthinknet.co.th): at a scale of 1:550,000, it's bilingual and fairly regularly updated, but costs B550. It's available at most bookshops in Thailand where English-language material is sold. They also have a newer *Thailand Handy Atlas* at 1:1,000,000 for B270, and their mapping is available online at ⓦmapguidethailand .com.

Trekking maps are hard to come by, except in the most popular national parks where you can usually pick up a free handout showing the main trails.

Money and banks

Thailand's unit of currency is the **baht** (abbreviated to "B"), divided into 100 satang – which are rarely seen these days. Coins come in B1 (silver), B2 (golden), B5 (silver) and B10 (mostly golden, encircled by a silver ring) denominations, notes in B20, B50, B100, B500 and B1000 denominations, inscribed with Western as well as Thai numerals, and generally increasing in size according to value.

At the time of writing, **exchange rates** were around B30 to US$1, B45 to €1 and B50 to £1. A good site for current exchange rates is ⓦxe.com. Note that Thailand has no black market in foreign currency.

Banking hours are Monday to Friday from 8.30am to 3.30 or 4.30pm, but exchange kiosks in the main tourist centres are always open till at least 5pm, sometimes 10pm, and upmarket hotels change money (at poor rates) 24 hours a day. The Suvarnabhumi Airport exchange counters also operate 24 hours, while exchange kiosks at overseas airports with flights to Thailand usually keep Thai currency.

Sterling and US dollar **travellers' cheques** are accepted by banks and exchange booths in every sizeable Thai town, and most places also deal in a variety of other currencies; everyone offers better rates for cheques than for straight cash. Generally, a total of B33 in commission and duty is charged per cheque – though kiosks and hotels in isolated places may charge extra – so you'll save money if you deal in larger cheque denominations. Note that Scottish and Northern Irish sterling notes may not be accepted in some places.

American Express, Visa and MasterCard **credit and debit cards** are accepted at top hotels as well as in some posh restaurants, department stores, tourist shops and travel agents, but surcharging of up to seven percent is rife, and theft and forgery are major industries – try not to let the card out of your sight, always demand any carbon copies, and never leave cards in baggage storage. With a debit or credit card and personal identification number (PIN), you can also withdraw cash from hundreds of 24-hour **ATMs** around the country. Almost every town now has at least one bank with an ATM that accepts overseas cards (all the banks marked on our maps throughout the Guide have ATMs), and there are a growing number of stand-alone ATMs in supermarkets. However, Thai banks now make a charge of B150 per ATM withdrawal (on top of whatever your bank at home will be charging you); to get around this, go into a bank with your card and passport instead and ask for a cash advance, or check out ⓦaeon.co.th, the website of a Japanese bank that operates in Thailand, for locations of their ATMs – they don't charge for ATM withdrawals from foreign bank accounts, though there have been reports of people not receiving cash from Aeon ATMs but having their accounts debited.

Opening hours and public holidays

Most shops **open** long hours, usually Monday to Saturday from about 8am to 8pm, while department stores operate daily from around 10am to 9pm. Private office hours are generally Monday to Friday 8am to 5pm and Saturday 8am to noon, though in tourist areas these hours are longer, with weekends worked like any other day. Government offices work Monday to Friday 8.30am to noon and 1 to 4.30pm, and national museums tend to stick to these hours too, but some close on Mondays and Tuesdays rather than at weekends. Temples generally open their gates every day from dawn to dusk.

Many tourists only register **national holidays** because trains and buses suddenly get extraordinarily crowded: although government offices shut on these days, most shops and tourist-oriented businesses carry on regardless, and TAT branches continue to dispense information. (Bank holidays vary slightly from the government office holidays given below: banks close on May 1 and

July 1, but not for the Royal Ploughing Ceremony nor for Khao Pansa.) Some national holidays are celebrated with theatrical festivals (see p.46). The only time an inconvenient number of shops, restaurants and hotels do close is during **Chinese New Year**, which, though not marked as an official national holiday, brings many businesses to a standstill for several days in late January or February. You'll notice it particularly in the south, where most service industries are Chinese-managed.

Thais use both the Western Gregorian **calendar** and a Buddhist calendar – the Buddha is said to have died (or entered Nirvana) in the year 543 BC, so Thai dates start from that point: thus 2013 AD becomes 2556 BE (Buddhist Era).

NATIONAL HOLIDAYS

Jan 1 Western New Year's Day

Feb (day of full moon) Makha Puja. Commemorates the Buddha preaching to a spontaneously assembled crowd of 1250.

April 6 Chakri Day. The founding of the Chakri dynasty.

April (usually 13–15) Songkhran. Thai New Year.

May 5 Coronation Day

May (early in the month) Royal Ploughing Ceremony. Marks the start of the rice-planting season.

May (day of full moon) Visakha Puja. The holiest of all Buddhist holidays, which celebrates the birth, enlightenment and death of the Buddha.

July (day of full moon) Asanha Puja. The anniversary of the Buddha's first sermon.

July (day after Asanha Puja) Khao Pansa. The start of the annual three-month Buddhist rains retreat, when new monks are ordained.

Aug 12 Queen's birthday and Mothers' Day

Oct 23 Chulalongkorn Day. The anniversary of Rama V's death.

Dec 5 King's birthday and Fathers' Day. Also now celebrated as National Day (instead of Constitution Day).

Dec 10 Constitution Day

Dec 31 Western New Year's Eve

Phones

Most foreign **mobile-phone** networks have links with Thai networks but you might want to check on roaming rates, which are often exorbitant, before you leave home. To get round this, most travellers purchase a Thai pre-paid SIM card – 1-2-Call (ⓦais.co.th) is the biggest network with the best coverage – for their mobile phone (*moe thoe*). Available for as little as B50 (sometimes free at airports, for example with True Move) and refillable at 7-Elevens around the country, they offer very cheap calls, both domestically and internationally (especially if you use low-cost international prefixes such as 1-2-Call's "005" or "009"). They also offer very

INTERNATIONAL DIALLING CODES

Calling from abroad, the international **country code** for Thailand is **66**, after which you leave off the initial zero of the Thai number.

Calling from Thailand, you'll need the relevant country code (see p.71 for information on prefixes):

Australia 61
Canada 1
Ireland 353
New Zealand 64
South Africa 27
UK 44
US 1

For **international directory enquiries** and operator services, call ☎ 100.

cheap texting and are free of charge for all incoming calls; mobile internet and wi-fi packages are also generally available.

Even cheaper international calls – less than B1/minute to most countries – can be made with a Zay Hi **phonecard** (Ⓦ zayhi.com), available in B300 and B500 denominations from post offices and branches of Family Mart. The cheapest option, of course, is to find a guesthouse or café with free wi-fi and **Skype** from your own device; Skype is also available on the computers in most internet cafés.

When **dialling** any number in Thailand, you must now always preface it with what used to be the area code, even when dialling from the same area. Where we've given several line numbers – eg ☎ 02 431 1802–9 – you can substitute the last digit, 2, with any digit between 3 and 9. For **directory enquiries** within Thailand, call ☎ 1133.

All mobile-phone numbers in Thailand have recently been changed from nine to ten digits, by adding the number "8" after the initial zero (you may still come across cards and brochures giving the old nine-digit number). Note also, however, that Thais tend to change mobile-phone providers – and therefore numbers – comparatively frequently, in search of a better deal.

One final local idiosyncrasy: Thai phone books list people by their first name, not their family name.

Photography

Most towns and all resorts have at least one **camera shop** where you will be able to get your digital pictures downloaded on to a CD for

B100–150; the shops all have card readers. In tourist centres many internet cafés also offer CD-burning services, though if you want to email your pictures bringing your own cable will make life easier.

Time

Thailand is in the same time zone year-round, with no daylight savings period. It's five hours ahead of South Africa, seven hours ahead of GMT, twelve hours ahead of US Eastern Standard Time, three hours behind Australian Eastern Standard Time and five hours behind New Zealand Standard Time.

Tipping

It is usual to **tip** hotel bellboys and porters B20–40, and to round up taxi fares to the nearest B10. Most guides, drivers, masseurs, waiters and maids also depend on tips, and although some upmarket hotels and restaurants will add an automatic ten percent service charge to your bill, this is not always shared out.

Tourist information

The **Tourism Authority of Thailand**, or **TAT** (Ⓦ tourismthailand.org), maintains offices in several cities abroad and has dozens of branches within Thailand (all open daily 8.30am–4.30pm, though a few close noon–1pm) plus counters at Suvarnabhumi International Airport. Regional offices should have up-to-date information on local festival dates and perhaps transport schedules, but none of them offers accommodation booking, and service can be variable. You can contact the TAT tourist assistance phoneline from anywhere in the country for free on ☎ 1672 (daily 8am–8pm). In Bangkok, the Bangkok Tourism Division is a better source of information on the capital (see p.142). In some smaller towns that don't qualify for a local TAT office, the information gap is filled by a **municipal tourist assistance office**, though at some of these you may find it hard to locate a fluent English-speaker.

TAT OFFICES ABROAD

Australia & New Zealand Suite 2002, Level 20, 56 Pitt St, Sydney, NSW 2000 ☎ 02/9247 7549, Ⓦ thailand.net.au.

South Africa Contact the UK office.

UK & Ireland 1st Floor, 17–19 Cockspur St, London SW1Y 5BL ☎ 020/7925 2511, ✉ info@tourismthailand.co.uk.

US & Canada 61 Broadway, Suite 2810, New York, NY 10006 ☎ 212/432-0433, ✉ info@tatny.com; 611 North Larchmont Blvd, 1st Floor, Los Angeles, CA 90004 ☎ 323/461-9814, ✉ tatla@tat.or.th.

Travellers with disabilities

Thailand makes few provisions for its disabled citizens and this obviously affects **travellers with disabilities**, but taxis, comfortable hotels and personal tour guides are all more affordable than in the West and most travellers with disabilities find Thais only too happy to offer assistance where they can. Hiring a local tour guide to accompany you on a day's sightseeing is particularly recommended: government tour guides can be arranged through any TAT office.

Most **wheelchair-users** end up driving on the roads because it's too hard to negotiate the uneven pavements, which are high to allow for flooding and invariably lack dropped kerbs. Crossing the road can be a trial, particularly in Bangkok and other big cities, where it's usually a question of climbing steps up to a bridge rather than taking a ramped underpass. Few buses and trains have ramps but in Bangkok some Skytrain stations and all subway stations have lifts.

Several **tour companies** in Thailand specialize in organizing trips featuring adapted facilities, accessible transport and escorts. The Bangkok-based Help and Care Travel Company (☎081 375 0792, ⓦwheelchair tours.com) designs **accessible holidays** in Thailand for slow walkers and wheelchair-users, as well as offering airport transfers and personal assistants. In Chiang Mai, Thai Focus (ⓦthaifocus.com) is used to designing trips for disabled travellers and can provide wheelchair rental. Mermaid's Dive Centre in Pattaya (☎038 232219, ⓦlearn-in-asia.com/handicapped _diving.htm) runs International Association of Handicapped Divers programmes for **disabled divers** and instructors (see p.389).

Bangkok

WAT PHRA KAEO

1

Bangkok

The headlong pace and flawed modernity of Bangkok match few people's visions of the capital of exotic Siam. Spiked with scores of high-rise buildings of concrete and glass, it's a vast flatness that holds an estimated population of eleven million, and feels even bigger. Yet under the shadow of the skyscrapers you'll find a heady mix of chaos and refinement, of frenetic markets, snail's-pace traffic jams and hushed golden temples, of dispiriting, zombie-like sex shows and early-morning alms-giving ceremonies. Plenty of visitors enjoy the challenge of taking on the "Big Mango", but one way or another, the place is sure to get under your skin.

Most budget travellers head for the **Banglamphu** district, where if you're not careful you could end up watching DVDs all day long and selling your shoes when you run out of money. The district is far from having a monopoly on Bangkok accommodation, but it does have the advantage of being just a short walk from the major sights in the **Ratanakosin** area: the dazzling ostentation of the **Grand Palace** and **Wat Phra Kaeo**, lively and grandiose **Wat Pho** and the **National Museum**'s hoard of exquisite works of art. Once those cultural essentials have been seen, you can choose from a whole bevy of lesser sights, including **Wat Benjamabophit** (the "Marble Temple"), especially at festival time, and **Jim Thompson's House**, a small, personal museum of Thai design.

For livelier scenes, explore the dark alleys of **Chinatown**'s bazaars or head for the water: the great **Chao Phraya River**, which breaks up and adds zest to the city's landscape, is the backbone of a network of **canals** that remains fundamentally intact in the west-bank Thonburi district. Inevitably the waterways have earned Bangkok the title of "Venice of the East", a tag that seems all too apt when you're wading through flooded streets in the rainy season. Back on dry land, **shopping** varies from touristic outlets pushing silks, handicrafts and counterfeit watches, through home-grown boutiques selling street-wise fashions and stunning contemporary decor, to thronging local markets where half the fun is watching the crowds. Thailand's long calendar of festivals (see p.46) is one of the few things that has been largely decentralized away from the capital, but Bangkok does offer the country's most varied **entertainment**, ranging from traditional dancing and the orchestrated bedlam of Thai boxing, through hip bars and clubs playing the latest imported sounds, to the farang-only sex bars of the

THE SKY BAR

Highlights

① The Grand Palace The country's least-missable sight, incorporating its holiest and most dazzling temple, Wat Phra Kaeo. **See p.84**

② Wat Pho Admire the Reclining Buddha and the lavish architecture, and leave time for a relaxing massage. **See p.90**

③ The National Museum The central repository of the country's artistic riches. **See p.95**

④ The canals of Thonburi See the Bangkok of yesteryear on a touristy but memorable longtail-boat ride. **See p.112**

⑤ Jim Thompson's House An elegant Thai design classic. **See p.120**

⑥ Chatuchak Weekend Market Eight thousand stalls selling everything from triangular pillows to secondhand Levis. **See p.129**

⑦ Thanon Khao San Legendary hangout for Southeast Asia backpackers; the place for cheap sleeps, baggy trousers and tall tales. **See p.143**

⑧ 63rd-floor sundowner Fine cocktails and jaw-dropping views, especially at sunset, at *The Sky Bar* and *Distil*. **See p.162**

⑨ Thai boxing Nightly bouts at the national stadia, complete with live musical accompaniment and frenetic betting. **See p.165**

HIGHLIGHTS ARE MARKED ON THE MAP ON P.79

1

Bangkok ("Krung Thep" in Thai) can be a tricky place to get your bearings as it's huge and ridiculously congested, with largely featureless modern buildings and no obvious centre. The boldest line on the map is the **Chao Phraya River**, which divides the city into Bangkok proper on the east bank, and **Thonburi**, part of Greater Bangkok, on the west (see map, p.82).

The historical core of Bangkok proper, site of the original royal palace, is **Ratanakosin**, cradled in a bend in the river. Three concentric canals radiate eastwards around Ratanakosin: the southern part of the area between the canals is the old-style trading enclave of **Chinatown** and Indian **Pahurat**, connected to the old palace by Thanon Charoen Krung (aka New Road); the northern part is characterized by old temples and the **Democracy Monument**, west of which is the backpackers' ghetto of **Banglamphu**. Beyond the canals to the north, **Dusit** is the site of many government buildings and the nineteenth-century Vimanmek Palace, and is linked to Ratanakosin by the three stately avenues, Thanon Rajdamnoen Nok, Thanon Rajdamnoen Klang and Thanon Rajdamnoen Nai.

"New" Bangkok begins to the east of the canals and beyond the main rail line and Hualamphong Station, and stretches as far as the eye can see to the east and north. The main business district is south of **Thanon Rama IV**, with the port of Khlong Toey at its eastern edge. The diverse area north of Thanon Rama IV includes the sprawling campus of Chulalongkorn University, huge shopping centres around **Siam Square** and a variety of other businesses. A couple of blocks northeast of Siam Square stands the tallest building in Bangkok, the 84-storey **Baiyoke II Tower**, whose golden spire makes a good point of reference. To the east lies the swish residential quarter off **Thanon Sukhumvit**.

notorious Patpong district, a tinseltown Babylon that's the tip of a dangerous iceberg. Even if the above doesn't appeal, you'll almost certainly pass through Bangkok once, if not several times – not only is it Thailand's main port of entry, it's also the obvious place to sort out **onward travel**, with good deals on international air tickets, as well as a convenient menu of embassies for visas to neighbouring countries.

Brief history

Bangkok is a relatively young capital, established in 1782 after the Burmese sacked Ayutthaya, the former capital. A temporary base was set up on the western bank of the Chao Phraya River, in what is now **Thonburi**, before work started on the more defensible east bank, where the French had built a grand, but short-lived, fort in the 1660s. The first king of the new dynasty, Rama I, built his palace at **Ratanakosin**, within a defensive ring of two (later expanded to three) canals, and this remains the city's spiritual heart.

Initially, the city was largely **amphibious**: only the temples and royal palaces were built on dry land, while ordinary residences floated on thick bamboo rafts on the river and canals; even shops and warehouses were moored to the river bank. A major shift in emphasis came in the second half of the nineteenth century, first under Rama IV (1851–68), who as part of his effort to restyle the capital along European lines built Bangkok's first roads, and then under Rama V (1868–1910), who constructed a new residential palace in Dusit, north of Ratanakosin, and laid out that area's grand boulevards.

The modern metropolis

Since World War II, and especially from the mid-1960s onwards, Bangkok has seen an explosion of **modernization**, which has blown away earlier attempts at orderly planning and left the city without an obvious centre. Most of the canals have been filled in, replaced by endless rows of cheap, functional concrete shophouses, high-rises and housing estates, sprawling across a built-up area of over 300 square kilometres. The benefits of Thailand's **economic boom** since the 1980s have been concentrated in

Bangkok, attracting migration from all over the country and making the capital ever more dominant: the population, over half of which is under 30 years of age, is now forty times that of the second city, Chiang Mai.

Every aspect of national life is centralized in the city, but the mayor of Bangkok is not granted enough power to deal with the ensuing problems, notably that of **traffic** – which in Bangkok now comprises four-fifths of the nation's automobiles. The Skytrain and the subway have undoubtedly helped, but the competing systems don't intersect properly or ticket jointly, and it's left to ingenious, local solutions such as the Khlong Saen Saeb canal boats and side-street motorbike taxis to keep the city moving. And there's precious little chance to escape from the pollution in green space: the city has only 0.4 square metres of public parkland per inhabitant, the lowest figure in the world, compared, for example, to London's 30.4 square metres per person.

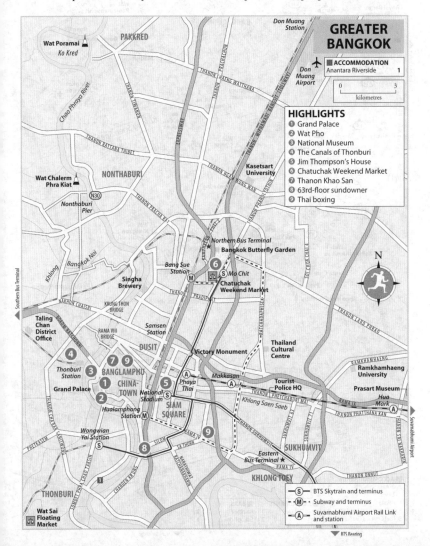

GREATER BANGKOK

■ **ACCOMMODATION**
Anantara Riverside — 1

0 ————— 3
kilometres

HIGHLIGHTS
❶ Grand Palace
❷ Wat Pho
❸ National Museum
❹ The Canals of Thonburi
❺ Jim Thompson's House
❻ Chatuchak Weekend Market
❼ Thanon Khao San
❽ 63rd-floor sundowner
❾ Thai boxing

—Ⓢ— BTS Skytrain and terminus
–Ⓜ·– Subway and terminus
—Ⓐ— Suvarnabhumi Airport Rail Link and station

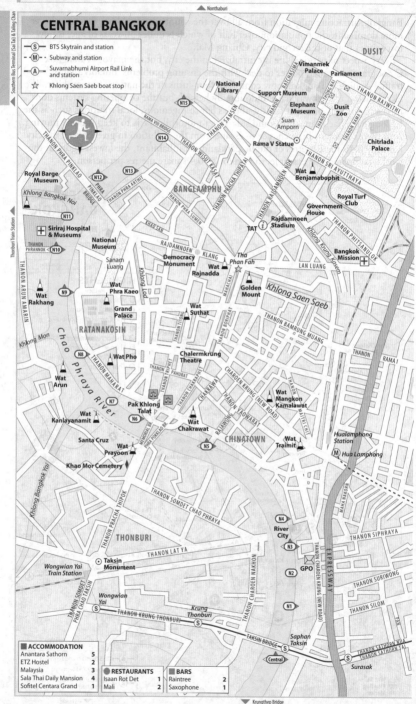

CENTRAL BANGKOK

- S BTS Skytrain and station
- M Subway and station
- A Suvarnabhumi Airport Rail Link and station
- ☆ Khlong Saen Saeb boat stop

ACCOMMODATION

Anantara Sathorn	5
ETZ Hostel	2
Malaysia	3
Sala Thai Daily Mansion	4
Sofitel Centara Grand	1

RESTAURANTS

Isaan Rot Det	1
Mali	2

BARS

Raintree	2
Saxophone	1

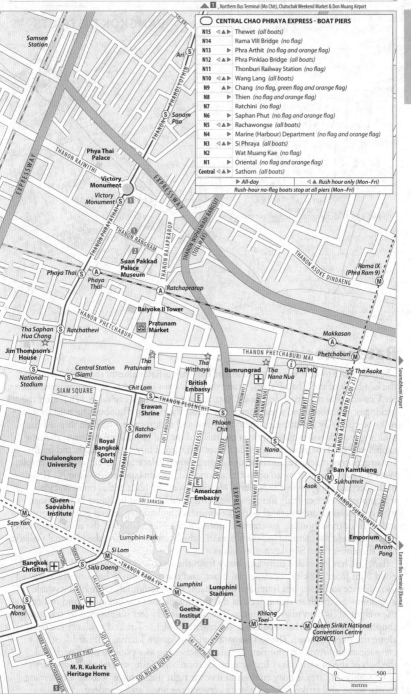

, Northern Bus Terminal (Mo Chit), Chatuchak Weekend Market & Don Muang Airport

CENTRAL CHAO PHRAYA EXPRESS - BOAT PIERS

N15	◁▲▷	Thewet *(all boats)*
N14		Rama VIII Bridge *(no flag)*
N13	▷	Phra Arthit *(no flag and orange flag)*
N12	◁▲▷	Phra Pinklao Bridge *(all boats)*
N11		Thonburi Railway Station *(no flag)*
N10	◁▲▷	Wang Lang *(all boats)*
N9	▲▷	Chang *(no flag, green flag and orange flag)*
N8	▷	Thien *(no flag and orange flag)*
N7		Ratchini *(no flag)*
N6	▷	Saphan Phut *(no flag and orange flag)*
N5	◁▲▷	Rachawongse *(all boats)*
N4	▷	Marine (Harbour) Department *(no flag and orange flag)*
N3	◁▲▷	Si Phraya *(all boats)*
N2		Wat Muang Kae *(no flag)*
N1	▷	Oriental *(no flag and orange flag)*
Central	◁▲▷	Sathorn *(all boats)*

▷ *All-day*	◁▲ *Rush hour only (Mon–Fri)*
Rush-hour no-flag boats stop at all piers (Mon–Fri)	

1

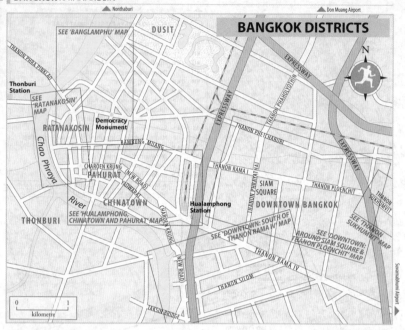

BANGKOK DISTRICTS

Ratanakosin

The only place to start your exploration of Bangkok is **Ratanakosin**, the royal island on the east bank of the Chao Phraya, where the city's most important and extravagant sights are located. When Rama I developed Ratanakosin for his new capital in 1782, after the sacking of Ayutthaya and a temporary stay across the river in Thonburi, he paid tribute to its precursor by imitating Ayutthaya's layout and architecture – he even shipped the building materials downstream from the ruins of the old city. Like Ayutthaya, the new capital was sited for protection beside a river and turned into an artificial island by the construction of defensive canals, with a central **Grand Palace** and adjoining royal temple, **Wat Phra Kaeo**, fronted by an open cremation field, **Sanam Luang**; the Wang Na (Palace of the Second King), now the **National Museum**, was also built at this time. **Wat Pho**, which predates the capital's founding, was further embellished by Rama I's successors, who have consolidated Ratanakosin's pre-eminence by building several grand European-style palaces (now housing government institutions); Wat Mahathat, the most important centre of Buddhist learning in Southeast Asia; the National Theatre; the National Gallery; and Thammasat and Silpakorn universities.

Bangkok has expanded eastwards away from the river, leaving the Grand Palace a good 5km from the city's commercial heart, and the royal family has long since moved its residence to Dusit, but Ratanakosin remains the ceremonial centre of the whole kingdom – so much so that it feels as if it might sink into the boggy ground under the weight of its own mighty edifices. The heavy, stately feel is lightened by traditional shophouses selling herbal medicines, pavement amulet-sellers and studenty canteens along the riverside road, **Thanon Maharat**; and by Sanam Luang, still used for cremations and royal ceremonies, but also functioning as a popular open park and the hub of the modern city's bus system. Despite containing several of the country's main sights, the area is busy enough in its own right not to have become a swarming tourist zone, and strikes a neat balance between liveliness and grandeur.

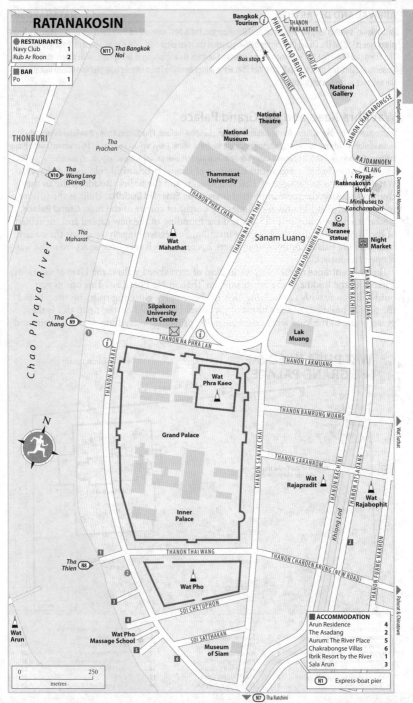

RATANAKOSIN

● RESTAURANTS
Navy Club   **1**
Rub Ar Roon   **2**

■ BAR
Po   **1**

Tha Bangkok Noi   **N11**

Bangkok Tourism ⓘ

Bus stop 5 ★

National Gallery

THONBURI

Tha Prachan

National Theatre

National Museum

RAJDAMNOEN KLANG

Royal Ratanakosin Hotel

Minibuses to Kanchanaburi

Tha Wang Lang (Siriraj)   **N10**

Thammasat University

THANON PHRA CHAN

Mae Toranee statue

Night Market

Tha Maharat

THANON NA PHRA THAT

Wat Mahathat

Sanam Luang

THANON RAJDAMNOEN NAI

THANON RACHINI

THANON ATSADANG

Chao Phraya River

Tha Chang   **N9**

Silpakorn University Arts Centre

THANON NA PHRA LAN

Lak Muang

THANON MAHARAT

THANON LAKMUANG

Wat Phra Kaeo

N

Grand Palace

THANON BAMRUNG MUANG

THANON SARANROM

Wat Rajapradit

Wat Rajabophit

THANON SANAM CHAI

Inner Palace

Khlong Lod

THANON CHAROEN KRUNG (NEW ROAD)

THANON FUANG NAKHON

Tha Thien   **N8**

THANON THAI WANG

Wat Pho

SOI CHETUPHON

Wat Arun

Wat Pho Massage School

SOI SATTHAKAN

Museum of Siam

■ ACCOMMODATION
Arun Residence   **4**
The Asadang   **2**
Aurum: The River Place   **5**
Chakrabongse Villas   **6**
Ibrik Resort by the River   **1**
Sala Arun   **3**

0   250
metres

N1   Express-boat pier

N7 Tha Ratchini

▶ Banglamphu
▶ Democracy Monument
▶ Wat Sathat
▶ Pahurat & Chinatown

1

Ratanakosin is within easy walking distance of Banglamphu, but is best approached from the river, via the **express-boat piers** (see p.138) of Tha Chang (the former bathing place of the royal elephants, which gives access to the Grand Palace) or Tha Thien (for Wat Pho). An extension of the subway line from Hualamphong is being built, with a new station at the Museum of Siam, five minutes' walk from Wat Pho, ten minutes from Tha Thien express boat pier and fifteen minutes from the entrance to the Grand Palace.

Wat Phra Kaeo and the Grand Palace

Thanon Na Phra Lan • Daily 8.30am–4pm, last admission 3.30pm (weapons museum, Phra Thinang Amarin Winichai and Dusit Maha Prasat interiors closed Sat & Sun) • B400, including a map and admission, within 7 days, to Dusit Park (see p.114) or Sanam Chandra Palace in Nakhon Pathom (see p.181); 2hr personal audioguide B200, with passport or credit card as deposit • Ⓦ palaces.thai.net

Hanging together in a precarious harmony of strangely beautiful colours and shapes, **Wat Phra Kaeo** is the apogee of Thai religious art and the holiest Buddhist site in the country, housing the most important image, the **Emerald Buddha**. Built as the private royal temple, Wat Phra Kaeo occupies the northeast corner of the huge **Grand Palace**, whose official opening in 1785 marked the founding of the new capital and the rebirth of the Thai nation after the Burmese invasion. Successive kings have all left their mark here, and the palace complex now covers 2 acres, though very little apart from the wat is open to tourists.

The only **entrance** to the complex in 2km of crenellated walls is the Gate of Glorious Victory in the middle of the north side, on Thanon Na Phra Lan. This brings you onto a driveway with a tantalizing view of the temple's glittering spires on the left and the dowdy buildings of the Offices of the Royal Household on the right: this is the powerhouse of the kingdom's ceremonial life, providing everything down to chairs and

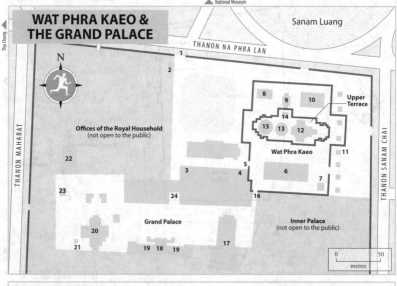

Gate of Glorious Victory	1	Porcelain viharn	9	Phra Thinang Amarin Winichai	17
Queen's Support Foundation Shop	2	Supplementary library	10	Chakri Maha Prasat	18
Ticket office	3	Prangs	11	Weapons museum	19
Royal Decorations & Coins Pavilion	4	Royal Pantheon	12	Dusit Maha Prasat	20
Entrance turnstiles to Wat Phra Kaeo	5	Phra Mondop	13	Mount Krailas model	21
The bot and Emerald Buddha	6	Angkor Wat model	14	Wat Phra Kaeo museum	22
Chapel of the Gandhara Buddha	7	Phra Si Ratana Chedi	15	Café	23
Royal mausoleum	8	Exit from Wat Phra Kaeo	16	Exit from Grand Palace	24

1

CITY OF ANGELS

When **Rama I** was crowned in 1782, he gave his new capital a grand 43-syllable name to match his ambitious plans for the building of the city. Since then, 21 more syllables have been added. Krungthepmahanakhornbowornrattanakosinmahintarayutthayamahadilokpopnopparatratcha-thaniburiromudomratchaniwetmahasathanamornpimanavatarnsathitsakkathattiyavis-nukarprasit is certified by the *Guinness Book of Records* as the longest place-name in the world, roughly translating as "Great city of angels, the supreme repository of divine jewels, the great land unconquerable, the grand and prominent realm, the royal and delightful capital city full of nine noble gems, the highest royal dwelling and grand palace, the divine shelter and living place of the reincarnated spirits". Fortunately, all Thais refer to the city simply as **Krung Thep**, "City of Angels", though plenty can recite the full name at the drop of a hat. **Bangkok** – "Village of the Plum Olive" – was the name of the original village on the Thonburi side; with remarkable persistence, it has remained in use by foreigners since the time of the French garrison.

catering, even lending an urn when someone of rank dies. A textile museum under the auspices of the queen, which it's claimed will show how she invented a new Thai national dress in the 1960s, is scheduled to open among these buildings, but for now you'll have to content yourself with some crafts shopping at the Queen's Support Foundation (see p.166). Turn left at the end of the driveway for the ticket office and entrance turnstiles.

As this is Thailand's most sacred site, you have to **dress in smart clothes:** no vests or see-through clothes; men must wear full-length trousers, women trousers or over-the-knee skirts. Suitable garments can be borrowed from the office to the right just inside the Gate of Glorious Victory (same building as the Queen's Support Foundation shop; free, deposit of B200 per item).

Wat Phra Kaeo

It makes you laugh with delight to think that anything so fantastic could exist on this sombre earth.
W. Somerset Maugham, *The Gentlemen in the Parlour*

Entering the temple is like stepping onto a lavishly detailed stage set, from the immaculate flagstones right up to the gaudy roofs. Reinforcing the sense of unreality, the whole compound is surrounded by arcaded walls, decorated with extraordinary murals of scenes from the *Ramayana*. Although it receives hundreds of foreign sightseers and at least as many Thai pilgrims every day, the temple, which has no monks in residence, maintains an unnervingly sanitized look, as if it were built only yesterday.

The approach to the bot

Inside the entrance turnstiles, you're confronted by 6m-tall **yaksha**, gaudy demons from the *Ramayana*, who watch over the Emerald Buddha from every gate of the temple and ward off evil spirits; the king of the demons, green, ten-faced Totsagan (labelled "Tosakanth"), stands to the left of the entrance by the southwest corner of the golden Phra Si Ratana Chedi. Less threatening is the toothless old codger, cast in bronze and sitting on a plinth immediately inside the turnstiles by the back wall of the bot, who represents a Hindu **hermit** credited with inventing yoga and herbal medicine. In front of him is a large grinding stone where previously herbal practitioners could come to grind their ingredients – with enhanced powers, of course. Skirting around the bot, you'll reach its **main entrance** on the eastern side, in front of which stands a cluster of grey **statues**, which have a strong Chinese feel: next to Kuan Im, the Chinese *bodhisattva* of mercy shown holding a bottle of *amritsa* (sacred elixir), are a sturdy pillar topped by a lotus flower, which Bangkok's Chinese community presented to Rama IV during his 27 years as a monk, and two handsome cows which commemorate Rama I's birth in the Year of the Cow. Worshippers make their offerings to the Emerald Buddha

1

A WORD OF WARNING

When you're heading for the Grand Palace or Wat Pho, you may well be approached by someone, possibly pretending to be a student or an official, who will tell you that the sight is closed when it's not, or some other lies to try to lead you away from the entrance, because they want to lead you on a shopping trip for souvenirs, tailored clothes or, if you seem really gullible, gems (see p.170). The opening hours of the Grand Palace – but not Wat Pho – are indeed sometimes erratic because of state occasions, but you can check the details out on its website, ⓦpalaces.thai.net – and even if it's closed on the day you want to visit, that's no reason to throw yourself at the mercy of these shysters.

at two small, stand-in Buddhas here, where they can look at the main image through the open doors of the bot without messing up its pristine interior with gold leaf, candle wax and joss-stick ash.

The bot and the Emerald Buddha

The **bot**, the largest building of the temple, is one of the few original structures left at Wat Phra Kaeo, though it has been augmented so often it looks like the work of a wildly inspired child. Eight *sema* stones mark the boundary of the consecrated area around the bot, each sheltering in a psychedelic fairy castle, joined by a low wall decorated with Chinese porcelain tiles, which depict delicate landscapes. The walls of the bot itself, sparkling with gilt and coloured glass, are supported by 112 golden garudas (birdmen) holding nagas, representing the god Indra saving the world by slaying the serpent-cloud that had swallowed up all the water. The symbolism reflects the king's traditional role as a rainmaker.

Of the bot's three doorways, the largest, in the middle, is reserved for the king himself. Inside, a 9m-high pedestal supports the tiny **Emerald Buddha**, a figure whose mystique draws pilgrims from all over Thailand – as well as politicians accused of corruption, who traditionally come here to publicly swear their innocence. Here especially you must act with respect, sitting with your feet pointing away from the Buddha. The spiritual power of the 60cm jadeite image derives from its legendary past. Reputed to have been created by the gods in India, it was discovered when lightning cracked open an ancient chedi in Chiang Rai in the early fifteenth century. The image was then moved around the north, dispensing miracles wherever it went, before being taken to Laos for two hundred years. As it was believed to bring great fortune to its possessor, the future Rama I snatched it back when he captured Vientiane in 1779, installing it at the heart of his new capital as a talisman for king and country.

Seated in the *Dhyana Mudra* (meditation), the Emerald Buddha has three **costumes**, one for each season: the crown and ornaments of an Ayutthayan king for the hot season; a gilt monastic robe for the rainy season, when the monks retreat into the temples; this is augmented with a full-length gold shawl in the cool season. To this day it's the job of the king himself to ceremonially change the Buddha's costumes – though in recent years, due to the present king's age, the Crown Prince has conducted proceedings. The Buddha was granted a new set of these three costumes in 1997: the old set is now in the Wat Phra Kaeo Museum (see p.90) while the two costumes of the new set that are not in use are on display among the blinding glitter of crowns and jewels in the Royal Decorations and Coins Pavilion, which lies between the ticket office and the entrance to Wat Phra Kaeo.

Among the paraphernalia in front of the pedestal sits the tiny, silver **Phra Chai Lang Chang** (Victory Buddha), which Rama I always carried into battle on the back of his elephant for luck and which still plays an important part in coronation ceremonies. Recently covered in gold, it occupies a prestigious spot dead centre, but is modestly

1

obscured by a fan and by the umbrella of a larger gold Buddha in front. The tallest pair of a dozen standing Buddha images, all made of bronze but encased in gold and raising both hands to dispel fear, are at the front: Rama III dedicated the one on the Emerald Buddha's left to Rama I, the one on his right to Rama II, and Rama IV enshrined relics of the Buddha in their crowns.

The Chapel of the Gandhara Buddha

Near the entrance to the bot, in the southeastern corner of the temple precinct, look out for the exquisite scenes of rice sheaves, fish and turtles painted in gold on blue glass on the doors and windows of the **Chapel of the Gandhara Buddha** (labelled "Hor Phra Kanthara Rat"). The decorations allude to the fertility of the ricefields, as this building was crucial to the old royal rainmaking ritual and is still used during the Royal Ploughing Ceremony (see p.94). Adorning the roof are thousands of nagas (serpents), symbolizing water; inside the locked chapel, among the paraphernalia used in the ritual, is kept the Gandhara Buddha, a bronze image in the gesture of calling down the rain with its right hand, while cupping the left to catch it. In times of drought the king would order a week-long rainmaking ceremony to be conducted, during which he was bathed regularly and kept away from the opposite sex while Buddhist monks and Hindu Brahmins chanted continuously.

The Royal Pantheon and minor buildings

On the north side of the bot, the eastern end of the **upper terrace** is taken up with the **Prasat Phra Thep Bidorn**, known as the **Royal Pantheon**, a splendid hash of styles. The pantheon has its roots in the Khmer concept of *devaraja*, or the divinity of kings: inside are bronze and gold statues, precisely life-size, of all the kings since Bangkok became the Thai capital. Constructed by Rama IV, the building is open only on special occasions, such as Chakri Day (April 6), when the dynasty is commemorated, and Coronation Day (May 5).

From here you get the best view of the **royal mausoleum**, the **porcelain viharn** and the **supplementary library** to the north (all of which are closed to tourists, though you can sometimes glimpse Thai Buddhists worshipping in the library), and, running along the east side of the temple, a row of eight bullet-like **prangs**, each of which has a different nasty ceramic colour. Described as "monstrous vegetables" by Somerset Maugham, they represent, from north to south, the Buddha, Buddhist scripture, the monkhood, the nunhood, the Buddhas who attained enlightenment but did not preach, previous emperors, the Buddha in his previous lives and the future Buddha.

The Phra Mondop and Phra Si Ratana Chedi

In the middle of the terrace, dressed in deep-green glass mosaics, the **Phra Mondop** was built by Rama I to house the *Tripitaka*, or Buddhist scripture, which the king had revised at Wat Mahathat in 1788, the previous version having been lost in the sack of Ayutthaya. It's famous for the mother-of-pearl cabinet and solid-silver mats inside, but is never open. Four tiny **memorials** at each corner of the mondop show the symbols of each of the nine Chakri kings, from the ancient crown representing Rama I to the present king's discus, while the bronze statues surrounding the memorials portray each king's lucky white elephants, labelled by name and pedigree. A contribution of Rama IV, on the north side of the mondop, is a **scale model of Angkor Wat**, the prodigious Cambodian temple, which during his reign (1851–68) was under Thai rule (apparently, the king had wanted to shift a whole Khmer temple to Bangkok but, fortunately, was dissuaded by his officials). At the western end of the terrace, you can't miss the golden dazzle of the **Phra Si Ratana Chedi**, which Rama IV erected, in imitation of the famous bell-shaped chedis at Ayutthaya's Wat Phra Si Sanphet (see p.219), to enshrine a piece of the Buddha's breastbone.

1

The murals

Extending for about a kilometre in the arcades that run inside the wat walls, the **murals of the Ramayana** depict every blow of this ancient story of the triumph of good over evil, using the vibrant buildings of the temple itself as backdrops, and setting them off against the subdued colours of richly detailed landscapes. Because of the damaging humidity, none of the original work of Rama I's time survives: maintenance is a never-ending process, so you'll always find an artist working on one of the scenes. The story is told in 178 panels, labelled and numbered in Thai only, starting in the middle of the northern side opposite the porcelain viharn: in the first episode, a hermit, while out ploughing, finds the baby Sita, the heroine, floating in a gold urn on a lotus leaf and brings her to the city. Panel 109 near the gate leading to the palace buildings shows the climax of the story, when Rama, the hero, kills the ten-headed demon Totsagan (Ravana), and the ladies of the enemy city weep at the demon's death. Panel 110 depicts his elaborate funeral procession, and in 113 you can see the funeral fair, with acrobats, sword-jugglers and tightrope-walkers. In between, Sita – Rama's wife – has to walk on fire to prove that she has been faithful during her fourteen years of imprisonment by Totsagan. If you haven't the stamina for the long walk round, you could sneak a look at the end of the story, to the left of the first panel, where Rama holds a victory parade and distributes thank-you gifts.

THE RAMAYANA/RAMAKIEN

The **Ramayana** is generally thought to have originated as an oral epic in India, where it appears in numerous dialects. The most famous version is that of the sage Valmiki, who is said to have drawn together the collection of stories as a tribute to his king over two thousand years ago. From India, the *Ramayana* spread to all the Hindu-influenced countries of Southeast Asia and was passed down through the Khmers to Thailand, where as the **Ramakien** it has become the national epic, acting as an affirmation of the Thai monarchy and its divine Hindu links. As a source of inspiration for literature, painting, sculpture and dance-drama, it has acquired the authority of holy writ, providing Thais with moral and practical lessons, while its appearance in the form of films and comic strips shows its huge popular appeal. The version current in Thailand was composed by a committee of poets sponsored by Rama I (all previous Thai texts were lost in the sack of Ayutthaya in 1767), and runs to three thousand pages – available in an abridged English translation by M.L. Manich Jumsai (see p.788).

The central story of the *Ramayana* concerns **Rama** (in Thai, Phra Ram), son of the king of Ayodhya, and his beautiful wife **Sita**, whose hand he wins by lifting, stringing – and breaking – a magic bow. The couple's adventures begin when they are exiled to the forest, along with Rama's good brother, **Lakshaman** (Phra Lak), by the hero's father under the influence of his evil stepmother. Meanwhile, in the city of Lanka (Longka), the demon king **Ravana** (Totsagan) has conceived a passionate desire for Sita and, disguised as a hermit, sets out to kidnap her. By transforming one of his demon subjects into a beautiful deer, which Rama and Lakshaman go off to hunt, Ravana catches Sita alone and takes her back to Lanka. Rama then wages a long war against the demons of Lanka, into which are woven many battles, spy scenes and diversionary episodes, and eventually kills Ravana and rescues Sita.

The Thai version shows some characteristic differences from the Indian, emphasizing the typically Buddhist virtues of filial obedience and willing renunciation. In addition, Hanuman, the loyal monkey general, is given a much more playful role in the *Ramakien*, with the addition of many episodes which display his cunning and talent for mischief, not to mention his promiscuity. However, the major alteration comes at the end of the story, when Phra Ram doubts Sita's faithfulness after rescuing her from Totsagan. In the Indian story, this ends with Sita being swallowed up by the earth so that she doesn't have to suffer Rama's doubts any more; in the *Ramakien* the ending is a happy one, with Phra Ram and Sita living together happily ever after.

The palace buildings

The exit in the southwest corner of Wat Phra Kaeo brings you to the palace proper, a vast area of buildings and gardens, of which only the northern edge is on show to the public. Though the king now lives in the Chitrlada Palace in Dusit, the Grand Palace is still used for state receptions and official ceremonies, during which there is no public access to any part of the palace.

Phra Maha Monthien

Coming out of the temple compound, you'll first of all see to your right a beautiful Chinese gate covered in innumerable tiny porcelain tiles. Extending in a straight line behind the gate is the **Phra Maha Monthien**, which was the grand residential complex of earlier kings.

Only the **Phra Thinang Amarin Winichai**, the main audience hall at the front of the complex, is open to the public. The supreme court in the era of the absolute monarchy, it nowadays serves as the venue for ceremonies such as the king's birthday speech. Dominating the hall are two gleaming, intricately carved thrones that date from the reign of Rama I: a white umbrella with the full nine tiers owing to a king shelters the front seat, while the unusual *busbok* behind is topped with a spired roof and floats on a boat-shaped base. The rear buildings are still used for the most important part of the elaborate coronation ceremony, and each new king is supposed to spend a night there to show solidarity with his forefathers.

Chakri Maha Prasat

Next door you can admire the facade of the "farang with a Thai hat", as the **Chakri Maha Prasat** is nicknamed. Rama V, whose portrait you can see over its entrance, employed an English architect to design a purely Neoclassical residence, but other members of the royal family prevailed on the king to add the three Thai spires. This used to be the site of the elephant stables: the large red tethering posts are still there and the bronze elephants were installed as a reminder. The building displays the emblem of the Chakri dynasty on its gable, which has a trident (*ri*) coming out of a *chak*, a discus with a sharpened rim. The only part of the Chakri Maha Prasat open to the public is the ground-floor **weapons museum**, which houses a forgettable display of hooks, pikes and guns.

The Inner Palace

The **Inner Palace** (closed to the public), which used to be the king's harem, lies behind the gate on the left-hand side of the Chakri Maha Prasat. Vividly described in M.R. Kukrit Pramoj's *Si Phaendin* (see p.788), the harem was a town in itself, with shops, law courts and an all-female police force for the huge population: as well as the current queens, the minor wives and their children (including pre-pubescent boys) and servants, this was home to the daughters and consorts of former kings, and the daughters of the aristocracy who attended the harem's finishing school. Today, the Inner Palace houses a school of cooking, fruit-carving and other domestic sciences for well-bred young Thais.

Dusit Maha Prasat

On the western side of the courtyard, the delicately proportioned **Dusit Maha Prasat**, an audience hall built by Rama I, epitomizes traditional Thai architecture. Outside, the soaring tiers of its red, gold and green roof culminate in a gilded *mongkut*, a spire shaped like the king's crown, which symbolizes the 33 Buddhist levels of perfection. Each tier of the roof bears a typical *chofa*, a slender, stylized bird's-head finial, and several *hang hong* (swans' tails), which represent three-headed nagas. Inside, you can still see the original throne, the **Phra Ratcha Banlang Pradap Muk**, a masterpiece of mother-of-pearl inlaid work. When a senior member of the royal family dies, the hall is used for the

1

THE ROYAL TONSURE CEREMONY

To the right and behind the Dusit Maha Prasat rises a strange model mountain, decorated with fabulous animals and topped by a castle and prang. It represents **Mount Krailas**, the Himalayan home of the Hindu god Shiva (Phra Isuan in Thai), and was built by Rama IV as the site of the **royal tonsure ceremony**, last held here in 1932, just three months before the end of the absolute monarchy. In former times, Thai children generally had shaved heads, except for a tuft or top-knot on the crown, which, between the age of eleven and thirteen, was cut in a Hindu initiation rite to welcome adolescence. For the royal children, the rite was an elaborate ceremony that sometimes lasted seven days, culminating with the king's cutting of the hair knot, which was then floated away on the Chao Phraya River. The child was then bathed at the model Krailas, in water representing the original river of the universe flowing down the central mountain.

lying-in-state: the body, embalmed and seated in a huge sealed urn, is placed in the west transept, waiting up to two years for an auspicious day to be cremated.

The Wat Phra Kaeo Museum

In the nineteenth-century Royal Mint in front of the Dusit Maha Prasat – next to a small, basic **café** and an incongruous hair salon – the **Wat Phra Kaeo Museum** houses a mildly interesting collection of artefacts donated to the Emerald Buddha, along with architectural elements rescued from the Grand Palace grounds during restoration in the 1980s. Highlights include the bones of various kings' white elephants, and upstairs, the Emerald Buddha's original costumes and two useful scale models of the Grand Palace, one as it is now, the other as it was when first built. Also on the first floor stands the grey stone slab of the Manangasila Seat, where Ramkhamhaeng, the great thirteenth-century king of Sukhothai, is said to have sat and taught his subjects. It was discovered in 1833 by Rama IV during his monkhood and brought to Bangkok, where Rama VI used it as the throne for his coronation.

Wat Pho (Wat Phra Chetuphon)

Soi Chetuphon, to the south of the Grand Palace • Daily 8am–9pm • B50 • ⓦ watpho.com

Where Wat Phra Kaeo may seem too perfect and shrink-wrapped for some, **Wat Pho** is lively and shambolic, a complex arrangement of lavish structures which jostle with classrooms, basketball courts and a turtle pond. Busloads of tourists shuffle in and out of the **north entrance**, stopping only to gawp at the colossal Reclining Buddha, but you can avoid the worst of the crowds by using the **main entrance** on Soi Chetuphon to explore the huge compound.

Wat Pho is the oldest temple in Bangkok and older than the city itself, having been founded in the seventeenth century under the name Wat Photaram. Foreigners have stuck to the contraction of this old name, even though Rama I, after enlarging the temple, changed the name in 1801 to **Wat Phra Chetuphon**, which is how it is generally known to Thais. The temple had another major overhaul in 1832, when Rama III built the chapel of the Reclining Buddha, and turned the temple into a public centre of learning by decorating the walls and pillars with inscriptions and diagrams on subjects such as history, literature, animal husbandry and astrology. Dubbed Thailand's first university, the wat is still an important centre for traditional medicine, notably **Thai massage** (see box, p.92), which is used against all kinds of illnesses, from backaches to viruses.

The eastern courtyard

The main entrance on Soi Chetuphon is one of a series of sixteen monumental gates around the main compound, each guarded by stone **giants**, many of them comic

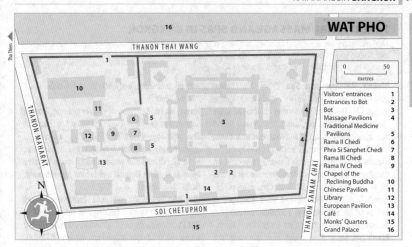

Legend for map:

Visitors' entrances	1
Entrances to Bot	2
Bot	3
Massage Pavilions	4
Traditional Medicine Pavilions	5
Rama II Chedi	6
Phra Si Sanphet Chedi	7
Rama III Chedi	8
Rama IV Chedi	9
Chapel of the Reclining Buddha	10
Chinese Pavilion	11
Library	12
European Pavilion	13
Café	14
Monks' Quarters	15
Grand Palace	16

Westerners in wide-brimmed hats – ships that exported rice to China would bring these statues back as ballast.

The entrance brings you into the eastern half of the main complex, where a courtyard of structures radiates from the bot in a disorientating symmetry. To get to the bot, the principal congregation and ordination hall, turn right and cut through the two surrounding cloisters, which are lined with hundreds of Buddha images. The elegant **bot** has beautiful teak doors decorated with mother-of-pearl, showing stories from the *Ramayana* (see p.88) in minute detail. Look out also for the stone bas-reliefs around the base of the bot, which narrate the story of the capture and rescue of Sita from the *Ramayana* in 152 action-packed panels. The plush interior has a well-proportioned altar on which ten statues of disciples frame a graceful, Ayutthayan Buddha image containing the remains of Rama I, the founder of Bangkok (Rama IV placed them there so that the public could worship him at the same time as the Buddha).

Back outside the entrance to the double cloister, keep your eyes open for a miniature mountain covered in statues of naked men in tall hats who appear to be gesturing rudely: they are *rishis* (hermits), demonstrating various positions of healing massage. Skirting the southwestern corner of the cloisters, you'll come to two pavilions between the eastern and western courtyards, which display plaques inscribed with the precepts of traditional medicine, as well as anatomical pictures showing the different pressure points and the illnesses that can be cured by massaging them.

The western courtyard

Among the 99 chedis strewn about the grounds, the four **great chedis** in the western courtyard stand out as much for their covering of garish tiles as for their size. The central chedi is the oldest, erected by Rama I to hold the remains of the most sacred Buddha image of Ayutthaya, the Phra Si Sanphet. Later, Rama III built the chedi to the north for the ashes of Rama II and the chedi to the south to hold his own remains; Rama IV built the fourth, with bright blue tiles, though its purpose is uncertain.

In the northwest corner of the courtyard stands the chapel of the **Reclining Buddha**, a 45m-long gilded statue of plaster-covered brick which depicts the Buddha entering Nirvana, a common motif in Buddhist iconography. The chapel is only slightly bigger than the statue – you can't get far enough away to take in anything but a surreal close-up view of the beaming 5m smile. As for the feet, the vast black soles are

1

TRADITIONAL MASSAGE AND SPAS IN BANGKOK

Thai massage sessions and courses are held most famously at Wat Pho, while luxurious and indulgent spa and massage treatments are available at many posh hotels across the city, as well as at the following stand-alone places.

Divana Massage and Spa 7 Soi 25, Thanon Sukhumvit ☎02 661 6784, ⓦdivanaspa.com; map p.124. Delightful spa serving up Thai massages (100min for B1150), foot, aromatherapy and herbal massages, as well as facials and Ayurvedic treatments. Mon–Fri 11am–11pm, Sat & Sun 10am–11pm.

Nicolie Sun Square, a small shopping arcade on the south side of Thanon Silom between soi 21 and 23 ☎02 233 6957, ⓦnicolie-th.com; map p.126. Superb Thai (B1600/90min) and other massages, as well as facials and scrubs, in a soothing environment decorated with Asian objets d'art. Daily 11am–10pm.

Pian's Soi Susie Pub, which runs between the east end of Thanon Khao San and Thanon Ram Bhuttri ☎02 629 0924; map pp.100–101. Uninvitingly clinical-looking but highly rated a/c massage centre, offering Thai massages (B200/hr) as well as foot, oil and herbal massages; you can also study Thai massage here. Daily 7.30am–12.30am.

Pimmalai Thanon Sukhumvit, 50m east of BTS On Nut, exit 1, between sois 81 and 83 ☎02 742 6452, ⓦpimmalai.com. In a nice old wooden house, Thai massages (B250/1hr), plus foot, herbal and oil massages, body scrubs and facials. Daily 10am–10pm.

Ruen Nuad 42 Thanon Convent, near Thanon Sathon Nua ☎02 632 2662–3; map p.126. Excellent Thai massages (B350/1hr, B600/2hr), as well as aromatherapy and foot massages and a juice bar, in an a/c, characterful wooden house, down an alley opposite the BNH Hospital and behind *Naj* restaurant. Daily 10am–9pm.

Wat Pho (see p.90); map p.83. Excellent massages are available in two a/c buildings on the east side of Wat Pho's main compound; allow two hours for the full works (B420/hr; foot reflexology massage B420/hr). There are often long queues here, however, so you might be better off heading over to the massage centre's other premises just outside the temple, at 392/25–28 Soi Pen Phat 1, Thanon Maharat (the soi is unmarked but look for the *Coconut Palm* restaurant on the corner; daily 8am–6pm; ☎02 622 3533 or ☎02 622 3550–1, ⓦwatpomassage.com). Here you can also enrol on a thirty-hour massage training course in English, over five days (B8500), and foot-massage courses for B6500. Daily 8am–7pm.

beautifully inlaid with delicate mother-of-pearl showing the 108 *lakshanas*, or auspicious signs, which distinguish the true Buddha. Along one side of the statue are 108 bowls: putting a coin in each will bring you good luck and a long life.

Museum of Siam (National Discovery Museum)

Thanon Sanam Chai • Tues–Sun 10am–6pm • B300, free after 4pm • ☎02 225 2777, ⓦmuseumsiam.com

The high-tech and mostly bilingual **Museum of Siam** is an excellent, recently developed attraction that occupies the century-old, European-style, former Ministry of Commerce. It looks at what it is to be Thai, with lots of humorous short films and imaginative touches such as shadow-puppet cartoons and war video games. In addition, the museum stages playful temporary exhibitions, which in the past have let visitors have a go at rice-growing, and examine Thailand's enduring love affair with foreign commodities. Generally, it's great fun for adults and kids, and there's a nice little indoor-outdoor **café-restaurant** in the grounds run by the Black Canyon chain.

It all kicks off with the prehistory of Southeast Asia, or Suvarnabhumi (Land of Gold) as ancient documents refer to it, and the legendary arrival of Buddhism via missionaries sent by the great Indian emperor, Ashoka (Asoke). Much space is devoted to Ayutthaya, where we learn that during that kingdom's four-hundred-year history, there were no less than twenty outbreaks of war with the Burmese states, before the final annihilation in 1767. Beyond this, look out for a fascinating map of Thonburi, King Taksin's new capital between 1768 and 1782, as drawn by a Burmese spy. In the Bangkok period, there's coverage of the Chinese in Thailand and of early

1

twentieth-century racialism, but next to nothing on the country's Muslims. Towards the end, under the banner of Westernization, visitors can wind up cartoon peep-shows and dress up in colonial-style uniform shirts.

Sanam Luang

Sprawling across 30 acres north of the Grand Palace, **Sanam Luang** is one of the last open spaces left in Bangkok, a bare field where residents of the capital gather in the early evening to meet, eat and play. The nearby pavements are the marketplace for some exotic spiritual salesmen (though, since splashing out on Sanam Luang's recent facelift, the city authorities have announced that they plan to further gentrify the place by moving the hawkers on): on the eastern side sit astrologers and palm-readers, and sellers of bizarre virility potions and contraptions; on the western side and spreading around Thammasat University and Wat Mahathat, scores of small-time hawkers sell amulets (see p.105), taking advantage of the spiritually auspicious location. In the early part of the year, especially in March, the sky is filled with **kite-fighting** contests (see box below).

The field is also the venue for national ceremonies, such as **royal cremations**, when huge, intricate, wooden *meru* or *phra mane* (funeral pyres) are constructed, representing Mount Meru, the Himalayan centre of the Hindu-Buddhist universe; and the **Ploughing Ceremony**, held in May at a time selected by astrologers to bring good fortune and rain to the coming rice harvest. Revived in 1960 to boost the status of the monarchy during the Cold War, the elaborate Brahmin ceremony is led by an official from the Ministry of Agriculture, who stands in for the king in case the royal power were to be reduced by any failure in the ritual. At the designated time, the official cuts a series of circular furrows with a plough drawn by two white oxen, and scatters rice from the king's experimental crop station at Chitrlada Palace, which has been sprinkled with lustral water by the Brahmin priests of the court. When the ritual is over, spectators rush in to grab handfuls of the rice, which they then plant in their own paddies for good luck.

The lak muang

Thanon Rajdamnoen Nai, southeast corner of Sanam Luang

At 6.54am on April 21, 1782 – the astrologically determined time for the auspicious founding of Bangkok – a pillar containing the city's horoscope was ceremonially driven

---

KITE FLYING

Flying intricate and colourful **kites** is now done mostly for fun in Thailand, but it has its roots in more serious activities. Filled with gunpowder and fitted with long fuses, kites were deployed in the first Thai kingdom at Sukhothai (1240–1438) as machines of war. In the same era, special *ngao* kites, with heads in the shape of bamboo bows, were used in Brahmin rituals: the string of the bow would vibrate in the wind and make a noise to frighten away evil spirits (nowadays noisy kites are still used, though only by farmers, to scare the birds). By the height of the Ayutthayan period (1351–1767) kites had become largely decorative: royal ceremonies were enhanced by fantastically shaped kites, adorned with jingling bells and ornamental lamps.

In the nineteenth century, Rama V, by his enthusiastic lead, popularized kite flying as a wholesome and fashionable recreation. **Contests** are now held all over the country between February and April, when winds are strong enough and farmers traditionally have free time after harvesting the rice. These contests fall into two broad categories: those involving manoeuvrable flat kites, often in the shapes of animals; and those in which the beauty of static display kites is judged. The most popular contest of all, which comes under the first category, matches two teams, one flying star-shaped *chula*s, 2m-high "male" kites, the other flying the smaller, more agile *pakpao*s, diamond-shaped "females". Each team uses its skill and teamwork to ensnare the other's kites and drag them back across a dividing line.

into the ground opposite the northeast corner of the Grand Palace. This phallic pillar, the **lak muang** – all Thai cities have one, to provide a home for their guardian spirits – was made from a 4m tree trunk carved with a lotus-shaped crown. In the nineteenth century, Rama IV had a new, shorter *lak muang* made, and the two pillars now amicably cohabit in an elegant shrine surrounded by immaculate gardens.

Hundreds of worshippers come every day to pray and offer flowers, particularly childless couples seeking the gift of fertility. In one corner of the gardens you can often see short performances of **classical dancing**, paid for by well-off families when they have a piece of good fortune to celebrate.

Silpakorn University Art Centre

Thanon Na Phra Lan, directly across the road from the entrance to the Grand Palace • Mon–Fri 9am–7pm, Sat 9am–4pm • Free • ☏ 02 623 6115 ext 1422, ⓦ art-centre.su.ac.th

Housed partly in the throne hall of a palace built during the reign of Rama I, the **Silpakorn University Art Centre** stages regular exhibitions by students, teachers, artists-in-residence and national artists. The country's first art school, Silpakorn was founded in 1935 by Professor Silpa Bhirasri, the much-revered, naturalized Italian sculptor; a charming, shady garden along the east wall of the art centre is dotted with his sculptures.

Wat Mahathat

Main entrance on Thanon Maharat, plus a back entrance on Thanon Na Phra That on Sanam Luang

Eighteenth-century **Wat Mahathat** provides a welcome respite from the surrounding tourist hype, and a chance to engage with the eager monks studying at **Mahachulalongkorn Buddhist University** here. As the nation's centre for the Mahanikai monastic sect (where Rama IV spent many years as a monk before becoming king in 1851), and housing one of the two Buddhist universities in Bangkok, the wat buzzes with purpose. It's this activity, and the chance of interaction and participation, rather than any special architectural features, that make a visit so rewarding. The many university-attending monks at the wat are friendly and keen to practise their English, and are more than likely to approach you: diverting topics might range from the poetry of Dylan Thomas to English football results.

Vipassana Meditation Centre

Section Five, Wat Mahathat • Practice daily 7–10am, 1–4pm & 6–8pm, dhamma talk daily 8–9pm • Donations welcome • ☏ 02 222 6011 or ☏ 02 222 4981, ⓦ udomwid.org

At the wat's **Vipassana Meditation Centre**, sitting and walking meditation practice is available in English (there's now a competing "Meditation Study and Retreat Center", nearby in Section One of the wat, but this is less geared towards foreign meditators). Participants generally stay in the simple surroundings of the meditation building itself, and must wear white clothes (available to rent at the centre) and observe the eight main Buddhist precepts (see p.748).

The National Museum

Thanon Na Phra That, northwest corner of Sanam Luang • Wed–Sun 9am–4pm, some rooms may close at lunchtime; usually some rooms are closed for restoration, as advertised at the ticket office • B200 • ☏ 02 224 1333, ⓦ thailandmuseum.com

The **National Museum** houses a colossal hoard of Thailand's chief artistic riches, ranging from sculptural treasures in the north and south wings, through bizarre decorative objects in the older buildings, to outlandish funeral chariots and the exquisite Buddhaisawan chapel, as well as sometimes staging worthwhile temporary exhibitions.

1

Guided tours It's worth making time for the free guided tours in English on Wed & Thurs 9.30am, Sat 10am, by the National Museum Volunteers (who also organize interesting lectures and excursions; ⓦmuseumvolunteers bkk.net): they're generally entertaining and their explication of the choicest exhibits provides a good introduction to Thai religion and culture.

Bookshop There's a well-stocked bookshop by the ticket office.

Eating Next to the bookshop is a pleasant a/c café, serving espressos, ice cream and a few lunch dishes, while the restaurant inside the museum grounds, by the funeral chariots building, dishes up decent, inexpensive Thai food.

History building

The first building you'll come to near the ticket office houses an overview of the authorized history of Thailand, including a small archeological gem: a black stone **inscription** (see also p.243), credited to King Ramkhamhaeng of Sukhothai, which became the first capital of the Thai nation (c.1278–99) under his rule. Discovered in 1833 by the future Rama IV, Mongkut, it's the oldest extant inscription using the Thai alphabet. This, combined with the description it records of prosperity and piety in Sukhothai's Golden Age, has made the stone a symbol of Thai nationhood. There's recently been much controversy over the stone's origins, arising from the suggestion that it was a fake made by Mongkut, but it seems most likely that it is indeed genuine, and was written partly as a kind of prospectus for Sukhothai, to attract traders and settlers to the underpopulated kingdom.

The main collection: southern building

At the back of the compound, two large modern buildings, flanking an old converted palace, house the museum's **main collection**, kicking off on the ground floor of the **southern building**. Look out here for some historic sculptures from the rest of Asia (S1), including one of the earliest representations of the Buddha, from Gandhara in modern-day Pakistan. Alexander the Great left a garrison at Gandhara, which explains why the image is in the style of Classical Greek sculpture: for example, the *ushnisha*, the supernatural bump on the top of the head, which symbolizes the Buddha's intellectual and spiritual power, is rationalized into a bun of thick, wavy hair.

Upstairs, the **prehistory** room (S6) displays axe heads and spear points from Ban Chiang in the northeast of Thailand (see p.483), one of the earliest Bronze Age cultures ever discovered. Alongside are many roughly contemporaneous metal artefacts from Kanchanaburi province, as well as some excellent examples of the developments of Ban Chiang's famous pottery. In the adjacent **Dvaravati** room (S7; sixth to eleventh centuries), the pick of the stone and terracotta Buddhas is a small head in smooth, pink clay from Wat Phra Ngam, Nakhon Pathom, whose downcast eyes and faintly smiling full lips typify the serene look of this era. At the far end of the first floor, you can't miss a voluptuous Javanese statue of elephant-headed Ganesh, Hindu god of wisdom and the arts, which, being the symbol of the Fine Arts Department, is always freshly garlanded. As Ganesh is known as the clearer of obstacles, Hindus always worship him before other gods, so by tradition he has grown fat through getting first choice of the offerings – witness his trunk jammed into a bowl of food in this sculpture.

Room S9 next door contains the most famous piece of **Srivijaya** art (seventh to thirteenth centuries), a bronze Bodhisattva Padmapani found at Chaiya (according to Mahayana Buddhism, a *bodhisattva* is a saint who has postponed his passage into Nirvana to help ordinary believers gain enlightenment). With its pouting face and sinuous torso, this image has become the ubiquitous emblem of southern Thailand. The rough chronological order of the collection continues back downstairs with an exhibition of **Khmer** and **Lopburi** sculpture (seventh to fourteenth centuries), most notably some dynamic bronze statuettes and stone lintels. Look out for an elaborate lintel from Ku Suan Tang, Buriram (S3), which depicts Vishnu reclining on the dragon Ananta in the sea of eternity, dreaming up a new universe after the old one has been annihilated in the Hindu cycle of creation and destruction. Out of his navel comes a lotus, and out of this emerges four-headed Brahma, who will put the dream into practice.

The main collection: northern building
The second half of the survey, in the northern building, begins upstairs with the **Sukhothai** collection (thirteenth to fifteenth centuries; N7–8), which features some typically elegant and sinuous Buddha images, as well as chunky bronzes of Hindu gods and a wide range of ceramics. The **Lanna** rooms (roughly thirteenth to sixteenth centuries; N5–6) include a miniature set of golden regalia, among them tiny umbrellas and a cute pair of filigree flip-flops, which would have been enshrined in a chedi. An ungainly but serene Buddha head, carved from grainy, pink sandstone, represents the **Ayutthaya** style of sculpture (fourteenth to eighteenth centuries; N9–10): the faintest incision of a moustache above the lips betrays the Khmer influences that came to Ayutthaya after its conquest of Angkor. A sumptuous scripture cabinet, showing a cityscape of old Ayutthaya, is a more unusual piece, one of a surviving handful of such carved and painted items of furniture.

Downstairs in the section on **Bangkok** or **Ratanakosin** art (eighteenth century onwards; N1), a stiffly realistic standing bronze brings you full circle. In his zeal for Western naturalism, Rama V had the statue made in the Gandhara style of the earliest Buddha image displayed in the first room of the museum.

The funeral chariots
To the east of the northern building, beyond the café on the left, stands a large garage where the fantastically elaborate **funeral chariots** of the royal family are stored. Pre-eminent among these is the Royal Chariot of Great Victory, built by Rama I in about 1789 for carrying the urn at his father's funeral. The 11m-high structure symbolizes heaven on Mount Meru, while the dragons and divinities around the sides – piled in five golden tiers to suggest the flames of the cremation – represent the mythological inhabitants of the mountain's forests. Each weighing around forty tonnes and requiring the pulling power of three hundred men, the teak chariots last had an outing in 2012, for the funeral of the only child of Rama VI, Princess Bejaratana.

Wang Na (Palace of the Second King)
The sprawling central building of the compound was originally part of the **Wang Na**, a huge palace stretching across Sanam Luang to Khlong Lod, which housed the "second king", appointed by the reigning monarch as his heir and deputy. When Rama V did away with the office in 1887, he turned the palace into a museum, which now contains a fascinating array of Thai objets d'art. As you enter (room 5), the display of sumptuous rare gold pieces behind heavy iron bars includes a well-preserved armlet taken from the ruined prang of fifteenth-century Wat Ratburana in Ayutthaya. In adjacent room 6, an intricately carved ivory seat turns out, with gruesome irony, to be a *howdah*, for use on an elephant's back. Among the masks worn by *khon* actors next door (room 7), look out especially for a fierce Hanuman, the white monkey-warrior in the *Ramayana* epic, gleaming with mother-of-pearl.

The huge and varied ceramic collection in room 8 includes some sophisticated pieces from Sukhothai, while the room behind (9) holds a riot of mother-of-pearl items, whose flaming rainbow of colours comes from the shell of the turbo snail from the Gulf of Thailand. It's also worth seeking out the display of richly decorated musical instruments in room 15.

The Buddhaisawan chapel
The second-holiest image in Thailand, after the Emerald Buddha, is housed in the **Buddhaisawan chapel**, the vast hall in front of the eastern entrance to the Wang Na. Inside, the fine proportions of the hall, with its ornate coffered ceiling and lacquered

1

window shutters, are enhanced by painted rows of divinities and converted demons, all turned to face the chubby, glowing **Phra Sihing Buddha**, which according to legend was magically created in Sri Lanka and sent to Sukhothai in the thirteenth century. Like the Emerald Buddha, the image was believed to bring good luck to its owner and was frequently snatched from one northern town to another, until Rama I brought it down from Chiang Mai in 1795 and installed it here in the second king's private chapel. Two other images (in Nakhon Si Thammarat and Chiang Mai) now claim to be the authentic Phra Sihing Buddha, but all three are in fact derived from a lost original – this one is in a fifteenth-century Sukhothai style. It's still much loved by ordinary people and at Thai New Year is carried out onto Sanam Luang, where worshippers sprinkle it with water as a merit-making gesture.

The careful detail and rich, soothing colours of the surrounding two-hundred-year-old **murals** are surprisingly well preserved; the bottom row between the windows narrates the life of the Buddha, beginning in the far right-hand corner with his parents' wedding.

Tamnak Daeng

On the south side of the Buddhaisawan chapel, the gaudily restored **Tamnak Daeng** (Red House) stands out, a large, airy Ayutthaya-style house made of rare golden teak, surmounted by a multi-tiered roof decorated with swan's-tail finials. Originally part of the private quarters of Princess Sri Sudarak, elder sister of Rama I, it was moved from the Grand Palace to the old palace in Thonburi for Queen Sri Suriyen, wife of Rama II; when her son became second king to Rama IV, he dismantled the edifice again and shipped it here to the Wang Na compound. Inside, it's furnished in the style of the early Bangkok period, with some of the beautiful objects that once belonged to Sri Suriyen, a huge, ornately carved box-bed, and the uncommon luxury of an indoor bathroom.

The National Gallery

4 Thanon Chao Fa, across from the National Theatre on the north side of Sanam Luang • Wed–Sun 9am–4pm • B200 • ☎ 02 282 2639–40, ⓦ thailandmuseum.com

If the National Museum hasn't finished you off, the **National Gallery** nearby probably will. In its upstairs gallery, it displays some rather beautiful early twentieth-century temple banners depicting Buddhist subjects, but the permanent collection of twentieth-century Thai art downstairs is largely uninspiring and derivative. Its temporary exhibitions can be pretty good, however. The fine old building that houses the gallery is also worth more than a cursory glance – it was constructed in typical early twentieth-century, neoclassical style, by Carlo Allegri, Rama V's court architect, as the Royal Mint.

Banglamphu and the Democracy Monument area

Immediately north of Ratanakosin, **Banglamphu**'s most notorious attraction is **Thanon Khao San**, a tiny sliver of a road whose multiple guesthouses and buzzing, budget-minded nightlife have made it an unmissable way-station for travellers through Southeast Asia. There is plenty of cultural interest too, in a medley of idiosyncratic temples within a few blocks of nearby landmark **Democracy Monument**, and in the typical Bangkok neighbourhoods that connect them, many of which still feel charmingly old-fashioned.

Banglamphu is served by plenty of public transport.

By boat Chao Phraya express-boat stops N13 (Phra Arthit), N14 (Rama VIII bridge) and N15 (Thewet) are nearby (see box, p.140). Banglamphu is also served by public boats along Khlong Saen Saeb to and from their Phan Fah terminus, which are useful for Siam Square and the Skytrain.

By BTS In addition to connecting to the Skytrain via Khlong Saen Saeb boat, the other fast way to get on to the BTS system is to take a taxi from Banglamphu to BTS National Stadium.

By bus Dozens of useful buses serve Banglamphu (see boxes, below & p.139).

Thanon Khao San

At the heart of Banglamphu is the legendary **Thanon Khao San**, almost a caricature of a travellers' centre, crammed with internet cafés and dodgy travel agents, the pavements lined with cheap backpackers' fashions, racks of bootleg PlayStation games, tattooists and hair-braiders. It's a lively, high-energy base: great for shopping and making travel arrangements – though beware the innumerable Khao San scams (see p.61) – and a good place to meet other travellers. It's especially fun at night when young Thais from all over the city gather here to browse the clothes stalls, mingle with the crowds of foreigners and squash into the bars and clubs that have made Khao San a great place to party. Even if you're staying elsewhere, the Khao San area is a cultural curiosity in its own right, a unique and continually evolving expression of global youth culture fuelled by Thai entrepreneurship.

Phra Arthit and the riverside walkway

Students from nearby Thammasat University inject an arty Thai vibe into the Banglamphu mix, particularly along **Thanon Phra Arthit**, which borders the Chao Phraya River. There's an attractive **riverside walkway** here too, which begins at the Bangkok Tourism Division's information centre beside Phra Pinklao Bridge and takes

---

BANGLAMPHU'S BUS STOPS AND ROUTES

The main bus stops serving Banglamphu are on Thanon Rajdamnoen Klang: with nearly thirty westbound and eastbound routes, you can get just about anywhere in the city from here. But there are some other useful routes running out of Banglamphu that have different pick-up points in the area. To make things simpler, we've assigned numbers to these **bus stops**, though they are not numbered on the ground. Where there are two stops served by the same buses they share a number. Bus stops are marked on the Banglamphu map (see p.100).

Bus stop 1: Thanon Krung Kasem, north side
#53 (clockwise) to Hualamphong train station (buses start from here)

Bus stop 2: Thanon Phra Sumen, south side, near Banglumpoo Place hotel; and Thanon Phra Arthit, east side, near Hemlock
#53 (anticlockwise) to the Grand Palace and Chinatown

Bus stop 3: Thanon Phra Arthit, west side, near New Siam Riverside; and Thanon Phra Sumen, north side, opposite Banglumpoo Place hotel
#3 & #9 to Chatuchak Weekend Market and Northern Bus Terminal
#53 (clockwise) to Hualamphong train station (change at Bus Stop 1, but same ticket)

Bus stop 4: Thanon Chakrabongse, near the 7-Eleven
#3 to the Museum of Siam, Pak Khlong Talat and Wongwian Yai train station
#9 to Wat Pho, Pak Khlong Talat
#15 to Jim Thompson's House, Siam Square and Thanon Silom

Bus Stop 5: Thanon Rajinee (Rachini), near Bangkok Tourism Information Centre
#124 to Southern Bus Terminal

1

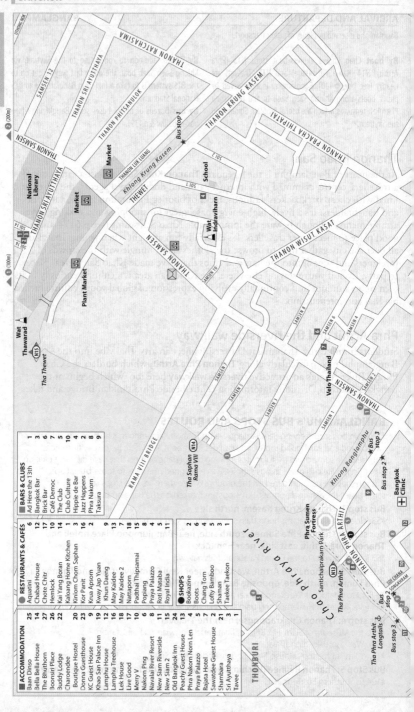

■ ACCOMMODATION

Baan Dinso	25
Bella Bella House	17
The Bhuthorn	24
Boonsiri Place	26
Buddy Lodge	22
Charoendee	
Boutique Hostel	20
Donna Guesthouse	23
KC Guest House	9
Khao San Palace Inn	19
Lamphu House	12
Lamphu Treehouse	16
Lek House	18
Live Good	17
Merry V	10
Nakorn Ping	6
Navalai River Resort	8
New Siam Riverside	11
New Siam 2	15
Old Bangkok Inn	24
Peachy Guest House	13
Phra Nakorn Norn Len	4
Praya Palazzo	5
Rajata Hotel	7
Sawatdee Guest House	2
Shambara	21
Sri Ayutthaya	3
Tavee	1

● RESTAURANTS & CAFÉS

Aquatini	6
Chabad House	12
Chote Chitr	17
Hemlock	10
Kai Yang Boran	14
Kaloang Home Kitchen	1
Kinlom Chom Saphan	3
Kor Panit	16
Krua Apsorn	2
Kway Jap Yuan	9
Khun Daeng	13
May Kaidee	7
May Kaidee 2	18
Nattaporn	15
Padthai Thipsamai	8
Popiang	4
Praya Palazzo	5
Roti Mataba	11
Royal India	11

■ BARS & CLUBS

Ad Here the 13th	1
Bangkok Bar	12
Brick Bar	6
Café Democ	7
The Club	10
Club Culture	4
Hippie de Bar	2
Jazz Happens	8
Phra Nakorn	9
Taksura	

● SHOPS

Bookazine	2
Boots	6
Chang Torn	4
Lofty Bamboo	5
Shaman	3
Taekee Taekon	1

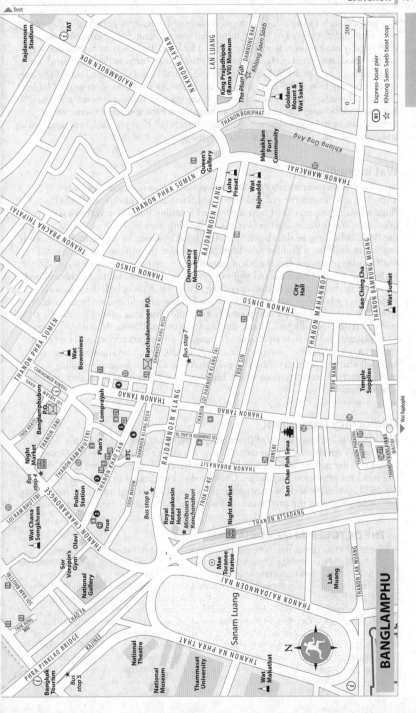

BANGLAMPHU

you past a couple of beautifully restored century-old mansions, currently occupied by Unicef and the UN's FAO; they show their most elegant faces to the river since in their heyday most visitors would have arrived by boat. The walkway terminates at the whitewashed, renovated octagonal tower of **Phra Sumen Fortress** (Phra Sumeru), one of fourteen built by Rama I in 1783 to protect the royal island of Ratanakosin. (The only other surviving tower, also renovated, is Phra Mahakhan Fortress, next to the Golden Mount.) Nowadays there's nothing to see inside the fort, but the area around it has been remodelled as grassy riverside **Santichaiprakarn Park** and retains some of the district's last remaining mangrove-like lamphu trees (*duabanga grandiflora*), after which Banglamphu, "the riverside place with lamphu trees", was named.

Wat Indraviharn

Thanon Wisut Kasat, about 20min walk north of Khao San • 10min walk from Chao Phraya express-boat stops N14 and N15

Though it can't match the graceful serenity of Ratanakosin's enormous Reclining Buddha, Banglamphu has its own super-sized Standing Buddha at **Wat Indraviharn** (also spelt Wat Intharawihan or Wat In), a glittering 32m-high mirror-plated statue of the Buddha bearing an alms bowl. Commissioned by Rama IV in the mid-nineteenth century to enshrine a Buddha relic from Sri Lanka (in the topknot), it's hardly the most elegant of images, but the 30cm-long toenails peep out prettily beneath offertory garlands of fragrant jasmine, and you can get reasonable views of the neighbourhood by climbing the stairways of the supporting tower; when unlocked, the doorways in the upper tower give access to the statue's hollow interior, affording vistas from shoulder level. The rest of the temple compound features the usual amalgam of architectural and spiritual styles, including a Chinese shrine and statues of Ramas IV and V.

Unfortunately, Wat In is an established hangout for **con-artists** (see p.61) offering tourists a tuk-tuk tour of Bangkok for a bargain B20, which invariably features a hard-sell visit to a jewellery shop (see p.170). Avoid all these hassles by hailing a passing metered taxi instead, or by catching one of the dozens of buses that run along Thanon Samsen.

Democracy Monument

The megalithic yellowy wings of **Democracy Monument** (*Anu Sawari Pracha Tippatai*) loom provocatively over Rajdamnoen Klang, the avenue that connects the Grand Palace and the new royal district of Dusit, and have since their erection in 1939 acted as a focus for pro-democracy rallies. Conceived as a testimony to the ideals that fuelled the 1932 revolution and the changeover to a constitutional monarchy, the monument's positioning between the royal residences is significant, as are its dimensions, which

---

THE OCTOBER 14 MEMORIAL

One of the biggest and most notorious demonstrations around Democracy Monument was the fateful student-led protest of October 14, 1973, when half a million people gathered on Rajdamnoen Klang to demand an end to the autocratic regime of the so-called "Three Tyrants". It was savagely quashed and turned into a bloody riot that culminated in the death of several hundred protesters at the hands of the police and the military. After three decades of procrastination, the events of this catastrophic day were finally commemorated with the erection of the **October 14 Memorial**, a small granite amphitheatre encircling an elegant modern chedi bearing the names of some of the dead; photographs and a bilingual account of the ten-day protest fill the back wall. The memorial stands in front of the former headquarters of Colonel Narong Kittikachorn, one of the Three Tyrants, 200m west of Democracy Monument, at the corner of Rajdamnoen Klang and Thanon Tanao.

allude to June 24, 2475 BE (1932 AD), the date the system was changed. In the decades since, Thailand's leaders have promulgated numerous interim charters and constitutions, the more repressive and regressive of which have been vigorously challenged in demonstrations on these very streets.

Thanon Tanao

A stroll down **Thanon Tanao** brings you into some engagingly old-fashioned neighbourhoods of nineteenth-century wooden shophouses, which are especially famous for their specialist **traditional Thai foods**. Many of these places have been making their specialities for generations, and there's all sorts that's fun to browse here, even if you're not inclined to taste, from beef noodles to pigs' brain soup, home-made ice cream to sticky rice with mango. See the "Eating" section for some recommendations (see p.153), but for an exhaustive survey consult the *Good Eats Ratanakosin* map (published by Pan Siam Publishing and available in major bookshops), which is especially handy given that few of these places have English-language signs or shop numbers.

The area around the south end of Thanon Tanao is also sometimes referred to as **Sao Ching Cha** (see p.104), after the **Giant Swing**, which is easily reached either by following any of the east-bound lanes off Tanao to Thanon Dinso, or by browsing the Buddhist paraphernalia stalls that take you there via Thanon Bamrung Muang. Alternatively, if you continue one block south along Tanao you'll reach the lovely little temple of Wat Rajabophit.

San Chao Poh Seua

Thanon Tanao • Daily 6am–5pm, till 9pm during the Vegetarian Festival (see p.154)

Not far south of Thanon Rajdamnoen Klang sits **San Chao Poh Seua** (San Jao Paw Sua), the **Tiger God Shrine**, an atmospheric, incense-filled Taoist shrine honouring the Chinese tiger guardian spirit and the God of the North Stars, whose image graces the centre of the main altar. It's a favourite with Chinese-Thais who come here to pray for power, prestige and successful pregnancy and offer in return pork rashers, fresh eggs, sticky rice, bottles of oil and sugar tigers.

Wat Rajabophit

Thanon Rajabophit, one block south of the Tanao/Bamrung Muang intersection, just to the east of Khlong Lod (see map, p.83)

One of Bangkok's prettiest temples, **Wat Rajabophit** is another example of the Chinese influence in this neighbourhood. It was built by Rama V and, typical of him, is unusual in its design, particularly the circular cloister that encloses a chedi and links the rectangular bot and viharn. Every external wall in the compound is covered in the pastel shades of Chinese *bencharong* ceramic tiles, creating a stunning overall effect, while the bot interior looks like a tiny banqueting hall, with gilded Gothic vaults and intricate mother-of-pearl doors.

Thanon Bamrung Muang

Thanon Bamrung Muang, which runs east from Thanon Tanao to Sao Ching Cha and Wat Suthat, is famous as the best place in Thailand to buy **Buddhist paraphernalia**, or *sanghapan*, and is well worth a browse. The road is lined with shops selling everything a good Buddhist might need, from household offertory tables to temple umbrellas and cellophane-wrapped Buddha images up to 2m high. They also sell special alms packs for donating to monks, which typically come in saffron-coloured plastic buckets (used by monks for washing their robes, or themselves), and include such necessities as soap, toothpaste, soap powder, toilet roll, candles and incense.

1

Sao Ching Cha

Midway along Thanon Bamrung Muang, just in front of Wat Suthat

You can't miss the towering, red-painted teak posts of **Sao Ching Cha**, otherwise known as the **Giant Swing**. This strange contraption was once the focal point of a Brahmin ceremony to honour the Hindu god Shiva's annual visit to earth, in which teams of young men competed to swing up to a height of 25m and grab a suspended bag of gold with their teeth. The act of swinging probably symbolized the rising and setting of the sun, though legend also has it that Shiva and his consort Uma were banned from swinging in heaven because doing so caused cataclysmic floods on earth – prompting Shiva to demand that the practice be continued on earth to ensure moderate rains and bountiful harvests. Accidents were so common with the terrestrial version that it was outlawed in the 1930s.

Wat Suthat

Thanon Bamrung Muang • Daily 9am–4pm • B20

Were the Giant Swing still in operation, you'd get a fine view over adjacent **Wat Suthat** and its towering central viharn, Bangkok's tallest. This is one of Thailand's six most important temples, built in the early nineteenth century to house the 8m-high statue of the meditating **Phra Sri Sakyamuni Buddha**, which was brought all the way down from Sukhothai by river. It now sits on a glittering mosaic dais surrounded with surreal murals that depict the last 24 lives of the Buddha rather than the more usual ten. The encircling galleries contain 156 serenely posed Buddha images, making a nice contrast to the **Chinese statues** dotted around the temple courtyards, most of which were brought over from China during Rama I's reign, as ballast in rice boats; there are some fun character studies among them, including gormless Western sailors and pompous Chinese scholars.

Wat Rajnadda

5min walk east of Democracy Monument, at the point where Rajdamnoen Klang meets Thanon Mahachai • Loha Prasat daily 9am–5pm • Free

Among the assortment of religious buildings known collectively as **Wat Rajnadda**, the most striking is the multi-tiered, castle-like, early nineteenth-century **Loha Prasat**, or "Iron Monastery", whose 37 forbidding metal spires represent the 37 virtues necessary for attaining enlightenment. Modelled on a Sri Lankan monastery, its tiers are pierced by passageways running north–south and east–west – fifteen in each direction at ground level – with small meditation cells at each point of intersection.

Amulet market

In the southeast (Thanon Mahachai) corner of the temple compound, Bangkok's biggest **amulet market**, the **Wat Rajnadda Buddha Centre**, comprises at least a hundred stalls selling tiny Buddha images of all designs. Alongside these miniature charms are statues of Hindu deities, dolls and carved wooden phalluses, also bought to placate or ward off disgruntled spirits, as well as love potions and CDs of sacred music.

Phra Mahakhan Fortress community

Thanon Mahachai

The **Phra Mahakhan Fortress community**, across the road from Wat Rajnadda, occupies the land between the whitewashed crenellations of the renovated eighteenth-century city walls and Khlong Ong Ang. It's a historic, working-class neighbourhood where some of the houses date from the early nineteenth century and has been the object of a recent urban renovation programme. It now welcomes visitors with informative signboards describing some of its traditions, including massage therapy, fish bladder soup and *likay* popular theatre. In the block of shops on Thanon Mahachai,

AMULETS

To invite good fortune, ward off malevolent spirits and gain protection from physical harm, many Thais wear or carry at least one **amulet** at all times. The most popular images are copies of sacred statues from famous wats, while others show revered monks, kings (Rama V is a favourite) or healers. On the reverse side, a yantra is often inscribed, a combination of letters and figures also designed to deflect evil, sometimes of a very specific nature: protecting your durian orchards from gales, for example, or your tuk-tuk from oncoming traffic. Individually hand-crafted or mass-produced, amulets can be made from bronze, clay, plaster or gold, and some even have sacred ingredients added, such as special herbs, or the ashes of burnt holy texts. But what really determines an amulet's efficacy is its history: where and by whom it was made, who or what it represents and who consecrated it. Stories of miracle cures and lucky escapes also prompt a rush on whatever amulet the survivor was wearing. Monks are often involved in the making of the images and are always called upon to consecrate them – the more charismatic the monk, the more powerful the amulet. Religious authorities take a relaxed view of the amulet industry, despite its anomalous and commercial functions, and proceeds contribute to wat funds and good causes.

The **belief in amulets** is thought to have originated in India, where tiny images were sold to pilgrims who visited the four holy sites associated with the Buddha's life. But not all amulets are Buddhist-related; there's a whole range of other enchanted objects to wear for protection, including tigers' teeth, rose quartz, tamarind seeds, coloured threads and miniature phalluses. Worn around the waist rather than the neck, the phallus amulets provide protection for the genitals as well as being associated with fertility, and are of Hindu origin.

For some people, amulets are not only a vital form of spiritual protection, but valuable **collectors' items** as well. Amulet-collecting mania is something akin to stamp collecting and there are at least half a dozen Thai magazines for collectors, which give histories of certain types, tips on distinguishing between genuine items and fakes, and personal accounts of particularly powerful amulet experiences. The most rewarding places to watch the collectors and browse the wares yourself are at Wat Rajnadda Buddha Centre (see opposite), probably the best place in Bangkok; along "Amulet Alley" on Trok Mahathat, between Wat Mahathat (see p.95) and the river, where streetside vendors will have cheaper examples; and at Chatuchak Weekend Market (see p.129). Prices start as low as B50 and rise into the thousands.

immediately south of the crenellations, are a famous traditional Thai perfume shop and several places specializing in Thai and Chinese antiques.

Wat Saket

Easiest access is along Thanon Boriphat (the specialist street for custom-carved wooden doors), 5min walk south from the khlong bridge and Phan Fah canal-boat stop at the eastern end of Rajdamnoen Klang

Beautifully illuminated at night, when it seems to float unsupported above the neighbourhood, the gleaming gold chedi of late eighteenth-century **Wat Saket** actually sits atop a structure known as the Golden Mount. Being outside the capital's city walls, the wat initially served as a crematorium and then a dumping ground for sixty thousand plague victims left to the vultures because they couldn't afford funeral pyres. There's no sign of this grim episode at modern-day Wat Saket of course, which these days is a smart, buzzing hive of religious activity at the base of the golden hilltop chedi. Wat Saket hosts an enormous annual **temple fair** in the first week of November, when the mount is illuminated with lanterns and the compound seethes with funfair rides and travelling theatre shows.

The Golden Mount

Daily 8am–5pm • B10

The **Golden Mount**, or **Phu Khao Tong**, dates back to the early nineteenth century, when Rama III commissioned a huge chedi to be constructed here, using building materials

1

from the ruined fortresses and walls of the former capital, Ayutthaya. However, the ground proved too soft to support the chedi. The whole thing collapsed into a hill of rubble, but as Buddhist law states that a religious building can never be destroyed, however tumbledown, fifty years later Rama V simply crowned it with the more sensibly sized chedi we see today, in which he placed some relics, believed by some to be the Buddha's teeth. These days the old rubbly base is picturesquely planted with shrubs and shady trees and dotted with gravestones and memorials. Winding stairways take you up to the chedi terrace and a fine view over Banglamphu and Ratanakosin landmarks, including the golden spires of the Grand Palace, the finely proportioned prangs of Wat Arun across the river beyond and, further upriver, the striking superstructure of the Rama VIII bridge.

The Queen's Gallery

North across Rajdamnoen Klang from Wat Rajnadda, on the corner of Thanon Phra Sumen • Daily except Wed 10am–7pm • B30 • ① 02 281 5360–1, ⓦ queengallery.org

The privately funded, five-storey **Queen's Gallery** hosts temporary shows of contemporary Thai art, plus the occasional exhibition by foreign artists, and makes a more stimulating alternative to the rather staid National Gallery down the other end of Rajdamnoen Klang. Its bookshop sells hard-to-find Thai art books.

Chinatown and Pahurat

When the newly crowned Rama I decided to move his capital across to the east bank of the river in 1782, the Chinese community living on the proposed site of his palace was obliged to relocate downriver, to the **Sampeng** area. Two centuries on, **Chinatown** has grown into the country's largest Chinese district, a sprawl of narrow alleyways, temples and shophouses packed between Charoen Krung (New Road) and the river, separated from Ratanakosin by the Indian area of **Pahurat** – famous for its cloth and dressmakers' trimmings – and bordered to the east by **Hualamphong** train station.

The **Chinese influence** on Thai culture and commerce has been significant ever since the first Chinese merchants gained a toehold in Ayutthaya in the fourteenth century. Following centuries of immigration and intermarriage, there is now some Chinese blood in almost every Thai citizen, including the king, and Chinese-Thai business interests play an enormous role in the Thai economy. This is played out at its most frantic in Chinatown, whose real estate is said to be among the most valuable in the country; there are over a hundred gold and jewellery shops along Thanon Yaowarat alone.

For the tourist, Chinatown is chiefly interesting for its **markets**, shophouses, open-fronted warehouses and remnants of colonial-style architecture, though it also harbours a few noteworthy **temples**. A meander through its most interesting neighbourhoods could easily soak up a whole day, allowing for frequent breaks from the thundering traffic and choking fumes. For the most authentic Chinatown experience, it's best to come during the week, as some shops and stalls shut at weekends; on weekdays they begin closing around 5pm, after which time the neighbourhood's other big draw – its **food** – takes centre stage.

GETTING THERE AND AROUND   **CHINATOWN**

Arrival The easiest way to reach Chinatown is either by subway to Hualamphong Station, or by Chao Phraya express boat to Tha Rachawongse (Rajawong; N5) at the southern end of Thanon Rajawong. A westward extension of the subway is being built, with new stations at Wat Mangkon Kamalawat and Pahurat. This part of the city is also well served by buses,

with Hualamphong a useful and easily recognized place to disembark (see box, p.139). Be warned that buses and taxis may take an unexpectedly circuitous route due to the many and complex one-way systems in Chinatown.

Getting around Orientation in Chinatown can be tricky: the alleys (often known as trok rather than the more usual

1

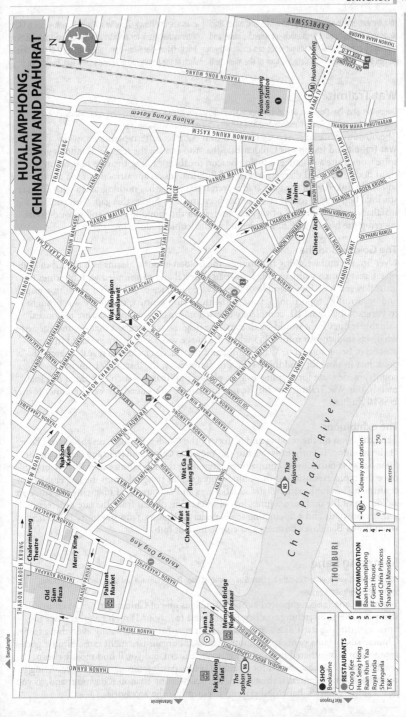

HUALAMPHONG, CHINATOWN AND PAHURAT

N

Chao Phraya River

THONBURI

- (M) - - Subway and station

| 0 | | 250 |
| metres | | |

ACCOMMODATION
Baan Hualamphong	3
FF Guest House	4
Grand China Princess	1
Shanghai Mansion	2

● SHOP
| Bookazine | 1 |

● RESTAURANTS
Chong Kee	6
Hua Seng Hong	3
Raan Khun Yaa	5
Royal India	2
Shangarila	1
T&K	4

soi) are extremely narrow, their turn-offs and other road signs often obscured by mounds of merchandise and thronging crowds, and the longer ones can change their names several times. For a detailed tour of the alleys and markets, use *Nancy Chandler's Map of Bangkok* (see p.142); alternatively, ask for help at the BMA tourist information booth (Mon–Sat 9am–5pm) just northwest of the Chinese Arch at the beginning of Thanon Yaowarat, beside Soi 5.

Wat Traimit

Thanon Mittaphap Thai-China, just west of Hualamphong train and subway stations (exit 1) • Daily 8am–5pm, exhibitions closed Mon • Golden Buddha only B40, Golden Buddha and exhibitions B100 • Ⓦ wattraimitr-withayaram.com

The obvious place to start a Chinatown tour is on its eastern perimeter, with **Wat Traimit** and its famous Golden Buddha. You can see the temple mondop's golden spire from quite a distance, a fitting beacon for the gleaming treasure housed on its third floor, the world's largest solid-gold Buddha. It's an apt attraction for a community so closely linked with the gold trade, even if the image has nothing to do with China's spiritual heritage. A recent attempt has been made to bridge this gap, with the installation of exhibitions of varying interest on the mondop's first and second floors, covering the history of Chinatown and of the iconic Buddha image.

The Golden Buddha

Over 3m tall and weighing five tonnes, the **Golden Buddha** gleams as if coated in liquid metal, seated on a white marble lotus-pad pedestal and surrounded with offerings of lotus flowers. It's a fine example of the curvaceous grace of Sukhothai art, slim-waisted and beautifully proportioned. Cast in the thirteenth century, the image was brought to Bangkok by Rama III, completely encased in stucco – a common ruse to conceal valuable statues from would-be thieves. The disguise was so good that no one guessed what was underneath until 1955 when the image was accidentally knocked in the process of being moved to Wat Traimit, and the stucco cracked to reveal a patch of gold. Just in time for Buddhism's 2500th anniversary, the discovery launched a country-wide craze for tapping away at plaster Buddhas in search of hidden precious metals, but Wat Traimit's is still the most valuable – it's valued, by weight alone, at over US$10 million.

The exhibitions

The exhibition on the making and history of the Golden Buddha, on the second floor of the mondop, is fairly missable but the **Yaowarat Chinatown Heritage Centre** on the floor below is rather more compelling. Interesting though sanitized, its display boards trace the rapid expansion of the Chinese presence in Bangkok from the late eighteenth century, first as junk traders, later as labourers and tax farmers. Enhancing the story are a diorama of life on board a junk, lots of interesting photos from the late nineteenth century onwards and a fascinating scale model of Thanon Yaowarat in its 1950s heyday, when it was Bangkok's business and entertainment hub.

Sampeng Lane

From Wat Traimit, walk northwest from the big China Gate roundabout along Thanon Yaowarat, and make a left turn onto Thanon Songsawat to reach Sampeng Lane

Sampeng Lane (also signposted as Soi Wanit 1) is one of Chinatown's most enjoyable shopping alleys. Stretching southeast–northwest for about 1km, it's a great place to browse, unfurling itself like a serpentine department store and selling everything from Chinese silk pyjama pants to computer games at bargain-basement rates. Similar goods are more or less gathered in sections, so at the eastern end you'll find mostly cheap jewellery and hair accessories, for example, before passing through stalls specializing in ceramics, Chinese lanterns, then shoes, clothes (west of Thanon Rajawong) and, as you near Pahurat, fabrics, haberdashery and irresistibly girlie accessories.

Soi Issaranuphap

For a rather more sensual experience, take a right about halfway down Sampeng Lane, into **Soi Issaranuphap** (also signed along its course as Yaowarat Soi 11 then Soi 6, and later Charoen Krung sois 16 and 21). Packed with people from dawn till dusk, this long, dark alleyway, which also traverses Charoen Krung, is where you come in search of ginseng roots (essential for good health), quivering fish heads, cubes of cockroach-killer chalk and a gastronome's choice of dried mushrooms and brine-pickled vegetables. Alleys branch off to florid Chinese temples and tiny squares before Soi Issaranuphap finally ends at the Thanon Plaplachai intersection amid a flurry of shops specializing in paper **funeral art**. Believing that the deceased should be well provided for in their afterlife, Chinese people buy miniature paper replicas of necessities to be burned with the body: especially popular are houses, cars, suits of clothing and, of course, money.

Wat Mangkon Kamalawat

Best approached via its dramatic multi-tiered gateway 10m up Thanon Charoen Krung from the Soi Issaranuphap junction

If Soi Issaranuphap epitomizes age-old Chinatown commerce, then **Wat Mangkon Kamalawat** (also known as **Wat Leng Noei Yee** or, in English, "Dragon Flower Temple") stands as a fine example of the community's spiritual practices. It receives a constant stream of devotees, who come to leave offerings at the altars inside this important Mahayana Buddhist temple. As with the Theravada Buddhism espoused by the Thais, Mahayana Buddhism fuses with other ancient religious beliefs, notably Confucianism and Taoism, and the statues and shrines within Wat Mangkon cover the spectrum. As you pass through the secondary gateway, under the glazed ceramic gables topped with undulating Chinese dragons, you're greeted by a set of four outsize statues of bearded and rather forbidding sages, each symbolically clasping either a parasol, a pagoda, a snake's head or a mandolin. Beyond them, a series of Buddha images swathed in saffron netting occupies the next chamber, a lovely open-sided room of gold paintwork, red-lacquered wood, lattice lanterns and pictorial wall panels inlaid with mother-of-pearl. Elsewhere in the compound are booths selling devotional paraphernalia, a Chinese medicine stall and a fortune-teller.

Wat Ga Buang Kim

Less than 100m up Thanon Charoen Krung from Wat Mangkon; take a left turn into Thanon Rajawong, followed by a right turn into Thanon Anawong and a further right turn into the narrow, two-pronged Soi Krai

The typical neighbourhood temple of **Wat Ga Buang Kim** is set around a tiny, enclosed courtyard. This particular wat is remarkable for its exquisitely ornamented "vegetarian hall", a one-room shrine with altar centrepiece framed by intricately carved wooden tableaux of gold-painted miniatures arranged as if in sequence, with recognizable characters reappearing in new positions and in different moods. The hall's outer wall is adorned with small tableaux, too, the area around the doorway at the top of the stairs peopled with finely crafted ceramic figurines drawn from Chinese opera stories. The other building in the wat compound is a stage used for Chinese opera performances.

Pahurat

The ethnic emphasis changes west of Khlong Ong Ang, where **Pahurat** begins, for here, in the small square south of the intersection of Chakraphet and Pahurat roads, is where the capital's sizeable Indian community congregates. Unless you're looking for *bindi* cigarettes, Punjabi sweets or Bollywood VCDs, curiosity-shopping is not as rewarding here as in Chinatown, but it's good for all sorts of **fabrics**, from shirting to curtain materials and saree lengths.

1

Also here, at the Charoen Krung/Thanon Triphet intersection, is the colonial-look mint-green and cream-painted **Old Siam Plaza**, whose nostalgia theme continues in part inside, with its ground-floor shopping concourse given over to stalls selling traditional, handmade Thai snacks, sweets and sticky desserts. The adjacent Sala Chalermkrung Theatre sometimes stages classical Thai drama for non-Thai speakers (see p.164).

Pak Khlong Talat

Pak Khlong Talat 24hr • **Memorial Bridge night bazaar** Tues–Sun roughly 8pm–midnight • Chao Phraya express boat to Tha Saphan Phut (N6)

A browse through the 24-hour flower and vegetable market, **Pak Khlong Talat**, is a fitting way to round off a day in Chinatown, though it's also a great place to come before dawn, when market gardeners from Thonburi and beyond boat and truck their freshly picked produce across the Chao Phraya ready for sale to shopkeepers, restaurateurs and hoteliers. The market has been operating from covered halls between the southern ends of Khlong Lod, Thanon Banmo, Thanon Chakraphet and the river bank since the nineteenth century and is the biggest wholesale market in the capital. The flower stalls, selling twenty different varieties of cut orchids and countless other tropical blooms, spill onto the streets along the riverfront as well and, though prices are lowest in the early morning, you can still get some good bargains in the afternoon. Most evenings, the riverside end of nearby Thanon Triphet and the area around the base of **Memorial Bridge** (Saphan Phut) hosts a huge **night bazaar** that's dominated by cheap and idiosyncratic fashions – and by throngs of teenage fashion victims.

For the most interesting **approach** to the flower market from the Old Siam Plaza, turn west across Thanon Triphet to reach Thanon Banmo, and then follow this road south down towards the Chao Phraya. As you near the river, notice the facing rows of traditional Chinese shophouses, still in use today, which retain their characteristic (peeling) pastel-painted facades, shutters and stucco curlicues. There's an entrance into the market on your right and just after sundown this southernmost stretch of Thanon Banmo fills with handcarts and vans unloading the most amazing mountains of fresh blooms.

Thonburi

For fifteen years between the fall of Ayutthaya in 1767 and the founding of Bangkok in 1782, the west-bank town of **Thonburi**, across the Chao Phraya from modern-day Bangkok, stood in as the Thai capital, under the rule of General Phraya Taksin. Its time in the spotlight was too brief for the building of the fine monuments and temples that graced earlier capitals at Sukhothai and Ayutthaya, but some of its centuries-old **canals**, which once transported everyone and everything, have endured; it is these and the ways of life that depend on them that constitute Thonburi's main attractions. In some quarters, life on this side of the river still revolves around these khlongs: vendors of food and household goods paddle their boats along the canals that crisscross the residential areas, and canalside factories use them to ferry their wares to the Chao Phraya River artery. Venture onto the backroads just three or four kilometres west of the river and you find yourself surrounded by market gardens and rural homes, with no hint of the throbbing metropolis across on the other bank. The most popular way to explore these old neighbourhoods is by **boat**, but joining a bicycle tour of the older neighbourhoods is also very rewarding (see p.138). Most boat trips also encompass Thonburi's imposing riverside Temple of the Dawn, **Wat Arun**, and often the **Royal Barge Museum** as well, though both are easily visited by yourself, as are the small but historic temple of **Wat Rakhang** and the surprisingly intriguing, and child-friendly, cemetery at **Wat Prayoon**.

Arrival Getting to Thonburi is generally just a matter of crossing the river. Either use Phra Pinklao or Memorial/Phra Pokklao bridge, take a cross-river ferry, or hop on one of the express boats, which make several stops on the Thonburi bank. The planned subway extension from Hualamphong will include a station near Wat Arun.

Getting around If you're not exploring Thonburi on a boat tour (see box, p.112), getting around the district can be complicated as the lack of footbridges over canals means that walking between sights often involves using the heavily trafficked Thanon Arun Amarin. A more convoluted alternative would be to leapfrog your way up or down the river by boat, using the various cross-river ferries that connect the Thonburi bank with the Chao Phraya express-boat stops on the other side.

Royal Barge Museum

Soi Wat Dusitaram, north bank of Khlong Bangkok Noi • Daily 9am–5pm • B100 • Ⓦ thailandmuseum.com • Chao Phraya express boat to Tha Phra Pinklao (N12), or cross-river ferry from under Pinklao Bridge in Banglamphu to Tha Phra Pinklao, then walk up the road 100m and take the first left down Soi Wat Dusitaram; if coming by bus from the Bangkok side (#507, #509 and #511 all cross the river here), get off at the first stop on the Thonburi side, which is at the mouth of Soi Wat Dusitaram – signs from Soi Wat Dusitaram lead you through a jumble of walkways and stilt-houses to the museum (10min)

Since the Ayutthaya era, kings of Thailand have been conveyed along their country's waterways in royal barges. For centuries, these slender, exquisitely elegant, black-and-gold wooden vessels were used on all important royal outings, and even up until 1967 the current king would process down the Chao Phraya to Wat Arun in a flotilla of royal barges at least once a year, on the occasion of Kathin, the annual donation of robes by the laity to the temple at the end of the rainy season. But the boats, some of which are a hundred years old, are becoming quite frail, so **royal barge processions** are now held only every few years to mark special anniversaries. However, if your trip happens to coincide with one of these magnificent events, you shouldn't miss it (see Ⓦ tourismthailand.org). Fifty or more barges fill the width of the river and stretch for almost 1km, drifting slowly to the measured beat of a drum and the hypnotic strains of ancient boating hymns, chanted by over two thousand oarsmen dressed in luscious brocades.

The eight beautifully crafted vessels at the heart of the ceremony are housed in the **Royal Barge Museum**. Up to 50m long and intricately lacquered and gilded all over, they taper at the prow into imposing mythical figures after a design first used by the kings of Ayutthaya. Rama I had the boats copied and, when those fell into disrepair, Rama VI commissioned exact reconstructions, some of which are still in use today. The most important is *Sri Suphanahongse*, which bears the king and queen and is graced by a glittering 5m-high prow representing the golden swan Hamsa, mount of the Hindu god Brahma. In front of it floats *Anantanagaraj*, fronted by a magnificent seven-headed naga and bearing a Buddha image. The newest addition to the fleet is *Narai Song Suban*, which was commissioned by the current king for his golden jubilee in 1996; it is a copy of the mid-nineteenth-century original and is crowned with a black Vishnu (Narai) astride a garuda figurehead. A display of miniaturized royal barges at the back of the museum re-creates the exact formation of a traditional procession.

Wat Rakhang

Cross-river ferry from Tha Chang (Grand Palace) express-boat pier to Wat Rakhang's pier, or a 5min walk from the Tha Wang Lang express-boat pier, south (left) through the Phrannok pierside market

The charming riverside temple of **Wat Rakhang** (Temple of the Bells) gets its name from the five large bells donated by King Rama I and is notable for the hundreds of smaller chimes that tinkle away under the eaves of the main bot and, more accessibly, in the temple courtyard, where devotees come to strike them and hope for a run of good luck. To be extra certain of having wishes granted, visitors also buy loaves of bread from the temple stalls and feed the frenzy of fat fish in the Chao Phraya River

1

EXPLORING THONBURI BY BOAT

The most popular way to explore the sights of Thonburi is by **boat**, taking in Wat Arun and the Royal Barge Museum, then continuing along Thonburi's network of small canals. The easiest option is to take a fixed-price trip from one of the piers on the Bangkok side of the Chao Phraya, most conveniently from Tha Chang near Wat Pho or the River City pier off Thanon Charoen Krung. You can also charter your own longtail from these piers and others such as Tha Phra Arthit in Banglamphu and Tha Sathorn, and from many five-star riverside hotels, but bear the prices listed below in mind when negotiating and be specific about your itinerary.

Many tours include visits to one of Thonburi's two main **floating markets**, both of which are heavily touristed and rather contrived. **Wat Sai** floating market is very small, very commercialized and worth avoiding; **Taling Chan** floating market is also fairly manufactured but more fun, though it only operates on Saturdays and Sundays (approx 9am–4pm). Taling Chan market is held on Khlong Chak Phra, in front of Taling Chan District Office, a couple of kilometres west of Thonburi train station, and can also be reached by taking bus #79 from Banglamphu. For a more authentic floating-market experience, consider heading out of Bangkok to Amphawa, in Samut Songkhram province (see p.186).

Arguably more photogenic, and certainly a lot more genuine, are the individual **floating vendors** who continue to paddle from house to house in Thonburi, touting anything from hot food to plastic buckets. You've a good chance of seeing some of them in action on almost any longtail boat tour on any day of the week, particularly in the morning.

Mitchaopaya Travel Service Tha Chang ☎02 623 6169, ⓦ mitchaophraya.co.th. Offers trips of varying durations: in 1hr (B1000/boat, or B400/person if you can join in with other people), you'll go out along Khlong Bangkok Noi and back via Khlong Mon, passing Wat Arun and the Royal Barge Museum without stopping; in 90min (B1300), you'd have time to stop at either or you could do a longer route, coming back along Khlong Bangkok Yai; while in 2hr (B1500) you'll have time to go right down the back canals on the Thonburi side and visit an orchid farm. On Sat & Sun, the 90min and 2hr trips take in Taling Chan floating market.
Real Asia ☎02 665 6364, ⓦ www.realasia.net. Runs guided full-day walking and boat tours of the Thonburi canals for B2000 per person, including lunch.
River City pier longtails ☎02 237 0077 ext 180.

Private longtail trips for B1500 per boat for two people for 1hr.

Tha Phra Arthit longtails Pier in front of *The Phra Arthit River Lounge*, 200m south of the N13 Tha Phra Arthit express-boat pier, Banglamphu. An enjoyable 90min loop (B1200 per boat) via Khlong Bangkok Noi, Khlong Chak Phra and Khlong Bangkok Yai that takes in a variety of different khlong-side residences, temples and itinerant floating vendors, with the possibility of stopping at Taling Chan floating market at weekends. One- (B800 per boat) and two-hour (B1500) trips also possible.

Wan Fah River City Shopping Centre pier ☎02 622 7657–61, ⓦ wanfahcruise.com. A 2hr cruise of the west-bank canals by a combination of ferry boat and converted rice barge. Daily 2.30pm; B800 per person.

below. Behind the bot stands an attractive eighteenth-century wooden *ho trai* (scripture library) that still boasts some original murals on the wooden panels inside, as well as exquisitely renovated gold-leaf paintwork on the window shutters and pillars.

Walking to Wat Rakhang from the Tha Wang Lang express-boat pier you'll pass through the enjoyable **Phrannok pierside market**, which is good for cheap clothes and tempting home-made snacks, especially sweet ones.

Wat Arun

Daily 8am–5pm • B50 • ⓦ watarun.org • Take the cross-river ferry from the pier adjacent to the Chao Phraya express-boat pier at Tha Thien

Almost directly across the river from Wat Pho rises the enormous, five-spired prang of **Wat Arun**, the Temple of Dawn, probably Bangkok's most memorable landmark and familiar as the silhouette used in the TAT logo. It looks particularly impressive from the river as you head downstream from the Grand Palace towards the *Oriental Hotel*, but is ornate enough to be well worth stopping off for a closer look.

1

A wat has occupied this site since the Ayutthaya period, but only in 1768 did it become known as the Temple of Dawn – when General Phraya Taksin reputedly reached his new capital at the break of day. The temple served as his royal chapel and housed the recaptured Emerald Buddha for several years until the image was moved to Wat Phra Kaeo in 1785. Despite losing its special status after the relocation, Wat Arun continued to be revered, and its corncob prang was reconstructed and enlarged to its present height of 81m by Rama II and Rama III.

The prang that you see today is classic Ayutthayan style, built as a representation of Mount Meru, the home of the gods in Khmer cosmology. By climbing the two tiers of the square base that supports the **central prang**, you not only enjoy a good view of the river and beyond, but also get a chance to examine the tower's distinctive decorations. Both this main prang and the four minor ones that encircle it are studded all over with bits of broken porcelain, ceramic shards and tiny bowls that have been fashioned into an amazing array of polychromatic flowers. The statues of mythical *yaksha* demons and half-bird, half-human *kinnari* that support the different levels are similarly decorated. The crockery probably came from China, possibly from commercial shipments that were damaged at sea, and the overall effect is highly decorative and far more subtle than the dazzling glass mosaics that clad most wat buildings. On the first terrace, the mondops at each cardinal point contain statues of the Buddha at birth (north), in meditation (east), preaching his first sermon (south) and entering Nirvana (west). The second platform surrounds the base of the prang proper, whose closed entranceways are guarded by four statues of the Hindu god Indra on his three-headed elephant Erawan. In the niches of the smaller prangs stand statues of Phra Pai, the god of the wind, on horseback.

Wat Prayoon

Off Thanon Pracha Thipok, 3min walk from Memorial Bridge; though on the Thonburi bank, it's easiest to reach from the Bangkok side, by walking over Memorial Bridge from the express ferry stop at Tha Saphan Phut (N6)

Just west of the Thonburi approach to Memorial Bridge, the unusual **Khao Mor cemetery** makes an unexpectedly enjoyable place to take the kids, with its miniaturized shrines and resident turtles. Its dollshouse-sized shrines are set on an artificial hillock, which was constructed by Rama III to replicate the pleasing shapes made by dripping candle wax. Wedged in among the grottoes, caverns and ledges of this uneven mass are numerous memorials to the departed, forming a not-at-all sombre gallery of different styles, from traditional Thai chedis, bots and prangs to more foreign designs like the tiny Wild West house complete with cacti at the front door. Turtles fill the pond surrounding the mound and you can feed them with the bags of banana and papaya sold nearby. The cemetery is part of **Wat Prayoon** (officially Wat Prayurawongsawat) but located in a separate compound to the southeast side of the wat.

Memorial Bridge

It wasn't until 1932 that Thonburi was linked to Bangkok proper by the **Memorial Bridge**, or **Saphan Phut**, built to commemorate the hundred and fiftieth anniversary of the foundation of the Chakri dynasty and of Bangkok, and dedicated to Rama I (or Phra Buddha Yodfa, to give him his official title), whose bronze statue sits at the Bangkok approach. It proved to be such a crucial river-crossing that the bridge has since been supplemented by the adjacent twin-track **Saphan Phra Pokklao**.

Dusit

Connected to Ratanakosin via the boulevards of Rajdamnoen Klang and Rajdamnoen Nok, the spacious, leafy area known as **Dusit** has been a royal district since the reign of

1

Rama V, King Chulalongkorn (1860–1910). The first Thai monarch to visit Europe, Rama V returned with radical plans for the modernization of his capital, the fruits of which are most visible in Dusit, notably at **Vimanmek Palace** and **Wat Benjamabophit**, the so-called "Marble Temple". Even now, **Rama V** still commands a loyal following and the statue of him, helmeted and on horseback, which stands at the Thanon U-Thong Nai–Thanon Sri Ayutthaya crossroads, is presented with offerings every week and is also the focus of celebrations on Chulalongkorn Day (Oct 23). On December 2, Dusit is also the venue for the spectacular annual **Trooping the Colour**, when hundreds of magnificently uniformed Royal Guards demonstrate their allegiance to the king by parading around Suan Amporn, across the road from the Rama V statue. Across from Chitrlada Palace, **Dusit Zoo** makes a pleasant enough place to take the kids.

Today, the Dusit area retains its European feel, and much of the country's decision-making goes on behind the high fences and impressive facades along its tree-lined avenues: the building that houses the National Parliament is here, as is Government House, and the king's official residence, Chitrlada Palace, occupies the eastern edge of the area. Normally a calm, stately district, in 2008 Dusit became the focus of the **mass anti-government protest** by the royalist PAD movement, whose thousands-strong mass of yellow-shirted supporters occupied Government House and part of Rajdamnoen Nok for an extraordinary three months, creating a heavily defended temporary village in this most refined of neighbourhoods.

ARRIVAL AND DEPARTURE   DUSIT

By bus From Banglamphu, you can get to Dusit by taking the #70 (non-expressway) bus from Rajdamnoen Klang and getting off outside the zoo and Elephant Museum on Thanon U-Thong Nai, or the #56 from Thanon Phra Sumen and alighting at the corner of Thanon Ratchasima and Thanon Rajwithi, near the main entrance to Vimanmek

Palace. From downtown Bangkok, easiest access is by bus from the Skytrain stop at Victory Monument; there are many services from here, including #28 and #108.

By boat Take the express boat to Tha Thewet and then walk.

Dusit Park

Main entrance on Thanon Rajwithi, with another ticket gate opposite Dusit Zoo on Thanon U-Thong Nai • Daily 9.30am–4pm, last admission 3.15pm • B100, or free with a Grand Palace ticket, which remains valid for one week • ⓦ vimanmek.com

The outstanding feature of what's known as **Dusit Park** is the breezy, elegant **Vimanmek Palace**, which was built by Rama V as a summer retreat on Ko Si Chang, from where it was transported here bit by bit in 1901. The ticket price also covers entry to a dozen other specialist collections in Dusit Park, which these days resembles a theme park, with piped muzak, cafés, souvenir shops and a huge coach park. Among these collections, which include antique textiles, photographs taken by the king, royal ceremonial paraphernalia and antique clocks, housed in handsome, pastel-painted, former royal residences, the most interesting are the Support Museum and Elephant Museum. Note that the same **dress rules** apply here as to the Grand Palace (see p.85).

Vimanmek Palace

Compulsory free guided tours every 30min, last tour 3.15pm

Built almost entirely of golden teak without a single nail, the coffee-coloured, L-shaped Vimanmek Palace is encircled by delicate latticework verandas that look out onto well-kept lawns, flower gardens and lotus ponds. Not surprisingly, this "Celestial Residence" soon became Rama V's favourite palace, and he and his enormous retinue of officials, concubines and children stayed here for lengthy periods between 1902 and 1906. All of Vimanmek's 81 rooms were out of bounds to male

1

visitors, except for the king's own apartments in the octagonal tower, which were entered by a separate staircase.

On display inside is Rama V's collection of **artefacts** from all over the world, including *bencharong* ceramics, European furniture and bejewelled Thai betel-nut sets. Considered progressive in his day, Rama V introduced many newfangled ideas to Thailand: the country's first indoor bathroom is here, as is the earliest typewriter with Thai characters, and some of the first portrait paintings – portraiture had until then been seen as a way of stealing part of the sitter's soul.

The Support Museum

Immediately behind (to the east of) Vimanmek Palace

The **Support Museum** is housed in a very pretty hundred-year-old building, the Abhisek Dusit Throne Hall, which was formerly used for meetings and banquets. It showcases the exquisite handicrafts produced under Queen Sirikit's charity project, Support, which works to revitalize traditional Thai arts and crafts. Outstanding exhibits include a collection of handbags, baskets and pots woven from the *lipao* fern that grows wild in southern Thailand; jewellery and figurines inlaid with the iridescent wings of beetles; gold and silver nielloware; and lengths of intricately woven silk from the northeast.

Chang Ton Royal Elephant National Museum

Just behind (to the east of) the Support Museum, inside the Thanon U-Thong Nai entrance to Dusit Park • ⓦ thailandmuseum.com

These two whitewashed buildings once served as the stables for the king's white elephants. Now that the sacred pachyderms have been relocated, the stables have been turned into the **Royal Elephant National Museum**. Inside you'll find some interesting pieces of elephant paraphernalia, including sacred ropes, mahouts' amulets and magic formulae, as well as photos of the all-important ceremony in which a white elephant is granted royal status (see below).

THE ROYAL WHITE ELEPHANTS

In Thailand, the most revered of all elephants are the so-called **white elephants** – actually tawny brown albinos – which are considered so sacred that they all, whether wild or captive, belong to the king by law. Their special status originates from Buddhist mythology, which tells how the previously barren Queen Maya became pregnant with the future Buddha after dreaming one night that a white elephant had entered her womb. The thirteenth-century King Ramkhamhaeng of Sukhothai adopted the beast as a symbol of the great and the divine, decreeing that a Thai king's greatness should be measured by the number of white elephants he owns. The present king, Rama IX, has eleven, the largest royal collection to date.

Before an elephant can be granted official "white elephant" status, it has to pass a stringent assessment of its physical and behavioural **characteristics**. Key qualities include a paleness of seven crucial areas – eyes, nails, palate, hair, outer edges of the ears, tail and testicles – and an all-round genteel demeanour, manifested, for instance, in the way in which it cleans its food before eating, or in a tendency to sleep in a kneeling position. Tradition holds that an elaborate ceremony should take place every time a new white elephant is presented to the king: the animal is paraded with great pomp from its place of capture to Dusit, where it's anointed with holy water in front of an audience of priests and dignitaries, before being housed in the royal stables. Recently though, the king has called time on this exorbitantly expensive ritual, and only one of the royal white elephants is now kept inside the palace compound; the others live in less luxurious, rural accommodation.

The expression "white elephant" probably derives from the legend that the kings used to present certain troublesome noblemen with one of these exotic creatures. The animal required expensive attention but, being royal, could not be put to work in order to pay for its upkeep. The recipient thus went bust trying to keep it.

Dusit Zoo (Khao Din)

Entrances on Thanon Rajwithi, on Thanon U-Thong Nai across from the Elephant Museum, and on Thanon Rama V, within walking distance of Wat Benjamabophit • Daily 8am–6pm • B100 • ⓦ dusitzoo.org or ⓦ zoothailand.org

Dusit Zoo, also known as **Khao Din**, was once part of the Chitrlada Palace gardens, but is now a public park. All the usual suspects are here in the zoo, including big cats, elephants, orang-utans, chimpanzees and a reptile house, but the enclosures are pretty basic. However, it's a reasonable place for kids to let off steam, with plenty of shade, a full complement of English-language signs, a lake with pedalos, tram rides, bicycles for rent and lots of foodstalls and cafés.

Wat Benjamabophit

Corner of Thanon Sri Ayutthaya and Thanon Rama V: 200m south of the zoo's east entrance, or about 600m from Vimanmek's U-Thong Nai gate • Daily 8.30am–6pm • B20 • Bus #70 from Banglamphu to the crossroads in front of the Rama V statue, then walk east along Thanon Sri Ayutthaya

Wat Benjamabophit (aka Wat Ben) is a fascinating fusion of classical Thai and nineteenth-century European design, with the Carrara-marble walls of its bot – hence the tourist tag "**The Marble Temple**" – pierced by unusual stained-glass windows, Neogothic in style but depicting figures from Thai mythology. Rama V commissioned the temple in 1899, at a time when he was keen to show the major regional powers, Britain and France, that Thailand was *siwilai* (civilized), in order to baulk their usual excuse for colonizing. The temple's sema stones are a telling example of the compromises involved: they're usually prominent markers of the bot's sacred area, but here they're hard to spot, decorative and almost apologetic – look for the two small, stone lotus buds at the front of the bot on top of the white, Italianate balustrade. Inside the unusually cruciform bot, a fine replica of the highly revered Phra Buddha Chinnarat image of Phitsanulok presides over the small room containing some of Rama V's ashes. The courtyard behind the bot houses a gallery of Buddha images from all over Asia, set up by Rama V as an overview of different representations of the Buddha.

Wat Benjamabophit is one of the best temples in Bangkok to see religious **festivals** and rituals. Whereas monks elsewhere tend to go out on the streets every morning in search of alms, at the Marble Temple the ritual is reversed, and merit-makers come to them. Between about 5.30 and 7 or 7.30am, the monks line up on Thanon Nakhon Pathom, their bowls ready to receive donations of curry and rice, lotus buds, incense, even toilet paper and Coca-Cola; the demure row of saffron-robed monks is a sight that's well worth getting up early for. The evening candlelight processions around the bot during the Buddhist festivals of Maha Puja (in Feb) and Visakha Puja (in May) are among the most entrancing in the country.

Downtown Bangkok

Extending east from the main rail line and south to Thanon Sathorn and beyond, **downtown Bangkok** is central to the colossal expanse of Bangkok as a whole, but rather peripheral in a sightseer's perception of the city. In this modern high-rise area, you'll find the main shopping centres around **Siam Square**, though don't come looking for an elegant commercial piazza here: the "square" is in fact a grid of small streets, sheltering trendy fashion shops, cinemas and inexpensive restaurants. It lies to the southeast of **Pathumwan intersection**, the junction of Thanon Rama I (in Thai, "Thanon Phra Ram Neung") and Thanon Phrayathai, and the name is applied freely to the surrounding area. Further east, you'll find yet more shopping malls around the noisy and glittering **Erawan Shrine**, where Rama I becomes Thanon Ploenchit, an intersection known as **Ratchaprasong**. It was here that the opposition redshirts set up a fortified camp for several months in early 2010, before the Democrat government sent in the troops, leading to the

1

deaths of 91 people. It's once more possible to stroll in peace here, using an elevated **walkway** that runs beneath the Skytrain lines but above the cracked pavements, noise and fumes of Thanon Rama I, all the way from the Siam Paragon shopping centre to the Erawan Shrine (further progress is blocked by Central and Chitlom Skytrain stations). East of Ratchaprasong, you pass under the expressway flyover and enter the farang hotel, shopping and entertainment quarter of **Thanon Sukhumvit**.

The area south of Thanon Rama I is dominated by Thailand's most prestigious centre of higher learning, Chulalongkorn University, and the green expanse of **Lumphini Park**. Thanon Rama IV (in Thai "Thanon Phra Ram Sii") then marks another change of character: downtown proper, centring around the high-rise, American-style boulevard of **Thanon Silom**, the heart of the financial district, extends from here to the river. Alongside the smoked-glass banks and offices, and opposite Convent Road, site of Bangkok's Carmelite nunnery, lies the dark heart of Bangkok nightlife, **Patpong**.

Surprisingly, among downtown's vast expanse of skyscraping concrete, the main attractions for visitors are four attractive museums housed in historic teak houses: **Jim Thompson's House**, the **Ban Kamthieng**, the **Suan Pakkad Palace Museum** and **M.R. Kukrit's Heritage Home**. The area's other tourist highlight is **Siam Ocean World**, a high-tech aquarium that both kids and adults can enjoy. The accounts of the sights below are arranged roughly north–south.

ARRIVAL AND DEPARTURE   **DOWNTOWN**

All of the sights reviewed here are within walking range of a **Skytrain** station; some are also served by the **subway**. Useful **buses** for getting here from Ratanakosin include #508 and #25; further details of bus routes are given on p.139. If you're heading downtown from Banglamphu, allow at least an hour to get to any of the places mentioned here by bus. A much faster way to cross town is by public **boat** along Khlong Saen Saeb, beginning near Democracy Monument. Depending on the time of day, taking an **express boat** downriver from Banglamphu, and then changing onto the **Skytrain**, may even be quicker than catching the bus downtown.

Victory Monument

Northern downtown is cut through by several major thoroughfares, including the original road to the north, Thanon Phaholyothin, which runs past the weekend market and doesn't stop until it gets to the Burmese border at Mae Sai, 900km away – though it's now more commonly known as Highway 1, at least in between towns. The start of Phaholyothin is marked by the stone obelisk of **Victory Monument** (*Anu Sawari Chaisamoraphum*, or just *Anu Sawari*), which can be seen most spectacularly from Skytrains as they snake their way round it. It was erected after the Indo-Chinese War of 1940–41, when Thailand pinched back some territory in Laos and Cambodia while the French government was otherwise occupied in World War II, but nowadays it commemorates all of Thailand's past military glories.

Suan Pakkad Palace Museum

352–4 Thanon Sri Ayutthaya • Daily 9am–4pm • B100 • ☎ 02 246 1775–6 ext 229, ⓦ suanpakkad.com • 5min walk from BTS Phaya Thai

The **Suan Pakkad Palace Museum** stands on what was once a cabbage patch but is now one of the finest gardens in Bangkok. Most of this private collection of beautiful Thai objects from all periods is displayed in four groups of traditional wooden houses, which were transported to Bangkok from various parts of the country.

In House no. 8, as well as in the Ban Chiang Gallery in the modern Chumbhot-Pantip Center of Arts in the palace grounds, you'll find a very good collection of elegant, whorled pottery and bronze jewellery, which the former owner of Suan Pakkad Palace, Princess Chumbhot, excavated from tombs at Ban Chiang, the major Bronze Age settlement in the northeast (see p.483). Scattered around the rest of the museum are some fine ceramics and attractive Thai and Khmer religious sculptures; an extensive

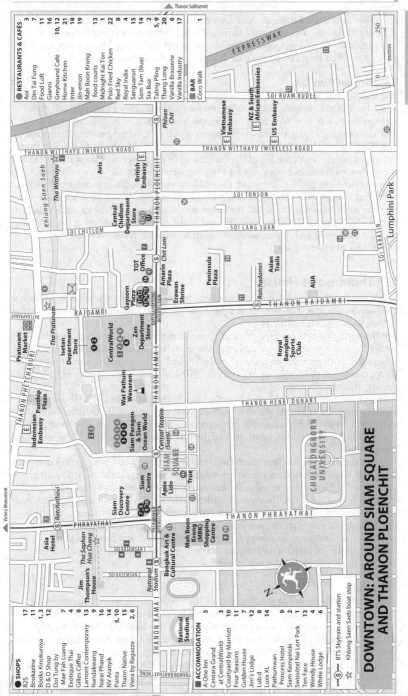

DOWNTOWN: AROUND SIAM SQUARE AND THANON PLOENCHIT

1

collection of colourful papier-mâché *khon* masks; beautiful betel-nut sets (see box, p.285); monks' elegant ceremonial fans; and some rich teak carvings, including a two-hundred-year-old temple door showing episodes from *Sang Thong*, a folk tale about a childless king and queen who discover a handsome son in a conch shell.

The Lacquer Pavilion

The highlight of Suan Pakkad is the renovated **Lacquer Pavilion**, across the reedy pond at the back of the grounds. Set on stilts, the pavilion is actually an amalgam of two eighteenth- or late seventeenth-century temple buildings, a *ho trai* (library) and a *ho khien* (writing room), one inside the other, which were found between Ayutthaya and Bang Pa-In. The interior walls are beautifully decorated with gilt on black lacquer: the upper panels depict the life of the Buddha while the lower ones show scenes from the *Ramayana*. Look out especially for the grisly details in the tableau on the back wall, showing the earth goddess drowning the evil forces of Mara. Underneath are depicted some European dandies on horseback, probably merchants, whose presence suggests that the work was executed before the fall of Ayutthaya in 1767. The carefully observed details of daily life and nature are skilful and lively, especially considering the restraints that the lacquering technique places on the artist, who has no opportunity for corrections or touching up.

Jim Thompson's House

Just off Siam Square at the north end of Soi Kasemsan 2, Thanon Rama I • Daily from 9am, viewing on frequent 30–40min guided tours in several languages, last tour 5pm • B100 • ☎ 02 216 7368, ⓦ jimthompsonhouse.com • BTS National Stadium, or via a canalside path from the Khlong Saen Saeb pier at Saphan Hua Chang

Jim Thompson's House is a kind of Ideal Home in elegant Thai style, and a peaceful refuge from downtown chaos. The house was the residence of the legendary American adventurer, entrepreneur, art collector and all-round character whose mysterious disappearance in the jungles of Malaysia in 1967 has made him even more of a legend among Thailand's farang community.

Apart from putting together this beautiful home, completed in 1959, Thompson's most concrete contribution was to turn traditional silk-weaving in Thailand from a dying art into the highly successful international industry it is today. The complex now includes a **shop** (closes 6pm), part of the Jim Thompson Thai Silk Company chain (see p.168).

Above the shop, the **Jim Thompson Center for the Arts** is a fascinating gallery that hosts both traditional and modern temporary exhibitions on textiles and the arts, such as royal maps of Siam in the nineteenth century or an interactive show that celebrates the hundredth anniversary of Thompson's birth and the vibrant evolution of Bangkok over the same period. There's also an excellent **bar-restaurant** (last food orders currently 6pm, though it may start to open in the evenings till 11pm), which serves a similar menu to *Jim Thompson's Saladaeng Café* (see p.158). Ignore any con-men at the entrance to the soi looking for mugs to escort on rip-off shopping trips, who'll tell you that the house is closed when it isn't.

The house

The grand, rambling **house** is in fact a combination of six teak houses, some from as far afield as Ayutthaya and most more than two hundred years old. Like all traditional houses, they were built in wall sections hung together without nails on a frame of wooden pillars, which made it easy to dismantle them, pile them onto a barge and float them to their new location. Although he had trained as an architect, Thompson had more difficulty in putting them back together again; in the end, he had to go back to Ayutthaya to hunt down a group of carpenters who still practised the old house-building methods. Thompson added a few unconventional touches of his own, incorporating the elaborately carved front wall of a Chinese pawnshop between the drawing room and the bedroom, and reversing the other walls in the drawing room so that their carvings faced into the room.

The impeccably tasteful **interior** has been left as it was during Jim Thompson's life, even down to the place settings on the dining table – Thompson entertained guests most nights and to that end designed the house like a stage set. Complementing the fine artefacts from throughout Southeast Asia is a stunning array of Thai arts and crafts, including one of the best collections of traditional Thai paintings in the world. Thompson picked up plenty of bargains from the Thieves' Quarter (Nakhon Kasem) in Chinatown, before collecting Thai art became fashionable and expensive. Other pieces were liberated from decay and destruction in upcountry temples, while many of the Buddha images were turned over by ploughs, especially around Ayutthaya. Some of the exhibits are very rare, such as a headless but elegant seventh-century Dvaravati Buddha and a seventeenth-century Ayutthayan teak Buddha.

THE LEGEND OF JIM THOMPSON

Thai silk-weavers, art dealers and conspiracy theorists all owe a debt to **Jim Thompson**, who even now, forty-odd years after his disappearance, remains Thailand's most famous farang. An architect by trade, Thompson left his New York practice in 1940 to join the Office of Strategic Services (later to become the CIA), a tour of duty that was to see him involved in clandestine operations in North Africa, Europe and, in 1945, the Far East, where he was detailed to a unit preparing for the invasion of Thailand. When the mission was pre-empted by the Japanese surrender, he served for a year as OSS station chief in Bangkok, forming links that were later to provide grist for endless speculation.

After an unhappy and short-lived stint as part-owner of the *Oriental Hotel*, Thompson found his calling with the struggling **silk-weavers** of the area near the present Jim Thompson House, whose traditional product was unknown in the West and had been all but abandoned by Thais in favour of less costly imported textiles. Encouragement from society friends and an enthusiastic write-up in *Vogue* convinced him there was a foreign market for Thai silk, and by 1948 he had founded the Thai Silk Company Ltd. Success was assured when, two years later, the company was commissioned to make the costumes for the Broadway run of *The King and I*. Thompson's celebrated eye for colour combinations and his tireless promotion – in the early days, he could often be seen in the lobby of the *Oriental* with bolts of silk slung over his shoulder, waiting to pounce on any remotely curious tourist – quickly made his name synonymous with Thai silk.

Like a character in a Somerset Maugham novel, Thompson played the role of Western exile to the hilt. Though he spoke no Thai, he made it his personal mission to preserve traditional arts and architecture (at a time when most Thais were more keen to emulate the West), assembling his famous Thai house and stuffing it with all manner of Oriental objets d'art. At the same time he held firmly to his farang roots and society connections: no foreign gathering in Bangkok was complete without Jim Thompson, and virtually every Western luminary passing through Bangkok – from Truman Capote to Ethel Merman – dined at his table (even though the food was notoriously bad).

If Thompson's life was the stuff of legend, his disappearance and presumed death only added to the mystique. On Easter Sunday, 1967, Thompson, while staying with friends in a cottage in Malaysia's Cameron Highlands, went out for a stroll and never came back. A massive search of the area, employing local guides, tracker dogs and even shamans, turned up no clues, provoking a rash of fascinating but entirely unsubstantiated theories. The grandfather of them all, advanced by a Dutch psychic, held that Thompson had been lured into an ambush by the disgraced former prime minister of Thailand, Pridi Panomyong, and spirited off to Cambodia for indeterminate purposes; later versions, supposing that Thompson had remained a covert CIA operative all his life, proposed that he was abducted by Vietnamese Communists and brainwashed to be displayed as a high-profile defector to Communism. More recently, an amateur sleuth claims to have found evidence that Thompson met a more mundane fate, having been killed by a careless truck driver and hastily buried.

1

After the guided tour, you're free to look again, at your leisure, at the former rice barn and gardener's and maid's houses in the small, jungly **garden**, which display some gorgeous traditional Thai paintings and drawings, as well as small-scale statues and Chinese ceramics.

Bangkok Art and Cultural Centre

Junction of Rama I and Phrayathai roads • Tues–Sun 10am–9pm • Free • ☎ 02 214 6630–1, ⓦ bacc.or.th • BTS National Stadium

A striking, white hunk of modernity, the prestigious **Bangkok Art and Cultural Centre** houses several galleries on its upper floors, connected by spiralling ramps like New York's Guggenheim, as well as several performance spaces. It hosts temporary shows by contemporary artists from Thailand and abroad across all media, from the visual arts to music and design, and there's usually something interesting on here – coming in from BTS National Stadium, there's a blackboard inside the entrance where the day's events and shows are chalked up in English.

Siam Ocean World

Basement of Siam Paragon shopping centre (east end), Thanon Rama I • Daily 10am–9pm, last admission 8pm • Shark feeds currently 1pm & 4pm • B900; B1000 including 10min glass-bottomed boat ride and 10min behind-the-scenes tour; shark walk B2000, shark dive from B5300, 4D films B250 • ☎ 02 687 2000, ⓦ siamoceanworld.com • BTS Siam

Spreading over two spacious floors, **Siam Ocean World** is a highly impressive, Australian-built aquarium. Despite the high admission price (though coupons for twenty-percent discounts are available in many Bangkok hotels), it gets crowded at weekends and during

---

BANGKOK FOR KIDS

The following theme parks and amusement centres are all designed for kids, the main drawbacks being that many are located a long way from the city centre. Other attractions kids should enjoy include the Museum of Siam (see p.92), feeding the turtles at Wat Prayoon (see p.113), Dusit Zoo (see p.117), Siam Ocean World aquarium (see above), the Snake Farm (see p.125), cycling around Muang Boran Ancient City (see p.133) and pedal-boating in Lumphini Park (see p.125). For general tips on kids' Thailand, see p.56.

Bangkok Butterfly Garden and Insectarium In Suan Rotfai (Railway Park), just north of Chatuchak Weekend Market; Tues–Sun 8.30am–4.30pm; free; ☎ 02 272 4359–60. Over 500 butterflies flutter within an enormous landscaped dome. There's also a study centre, plus family-oriented cycle routes and bikes (and pedalos) for rent in the adjacent park, which also has a kids' playground. BTS Mo Chit or Chatuchak Park subway.

Dream World Ten minutes' drive north of Don Muang Airport at kilometre-stone 7 Thanon Rangsit–Ongkarak; Mon–Fri 10am–5pm, Sat & Sun 10am–7pm; B500, children under 90cm free, or B1000 per person including lunch and transfers; ☎ 02 533 1152, ⓦ dreamworld-th.com. Theme park with different areas such as Snow Town and Fairytale Land, including water rides, a hanging coaster and other amusements. A/c bus #538 from Victory Monument.

Funarium Soi 26, Thanon Sukhumvit, down towards Thanon Rama IV; Mon–Thurs 9am–7pm, Fri–Sun 8.30am–8.30pm; B90–300, depending on size of visitor; ☎ 02 665 6555, ⓦ funarium.co.th. Huge

indoor playground, with an arts and crafts room, cooking classes and a restaurant. BTS to Prom Pong, then a taxi.

Safari World On the northeastern outskirts at 99 Thanon Ramindra, Minburi; daily 9am–5pm; joint ticket to both parks B600, children B500; ☎ 02 518 1000, ⓦ safariworld.com. Drive-through safari park, with monkeys, lions, giraffes and zebras, and separate marine park with dolphins and sea lions, as well as various animal shows (phone for times). If you don't have your own car, you can be driven through the park in a Safari World coach. Take a/c bus #60 from Rajdamnoen Klang in Banglamphu or a/c #26 from Victory Monument, then a songthaew to Safari World.

Siam Park On the far eastern edge of town at 101 Thanon Sukhapiban 2; daily 10am–6pm; B300, children 100–130cm B100, under 100cm free, with extra charges for some rides, or B900 for an unlimited day pass; ☎ 02 919 7200, ⓦ siamparkcity .com. Waterslides, whirlpools and artificial surf, plus roller coasters and other rides, and a safari zone. Bus #60 from Rajdamnoen Klang in Banglamphu.

holidays, and can be busy with school groups on weekday afternoons. Among outstanding features of this US$30-million development are an 8m-deep glass-walled tank, which displays the multicoloured variety of a coral reef drop-off to great effect, touch tanks for handling starfish, and a long, under-ocean tunnel where you can watch sharks and rays swimming over your head. In this global piscatorial display of around four hundred species, locals such as the Mekong giant catfish are not forgotten, while regularly spaced touch-screen terminals provide information in English about the creatures on view. It's even possible to walk with the sharks (wearing a diving helmet) for fifteen minutes, or dive with them for thirty minutes. You can also watch – through 3D glasses – underwater cartoons in "4D X-venture", where the chairs move and there are occasional sprays of water.

The Erawan Shrine

Corner of Thanon Ploenchit and Thanon Rajdamri • 24hr • Free • BTS Chit Lom

For a glimpse of the variety and ubiquity of Thai religion, drop in on the **Erawan Shrine** (*Saan Phra Prom* in Thai). Remarkable as much for its setting as anything else, this shrine to Brahma, the ancient Hindu creation god, and Erawan, his elephant, squeezes in on one of the busiest and noisiest intersections in modern Bangkok. And it's not the only one: half a dozen other Hindu shrines are dotted around Ratchaphrasong intersection, most notably **Trimurti**, who combines the three main gods, Brahma, Vishnu and Shiva, on the opposite corner outside Central World Plaza. Modern Bangkokians see Trimurti as a sort of Cupid figure, and those looking for love bring red offerings.

The *Grand Hyatt Erawan Hotel*, towering over the Erawan Shrine, is the reason for its existence and its name. When a string of calamities held up the building of the original hotel in the 1950s, spirit doctors were called in, who instructed the owners to build a new home for the offended local spirits: the hotel was then finished without further mishap. Ill fortune struck the shrine itself, however, in early 2006, when a young, mentally disturbed, Muslim man smashed the Brahma statue to pieces with a hammer – and was then brutally beaten to death by an angry mob. An exact replica of the statue was quickly installed, incorporating the remains of the old statue to preserve the spirit of the deity.

Be prepared for sensory overload here: the main structure shines with lurid glass of all colours and the overcrowded precinct around it is almost buried under scented garlands and incense candles. You might also catch a group of traditional dancers performing here to the strains of a small classical orchestra – worshippers hire them to give thanks for a stroke of good fortune. To increase their future chances of such good fortune, visitors buy a bird or two from the flocks incarcerated in cages here; the bird-seller transfers the requested number of captives to a tiny hand-held cage, from which the customer duly liberates the animals, thereby accruing merit. People set on less abstract rewards will invest in a lottery ticket from one of the physically disabled sellers: they're thought to be the luckiest you can buy.

Ban Kamthieng (Kamthieng House)

131 Soi 21, Thanon Asok Montri, off Thanon Sukhumvit • Tues–Sat 9am–5pm • B100 • ⓦ siam-society.org • BTS Asok or Sukhumvit subway

Another reconstructed traditional Thai residence, **Ban Kamthieng** was moved in the 1960s from Chiang Mai to just off Thanon Sukhumvit and set up as an ethnological museum by the Siam Society. The delightful complex of polished teak buildings makes a pleasing oasis beneath the towering glass skyscrapers that dominate the rest of Sukhumvit. It differs from Suan Pakkad, Jim Thompson's House and M.R. Kukrit's Heritage Home in being the home of a rural family, and the objects on display give a fair insight into country life for the well-heeled in northern Thailand.

The house was built on the banks of the Ping River in the mid-nineteenth century, and the ground-level display of farming tools and fish traps evokes the upcountry

1

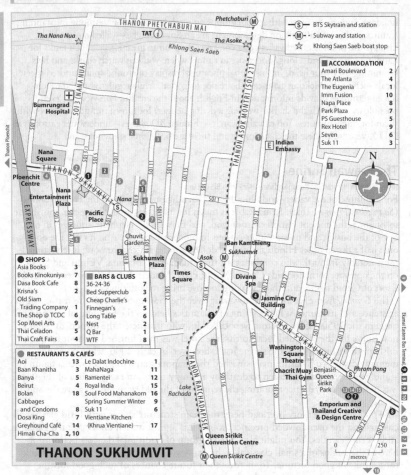

practice of fishing in flooded rice paddies to supplement the supply from the rivers. Upstairs, the main display focuses on the ritual life of a typical Lanna household, explaining the role of the spirits, the practice of making offerings, and the belief in talismans, magic shirts and male tattoos. The rectangular lintel above the door is a *hum yon*, carved in floral patterns that represent testicles and designed to ward off evil spirits. Walk along the open veranda to the authentically equipped kitchen to see a video lesson in making spicy frog soup, and to the granary to find an interesting exhibition on the ritual practices associated with rice farming. Elsewhere in the compound you'll find a tiny bookshop selling the Siam Society's and Silkworm's publications on Thailand, and a *Black Canyon* café.

Thailand Creative and Design Centre (TCDC)

6th floor of the Emporium Shopping Centre, Thanon Sukhumvit between sois 22 and 24 • Tues–Sun 10.30am–9pm • Free • ⓦ tcdc.or.th • BTS Phrom Phong

Appropriately located in the Emporium, one of Bangkok's most fashion-conscious shopping plazas, the **Thailand Creative and Design Centre** seeks to celebrate, promote and inspire innovative design through exhibitions, talks, a resource centre and shop (see p.168). Alongside often fascinating temporary exhibitions, the concise but thought-provoking permanent bilingual display focuses on the cultural contexts of design classics from around the world, beginning with the Louis Vuitton trunk of 1854 and including Thai fabrics and playful household items.

The Queen Saovabha Memorial Institute (Snake Farm)

Corner of Thanon Rama IV and Thanon Henri Dunant • Live shows Mon–Fri 2.30pm, Sat, Sun & hols 11am • B200 • ☎ 02 252 0161–4, ⓦ saovabha.com • 10min walk from BTS Sala Daeng, or from Sam Yan or Si Lom subway stations

The **Queen Saovabha Memorial Institute** (*Sathan Saovabha*) is a bit of a circus act, but an entertaining, informative and worthy one at that. It's often simply known as the **Snake Farm**, but takes its formal name from one of Rama V's wives, who was a notable campaigner. Run by the Thai Red Cross, the institute has a double function: to produce snake-bite serums, and to educate the public on the dangers of Thai snakes. The latter mission involves putting on live demonstrations of snake handling and feeding. Well presented and safe, these displays gain a perverse fascination from the knowledge that the strongest venoms of the snakes on show can kill in only three minutes. If you're still not herpetologically sated, you can look round the attached exhibition space, where dozens of Thai snakes live in cages.

Lumphini Park

Thanon Rama IV • Daily 4.30am–9pm • Free • BTS Saladaeng or Si Lom or Lumphini subway stations

If you're sick of cars and concrete, head for **Lumphini Park** (*Suan Lum*), where the air is almost fresh and the traffic noise dies down to a low murmur. Named after the town in Nepal where the Buddha was born, it was the country's first public park, donated by Rama VI, whose statue by Silpa Bhirasri (see p.759) stands at the main, southwest entrance. The park is arrayed around two lakes, where you can join the locals in feeding the turtles and fish with bread or take out a pedalo or rowing boat, and is landscaped with a wide variety of local trees and numerous pagodas and pavilions, usually occupied by chess-players. In the early morning and at dusk, people hit the outdoor gym on the southwest side of the park, or en masse do aerobics, balletic t'ai chi or jogging along the yellow-marked circuit, stopping for the twice-daily broadcast of the national anthem. On late Sunday afternoons in the cool season (usually mid-Dec to mid-Feb), free classical concerts by the Bangkok Symphony Orchestra (☎ 02 255 6617–8, ⓦ bangkoksymphony.org) draw in scores of urban picnickers.

Patpong

Concentrated into two lanes running between the eastern ends of Thanon Silom and Thanon Suriwong, the neon-lit go-go bars of the **Patpong** district loom like rides in a tawdry sexual Disneyland. In front of each bar, girls cajole passers-by with a lifeless sensuality while insistent touts proffer printed menus and photographs detailing the degradations on show. Inside, bikini-clad women gyrate to Western music and play hostess to the (almost exclusively male) spectators; upstairs, live shows feature women who, to use Spalding Gray's phrase in *Swimming to Cambodia*, "do everything with their vaginas except have babies".

Patpong was no more than a sea of mud when the capital was founded on the marshy river bank to the west, but by the 1960s it had grown into a flash district of dance halls for rich Thais, owned by a Chinese millionaire godfather, educated at the London School of Economics and by the OSS (forerunner of the CIA), who gave his name to the area. In 1969, an American entrepreneur turned an existing teahouse into a luxurious nightclub to satisfy the tastes of soldiers on R&R trips from Vietnam, and

1

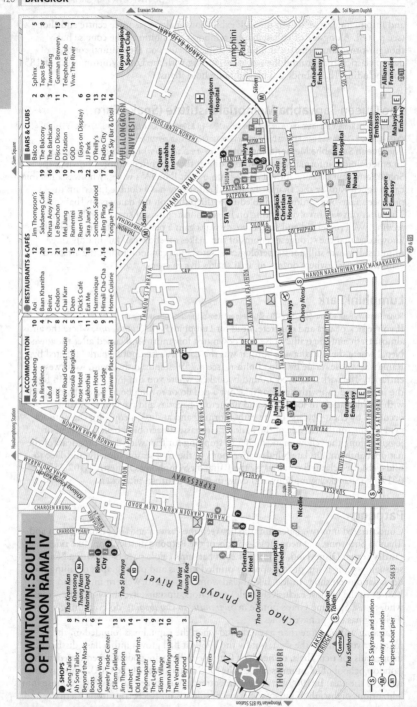

DOWNTOWN: SOUTH OF THANON RAMA IV

SHOPS
A Song Tailor	8
Ah Song Tailor	7
Beyond the Masks	2
Boots	6
Golden Wool	11
Jewelry Trade Center (Silom Galleria)	13
Jim Thompson	5
Lambert	14
Old Maps and Prints	1
Khomapastr	4
The Legend	9
Silom Village	12
Taman Mingmuang	10
The Verandah and Beyond	3

ACCOMMODATION
Baan Saladaeng	10
La Residence	4
Lub.d	7
Luxx	8
New Road Guest House	5
Peninsula Bangkok	1
Rose Hotel	11
Sukhothai	6
Swan Hotel	9
Swiss Lodge	2
Tarntawan Place Hotel	3

RESTAURANTS & CAFÉS
Aoi	12
Baan Khanitha	20
Beirut	7
Celadon	8
Chai Karr	5
Deen	2
Dick's Café	1
Eat Me	18
Harmonique	9
Himali Cha-Cha	6
Home Cuisine	3
Jim Thompson's	12
Saladaeng Café	19
Khrua Aroy Aroy	16
Le Bouchon	21
Mei Jiang	13
Ramentei	15
Ruen Urai	22
Sara Jane's	18
Somboon Seafood	1
Taling Pling	4, 14
Tongue Thai	5

BARS & CLUBS
Balco	2
The Balcony	9
The Barbican	11
Disco Disco	7
DJ Station	10
GOD (Guys on Display)	3
JJ Park	6
O'Reilly's	13
Radio City	12
The Sky Bar & Distil	14
Sphinx	5
Tapas Bar	8
Tawandang	11
German Brewery	15
Telephone Pub	4
Viva: The River	1

BTS Skytrain and station
Subway and station
Express-boat pier

1

THAILAND'S SEX INDUSTRY

Bangkok owes its reputation as the carnal capital of the world to a **sex industry** adept at peddling fantasies of cheap thrills on tap. More than a thousand sex-related businesses operate in the city, but the gaudy neon fleshpots of Patpong and Sukhumvit's Soi Nana and Soi Cowboy give a misleading impression of an activity that is deeply rooted in Thai culture: the overwhelming majority of Thailand's prostitutes of both sexes (estimated at anywhere between 200,000 and 700,000) work with Thai men, not farangs.

Prostitution and polygamy have long been intrinsic to the Thai way of life. Until Rama VI broke with the custom in 1910, Thai kings had always kept concubines, only a few of whom would be elevated to royal mothers. The practice was aped by the nobility and, from the early nineteenth century, by newly rich merchants keen to have lots of sons. Though the monarch is now monogamous, many men of all classes still keep **mistresses**, known as *mia noi* (minor wives), or have casual girlfriends (*gig*); the common view is that an official wife (*mia luang*) should be treated like the temple's main Buddha image – respected and elevated upon the altar – whereas the minor wife is like an amulet, to be taken along wherever you go. For less wealthy men, prostitution is a far cheaper option: at least two-fifths of sexually active Thai men are thought to visit brothels twice a month.

The **farang sex industry** is a relatively new development, having started during the Vietnam War, when the American military set up seven bases around Thailand. The GIs' appetite for "entertainment" attracted women from surrounding rural areas to cash in on the boom, and Bangkok joined the fray in 1967. By the mid-1970s, the GIs had left, but tourists replaced them, lured by advertising that diverted most of the traffic to Bangkok and Pattaya. Sex tourism has since grown to become an established part of the Thai economy and has spread to Phuket, Hat Yai, Ko Samui and Chiang Mai.

The majority of the women who work in the country's go-go bars and "bar-beers" (outdoor hostess bars) come from the poorest areas of north and northeast Thailand. **Economic refugees**, they're easily drawn into an industry in which they can make in a single night what it takes a month to earn in the rice fields. Many women opt for a couple of years in the sex bars to help pay off family debts and improve the living conditions of parents stuck in the poverty trap.

Many bar girls, and male prostitutes too, are looking for longer-term **relationships** with their farang customers, bringing a temporary respite from bar work and perhaps even a ticket out. A surprising number of one-night transactions do develop into some sort of holiday romance, with the young woman accompanying her farang "boyfriend" (often twice her age) around the country and maintaining contact after he's returned home. It's a common joke that some bar girls field half a dozen mobile phones so they can juggle all their various "sponsors". An entire sub-genre of novels and confessional memoirs (among them the classic *Hello, My Big Big Honey!: Letters to Bangkok Bar Girls and Their Revealing Interviews*) testifies to the role money plays in all this, and highlights the delusions common to both parties, not to mention the cross-cultural incomprehension.

Despite its ubiquity, prostitution has been **illegal** in Thailand since 1960, but sex-industry bosses easily circumvent the law by registering their establishments as clubs, karaoke bars or massage parlours, and making payoffs to the police and politicians. Sex workers, on the other hand, often endure exploitation and violence from pimps and customers rather than face fines and long rehabilitation sentences. Hardly surprising that many prefer to go freelance, working the clubs and bars in non-red-light zones such as Thanon Khao San. Life is made even more difficult because abortion is illegal in Thailand. The **anti-prostitution law**, however, does attempt to treat sex workers as victims rather than criminals and penalizes parents who sell their children. A high-profile voice in the struggle to improve the **rights of sex workers** is the Empower Foundation (ⓦempowerfoundation.org), which not only organizes campaigns and runs education centres for bar workers but also manages its own bar in Chiang Mai.

Inevitably, **child prostitution** is a significant issue in Thailand, but NGOs such as ECPAT (ⓦecpat.net) say numbers have declined over the last decade, due to zero-tolerance and awareness campaigns. The government has also strengthened legislation against hiring a prostitute under the age of 18, and anyone caught having sex with an under-15 is now charged with rape. The disadvantaged are still targeted by traffickers however, who "buy" children from desperately poor hill-tribe and other minority families and keep them as bonded slaves until the debt has been repaid.

1

so Patpong's transformation into a Western sex reservation began. At first, the area was rough and violent, but over the years it has wised up to the desires of the affluent farang, and now markets itself as a packaged concept of Oriental decadence.

The centre of the skin trade lies along the interconnected sois of **Patpong 1 and 2**, where lines of go-go bars share their patch with respectable restaurants, a 24-hour supermarket and an overabundance of pharmacies. Even the most demure tourists – of both sexes – turn out to do some shopping at the night market down the middle of Patpong 1, where hawkers sell fake watches, bags and designer T-shirts. By day, a relaxed hangover descends on the place. Farang men slump at the bars on Patpong 2, drinking and watching videos, unable to find anything else to do in the whole of Bangkok. Running parallel to the east, **Soi Thaniya** is Patpong's Japanese counterpart, lined with hostess bars and some good restaurants, while the focus of Bangkok's gay scene, **Silom 2** (ie Soi 2, Thanon Silom) and the more mixed **Silom 4**, flank Thaniya.

The west end of Thanon Silom

Further west along Silom from Patpong, in a still-thriving South Indian enclave, lies the colourful landmark of the **Maha Uma Devi Temple**. Also known as **Sri Mahamariamman** or **Wat Khaek**, this vibrant, gaudy Hindu shrine was built in 1895 in honour of Shiva's consort, Uma. Carrying on to the river, the strip west of Charoen Krung (New Road) reveals some of the history of Bangkok's early dealings with foreigners in the fading grandeur of the old trading quarter. Here you'll find the only place in Bangkok where you might be able to eke out an architectural walk, though it's hardly compelling. Incongruous churches and "colonial" buildings – the best being the Authors' Wing of the *Oriental Hotel*, where nostalgic afternoon teas are served – are hemmed in by the spice shops and *halal* canteens of the growing Muslim area around Thanon Charoen Krung.

M.R. Kukrit's Heritage Home

19 Soi Phra Pinit (Soi 7, Thanon Narathiwat Ratchanakharin), a 10min walk south then east from Thanon Sathorn • Daily 10am–4pm, though it's often closed for social engagements, so worth phoning ahead to check • B50 • ☎ 02 286 8185, ✆ kukritshousefund.com • 20min walk from BTS Chong Nonsi

M.R. Kukrit's Heritage Home (*Baan Mom Kukrit*) is the beautiful traditional house and gardens of one of Thailand's leading figures of the twentieth century. M.R. (*Mom Rajawongse*, a princely title) **Kukrit Pramoj** (1911–95) was a remarkable all-rounder, descended from Rama II on his father's side and, on his mother's side, from the influential ministerial family, the Bunnags. Kukrit graduated in Philosophy, Politics and Economics from Oxford University and went on to become a university lecturer back in Thailand, but his greatest claim to fame is probably as a writer: he founded, owned and penned a daily column for *Siam Rath*, the most influential Thai-language newspaper, and wrote short stories, novels, plays and poetry. He was also a respected performer in classical dance-drama (*khon*), and he starred as an Asian prime minister, opposite Marlon Brando, in the Hollywood film, *The Ugly American*. In 1974, during an especially turbulent period for Thailand, life imitated art, when Kukrit was called on to become Thailand's prime minister at the head of a coalition of seventeen parties. However, just four hundred days into his premiership, the Thai military leadership dismissed him for being too anti-American.

The **residence**, which has been left just as it was when Kukrit was alive, reflects his complex character. In the large, open-sided *sala* (pavilion) for public functions, near the entrance, is an attractive display of *khon* masks, including a gold one that Kukrit wore when he played the demon king, Totsagan (Ravana). In and around the adjoining Khmer-styled garden, keep your eyes peeled for the *mai dut*, sculpted miniature trees similar to bonsai, some of which Kukrit worked on for decades. The living quarters

1

beyond are made up of five teak houses on stilts, assembled from various parts of central Thailand and joined by an open veranda. The bedroom, study and various sitting rooms are decked out with beautiful objets d'art; look out especially for the carved bed that belonged to Rama II and the very delicate, two-hundred-year-old nielloware (gold inlay) from Nakhon Si Thammarat in the formal reception room. In the small family prayer room, Kukrit Pramoj's ashes are enshrined in the base of a reproduction of the Emerald Buddha.

The city outskirts

The amorphous clutter of Greater Bangkok doesn't harbour many attractions, but there are a handful of places that make pleasant half-day escapes, principally **Chatuchak Weekend Market**, the cultural theme-park of **Muang Boran**, the rather more esoteric **Prasart Museum**, the upstream town of **Nonthaburi** and the tranquil artificial island of **Ko Kred** (see map, p.79).

Chatuchak Weekend Market (JJ)

Occupies a huge patch of ground extending northwest from the corner of Phaholyothin and Kamphaeng Phet roads • Sat & Sun roughly 9am–6/7pm, though many stalls open earlier and some close later

With over eight thousand open-air stalls to peruse, and wares as diverse as Lao silk, Siamese kittens and designer lamps, the enormous **Chatuchak Weekend Market**, or **JJ** as it's usually abbreviated (from "Jatu Jak"), is Bangkok's most enjoyable – and exhausting – shopping experience.

The market also contains a controversial **wildlife** section that has long doubled as a clearing house for protected and endangered species such as gibbons, palm cockatoos and Indian pied hornbills, many of them smuggled in from Laos and Cambodia and sold to private animal collectors and foreign zoos. The illegal trade goes on beneath the counter, despite occasional crackdowns, but you're bound to come across fighting cocks around the back, miniature flying squirrels being fed milk through pipettes, and iridescent red-and-blue Siamese fighting fish, kept in individual jars and shielded from each other's aggressive stares by sheets of cardboard.

Where to shop
Chatuchak is divided into 27 numbered **sections**, plus a dozen unnumbered ones, each of them more or less dedicated to a particular genre, for example household items, plants and secondhand books, and if you have several hours to spare, it's fun just to browse at whim. The market's primary customers are Bangkok residents in search of idiosyncratic fashions (try sections 5 and 6) and homewares (sections 2, 3, 4, 7 and 8), but Chatuchak also has plenty of collector- and tourist-oriented **stalls**; best buys include antique lacquerware, unusual sarongs, traditional cotton clothing and crafts from the north, silver jewellery, and ceramics, particularly the five-coloured *bencharong*. For handicrafts and traditional textiles, you should start with sections 22, 24, 25 and 26, which are all in a cluster at the southwest (Kamphaeng Phet subway) end of the market; sections A, B and C, behind the market's head office and information centre, are also full of interesting artefacts.

Foodies will want to check out **Talat Or Tor Khor** (the Agricultural Market Organization), a covered market that sells a fantastic array of fruit, veg and other produce from around the country, as well as prepared dishes to take away or to eat at the food court; it's on the south side of Thanon Kamphaeng Phet, next to Kamphaeng Phet subway station. There are a number of other places to eat and drink inside the market (see p.160 and p.164).

GETTING THERE AND AROUND

Arrival Kamphaeng Phet subway station exits right into the most interesting, southwestern, corner of the market; on the northeast side of the market are Chatuchak Park subway and Mochit BTS stations. Coming from Banglamphu, either get a bus to BTS National Stadium or Ratchathewi, or take the #159, #503 (non-expressway version) or #509 bus all the way from Rajdamnoen Klang (about 1hr; see p.139 for details); once the MRT extension has opened, it should be possible to catch an express-boat to Tha Tien, then walk 5min to Sanam Chai station, for subway trains to Chatuchak Park or Kamphaeng Phet stations.

Getting around A few very small electric trams circulate around the market's main inner ring road, transporting weary shoppers for free, though they always seem to be full.

CHATUCHAK WEEKEND MARKET

INFORMATION

Maps *Nancy Chandler's Map of Bangkok* has a fabulously detailed and informatively annotated map of all the sections in the market. Maps are also posted at various points around the market, including in the subway stations. For specific help you can ask at the market office, on the main inner ring road near Gate 1 off Thanon Kamphaeng Phet 2, which also has ATMs and currency exchange booths.

The Prasart Museum

9 Soi 4A, Soi Krungthep Kreetha, Thanon Krungthep Kreetha • Tues–Sun 10am–3pm • B1000 for 1 or 2 people • Call ☎ 02 379 3601 to book the compulsory tour

Located on the far eastern edge of the city, the **Prasart Museum** is an unusual open-air exhibition of traditional Asian buildings, put together by wealthy entrepreneur and art-lover Khun Prasart. The museum is rarely visited by independent tourists – partly because of the intentionally limited opening hours and inflated admission price, and partly because it takes a long time to get there by public transport – but it makes a pleasant day out and is worth the effort.

Set in a gorgeously lush tropical garden, the museum comprises about a dozen beautifully crafted replicas of **traditional buildings**, including a golden teak palace inspired by the Tamnak Daeng at the National Museum, a Chinese temple and water garden, a Khmer shrine and a Sukhothai-era teak library set over a lotus pond. Some have been pieced together from ruined originals, while others were constructed from scratch. Many are filled with antique **artefacts**, including Burmese woodcarvings, prehistoric pottery from Ban Chiang and Lopburi-era statuettes. There's also an exquisite collection of *bencharong* ceramics. Khun Prasart also owns the Prasart Collection, on the second floor of the Peninsula Plaza shopping centre on Thanon Rajdamri (☎02 253 9772), a shop selling objets d'art, including reproductions of his collection.

ARRIVAL AND DEPARTURE

PRASART MUSEUM

By bus Regular and a/c bus #93 runs almost to the door: pick it up near its starting point on Thanon Si Phraya near River City and the GPO, or anywhere along its route on Phetchaburi and Phetchaburi Mai roads (both the Khlong Saen Saeb canal boats and the subway have potentially useful stops at the Thanon Asok Montri/Sukhumvit Soi 21 junction with Thanon Phetchaburi Mai). The #93 terminates on Thanon Krungthep Kreetha, but you should get off a couple of stops before the terminus, at the first stop on Thanon Krungthep Kreetha, as soon as you see the sign for the Prasart Museum (about 1hr

15min by bus from Si Phraya). Follow the sign down Soi Krungthep Kreetha, go past the golf course and, after about a 15min walk, turn off down Soi 4A.

By boat and train To speed things up, you could instead take the Khlong Saen Saeb canal boat all the way to Tha The Mall Bangkapi (about 40min from Phan Fah, four stops after the confusingly similar Tha The Mall 3 stop), or a stopping City Line train on the Suvarnabhumi Airport Rail Link from Phaya Thai to Hua Mark station, either of which leaves you within a very short taxi-ride of the museum.

Nonthaburi

Chao Phraya Express Boat to Nonthaburi, the last stop upriver for most (N30), under an hour from Central Pier (Sathorn) on an orange-flag boat

A trip to **NONTHABURI**, the first town and province beyond the northern boundary of Bangkok, is the easiest excursion you can make from the centre of the city and affords a perfect opportunity to recharge your batteries. Nonthaburi is the last stop upriver for most express boats and the ride itself is most of the fun, weaving round huge, crawling sand barges and tiny canoes, and the slow pace of the boat gives you plenty of time to take in the sights on the way. On the north side of Banglamphu, beyond the elegant, new **Rama VIII Bridge**, which shelters the Mekong whisky distillery on the west bank, you'll pass in turn, on the east bank: the Bangkhunprom Palace and the adjacent Devaves Palace, two gleamingly restored former princely residences in the Bank of Thailand compound; the royal boathouse at Tha Wasukri in front of the National Library, where you can glimpse the minor ceremonial boats that escort the grand royal barges; the city's first Catholic church, Holy Conception, founded in the seventeenth century during King Narai of Ayutthaya's reign and rebuilt in the early nineteenth; and, beyond Krungthon Bridge, the Singha brewery. Along the route are dazzling Buddhist temples and drably painted mosques, catering for Bangkok's growing Muslim population, as well as a few remaining communities who still live in houses on stilts or houseboats – around Krungthon Bridge, for example, you'll see people living on the huge teak vessels used to carry rice, sand and charcoal.

Disembarking at suburban Nonthaburi, on the east bank of the river, you won't find a great deal to do, in truth. There's a market that's famous for the quality of its fruit, while the attractive, old Provincial Office across the road is covered in wooden latticework. To break up your trip with a slow, scenic drink or lunch, you'll find a floating seafood restaurant, *Rim Fang*, to the right at the end of the prom.

Wat Chalerm Phra Kiat

1km north of Nonthaburi pier on the west bank of the river • From the express-boat pier take the ferry straight across the Chao Phraya and then catch a motorbike taxi or walk

Set in relaxing grounds on the west bank of the river, elegant **Wat Chalerm Phra Kiat** injects a splash of urban refinement among a grove of breadfruit trees. The beautifully proportioned temple, which has been lavishly restored, was built by Rama III in memory of his mother, whose family lived and presided over vast orchards in the area. Inside the walls of the temple compound, you feel as if you've come upon a stately folly in a secret

---

DURIANS

The naturalist Alfred Russel Wallace, eulogizing the taste of the **durian**, compared it to "rich butter-like custard highly flavoured with almonds, but intermingled with wafts of flavour that call to mind cream cheese, onion sauce, brown sherry and other incongruities". He neglected to discuss the smell of the fruit's skin, which is so bad – somewhere between detergent and dog shit – that durians are barred from Thai hotels and aeroplanes. The different **varieties** bear strange names that do nothing to make them more appetizing: "frog", "golden pillow", "gibbon" and so on. However, the durian has fervent admirers, perhaps because it's such an acquired taste, and because it's considered a strong aphrodisiac. Aficionados discuss the varieties with as much subtlety as if they were vintage Champagnes, and treat the durian as a social fruit, to be shared around, despite a price tag of up to B3000 each. They also pour scorn on the Thai government scientists who have recently genetically developed an odourless variety, the Chanthaburi 1 durian.

The most famous durian orchards are around Nonthaburi, where the fruits are said to have an incomparably rich and nutty flavour due to the fine clay soil. To see these and other plantations such as mango, pomelo and jackfruit, your best bet is to hire a longtail from Nonthaburi pier to take you west along Khlong Om Non. If you don't smell them first, you can recognize durians by their sci-fi appearance: the shape and size of a rugby ball, but slightly deflated, they're covered in a thick, pale-green shell which is heavily armoured with short, sharp spikes (*duri* means "thorn" in Malay). By cutting along one of the faint seams with a good knife, you'll reveal a white pith in which are set a handful of yellow blobs with the texture of a wrinkled soufflé: this is what you eat. The taste is best when the smell is at its highest, about three days after the fruit has dropped. Be careful when out walking near the trees: because of its great weight and sharp spikes, a falling durian can lead to serious injury, or even an ignominious death.

1

garden, and a strong Chinese influence shows itself in the unusual ribbed roofs and elegantly curved gables, decorated with pastel ceramics. The restorers have done their best work inside: look out especially for the simple, delicate landscapes on the shutters.

Ko Kred

The tiny island of **KO KRED** lies in a particularly sharp bend in the Chao Phraya, about 7km north of Nonthaburi pier, cut off from the east bank by a waterway created in the eighteenth century to make the cargo route from Ayutthaya to the Gulf of Thailand just that little bit faster. Although it's been discovered by day-trippers from Bangkok, this artificial island remains something of a time capsule, a little oasis of village life completely at odds with the metropolitan chaos downriver. Roughly ten square kilometres in all, Ko Kred has no roads, just a concrete path that follows its circumference, with a few arterial walkways branching off towards the interior. Villagers, the majority of whom are Mon (see box, p.211), descendants of immigrants during the reigns of Taksin and Rama II, use a small fleet of motorbike taxis to cross their island, but as a sightseer you're much better off on a rental bicycle or just on foot: a round-island walk takes less than an hour and a half.

There are few sights as such on Ko Kred, but its lushness and comparative emptiness make it a perfect place in which to wander. You'll no doubt come across one of the island's potteries and kilns, which churn out the regionally famous earthenware flower-pots and small water-storage jars and employ a large percentage of the village workforce. The island's clay is very rich in nutrients and therefore excellent for fruit-growing, and banana trees, coconut palms, pomelo, papaya, mango and durian trees all grow in abundance on Ko Kred, fed by an intricate network of irrigation channels that crisscrosses the interior. In among the orchards, the Mons have built their wooden houses, mostly in traditional style and raised high above the marshy ground on stilts.

Wat Paramaiyikawat

Ko Kred boasts a handful of attractive riverside wats, most notably **Wat Paramaiyikawat** (also called **Wat Poramai**), at the main pier at the northeast tip of the island. This engagingly ramshackle eighteenth-century temple was restored by Rama V in honour of his grandmother, with a Buddha relic placed in its white, riverside chedi, which is a replica of the Mutao Pagoda in Hanthawadi, capital of the Mon kingdom in Burma. Among an open-air scattering of Burmese-style alabaster Buddha images, the tall bot shelters some fascinating nineteenth-century murals, depicting scenes from temple life at ground level and the life of the Buddha above, all set in delicate imaginary landscapes.

ARRIVAL AND DEPARTURE   KO KRED

The easiest but busiest time to visit Ko Kred is at the weekend, when you can take a boat tour from central Bangkok. At other times, getting there by public transport is a bit of a chore.

By boat tour The Mitchaopaya Travel Service (B300; ☏ 02 623 6169) runs boat tours to Ko Kred on Sat, Sun and public holidays, leaving Tha Chang in Ratanakosin at 9am, returning at about 4pm. On the way, you'll cruise along Khlong Bangkok Noi and Khlong Om, and call in at the Royal Barge Museum (see p.111), Wat Chalerm Phra Kiat in Nonthaburi (see p.131), and Wat Poramai and Ban Khanom Thai on Ko Kred, where you can buy traditional sweets and watch them being made.

By public transport Your best option is to take a Chao Phraya Express Boat to Nonthaburi, then bus #32 (ordinary and a/c, coming from Wat Pho via Banglamphu) or a taxi

(about B100) to Pakkred or a chartered longtail boat direct to Ko Kred (about B300). There are also fast, a/c #166 buses from Victory Monument (accessible by Skytrain) to Pakkred, which are your best option for getting back as the #32 stops a fair way from Nonthaburi pier on its inbound journey. From Pakkred, the easiest way of getting across to the island is to hire a longtail boat, although shuttle boats cross at the river's narrowest point to Wat Poramai from Wat Sanam Neua, about 1km walk or motorbike-taxi ride south of the Pakkred pier (getting off the bus at Tesco Lotus in Pakkred will cut down the walk to Wat Sanam Neua).

Muang Boran Ancient City

1

33km southeast of Bangkok • Daily 8am–5pm • B400 • ⓦ ancientcity.com • A/c bus #511 to Samut Prakan on the edge of built-up Greater Bangkok, then songthaew #36 to Muang Boran; bus #511 runs from Banglamphu via Thanon Rama I and Thanon Sukhumvit, but it's much faster to cross downtown Bangkok by Skytrain and boat/subway if necessary and pick up the #511 at Bearing Skytrain station

A day-trip out to the **Muang Boran Ancient City** open-air museum is a great way to enjoy the best of Thailand's architectural heritage in relative peace and without much effort. Occupying a huge park shaped like Thailand itself, the museum comprises more than 116 traditional Thai buildings scattered around pleasantly landscaped grounds and is best toured by rented **bicycle** (B50), though doing it on foot is just about possible. Many of the buildings are copies of the country's most famous monuments, and are located in the appropriate "region" of the park, with everything from Bangkok's Grand Palace (central region) to the spectacularly sited, hilltop Khmer Khao Phra Viharn sanctuary (northeast) represented here. There are also some original structures, including a rare scripture library rescued from Samut Songkhram (south), as well as some painstaking reconstructions from contemporary documents of long-vanished gems, of which the Ayutthaya-period Sanphet Prasat Palace (central) is a particularly fine example. A sizeable team of restorers and skilled craftspeople maintains the buildings and helps keep some of the traditional techniques alive; if you come here during the week you can watch them at work.

ARRIVAL AND DEPARTURE
BANGKOK

Unless you arrive in Bangkok by train, be prepared for a long trip into the city centre. Suvarnabhumi Airport is 25km out and the three bus stations are not much closer in, though at least the Eastern Terminal is close to a Skytrain stop.

BY PLANE

SUVARNABHUMI

Suvarnabhumi is Bangkok's main airport (coded "BKK" and pronounced "soo-wanna-poom"; ☎02 132 8888; ⓦ suvarnabhumiairport.com), situated 25km east of central Bangkok between highways 7 and 34. The large airport is well stocked with 24hr exchange booths, ATMs, places to eat, pharmacies and a post office. 24-hour information is available at the TAT desks at Gates 3 and 10 (☎02 134 0040–1) and there's a tourist police booth in the arrivals hall on Floor 2; there are 24hr left-luggage depots (B100/item/day) in arrivals and in the departures hall on Floor 4. Car-rental companies here include Avis and Budget (see p.142), though you'll have to pick your car up from the Public Transportation Centre (see below). There are a number of accommodation options near Suvarnabhumi (see p.151). When departing Bangkok, leave plenty of time to get to Suvarnabhumi, as getting there by bus, minibus or taxi can be severely hampered by traffic jams.

Public Transportation Centre Situated on the other side of the huge airport complex from the terminal building, the Public Transportation Centre is reached by a free, 10min ride on an "Express" shuttle bus from Gate 5 outside arrivals or Gate 5 outside departures – be sure not to confuse these with the much slower "Ordinary" shuttle buses, which ferry airport staff around the complex. However, because of the inconvenience involved, many long-distance buses now pick up and drop off at the terminal building.

Suvarnabhumi Airport Rail Link The high-speed rail link (SARL; ⓦ airportraillink.railway.co.th; daily 6am–midnight) from the basement of Suvarnabhumi is the quickest means of getting downtown. There's only one set of elevated tracks, ending at Phaya Thai station (an interchange with the Skytrain system, and served by a/c and non-a/c #59 and a/c #79 buses to Thanon Rajadamnoen Klang, for Banglamphu), but three services run on them: stopping, often crowded "City Line" services to Phaya Thai (every 12–20min; 24min; B45), via Makkasan, Ratchaprarop and four other stations; non-stop "Express" trains to Phaya Thai (every 30min; 17min; currently on promotion at B90 single, B150 return); and nonstop "Express" trains to Makkasan Station (every 40min; 15min; B150 single), which is inconveniently located although it's within walking distance of Phetchaburi subway station and served by a/c bus #556 to Thanon Rajadamnoen Klang (for Banglamphu) and the Southern Bus Terminal. Makkasan also offers a luggage check-in facility for most Thai Airways flights (3–12hr before departure).

Taxis Taxis to the centre are comfortable, a/c and reasonably priced, although the driving can be hairy. Walk past the pricey taxis and limousines on offer within the baggage hall and arrivals hall, and ignore any tout who may offer a cheap ride in an unlicensed and unmetered vehicle, as newly arrived travellers are seen as easy prey for robbery and the cabs are untraceable. Licensed and metered public taxis are operated from clearly signposted and well-regulated counters, outside Floor 1's Gates 4 and 7. Including the B50 airport pick-up fee and around B70

1

tolls for the overhead expressways, a journey to Thanon Silom downtown, for example, should set you back around B300–350, depending on the traffic. Heading back to the airport, drivers will nearly always try to leave their meters off and agree an inflated price with you – say "*poet meter, dai mai khrap/kha?*" to get them to switch the meter on. If you leave the downtown areas before 7am or after 9pm you can get to the airport in half an hour, but at other times you should set off about an hour and a half before you have to check in.

City buses and minibuses The most economical way of getting into the city is by public a/c bus (B22–35) or pricier minibus from the Public Transportation Centre, but only the following routes are likely to be useful to visitors: #552 along Thanon Sukhumvit via On Nut (for the Skytrain); and #554 (also available from Gate 8, Floor 1 of the terminal building) and #555 to Don Muang. On departure, many travellers opt for one of the private minibus services to Suvarnabhumi (at least every 2hr; B130–150; at least 90min) organized through guesthouses and travel agents in Banglamphu and elsewhere around the city.

Long-distance buses From Gate 8, Floor 1 of the terminal building, there are long-distance buses to Pattaya, Aranyaprathet, Khorat, Khon Kaen, Udon Thani and Nong Khai, and minibuses to Chanthaburi and Ko Chang. From the Public Transportation Centre, there are also long-distance buses to Rayong, Chanthaburi, Laem Ngop (for Ko Chang) and Trat. In the opposite direction, some of these buses continue to Bangkok's Northern Bus Terminal (Mo Chit).

Destinations Buriram (7 weekly; 1hr); Chiang Mai (25 daily; 1hr); Chiang Rai (4–5 daily; 1hr 15min); Chumphon (daily; 1hr); Khon Kaen (2 daily; 55min); Ko Samui (20 daily; 1hr–1hr 30min); Krabi (15 daily; 1hr 20min); Lampang (5 weekly; 1hr); Mae Sot (5 weekly; 1hr 15min); Nakhon Phanom (1–2 daily; 1hr 5min); Nakhon Si Thammarat (3 daily; 1hr 5min); Nan (daily; 1hr 20min); Phitsanulok (2 daily; 55min); Phrae (2–3 weekly; 1hr); Phuket (21 daily; 1hr 20min); Sukhothai (2 daily; 40min); Surat Thani (4 daily; 1hr 15min); Trang (2 daily; 1hr 30min); Trat (3 daily; 1hr 5min); Ubon Ratchathani (7 daily; 1hr 5min); Udon Thani (7 daily; 1hr).

DON MUANG

The old **Don Muang Airport** (coded "DMK"; ☏ 02 535 1253; ⊛ donmuangairportonline.com), 25km north of the city, is currently used only by Nok Air's domestic services (Orient Thai may also move back there from Suvarnabhumi). If you do wind up at Don Muang, which has its own train station on the North and Northeastern lines and is handy for the Northern Bus Terminal, the best way to get into the city centre is by licensed, metered taxi from the desk outside Arrivals (about B300–350, including B50 airport fee and expressway fees); depending on your destination

in the city, you may save some time during rush hours by hopping out of the taxi at Mo Chit Skytrain station or Phahon Yothin subway station.

BY TRAIN

Travelling to Bangkok by train from Malaysia and most parts of Thailand, you arrive at the main Hualamphong Station. Trains from Kanchanaburi, however, plus a handful from Nakhon Pathom, Hua Hin and other slow, local trains on the Southern line, pull in at Thonburi Station, while Samut Sakhon trains use Wongwian Yai Station (see p.185), also in Thonburi.

HUALAMPHONG STATION

Hualamphong Station is centrally located at the edge of Chinatown and is on the subway line. The most useful of the city buses (see box, p.139) serving Hualamphong is the #159 (non-a/c), which runs west to Democracy Monument, Rajdamnoen Klang (for Banglamphu) and the Southern Bus Terminal, and east to MBK, Siam Square, Chatuchak and the Northern Bus Terminal. Station facilities include an exchange booth, several ATMs, an internet centre and a left-luggage office at the front of the main concourse (daily 4am–11pm; B30–100/day). The 24-hour State Railways (SRT) information booth in the main concourse, on the right, keeps English-language time-tables. Between 8.30am and 4pm, advance tickets can be bought from the clearly signed Advance Booking counters #15–20 under the main departures board; at other times, check availability at the SRT information booth, then buy your ticket at any ticket counter (daily 4.30am–midnight). Train tickets can also be bought through almost any travel agent and through some hotels and guesthouses for a booking fee of about B50. See "Basics" for more information on tickets and timetables (see p.30). The station area is fertile ground for con-artists, looking to prey on new arrivals. Anyone who comes up to you in or around the station concourse and offers help/information/transport or ticket-booking services is probably a scammer, however many official-looking ID tags are hanging round their neck. Hualamphong also nurtures plenty of dishonest tuk-tuk drivers – take a metered taxi or public transport instead.

Destinations Aranyaprathet (2 daily; 5–6hr); Ayutthaya (23 daily; 1hr 30min–2hr); Butterworth (Malaysia; 1 daily; 21hr); Cha-am (5 daily; 3hr 10min–3hr 50min); Chiang Mai (6 daily; 12–14hr); Chumphon (12 daily; 7hr–9hr 30min); Hua Hin (12 daily; 4–5hr); Khon Kaen (5 daily; 7hr 30min–10hr 30min); Khorat (11 daily; 4–5hr); Lampang (6 daily; 10–12hr); Lamphun (6 daily; 12–14hr); Lopburi (15 daily; 2hr 30min–3hr); Nakhon Pathom (12 daily; 1hr 30min); Nakhon Si Thammarat (2 daily; 15–16hr); Nong Khai (3 daily; 10hr 30min–12hr 30min); Pak Chong (for Khao Yai National Park; 10 daily; 2hr 45min–3hr 30min); Pattaya (1 daily; 3hr 45min); Phetchaburi (11 daily; 2hr 45min–3hr

45min); Phitsanulok (12 daily; 5hr 15min–8hr); Prachuap Khiri Khan (11 daily; 5–7hr); Pranburi (daily; 5hr 30min); Si Racha (1 daily; 3hr 15min); Surat Thani (10 daily; 9–12hr); Surin (10 daily; 7–10hr); Tha Naleng (near Vientiane, Laos; 1 daily; 13hr 30min); Trang (2 daily; 15–16hr); Ubon Ratchathani (7 daily; 8hr 35min–12hr 15min); Udon Thani (4 daily; 10–12hr).

THONBURI STATION

Thonburi Station (sometimes still referred to by its former name, Bangkok Noi Station) is a short ride in a red public songthaew or an 850m walk west from the N11 express-boat pier (Mon–Fri rush hours only), just across the Chao Phraya River from Banglamphu and Ratanakosin; at other times you'll need to use the N10 Tha Wang Lang express-boat stop instead, which is 500m south of N11, through the Siriraj hospital compound.

Destinations Hua Hin (4 daily; 4hr–4hr 30min); Kanchanaburi (2 daily; 2hr 40min); Nakhon Pathom (6 daily; 1hr 10min); Nam Tok (2 daily; 4hr 35min); Phetchaburi (3 daily; 2hr 45min–3hr 45min); Pranburi (2 daily; 5hr 30min).

BY BUS

Bangkok's three main bus terminals, all of which have left-luggage facilities of some kind, are distributed around the outskirts of town. On departure, leave plenty of time to reach them, especially if setting off from Banglamphu, from where you should allow at least an hour and a half (outside rush hour) to get to the Eastern Bus Terminal, and a good hour to get to the Northern or Southern terminals. Seats on the most popular long-distance a/c bus services (such as to Chiang Mai, Krabi, Phuket and Surat Thani) should be reserved ahead of time, either at the relevant bus station or in any of the ways described in Basics (see p.29), as guesthouses may book you on to one of the dodgy tourist services (see p.136).

NORTHERN AND NORTHEASTERN BUS TERMINAL (MO CHIT)

All services from the north and northeast terminate at Bangkok's biggest bus station, the Northern and Northeastern Bus Terminal (Mo Chit) on Thanon Kamphaeng Phet 2; some buses from the south and the east coast also use Mo Chit. The quickest way to get into the city centre from Mo Chit is to hop onto the Skytrain at Mo Chit Station on Thanon Phaholyothin, or the subway at the adjacent Chatuchak Park Station or at Kamphaeng Phet Station (at the bottom of Thanon Kamphaeng Phet 2), all of which are about a 15min walk from the bus terminal, and then change onto a city bus if necessary. Otherwise, it's a long bus or taxi ride into town: city buses from the Northern Bus Terminal include ordinary #159 to Siam Square, Hualamphong Station, Banglamphu and the Southern Bus Terminal; and ordinary and a/c #3, and a/c #509 and #512 to Banglamphu (see p.139).

Destinations Aranyaprathet (hourly; 4hr 30min); Ayutthaya (every 20min; 2hr); Chanthaburi (13 daily; 3–4hr); Chiang Khan (2 daily; 9hr); Chiang Khong (10 daily; 13–14hr); Chiang Mai (20 daily; 10–11hr); Chiang Rai (21 daily; 11–13hr); Chong Mek (daily; 11hr); Kamphaeng Phet (7 daily; 6hr 30min); Kanchanaburi (9 daily; 2hr 30min); Khon Kaen (29 daily; 6–7hr); Khorat (every 30min; 2hr 30min–3hr); Kong Chiam (4 daily; 11hr); Lampang (18 daily; 8hr 30min); Loei (20 daily; 8hr); Lopburi (every 20min; 2hr 30min–3hr); Mae Hong Son (2 daily; 18hr); Mae Sai (13 daily; 13hr); Mae Sariang (2 daily; 15hr); Mae Sot (11 daily; 8hr 30min); Mukdahan (13 daily; 11hr);

OVERLAND TO OTHER ASIAN COUNTRIES

Most travellers who choose to make their way **overland from Thailand** to Laos, Cambodia or Malaysia (see also p.27) do so slowly, but it is possible to do the border-hop in one swoop from Bangkok, though in most cases you'll need to spend a night somewhere on the way. To get **from Bangkok to Laos**, you have to take a bus to the border at Chiang Khong, Nong Khai (which also has a train service from the capital), Nakhon Phanom (which also has an airport), Mukdahan or Chong Mek. For transport **to Cambodia**, it's best to begin by either taking a bus from Bangkok to Trat or a train or bus from Bangkok to Aranyaprathet. Khao San travel agents also run direct buses to Siem Reap for as little as B200, but scams and discomfort on these services are common (see p.383). The easiest way of travelling from Bangkok **to Malaysia** is by train to the west coast of the peninsula. There is one train a day from Bangkok's Hualamphong Station to Butterworth (for Penang; 21hr), which costs about B1200 in a second-class sleeper; it's possible to make onward train connections to Kuala Lumpur and Singapore.

All the **foreign embassies and consulates** in Bangkok are located in the downtown area (see p.171). Phone ahead to check the opening hours (usually very limited) and documentation required. Some travellers prefer to avoid the hassle of trudging out to the relevant embassy by paying one of the Khao San travel agencies to get their visa for them; beware of doing this, however, as some agencies are reportedly **faking the stamps**, which causes serious problems at immigration.

1

Nakhon Phanom (17 daily; 12hr); Nan (10 daily; 12hr); Nong Khai (24 daily; 11hr); Pak Chong (for Khao Yai National Park; every 30min; 3hr); Pattaya (every 30min; 2–3hr); Phitsanulok (up to 19 daily; 5–6hr); Phrae (11 daily; 8hr 30min); Rayong (every 30min; 2hr 30min–3hr 30min); Si Racha (every 30min; 2hr); Sukhothai (17 daily; 6–7hr); Surin (up to 20 daily; 8–9hr); Tak (13 daily; 7hr); That Phanom (3 daily; 12hr); Trat (5 daily; 4hr 30min); Ubon Ratchathani (19 daily; 10–12hr); Udon Thani (every 30min; 9hr).

EASTERN BUS TERMINAL (EKAMAI)

Most buses to and from east-coast destinations such as Pattaya, Ban Phe (for Ko Samet) and Trat (for Ko Chang) use the Eastern Bus Terminal (Ekamai; ☎ 02 391 2496) between sois 40 and 42 on Thanon Sukhumvit. This bus station is right beside the Ekamai Skytrain stop (see p.141), and is also served by lots of city buses, including a/c #511 to and from Banglamphu and the Southern Bus Terminals. Alternatively, you can use the Khlong Saen Saeb canal-boat service, which runs westwards almost as far as Banglamphu (see p.140); there's a pier called Tha Ekamai, at the northern end of Sukhumvit Soi 63, which is easiest reached from the bus station by taxi.

Destinations Ban Phe (for Ko Samet; 12 daily; 3hr–3hr 30min); Chanthaburi (hourly; 4–5hr); Laem Ngop (for Ko Chang; 3–4 daily; 5hr 15min); Pattaya (every 30min; 2hr 30min–3hr 30min); Rayong (every 40min; 2hr 30min–3hr); Si Racha (every 30min; 2–3hr); Trat (6 daily; 5–6hr).

SOUTHERN BUS TERMINAL (SATHAANII SAI TAI)

The huge, airport-like Southern Bus Terminal, or Sathaanii Sai Tai (☎ 02 434 7192), handles transport to and from all points south of the capital, including Hua Hin, Chumphon (for Ko Tao), Surat Thani (for Ko Samui), Phuket and Krabi, as well as buses for destinations west of Bangkok, such as Amphawa, Nakhon Pathom and Kanchanaburi. The terminal has recently been relocated to the junction of Thanon Borom Ratchonni and Thanon Phutthamonthon Sai 1 in Taling Chan, an interminable 11km west of the Chao Phraya River and Banglamphu, so access to and from city accommodation can take an age, even in a taxi. City buses serving Sathaanii Sai Tai include #124 for Banglamphu, #159 to Banglamphu, Hualamphong Station, Siam Square and the Northern Bus Terminal, #511 for Banglamphu, Thanon Sukhumvit and Ekamai, and #516 for Thewet and Banglamphu, but note that when arriving in Bangkok most long-distance bus services make a more convenient stop before reaching the terminus (via a time-consuming U-turn), towards the eastern end of Thanon Borom Ratchonni, much nearer Phra Pinklao Bridge and the river; the majority of passengers get off here and it's highly recommended to do the same rather than continue to the terminal. The above-listed city buses all cross the

river from this bus drop, as do many additional services, and this is also a faster and cheaper place to grab a taxi into town.

Destinations Amphawa (every 40min; 2hr); Cha-am (every 40min; 2hr 45min–3hr 15min); Chumphon (roughly hourly; 7–9hr); Damnoen Saduak (every 40min; 2hr); Hat Yai (13 daily; 12hr); Hua Hin (every 40min; 3–4hr); Kanchanaburi (every 15min; 2hr); Khao Lak (3 daily; 12hr); Ko Pha Ngan (2 daily; 14hr); Ko Samui (8 daily; 13hr); Krabi (12 daily; 12–14hr); Nakhon Pathom (every 10min; 40min–1hr 20min); Nakhon Si Thammarat (19 daily; 12hr); Phang Nga (6 daily; 12hr); Phetchaburi (4–7 daily; 2hr 15min); Phuket (15 daily; 12hr); Prachuap Khiri Khan (every 30min; 4–5hr); Pranburi (every 40min; 3hr 30min); Ranong (15 daily; 9hr); Samut Songkhram (every 20min; 1hr 30min); Satun (5 daily; 16hr); Surat Thani (10 daily; 10–12hr); Trang (11 daily; 12–14hr).

BY AIR-CONDITIONED MINIBUS

A faster, more convenient alternative to traipsing out to the bus terminals is to make use of the licensed, a/c minibus services (*rot tuu*; see p.30) that depart from central downtown locations. The Kanchanaburi service leaves from outside the *Royal Hotel* at the west end of Ratchadamnoen Klang in Banglamphu, but most other services depart from the Victory Monument roundabout (*Anu Sawari*), most easily reached via the Victory Monument Skytrain station. See the accounts of the relevant destinations for details.

BY TOURIST BUS

Many Bangkok tour operators sell tickets for unlicensed budget tourist buses and minibuses to popular long-distance destinations such as Chiang Mai, Surat Thani (for Ko Samui) and Krabi (for Ko Phi Phi), and to places closer at hand such as Kanchanaburi, Ko Samet and Ko Chang. Their only advantage is convenience, as they mostly leave from the Khao San area in Banglamphu. Prices, however, can vary considerably but rarely work out cheaper than buses from the public terminals or licensed a/c minibuses. The big drawbacks, however, are the lack of comfort and poor safety, which particularly applies to the long-distance overnight services. It is standard practice for budget tour operators, especially those on Thanon Khao San, to assure you that overnight transport will be in a large, luxury VIP bus despite knowing it's actually a clapped-out old banger. Security on overnight tourist buses is a serious problem, and because they're run by unlicensed private companies there is no insurance against loss or theft of baggage: don't keep anything of value in luggage that's stored out of sight, even if it's padlocked, as luggage sometimes gets slashed and rifled in the roomy baggage compartment. In addition, passengers often find themselves dumped on the outskirts of their destination city, at the mercy of unscrupulous touts. Services to Kanchanaburi (around B250), Ko Samet

(B350 including boat transfer) and Ko Chang (B350 including boat) are usually by a/c minibus; these are usually cramped and can go scarily fast but luggage is generally secure. Bear in mind that Khao San tour operators open up and go bust all the time; never hand over any money until you see the ticket. One tourist company that is licensed and reliable is Lomprayah, who operate catamarans to Ko Tao, Ko Pha Ngan and Ko Samui and connecting buses from Banglamphu to Chumphon. They have an office at 154 Thanon Ram Buttri (☏ 02 629 2569–70, ⓦ lomprayah.com). Recommended travel agents are listed in the Directory (see p.173).

GETTING AROUND

Getting around can undoubtedly be a headache in a city where it's not unusual for residents to spend three hours getting to work. The main form of transport is **buses**, and once you've mastered the labyrinthine complexity of the route maps you'll be able to get to any part of the city, albeit slowly. Catching the various kinds of **taxi** is more expensive, and you'll still get held up by the daytime traffic jams. **Boats** are obviously more limited in their range, but they're regular and as cheap as buses, and you'll save a lot of time by using them whenever possible – a journey between Banglamphu and the GPO, for instance, will take around thirty minutes by water, half what it would usually take on land. The **Skytrain** and **subway** each have a similarly limited range but are also worth using whenever suitable for all or part of your journey; their networks roughly coincide with each other at the east end of Thanon Silom, at the corner of Soi Asoke and Thanon Sukhumvit, and on Thanon Phaholyothin by Chatuchak Park (Mo Chit), while the Skytrain joins up with the Chao Phraya

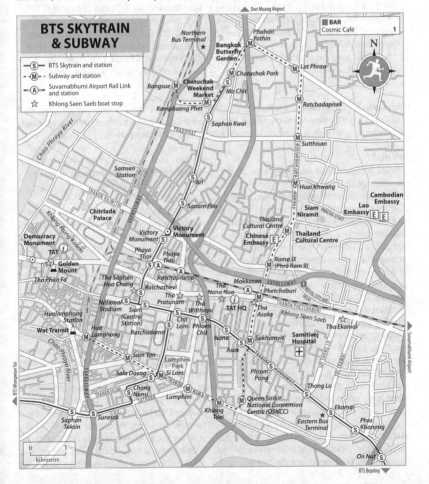

1

TOURS OF THE CITY

Unlikely as it sounds, the most popular organized **tours** in Bangkok for independent travellers are by bicycle, heading to the city's outer neighbourhoods and beyond; these are an excellent way to gain a different perspective on Thai life and offer a unique chance to see traditional communities close up. In addition to those listed below, other tour options include Thonburi canal tours (see p.112), Chao Phraya Express tourist boats (see p.140) and dinner cruises along the Chao Phraya River (see p.151).

ABC Amazing Bangkok Cyclist Tours and **Real Asia** 10/5–7 Soi Aree, Soi 26, Thanon Sukhumvit ☎ 02 665 6364, ⓦ realasia.net. ABC's are the most popular and longest-running bicycle tours, starting in the Sukhumvit area and taking you across the river to surprisingly rural khlong- and riverside communities (including a floating market at weekends); they also offer cycle-and-dine tours in the evening. Tours operate every day year-round, cover up to 30km depending on the itinerary, and need to be reserved in advance (B1000–2000 including bicycle). Part of the same company, Real Asia does full-day canal and walking tours through Thonburi and leads outings by train to the historic fishing port of Samut Sakhon (both B2000, including lunch and boat trips).

Bangkok Bike Rides 14/1 Soi Promsi 2, Soi 39, Thanon Sukhumvit ☎ 02 712 5305, ⓦ bangkok bikerides.com or ⓦ spiceroads.com. Runs a programme of different day and half-day tours within Greater Bangkok (B1000–2650 per person, minimum two people), including Ko Kred, as well as to the floating markets and canalside neighbourhoods of Damnoen Saduak and Ayutthaya. Also offers multi-day trips out of the city.

Velo Thailand Soi 4, Thanon Samsen ☎ 02 628 8628, ⓦ velothailand.com. Runs half a dozen different bike tours of the capital out of its cycle shop on the edge of Banglamphu, including an after-dark tour (6–10pm; B1100) that takes in floodlit sights including Wat Pho, Wat Arun and the Pak Khlong Talat flower market.

River express boats at the vital hub of Sathorn/Saphan Taksin (Taksin Bridge). At each Skytrain and subway station, you'll find a useful map of the immediate neighbourhood. Also under construction in the north of the city are the elevated metro lines known as the SRT Red Lines from Bang Sue, one of which will stop at Don Muang airport.

BY BUS

Bangkok has reputedly the world's largest bus network, on which operate three main types of bus service. On ordinary (non-a/c) buses, which are either red and white, blue and white, or small and green, fares range from B6.50 to B8.50; most routes operate from about 5am to 11pm, but some maintain a 24-hour service (see box opposite). A/c buses are either blue, orange or yellow (some are articulated) and charge between B12 and B36 according to distance travelled; most stop in the late evening, but a few of the more popular routes run 24-hour services. As buses can only go as fast as the car in front, which at the moment is averaging 4km per hr, you'll probably be spending a long time on each journey, so you'd be well advised to pay the extra for cool air – and the a/c buses are usually less crowded, too. For a comprehensive roundup of bus routes in the capital, buy a bus map or log onto the Bangkok Mass Transit Authority website (ⓦ bmta.co.th), which gives details of all city-bus routes.

Maps To get around Bangkok on the cheap, you'll need to buy a bus map. Of the several available, the most useful and reliable are Bangkok Guide's *Bus Routes & Map*, which not only charts all major a/c and non-a/c bus routes but also carries detailed written itineraries of some two hundred routes; and Thinknet's more user-friendly *Bangkok*

Bus Guide, which also charts a/c and non-a/c buses, with close-up maps of Banglamphu and Victory Monument.

BY BOAT

Bangkok was built as an amphibious city around a network of canals (khlongs) and the first streets were constructed only in the second half of the nineteenth century. Many canals remain on the Thonburi side of the river, but most of those on the Bangkok side have been turned into roads. The Chao Phraya River itself is still a major transport route for residents and non-residents alike, forming more of a link than a barrier between the two halves of the city.

EXPRESS BOATS

The Chao Phraya Express Boat Company operates the vital express-boat (*reua duan*; ⓦ chaophrayaexpressboat.com) services, using large water buses to plough up and down the river, between clearly signed piers (*tha*), which appear on all Bangkok maps. Tha Sathorn, which gives access to the Skytrain network at Saphan Taksin Station, has been designated "Central Pier", with piers to the south of here numbered S1, S2, etc, those to the north N1, N2 and so on (see box, p.140 and map, pp.80–81). Boats do not necessarily stop at every landing – they only pull in if people want to get on or off, and when they do stop, it's not

USEFUL BUS ROUTES

In addition to those listed below, there are also bus routes from Suvarnabhumi Airport (see p.134). In Banglamphu, finding the right bus stop can sometimes be tricky (see p.99).

#3 (ordinary and a/c)
Northern Bus Terminal–Chatuchak Weekend Market–Thanon Phaholyothin–Thanon Samsen–Thanon Phra Arthit (for Banglamphu guesthouses)–Thanon Sanam Chai (for Museum of Siam)–Thanon Triphet–Memorial Bridge (for Pak Khlong Talat)–Taksin Monument (for Wongwian Yai)–Wat Suwan.

#15 (ordinary)
Thanon Ratchadaphisek–Krung Thep Bridge–Thanon Charoen Krung–Thanon Silom–Thanon Rajdamri–Siam Square–Thanon Lan Luang–Sanam Luang–Thanon Phra Arthit (for Banglamphu guesthouses).

#16 (ordinary and a/c)
Thanon Srinarong–Thanon Samsen–Thewet (for guesthouses)–Thanon Phitsanulok–Thanon Phrayathai–Siam Square–Thanon Suriwong.

#25 (ordinary and a/c, 24hr)
Pak Nam (for Ancient City buses)–Thanon Sukhumvit–Eastern Bus Terminal–Siam Square–Hualamphong Station–Thanon Yaowarat (for Chinatown)–Pahurat–Wat Pho–Tha Chang (for the Grand Palace); some #25 buses (ordinary only) only go as far as Hualamphong Station.

#53 circular (also anticlockwise; ordinary)
Thewet–Thanon Krung Kasem–Hualamphong Station–Thanon Yaowarat (for Chinatown)–Pahurat–Pak Khlong Talat–Thanon Maharat (for Wat Pho and the Grand Palace)–Sanam Luang (for National Museum)–Thanon Phra Arthit and Thanon Samsen (for Banglamphu guesthouses)–Thewet.

#56 circular (also clockwise; ordinary)
Thanon Phra Sumen–Wat Bowoniwes–Thanon Pracha Thipatai–Thanon Ratchasima (for Vimanmek Palace)–Thanon Rajwithi–Krung Thon Bridge–Thonburi–Phrapokklao Bridge–Thanon Chakraphet (for Chinatown)–Thanon Mahachai–Democracy Monument–Thanon Tanao (for Khao San guesthouses)–Thanon Phra Sumen.

#124 (ordinary)
Sanam Luang–Thanon Rajinee, near Information Centre (for Banglamphu guesthouses)–Phra Pinklao Bridge–Southern Bus Terminal–Mahidol University.

#159 (ordinary)
Southern Bus Terminal–Phra Pinklao Bridge–Democracy Monument–Hualamphong Station–MBK Shopping Centre–Thanon Ratchaprarop–Victory Monument–Chatuchak Weekend Market–Northern Bus Terminal.

#503 (a/c)
Sanam Luang–Democracy Monument (for Banglamphu guesthouses)–Thanon Rajdamnoen Nok (for TAT and boxing stadium)–Wat Benjamabophit–Thanon Sri Ayutthaya (for Thewet guesthouses)–Victory Monument–Chatuchak Weekend Market–Rangsit. Note, however, that during rush hours, some #503 buses take the expressway, missing out Chatuchak Weekend Market.

#508 (a/c)
Thanon Maharat–Grand Palace–Thanon Charoen Krung–Siam Square–Thanon Sukhumvit–Eastern Bus Terminal–Pak Nam (for Ancient City buses). Note, however, that during rush hours, some #508 buses take the expressway, missing out the Eastern Bus Terminal.

#509 (a/c)
Northern Bus Terminal–Chatuchak Weekend Market–Victory Monument–Thanon Rajwithi–Thanon Sawankhalok–Thanon Phitsanulok–Thanon Rajdamnoen Nok (for TAT and boxing stadium)–Democracy Monument–Thanon Rajdamnoen Klang (for Banglamphu guesthouses)–Phra Pinklao Bridge–Thonburi.

#511 (a/c, 24hr)
Southern Bus Terminal–Phra Pinklao Bridge (for Banglamphu guesthouses)–Democracy Monument–Thanon Lan Luang–Thanon Phetchaburi–Thanon Sukhumvit–Eastern Bus Terminal–Pak Nam (for Ancient City buses). Note, however, that between 4am and 11pm, some #511 buses take the expressway, missing out the Eastern Bus Terminal.

#512 (a/c)
Northern Bus Terminal–Chatuchak Weekend Market–Thanon Phetchaburi–Thanon Lan Luang–Democracy Monument (for Banglamphu guesthouses)–Sanam Luang–Tha Chang (for Grand Palace)–Pak Khlong Talat.

1

CENTRAL STOPS FOR THE CHAO PHRAYA EXPRESS BOATS

N15 Thewet (all express boats) – for Thewet guesthouses.

N14 Rama VIII Bridge (no flag) – for Samsen Soi 5.

N13 Phra Arthit (no flag and orange flag) – for Thanon Phra Arthit, Thanon Khao San and Banglamphu guesthouses.

N12 Phra Pinklao Bridge (all boats) – for Royal Barge Museum.

N11 Thonburi Railway Station (or Bangkok Noi; no flag) – for trains to Kanchanaburi.

N10 Wang Lang (aka Siriraj or Prannok; all boats) – for Wat Rakhang.

N9 Chang (no flag, green flag and orange flag) – for the Grand Palace, Sanam Luang and the National Museum.

N8 Thien (no flag and orange flag) – for Wat

Pho, and the cross-river ferry to Wat Arun.

N7 Ratchini (aka Rajinee; no flag).

N6 Saphan Phut (Memorial Bridge; no flag and orange flag) – for Pahurat, Pak Khlong Talat and Wat Prayoon.

N5 Rachawongse (aka Rajawong; all boats) – for Chinatown.

N4 Harbour (Marine) Department (no flag and orange flag).

N3 Si Phraya (all boats) – walk north past the *Sheraton Royal Orchid Hotel* for River City shopping complex, head south for the GPO.

N2 Wat Muang Kae (no flag) – for the GPO.

N1 Oriental (no flag and orange flag) – for Thanon Silom.

Central Sathorn (all boats) – for the Skytrain (Saphan Taksin Station) and Thanon Sathorn.

for long – so when you want to get off, be ready at the back of the boat in good time for your pier. No-flag, local-line boats call at every pier between Wat Rajsingkorn, just upriver of Krung Thep Bridge, in the south, and Nonthaburi, 90min away to the north, but only operate during rush hour (Mon–Fri roughly 6.20–8am & 3–5.30pm, every 20–25min; B10–14). The only boats to run all day, every day, are on the limited-stop orange-flag service (Nonthaburi to Wat Rajsingkorn in 1hr; roughly 6am–7pm, every 5–20min; B15). Other limited-stop services run during rush hour, flying either a yellow flag (Nonthaburi to Tha Sathorn or Rajburana, far downriver beyond Krung Thep Bridge, in about 50min; Mon–Fri roughly 6.15–8.30am & 3.30–8pm; B20–29) or a green flag (Pakkred to Tha Sathorn Mon–Fri 6.15–8.10am & 5–6pm, Tha Sathorn to Pakkred Mon–Fri 3.30–6.05pm; about 50min; B13–32). Tickets can be bought on board; don't discard your ticket until you're off the boat, as the staff at some piers impose a B1 fine on anyone disembarking without one.

TOURIST BOATS

The Chao Phraya Express Boat Company also runs tourist boats, distinguished by their light-blue flags, between Sathorn (every 30min; 9.30am–4pm) and Phra Arthit piers (every 30min; 10am–4.30pm). In between (in both directions), these boats call in at Oriental, Si Phraya, Rachawongse, Thien, Maharat (near Wat Mahathat and the Grand Palace) and Wang Lang. On-board guides provide running commentaries, and a one-day ticket for unlimited trips, which also allows you to use other express boats within the same route on the same day, costs B150; one-way tickets are also available, costing, for example, B30 from Si Phraya to Thien.

CROSS-RIVER FERRIES

Smaller than express boats are the slow cross-river ferries (*reua kham fak*), which shuttle back and forth between the same two points. Found at or beside every express-boat stop and plenty of other piers in between, they are especially useful for exploring Thonburi. Fares are generally B3–4, payable at the entrance to the pier.

CANAL BOATS

Longtail boats (*reua hang yao*) ply the canals of Thonburi like commuter buses, stopping at designated shelters (fares are in line with those of express boats), and are available for individual rental here and on the river (see box, p.112). On the Bangkok side, Khlong Saen Saeb is well served by passenger boats, which run at least every 15min during daylight hours from the Phan Fah pier at the Golden Mount (handy for Banglamphu, Ratanakosin and Chinatown), and head way out east to Wat Sribunruang, with useful stops at Thanon Phrayathai, aka Saphan Hua Chang (for Jim Thompson's House and Ratchathevi Skytrain stop); Pratunam (for the Erawan Shrine); Thanon Witthayu (Wireless Road); and Soi Nana Nua (Soi 3), Thanon Asok Montri (Soi 21, for TAT headquarters and Phetchaburi subway stop), Soi Thonglo (Soi 55) and Soi Ekamai (Soi 63), all off Thanon Sukhumvit. This is your quickest and most interesting way of getting between the west and east parts of town, if you can stand the stench of the canal. You may have trouble actually locating the piers as few are signed in English and they all look very unassuming and rickety (see map, p.137); keep your eyes peeled for a plain wooden jetty – most jetties serve boats running in both directions. Once on the boat, state your destination to the conductor when he collects your fare, which will be between B10 and B24. Due to the construction of some low bridges, all passengers change onto a different boat at Tha Pratunam – just follow the crowd.

BY SKYTRAIN

Although its network is limited, the BTS Skytrain, or *rot fai faa* (⊕ bts.co.th), provides a much faster alternative to the bus, and is clean, efficient and over-vigorously air-conditioned. There are only two Skytrain lines, which interconnect at Siam Square (Central Station). Both run every few minutes from around 6am to midnight, with fares of B15–55 per trip depending on distance travelled. You buy tickets from machines that accept only coins, but you can change notes at staffed counters. You'd really have to be motoring to justify buying a day pass at B120, while the various multi-trip cards are designed for long-distance commuters. The Sukhumvit Line runs from Mo Chit (stop N8) in the northern part of the city, via the interchange at Phayathai (N2) with the airport rail line, to Bearing (Soi 105, Thanon Sukhumvit; E14) in around 40min. The Silom Line runs from the National Stadium (W1) via Saphan Taksin (Taksin, or Sathorn, Bridge; S6), to link up with the full gamut of express boats on the Chao Phraya River (though there are plans to close down Saphan Taksin Station and build a moving walkway between the river and Surasak Station), to Wongwian Yai (S8) in Thonburi (a continuation to Bang Wa station on Thanon Phetkasem is being built).

BY SUBWAY

Bangkok's underground rail system, the MRT subway (or metro; in Thai, *rot fai tai din*; ⊕ bangkokmetro.co.th), has similar advantages to the Skytrain, though its current single line connects few places of interest for visitors. It runs every few minutes between around 6am and midnight from Hualamphong train station, via Silom (near Sala Daeng Skytrain station), Sukhumvit (near Asoke Skytrain) and Chatuchak Park (near Mo Chit Skytrain), to Bang Sue train station in the north of the city. Building work is under way to continue the line westwards from Hualamphong to Wat Mangkon Kamalawat in Chinatown, Pahurat, Thanon Sanam Chai in Ratanakosin, then across to Thonburi, the eventual plan being to complete a loop back to Bang Sue. Pay your fare (B15–40) at a staffed counter or machine, where you'll receive a token to put through an entrance gate (the various day-passes and stored-value cards available are unlikely to be worthwhile for visitors).

BY TAXI

Bangkok taxis come in three forms, and are so plentiful that you rarely have to wait more than a couple of minutes before spotting an empty one of any description. Neither tuk-tuks nor motorbike taxis have meters, so you should agree on a price before setting off, and expect to do a fair amount of haggling.

METERED TAXIS

For nearly all journeys, the best and most comfortable option is to flag down one of Bangkok's metered, a/c taxi cabs; look out for the "TAXI METER" sign on the roof, and a red light in the windscreen in front of the passenger seat, which means the cab is available for hire. Starting at B35, fares are displayed on a clearly visible meter that the driver should reset at the start of each trip (say *"poet meter, dai mai khrap/kha?"* to ask him to switch it on), and increase in stages on a combined distance/time formula; as an example, a medium-range journey from Thanon Ploenchit to Thanon Sathorn will cost around B50 at a quiet time of day. Try to have change with you as cabs tend not to carry a lot of money; tipping of up to ten percent is common, though occasionally a cabbie will round down the fare on the meter. If a driver tries to quote a flat fare rather than using the meter, let him go, and avoid the now-rare unmetered cabs (denoted by a "TAXI" sign on the roof). Getting a metered taxi in the middle of the afternoon when the cars return to base for a change of drivers can sometimes be a problem. If you want to book a metered taxi (B20–50 surcharge), try Siam Taxi Co-operative on ☎ 1661 or Taxi Radio on ☎ 1681.

TUK-TUKS

Somewhat less stable though typically Thai, tuk-tuks have very little to recommend them. These noisy, three-wheeled, open-sided buggies, which can carry three medium-sized passengers comfortably, fully expose you to the worst of Bangkok's pollution and weather. You'll have to bargain very hard to get a fare lower than the taxi-cab flagfall of B35; for a longer trip, for example from Thanon Convent to Siam Square, drivers will ask for as much as B200. Be aware, also, that tuk-tuk drivers tend to speak less English than taxi drivers – and there have been cases of robberies and attacks on women passengers late at night. During the day it's quite common for tuk-tuk drivers to try and con their passengers into visiting a jewellery, tailor's or expensive souvenir shop with them (see p.61).

MOTORBIKE TAXIS

Motorbike taxis generally congregate at the entrances to long sois – pick the riders out by their numbered, coloured vests – and charge from B10 for short trips down into the side streets. If you're short on time and have nerves of steel, it's also possible to charter them for hairy journeys out on the main roads (a short trip from Sanam Luang to Thanon Samsen will cost around B40). Crash helmets are compulsory on all main roads in the capital (traffic police fine non-wearers on the spot), though they're rarely worn on trips down the sois.

1

CAR RENTAL

You'd be mad to rent a self-drive car for getting around Bangkok, especially as taxis are so cheap, but you may want to start a driving tour around the country here.

Avis 2/12 Thanon Witthayu (Wireless Road), Suvarnabhumi and Don Muang airports (☎ 02 251 1131–2, ⓦ avisthailand .com).

Budget 19/23 Building A, Royal City Avenue, Thanon Phetchaburi Mai, Suvarnabhumi Airport and Don Muang Airport (☎ 02 203 9222, ⓦ budget.co.th).

National 727 Thanon Srinakharin, Suvarnabhumi Airport and Don Muang Airport (☎ 02 722 8487, ⓦ national carthailand.com).

INFORMATION

Bangkok Tourism Division The official source of information on the capital, whose main office is next to Phra Pinklao Bridge at 17/1 Thanon Phra Arthit in Banglamphu (Mon–Fri 8.30am–7pm, Sat & Sun 9am–5pm; ☎ 02 225 7612–4, ⓦ bangkoktourist.com). This is supported by about twenty strategically placed satellite booths around the capital (most daily 9am–5pm, though some closed Sun), including in front of the Grand Palace, at River City and Mah Boon Krong shopping centres, and in front of Banglamphu's Wat Chana Songkhram.

Tourism Authority of Thailand (**TAT**) For advice on destinations further afield, TAT maintains a Tourist Service Centre within walking distance of Banglamphu, at 4 Rajdamnoen Nok (daily 8.30am–4.30pm; ☎ 02 356 0650; freephone tourist assistance 8am–8pm ☎ 1672; ⓦ tourismthailand.org); it's a 20min stroll from Thanon Khao San, or a short ride in a/c bus #503. TAT also has booths at Suvarnabhumi Airport. Note, however, that the many other travel agents, shops and private offices across the capital displaying "TAT Tourist Information" signs or similar are not official Tourism Authority of Thailand information centres and will not be dispensing impartial advice (they may be licensed by TAT to run their business,

but that doesn't make them government information offices). The Tourism Authority of Thailand never uses the acronym TAT on its office-fronts or in its logo, and doesn't book hotels or sell transport tickets.

Listings Listings magazines rise and fall with confusing rapidity in Bangkok; the best of the current publications is the free, weekly *Bk Magazine*, which comes out on Friday and gives a decent rundown of the art and drama scenes, live music and club nights for the week ahead. If you're interested in Bangkok's contemporary art scene, check out ⓦ bangkokartmap.com or pick up a copy of their free, monthly map for exhibition listings.

City maps For a personal guide to Bangkok's most interesting shops, markets, restaurants and backstreets, look for the famously idiosyncratic hand-drawn *Nancy Chandler's Map of Bangkok* and *Nancy Chandler's Map of Khao San and Old Bangkok*. Both carry a mass of annotated recommendations, are impressively accurate and regularly reissued; they're sold in most tourist areas, and copies and interim updates, as well as information about current events in Bangkok, are also available at ⓦ nancychandler .net. Maps are also available for Bangkok's bus routes (see p.138).

ACCOMMODATION

If your time in Bangkok is limited, you should think especially carefully about what you want to do in the city before deciding which part of town to stay in. Traffic jams are so appalling here that easy access to Skytrain, subway or river transport can be crucial. Advance reservations are recommended where possible during high season (Nov–Feb), though some guesthouses will only take cash deposits. For ultra-cheap double rooms under B400, your widest choice lies on and around **Banglamphu's** Thanon Khao San. The most inexpensive rooms here are no-frills crash-pads – small and often windowless, with thin walls and shared bathrooms – but Banglamphu also offers plenty of well-appointed mid-priced options with a/c and swimming pools. Other, far smaller and less interesting travellers' ghettoes that might be worth bearing in mind are the generally dingy **Soi Ngam Duphli**, off the south side of Thanon Rama IV, which nevertheless harbours a couple of decent shoestring options; and **Soi Kasemsan I**, which is very handily placed next to Siam Square and firmly occupies the moderate range, though with a few rooms for B500. Otherwise, the majority of the city's moderate and expensive rooms are scattered widely across the **downtown areas**, around Siam Square and Thanon Ploenchit, to the south of Thanon Rama IV and along **Thanon Sukhumvit**, and to a lesser extent in **Chinatown**. As well as easy access to transport links and shops, the downtown views from accommodation in these areas are a real plus, especially from the deluxe hotels that are scenically sited along the banks of the Chao Phraya River.

BANGLAMPHU

Nearly all backpackers head straight for Banglamphu, Bangkok's long-established travellers' ghetto just north of the Grand Palace, location of the cheapest accommodation,

the best traveller-oriented facilities and some of the most enjoyable bars and restaurants in the city. A growing number of Khao San guesthouses are reinventing themselves as good-value mini-hotels boasting chic decor, swimming pools, and even views from the windows, but the cheap sleeps are still there, particularly immediately west of Khao San, around the neighbourhood temple Wat Chana Songhkram, and along riverside Thanon Phra Arthit – where you'll also find some upscale places offering prime views over the Chao Phraya. About a 10min walk north from Thanon Khao San, the handful of guesthouses scattered among the shophouses of the Thanon Samsen sois enjoy a more authentically Thai environment, while the Thewet area, a further 15min walk in the same direction or a 7min walk from the Thewet express-boat stop, is more local still. Heading south from Khao San, across multi-laned Rajdamnoen Klang, to the upscale guesthouses in the area immediately south of Democracy also puts you plumb in the middle of an interesting old neighbourhood, famous for its traditional shophouse restaurants. Theft is a problem in Banglamphu, particularly at the cheaper guesthouses, so don't leave anything valuable in your room and heed the guesthouses' notices about padlocks and safety lockers.

THANON KHAO SAN AND AROUND

Buddy Lodge 265 Thanon Khao San ☎ 02 629 4477, ⓦ buddylodge.com; map pp.100–101. The most stylish hotel on Khao San and right in the thick of the action. The charming, colonial-style rooms are done out in cream, with louvred shutters, balconies, marble bathrooms, a/c and polished dark-wood floors, though they aren't as pristine as you might expect for the price. There's a beautiful rooftop pool, a spa, a gym, in-room wi-fi and several bars downstairs in the *Buddy Village* complex. Specify an upper-floor location away from Khao San to ensure a quieter night's sleep. Buffet breakfast included. B2800

Charoendee Boutique Hostel 189 Thanon Khao San ☎ 02 629 1980, ⓦ charoendee.com; map pp.100–101. Pleasantly surprising compound of pretty, colonial-style edifices with wooden shutters and latticework around a small, plant-strewn courtyard, hemmed in by a mess of surrounding buildings. Bedrooms are light and clean, bathrooms generally small but with hot showers. Good rates available for singles, which are fan-cooled and share bathrooms. Internet access, plus free coffee and toast for breakfast. At the bottom of a narrow alley, so quieter than many. Fan (shared bathroom) B450, a/c (en-suite) B650

Donna Guesthouse 75 Thanon Ratchadamnoen Klang ☎ 02 281 9374; map pp.100–101. Down a tiny alley and hemmed in by other buildings, this friendly, bright, and very clean establishment occupies a cute, white, clapboard house opposite the west wall of Ratchadamnoen post office. Downstairs, the tile-floored, a/c rooms with en-suite cold showers are small but manageable, while upstairs, the seven wood-floored, fan rooms share three cold-water bathrooms. Fan B250, a/c B350

Khao San Palace Inn 139 Thanon Khao San ☎ 02 282 0578, ⓦ khaosanpalace.com; map pp.100–101. Clean and well-appointed hotel, hung with appealing black-and-white photos of Bangkok, with a rooftop pool. Even the cheapest rooms have bathrooms, windows, a/c and satellite TV and are nicely tiled, making them good value, while some have panoramic views. B720

Lek House 125 Thanon Khao San ☎ 02 281 8441; map pp.100–101. Classic old-style Khao San guesthouse, in a stand-alone, multi-storey, yellow building, so most of the twenty rooms have windows; go for one on the front with a balcony, if you want the full Khao San blast. Bedrooms are small and basic, with thin partition walls but thick mattresses; bathrooms are shared and cold-water. Less shabby than many others in the same price bracket and friendlier than most. Can get noisy at night as it's right next to the popular *Silk Bar*. B240

Live Good East off Thanon Tanao ☎ 02 282 5092; map pp.100–101. Cheap, small and simple rooms in this friendly, back-alley guesthouse in a modern block, just off the veggie-restaurants soi, 1min from Khao San. Budget options have fans, wall views and shared cold-water bathrooms. En-suite (hot showers) fan rooms are larger and most have outlooks of sorts. Shared bathroom B200, en suite B350

Shambara 138 Thanon Khao San ☎ 02 282 7968, ⓦ shambarabangkok.com; map pp.100–101. This calm little hideaway is set down a tiny soi at the eastern end of Khao San and has just nine simple but individually designed fan and a/c rooms, most with windows, sharing two shower rooms and two toilets. Good single rates. Very popular, especially with solo women travellers, so book well ahead. Fan B450, a/c B560

WEST: AROUND WAT CHANA SONGKHRAM, PHRA ARTHIT AND THE RIVER

Bella Bella House Soi Ram Bhuttri ☎ 02 629 3090; map pp.100–101. Above an attractive, plant-strewn café, the pastel-coloured rooms here are no frills but well priced, and a few boast lovely views over Wat Chana Songkhram. The cheapest share cold-water bathrooms, a notch up gets you an en-suite hot shower, while the most expensive have a/c. In-room wi-fi available throughout. Shared bathroom B300, en suite B410, a/c B490

KC Guest House 64 Trok Kai Chae, corner of Thanon Phra Sumen ☎ 02 282 0618, ⓦ kc64guesthouse.com; map pp.100–101. Friendly, family-run guesthouse offering exceptionally clean, colourful rooms, either en suite (with hot water) or with shared, cold-water bathrooms. There's also a rooftop terrace and a decked eating area on the soi in front of 7-Eleven. Shared bathroom B300, en suite B420, a/c B520

Lamphu House 75 Soi Ram Bhuttri ☎ 02 629 5861–2, ⓦ lamphuhouse.com; map pp.100–101. With smart

1

bamboo beds, coconut-wood clothes rails, and elegant rattan lamps in all the rooms, this travellers' hotel set round a quiet courtyard has a calm, modern feel. Cheapest fan rooms share facilities and have no outside view, while the triples and four-bed rooms are popular with families. Wi-fi is available throughout. Shared bathroom B400, en suite B520, a/c B630

Merry V Soi Ram Bhuttri ✆02 282 9267; map pp.100–101. Large, efficiently run guesthouse offering some of the cheapest accommodation in Banglamphu. Bottom-end rooms are basic and small, many share bathrooms and it's pot luck whether you get a window or not. Better en-suites with hot showers and a/c versions are also available. Decent rates for singles. B200

Navalai River Resort 45/1 Thanon Phra Arthit ✆02 280 9955, ⓦnavalai.com; map pp.100–101. Style-conscious riverfront hotel, with an elegant rooftop pool, modishly furnished rooms, and river views from the most desirable. There's a/c, DVDs, bathtubs, private balconies and free wi-fi throughout, and the excellent riverside *Aquatini* restaurant is at ground level (see p.152). Buffet breakfast included. B2900

★ **New Siam 2** 50 Trok Rong Mai ✆02 282 2795, ⓦwww.newsiam.net; map pp.100–101. Very pleasant and well-run small hotel whose en-suite rooms with fan and cold shower or a/c and hot shower stand out for their thoughtfully designed extras such as in-room safes, cable TV and drying rails on the balconies. Occupies a quiet but convenient location and has a small streetside pool. Popular with families, and triple rooms are also available. Fan B690, a/c B790

New Siam Riverside 21 Thanon Phra Arthit ✆02 629 3535, ⓦnewsiam.net; map pp.100–101. Occupying a prime riverside spot, the latest in the *New Siam* empire offers well-designed, good-value rooms. Even the cheapest have a/c, full amenities and wi-fi, while the best of them boast fabulous river views from windows or private balconies. Also has a large riverside swimming pool and terrace restaurant. Breakfast included. B1390

Peachy Guest House 10 Thanon Phra Arthit ✆02 281 6471; map pp.100–101. Popular, good-value, long-running Bangkok institution set round a small, late-night courtyard bar. Offers lots of clean, simple, wooden-floored rooms, most with shared bathrooms but some with a/c. Very good rates for singles. Fan and shared bathroom B200, a/c and shared bathroom B300, a/c en suite B400

★ **Praya Palazzo** 757/1 Soi 2, Thanon Somdet Phra Pinklao ✆02 883 2998, ⓦprayapalazzo.com; map pp.100–101. A peaceful riverside sanctuary right opposite Banglamphu, this large, graceful, Italianate mansion has been lovingly restored by an architecture professor, with great attention to detail – right down to the wallpaper and lampshades – to give the feel of its 1920s origins. Twenty-first century luxuries have been overlaid, of course, such as

DVDs, free wi-fi and, in the bathrooms, big-head showers to go alongside the brass taps and swathes of coloured marble. There's a lovely pool in the garden and an excellent restaurant too (see p.152), where complimentary breakfast and afternoon tea are served; a spa is planned. Access is by the free hotel boat, which shuttles across to Phra Arthit express-boat pier (where a satellite hotel office operates in high season) and up to Tha Wasukri (for Dusit) on demand. Discounts for longer stays. B7900

NORTH: SAMSEN SOIS AND THEWET

Lamphu Treehouse 155 Saphan Wanchat, Thanon Phracha Thipatai ✆02 282 0991–2, ⓦlamphu treehotel.com; map pp.100–101. Named after the *lamphu* trees that line the adjacent canal, this attractively turned-out guesthouse offers smart, a/c rooms, all with balconies and plenty of polished teakwood fittings, among other traditional Thai decorative elements. There's a pool, an inviting rooftop terrace, and wi-fi in the lobby. It's in a quiet neighbourhood but just a few minutes' walk from Democracy. Breakfast included. B1450

Nakorn Ping 9/1 Soi 6, Thanon Samsen ✆02 281 6574, ⓦnakornpinghotel.com; map pp.100–101. In a low-rise, orange building dotted with plants on a fairly quiet soi, this place sports some classic elements of a Thai-Chinese hotel: spittoons for waste baskets, gnarly wooden furniture and little natural light. However, it's very clean, efficiently run and good value, offering fridges, cable TV and bathrooms in all rooms, and hot showers in the a/c options. Fan B400, a/c B500

★ **Old Bangkok Inn** 609 Thanon Phra Sumen ✆02 629 1787, ⓦoldbangkokinn.com; map pp.100–101. This chic little boutique guesthouse with an eco-friendly philosophy has just ten a/c rooms, each of them individually styled in dark wood, with antique northern Thai partitions, Burmese doors, beds and ironwork lamps, plus elegant contemporary-accented bathrooms. All rooms have a PC with free internet access, and a DVD player. Some also have a tiny private garden. A 10min walk from Khao San. B3200

★ **Phra Nakorn Norn Len** 46 Thewet Soi 1, Thewet ✆02 628 8188, ⓦphranakorn-nornlen.com; map pp.100–101. What was once a seedy short-time motel has been transformed into a bohemian haven with genuine eco-conscious and socially engaged sensibilities and a tangible fair-trade philosophy. Every one of the comfortable, though not luxurious, rooms has been hand-painted to a different retro Thai design, and each has a cute bathroom, balcony, free wi-fi and a/c. Public areas include a kids' play area and a washing machine and dryer; the rooftop enjoys unrivalled views of Wat Indraviharn's huge standing Buddha and is partly given over to growing organic veg for the restaurant. Mostly organic vegetarian breakfast included. B2400

★ **Rajata** Soi 6, Thanon Samsen ☎02 628 8084, ⓦrajatahotel.com; map pp.100–101. This traditional motel of large bedrooms and bathrooms around a quiet courtyard has been subtly transformed with retro furniture, hundreds of plants and a friendly welcome. All of the shining white, spotlessly clean accommodation has a/c and satellite TV; B200 extra gets you a hot shower, mini-bar and a complimentary breakfast in the courtyard café. Computers available, free wi-fi. B650

Sawatdee 71 Thanon Sri Ayutthaya (at Soi 16), Thewet ☎02 281 0757; map pp.100–101. Cheap and basic, but friendlier than many in the Thewet area, this long-running old-style guesthouse offers no-frills fan rooms with partition walls. Shared bathroom B200, en suite B400

Sri Ayutthaya 23/11 Thanon Sri Ayutthaya (at Soi 14), Thewet ☎02 282 5942; map pp.100–101. The most attractive guesthouse in Thewet, where most of the good-sized rooms (choose between fan rooms without private bathroom and en suites with a/c) are elegantly done out with wood-panelled walls and beautiful polished wood floors; these have now been augmented by a few modern, "Superior" rooms (B1000) done out in bright, fetching colours. Hot showers throughout. Fan B450, a/c B650

★ **Tavee** 83 Soi 14, Thanon Sri Ayutthaya, Thewet ☎02 280 1447; map pp.100–101. Down a pedestrian alley behind *Sri Ayutthaya* and owned by the same family, but quieter and friendlier. Behind the stylish little café, with its chillout music, computers and free wi-fi, the fan rooms sport attractive wood floors and share chic hot-water bathrooms, while the en-suite a/c options are larger and enjoy a few more decorative touches. Fan B450, a/c B700

SOUTH: SOUTH OF DEMOCRACY

Baan Dinso 113 Trok Sin, Thanon Dinso ☎02 622 0560, ⓦbaandinso.com; map pp.100–101. This tasteful, upmarket little guesthouse occupies an elegant 1920s Thai house all done out in cool buttermilk paintwork and polished teak floors. Prices are a little steep considering that all but the deluxe rooms have to use shared ground-floor, hot-water bathrooms, but they all have a/c and DVD players and there's free wi-fi. Hostelling International members get a ten percent discount. Breakfast included. Very good single rates. B2200

★ **The Bhuthorn** 96 Thanon Phraeng Phuthon, just off Thanon Kanlayana Maitri ☎02 622 2270, ⓦthebhuthorn.com; map pp.100–101. The architect-owners have beautifully converted this hundred-year-old shophouse into a B&B. Behind the small lobby lie just three elegant rooms (including a junior suite with a mezzanine for B5000), fitted with Chinese, Thai and Western dark-wood antique furniture, chandeliers, *khon* masks and other objets d'art, as well as DVDs and additional modern comforts. Full breakfast (including daily Thai specials), afternoon tea and wi-fi included. B3600

Boonsiri Place 55 Thanon Buranasart ☎02 622 2189, ⓦboonsiriplace.com; map pp.100–101. Run by two charming sisters, this mid-sized hotel is notable for its good value, environmentally conscious policies and location in a lively, seedy old neighbourhood, just a 10min walk from the Grand Palace. Each of its 48 large a/c rooms (an extra B200 buys you considerably more space in a "Deluxe" room) is hung with a different painting commissioned from the late Thai traditional temple artist Chanok Chunchob. Wi-fi and computers available. Buffet breakfast included. B1400

RATANAKOSIN AND AROUND

Several small, upmarket hotels have recently opened on the west side of Ratanakosin, which put you in a peerless location, in a quiet, traditional, heavily Chinese neighbourhood of low-rise shophouses, overlooking the river and on the doorsteps of Wat Pho and the Grand Palace. The restaurants and nightlife of Banglamphu are within walking distance if you fancy a bit more of a buzz, while the sights of Thonburi and Chinatown, and Saphan Taksin Skytrain station are just a public boat ride away. It's also well worth considering *Ibrik Resort*, a small, appealing hotel directly opposite Ratanakosin on the Thonburi bank of the Chao Phraya, whose main link with the rest of the city is by cross-river boat.

Arun Residence 36 Soi Pratu Nokyung, Thanon Maharat ☎02 221 9158, ⓦarunresidence.com; map p.83. Stunning views of Wat Arun and charming, wooden-floored rooms and suites that mix traditional and contemporary Thai styles. Occupying an eccentrically converted shophouse (plumbing can sometimes be a problem), the hotel also has an attractive lounge with internet access, a rooftop bar and a good European and Thai restaurant, *The Deck*, where breakfast (included in the price) is served. B3500

The Asadang Thanon Atsadang, corner of Thanon Phraya Si ☎085 180 7100, ⓦtheasadang.com; map p.83. In an early-twentieth-century neoclassical mansion on Ratanakosin's doorstep, this very upscale B&B is perhaps a little truer to Thai roots than its sister, *The Bhuthorn* (see above), showcasing antique Thai furniture, carved lintels and attractive local fabrics; it's certainly airier and more spacious, with white wooden walls throughout. If you can manage the narrow, steep spiral staircase (and the higher rate, B4500), plump for the cute roof-top "Ratchabopit" overlooking the eponymous temple, which boasts a rocking chair, full-length windows and a plant-strewn private terrace. Free wi-fi throughout. Full breakfast (including daily Thai specials) included. B3600

Aurum: The River Place 394/27–29 Soi Pansook, Thanon Maharat ☎02 622 2248, ⓦaurum-bangkok .com; map p.83. Modelled on a French townhouse, with wooden shutters and wrought-iron balconies, this spruce, four-storey hotel is set back very slightly from the river and

1

four of the rooms are "City View" only, but the other eight offer at least partial views of the water. Splashed with colourful Thai fabrics and sporting heavily varnished wooden floors, the well-equipped rooms are a little on the small side, apart from those on the top floor. There's free wi-fi and a daytime riverside café, *Vivi The Coffee Place*, where complimentary breakfast is served. B3700

Chakrabongse Villas 396 Thanon Maharat ☎ 02 222 1290, ⌨ thaivillas.com; map p.83. Upmarket riverside accommodation with a difference: nine tranquil rooms, suites and villas beautifully furnished in a choice of Thai, Chinese and Moroccan styles, set in the luxuriant gardens of hundred-year-old Chakrabongse House overlooking Wat Arun. All have a/c, free wi-fi and cable TV, and there's a small, attractive swimming pool and a riverfront pavilion for relaxing or dining (if ordered in advance). Canoes and bicycles available for guests. B5850

★ **Ibrik Resort by the River** 256 Soi Wat Rakang ☎ 02 848 9220, ⌨ ibrikresort.com; map p.83. With just three rooms, this is the most bijou of boutique resorts. Each room is beautifully appointed in boho-chic style, with traditional wood floors, modernist white walls and sparkling silk accessories – and two of them have balconies right over the Chao Phraya River. It's just like staying at a trendy friend's home, in a neighbourhood that sees hardly any other tourists. Located next door to *Supatra River House* restaurant and 5min walk from either express-boat stop Tha Wang Lang or the cross-river pier at Wat Rakhang (for Tha Chang and the Grand Palace). Breakfast included. B4000

Sala Arun 47 Soi Tha Thien, Thanon Maharat ☎ 02 622 2932–3, ⌨ salaarun.com; map p.83. Sister property to *Arun Residence*, also on the river, two blocks up. The six teak-floored rooms (and one suite) feature objets d'art from the owners' worldwide travels, DVDs, iPod docks and free wi-fi, while complimentary breakfast is served in the boldly coloured ground-floor café, which has computers and a small terrace with armchairs facing Wat Arun. All bedrooms come with balconies and all are the same price, so it's best to avoid city-view "Krungthep" and "Sukhothai". B3500

CHINATOWN AND HUALAMPHONG STATION AREA

Set between the Ratanakosin sights and downtown, Chinatown (Sampeng) is among the most frantic and fume-choked parts of Bangkok – and there's quite some competition. If you're in the mood, however, it's got plenty of interest, sees barely any Western overnighters, and is also very handy for Hualamphong Station, which is on the subway system.

Baan Hualamphong 336/20 Soi Chalong Krung ☎ 02 639 8054, ⌨ baanhualampong.com; map p.107. Just 5min from Hualamphong, this stylish wooden guesthouse

is the most welcoming of several similar places in the soi, with a traveller-friendly vibe. There are big, bright, twin rooms plus five-person dorms, but most bedrooms share bathrooms. Has kitchen, internet and laundry facilities, inviting lounging areas and a left-luggage service, and is open 24hr. Very good single rates. Dorm B220, fan double B520, a/c double B720

FF Guest House 338/10 Trok La-O, off Thanon Rama IV ☎ 02 233 4168; map p.107. Tiny, family-run guesthouse offering ten cheap, cell-like but perfectly acceptable wooden-floored fan rooms with shared, cold-water bathrooms. No other facilities. A 5min walk from the train and subway stations. Decent single rates. B250

Grand China Princess 215 Thanon Yaowarat ☎ 02 224 9977, ⌨ grandchina.com; map p.107. The poshest hotel in Chinatown, part of the reliable, local Dusit chain, boasts fairly luxurious accommodation in its 25-storey tower close to the heart of the bustle, with stunning views over all the city landmarks (the best take in the river), a small rooftop swimming pool, revolving panoramic restaurant and internet in every room. B2925

★ **Shanghai Mansion** 479 Thanon Yaowarat, next to *Scala* shark's fin restaurant ☎ 02 221 2121, ⌨ shanghaimansion.com; map p.107. The most design-conscious accommodation in Chinatown has embraced the modern Chinoiserie look with gusto. It's not actually an historic mansion, but has been purpose-built on the site of a former Beijing opera house, with most bedrooms (and their windows and private terraces) facing onto an appealing, four-storey atrium, and thus cosily isolated from the Chinatown frenzy. Rooms are prettily done out in silks, lacquer-look furniture and lanterns, featuring a lot of sumptuous reds and purples, as well as a/c, hot showers and free wi-fi. Breakfast included. B2500

SIAM SQUARE, THANON PLOENCHIT AND NORTHERN DOWNTOWN

Siam Square and nearby Thanon Ploenchit are as central as Bangkok gets: all the accommodation listed here is within walking distance of a Skytrain or subway station. On hand are the city's best shopping possibilities – notably the phalanx of malls along Thanon Rama I – and a wide choice of Thai and international restaurants and food courts. There's no ultra-cheap accommodation around here, but a few scaled-up guesthouses complement the expensive hotels. Concentrated in their own small "ghetto" on Soi Kasemsan 1, which runs north off Thanon Rama I, between the Bangkok Art and Cultural Centre and Jim Thompson's House, these offer typical travellers' facilities and basic hotel comforts – a/c and en-suite hot-water bathrooms – at moderate prices; the Khlong Saen Saeb canal-boat pier, Tha Saphan Hua Chang (easily accessed via Thanon Phrayathai), is especially handy for heading west to the Golden Mount and beyond, to Ratanakosin.

A-One Inn 25/13 Soi Kasemsan 1, Thanon Rama I ☎02 215 3029 or ☎02 216 4770, ⓦaoneinn.com; map p.119. The original upmarket guesthouse, and still justifiably popular, with a 24hr internet café, wi-fi and a reliable left-luggage room. All bedrooms have fridges and satellite TV and come in a variety of sizes, including triples; discounts for longer stays. B970

Centara Grand at Central World 999/99 Thanon Rama I ☎02 100 1234, ⓦcentarahotelsresorts.com; map p.119. Occupying floors 23 to 55 atop the north end of the huge, glossy Central World Plaza mall with its fifty restaurants and fifteen cinema screens, this is a luxurious cocoon high above the hot, noisy city. Views from the brightly coloured, contemporary rooms and the restaurants – particularly *Red Sky* (see p.155) and the appealingly laid-back, indoor-outdoor *Globe* lounge bar – are panoramic, and shared by the invitingly large swimming pool. A spa, gym and floodlit tennis courts flesh out the picture. B4450

Courtyard by Marriott 155/1 Soi Mahadlekluang 1, Thanon Rajdamri ☎02 690 1888, ⓦmarriott.com; map p.119. On a quiet, but very handy soi, this hotel offers most of the facilities of a five-star, but at more manageable prices. The modern design is seductive, gleaming white outside, candy colours and plenty of natural light inside, and there's a long, narrow, infinity pool, a fitness centre and reasonably priced massage rooms. Free wi-fi. B4200

★ **Four Seasons** 155 Thanon Rajdamri ☎02 126 8866, ⓦfourseasons.com; map p.119. The stately home of Bangkok's top hotel, formerly the *Regent*. Afternoon tea is still served in the monumental lobby, which is adorned with magnificent, vibrant eighteenth-century-style murals depicting the Thai cosmology, and flanked by acclaimed Thai, Italian and Japanese restaurants, a steakhouse and an opulent spa by MSpa. The large and luxurious rooms are decorated in warm Thai colours and dark wood, and there's an excellent concierge service. Discounts for longer stays. B8030

Golden House 1025/5–9 Thanon Ploenchit ☎02 252 9535–7, ⓦgoldenhousebangkok.com; map p.119. A very clean and welcoming small hotel in a peerless location, down a short soi by Chit Lom BTS. The plain but attractive, parquet-floored bedrooms are equipped with a/c, hot water, cable TV, free wi-fi and mini-bar – ask for one of the larger front rooms with bay windows, which leave just enough space for a couple of armchairs. Breakfast included. Long-term discounts available. B1650

Jim's Lodge 125/7 Soi Ruam Rudee, Thanon Ploenchit ☎02 255 3100, ⓦjimslodge.com; map p.119. In a relatively peaceful residential area, with friendly and helpful staff, offering international standards, including satellite TV, wi-fi and mini-bars, on a smaller scale and at bargain prices. There's no swimming pool, but there is a roof garden with outdoor jacuzzi. B1550

Lub.d 925/9 Thanon Rama I ☎02 612 4999, ⓦlubd

.com; map p.119. New branch of the hip, well-run Silom hostel (see p.148), with similar style and facilities (including women-only dorms). It's right on Thanon Rama I, under BTS National Stadium, so handy for just about everything but rather noisy. Dorm B550, double with shared bathroom B1400, en-suite double B1900

Luxx XL 82/8 Soi Lang Suan ☎02 684 1111, ⓦstaywithluxx.com/xl; map p.119. Quietly set back behind *Thang Long* restaurant, this hip boutique hotel (younger, but bigger brother of the original Silom *Luxx*) shelters large, balconied "Studio" rooms in a seductive contemporary style, all red wood and grey stone. As well as a 13m, infinity-edge, slate pool, all kinds of thoughtful extras are on offer: bicycles for use in nearby Lumphini Park; an honesty bar; and in the rooms, DVD players (with iPod and iPhone connections) and free wi-fi. Discounts for longer stays. B2600

Pathumwan Princess Hotel 444 Thanon Phrayathai ☎02 216 3700, ⓦpprincess.com; map p.119. Central luxury hotel, at the southern end of MBK Shopping Centre, that's recently been refurbished in a crisp, modern style. Service is of a high standard, and the facilities include a very good Italian restaurant, overlooking a large, saltwater swimming pool on the 8th floor, a spa and a huge, popular fitness club, The Olympic, that encompasses squash and tennis courts and a 400m jogging track. B5850

Siam Kempinski 991/9 Thanon Rama I ☎02 162 9000, ⓦkempinski.com/bangkok; map p.119. Though it's in downtown's throbbing heart, right behind Paragon shopping centre, this new, top-of-the-range offering from Europe's oldest luxury hotel group styles itself as a resort: all rooms turn in on a triangular garden, artfully landscaped with three pools, a kids' pool, trees, lawns, fountains and a beach-style rotunda bar (some ground-floor rooms even have direct access to one of the pools). As the site used to be part of the "lotus-pond palace", Wang Sra Pathum, the interior designers have made subtle but striking use of lotus motifs, complemented by over two hundred specially commissioned paintings and sculptures by Thai artists, amid the Art Deco-inspired architecture. There's also a beautiful spa, an impressive kids' club and an excellent contemporary Thai restaurant, *Sra Bua* (see p.156). B8775

Sofitel Centara Grand 1695 Thanon Phaholyothin ☎02 541 1234, ⓦcentarahotelsresorts.com; map pp.80–81. The 560-room flagship of the luxury Centara group still boasts seven restaurants from around the world and a fine spa but has had a highly successful recent makeover in a sleek, sharp modern idiom. It's handy for Don Muang airport, near Chatuchak Market and Mo Chit BTS (connected to both by shuttle buses), and 5min walk from Phahon Yothin subway. B4000

★ **Swissôtel Nai Lert Park** 2 Thanon Witthayu ☎02 253 0123, ⓦswissotel.com; map p.119. This welcoming, low-rise hotel is distinguished by its lushly beautiful

1

gardens, overlooked by many of the chic and spacious, balconied bedrooms; set into the grounds are a landscaped swimming pool, tennis courts, squash court and popular spa and health club. Good deli-café, cool bar and fine Japanese, French and Chinese restaurants. B4000

Ten Face 81 Soi 2, Soi Ruam Rudee ☎02 695 4242, ⓦtenfacebangkok.com; map p.119. The name comes from Totsagan, the ten-faced demon of the *Ramakien* (see p.88); this place ingeniously combines sleek, contemporary design with striking artworks inspired by the national myth, without being gimmicky. All the rooms are spacious suites with espresso machines, free wi-fi, SIM cards and iPods, some with small kitchens; ask for a room at the back if you're worried about noise from the nearby expressway. There's a fusion restaurant, fitness centre, long, narrow "dipping" pool and shuttle service to Ploen Chit Skytrain, plus a special concierge, who DJs in the ultra-hip *Sita Bar* and dispenses the lowdown on Bangkok parties and happenings. B3200

Wendy House 36/2 Soi Kasemsan 1, Thanon Rama I ☎02 214 1149, ⓦwendyguesthouse.com; map p.119. Friendly and well-run guesthouse, with smart, clean and comfortable rooms, all with fridge, cable TV and free wi-fi. There are internet terminals in the ground-floor café, where breakfast (included in the price) is served. Reliable luggage storage, and long-stay discounts available. B1100

White Lodge 36/8 Soi Kasemsan 1, Thanon Rama I ☎02 216 8867 or ☎02 215 3041, 🖷02 216 8228; map p.119. Cheapest guesthouse on the soi, and not always the cleanest, with plain white cubicles and a lively, welcoming atmosphere – the best rooms, bright and quiet, are on the upper floors. B500

DOWNTOWN: SOUTH OF THANON RAMA IV

South of Thanon Rama IV, the area sometimes known as Bangrak contains a full cross section of accommodation. Tucked away at its eastern edge, there are a few cheap places that are worth recommending in the small travellers' ghetto of Soi Ngam Duphli and adjacent Soi Sri Bamphen and Soi Saphan Khu. The neighbourhood is often traffic-clogged and occasionally seedy, but is close to Lumphini Park and subway station and handy for Suvarnabhumi Airport. As well as a fair scattering of medium-range places, the arc between Thanon Rama IV and the river also lays claim to the capital's biggest selection of top hotels, which are among the most opulent in the world. Traversed by the Skytrain, this area is especially good for eating and for gay and straight nightlife, mostly near the east end of Thanon Silom (around which several gay-friendly hotels are scattered). Staying by the river itself in the atmospheric area around Thanon Charoen Krung, also known as New Road, has the added advantage of easy access to express boats.

★ **Anantara Riverside** 257 Thanon Charoennakorn ☎02 476 0022, ⓦanantara.com; map p.79. A luxury retreat from the frenetic city centre, well to the south on the Thonburi bank, but connected to Taksin Bridge (for the Skytrain and Chao Phraya express boats), 15min away, by hotel ferries every 20min. Arrayed around a highly appealing, landscaped swimming pool, the tranquil, riverside gardens are filled with birdsong, while the stylish and spacious bedrooms come with varnished hardwood floors and balconies. There's a fitness centre, tennis courts, kids' club, a branch of the classy Mandara Spas, and among a wide choice of eateries, a good Japanese teppanyaki house. B5900

Anantara Sathorn 36 Thanon Narathiwat Ratchanakharin ☎02 210 9000, ⓦanantara.com; map pp.80–81. With its enclosed, 32m outdoor pool at the centre of activity, toddlers' pool, children's play room and wide choice of suites, this new high-rise hotel is very popular with families. There's also a gym, a tennis court and a very good spa, while the spacious, balconied rooms show restrained contemporary decor. Hotel minibuses run to BTS Chong Nonsi hourly during the day, which is otherwise a 15min walk away. B3000

Baan Saladaeng 69/2 Soi 3, Thanon Saladaeng ☎02 636 3038, ⓦbaansaladaeng.com; map p.126. On a tiny, central alley, this chic designer guesthouse offers eleven individually styled and priced rooms, such as the Pop Art Mania Room and the Moroccan Suite, some with bathtubs and balconies and one with its bath on the balcony. A/c, rain showers, mini-bars, cable TV, comfy beds and free wi-fi throughout. No children. Breakfast included. B1000

ETZ Hostel 5/3 Soi Ngam Duphli ☎02 286 9424, ⓦetzhostel.com; map pp.80–81. Above a branch of the recommended ETC travel agent, and very handy for Lumphini subway and Thanon Rama IV, though conse-quently a little noisy. Helpful and very clean, the hostel sports playful contemporary decor in primary colours, a popular roof terrace and a large, attractive lounge with free computers. The a/c dorms share hot showers and fit four to twelve people, or you could upgrade to a bright white double with large, en-suite, hot-water bathroom. Breakfast and luggage storage are available; free wi-fi throughout. Dorm B200, double B900

La Residence 173/8–9 Thanon Suriwong ☎02 266 5400–1, ⓦlaresidencebangkok.com; map p.126 A small, intimate boutique hotel where the tasteful, indi-vidually decorated bedrooms – including proper single rooms at proper single rates – stretch to mini-bars, safes, wi-fi and cable TV. Continental breakfast included. B2350

Lub.d 4 Thanon Decho ☎02 634 7999, ⓦlubd.com; map p.126. Meaning "sleep well" (*lap dii*), this buzzing, upmarket hostel has a/c and hot water throughout and an industrial feel to its stylishly lit decor. This crisp modernity extends to the bedrooms, among which the dorms (some women-only) and the bunk-bedded "Railway" private rooms share large bathroom areas, while the top-of-the-range en-suite doubles boast TVs. The hostel lays on some interesting activities and tours, and there's free wi-fi throughout, a popular bar and café, washing machines, free storage facilities and free internet terminals, but no kitchen. Dorm B350, "Railway" B1100, double B1500

Luxx 6/11 Thanon Decho ☎02 635 8800, ⓦstaywithluxx.com; map p.126. Welcoming boutique hotel offering a good dose of contemporary style at reasonable prices. Decorated in white, grey and natural teak, the rooms feature DVD players, free wi-fi and cute wooden baths surmounted by rain showers. Discounts for longer stays. Breakfast included. B2200

Malaysia 54 Soi Ngam Duphli ☎02 679 7127–36, ⓦmalaysiahotelbkk.com; map pp.80–81. Once a travellers' legend famous for its compendious noticeboard, now better known for its seedy 24hr coffee shop and massage parlour. The accommodation itself is reasonable value though: the rooms are large and have a/c, mini-bars and hot-water bathrooms; some have cable TV. There's also a swimming pool and internet access. Gay-friendly. B798

★ **New Road Guest House** 1216/1 Thanon Charoen Krung, between sois 34 and 36 ☎02 630 9371, ⓦvisitbeyond.com/Thailand; map p.126. Thai head-quarters of Danish backpacker tour operator, Visit Beyond, offering a wide choice of accommodation around a court-yard off New Road, as well as a helpful service centre and travel agent, and interesting Thailand tours (see p.173). There are fan and a/c dorms, as well as "Backpacker" fan rooms with mini-bars and well-equipped, hot-water bathrooms; a/c rooms sport attractive wooden floors, Thai decorative touches and cable TV. Guests can hang out in the restaurant, the sociable bar with pool table or the DVD room; computers, free wi-fi and free baggage storage are available. Dorm B160, fan double B450, a/c double B900

★ **Peninsula Bangkok** 333 Thanon Charoennakorn ☎02 861 2888, ⓦpeninsula.com; map p.126. On the Thonburi bank, with shuttle boats down to Taksin Bridge and its BTS station. Superb top-class hotel: service is flawless, the ultra-luxurious decor stylishly blends traditional Western and Asian design, and every room has a panoramic view of the Chao Phraya. The lovely riverside gardens shelter a three-tiered pool, a beautiful spa run by ESPA, a fitness centre and tennis courts. B12,500

Rose 118 Thanon Suriwong ☎02 266 8268–72, ⓦrosehotelbkk.com; map p.126. Set back from the main road but very handy for the city's nightlife, this 30-year-old hotel has been cleverly refurbished: the compact rooms (all with bathtubs and wi-fi) now boast a simple but stylish, modernist look, in keeping with the age of the place. The ground-floor public rooms, where breakfast (included in the price) is served, are more elegant again, and there's

a beautiful swimming pool (with a small gym and dry saunas) at the back. B2150

★ **Sala Thai Daily Mansion** 15 Soi Saphan Khu ☎02 287 1436; map pp.80–81. The last and best of several budget guesthouses on this quiet, narrow alleyway off Soi Saphan Khu, near Soi Sri Bamphen. A clean and efficiently run place, with bright, cheerful rooms with wall fans, sharing hot-water bathrooms, and a large, leafy roof garden. Decent rates for single rooms. Fan B400, a/c B600

★ **Sukhothai** 13/3 Thanon Sathorn Tai ☎02 344 8888, ⓦsukhothai.com; map p.126. The most elegant of Bangkok's top hotels, its decor inspired by the walled city of Sukhothai, offers low-rise accommodation, as well as a beautiful garden spa, all coolly furnished in silks, teak and granite. Service is of the highest standard and the architecture makes the most of the views of the surrounding six acres of gardens, lotus ponds and pools dotted with statuary. There's also a health club, 25m infinity pool, squash and tennis courts, and excellent restaurants including *Celadon* (see p.156). B9180

Swan 31 Soi 36, Thanon Charoen Krung ☎02 235 9271–3, ⓦswanhotelbkk.com; map p.126. Next to the stately residence of the French ambassador, this good-value, well-run and welcoming Chinese hotel has successfully upgraded, with regular renovations, to keep up with the times. Arrayed around a 15m pool, the rooms are bright, clean and spacious (though bathrooms in the standard rooms are small), with a/c, hot water, cable TV, mini-bars and armchairs; some have balconies with armchairs. Computers and wi-fi available. Breakfast included. B1500

Swiss Lodge 3 Thanon Convent ☎02 233 5345, ⓦswisslodge.com; map p.126. Swish, friendly, good-value boutique hotel, with high standards of service, just off Thanon Silom and ideally placed for business and nightlife. The tiny terrace swimming pool confirms the national stereotypes of neatness and clever design, while the restaurant offers a range of savoury and sweet fondues. Free wi-fi throughout; buffet breakfast included. B1990

Tarntawan Place 119/5–10 Thanon Suriwong ☎02 238 2620, ⓦtarntawan.com; map p.126. Set back from the main road, a pretty, flower-strewn lobby announces this welcoming and well-run, gay-friendly hotel. The decent-sized, well-equipped rooms are gracefully furnished in natural colours, with free wi-fi. Guests also receive free breakfast, as well as reduced-price entry to a gym and swimming pool on Soi Thaniya. Discounts for longer stays. B2900

THANON SUKHUMVIT

Thanon Sukhumvit is Bangkok's longest road – it keeps going east all the way to Cambodia – but for such an important artery it's far too narrow for the volume of traffic that needs to use it, and is further hemmed in by the Skytrain line that runs above it. Packed with high-rise

1

hotels and office blocks, an impressive array of specialist restaurants (from Lebanese to Lao), and stall after stall selling cheap souvenirs and T-shirts, it's a lively place that attracts a high proportion of single male tourists to its enclaves of girlie bars on Soi Nana Tai and Soi Cowboy. But for the most part it's not a seedy area, and is home to many expats and middle-class Thais. The majority of overnighters are business travellers, though Sukhumvit also has several very good mid-priced guesthouses. Even at the west end of Sukhumvit, many of the sois are refreshingly quiet, even leafy; transport down the longer sois is provided by motorbike-taxi (*mohtoesai*) drivers who wait at the soi's mouth, clad in numbered waistcoats. Hotels further east are quite convenient for Suvarnabhumi Airport but far from the main shopping and eating hubs. Odd-numbered sois run off the north side of Thanon Sukhumvit, even-numbered off the south side; many of the sois are long enough to have sub-sois running off them, which usually have their own names.

Amari Boulevard Soi 5 ☎ 02 255 2930, ⓦ amari.com; map p.124. At this long-running but modernized four-star tourist hotel, it's worth paying a little extra for a deluxe room to enjoy fine views of the Bangkok skyline and have a bit more space and a DVD player. The attractive sixth-floor rooftop swimming pool and garden terrace becomes the Thai-food restaurant *Season* in the evenings. Substantial discounts in low season. B3800

The Atlanta At the far southern end of Soi 2 ☎ 02 252 1650, ⓦ theatlantahotelbangkok.com; map p.124. A Bangkok institution, this classic, five-storey budget hotel was built in 1952 around a famously photogenic Art Deco-style lobby and continues to emphasize an old-fashioned hospitality. It offers some of the cheapest accommodation on Sukhumvit: rooms are plain and simple, though they are all en suite and some have a/c and hot water; many have small balconies. There's a swimming pool and kids' pool in the garden, wi-fi and internet access, a good restaurant and a free left-luggage facility. Fan B700, a/c B800

The Eugenia 267 Soi 31 ☎ 02 259 9017, ⓦ theeugenia.com; map p.124. This cosy little Relais & Chateaux hideaway of just twelve rooms in a late nineteenth-century mansion re-creates an ambience of old-fashioned Indochinese charm with four-poster beds, freestanding copper bathtubs, mellow colour schemes and a bijou courtyard pool. It's a good 15min walk from BTS Phrom Pong but free hotel transport is offered from here. Discounts for stays of two nights or more. B6800

Imm Fusion 1594/50 Thanon Sukhumvit, 30m walk west along Thanon Sukhumvit from BTS On Nut, exit 2, beyond Soi 50 ☎ 02 331 5555, ⓦ immhotel.com; map p.124. Step through the entrance of this attractively themed hotel and you could be in Morocco, with its rich earthy colours, wrought ironwork, pretty tiles and plenty of Moorish arches. Rooms are comfortable and equally tasteful, and come with a/c, hot showers, TV, free wi-fi and breakfast. There's a gorgeous indoor pool, spa and restaurant, and the staff are charming. B1530

Napa Place 11/3 Soi Naphasap 2, off Soi 36 ☎ 02 661 5525, ⓦ napaplace.com; map p.124. Down a quiet sub-soi (second right off Soi 36), a 10min walk from BTS Thong Lo, this welcoming, family-friendly guesthouse offers plenty of cosy public spaces and large bedrooms, all with their own sitting areas. Teak floors and furniture are set off by cream furnishings and other natural colours in the very clean rooms, which feature a/c, hot water, mini-bars, cable TV and free broadband (free computers also available). Discounted weekly rates. B2825

Park Plaza 9 Soi 18 ☎ 02 658 7000, ⓦ parkplaza.com/bangkokth_soi18; map p.124. The quieter and newer of two nearby Park Plazas, this small hotel is topped by an appealing, open-air 20m pool, gym and bar-restaurant on the eighth floor. Fitted with DVD players, the rooms sport a perky contemporary look, with bright colours set against businessman's black; the superior rooms enjoy better views than the pricier deluxe options. B3295

★ **PS Guesthouse** 26/1 Soi 8 ☎ 02 255 2309, ⓔ psguesthouse@hotmail.com; map p.124. This small, calm, friendly guesthouse offers huge, airy and very well-equipped rooms, each with a/c, hot showers, TV, safety box, fridge, free tea and coffee, and refreshingly green, plant-screened balconies. Pay a little extra for in-room kitchen facilities. Complimentary wi-fi throughout. B900

Rex Hotel Between sois 32 and 34 (opposite Soi 49), about 300m west from BTS Thong Lo, exit 2 ☎ 02 259 0106–15, ⓦ rexhotelbangkok.com; map p.124. The best-value accommodation close to the Eastern Bus Terminal (one stop on the BTS), this old-fashioned but attractively refurbished hotel is comfortable and run with an old-world graciousness. A rooftop pool and a restaurant complement the spacious a/c rooms. B1150

Seven 3/15 Soi Sawasdee 1, off Soi 31 ☎ 02 662 0951, ⓦ sleepatseven.com; map p.124. A personable welcome and plenty of local advice awaits once you head down the quiet alley to this super-stylish B&B. Bold, cartoon-like murals, as well as DVDs, iPod docks, big-head showers and balconies, enhance the six rooms, which are priced according to size. All include a good, free, continental breakfast, wi-fi, local calls and the loan of a local mobile phone. B3000

Suk 11 Behind the 7-Eleven store at 1/33 Soi 11 ☎ 02 253 5927, ⓦ suk11.com; map p.124. One of the most unusual little hotels in Bangkok, this is also the most backpacker-orientated guesthouse in the area. The interior of the apparently ordinary apartment-style building has been transformed to resemble a village of traditional wooden houses, accessed by a dimly lit plankway that winds past a variety of guest rooms, terraces and lounging areas. The rooms themselves are simple but comfortable, all with a/c, and some are en suite; all showers are hot. It's well run and thoughtfully appointed, provides free breakfast, has pay wi-fi (in the lobby), computers and washing machines, and stores left luggage (B20/day). Good rates for singles; triples and family rooms also available. Shared bathroom B749, en suite B963

SUVARNABHUMI AIRPORT

Novotel Suvarnabhumi 02 131 1111, novotel .com. The official airport hotel, set within the complex and a 10min walk from arrivals via a walkway in the basement (or catch the shuttle bus from outside arrivals Gate 4). Offering smart, contemporary rooms with marble bathrooms, Thai, Japanese, Cantonese and international restaurants, a swimming pool and fitness centre, the *Novotel* operates on a 24hr basis – you can check in at any time, and check out 24hr later. B6000

Queens Garden Resort 5min drive from the airport complex, to the north near Highway 7 02 172 6114, queensgardenresort.net. Hot water, a/c, mini-bar and satellite TV in all of the plain bedrooms, which include triples and connecting rooms. Facilities include a restaurant, beer garden, pool table, computers and wi-fi. 24-hour pick-ups (B150 each way per room) are available, but a regular metered taxi from the airport will be cheaper, even with the B50 airport tax. B1000

EATING

As you'd expect, nowhere in Thailand can compete with Bangkok's diversity when it comes to food: it boasts an astonishing fifty thousand places to eat, almost one for every hundred citizens. Although prices are generally higher here than in the provinces, it's still easy to dine well on a budget. For **Thai** food, the best gourmet restaurants in the country operate from the downtown districts, proffering wonderful royal, traditional and regional cuisines that definitely merit a visit. At the lower end of the price scale, one-dish meals from around the country are rustled up at the **food courts** of shopping centres and department stores, as well as at **night markets** and **street stalls**, which are so numerous in Bangkok that we can only flag the most promising areas. For the non-Thai cuisines, Chinatown naturally rates as the most authentic district for pure **Chinese** food; likewise neighbouring Pahurat, the capital's Indian enclave, is best for unadulterated **Indian** dishes, while there's a sprinkling of Indian and (mostly southern Thai) **Muslim** restaurants around Silom's Maha Uma Devi Temple and nearby Thanon Charoen Krung. Sukhumvit's Soi 3 is a hub for **Middle Eastern** cafés, complete with hookah pipes at the outdoor tables; good, comparatively cheap **Japanese** restaurants are concentrated on Soi Thaniya, at the east end of Thanon Silom; and there's a Korean enclave in Sukhumvit Plaza, at the corner of Soi 12. In the more expensive restaurants listed below you may have to pay a ten percent **service charge** and seven percent VAT.

BANGLAMPHU AND THE DEMOCRACY MONUMENT AREA

Copycat entrepreneurship means that Khao San is stacked full of backpacker restaurants serving near-identical Western and (mostly) watered-down Thai food; there's even a lane, one block east, parallel to Thanon Tanao (behind *Burger King*), that's dominated by vegetarian cafés, following a trend started by *May Kaidee*. Hot-food stalls selling very cheap night-market snacks operate until the early hours. Things are more varied down on Thanon Phra Arthit, with its arty little café-restaurants favoured by Thammasat University students, while the riverside places,

---

DINNER CRUISES

The **Chao Phraya River** looks fabulous at night, when most of the noisy longtails have stopped terrorizing the ferries, and the riverside temples and other grand monuments – including the Grand Palace and Wat Arun – are elegantly illuminated. Joining one of the nightly **dinner cruises** along the river, especially one of the converted, wooden rice-barges listed below, is a great way to appreciate it all. Call ahead to reserve a table and check departure details – some cruises may not run during the rainy season (May–Oct).

Loy Nava 02 437 4932, loynava.com. The original, 40-year-old converted rice-barge service still departs Si Phraya pier twice nightly, at 6pm and 8.10pm, with pick-ups at Tha Sathorn possible. Thai, seafood or vegetarian meal, accompanied by live traditional music and dancing. B1300, including hotel pick-up in central Bangkok.

Manohra 02 476 0022 ext 1416, manohra cruises.com. Beautiful converted rice-barge operated by the *Anantara Riverside Resort*, south of Taksin Bridge in Thonburi, serving Thai set dinners. Departs hotel at 7.30pm, returning 10pm, with pick-ups at Tha Sathorn possible. From B1400.

Wan Fah 02 222 8679, wanfahcruise.com. Wooden rice-barge-style boat that departs River City at 7pm, returning at 9pm, with Thai classical dancing, and a choice of a Thai or seafood set menu. B1200, including hotel pick-up in central Bangkok.

1

on Phra Arthit and further north off Thanon Samsen and in Thewet, tend to be best for seafood with a view. For the real old-fashioned Thai taste though, browse southern Thanon Tanao, where traditional shophouses have been selling specialist sweets and savouries for generations.

AROUND KHAO SAN

Chabad House 96 Thanon Ram Bhuttri ⓦchabadthailand.com; map pp.100–101. A little piece of Israel, run by the Bangkok branch of the Jewish outreach Chabad-Lubavitch movement. Serves a well-priced, tasty kosher menu of schnitzels (B160), baba ganoush, falafels, hummus, salads and Jewish breads in a/c calm, on the ground floor of a long-established community centre and guesthouse; the best deal is five taster plates for B60. Sun–Thurs 10am–11pm, Fri 10am–3pm, Sat 8–11pm.

★ **May Kaidee** East off Thanon Tanao ⓦmaykaidee .com; map pp.100–101. Simple, neighbourhood Thai vegetarian restaurant, with two outlets on opposite sides of the soi, that still serves some of the best veggie food in Banglamphu despite having spawned several competitors on the same alley. Come for Western breakfasts or try the tasty green curry, the Vietnamese-style veggie spring rolls or the sticky black-rice pudding with mango or banana. Most dishes B60–70. All-you-can-eat buffet party with Thai dancing on Sat nights (B120). Daily 9am–10pm.

Popiang 43 Soi Ram Bhuttri; map pp.100–101. Popular, friendly place for cheap seafood: mussels cost just B80 per plate, squid B100, or you can get a large helping of seafood noodles for B110. Eat in the low-rent restaurant area or on the street beneath the temple wall. Daily 7am–1am.

Royal India Rambuttri Village complex, 95 Soi Ram Bhuttri ⓣ02 282 6688; map pp.100–101. Branch of the famous Pahurat restaurant (see p.154), by a carp pond in a pleasant courtyard. Daily 6am–midnight.

PHRA ARTHIT AREA

Aquatini Navalai River Resort, 45/1 Thanon Phra Arthit ⓣ02 280 9955; map pp.100–101. Occupying a nice wooden deck in a perfect breezy riverfront spot beside the express-boat pier (even better after sunset when the boats stop running), this hotel restaurant does exceptionally good mid-priced Thai food. Seafood's a speciality: the deep-fried ruby fish served with cashew nuts and bell peppers is very good, and their tangy coconut-milk *tom kha kai* soup is especially delicious. Most seafood mains B200–300. Daily 6.30am–1am.

★ **Hemlock** 56 Thanon Phra Arthit ⓣ02 282 7507; map pp.100–101. Small, stylish, a/c restaurant that's very popular with students and young Thai couples. Offers a long and interesting menu of unusual Thai dishes, including banana-flower salad (B95) and several kinds of *laap*. The traditional *miang* starters (shiny green wild tea leaves filled with chopped vegetables, fish, prawn or

meat) are also very tasty, and there's a good vegetarian selection. Worth reserving a table on Fri and Sat nights. Mon–Sat 4–11pm.

Kway Jap Yuan Khun Daeng Thanon Phra Arthit ⓣ085 246 0111; map pp.100–101. This basic, bustling canteen does a roaring trade with Thammasat University students, who come for the delicious *kway jap yuan*, noodle soup similar to Vietnamese *pho* but a little starchier – go for the version with egg (B40–50) and a baguette (B29) and you're set up for the day. Find it in an historic shophouse, unmistakably painted white and green – colours which the flamboyant owner often sports himself. Mon–Sat 11am–10pm.

★ **Praya Palazzo** 757/1 Soi 2, Thanon Somdet Phra Pinklao ⓣ02 883 2998, ⓦprayapalazzo.com; map pp.100–101. Superb royal Thai cuisine, using hard-to-find recipes that came out of Rama V's palace. Complex flavours come together in perfect harmony, in roast shrimp dip with crispy catfish, spicy beef soup with shrimp paste, and pork with young aubergines, yellow chilli paste and sour sauce (all B350). Or make the most of the boat ride and the historic architecture of this small garden hotel by coming for afternoon tea (B800), which features delicious Thai sweets alongside sandwiches and scones. Call to make a booking and arrange a free pick-up from Tha Phra Arthit express-boat pier. Daily 11.30am–2pm, 2.30–5pm & 6–9.30pm.

Roti Mataba 136 Thanon Phra Arthit ⓣ02 282 2119; map pp.100–101. Famous 70-year-old outlet for the ever-popular fried Indian breads, or *rotis*, served here in lots of sweet and savoury varieties, including with vegetable and meat curries (from B51), stuffed with meat and veg (*mataba*), and with bananas and condensed milk (from B15); biryanis (*khao mok*) are also on offer. Choose between pavement tables and a basic upstairs a/c room. Tues–Thurs 10am–9pm, Fri–Sun 10am–9.30pm.

THANON SAMSEN AND THEWET

Kaloang Home Kitchen Beside the river at the far western end of Thanon Sri Ayutthaya ⓣ02 281 9228; map pp.100–101. Flamboyant service and excellent seafood attracts an almost exclusively Thai clientele to this open-air, no-frills, bare-wood restaurant that perches on stilts over the river. Dishes well worth sampling include the fried rolled shrimps served with a sweet dip and any of the host of Thai salads; there's a selection of traditional desserts to finish (you) off with. Most mains are B100–150, more for crab, shrimp and some fishes. Daily 11am–10pm.

Kinlom Chom Saphan Riverside end of Thanon Samsen Soi 3 ⓣ02 628 8382, ⓦkhinlomchomsaphan; map pp.100–101. This sprawling, waterside restaurant boasts close-up views of the lyre-like Rama VIII Bridge and is always busy with a youngish Thai crowd. The predominantly seafood menu (B150–300) features

THAI COOKERY CLASSES IN BANGKOK

As well as the places listed below, nearly all the luxury hotels in Bangkok offer cookery classes.

Baipai 8/91 Soi 54, Thanon Ngam Wongwan ☏ 02 561 1404, ⓦ baipai.com. Thorough, four-hour classes in a quiet, suburban house in northern Bangkok. B2200, including transfers from central hotels. Closed Sun.

Blue Elephant 233 Thanon Sathorn Tai (BTS Surasak) ☏ 02 673 9353–4, ⓦ blueelephant.com. In a grand, century-old building, courses that range from B3300 for a half-day to a five-day private course for professional chefs for B90,000.

Helping Hands Klong Toey ⓦ cookingwithpoo .com. Set up with the help of a Christian charity, a chance to experience the slums of Klong Toey and spend a morning learning to cook. B1200, including a market tour and free transfers from next to Phrom Pong BTS station. Closed Sun.

May Kaidee 33 Thanon Samsen, ☏ 089 137 3173, ⓦ maykaidee.com. Banglamphu's famous vegetarian cook shares her culinary expertise at the Samsen branch of her restaurant chain for B1200 per half-day, including making raw food dishes and a market visit. Also available are shorter "cooking parties" for B600 and special classes such as fruit carving for B1500.

Thai House 22km from central Bangkok in Bangmuang ☏ 02 903 9611 or ☏ 02 997 5161, ⓦ thaihouse.co.th. Set in a rural part of Nonthaburi province, one- (B3800) to three-day (B16,650) cooking courses, all including transfers from downtown, the latter including vegetable and fruit-carving, all meals and homestay accommodation in traditional wooden houses.

everything from crab to grouper cooked in multiple ways, including with curry, garlic or sweet basil sauces, but never with MSG. Daily 11am–2am.

Krua Apsorn Thanon Samsen, opposite Thanon Uthong Nok on the southwestern edge of Dusit ☏ 02 668 8788, ⓦ kruaapsorn.com; map pp.100–101. Very good, spicy and authentic food and a genteel welcome make this unpretentious, a/c restaurant popular with the area's civil servants – as well as the royalty whom they serve. Try the green fish-ball curry (B100) or the yellow curry with river prawns and lotus shoots (B110), both recommended by the leading Thai restaurant guide, and put the fire in your mouth out with home-made coconut sorbet. Mon–Sat 10.30am–7.30pm.

May Kaidee 2 33 Thanon Samsen, between the khlong and Soi 1 ⓦ maykaidee.com; map pp.100–101. A/c branch of Banglamphu's best-loved Thai veggie restaurant (see opposite), which also runs vegetarian cookery classes (see box above). Daily 9am–10pm.

SOUTH: THANON TANAO AND THANON MAHACHAI

Chote Chitr 146 Thanon Phraeng Phuton ☏ 02 221 4082; map pp.100–101. The word's out about this unreconstructed, 80-year-old, shophouse restaurant of just half-a-dozen tables – it's been featured in the *New York Times* and the *FT*. However, the wide-ranging menu of Thai dishes (most about B100) in large, homely portions is still excellent. The formidable owner will explain what's good today, perhaps a deep-fried whitefish with mango salad (B200). Shame about the pet dogs running around the tables, though. Mon–Sat 11am–9pm.

Kai Yang Boran 474–476 Thanon Tanao, immediately to the south of the Chao Poh Seua Chinese shrine; map

pp.100–101. Locally famous grilled chicken (B180 for a small bird) and *som tam* (from B40) restaurant (with a/c), wallpapered with photos of celebrities who have eaten here. *Nam tok* with roast pork and several kinds of *laap* round out the northeastern menu. Daily 8am–9pm.

Kor Panit 431–433 Thanon Tanao, on the east side, directly opposite Thanon Phraeng Phuton; map pp.100–101. Outstanding takeaway coconut-laced sticky rice (currently B140/kg) has been sold here since 1932. No English sign, but look for the mango vendors outside, where you choose your variety to accompany the delicious *khao niaw*. Mon–Sat 7am–6pm.

Nattaporn 94 Thanon Phraeng Phuton, just off Thanon Kanlayana Maitri; map pp.100–101. This family has been specializing in its famous home-made fresh coconut ice cream for over sixty years, topping it with classic Thai condiments like sweetcorn, red beans and taro balls. They also have chocolate, coffee and tea flavours. No English sign, but it's a basic shophouse, right next door to *The Bhuthorn* guesthouse. Mon–Sat 9am–4pm.

Padthai Thipsamai 313 Thanon Mahachai (no English sign), near Wat Rajnadda ☏ 02 221 6280 ⓦ thipsamai .com; map pp.100–101. The most famous *phat thai* in Bangkok, flash-fried by the same husband-and-wife team since 1966. The "special" option is huge, comes with especially juicy prawns, and is wrapped in a translucent, paper-thin omelette. Best washed down with fresh coconut juice. Daily except alternate Wed, from 5.30pm until late.

RATANAKOSIN

The places reviewed below are especially handy for sightseers, but there are also plenty of street stalls around Tha Chang and a load of simple, studenty restaurants off the north end of Thanon Maharat near Thammasat

University, as well as a decent restaurant at *Arun Residence* and a daytime café at *Aurum* (see p.145).

Navy Club Tha Chang ☎02 222 0081; map p.83. Walk on by the prominent but overpriced *Navy Club 77 Café* on the corner of Na Phra Lan and Maharat roads, to find this place just beyond an ATM on the south side of the express-boat pier, announced by an English sign and a navy guard (don't be put off – anyone can eat here, even farangs). The decor's deeply institutionalized but the real draw is the shaded terrace built over the river, where you can enjoy tasty dried prawn and lemon-grass salad (B120) and other marine delights. Mon–Fri 11am–2pm & 4–10pm, Sat & Sun 11am–10pm.

Rub Ar Roon Opposite Wat Pho at 310–2 Thanon Maharat ☎02 622 2312; map p.83. Among many open-fronted, century-old shophouses on this stretch, this cosy, congenial café used to be a dispensary and still has its original teak cabinets. The Thai food is varied and very reasonably priced, and there are sandwiches (B75–85), espressos, Thai herbal teas and fruit shakes. Daily 8am–6pm.

CHINATOWN AND PAHURAT

Much of the fun of Chinatown dining is in the browsing of the night-time hot-food stalls that open up all along Thanon Yaowarat, around the mouth of Soi Issaranuphap (Yaowarat Soi 11) and along Soi Phadungdao (Soi Texas); wherever there's a crowd you'll be sure of good food. Pan Siam's *Good Eats: Chinatown* map, available from major bookshops, is also a great resource for the weirder local specialities.

Chong Kee 84 Soi Sukon 1, near Wat Traimit; map p.107. Famous, basic café serving nothing but delicious pork satay (B65 for 10 sticks) and sweet toast. No English sign, but look for the Shell sign (proof of a "Shell Chuan Chim" recommendation, a respected accolade for restaurants in Thailand). Tues–Sun 9.30am–6pm, Mon 9.30am–2pm.

Hua Seng Hong 371 Thanon Yaowarat ☎02 222 7053, ⓦhuasenghong.co.th; map p.107. Vibrant, ever-popular, few-frills restaurant, with an open kitchen out front alongside a stall that does a brisk, all-day trade in dim sum. Dishes from around B100, less for noodle soup, more for delicacies such as braised geese's feet. Daily 9am–1am.

Raan Khun Yaa Wat Traimit; map p.107. Just to the right inside the temple's Thanon Mittaphap entrance, this basic, very traditional restaurant, now in its third generation of operation, is especially famous for its delicious and cheap *kaeng khiaw wan neua* (green beef curry; B35), on a menu that otherwise changes daily. Mon–Sat 6am–1pm.

Royal India Just off Thanon Chakraphet at 392/1 ☎02 221 6565; map p.107. Great dhal, perfect parathas and famously good North Indian curries (from around B100), served in a dark little café in the heart of Bangkok's most Punjabi of neighbourhoods to an almost exclusively South Asian clientele. Daily 10am–10pm.

Shangarila 306 Thanon Yaowarat (corner of Thanon Rajawong) ☎02 224 5933; map p.107. Cavernous banquet hall serving Cantonese classics, including lots of seafood (mostly sold by weight), and lunchtime dim sum. Very popular, especially for family gatherings. Try the huge, very tasty, seared scallops with XO sauce (chillies, dried shrimps and brandy) for B500. Daily 10am–10pm.

T&K (Toi & Kid's Seafood) 49 Soi Phadungdao, corner of Thanon Yaowarat; map p.107. Known for their barbecued seafood, with everything from prawns (from B150 a serving) to oysters (B40 each) on offer. Eat at streetside tables or inside with a/c. Daily 4.30pm–2am.

SIAM SQUARE, THANON PLOENCHIT AND NORTHERN DOWNTOWN

In this area, there are also branches of *Taling Pling* (see p.158), on the ground floor of Siam Paragon (☎02 129

YELLOW-FLAG HEAVEN FOR VEGGIES

Every autumn, for nine days during the ninth lunar month (between late Sept and Nov), Thailand's Chinese community goes on a **meat-free** diet to mark the onset of the Vegetarian Festival (Ngan Kin Jeh), a sort of Taoist version of Lent. Though the Chinese citizens of Bangkok don't go in for skewering themselves like their compatriots in Trang and Phuket (see p.629), they do celebrate the Vegetarian Festival with gusto: some people choose to wear only white for the duration, all the temples throng with activity, and nearly every restaurant and foodstall in Chinatown turns vegetarian for the period, flying small yellow flags to show that they are upholding the tradition and participating in what's essentially a nightly veggie food jamboree. For vegetarian tourists this is a great time to be in town – just look for the yellow flag and you can be sure all dishes will be one hundred percent vegetarian. Soya substitutes are a popular feature on the vegetarian Chinese menu, so don't be surprised to find pink prawn-shaped objects floating in your noodle soup or unappetizingly realistic slices of fake duck. Many hotel restaurants also get in on the act during the Vegetarian Festival, running special veggie promotions for a week or two.

4353; daily 11am–10pm) and Floor 3, Central World (☎02 613 1360–1; daily 11am–9.30pm); *Royal India* (see opposite; basement; ☎02 610 7667; daily 10am–10pm) and *Aoi* (see p.156; ground floor; ☎02 129 4348–50; Mon–Fri 11.30am–2.30pm & 5.30–10.30pm, Sat & Sun 11am–10.30pm), both in Siam Paragon; and *Greyhound Café* (see p.159), in the Siam Centre (☎02 658 1129; daily 10am–9pm) and in Central Chidlom department store on Thanon Ploenchit (☎02 255 6964; daily 10am–9pm).

Din Tai Fung Floor 7, Central World ☎02 646 1282, ⓦdintaifung.com.sg; map p.119. Among Central World's fifty-odd restaurants, this attractive and efficient all-day dim sum place stands out, not least because its Hong Kong branch has a Michelin star. Its superb speciality is steamed pork dumplings with clear broth inside each one (B145), but other dishes such as spring rolls with duck and spring onion (B160) are also very tasty. Sit at the big windows overlooking Ratchaprasong or watching the chefs beavering away in the open kitchen. Daily 11am–9pm.

Food Loft Floor 7, Central Chidlom, Thanon Ploenchit; map p.119. Bangkok's top department store lays on a suitably upscale food court of all hues – Thai, Vietnamese, Chinese, Japanese, Korean, Indian, Greek, Italian (by *Gianni* – see below). Choose your own ingredients and watch them cooked in front of you, eat by the huge windows in the stylish, minimalist seating areas and then ponder whether you have room for a Thai or Western dessert. Daily 10am–10pm.

Gianni 34/1 Soi Tonson, Thanon Ploenchit ☎02 252 1619, ⓦgiannibkk.com; map p.119. Probably Bangkok's best independent Italian restaurant, offering a sophisti-cated blend of traditional and modern in both its decor and food, with main courses starting at around B350. Twice-weekly shipments of artisan ingredients from the old country are used in dishes such as lobster and artichoke risotto and squid-ink spaghetti with clams, prawns and asparagus. Daily 11.30am–2pm & 6–10pm.

★ **Home Kitchen (Khrua Nai Baan)** 94 Soi Lang Suan ☎02 253 1888, ⓦkhruanaibaan.com; map p.119. Like an upcountry restaurant in the heart of the city, this congenial, unpretentious spot offers a choice between a/c and outdoor tables behind a huge open kitchen. On the inexpensive Thai and Chinese picture menu, you're bound to find something delicious, including dozens of soups – try the *kaeng som*, with shrimp and mixed vegetables, for B150 – six kinds of *laap* and a huge array of seafood. Success has spawned a smarter new branch with the same menu, in an attractive villa just two doors away. Daily 8am–midnight.

Inter 432/1–2 Soi 9, Siam Square; map p.119. Honest, efficient Thai restaurant that's popular with students and shoppers, serving good one-dish meals from B55, as well as curries, soups, salads and seafood, in a no-frills, fluorescent-lit canteen atmosphere. Daily 10am–10pm.

Isaan Rot Det 3/5–6 Thanon Rangnam; map pp.80–81. On a street that's well-known for its Isaan cafés, this is perhaps the most famous. The decor's weather-beaten, scruffy even, with a few basic pavement tables, but the name, "Northeast Very Tasty", says it all: delicious *nam tok* with duck (B60), many kinds of *laap*, *kai yaang*, the works. No English sign, but you'll pick it out by the Pepsi sign, the oversized fish basket over the open kitchen or the deadly serious *som tam*-basher. Daily 11am–10pm.

Jin-emon Ground floor, MBK Shopping Centre, near the Pathumwan Princess Hotel ☎02 626 0151; map p.119. Multiculturalism's gone mad at this welcoming Japanese spaghetti house, but the results are very tasty (mains around B100–150). Some of the sauces are frankly weird but they all come on delicious, high-quality pasta, and there are good-value set menus of extras (drinks, garlic bread, salads and the like). Leave room, or – more likely – come back for "big toast", a loaf of bread scooped out and filled with ice cream. Daily 10am–10pm.

Mah Boon Krong Shopping Centre Corner of Rama I and Phrayathai rds; map p.119. Two decent food-courts at the north end of MBK: the long-running area on Floor 6, operating on a coupon system, is a good introduction to Thai food, with English names and pictures of a huge variety of tasty, cheap one-dish meals from all over the country displayed at the various stalls, as well as fresh juices and a wide range of desserts; the upmarket version on Floor 5 is an international affair, spanning India, Italy, Vietnam, China and Japan, plus vegetarian food at *Tamarind Café* and good moussaka at *Olive*. Floor 6 daily 10am–8.30pm, Floor 5 daily 10am–10pm.

Midnight Kai Ton Unmarked soi between Soi 30 and Soi 32, Thanon Phetchaburi; map p.119. Famous, late-night, anti-hangover refuge that serves just one dish: delicious *khao man kai*, boiled chicken breast with broth, dipping sauces and rice that's been cooked in chicken stock. It'll set you back just B30–40, more if you ask for liver and other innards (*khreuang nai*, literally "the inner workings"). More choice is offered by the string of other popular foodstalls between here and the corner of Phetchaburi and Rajdamri roads. Daily 7pm–4.30am.

Polo Fried Chicken (Kai Thawt Jay Kee Soi Polo) Soi Polo, Thanon Witthayu ☎02 655 8489; map p.119. On the access road to the snobby polo club, this is Bangkok's most famous purveyor of the ultimate Thai peasant dish, fried chicken. All manner of northeastern dishes, including fish, sausages and loads of salads, fill out the menu, but it would be wrong to come to this basic, a/c restaurant and not have the classic combo of finger-licking chicken (B80 for a half), *som tam* and sticky rice. Daily 7am–10pm.

Red Sky *Centara Grand*, 999/99 Thanon Rama 1 ☎02 100 1234, ⓦcentarahotelsresorts.com; map p.119. Opulent, blow-out restaurant, named for the great sunset views from its indoor-outdoor, 55th-floor

1

perch. It purveys "the best of the land, sky and water" – be that Maine lobster, Dutch veal or Kobe beef – beautifully presented in complex, meticulous preparations, with a signature splash of red in each dish (B1000 upwards). Daily 5pm–1am.

Sanguansri 59/1 Thanon Witthayu (no English sign, but the house number's in Arabic numerals) ☎02 251 9378; map p.119. The rest of the street may be a multi-storey building site but this low-rise, canteen-like old-timer, run by a friendly bunch of middle-aged women, clings on. And where else around here can you lunch on a sweet, thick and toothsome *kaeng matsaman* for B60? It goes well with *kung pla*, a tasty, fresh prawn and lemon-grass salad that can be spiced to order. Mon–Sat 10am–3pm.

Som Tam (Nua) 392/14 Soi 5, Siam Square ☎02 251 4880; map p.119. This basic but lively modern restaurant on a pedestrian alley is a great place to get to know the full range of Thai spicy salads. The house *som tam*, with pork crackling and sausage, goes well with the very tasty deep-fried chicken (B90), or there's northeastern *laap* and *nam tok*, and central Thai *yam* by the dozen. Daily 10.45am–9.30pm.

Sra Bua *Siam Kempinski Hotel* (see p.147); map p.119. Molecular gastronomy comes to Bangkok, with great success. Operated by Copenhagen's Thai Michelin one-star, *Kiin Kiin*, this place applies some serious creativity and theatricality to Thai cuisine, in dishes such as frozen red curry with lobster salad, which perfectly distils the taste of the *kaeng daeng*. The grand decor, which encompasses two lotus ponds (*sra bua*), is matched by the prices: multi-course set menus cost B1800–2400 for dinner, B1500 for lunch. Mon–Fri noon–2pm & 6–10pm, Sat & Sun 6–10pm.

Thang Long 82/5 Soi Lang Suan ☎02 251 3504, ⓦthanglongsince1987.com; map p.119. Excellent Vietnamese food, such as whole, deep-fried, lemon-grass fish (B275), in this stylish, minimalist and popular restaurant. Eat in the front garden, which is all black stone and ornamental plants, or inside where these motifs are complemented with red wood and brown leather. Daily 11am–2pm & 5–11pm.

Vanilla Brasserie Ground floor, Siam Paragon shopping centre ☎02 610 9383; and *Vanilla Industry*, Soi 11, Siam Square ☎02 658 4720, ⓦvanillaindustry .com; map p.119. Two sophisticated shrines to Western gourmet delights that combine restaurant, patisserie, crêperie and chocolatier (and in Siam Square, a cooking school). On offer are delicious parma ham and mascarpone crêpes (B390), salads and other main courses, spot-on desserts, and excellent teas and coffees. Both daily 10am–10pm.

DOWNTOWN: SOUTH OF THANON RAMA IV

Several popular groupings of street stalls are worth noting here: the top end of Thanon Convent, just off Thanon Silom; away to the west opposite the Maha Uma Devi Temple, Silom Soi 20; and the late-night noodle soup stalls on the east end of Thanon Suriwong. In this area, there are also branches of *Baan Khanitha* (see p.159) at 69 Thanon Sathorn Tai, at the corner of Soi Suan Phlu (☎02 675 4200–1; daily 11am–11pm); and *Beirut* (see p.159), in the Silom 64 building, set back off Thanon Silom behind *Sabushi*, opposite the Silom Complex (☎02 266 7150–1; daily 10am–9pm).

★ **Aoi** 132/10–11 Soi 6, Thanon Silom ☎02 235 2321–2, ⓦaoi-bkk.com; map p.126. The best place in town for a Japanese blowout, justifiably popular with the expat community. Excellent authentic food and elegant decor. Good-value lunch bento boxes (from B350) available and a superb sushi bar. Daily 11.30am–2.30pm & 5.30/6pm–10.30/11pm.

★ **Celadon** *Sukhothai Hotel*, 13/3 Thanon Sathorn Tai ☎02 344 8888; map p.126. Consistently rated as one of the best hotel restaurants in Bangkok and a favourite with locals, serving outstanding traditional and contemporary Thai food – try the banana-flower salad and the red curry with chicken rolls and salted egg – in an elegant setting surrounded by lotus ponds. Daily noon–3pm & 6.30–11pm.

Chai Karr 312/3 Thanon Silom, opposite *Holiday Inn* ☎02 233 2549; map p.126. Folksy, traditional-style wooden decor is the welcoming setting for a wide variety of well-prepared, modestly priced Thai and Chinese dishes, followed by home-made coconut ice cream and freshly ground coffee. Mon–Sat 11.30am–10pm.

Deen 761 Thanon Silom, almost opposite Silom Village ☎02 635 0441; map p.126. Small, basic, a/c Muslim café (espresso coffee, but no alcohol), which offers mostly Malay-Thai dishes, including green chicken curry with *roti* (flatbread; B100), crispy grouper fish with pepper and garlic, and *ikan kambung* (in Thai, *nam phrik pla thu*, a kind of mackerel salad). Daily except Wed 11.30am–9.15pm.

Eat Me 1/6 Soi Phiphat 2, Thanon Convent ☎02 238 0931, ⓦeatmerestaurant.com; map p.126. Justly fashionable art gallery and restaurant in a striking, white, modernist building, with changing exhibitions on the walls and a temptingly relaxing balcony. The eclectic, far-reaching menu features such mains as Tasmanian salmon with salsa verde (B690), and the lemon-grass *crème brûlée* is not to be missed. Daily 3pm–1am.

Harmonique 22 Soi 34, Thanon Charoen Krung, on the lane between Wat Muang Kae express-boat pier and

ร้านสายฝนผ้าไหม
Sai Fon Silk Shop

1

the GPO ☎02 237 8175; map p.126. A relaxing, welcoming, moderately priced restaurant that's well worth a trip: tables are scattered throughout several converted shophouses, decorated with antiques and bric-a-brac, and a quiet, leafy courtyard, and the Thai food is varied and excellent – among the seafood specialities, try the crab (B180) or red shrimp (B85) curries. Mon–Sat 11am–10pm.

Himali Cha-Cha 1229/11 Soi 47/1, Thanon Charoen Krung, south of GPO ☎02 235 1569, ⓦhimalichacha .com; map p.126. Fine, moderately priced North Indian restaurant, founded by a character who was chef to numerous Indian ambassadors, and now run by his son. Tasty chicken tikka masala (B195) and a good vegetarian selection, with a homely atmosphere and attentive service. There's also a branch down a short alley off the north end of Thanon Convent (☎02 238 1478; same hours), opposite *Molly Malone's* Irish pub. Daily 11am–3.30pm & 6–10.30pm.

Home Cuisine Islamic Restaurant 186 Soi 36, Thanon Charoen Krung ☎02 234 7911; map p.126. The short, cheap menu of Indian and southern Thai dishes here has proved popular enough to warrant a refurbishment in green and white, with comfy booths, pot plants and a few outdoor tables overlooking the colonial-style French embassy. The *khao mok kai* (B85), a typical hybrid version of a chicken biryani, served with aubergine curry, is delicious. Mon–Sat 11am–10pm, Sun 6–10pm.

Jim Thompson's Saladaeng Café 120/1 Soi 1, Thanon Saladaeng ☎02 266 9167, ⓦsaladaengcafe.com; map p.126. A civilized, reasonably priced haven with tables in the elegantly informal a/c interior or out in the leafy garden. The Thai food stretches to one or two unusual dishes such as grilled pork neck with garlic and tamarind dip (B180), and there's pasta, salads and a few other Western dishes. The array of desserts is mouthwatering, rounded off by good coffee and a wide choice of teas. Daily 11am–11pm.

★ **Khrua Aroy Aroy** 3/1 Thanon Pan ☎02 635 2365; map p.126. Aptly named "Delicious, Delicious Kitchen", this simple shophouse restaurant stands out for its choice of cheap, tasty, well-prepared dishes from all around the kingdom, notably *khao soi, kaeng matsaman* and *khanom jiin*. Daily 7am–about 8pm, or earlier if the food runs out.

Le Bouchon 37/17 Patpong 2, near Thanon Suriwong ☎02 234 9109; map p.126. Cosy bar-bistro that's much frequented by the city's French expats, offering home-cooking such as lamb shank in a white bean sauce (B580); booking is strongly recommended. Mon–Sat noon–3pm & 6.30–11pm.

Mali Soi 1, Thanon Sathorn, just off Soi Ngam Duphli ☎02 679 8693; map pp.80–81. Cosy, informal, low-lit restaurant, mostly a/c with a few cramped tables

out front. The Thai menu specializes in salads and northeastern food, with plenty of veggie dishes, while pricier Western options run as far as tasty burgers (B180), potato salad, all-day breakfasts, delicious banana or chocolate pancakes and a few Mexican dishes. Daily 8.30am–11pm.

Mei Jiang Peninsula Hotel, 333 Thanon Charoennakorn ☎02 861 2888, ⓦpeninsula.com; map p.126. Probably Bangkok's best Chinese restaurant, with beautiful views of the hotel's riverside gardens, and very attentive and graceful staff. Cantonese specialities include delicious teas, lobster rolls, smoked duck with tea and excellent lunchtime dim sum such as crystal prawn dumplings, starting at around B100 a dish. Daily 11.30am–2.30pm & 6–10.30pm.

★ **Ramentei** 23/8–9 Soi Thaniya ☎02 234 8082; map p.126. Excellent Japanese noodle café, bright, clean and welcoming, under the same ownership as *Aoi* (see p.156). The open kitchen turns out especially good, huge bowls of miso ramen, which goes very well with the gyoza dumplings. Most dishes B150–200. Daily 11am–2am.

Ruen Urai *Rose Hotel*, 118 Thanon Suriwong ☎02 266 8268–72, ⓦruen-urai.com; map p.126. Set back behind the hotel, this peaceful, hundred-year-old, traditional house, with fine balcony tables overlooking the beautiful hotel pool, comes as a welcome surprise in this full-on downtown area. The varied Thai food is of a high quality (though you can forget the house wine): try the *tom khlong talay* (B250) and don't be misled by the name, which means "seafood canal soup" – it's a delicious, refined, spicy and sour soup from the northeast, with tamarind juice and herbs. Daily noon–11pm.

Sara Jane's 55/21 Thanon Narathiwat Ratchanakharin, between sois 4 & 6 ☎02 676 3338–9; map p.126. Long-standing, basic, a/c restaurant, popular with Bangkok's Isaan population, serving good, simple northeastern dishes, including a huge array of *nam tok* (B95), *laap* and *som tam*, as well as Italian food. Daily 11am–2pm & 5.30–10pm.

Somboon Seafood Thanon Suriwong, corner of Thanon Narathiwat Ratchanakharin ☎02 233 3104, ⓦsomboonseafood.com; map p.126. Highly favoured, bustling seafood restaurant, known especially for its crab curry (B250), with simple, functional, modern decor and an array of marine life lined up in tanks outside awaiting its gastronomic fate. Daily 4–11.30pm.

★ **Taling Pling** 60 Thanon Pan ☎02 234 4872; map p.126. One of the best Thai restaurants in the city outside of the big hotels, specializing in classic dishes from the four corners of the kingdom. The house deep-fried fish salad (B135) is delicious and refreshing, while the deeply flavoured green beef curry (B145) with roti is recommended by the leading Thai restaurant guides. The atmosphere's convivial and relaxing, too. Daily 11am–10pm.

★ Tongue Thai 18–20 Soi 38, Thanon Charoen Krung, in front of the Oriental Place shopping mall ☎02 630 9918–9; map p.126. Very high standards of food and cleanliness, with charming, unpretentious service, in a hundred-year-old shophouse elegantly decorated with Thai and Chinese antiques. Veggies are very well catered for with delicious dishes such as tofu in black bean sauce and deep-fried banana-flower and corn cakes, while carnivores should try the fantastic beef curry (*panaeng neua*; B170). Daily 11am–2pm & 5.30–10.30pm.

THANON SUKHUMVIT

In this area, there are also branches of Japanese *Aoi* (see p.156; Floor 4; ☎02 664 8590; daily 11/11.30am–2.30/3pm & 5/5.30–10.30pm) and *Royal India* (see p.154; Floor 5; ☎081 633 0737; daily 10am–10pm), both in the Emporium shopping centre; *Ramentei* Japanese noodle café on Soi 33/1 (see opposite; ☎02 662 0050; daily 11am–midnight); and the North Indian *Himali Cha-Cha* (see opposite), on Soi 31 (☎02 259 6677) and at the mouth of Soi 3/1 (☎02 655 6223; both daily 11am–3.30pm & 6–10.30pm). For street food, check out the night market at the mouth of Soi 38 (BTS Thong Lo).

Baan Khanitha 36/1 Soi 23 ☎02 258 4128, ⓦbaan -khanitha.com; map p.124. The big attraction at this long-running favourite haunt of Sukhumvit expats is the setting in a traditional Thai house. The food is upmarket Thai and fairly pricey, and includes lots of fiery salads (*yam*), and a good range of *tom yam* soups, green curries and seafood curries. Most mains cost B200–500. Daily 11am–11pm.

Banya 12 Soi 7 ☎02 251 6468; map p.124. The decor in this white villa is unexceptional, but it stands out on this section of Sukhumvit because it's spacious (with outdoor tables at the front), quiet and low-rise and offers good, reasonably priced Thai food. Try the spicy green chicken curry with roti (B130) or the zesty Thai mushroom salad with prawns, squid and minced pork (B120). Daily noon–10pm.

★ Beirut Basement, Ploenchit Centre, at the mouth of Soi 2 ☎02 656 7377; map p.124. It's worth crossing the road from Bangkok's main Middle Eastern ghetto (Soi 3 and Soi 3/1) for the top-notch Lebanese food in this comfortable, a/c restaurant. Among dozens of salads and stuffed breads, the superb *motabel* (*baba ganoush*) is fluffy and smoky, while the falafels are suitably moist inside and crunchy out. These are best sampled on a B280 set menu, which gets you three dishes plus pitta bread. Good baklava, too. Daily 10am–10pm.

★ Bolan 42 Soi Pichai Rongnarong, Soi 26 ☎02 260 2962, ⓦbolan.co.th; map p.124. Meticulous and hugely successful attempt to produce authentic traditional food in all its complexity – while upholding the "Slow Food" philosophy – that'll give you a lipsmacking education in Thai cuisine. Delights on the seasonal menu might include duck jungle curry with green banana (B580) and clear soup of jackfruit seed and chicken (B250), or let the chefs design a harmonious "Bolan Balance" menu for you (B1680). In a garden villa with especially attractive veranda tables, 15min walk from Phrom Pong BTS behind *Four Wings Hotel*. Tues–Sun 6pm–late.

Cabbages and Condoms 6–8 Soi 12 ☎02 229 4610, ⓦpda.or.th/restaurant; map p.124. The Population and Community Development Association of Thailand (PDA) runs this relaxing restaurant, decorated with condoms from around the world and the slogan "our food is guaranteed not to cause pregnancy". Try the deep-fried, fluffy catfish with mango sauce (B130) or the seafood *haw mok* (B200); there's also a varied vegetarian menu. Daily 11am–10pm.

Dosa King Soi 11/1, with a back entrance on Soi 11 ☎02 651 1700, ⓦdosaking.net; map p.124. Usually busy with expat Indian diners, this vegetarian Indian restaurant serves good food from both north and south, including over a dozen different dosa (southern pancake) dishes, tandooris and the like. It's an alcohol-free zone so you'll have to make do with sweet lassi instead. Most dishes B100–200. Daily 11am–11pm.

Greyhound Café Floor 2, Emporium shopping centre ☎02 664 8663, ⓦgreyhoundcafe.co.th; map p.124. Next to a branch of the hip, Thai fashion outlet that owns it, this café clothes itself head to toe in black and white industrial chic, including the blackboards advertising regular specials and the shining tablecloths and napkins. The menu is mostly comfort food, such as tasty and well-prepared egg and bacon fried rice with pork soup (B150), plus a few more ambitious, fusion main courses, and some wicked Western and Thai desserts. Daily 11am–10pm.

Le Dalat Indochine 57 Soi 23 (Soi Prasanmitr) ☎02 259 9593, ⓦledalatbkk.com; map p.124. There's Indochinese romance aplenty at this delightful, re-created Vietnamese brick mansion decked out with pot plants, plenty of photos and eclectic curiosities. The extensive, high-class Vietnamese menu features favourites such as a *goi ca* salad of aromatic herbs and raw fish (B260) and *chao tom* shrimp sticks on sugar cane (B360). Good-value lunchtime sets. Daily 11.30am–2.30pm & 5.30–10pm.

MahaNaga 2 Soi 29 ☎02 662 3060, ⓦmahanaga.com; map p.124. The dining experience at this tranquil enclave is best appreciated after dark, when the fountain-courtyard tables are romantically lit and the a/c interior seduces with its burgundy velvet drapes. Cuisine is Thai fine dining, featuring such tasty delights as *nam tok* made with grilled sirloin steak (B350) and *tom yam* with river prawns (B200). Daily 5.30–10.45pm.

1

Soul Food Mahanakorn 56/10 Soi 55 (Soi Thong Lo; Exit 3 from BTS Thong Lo, then it's 100m up the soi on the right) ☏ 02 714 7708, ⓦ soulfoodmahanakorn .com; map p.124. If you already have your favourite stall for *som tam* or *laap*, this is not for you, but if not, this trim, welcoming, American–Thai bistro makes a great introduction to street food from around Thailand, using top-quality ingredients. The beef *khao soi* (curried noodle soup; B180) is thick, creamy and toothsome, and the *som tam* (B140) can be spiced to order. Daily blackboard specials, and a huge selection of creative cocktails. Daily 5.30pm–midnight.

Spring Summer Winter 199 Soi Promsri 1, about 15min walk from BTS Phrom Pong, 700m north up Soi 39 then 350m east along Soi Promsri 1 ☏ 02 392 2747, ⓦ springsummer.com; map p.124. A fashionable three-in-one experience occupying a pair of chic modernist buildings set round a grassy lawn in a residential soi. *Spring* (dishes from around B300) serves delicious fusion cuisine (Thai with strong influences from Japan and India), with an emphasis on seafood, in dishes such as scrumptiously tangy pomelo and wingbean salad, and fried rice with seared salmon and avocado; *Summer* indulges chocoholics with all manner of treats from frozen tiramisu to cheesecakes and chocolate hotpots; and *Winter* sets up a bar on the lawn in between, with food from *Spring* and *Summer*, and lounging cushions. Spring daily 11.30am–2.30am & 6–11pm; Summer daily noon–midnight; Winter 7pm–midnight, weather permitting.

Suk 11 Soi 11 ☏ 02 253 5468, ⓦ suk11.com; map p.124. Part of the idiosyncratic *Suk 11* guesthouse (see p.150), with which it shares a traffic-free sub-soi, this restaurant also re-creates an atmosphere of old-fashioned village Thailand, with its wooden building, lamplight and

plentiful foliage. The food is good, authentic, mid-priced Thai (mostly B100–200), with plenty of spicy *yam* salads, delicious chicken *laap*, tasty *phanaeng* curry plus cocktails and imported wines by the glass. It all adds up to a special-occasion ambience, but without the pretension or high prices of its better-known competitors. Daily 3.30–11pm.

★ **Vientiane Kitchen (Khrua Vientiane)** 8 Soi 36, about 50m south off Thanon Sukhumvit ☏ 02 258 6171, ⓦ vientianekitchen.com; map p.124. Just a 3min walk west then south from BTS Thong Lo (Exit 2) and you're transported into a little piece of Isaan, where the menu's stocked full of northeastern delicacies, a live band sets the mood with heart-felt, sometimes overamplified folk songs, and there are even performances by a troupe of traditional dancers (daily at 8pm). The Lao- and Isaan-accented menu (mostly B100–300) includes vegetable soup with ants' eggs, spicy-fried frog, jackfruit curry and snakehead fish (from B300), plus there's a decent range of veggie options such as *som tam* and sweet and sour dishes, and Thai desserts. With its airy, barn-like interior and mixed clientele of Thais and expats, it's a very enjoyable dining experience. Daily noon–midnight.

CHATUCHAK WEEKEND MARKET

There's no shortage of foodstalls inside the market compound, particularly at the southern end, where you'll find plenty of places serving inexpensive *phat thai* and Isaan dishes.

Toh Plue ☏ 02 272 5283. The biggest and most famous restaurant in Chatuchak, whose main branch is on the eastern edge of the block containing the market office; there's a second branch near Kamphaeng Phet subway station's exit 1. Both have a/c rooms and serve tasty standards such as chicken with cashew nuts (B120). Market hours.

DRINKING AND NIGHTLIFE

For many of Bangkok's male visitors, nightfall is the signal to hit the city's sex bars, most notoriously in the area off the east end of Thanon Silom known as Patpong (see p.125). Fortunately, Bangkok's **nightlife** has thoroughly grown up in the past ten years to leave these neon sumps behind, and now offers everything from microbreweries and vertiginous, rooftop cocktail bars to fiercely chic clubs and dance bars, hosting top-class DJs. The high-concept bars of Sukhumvit and the lively,

---

OPENING HOURS AND ID CHECKS

Most bars and clubs in Bangkok are meant to **close** at 1am, while those at the east end of Silom and on Royal City Avenue can stay open until 2am. In previous years, there have been regular "social order" clampdowns by the police, strictly enforcing these closing times, conducting occasional urine tests for drugs on bar customers, and setting up widespread ID checks to curb under-age drinking (you have to be 20 or over to drink in bars and clubs). However, at the time of writing, things were much more chilled, with many bars and clubs staying open into the wee hours on busy nights and ID checks in only a few places. It's hard to predict how the situation might develop, but you'll soon get an idea of how the wind is blowing when you arrive in Bangkok – and there's little harm in taking a copy of your passport out with you, just in case.

teeming venues of Banglamphu, in particular, pull in the style-conscious cream of Thai youth and are tempting an increasing number of travellers to stuff their party gear into their rucksacks. During the cool season (Nov–Feb), an evening out at one of the seasonal **beer gardens** is a pleasant way of soaking up the urban atmosphere (and the traffic fumes). You'll find them in hotel forecourts or sprawled in front of dozens of shopping centres all over the city, most notably Central World Plaza. Among the city's **club nights**, look out for the interesting regular events organized by Zudrangma Record Store (ⓦ zudrangmarecords.com) at venues such as *Cosmic Café* (see p.162), which mix up dance music from all around Thailand and from all over the world. Getting back to your lodgings should be no problem in the small hours: many bus routes run a (reduced) service throughout the night, and tuk-tuks and taxis are always at hand – though it's probably best for unaccompanied women to avoid using tuk-tuks late at night.

BANGLAMPHU AND RATANAKOSIN

The travellers' enclave of Banglamphu takes on a new personality after dark, when its hub, Thanon Khao San, becomes a "walking street," closed to all traffic but open to almost any kind of makeshift stall, selling everything from fried bananas and buckets of "very strong" cocktails to share, to bargain fashions and one-off artworks. Young Thais crowd the area to browse and snack before piling in to Banglamphu's more stylish bars and indie live-music clubs, most of which are free to enter (though some ask you to show ID first).

Ad Here the 13th (Blues Bar) 13 Thanon Samsen, opposite Soi 2; map pp.100–101. Relaxed, little neighbourhood live-music joint with sociable seats out on the pavement, where musos congregate nightly to listen to Thai and expat blues and jazz bands (from about 9.30pm onwards). Well-priced beer and plenty of cocktails. Daily 6pm–midnight.

Bangkok Bar 100 Thanon Ram Bhuttri ☏ 02 281 2899, ⓦ bkkbar.com; map pp.100–101. By far the most ambitious and best of several live-music places on this street, whose Thai indie-rock bands and DJs – including occasional big-name appearances – are popular with young locals. In a multi-tiered bar-restaurant around a fountain courtyard, the stage is on the first floor but can also be viewed from the second-floor balconies. B100 including one drink. Daily 6pm–3am.

Brick Bar Buddy Village complex, 265 Thanon Khao San ⓦ brickbarkhaosan.com; map pp.100–101. Massive red-brick vault of a live-music bar whose regular roster of reggae, ska, soul and blues bands, and occasional one-off appearances, are hugely popular with Thai twenty-somethings and teens. Big, sociable tables are set right under the stage and there's food too. The biggest nights are Fri and Sat when there's a B150 entry charge, which includes one drink. Daily 7pm–1.30am.

Café Democ 78 Thanon Rajdamnoen Klang ⓦ cafe -democ.com; map pp.100–101. Fashionable, dark and dinky bar in a turret-like building that overlooks Democracy Monument from its huge windows and is spread over one and a half cosy floors, with extra seating on the semi-circular mezzanine. Almost-nightly sessions from Thai and international DJs, sometimes as a warm-up for nearby *Club Culture* (see below), plus occasional gigs by up-and-coming

Thai bands. By day, it's a relaxed café. Daily 11am/ noon–2am.

The Club 123 Thanon Khao San ☏ 02 629 1010, ⓦ the clubkhaosan.com; map pp.100–101. High ceilings, an elevated, central DJ station spinning electronic dance music, and state-of-the-art lighting draw a sophisticated young Thai and international crowd. B100 including one drink. Daily 10pm–3am.

Club Culture Unmarked soi just off the south side of Thanon Rajdamnoen Klang, southeast of Democracy Monument ☏ 089 497 8422, ⓦ club-culture-bkk.com; map pp.100–101. Popular with both Thai and expat hipsters, this converted four-storey shophouse with three separate rooms hosts an assortment of international and local DJs playing house music of all hues, plus techno, electronica, drum'n'bass, as well as live indie bands, depending on the night. Admission depends on what's on but is usually at least B150 including one drink. Wed– Sat 10pm–late.

★ **Hippie de Bar** 46 Thanon Khao San ☏ 02 629 3508; map pp.100–101. Inviting courtyard bar set away from the main fray, surrounded by graffitied walls, TV screens and its own-brand fashion boutique. Attracts a mixed studenty/arty/high society, mostly Thai crowd, to drink cheapish beer at its wrought-iron tables and park benches. Indoors is totally given over to kitsch, with plastic armchairs, Donny Osmond posters and ancient TVs. Sun–Thurs 4pm–2am, Fri & Sat 4pm–3am.

Jazz Happens Thanon Phra Arthit ☏ 02 282 9934, ⓦ facebook.com/jazzhappens; map pp.100–101. Typical Phra Arthit bar, full of students, with just one small room and a few sociable pavement tables, but what sets this place apart is that some of the students are from Silpakorn University's Faculty of Jazz, playing here in a self-styled jazz commune. Tuck into a decent selection of well-priced cocktails and a short menu of drinking food while you're listening. Daily 7pm–midnight.

Phra Nakorn 58/2 Soi Damnoen Klang Tai ☏ 02 622 0282; map pp.100–101. Styles itself as "a hangout place for art lovers", and it successfully pulls in the capital's artists and art students, who can admire the floodlit view of the Golden Mount from the rooftop terrace, play pool on the second floor or browse one of the regular exhibitions on the first floor. Daily 6pm–1am.

1

Po 203/1 Tha Thien, Thanon Maharat ☎02 622 3081; map p.83. When the Chao Phraya express boats start to wind down, this bar takes over the rustic wooden pier and the balcony above with their great sunset views across the river to Wat Arun. It's popular with local students and office workers, hence the loud Thai pop music; avoid the food in favour of beer and Thai whisky. Daily 6–11pm.

★ **Taksura** Thanon Tanao ☎02 622 0708; map pp.100–101. This run-down but cinematically lit, hundred-year-old mansion, its wooden shutters flung wide open, is set back but visible from Tanao down a very short alley. Behind the large, sheltered garden, the interior is your archetypal students' common room, with a hodge-podge of retro chairs, indie music on the CD player and reasonably priced drink and food. Daily 5pm–1am.

SIAM SQUARE, THANON PLOENCHIT AND NORTHERN DOWNTOWN

Downtown, Siam Square has much less to offer after dark than Thanon Silom, further south. Out to the northeast, running south off Thanon Rama IX, lies RCA (Royal City Avenue), an officially sanctioned "nightlife zone" that's allowed to stay open until 2am. It's lined mostly with warehouse-like clubs that have a reputation as meat markets, but if there's something interesting on at *Cosmic Café*, it's worth the taxi ride out here.

Coco Walk Thanon Phrayathai; map p.119. It would be hard not to enjoy yourself at this covered parade of loosely interchangeable but buzzing, good-time bars, right beside Ratchathevi BTS. Popular with local students, they variously offer pool tables, live musicians, DJs and cover bands, but all have reasonably priced beer and drinking food. Daily roughly 6pm–1am.

Cosmic Café Block C, Royal City Avenue (RCA) ☎081 304 6907; map p.137. The look's nothing special, just several floors of bars and a large outdoor terrace, but this place stands out for its imaginative programming, ranging from poetry and art installations to live indie bands and DJs playing anything from ska to *mor lam*. Roughly daily 7pm–2am.

Raintree 116/63–4 Soi Ruamjit, Thanon Rangnam ☎02 245 7230, ⓦraintreepub.com; map pp.80–81. Near Victory Monument, two ordinary shophouses have been converted into this friendly, typical "good ol' boys" bar, with lots of rough timber furniture and the biggest water-buffalo skulls you've ever seen. Live, nightly music is mostly Songs for Life, mixed in with some *luk thung*, starting out low-key and soothing, and getting more raucous and danceworthy as the night hots up. Daily 6pm–1am.

Saxophone 3/8 Victory Monument (southeast corner), just off Thanon Phrayathai ☎02 246 5472, ⓦsaxophonepub.com; map pp.80–81. Lively, easy-going, spacious venue with decent Thai and Western food and a diverse roster of bands – mostly jazz (Mon–Thurs &

Sun) and blues (Fri & Sat), plus acoustic guitar, funk, rock and reggae – which attracts a good mix of Thais and foreigners. Daily 6pm–2am.

SOUTHERN DOWNTOWN: SOUTH OF THANON RAMA IV

Most of the action here happens around the east end of Thanon Silom, though a few bars further west lay on great views of the river or the vast cityscape. If, among all the choice of nightlife around Silom, you do end up in one of Patpong's sex shows, watch out for hyper-inflated bar bills and other cons – plenty of customers get ripped off in some way, and stories of menacing bouncers are legion.

Balco 5th floor, River City shopping centre ☎084 928 6161; map p.126. Welcoming rooftop bar with reasonably priced beers and cocktails, whose armchairs and sofas provide a good view of the river, up towards Chinatown and down to Saphan Taksin. Tues–Sun 6pm–2am.

The Barbican 9/4–5 Soi Thaniya, east end of Thanon Silom ☎02 233 4141–2, ⓦgreatbritishpub.com; map p.126. Stylishly modern fortress-like decor to match the name: dark woods, metal and undressed stone. With Guinness on tap and a long menu of imported beers, it could almost be a smart City of London pub – until you look out of the windows onto the soi's incongruous Japanese hostess bars. Good food, and happy hours daily 4–7pm. Daily 11am–1am.

O'Reilly's Corner of Silom and Thaniya rds ☎02 632 7515; map p.126. Welcoming Irish bar that's especially good for watching TV sport. Guinness and Kilkenny bitter on draught, multifarious drinks offers including 4–7pm happy hours, popular food and varied live music Tues, Thurs & Fri evenings. Daily 10am–1am.

Radio City 76/1–3 Patpong 1 ☎02 266 4567; map p.126. Raucous bar, with jumping live bands (Mon–Sat 10pm) – including a famous Elvis impersonator (Thurs–Sat) – and tables out on the sweaty, sleazy pavement. Daily 6pm–2am.

★ **The Sky Bar & Distil** Floor 63, State Tower, 1055 Thanon Silom, corner of Thanon Charoen Krung ☎02 624 9555; map p.126. Thrill-seekers and view addicts shouldn't miss forking out for an alfresco drink here, 275m above the city's pavements – come around 6pm to enjoy the stunning panoramas in both the light and the dark. It's standing-only at *The Sky Bar*, a circular restaurant-bar on the edge of the building with almost 360 degree views, but for the sunset itself, you're better off on the outside terrace of *Distil* on the other side of the building (where bookings are accepted), which has a wider choice of drinks, charming service and huge couches to recline on. Daily 5/6pm–1am.

Tapas Bar Soi 4, Thanon Silom ☎02 234 4737; map p.126. Vaguely Spanish-oriented, pricey bar (but no tapas) with Moorish-style decor, whose outside tables are probably the best spot for checking out the comings and goings on this pedestrianized, partly gay soi. In the multi-roomed interior, which stretches up to a third-floor roof terrace, the music is mostly house. Admission pricing policy changes regularly but is currently Fri & Sat B200 including one drink, Sun–Thurs free. Daily 7pm–2am.

★**Tawandang German Brewery** 462/61 Thanon Rama III ☎02 678 1114–6; map p.126. A taxi-ride south of Chong Nonsi BTS down Thanon Narathiwat Ratchanakharin – and best to book a table in advance – this vast all-rounder is well worth the effort. Under a huge dome, up to 1600 revellers enjoy good food, great micro-brewed German beer and a mercurial, hugely entertaining cabaret, featuring Fong Naam, who blend Thai classical and popular with Western styles of music, as well as magic shows, ballet and hip-hop dancing. Daily 5pm–1am.

Viva: The River Ground floor, River City shopping centre ☎02 639 6305; map p.126. Recently opened branch of the famous Chatuchak Market bar (see p.164), with a lovely terrace on the river and a gnarly interior decor of hide-bound chairs and ships' winches. On offer are some serious cocktails, good coffees and smoothies, as well as breakfasts and comfort food (till midnight) such as gourmet hot dogs, pizzas and salads; chilled DJs play every night, plus occasional live music. Daily 8am–1am.

THANON SUKHUMVIT

A night out on Thanon Sukhumvit could be subsumed by the girlie bars and hostess-run bar-beers (open-sided drinking halls with huge circular bars) on sois Nana and Cowboy, but there's plenty of style on Sukhumvit too, especially in the rooftop bars and enjoyably trendy clubs.

36-24-36 23 Soi Naphasap 2, Soi 36 ☎02 661 5636, ⓦ362436kitchenbar.com; map p.124. At the end of a quiet sub-soi (second right off Soi 36), 15min walk from BTS Thong Lo, this friendly, unpretentious bar occupies a large, modernist villa that's all windows. Sit on the retro furniture inside, or under the trees in the large garden, and enjoy cheap beer and a varied menu of Thai food. DJs every night, plus live acoustic or indie music Fri and Sat. Tues–Sun 5pm–1am.

★**Bed Supperclub** 26 Soi 11 ☎02 651 3537, ⓦbedsupperclub.com; map p.124. Worth visiting for the futuristic visuals alone, this seductively curvaceous space-pod bar is still the top nightspot in this trendy soi. Inside, the all-white interior is dimly lit and surprisingly cosy, with deep couches inviting drinkers to recline around the edges of the upstairs gallery, getting a good view of the downstairs bar and DJ. The vibe is always welcoming and a lot less pretentious than you might expect; some nights are themed, with regular promotions and international guest DJs. The starker restaurant section serves a global fusion menu, accompanied by lounge DJs and contemporary shows of music, dance and performance art (closed Mon;

Fri & Sat set four-course menu). ID required; admission depends on what's on, but is typically B600 including two drinks after 10pm. Bar daily 8pm–2am.

Cheap Charlie's Soi 11; map p.124. Idiosyncratic, long-running, low-tech, open-air bar that's famous for its cheap beer and customers' hall-of-fame gallery. It now offers the luxury of plastic tables and chairs, on a quiet, pedestrianized side-alley. Mon–Sat 5.30pm–midnight.

Finnegan's 23/1 Soi 4 (Nana Tai) ☎02 656 8160, ⓦfinnegansthailand.com; map p.124. Probably the most authentically Irish of Bangkok's many "Oirish" bars, friendly *Finnegan's* offers draught Guinness, homely wood and leather decor, popular food and a wide array of TV sports, including rugby and Gaelic games. Happy hour till 8pm. Daily 9am–1am.

Long Table Column Tower, 48 Soi 16 ☎02 302 2557–9, ⓦlongtablebangkok.com; map p.124. This achingly fashionable 25th-floor restaurant is named for its 25m-long communal centrepiece table, which seats seventy and serves contemporary Thai cuisine. But the real attraction is the sleek, Shanghai-style open-sided balcony bar whose "long-tail" cocktails give you ample time to lounge glamorously on the leather sofas and soak up the wraparound panoramas across downtown skyscrapers. Daily 5pm–2am.

Nest 9th Floor, *Le Fenix* hotel, Soi 11 ☎02 255 0638, ⓦnestbangkok.com; map p.124. Whether you unfurl on a daybed, curl up in a basket-chair or recline under a hooded chaise longue at this aptly named, leafy, rooftop eyrie you'll get an airy view of the condo-spiked skyline (there are covers for wet days) and a decent choice of cocktails (mostly B300). There's music every night, be it DJs, singer-songwriters, Latin nights or occasional parties. Not as slick or spectacular as the more famous downtown sky bars but very pleasant. Sun–Thurs 5pm–2am, Fri & Sat 5pm–3am.

Q Bar 34 Soi 11 ☎02 252 3274, ⓦqbarbangkok.com; map p.124. Very dark, very trendy, New York-style bar-club occupying two floors and a terrace. Famous for its wide choice of chilled vodkas, and for its music from local and international DJs, *Q Bar* appeals to a mixed crowd of fashionable people, particularly on Fri and Sat nights. Admission price depends on who's on, but count on B500 including two free drinks (currently free Mon & Tues); don't turn up in shorts, singlets or sandals if you're male. ID required. Daily 8pm–late.

WTF 7 Soi 51 ☎02 662 6246, ⓦwtfbangkok.com; map p.124. Small, hip, Spanish-influenced bar-café and art gallery, which hosts occasional poetry nights, left-field DJs and gigs. Adorned with luridly coloured Thai film posters and a great soundtrack, it offers tapas (from B70), pizzas and a tempting variety of cocktails and wines. It's 5min walk west of BTS Thong Lo, 100m up Soi 51, near the mouth of a small sub-soi on the left. Tues–Sun 7pm–12.30am.

1

CHATUCHAK WEEKEND MARKET

Viva Soi 6, Section 26 ☎02 272 4783. Classy, relaxing little juice bar that also serves coffees and cocktails, where you can rest your feet while listening to jazz on the sound system, or live music in the evening (until 9pm). There's another handy branch in Section 8, with a DJ in the evening. Sat & Sun 8am–9pm.

GAY BANGKOK

The bars, clubs and café-restaurants listed here, located around the east end of Thanon Silom and especially in the narrow alleys of Soi 2 and Soi 4 (see map, p.126), are the most notable of Bangkok's **gay nightlife** venues. More general background on gay life in Thailand, plus contacts and sources of information, most of them concentrated in Bangkok, can be found in Basics (see p.65). Advice on opening hours and on carrying ID is given in Drinking and Nightlife (see p.160).

The Balcony Soi 4, Thanon Silom ☎02 235 5891, ⓦbalconypub.com. Unpretentious, fun place with plenty of outdoor seats for people-watching, welcoming staff, reasonably priced drinks, upstairs karaoke and decent Thai and Western food. Happy hour till 8pm. Daily 5.30pm–2am.

Dick's Café Duangthawee Plaza, 894/7–8 Soi Pratuchai, Thanon Suriwong ☎02 637 0078, ⓦdicks cafe.com. Elegant day-and-night café-bar-restaurant, with a *Casablanca* theme to the decor (styling itself on Rick's Café Americain). On a traffic-free soi of go-go bars off the north side of Suriwong, it's ideal for drinking, eating decent Thai and Western food or just chilling out. Daily 10.30am–2am.

Disco Disco Soi 2, Thanon Silom. Small, pared-down bar-disco with a minimalist, retro feel, playing good dance music to a fun young crowd. Daily 10.30pm–3am.

DJ Station Soi 2, Thanon Silom ☎02 266 4029, ⓦdj-station.com. Highly fashionable but unpretentious three-storey club, packed at weekends, attracting a mix of Thais and farangs; popular cabaret show nightly at 11.30pm. B100 including one drink (B200 including two drinks Fri & Sat). Daily 10.30pm–3am.

GOD (Guys on Display) 60/18–21 Soi 2/1, Thanon Silom, in a small pedestrianized alley between Soi Thaniya and Soi 2 ☎02 632 8033. Large, busy club with go-go dancers, somewhat more Thai-oriented and with later hours than *DJ Station*. B150 including one drink. *Diamond* next door is a smart bar-restaurant that's open till 2am. Daily roughly midnight–6am.

JJ Park 8/3 Soi 2, Thanon Silom ☎02 235 1227. Classy, Thai-oriented bar, for relaxed socializing rather than raving, with nightly singers and cabaret acts, and a chill-out annexe, *Club Café*, next door. Daily 10.30pm–3am.

Sphinx 98–104 Soi 4, Thanon Silom ☎02 234 7249, ⓦsphinxpub.com. Plush decor with a vaguely Egyptian theme, terrace seating and very good Thai and Western food attract a sophisticated crowd to this ground-floor bar and restaurant; karaoke upstairs at *Pharoah's* on Fri & Sat. Daily 6pm–1am.

Telephone Pub 114/11–13 Soi 4, Thanon Silom ☎02 234 3279, ⓦtelephonepub.com. Bangkok's first Western-style gay bar when it opened in 1987, this cruisy, dimly lit eating and drinking venue has a terrace on the alley, telephones on the tables inside for making new friends and karaoke upstairs. Daily 6pm–2am.

ENTERTAINMENT

On the cultural front, the most accessible of the capital's performing arts is **Thai dancing**, particularly when served up in bite-size portions in tourist shows. **Thai boxing** is also well worth watching: the raucous live experience at either of Bangkok's two main national stadia far outshines the TV coverage.

CULTURE SHOWS AND PERFORMING ARTS

Because of the language barrier, most Thai theatre is inaccessible to foreigners and so, with a few exceptions, the best way to experience the traditional performing arts is at shows designed for tourists, most notably at Siam Niramit. You can, however, witness Thai dancing being performed for its original ritual purpose, usually several times a day, at the Lak Muang Shrine behind the Grand Palace (see p.94) and the Erawan Shrine on the corner of Thanon Ploenchit (see p.123). For background on Thai classical dance and traditional theatre, see p.47.

Meanwhile, more glitzy and occasionally ribald entertainment is the order of the day at the capital's ladyboy cabaret shows.

Chalermkrung Theatre (Sala Chalermkrung) 66 Thanon Charoen Krung, on the intersection with Thanon Triphet in Pahurat, next to Old Siam Plaza ☎02 224 4499, ⓦsalachalermkrung.com or ⓦthaiticket major.com; map p.107. Mainstream traditional and contemporary theatre, plus regular *khon* performances with English subtitles. Thurs & Fri 7.30pm; from B800.

National Theatre Sanam Luang, Ratanakosin ☎02 224 1342; map p.83. Roughly weekly shows of traditional performing arts such as *khon*, plus twice-monthly medley shows of music, dancing and *lakhon* (classical dance-drama) for tourists and other beginners (usually the first and last Fri of the month at 5pm; B60–100), as well as outdoor shows of classical music and dancing on dry-season weekends. However, it's difficult to get information about what's on in English – try the nearby Bangkok Tourism Division (see p.142).

New Calypso Cabaret About to move to Asiatique shopping centre, Thanon Charoen Krung, 2km south of Saphan Taksin BTS (ⓦcalypsocabaret.com or ⓦthaiasiatique.com). A bevy of luscious transvestites don glamorous outfits and perform over-the-top song-and-dance routines. B1200, or B900 if booked online three days ahead. Shows every evening, tickets about B1000.

Siam Niramit 19 Thanon Tiam Ruammit, 5min walk (or a free shuttle ride from Exit 1) from Thailand Cultural Centre subway, following signs for the South Korean embassy ☎02 649 9222, ⓦsiamniramit.com; map p.137. Unashamedly tourist-oriented but the easiest place to get a glimpse of the variety and spectacle intrinsic to traditional Thai theatre. The 80min show presents a history of regional Thailand's culture and beliefs in a high-tech spectacular of fantastic costumes and huge chorus numbers, enlivened by acrobatics and flashy special effects. The complex also includes crafts outlets and a buffet restaurant (dinner plus show B1850). Tickets (from B1500) can be bought on the spot, online or through most travel agents. Daily 8pm.

Silom Village Thanon Silom ☎02 234 4581, ⓦsilomvillage.co.th; map p.126. This complex of tourist shops stages a nightly 50min show at its Ruen Thep theatre (8.30pm; B650) to accompany a set menu of Thai food (available from 7pm), as well as rather desultory free 15min shows at 7.50pm and 8.50pm at its outdoor restaurant.

Thailand Cultural Centre Thanon Ratchadapisek ☎02 247 0028, ⓦthaiticketmajor.com; Thailand Cultural Centre subway; map p.79. All-purpose venue, under the control of the Ministry of Culture, that hosts mainstream classical concerts, traditional and contemporary theatre, and visiting international dance and theatre shows.

CINEMAS

Central Bangkok has more than forty cinemas, many of them on the top floors of shopping centres. Most show recent American and European releases with their original dialogue and Thai subtitles, screening shows around four times a day. For programme details, your best bet is to go to ⓦmovieseer.com, which allows you to search by movie or by area in Bangkok (or indeed around the country), up to a week ahead; cinema locations are printed on *Nancy*

Chandler's Map of Bangkok. Whatever cinema you're in, you're expected to stand for the king's anthem, which is played before every performance.

Alliance Française 29 Thanon Sathorn Tai ☎02 670 4200, ⓦalliance-francaise.or.th; map p.126. Movies at the French cultural centre (every Wed 7.30pm; free) are usually subtitled in English. Scheduled to move locations soon, so check the website.

Apex Lido Thanon Rama I, Siam Square ☎02 252 6498, ⓦapexsiam-square.com; map p.119. Among half-a-dozen cinemas in and around Siam Square, this is your best bet for independent foreign films.

Goethe Institut 18/1 Soi Goethe, between Thanon Sathorn Tai and Soi Ngam Duphli ☎02 287 0942, ⓦgoethe.de; map pp.80–81. In the cool season (Dec–Feb), the German cultural centre screens an interesting programme of recent movies from German-speaking countries, always subtitled in English, outdoors in the garden; check their website for a detailed map. Wed 7.30pm; free.

House Royal City Avenue (RCA) ☎02 641 5177–8, ⓦhouserama.com; map p.137. Bangkok's only art-house cinema, well to the northeast of the centre. The nearest subway station, Phetchaburi, is a long walk away, so it's best to come by taxi (though an RCA stop on the Suvarnabhumi Airport Rail Link is planned).

Pridi Banomyong Library Thammasat University, Ratanakosin ☎02 613 3544; map p.83. Hosts regular free shows of foreign films.

THAI BOXING

The violence of the average Thai boxing match (see p.49) may be off-putting to some, but spending a couple of hours at one of Bangkok's two main stadia can be immensely entertaining, not least for the enthusiasm of the spectators and the ritualistic aspects of the fights. Seats for foreigners cost B1000–2000 (cheaper, standing tickets are reserved for Thais), though at Rajdamnoen the view from the B1000 section is partially obscured. Sessions usually feature ten bouts, each consisting of five three-minute rounds with two-minute rests in between each round, so if you're not a big fan it may be worth turning up an hour late, as the better fights tend to happen later in the billing. To engage in a little *muay thai* yourself, visit one of several gyms around Bangkok that offer classes to foreigners.

Chacrit Muay Thai School Next to Washington Square Theatre on Sukhumvit, between sois 22 and 24 ☎02 260 5816, ⓦchacritmuaythaischool.com; map p.124. Drop-in sessions B800/hr; longer courses available. Closed Sun.

Lumphini Stadium Thanon Rama IV, next to Lumphini subway ☎02 251 4303, ⓦmuaythailumpini.com; map pp.80–81. Tues & Fri 6.30pm, Sat 4pm & 8.15pm.

1

Rajdamnoen Stadium Next to the TAT office on Thanon Rajdamnoen Nok ☎02 281 4205; map pp.100–101. Mon, Wed, Thurs & Sun 6.30pm.

Sor Vorapin's Gym 13 Trok Kasap, off Thanon Chakrabongse in Banglamphu ☎02 282 3551, ⓦ thaiboxings.com; map pp.100–101. Holds *muay thai* classes twice daily (B500 per session). Sor Vorapin also offers extended training and a homestay at a second gym in Thonburi (B6500 all-in for 1 week) – see the website for details.

SHOPPING

Bangkok has a good reputation for shopping, particularly for antiques, gems, contemporary interior design and fashions, where the range and quality are streets ahead of other Thai cities. Silk and handicrafts are good buys too, though shopping for these in Chiang Mai has many advantages. As always, watch out for **fakes**: cut glass masquerading as precious stones, old, damaged goods being passed off as antiques, counterfeit designer clothes and accessories, pirated CDs and DVDs, even mocked-up international driver's licences (though Thai travel agents and other organizations aren't that easily fooled). Bangkok also has the best English-language bookshops in the country. Downtown is full of smart, multi-storey **shopping plazas** like Siam Centre, Siam Paragon and Central World on Thanon Rama I and Emporium on Thanon Sukhumvit, which is where you'll find the majority of the city's fashion stores, as well as designer lifestyle goods and bookshops. The plazas tend to be pleasantly air-conditioned and thronging with trendy young Thais, but don't hold much interest for tourists unless you happen to be looking for a new outfit. Shopping centres, department stores and tourist-oriented shops in the city keep late **hours**, opening daily at 10 or 11am and closing at about 9pm; many small, upmarket boutiques, for example along Thanon Charoen Krung and Thanon Silom, close on Sundays, one or two even on Saturdays. Monday is meant to be no-street-vendor day throughout Bangkok, a chance for the pavements to get cleaned and for pedestrians to finally see where they're going, but plenty of stalls manage to flout the rule.

MARKETS

For travellers, spectating, not shopping, is apt to be the main draw of Bangkok's neighbourhood markets – notably the bazaars of Chinatown and the blooms and scents of Pak Khlong Talat, the flower and vegetable market just west of Memorial Bridge (see p.110). The massive Chatuchak Weekend Market is an exception, being both a tourist attraction and a marvellous shopping experience (see p.129). With the chief exception of Chatuchak, most markets operate daily from dawn till early afternoon; early morning is often the best time to go to beat the heat and crowds.

HANDICRAFTS, TEXTILES AND CONTEMPORARY DESIGN

Samples of nearly all regionally produced handicrafts end up in Bangkok, so the selection is phenomenal. Many of the shopping plazas have at least one classy handicraft outlet, and competition keeps prices in the city at upcountry levels, with the main exception of household objects – particularly wickerware and tin bowls and basins – which get palmed off relatively expensively in Bangkok. Several places on and around Thanon Khao San sell reasonably priced triangular "axe" pillows (*mawn khwaan*) in traditional fabrics, which make fantastic souvenirs but are heavy to post home; some places sell unstuffed versions which are simple to mail home, but a pain to fill when you return. The cheapest outlet for traditional northern and northeastern textiles is Chatuchak Weekend Market (see p.129), where you'll also be able to nose out some interesting handicrafts. Most Thai silk, which is noted for its thickness and sheen, comes

from the northeast and the north, where shopping for it is probably more fun. However, there is a decent range of outlets in the capital, including many branches of Jim Thompson (see p.168). Bangkok is also rapidly establishing a reputation for its contemporary interior design, fusing minimalist Western ideals with traditional Thai and other Asian craft elements. The best places to sample this, as detailed in the reviews below, are on Floor 4 of the Siam Discovery Centre and Floor 4 of the Siam Paragon shopping centre, both on Thanon Rama I, and Floor 3 of the Gaysorn Plaza on Thanon Ploenchit.

BANGLAMPHU AND RATANAKOSIN

Lofty Bamboo Buddy Hotel shopping complex, 265 Thanon Khao San ⓦ loftybamboo.com; map pp.100–101. Fair-trade outlet for Thai crafts, accessories and jewellery, including silver made by Karen people from north and west Thailand, recycled textile products from tsunami-affected communities in Phang Nga, and Sop Moei Arts products (see p.303). Daily 10.30am–7.30pm.

Queen's Support Foundation Grand Palace (on the right just inside the Gate of Glorious Victory); map p.84. Not-for-profit shop that's especially good for beautiful, top-quality *yan lipao*, traditional basketware made from delicately woven fern stems. Under renovation at the time of writing, but should have reopened by the time you read this.

Taekee Taekon 118 Thanon Phra Arthit; map pp.100–101. Tasteful assortment of handicraft gifts and souvenirs, plus a selection of Thai art cards, black-and-white photocards and Nancy Chandler greetings cards. Mon–Sat 9am–6pm.

SHOPPING FOR EVERYDAY STUFF

You're most likely to find useful everyday items in one of the city's numerous **department stores**: seven-storey Central Chidlom on Thanon Ploenchit (daily 10am–10pm), which boasts handy services like watch-, garment- and shoe-repair booths as well as a huge product selection (including large sizes), is probably the city's best. For **children's stuff**, Central Chidlom also has a branch of Mothercare, as do the Emporium and Siam Paragon shopping centres. Meanwhile, the British chain of **pharmacies**, Boots the Chemist, has scores of branches across the city, including on Thanon Khao San, in Siam Paragon, in Central World, in Emporium and a late-night branch at the Thanon Suriwong end of Patpong 1.

The best place to buy anything to do with **mobile phones** (see p.71) is the scores of small booths on the third floor of Mah Boon Krong (MBK) Shopping Centre at the Rama I/Phrayathai intersection. For **computer** hardware and genuine and pirated software, as well as digital cameras, Panthip Plaza, at 604/3 Thanon Phetchaburi, is the best place; it's slightly off the main shopping routes, but handy for Khlong Saen Saeb boat stop Tha Pratunam, or a longer walk from BTS Ratchathevi. Mac-heads are catered for here, including authorized resellers, and there are dozens of repair and secondhand booths, especially towards the back of the shopping centre and on the upper floors.

DOWNTOWN: AROUND SIAM SQUARE AND THANON PLOENCHIT

D & O Shop Floor 3, Gaysorn Plaza ⓦdandoshop.com; map p.119. A dozen enterprising local designers have formed the Design and Objects Association to showcase their diverse contemporary wares here: vases, lamps, tableware, jewellery, bags, stationery. Daily 10am–8pm.

Doi Tung by Mae Fah Luang Floor 4, Siam Discovery Centre ⓦdoitung.org; map p.119. Part of the late Princess Mother's development project based at Doi Tung, selling very striking and attractive cotton and linen in warm colours, made up into clothes, cushion covers, rugs and so on, as well as rustic ceramics. Mon–Thurs 11am–8pm, Fri–Sun 11am–9pm.

Exotique Thai Floor 4, Siam Paragon; map p.119. A collection of small outlets from around the city and the country – including silk-makers and designers such as Vila Cini (see p.303) from Chiang Mai – that makes a good, upmarket one-stop shop, much more interesting than Narai Phand (see below). There's everything from jewellery, through celadons, to beauty products, with a focus on contemporary adaptations of traditional crafts. Daily 10am–10pm.

Gilles Caffier Floor 4, Siam Discovery Centre ⓦgilles caffier.com; map p.119. Cushion covers and other items made from leather and hides, plus some frankly uncategorizable, but therefore very striking, objets d'art, from a French designer based in Nakhon Pathom, who has spent time in Japan but takes his influences from around the world. Daily 10am–8pm.

Lamont Contemporary Floor 3, Gaysorn Plaza ⓦlamont-design.com; map p.119. Beautiful lacquer-ware bowls, vases and boxes, as well as bronze, glass, crystal and ceramic objects, all in imaginative contemporary styles. Lamont also have a pan-Asian

antique and repro shop opposite, and branches in the Sukhothai (both contemporary and antique lines), Oriental (mostly antiques) and Four Seasons (mostly contemporary) hotels. All daily 10am–8pm.

Nandakwang Floor 4, Siam Discovery Centre ⓣ02 658 0407; map p.119. Outlet of a famous cotton company from Pasang in northern Lamphun province, whose main draws are cushion covers (including axe cushions) and bags in sumptuous colours, often featuring floral motifs. Daily 10am–9pm.

Narai Phand Ground floor, President Tower Arcade, just east of Gaysorn Plaza, Thanon Ploenchit ⓦnaraiphand.com; map p.119. This souvenir centre was set up to ensure the preservation of traditional crafts and to maintain standards of quality, as a joint venture with the Ministry of Industry in the 1930s, and has a duly institutional feel, though it makes a reasonable one-stop shop for last-minute presents. It offers a huge assortment of reasonably priced goods from all over the country, including silk and cotton, khon masks, bencharong, celadon, woodcarving, silver, yan lipao basketware and axe cushions. Daily 10am–8pm.

NV Aranyik Floor 3, Gaysorn Plaza ⓦnv-aranyik.com; map p.119. A good place to buy that chunky, elegant Thai-style cutlery you may have been eating your dinner with in Bangkok's posher restaurants, with both traditional and contemporary handmade designs; plus lovely, handmade stainless-steel bowls. Daily 10am–8pm.

Panta Floor 4, Siam Discovery Centre, and Floor 4, Siam Paragon ⓦpantathailand.net; map p.119. Modern design store that stands out for its experimental furniture, including way-out-there cushions and other items made of woven rattan, wood and dried water-hyacinth stalks. Discovery daily 10am–9pm; Paragon daily noon–8/9pm.

1

Thann Native Floor 3, Gaysorn Plaza ⓦthann.info; map p.119. Striking contemporary rugs, cushion covers and other furnishings, plus famous spa and beauty products (with a high-concept modern spa next door). Daily 10am–8pm.

DOWNTOWN: SOUTH OF THANON RAMA IV

Jim Thompson 9 Thanon Suriwong, corner of Thanon Rama IV; branches at the Jim Thompson House Museum (see p.120), Suvarnabhumi Airport and many department stores, malls and hotels around the city; ⓦjimthompson.com; map p.126. A good place to start looking for traditional Thai fabric, or at least to get an idea of what's out there. Stocks silk, linen and cotton by the metre and ready-made items from shirts to cushion covers, which are well designed and of good quality, but pricey. They also have a home-furnishings section and a good dressmaking service. A couple of hundred metres along Thanon Suriwong from the main branch, at no. 149/4–6, a Jim Thompson Factory Sales Outlet (daily 9am–6pm) sells remnant home-furnishing fabrics and home accessories at knock-down prices (if you're really keen on a bargain, they have a much larger factory outlet way out east of the centre on Soi 93, Thanon Sukhumvit; daily 9am–6pm). Daily 9am–9pm.

Khomapastr 56–58 Thanon Naret, between Suriwong and Si Phraya ⓦkhomapastrfabrics.com; map p.126. Branch of the famous Hua Hin cotton shop (see p.525). Mon–Sat 9am–5.30pm.

The Legend Floor 3, Thaniya Plaza, corner of Soi Thaniya and Thanon Silom ☏02 231 2170; map p.126. Stocks a small selection of well-made Thai handicrafts, from wood and wickerware to pretty fabrics and celadon and other ceramics, at reasonable prices. Daily 11am–8pm.

Silom Village 286/1 Thanon Silom ⓦsilomvillage .co.th; map p.126. An open-air complex of low-rise shops that attempts to create a relaxing, upcountry atmosphere as a backdrop for its diverse, fairly pricey handicrafts. Most shops daily 10am–9/10pm.

Tamnan Mingmuang Floor 3, Thaniya Plaza, corner of Soi Thaniya and Thanon Silom ☏02 231 1220; map p.126. Subsidiary of The Legend (see above), which sells clay figurines but concentrates on basketry from all over the country: among the unusual items on offer are trays and boxes for tobacco and betel nut made from yan lipao (intricately woven fern vines), and bambooware sticky-rice containers, baskets and lampshades. Daily 11am–8pm.

THANON SUKHUMVIT

Krisna's Just west of Soi 11 ⓦkrishnaasianarts.com; map p.124. Five-floor emporium of mostly mass-produced but good-quality artefacts from Thailand and beyond, especially figurines and Buddha statues in wood, lacquer and silver plus some jewellery and trinkets. Mon–Sat 9am–7.30pm, Sun 3–7pm.

The Shop @ TCDC Thailand Creative and Design Centre, Floor 6, Emporium, Thanon Sukhumvit, between sois 22 and 24 ⓦtcdc.or.th; map p.124. The retail outlet at Bangkok's design centre sells innovative products dreamt up by local creatives, mostly fairly funky stocking-fillers, bags and household items, with just a whiff of kitsch. Tues–Sun 10.30am–9pm.

Sop Moei Arts 8 Soi 49 ⓦsopmoeiarts.com; map p.124. If you're not going up to Chiang Mai, it's well worth checking out the lovely fabrics and basketware at this small branch shop, which also sells Studio Naenna textiles (see p.303). Daily except Sat 9.30am–6pm.

Thai Celadon Soi 16 (Thanon Ratchadapisek) ⓦthaiceladon.thailand.com; map p.124. Classic celadon stoneware made in Chiang Mai without commercial dyes or clays and glazed with the archetypal blues and greens that were invented by the Chinese to emulate the colour of precious jade. Mainly crockery, vases and lamps, plus some figurines. Daily 9am–5pm.

Thai Craft Fairs Floor 3, Jasmine City Building, corner of Thanon Sukhumvit and Soi 23 ⓦthaicraft.org; map p.124. Roughly monthly craft sales and demonstrations, involving about seventy groups of artisans from all over the country, run by the Thai Craft Association, an independent development organization; plus occasional smaller fairs around the city.

TAILORED CLOTHES

Inexpensive tailoring shops crowd Silom, Sukhumvit and Khao San roads, but the best single area to head for is the short stretch of Thanon Charoen Krung between the GPO and Thanon Silom (near the Chao Phraya express-boat stops at Tha Oriental and Tha Wat Muang Kae, or a 10min walk from Saphan Taksin Skytrain station), where most of the recommended tailors below are. It's generally advisable to avoid tailors in tourist areas such as Thanon Khao San, shopping malls and Thanon Sukhumvit's Soi Nana and Soi 11, although if you're lucky it's still possible to come up trumps here. For cheap and reasonable shirt and dress material other than silk go for a browse around Pahurat market (see p.109), though the suit materials are mostly poor, and best avoided.

A Song Tailor 8 Trok Chartered Bank, just round the corner from Tongue Thai restaurant off Thanon Charoen Krung, near the Oriental Hotel ☏02 630 9708; map p.126. Friendly, helpful small shop that's a good first port of call if you're on a budget. Men's and women's suits and shirts; ideally three to four days with two fittings, but can turn work around in two days. Mon–Sat 10am–7.30pm, Sun 8–10am.

Ah Song Tailor 1203 Thanon Charoen Krung, opposite

HAVING CLOTHES TAILOR-MADE

Bangkok can be an excellent place to get tailor-made suits, dresses, shirts and trousers at a fraction of the price you'd pay in the West. Tailors here can copy a sample brought from home and will also work from any photographs you can provide; most also carry a good selection of catalogues. The bad news is that many tourist-oriented tailors aren't terribly good, often attempting to get away with poor work and shoddy materials (and sometimes trying to delay delivery until just before you leave the city, so that you don't have time to complain). However, with a little effort and thought, both men and women can get some fantastic clothes made to measure.

Choosing a tailor can be tricky, and unless you're particularly knowledgeable about material, shopping around won't necessarily tell you much. However, don't make a decision wholly on prices quoted – picking a tailor simply because they're the cheapest usually leads to poor work, and cheap suits don't last. Special deals offering two suits, two shirts, two ties and a kimono for US$99 should be left well alone. Above all, ignore recommendations by anyone with a vested interest in bringing your custom to a particular shop.

Prices vary widely depending on material and the tailor's skill. As a very rough guide, for labour alone expect to pay B5000–6000 for a two-piece suit, though some tailors will charge rather more (check whether or not the price you're quoted includes the lining). For middling **material**, expect to pay about B3000–5000, or anything up to B20,000 for top-class cloth. With the exception of silk, local materials are frequently of poor quality and for suits in particular you're far better off using English or Italian cloth. Most tailors stock both imported and local fabrics, but bringing your own from home can work out significantly cheaper.

Give yourself as much **time** as possible. For suits, insist on two fittings. Most good tailors require around three days for a suit (some require ten days or more), although a few have enough staff to produce good work in a day or two. The more **detail** you can give the tailor the better. As well as deciding on the obvious features such as single- or double-breasted and number of buttons, think about the width of lapels, style of trousers, whether you want the jacket with vents or not, and so forth. Specifying factors like this will make all the difference to whether you're happy with your suit, so it's worth discussing them with the tailor; a good tailor should be able to give good advice. Finally, don't be afraid to be an awkward customer until you're completely happy with the finished product – after all, the whole point of getting clothes tailor-made is to get exactly what you want.

Soi 36 ☎02 233 7574; map p.126. Younger brother of the above (neither of them should be confused with the nearby Ah Sun Tailor), a meticulous tailor who takes pride in his work. Men's and women's suits and shirts in around four days, with two fittings. Mon–Sat 10am–7pm.

Chang Torn 95 Thanon Tanao ☎02 282 9390; map pp.100–101. Well-regarded, traditional tailor in Banglamphu, who prefers ten days to make a suit. Mon–Sat 10am–5pm.

Golden Wool 1340–2 Thanon Charoen Krung ☎02 233 0149, ⓦgolden-wool.com; map p.126. Larger operation than all of the above, which can turn around decent work for men and women in two days, though prices are slightly on the high side. Mon–Sat 9am–8pm.

FASHION

Thanon Khao San is lined with stalls selling low-priced fashion: the tie-dyed vests, baggy cotton fisherman's trousers and embroidered blouses are all aimed at backpackers, but they're supplemented by cheap contemporary fashions that appeal to urban Thai trendies as well. Downtown, the most famous area for low-cost,

low-quality casual clothes is the warren-like Pratunam Market and surrounding malls such as Platinum Fashion Mall around the junction of Phetchaburi and Ratchaprarop roads (see map, p.119), but for the best and latest trends from Thai designers, you should check out the shops in Siam Square and across the road in the more upmarket Siam Centre. Prices vary considerably: street gear in Siam Square is undoubtedly inexpensive (and look out for outlet stores such as Jaspal's in Emporium), while genuine Western brand names are generally competitive but not breathtakingly cheaper than at home; larger sizes can be hard to find. Shoes and leather goods are good buys in Bangkok, being generally handmade from high-quality leather and quite a bargain.

Central World Ratchaprasong Intersection, corner of Rama I and Rajdamri ⓦcentralworld.co.th; map p.119. This shopping centre – recently refurbished after it was torched during the suppression of the red-shirt street protests in 2010 – is so huge that it defies easy classification, but you'll find plenty of Thai and international fashions on its lower floors and in the attached Zen department store at its southern end. Daily 10am–9/10pm.

1

Emporium Thanon Sukhumvit, between sois 22 and 24 ⓦemporiumthailand.com; map p.124. Enormous and rather glamorous shopping plaza, with its own department store and a good range of fashion outlets, from exclusive designer wear to trendy high-street gear. Genuine brand-name shops include Prada, Chanel, Louis Vuitton, as well as established local labels such as Soda and Jaspal. Daily 10am–8/10pm.

Gaysorn Plaza Thanon Ploenchit ⓦgaysorn.com; map p.119. The most chic of the city's shopping plazas: in among Prada, Emporio Armani and Louis Vuitton, a few Thai names have made it onto the second floor, notably Fly Now, which mounts dramatic displays of women's party and formal gear, alongside more casual wear, and Myth, a gathering of seven cutting-edge local designers for men and women in one store. Daily 10am–8pm.

Mah Boon Krong (MBK) At the Rama I/Phrayathai intersection ⓦmbk-center.co.th; map p.119. Vivacious, labyrinthine shopping centre which most closely resembles a traditional Thai market that's been rammed into a huge mall. It houses hundreds of small, mostly fairly inexpensive outlets, including plenty of high-street fashion shops. Daily 10am–8/9pm.

Siam Centre Thanon Rama I ⓦsiamcenter.co.th; map p.119. Particularly good for hip local labels, many of which have made the step up from the booths of Siam Square across the road – look out for Greyhound, Jaspal and Theatre – as well as international names like FCUK and Quiksilver. Daily 10am–9pm.

Siam Square map p.119. Worth poking around the alleys here, especially near what's styled as the area's "Centerpoint" between sois 3 and 4. All manner of inexpensive boutiques, some little more than booths, sell colourful street-gear to the capital's fashionable students and teenagers.

Viera by Ragazze Floor 2, Central World and in the attached Isetan department store ⓦragazze.co.th; map p.119. Stylish, Italian-influenced leather goods. Daily 10am–9/9.30pm.

BOOKS

English-language bookshops in Bangkok are always well stocked with everything to do with Thailand, and most carry fiction classics and popular paperbacks as well. The capital's secondhand bookshops are not cheap, but you can usually part-exchange your unwanted titles.

Asia Books Branches include on Thanon Sukhumvit between sois 15 and 19 (see map p.124), in Times Square between sois 12 and 14, and in Emporium between sois 22 and 24; in Peninsula Plaza and in Central World, both on Thanon Rajdamri; in Siam Discovery Centre and Siam Paragon, both on Thanon Rama I; and in Thaniya Plaza on Soi Thaniya off Thanon Silom ⓦasiabooks.com. English-language bookshop (and publishing house) that's

especially recommended for its books on Asia – everything from guidebooks to cookery books, novels to art (the Sukhumvit 15–19 branch has the very best Asian selection). Also stocks bestselling novels and coffee-table books.

B2S Floor 7, Central Chidlom, Thanon Ploenchit, among dozens of branches around town ⓦb2s.co.th; map p.119. Decent selection of English-language books, but most notable for its huge selection of magazines, newspapers and stationery. Daily 10am–10pm.

Bookazine 62 Thanon Khao San; Hualamphong train station; Gaysorn Plaza, Thanon Ploenchit ⓦasiabooks .com; maps pp.100–101, p.107 & p.119. Alongside a decent selection of English-language books about Asia and novels, these shops stock a wide range of foreign newspapers and magazines.

Books Kinokuniya 3rd Floor, Emporium Shopping Centre, Thanon Sukhumvit, with branches at Floor 6, Isetan, in the Central World Plaza, and Floor 3, Siam Paragon, Thanon Rama I ⓦkinokuniya.com/th; map p.119 & p.124. Huge, efficient, Japanese-owned, English-language bookshop with a wide selection of books ranging from bestsellers to travel literature and from classics to sci-fi; not so hot on books about Asia though.

Dasa Book Cafe Between sois 26 and 28, Thanon Sukhumvit ⓦdasabookcafe.com; map p.124. Bangkok's best secondhand bookshop, Dasa is appealingly calm and intelligently, and alphabetically, categorized, with sections on everything from Asia to chick lit, health to gay and lesbian interest. Browse its stock online, or enjoy coffee and cakes *in situ*. Daily 10am–8pm.

Shaman Books 71 Thanon Khao San, Banglamphu; map pp.100–101. Well-stocked secondhand bookshop where all books are logged on the computer. Lots of books on Asia (travel, fiction, politics and history) as well as a decent range of novels and general-interest books. Daily 10am–11pm.

JEWELLERY AND GEMS

Bangkok boasts the country's best gem and jewellery shops, and some of the finest lapidaries in the world, making this *the* place to buy cut and uncut stones such as rubies, blue sapphires and diamonds. However, countless gem-buying tourists get badly ripped off, so be extremely wary.

Asian Institute of Gemological Sciences 48th floor, Jewelry Trade Center, 919/539 Thanon Silom ☎02 267 4325, ⓦaigsthailand.com; map p.126. Independent professional advice and precious stones certification from its laboratory. Also runs reputable courses, such as a five-day (15hr) introduction to gems and gemology (US$280).

Jewelry Trade Center (Silom Galleria) West end of Thanon Silom ⓦsilomgalleria.net; map p.126. Dozens of members of the Thai Gem and Jewelry Traders Association have outlets in this shopping mall (and on the surrounding streets). Mon–Sat roughly 10.30am–6pm.

GEM SCAMS

Gem scams are so common in Bangkok that TAT has published a brochure about it and there are several websites on the subject, including the very informative ⓦ 2bangkok.com/2bangkok -scams-sapphire.html, which describes typical scams in detail. Never buy anything through a tout or from any shop recommended by a "government official"/"student"/"businessperson"/ tuk-tuk driver who just happens to engage you in conversation on the street, and note that there are no government jewellery shops, despite any information you may be given to the contrary, and no special government promotions or sales on gems.

The basic **scam** is to charge a lot more than what the gem is worth based on its carat weight – at the very least, get it **tested** on the spot, ask for a written guarantee and receipt. Don't even consider **buying gems in bulk** to sell at a supposedly vast profit elsewhere: many a gullible traveller has invested thousands of dollars on a handful of worthless multicoloured stones, believing the vendor's reassurance that the goods will fetch at least a hundred percent more when resold at home.

If you're determined to buy precious stones, check that the shop is a member of the **Thai Gem and Jewelry Traders Association**, by visiting their website which has a directory of members (ⓦthaigemjewelry.or.th). To be doubly sure, you may want to seek out shops that also belong to the TGJTA's **Jewel Fest Club** (ⓦjewelfest.com), which guarantees quality and will offer refunds; see their website for a directory of members.

Lambert Floor 4, Silom Shanghai Building, Soi 17, 807–9 Thanon Silom ☎02 236 4343, ⓦlambertgems .com; map p.126. Thoroughly reputable, thirty-year-old, American-owned outlet, offering a full service: loose stones and pearls, including collectors' stones, ready-made pieces, cutting, design, redesign and repairs. Mon–Fri 9am–5pm, Sat 9am–4pm.

ANTIQUES

Bangkok is the entrepôt for the finest Thai, Burmese and Cambodian antiques, but the market has long been sewn up, so don't expect to happen upon any undiscovered treasure. Even experts admit that they sometimes find it hard to tell real antiques from fakes, so the best policy is just to buy on the grounds of attractiveness. The River City shopping complex (ⓦrivercity.co.th) off Thanon Charoen Krung, which is near Si Phraya and Harbour Department express-boat piers and operates a shuttle boat every 30min from Saphan Taksin BTS, devotes its third, fourth and some of its second floors to a bewildering array of pricey treasures, as well as holding an auction on the first Saturday of every month (viewing during the preceding week; ☎02 237 0077). The other main area for antiques is the nearby section of Charoen Krung that runs between the GPO and the bottom of Thanon Silom, and the stretch of Silom running east from here up to and including the multistorey Silom Galleria. Here you'll find a good selection of largely reputable individual businesses specializing in woodcarvings, ceramics, bronze statues and stone sculptures culled from all parts of Thailand and neighbouring countries as well. Remember that most antiques require an export permit (see p.63).

Beyond the Masks Floor 3, River City; map p.126. True to its name: Asian tribal masks plus a miscellany of ornamental coconut scrapers, silver jewellery and fabrics. Daily 10.30am–7.30pm.

Old Maps and Prints Floor 4, River City ☎081 424 4425, ⓦclassicmaps.com; map p.126. Lovely old prints of Thailand and Asia, as well as rare maps. Mon–Sat 11am–7pm, Sun 1–6pm, but best to make an appointment.

Old Siam Trading Company Nailert Building at the mouth of Soi 5, Thanon Sukhumvit ⓦoldsiamtrading .com; map p.124. Old prints, books and maps of Asia. Mon–Fri 8.30am–6pm, Sat 11am–6pm.

The Verandah and Beyond Floor 3, River City; map p.126. Lacquerware, silver jewellery, Buddha images and other statuary, including pieces from Burma. Daily 10.30am–7.30pm.

DIRECTORY

Couriers DHL Worldwide (☎02 345 5000, ⓦdhl.co.th) has several Bangkok depots.

Embassies and consulates Australia, 37 Thanon Sathorn Tai ☎02 344 6300, ⓦthailand.embassy.gov.au; Burma (Myanmar), 132 Thanon Sathorn Nua ☎02 234 4789; Cambodia, 518/4 Thanon Pracha Uthit (Soi Ramkamhaeng 39) ☎02 957 5851–2; Canada, 15th floor, Abdulrahim Place, 990 Thanon Rama IV ☎02 636 0540, ⓦthailand.gc.ca; China, 57 Thanon Rajadapisek ☎02 245 7033 or ☎02 245 7036; India, 46 Sukhumvit Soi 23 ☎02 258 0300–6, ⓦindianembassy.in.th; Indonesia, 600–602 Thanon Phetchaburi ☎02 252 3135–9; Ireland (honorary consul), Room 407, Thaniya Building, 62 Thanon Silom ☎02 632 6720, ⓦirelandinthailand.com; Laos, 502/1–3

Soi Sahakarnpramoon, Thanon Pracha Uthit ☎02 539 6667–8 ext 106, ⓦbkklaoembassy.com; Malaysia, 35 Thanon Sathorn Tai ☎02 629 6800; New Zealand, 14th Floor, M Thai Tower, All Seasons Place, 87 Thanon Witthayu ☎02 254 2530; Singapore, 129 Thanon Sathorn Tai ☎02 286 2111; South Africa, Floor 12A, M Thai Tower, All Seasons Place, 87 Thanon Witthayu ☎02 659 2900, ⓦsaembbangkok.com; UK, 14 Thanon Witthayu ☎02 305 8333; US, 120 Thanon Witthayu ☎02 205 4000; Vietnam, 83/1 Thanon Witthayu ☎02 650 8979.

Emergencies For English-speaking help in any emergency, call the tourist police on their free 24hr phoneline ☎1155. The tourist police headquarters is on the eastern edge of town at 2107 Bangkok Tower, Thanon Phetchaburi Mai (east of the Wat Mai Chong Lom stop on the Saen Saeb canal-boat service and well to the east of Phetchaburi subway station; ☎02 308 0333), or drop in at the more convenient Chana Songkhram Police Station at the west end of Thanon Khao San in Banglamphu (☎02 282 2323). In the evenings, you'll also find tourist police at the Silom end of Patpong 1.

Exchange The Suvarnabhumi Airport exchange desks and those in the upmarket hotels are open 24hr, while many other exchange booths stay open till 8pm or later, especially along Khao San, Sukhumvit and Silom roads and in the major shopping malls. You can also withdraw cash from hundreds of ATMs around the city and at the airports.

Hospitals, clinics and dentists Most expats rate the private Bumrungrad International Hospital, 33 Sukhumvit Soi 3 (☎02 667 1000, emergency ☎02 667 2999, ⓦbumrungrad.com), as the best and most comfortable in the city, followed by the BNH (Bangkok Nursing Home) Hospital, 9 Thanon Convent (☎02 686 2700, emergency ☎02 632 1000, ⓦbnhhospital.com); and the Bangkok Hospital Medical Centre, 2 Soi Soonvijai 7, Thanon Phetchaburi Mai (☎02 310 3000, emergency ☎1719, ⓦbangkokhospital.com). You can get vaccinations and malaria advice, as well as rabies advice and treatment, at the Thai Red Cross Society's Queen Saovabha Memorial Institute (QSMI) and Snake Farm on the corner of Thanon Rama IV and Thanon Henri Dunant (Mon–Fri 8.30am–4.30pm, Sat 8.30am–noon; ☎02 252 0161–4 ext 125 or 132, ⓦsaovabha.com). Among general clinics, there's one in Banglamphu in the Rambuttri Village complex on Soi Rambuttri run by the Bangkok Hospital (☎02 629 5260; daily 10am–8pm), and Global Doctor, Ground Floor, *Holiday Inn Hotel*, 981 Thanon Silom (corner of Thanon Surasak; ☎02 236 8442–4, ⓦglobaldoctorclinic .com), is recommended. For dental problems, try the Bumrungrad Hospital's dental department on ☎02 667 2300; the Dental Hospital, 88/88 Sukhumvit Soi 49 (☎02 260 5000–15, ⓦdentalhospitalbangkok.com); or Siam Family Dental Clinic, 292/6 Siam Square Soi 4 (☎081 987 7700, ⓦsiamfamilydental.com).

Immigration office North of the centre off Thanon Wiphawadi Rangsit at Floor 2, B Building, Government Complex, Soi 7, Thanon Chaengwattana (Mon–Fri 8.30am–noon & 1–4.30pm; ☎02 141 9889, ⓦbangkok .immigration.go.th, which includes a map); see p.64 for information on visa extensions. Be very wary of any Khao San tour agents who offer to organize a visa extension for you: some are reportedly faking the relevant stamps and this has caused problems at immigration.

Internet access Most hotels, an increasing number of guesthouses and a few restaurants and bars offer wi-fi, usually free to customers, sometimes for a fee. For a list of hot spots, try ⓦjiwire.com; for free locations, go to ⓦstickmanweekly.com. Banglamphu is packed with places offering internet access, in particular along Thanon Khao San, where competition keeps prices very low; to surf in a/c style, head for *True*, off the western end of Thanon Khao San (daily 9.30am–11pm). The Ratchadamnoen Post Office on Banglamphu's Soi Damnoen Klang Neua (daily 10am–10pm) has cheap public internet booths. Downtown, the TAT office on the north side of Thanon Ploenchit near Central Chidlom offers cheap surfing (daily 8am–9pm), while the flagship branch of *True* on Floor 3 of Siam Paragon shopping centre, Thanon Rama I, is only a little more expensive and offers wi-fi. Elsewhere in the downtown area, during the day, there are several, rather noisy, places on Floor 7 of the MBK Shopping Centre (Zone D, towards the *Pathumwan Princess Hotel*). There's also an internet centre in the public telephone office on Thanon Charoen Krung (see opposite) and on Floor 3 of the Emporium shopping centre on Thanon Sukhumvit (roughly daily 8am–8pm).

Laundry Nearly all guesthouses and hotels offer same-day laundry services (about B35/kg at a guesthouse, much more at a hotel), or there are several self-service laundries on and around Thanon Khao San.

Left luggage At Suvarnabhumi Airport (B100/day); Don Muang Airport (B75/day); Hualamphong train station (B30–100/day); the bus terminals and most hotels and guesthouses.

Post offices The GPO is at 1160 Thanon Charoen Krung (postcode 10501), near Wat Muang Kae express-boat pier and walkable from Si Phraya pier. Poste restante, which is kept for two months, can be collected here. This and most other services at the GPO are open Mon–Fri 8am–8pm, Sat & Sun 8am–1pm; the parcel-packing service, however, operates Mon–Fri 8am–5pm, Sat 9am–noon. If you're staying on or near Thanon Khao San in Banglamphu, it's more convenient to use the local postal, packing and poste restante services at either Ratchadamnoen Post Office, Soi Damnoen Klang Neua, Bangkok 10200 (Mon–Fri 8am–5pm, Sat 9am–noon); or Banglamphubon PO, Soi Sibsam Hang, Bangkok 10203 (daily 8am–5pm). On Thanon Sukhumvit, use Nana PO, between sois 4 and 6, Thanon Sukhumvit, Bangkok 10112 (Mon–Fri 8.30am–6pm, Sat, Sun & hols 9am–5pm).

Telephones It's best to buy a Thai SIM card for both international and domestic calls (see p.71), but otherwise there are international cardphones dotted around the city, including at the CAT office in the compound of the GPO on Thanon Charoen Krung (see opposite; Mon–Fri 8am–8pm, Sat & Sun 8am–4pm), which also offers a fax service and a free collect-call service. Many internet cafés have facilities for making cheap or free international calls over the internet.

Travel agents If buying onward international air tickets, be warned that there are many dodgy, transient travel agents in Bangkok, particularly on and around Thanon Khao San, which is known for its shady operators who display fake TAT licences, issue false tickets and flee with travellers' money overnight. The best advice is to use one of the tried and tested agents listed here. Never hand over any money until you've been given the ticket and checked it carefully. Asian Trails, 9th Floor, SG Tower, 161/1 Soi Mahadlek Luang 3, Thanon Rajdamri (☎ 02 626 2000, ⓦ asiantrails.net), sells flights, does interesting Thailand tours and runs scheduled and private transfers to many coastal destinations from Bangkok hotels and the airport; Educational Travel Centre (ETC) sells air and bus tickets, Thailand tours and day-trips, and has offices inside the *Royal Ratanakosin Hotel*, 2 Thanon Rajdamnoen Klang, Banglamphu (☎ 02 224 0043, ⓦ etc .co.th), at 180 Thanon Khao San, Banglamphu (☎ 02 629 1885), and at 5/3 Soi Ngam Duphli (underneath *ETZ Hostel*), off Thanon Rama IV (☎ 02 286 9424); *New Road Guest House* (see p.149) is a reliable agent for train, bus and minibus tickets, as well as their own unusual tours; Olavi Travel sells air tickets and budget transport within Thailand and is opposite the west end of Thanon Khao San at 53 Thanon Chakrabongse, Banglamphu (☎ 02 629 4711–3, ⓦ olavi .com); and the Bangkok branch of the worldwide STA Travel is a reliable outlet for cheap international flights and local tours: 14th Floor, Wall Street Tower, 33 Thanon Suriwong (☎ 02 236 0262, ⓦ statravel.co.th).

The central plains

WAT PHRA SI SANPHET, AYUTTHAYA

The central plains

North and west of the capital, the unwieldy urban mass of Greater Bangkok peters out into the vast, well-watered central plains, a region that for centuries has grown the bulk of the nation's food and been a tantalizing temptation for neighbouring power-mongers. The most densely populated region of Thailand, with sizeable towns sprinkled among patchworks of paddy, orchards and sugar-cane fields, the plains are fundamental to Thailand's agricultural economy. Its rivers are the key to this area's fecundity, especially the Nan and the Ping, whose waters irrigate the northern plains before merging to form the Chao Phraya, which meanders slowly south through Bangkok and out into the Gulf of Thailand. Further west, the Mae Khlong River sustains the many market gardens and fills the canals that dominate the hinterlands of the estuary at Samut Songkhram, a centre for some of the most authentic floating markets in the country.

Sited at the confluence of the Kwai Yai and Kwai Noi rivers, the town of **Kanchanaburi** has long attracted visitors to the notorious **Bridge over the River Kwai** and is now well established as a travellers' hangout, with everything from floating raft-house accommodation to waterside boutique hotels. Few tourists venture much further upriver, except as passengers on the remaining stretch of the **Death Railway** – the most tangible wartime reminder of all – but the remote little hilltop town of **Sangkhlaburi** holds enough understated allure to make the extra kilometres worthwhile.

On the plains north of Bangkok, the historic heartland of the country, the major sites are the **ruined ancient cities**, most of which are conserved as historical parks, covering the spectrum of Thailand's art and architecture. Closest to Bangkok, **Ayutthaya** served as the country's capital for the four hundred years prior to the 1782 foundation of Bangkok, and its ruins evoke an era of courtly sophistication. A short hop to the north, the remnants of **Lopburi** hark back to an earlier time, when the predominantly Hindu Khmers held sway over this region.

ERAWAN WATERFALL, KANCHANABURI

Highlights

❶ Kanchanaburi and the River Kwai Stay in a raft house, take a scenic train ride along the Death Railway and visit some moving World War II memorials. **See p.188**

❷ Erawan Waterfall Seven breathtakingly beautiful crystal pools in a jungle setting. **See p.199**

❸ Sangkhlaburi Search for the sunken temple of Wat Sam Phrasop at this peaceful lakeside town near the Burmese border. **See p.209**

❹ Ayutthaya Atmospheric ruined temples, three fine museums and laidback guesthouses in the broad, grassy spaces of the former capital. **See p.215**

❺ Wat Phra Phutthabat A vibrant introduction to Thai religion at the Temple of the Buddha's Footprint. **See p.230**

❻ Sergeant Major Thawee Folklore Museum, Phitsanulok Housed in a series of wooden pavilions, this is one of the country's best ethnology museums, offering a fascinating insight into rural life. **See p.236**

❼ Sukhothai The nation's first capital is packed with elegant thirteenth-century ruins and inviting guesthouses. **See p.240**

❽ Trekking from Umphang A remote border region with spectacular waterfalls, river-rafting and Karen villages. **See p.267**

HIGHLIGHTS ARE MARKED ON THE MAP ON PP.178–179

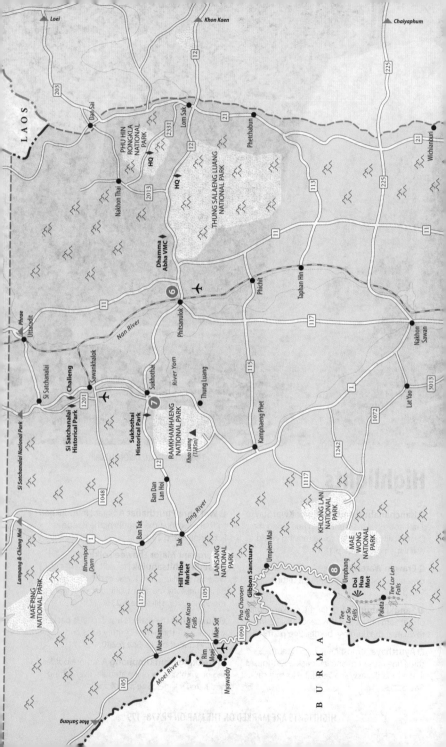

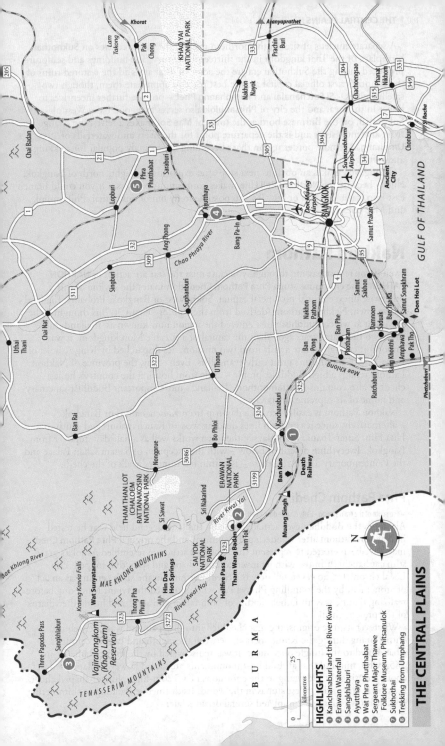

THE CENTRAL PLAINS

Khorat
Lam Takong
Pak Chong
Aranyaprathet
Prachin Buri

KHAO YAI NATIONAL PARK

Nakhon Nayok

Phanat Nikhom
Chachoengsao
Si Racha

Chai Badan

Lopburi

Phra Phutthabat

Saraburi

Suvarnabhumi Airport

Chonburi

Ancient City

Don Muang Airport

BANGKOK

Samut Prakan

GULF OF THAILAND

Ayutthaya

Ang Thong

Bang Pa-In

Singburi

Chao Phraya River

Suphanburi

Samut Sakhon

Nakhon Pathom

Ban Phe

Photharam

Bamroen Saduak

Samut Songkhram

Don Hoi Lot

Uthai Thani

Chai Nat

U Thong

Ban Pong

Mae Khlong

Ban Tha To

Ban Khonthi

Amphawa

Pak Tho

Ban Rai

Ratchaburi

Phetchaburi

Nongrue

Bo Phloi

Kanchanaburi

Ban Kao

Death Railway

Si Sawat

Sri Nakarind

River Kwai Yai

ERAWAN NATIONAL PARK

Muang Singh

THAM THAN LOT (CHALOEM RATTANAKOSIN) NATIONAL PARK

Nam Tok

Tham Wang Badan

Kraeng Kravia Falls

SAI YOK NATIONAL PARK

Hin Dat Hot Springs

Hellfire Pass

Wat Sunyataram

Thong Pha Phum

River Kwai Noi

Mae Khlong River

Three Pagodas Pass

Sangkhlaburi

Vajiralongkom (Khao Laem) Reservoir

MAE KHLONG MOUNTAINS

TENASSERIM MOUNTAINS

BURMA

N

0   kilometres   25

HIGHLIGHTS
1 Kanchanaburi and the River Kwai
2 Erawan Waterfall
3 Sangkhlaburi
4 Ayutthaya
5 Wat Phra Phutthabat
6 Sergeant Major Thawee Folklore Museum, Phitsanulok
7 Sukhothai
8 Trekking from Umphang

A separate nucleus of sites in the northern neck of the plains centres on **Sukhothai**, birthplace of the Thai kingdom in the thirteenth century. The buildings and sculpture produced during the Sukhothai era are the acme of Thai art, and the restored ruins of the country's first official capital are the best place to appreciate them, though two satellite cities – **Si Satchanalai** and **Kamphaeng Phet** – provide further incentives to linger in the area, and the city of **Phitsanulok** also serves as a good base. West of Sukhothai, on the Burmese border, the town of **Mae Sot** makes a refreshing change from ancient history and is the departure point for the rivers and waterfalls of **Umphang**, a remote border region that's becoming increasingly popular for trekking and rafting.

Chiang Mai makes an obvious next stop after exploring the sights north of Bangkok, chiefly because the **Northern Rail Line** makes connections painless. Or you could branch east into Isaan, by train or bus. It's also possible to **fly** out of Sukhothai, Phitsanulok and Mae Sot.

Nakhon Pathom

Even if you're just passing through, you can't miss the star attraction of **NAKHON PATHOM**: the enormous stupa **Phra Pathom Chedi** dominates the skyline of this otherwise unexceptional provincial capital, 56km west of Bangkok. Probably Thailand's oldest town, Nakhon Pathom (derived from the Pali for "First City") is thought to be the point at which **Buddhism** first entered the region now known as Thailand, more than two thousand years ago. Then the capital of a sizeable Mon kingdom, it was important enough to rate a visit from two missionaries dispatched by King Ashoka of India, one of Buddhism's great early evangelists. Even today, the province of Nakhon Pathom retains a high Buddhist profile – aside from housing the country's holiest chedi, it also contains **Phuttamonthon**, Thailand's most important Buddhist sanctuary and home of its supreme patriarch.

Nakhon Pathom is easily seen on a day-trip from Kanchanaburi or Bangkok – alternatively, since it's on train lines heading west to Kanchanaburi and south to Hua Hin, Surat Thani and Malaysia, the town works well as a half-day stopover from Bangkok. Everything described below – with the exception of Sanam Chan Palace and the Contemporary Thai Art Centre – is within ten minutes' walk of the chedi.

Phra Pathom Chedi

400m south of the train station • Daily dawn–dusk • B40

Although the Buddha never actually came to Thailand, legend held that he rested in Nakhon Pathom after wandering the country, and the original **Phra Pathom Chedi** may have been erected to represent this. The first structure resembled Ashoka's great stupa at Sanchi in India, with its inverted bowl shape and spire that topped 39m. Local chronicles, however, tell how the chedi was built in the sixth century as an act of atonement by the foundling Phraya Pan who murdered the tyrant Mon king before realizing that he was his father. Statues of both father and son stand inside the viharns of the present chedi.

Whatever its true origins, the first chedi fell into disrepair and was later rebuilt with a prang during the Khmer period, between the eighth and twelfth centuries. Abandoned to the jungle once more, it was rediscovered by the future Rama IV in 1853 who, mindful that all Buddhist monuments are sacred however dilapidated, set about encasing the old prang in the enormous new 120m-high plunger-shaped chedi, making it one of the tallest stupas in the world. Its distinctive cladding of shimmering golden-brown tiles was completed several decades later.

The present-day chedi is much revered and holds its own week-long Phra Pathom Chedi **fair**, around the time of Loy Krathong (see p.47) in mid-November, which attracts musicians, fortune-tellers and of course plenty of food stalls.

Around the chedi

Approaching the chedi from the main (northern) staircase, you're greeted by the 8m-high Sukhothai-style Buddha image known as **Phra Ruang Rojanarit**, installed in front of the north viharn. There's a viharn at each of the cardinal points and they all have an inner and an outer chamber containing tableaux of the life of the Buddha. The figures in the outer chamber of the **north viharn** depict two princesses paying homage to the newly born Prince Siddhartha (the future Buddha), while the inner one shows a monkey and an elephant offering honey and water to the Buddha at the end of a forty-day fast.

Proceeding clockwise around the chedi, as is the custom at all Buddhist monuments, you can weave between the outer promenade and the inner cloister via ornate doors that punctuate the dividing wall; the promenade is dotted with **trees**, many of which have religious significance, such as the bodhi tree (*ficus religiosa*) under one of which the Buddha was meditating when he achieved enlightenment. The wall of the **east viharn** features a diagrammatic cross section of the chedi showing the encased original at its core, while beside the **south viharn** staircase is a three-dimensional replica of the original chedi with its Khmer prang (east side) and a model of the venerated chedi at Nakhon Si Thammarat (west side). The **west viharn** houses two reclining Buddhas: a sturdy, 9m-long figure in the outer chamber and a more delicate portrayal in the inner one.

Phra Pathom Chedi National Museum

Just east from the bottom of the chedi's south staircase • Wed–Sun 9am–noon & 1–4pm • B100 • ⓦ thailandmuseum.com

Within the chedi compound are a couple of similarly named museums. The newer, more formal setup, the **Phra Pathom Chedi National Museum**, displays a good collection of Dvaravati-era (sixth to eleventh centuries) artefacts excavated nearby, including Wheels of Law – an emblem introduced by Theravada Buddhists before naturalistic images were permitted – and Buddha statuary with the U-shaped robe and thick facial features characteristic of Dvaravati sculpture. Together, the exhibits tell the story of how external influences, particularly those from India, shaped local beliefs.

Phra Pathom Chedi Museum

Halfway up the steps near the east viharn • Wed–Sun 9am–noon & 1–4pm • Free

The **Phra Pathom Chedi Museum** is a magpie's nest of a collection, offering a broader, more domestic introduction to Nakhon Pathom's history than the National Museum. More a curiosity shop than a museum, the small room and entranceway are filled with Buddhist amulets, seashells, gold and silver needles, Chinese ceramics, Thai musical instruments and ancient statues – enough for a short but satisfying browse.

Sanam Chandra Palace

A 10min walk west of the chedi along Thanon Rajdamnoen (or a B20 ride on a motorbike taxi) • Daily 9am–4pm (ticket office closes at 3.30pm) • B50 or free with ticket for Bangkok's Grand Palace • ⓦ palaces.thai.net/day/index_sc.htm

Before ascending to the throne in 1910, Rama VI made several pilgrimages to the Phra Pathom Chedi, eventually choosing this 335-acre plot west of the pagoda as the location for a convenient new country retreat. The resulting complex of elegant wooden buildings, known as **Sanam Chandra Palace**, was designed to blend Western and Eastern styles, and half a dozen of its main buildings are now open to the public. Its principal structure, the **Chaleemongkolasana Residence**, evokes a miniature

2

Bavarian castle, complete with turrets and red-tiled roof; the **Mareerajaratabulung Residence** is a more oriental-style pavilion, built of teak and painted a deep rose colour inside and out; and the **Thub Kwan Residence** is an unadorned traditional Thai-style house of polished, unpainted golden teak. They each contain royal artefacts and memorabilia and, as such, visitors should take care to dress appropriately. If you happen to be here at the weekend, check out one of the free classical dance performances, which take place every Saturday and Sunday at 1.30pm.

Contemporary Thai Art Centre

Just outside Sanam Chandra's southern perimeter, behind the Thub Kwan Residence on Thanon Rajamanka Nai • Tues–Sun 9am–4pm • Free • ⓦ su.ac.th • If coming from the chedi, expect to pay around B20 for a motorbike taxi

If you're interested in modern Thai art it's well worth seeing what's on at the **Contemporary Thai Art Centre**. A purpose-built art centre set among outlying Sanam Chandra villas, it's the exhibition space for Bangkok's premier art school, Silpakorn University, whose satellite campus is just across the road. Their annual student show, held here every September and October, is usually very interesting.

ARRIVAL AND DEPARTURE   NAKHON PATHOM

BY TRAIN

To get to the chedi compound's northern gate from the train station, walk south for 200m down Thanon Rotfai, across the khlong and past the covered market.

Destinations Bangkok Hualamphong (13 daily; 1hr 35min); Bangkok Thonburi (5 daily; 1hr 10min); Butterworth (Malaysia; 1 daily; 19hr); Chumphon (12 daily; 5hr 40min–8hr 30min); Hat Yai (5 daily; 12hr 15min–16hr); Hua Hin (14 daily; 2hr 15min–3hr 15min); Kanchanaburi (2 daily; 1hr 25min); Nakhon Si Thammarat (2 daily; 14–15hr); Nam Tok (2 daily; 3hr 30min); Phetchaburi (14 daily; 1hr 20min–2hr 20min); Surat Thani (10 daily; 8hr–11hr 30min); Trang (2 daily; 13hr 30min–14hr 30min).

BY BUS

Bus connections to Nakhon Pathom are good, especially from Bangkok's Southern Bus Terminal, Damnoen Saduak

and Kanchanaburi.

Arrival On arrival, try to avoid being taken to the main bus terminal, which is about 1km east of the town centre: most buses pass the chedi first, dropping passengers either in front of the police station across from the chedi's southern entrance, or beside the khlong, 100m from the northern gate.

Moving on Buses heading for Kanchanaburi, Damnoen Saduak and Phetchaburi collect passengers outside the police station across Thanon Kwaa Phra from the chedi's southern gate. Buses bound for Bangkok pick up from Thanon Phaya Pan on the north bank of the khlong, across from the *Mitpaisal Hotel*.

Destinations Bangkok (every 10min; 40min–1hr 20min); Damnoen Saduak (every 20min; 1hr); Kanchanaburi (every 20min; 1hr 45min–2hr).

ACCOMMODATION AND EATING

Boncafé Tongmesang Beside Soi 3 on Thanon Rajdamnoen, about 300m west of the chedi's west gate ☎034 217995. For a quality cappuccino or iced mocha, head for this a/c coffee salon. Internet access available. Daily 8am–9pm.

Hot-food stalls Just outside the chedi compound's southern wall, near the museum. The obvious place to eat during the day. There are most options here, from noodle soup to grilled chicken and rice dishes. Usually open from early morning until dusk.

Market In front of the station. Serves the usual takeaway

goodies, including reputedly the tastiest *khao laam* (bamboo cylinders filled with steamed rice and coconut) in Thailand. The market really hits its stride after sunset. Hours vary, but usually at least mid-morning until around 8pm.

Mitpaisal Hotel 120/30 Thanon Phaya Pan ☎034 242422, ✉ mitpaisal@hotmail.com. This Chinese-Thai hotel has seen better days, but is still reasonable value and enjoys a convenient location, close to the train station and less than 200m from the chedi's north gateway. Rooms are a good size and are all en suite. Fan **B300**, a/c **B400**

DIRECTORY

Banks, exchange and ATMs You can change money at the exchange booth (open banking hours only) on Thanon

Rotfai, beside the bridge over the khlong, one block south of the train station; several nearby banks also have ATMs.

Damnoen Saduak floating markets

To get an idea of what shopping in Bangkok used to be like before all the canals were tarmacked over, many people take an early-morning trip to the **floating markets** (*talat khlong*) of **DAMNOEN SADUAK**, 60km south of Nakhon Pathom and easily accessible from Bangkok on a day-trip. Vineyards and orchards here back onto a labyrinth of narrow canals, and every morning between 6am and 11am local market gardeners ply these waterways in paddleboats full of fresh fruit, vegetables and tourist-tempting soft drinks and souvenirs. Most dress in the deep-blue jacket and high-topped straw hat traditionally favoured by Thai farmers, so it all looks very picturesque, but the setup feels increasingly manufactured, and some visitors have complained of seeing more tourists than vendors, however early they arrive. The best way to see the markets is to stay overnight in Damnoen Saduak and get up at dawn, well before the buses and coach tours from Bangkok arrive. But for a more authentic version, consider going instead to the floating markets of Amphawa, 10km south of Damnoen Saduak (see p.186 & p.188).

The markets

Daily 6–11am

The target for most tourists is the main **Talat Khlong Ton Kem**, 2km west of Damnoen Saduak's tiny town centre at the intersection of Khlong Damnoen Saduak and Khlong Thong Lang. Many of the wooden houses here have been converted into warehouse-style souvenir shops and tourist restaurants, diverting trade away from the khlong vendors and into the hands of large commercial enterprises. But, for the moment at least, a semblance of the traditional water trade continues, and the two bridges between Ton Kem and **Talat Khlong Hia Kui** (a little further south down Khlong Thong Lang) make decent vantage points.

Touts invariably congregate at the Ton Kem pier to hassle you into taking a **rowing boat trip** around the khlong network (asking an hourly rate of around B300/person) – worth considering, and far preferable to being propelled between markets at top speed in one of the noisy motorized boats, which cost far more to charter. For a less hectic and more sensitive look at the markets, explore via the walkways beside the canals.

ARRIVAL AND DEPARTURE — DAMNOEN SADUAK

BY BUS

From/to Bangkok Damnoen Saduak is 109km from Bangkok, so to reach the market in good time you have to catch one of the earliest a/c buses from the capital's Southern Bus Terminal (#78; every 40min in both directions from 6am; 2hr). Alternatively you can join one of the day-trips from Bangkok, which generally give you two hours at the market, then stop at a handicraft village before dropping you back in the capital.

From Kanchanaburi Take a Ratchaburi-bound bus as far as Ban Phe (#461; every 15min from 5.10am; 1hr 15min), then change to bus #78 or minibus #1733 for the 30min journey to Damnoen Sakuak.

From Phetchaburi and beyond To get to Damnoen Saduak from Phetchaburi or points further south, catch any Bangkok-bound bus and change either at Samut Songkhram or at the Photharam intersection.

Getting into town Damnoen Saduak's bus terminal is just north of Thanarat Bridge and Khlong Damnoen Saduak, on the main Nakhon Pathom–Samut Songkhram road, Highway 325. Frequent yellow songthaews cover the 2km to Ton Kem, but walk if you've got the time: a walkway follows the canal, which you can get to from Thanarat Bridge, or you can cross the bridge and take the road to the right (west), Thanon Sukhaphiban 1, through the orchards. Drivers on the earliest buses from Bangkok sometimes do not terminate at the bus station but instead cross Thanarat Bridge and then drop tourists at a pier closer to the market, a few hundred metres along Thanon Sukhaphiban 1.

ACCOMMODATION

Nok Noi Hotel (also known as **Little Bird**) 1 Moo 8 ☎ 032 254382, ⓦ noknoihotel.com. The "hotel" sign is clearly visible from the main road and Thanarat Bridge. Rooms here are reasonable value with enormous en-suite bathrooms and a/c if you want it. Staff can also arrange floating-market boat trips. Fan B220, a/c B380

Samut Songkhram

Rarely visited by foreign tourists and yet within easy reach of Bangkok, the tiny estuarine province of **Samut Songkhram** is nourished by the Mae Khlong River as it meanders through on the last leg of its route to the Gulf. Fishing is an important industry round here, and big wooden boats are still built in riverside yards near the estuary; further inland, fruit is the main source of income, particularly pomelos, lychees, guavas and coconuts. But for visitors it is the network of three hundred **canals** woven around the river, and the traditional way of life the waterways still support, that makes a stay of a few days or more appealing. As well as some of the most interesting **floating markets** in Thailand – notably at **Amphawa** and **Tha Ka** – there are chances to witness traditional cottage industries such as palm-sugar production and *bencharong* ceramic-painting, plus more than a hundred historic temples to admire, a number of

ENG AND CHANG, THE SIAMESE TWINS

Eng (In) and Chang (Chan), the "original" **Siamese twins**, were born in Samut Songkhram in 1811, when Thailand was known as Siam. The boys' bodies were joined from breastbone to navel by a short fleshy ligament, but they shared no vital organs and eventually managed to stretch their connecting tissue so that they could stand almost side by side instead of permanently facing each other.

In 1824 the boys were spotted by entrepreneurial Scottish trader Robert Hunter, who returned five years later with an American sea merchant, Captain Abel Coffin, to convince the twins' mother to let them take her sons on a world tour. Hunter and Coffin anticipated a lucrative career as producer-managers of an exotic **freak show**, and were not disappointed. They launched the twins in Boston, advertising them as "the Monster" and charging the public 50 cents to watch the boys demonstrate how they walked and ran. Though shabbily treated and poorly paid, the twins soon developed a more theatrical show, enthralling their audiences with acrobatics and feats of strength, and earning the soubriquet "the eighth wonder of the world". At the age of 21, having split from their exploitative managers, the twins became self-employed, but continued to tour with other companies across the world. Wherever they went, they would always be given a thorough examination by local **medics**, partly to counter accusations of fakery, but also because this was the first time the world and its doctors had been introduced to conjoined twins. Such was the twins' international celebrity that the term "Siamese twins" has been used ever since. Chang and Eng also sought advice from these doctors on surgical separation – an issue they returned to repeatedly right until their deaths but never acted upon, despite plenty of gruesome suggestions.

By 1840 the twins had become quite wealthy and decided to settle down. They were granted American citizenship, assumed the family name Bunker, and became slave-owning **plantation farmers** in North Carolina. Three years later they married two local sisters, Addie and Sally Yates, and between them went on to father 21 children. The families lived in separate houses and the twins shuttled between the two, keeping to a strict timetable of three days in each household; for an intriguing imagined account of this bizarre state of affairs, read Darin Strauss's novel *Chang and Eng* (see p.789). Chang and Eng had quite different personalities, and relations between the two couples soured, leading to the division of their assets, with Chang's family getting most of the land, and Eng's most of the slaves. To support their dependants, the twins were obliged to take their show back on the road several times, on occasion working with the infamous showman P.T. Barnum. Their final tour was born out of financial desperation following the 1861–65 Civil War, which had wiped out most of the twins' riches and led to the liberation of all their slaves.

In 1874, Chang succumbed to bronchitis and died; Eng, who might have survived on his own if an operation had been performed immediately, died a few hours later, possibly of shock. They were 62. The twins are buried in White Plains in North Carolina, but there's a **memorial** to them near their birthplace in Samut Songkhram, where a statue and the small, makeshift In-Chan Museum (Mon–Fri 8.30am–4.30pm; free) have been erected 4km north of the provincial capital's centre on Thanon Ekachai (Route 3092).

them dating back to the reign of Rama II, who was born in the province. The other famous sons of the region are Eng and Chang, the "original" Siamese twins, who grew up in the province (see box opposite).

Samut Songkhram town

The provincial capital – officially called **SAMUT SONGKHRAM** but often referred to by locals as **Mae Khlong**, after the river that cuts through it – is a useful jumping-off point for trips to the floating markets at Amphawa and Tha Ka. It's a pleasant enough market town, which, despite its proximity to Bangkok, remains relatively unaffected by Western influences. However, there's little reason to linger here as all the local sights are out of town, mainly in **Amphawa** district a few kilometres upriver (see p.186).

2

ARRIVAL AND DEPARTURE
SAMUT SONGKHRAM TOWN

BY TRAIN

Samut Songkhram's train station is in the middle of town, on the eastern side of the Mae Klong River, with four trains a day making the 1hr trip from and to Ban Laem, where you can connect with trains from/to Bangkok (see box below).

off Thanon Ratchayadruksa. When returning to Bangkok, there's also a minibus service to the Northern Mo Chit bus terminal (approximately hourly; about 1hr 30min), which departs from Thanon Si Jumpa, about 100m east of the *Maeklong Hotel*.

BY BUS OR MINIBUS

The journey to Samut Songkhram from Bangkok's Southern Bus Terminal (every 20min in both directions; 1hr 30min) is faster than the train, but the views are mostly dominated by urban sprawl. Samut Songkhram's bus station is south of the market, across from the Siam Commercial Bank

CONNECTIONS TO AMPHAWA AND DAMNOEN SADUAK

By songthaew or bus Songthaews to Amphawa (approximately every 30min; 15min) and local buses to Amphawa and Damnoen Saduak, via Highway 325, leave from the north edge of the central market and from the bus station.

THE SLOW ROUTE TO SAMUT SONGKHRAM

The most enjoyable way of travelling to Samut Songkhram is by **train** from Bangkok – a scenic, albeit rather convoluted, route that has three stages, involves going via Samut Sakhon and could take up to three hours. It's a very unusual line, being single track and for much of its route literally squeezed in between homes, palms and mangroves, and, most memorably, between market stalls, so that at both the Samut Sakhon and Samut Songkhram termini the train really does chug to a standstill amid the trays of seafood.

Trains to Samut Sakhon leave approximately hourly from Bangkok's **Wongwian Yai station** in southern Thonburi (which is within walking distance of Wongwian Yai Skytrain station), but for the fastest onward connections catch the 5.30am, 8.35am, 12.15pm or 3.25pm (1hr). The train pulls up right inside the wet market at **Samut Sakhon**, also known as **Mahachai**, where you need to take a ferry across the Maenam Tha Chin to get the connecting train from **Ban Laem** on the other bank. Once you've left the train, cross the track and continue in the same direction as the train was going, through a clothes market, until you emerge onto a shopping street. Cross the street to the five-storey, blue-painted *Tarua Restaurant*, right on the estuary, adjacent to the busy fishing port, where you'll find two piers. Boats from both piers will get you across the river: those departing from the pier on the right of the restaurant are frequent but drop you directly across on the other bank, from where it's a twenty-minute walk to Ban Laem station (turn right and walk upriver, past a Thai temple); boats from the pier on the left of the restaurant go direct to Ban Laem station (5min), but leave infrequently, being timed to coincide with the Ban Laem trains. There are only four trains a day in each direction from Ban Laem to Samut Songkhram at the end of the line (1hr), a journey through marshes, lagoons, prawn farms, salt flats and mangrove and palm growth. Once again, at **Samut Songkhram**, the station is literally enveloped by the town-centre market, with traders gathering up their goods and awnings from the trackside for the arrival and departure of the service.

2

DON HOI LOT'S SEAFOOD RESTAURANTS

Seafood is the obvious regional speciality in these parts, with the most famous local dish being **hoi lot pat cha**, a spicy stir fry that centres round the tubular molluscs, known as hoi lot or "worm shells", that are harvested in their sackloads at low tide from a muddy sandbank known as **Don Hoi Lot** at the mouth of the Mae Khlong estuary. This is probably the most famous spot in the province to eat seafood, and a dozen **restaurants** occupy the area around the nearby pier, many offering views out over the Gulf and its bountiful sandbar. Don Hoi Lot is served by frequent songthaews from Samut Songkhram market (15–20min); the restaurants are usually open daily during daylight hours.

By taxi-boat Taxi-boats operate from the Mae Khlong River pier, 50m west of the train station and market in the town centre. The journey upstream to Amphawa should take 20–30min.

By motorbike taxi At the Mae Khlong River pier, ferries (B2) take passengers across to the other side of the river, where motorbike taxis are available for the short ride to Amphawa (B20).

ACCOMMODATION

Few people choose to stay in the town itself (though we list a couple of options below). Just a short ride from the pier, however, takes you to one of the best places to stay in the province.

★ **Baan Tai Had Resort** Beside the Mae Khlong River, a couple of kilometres northwest of town ☎034 767220, ⓦbaantaihad.com. To get the most out of the area, it's worth splashing out on this luxurious but good-value resort, 15min by taxi-boat from Samut Songkhram's pier (alternatively, take the ferry across the river, then a 10min ride on a motorbike taxi). With its stylish, comfortable bungalows and rooms set around a Bali-style garden, swimming pool and restaurant, *Baan Tai Had* makes a good base, not least because of its local tour programmes and English-speaking guides (book in advance). Also offers bicycle, kayak and jetski rental. Breakfast included. B1600
The Legend Maeklong 1285 Thanon Pathummalai ☎034 701121 ⓦthelegendmaeklong.com. Located

100m north of the ferry landing on the western edge of the river, this is the classiest place in town, with rooms in three beautiful wooden houses, including a shuttered colonial building by the waterfront that dates back to the early 1900s. As well as free wi-fi and quality wooden furnishings throughout, there's a riverside restaurant with excellent river views. Breakfast included. B1840
Maeklong Hotel 526/10–13 Thanon Si Jumpa ☎034 711150. If you want cheap accommodation then this welcoming place in the town centre (150m due north of the train station, beyond the edge of the market) is a decent choice with its large fan and a/c rooms. Fan B250, a/c B350

EATING

The **foodstalls** near the pier, in the centre of town, make a pleasant spot for a cheap seafood lunch – and for dessert, head to the **market**, near the train station, where you can buy fresh bananas, rambutans and watermelon slices.

DIRECTORY

Banks and ATMs Currency exchange and ATMs are available at all the central branches of the main banks around the edge of Samut Songkhram market.

Amphawa

The district town of **AMPHAWA** is smaller and more atmospheric than Samut Songkhram, retaining original charm alongside modern development. Its old neighbourhoods hug the banks of the Mae Khlong River and the Khlong Amphawa tributary, the wooden homes and shops facing the water and accessed either by boat or on foot along one of the waterfront walkways. The tradition of holding a **floating market** on the canal near Wat Amphawan has recently been revived for tourists, with traders setting up at around noon and staying out until after sunset every Friday, Saturday and Sunday.

2

LONGTAIL BOAT TOURS AROUND AMPHAWA

On market days and during the week, when the waterways are far quieter, you can take a longtail boat tour around Amphawa (around B500/boat/hr) – boats wait on the canal, just over the bridge from the memorial park. If you get the chance, it's well worth venturing out onto the canals after dark to **watch the fireflies** twinkling romantically in their favourite lamphu trees like delicate strings of fairylights; any boatman will ferry you to the right spot for around B60 per head, but you may need to link up with others to get a good price. For boat tours in quiet areas further from the town, contact staff at *Baan Tai Had Resort* (see opposite) or one of the nearby homestays.

King Rama II Memorial Park

5min walk west of Amphawa market and khlong • **Park** daily 9am–6pm • Free • **Museum** Wed–Sun 9am–4pm • B20 • Accessible both by boat and by road

King Rama II was born in Amphawa (his mother's home town) in 1767 and is honoured with a memorial park and temple erected on the site of his probable birthplace, beside the Mae Khlong River on the western edge of Amphawa town.

Rama II, or Phra Buddhalertla Naphalai as he is known in Thai, was a famously cultured king and a respected poet and playwright, and the **museum** at the heart of the **King Rama II Memorial Park** displays lots of rather esoteric Rama II memorabilia, including a big collection of nineteenth-century musical instruments and a gallery of *khon* masks used in traditional theatre.

On the edge of the park, **Wat Amphawan** is graced with a statue of the king and decorated with murals that depict scenes from his life, including a behind-the-altar panorama of nineteenth-century Bangkok, with Ratanakosin Island's Grand Palace, Wat Pho and Sanam Luang still recognizable to modern eyes.

Wat Chulamani

Beside Khlong Amphawa, a 20min walk east of Amphawa market, or a 5min boat ride

The canalside **Wat Chulamani** was until the late 1980s the domain of the locally famous abbot Luang Pho Nuang, a man believed by many to possess special powers, and followers still come to the temple to pay respects to his body, which is preserved in a glass-sided coffin in the main viharn. The breathtakingly detailed decor inside the viharn is testament to the devotion he inspired: the intricate black-and-gold lacquered artwork that covers every surface took years and cost millions of baht to complete. Across the temple compound, the bot's modern, pastel-toned murals tell the story of the Buddha's life, beginning inside the door on the right with a scene showing the young Buddha emerging from a tent (his birth) and being able to walk on lilypads straight away. The death of the Buddha and his entry into Nirvana is depicted on the wall behind the altar.

Ban Pinsuwan bencharong workshop

A few hundred metres down the road from Wat Chulamani • Daily 8am–5pm • Free • Accessible on foot, by bus or by canal

The Ban Pinsuwan **bencharong workshop** specializes in reproductions of famous antique *bencharong* ceramics, the exquisite five-coloured pottery that used to be the tableware of choice for the Thai aristocracy and is now a prized collectors' item. Here you can watch the manufacturing process in action, and even order your own glittering, custom-made bowls, which can then be shipped back home.

ARRIVAL AND DEPARTURE   AMPHAWA

From/to Bangkok Direct buses connect Amphawa with Bangkok's Southern Bus Terminal (every 20min; 2hr). Returning to Bangkok, hourly buses head for the Southern Bus Terminal, while several buses a day make the journey to the Northern Mo Chit terminal.

From/to Samut Songkhram Frequent songthaews and local buses (both approximately every 30min; 15min) connect Amphawa market, which sets up beside the khlong, just back from its confluence with the river, with the market in Samut Songkhram.

2

GETTING AROUND

By boat The most appealing way to explore the area is by boat – see the box (p.187) for more details.

By bicycle You can rent bicycles from *Baan Tai Had Resort*

(see p.186). Alternatively, you could join a one-day cycling tour of the area from Bangkok with Bangkok Bike Rides (see p.138) for B2650 per person.

ACCOMMODATION AND EATING

Baan Amphawa Resort & Spa 22 Thanon Bangkapom Kaewfah ☎034 752222, ⓦbaanamphawa.com. A large, business-friendly resort hotel with attractive rooms in a series of traditional-style wooden buildings. There's a pool, a spa, and a reasonable restaurant (see below) but prices are high. B2700

Plai Phong Pang collective Contact Nathawut Boonpad in Plai Phong Pang, around 7km southwest of Amphawa on Route 3093 ☎034 717510, ⓦthaitambon .com/SS/Ampawa1A.htm. A small collection of homestays

grouped together to form a special "tourism village", which allows visitors a taste of life along the canals. Price per person B700

Saban-Nga Baan Amphawa Resort & Spa, 22 Thanon Bangkapom Kaewfah ☎034 752222, ⓦbaanamphawa .com. The fresh fish dishes at this spa hotel's upmarket restaurant are tasty enough, and the riverfront terrace is a great spot for an evening drink. However, the service sometimes struggles to match up to the surroundings. Daily 7am–10pm.

Tha Ka floating market

On Khlong Phanla in Ban Tha Ka • Weekends from 7am to around noon, plus the second, seventh and twelfth mornings of every fifteen-day lunar cycle (contact any TAT office for exact dates) • By boat, it's reached in 10–40min from the homestays in Amphawa district, 30min from Baan Tai Had Resort (see p.186) or about 1hr from Damnoen Saduak

Unlike at the over-touristed markets of nearby Damnoen Saduak, the **floating market** in the village of **Tha Ka** is still largely the province of local residents. Visits here are often incorporated into larger day-trips, but it's possible to get here alone. The most fun option is taking a boat trip to the market from your accommodation, though you can also get here by road, following Highway 325 out of Samut Songkhram for 10km, then taking a 5km access road to the village of **Ban Tha Ka**. Market gardeners paddle up here in their small wooden sampans, or motor along in their noisy longtails, the boats piled high either with whatever's in season, be it pomelos or betel nuts, rambutans or okra, or with perennially popular snacks like hot noodle soup and freshly cooked satay. Their main customers are canalside residents and other traders, so the atmosphere is still pleasingly but not artificially traditional. The Tha Ka market used to operate just six times a month, on a **timetable** dictated by the waxing and waning of the moon, but now it's also open on weekends, when Thai tourist groups come to browse.

Kanchanaburi

Set at the confluence of two rivers, the Kwai Noi and the Kwai Yai, the provincial capital of **KANCHANABURI** makes the perfect getaway from Bangkok, a two- to three-hour bus ride away. With its plentiful wartime history, plentiful supply of traveller-oriented accommodation and countless possibilities for easy forays into the surrounding countryside, there are plenty of reasons to linger here, and many visitors end up staying longer than planned. The big appeal is the river: that it's the famous River Kwai is a bonus, but the more immediate attractions are the guesthouses whose rooms overlook the waterway, many of them offering fine views of the jagged limestone peaks beyond.

The heart of Kanchanaburi's ever-expanding travellers' scene dominates the southern end of **Thanon Maenam Kwai** (also spelt Kwae) and is within easy reach of the train station, but the real town centre is some distance away, running north from the bus station up the town's main drag, **Thanon Saeng Chuto**. Between this road and the river you'll find most of the town's **war sights**, with the infamous **Bridge over the River Kwai**

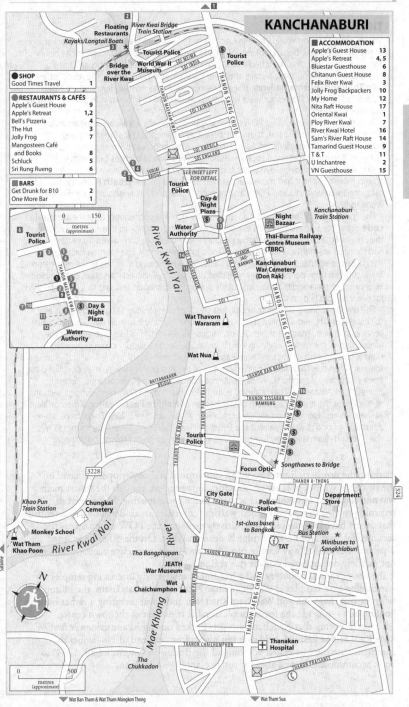

KANCHANABURI

ACCOMMODATION
Apple's Guest House	13
Apple's Retreat	4, 5
Bluestar Guesthouse	6
Chitanun Guest House	8
Felix River Kwai	3
Jolly Frog Backpackers	10
My Home	12
Nita Raft House	17
Oriental Kwai	1
Ploy River Kwai	7
River Kwai Hotel	16
Sam's River Raft House	14
Tamarind Guest House	9
T & T	11
U Inchantree	2
VN Guesthouse	15

SHOP
Good Times Travel	1

RESTAURANTS & CAFÉS
Apple's Guest House	9
Apple's Retreat	1, 2
Bell's Pizzeria	4
The Hut	3
Jolly Frog	7
Mangosteen Café and Books	8
Schluck	5
Sri Rung Rueng	6

BARS
Get Drunk for B10	2
One More Bar	1

THE DEATH RAILWAY

Shortly after entering World War II in December 1941, Japan, fearing an Allied blockade of the Bay of Bengal, began looking for an alternative supply route to connect its newly acquired territories that stretched from Singapore to the Burma–India border. In spite of the almost impenetrable terrain, the River Kwai basin was chosen as the route for a new **Thailand–Burma Railway**, the aim being to join the existing terminals of Nong Pladuk in Thailand (51km southeast of Kanchanaburi) and Thanbuyazat in Burma – a total distance of 415km.

About sixty thousand Allied POWs were shipped up from captured Southeast Asian territories to work on the link, their numbers later augmented by as many as two hundred thousand conscripted Asian labourers. Work began at both ends in June 1942. Three million cubic metres of rock were shifted and 14km of bridges built with little else but picks and shovels, dynamite and pulleys. By the time the line was completed, fifteen months later, it had more than earned its nickname, the **Death Railway**: an estimated sixteen thousand POWs and hundred thousand Asian labourers died while working on it.

The appalling conditions and Japanese brutality were the consequences of the **samurai code**: Japanese soldiers abhorred the disgrace of imprisonment – to them, ritual suicide was the only honourable option open to a prisoner – and therefore considered that Allied POWs had forfeited any rights as human beings. Food rations were meagre for men forced into backbreaking eighteen-hour shifts, often followed by night-long marches to the next camp. Many suffered from beriberi, many more died of dysentery-induced starvation, but the biggest killers were cholera and malaria, particularly during the monsoon. It is said that one man died for every sleeper laid on the track.

The two lines finally met at Konkuita, just south of present-day Sangkhlaburi. But as if to underscore its tragic futility, the Thailand–Burma link saw less than two years of active service: after the Japanese surrender on August 15, 1945, the railway came under the jurisdiction of the British who, thinking it would be used to supply Karen separatists in Burma, tore up 4km of track at Three Pagodas Pass, thereby cutting the Thailand–Burma link forever. When the Thais finally gained control of the rest of the railway, they destroyed the track all the way down to Nam Tok, apparently because it was uneconomic. Recently, however, an Australian–Thai group of volunteers and former POWs has salvaged sections of track near the fearsome stretch of line known as **Hellfire Pass**, clearing a memorial walk at the pass and founding an excellent museum at the site (see p.206). There have been a number of books written about the Death Railway, including several by former POWs; the Thailand–Burma Railway Centre stocks a selection, as do the town's bookshops.

marking the northern limit. Every day, tour groups and day-trippers descend on the Bridge, a symbol of Japanese atrocities in the region, though the town's main **war museums** and **cemeteries** are actually much more moving. Many veterans returning to visit the graves of their wartime comrades are understandably resentful that others have in some cases insensitively exploited the POW experience – the commercial buzz around the Bridge is a case in point. On the other hand, the Thailand–Burma Railway Centre provides shockingly instructive accounts of a period not publicly documented outside this region.

The **Chungkai war cemetery** and a handful of moderately interesting temples – including cave temples at **Wat Tham Khao Poon** and **Wat Ban Tham**, the hilltop twins of **Wat Tham Sua** and **Wat Tham Khao Noi**, and a wat featuring a rather bizarre **floating nun** – provide the focus for pleasurable trips west of the town centre.

It's worth noting that Kanchanaburi gets packed during its annual *son et lumière* **River Kwai Bridge Festival**, held over ten nights from the end of November to commemorate the first Allied bombing of the Bridge on November 28, 1944, so book accommodation well ahead if you're planning a visit then.

Thailand–Burma Railway Centre

Opposite the train station, next to the Don Rak Kanchanaburi War Cemetery on Thanon Jaokannun • Daily 9am–5pm • B100 • Ⓦ tbrconline.com

The modern Thailand–Burma Railway Centre is the best place to start any tour of Kanchanaburi's World War II memorials. It was founded to provide an informed context and research centre for the thousands who visit the POW graves every week. The result is a comprehensive and sophisticated history of the entire Thailand–Burma Railway line, with plenty of original artefacts, illustrations and scale models, and particularly strong sections on the planning and construction of the railway, and on the subsequent operation, destruction and decommissioning of the line. There is more of a focus on the line itself here than at the more emotive Hellfire Pass Memorial Museum, but the human stories are well documented too, notably via some extraordinary original photographs and video footage shot by Japanese engineers, as well as through unique interviews with surviving Asian labourers on the railway.

The shop inside the entrance stocks some interesting books on the railway and also sells products made by the Weaving for Women project in Sangkhlaburi. Admission includes a free tea or coffee in the upstairs café.

Kanchanaburi War Cemetery (Don Rak)

Opposite the train station on Thanon Saeng Chuto • Daily 8am–4pm • Free

Thirty-eight Allied POWs died for each kilometre of track laid on the Thailand–Burma Railway, and many of them are buried in Kanchanaburi's two war cemeteries, **Don Rak Kanchanaburi War Cemetery** and Chungkai Cemetery (see p.192). Of all the region's war sights, the cemeteries are the only places to have remained untouched by commercial enterprise. Of the two, Don Rak is the bigger with 6982 POW graves laid out in straight lines amid immaculate lawns and flowering shrubs. It was established after the war, on a plot adjacent to the town's Chinese cemetery, as the final resting place for the remains that had been hurriedly interred at dozens of makeshift POW-camp gravesites all the way up the line. Many of the identical stone memorial slabs in Don Rak state simply, "A man who died for his country"; others, inscribed with names, dates and regiments, indicate that the overwhelming majority of the dead were under 25 years old. A commemorative service is held here, and at Hellfire Pass (see p.206), every year on April 25, Anzac Day.

The Bridge over the River Kwai

Just west of the River Kwai Bridge Train Station • A 15–20min walk north of the main Thanon Maenam Kwai guesthouse area; alternatively cycle or take a tuk-tuk

For most people, the plain steel arches of the **Bridge over the River Kwai** come as a disappointment: as a war memorial it lacks both the emotive punch of the museums and the perceptible drama of spots further up the line, and as a bridge it looks nothing out of the ordinary – certainly not as awesomely hard to construct as it appears in David Lean's famous 1957 film, *Bridge on the River Kwai* (which was in fact shot in Sri Lanka). But it is the link with the multi-Oscar-winning film, of course, that draws tour buses by the dozen, and makes the Bridge approach seethe with trinket-sellers and touts. For all the commercialization of the place, however, you can't really come to the Kwai and not see it.

The fording of the Kwai Yai at the point just north of Kanchanaburi known as Tha Makkham was one of the first major obstacles in the construction of the Thailand–Burma Railway. Sections of a steel bridge were brought up from Java and reassembled by POWs using only pulleys and derricks. A temporary **wooden bridge** was built alongside it, taking its first train in February 1943; three months later the steel bridge was finished. Both bridges were severely damaged by Allied bombers (rather than commando-saboteurs as in the film) in 1944 and 1945, but the steel bridge was repaired after the war and is still in use today. The best way to see the Bridge is by walking gingerly across the tracks, or taking the **train** right over it: the Kanchanaburi–Nam Tok service crosses it three times a day in each direction, stopping briefly at the River Kwai Bridge station on the east bank of the river.

World War II Museum and Art Gallery

A few metres south of the Bridge • Daily 8am–6.30pm • B40

You're strongly advised to avoid the poorly designed and in some places distasteful **World War II Museum**, just steps from the Bridge, and to head instead for one of the far better informed commemorations of the war at either the Thailand–Burma Railway Centre or the Hellfire Pass Memorial Museum. The bizarre private collection here features all sorts of oddities, from coins, stamps and an incongruous Miss Thailand exhibition, to unsympathetic tableaux of dying POWs. Note that there are signs around the building claiming this to be the JEATH War Museum (see below), which is in fact at the opposite end of town.

The JEATH War Museum

Beside the Mae Khlong on Thanon Pak Praek, at the southern end of town, about 700m from the TAT office, or 5km from the Bridge • Daily 8.30am–4.30pm • B30 • 5–10min by tuk-tuk from the main Thanon Maenam Kwai guesthouse area

Founded by the chief abbot of Wat Chaichumpon in 1977 and housed within the temple grounds in a reconstructed Allied POW hut of thatched palm, the ramshackle and unashamedly low-tech **JEATH War Museum** was the town's first public repository for the photographs and memories of the POWs who worked on the Death Railway. The name JEATH is an acronym of six of the countries involved in the railway: Japan, England, Australia, America, Thailand and Holland. The museum has since been surpassed by the slicker and more informative exhibitions at the Thailand–Burma Railway Centre and the Hellfire Pass Memorial Museum and is now of most interest for its small collection of wartime photographs and for its archive of newspaper articles about and letters from former POWs who have revisited the River Kwai.

Chungkai Cemetery

On the west bank of the Kwai Noi, 2km from Rattanakarn Bridge, along Route 3228 • 5–10min by tuk-tuk from the main Thanon Maenam Kwai guesthouse area

Scrupulously well-trimmed **Chungkai Cemetery** occupies a fairly tranquil roadside spot on the west bank of the Kwai Noi, at the site of a former POW camp. Some 1750 POWs are buried here; most of the gravestone inscriptions include a name and regimental insignia, but a number remain unnamed – at the upcountry camps, bodies were thrown onto mass funeral pyres, making identification impossible. The cemetery makes a pleasant cycle ride from Rattanakarn Bridge – much of the land in this area is sugar-cane country, for which Kanchanaburi has earned the title "sugar capital of Thailand".

Wat Tham Khao Poon

On the west bank of the Kwai Noi, 2km west along Route 3228 from Chungkai Cemetery, or 4km from Rattanakarn Bridge • Daily 8am–6pm • B20 • Can be reached by boat in around 15min from the centre

At the top of Route 3228's only hill sits the cave temple **Wat Tham Khao Poon**. The attraction here is a nine-chambered cave connected by a labyrinth of dank stalactite-filled passages, where almost every ledge and knob of rock is filled with religious icons, the most important being the Reclining Buddha in the main chamber. Once out of the cave system, follow the track through the temple compound for 150m to reach a good vantage point over the Kwai Noi, just above the train tracks, presided over by an outsized, pot-bellied golden Buddha statue; if arriving by boat, you enter the wat compound via the cliff-side steps here.

Wat Tham Mangkon Thong (Floating Nun Temple)

Around 5km west of town • Daily 8am–6pm • "Show" times and prices dependent on number of tourists • Travelling by bicycle or motorbike, take the ferry across the Mae Khlong River at Tha Chukkadon then follow the road on the other side for about 4km; by car, turn west off Thanon Saeng Chuto (Highway 323) about 3km south of TAT onto Route 3429, which bridges the river and takes you north then west to the temple; alternatively take bus #8191 (every 30min; 20min) from Kanchanaburi bus station – the last return bus passes the temple at about 4.15pm

The impressive scenery across on the east of the River Kwai Noi makes for a worthwhile bike trip, but the cave temple on this side – **Wat Tham Mangkon Thong**, otherwise known as the **Floating Nun Temple** – is fairly tacky. The draw here is a Thai nun who, clad in white robes, will get into the temple pond and float there, meditating – if tourists give her enough money to make it worth her while. It's difficult not to be cynical about such a commercial stunt, though Taiwanese visitors are said to be particularly impressed. The floating takes place on a round pond at the foot of the enormous dragon staircase that leads up to the temple embedded in the hillside behind. The temple comprises an unexceptional network of low, bat-infested limestone caves, punctuated at intervals with Buddha statues.

There's no direct access from the west to the east bank of the Kwai Noi, so to get to Wat Tham Mangkon Thong from Chungkai and Wat Tham Khao Poon you have to return to town and start again.

Wat Ban Tham

12km south of town • Cross the Mae Khlong River at Thanon Mae Khlong, then turn left for the 6km ride along a partially unmade road or, if combining with Wat Tham Mangkon Thong, see directions above and then head south; alternatively, it can be reached by boat in around 30min from the centre

Because of the limestone landscape, caves are found right around Kanchanaburi and many of them have been sanctified as shrines. **Wat Ban Tham** is one such place, and is intriguing enough to make the 12km trip from the town centre worthwhile. Travelling south down the Mae Khlong to get to the temple is especially pleasant by longtail or kayak, but can also be done by road.

Wat Ban Tham was founded around six hundred years ago but its fame rests on the seventeenth-century love story that was supposedly played out in a cave on this site. A young woman called Nang Bua Klee was forced to choose between duty to her criminal father and love for the local hero by whom she had fallen pregnant; her father eventually persuaded Bua Klee to poison her sweetheart's food, but the soldier learned of the plot and killed both Bua Klee and their unborn son, whose souls are now said to be trapped in the cave at Wat Ban Tham. The cave is approached via an ostentatious Chinese-style dragon's mouth staircase, whose upper levels relate the legend in a gallery of brightly painted modern murals on the right-hand walls. Inside the cave, a woman-shaped stone has been painted in the image of the dead mother and is a popular object of worship for women trying to conceive: hopeful devotees bring pretty dresses and shoes for the image, which are hung in wardrobes to the side of the shrine, as well as toys for her son.

Wat Tham Sua and Wat Tham Khao Noi

5km south of Wat Ban Tham • Coming by car, head south out of town along Highway 323 and cross the river via the signed Mae Khlong Dam; otherwise, take any local bus as far as Tha Muang, 12km south along Highway 323, then change to a motorbike taxi to the temples (about B40)

If you're in the mood for more temples, the modern hilltop wats of Tham Sua and Tham Khao Noi – around 16km south of the town centre – both afford expansive views over the Mae Khlong river valley and out to the mountains beyond. Designed

2

by a Thai architect at the end of the twentieth century, **Wat Tham Sua** was conceived in typical grandiose style around a massive chedi covered with tiles similar to those used at Nakhon Pathom. Inside, a placid seated Buddha takes centre stage, his huge palms raised to show the Wheels of Law inscribed like stigmata across them; a conveyor belt transports devotees' offerings into the enormous alms bowl set into his lap. The neighbouring Chinese-designed **Wat Tham Khao Noi** was built at the same time and is a fabulously gaudy, seven-tiered Chinese pagoda within which a laughing Buddha competes for attention with a host of gesturing and grimacing statues and painted characters.

ARRIVAL AND DEPARTURE   KANCHANABURI

BY TRAIN

The main Kanchanaburi train station (☎034 511285), not to be confused with the station at the Bridge, is on Thanon Saeng Chuto, about 2km north of the town centre, but within walking distance of some of the Thanon Maenam Kwai accommodation. A samlor or tuk-tuk ride from here to Thanon Maenam Kwai accommodation will cost around B50.

Services to Kanchanaburi Trains are the most scenic way to get to Kanchanaburi, but there are only two daily from Bangkok's Thonburi station via Nakhon Pathom (7.50am and 1.55pm). If coming from Hua Hin, Chumphon and points further south, take the train to Ban Pong and then change to a Kanchanaburi-bound train (or bus – the bus stop is at the clocktower, about 1km from Ban Pong train station).

Moving on The easiest way to get to northern Thailand is to take a minibus to Ayutthaya (see below), where you can pick up the Northern Rail Line. For southern Thailand, take a train (or chartered minibus or public bus #81) to Ban Pong and change to a night train headed for Chumphon, Surat Thani or beyond.

Reservations and tickets Reservations for any rail journey can be made at Kanchanaburi train station, or through Good Times tour agency (see p.197) for an extra B50. Tickets for the train ride to Bangkok or along the Death Railway to Nam Tok (see p.204) don't need advance booking.

Destinations Bangkok Thonburi (2 daily; 3hr); Nakhon Pathom (2 daily; 1hr 40min–2hr); Nam Tok (3 daily; 2hr 20min).

BY BUS

Kanchanaburi's bus station (☎034 511182) is at the southern edge of the town centre, a good 2km from most accommodation. Tuk-tuks and samlors wait here and will run you into the main Thanon Maenam Kwai accommodation area for around B50.

Services to Kanchanaburi Faster than the train are the

buses from Bangkok's Southern Bus Terminal and Northern Mo Chit terminal. From Lopburi, Ayutthaya (connecting with trains from Chiang Mai), or points further north, you'll have to return to Bangkok, use a minibus service (see below) or change buses (onto #411) at Suphanburi, about 90km north of Kanchanaburi. Coming from Phetchaburi and Hua Hin, you need to change buses (onto #461) at Ratchaburi.

Moving on Government buses run from the bus station to Bangkok's Northern Mo Chit bus terminal, the Southern Bus Terminal, and to all destinations listed below. The first-class ticket office and departure point is beside the main road on the edge of the bus station, while the office for all other services is in the middle of the depot.

Destinations Bangkok (Northern Mo Chit terminal; 8 daily; 3hr); Bangkok (Southern Bus Terminal; every 10–15min; 2hr); Erawan (9 daily; 1hr 30min); Nam Tok (every 30min; 1hr 30min); Ratchaburi (every 15min; 2hr); Sai Yok (every 30min; 2hr 30min); Sangkhlaburi (14 daily; 3–4hr); Suphanburi (every 20min; 2hr); Thong Pha Phum (every 20–30min; 3hr); Three Pagodas Pass (6 daily; 4hr).

BY MINIBUS

From/to Bangkok Fast tourist a/c minibuses from Thanon Khao San get to Kanchanaburi in just 2hr, though they generally only drop passengers at *Jolly Frog* on Thanon Maenam Kwai (see p.196), despite advertising otherwise. Licensed a/c minibuses departing from outside Bangkok's *Royal Ratanakosin Hotel* on Ratchadamnoen Klang in Banglamphu, a 5min walk from Khao San, will drop you wherever you want.

Tickets You can buy tickets for a/c minibuses from travel agents and guesthouses in Kanchanaburi.

Destinations Ayutthaya (1 daily; 3hr, timed to connect with the night trains to Chiang Mai); Bangkok, Khao San, or the nearby *Royal Ratanakosin Hotel* (hourly; 2hr); Bangkok, Victory Monument (hourly; 2hr); Sangkhlaburi (10 daily; 3hr; tickets available from a booth at the back of the bus station); Suvarnabhumi Airport (6 daily; 2hr 30min–3hr).

GETTING AROUND

With tuk-tuks plying the main route between the bus station and the Bridge, and boatmen waiting to ferry you along the waterways, it's easy to get to and from Kanchanaburi's main sights.

By tuk-tuk From the guesthouses up to the Bridge, for example, you should easily be able to charter a tuk-tuk for B30–40.

By songthaew Orange public songthaews run along Thanon Saeng Chuto, originating from outside the Focus Optic optician's, three blocks north of the bus station, and travelling north via the Kanchanaburi War Cemetery (Don Rak), Thai–Burma Railway Centre, train station and access road to the Bridge (#2; every 15min until 6pm; 15min to the Bridge turn-off; B10).

By car, jeep or motorbike Many outlets rent out motorbikes for around B200 per day. Mek and Mee (☎081 757119), next to *Jolly Frog* on Thanon Maenam Kwai, is one of the few places that will provide first-class (fully comprehensive) insurance with rental cars.

By longtail boat Boats wait beside the Bridge for trips to the JEATH War Museum or out to sights along the Kwai Noi. To save yourself a couple of hundred baht, cross over to the western bank on foot and talk with the boatmen there instead – they charge around B600 for an hour-long outing.

By bicycle Guesthouses and tour agencies rent out bicycles for B50 a day– ideal for exploring the main town sights and the quiet rural backroads.

By kayak A green and sedate way of exploring the area is by kayak; you can rent one just north of the Bridge or from further upstream at Nong Bua (available from B300/person from several tour agencies on Maenam Kwai). Alternatively, try specialists Safarine, who charge B350 for 1hr 30min (see p.198).

INFORMATION

Tourist information The helpful TAT office (daily 8.30am–4.30pm; ☎034 511200, ✉tatkan@tat.or.th) is just south of the bus station on Thanon Saeng Chuto and keeps up-to-date bus and train timetables.

ACCOMMODATION

Many people choose to make the most of the inspiring scenery by staying on or near the river, in either a **raft house** (often just a rattan hut balanced on a raft of logs) or a **guesthouse**. The most popular area is around **Thanon Maenam Kwai**, which stretches 2km from Soi Rongheabaow to the Bridge, and is *the* backpackers' hub, crammed with bars, restaurants and tour agents; most guesthouses are at the riverside end of the small sois running off this thoroughfare. Despite the tranquil views, Kwai-side accommodation can be plagued by roaring longtail engines during the day, so you might want to book in for just one night until you've experienced the decibel levels for yourself. Bring mosquito repellent too, as many huts float in among lotus swamps.

Details of raft-house accommodation further **upstream** are given under the relevant accounts: Tham Lawa on p.206 and Sai Yok on p.207.

KANCHANABURI

Apple's Guest House East off Thanon Maenam Kwai across Sudjai Bridge ☎034 512017, ⱳapplenoi -kanchanaburi.com. The more central of two similarly named mid-range options run by friendly local women Apple and Noi, *Apple's Guest House* sits between the train station and Thanon Maenam Kwai. Set round a quiet garden, it offers smart, modern fan and a/c rooms behind the airy restaurant, plus wi-fi. Fan B490, a/c B590

Apple's Retreat Across the river, 600m from Thanon Maenam Kwai ☎034 512017, ⱳapplenoi -kanchanaburi.com. *Apple's Retreat* sits in a green and tranquil spot, with a lovely Kwai-side restaurant and terrace. Rooms are across the road in a two-storey building, with views across farmland to the hills beyond, and there's a peaceful garden. Offers wi-fi throughout, plus free transport to and from *Apple's Guest House*. Fan B490, a/c B590

Bluestar Guesthouse 241 Thanon Maenam Kwai ☎034 512161, ⱳbluestar-guesthouse.com. Popular, clued-up guesthouse with a wide range of good-value accommodation including very cheap, basic fan rooms in a row house; attractive, well-priced a/c bungalows set over a lotus swamp; and cabins raised on elevated piles with downstairs bathrooms and high-level bedrooms or private upper-level terraces. The land runs down to the riverside area, though views are dominated by the overgrown islet in front. Call for free pick-up from transport terminals. Fan rooms B150, a/c rooms B350, bungalows B650

Chitanun Guest House 47/3 Thanon Maenam Kwai, on the opposite side of the road from the river ☎034 624785. A range of en-suite rooms – from basic white-walled crash pads to quite luxurious affairs with a/c and TV – set in a private compound full of tropical plants. It's a friendly place; the only downside is that there aren't any river views. Fan B250, a/c B600

Felix River Kwai On the west bank of the Kwai Yai ☎034 551000, ⱳfelixriverkwaihotel.com. Occupying a lovely riverside spot within walking distance of the Bridge (get off at the River Kwai Bridge train station if arriving by train; otherwise it's a 2km drive from Thanon Maenam Kwai – transfers can be arranged), this is one of the top hotels in the area, though it's starting to look dated and a little faded, particularly in the public areas. It has over two hundred large a/c rooms, plus two swimming pools. Rates depend on whether you want a river view, and are sometimes discounted during the week. Breakfast included. B5300

2

Jolly Frog Backpackers 28 Soi China, Thanon Maenam Kwai ☎034 514579. Many backpackers' first choice, this large complex occupies a lovely stretch of the riverfront and has a popular restaurant serving cheap traveller grub. Unfortunately, the staff aren't all that jolly, and nowadays it struggles to live up to its reputation. Apart from some very cheap single rooms and a few doubles with shared bathrooms, accommodation mostly comprises comfy en-suite rooms in bamboo-walled blocks built around a shady garden. You can swim off the jetty, though be careful of the strong current. Free wi-fi and nightly film screenings at 7pm. Fan B150, a/c B290

★ **My Home** 18/1 Thanon Maenam Kwai, signposted down an unnamed soi just north of the Water Authority building ☎034 625555, ⓦmyhomekan.com. This clean new place, on a quiet soi between Thanon Maenam Kwai and the river, is far enough away from all of the noisy bars to ensure a restful sleep, but still relatively central. The great-value en-suite rooms occupy a modern single-storey block, which backs onto a courtyard, and have brightly painted walls. TV and free wi-fi. Fan B350, a/c B550

Nita Raft House 271/1 Thanon Pak Praek ☎034 514521, ⓦnitarafthouse.com. Located away from the main Thanon Song Kwai fray, near the JEATH Museum, this is a genuine, old-style guesthouse with a very laidback atmosphere. The fourteen simple, floating rooms (some en suite) are among the cheapest in town and all offer some sort of river view. There's a lounge for watching DVDs and sampling the tasty guesthouse food. Good rates for singles. Fan B250, a/c B650

Ploy River Kwai Thanon Maenam Kwai, just north of Jolly Frog Backpackers ☎034 515804, ⓦploygh.com. Strikingly different in style from other guesthouses on this road, this is a smart little enclave set back off the road but with distant river views only from the restaurant. The chic, sleek, contemporary-look rooms have platform beds and a/c, with extra charged for those with garden-style bathrooms or TVs. Good discounts if you book online. B900

River Kwai Hotel 284/3–16 Thanon Saeng Chuto ☎034 510111, ⓦriverkwai.co.th. The town centre's top hotel is nowhere near the river, but it's very good value even if it lacks the atmosphere of its riverside competitors. Rooms are of a high standard, and all have a/c and cable TV. Facilities include a pool, spa, nightclub and free wi-fi. B1800

Sam's River Rafthouse 48 Soi Rongheabaow ☎034 624231, ⓦsamsguesthouse.com. Unfussy a/c rooms on a shabby, creaking pontoon that floats on the edge of the river, plus cheaper stone-built bungalows with fans and cold-water showers. Compared to its neighbour, *VN Guesthouse* (see below), it seems poor value, but it's a decent enough fallback option. Fan B250, a/c B600

Tamarind Guest House 29/1 Thanon Maenam Kwai ☎034 518790, ⓔtamarind_guesthouse@yahoo.co.th. Smaller rooms than in some of the other waterfront guesthouses, but the place is very clean throughout and managed by considerate, friendly staff. Sleep in the two-storey house, or down by the waterfront in one of the rafthouse rooms, which share a breezy terrace. Wi-fi and free internet available. Fan B350, a/c B550

T & T 1/14 Thanon Maenam Kwai, just north of My Home, on a soi leading down towards the river ☎034 514846, ⓦtandt-kanchanaburiguesthouse.com. A friendly and relaxing budget choice, with a small but attractive terrace overlooking the Kwai Yai. Sleeping options include small, fan-cooled singles with clean shared bathrooms, doubles in a floating raft house which have mattresses on the floor (also with shared bathrooms), and more luxurious rooms with a/c and private bathrooms. TV B50 extra per room. Fan B250, a/c B500

★ **U Inchantree** 443 Thanon Maenam Kwai ☎034 521584, ⓦukanchanaburi.com. Spectacularly located on a bend in the Kwai Yai River, a 5min walk north of the Bridge (get off at the River Kwai Bridge train station if arriving by train), this luxurious, 26-room retreat has charming staff and what must be Kanchanaburi's most style-conscious rooms. They're not huge, but the powerful rain showers, snuggly white duvets and in-room iPod docks more than compensate. Outside, facilities include a riverside pool, a peaceful glass-fronted library and a restaurant serving superb buffet breakfasts. Best of all, you can keep your room for a full 24 hours, regardless of when you check in. B2500

VN Guesthouse 44 Soi Rongheabaow ☎034 514082, ⓦvnguesthouse.net. In a pretty location on a quiet stretch of the river just south of the Maenam Kwai hub (along from *Sam's River Rafthouse*), this place offers decent raft-house rooms: they're large, en suite, and come with either fan or a/c; the best have lovely outlooks and they all have terraces and wi-fi. Rooms on dry land are unexceptional. Fan B250, a/c B400

OUT OF TOWN

Oriental Kwai Off Route 3199, Ladya ☎034 588168, ⓦorientalkwai.com; map p.199. In a quiet spot beside the Kwai Yai, 15km north of town, this Dutch–Thai-run little hotel offers just twelve thoughtfully designed cottages in a garden with pool, pétanque, volleyball and a miniature driving range. Cottages are a/c, have wi-fi and DVD players and are tastefully decorated in modern Asian accents; some are wheelchair accessible. There's nothing to see in the immediate area but you can rent cars, motorbikes, kayaks and bicycles or join tours to all Kanchanaburi attractions. B2400

★ **Xanadu 2008** 19/5 Moo 1, Tambon Nong Bua ☎080 021 3346, ⓦxanaduresort2008.com; map p.199. With just ten en-suite bungalows in a sloping, tropical garden that leads down towards an undeveloped section of the river, this welcoming place is ideal for families in search of peace and quiet. The flowery decor might not be to everyone's taste, but there's a well-maintained pool and English–Thai owners Dennis and Nee do everything they can to fill guests in on local happenings. Nee is an excellent cook, and the spring rolls served in the

poolside restaurant are the subject of rave reviews. It's a 9km drive from the Bridge, on the northern bank of the River Kwai Yai; join Route 3199 as you head north out of town, then turn left towards Nong Bua. B1000

EATING

Almost all of Kanchanaburi's guesthouses and raft houses have **restaurants**, and there's a cluster of floating restaurants beside the Bridge, serving good if rather pricey seafood to accompany the river views. A cheaper place to enjoy genuine local food is at the ever-reliable **night market**, which sets up alongside Thanon Saeng Chuto on the edge of the bus station. There are also a few foodstalls at the **night bazaar**, which operates in front of the train station (Thurs–Tues 6–10pm).

Apple's Guest House East off Thanon Maenam Kwai ☎034 512017, ⓦapplenoi-kanchanaburi.com. Reliably tasty food both here and at *Apple's Retreat* (same hours; see p.195), across Sudjai Bridge, prepared to traditional Thai recipes by Kanchanaburi's most famous cooking school. The extensive menu (B65–180) includes coconut- and cashew-laced *matsaman* curries – both meat and vegetarian varieties – as well as outstanding yellow curries and multi-course set dinners. Every dish is prepared to order, so service can be slow. Also offers cookery classes (see p.198). Daily 7am–9pm.

Bell's Pizzeria Thanon Maenam Kwai ☎081 010 6614, ⓦbellspizzeria.com. This insanely popular Italian place has tables inside and out, and the menu, which runs from carbonara right through to *phanaeng* curries, is actually quite diverse. If you'd rather not decide at the restaurant, you can pre-order online. Pizzas from B160. Daily 4–11pm.

Jolly Frog At Jolly Frog Backpackers on Thanon Maenam Kwai ☎034 514579. There's a huge menu of cheap backpacker grub at this big, open-sided restaurant, including burgers, sandwiches and the like, but service can be very slow. Daily 7am–10.30pm.

★ **Mangosteen Café and Books** 13 Thanon Maenam Kwai ☎081 793 5814, ⓦmangosteencafe.net. Plants edge the entranceway to this bright and cheery café, where you'll find bookshelves bursting with free-to-borrow paperbacks. The food (most dishes B60–100) is worth sticking around for too, with a lively mix of soups, pasta salads and Thai dishes. Daily 8am–9pm; closed on the first and third Mon of every month.

Schluck Thanon Maenam Kwai ☎034 624 599. Cosy a/c restaurant that entices a regular crowd of expats with its menu of pizzas, salads and steaks (from B150), plus its decent selection of authentically spicy fish and yam dishes. Also has a few tables outside. Daily 4pm–2am.

Sri Rung Rueng Thanon Maenam Kwai. Popular, well-priced, bamboo-roofed restaurant with a huge menu of *tom kha*, *tom yam* and curries (yellow, red, green, *phanaeng* and *matsaman*), lots of which are available in veggie and non-veggie versions (from B60), plus steaks, seafood and cocktails. Daily until midnight.

The Hut Thanon Maenam Kwai. Good-value steaks and salads draw big groups, solo travellers and loved-up couples to this popular place facing Kanchanaburi's busiest tourist street. The garden area out front, partially sheltered from the rain by an attractive thatched roof, is a pleasant spot for a beer (B60). Daily 7am–11pm.

DRINKING

Nightlife in Kanchanaburi is still relatively low-key, but in recent years there's been an influx of farang-managed **bars** competing for attention along the southern stretch of Thanon Maenam Kwai. Most of the new places offer a similar diet of loud music and cheapish beer, with bar girls and/or sports TV as an added attraction.

Get Drunk for B10 Thanon Maenam Kwai, across from Sri Rung Rueng. This tiny streetside booth opens up when the sun goes down, attracting a fun crowd of mostly young backpackers. Buckets seem to be *de rigueur* here (you sit on them and drink from them), but to save cash it's best to drink shorts: single shots of almost every spirit are just B10.

Usually open from dusk until after midnight.

One More Bar Thanon Maenam Kwai ☎084 801 3933. A lively, sociable place to head to after dark, not least because it has a refreshing no-bar-girls policy, hosts regular free barbecues and occasional parties, and has Nintendo Wii and DVDs in its backroom lounge. Daily 8am–2am.

DIRECTORY

Airline tickets Domestic and international tickets from Good Times Travel, 63/1 Thanon Maenam Kwai ☎034 624441, ⓦgood-times-travel.com.

Banks and ATMs There are several banks with money-changing facilities and ATMs on Thanon Saeng Chuto,

immediately to the north of the Thanon U Thong junction, and around the bridge.

Books Several secondhand bookshops on Thanon Maenam Kwai.

2

Cookery classes Most famously at *Apple's Guest House*: shop at the morning market and learn how to cook the basic Thai dishes (9.30am–3pm; B1250).

Hospitals The private Thanakan Hospital (☎034 622366–75) is at 20/20 Thanon Saeng Chuto, at the southern end of town, near the junction with Thanon Chukkadon; the government-run Phahon Phonphayulasena Hospital (☎034 511507 or ☎034 622999) is further south at 572/1 Thanon Saeng Chuto, near the junction with Thanon Mae Khlong.

Immigration office At 100/22 Thanon Mae Khlong ☎034 564279.

Internet access Almost all of Kanchanaburi's guest-houses and hotels have free-to-use computers, free wi-fi, or both. If you're looking for an internet café where you can use Skype, print documents, etc, your best option is Thanon Maenam Kwai.

Massage UK-owned Suan Nanachat (☎081 908 0201, ☎suan-nanachaat.com) is an invitingly secluded boutique-style massage centre and day-spa in the Nong Bua area, 10km north of town on the way to Nam Tok (phone for free transport). Offers high-quality masseurs and a wide choice of (quite pricey) treatments (90min massage B500), as well as wholemeal sandwiches, salads and herbal teas. Reservations essential as numbers are restricted to six at a time.

Post office The GPO is 1km south of the TAT office on Thanon Saeng Chuto, but there are a couple of more central postal agents on Thanon Maenam Kwai.

Swimming pool Non-guests can use the two huge pools at the *Felix River Kwai* (☎034 551000, ☎felixriverkwaihotel .com) for B300 per day including towel (6am–8pm).

Tourist police For all emergencies, call the tourist police on the free, 24hr phone line (☎1155), or contact them at one of their booths in town (daily 9am–6pm): right beside the Bridge (☎034 512795); on Thanon Song Kwai; and on Thanon Saeng Chuto (☎034 512668).

Around Kanchanaburi

The parallel valleys of the Kwai Noi and the Kwai Yai, northwest of Kanchanaburi, are stacked full of great day-tripping opportunities, from the exceptionally beautiful **Erawan Falls** to the drama of a ride on the **Death Railway** and the pathos of the World War II museum at **Hellfire Pass**. There are Stone Age artefacts at the **Ban Kao Museum**, twelfth-century Khmer temple ruins at **Prasat Muang Singh**, the (controversial)

DAY-TRIPS, RAFTING AND TREKKING AROUND KANCHANABURI

All the places listed below advertise **day- and overnight trips** around the Kanchanaburi and Sangkhlaburi areas, including infinite permutations of rafting, elephant-riding, Erawan Falls, Hellfire Pass and the Death Railway, sometimes with a short trek thrown in. Prices listed are per person, usually for a minimum of four. They all also do tailor-made guided tours to the war sights (often by boat or raft) and to Damnoen Saduak floating markets, and will also provide a cheap transport service – car plus driver but no guide – for the more accessible attractions. If you're given the opportunity to visit Kanchanaburi's "**Monkey School**" as part of your tour, you're strongly advised to turn it down. The monkeys here are said to have been rescued from abusive owners, but now they spend their days chained up by the neck until they are coerced into performing circus tricks like shooting hoops and riding children's bicycles.

A.S. Mixed Travel Apple's Guest House, east off Thanon Maenam Kwai ☎034 512017, ☎applenoi-kanchanaburi.com. In addition to the standard tours and treks in and around Kanchanaburi, the speciality here is village cycle tours through the rice fields and traditional rural hinterland around *Apple's Retreat* across the Sudjai Bridge.

Good Times Travel 63/1 Thanon Maenam Kwai ☎034 624441, ☎good-times-travel.com. Energetically run, with competitively priced day-trips (B900–1550/person) and longer treks that get good reviews. Especially popular for its two-day trip to a Karen area near Hin Dat hot springs, which includes four hours' trekking each day (B3450/person, based on two sharing). Also offers cycle

tours around Thong Pha Phum and Sangkhlaburi and can arrange for joint cycle tours to Ayutthaya.

KTC Travel 99–101 Thanon Maenam Kwai ☎086 396 7349 or ☎087 153 4147, ☎tourkanchanaburi .com. Offers a twice-daily trip out to bathe elephants in the river (B650) as well as short bamboo rafting trips (B350). Longer full-day trips are also available (B750–1090) and for your fee you're promised lunch, fruit, drinking water and an English-speaking guide.

Safarine To the west of town at 120/5 Moo 4, Tambon Nongbua ☎086 049 1662, ☎safarine.com. French-run kayaking specialist offering short, full-day and overnight kayaking trips in the Kanchanaburi area for B300–2850.

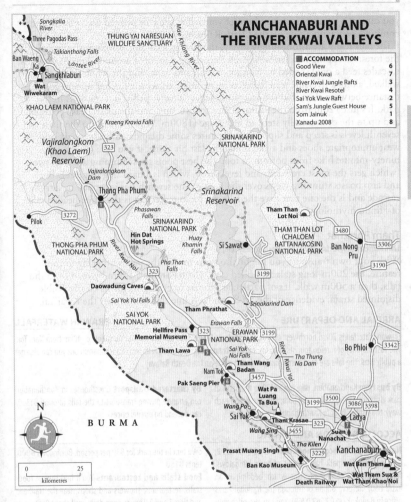

KANCHANABURI AND THE RIVER KWAI VALLEYS

ACCOMMODATION	
Good View	6
Oriental Kwai	7
River Kwai Jungle Rafts	3
River Kwai Resotel	4
Sai Yok View Raft	2
Sam's Jungle Guest House	5
Som Jainuk	1
Xanadu 2008	8

2

Songkalia River
Three Pagodas Pass
THUNG YAI NARESUAN WILDLIFE SANCTUARY
Mae Khlong River
Takianthong Falls
Ban Waeng
Ka
Lantee River
Sangkhlaburi
Wat Wiwekaram
KHAO LAEM NATIONAL PARK
Kraeng Kravia Falls
SRINAKARIND NATIONAL PARK
Vajiralongkom (Khao Laem) Reservoir
323
Vajiralongkom Dam
Thong Pha Phum
Srinakarind Reservoir
Tham Than Lot Noi
Phasawan Falls
SRINAKARIND NATIONAL PARK
3480
THAM THAN LOT (CHALOEM RATTANAKOSIN) NATIONAL PARK
3272
Pilok
Hin Dat Hot Springs
Huay Khamin Falls
Si Sawat
Ban Nong Pru
3306
THONG PHA PHUM NATIONAL PARK
Pha That Falls
River Kwai Noi
3199
3190
Daowadung Caves
Sai Yok Yai Falls
323
Tham Phrathat
Srinakarind Dam
SAI YOK NATIONAL PARK
Erawan Falls
ERAWAN NATIONAL PARK
3199
Bo Phloi
3342
Hellfire Pass Memorial Museum
323
Tham Lawa
Sai Yok Noi Falls
Tham Wang Badan
Tha Thung Na Dam
River Kwai Yai
Nam Tok
3457
Pak Saeng Pier
Wat Pa Luang Ta Bua
3199
3500
3086
3398
Wang Po
Sai Yok
Tham Krasae
323
Ladya
N
BURMA
Wang Sing
3455
Tha Kilen
Suan Nanachat
Prasat Muang Singh
3229
Kanchanaburi
0 25 kilometres
Ban Kao Museum
Wat Ban Tham
Death Railway
Wat Tham Sua & Wat Tham Khao Noi

opportunity to get up close to a tiger at the **Tiger Sanctuary Temple** and several good caves, including at **Tham Than Lot National Park** and the riverside **Tham Lawa**.

Many of these attractions are served by public **transport**, the train being an obvious option along the Kwai Noi valley as far as its **Nam Tok** terminus, with buses useful along both valleys. But train schedules are unreliable and bus connections can be time-consuming so many people either opt instead to join one of the many mix-and-match **tours** offered by Kanchanaburi agents (see opposite) or rent their own wheels for a day. Distances are not large, and there's a handy connecting road between the two valleys just south of Nam Tok.

Erawan Waterfall

Daily 8am–4pm, tiers 1 and 2 until 5pm • National park admission B200 • ☎ 034 574222, ⓦ dnp.go.th

Considered by many to be the most beautiful falls in Thailand, **Erawan Waterfall** is the star attraction of **Erawan National Park**. It's a great day out – so popular, in fact, that

2

you can get a commemorative photo of yourself at the falls printed on a plate – and combines well with a ride on the Death Railway.

The falls really are astonishingly lovely: the clear glacial-blue waters gush through the forest, dropping in a series of seven tiers along a route of around 2km. At each tier, cascades feed a pool shaded by bamboo, rattan and liana, and the whole course can be walked, along a riverside trail that gets increasingly tricky the further up you go. The distance between tiers, and the ascent to each, is clearly spelled out on signs in the park. It's just 720m from the visitor centre to level one, and then fairly easy going on and up to the dramatically stepped fifth stage (1800m). The route on to the sixth and seventh levels is steep and slippery and features some dilapidated bridges and ladders: wear appropriate shoes and avoid doing the last bit alone, if you can; it's about a ninety-minute hike from bottom to top. The best pools for swimming are level two (which gets the most crowded) and level seven, which is a hard slog but rarely busy, and also boasts stunning views over the jungle. The seventh tier is topped by a triple cascade and is the one that gave the falls their name: Erawan is the three-headed god of Hindu mythology.

Tham Phrathat

12km from Erawan Waterfall • Daily 8am–4pm (last entry 3pm)

With your own transport you might also want to visit the park's other significant feature, the 200m-long stalactite-filled cave, **Tham Phrathat**, 12km by road from the falls, then a 500m walk. It's of particular interest to geologists for its clearly visible disjointed strata, evidence of the Sri Sawat fault line that runs under the Kwai Yai.

ARRIVAL AND DEPARTURE   ERAWAN WATERFALL

Erawan Waterfall is 70km northwest of Kanchanaburi, via Route 3199 along the Kwai Yai valley, or 40km from Nam Tok. The vast majority of foreign tourists **charter return transport** to Erawan Falls from Kanchanaburi but you can also get a public **bus**. The falls are commonly combined with a ride on the Death Railway.

By bus From Kanchanaburi, take bus #8170 to the national park visitor centre (roughly every hour; 1hr 30min; B50 each way); the last bus back to Kanchanaburi departs at 4pm.

By chartered transport Guesthouses in Kanchanaburi can arrange private transport to the falls (around B1300/car, depending on fuel prices).

ACCOMMODATION AND EATING

National park accommodation ☎ 034 574222, ⓦ dnp.go.th. The park has a series of basic bungalows, terraced "houses" and tents (for which bedding is an extra B50). Reserve online or through the National Parks office in Bangkok (☎ 02 562 0760). You can also pitch your own tent in the park for B30 per person. Bungalows B800, tents B150

Food stalls and restaurants You'll find several food-stalls, restaurants, showers and shops near the trailhead and tiers 1 and 2. They're open daily until about 8pm.

Srinakarind National Park

105km northwest of Kanchanaburi via Route 3199 • B200 • ☎ 034 516667, ⓦ dnp.go.th

A few kilometres north of the turn-off to Erawan, the landscape is dominated by the scenic **Srinakarind Reservoir**, which is fed by the dammed waters of the Mae Khlong and the Kha Khaeng and gives rise to the Kwai Yai. It's a popular recreation spot and site of several resorts, all of which lie within the **Srinakarind National Park** (also known as **Khuean Srinagarindra National Park**). From the dam you can hire boats (about B1800) to make the two-hour journey northwest across the reservoir to **Huay Khamin Falls**, which are said to be the most powerful in the district, and reputedly get the name "Turmeric Streak" from the ochre-coloured limestone rockface. However, it's quicker and less hassle to join one of the tours from Kanchanaburi.

CLOCKWISE FROM TOP WAT WANG WIWEKARAM, SANGKHLABURI (P.211); SUNKEN TEMPLE, SANGKHLABURI (P.210); WAT WANG WIWEKARAM >

2

Tham Than Lot (Chaloem Rattanakosin) National Park

B200 • ☎ 034 519606, ⓦ dnp.go.th

Tiny **Tham Than Lot National Park** (also known as **Chaloem Rattanakosin National Park**) covers just 59 square kilometres but boasts two stalactite-strewn **caves** (bring a torch), a decent **waterfall** and an enjoyable hiking trail that links them.

From the visitor centre, follow the signed trail for about ten minutes to reach the first cave, **Tham Than Lot Noi**, which is 400m deep and illuminated if there are enough people (for example at weekends). A very picturesque 2.5km, two-hour **trail** runs on from the other side of Tham Than Lot Noi, along a stream and through a ravine to the first of three **waterfalls**, about an hour and a half's easy walk away and passing towering dipterocarps, fine jungle views and plenty of butterflies en route. The path gets more difficult after the first waterfall, and dangerously slippery in the wet season, running via another couple of waterfalls before coming to the larger of the park's two caves, the impressively deep sink-hole **Tham Than Lot Yai**, site of a small Buddhist shrine. Another ten minutes along the trail brings you to a small forest temple, from where you'll need to retrace your steps to return to the visitor centre.

ARRIVAL AND DEPARTURE   THAM THAN LOT NATIONAL PARK

The park entrance is 97km north of Kanchanaburi, off Route 3086. If you'd rather not drive, your best bet is to organize a private tour from Kanchanaburi.

By car From the city, follow Route 3199 until you reach Ladya, and then join Route 3086. Turn left at Amphoe Nongprue and then follow the road for 18km until you reach the park.

ACCOMMODATION AND EATING

A handful of simple, government-owned **bungalows** (B1200) sit within the park – bedding and fan are provided. For eating, there's a very basic **restaurant** at the park's headquarters.

Ban Kao Museum

35km west of Kanchanaburi and 8km from Prasat Muang Singh • Wed–Sun 9am–4pm • B50 • ☎ 034 654058 • No public transport; follow Highway 323 north out of Kanchanaburi until you get to the junction with minor road 3229, then follow this road southwest for about 16km before joining minor road 3445 for the last 2km

The **Ban Kao Museum** is devoted to relics from an advanced prehistoric civilization (8000 to 1000 BC) that once settled on the banks of the Kwai Noi. Items on display include unique, curiously designed pots dated to around 1770 BC that were found buried at the head and feet of fifty skeletons; polished stone tools from around 8000 BC; and inscribed bronze pots and bangles transferred from a nearby bronze-culture site, which have been placed at around 1000 BC – somewhat later than the bronze artefacts from Ban Chiang in the northeast (see p.483). The hollowed-out tree trunks in front of the museum are also unusual: they may have been used as boats or as coffins – or possibly as a metaphorical combination of the two.

Prasat Muang Singh

Daily 8.30am–4.30pm • B100, plus B50 per car, B30 per motorbike or B10 per bicycle • ☎ 034 591122

Eight hundred years ago, the Khmer empire extended west as far as Muang Singh (City of Lions), an outpost strategically sited on the banks of the River Kwai Noi, 43km west of present-day Kanchanaburi. Thought to have been built at the end of the twelfth century, the temple complex of **Prasat Muang Singh** follows Khmer religious and architectural precepts, but its origins are obscure – the City of Lions gets no mention in any of the recognized chronicles until the nineteenth century.

Prasat Muang Singh covers one-third of a square kilometre, bordered by moats and ramparts that probably had cosmological as well as defensive significance, and with an enclosed **shrine complex** at its heart. Restorations now give an idea of the crude grandeur of the original structure, which was constructed entirely from blocks of rough, russet laterite.

As with all Khmer prasats, the pivotal feature of Muang Singh is the main prang, surrounded by a series of walls and a covered gallery, with gateways marking the cardinal points. The prang faces east, towards Angkor, and is guarded by a fine sandstone statue of **Avalokitesvara**, one of the five great *bodhisattvas* of Mahayana Buddhism, would-be Buddhas who have postponed their entrance into Nirvana to help others attain enlightenment. He's depicted here in characteristic style, his eight arms and torso covered with tiny Buddha reliefs and his hair tied in a topknot. In Mahayanist mythology, Avalokitesvara represents mercy, while the other statue found in the prasat, the female figure of **Prajnaparamita**, symbolizes wisdom – when wisdom and mercy join forces, enlightenment ensues. Just visible on the inside of the north wall surrounding the prang is the only intact example of the stucco carving that once ornamented every facade. Other fragments and sculptures found at this and nearby sites are displayed beside the north gate; especially tantalizing is the single segment of what must have been a gigantic face hewn from several massive blocks of stone.

ARRIVAL AND DEPARTURE	**PRASAT MUANG SINGH**

Prasat Muang Singh is 8km northwest of Ban Kao Museum, on minor road 3445.

By car From Kanchanaburi either follow directions given for Ban Kao Museum, opposite, or continue along Highway 323 as far as kilometre-stone 15 to take Route 3445 southwest to Muang Singh.

By train You can get to Muang Singh by taking the Death

Railway train: get off at Tha Kilen (1hr 15min from Kanchanaburi), walk straight out of the station for 500m, turn right at the crossroads and continue for another 1km to reach the ruins.

EATING

You'll find a handful of **food outlets** and souvenir stalls towards the northern end of the compound.

Wat Pa Luang Ta Bua Yannasampanno: the Tiger Temple

37km from Kanchanaburi, signed off Highway 323 at kilometre-stone 21 • Daily noon–4.45pm (last admission 3.15pm); also opens for private visits 7.30–11am • B600 (afternoon), or B5000 for private visits • ☎ 085 561 9555, ⓦ tigertemple.org • No vests or shorts, and no red clothing (which antagonizes the tigers) • Transport arranged through Kanchanaburi tour operators costs around B130 return per person

The region's oddest and most controversial attraction is the chance to have your photo taken with a tiger at the so-called "Tiger Temple", **Wat Pa Luang Ta Bua Yannasampanno**. Temples are traditionally regarded as sanctuaries for unwanted and illegally captured animals, and Wat Pa Luang Ta Bua has been taking in tigers since 1999, when a distressed young tiger cub was brought here. Since then, the temple's tiger population has grown to an incredible 96, attracting hundreds of Thai and foreign visitors a day. However, a lot of people return discouraged by the experience, not least because the animals are housed in small, bare cages and only let out to be paraded in front of visitors in the afternoons. Moreover, the temple has been accused of exploiting the animals as a money-making tourist attraction. Undercover investigators sent by the British animal welfare charity Care for the Wild International (ⓦ careforthewild.org) have alleged a range of **welfare problems** and other malpractices, including unauthorized trading of tigers with a breeding centre in Laos.

Controversy aside, our advice is not to bother with the Tiger Temple. Visitors who pay B600 for the regular afternoon visit enter the park en masse, only to be huddled together by staff, who quickly try to sell you a variety of optional "experiences", such as tiger cub feeding (B1000). Meanwhile, the tired- and bored-looking tigers are brought down to a shady gravel area and chained up with little room to move, as queues of tourists crowd around for their chance to take photos.

Nam Tok

There's not much more to the tiny town of **NAM TOK** than the terminus of the Death Railway line. On rainy-season weekends, Thais flock to the roadside **Sai Yok Noi Falls**, 2km north, but if you're filling time between trains, you'd be better off stretching your legs on the short trek to the nearby Wang Badan cave or taking a boat trip to Tham Lawa or Sai Yok Yai Falls. It's also straightforward to get a bus on to Hellfire Pass.

Tham Wang Badan

1.5km north of Nam Tok train station • Daily 8.30am–4.30pm • National park admission B200

Impressive stalactites, fathomless chambers and unnerving heat make **Tham Wang Badan**, part of the Erawan National Park, one of the more interesting underground experiences in the region. It's easily reached by a **trail** that's signposted east off Highway 323, 600m northwest from the station road T-junction, 1.5km from the station itself. About 1km into the trail, you arrive at the park warden's office where you can rent feeble **torches**; it's better to bring your own or to pay the warden a nominal fee to accompany you and turn on the cave lights. From the office it's 2km of easy walking to the cave, and as most tourists bypass Tham Wang Badan in favour of Erawan Falls, in another area of the park (see p.199), it's usually quiet here.

ARRIVAL AND DEPARTURE
NAM TOK

By train The train station is at the top of the town, 900m north of Highway 323, and a further 2km from the Kwai

Noi. To reach the highway from the station, walk up the station approach road, cross the tracks, turn left at the

---

RIDING THE DEATH RAILWAY

The two-hour journey along the notorious Thailand–Burma **Death Railway** from Kanchanaburi to Nam Tok is one of Thailand's most scenic and most popular train rides. Though the views are lovely, it's the history that makes the ride so special, so it's worth visiting the Thailand–Burma Railway Centre in Kanchanaburi before making the trip, as this provides a context for the enormous loss of human life and the extraordinary feat of engineering behind the line's construction (see p.191). Alternatively, take the bus straight up to the **Hellfire Pass Memorial Museum** (see p.206), just north of the line's current Nam Tok terminus, which provides an equally illuminating introduction to the railway's history, then return to Kanchanaburi by train. A good tip, to get the best views, is to make sure you sit (or stand) on the right-hand side of the train on the journey back to Kanchanaburi, and on the left-hand side when travelling towards Nam Tok.

Leaving Kanchanaburi via the Bridge over the River Kwai, the train chugs through the Kwai Noi valley, stopping frequently at country stations decked with frangipani and jasmine. The first stop of note is Tha Kilen (1hr 15min), where you can alight for Prasat Muang Singh (see p.202). About twenty minutes later the most hair-raising section of track begins: at **Wang Sing**, also known as Arrow Hill, the train squeezes through 30m-deep solid rock cuttings, dug at the cost of numerous POW lives; 6km further, it slows to a crawl at the approach to the **Wang Po viaduct**, where a 300m-long trestle bridge clings to the cliff face as it curves with the Kwai Noi – almost every man who worked on this part of the railway died. The station at the northern end of the trestle bridge is called **Tham Krasae**, after the cave that's hollowed out of the rock face beside the bridge; you can see the cave's resident Buddha image from the train. North of Tham Krasae, the train pulls in at **Wang Po Station** before continuing alongside a particularly lovely stretch of the Kwai Noi, its banks thick with jungle and not a raft house in sight, the whole vista framed by distant tree-clad peaks. Thirty minutes later, the train reaches **Nam Tok**, a small town that thrives chiefly on its position at the end of the line (see above).

Three trains operate daily along the Death Railway in both directions, but they often run very late. At the time of writing, they're scheduled to leave Kanchanaburi at 6.07am, 10.35am and 4.26pm and to return from Nam Tok at 5.20am, 12.55pm and 3.30pm; Kanchanaburi TAT keeps up-to-date timetables. If you're up at the Bridge, you can join the train five minutes later.

BOAT TRIPS FROM NAM TOK

You can rent a longtail **boat** (plus driver) from the restaurant beside Nam Tok's **Pak Saeng pier** for the forty-minute boat ride upstream to **Tham Lawa** and its nearby riverside accommodation (see below). To reach the pier from the Highway 323 T-junction, cross the road, turn southeast towards Kanchanaburi, then take the first road on your right; it's 2km from here to the river. The return journey to the cave takes roughly two hours, including half an hour there, and costs B1000 for the eight-seater boat; for B2000 you can continue to **Sai Yok Yai Falls**, a six-hour return trip (see p.207).

spirit-house roundabout, then first right through the small town, passing a water tower and market on your left. Return trains to Kanchanaburi currently depart at 5.20am, 12.55pm and 3.30pm.

By bus All Kanchanaburi–Hellfire Pass–Thong Pha Phum buses pass through Nam Tok, generally making a stop near the T-junction of the highway and the station road (#8203; every 20–30min; last bus back to Kanchanaburi at 5pm); it's about 30min from Nam Tok to Hellfire Pass.

ACCOMMODATION AND EATING

There are several tourist-oriented **restaurants** at the station, and cheap **hot-food stalls** in the market, halfway along the station road.

Good View Resort & Camping 199/1 Moo 3, Thasao, Sai Yok ☎089 516 7614, ⓦgoodview-river.com. Few tourists stay in Nam Tok, but should you get stuck here, head for this good all-rounder in a beautiful spot by the river, 2km southwest of the station. There's (expensive) camping in pre-erected "tents" built on wooden platforms, and A-shaped riverside villas (complete with a/c and private bathrooms) for those in need of a little more luxury. Two-man tents B1000, a/c villas B2000

DIRECTORY

ATM There's an ATM on the station road, near the T-junction.

Upriver on the Kwai Noi

About 10km north of Nam Tok, a side road turns off Highway 323 at kilometre-stone 54 and runs down to the river, giving access to a beautiful stretch of the Kwai Noi, the **Resotel pier** and several pleasant places to stay. There's no development along the banks apart from a few raft houses and shore-bound little hotels.

Tham Lawa

60km northwest of Kanchanaburi, just south of Route 323 • B200 • Can be reached via a 10min longtail ride upriver from the Resotel pier (B700/return trip)

The most famous attraction around here is **Tham Lawa**, the largest stalactite cave in the area and home to three species of bat, easily reached via longtail boat from the pier. The river is about 50m wide at this point, embraced by sheer limestone cliffs that are artistically pitted, dramatically streaked in red and white, and grown thick with lianas and bamboos tumbling down to the water's edge – be careful when swimming as the current is very strong (hotels should have lifejackets available). Beyond the cave's entrance are several large and impressive chambers, resplendent with stalactites and stalagmites that look like molten candle wax.

The Mon village

You can visit the **Mon village** behind the *River Kwai Jungle Rafts* resort, where you're encouraged to browse the sarongs and other artefacts made and sold by the villagers, take an elephant ride and visit the school. The Mon villagers fled here from Burma in the late 1950s but have still not been granted Thai ID papers, which means the children can't study at Thai secondary schools and adults have difficulty finding work.

2

This village has close links with *Jungle Rafts* and many of its residents work at the hotel. For more on the Mon people, see the box later in this chapter (p.211).

ARRIVAL AND GETTING AROUND

By bus Any Kanchanaburi–Thong Pha Phum bus will drop you at the turn-off to the Resotel pier. Heading back to Kanchanaburi, you should be able to flag down buses on the main road.

By boat There's boat rental at the Resotel pier (for up to

UPRIVER ON THE KWAI NOI

eight people, prices quoted are per boat, for return trips) to Tham Lawa cave (10min; B700), Hellfire Pass (B900 to the nearest pier, then a 4km walk) and Sai Yok Yai Falls (1hr 30min; B1800).

ACCOMMODATION

River Kwai Jungle Rafts A short boat ride upstream from the River Kwai Resotel (see below) ☎ 02 642 5497, ⓦ riverkwaijunglerafts.com; map p.199. More rustic than the *Resotel*, which is owned by the same people, this "floatel" is still very popular, with simple yet tasteful floating rooms snaking along a bend in the river. Along with the obligatory hammocks there's a swimming area, canoe rental and a bar. Rooms have no electricity so there are no fans or a/c and only oil-lamps at night. Breakfast, dinner and boat transfers included. B4300

River Kwai Resotel On the west bank of the river (take a boat from the Resotel pier) ☎ 081 734 5238, ⓦ riverkwairesotel.net; map p.199. A classy, upmarket

spot, comprising an open-air restaurant, some charming thatched riverside chalets (some with their own private hot tubs) and a brilliant-blue swimming pool. B2500

Sam's Jungle Guest House About 1km off the highway at kilometre-stone 54 ☎ 081 948 3448, ⓦ samsguesthouse.com; map p.199. Occupying a large swathe of steep and densely grown river bank, this friendly place offers a range of well-priced fan and a/c accommodation, plus a swimming pool, in a strange and rather unstylish assortment of buildings that nonetheless enjoy an exceptionally tranquil setting; there's kayak rental too. Staff keep the front gate closed while working down by the river, so call ahead if you can. Fan B400, a/c B500

Hellfire Pass

Although the rail line north of Nam Tok was ripped up soon after the end of World War II, it casts its dreadful shadow all the way up the Kwai Noi valley into Burma. The remnants of track are most visible at **Hellfire Pass**, and many of the villages in the area are former POW sites – locals frequently stumble across burial sites, now reclaimed by the encroaching jungle. To keep the Death Railway level through the uneven course of the Kwai valley, the POWs had to build a series of embankments and trestle bridges and, at dishearteningly frequent intervals, gouge deep cuttings through solid rock. The most concentrated digging was at **Konyu**, 18km beyond Nam Tok, where seven separate cuttings were made over a 3.5km stretch. The longest and most brutal of these was Hellfire Pass, which got its name from the hellish-looking lights and shadows of the fires the POWs used when working at night. The job took three months of round-the-clock labour with the most primitive tools.

Hellfire Pass Memorial Museum

Daily 9am–4pm • Donation requested

The story of the POWs who died on the Hellfire Pass is documented at the beautifully designed **Hellfire Pass Memorial Museum**, the best and most informative of all the World War II museums in the Kanchanaburi region. Inside, wartime relics, POW memorabilia, photos and first-hand accounts tell the sobering history of the construction of this stretch of the Thailand–Burma Railway. Founded by an Australian–Thai volunteer group, the museum now serves as a sort of pilgrimage site for the families and friends of Australian POWs.

Hellfire Pass Memorial Walk

The same Australian–Thai group responsible for the Hellfire Pass Memorial Museum has also cleared a 4km-long, ninety-minute circular **memorial walk**, which begins at the museum and follows the old rail route through the 18m-deep cutting and on to Hin Tok creek along a course relaid with some of the original narrow-gauge track.

The creek was originally forded by a trestle bridge so unstable that it was nicknamed the Pack of Cards Bridge, but this has long since crumbled away. The trail doubles back on itself, passing through bamboo forest and a viewpoint that gives some idea of the phenomenal depth of rock the POWs had to dig through.

ARRIVAL AND DEPARTURE   HELLFIRE PASS

Hellfire Pass is 18km north of Nam Tok, on the west side of Highway 323 just after kilometre-stone 64. Most Kanchanaburi tour-operators offer **day-trips** featuring Hellfire Pass. It's also quite easy to get here on your own, and to combine it with a trip on the Death Railway.

By bus From Kanchanaburi or Nam Tok, take any bus bound for Thong Pha Phum or Sangkhlaburi and ask to be dropped off at Hellfire Pass, which is signposted on the west side of Highway 323 just after kilometre-stone 64; it's about a 75min journey from Kanchanaburi or 20min from Nam Tok. The last return bus to Kanchanaburi passes Hellfire Pass at about 4.45pm; if you're continuing to Sangkhlaburi, the last onward bus comes past at about 1.15pm.

Sai Yok National Park

B200 • ☎ 034 686024, ⓦ dnp.go.th

Expanses of impenetrable mountain wilderness characterize the Kwai Noi valley to the north of Hellfire Pass, a landscape typified by the dense monsoon forests of **Sai Yok National Park**, which stretches all the way to the Burmese border. The park makes a refreshing enough stopover between Nam Tok and Sangkhlaburi, particularly if you have your own transport. Its teak forests are best known for the much-photographed though unexceptional **Sai Yok Yai Falls** and for the eight stalactite-filled chambers of **Daowadung Caves**. It's also home to the smallest-known mammal in the world, the elusive hog-nosed or bumblebee bat, which weighs just 1.75g and has a wingspan of 1.6cm. Short trails to these attractions start from near the park's visitor centre.

ARRIVAL AND DEPARTURE   SAI YOK NATIONAL PARK

The park is 104km north of Kanchanaburi, signed off Highway 323 between kilometre-stones 80 and 81.

By bus Any of the Kanchanaburi–Thong Pha Phum buses will stop at the road entrance to Sai Yok, from where it's a 3km walk to the visitor centre, trailheads and river (motorbike taxis sometimes hang around the road entrance). The last buses in both directions pass the park at about 4.30pm.
By boat The most scenic approach to Sai Yok is by longtail from Nam Tok, a 6hr return trip (see p.205).

ACCOMMODATION AND EATING

Within the park, your main decision is whether to stay in one of the government-owned bungalows, or one of the more luxurious (and more expensive) raft houses near the waterfall. There are plenty of **hot-food stalls** (daily 6am–8pm) near the visitor centre.

National park accommodation ☎ 034 686024, ⓦ dnp.go.th. You can stay in the national park's simple, fan-cooled bungalows, which sleep between four and seven people, but it's worth booking ahead online. From B800

Sai Yok View Raft Near the waterfall ☎ 081 857 2284, ⓦ saiyokviewraft.com; map p.199. More inviting than the government bungalows and popular with tour groups are the floating timber cabins at *Sai Yok View Raft*, which have balconies overlooking the water. B2800

Pha Tad Falls and Hin Dat hot springs

North of Sai Yok National Park, signs off Highway 323 direct you to the two long, gently sloping cascades of **Pha Tad Falls** and to **Hin Dat** (Hindad) **hot springs**, where, after paying the B40 entry fee, you can immerse yourself in a big pool of soothingly warm water. Close by is a much cooler stream – perfect for leaping into after a good soak in the springs – and you can make use of the nearby showers and foodstalls.

ARRIVAL AND DEPARTURE

PHA TAD FALLS AND HIN DAT HOT SPRINGS

Both Pha Tad Falls and Hin Dat hot springs are off Highway 323.

To/from Pha Tad Falls The falls are 12km east from kilometre-stone 103 and can only be reached with your own transport or on a tour.

To/from Hin Dat The hot springs are 1km east from kilometre-stone 105; any Thong Pha Phum bus from

Kanchanaburi will drop you at the Hin Dat access track, from where it's an easy walk across to the springs. Returning in the afternoon, it should be possible to flag down a bus from Thong Pha Phum or Sangkhlaburi for the trip back to Kanchanaburi.

Thong Pha Phum and around

The first significant town northwest of Sai Yok is **Thong Pha Phum** (147km from Kanchanaburi), which sits at the southern edge of the massive Vajiralongkorn Reservoir and features some pleasant waterside accommodation. It's a mid-sized market town with bus connections to Sangkhlaburi and Kanchanaburi and plenty of small food shops.

Vajiralongkorn Reservoir

12km west of Thong Pha Phum market

With your own transport, a much more scenic overnight option than staying in town is to drive 12km west of Thong Pha Phum market to the southeastern fringes of nearby **Vajiralongkorn Reservoir** (formerly Khao Laem Reservoir). This vast body of water stretches all the way to Sangkhlaburi 73km to the north and, when created in the early 1980s, flooded every village in the vicinity. Hotels make the most of the refreshing, almost Scandinavian, landscape of forested hills and clear, still water that's perfect for swimming.

ACCOMMODATION

THONG PHA PHUM

THONG PHA PHUM TOWN

Som Jainuk 29/9 Moo 1, between the police station and the main market ☏ 034 599067. Forty or so fan and a/c motel-style rooms around a car park on Thong Pha Phum's main street. Look for the wooden "Hotel" sign (no English name). Fan B200, a/c B350

VAJIRALONGKORN RESERVOIR

Ban Suan Thaveechaiphaphum 401/8 Moo 1 Thakanun, about 10km from Thong Pha Phum town ☏ 034 599841, ⊛ thaveechaiphaphum.com. The nicest

of the English-speaking hotels by the water, *Ban Suan* offers stylishly decorated fan and a/c rooms overlooking the garden or lake. The best rooms have private, stilted chill-out pavilions built over the water. The location is great and they can also arrange boat trips around the lake. To drive here, follow signs for the Vajiralongkorn Dam, then instead of turning right for the dam continue along the left-hand branch of the road for another 6km. Occasional yellow songthaews travel this route from Thong Pha Phum market. Fan B1200, a/c B1600

Thong Pha Phum National Park

About 70km from Thong Pha Phum along Route 3272 • B200 • ☏ 081 382 0359, ⊛ dnp.go.th

The final 30km of the road to **Thong Pha Phum National Park** twists like a roller coaster and is slow but surfaced. If you have your own wheels the effort is worth it; this is a remote and lovely place to escape to, barely visited by foreign tourists and home to a population of mountain goats, buffalo and barking deer. If you stay overnight (there's no permanent accommodation, so you have to camp) the big pleasure here is waking to see the foggy jungle below. During the day you can follow several **trails** that lead to the park's waterfalls.

ACCOMMODATION AND EATING

THONG PHA PHUM NATIONAL PARK

Camping At the time of writing there was no option to reserve a tent online. You can, however, rent one on arrival (B150), or you can bring your own and use that instead;

expect to pay a small fee.

Eating There's a restaurant on site but options are limited, so it's worth bringing some of your own supplies.

Sangkhlaburi and around

Beyond Thong Pha Phum the views get increasingly spectacular as Highway 323 climbs through the remaining swathes of montane rainforest, occasionally hugging the eastern shore of the Vajiralongkorn Reservoir until 73km later it comes to an end at **Sangkhlaburi** (often called **Sangkhla** for short). In the early 1980s, the old town was lost under the rising waters of the newly created Khao Laem (now Vajiralongkorn) Reservoir. Its residents were relocated to the northeastern tip of the lake, beside the Songkalia River, where modern-day Sangkhla now enjoys an eerily beautiful view of semi-submerged trees and raft houses. It's a tiny town with no unmissable attractions, but the atmosphere is pleasantly low-key and the best of the accommodation occupies scenic lakeside spots so it's a great place to slow down for a while.

Cultural interest is to be found in the villages, markets and temples of the area's Mon, Karen and Thai populations, including at **Ban Waeng Ka** across the water, and there's natural beauty in various waterfalls, whitewater rivers and the remote Thung Yai Naresuan Wildlife Sanctuary. It sees relatively few farang tourists, but it's a popular destination for weekending Thais (come during the week for better deals on accommodation) and resident NGO volunteers add a positive vibe. Though the Burmese border is just 22km away at **Three Pagodas Pass**, at the time of writing it was closed to foreigners.

SANGKHLABURI AND BAN WAENG KA

ACCOMMODATION
Burmese Inn	2
J Family Bed and Breakfast	1
P Guest House	3
Pornpailin Riverside	4

RESTAURANTS & CAFÉS
Bakery	2
Blend	1
Graph Café	3
P Guest House	4

2

> ## WEAVING FOR WOMEN
>
> A community project worth supporting in Sangkhlaburi is **Weaving for Women**, set up by a group of Karen refugees in 1989. Their Hilltribe Handicrafts **shop** (450m down the hill from the post office, or 150m up the hill from the turn-off to *Burmese Inn*; ⓦweavingforwomen.org) carries a huge selection of hand-woven items, much of it in *mut mee* design and all of it made from good-quality Chiang Mai cotton, including tablecloths, sarongs, shirts and bags. For more on the Karen, see our box later in this chapter (p.262).

Wat Sam Phrasop

Aside from crossing the famous wooden bridge over the lake to the Mon village of Ban Waeng Ka (see below), the main pastime in Sangkhlaburi is **boating** across the reservoir in search of **Wat Sam Phrasop**, the **sunken temple** which was all but submerged when the valley was flooded; by the end of the dry season its upper storey usually reappears. *P Guest House* rents out two-person **canoes** for independent exploring (B150/hr, or B300 for half a day), or you can join a longtail boat trip from either of the town's two guesthouses.

Baan Unrak

99-1 Moo 1 Nonglu • ☎ 034 595428, ⓦ baanunrak.org

Sangkhla's location so close to the Burmese border, along with the upheavals caused by the creation of the reservoir, mean that the town is full of displaced people, many of whom are in dire straits. Several organizations work with refugees in the area, including **Baan Unrak**, a farang-managed programme founded by the Neo Humanist Foundation that has run an orphans' home here since 1991 and has also established a school and a weaving project for destitute women and children. To help support the project you can buy handicrafts at the Baan Unrak shop next to *P Guest House*, and visit their *Bakery* café (see p.213) to make donations of books, clothes and money, and get directions to the orphanage, which welcomes visitors and stages a yoga show every Wednesday during term-time at 6pm. Volunteer placements are also possible.

Ban Waeng Ka

The Mon village of **BAN WAENG KA**, across the reservoir from Sangkhlaburi, was founded in the late 1940s after the outbreak of civil war in Burma forced many to flee across the Thai border (see box opposite). The **Mon** people's homeland, Mon State, lies just west of the Tenasserim Mountains, so thousands of Mon ended up in Sangkhlaburi, illegal immigrants whose presence was permitted but not officially recognized. Most now have official Sangkhlaburi residency, but still endure limited rights and must apply for expensive seven-day permits if they wish to travel out of the district, a system that lends itself to corruption.

The wooden bridge

Getting to Ban Waeng Ka is simply a matter of crossing the narrow northern neck of the lake, near the influx of the Songkalia River. Pedestrians can use the spider's web of a **wooden bridge** that is Sangkhla's unofficial town symbol: at almost 400m it is said to be the longest hand-built wooden bridge in the world and can be reached either by following signs from near the post office to *Samprasop Resort*, which overlooks the structure, or by using the newer connecting footbridge near the *Burmese Inn*. The concrete road bridge is several hundred metres further north. Once across the wooden bridge, turn left to get into the village – a sprawling collection of traditional wooden houses lining a network of steep tracks, with a small but lively dry-goods market at its heart.

THE MON IN THAILAND

Dubbed by some "the Palestinians of Asia", the **Mon** people – numbering between two and four million in Burma and an estimated fifty thousand to two hundred thousand in Thailand (chiefly in the western provinces of Kanchanaburi and Ratchaburi, in the Gulf province of Samut Sakhon and in Nonthaburi and Pathum Thani, just north of Bangkok) – have endured centuries of persecution, displacement and forced assimilation.

Ethnologists speculate that the Mon originated either in India or Mongolia, travelling south to settle on the western banks of the Chao Phraya valley in the first century BC. Here they founded the **Dvaravati kingdom** (sixth to eleventh centuries AD), building centres at U Thong, Lopburi and Nakhon Pathom and later consolidating a northern kingdom in Haripunchai (modern-day Lamphun). They probably introduced Theravada Buddhism to the region, and produced some of the earliest Buddhist monuments, particularly Wheels of Law and Buddha footprints.

Over on the Burmese side of the border, the Mon kingdom had established itself around the southern city of Pegu well before **the Burmese** filtered into the area in the ninth century, but by the mid-eighteenth century they'd been stripped of their homeland and were once again relocating to Thailand. The Thais welcomed them as a useful source of labour, and in 1814 the future Rama IV arrived at the Kanchanaburi border with three royal warboats and a guard of honour to chaperone the exiles. Swathes of undeveloped jungle were given over to them, many of which are still Mon-dominated today.

The **persecution** of Burmese Mon continues to this day under Burma's repressive regime (see box, p.262), and the Mon continue to struggle for the right to administer their own independent Mon State in their historical homelands opposite Kanchanaburi province in lower Burma. As one commentator has described it, while some of Burma's ethnic minority groups seek to *establish* autonomy, the Mon are attempting to *reclaim* it. Though the New Mon State Party (NMSP) entered into a ceasefire agreement with the Burmese junta in June 1995, international human-rights organizations continue to report gross violations against civilian Mon living in Burma. Thousands of Mon men, women and children have been press-ganged into unpaid labour, soldiers occupy certain Mon villages and commandeer produce and livestock, and reports of beatings and gang rapes are not uncommon. In an attempt to wipe out Mon culture, the junta has also banned the teaching of Mon language, literature and history in government schools, and outlawed the wearing of Mon national dress at official institutions.

Not surprisingly, Mon have been fleeing these atrocities in droves, the majority ending up in three **resettlement camps** in a Mon-controlled area along the Thai–Burma border, the biggest being Halockhani near Sangkhlaburi; the 11,000 Mon estimated to be living in these camps as of October 2011 have no right of entry into Thailand. For more information, see the website of the Human Rights Foundation of Monland (HURFOM; ❿ rehmonnya.org).

Like Thais, the Mon are a predominantly Buddhist, rice-growing people, but they also have strong animist beliefs. All Mon families have totemic **house spirits**, such as the turtle, snake, chicken or pig, which carry certain taboos; if you're of the chicken-spirit family, for example, the lungs and head of every chicken you cook have to be offered to the spirits, and although you're allowed to raise and kill chickens, you must never give one away. Guests belonging to a different spirit group from their host are not allowed to stay overnight. Mon **festivals** also differ slightly from Thai ones – at Songkhran (Thai New Year), the Mon spice up the usual water-throwing and parades with a special courtship ritual in which teams of men and women play each other at bowling, throwing flirtatious banter along with their wooden discs.

Wat Wang Wivekaram

About 2km west from the bridgehead

Wat Wang Wivekaram (also known as **Wat Luang Pho Uttama**) is Ban Waeng Ka's most dramatic sight, its massive, golden **chedi** clearly visible from Sangkhlaburi. Built in a fusion of Thai, Indian and Burmese styles, the imposing square-sided stupa is modelled on the centrepiece of India's Bodh Gaya, the sacred site of the Buddha's enlightenment, and contains a much-prized Buddha relic (said to be a piece of his skeleton) brought to Ban Waeng Ka from Sri Lanka. It's a focal point for the Mon community on both sides

2

of the Thai–Burma border, particularly at Mon New Year in April. There's a good **tourist market** in the covered cloisters at the chedi compound, with plenty of reasonably priced Burmese woodcarvings, checked *longyis* and jewellery.

The wat is spread over two compounds (you might want to hail a motorbike taxi to get here from the bridgehead), with the gleaming new bot, **viharn** and monks' quarters about 1km away from the chedi, at the end of the right-hand fork in the road. The interior of the viharn is decorated with murals showing tableaux from the five hundred lives of the Buddha, designed to be viewed in anticlockwise order.

Three Pagodas Pass and the Burmese border

22km north of Sangkhlaburi • Songthaews leave Sangkhla bus station every 40min from 6am until about 5pm and take 40min; the last songthaew back to Sangkhla leaves at 6pm

All border trade for hundreds of kilometres north and south has to come through **Three Pagodas Pass** (signed as **Jadee Sam Ong**), but at the time of writing the border was **closed** to foreigners. Small skirmishes also continued to break out between Burmese government troops and the Karen National Liberation Army (KNLA).

Unless you're looking for heavy teak furniture or orchids, that means it's currently not worth making the trip as there's nothing more than a small market on the Thai side, in the village of **Ban Chedi Sam Ong**, plus the three eponymous little **chedis** said to have been erected in the eighteenth century by the kings of Burma and Thailand as a symbolic peace gesture. If and when full border operations resume, foreigners will probably once again be allowed very limited access to the Burmese border village of **Payathonzu**, whose main attraction is the Mon temple **Wat Sao Roi Ton**, known in Burmese as **Tai Ta Ya temple**, or the Temple of One Hundred Teakwood Posts.

ARRIVAL AND DEPARTURE   SANGKHLABURI

BY BUS OR MINIBUS

By bus A/c buses run from Bangkok's Northern Mo Chit bus terminal via Kanchanaburi to the bus station on the western edge of Sangkhla (4 daily; 7hr).

By minibus The fastest way to get to Sangkhlaburi from Kanchanaburi is by a/c minibus (10 daily 7.30am–4.30pm; 3hr; reserve a few hours ahead and be prepared to buy an extra seat if you have luggage); they also pick up from Thong Pha Phum. Minibuses terminate on the northern edge of Sangkhla, with services in the opposite direction departing from the same spot (8 daily 11.30am–4pm; 3hr; reserve ahead if possible).

BY CAR OR MOTORBIKE

Driving from Kanchanaburi to Sangkhlaburi can be tiring as the road is full of twists after Thong Pha Phum; the last 25km are particularly nerve-wracking for bikers because of the gravel spots in the many bends. Nonetheless, the scenery is fabulous, particularly at the lakeside viewpoint just north of kilometre-stone 35 (about 40km south of Sangkhlaburi). Be aware that you are likely to be pulled over at numerous police checkpoints en route – after a quick look at your passport, the officers should wave you through.

GETTING AROUND

Sangkhlaburi itself is small enough to walk round in an hour, but if the sun is beating down hard, you might want to look for an alternative.

> ## ORGANIZED TRIPS OUT OF SANGKHLABURI
>
> The two guesthouses in Sangkhlaburi both run **organized trips** in the area for their guests. *P Guest House* does good-value accommodation packages featuring various combinations of elephant-riding, bamboo-rafting and boat trips on the lake (from B950/person). *Burmese Inn* does one-day rafting excursions on the Songkalia River (B500); two- and three-day treks in the Thung Yai Naresuan Wildlife Sanctuary, around the Karen village of Ban Sane Pong (B1800–3200); and two-day cooking classes (B500). They also keep a book of useful information on **motorbike routes** in the area, including to Takianthong waterfall and Sawan Badan cave, both accessed via the road to Three Pagodas Pass, and a back route to Erawan Waterfall.

By motorbike taxi or songthaew Motorbikes usually charge B20 from the bus station to the guesthouses and around B50 for a ride from the guesthouses to Wat Wang Wiwekaram across the water. If you're travelling in a group, you should be able to charter a whole songthaew from the bus station to one of the guesthouses for around B50.

By bicycle or motorbike *P Guest House* rents out bicycles (B20/hr; B70/day) and motorbikes (B50/hr; B200/day).

By kayak Decent kayaks are available by the hour (B150) and half-day (B300) at *P Guest House*.

By pick-up truck *Burmese Inn* should be able to arrange a pick-up truck and driver; prices depend on the length of hire and distances travelled.

ACCOMMODATION

The two guesthouses are used by backpacking tour groups, so it's worth booking ahead; **reservations** are essential at all accommodation for weekends and national holidays.

Burmese Inn Soi 1 086 168 1801, sangkhlaburi .com. This rambling, traveller-oriented guesthouse overlooks the northeastern spur of the lake just behind the newer bridge, offering easy access to the Mon village, but slightly truncated lake views. Most of the rooms and bungalows feel run-down, but they look right over the water and nearly all are en suite; some have a/c and TV. Fan B400, a/c B800

★ **J Family Bed and Breakfast (Kumsai Soonploy)** 17/1 Soi 2 034 595511. A genuine homestay offering four big rooms with fan and shared bathroom in the large family home of the Mon woman, Kumsai Soonploy, who runs the Baan Unrak shop. She speaks great English, is very welcoming, and (if you're lucky) will even make coffee for you in the mornings. B150

P Guest House West of soi 3 034 595061, p-guesthouse.com. Large, popular, efficiently run, clued-up Mon-owned place that sits prettily on the banks of the lake. There's spacious, comfortable travellers' accommodation in sturdy, terraced stone-studded rooms with shared bathrooms, and en-suite rooms with a/c – although it's doubtful whether these justify the extra expense. Wi-fi in the restaurant. Reservations strongly advised. Fan and shared bathroom B250, a/c B950

Pornpailin Riverside About 2km down the hill from the bus station 034 595355, ppailin.com. Resort-style place at the bottom of town whose a/c rooms nearly all offer fabulous lake views from their large glass windows and private terraces. Although rooms here are large, they're in a state of neglect, and you'll have to pass through the dark and scruffy hallways to get to them. Includes breakfast. B1000

EATING

Day and night, the cheapest places to eat are at and around the **market** in the town centre. If you're hankering after a decent latte, however, drop into one of the new a/c coffee shops that have popped up across town.

Bakery Opposite Soi 3. The sociable *Bakery* does brown-bread sandwiches, hot veggie meals, pizzas and banana cake, and is staffed by volunteers from the nearby Baan Unrak orphans' home; it has internet access too. Daily 7am–8pm.

Blend Tessaban 1, just across from the bus station. More central than *Graph Café*, and a handy place to wait before catching a bus, this diddy café serves scrummy home-baked cakes and good, strong Arabica coffee (B35). Mon–Fri 8am–8pm, Sat & Sun 7am–8pm.

Graph Café Opposite P Guest House facebook.com /graphcafe. A neatly manicured lawn leads the way to this chilled modern café serving a wide range of teas, chais and speciality coffees (B35–40). Free wi-fi. Daily 8.30am–2pm.

P Guest House The large restaurant at *P Guest House* offers fine lake views from its terrace and serves reasonable Thai, Burmese and European food, along with bottles of Kanchanaburi-made pineapple wine. Open for breakfast, lunch and dinner.

DIRECTORY

Banks and ATMs Travellers' cheques and dollars can be changed at the bank, on the edge of the market in the town centre, which also has an ATM.

Internet access You can access the net at *P Guest House*, Baan Unrak's *Bakery*, *Blend* or *Graph Café*.

Bang Pa-In

Little more than a roadside market, the village of **BANG PA-IN**, 60km north of Bangkok, has been put on the tourist map by its extravagant and rather surreal **Royal Palace**, even though most of the buildings can be seen only from the outside. King Prasat Thong of

Ayutthaya first built a palace on this site, 20km downstream from his capital, in the middle of the seventeenth century, and it remained a popular country residence for the kings of Ayutthaya. The palace was abandoned a century later when the capital was moved to Bangkok, only to be revived in the middle of the nineteenth century when the advent of steamboats shortened the journey time upriver. Rama IV (1851–68) built a modest residence here, which his son Chulalongkorn (Rama V), in his passion for Westernization, knocked down to make room for the eccentric melange of European, Thai and Chinese architectural styles visible today.

The palace

Daily 8am–4pm, ticket office closes 3.30pm • B100 • ⓦ palaces.thai.net • Visitors are asked to dress respectfully, so no vests, shorts or sandals

Set in manicured grounds on an island in the Chao Phraya River, and based around an ornamental lake, the palace complex is flat and compact. Exploring slowly is the best approach, following walkways that crisscross the lake.

The lakeside and covered bridge

On the north side of the lake stand a two-storey, colonial-style residence for the royal relatives and the Italianate **Varobhas Bimarn** (**Warophat Phiman**, "Excellent and Shining Heavenly Abode"), which housed Chulalongkorn's throne hall and still contains private apartments where the present royal family sometimes stays. A covered bridge links this outer part of the palace to the **Pratu Thewarat Khanlai** ("The King of the Gods Goes Forth Gate"), the main entrance to the inner palace, which was reserved for the king and his immediate family. The high fence that encloses half of the bridge allowed the women of the harem to cross without being seen by male courtiers.

Aisawan Thiphya-art

You can't miss the glittering **Aisawan Thiphya-art** ("Divine Seat of Personal Freedom") in the middle of the lake: named after King Prasat Thong's original palace, it's the only example of pure Thai architecture at Bang Pa-In. The elegant tiers of the pavilion's roof shelter a bronze statue of Chulalongkorn.

The inner palace

In the inner palace, the **Uthayan Phumisathian** ("Garden of the Secured Land"), recently rebuilt by Queen Sirikit in grand, neocolonial style, was Chulalongkorn's favourite house. After passing the candy-striped **Ho Withun Thasana** ("Sage's Lookout Tower"), built so that the king could survey the surrounding countryside, you'll come to the main attraction of Bang Pa-In, the **Phra Thinang Wehart Chamrun Residential Hall** ("Palace of Heavenly Light"). A masterpiece of Chinese design, the mansion and its contents were shipped from China and presented as a gift to Chulalongkorn in 1889 by the Chinese Chamber of Commerce in Bangkok. The sumptuous interior gleams with fantastically intricate lacquered and gilded wooden screens, hand-painted porcelain floor tiles and ebony furniture inlaid with mother-of-pearl.

The obelisk

The simple marble **obelisk** behind the Uthayan Phumisathian was erected by Chulalongkorn to hold the ashes of Queen Sunandakumariratana, his favourite wife. In 1881, Sunanda, who was then 21 and expecting a child, was taking a trip on the river here when her boat capsized. She could have been rescued quite easily, but the laws concerning the sanctity of the royal family left those around her no option: "If a boat founders, the boatmen must swim away; if they remain near the boat [or] if they lay hold of him [the royal person] to rescue him, they are to be executed." Following the tragedy, King Chulalongkorn became a zealous reformer of Thai customs and strove to make the monarchy more accessible.

ARRIVAL AND DEPARTURE   **BANG PA-IN**

Bang Pa-In can easily be visited on a day-trip from Bangkok or Ayutthaya. Many day-tours from Bangkok to Ayutthaya feature a stop at Bang Pa-In (see p.218).

BY TRAIN
The best route from Bangkok is by train from Hualamphong station, which takes just over an hour to reach Bang Pa-in (on arrival, note the separate station hall built by Chulalongkorn for the royal family). All trains continue to Ayutthaya, with half going on to Lopburi. Note that trains from Ayutthaya are more frequent than the English-language timetable implies (most Ayutthaya guesthouses keep the full Thai timetable).
To/from the palace From Bang Pa-In's train station it's a 2km hike to the palace, or you can take a motorbike taxi for about B30. Returning to the station, catch a motorized samlor from the market, about 300m southwest of the palace entrance.

Destinations Ayutthaya (7 daily; 15min); Bangkok Hualamphong (8 daily; 1hr 30min).

BY BUS
Slow buses leave Bangkok's Northern Mo Chit terminal (roughly every 30min; 2hr) and stop at Bang Pa-In market, about 300m southwest of the palace entrance. This is also the easiest place to catch a bus back to Bangkok.

BY SONGTHAEW
From Ayutthaya, large songthaews leave Thanon Naresuan roughly every half hour for the 40min journey to Bang Pa-In market, returning from the same spot.

EATING

There are **foodstalls** just outside the palace gates, at the back of the parking lot and at Bang Pa-In market.

Ayutthaya

In its heyday as the booming capital of the Thai kingdom, **AYUTTHAYA**, 80km north of Bangkok, was so well-endowed with temples that sunlight reflecting off their gilt decoration was said to dazzle from 5km away. Wide, grassy spaces today occupy much of the atmospheric site, which now resembles a graveyard for temples: grand, brooding red-brick ruins rise out of the fields, satisfyingly evoking the city's bygone grandeur while providing a soothing contrast to flashy modern temple architecture. A few intact buildings help form an image of what the capital must have looked like, while three fine museums flesh out the picture.

The core of the ancient capital was a 4km-wide **island** at the confluence of the Lopburi, Pasak and Chao Phraya rivers, which was once encircled by a 12km-long wall, crumbling parts of which can be seen at the Phom Phet fortress in the southeast corner. A grid of broad roads now crosses the island, known as **Ko Muang**: the hub of the small modern town occupies its northeast corner, around the Thanon U Thong and Thanon Naresuan junction, but the rest is mostly uncongested and ideal for exploring by bicycle.

VISITING AYUTTHAYA – ORIENTATION AND TEMPLE PASS

The majority of Ayutthaya's ancient remains are spread out across the western half of the island in a patchwork of parkland: **Wat Phra Mahathat** and **Wat Ratburana** stand near the modern centre, while a broad band runs down the middle of the parkland, containing the **Royal Palace** (Wang Luang) and temple, the most revered Buddha image, at **Viharn Phra Mongkol Bopit**, and the two main **museums**. To the north of the island you'll find the best-preserved temple, **Wat Na Phra Mane**, and **Wat Phu Khao Thong**, the "Golden Mount"; to the west stands the Khmer-style **Wat Chai Watthanaram**, while to the southeast lie the giant chedi of **Wat Yai Chai Mongkol** and **Wat Phanan Choeng**, still a vibrant place of worship. The city's main temples can be visited for a reduced rate when you buy the special six-in-one **pass** (B220; valid for 30 days; participating temples marked below), which is available from most temple ticket offices.

2

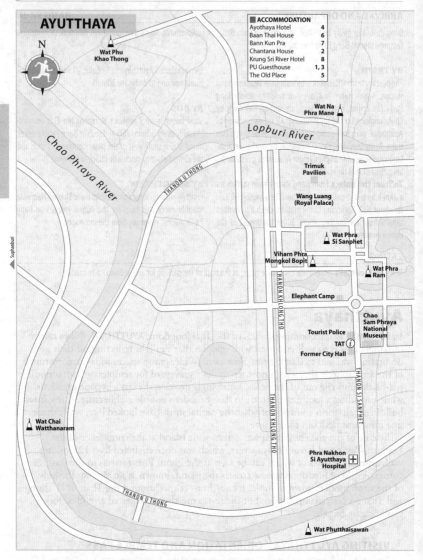

AYUTTHAYA

N

Wat Phu Khao Thong

ACCOMMODATION	
Ayothaya Hotel	4
Baan Thai House	6
Bann Kun Pra	7
Chantana House	2
Krung Sri River Hotel	8
PU Guesthouse	1, 3
The Old Place	5

Chao Phraya River

Lopburi River

Wat Na Phra Mane

THANON U THONG

Trimuk Pavilion

Wang Luang (Royal Palace)

Wat Phra Si Sanphet

Viharn Phra Mongkol Bopit

Wat Phra Ram

Elephant Camp

Chao Sam Phraya National Museum

Tourist Police

TAT (i)

Former City Hall

THANON KHLONG THO

THANON SI SANPHET

Wat Chai Watthanaram

Phra Nakhon Si Ayutthaya Hospital

THANON U THONG

Wat Phutthaisawan

Suphanburi

There is much pleasure to be had, also, from soaking up life on and along the encircling **rivers**, either by taking a boat tour or by dining at one of the waterside restaurants. It's very much a working waterway, busy with barges carrying cement, rice and other heavy loads to and from Bangkok and the Gulf and with cross-river ferry services that compensate for the lack of bridges.

Ayutthaya comes alive each year for a week in mid-December, with a **festival** that commemorates the town's listing as a **World Heritage Site** by UNESCO on December 13, 1991. The highlight is the nightly *son et lumière* show, featuring fireworks and elephant-back fights, staged around the ruins.

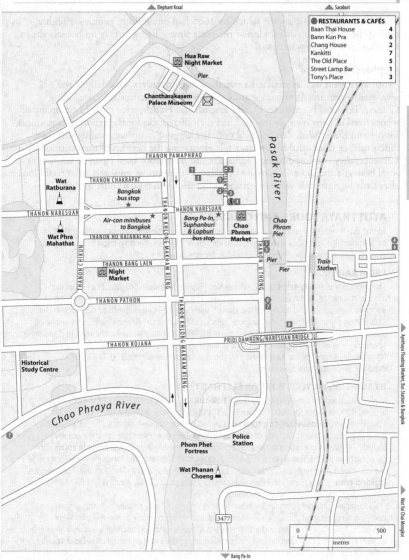

● RESTAURANTS & CAFÉS	
Baan Thai House	4
Bann Kun Pra	6
Chang House	2
Kankitti	7
The Old Place	5
Street Lamp Bar	1
Tony's Place	3

Brief history

Ayutthaya takes its name from the Indian city of Ayodhya (Sanskrit for "invincible"), the legendary birthplace of Rama, hero of the *Ramayana* epic. It was founded in 1351 by U Thong – later **Ramathibodi I** – after Lopburi was ravaged by smallpox, and it rose rapidly through exploiting the expanding trade routes between India and China. Stepping into the political vacuum left by the decline of the Khmer empire at Angkor and the first Thai kingdom at Sukhothai, by the mid-fifteenth century Ayutthaya controlled an empire covering most of the area of modern-day Thailand. Built entirely on canals, few of which survive today, Ayutthaya grew into an enormous amphibious city, which by 1685 had one million people – roughly double the population of London at the same time – living largely on houseboats in a 140km network of waterways.

Ayutthaya's golden age

Ayutthaya's great wealth attracted a swarm of **foreign traders**, especially in the seventeenth century. At one stage around forty different nationalities, including Chinese, Persians, Portuguese, Dutch, English and French, were settled here, many of whom lived in their own ghettos and had their own docks for the export of rice, spices, timber and hides. With deft political skill, the kings of Ayutthaya maintained their independence from outside powers, while embracing the benefits of their cosmopolitan influence: they employed foreign architects and navigators, used Japanese samurai as royal bodyguards, and even took on outsiders as their prime ministers, who could look after their foreign trade without getting embroiled in the usual court intrigues.

AYUTTHAYA TOURS AND CRUISES

Ayutthaya is relatively spread out, so if you're pushed for time and want to make the most of its historic ruins and busy waterways, consider joining one of the **day-trips** from Bangkok. With more time, you can explore by tuk-tuk, bicycle, boat or elephant.

FROM BANGKOK

The most popular **day-trips** to Ayutthaya from Bangkok feature only the briefest whizz around the old city's three main temples, making a stop at the Bang Pa-In summer palace en route (see p.213) and rounding the day off with a three-hour river cruise back down the Chao Phraya from the northern Bangkok suburb of Nonthaburi; Grand Pearl Cruise is one of the main operators (Ⓦgrandpearlcruise.com; B1900). You can also cruise the river in more style, spending one or more nights on plushly converted teak rice-barges such as the *Mekhala* (Ⓦasian-oasis.com) or the two owned by the *Anantara Riverside Hotel* (Ⓣ02 477 0770, Ⓦbangkok-cruises.anantara.com).

BY TUK-TUK, BICYCLE, BOAT OR ELEPHANT

If you're pushed for time you could hire a **tuk-tuk** for a whistle-stop tour of the old city for around B200 an hour (or B600 for four hours), either from the train station or from Chao Phrom market. **Sunset tuk-tuk tours** organized by guesthouses (about 2hr; B300/vehicle) are also popular, taking in some of the illuminated ruins (the main five central ruins are lit nightly 7–9pm) and ending at the night market, or there are the guided **bicycle tours** run by Ayutthaya Boat & Travel (Ⓣ081 733 5687, Ⓦayutthaya-boat.com), whose itineraries include the ruins by day or night, a combination cycle and boat tour and a dinner cruise. For a serious **guided tour** of the ruins, local expert Professor Monton at Classic Tour (Ⓣ081 832 4849; B1600/day) comes highly recommended.

Circumnavigating Ayutthaya by boat is a very enjoyable way to take in some of the outlying temples, and possibly a few lesser-visited ones too; many of the temples were designed to be approached and admired from the river, and you also get a leisurely look at twenty-first-century riverine residences. All guesthouses and agencies offer **boat tours**, typically charging B300 per person for a two-hour trip; they can also be chartered from the pier outside the Chantharakasem Palace museum.

It's also possible to take a brief **elephant ride** (B400/person for 20min, B500 for 30min) past a couple of the central ruins from the roadside elephant "camp" on Thanon Pathon. The elephants and their mahouts are photogenically clad in period costume and you can buy the elephants bananas while they wait for custom, or simply watch them return home after 6pm when they rumble across to the northeast side of town to bathe and bed down in the restored sixteenth-century kraal. You can take a photo with one of the baby elephants for B40. Wild elephants were formerly driven to the kraal for capture and taming but these days it's the headquarters of Elephantstay (Ⓦelephantstay.com), an organization that runs three- to fourteen-day residential packages for visitors who want to ride, feed, water and bathe the ninety resident elephants.

In decline

In 1767, this four-hundred-year-long golden age of stability and prosperity came to an abrupt end. After more than two centuries of recurring tensions, the Burmese captured and ravaged Ayutthaya, taking tens of thousands of prisoners back to Burma. With even the wats in ruins, the city had to be abandoned to the jungle, but its memory endured: the architects of the new capital on Ratanakosin island in Bangkok perpetuated Ayutthaya's layout in every possible way.

Wat Phra Mahathat

1km west of the new town centre along Thanon Naresuan • Daily 8am–5pm • B50, or included with the B220 six-in-one pass

Heading west out of the new town centre brings you to the first set of ruins – a pair of temples on opposite sides of the road. The overgrown **Wat Phra Mahathat**, on the left, is the epitome of Ayutthaya's nostalgic atmosphere of faded majesty. The name "Mahathat" (Great Relic Chedi) indicates that the temple was built to house remains of the Buddha himself: according to the royal chronicles – never renowned for historical accuracy – King Ramesuan (1388–95) was looking out of his palace one morning when ashes of the Buddha materialized out of thin air here. A gold casket containing the ashes was duly enshrined in a grand 38m-high prang. The prang later collapsed, but the reliquary was unearthed in the 1950s, along with a hoard of other treasures, including a gorgeous marble fish, which opened to reveal gold, amber, crystal and porcelain ornaments – all now on show in the Chao Sam Phraya National Museum (see p.220).

You can climb what remains of the prang to get a good view of the broad, grassy complex, with dozens of brick spires tilting at impossible angles and headless Buddhas scattered around like spare parts in a scrapyard; look out for the serene (and much photographed) head of a stone Buddha that has become nestled in the embrace of a bodhi tree's roots.

Wat Ratburana

Across the road from Wat Phra Mahathat • Daily 8am–5pm • B50, or included with the B220 six-in-one pass

The towering **Wat Ratburana** was built in 1424 by King Boromraja II to commemorate his elder brothers, Ay and Yi, who managed to kill each other in an elephant-back duel over the succession to the throne, thus leaving it vacant for Boromraja. Here, four elegant Sri Lankan chedis lean outwards as if in deference to the main prang, on which some of the original stuccowork can still be seen, including fine statues of garudas swooping down on nagas. It's possible to descend steep steps inside the prang to the crypt, where on two levels you can make out fragmentary murals of the early Ayutthaya period.

Wat Phra Ram

West of Wat Phra Mahathat • Daily 8am–6pm • B50, or included with the B220 six-in-one pass

West of Wat Phra Mahathat you'll see a lake, now surrounded by a popular park, and the slender prang of **Wat Phra Ram**, built in the late fourteenth century on the site of Ramathibodi's cremation by his son and successor as king, Ramesuan. Sadly not much of the prang's original stuccowork remains, but you can still get an idea of how spectacular it would have looked when the city was at its zenith.

Wat Phra Si Sanphet and the Wang Luang (Royal Palace)

Across Thanon Si Sanphet from Wat Phra Ram • Daily 8am–6.30pm • B50, or included with the B220 six-in-one pass

Wat Phra Si Sanphet was built in 1448 by King Boromatrailokanat as a private chapel, and was formerly the grandest of Ayutthaya's temples. Even now, it's one of the best preserved.

The wat took its name from one of the largest standing metal images of the Buddha ever known, the **Phra Si Sanphet**, erected here in 1503. Towering 16m high and covered in 173kg of gold, it did not survive the ravages of the Burmese, though Rama I rescued the pieces and placed them inside a chedi at Wat Pho in Bangkok. The three remaining grey chedis in the characteristic style of the old capital were built to house the ashes of three kings, and have now become the most familiar image of Ayutthaya.

The site of this royal wat was originally occupied by Ramathibodi I's wooden palace, which Boromatrailokanat replaced with the bigger **Wang Luang** (Royal Palace; same hours and ticket as Wat Phra Si Sanphet), stretching to the Lopburi River on the north side. Successive kings turned the Wang Luang into a vast complex of pavilions and halls, with an elaborate system of walls designed to isolate the inner sanctum for the king and his consorts. The palace was destroyed by the Burmese in 1767 and plundered by Rama I for its bricks, which he needed to build the new capital at Bangkok. Now you can only trace the outlines of a few walls in the grass and inspect an unimpressive wooden replica of an open pavilion – better to consult the model of the whole complex in the Historical Study Centre (see p.222).

Viharn Phra Mongkol Bopit and the cremation ground

On the south side of Wat Phra Si Sanphet • Mon–Fri 8.30am–4.30pm, Sat & Sun 8.30am–5.30pm • Free

Viharn Phra Mongkol Bopit attracts tourists and Thai pilgrims in about equal measure. The pristine hall – a replica of a typical Ayutthayan viharn, with its characteristic chunky lotus-capped columns around the outside – was built in 1956, with help from the Burmese to atone for their flattening of the city two centuries earlier, in order to shelter the revered **Phra Mongkol Bopit**, which, at 12.45m high (excluding the base), is one of the largest bronze Buddhas in Thailand. The powerfully austere image, with its flashing mother-of-pearl eyes, was cast in the fifteenth century, then sat exposed to the elements from the time of the Burmese invasion until its new home was built. During restoration, the hollow image was found to contain hundreds of Buddha statuettes, some of which were later buried around the shrine to protect it.

The cremation ground

The car park in front of the viharn used to be the **cremation site** for Ayutthayan kings and high-ranking members of the royal family. Here, on a propitious date decided by astrologers, the embalmed body was placed on a towering *meru* (funeral pyre), representing Mount Meru, the centre of the Hindu-Buddhist universe. These many-gabled and -pinnacled wooden structures, which had all the appearance of permanent palaces, were a miracle of architectural technology: the *meru* constructed for King Phetracha in 1704, for example, was 103m tall and took eleven months to raise, requiring thousands of tree trunks and hundreds of thousands of bamboo poles. The task of building at such great heights was given to *yuan-hok*, a particular clan of acrobats who used to perform at the tops of long poles during special festivals. Their handiwork was not consigned to the flames: the cremation took place on a pyramid erected underneath the central spire, so as not to damage the main structure, which was later dismantled and its timber used for building temples. The cremation ground is now given over to a picnic area and a clutch of souvenir and refreshment stalls.

Chao Sam Phraya National Museum

10min walk south of Viharn Phra Mongkol Bopit • Wed–Sun 9am–4pm, last admission 3.30pm • B150 • ⓦ thailandmuseum.com

The largest of the town's three museums is the **Chao Sam Phraya National Museum**, where most of the moveable remains of Ayutthaya's glory – those that weren't

CLOCKWISE FROM TOP LEFT WAT PHU KHAO THONG, AYUTTHAYA (P.222); WAT YAI CHAI MONGKOL, AYUTTHAYA (P.223); AISAWAN THIPHYA-ART, BANG PA-IN (P.214) >

plundered by treasure-hunters or taken to the National Museum in Bangkok – are exhibited. Apart from numerous Buddhas and some fine woodcarving, the museum is bursting with **gold treasures**, including the original relic casket from Wat Mahathat, betel-nut sets and model chedis, and a gem-encrusted fifteenth-century crouching elephant found in the crypt at Wat Ratburana.

Historical Study Centre

Thanon Rotchana, a 5min walk from Chao Sam Phraya National Museum • Daily 9am–4.30pm • B100

It's worth paying a visit to the **Historical Study Centre**, if only to check out its scale model of the Royal Palace before you set off to wander around the real thing. The visitors' exhibition upstairs puts Ayutthaya's ruins in context, dramatically presenting a broad social history of the city through videos, sound effects and reconstructions of temple murals. Other exhibits include model ships and a peasant's wooden house.

Chantharakasem Palace Museum

In the northeast corner of the island • Wed–Sun 9am–4pm • B100 • ⓦ thailandmuseum.com

The **Chantharakasem Palace** was traditionally the home of the heir to the Ayutthayan throne. The Black Prince, Naresuan, built the first *wang na* (palace of the front) here in about 1577 so that he could guard the area of the city wall that was most vulnerable to enemy attack. Rama IV (1851–68) had the palace rebuilt and it now houses a **museum** displaying many of his possessions, including a throne platform overhung by a white *chat*, a ceremonial nine-tiered parasol that is a vital part of a king's insignia. The rest of the museum features beautiful ceramics and Buddha images, and a small arsenal of cannon and musketry.

Wat Na Phra Mane

On the north bank of the Lopburi River, opposite the Wang Luang • Daily 8am–6pm • B20

Wat Na Phra Mane is Ayutthaya's most rewarding temple as it's the only one from the town's golden age that survived Burmese attacks.

The main **bot**, built in 1503, shows the distinctive features of Ayutthayan architecture – outside columns topped with lotus cups, and slits in the walls instead of windows to let the wind pass through. Inside, underneath a rich red-and-gold coffered ceiling that represents the stars around the moon, sits a powerful 6m-high Buddha in the disdainful, over-decorated royal style characteristic of the later Ayutthaya period.

In sharp contrast is the dark-green **Phra Khan Thavaraj** Buddha, which dominates the tiny viharn behind to the right. Seated in the "European position", with its robe delicately pleated and its feet up on a large lotus leaf, the gentle figure conveys a reassuring serenity. It's advertised as being from Sri Lanka, the source of Thai Buddhism, but more likely is a seventh- to ninth-century Mon image from Wat Phra Mane at Nakhon Pathom.

Wat Phu Khao Thong

2km northwest of Wat Na Phra Mane

Head northwest of Wat Na Phra Mane and you're in open country, where the 50m-high chedi of **Wat Phu Khao Thong** rises steeply out of the fields. In 1569, after a temporary occupation of Ayutthaya, the Burmese erected a Mon-style chedi here to commemorate their victory. Forbidden by Buddhist law from pulling down a sacred monument, the Thais had to put up with this galling reminder of the enemy's success until it collapsed nearly two hundred years later, when King Borommakot promptly built a truly Ayutthayan chedi on the old Burmese base – just in time for the

Burmese to return in 1767 and flatten the town. This "Golden Mount" has recently been restored and painted toothpaste-white, with a colossal equestrian statue of King Naresuan, conqueror of the Burmese, to keep it company. You can climb 25m of steps up the side of the chedi to look out over the countryside and the town, with glimpses of Wat Phra Si Sanphet and Viharn Phra Mongkok Bopit in the distance.

Wat Chai Watthanaram

Across the river, southwest of the island • Daily 8am–6.30pm • B50, or included with the B220 six-in-one pass

It's worth the ride to reach the elegant brick-and-stucco latticework of Khmer-style stupas at **Wat Chai Watthanaram**. These graceful ruins used to be a common stop on boat tours, but because of recurrent flooding a wall now protects them from the river and access is only viable by road. Late afternoon is a popular time to visit, as the sun sinks photogenically behind the main tower.

King Prasat Thong built Wat Chai Watthanaram in 1630, possibly to commemorate a victory over Cambodia, designing it as a sort of Angkorian homage, around a towering central Khmer corncob **prang** encircled by a constellation of four minor prangs and eight tiered and tapered chedis. Most of the stucco facing has weathered away to reveal the red-brick innards in pretty contrast, but a few tantalizing fragments of stucco relief remain on the outside of the chedis, depicting episodes from the Buddha's life. Around the gallery that connects them sits a solemn phalanx of 120 headless seated Buddhas, each on its own red-brick dais but showing no trace of their original skins, which may have been done in black lacquer and gold-leaf. To the east a couple of larger seated Buddhas look out across the river from the foundations of the old bot. Just a few years ago, it was possible to climb the steep steps of the central prang behind them, but visitors are now asked to refrain from doing so to help preserve the structure.

Ayothaya Floating Market

East of the railway station • Daily 10am–9pm

Not to be confused with Klong Sa Bua Floating Market in the north of town, **Ayothaya Floating Market** is a new, purpose-built complex with around two hundred shops and restaurants. The majority of traders here operate from traditional-style shops set around a lake, rather than from boats, but it still makes a pleasant enough break from tramping around temples. There are relatively few foreigners here, and it's easy to while away a couple of hours browsing through the T-shirts, straw hats and other trinkets offered for sale. Worth trying are the tasty black bean-, orange- and chocolate-flavoured ice-lollies you'll see locals devouring (B5). Other diversions include theatre shows, fish spas and massages, plus elephant rides at the nearby Ayothaya Elephant Camp (B100/10 min).

Wat Yai Chai Mongkol

Southeast of the island, about 2km from the station • Daily 8am–5pm • B20 • If cycling here, avoid the multi-laned Pridi Damrong/ Naresuan Bridge and Bangkok road by taking the river ferry across to the train station and then heading south 1.5km before turning east to the temple

Across the Pasak River southeast of the island, you pass through Ayutthaya's new business zone and some rustic suburbia before reaching the ancient but still functioning **Wat Yai Chai Mongkol**. Surrounded by formal lawns, flowerbeds and much-photographed saffron-draped Buddhas, the wat was established by Ramathibodi I in 1357 as a meditation site for monks returning from study in Sri Lanka. King Naresuan put up the beautifully curvaceous **chedi** to mark the decisive victory over the Burmese at Suphanburi in 1593, when he himself had sent the enemy packing by slaying the Burmese crown prince in an elephant-back duel. Built on a colossal scale to outshine the Burmese Golden Mount on the opposite side of Ayutthaya, the chedi has come to symbolize the prowess and devotion of Naresuan and, by implication, his descendants right down to the present king. By the entrance, a **reclining Buddha**, now gleamingly restored in white, was also constructed by Naresuan. A huge modern glass-walled shrine to the revered king dominates the back of the temple compound.

Wat Phanan Choeng

Near the confluence of the Chao Phraya and Pasak rivers, to the west of Wat Yai Chai Mongkol • Daily 8am–5pm • B20

In Ayutthaya's most prosperous period, the docks and main trading area were located near the confluence of the Chao Phraya and Pasak rivers, to the west of Wat Yai Chai Mongkol. This is where you'll find the oldest and liveliest working temple in town, **Wat Phanan Choeng**. The main viharn is often filled with the sights, sounds and smells of an incredible variety of merit-making activities, as devotees burn huge pink Chinese incense candles, offer food and rattle fortune sticks. It's even possible to buy tiny golden statues of the Buddha to be placed in one of the hundreds of niches that line the walls, a form of votive offering peculiar to this temple. If you can get here during a festival, especially Chinese New Year, you're in for an overpowering experience.

The 19m-high Buddha, which almost fills the hall, has survived since 1324, shortly before the founding of the capital, and tears are said to have flowed from its eyes when Ayutthaya was sacked by the Burmese. However, the reason for the temple's popularity with the Chinese is to be found in the early eighteenth-century shrine by the pier, with its image of a beautiful Chinese princess who drowned herself here because of a king's infidelity: his remorse led him to build the shrine at the place where she had walked into the river.

ARRIVAL AND DEPARTURE
AYUTTHAYA

BY TRAIN
The best way of getting to Ayutthaya from Bangkok is by train (with departures mostly in the early morning and evening); trains continue on to Nong Khai and Ubon Ratchathani in the northeast, and to the north and Chiang Mai. The station has a useful left-luggage service (24hr; B20 per piece per day).

Getting into town The station is on the east bank of the Pasak; to get to the centre of town, take a ferry from the jetty 100m west of the station (last ferry around 8pm; B3) across and upriver to Chao Phrom pier; it's then a 5min walk to the junction of Thanon U Thong and Thanon Naresuan, near most guesthouses (if you're going to stay at *Bann Kun Pra*, however, take the ferry from the neighbouring jetty, which runs directly across the river and back).

Destinations Bangkok Hualamphong (around 38 daily; 1hr 30min–2hr); Chiang Mai (6 daily; 10hr 45min–13hr 10min); Lopburi (20 daily; 45min–1hr 30min); Nong Khai (3 daily; 9hr 30min); Phitsanulok (11 daily; 3hr 30min–6hr 20min); Ubon Ratchathani (7 daily; 7hr 20min–10hr 30min).

BY BUS OR MINIBUS
From/to Bangkok Frequent buses to Ayutthaya depart Bangkok's Northern Mo Chit terminal. Most pull in at the bus stop on Thanon Naresuan, near the main accommodation area, though some long-distance services only stop at Ayutthaya's bus terminal, 5km to the east of the centre on Highway 1, from where you'll need a tuk-tuk (B100–150). Private a/c minibuses from Bangkok's Victory Monument and Southern Bus Terminal finish their routes opposite the Thanon Naresuan bus stop (both about every 20min during daylight hours). Services in the opposite direction, returning to Bangkok, leave from all the above-mentioned drop-off points. There are also tourist minibuses that connect Ayutthaya with Suvarnabhumi Airport and with Thanon Khao San.

From/to Kanchanaburi Travelling from Kanchanaburi, it's possible to bypass the Bangkok gridlock, either by hooking up with an a/c tourist minibus (1 daily; 3hr) arranged through guesthouses in Kanchanaburi or, under your own steam, by taking a public bus to Suphanburi (every 20min; 1hr 30min), then changing to an Ayutthaya bus, which will drop you off on Thanon Naresuan. To travel from Ayutthaya to Kanchanaburi, the easiest option is to arrange a minibus through one of the guesthouses.

Other services Fast but cramped tourist minibuses serve Sukhothai, and there are also connecting minibuses for Ko Samet and Ko Chang, an overnight bus service to Chiang Mai and another to Siem Reap in Cambodia.

AYUTTHAYA EXHIBITIONS

While visiting the branch of the **Tourist Information Centre** located in the old city hall (see below), it's well worth heading upstairs to the smartly presented multi-media **exhibition** on Ayutthaya (daily except Wed 8.30am–4.30pm; free), which provides an engaging introduction to the city's history, an overview of all the sights, including a scale-model reconstruction of Wat Phra Si Sanphet, and insights into local traditional ways of life. On the other side of the staircase, there's the **Ayutthaya National Art Museum** (daily except Wed 8.30am–4.30pm; free), which has depictions of animals, people and landscapes by Thai artists including a drawing in black ink by former Prime Minister Chuan Leekpai.

2

Destinations Bangkok (every 20min; 1hr 30min–2hr); Chiang Mai (9 daily; 9hr); Chiang Rai (12 daily; 12hr); Kamphaeng Phet (9 daily; 5hr); Lampang (11 daily; 8hr); Lamphun (7 daily; 9hr); Lopburi (every 20min; 2hr); Phitsanulok (9 daily; 5hr); Sukhothai (12 daily; 4hr 30min–6hr); Suphanburi (every 30min; 1hr); Tak (1 daily; 6hr).

GETTING AROUND

Busloads of tourists descend on Ayutthaya's sights during the day, but the area covered by the old capital is large enough not to feel swamped. Distances are deceptive, so it's best not to walk everywhere.

By bicycle or motorbike Bicycles can be rented at guesthouses, around the train station and from the tourist police. Watch out though, as some places try to charge up to B100 per day – double the usual rate. Some guesthouses and a few cheaper outlets in front of the station rent small motorbikes.

By tuk-tuk Tuk-tuks are easy enough to flag down on the street. Their set routes for sharing passengers are more useful for locals than for tourists, but a typical journey in town on your own should only cost B50. If you want to hire a tuk-tuk for the day, it's best to head for the ferry landing or the area around Naresuan Soi 2 (see below).

By motorbike taxi Motorbikes charge around B40 for medium-range journeys.

INFORMATION

Tourist information TAT's helpful Ayutthaya Tourist Information Centre (daily 8.30am–4.30pm; ☎ 035 322730, ✉ tatyutya@tat.or.th) is split between a room on the ground floor of the former city hall (on the west side of Thanon Si Sanphet, opposite the Chao Sam Phraya National Museum), and an ornate wooden building a short walk further north on the same stretch of road.

ACCOMMODATION

Ayutthaya offers a good choice of accommodation, including a small ghetto of **budget guesthouses** on and around the soi that runs north from Chao Phrom market to Thanon Pamaphrao; it's sometimes known as Soi Farang but is actually signed as Naresuan Soi 2 at the southern end and Pamaphrao Soi 5 at the northern.

Ayothaya Hotel Thanon Naresuan ☎ 035 232855, ⓦ ayothayahotel.com. Central, good-value hotel with unexciting a/c motel rooms in the "standard" wing behind the car park and much more salubrious superior rooms in the hotel building. All guests can use the outdoor swimming pool. Helpful staff and a handy location, plus bike rental. Budget B650, superior B1500

Bann Kun Pra Thanon U Thong, just north of Pridi Damrong Bridge ☎ 035 241978, ⓦ bannkunpra.com. The best rooms in the rambling, hundred-year-old teak house here have shared bathrooms and gorgeous river-view balconies. There are also two newer and slightly noisier blocks near the road, where you can choose between cheap, single-sex dorm rooms (B250) with individual lockable tin trunks, or newly renovated en-suite doubles with a/c, attractive wooden floors and private terraces overlooking the waterway. Internet access, bike rental, river tours and a warm welcome. Fan B500, a/c B1100

★ **Baan Thai House** Soi Ban Bat, 600m east of the train station ☎ 035 245555, ⓦ baanthaihouse.com. Twelve immaculate a/c villas with sloping pitched roofs, set around manicured tropical gardens and a huge artificial pond with its own wooden water wheel and rowing boats (free for guests to use). Rooms have flatscreen TVs, wooden floors and delicately carved furnishings, plus classy outdoor showers. In cheaper garden-view rooms, the toilet is separated from the room by a thin curtain, so if you're prudish, consider upgrading. Perks include personal service, a spa, an outdoor pool and an excellent restaurant (see p.226). B2400

Chantana House Naresuan Soi 2 ☎ 035 323200, ✉ chantanahouse@yahoo.com. At the quieter end of the

2

travellers' soi, this low-key guesthouse has simple, boxy but spotlessly clean en-suite fan and a/c rooms, though not all have outward-facing windows. Kind, friendly staff, but not much English spoken. Fan **B400**, a/c **B500**

Krung Sri River 27/2, Thanon Rojana ☏035 244333, ⓦ krungsririver.com. Ayutthaya's most prominent hotel occupies nine storeys in a prime if noisy position beside the Pridi Damrong Bridge, with some standard rooms and all suites enjoying river views. Furnishings aren't exactly chic, but there's a/c and TVs throughout, an attractive third-floor pool and a car park. Standard rooms are good value. Free wi-fi. **B1700**

The Old Place Guest House Thanon U Thong, just south of the Chao Phrom Pier ☏035 211161. Plain fan and a/c rooms in the same spot as the popular riverside restaurant, with stark white walls and en-suite bathrooms. Free wi-fi throughout. Fan **B350**, a/c **B500**

PU Guesthouse 20/1 Moo 4, down an alley off Naresuan Soi 2 ☏035 251213, ⓦ puguesthouse.com. More peaceful than the guesthouses on Naresuan Soi 2 but still very central, this backpacker favourite has a great selection of cheap singles (from B180), doubles, and triples, many with a/c and en-suite bathrooms. Rooms aren't as stylish as others in the same price range, but it's worth staying here for the sociable lounge area and the cheap fried rice and fruit shakes. The friendly owner, Pu, is a fountain of knowledge, and can provide you with maps, train timetables and plenty of sightseeing tips. A second building with its own outdoor pool is being built across the street. Fan **B250**, a/c **B500**

EATING AND DRINKING

Other than the restaurants listed below, the *roti* (Muslim pancake) stalls near the hospital around the southern end of Thanon Si Sanphet are good for daytime snacks and after dark there are a couple of **night markets**: beside the river at Hua Raw, about ten minutes' walk north of Naresuan Soi 2, and at the west end of Thanon Bang Laen, 150m south of Wat Phra Mahathat. Competing singers at the clutch of **bar-restaurants** can make Naresuan Soi 2 a bit of a battle of the bands after 9pm but it's fun and lively, and free with your beer.

Baan Thai House Soi Ban Bat, 600m east of the train station ☏035 245555, ⓦ baanthaihouse.com. Slick and stylishly presented Thai food served right next to this hotel's private lotus pond. Try the chicken with chilli and cashew nuts, which tastes just perfect with a plate of steamed rice. Open daily for breakfast, lunch and dinner.

Bann Kun Pra Thanon U Thong, just north of Pridi Damrong Bridge ☏035 241978. The riverside dining terrace is just as atmospheric as the lovely guesthouse upstairs, and enjoys fine views. It specializes in reasonably priced fish and seafood, notably prawns, and the pork and pumpkin curry is good too. Most mains about B100. Daily 7am–10.30pm.

Chang House Naresuan Soi 2 ☏089 414 1448. A small but inviting streetside travellers' restaurant that lives up to its motto "Good food, good beer and good cheer" by serving tasty burgers, Thai standards and lots of veggie-friendly Indian dishes (most mains B80). The drinks menu includes imported wine and cocktails, and the tunes – mostly indie and grunge – aren't bad either. Daily from lunchtime until midnight.

Kankitti Thanon U Thong on the south side of town ☏035 241971. Congenial spot where, on a river-bank terrace or a moored boat with views of Wat Phutthaisawan's

white prang, you can dine on Ayutthaya's most famous delicacy, river prawns (B500), or on less expensive but nevertheless very tasty dishes such as green curry with fishballs (B120). Daily 9am–9.30pm.

★ **The Old Place** Thanon U Thong ☏035 211161. Great Thai food and a breezy, always interesting riverside location just south of the Chao Phrom Pier make this place a hit with locals and tourists alike. Tables are on a wooden deck over the water, shaded by a venerable century-old kapok tree. Seafood is tip-top and there's a good spicy sausage salad; cheap cocktails too. Mains B80–200. Open for breakfast, lunch and dinner.

Street Lamp Bar Naresuan Soi 2. The most crowded place on the street, with regular live music (usually guitar covers of the oldies) and cheap, ice-cold beer. Simple dishes like fried rice from B40. Daily 7am–midnight.

Tony's Place Naresuan Soi 2 ☏035 252578, ⓦ tonyplace-ayutthaya.com. The size of this cavernous timbered restaurant on the ground floor of the guesthouse, plus its cushioned chill-out areas, blasting music and free internet access, make this a popular travellers' meeting place; the typical food and beer are cheap enough but nothing special. Open daily for breakfast, lunch and dinner, with live music 7–11pm on Fri & Sat.

DIRECTORY

Banks and ATMs There are plenty of banks with exchange services and ATMs around the junction of Thanon Naresuan and Naresuan Soi 2.

Hospital The government Phra Nakhon Si Ayutthaya hospital is at the southern end of Thanon Si Sanphet

(☏035 241888).

Internet access At several places along Naresuan Soi 2. For free wi-fi, head to the restaurant at *Tony's Place*.

Tourist police Based just to the north of the TAT office on Thanon Si Sanphet (☏035 242352 or ☏1155).

Lopburi and around

Mention the name **LOPBURI** to a Thai and the chances are that he or she will start telling you about monkeys – the central junction in the old town of this unexceptional provincial capital, 150km due north of Bangkok, swarms with **macaques**. So beneficial are the beasts to the town's tourist trade that a local hotelier treats six hundred of them to a sit-down meal at Phra Prang Sam Yod temple every November, complete with menus, waiters and napkins, as a thank you for their help. In fact, the monkeys can be a real nuisance, but at least they add some life to the town's central **Khmer buildings**, which, though historically important, are rather unimpressive. More illuminating is the **Narai National Museum**, housed in a partly reconstructed seventeenth-century palace complex, and distant **Wat Phra Phutthabat**, a colourful eye-opener for non-Buddhists. Lopburi's main festival is the five-day **King Narai Reign Fair** in February, which commemorates the seventeenth-century king's birthday with costumed processions, cultural performances, traditional markets and a *son et lumière* show at Phra Narai Ratchanivet.

The old centre of Lopburi sits on an egg-shaped island between canals and the Lopburi River, with the rail line running across it from north to south. **Thanon Vichayen**, the main street, crosses the rail tracks at the town's busiest junction before heading east – now called Thanon Narai Maharat – through the newest areas of development, via Sakeo roundabout and the bus station, towards Highway 1. All of the sights below are easily walkable from the train station; the best accommodation and most restaurants are

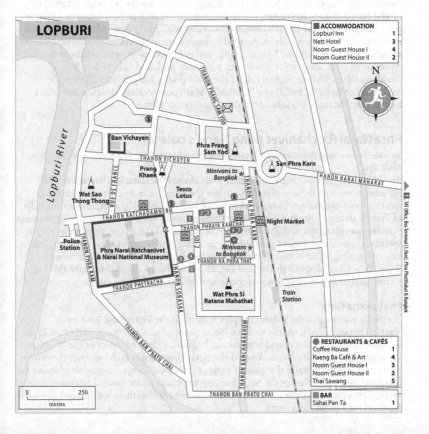

LOPBURI

ACCOMMODATION	
Lopburi Inn	1
Nett Hotel	3
Noom Guest House I	4
Noom Guest House II	2

Lopburi River

Ban Vichayen

THANON PRANG SAM YOD

Phra Prang
Sam Yod

San Phra Karn

THANON VICHAYEN

Prang
Khaek

Minivans to
Bangkok

THANON NARAI MAHARAT

RUE DE FRANCE

Wat Sao
Thong Thong

Tesco
Lotus

THANON NA PHRA KARN

Night Market

THANON RATCHADAMNERN

THANON PHRAYA KANCHAI

SOI 2

Police
Station

THANON PHRA RAM

Phra Narai Ratchanivet
& Narai National Museum

@

Minivans
to Bangkok

THANON NA PHRA THAT

THANON PHETRACHA

THANON SORASAK

Wat Phra Si
Ratana Mahathat

Train
Station

THANON BAN PRATU CHAI

THANON KANCHANAKHOM

0 — 250
metres

THANON BAN PRATU CHAI

RESTAURANTS & CAFÉS	
Coffee House	1
Kaeng Ba Café & Art	4
Noom Guest House I	3
Noom Guest House II	2
Thai Sawang	5

BAR	
Sahai Pan Ta	1

TAT Office, Bus Terminal (1.5km), Phra Phutthabat & Bangkok

set within the quiet, partly residential core between Phra Narai Ratchanivet to the west and Thanon Na Phra Karn to the east.

Brief history

Originally called Lavo, Lopburi is one of the longest-inhabited towns in Thailand, and was a major centre of the Mon (Dvaravati) civilization from around the sixth century. It maintained a tenuous independence in the face of the advancing Khmers until as late as the early eleventh century, when it was incorporated into the empire as the provincial capital for much of central Thailand. Increasing Thai immigration from the north soon tilted the balance against the Khmers, and Lopburi was again independent from some time early in the thirteenth century until the rise of Ayutthaya in the middle of the fourteenth. Thereafter, Lopburi was twice used as a second capital, first by King Narai of Ayutthaya in the seventeenth century, then by Rama IV of Bangkok in the nineteenth, because its remoteness from the sea made it less vulnerable to European expansionists. Rama V downgraded the town, turning the royal palace into a provincial government office and museum; Lopburi's modern role is as the site of several huge army barracks.

Wat Phra Si Ratana Mahathat

Just south of Thanon Na Phra That • Daily 7am–5pm • B50

As you come out of the station, the first thing you'll see are the sprawled grassy ruins of **Wat Phra Si Ratana Mahathat**, where the impressive centrepiece is a laterite prang in the Khmer style of the twelfth century, decorated with finely detailed stuccowork and surrounded by a ruined cloister. Arrayed in loose formation around this central feature are several more rocket-like Khmer prangs and a number of graceful chedis in the Ayutthayan style, among them one with a bulbous peak and faded bas-reliefs of Buddhist saints. On the eastern side of the main prang, King Narai added to the mishmash of styles by building a "Gothic" viharn, now roofless, which is home to a lonely, headless stone Buddha, draped in photogenic saffron.

Phra Narai Ratchanivet (King Narai's palace)

Sandwiched between Thanon Ratchadamnern and Thanon Phetracha; main entrance on Thanon Sorasak • Palace grounds open daily 7am–5.30pm

The imposing gates and high crenellated walls of the **Phra Narai Ratchanivet** might promise more than the complex delivers, but the museum in its central courtyard is worth a look, and the grounds are a green and relaxing spot. King Narai, with the help of French architects, built the heavily fortified palace in 1666 as a precaution against any possible confrontation with the Western powers, and for the rest of his reign he was to spend eight months of every year here, entertaining foreign envoys and indulging his love of hunting. After Narai's death, Lopburi was left forgotten until 1856, when Rama IV – worried about British and French colonialism – decided to make this his second capital and lavishly restored the central buildings of Narai's palace.

Phayakkha Gate

The main entrance to the palace complex is through the **Phayakkha Gate** on Thanon Sorasak. You'll see the unusual lancet shape of this arch again and again in the seventeenth-century doors and windows of Lopburi – just one aspect of the Western influences embraced by Narai. Around the **outer courtyard**, which occupies the eastern half of the complex, stand the walls of various gutted buildings – twelve warehouses for Narai's treasures, stables for the royal hunting elephants and a moated reception hall for foreign envoys. With their lily ponds and manicured lawns, these well-shaded grounds are ideal for a picnic or a siesta.

The Chanthara Phisan Pavilion

Straight ahead from the Phayakkha Gate another arch leads into the **central courtyard**, where the typically Ayutthayan **Chanthara Phisan Pavilion** contains a fascinating exhibition on Narai's reign – check out the pointed white cap typical of those worn by noblemen of the time, which increased their height by no less than 50cm.

Somdet Phra Narai National Museum

Wed–Sun 8.30am–4pm • B150 (payable at Phayakkha Gate) • ⓦ thailandmuseum.com

The colonial-style Phiman Mongkut Hall houses the **Somdet Phra Narai National Museum**, whose exhibits concentrate on the period following the Khmer subjugation of Lopburi in the eleventh century. Inevitably there's a surfeit of Buddhas, most of them fine examples of the Khmer style and the distinctive **Lopburi style**, which emerged in the thirteenth and fourteenth centuries, mixing traditional Khmer elements – such as the conical *ushnisha*, or flame on the crown of the Buddha's head – with new features such as a more oval face and slender body. On the top floor is **King Mongkut's bedroom**, filled with his furniture and assorted memorabilia of his reign, including his very short and uncomfortable-looking bed and eerie painted statues of his equally vertically challenged near-contemporaries, Napoleon and Queen Victoria.

Dusit Sawan Hall

On the south side of the museum lies the shell of the **Dusit Sawan Hall**, where foreign dignitaries came to present their credentials to King Narai. Inside you can still see the niche, raised 3.5m above the main floor, where the throne was set; beneath the niche, a modern plaque showing Narai receiving the French envoy, the Chevalier de Chaumont, in 1685 is revered as an icon of the king, with offerings of gold leaf, joss sticks and garlands. The whole building is divided in two around the throne: the front half has "foreign" doors and windows with pointed arches; the rear part, from where the king would have made his grand entrance, has traditional Thai openings. The hall used to be lined with French mirrors in imitation of Versailles, with Persian carpets and a pyramidal roof of golden glazed tiles rounding off the most majestic building in the palace.

The private courtyards

King Narai's private courtyard, through whose sturdy walls only the trusted few were admitted, occupied the southwest corner of the complex. During Narai's time, hundreds of lamps were placed in niches around the walls of this courtyard by night, shedding a fairy-like light on the palace. Now there's not much more than the foundations left of his residence, the **Sutha Sawan Hall** and its bathing ponds and artificial grotto.

Rama IV's private courtyard was built to house his harem in the northwest corner of the grounds, behind the present site of the museum. In what used to be the kitchen there's now a small folk museum of central Thai life, containing a loom and various pieces of farming and fishing equipment. In front, you can consult a crude model of the palace as it looked in Narai's time.

Wat Sao Thong Thong

Rue de France

Halfway along Rue de France, set back on the left, you'll pass a building whose plain terracotta roof tiles and whitewashed exterior give it a strangely Mediterranean look. This is in fact the viharn of **Wat Sao Thong Thong**, and is typical of Narai's time in its combination of Thai-style tiered roof with "Gothic" pointed windows. Erected as either a Christian chapel or a mosque for the Persian ambassador's residence, it was later used as a Buddhist viharn and has now been tastefully restored, complete with brass door-knockers and plush red carpet. Inside there's an austere Buddha image of the Ayutthaya period and, in the lamp niches, some fine Lopburi-style Buddhas.

Ban Vichayen

Thanon Vichayen • Daily 8.30am–4pm • B50

The complex of **Ban Vichayen** was originally built by Narai as a residence for foreign ambassadors, with a Christian chapel incongruously stuccoed with Buddhist flame and lotus-leaf motifs. Though now just a nest of empty shells, it still conjures up the atmosphere of court intrigue and dark deeds which, towards the end of Narai's reign, centred on the colourful figure of its most famous resident, **Constantine Phaulkon**, a Greek adventurer who came to Ayutthaya with the English East India Company in 1678. He entered the royal service as interpreter and accountant, rapidly rising to the position of prime minister. It was chiefly due to his influence that Narai established close ties with Louis XIV of France, a move that made commercial sense but also formed part of Phaulkon's secret plan to turn Narai and his people to Christianity, with the aid of the French. (It was around this time that the word for Westerner, *farang*, entered the Thai language, from the same derivation as *français*, which the Thais render *farangset*.) In 1688, a struggle for succession broke out, and leading officials persuaded the dying Narai to appoint as regent his foster brother, Phetracha, a great rival of Phaulkon's. Phetracha promptly executed Phaulkon on charges of treason, and took the throne himself when Narai died. Under Phetracha, Narai's open-door policy towards foreigners was brought to a screeching halt and the Thai kingdom returned to traditional, smaller-scale dealings with the outside world.

Prang Khaek

The junction of Thanon Vichayen and Thanon Sorasak is marked by an unusual traffic island on which perch the three stubby red-brick towers of **Prang Khaek**, a well-preserved Hindu shrine, possibly to the god Shiva, dating from as early as the eighth century. The three towers, which face east and are aligned in a row, have been restored on several occasions – most notably in the seventeenth century under the auspices of King Narai.

Phra Prang Sam Yod and San Phra Karn

On the corner of Thanon Prang Sam Yod and Thanon Vichayen • Daily 6am–6pm • B50

Like nearby Prang Khaek, **Phra Prang Sam Yod**, at the top of Thanon Na Phra Karn, seems to have been a Hindu temple, later converted to Buddhism under the Khmers. The three chunky prangs, made of dark laterite with some restored stuccowork, and symbolizing the Hindu triumvirate of Brahma, Vishnu and Shiva, are Lopburi's most photographed sight, though they'll only detain you for a minute or two – at least check out some carved figures of seated hermits at the base of the door columns.

The shrine's grassy knoll is a good spot for **monkey-watching** – monkeys run amok all over this area (there's even a warning sign: "Beware Monkey Zone"), so keep an eye on your bags and pockets. Across the rail line at the modern red-and-gold shrine of **San Phra Karn**, there's even a monkey's adventure playground for the benefit of tourists, beside the base of what must have been a huge Khmer prang.

Wat Phra Phutthabat (Temple of the Buddha's Footprint)

17km southeast of Lopburi, off Highway 1 • Any of the frequent buses to Saraburi or Bangkok from Lopburi's Sakeo roundabout will get you there in 30min

The most important pilgrimage site in central Thailand, **Wat Phra Phutthabat** is believed to house a footprint made by the Buddha.

The **legend** of Phra Phutthabat dates back to the beginning of the seventeenth century, when King Song Tham of Ayutthaya sent some monks to Sri Lanka to worship the famous Buddha's footprint of Sumankut. To the monks' surprise,

2

THE FESTIVAL OF THE HOLY FOOTPRINT

During the dry season in January, February and March, a million pilgrims from all over the country flock to Wat Phra Phutthabat for the **Ngan Phrabat** (**Festival of the Holy Footprint**), when other pilgrims are making their way to the other major religious sites at Doi Suthep, Nakhon Si Thammarat and That Phanom. During the fair, which reaches its peak in two week-long lunar periods, one usually at the beginning of February, the other at the beginning of March, stalls selling souvenirs and traditional medicines around the entrance swell to form a small town, and traditional entertainments, magic shows and a Ferris wheel are laid on. The fair is still a major religious event, but before the onset of industrialization it was the highlight of social and cultural life for all ages and classes; it was an important place of courtship, for example, especially for women at a time when their freedom was limited. Another incentive for women to attend the fair was the belief that visiting the footprint three times would ensure a place in heaven – for many women, the Phrabat Fair became the focal point of their lives, as Buddhist doctrine allowed them no other path to salvation. Up to the reign of Rama V (1868–1910) even the king used to come, performing a ritual lance dance on elephant-back to ensure a long reign.

---

the Sri Lankans asked them why they had bothered to travel all that way when, according to the ancient Pali scriptures, the Buddha had passed through Thailand and had left his footprint in their own backyard. As soon as Song Tham heard this he instigated a search for the footprint, which was finally discovered in 1623 by a hunter named Pram Bun, when a wounded deer disappeared into a hollow and then emerged miraculously healed. The hunter pushed aside the bushes to discover a foot-shaped trench filled with water, which immediately cured him of his terrible skin disease. A temple was built on the spot, but was destroyed by the Burmese in 1765 – the present buildings date from the Bangkok era.

A staircase flanked by nagas leads up to a marble platform, where an ornate mondop with mighty doors inlaid with mother-of-pearl houses the **footprint**, which in itself is not much to look at. Sheltered by a mirrored canopy, the stone print is nearly 2m long and obscured by layers of gold leaf presented by pilgrims; people also throw money into the footprint, some of which they take out again as a charm or merit object. The hill behind the shrine, which you can climb for a fine view over the gilded roofs of the complex to the mountains beyond, is covered in shrines. The souvenir village around the temple includes plenty of **foodstalls** for day-trippers.

ARRIVAL AND DEPARTURE   LOPBURI

BY TRAIN

As it's on the main line north to Chiang Mai, Lopburi is best reached by train from Bangkok's Hualamphong Station (most departures early morning and evening), via Ayutthaya. A popular option is to arrive in Lopburi in the morning, leave your bags at the conveniently located station while you look around the old town, then catch one of the night trains to the north.

Destinations Ayutthaya (19 daily; 45min–1hr 30min); Bangkok Hualamphong Station (14 daily; 2hr 30min–3hr); Chiang Mai (6 daily; 10–12hr); Phitsanulok (12 daily; 3hr–5hr 15min).

BY BUS OR MINIBUS

The long-distance bus terminal is on the southwest side of the huge Sakeo roundabout, 2km east of the old town: any blue city bus or red songthaew heading west on Thanon

Narai Maharat to Narai's Palace will save you the walk (B10).

From/to Bangkok Besides regular buses from the Northern Mo Chit terminal, a couple of companies operate fast a/c minibuses between Bangkok's Victory Monument (west side, near Ratchawithi Hospital) and Lopburi, which leave when full (from Bangkok 5am–8pm; from Lopburi 3.30am–8pm) and terminate outside their offices on Thanon Na Phra Karn, 200m north of the Lopburi train station.

From/to Kanchanaburi Coming from Kanchanaburi, it's possible to bypass Bangkok by taking a public bus to Suphanburi (every 20min; 1hr 30min), then changing to a Lopburi bus; the same applies heading in the opposite direction.

Destinations Ayutthaya (every 20min; 2hr); Bangkok (every 20min; 2–3hr), via Wat Phra Phutthabat (30min); Chiang Mai (5 daily; 9hr); Khorat (15 daily; 3hr 30min); Phitsanulok (3 daily; 4hr); Suphanburi (hourly; 3hr).

2

GETTING AROUND

By motorbike Lopburi itself is easily explored on foot, but if you want to get further afield, *Noom Guesthouse I* (see below) rents out automatic motorbikes for B300/day.

INFORMATION AND TOURS

Tourist information TAT has a new office east of San Phra Karn on Highway 311 (Thanon Narai Maharat) near the city hall (daily 8.30am–4.30pm; ⓣ036 422768–9, ⓔtatlobri@tat.or.th) but it's too far from the city's main sights to be of much use.

Tours *Noom Guesthouse I* (see below) runs rock-climbing trips to the cliff-face at Khao Chin Lae, about 20km east of town, behind Wat Pa Suwannahong (from B1000 excluding equipment), while a trip to swim in a nearby lake and see a cave packed with bats (also with *Noom I*) costs B600 for up to five people.

ACCOMMODATION

Lopburi Inn Resort Around 9km east of the old town at 144 Thanon Phahonyothin ⓣ036 420777, ⓦlopburiinnresort.com. The a/c rooms here are more luxurious than anything you'll find in town, but the resort is a long way from the centre, which is a definite drawback if you want to see the ruins. On the plus side there's a popular on-site restaurant and an inviting outdoor pool. B1800

Nett Hotel Soi 2, Thanon Ratchadamnern ⓣ036 411738. The best alternative to *Noom* is this clean and friendly place, announced by a multicoloured mosaic of a dragon and a cock. It offers unadorned en-suite fan or a/c rooms, the latter with hot water, TVs and fridges, though don't expect a view. Fan B200, a/c B350

Noom Guesthouse I Thanon Praya Kumjud ⓣ036 427693, ⓦnoomguesthouse.com. Most travellers make a beeline for the rooms at *Noom Guesthouse I*, whose centrally located old wooden house is fronted by a street-side restaurant and bar. There's a good mix of teak-floored rooms in the main house, which shared bathrooms, or you can stay in one of the en-suite bungalows out back. Facilities are very good and include free wi-fi, plus TV in the bungalows. Fan B350, a/c B450

Noom Guesthouse II Soi 2, Thanon Ratchadamnern ⓣ036 427693, ⓦnoomguesthouse.com. Offering more up-to-date rooms than *Noom I* and decent Western breakfasts, the owners' new spot is a good standby option. Free wi-fi. Fan B350, a/c B450

EATING AND DRINKING

Lopburi's dining scene is pretty limited, but the **night market**, which sets up all along the west side of the railway tracks, is a reliable choice for cheap eats. The most popular places for a **beer**, day or night, are *Sahai Pan Ta* and the sociable pavement tables at *Noom Guesthouse I*.

Coffee House Thanon Ratchadamnern ⓣ081 587 7606. Good espressos, lattes and cappuccinos (around B30) in this fairly comfortable little café near the northern end of Soi 1. Noodles and Western breakfasts are also on offer. Daily 8am–8pm.

★ **Keang Ba Café & Art** Thanon Na Phra That ⓔclayman_lm@hotmail.com. Tall, wonderfully detailed canvases hang from the white walls in this artfully put together café just across from Wat Phra Si Ratana Mahathat. Look out for the stencilled black birds, cats and bats stuck to the walls above the tables. The blueberry smoothie (B30) is excellent but don't expect gourmet food – the menu is as minimalist as the interior design. Free wi-fi. Daily mid-morning until evening.

Noom Guesthouse I & II Thanon Praya Kumjud and Soi 2, Thanon Ratchadamnern ⓣ036 427693, ⓦnoomguesthouse.com. The original *Noom Guesthouse* on Thanon Praya Kumjud does travellers' fare throughout the day and cocktails by night, while the second property serves up good Western breakfasts. Noom II 8am–11am, Noom I open for lunch and dinner (bar closes at 1am).

Sahai Pan Ta Near the northwest corner of Wat Mahathat ⓣ036 783432. Lit up by neon lights, this is a rowdy Wild-West-style watering hole, with food and live music. There's no English sign, but look out for the huge *Ben More* billboard. Daily 7pm–late.

Thai Sawang Thanon Sorasak ⓣ036 411881. This cheap, a/c café offers simple Western breakfasts, but is best known for its recommended Vietnamese food, especially roll-your-own fresh spring rolls stuffed with herbs, salad leaves and pork or Vietnamese sausage. Most dishes B40–80. Daily 6am–8pm.

SHOPPING

Lopburi's busy **market** sets up on Thanon Praya Kumjud every Wednesday evening, selling everything from sunglasses and Thai pop CDs to freshly made doughnuts.

DIRECTORY

ATMs There are several ATMs on Thanon Ratchadamnern, east of Thanon Sorasak.

Internet access Available at Connect, on Thanon Praya

Kumjud, near *Noom Guesthouse I*, and at dozens of games centres across town.

Phitsanulok

Handily located midway up the railway line between Bangkok and Chiang Mai, the likeable provincial capital of **PHITSANULOK** makes a useful and pleasant stopover with reasonable hotels and good transport connections, especially to the historical centres of Sukhothai and Kamphaeng Phet. The main sight in town is the country's second-most important Buddha image, enshrined in historic **Wat Mahathat** and the focus of pilgrimages from all over Thailand; it is complemented by one of the best ethnology collections in Thailand, at the **Sergeant Major Thawee Folklore Museum**. There are also several potentially rewarding national parks within an hour or two's drive along Highway 12, the so-called "**Green Route**".

Typically for a riverside town, "Phit'lok" as it's often nicknamed, is long and narrow. The heart of the city, which occupies the east bank of the Nan River, is easily walkable and still feels quite old-fashioned with its shophouses, traditional restaurants and foodstalls, particularly along Thanon Boromtrailoknat between the police station and the *Pailyn Hotel*. The two main sights, however, lie at opposite extremities: Wat Mahathat to the north, and the folklore museum 2.5km south.

Brief history

Huge swathes of Phitsanulok were destroyed by fire in 1957, but the town's history harks back to a heyday in the late fourteenth and early fifteenth centuries when, with Sukhothai waning in power, it rose to prominence as the favoured home of the crumbling capital's last rulers. After supremacy was finally wrested by the emerging state of Ayutthaya in 1438, Phitsanulok was made a provincial capital, subsequently becoming a strategic army base during Ayutthaya's wars with the Burmese, and adoptive home to Ayutthayan princes. The most famous of these was **Naresuan**, a famously courageous warrior who was governor of Phitsanulok before he assumed the Ayutthayan crown in 1590. The ruins of Naresuan's Chandra Palace, where both he and his younger brother Akkathasaroth were born, are currently under excavation in the grounds of a former school northwest of the bridge that bears his name; the tramway tour makes a stop there.

Wat Mahathat (Wat Yai)

At the northern limit of the town on the east bank of the Nan River; **Wat Mahathat** Daily 6.30am–6pm • B50 • **Gallery of Buddha Images** Wed–Sun 9am–4pm • Free • Can be reached on city buses #1, #5, #8, #12 and #13 • No shorts or skimpy clothing

Officially called Wat Phra Si Ratana Mahathat (and known locally as **Wat Mahathat** or **Wat Yai**), this fourteenth-century temple was one of the few buildings miraculously to

---

FESTIVALS AND EVENTS IN PHIT'LOK

Phitsanulok hosts two lively **food festivals** every year, once during the Western New Year period (Dec 25–Jan 1) and again at Songkhran, the Thai New Year (April 9–15). Almost every restaurant in town participates, selling their trademark dishes from special stalls set up along the east bank of the river, and there's traditional Thai dance and other entertainments. In February, Phitsanulok honours the **Phra Buddha Chinnarat** with a **week-long festival**, which features *likay* folk-theatre performances and dancing (see p.48) Then, later in the year, on the third weekend of September, traditional **longboat races** are staged on the Nan River, in front of Wat Mahathat.

escape Phitsanulok's great 1957 fire. It receives a constant stream of worshippers eager to pay homage to the highly revered Buddha image inside the viharn. Because the image is so sacred, a **dress code** is strictly enforced here, forbidding shorts and skimpy clothing. When you're done with the temple, take a look at the riverside stalls outside, which offer visitors the chance to make merit by buying their live **eels**, **fish** and **baby turtles** (kept in plastic bags) and releasing them into the Maenam Nan.

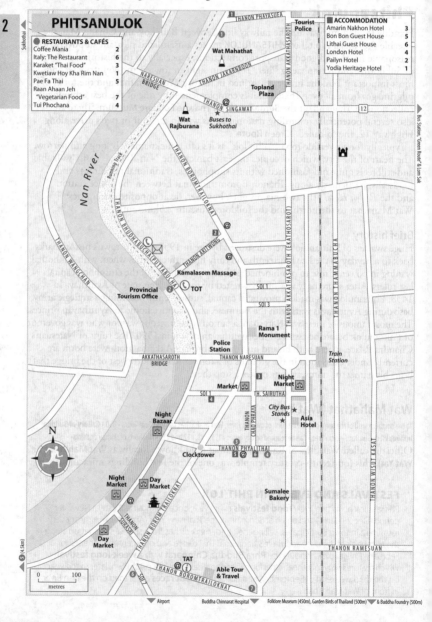

PHITSANULOK

● **RESTAURANTS & CAFÉS**
Coffee Mania	2
Italy: The Restaurant	6
Karaket "Thai Food"	3
Kwetiaw Hoy Kha Rim Nan	5
Pae Fa Thai	1
Raan Ahaan Jeh "Vegetarian Food"	7
Tui Phochana	4

■ **ACCOMMODATION**
Amarin Nakhon Hotel	3
Bon Bon Guest House	5
Lithai Guest House	6
London Hotel	4
Pailyn Hotel	2
Yodia Heritage Hotel	1

TOURS OF PHITSANULOK

For a cheap whizz around some of the town's main sights you could take the thirty-minute **tramway tour** that starts in front of the tourist information booth in the car park at Wat Mahathat (9am–3pm; departs when full, approximately every 30min on busy days; B30). Commentary is in Thai but there's an English-language summary available and the route takes in a trio of partially excavated ruins across the river – King Naresuan's shrine and place of birth, Chandra Palace, plus the Sukhothai-era Wat Wihanthong – none of which is as yet sufficiently restored to be worth making the effort to walk to.

At night a fleet of samlors twinkling with fairy lights takes tourists on an hour-long **evening tour** of Phitsanulok and its night bazaar; arrange the trip (B250) through any hotel.

Phra Buddha Chinnarat

Delicately inlaid mother-of-pearl doors mark the entrance to the viharn, opening onto the low-ceilinged interior, painted mostly in dark red and black, with gold leaf motifs, and dimly lit by narrow slits along the upper walls. In the centre of the far wall sits the much-cherished **Phra Buddha Chinnarat**: late Sukhothai in style and probably cast in the fourteenth century, this gleaming, polished-bronze Buddha is one of the finest of the period and, for Thais, second in importance only to the Emerald Buddha in Bangkok. Tales of the statue's miraculous powers have fuelled the devotion of generations of pilgrims – one legend tells how the Buddha wept tears of blood when Ayutthayan princes arrived in Phitsanulok to oust the last Sukhothai regent. The Phra Buddha Chinnarat stands out among Thai Buddha images because of its *mandorla*, the flame-like halo that symbolizes extreme radiance and frames the upper body and head like a chair-back, tapering off into nagas at the arm rests. There's an almost perfect replica of the Phitsanulok original in Bangkok's Marble Temple, commissioned by Rama V in 1901.

The prang

Behind the viharn, the gilded mosaic **prang** houses the holy relic that gives the wat its name (Mahathat means "Great Relic Stupa") – though which particular remnant lies entombed here is unclear – and the cloister surrounding both structures contains a gallery of Buddha images of different styles.

The east bank

South of Wat Mahathat and Naresuan Bridge, **the east bank** of the Nan River has been landscaped into a pleasant riverside park that runs all the way down to Akkathasaroth (Ekathosarot) Bridge. There are no exceptional attractions along its course, but you may want to make a stop at Wat Rajburana. Beyond Akkathasaroth Bridge, the river bank is dominated by the permanent stalls of the **night bazaar**, the place for locals and tourists to shop for bargain-priced fashions and a cheap meal.

Wat Rajburana

Around 150m southwest of Wat Mahathat

Just south of Naresuan Bridge is Wat Rajburana, which, like Wat Mahathat, survived the 1957 fire. Recognizable by the dilapidated brick-based chedi that stands in the compound, the wat is chiefly of interest for the *Ramakien* **murals** (see p.88) that cover the interior walls of the bot. Quite well preserved, they were probably painted in the mid-nineteenth century. Traditional Thai massage is available in the open-sided *sala* at the heart of the wat compound.

The Sergeant Major Thawee Folklore Museum

Thanon Wisut Kasat, 1.3km southeast of the train station • Tues–Sun 8.30am–4.30pm • B100 • Local bus #8 will drop you close by

The **Sergeant Major Thawee Folklore Museum** (Jatawee Buranaket) puts a different slant on the region's culture. Its fascinating look at traditional rural life makes this one of the best ethnology museums in the country. The collection, which is housed in a series of wooden pavilions, belongs to former sergeant major Dr Thawee, who has pursued a lifelong personal campaign to preserve and document a way of life that's gradually disappearing. Highlights include the reconstructed kitchen, veranda and birthing room of a typical village house, known as a "tied house" because its split-bamboo walls are literally tied together with rattan cane; and an exceptionally comprehensive gallery of traps: dozens of specialized contraptions designed to ensnare everything from cockroaches to birds perched on water buffaloes' backs. There's also a display on weaving and natural dyes, a collection of traditional toys and some fearsome-looking wooden implements for giving yourself a massage.

Buddha Foundry

26/43 Thanon Wisut Kasat, 1.35km southeast of the train station, about 50m south of the Folklore Museum • Open during working hours (usually daily 8am–5pm) but appointments advisable • Free • ☎ 055 258715 • Local bus #8 will drop you close by

For a rare chance to see Buddha images being forged, head to the **Buranathai Buddha Bronze-Casting Foundry**. Anyone can drop in to see the fairly lengthy procedure, which is best assimilated from the illustrated explanations inside the foundry. Images of all sizes are made here, from 30cm-high household icons to mega models destined for wealthy temples. The Buddha business is quite a profitable one: worshippers can earn a great deal of merit by donating a Buddha statue, particularly a precious one, to their local wat, so demand rarely slackens. There's a gift shop on site.

Garden Birds of Thailand

Adjacent to the Buddha Foundry on Thanon Wisut Kasat • Daily 8.30am–5pm • B50 • Accessible from the foundry or via Soi 17

Garden Birds of Thailand (Suan Nok) is Dr Thawee's most recent enthusiasm: a zoo containing hundreds of breathtakingly beautiful Thai birds, each one segregated and informatively described. It's an astonishing collection that offers a unique chance to admire at close range such beauties as a silver pheasant, an Asian fairy bluebird and a rhinoceros hornbill, as well as highly endangered species such as the jambu fruit dove and the helmeted hornbill. As is often the case in such places, however, the cages are very small and few of the birds are in pairs or groups.

ARRIVAL AND DEPARTURE   PHITSANULOK

Phitsanulok stands at the hub of an efficient transport network that works well as a transit point between Bangkok, the far north and Isaan. Nearly every Bangkok–Chiang Mai **train** stops here, and assorted **buses** head east towards the Isaan towns of Loei and Khon Kaen.

BY PLANE

Thai Airways runs flights to Bangkok (2 daily; 50min), Nok Air to Chiang Mai (3 weekly; 1hr) from Phitsanulok airport (☎ 055 301010), 7km south of town and about B150 by taxi from the centre.

BY TRAIN

Phitsanulok train station (☎ 055 258005) is in the town centre; tuk-tuk rates from here to hotels and attractions are posted outside (mostly B60).

Connections to Sukhothai If you've arrived at the train station and want to make an immediate bus connection to Sukhothai, you can either take a samlor or local bus to the regional bus station, 2km east, where the Sukhothai buses originate, or join the bus at a pick-up point opposite the Topland Plaza shopping centre on Thanon Singawat (B60 by samlor, or take a/c local bus #5 – non-a/c #5 goes elsewhere – to the Plaza, then cross the road).

Destinations Ayutthaya (11 daily; 4hr 30min–5hr 30min); Bangkok Hualamphong (11 daily; 5hr 30min–8hr); Chiang

THE BUDDHA'S FOOTPRINT, WAT PHRA PHUTTHABAT, NEAR LOPBURI (P.231) >

2

THE GREEN ROUTE

East of Phitsanulok, Highway 12 has been tagged "**the Green Route**" by TAT because it gives access to several national parks and rapids, and provides an excuse for a pleasant day or two's excursion from the city. TAT has produced a sketch map outlining car and motorbike routes.

The first highlight is the chance to go **whitewater rafting** on the Class 1–5 rapids of the Khek River; the Sappraiwan Resort (☎055 293293, ⓦresort.co.th; rooms B2000) at kilometre-marker 53 on Highway 12 arranges an overnight trip (June–Oct; B1699/person including three meals and one night's accommodation).

Next up is **Phu Hin Rongkla National Park** (B200; ☎055 233527, ⓦdnp.go.th), about 100km northeast of Phitsanulok: turn north off Highway 12 at kilometre-stone 68 onto Route 2013, then east onto Route 2331 to reach the visitor centre. Formerly the notorious stronghold of the insurgent Communist Party of Thailand from 1967 to 1982, the park still contains some relics from that period, though its short trails through montane forests and natural rock gardens are now its main point of interest. Should you want to stay, the park offers accommodation (dorm beds B100, en-suite rooms B800).

Also on the Green Route is **Thung Salaeng Luang National Park** (B200–400 depending on which areas you want to visit; ☎055 268019, ⓦdnp.go.th), 82km east of Phitsanulok (turn south off Highway 12 at kilometre-stone 79). Thung Salaeng is famous for the flowers that carpet its grasslands after the end of the rainy season (the flower meadows are only open Oct 23–Dec) and has two designated mountain-bike trails as well as rafting opportunities. Bungalows are available in the park from B1000.

The Dhamma Abha Vipassana meditation centre (☎081 646 4695, ⓦdhamma.org/schthaia .htm), which holds two ten-day **meditation** courses every month, is also in this area, in Ban Huayplu; turn north off Highway 12 at kilometre-stone 49.

Mai (6 daily; 5hr 50min–8hr 15min); Lamphun (6 daily; 5hr 40min–7hr 20min); Lopburi (12 daily; 3hr–5hr 15min).

BY BUS

The regional bus station (☎055 242430) is 2km east of the city on Highway 12, from where it's B60 by tuk-tuk to the centre or a ride on local bus #1 or #6 (see below). If coming from Sukhothai or the north, you should be able to get off somewhere more central, near Topland Plaza,

before the bus continues to the terminus.

Destinations Bangkok (up to 40 daily; 5–6hr); Chiang Mai (up to 18 daily; 5–6hr); Chiang Rai (17 daily; 6–7hr); Kamphaeng Phet (hourly; 3hr); Khon Kaen (10 daily; 5–6hr); Khorat/Nakhon Ratchasima (21 daily; 6–7hr); Loei (15 daily; 5hr); Lomsak (hourly; 2hr); Mae Sot (7 daily; 3hr 15min–5hr); Phrae (7 daily; 2–3hr); Sukhothai (at least every 40min; 1hr 30min); Tak (every 30min; 3hr); Ubon Ratchathani (7 daily; 12hr); Udon Thani (5 daily; 7hr).

GETTING AROUND

BY BUS

Several local city bus routes (about every 30min 5am–9pm) crisscross the city, most running via the city-centre bus stands on Thanon Akkathasaroth, 150m south of the train station, where southbound buses pick up outside the *Asia Hotel* and northbound ones from across the road.

Useful routes #1, from the regional bus station to Wat Mahathat and the train station; #5 and #11, from the train station to Topland Plaza (for Sukhothai buses) and Wat Mahathat; #6, from the regional bus station to the

Pailyn Hotel; and #8, from the regional bus station to the Folklore Museum, train station, Topland Plaza and Wat Mahathat.

BY CAR OR MOTORBIKE

Avis (☎089 9698672) and Budget (☎055 301020) have desks at the airport. Motorbike rental is available for around B200 per day at PN Motor (☎055 303222), inside the bus terminal complex on Thanon Mittraphap, then one block west.

INFORMATION

Tourist information The helpful and well-informed TAT office (daily 8.30am–4.30pm; ☎055 252742, ⓔtatphlok @tat.or.th) is on the eastern arm of Thanon Boromtrailoknat (known to local taxi drivers as Surasi Trade Centre). At the

time of writing it was closed for refurbishment, and could be for some time, so as a backup try the Provincial Tourism Office beside the river next to *Coffee Mania* (daily 8.30am–4.30pm).

2

ACCOMMODATION

Amarin Nakorn Hotel 3/1 Thanon Chao Phraya ☏ 055 219069. Very central, good value but dated, this tourist-oriented hotel has compact a/c rooms, all with wi-fi and nicely tiled bathrooms; those on the uppermost of the hotel's eleven floors enjoy panoramic views of the city. In-house massage service and restaurant. Rates include a simple breakfast. B600

Bon Bon Guest House 77 Thanon Phayalithai ☏ 055 219058. The only genuine guesthouse in town, this place is set back from the road with three storeys of rooms set around a little yard. The twenty rooms are all en suite and kept nice and clean; some have a/c. Not as cheap as the *Lithai* next door, but friendlier and more sociable. Fan B350, a/c B450

Lithai Guest House 73/1–5 Thanon Phayalithai ☏ 055 219629, ✉ lithaiphs@yahoo.com. Centrally located, and sharing the Lithai Building with a travel agency and a couple of restaurants, this is a good lower- to mid-range option, used mainly by salespeople so not especially cosy and much more of a hotel than a guesthouse. The big, clean, bright rooms come with either fan or a/c, the cheapest sharing bathrooms; there's wi-fi here too. Breakfast included. Fan B250, a/c B460

London Hotel 21–22 Soi Buddhabucha (Puttabucha) 1 ☏ 055 225145. The cheapest and most basic place in town, this converted family home – its downstairs filled with bikers' memorabilia and other curios – has just eight small, bare-bones, fan rooms upstairs, all painted to a funky mint-green-and-yellow colour scheme and all sharing bathrooms. B150

Pailyn Hotel 38 Thanon Boromtrailoknat ☏ 055 252411. Central, long-running three-star tourist hotel that's old-fashioned and unstylish but offers good-sized a/c rooms with comfortable beds. Upper-floor rooms in the thirteen-storey tower enjoy long-range river views from their balconies. Has a massage centre, restaurant and nightclub and runs tours to Sukhothai. Breakfast included. B765

Yodia Heritage Hotel Thanon Buddhabucha (Puttabucha) ☏ 055 214677, ⊛ yodiaheritage.com. The only proper boutique hotel in Phitsanulok, with just 25 upmarket, contemporary-styled rooms, all with a/c, wooden floors, elegantly restrained decor, bathtubs, free wi-fi, and a balcony overlooking the small garden. Located beside the hotel, 250m north of Wat Mahathat. The on-site *Amore* restaurant enjoys river views, and there's also a library and free transfers from the airport. B2300

EATING

In the evening, **night market** stalls set up within the night bazaar along the east bank of the river, south of Akkathasaroth Bridge. Fish and mussels are a speciality, but the most famous dish is "flying vegetables", in which strong-tasting morning-glory (*phak bung*) is stir-fried before being tossed flamboyantly in the air towards the plate-wielding waiter or customer.

Coffee Mania Thanon Buddhabucha, just south of the Provincial Tourism Office. The best of Phitsanulok's new coffee shops, with a great riverside location and delicious milky cappuccinos. Daily from 11am: Mon–Wed to 8pm, Thurs to midnight, Fri–Sun to 9pm.

Italy: The Restaurant Thanon Boromtrailoknat Soi 7 ☏ 055 219 177. Offers a huge choice of pizzas, calzones and pastas, plus wines and Thai dishes (B110–290), in a slightly quieter part of town, away from the worst of the traffic noise. Daily 11am–10pm.

Karaket "Thai Food" Thanon Phyalithai. Tasty Thai curry shop, where you make your selection from the metal trays set out on the pavement trestle, then eat in a/c comfort inside. Popular for family takeaways and very cheap: most savouries sell for just B30 a serving. Daily lunchtime until around 8.30pm.

Kwetiaw Hoy Kha Rim Nan 100m north of Wat Mahathat ☏ 081 379 3172. The noodles here are so famously tasty they've been featured on three local TV channels. Choose from *phat thai*, Sukhothai noodles with red pork in chilli-hot broth, *tom yam* soup with noodles, or yellow noodles with pork; tofu versions are also available

(B25–40). There's no English sign but it's got a brown awning, counter seating (with some river views), and is always packed. Daily 9am–4pm.

Pae Fa Thai About 5km south of the night bazaar down riverside Thanon Buddhabucha (Puttabucha); just upriver from the Supanganlaya Bridge. Many locals rate this as the best of the several floating restaurants that capitalize on the romance and breeziness of Phitsanulok's river setting, though the views here, near the bridge, aren't especially gripping. The menu (mostly B100–200) naturally features lots of fish and seafood as well as curries – their *phanaeng* tofu is especially good. Daily 11am–11pm.

Raan Ahaan Jeh "Vegetarian Food" Thanon Sithamtraipidok. Tiny, ultra-cheap vegetarian canteen near the TAT office, where you get a plate of brown rice plus B10 servings from a selection of veggie stir-fries and curries. Daily 6am–3pm.

Tui Phochana 90 Thanon Phayalithai. One of several cheap and cheerful Thai curry shops on this road, this one is famous for its tasty curries made with jackfruit (B20–40). Daily lunchtime until about 7pm.

2

DIRECTORY

ATMs ATMs are found across town, including at the corner of Soi 7 and Thanon Boromtrailokanat.

Hospitals Rattanavej Hospital on Thanon Phra Ong Dam (📞055 210819–28) is private, and Buddha Chinnarat Hospital, Thanon Sithamtraipidok (📞055 219844–52), is government-run.

Internet access There's a cluster of internet cafés on Thanon Phyalithai. In addition, most hotels and guesthouses have wi-fi.

Left luggage At the train station (24hr; B20 per item).

Massage At many hotels and the recommended

Kamalasom Massage on Thanon Akitwong (Mon–Sat 8.30am–4.30pm; B200/90min).

Tourist police For all emergencies, call the tourist police on the free 24hr phoneline 📞1155, or contact them at their office north of Wat Mahathat on Thanon Akkathasaroth (📞055 245358).

Travel agent Able Tour and Travel (Mon–Fri 8am–6pm, Sat 8am–4pm; 📞055 242206, ✉ablegroup@hotmail .com), near the TAT office on Thanon Boromtrailoknat, sells air tickets and can arrange minibuses to Sukhothai or Kamphaeng Phet (B1800, plus B1200 for optional guide).

Sukhothai

For a brief but brilliant period (1238–1376), the walled city of **SUKHOTHAI** presided as the capital of Thailand, creating the legacy of a unified nation of Thai peoples and a phenomenal artistic heritage. Some of Thailand's finest buildings and sculpture were produced here, but by the sixteenth century the city had been all but abandoned to the jungle. Now an impressive assembly of elegant ruins, the Old City, 58km northwest of

NEW SUKHOTHAI

ACCOMMODATION
At Home	3
Ban Thai Guest House	8
EZ House	6
J&J Guest House	5
Lotus Village	4
Ruean Thai Hotel	2
Sukhothai Heritage Resort	1
TR Guest House	7

RESTAURANTS & CAFÉS
Dream Café	5
J&J Guest House	2
Khun Tanode	3
Kru Iew	1
Poo Restaurant	6
Rom Poa	4

BAR
| Chopper Bar | 1 |

Phitsanulok, has been preserved as **Sukhothai Historical Park** and is one of Thailand's most visited ancient sites.

There are several sleepy accommodation options near the historical park, but travellers longing for urban comforts tend to stay in so-called **NEW SUKHOTHAI**, a modern market town 12km to the east, which has good travel links with the Old City and is also better for restaurants and long-distance bus connections. Straddling the Yom River, it's a small, friendly town, used to seeing tourists but by no means overrun with them. The new town also makes a peaceful and convenient base for visiting Ramkhamhaeng National Park, as well as the ruins of Si Satchanalai and Kamphaeng Phet which, while not as extensively renovated, are still worth visiting – if only for their relative wildness and lack of visitors. Most of these outlying places can be reached fairly easily by public transport, but for trips to Wat Thawet and Ramkhamhaeng National Park you'll need to rent your own vehicle or arrange a driver through your accommodation.

The Historical Park (Muang Kao Sukhothai)

12km west of New Sukhothai • Daily 6am–6pm, floodlit every, Fri, Sat & Sun 7–8pm • B100 per zone, or B350 inclusive, plus B10–50 per vehicle

In its prime, the Old City boasted around forty separate temple complexes and covered an area of about seventy square kilometres between the Yom River and the low range of hills to the west. At its heart stood the walled royal city, protected by a series of moats and ramparts. **SUKHOTHAI HISTORICAL PARK**, or **Muang Kao Sukhothai**, covers all this area and is divided into five **zones**: all the most important temples lie within the central zone, with the Ramkhamhaeng Museum just outside it; the ruins outside the city walls are spread out over a sizeable area and divided into north, south, east and west zones.

With the help of UNESCO, the Thai government's Fine Arts Department has restored the most significant ruins and the result reveals the original town planners' keen aesthetic sense, especially their astute use of water to offset and reflect the solid monochrome contours of the stone temples. Although there is a touch of the too perfectly packaged theme park about the central zone (and, in some critics' opinions, too liberal an interpretation of thirteenth-century design), it's a serene and rewarding site, with plenty to investigate should you want to look more closely. It does, however, take a determined imagination to visualize the ancient capital as it must once have looked, not least because houses and palaces would have filled the spaces between the wats – like their Khmer predecessors, the people of Sukhothai constructed their secular buildings from perishable materials such as wood, only using expensive, durable stone for their sacred structures. The **central zone** covers three square kilometres so a bike is recommended, though not essential. Of the eleven ruins here, Wat Mahathat is the one that should definitely not be missed.

There's a much less formal feel to the ruins in the four **outer zones**, where you're as likely to find cows trampling through the remains as tourists. You'll need a bicycle or car to get around, but all sites are clearly signposted from the gates encircling the central zone. The **north** zone is the closest and most rewarding, followed by the **east** zone just off the road to New Sukhothai. If you're feeling energetic, head for the **west** zone, which requires a much longer bike ride and some hill climbing. The ruins to the **south** aren't worth a special effort but you'll pass a few of them, including Wat Chetuphon, if you take the quiet, rural back route between the accommodation on Route 1272 and Wat Mahathat.

Brief history

Prior to the thirteenth century, the land now known as Thailand was divided into a collection of petty principalities, most of which owed their allegiance to the Khmer empire and its administrative centre Angkor (in present-day Cambodia). With the Khmers' power on the wane, two Thai generals joined forces in 1238 to oust the Khmers from the northern plains, founding the kingdom of **Sukhothai** ("Dawn of Happiness" in Pali) under the regency of one of the generals, Intradit. In short order

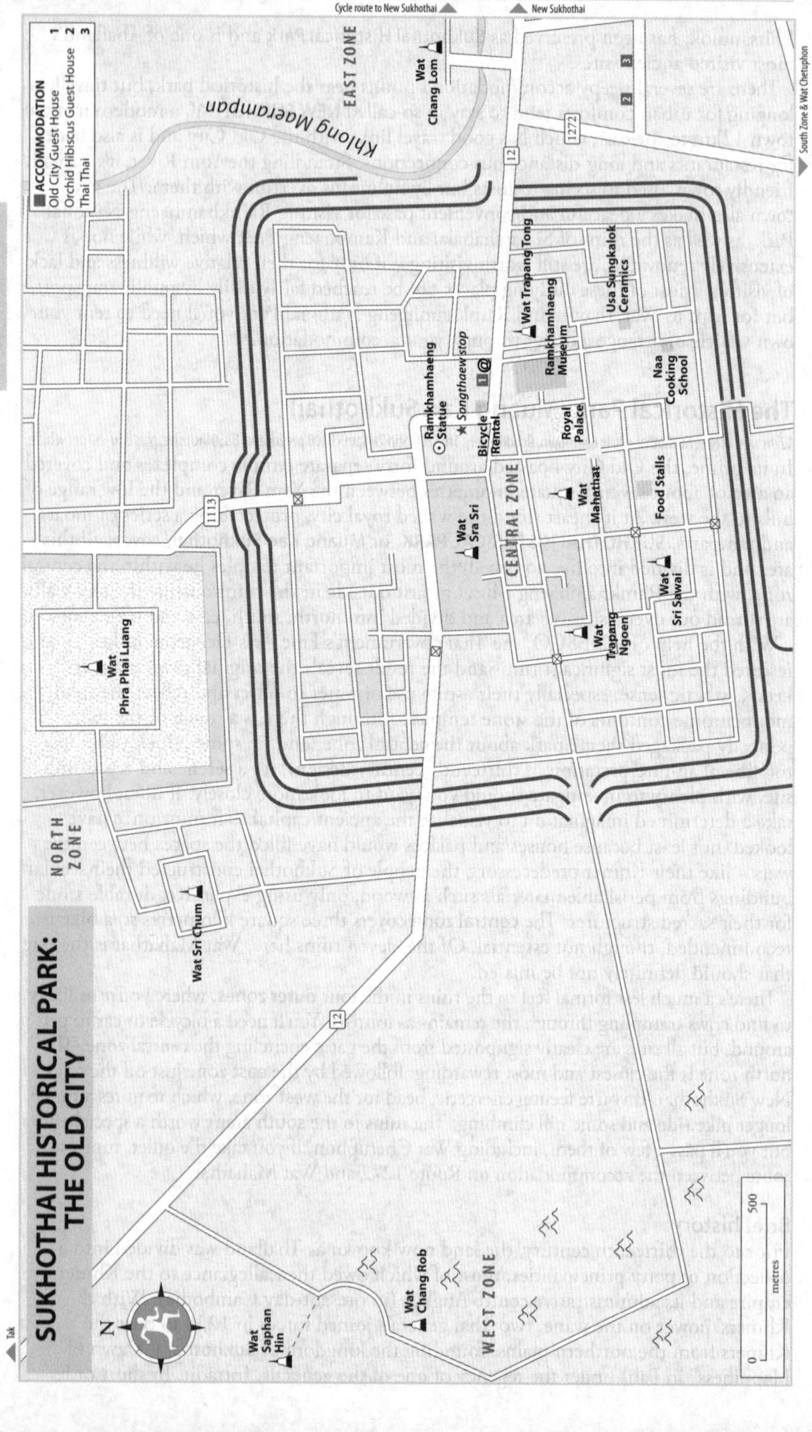

2

SUKHOTHAI HISTORICAL PARK: THE OLD CITY

N

Tak ▲

▲ Cycle route to New Sukhothai   ▲ New Sukhothai

Khlong Maeramphan

EAST ZONE

▲ Wat Chang Lom

12

272

ACCOMMODATION
Old City Guest House   1
Orchid Hibiscus Guest House   2
Thai Thai   3

2
3

South Zone & Wat Chetuphon ▶

▲ Wat Trapang Tong

Usa Sungkalok Ceramics

Ramkhamhaeng Museum

Naa Cooking School

Ramkhamhaeng Statue ⊙

★ Songthaew stop

Bicycle Rental ⊙

Royal Palace

Food Stalls

▲ Wat Mahathat

1113

▲ Wat Sra Sri

CENTRAL ZONE

▲ Wat Sri Sawai

▲ Wat Trapang Ngoen

NORTH ZONE

▲ Wat Sri Chum

▲ Wat Phra Phai Luang

12

WEST ZONE

▲ Wat Chang Rob

▲ Wat Saphan Hin

0   500
metres

THE SUKHOTHAI BUDDHA

The classic Buddha images of Thailand were produced towards the end of the Sukhothai era. Ethereal, androgynous figures with ovoid faces and feline expressions, they depict not a Buddha meditating to achieve enlightenment – the more usual representation – but an already **enlightened Buddha**: the physical realization of an abstract, "unworldly" state. Though they produced mainly seated Buddhas, Sukhothai artists are renowned for having pioneered the **walking Buddha**, one of four postures described in ancient Pali texts but without precedent in Thailand.

2

they had extended their control over much of present-day Thailand, as well as parts of Burma and Laos.

King Ramkhamhaeng

The third and most important of Sukhothai's eight kings, Intradit's youngest son **Ramkhamhaeng** (c.1278–99) laid the foundations of a unique Thai identity by establishing Theravada (Hinayana) Buddhism as the common faith and introducing the forerunner of the modern Thai alphabet; of several inscriptions attributed to him, the most famous, found on what's known as Ramkhamhaeng's Stele and housed in Bangkok's National Museum (with a copy kept in Sukhothai's Ramkhamhaeng Museum), tells of a utopian land of plenty ruled by a benevolent monarch.

Ramkhamhaeng turned Sukhothai into a vibrant spiritual and commercial centre, inviting Theravada monks from Nakhon Si Thammarat and Sri Lanka to instruct his people in the religion that was to supplant Khmer Hinduism and Mahayana Buddhism, and encouraging the growth of a ceramics industry with the help of Chinese potters. By all accounts, Ramkhamhaeng's successors lacked his kingly qualities and so, by the second half of the fourteenth century, Sukhothai had become a vassal state of the newly emerged kingdom of Ayutthaya; finally, in 1438, it was forced to relinquish all vestiges of its independent identity.

Ramkhamhaeng National Museum

Just outside the main entrance to the central zone • Daily 9am–4pm • B150 • ⓦ thailandmuseum.com

The well-presented **Ramkhamhaeng National Museum** features several illuminating exhibitions and contains some of the finest **sculptures** and reliefs found at the temples of Sukhothai's Old City and nearby Si Satchanalai. Outstanding artefacts in the downstairs gallery of the main building include the fourteenth-century bronze statue of a walking Buddha, and the large Buddha head that was found at Wat Phra Phai Luang in the north zone of Sukhothai Historical Park. Also here is a useful guide to the many different **stucco motifs** that once decorated every Sukhothai-era temple, along with a copy of one of the finest local examples of stucco relief, depicting the Buddha being sheltered by a naga, whose original is still *in situ* at Si Satchanalai's Wat Chedi Jet Taew. The wide-ranging section on Ramkhamhaeng's famous **stele** features a complete translation of the inscription, plus a detailed look at the origins and evolution of the original "Tai" script. The upstairs gallery concentrates on **Sangkhalok ceramics** and provides a much more informative introduction than the kiln museum in Si Satchanalai.

Statue of King Ramkhamhaeng

A modern **statue** of King Ramkhamhaeng sits to the right just inside the zone entrance: cast in bronze, he holds a palm-leaf book in his right hand – a reference to his role as founder of the modern Thai alphabet. Close by stands a large bronze **bell**, a replica of the one referred to on the famous stele (also reproduced here), which told how the king had the bell erected in front of his palace so that any citizen with a grievance could come by and strike it, whereupon the king himself would emerge to investigate the problem.

2

LOY KRATHONG

Every year on the evening of the full moon of the twelfth lunar month (usually in November), Thais all over the country celebrate the end of the rainy season with **Loy Krathong**, also known as the Festival of Light. One of Thailand's most beautiful festivals, it's held to honour and appease the spirits of the water at a time when all the fields are flooded and the canals and rivers are overflowing their banks. The festival is said to have originated seven hundred years ago, when **Nang Noppamas**, the consort of a Sukhothai king, adapted an ancient Brahmin tradition of paying homage to the water goddess.

At this time, nearly everyone makes or buys a **krathong** and sets it afloat (*loy*) on the nearest body of water, to cast adrift any bad luck that may have accrued over the past year. *Krathongs* are miniature basket-boats made of banana leaves that have been elegantly folded and pinned, origami style, and then filled with flowers, three sticks of incense and several lighted candles; the traditional base is a slice of banana tree trunk, but it's increasingly popular to buy your *krathong* ready-made from the market, sometimes with an eco-unfriendly polystyrene bottom. Some people slip locks of hair and fingernail clippings between the flowers, to represent sinful deeds that will then be symbolically released along with the *krathong*; others add a coin or two to persuade the spirits to take away their bad luck (swiftly raided by opportunist young boys looking for small change). It's traditional to make a wish or prayer as you launch your *krathong* and to watch until it disappears from view: if your candle burns strong, your wishes will be granted and you will live long.

Chiang Mai goes to town over Loy Krathong (see p.286), but **Sukhothai Historical Park** is the most famous place in Thailand to celebrate the festival, and the ruins are the focus of a spectacular festival held over several nights around the full moon. The centrepiece is a charming *son et lumière* performance at Wat Mahathat, complemented by firework displays, the illumination of many Old City ruins, thousands of candles floating on the shimmering lotus ponds, a parade of charming Nang Noppamas (Miss Loy Krathong) lookalikes and all sorts of concerts and street-theatre shows. All accommodation gets packed out during the festival, so book ahead if possible.

Wat Mahathat
Central zone

Your first stop in the central zone should be Sukhothai's most important site, the enormous **Wat Mahathat** compound. It's packed with the remains of scores of monuments and surrounded, like a city within a city, by a moat. This was the spiritual focus of the city, the king's temple and symbol of his power; successive regents, eager to add their own stamp, restored and expanded it so that by the time it was abandoned in the sixteenth century it numbered ten viharns, one bot, eight mondops and nearly two hundred small chedis. Looking at the wat from ground level, it's hard to distinguish the main structures from the minor ruins. Remnants of the viharns and the bot dominate the present scene, their soldierly ranks of pillars, which formerly supported wooden roofs, directing the eye to the Buddha images seated at the far western ends.

The principal chedi complex, which houses the Buddha relic, stands grandly, if a little cramped, at the heart of the compound, built on an east–west axis in an almost continuous line with two viharns. Its elegant centrepiece follows a design termed **lotus-bud chedi** (after the bulbous finial ornamenting the top of a tower), and is classic late Sukhothai in style. This lotus-bud reference is an established religious symbol: though Sukhothai architects were the first to incorporate it into building design – since when it's come to be regarded as a hallmark of the era – the lotus bud had for centuries represented the purity of the Buddha's thoughts nudging through the muddy swamp and finally bursting into flower. The chedi stands surrounded by eight smaller towers – some with their stucco decoration partially reapplied, and some with a Buddha image in one of their four alcoves – on a square platform decorated with a procession of walking Buddha-like monks, another artistic innovation of the Sukhothai school, here depicted in stucco relief. Flanking the chedi platform are two square mondops, built for the colossal standing Buddhas still inside them today.

The grassy patch across the road from Wat Mahathat marks the site of the former palace, of which nothing now remains.

Wat Sri Sawai
300m southwest of Wat Mahathat, central zone

The triple corn-cob-shaped prangs of **Wat Sri Sawai** make for an interesting architectural comparison with Wat Mahathat. Just as the lotus-bud chedi epitomizes Sukhothai aspirations, the prang represents Khmer ideals: Wat Sri Sawai was probably conceived as a Hindu shrine several centuries before the Sukhothai kingdom established itself here. The stucco reliefs decorating the prangs feature a few weatherworn figures from both Hindu and Buddhist mythology, which suggests that the shrine was later pressed into Buddhist service; the square base inside the central prang supported the Khmer Shiva lingam (phallus), while the viharn out front is a later, Buddhist, addition.

Wat Trapang Ngoen
Just west of Wat Mahathat, central zone

The particularly fine lotus-bud chedi of **Wat Trapang Ngoen** rises gracefully against the backdrop of distant hills. Aligned with the chedi on the symbolic east–west axis are the dilapidated viharn and, east of that, on an island in the middle of the "silver pond" after which the wat is named, the remains of the bot. Walk the connecting plank to the bot to appreciate the setting from the water. North of the chedi, notice the fluid lines of the walking Buddha mounted onto a brick wall – a classic example of Sukhothai sculpture.

Wat Sra Sri
North of Wat Trapang Ngoen, central zone

Taking the water feature one step further than its neighbour, **Wat Sra Sri** commands a fine position on two connecting islands north of Wat Trapang Ngoen. The bell-shaped chedi with a tapering spire and square base shows a strong Sri Lankan influence, and the metallic replica of a freestanding walking Buddha is typical Sukhothai.

Wat Phra Phai Luang
North zone, about 500m north of the old city walls: exit the central zone north of Wat Sra Sri

About 500m north of the earthen ramparts of the old city walls, a footbridge (also accessible to bicycles and motorbikes) leads you across to **Wat Phra Phai Luang**, one of the ancient city's oldest structures. The three prangs, only one of which remains intact, were built by the Khmers before the Thais founded their own kingdom here and, as at the similar Wat Sri Sawai, you can still see some of the stucco reliefs showing both Hindu and Buddhist figures. Others are displayed in Ramkhamhaeng National Museum. It's thought that Wat Phra Phai Luang was at the centre of the old Khmer town and that it was as important then as Wat Mahathat later became to the Thais. When the shrine was converted into a Buddhist temple, the viharn and chedi were built to the east of the prangs: the reliefs of the (now headless and armless) seated Buddhas are still visible around the base of the chedi. Also discernible among the ruins are parts of a large reclining Buddha and a mondop containing four huge standing Buddhas in different postures.

Wat Sri Chum
About 750m southwest from the Wat Phra Phai Luang compound, north zone

Wat Sri Chum boasts Sukhothai's largest surviving Buddha image. The enormous, heavily restored brick-and-stucco seated Buddha, measuring more than 11m from knee to knee and almost 15m high, peers through the slit in its custom-built mondop. Check out the elegantly tapered fingers, complete with gold-leaf nail varnish. A passageway – rarely opened up, unfortunately – runs inside the mondop wall, taking you from ground level on the left-hand side to the Buddha's eye level and then up again to the roof, affording a

2

bird's-eye view of the image. Legend has it that this Buddha would sometimes speak to favoured worshippers, and this staircase would have enabled tricksters to climb up and hold forth, unseen; one of the kings of Sukhothai is said to have brought his troops here to spur them on to victory with encouraging words from the Buddha.

Wat Chang Lom

East zone, about 1.5km east of the main entrance

The only temple of interest in the **east zone** is canalside **Wat Chang Lom**, beside the bicycle track to New Sukhothai and just off the road to the new city. Chang Lom means "surrounded by elephants" and the main feature here is a large Sri Lankan-style, bell-shaped chedi encircled by a frieze of elephants.

Wat Saphan Hin

West zone, almost 5km west of the Ramkhamhaeng National Museum

Be prepared for a long haul out to the **west zone**, in the forested hills off the main road to Tak. Marking the western edge of the Old City, the hilltop temple of **Wat Saphan Hin** should – with sufficiently powerful telescopic lenses – give a fantastic panorama of the Old City's layout, but with the naked eye conjures up only an indistinct vista of trees and stones. If you make it this far, chances are you'll share the view only with the large standing Buddha at the top. The wat is reached via a steep 300m-long pathway of stone slabs (hence the name, which means "Stone Bridge") that starts from a track running south from the Tak road. This is the easiest approach if you're on a bike as it's completely flat; the other route, which follows a lesser, more southerly, road out of the Old City, takes you over several hills and via the elephant temple of **Wat Chang Rob**, 3km south of Saphan Hin.

Sangkhalok Museum

2km east of New Sukhothai on Highway 101, close to the junction with Highway 12, the road to Phitsanulok • Mon–Fri 8am–6pm, Sat & Sun 10am–8pm • B100 • Samlor ride from central New Sukhothai should cost no more than B40–50

If you have a serious interest in ceramics you'll probably enjoy the Sukhothai-era exhibits at the privately owned **Sangkhalok Museum** – ask for one of the informative museum booklets at the ticket desk to get the most out of a visit. The ground floor of the museum displays ceramic artefacts from twelfth- to sixteenth-century Sukhothai, including **water pipes** used in the city's widely admired irrigation system, and the lotus-bud **lamps** whose gracefully shaped perforations both shield the flame and diffuse its light and are still as popular in Thailand today. Some of the finest pieces are the **bowls** with scalloped rims and bluish-green patterns and the characteristically expressive **figurines**; unusually, many of these works are signed by the potter. This style of pottery has become known as Sangkhalok, after the prosperous city of Sawankhalok, near Si Satchanalai (see p.254), which was part of the kingdom of Sukhothai at that time. Also on show are ceramics from twelfth-century Burma, China and Vietnam, all of which were found in the area and so show who the citizens of Sukhothai were trading with at that time, as well as some of the most exquisite ceramics produced in northern Thailand during the Lanna era (thirteenth to sixteenth centuries). Upstairs, the focus is on the cultural significance of certain artefacts and their recurring motifs.

Wat Thawet

8km north of New Sukhothai along the River Yom • Donation requested • Best reached by bicycle (taking a tuk-tuk would mean having to travel along the busy main road)

Famous for its one hundred different, brightly painted, concrete statues depicting morality tales and Buddhist fables, **Wat Thawet** is quite a popular sight for Thai tourists, though farangs tend to find it a bit tacky. The temple **sculpture park** was conceived by a local monk in the 1970s, with the aim of creating a "learning garden" where visitors could learn about the Buddhist ideas of hell and karmic retribution. For example, people who have spent their lives killing animals are depicted here with the head of a buffalo, pig, cock or elephant, while those who have been greedy and materialistic stand naked and undernourished, their ribs and backbones sticking out. Then there's the alcoholic who is forced to drink boiling liquids that make his concrete guts literally explode on to the ground.

Part of the appeal of Wat Thawet is that it makes a good focus for a very pleasant **bicycle trip** from Sukhothai, a 16km round-trip that is almost entirely along peaceful canalside tracks. From New Sukhothai, follow riverside Thanon Ratchathani north beyond *Lotus Village* until you hit the bypass. Cross the bypass and take the concrete path from the west edge of the bridge. Stay on this calm, scenic track for the next 8km, passing typical wooden houses, several banana plantations, a wooden suspension bridge and, about 1km before the temple, going beneath a major flyover; Wat Thawet is beside the second wooden suspension bridge. Cycling Sukhothai leads bike trips here too (see p.248).

Ramkhamhaeng National Park

Around 30km southwest of Sukhothai • B100 • ☎ 055 619200, ⓦ dnp.go.th • To get to the main park entrance from New Sukhothai, follow Highway 101 towards Kamphaeng Phet for 19km, then take side road 1319 (signed to Khao Luang) for the final 16km to park headquarters; Kamphaeng Phet-bound buses will take you to the junction, but you'll have trouble hitching to the park from here, so renting private transport is advised

The forested area immediately to the southwest of Sukhothai is protected as **Ramkhamhaeng National Park** and makes a pleasant enough day-trip on a motorbike. The park is home to waterfalls and herbal gardens and, if you're feeling sufficiently energetic, there's the possibility of a challenging mountain climb.

The headquarters stands at the foot of the eastern flank of the highest peak, **Khao Luang** (1185m), which can be climbed in around four hours, but only safely from November to February. Several very steep trails run up to the summit from here, but they are not very clearly marked; the first couple of kilometres are the worst, after which the incline eases up a little. From the top you should get a fine view over the Sukhothai plains. If you want to camp on the summit, simply alert the rangers at the park headquarters, and they will arrange for their colleague at the summit to rent you a tent; you need to take your own food and water. Fan-cooled **bungalows** in the area around the park headquarters can be rented for B1200.

Thung Luang Pottery Village

16km south of New Sukhothai on Highway 101

En route to or from Ramkhamhaeng National Park you could make a detour to **Thung Luang Pottery Village** (signposted), where nearly every household is involved in the production of earthenware pots, vases and statuary. Originally people here made basic pots for storing rice and water – crucial at a time when the community's livelihood depended on farming – but in recent years artisans have diversified their trade. Their lamps and table decorations are often purchased by Thai resort hotels and used to add colour to outdoor restaurants. Once you've turned off the main road, you'll pass a line of roadside stalls, but to enter the heart of the pottery neighbourhoods continue for another kilometre or so, past a school and two temples.

ARRIVAL AND DEPARTURE **SUKHOTHAI**

BY PLANE
Bangkok Airways has two daily flights in each direction between Bangkok and Sukhothai (1hr 20min).

From/to the airport The tiny airport is about 25km north of town (half way to Si Satchanalai). Shuttle buses transfer passengers to New Sukhothai hotels for B180 per person and to the Old City for B300; the return shuttle to the airport departs from the Sukhothai Travel Agency in New Sukhothai only (see p.251), and from the Old City hotels, though most New Sukhothai guesthouses do their own airport transfer for about B250–300 per person.

Reservations and tickets The local Bangkok Airways office (☎ 055 647224) is at the airport, though you can also buy air tickets from the more central Sukhothai Travel Agency (see p.251).

BY BUS

New Sukhothai has direct bus connections with many major provincial capitals and makes a good staging point between Chiang Mai and Bangkok, as well as an easy day-trip from Phitsanulok. All buses use the Sukhothai bus terminal, located about 3km west of New Sukhothai's town centre, just off the bypass (note that buses from Mae Sot and Tak pass the Old City en route).

Destinations Ayutthaya (14 daily; 6hr); Bangkok (up to 23 daily; 6–7hr); Chiang Mai (up to 19 daily; 5–6hr); Chiang Rai (4 daily; 8–9hr); Kamphaeng Phet (14 daily; 1hr–1hr 30min); Khon Kaen (5 daily; 6–7hr); Lampang (16 daily; 4hr); Mae Sot (8 daily; 2hr 30min–3hr); Nan (2 daily; 7hr); Phitsanulok (every 30min; 1hr); Phrae (2 daily; 4hr); Si Satchanalai (every 30min; 1hr–1hr 45min); Tak (every 30min; 1hr 30min).

BY TRAIN AND BUS

If you're coming from Bangkok, Chiang Mai or anywhere in between, one option is to take the train to Phitsanulok and then change onto one of the half-hourly buses to New Sukhothai (1hr). For details on getting from the train station to the bus pick-up point, see the Phitsanulok "Arrival and departure" section (p.236).

GETTING AROUND

FROM THE BUS STATION TO THE NEW SUKHOTHAI GUESTHOUSES

To get from the bus station to the New Sukhothai guesthouses listed here, you can either use the public songthaew (B10) and get off by the river, which puts you less than a 10min walk from most accommodation, or you can charter a motorbike taxi, tuk-tuk, samlor or songthaew (B50–60/vehicle); rates are posted in the bus terminal. Otherwise, many guesthouses will pick you up for free – just ring ahead.

GETTING TO AND AROUND THE OLD CITY

By bus Public buses from the bus terminal pass by the Old City (approximately hourly 6.30am–6.20pm).

By songthaew Songthaews from New Sukhothai (every 15min; 15min; B30; see map p.240 for location) terminate around 500m northeast of the central zone entrance point, beside a couple of cycle-rental outlets.

By tuk-tuk New Sukhothai guesthouses can organize a tuk-tuk to drop you in Old Sukhothai for B150. Tuk-tuks at the New Sukhothai bus station and in the town offer a 4hr tour of the ruins plus return transport for about B600.

By bicycle Cycling makes a peaceful and pleasant way to see Sukhothai and its surroundings – see our box below for more details.

By trolley bus During busy times, a trolley bus takes visitors round the central zone for B20 per person, starting from near the museum and passing all the main sites.

CYCLING AROUND SUKHOTHAI

You can **cycle** from New Sukhothai to the historical park along a peaceful canalside track. To pick up the track, start from the bridge in New Sukhothai, cycle west along the main road to the historical park for about 3km (beyond Sukhothai Hospital, just before the Big C hypermarket) until you reach a temple with an impressive gold-and-white-decorated gateway on the right-hand side. A narrow track between this temple and the adjacent little petrol station takes you via a small bridge to a track that runs along the north bank of Khlong Maerampan, nearly all the way to the Old City. It's an easy 14km ride. Near the end you cross a major road to pick up the final stretch of track; then, after reaching the elephant statues at the ruins of Wat Chang Lom (see p.246), cross the bridge on your left to regain the main road into the historical park, about 1.5km away. **Bicycle rental** is available from a few guesthouses in New Sukhothai and in great numbers at the historical park where outlets near the songthaew stop rent them out for B30.

Alternatively, join a **guided cycle tour** around the historical park (B750) with Belgian–Thai-run Cycling Sukhothai (☎085 083 1864, ⓦ cycling-sukhothai.com). They also offer recommended **sunset bicycle tours** around local villages and countryside most afternoons from 4pm (B300) plus longer half-day tours (B600). All trips include mountain bike and transfers, and are bookable through most guesthouses.

2

BY MOTORBIKE

For getting around the wider area, motorbike rental is available at several places on Thanon Pravetnakorn and at nearby *Poo Restaurant*. Alternatively try *J&J Guest House* (B250/day).

INFORMATION

Tourist information The TAT office at 139 Thanon Charodvithitong (daily 8.30am–4.30pm; ☎055 616228, ✉tatsukho@tat.or.th) is the best place to come for maps and information on the historical park. Alternatively, friendly tour guide Naa offers free information and advice by phone or in person at her cookery school (see p.251).

Guidebook Dawn F. Rooney's lively and beautifully photographed *Ancient Sukhothai* is a great guidebook, not only to Sukhothai's Old City but also to those of Si Satchanalai and Kamphaeng Phet; you'll need to buy it before you arrive though (see p.789).

ACCOMMODATION

There's plenty of attractive accommodation in Sukhothai; just be wary of commission-hungry tuk-tuk drivers falsely claiming places are full, no good or no longer in business.

NEW SUKHOTHAI

At Home 184/1 Thanon Wichien Chamnong ☎055 610172, ⊛athomesukhothai.com. Delightful, genuinely welcoming guesthouse that's been converted from a fifty-year-old family home to accommodate eleven large, attractive en-suite rooms. The most atmospheric are upstairs in the teak-walled, teak-floored part of the house, which is set back from the road in a garden with a large pond. Free internet and wi-fi. **B850**

Ban Thai Guest House 38 Thanon Pravetnakorn ☎055 610163, ✉banthai_guesthouse@yahoo.com. On the west bank of the Yom River, this comfortable, traveller-oriented budget option comprises several attractive wood-floored rooms in a single-storey house with shared bathrooms and an inviting terrace out front, plus some wooden bungalows with private bathroom in a little garden to the back. Home-made yoghurt is a breakfast favourite, and the *matsaman* curry is popular too. Wi-fi, internet access and free pick-up from the bus station. Shared bathroom **B200**, fan bungalows **B350**, a/c bungalows **B500**

EZ House 240/4 Thanon Charodvithitong, opposite the Shell garage ☎055 611711, ⊛ezhouse.multiply.com. The six hotel-style rooms here are on the third floor, above the mobile phone shop – not the most inspiring location, but with TV, a/c, a fridge and an en-suite bathroom in every room, it represents good value. It's a long walk from town though, with few decent places to eat or drink nearby. **B350**

J&J Guest House 15 Soi Kuhasuwan, around 100m north of the bridge ☎055 620095. Located right by the River Yom, J&J has eight comfortably furnished bungalows with attractive en-suite bathrooms, TVs and handbasins in the shape of blooming flowers. The rooms are set around a quiet lawned area, while the restaurant, which serves delicious home-baked bread, faces the water. Thai–Belgian owners Jacqui and Jim are kind and welcoming, and can help out with tours and motorbike hire (B250/day). Fan **B600**, a/c **B700**

Lotus Village 170 Thanon Ratchathani, also accessible from Thanon Rajuthit ☎055 621484, ⊛lotus-village .com. Elegantly simple mid-priced accommodation in a traditional Thai compound of beautiful teak houses set around a mature tropical garden with lotus ponds. All but the superior rooms have polished teak floors: some are in detached bungalows, others have either fan or a/c and there's also a family house that can sleep six. There's wi-fi, internet and a charming spa here too (see p.251). Reception shuts at 9pm. Fan rooms **B950**, a/c **B1250**

Ruean Thai Hotel 181/20 Soi Praharuammit, off Thanon Charodvithitong ☎055 612444, ⊛rueanthai hotel.com. This idiosyncratic thirty-room hotel has been painstakingly assembled from ten century-old teak houses from the Sukhothai area. The main two-storey complex is built around a central swimming pool, its attractive facades fashioned from salvaged teak walls, windows and doors, and steeply gabled roofs; the interiors are modern, individually furnished and with good-quality contemporary bathrooms. The rooms with most character are the three large, homely doubles in a separate building above the restaurant. All rooms have a/c, fridges and wi-fi; price depends on the size. There are two restaurants, free bicycle rental and free transfers from the bus station and around town. **B1200**

★ **TR Guest House** 27/5 Thanon Pravetnakorn ☎055 611663, ⊛sukhothaibudgetguesthouse.com. Large a/c doubles in a spotlessly clean concrete block, plus slightly less stylish but otherwise identical fan rooms for B150 less. There's also a handful of en-suite bungalows out back, reached through a car park; these have mozzy nets but not much else in the way of decoration. Toh and Long, the helpful and knowledgable couple who run the place, can provide you with an excellent map of the area, and will pick you up from the bus station if you arrive during the daytime. Motorbikes for rent (B150–250/day). Fan **B250**, a/c **B400**, bungalows **B400**

2

THE OLD CITY AREA

Old City Guest House Thanon Charodvithitong, a few metres from the access road to the museum and central zone ☎ 055 697515; map p.242. Good-value guesthouse offering a big range of options in two-storey buildings around a yard (with parking), set back from the road. Choose between small, rather dark but very cheap rooms with shared bathrooms; attractive, well-priced, en-suite fan rooms; and large, quite plush, a/c doubles with TV. Possibly the best location for seeing the main ruins. Fan B300, a/c B500

Orchid Hibiscus Guest House Just off Route 1272, about 1.5km southeast of the main entrance to the historical park ☎ 081 962 7698, ⓦ orchidhibiscus -guesthouse.com; map p.242. Tranquil Italian–Thai-managed garden haven within easy cycling reach of the Old City. The brick bungalows are furnished with four-poster beds, a/c and mosquito nets and are ranged around a pretty tropical flower garden and swimming pool. It also has a couple of more private teak bungalows, plus, in a compound across the road, three- and four-bed family houses for rent. Email for cheapest rates. Room B1000, bungalows B1850, family room B2000

Thai Thai Near Route 1272, just east of Orchid Hibiscus Guest House ☎ 084 932 1006, ⓦ thaithaisukhothai .com; map p.242. Ten big and luxurious bungalows, each with its own breezy balcony; inside, mosquito nets are bunched around the four-poster beds with posies of fake flowers, and the en-suite bathrooms have attractive emerald-coloured tiles. Other nice touches include towels arranged into the shape of swans. Every room has wi-fi, TV and a fridge. Bikes for hire (B50) and breakfast included. B1200

SUKHOTHAI AIRPORT

Sukhothai Heritage Resort Just outside the airport compound ☎ 055 647564, ⓦ sukhothaiheritage.com. Calm, tastefully designed four-star hotel owned by Bangkok Airways and set in lovely rural surrounds of organic rice fields, an orchid farm and lotus ponds. The hotel garden is artfully planted with shrubs and hedges, just like the airport, and there are two pools, a restaurant and a library. Rooms are modern with verandas over-looking the pool, flat-screen TVs and DVD players; there's wi-fi throughout and local cycling tours are encouraged. There's little in the immediate vicinity, however. B2900

EATING AND DRINKING

The local speciality is a pungent bowl of **Sukhothai noodles**: thin rice noodles served in a dark, slightly sweet broth flavoured with soy sauce, coriander and chilli and spiked with chunks of pork crackling, green beans and peanuts. In New Sukhothai you should be able to find them, and many other good cheap dishes, at the **hot-food stalls** and streetside tables that set up every evening in front of Wat Ratchathani on Thanon Charodvithitong and further west near *Poo Restaurant*. There's also a permanent covered area for night-market-style **restaurants** on the soi between Thanon Ramkhamhaeng and Thanon Nikhon Kasem. In the Old City, handy for Wat Mahathat, are the stalls and restaurants serving hot food and fresh coffee in the lot just south of the main central zone entrance.

Chopper Bar Thanon Pravetnakorn. Farang-oriented upstairs terrace and bar with occasional live music and a vague biker theme. The menu runs to steak as well as seafood. Cocktails from B70. Daily 5pm–12.30am.

★ **Dream Café** 88/1 Thanon Singhawat. Dark and cosy, with walls and windowsills full of curios and Thai antiques, this rather cool, long-running Sukhothai insti-tution serves great food (two courses for around B300) and is very popular. Highlights include *tom yam* with pork spare ribs and young tamarind, fresh Vietnamese-style spring rolls, and deep-fried banana-flower fritters. Choose also from twenty different ice-cream sundaes and a range of stamina-enhancing herbal drinks (B35) – plus gin-and-tonics. Daily 10am–11pm.

J&J Guest House 15 Soi Kuhasuwan, around 100m north of the bridge ☎ 055 620095. Fresh home-made baguettes are served until stocks last at *J&J's* peaceful restaurant, which overlooks the river. Other favourites include a mean spaghetti bolognese. Open for breakfast, lunch and dinner.

Khun Tanode Thanon Charodvithitong. Low-key, laidback, well-priced little riverside restaurant that's

popular with locals and is prettily illuminated at night. Try the local speciality – crispy-fried chicken drumsticks in Sukhothai sauce – or mussels cooked in a herb sauce. Most mains B60–100. Daily 10am–midnight.

Kru lew Thanon Wichien Chamnong, corner of Soi Mahasaranon 1, about 75m north of At Home guest-house. An "OTOP" ("One Tambon One Product") sign, signifying traditional rural produce, announces this award-winning, folksy lunch spot that's locally famous for its aromatic parcels of *phat thai* wrapped in thin omelette (from B20), its fresh Vietnamese-style *naem nueng* herb and pork spring rolls (B70) – and its Sukhothai noodles. Watch the white-capped cooks in their open-plan kitchens. Daily 10am–3pm.

Poo Restaurant Thanon Charodvithitong. Streetside travellers' bar-restaurant that serves all the standard Thai dishes plus cheap draught Chang beer, Belgian beer (from B120) and cocktails (from B80). Also rents motorbikes and gives Thai massages. Daily 8am–late.

Rom Poa At the edge of the covered night market between Thanon Ramkhamhaeng and Thanon Nikhon

Kasem. Popular place with pushy touts but a perfectly decent menu of spicy jelly-thread noodle salads (*yam wun sen*), curries, lots of seafood dishes, fruit shakes and a reasonable vegetarian selection. Most dishes B50–70, though that's still more expensive than many other stalls in the night market. Evenings only.

SHOPPING

In the Old City, several shops just outside the park entrance sell reproduction antique furniture and ceramics.

Usa Sungkalok Sukhothai Just outside the central zone on the narrow road that runs between the museum and Wat Trapang Tong ☎ 055 633058. For the best range of traditional-style ceramics, especially copies of historic Sangkhalok and Sukhothai designs and glazes, visit this friendly ceramics factory.

DIRECTORY

Banks, exchange and ATMs In the Old City there's a currency exchange booth (daily 8.30am–12.30pm) next to the museum, and several ATMs on the approach road. New Sukhothai has many banks and ATMs.

Cookery courses One- and two-day courses led by excellent tour guide Naa at her new cooking school in the Old City (423/6 Moo 3, 300m south of the museum; ☎ 089 858 9864; B750/person/day). Accommodation is available for those on longer courses.

Hospital The government-run Sukhothai Hospital (☎ 055 611782) is west of New Sukhothai on the road to Sukhothai Historical Park; there's a more central 24hr clinic on Thanon Singhawat.

Internet access At many guesthouses and some internet centres in New Sukhothai, including Oka-ne Online II on Thanon Prasertpong, and on the approach road just outside the Old City.

Massage and spa treatments Most luxuriously at Baan Spa, part of *Lotus Village* (see p.249), where treatments take place in a lovely teak house and include turmeric body scrubs, herbal saunas, waxing and Thai massage (B500/1hr). There are many other cheaper massage places at guesthouses in the New City.

Post Office Thanon Nikhon Kasem, about 1km south of the bridge (Mon–Fri 8.30am–4.30pm).

Tourist police For all emergencies, call the tourist police on ☎ 1155, or go to the local police station on Thanon Singhawat.

Travel agent Domestic and international air tickets can be bought through Sukhothai Travel Service, 10–12 Thanon Singhawat (Mon–Fri 8am–5pm, Sat 8am–noon; ☎ 055 613075, ✉ sukhothai_travel@hotmail.com).

Visa run *J&J Guest House* does a day-trip visa run to the Burmese border near Mae Sot (B1600/person excluding entry into Burma; min 2 people).

Si Satchanalai

In the mid-thirteenth century, Sukhothai cemented its power by establishing several satellite towns, of which the most important was **SI SATCHANALAI**, 57km upriver from Sukhothai on the banks of the Yom. Now a UNESCO-listed **historical park**, the partially restored ruins of **Muang Kao Si Satchanalai** have a quieter ambience than the grander models at Sukhothai Historical Park, and the additional attractions of the riverside wat in nearby **Chalieng**, the **Sangkhalok pottery kilns** in Ban Ko Noi and the **Sathorn Textile Museum** in New Si Satchanalai combine to make the area worth exploring.

The Historical Park (Muang Kao Si Satchanalai)

Daily 6am–6pm • B100 or B240 for a ticket that includes entry to the Chalieng area (Wat Phra Si Ratana Mahathat) and the kilns; vehicles charged at B10–50, depending on size

Just across the Yom River from Route 101 sits **Si Satchanalai Historical Park**, or **Muang Kao Si Satchanalai**, where you'll find most of the main monuments. At the entrance on the park's eastern side, there are foodstalls and a trolley bus (operates during busy times only).

Muang Kao Si Satchanalai Information Centre

South of Wat Nang Phya, on the road that skirts around the central area of ruins • Daily 8am–5pm

Once inside the park it's worth heading to this friendly information centre, set around tranquil gardens, which provides useful background information on the area and shows

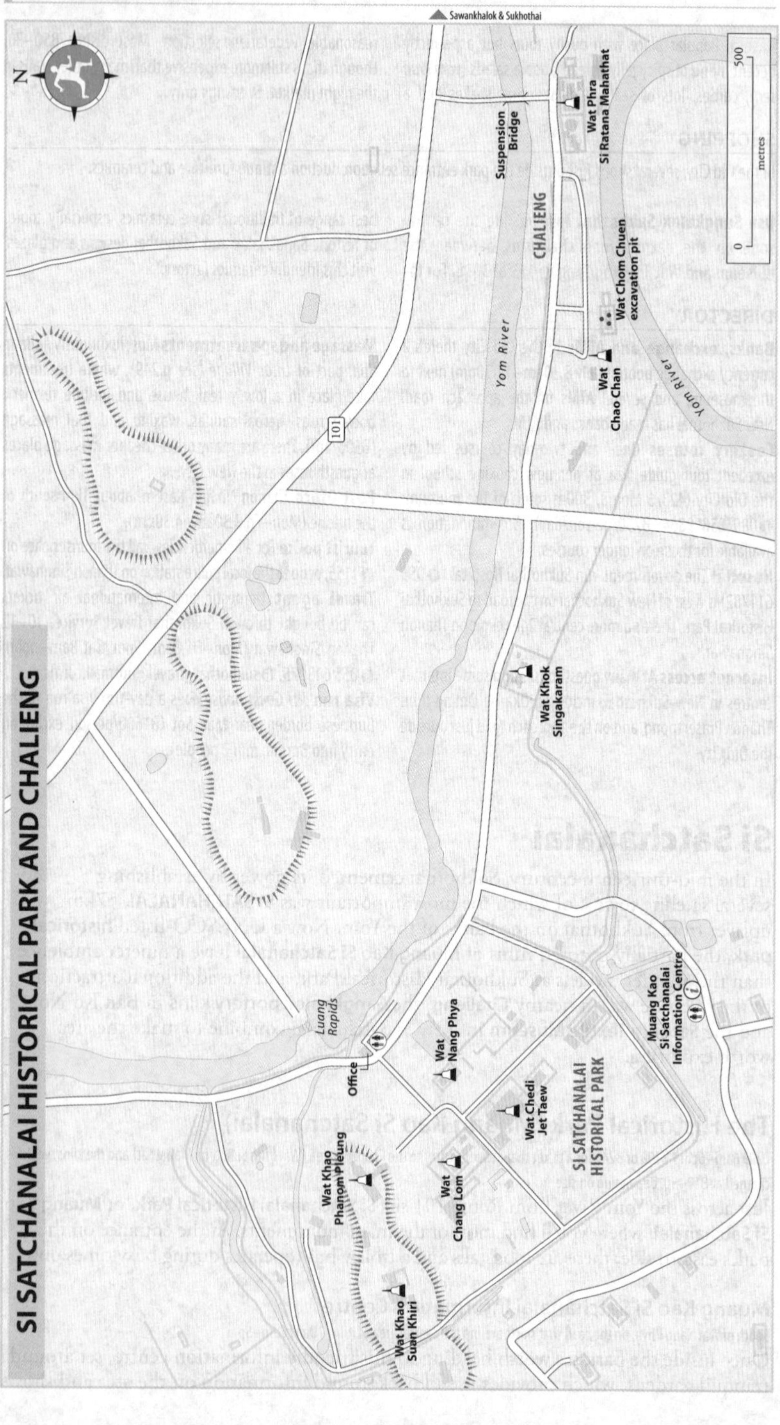

2

SI SATCHANALAI HISTORICAL PARK AND CHALIENG

Sawankhalok & Sukhothai

N

Yom River

Yom River

Suspension Bridge

CHALIENG

Wat Phra Si Ratana Mahathat

Wat Chom Chuen excavation pit

Wat Chao Chan

101

Wat Khok Singakaram

New Si Satchanalai & Sathorn Textile Museum

Ban Ko Noi Kilns

Luang Rapids

Office

Wat Nang Phya

Wat Chedi Jet Taew

Muang Kao Si Satchanalai Information Centre

SI SATCHANALAI HISTORICAL PARK

Wat Khao Phanom Pleung

Wat Chang Lom

Wat Khao Suan Khiri

0   500
metres

how its location, on a plain between the Yom River and the Khao Phra Sri ridge, made it ideal for human habitation. Exhibits include shards of pottery from the excavation at nearby Wat Chom Chuen and some polished stone tools from Tha Chai subdistrict. There's also a large-scale model of the entire UNESCO World Heritage Site, showing how the temples hug the bend in the river.

Wat Chang Lom
Towards the centre of the park, southwest of the main entrance

Most circuits begin with the most striking set of ruins, the elephant temple of **Wat Chang Lom**, whose centrepiece is a huge, Sri Lankan-style, bell-shaped chedi set on a square base studded with 39 life-sized elephant buttresses (those in Sukhothai and Kamphaeng Phet are smaller). A mahout and his elephant sometimes hang out here to prove the point. Many of the elephant reliefs are in good repair, with much of their stucco flesh still intact; others now have their bulky laterite-brick innards exposed.

Wat Chedi Jet Taew
Just across from Wat Chang Lom

Wat Chedi Jet Taew has seven rows of small chedis thought to enshrine the ashes of Si Satchanalai's royal rulers, which makes it the ancient city's most important temple. One of the 34 chedis is an elegant scaled-down replica of the hallmark lotus-bud chedi at Sukhothai's Wat Mahathat; some of the others are copies of other important wats from the vicinity. Several have fine stucco-covered Buddha images in their alcoves, including a famously beautiful one of the Buddha sheltered by a naga (now with restored head), also reproduced in Ramkhamhaeng National Museum.

Wat Nang Phya
A few hundred metres south of Wat Chedi Jet Taew

Wat Nang Phya is remarkable for the original stucco reliefs on its viharn wall, which remain in fine condition; stucco is a hardy material that sets soon after being first applied, and becomes even harder when exposed to rain – hence its ability to survive seven hundred years in the open. The balustraded wall has slit windows and is entirely covered with intricate floral motifs.

Wat Khao Phanom Pleung and Wat Khao Suan Khiri

About 600m north of Wat Chang Lom, the hilltop ruins of Wat Khao Phanom Pleung and nearby Wat Khao Suan Khiri afford splendid aerial views of different quarters of the ancient city. The sole remaining intact chedi of **Wat Khao Phanom Pleung** sits on top of the lower of the hills and used to be flanked by a set of smaller chedis built to entomb the ashes of Si Satchanalai's important personages – the ones who merited some special memorial, but didn't quite make the grade for Wat Chedi Jet Taew. The temple presumably got its name, which means "mountain of sacred fire", from the cremation rituals held on the summit.

Wat Khao Suan Khiri's huge chedi, which graces the summit 200m northwest, has definitely seen better days, but the views from its platform – south over the main temple ruins and north towards the city walls and entrance gates – are worth the climb.

Wat Phra Si Ratana Mahathat
Just over 2km southeast of the Historical Park • B100 for Chalieng area plus B20 for admission to the temple, or B240 for a ticket that includes entry to Chalieng, the Historical Park and the kilns; vehicles charged at B10–50, depending on size

Before Sukhothai asserted control of the region and founded Si Satchanalai, the Khmers governed the area known as **Chalieng**, which is cradled in a bend in the Yom River. Just about all that now remains of Chalieng is **Wat Phra Si Ratana Mahathat**, whose compound, aligned east–west and encircled by a now sunken wall of laterite blocks, contains structures thought to date back to the Khmer era, but with later additions by Sukhothai and Ayutthayan builders. If you approach from the wooden suspension bridge you'll enter via the semi-submerged eastern gateway, passing beneath a hefty Khmer-style carved lintel that was hewn from a single block of stone. Inside, the compound is dominated by a towering corncob prang, the main shrine, which was likely remodelled during the Ayutthayan era and whose exterior has recently been renovated with all-over stucco decorations. The ruined viharn in front of the prang enshrines a large seated Buddha sculpted in typical Sukhothai style, with hand gestures symbolizing his triumph over temptation. The tall stucco relief of a walking Buddha to the left is also classic Sukhothai and is regarded as one of the finest of its genre. Immediately to the west of the prang, the remains of the octagonal laterite platform and its bell-shaped chedi are believed to date from a different era, possibly considerably earlier. A mondop containing a large standing Buddha guards one side and looks towards the River Yom; a second viharn, containing two Buddha images, occupies the other flank.

Ban Ko Noi Kilns

7km upstream from Si Satchanalai Historical Park • Daily 8am–4.30pm • B100 or B240 for a ticket that includes entry to Chalieng and the Historical Park

Endowed with high-quality clay, the area around Si Satchanalai – known as Sawankhalok or Sangkhalok during the Ayutthaya period – commanded an international reputation as a ceramics centre from the mid-fourteenth to the end of the fifteenth century, producing pieces still rated among the finest in the world. More than two hundred **kilns** have been unearthed in and around Si Satchanalai to date, and it's estimated that there could once have been a thousand in all. One of the main groups of kilns is in the village of **BAN KO NOI**, which is about 7km upstream from the park entry point and can be reached by bicycle by following the very pleasant, almost traffic-free road beside the river (not the one going into the park) through hamlets fringed with flowering shrubs and fruit trees.

Sangkhalok Kiln Preservation Centre

Daily 9am–4pm • B30

At Ban Ko Noi, four excavated kilns have been roofed and turned into the **Sangkhalok Kiln Preservation Centre**, but, unfortunately, they are poorly served by almost nonexistent English-language captions (you'll have a much better idea of what you're looking at if you've already been to the Ramkhamhaeng National Museum in Sukhothai Historical Park).

Two of the kilns are up-draught kilns and two are cross-draught kilns, the latter generating a greater and more consistent heat, which enabled the production of glazed ware. Most Sangkhalok ceramics were glazed – the grey-green celadon, probably introduced by immigrant Chinese potters, was especially popular – and typically decorated with fish or chrysanthemum motifs. A small display of **Sangkhalok ceramics** gives a hint of the pieces that were fired here: domestic items such as pots, decorated plates and lidded boxes; decorative items like figurines, temple sculptures and temple roof tiles; and items for export, particularly to Indonesia and the Philippines, where huge Sangkhalok storage jars were used as burial urns.

At busy times, stalls across the road from the Preservation Centre sell reproduction ceramics and "antiques". Several of Thailand's major museums feature collections of ceramics from both Si Satchanalai and Sukhothai under the umbrella label of Sangkhalok, and there's a dedicated collection of Sangkhalok wares just outside New Sukhothai (see p.246).

The Sathorn Textile Museum

11km north of the Historical Park, at the northern end of the modern town of Si Satchanalai, on the east side of Highway 101 • Daily 9am–5pm • Free • Any Sukhothai guesthouse can include a visit to the museum in a Si Satchanalai day-trip, or you can come here on the bus from New Sukhothai, getting off in modern Si Satchanalai rather than at the ruins

The **Sathorn Textile Museum** houses the private collection of Khun Sathorn, who also runs the adjacent textile shop, and he or his staff open up the one-room exhibition for anyone who shows an interest.

Most of the **textiles** on show come from the nearby village of Hat Siew, whose weavers have long specialized in the art of *teen jok*, or hem embroidery, whereby the bottom panel of the sarong or *phasin* (woman's sarong) is decorated with a band of supplementary weft, usually done in exquisitely intricate patterns. Some of the textiles here are almost a hundred years old and many of the *teen jok* **motifs** have symbolic meaning showing what the cloths would have been used for – a sarong or *phasin* used for a marriage ceremony, for example, tends to have a double image, such as two birds facing each other. Elephants also feature quite a lot in Hat Siew weaving, probably a reference to the village custom in which young men who are about to become monks parade on elephants to their ordination ceremony. The tradition continues to this day and elephant parades are held at the mass ordination ceremony every year on April 7 and 8. Modern Hat Siew textiles are sold at the adjacent Sathorn **shop** and at other outlets further south along the main road.

ARRIVAL AND DEPARTURE   SI SATCHANALAI

Si Satchanalai works best as a day-trip from Sukhothai (60km away). The easiest option is to travel with a **car** or **motorbike** from New Sukhothai, or join an organized **tour** from there, which can be organized through many of the guesthouses.

BY BUS
Travelling by public transport, the fastest way to get here from Sukhothai is on one of the a/c buses bound for Chiang Rai; these depart New Sukhothai bus station at 6.40am, 9am, 10.30am and 11.30am and take just over an hour. Local buses depart about every half-hour (also from the bus station), but take almost two hours and sometimes require a change of bus in Sawankhalok. All buses drop passengers on Highway 101 at the signpost for Wat Phra Si Ratana Mahathat, beside a pink archway gate. Pass through it, follow the narrow road and cross the suspension

bridge to the temple, from where it's a further 2km to Si Satchanalai Historical Park. Heading back, the last conveniently timed a/c bus to New Sukhothai passes Old Si Satchanalai at about 4.30pm.

BY TRAIN
One train a day leaves Bangkok for the modern town of Sawankhalok, 20km south of Si Satchanalai, passing Ayutthaya, Lopburi and Phitsanulok en route. On arrival it should be possible to charter a songthaew or motorbike taxi for the rest of the journey to the ruins.

GETTING AROUND

By bicycle The best place to rent a bike (B30) is the small hut at the far end of the suspension bridge, close to Wat Phra Si Ratana Mahathat; otherwise, it's almost another

2km to the next rental place, at the entry to Si Satchanalai Historical Park.

Kamphaeng Phet

KAMPHAENG PHET, 77km south of Sukhothai, was probably founded in the fourteenth century by the kings of Sukhothai as a buffer city between their capital and the increasingly powerful city-state of Ayutthaya. Strategically sited 100m from the east bank of the Ping, the ruined old city has, like Sukhothai and Si Satchanalai before it, been partly restored and opened to the public as a **historical park** and is similarly listed as a UNESCO World Heritage Site. The least visited of the three, it rivals Si Satchanalai for your attention mainly because of the untamed setting and the gracefully weathered statues of its main temple. A new city has grown up on the southeastern boundaries of the old, the usual commercial blandness offset by a riverside park, plentiful flowers and an unusual number of historic wooden houses dotted along the main thoroughfares.

You can even swim off an island in the middle of the river, accessible via a footbridge near Soi 21, a few hundred metres south of the night market. With a few days in the area, you can spend time bird-watching or rafting in the nearby national parks.

The Historical Park (Muang Kao Kamphaeng Phet)

Daily 6am–6pm • B150 for both main zones or B100 for one zone, plus B10–50 per vehicle

Ruins surround modern Kamphaeng Phet on all sides, but the **Historical Park** – or **Muang Kao Kamphaeng Phet** – takes in the two most interesting areas: the oblong zone inside the old city walls, and the forested ("*arunyik*") area just north of that. A tour of both areas involves a 5km round-trip, so you'll need transport. The ruins that dot the landscape across the Ping River, west of the Thanon Tesa roundabout, belong to the even older city of Nakhon Chum, but are very dilapidated.

Parts of the **city walls** that gave Kamphaeng Phet its name are still in good condition, though Highway 101 to Sukhothai now cuts through the enclosed area and a few shops have sprung up along the roadside, making it hard to visualize the fortifications as a whole. Approaching from the Thanon Tesa roundabout, you can either head up Thanon Pin Damri and start your tour at **Wat Phra That** and the **Provincial Museum**, or you enter the compound from the western gate and come in at the back end of **Wat Phra Kaeo**.

The dozen or so ruins in the forested area north of the city walls – east 100m along Highway 101 from behind Wat Phra Kaeo, across the moat and up a road to the left – are all that remains of Kamphaeng Phet's **arunyik** (forest) temples, built here by Sukhothai-era monks in a wooded area to encourage meditation. It's an enjoyably tranquil and atmospheric area to explore if you have your own wheels, with the tumbledown structures peeking out of the thinly planted groves that line the access road; the road winds around a fair bit before eventually rejoining the Sukhothai–Kamphaeng Phet highway to the north of the walled city.

Wat Phra Kaeo
Inside the city walls

Built almost entirely of laterite and adorned with laterite Buddhas, **Wat Phra Kaeo** was the city's central and most important structure, and given the name reserved for temples that have housed the kingdom's most sacred image: the Emerald Buddha, now in the wat of the same name in Bangkok, is thought to have been set down here to rest at some point. Seven centuries later, the Buddha images have been worn away into attractive abstract shadows, often aptly compared to the pitted, spidery forms of Giacometti sculptures, and the slightly unkempt feel to the place makes a perfect setting. Few tools have been unearthed at any of the Kamphaeng Phet sites, giving weight to the theory that the sculptors moulded their statues from the clay-like freshly dug laterite before leaving it to harden. Small, overgrown laterite quarry pits are still visible all over the old city. The statues would originally have been faced with stucco, and restorers have already patched up the central tableau of one reclining and two seated Buddhas. The empty niches that encircle the principal chedi were once occupied by statues of bejewelled lions.

Wat Phra That
Adjoining Wat Phra Kaeo, inside the city walls

Just east of Wat Phra Kaeo is Kamphaeng Phet's second-biggest temple, **Wat Phra That**. Together, Wat Phra That and Wat Phra Kaeo represented the religious centre of the ancient city. Here the central bell-shaped chedi, now picturesquely wreathed in lichen and stray bits of vegetation, is typical of the Sri Lankan style and was built to house a sacred relic.

Kamphaeng Phet National Museum
Just east of Wat Phra That, inside the city walls • Wed–Sun 9am–4pm • B100 • ⊕ thailandmuseum.com

Kamphaeng Phet National Museum takes a look at the fascinating development of the ancient city. The prize exhibit in its upstairs sculpture gallery is the bronze standing **Shiva**: cast in the sixteenth century in Khmer-Ayutthayan style, the statue has had a chequered history – including decapitation by a nineteenth-century German admirer. Also on this floor is an unusual wooden, seventeenth- or eighteenth-century Ayutthayan-style standing Buddha, whose diadem, necklace and even hems are finely carved.

Kamphaeng Phet Ruan Thai Provincial Museum

Next to Kamphaeng Phet National Museum, inside the city walls • Daily 9am–4.30pm • B10

While you're at the National Museum you can't miss the alluring group of recently built traditional-style teak wood *salas* in the adjacent compound. This is the **Kamphaeng Phet Ruan Thai Provincial Museum**, whose captivating exhibits and scale models introduce the history, traditions and contemporary culture of Kamphaeng Phet province.

Wat Phra Non

Arunyik area: the first temple on the left once through the entrance

Wat Phra Non is otherwise known as the Temple of the Reclining Buddha, though you need a good imagination to conjure up the indistinct remains into the once enormous Buddha figure. Gigantic laterite pillars support the viharn that houses the statue; far more ambitious than the usual brick-constructed jobs, these pillars were cut from single slabs of stone from a nearby quarry and would have measured up to 8m in height.

Wat Phra Sri Ariyabot

Arunyik area: immediately to the north of Wat Phra Non

The four Buddha images of **Wat Phra Sri Ariyabot** are in better condition than Wat Phra Non's reclining Buddha. With cores of laterite and skins of stucco, the restored standing and walking images tower over the viharn, while the seated (south-facing) and reclining (north-facing) Buddhas have been eroded into indistinct blobs. The full-grown trees rooted firmly in the raised floor are evidence of just how old the place is.

Wat Chang Rob

Arunyik area: 1km from the entrance gate • Follow the road around the bend from Wat Phra Sri Ariyabot

Wat Chang Rob is crouched on top of a laterite hill. Built to the same Sri Lankan model as its sister temples of the same name in Sukhothai and Si Satchanalai, this "temple surrounded by elephants" retains only the square base of its central bell-shaped chedi. Climb one of its four steep staircases for a view out over the mountains in the west, or just for a different perspective of the 68 elephant buttresses that encircle the base. Sculpted from laterite and stucco, they're dressed in the ceremonial garb fit for such revered animals; floral reliefs can just be made out along the surfaces between neighbouring elephants – the lower level was once decorated with a stucco frieze of flying birds.

ARRIVAL AND DEPARTURE

KAMPHAENG PHET

Most people visit Kampheng Phet as a **day-trip** from Sukhothai, either on one of the direct buses or by arranging a tour and driver through their guesthouse – though there are buses here from other towns, too.

By bus Arriving by bus from Sukhothai or Phitsanulok, you'll enter Kamphaeng Phet from the east and should get off either inside the old city walls or at the Thanon Tesa roundabout rather than wait to be deposited across the river at the terminal, 2km west of town on Highway 1. From the bus terminal, you'll need to hop on a red town songthaew, which will take you to the Thanon Tesa roundabout just east of the river (the most convenient disembarkation point for the ruins), or further into the town centre for most of the hotels and restaurants.

Destinations Bangkok (7 daily; 6hr 30min); Chiang Mai (9 daily; 6hr); Phitsanulok (hourly; 3hr); Sukhothai (hourly; 1hr–1hr 30min); Tak (hourly; 1hr).

GETTING AROUND AND TOURS

By songthaew From the Thanon Tesa roundabout, songthaews generally do a clockwise circle around the new town, running south along Thanon Rajdamnoen (get off at the intersection with Rajdamnoen Soi 4 for *Three J Guest House*), then west along Bumrungrat, north up Thanon Tesa 1 and west out to the bus station.

By bicycle or motorbike *Three J Guest House* is the only place that rents out bicycles and motorbikes – not very convenient for day-trippers.

Tours Should you decide to linger for a few days, *Three J Guest House* not only makes a pleasant base but can also arrange rafting and bird-watching trips in nearby national parks.

ACCOMMODATION

Kor Chok Chai 19/43 Rajdamnoen Soi 8, east of the fruit and veg market ☎ 055 711247. The main budget alternative to *Three J Guest House*, with decent fan and a/c rooms, this hotel is recognizable by its pair of Chinese stone lions guarding the door. Most of its customers are salespeople, so there's some call-girl activity after hours, but it's clean, comfortable and friendly – you'll just have to put up with the old-fashioned brown blankets. Fan B260, a/c B320

Phet Hotel 189 Thanon Bumrungrat, on the southeastern edge of town ☎ 055 712810, ⓦ phethotel .com. The best of the town's central hotels, and the usual choice of tour groups. Though it's dated and rather faded, the a/c rooms are fine and all have TVs and wide views over

the town's skyline; there's wi-fi and internet in the lobby, competent English-speaking staff and a restaurant, bar and nightclub on the premises. Breakfast included. B700

Three J Guest House 79 Thanon Rajwithee, 600m east of the main drag ☎ 081 887 4189, ⓦ threejguesthouse .com. The most traveller-oriented place in Kamphaeng Phet, this pleasant, secluded homestay with a dozen comfortable bungalows is built from rough-cut logs and set in a Chinese-style rock garden at the back of a family home. All rooms have cosy verandas; the cheapest options share bathrooms and the priciest have a/c, and there are family rooms sleeping four people. There's bicycle and motorbike rental, internet access and tours to national parks at weekends. Fan B320, a/c B450, family rooms B800

EATING AND DRINKING

From late afternoon the **night market** is the most enjoyable place to eat. Occupying a covered area in the southern part of the new town between the river and Thanon Tesa 1, it offers a mouthwateringly wide selection of specialist sweet and savoury stalls; try asking for the special local noodle dish, *kway tiaw cha kang rao*, made with cowpeas and pork.

Eagle Pub One block south and east of Kor Chok Chai on Thanon Bumrungrat. For beer, whisky and live music (from 9pm), this is one of the livelier spots in town. Daily until late.

J Café Signed just off Thanon Bumrungrat on Soi 2 at 68/3. For cheap Thai vegetarian food – rice plus a couple of stews, curries or stir-fries for B20–30 – head to this

welcoming streetside café. Daily 7am–2pm.

Ruam Thai South of the Charoensuk intersection on Thanon Wijit. The huge range of cheap noodles, stir-fries and rice dishes served here makes this popular, unpretentious restaurant a reliable choice at any time of day. Usually open daily from lunchtime until around 10pm.

Mae Sot and the border

Located just 6km from Burma, and 100km west of Tak, **MAE SOT** is very much a border town, populated by a rich ethnic mix of Burmese, Karen, Hmong and

HELPING MAE SOT'S BURMESE REFUGEES

There are currently five camps for **refugees** from Burma along the border to the north and south of Mae Sot, and Mae Sot itself is the headquarters for many related international **aid projects**; most of these organizations welcome donations and some are happy to receive visitors and even short-term volunteers; ask at *Ban Thai* guesthouse, Borderline shop and at *Krua Canadian* and *Bai Fern* restaurants. One of the most famous organizations in Mae Sot is the **Mae Tao clinic**, which provides free medical care for around 150,000 Burmese migrants and refugees a year, focusing on those who fall outside the remit of the camps and cannot use the Thai health system. The clinic was founded in 1989 by a Karen refugee, Dr Cynthia, who has won several prestigious international awards for her work; her clinic also trains and equips "backpack teams" of mobile medics who spend months travelling through the Burmese jungle providing healthcare to internally displaced peoples. To help the clinic by giving blood or financial aid, visit the office inside the clinic compound on Thanon Indharakiri (mornings are preferable but the office opens Mon–Sat 9am–4pm; ☎ 055 563644, ⓦ maetaoclinic.org); it's about 1km west of *Ban Thai*, or 350m east of the bus station. The clinic also runs a primary and secondary school and welcomes volunteer health-workers and teachers who can commit for several months.

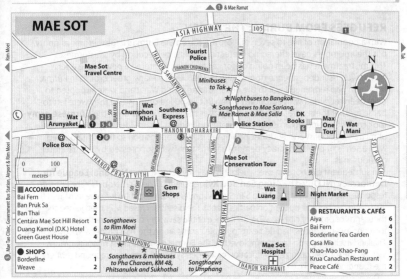

Thais (plus a lively injection of committed NGO expats). It is dependent on its thriving trade in Burmese gems and teak as well as, reportedly, on an even more lucrative cross-border black market in drugs, labourers and sex workers. For the casual visitor, however, it's a relaxed place to hang out, with a burgeoning number of good restaurants to enjoy, albeit no real sights. The short ride to the border market provides additional, if low-key, interest, and there are several caves and waterfalls within day-tripping distance.

Mae Sot's main selling point, though, is as a stopover on the way to **Umphang**, a remote village 164km further south, which is starting to get a name as a centre for interesting rafting and trekking adventures. The journey to Umphang takes at least four hours in a bumpy songthaew, so it's usually worth staying the night in Mae Sot; you can also organize treks to Umphang through Mae Sot tour operators. If you need to change money for the trip, you should do so in Mae Sot as there are no exchange facilities anywhere in Umphang.

Over the last two decades the **Burmese population** of Mae Sot and its environs has swelled enormously (see box, p.262) and the Burmese influence in Mae Sot is palpable in everything from food to fashions; many of the guesthouses are run by Burmese staff, who often speak good English, and the only real sights in the town are its handful of glittering Burmese-style temples.

Rim Moei market

Frequent songthaews (B15) ferry Thai traders and a meagre trickle of tourists the 6km from Mae Sot's government bus station (and bus stop "E", marked on our map) to the border at **RIM MOEI**, where a market for Burmese goods has grown up along the high street and beside the banks of the Moei River. It's a bit tacky, and not as fun to browse as Mae Sot's markets, but it's not a bad place to pick up Burmese **handicrafts**, particularly wooden artefacts such as boxes and picture frames, woven Karen shoulder-bags and checked *longyis*. The best buys are chunky teak tables and chairs, most of them polished up to a fine, golden brown sheen; vendors will arrange shipping.

2

REFUGEES FROM BURMA: THE KAREN

With a population of five to seven million, the **Karen** are Burma's largest ethnic minority, but their numbers have offered no protection against persecution by the Burmese. This mistreatment has been going on for centuries, and entered a new phase after Burma won its independence from Britain in 1948. Unlike many other groups in Burma, the Karen had remained loyal to the British during World War II and were supposed to have been rewarded with autonomy when Britain pulled out; instead they were left to battle for that themselves. Fourteen years after the British withdrawal, the **Burmese army** took control, setting up an isolationist state run under a bizarre ideology compounded of militarist, socialist and Buddhist principles. In 1988, opposition to this junta peaked with a series of pro-democracy demonstrations that were suppressed by the slaughter of thousands.

In subsequent elections an overwhelming majority voted for the **National League for Democracy (NLD)**, led by **Aung San Suu Kyi**, recipient of the 1991 Nobel Peace Prize. In response, the military placed Aung San Suu Kyi under house arrest (where she remained until 2010) and declared all opposition parties illegal. The disenfranchised MPs then joined the thousands of ordinary citizens who, in the face of the savagery of the Burmese militia against the country's minorities, had fled east to jungle camps along the Thai border and beyond, into Thailand itself. Common tactics employed by the Burmese army against minority groups include the forcible razing and relocation of villages, systematic murder, rape and robbery, and the rounding-up of slave labour.

Despite positive steps in a nationwide peace process, which has seen numerous ceasefires signed since late 2011, clashes continue to erupt between government forces and armed factions of some minority groups. The Karen people, whose homeland state of Kawthulay borders northwest Thailand from Mae Sariang down to Three Pagodas Pass, are among those affected. Despite signing a ceasefire, the Karen National Union (KNU), which has an armed wing, was involved in skirmishes with Burmese government troops as recently as March 2012. (The Karen are distinct from the Karenni, or Red Karen, whose homeland is north of Kawthulay and borders Thailand's Mae Hong Son province.)

As a result of these conflicts, as many as one thousand Burmese are thought to flee across the Thai border every month, the majority of them Karen. For many years **Thai government policy** has been to admit only those who are fleeing active fighting, not human rights violations. Thailand is not a signatory to the 1951 Convention Relating to the Status of Refugees and has no legal framework for processing asylum seekers. The hundreds of thousands who have left their homeland because of politically induced economic hardship – forced labour, theft of their land and livestock, among other factors – must therefore either try to enter the refugee camps illegally, or attempt to make a living as **migrant workers**. There are between two and three million migrants from Burma currently in Thailand. Without refugee status, these exiles are extremely vulnerable to abuse, both from corrupt officials and from exploitative employers. In Mae Sot, for example, where Burmese migrants are a mainstay of the local economy, many of them are reportedly paid as little as B70 a day (less than half the regional minimum wage) to work in the worst jobs available, in gem and garment factories, and as prostitutes. Demands for better wages and improved conditions, however, nearly always result in deportation.

Reactions in the **Thai press** to Burmese refugees are mixed, with humanitarian concerns tempered by economic hardships in Thailand and by high-profile cases of illegal Burmese workers involved in violent crimes and drug-smuggling (Burma is now one of the world's leading producers and smugglers of methamphetamines, also known as *ya baa*, or Ice, much of which finds its way into Thailand).

For recent **news** and archive reports on the situation in Burma and on its borders, see ⓦ bnionline.net. For information on how to offer **support** to refugees from Burma, see the website of the Thai Burma Border Consortium (TBBC; ⓦ tbbc.org), and further leads on p.58. A good book about the Karen struggle and the refugee situation in Mae Sot is *Restless Souls: Rebels, Refugees, Medics and Misfits* by Phil Thornton, a Mae Sot-based journalist (see p.787).

Myawaddy and the Burmese border

Thai customs daily 6.30am–6.30pm • Fee to enter Burma B500 • Last exit from Burma at 5.30pm Thai time, 5pm Burmese time, and last entry into Thailand at 6pm

At the time of writing, access to the Burmese village of **MYAWADDY**, across the Thailand–Burma Friendship Bridge on the opposite bank of the Moei River, is open to any foreign national for a fee, payable at the bridge, though foreign visitors are allowed no further **into Burma** than this, and must return to Thailand on the same day. When coming back through Thai customs you will automatically be given a new Thai visa on the spot, currently only for fifteen days. There's nothing much to see in Myawaddy save for an awful lot of samlor drivers touting for business, a few places to eat and a number of clothes stalls and the odd lacquerware outlet.

Waterfalls, springs and caves near Mae Sot

There are several minor caves and waterfalls around Mae Sot, which are easy enough to explore if you have your own transport, though none can compare with Umphang's far mightier Tee Lor Su Falls. Borderline (see p.265) rents good mountain bikes (B70, plus a B1000 deposit), and staff should be able to provide you with route maps and information.

To reach the three-tier **Mae Kasa Falls** (rainy season only) and hot springs (around 10km from town) head north out of Mae Sot, along Highway 105 towards Mae Ramat, then take a side road at around kilometre-stone 13 for 7km. Much further north, just after kilometre-stone 95 on Highway 105, a sign directs you the 2km off the highway to the enormous 800m-deep bat-cave, **Tham Mae Usu** (inaccessible July–Oct because of flooding).

South out of town, off Route 1090 to Umphang, the 97 tiers of **Pha Charoen Falls** are 41km from Mae Sot; take any songthaew bound for kilometre-stone 48 from the depot on the southern edge of Mae Sot. The falls drop down through the jungle like a wonky staircase, and are a popular photo spot for day-tripping Thais.

Highland Farm Gibbon Sanctuary

43km south of Mae Sot at kilometre-stone 42.8 on Route 1090 to Umphang • ☎ 089 958 0821, ⊛ highland-farm.org • Take any songthaew bound for kilometre-stone 48 from the depot on the southern edge of Mae Sot

A couple of kilometres on from Pha Charoen Falls, **Highland Farm Gibbon Sanctuary** (known as Baan Farang) cares for over forty injured and abandoned gibbons, most of which have been rescued from abusive owners and are unable to live in the wild. The sanctuary welcomes day-trippers and homestay visitors (minimum stay 3 nights full-board; $25 per person per day), and also offers one-month placements ($750 all-inclusive).

ARRIVAL AND DEPARTURE   **MAE SOT**

BY PLANE
Nok Air operates flights from Bangkok (Don Muang; 5 weekly; 1hr 15min) to Mae Sot's airport, 3km west of town.

Motorbike taxis are on hand for the run into the centre. Domestic and international air tickets can be bought at SE Southeast Express internet centre and shipping agent,

---

TOURS AROUND MAE SOT

Eco-conscious Mae Sot Conservation Tour (see p.264) runs **tours** to the upland jungle around Mae Lamao, home to Karen and Hmong hill tribes, about 25km east of Mae Sot off Highway 105. The jungle-craft day-trip includes a two-hour trek and whitewater rafting (B2100, minimum four people); the overnight version adds a stay in a Karen village plus a side-trip to the gibbon sanctuary (B3900). They also do a day-trip featuring the Karen village of Mae Salao, a two-hour trek, and the Mae Kasa hot springs (B2100). A cheaper one-day tour by Max One Tour (see p.264) combines a trip to the Karen village with some river rafting and the chance to go shopping at Rim Moei market (B1500).

2

522 Thanon Indharakiri ☎055 547048, ✉se.southeast express@gmail.com.

BY BUS, MINIBUS OR SONGTHAEW

Mae Sot's buses, a/c minibuses and songthaews use various transport terminals (see map, p.261), as well as the government bus station west of town at the Thanon Indharakiri/Highway 105 intersection. Arriving from (or heading to) far-away towns other than Bangkok, it's often

more convenient to go via Tak bus station, which operates more frequent long-distance buses.

Destinations Bangkok (13 daily; 8hr 30min); Chiang Mai (2 daily; 6hr 30min–7hr 30min); Chiang Rai (2 daily; 11hr); Mae Ramat (songthaews every 30min; 45min); Mae Sai (2 daily; 12hr); Mae Sariang (hourly songthaews 6am–noon; 5hr); Phitsanulok (9 daily; 4–5hr); Sukhothai (9 daily; 2hr 30min–3hr); Tak (minibuses every 30min; 2hr); Umphang (hourly songthaews 7.30am–3pm; 4–5hr).

GETTING AROUND

By bicycle or motorbike Most guesthouses have rental bicycles for guests. *Bai Fern* restaurant rents motorbikes (B150/day) and bicycles (B50/day) and Borderline shop has

good mountain bikes (see opposite).

By car Mae Sot Travel Centre can arrange a car-plus-driver service to Umphang and back (B5000/three days).

INFORMATION

Tourist information There is no TAT office here, but both *Bai Fern* and *Krua Canadian* restaurants are good sources of

local information, as are the guesthouses.

TREKKING OPERATORS

Khun Om Ask at No. 4 Guesthouse, 736 Thanon Indharakiri ☎081 785 2095, ✉no4guesthouse@yahoo .com. The treks run by the taciturn Khun Om get good reviews. As well as the standard Tee Lor Su programme (see p.267) he does an extended five-day, four-night version featuring a hearty climb up Doi Phuwatoo (B6000/person, based on four people sharing the trip) as well as – his *pièce de résistance* – a seven-day expedition all the way down to Sangkhlaburi for US$400 per person.

Mae Sot Conservation Tour 415/17 Thanon Tang Kim Chang ☎055 532818 (Mon–Sat 9am–5pm), ☎087 842 8031 (Sun), ✉maesotco@hotmail.com. Standard Tee Lor Su programmes.

Max One Tour In the DK Hotel plaza at 296/1 Thanon Indharakiri ☎055 542942, ⊕maxonetour.com. A Mae Sot outlet for the Umphang-based Umphang Hill trek operator (see p.268).

ACCOMMODATION

Because of the many volunteers in town, most guesthouses offer weekly and monthly discounts.

Bai Fern 660/ Thanon Indharakiri ☎055 531349, ⊕bai -fern.com. Well-run, traveller-oriented guesthouse that's attached to a great restaurant. The simple rooms have shared bathrooms and some have a/c – a few also show signs of damp, so look around before checking in. Good rates for singles and wi-fi throughout (B50/day). Fan **B250**, a/c **B300**

Ban Pruk Sa Thanon Indharakiri, just across from Ban Thai ☎055 532656, ⊕banpruksa.com. A good fallback option for when *Ban Thai* (see below) is fully booked, with comfortably furnished rooms (some with shared bathrooms) in a spacious modern building. There's free wi-fi and a nice garden area to sip cups of coffee in. **B500**

★ **Ban Thai** 740/1 Thanon Indharakiri ☎055 531590, ✉banthai_mth@hotmail.com. The most appealing guesthouse in Mae Sot occupies several traditional-style, wooden-floored houses in a peaceful garden compound (with wi-fi) at the west end of town. All rooms are tastefully and comfortably furnished; those in the main house share bathrooms, while those in the more expensive compound houses are en suite and have cable TV. Many NGO volunteers board here long-term, which makes for sociable and

interesting encounters in the communal garden room but also means it's a good idea to phone ahead and check for vacancies. Fan **B400**, a/c **B700**

Centara Mae Sot Hill Resort 100 Asia Highway/ Highway 105 ☎055 532601, ⊕centarahotelsresorts .com. The top business hotel in the area has tennis courts and a pool, though rooms are unexceptional and it's a 10min drive from the town centre. **B850**

Duang Kamol (D.K.) Hotel 298 Thanon Indharakiri ☎055 531699. The nicest and best value of the town-centre hotels has huge, clean rooms, many of them with little balconies and some with a/c and TVs. The entrance is on the first floor, above a series of shops. Fan **B250**, a/c **B350**

Green Guest House Across the stream from the Tak/ Mae Sariang bus station at 460/8 Thanon Indharakiri ☎055 533207. Small, central, friendly little complex of sixteen good, clean rooms, all of them en suite. Those upstairs are nicest: large, light and with wooden floors, hot water and TV; downstairs ones are slightly cheaper and have cold water, no TV and concrete floors. Popular with long-stay NGOs. Fan **B270**, a/c **B350**

EATING AND DRINKING

Thanon Prasat Vithi is well stocked with noodle shops and **night-market stalls**, there's lots of Muslim and Burmese food for sale in the market, and the NGO presence ensures a good spread of **restaurants** catering to Western palates. The NGO **bars** tend to change names and owners quite frequently, but are generally convivial places with garden seating and perhaps big-screen sports, wi-fi, regular live music, quiz nights or similar: you should find several along the stretch of Thanon Indharakiri running west from Wat Arunyaket to Thanon Don Kaew.

★ **Aiya** Thanon Indharakiri, across from Bai Fern. Famous for its great Thai and Burmese food, including especially good, spiced Burmese curries (from B80), and chopped watercress and fried onion salad. Live music some evenings. Daily 4–10pm.

Bai Fern 660/2 Thanon Indharakiri ☎ 055 531349. Recommended restaurant attached to the guesthouse of the same name, which serves some of the most imaginative food in the region. The menu (most dishes B60–80) includes pepper steaks served with a variety of unusual sauces, salmon salad, authentic Italian carbonara (B100), traditional Thai curries and lots of vegetarian options, as well as brownies, apple pie, chocolate cake and mixed-grain bread. Daily 7am–10pm.

Borderline Tea Garden Thanon Indharakiri. In the garden at the back of their fair-trade handicrafts shop, this very relaxed café serves cheap Burmese snacks (B30–40), – including vegetable wraps with lime sauce, and potato curry with flat bread – washed down by Burmese tea, lemon grass and other juices. Also sells secondhand books and runs cookery classes (see below). Daily 9am–6pm.

Casa Mia Thanon Don Kaew, 5min walk past Ban Thai guesthouse. A favourite with NGOs for its twenty different home-made pastas, including an especially delicious spicy tortellini pomodoro and another twenty pizzas. Also does a big range of Thai dishes, salads, veggie options and a daily roster of cakes and desserts – lime cheesecake, banoffee pie and the like. Delivery to guesthouses available for B20 per order. Most mains B30–90. Daily 8am–10pm.

Khao-Mao Khao-Fang Out of town, 2km north towards Mae Ramat up Highway 105. A garden restaurant extraordinaire, where the artfully landscaped cascades, rivulets, rock features and mature trees make you feel as if you're sitting in a primeval forest film set, especially at night when sea-green lighting adds to the effect. A popular spot for dates and VIP lunches, it serves fairly pricey food that's nothing special, but the cocktails are fun and as one of Mae Sot's most famous attractions, it's worth the hassle to get here. During the day you could use the Mae Ramat/Mae Sariang songthaew service, but after dark you'll need your own transport. Daily 11am–10pm.

Krua Canadian Restaurant Near the police station, just off Thanon Indharakiri. There's a great menu of delicious dishes (mostly B90–120) at this NGO favourite, including local specialities such as stir-fried frog and bird curry, mango catfish salad and *matsaman* curries, plus tofu steak, imported steaks and Mexican enchiladas. Also serves several blends of local hill-tribe coffee, plus a long menu of veggie options. DVD screenings in the evening. Daily 7am–9pm.

Peace Café Thanon Sawanwithi, just north of the junction with Thanon Indharakiri. Tiny streetside café set up by two Burmese monks to raise awareness about the issues facing Burmese migrants along the Thai–Burmese border. The food is simple but fresh, with excellent Burmese tea on offer and plenty of tasty vegetarian dishes. There is a Karen buffet (B99) from 7pm on some Friday evenings. Daily 9am–9pm.

SHOPPING

For fashions, Burmese sarongs and daily necessities, you can't beat the well-stocked **day market** that runs south off Thanon Ruamchit. Mae Sot is most famous, however, as a good place to buy jewellery: the **gem and jade shops** on central Thanon Prasat Vithi offer a larger and less expensive selection than the stalls at the Rim Moei border market, and even if you don't intend to buy, just watching the theatrical haggling is half the fun.

Borderline Next to Wat Arunyaket on Thanon Indharakiri, just in front of the Tea Garden ⓦ borderlinecollective.org. One of a number of places in town selling Karen crafts, including sarongs, yoga mats and bags that are designed for laptops. Most items are made by Karen women living in refugee camps along the border. Daily 2–6pm.

Weave Opposite Bai Fern on Thanon Indharakiri ⓦ weave-women.org. A similar operation to Borderline, with a name that's short for "Women's Education for Advancement and Empowerment". Traditional patterns, dyes and colour combinations are used to create a variety of woven products, thus helping to preserve Karen culture and give local refugee women an income. Mon–Sat 9am–6pm.

DIRECTORY

Cookery lessons Learn how to rustle up Shan, Karen and Burmese dishes at *Borderline Tea Garden* (8am–noon;

B450–1000, depending on group size).
Hospitals Mae Sot Hospital is on the southeastern edge of

town (☎ 055 531970) and Pha Wawa Hospital is on the southwestern edge (☎ 055 533912).

Immigration office At Rim Moei border crossing.

Internet access You can access the internet at guesthouses or in the lobby of the *Duang Kamol* hotel (B15/hr).

Language lessons Thai lessons through *Krua Canadian Restaurant*. Burmese lessons available through most guesthouses and several restaurants.

Massage Herbal saunas (3–7pm) at Wat Mani, on Thanon Indharakiri.

Tourist police For all emergencies, call the tourist police on the free, 24hr phoneline ☎ 1155, or contact them at the police station on Thanon Indharakiri (☎ 055 533523).

Umphang

Even if you don't fancy doing a trek, consider making the spectacular trip 164km south from Mae Sot to the village of **UMPHANG**, both for the stunning mountain scenery you'll encounter along the way, and for the buzz of being in such an isolated part of Thailand. Surrounded by mountains and situated at the confluence of the Mae Khlong and Umphang rivers, Umphang itself is small and very quiet, made up of little more than a thousand or so wooden houses and a wat. It won't take long to explore the minute grid of narrow roads that bisects the village, but independent tourists are still relatively rare here, so communication could be a challenge. Bring some warm clothes as it can get pretty cool at night and in the early mornings – and the songthaew ride along the Sky Highway from Mae Sot is often windy.

Riding the Sky Highway

The drive from Mae Sot to Umphang generally takes about four hours and for the first hour proceeds in a fairly gentle fashion through the maize, cabbage and banana plantations of the Moei valley. The fun really begins when you start climbing into the mountains and the road – accurately dubbed the "**Sky Highway**" – careers round the edges of steep-sided valleys, undulating like a fairground rollercoaster (there are said to

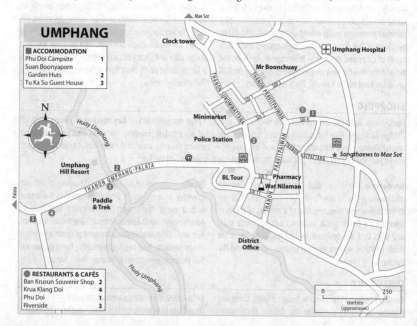

TREKKING AROUND UMPHANG

Unlike treks further north around Chiang Mai, **treks around Umphang** are more about wilderness than hill-tribe villages and are far more popular with Thai tourists than farangs. The big highlight is the three-tiered, 200m-high **Tee Lor Su Waterfall** (Nam Tok Thilawsu), star feature of the Umphang Wildlife Sanctuary (entry B200), which, unusually for Thailand, flows all year round. It's at its most thunderous just after the rainy season in November, when it can extend to a dramatic 400m across. During this period you can swim in the beautifully blue lower pool, but trails can still be muddy, which makes for tough going; trek leaders recommend wearing rubber boots (best bought in Mae Sot, as they're hard to find in Umphang). One stretch of the route becomes so muddy during and just after the rainy season that it's impassable to human feet and needs to be done on elephant-back, a pretty uncomfortable ride of three to four hours. Nonetheless, the best **season** for trekking is November through February, even if the nights get pretty chilly. From December to April (the dry season), it's usually possible to climb to one of the waterfall's upper tiers, mud permitting. Around the falls, the vegetation is mainly montane forest, home to numerous varieties of orchid, and plenty of commonly encountered monkeys and hornbills, plus an elusive band of wild elephants.

Access to the falls is strictly controlled by national park rangers, who forbid people from taking food or plastic water bottles beyond the ranger station and campsite, which is 1.5km from the falls. As yet, the number of visitors is reasonably small – except on public holidays, during school holidays and on some weekends, when Thai trippers flood the area. Visitors reach Tee Lor Su Falls either via a fairly challenging combination of rafting and walking, or by using the **road** to the ranger station (4WD only), which may be impassable between June and November. If you can take this road route, you'll only have to walk the 1.5km route from the station to the falls. Some tour operators offer the car-plus-hike option as a day-trip from Umphang, usually throwing in a rafting session as well.

A **typical trek** to Tee Lor Su lasts three days and follows something like this increasingly standard itinerary. Day one: rafting down the Mae Khlong River via Tee Lor Jor Falls and some striking honeycombed cliffs; then a 9km trek (3hr) to the official campsite near Tee Lor Su Falls. Day two: morning at the falls, then a two-hour trek to a homestay at the Karen village of Khotha. Day three: a three-hour elephant ride (or trek) to Mae Lamoong junction; return to Umphang by car. Some trekkers find the three-day itinerary too baggy, with quite a lot of empty time at day's end (bring a book), so if you want a more challenging experience try to persuade your trekking agency to cover the same itinerary in two days. **Prices** start at about B2700 per person (B3200 with elephant riding) for the two-day Tee Lor Su trek (minimum two people) or B3000/3500 for three days. Add about B1000 per person for treks arranged in Mae Sot (see p.264). Prices do vary between operators: smaller outfits can't afford to undercut the big operators and cost savings can mean lower wages – and morale – for guides. In Umphang the best time to contact **trek leaders** at the smaller outfits is often after about 4pm, when they've returned from their last trip. Guides should provide tents, bedrolls, mosquito nets and sleeping bags, plus food and drinking water; trekkers may be asked to help carry some of the gear.

Although Tee Lor Su is the most famous destination in the Umphang area, other programmes are available on request. From June to October there's **whitewater rafting** from the Karen village of **Umphang Khi** via the forty-plus rapids of the Umphang River, which can also include a fairly long trek and a night in the village. Alternatively, there are one- and two-day rafting trips to **Thi Lor Leh Falls**, which involve four to eight hours' rafting (depending on water levels) via a series of cataracts along the Mae Khlong River, and the possibility of a seven-hour trek on the second day. For bird-spotting, ask about trips to Thung Yai Naresuan.

be 1219 bends in all). The scenery is glorious, but if you're prone to car sickness, dose up on preventative tablets as the ride can be very unpleasant: the songthaews (see p.268) get so crammed with people and produce that there's often no possibility of distracting yourself by staring out of the window.

Karen, Akha, Lisu and Hmong people live in the few hamlets along the route, many growing cabbages along the cleared lower slopes with the help of government incentives (part of a national campaign to steer upland farmers away from the opium trade). The **Hmong** in particular are easily recognized by their distinctive embroidered jackets and skirts edged in bright pink, red and blue bands (see p.779). In 2000, the local **Karen** population mushroomed when three refugee camps from the Rim Moei area were relocated to the purpose-built village of Umpiem Mai alongside the Sky Highway midway between Mae Sot and Umphang (see box, p.262). Umpiem Mai is currently home to around fifteen thousand Karen refugees.

In fact the Umphang region was inhabited by Karen hill tribes before the Thais came to settle in the area in the early twentieth century; later when the Thais began trading in earnest with their neighbours across the Burmese border, the Karen traders from Burma used to carry their identification documents into Thailand in a bamboo container which they called an "umpha" – this is believed to be the origin of the name Umphang.

ARRIVAL AND DEPARTURE   UMPHANG

When it comes to public transport, Umphang is effectively a dead end, so the only way to travel on from here is to go back to **Mae Sot** first.

By songthaew The only public transport access to Umphang is by songthaew along the Sky Highway from Mae Sot (hourly 7.30am–3.30pm; 4–5hr; B140, or B170 if you're lucky enough to get the front seat). Heading back to Mae Sot, songthaews leave at least hourly until noon from the top of the town, but it's usual for guesthouses to phone ahead and get the songthaew to pick you up. After noon you'll probably need to charter the whole vehicle.

GETTING AROUND

By car or motorbike *Tu Ka Su Guest House* can arrange a 4WD with driver for exploring the area (price dependent on destination). There's no official motorbike rental in Umphang, but it's worth asking around as guesthouse owners may be able to help you.

TREKKING OPERATORS

The main English-speaking trek leaders operating out of Umphang at the time of writing are listed below, but you can also arrange treks through staff at *Suan Boonyaporn Garden Huts* (phone English-speaker Dac on ☎ 089 568 5273, or see the website ⊛ boonyapornresort.com for more information) and *Phu Doi Campsite*.

BL Tour 1/438 Thanon Umphang-Palata ☎ 055 561021, ⊛ boonlumtour.com. Ask for English-speakers Oi or Johnny. Very well-priced two- and three-day trips to Tee Lor Su, including all extras such as food and sleeping bags; happy to do the two-day version, omitting the Khotha homestay.

Mr Boonchuay 360 Thanon Pravitpaiwan ☎ 055 561020, ⊛ boonchuaytour.com. Umphang-born and bred, Mr Boonchuay knows the area well and has a good reputation; his English is not perfect, but he has English-speaking guides. Offers standard Tee Lor Su programme. Trekkers can stay in the basic concrete rooms behind his office (B200/double) or in nicer bungalows down by the river (B250/double).

Paddle & Trek Thanon Umphang-Palata ☎ 089 958 9374, ✉ tom_trek@hotmail.com. Well-thought-out itineraries in addition to the Tee Lor Su classic include two-nighters based in the Karen village of Khotha that feature a trek to the twin lakes near Thipoji in addition to Tee Lor Su. Also does kayaking on the Bhumipol Dam reservoir north of Mae Sot and tailor-made itineraries on request.

Umphang Hill At Umphang Hill Resort, 99 Thanon Umphang-Palata ☎ 055 561063, ⊛ umphanghill.com. The biggest outfit in the area offers eleven itineraries and tailor-made permutations. From Dec–May, with advance notice, they can also arrange a challenging seven-day trek to Sangkhlaburi (B15,000/person).

ACCOMMODATION

As most of the accommodation in Umphang is geared towards trekkers in transit, charges are often per person rather than per room; the prices listed below are for two people sharing, so expect to pay half if you're on your own. Many trekking companies have their own accommodation (see above).

Phu Doi Campsite Thanon Pravitpaiwan Soi 4 ☎ 055 561049, ⊛ phudoi.com. Decent set of comfortable en-suite fan rooms in a couple of wooden houses with verandas overlooking a pond, plus some rooms above the office. **B600**

Suan Boonyaporn Garden Huts 106 Thanon Umphang-Palata ☎ 055 561093, ⊛ boonyapornresort .com. A spread of accommodation options, set around a pretty riverside flower garden, ranging from fairly simple wooden huts with shared facilities to quite attractive wooden bungalows with pretty basic bathrooms but fronted by decks and partial river-views. Shared bathroom B300, en-suite B400

Tu Ka Su Guest House 129 Thanon Umphang-Palata ☎055 561295, ⓦtukasu.net. In a pretty garden up the hill from the river, this quite stylish place is the most attractive in Umphang and offers nicely designed en-suite wooden cabins, with TV; some have cute, semi-garden-style bathrooms. B600

EATING

The town's best places to eat are strung out along Thanon Umphang-Palata, and there are cheap **food stalls** that set up close to the temple at dusk.

Ban Krusun Souvenir Shop Thanon Sukomwattana. Along with CDs and local arts and crafts, this souvenir shops sells good cappuccinos and lattes (B30). Daily 6.30am–8.30pm.

Krua Klang Doi Just east of Tu Ka Su. Popular with locals and visitors, this simple restaurant serves good cheap Thai standards (from B30), including some fresh and spicy salads. Open from mid-morning until after 8pm.

Phu Doi Restaurant Adjacent to Phu Doi Campsite. Popular with Thais, this place has an English-language menu of curries and meat-over-rice dishes (around B60). Open for breakfast, lunch and dinner; high season only.

Riverside Restaurant Opposite Boonyaporn Garden Huts. Similar to *Krua Klang Doi* but right next to the twisting Huay Umphang River and a popular spot for a beer in the evening. Daily mid-morning to late evening.

2

The north

PAINTING UMBRELLAS NEAR CHIANG MAI

The north

Travelling up by rail through the central plains, there's no mistaking when you've reached the north of Thailand: somewhere between Uttaradit and Den Chai, the train slows almost to a halt, as if approaching a frontier post, to meet the abruptly rising mountains that continue largely unbroken to the borders of Burma and Laos. Beyond this point the climate becomes more temperate (downright cold at night between December and February), nurturing the fertile land that gave the old kingdom of the north the name of Lanna, "the land of a million rice fields". Although only one-tenth of the land can be used for rice cultivation, the valley rice fields here are three times more productive than those in the dusty northeast, and the higher land yields a great variety of fruits, as well as beans, groundnuts and tobacco.

Until the beginning of the last century, Lanna was a largely independent region. On the back of its agricultural prosperity, it developed its own styles of art and architecture, which can still be seen in its flourishing temples and distinctive handicraft traditions. The north is also set apart from the rest of the country by its exuberant festivals, a cuisine which has been heavily influenced by Burma and a dialect quite distinct from central Thai. Northerners proudly call themselves *khon muang*, "people of the principalities", and their gentle sophistication is admired by the people of Bangkok, whose wealthier citizens build their holiday homes in the clean air of the north's forested mountains.

Chiang Mai, the capital and transport centre of the north, is a great place just to hang out or prepare for a journey into the hills. For many tourists, this means joining a trek (see p.54) to visit one or more of the **hill tribes**, who comprise one-tenth of the north's

THE MAE HONG SON LOOP

Highlights

❶ Hill-tribe trekking A chance to visit the diverse hill tribes of northern Thailand and explore dramatic countryside along the way. **See p.54**

❷ Chiang Mai Old-town temples, the best of Thai crafts, cookery courses and fine restaurants – the north's sophisticated capital is a great place to hang out. **See p.277**

❸ Festivals Exuberant Songkhran, glittering Loy Krathong and colourful Poy Sang Long are the pick of many. **See p.286 & p.340**

❹ Khao soi Delicious, spicy, creamy noodle soup, the northern Thai signature dish. **See p.295**

❺ Wat Phra That Doi Suthep Admire the towering views from this stunning example of temple architecture, just outside Chiang Mai. **See p.304**

❻ Nan A welcoming riverside town offering fascinating temple murals, attractive handicrafts and dramatic mountainscapes. **See p.324**

❼ The Mae Hong Son loop A rollercoaster journey – with a chill-out break in laidback Pai – through the country's wildest mountain scenery. **See p.330**

❽ Whitewater rafting on the Pai River Well-organized excitement taking in rapids, gorges and beautiful waterfalls. **See p.349**

HIGHLIGHTS ARE MARKED ON THE MAP ON PP.274–275

THE NORTH

HIGHLIGHTS
1. Hill-tribe trekking
2. Chiang Mai
3. Festivals
4. Khao soi
5. Wat Phra That Doi Suthep
6. Nan
7. The Mae Hong Son loop
8. Whitewater rafting on the Pai River

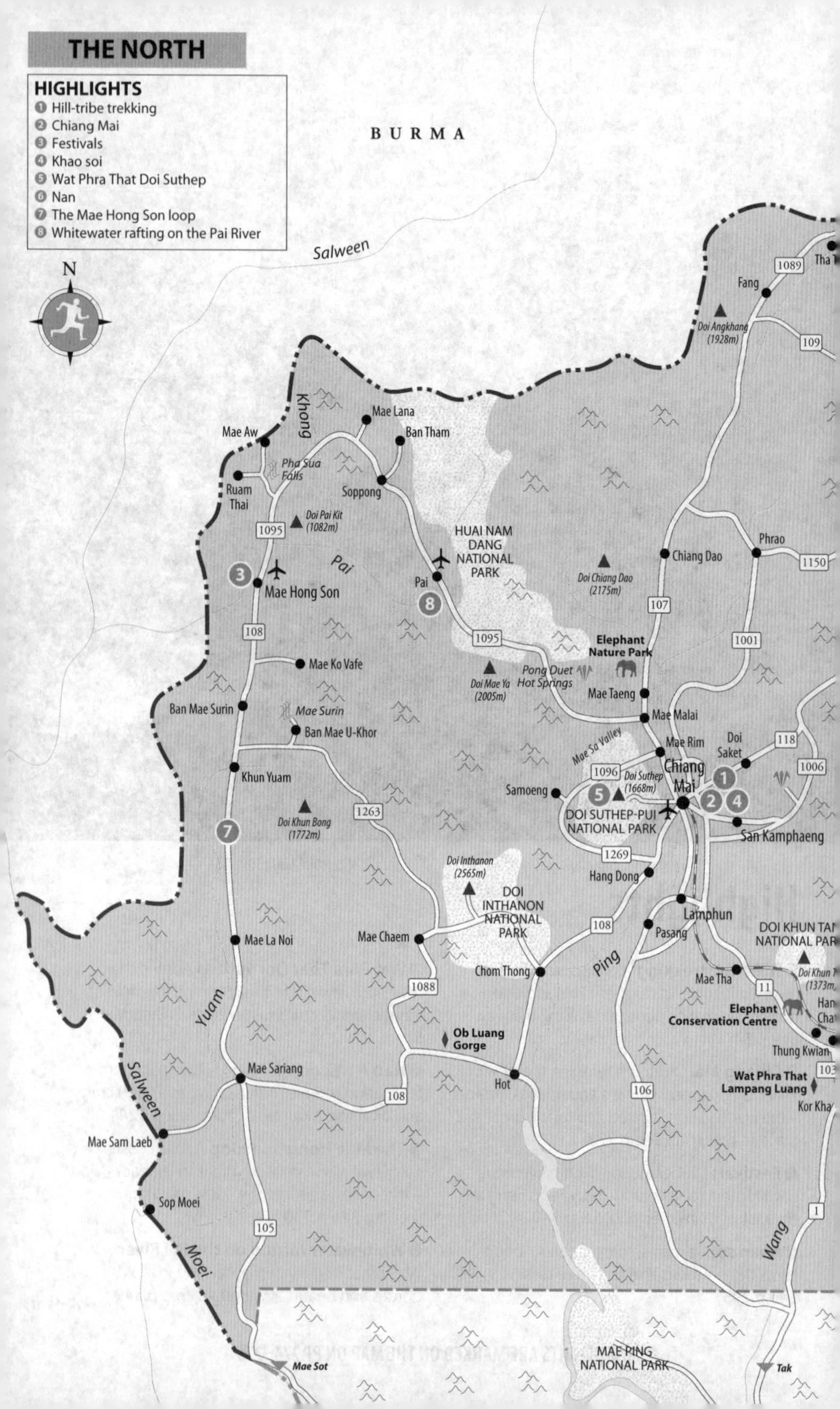

N

BURMA

Salween

Khong

Mae Aw
Ruam Thai
Pha Sua Falls
1095
Doi Pai Kit (1082m)
Pai
Mae Hong Son
3
108
Mae Ko Vafe
Ban Mae Surin
Mae Surin
Ban Mae U-Khor
Khun Yuam
Doi Khun Bong (1772m)
7
1263
Mae La Noi
Yuam
Salween
Mae Chaem
1088
Chom Thong
Ob Luang Gorge
Mae Sariang
108
Hot
Mae Sam Laeb
Sop Moei
105
Moei
Mae Sot

Mae Lana
Ban Tham
Soppong
Pai
8
1095

HUAI NAM DANG NATIONAL PARK

Doi Chiang Dao (2175m)
Chiang Dao
107

Pong Duet Hot Springs
Doi Mae Ya (2005m)
Elephant Nature Park
Mae Taeng
Mae Malai
Mae Rim
Moe Sa Valley
1096 Doi Suthep (1668m)
Samoeng
5
DOI SUTHEP-PUI NATIONAL PARK
Doi Inthanon (2565m)
DOI INTHANON NATIONAL PARK
Hang Dong
1269
108
Ping
Lamphun
Pasang
Mae Tha
11
Elephant Conservation Centre
Wat Phra That Lampang Luang

Fang
1089 Tha
Doi Angkhang (1928m)
109

Phrao
1150

1001

Doi Saket
118
Chiang Mai
1
2 4
San Kamphaeng
1006

DOI KHUN TAN NATIONAL PARK
Doi Khun (1373m)
Han Cha
Thung Kwian
103
Kor Kha
Wong
1

MAE PING NATIONAL PARK
Tak

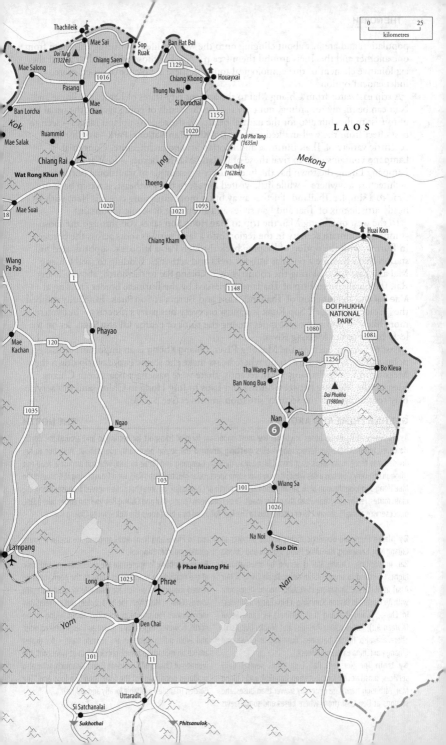

population and are just about clinging onto the ways of life that distinguish them from one another and the Thais around them (see p.777). For those with qualms about the exploitative element of this ethnological tourism, there are plenty of other, more independent options.

A trip eastwards from Chiang Mai to the ancient city-states of Lampang, Phrae and Nan can be highly rewarding, not only for the dividends of going against the usual flow of tourist traffic, but also for the natural beauty of the region's upland ranges – seen to best effect from the well-marked trails of **Doi Khun Tan National Park** – and for its eccentric variety of Thai, Burmese and Laotian art and architecture. Congenial **Lampang** contains wats to rival those of Chiang Mai for beauty – in Wat Phra That Lampang Luang the town has the finest surviving example of traditional northern architecture anywhere – while little-visited **Phrae**, to the southeast, is a step back in time to a simpler Thailand. Further away but a more intriguing target is **Nan**, with its heady artistic mix of Thai and Lao styles and steep ring of scenic mountains.

To the west of Chiang Mai, the trip to **Mae Hong Son** takes you through the most stunning mountain scenery in the region into a land with its roots across the border in Burma, with the option of looping back through **Pai**, a laidback, sophisticated hill station that's become a popular hub for treks and activities. Bidding to rival Chiang Mai as a base for exploring the countryside is **Chiang Rai** to the north; above Chiang Rai, the northernmost tip of Thailand is marked by the Burmese border crossing at **Mae Sai** and the junction of Thailand, Laos and Burma at **Sop Ruak**. Fancifully dubbed the "Golden Triangle", Sop Ruak is a must on every bus party's itinerary – but you're more likely to find peace and quiet among the ruins of nearby **Chiang Saen**, set on the leafy banks of the Mekong River.

East of Chiang Saen on the Mekong River, **Chiang Khong** is an important crossing point to Houayxai in Laos, from where boats make the scenic two-day trip down the Mekong to Luang Prabang. Until recently, there were passenger boats from Chiang Saen up the Mekong between Burma and Laos to Jing Hong in China, and this service may resume again if the security situation improves (see p.373).

GETTING THERE AND AROUND THE NORTH

As elsewhere in Thailand, buses are by far the most important form of transport for getting to and around the north. However, the mountainous topography makes **getting around** the region necessarily roundabout, with bus routes divided into three main areas: east from Chiang Mai, through Lampang and Phrae to Nan, which is almost a dead end (though one very slow bus a day winds its way over some spectacular hills to Chiang Rai); west from Chiang Mai around the Mae Hong Son loop through Mae Sariang and Pai; and north of Chiang Rai, an area that is well served by buses along the main routes, fed by songthaews on the minor roads. To get between Chiang Mai and Chiang Rai, you can either take a fast, direct service along Highway 118 or catch a bus to Tha Ton, followed by a boat down the Kok River to Chiang Rai.

By plane There are domestic flights to the airports at Chiang Mai, Lampang, Nan, Mae Hong Son, Pai and Chiang Rai. In addition, Chiang Mai is served by international flights from and to several Asian cities: Kuala Lumpur (Air Asia) in Malaysia, Singapore (Silk Air), Yangon (Rangoon; with Air Bagan) in Burma, Kunming (China Eastern Airlines) in China, Luang Prabang (Lao Airlines) in Laos, Seoul (Korean Air), Taipei (China Airlines) and Macau (Air Asia). There are also flights between Kunming in China and Chiang Rai (China Eastern Airlines).

By train The Northern Rail Line offers several daily services, mostly overnight, between Bangkok and Chiang Mai. Although trains are generally slower than buses, the stations at Den Chai (from where buses and songthaews run to Phrae and Nan) and Lampang are useful if you're coming up from Bangkok.

By motorbike To appreciate the mountainous landscape of the north fully, many people take to the open roads on rented motorbikes, which are available in most northern towns (Chiang Mai offers the best choice) and are relatively inexpensive. You should be cautious about biking in the north, however, especially if you're an inexperienced rider, and avoid riding alone on any remote trails – for expert advice on motorbike travel, check out ✆ gt-rider.com, the website of Chiang Mai resident David Unkovich, who also produces good maps of the Mae Hong Son loop and "The Golden Triangle" (available locally and online).

Brief history

The first civilization to leave an indelible mark on the north was **Haripunjaya**, the Mon (Dvaravati) state that was founded at Lamphun in the late eighth or early ninth century. Maintaining strong ties with the Mon kingdoms to the south, it remained the cultural and religious centre of the north for four centuries. The Thais came onto the scene after the Mon, migrating down from China between the seventh and the eleventh centuries and establishing small principalities around the north.

King Mengrai and the founding of Chiang Mai

The prime mover for the Thais was **King Mengrai** of Ngon Yang (around present-day Chiang Saen), who, shortly after the establishment of a Thai state at Sukhothai in the middle of the thirteenth century, set to work on a parallel unified state in the north. By 1296, when he began the construction of Chiang Mai, which has remained the capital of the north ever since, he had brought the whole of the north under his control, and at his death in 1317 he had established a dynasty which was to oversee a two-hundred-year period of unmatched prosperity and cultural activity.

The Burmese occupation

After the expansionist reign of Tilok (1441–87), who hosted the eighth world council of Theravada Buddhism in Chiang Mai in 1477, a series of weak, squabbling kings came and went, while Ayutthaya increased its unfriendly advances. But it was the **Burmese** who finally snuffed out the Mengrai dynasty by capturing Chiang Mai in 1558, and for most of the next two centuries they controlled Lanna through a succession of puppet rulers. In 1767, the Burmese sacked the Thai capital at Ayutthaya, but the Thais soon regrouped under King Taksin, who with the help of **King Kawila** of Lampang gradually drove the Burmese northwards. In 1774 Kawila recaptured Chiang Mai, then deserted and in ruins, and set about rebuilding it as his new capital.

The colonial period

Kawila was succeeded as ruler of the north by a series of incompetent princes for much of the nineteenth century, until colonialism reared its head. After Britain took control of Upper Burma, **Rama V** of Bangkok began to take an interest in the north – where, since the Bowring Treaty of 1855, the British had established lucrative logging businesses – to prevent its annexation. He forcibly moved large numbers of ethnic Thais northwards, in order to counter the British claim of sovereignty over territory occupied by Thai Yai (Shan), who also make up a large part of the population of Upper Burma. In 1877 Rama V appointed a commissioner over Chiang Mai, Lamphun and Lampang to better integrate the region with the centre, and links were further strengthened in 1921 with the arrival of the railway from Bangkok.

The north today

Since the early twentieth century, the north has built on its agricultural richness to become relatively prosperous, though the economic booms of the last thirty years have been concentrated, as elsewhere in Thailand, in the towns, due in no small part to the increase in tourism. The eighty percent of Lanna's population who live in rural areas – of which the vast majority are subsistence farmers – are finding it increasingly difficult to earn a living off the soil, due to rapid population growth and land speculation for tourism and agro-industry.

Chiang Mai

Although rapid economic progress in recent years has brought problems such as pollution and traffic jams, **CHIANG MAI** still manages to preserve some of the atmosphere of an ancient village alongside its modern urban sophistication. It's the kingdom's second city, with a youthful population of about 400,000 (over 60,000 of them are students), and the contrast with the maelstrom of Bangkok is pronounced: the people here are famously easy-going and even speak more slowly than their cousins in the capital, a lilting dialect known as *kham muang*. Chiang Mai's moated old quarter, where new buildings are limited to a height of four storeys, has retained many

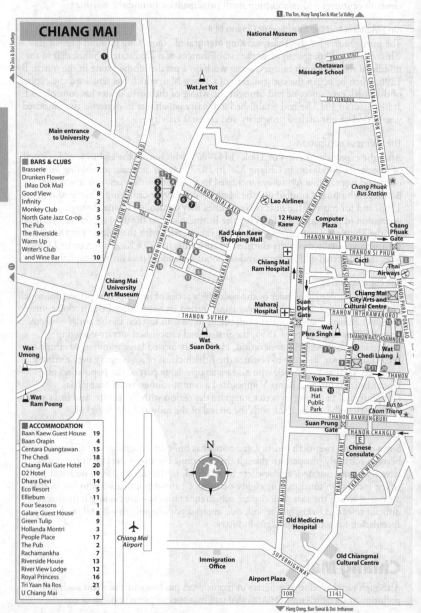

CHIANG MAI

National Museum

Tha Ton, Huay Tung Tao & Mae Sa Valley

Chetawan
Massage School

Wat Jet Yot

Main entrance
to University

■ BARS & CLUBS
Brasserie	7
Drunken Flower	
(Mao Dok Mai)	6
Good View	8
Infinity	2
Monkey Club	3
North Gate Jazz Co-op	5
The Pub	1
The Riverside	9
Warm Up	4
Writer's Club	
and Wine Bar	10

Lao Airlines

Chang Phuak
Bus Station

12 Huay
Kaew

Computer
Plaza

Chang
Phuak
Gate

Kad Suan Kaew
Shopping Mall

Chiang Mai
Ram Hospital

Cacti

Thai
Airways

Chiang Mai
University
Art Museum

Chiang Mai
City Arts and
Cultural Centre

Maharaj
Hospital

Suan
Dork
Gate

Wat
Phra Singh

Chedi
Luang

THANON SUTHEP

Wat
Suan Dork

Yoga Tree

Buak
Hat
Public
Park

Wat
Umong

Bus to
Chom Thong

Wat
Ram Poeng

Suan Prung
Gate

Chinese
Consulate

■ ACCOMMODATION
Baan Kaew Guest House	19
Baan Orapin	4
Centara Duangtawan	15
The Chedi	18
Chiang Mai Gate Hotel	20
D2 Hotel	10
Dhara Devi	14
Eco Resort	5
Elliebum	11
Four Seasons	8
Galare Guest House	1
Green Tulip	9
Hollanda Montri	3
People Place	17
The Pub	2
Rachamankha	7
Riverside House	13
River View Lodge	12
Royal Princess	16
Tri Yaan Na Ros	21
U Chiang Mai	6

Chiang Mai
Airport

N

Old Medicine
Hospital

Immigration
Office

Old Chiangmai
Cultural Centre

Airport Plaza

108   1141

Hang Dong, Ban Tawai & Doi Inthanon

of its traditional wooden houses and quiet, leafy gardens, as well as the most famous and interesting **temples** in the city – Wat Phra Singh, Wat Chedi Luang and Wat Chiang Man – clustered conveniently close to each other. These elegant wats may be Chiang Mai's primary tourist sights, but they're no pre-packaged museum pieces – they're living community centres, where you're quite likely to be approached by monks keen to chat and practise their English. Inviting handicraft **shops**, a couple of

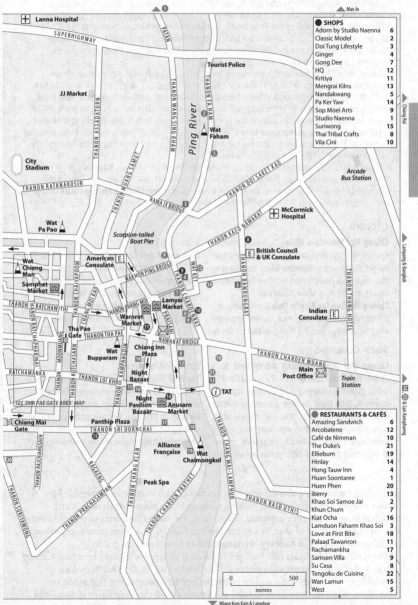

SHOPS

Adorn by Studio Naenna	6
Classic Model	2
Doi Tung Lifestyle	3
Ginger	4
Gong Dee	7
HQ	12
Kritiya	11
Mengrai Kilns	13
Nandakwang	5
Pa Ker Yaw	14
Sop Moei Arts	9
Studio Naenna	1
Suriwong	15
Thai Tribal Crafts	8
Vila Cini	10

RESTAURANTS & CAFÉS

Amazing Sandwich	6
Arcobaleno	12
Café de Nimman	10
The Duke's	21
Elliebum	19
Hinlay	14
Hong Tauw Inn	4
Huan Soontaree	1
Huen Phen	20
iberry	13
Khao Soi Samoe Jai	2
Khun Churn	7
Kiat Ocha	16
Lamduon Faharm Khao Soi	3
Love at First Bite	18
Palaad Tawanron	11
Rachamankha	17
Samsen Villa	9
Su Casa	8
Tengoku de Cuisine	22
Wan Lamun	15
West	5

3

TREKKING AND OTHER OUTDOOR ACTIVITIES IN CHIANG MAI

The **trekking** industry in Chiang Mai offers an impressive variety of itineraries, with over two hundred agencies covering nearly all trekkable areas of the north – see Basics (p.56) for general advice on how to choose an agency. Most treks include a ride on an elephant and a bamboo-raft excursion, though the amount of actual walking included can vary greatly. A few operators offer something a little different. Eagle House (see p.291) runs the standard type of trek, with elephants and rafting, but to carefully chosen quiet areas and with an educational bent, and passes on a proportion of costs towards funding projects in hill-tribe villages. Moving upmarket, the Trekking Collective (3/5 Soi 1, Thanon Loi Khro T 053 208340, W trekkingcollective.com) can arrange pricey but high-quality customized treks from one to five days and can cater for specific interests such as bird-watching; it too is involved in community programmes to help tribal people.

Meanwhile, Chiangmai Green Alternative Tours, an eco-friendly and culturally sensitive operation 100m north of TAT at 31 Thanon Chiangmai–Lamphun (T 053 247374 or T 084 611 1711, W chiangmaigreen.com), offers a fascinating diversity of worthwhile **nature field trips**. Sharing the proceeds with knowledgeable local guides, they can take you up Doi Suthep, Doi Inthanon or Doi Chiang Dao on one-day or multi-day trips, including bird-watching specialities.

For a wide range of **adventure tours**, including whitewater rafting on the Pai River, trekking, cycling and kayaking, a long-standing, general agency is Contact Travel, based at Tasala to the east of town (T 053 850160, W activethailand.com).

If you just fancy a gentle paddle up and down the Ping River in town, **kayaks** can be rented from Wat Faham on Thanon Fa Ham (B100). For those with a head for heights, Flight of the Gibbon (T 089 970 5511, W treetopasia.com) offers full-day **rainforest canopy tours** on zip lines and sky bridges in the hills to the east of town.

CYCLING

Chiang Mai Mountain Biking 1 Thanon Samlarn, opposite Wat Phra Singh T 081 024 7046, W mountainbikingchiangmai.com. Mountain-biking tours, ranging from single-track downhill rides, mostly on Doi Suthep, to cross-country leisure or hike-and-bike trips.

Chiang Mai Sunday Bicycle Club W cmcycling.org. Interesting rides (part of a local cycling campaign) every Sun morning from Tha Phae Gate that are free to anyone to join in.

Click and Travel 158/40 Thanon Chiang Mai–Hod T 053 281553, W clickandtravelonline.com. Belgian–Thai company that runs cycling tours of Chiang Mai and the north, lasting from a few hours to four days, and maintains a useful website, W chiangmaicycling.org, full of all manner of information for cyclists.

ROCK-CLIMBING

Chiang Mai Rock Climbing Adventures 55/3 Thanon Ratchaphakinai T 053 207102 or T 086 911 1470, W thailandclimbing.com. Climbing trips and courses to Crazy Horse Buttress, a limestone outcrop in the San Kamphaeng area, 50km east of town, which offers highly varied climbing with more than seventy routes. Also caving and bouldering courses, as well as equipment rental and sales, private guides and a partner-finding service.

The Peak 302/4 Thanon Chiang Mai–Lamphun T 053 800567–8, W thepeakadventure.com. Climbing trips and courses to Crazy Horse, climbing, camping and kayaking at Kiew Lom Reservoir near Lampang, and climbing and caving trips in the Soppong area, as well as whitewater rafting, trekking and jungle survival cooking.

fascinating **museums**, good-value accommodation, rich cuisine and riverside bars further enhance the city's allure, making Chiang Mai a place that detains many travellers longer than they expected. These days, increasing numbers of travellers are also taking advantage of the city's relaxed feel to indulge in a burst of self-improvement, enrolling for **courses** in **cookery**, **massage** and the like (see box, p.283).

Many colourful **festivals** (see box, p.286) attract throngs of visitors here too: Chiang Mai is one of the most popular places in Thailand to see in the Thai New Year – Songkhran – in mid-April, and to celebrate Loy Krathong at the full moon in November, when thousands of candles are floated down the Ping River in lotus-leaf boats. And a pilgrimage to **Doi Suthep**, the mountain to the west of town, should not be missed, to see the sacred, glittering temple and the towering views over the valley of the Ping River, when weather permits. Beyond the city limits (see p.304), a number of other day-trips can be made, such as to the ancient temples of Lamphun – and, of course, Chiang Mai is the main centre for hill-tribe **trekking**, as well as all sorts of other outdoor activities (see box opposite). **Orientation** is simple in central Chiang Mai, which divides roughly into two main parts: the **old town**, surrounded by the well-maintained moat and occasional remains of the city wall, where you'll find most of the temples, and the **new town centre**, between the moat and the Ping River to the east, the main market and shopping area. The biggest concentration of guesthouses and restaurants hangs between the two, centred on the landmark of **Tha Pae Gate** (*Pratu Tha Pae*) in the middle of the east moat. On the outskirts, the town is bounded to the north, east and south by the Superhighway and two further huge but incomplete ring roads, with Thanon Chon Prathan (Canal Road) providing a western bypass.

Brief history

Founded as the capital of Lanna in 1296, on a site indicated by the miraculous presence of deer and white mice, Chiang Mai – "New City" – has remained the north's most important settlement ever since. Lanna's golden age under the Mengrai dynasty, when most of the city's notable temples were founded, lasted until the Burmese captured the city in 1558. Two hundred years passed before the Thais pushed the Burmese back beyond Chiang Mai to roughly where they are now, and the **Burmese influence** is still strong – not just in art and architecture, but also in the rich curries and soups served here. After the recapture of the city, the *chao* (princes) of Chiang Mai remained nominal rulers of the north until 1939, but, with communications rapidly improving from the beginning of the last century, Chiang Mai was brought firmly into Thailand's mainstream as the region's administrative and service centre.

Wat Phra Singh

At the far western end of Thanon Ratchdamnoen in the old town

If you see only one temple in Chiang Mai it should be **Wat Phra Singh**, perhaps the single most impressive array of buildings in the city. Just inside the gate to the right, the wooden scripture repository is the best example of its kind in the north, inlaid with glass mosaic and set high on a base decorated with stucco angels. The largest building in the compound, a colourful modern viharn fronted by naga balustrades, hides from view a rustic wooden bot, a chedi with a typical northern octagonal base constructed in 1345 to house the ashes of King Kam Fu, and – the highlight of the whole complex – the beautiful **Viharn Lai Kam**. This wooden gem is a textbook example of Lanna

---

CHIANG MAI BOAT TRIPS

A pleasant way to get a feel for the city and its layout is to take a **boat trip** on the Ping River. Frequent two-hour cruises operated by Mae Ping River Cruises (☎053 274822 or ☎081 884 4621, ⓦmaepingrivercruise.com) depart from Wat Chaimongkol on Thanon Charoen Prathet, sailing 8km upstream through lush countryside to a riverside farmhouse for a look around the fruit, herb and flower gardens, plus refreshments and fruit-tasting (B450/person, or B550 including *khao soi* lunch; minimum two people, includes pick-up from your accommodation). Mae Ping River Cruises also offer trips to Wiang Kum Kam (see p.307) and dinner cruises (see p.295). Another alternative is to take a trip on a scorpion-tailed boat (currently at 9am, 11am, 1pm, 3pm and 5pm; 1hr 30min; B500/person, minimum two people; ☎081 960 9398, ⓦscorpiontailed.com), a reconstruction of vessels that plied the river a century ago. This cruise heads downriver from a pier on Thanon Charoenrat, north of Nakhon Ping Bridge, and includes a commentary (in English) on historic places beside the river.

architecture, with its squat, multi-tiered roof and exquisitely carved and gilded pediment: if you feel you're being watched as you approach, it's the sinuous double arch between the porch's central columns, which represents the Buddha's eyebrows.

Inside sits one of Thailand's three **Phra Singh** (or Sihing) Buddha images (see p.98), a portly, radiant and much-revered bronze in a fifteenth-century Lanna style. Its setting is enhanced by the partly damaged but colourful **murals** of action-packed tableaux, which give a window on life in the north a hundred years ago. The murals illustrate two different stories: on the right-hand wall is an old folk tale, the *Sang Thong*, about a childless king and queen who are miraculously given a beautiful son, the "Golden Prince", in a conch shell. The murals on the left show the story of the mythical swan Suwannahong, who forms the magnificent prow of the principal royal barge in Bangkok. Incidentally, what look like Bermuda shorts on the men are in fact **tattoos**: in the nineteenth century, all boys in the north were tattooed from navel to kneecap, an agonizing ordeal undertaken to show their courage and to enhance their appeal to women. On one side of the wat is a high school for young yellow-sashed novices and schoolboys in blue shorts, who all noisily throng the temple compound during the day. Dally long enough and you'll be sure to have to help them with their English homework.

Wat Chedi Luang

Main entrance on Thanon Phra Pokklao, 10min walk east along Thanon Ratchdamnoen from Wat Phra Singh, with side entrances on Thanon Ratchamanka, Thanon Jhaban and Thanon Ratchdamnoen • Monk Chat daily 9am–6pm, with talks on Buddhism Sat 1pm

At **Wat Chedi Luang**, an enormous chedi, built in 1421 to house the ashes of King Ku Na but toppled from 90m to its present 60m by an earthquake in 1545, is the temple's most striking feature. You'll need a titanic leap of the imagination, however, to picture the beautifully faded pink-brick chedi, in all its crumbling grandeur, as it was in the fifteenth century, when it was covered in bronze plates and gold leaf, and housed the Emerald Buddha (see p.86) for eighty years. Recent attempts to rebuild the entire chedi to its former glory, now abandoned, have nevertheless led to modern replacements of the elephants at the base, the nagas that line the lengthy staircases and

---

MENGRAI MANIA

The spirit of **King Mengrai**, the heroic founder of the Lanna kingdom (see p.731), is still worshipped at dozens of shrines in Chiang Mai and the north eight hundred years after his death, but three in the old city stand out. About halfway between Wat Phra Singh and Wat Chedi Luang, Wat Kawt Kala was the second temple founded by the king in Chiang Mai (after Wat Chiang Man) and had its name changed to **Wat Phra Chao Mengrai** (or just **Wat Mengrai**) in the 1950s. The standing Buddha in its own *sala* just to the right of the main viharn here is said to replicate exactly King Mengrai's dimensions – and no wonder he was capable of such heroic deeds, as the image is 4m tall. By the beautiful, stately *bo* tree at the back of the compound stands a more plausible life-size modern statue of the king himself holding an elephant hook, where people leave all kinds of offerings, including swords.

Between Wat Chedi Luang and Chiang Mai City Arts and Cultural Centre stand two further monument-shrines to the great king. The site where he was killed by lightning, aged 80, is marked by a glittering, much-venerated **shrine** in its own small piazza on the corner of Thanon Ratchdamnoen and Thanon Phra Pokklao. A few minutes on up Thanon Phra Pokklao, Mengrai features again in the bronze **Three Kings Monument** in front of the arts and cultural centre, showing him discussing the auspicious layout of his "new city", Chiang Mai, with his allies, Ramkhamhaeng of Sukhothai and Ngam Muang of Phayao. The three kings had studied together under a religious teacher in Lopburi, but when they met up again, things were actually rather different from the harmonious picture portrayed by the monument: on a visit to Phayao, Ramkhamhaeng had an affair with Ngam Muang's wife, and Mengrai had to step in and mediate.

COURSES IN CHIANG MAI

The most popular course on offer is how to **cook** Thai food (especially at the cluster of small schools on and around Soi 5, Thanon Ratchdamnoen), followed by **Thai massage**. Chiang Mai is also a popular place for meditation retreats (see p.288), while other skills to be tackled, besides rock-climbing (see p.280), include: **t'ai chi**, on an eight-day introductory programme at Naisuan House, off Thanon Doi Saket Kao (☎085 714 5537, ⒲taichithailand.com); **yoga** at the Yoga Tree, 65/1 Thanon Arak (⒲theyogatree.org); **Thai boxing** at Lanna Muay Thai, 161 Soi Changkhian, Thanon Huai Kaeo (☎053 892102 or ☎081 951 3164, ⒲lannamuaythai.com); **Thai dance** at the Thai Dance Institute, 53 Thanon Kohklong (☎053 801375–6, ⒲thaidanceinstitute.com); one- to five-day workshops in **jewellery-making** through Nova, 179 Thanon Tha Pae (☎053 273058, ⒲nova-collection.com); and **Lanna arts and culture** with Origin Asia (see p.26).

COOKERY COURSES

Baan Thai 11 Soi 5, Thanon Ratchdamnoen ☎053 357339, ⒲cookinthai.com. Full-day (B900) or short evening course (B700); both include a market tour, and vegetarians are welcome.

Chiang Mai Thai Cookery School 47/2 Thanon Moonmuang ☎053 206388, ⒲thaicookeryschool .com. The original – and still the best – offering courses of one to five days as well as more advanced evening masterclasses. Each day begins with either an introduction to Thai ingredients, shopping in the market, making curry pastes or vegetable carving.

Courses are held at the owners' house, a 30min drive out of town (transport provided). B1450–6700, including a recipe book.

Thai Farm Cooking School 38 Soi 9, Thanon Moonmuang ☎081 288 5989, ⒲thaifarmcooking .com. Offers something slightly different, with the chance to pick your own organic vegetables, herbs and fruits for cooking on their farm, a 30min drive from town (transport provided). B1000/day; vegetarian, vegan and three-day courses also possible.

THAI MASSAGE COURSES

We give details on having a massage in Chiang Mai later in the chapter (see p.291).

Baan Hom Samunprai 9km south of town beyond Wiang Kum Kam ☎053 817362, ⒲homprang.com. Live-in massage courses out in the countryside costing B2100/day, including accommodation in a traditional village-style house with en-suite bathrooms, full board and the use of a plunge pool and bicycles; live-out courses from B1100/day.

Chetawan Massage School 7/1–2 Soi Samud Lanna, Thanon Pracha Uthit, off Thanon Chotana ☎053 410360, ⒲watpomassage.com. A branch of the massage school at Bangkok's Wat Pho (see p.92), which is considered to be the best place to study Thai massage in Thailand. Thirty-hour courses (6hr/day for 5 days) in traditional Thai (B9500) or foot (B7500) massage.

Old Medicine Hospital Off Thanon Wualai, opposite the Old Chiangmai Cultural Centre ☎053 201663 or ☎053 275085, ⒲thaimassageschool .ac.th. The longest-established centre in Chiang Mai, aka Shivagakomarpaj after the Indian hermit who is said to have founded the discipline over two thousand years ago. Highly respected week-long courses (B5000)

with dorm accommodation available; foot, oil and herbal compress courses are also offered.

Sunshine Network ☎089 835 5312, ⒲thaiyogamassage.infothai.com. An international group of practitioners and teachers founded by the highly respected German teacher, Harald Brust, aka Asokananda, who died in June 2005. Asokananda emphasized the spiritual aspect of what he called Thai yoga massage or Ayurvedic bodywork. Led by one of Asokananda's followers, twelve-day beginners' courses (B12,800, including basic accommodation, simple vegetarian rice meals and transportation) are held at a rural retreat in a Lahu village between Chiang Mai and Chiang Rai, often with optional yoga, t'ai chi and Vipassana meditation classes.

Thai Massage School of Chiangmai Northeast of town on the Mae Jo road, 2km beyond the Superhighway ☎053 854330, ⒲tmcschool.com. Accredited by the Ministry of Education and highly recommended by past pupils. Five-day courses (B7500), as well as longer professional courses. All courses include transportation.

the Buddha images in its four niches, including an oversized replica of the Emerald Buddha, funded by the present king for Chiang Mai's seven-hundredth anniversary, in its old spot on the eastern side.

In an unprepossessing modern building (which women are not allowed to enter) by the main entrance stands the city's *lak muang* or foundation pillar, here called the **Sao Inthakin** (Pillar of Indra), a brick structure covered in coloured glass and topped by a Buddha. Built by King Mengrai at Wat Sadeu Muang (on the site of the present-day Arts and Cultural Centre) when he established Chiang Mai, the pillar was moved here to the city's geographical centre by King Kawila in 1800, while he was re-founding the city after the ravages of the wars with the Burmese. The *Sao Inthakin* is sheltered by a stately gum tree which, the story has it, will stand for as long as the city's fortunes prosper. On the northeast side of the chedi, **Monk Chat** is advertised, giving you a chance to meet and talk to the monks in English.

Wat Pan Tao

Thanon Phra Pokklao, next door to Wat Chedi Luang on the north side

While you're in the vicinity, pop in on **Wat Pan Tao**, to see the recently renovated, fourteenth-century, all-teak viharn, constructed of unpolished panels, supported on enormous pillars and protected by carved wooden bars on the windows, a classic of graceful Lanna architecture.

Chiang Mai City Arts and Cultural Centre

Thanon Phra Pokklao • Tues–Sun 8.30am–5pm • B90 • ☎ 053 217793, ⓦ cmocity.org

Behind the Three Kings Monument, the elegant 1920s former provincial office has been turned into the **Chiang Mai City Arts and Cultural Centre** by the municipality – essentially a museum with the aim of conveying the history, customs and culture of the city and the region. To this end, scale models and plenty of high-quality English-language audiovisuals are thoughtfully deployed, with some nice touches such as vivid reminiscences by Chiang Mai's older inhabitants about what the city was like in the early twentieth century. Upstairs, the interest tails off, though there is an engaging audiovisual and exhibit on the hill tribes. The back half of the building shelters cultural activities such as weaving demonstrations, temporary exhibitions, a souvenir shop and a small café. A new Lanna history museum is planned behind the Arts and Cultural Centre, while the colonial-style former courthouse opposite the Three Kings Monument is slowly being converted into a museum focusing on Lanna arts.

Wat Chiang Man

Thanon Ratchaphakinai (carry on from the Arts and Cultural Centre up Thanon Phra Pokklao and turn right along Thanon Wiang Kaeo)

Erected by Mengrai on the site where he first pitched camp, **Wat Chiang Man** is the oldest temple in Chiang Mai and most notable for two dainty and very holy Buddha images housed in the viharn to the right of the entrance: the **Phra Sila**, a graceful marble bas-relief carved in northern India, supposedly in the sixth century BC, stands in the typical *tribunga*, or hip-shot stance; its partner, the **Phra Setangamani** (or Crystal Buddha), made four centuries later, probably in Lavo (modern Lopburi), is much revered by the inhabitants of Chiang Mai for its rainmaking powers and is carried through the streets during the Songkhran festival to help the rainy season on its way. Neither image is especially beautiful, but a powerful aura is created by making them difficult to see, high up behind two sets of iron bars.

Chiang Mai National Museum

On the northwestern outskirts on the Superhighway • Wed–Sun 9am–4pm • B100 • ⓦ thailandmuseum.com

In telling the history of Lanna art and culture, the **National Museum** has far fewer bells and whistles than its rival, the Chiang Mai Arts and Cultural Centre, but in terms of the quality of artefacts on display, it wins hands down. Inside, the airy rooms are cool enough for a long browse, and the collection is liberally labelled in English. There's an excellent spot for lunch, a branch of *Lamduon Faharm Khao Soi* (see p.298), just east of the museum on the north side of the Superhighway.

The history sections

As you enter, you're greeted on the left by the head of a smiling bronze Buddha that's as tall as a man, but you need to go right to follow the displays, which are grouped into six sections. The first of these displays artefacts and skeletons unearthed by local archeological digs, as well as photographs of cave paintings found in the area. The second section focuses on the golden age of the Lanna kingdom, from the fourteenth to the sixteenth centuries, including beautiful ceremonial betel sets (see box below) and some lovely ceramics from San Kamphaeng, while the third, fourth (upstairs) and fifth sections bring the history of the north up to date.

The religious art section

3

The biggest section is given over to **Thai religious art**, with a particular focus on **Lanna art**. Hundreds of Buddha images are on display, ranging from a humble, warmly smiling sandstone head of the Haripunjaya (Lamphun) era, representing the earliest northern style, to gleaming images in the Ratanakosin (Bangkok) style. In the golden age of Lanna, images were produced in two contrasting styles. One group, which resembles images from northern India, has been called the **lion-type**, after the Shakyamuni (Lion of the Shakyas) archetype at the great Buddhist temple at Bodh Gaya, the site of the Buddha's enlightenment. It's been conjectured that a delegation sent by King Tilok to Bodh Gaya in the 1450s brought back a copy of the statue, which became the model for hundreds of Lanna images. These broad-shouldered, plump-bellied Buddhas are always seated with the right hand in the touching-the-earth gesture, while the face is well rounded with pursed lips and a serious, majestic demeanour. The second type is the **Thera Sumana** style named after the monk Mahathera Sumana, who came from Sukhothai in 1369 to establish his Sri Lankan sect in Lanna. The museum is well stocked with this type of image, which shows strong Sukhothai influence, with an oval face and a flame-like *ushnisha* on top of the head.

BETEL

Betel-chewing today is popular only among elderly Thais, particularly country women, but it used to be a much more widespread social custom, and a person's betel tray set was once a Thai's most prized possession and an indication of rank: royalty would have sets made in gold, the nobility's would be in silver or nielloware, and poorer folk wove theirs from rattan or carved them from wood. A set comprises at least three small covered receptacles, and sometimes a tray to hold these boxes and the knife or nutcracker used to split the fruit.

The three essential ingredients for a good chew are betel leaf, limestone ash and areca palm fruit. You chew the coarse red flesh of the narcotic fruit (best picked when small and green-skinned) first, before adding a large heart-shaped betel leaf, spread with limestone-ash paste and folded into manageable size; for a stronger kick, you can include tobacco and/or marijuana at this point. An acquired and bitter taste, betel numbs the mouth and generates a warm feeling around the ears. Less pleasantly, constant spitting is necessary – which is why you'll often see spittoons in old-fashioned hotels in Thailand, re-used as waste baskets. It doesn't do much for your looks either: betel-chewers are easily spotted by their rotten teeth and lips stained scarlet from the habit.

3

CHIANG MAI FESTIVALS

Chiang Mai is the best and busiest place in the country to see in the Thai New Year, **Songkhran**, which takes over the city roughly between April 12 and 15. The most obvious role of the festival is as an extended "rain dance" in the driest part of the year, when huge volumes of canal water are thrown about in a communal water-fight that spares no one a drenching. The other elements of this complex festival are not as well known but no less important. In the temple compounds, communities get together to build sandcastles in the shape of chedis, which they cover with coloured flags – this bestows merit on any ancestors who happen to find themselves in hell and may eventually release them from their torments, and also shows an intent to help renovate the wat in the year to come. Houses are given a thorough spring-clean to see out the old year, while Buddha images from the city's main temples are cleaned, polished and sprinkled with lustral water, before being ceremonially carried through the middle of the water-fight to give everyone the chance to throw water on them and receive the blessing of renewal. Finally, younger family members formally visit their elders during the festival to ask for their blessings, while pouring scented water over their hands.

Loy Krathong, on and around the night of the full moon in November, has its most showy celebration at Sukhothai (see box, p.244), but Chiang Mai – where it is also known as **Yipeng** – is not far behind. While a spectacular but unnerving firework fiesta rages on the banks, thousands of candles are gently floated down the Ping River in beautiful lotus-leaf boats. As well as floating krathongs, people release **khom loy**, paper hot-air balloons that create a magical spectacle as they float heavenward, sometimes with firecrackers trailing behind. As with krathongs, they are released to carry away sins and bad luck, as well as to honour the Buddha's topknot, which he cut off when he became an ascetic (according to legend, the topknot is looked after by the Buddha's mother in heaven).

Chiang Mai's brilliantly colourful **flower festival**, centred on Buak Hat Park at the southwest corner of the old town usually on the first weekend of February, also attracts huge crowds. The highlight is a procession of floats, modelled into animals, chedis and even scenes from the *Ramayana*, and covered in flowers. In early April, the **Poy Sang Long** festival, centred around Wat Pa Pao near the northeast corner of the old city, is an ordination ritual for young Shan men, who are paraded round town on the shoulders of relatives. The boys are dressed in extravagant, colourful clothing with huge floral headdresses, which they symbolically cast off at the end of the festival to don a saffron robe – its most elaborate manifestation in Thailand is in Mae Hong Son (see box, p.340). In late May or early June, the **Inthakin Festival**, a life-prolonging ceremony for the city of Chiang Mai, using holy water from Doi Luang Chiang Dao, is focused around the city foundation pillar at Wat Chedi Luang, which throngs with locals making offerings.

Wat Jet Yot

Set back from the Superhighway, a 5min walk west of the National Museum

The peaceful garden temple of **Wat Jet Yot** is named after the "seven spires" of its unusual chedi. It was built in 1455 by King Tilok, after a model of the great temple at Bodh Gaya in India, and represents the seven places around Bodh Gaya which the Buddha visited in the seven weeks following his enlightenment; it also houses the king's ashes. Around the base of the chedi, delicate stuccos portray cross-legged deities serenely floating in the sky, a role model for all yogic fliers; their faces are said to be those of Tilok's relatives.

Chiang Mai Zoo and Aquarium

Thanon Huai Kaeo

About 1km beyond Wat Jet Yot, the Superhighway meets Thanon Huai Kaeo, a broad avenue of posh residences and hotels that starts out from the northwest corner of the moat and ends at the foot of Doi Suthep. Heading out up Thanon Huai Kaeo, past the sprawling campus of Chiang Mai University (CMU or "*Mor Jor*"), brings you to **Chiang Mai Zoo and Aquarium**, in an attractive park at the base of the mountain.

The zoo

Daily 8am–5pm • B100, children B50 • ⓦ chiangmaizoo.com

Originally a menagerie of a missionary family's pets, the **zoo** now houses an impressive collection of about eight thousand animals in modern, relatively comfortable conditions. There's a children's zoo and a colourful walk-through aviary, while larger mammals include elephants, giraffes, Humboldt penguins, koalas, a rhino and the current favourites, two **giant pandas** and a cub, born here in 2009 (B100 extra, children B50). Despite a disorientating layout, it makes a diverting visit, especially for kids. Feeding times for animals are posted clearly, and refreshment stalls for humans are never far away.

The zoo is better visited in the morning to avoid the afternoon heat. The grounds are too big to walk round, but "**service cars**" (small open-sided buses; B20, children B10) and a **monorail** (B150, children B50) are available to take you around.

The aquarium

Mon–Fri 10am–5pm, Sat & Sun 9am–5pm • B520, children B390 (includes admission to zoo) • ⓦ chiangmaiaquarium.com

Towards the western side of the zoo, the recently built **aquarium** is the biggest in Southeast Asia, with what's said – at 130m – to be the longest underwater viewing tunnel in the world. With the aim of showing landlocked Chiang Mai some rarely seen species, the huge edifice is strictly divided in half: in the freshwater section, you can see not only the Mekong giant catfish (see p.374), but also *thae pha*, the Chao Phraya giant catfish; while the salty half displays rare white-tip reef sharks, a double-headed Maori wrasse and a giant guitarfish, which is somewhere between a ray and a shark, and a precursor of the latter. There's a saltwater touch pool, and a long menu of feeding times, detailed on the website; it's also possible to snorkel (B1000) and scuba-dive (B4290) with the fishes.

Wat Suan Dork

Thanon Suthep • Monk Chat Mon, Wed & Fri 5–7pm • ⓦ monkchat.net

Wat Suan Dork, the "Flower Garden Temple", is surrounded by walls as part of Chiang Mai's fortifications. Legend says that Mahathera Sumana, when he was invited to establish his Sri Lankan sect here in 1369, brought with him a miraculous glowing relic. Ku Na, the king of Chiang Mai, ordered a huge chedi – the one you see today – to be built in his flower garden, but as the pea-sized relic was being placed inside the chedi, it split into two parts: one half was buried here, the other found its way to Doi Suthep, after further adventures (see p.304).

The brilliantly whitewashed chedi now sits next to a garden of smaller, equally dazzling chedis containing the ashes of the Chiang Mai royal family; framed by Doi Suthep to the west, this makes an impressive and photogenic sight, especially at sunset. At the back of the dusty compound, the bot is decorated with lively *Jataka* murals and enshrines a beautifully illuminated, 500-year-old bronze Buddha image. Nearby signs point the way to **Monk Chat**, organized by the Mahachulalongkorn Buddhist University based at the temple, which gives the monk-students the opportunity to meet foreigners and practise their English, and you the chance to talk to monks about anything from Buddhism to the weather – or about the university's overnight Buddhist culture and meditation courses (see box, p.288).

Chiang Mai University Art Museum

Thanon Nimmanhemin, near the corner of Thanon Suthep • Tues–Sun 9am–5pm • Free • ☎ 053 944833 or ☎ 053 218280, ⓦ cmuartcenter.org or ⓦ cmumuseum.org

The modern **Chiang Mai University Art Museum** is not only confirmation of the city's growing importance, but also a boon to the large local artistic community. The large,

MEDITATION IN CHIANG MAI

The peace and quiet of the northern capital make it ideally suited to **meditation** sessions, short courses and longer retreats, many of which are conducted in English. General information and advice about meditation is given in Basics (see p.50), where you'll also find details of the famous retreats at Wat Phra That Chom Thong, 60km south of Chiang Mai.

Green Papaya Sangha ⓦ greenpapayasangha.org. Offers meditation in the tradition of Vietnamese Zen Master, Thich Nhat Hanh, on Thursday evenings at 7.30pm at the Yoga Tree (see p.283), who also host dhamma talks from teachers of other Buddhist traditions. By donation.

International Buddhist Meditation Centre Wat Phra That Doi Suthep ⓣ 053 295012, ⓦ fivethousandyears.org. A variety of Vipassana meditation courses for beginners and experienced students, from four to 21 days. Registration must be made in advance (courses are often full). By donation.

International Meditation Centre Wat Umong ⓣ 053 810965, ⓦ watumong.org. Offers "open in, open out" meditation retreats, with a minimum three-day stay. Retreatants are asked to arrive at 8am. The meditation teacher, Phra Uttara, is a Vietnamese monk fluent in English who studied in Burma. By donation.

Mahachulalongkorn Buddhist University Wat Suan Dork ⓦ monkchat.net. Introductory retreat courses on meditation and Thai Buddhist culture, for which you need to wear white clothes, available for B300. Including yoga, chanting and almsgiving, they begin at about 2pm on a Tuesday, before departure to the training centre on Doi Suthep, returning to Wat Suan Dork at 2pm the next day (B500); in the fourth week of the month, the courses last three nights, returning on Friday (B1000). Courses are sometimes cancelled so check the schedule on the website.

Northern Insight Meditation Centre Wat Ram Poeng (aka Wat Tapotaram), off Thanon Chon Prathan near Wat Umong ⓣ 053 278620, ⓦ palikanon.com/vipassana/tapotaram/tapotaram.htm. Disciplined Vipassana courses (with a rule of silence, no food after noon and so on), taught by Thai monks with translators. The minimum stay is ten days, with a basic course lasting 26 days, and payment is by donation.

purpose-built exhibition areas are well designed and lit, and the exhibitions generally change each month, giving visitors an insight into modern Thai art, as well as anything from Japanese lacquerware sculpture to Iranian carpetry art. There's a café and shop, and films and concerts are regularly put on here.

Wat Umong

Off Thanon Suthep: turn left (south) after Wang Nam Gan (a royal agricultural produce project), then follow the signs to the Wat for about 1km along a winding lane

More of a park than a temple, **Wat Umong** makes an unusual, charming place for a stroll in the western suburbs. According to legend, the wat was built by King Mengrai, but renovated in the 1380s by King Ku Na for a brilliant but deranged monk called Jan, who was prone to wandering off into the forest to meditate. Because Ku Na wanted to be able to get Jan's advice at any time, he founded this wat and decorated the **tunnels** (*umong*) beneath the chedi with paintings of trees, flowers and birds to simulate the monk's favoured habitat. Some of the old tunnels can still be explored, where obscure fragments of paintings and one or two small modern shrines can be seen. Above the tunnels, frighteningly lavish nagas guard the staircase up to the overgrown **chedi** and a grassy platform that supports a grotesque black statue of the fasting Buddha, all ribs and veins: he is depicted as he was during his six years of self-mortification, before he realized that he should avoid extremes along the Middle Path to enlightenment. Behind the chedi, the ground slopes away to a **lake** inhabited by hungry carp, where locals come to relax and feed the fish. On a tiny island here, reached by a concrete bridge, stands a statue of the late Buddhadasa Bhikkhu (see p.536), a famous southern Thai monk who re-established the monastic community here in the 1960s.

Throughout the tranquil wooded grounds, the temple's diverse education-focused philosophy comes vividly alive: as you enter the compound you pass through a shady grove where signs are pinned to nearly every tree, displaying simple Buddhist maxims in Thai and English and the botanical name of the species. There's a library, in the centre of the temple grounds, with some books in English, and an adjacent bookshop; outside at tables and covered seating areas local people read, study and conduct discussions. The wat also holds meditation retreats (see box opposite).

ARRIVAL AND DEPARTURE
CHIANG MAI

On arrival at the train station or one of the bus stations, you can either flag down a red songthaew on the road or charter a tuk-tuk or songthaew (see p.290) to get to the centre. To **book tickets** for departure, there are several ways to dodge a long, extra trip out to the train station or Arcade (see p.29, p.31 and below), including just asking your guesthouse or hotel. Queen Bee, 5 Thanon Moonmuang (☎053 275525, ⓦqueenbeetours.com), is a reliable **travel agent** for train tickets and all manner of minibus and bus tickets, as well as for a wide range of tours. Global Union Express, near Warorot Market at 35 Thanon Chang Moi (☎053 234400 ⓦguetravel.com), is a good agent for domestic and international plane tickets.

BY PLANE

Chiang Mai Airport (☎053 270222–33) is 3km southwest of the centre. Its busiest route is Bangkok, which is served by all five of the main Thai carriers, while Bangkok Airways does Ko Samui, Thai Airways and Air Asia Phuket, Air Asia Hat Yai and Ubon Ratchathani, and Nok Air Mae Hong Son, Phitsanulok and Udon Thani. There are also half a dozen international routes (see p.276), while the new Kan Airlines (ⓦkanairlines.com) operates small propeller planes out of Chiang Mai on a constantly changing schedule of domestic routes.

Airport facilities You'll find currency exchange booths and ATMs, a post office (daily 8.30am–8pm), a Silkworm bookshop on the ground floor near domestic arrivals and Bookazine in the domestic departure lounge, cafés, left-luggage lockers (B140/day) and car rental offices such as Avis (☎053 201574, ⓦavisthailand.com).

Getting to/from the centre Both metered and unmetered licensed taxis are available in the baggage hall, and there's very little between them; the former, even with a B50 airport pick-up fee, are probably slightly cheaper to the city centre, at around B110 to Tha Pae Gate. Tuk-tuks and red songthaews can bring departing passengers to the airport (around B100 from the city centre), but are not allowed to pick up fares there.

Destinations Bangkok (25 daily; 1hr); Hat Yai (daily; 2hr); Ko Samui (2 daily; 1hr 40min); Mae Hong Son (2 daily; 35min); Phitsanulok (3 weekly; 1hr); Phuket (3 daily; 2hr); Ubon Ratchathani (2 weekly; 1hr 15min); Udon Thani (2 daily; 1hr 20min).

BY TRAIN

Many people arrive – often an hour or two later than scheduled – at the train station (which has a left-luggage office) on Thanon Charoen Muang, just over 2km from Tha Pae Gate on the eastern side of town (☎1690, ☎053 244795 or ☎053 245364). There's usually a welcoming committee of guesthouse staff, plugging their accommodation and offering free lifts.

Destinations Bangkok (6 daily; 12hr–14hr 30min); Den Chai (for Phrae and Nan; 7 daily; 4–5hr); Doi Khun Tan (5 daily; 1hr 30min); Lampang (7 daily; 2hr–2hr 30min).

BY BUS

Arcade bus station Chiang Mai's main bus station is off the south side of Thanon Kaeo Nawarat (☎053 243669 or ☎053 247020), about 3km from Tha Pae Gate to the northeast.

Chang Phuak bus station This small station off the east side of Thanon Chotana handles services from the rest of Chiang Mai province (including Tha Ton); buses from Lamphun also end up here.

Bus companies The main Chiang Mai-based long-distance bus company, Green Bus (☎053 266480, ⓦgreenbusthailand.com), maintains a ticket office in the centre of town, on Thanon Singharat, just north of Wat Phra Singh. If you insist on travelling here with one of the low-cost tourist bus companies on Bangkok's Thanon Khao San despite our warnings (see p.136), try to find out exactly where you'll be dropped in Chiang Mai before making a booking: these companies' buses have been known to stop on a remote part of the Superhighway, where they "sell" their passengers to various guesthouse touts.

Destinations Bangkok (20 daily; 10–11hr); Chiang Khong (3 daily; 6hr); Chiang Rai (every 30min; 3–4hr); Chiang Saen (2 daily; 5hr); Chom Thong (11 daily; 1hr); Fang (every 30min; 3hr 30min); Khon Kaen (10 daily; 12hr); Khorat (12 daily; 12hr); Lampang (every 30min; 1hr 30min); Lamphun (every 10min; 1hr); Mae Hong Son (5 daily via Mae Sariang, 8–9hr; 3 daily via Pai, 8hr); Mae Sai (6 daily; 4–5hr); Mae Sot (2 daily; 6hr); Nan (8 daily; 6hr); Pai (5 daily; 4hr); Phitsanulok (up to 18 daily; 5–6hr); Phrae (hourly; 4hr); Rayong (8 daily; 17hr); Sukhothai (up to 19 daily; 5–6hr); Tha Ton (4 daily; 4hr); Ubon Ratchathani (6 daily; 17hr); Udon Thani (4 daily; 12hr).

3

GETTING AROUND

BY BICYCLE

Although you can comfortably walk between the most central temples, bicycles are the best way of getting around the old town and, with a bit of legwork, out to the attractions beyond the moat too. Sit-up-and-beg models and basic mountain bikes are available at many outlets on the roads along the eastern moat for B30–50/day, while Cacti, 94/1 Thanon Singharat, near the corner of Si Phum (☎ 053 212979 or ☎ 089 757 9150), rents (B80–350/day) and sells good-quality, well-maintained road and mountain bikes.

BY SONGTHAEW

There's been talk about setting up a comprehensive bus system in Chiang Mai for years, but for now people make do with red songthaews, which act as shared taxis within the city, picking up a number of passengers headed in roughly the same direction and taking each to their specific destination. A journey in the centre of town, for example from Tha Pae Gate to Wat Phra Singh, will set you back B20, but it'll naturally cost more to go somewhere off the beaten track or if the driver thinks you want to charter (*mao*) the whole vehicle.

BY TAXI, TUK-TUK OR SAMLOR

Chiang Mai's taxis only ever switch on their meters when leaving the airport; otherwise, they quote flat fares, typically B150 for a 2km journey. You can't flag them down on the street – call ☎ 053 922128 or ☎ 053 218271 for a

pick-up. More prevalent are tuk-tuks, for which heavy bargaining is expected – allow around B50 for a short journey, say from the Night Bazaar to Tha Pae Gate. The town still has a few samlors, which are cheap when used by locals to haul produce home from the market, but not so cheap when chartered by groups of upmarket tourists on sightseeing tours from their hotel.

BY MOTORBIKE

Motorbikes – most useful for exploring places outside of Chiang Mai – are available to rent in all shapes and sizes around Tha Pae Gate, starting from about B130–150/day for an 80cc step-through. Among reliable rental outlets, Queen Bee, 5 Thanon Moonmuang (☎ 053 275525, ⓦ queen-bee.com), and Mr Mechanic, Thanon Moonmuang, near the corner of Thanon Ratchawithi (☎ 053 214708, ⓦ mr-mechanic1994.com), who has bikes of all sizes and leads biking tours, can also offer insurance.

BY CAR

Many outlets in the Tha Pae Gate area rent out cars and four-wheel drives, from as little as B800/day: reliable companies offering insurance and breakdown recovery include Avis (ⓦ avisthailand.com), at Chiang Mai airport (☎ 053 201798–9) and *Royal Princess Hotel* (see p.295); Journey, 283 Thanon Tha Pae (☎ 053 208787, ⓦ journeycnx.com); North Wheels, 70/4–8 Thanon Chaiyapoom (☎ 053 874478, ⓦ northwheels .com); and Queen Bee, 5 Thanon Moonmuang (☎ 053 275525, ⓦ queenbeetours.com).

INFORMATION

Tourist information The TAT office is at 105/1 Thanon Chiang Mai–Lamphun, on the east bank of the river, south of Nawarat Bridge (daily 8.30am–4.30pm; ☎ 053 248604 or ☎ 053 302500, ⓔ tatchmai@tat.or.th), where you can pick up handouts and a simple free map of the city. It's not to be confused with T&T Travel and Tours on Thanon Ratchaphakinai, which pretends to be a government information office but is in fact a private travel agent.

Maps *Nancy Chandler's Map of Chiang Mai*, sold in many outlets in the city (B250), is very handy for a detailed exploration: like her brightly coloured Bangkok map, it

gives a personal choice of sights, shops, restaurants and various oddities. Regular updates are posted at ⓦ nancy chandler.net.

Listings Several free, monthly, locally published magazines, the best of which are *Guidelines* and *Citylife*, contain information about upcoming events in town and articles about local culture; they're distributed in spots where tourists tend to congregate, including money-exchange booths and hotel lobbies. *Citylife* also has a website at ⓦ chiangmainews .com and produces a fortnightly map with events listings, *City Now*.

ACCOMMODATION

Chiang Mai is well stocked with every kind of accommodation to suit all budgets. Its **basic guesthouses**, often friendly, quiet affairs with their own outdoor cafés, are gathered on the narrow sois inside the old city. Situated close to the eastern side of the moat and Tha Pae Gate, **Thanon Moonmuang's Soi 9** and the **south end of Thanon Ratchaphakinai** almost warrant being called travellers' ghettoes (though nothing like on the scale of Bangkok's Thanon Khao San), but there are plenty of other, quieter options within the moat where you can better soak up the old town's charm. In the moderate price range, by far the best options are the **upmarket guesthouses and lodges**, which, as well as good facilities, generally offer more appealing decor and atmosphere than similarly priced hotels. At the top end, there has been a recent explosion of **luxury accommodation** in Chiang Mai, ranging from small boutique hotels to massive projects like the Mandarin Oriental's *Dhara Devi*, most of them enhanced by traditional Lanna architectural touches.

MASSAGES AND SPAS IN CHIANG MAI

Many of Chiang Mai's top hotels now have full-service **spas**, and there are several upmarket stand-alones. However, the best traditional **massages** in town – no frills but highly skilled and good value – are likely to be had at the massage schools (see p.283): the Old Medicine Hospital offers consistently good Thai (B250/90min), herbal and foot massages; on the opposite side of town, the offshoot of Wat Pho, Chetawan, charges B360 per hour for traditional massage (daily 4–6pm; closed first and third Sun of every month); while out in the countryside at Baan Hom Samunprai, two-hour massages cost B600 (foot massage B300).

Chiangmai Oasis Spa 4 Thanon Samlan, just south of Wat Phra Singh, & 103 Thanon Sirimuangkarajan ☎053 920111, ⓦchiangmaioasis.com. Upmarket spa with a good reputation (B2000 for a 2hr traditional massage).

Let's Relax Night Bazaar Pavilion, Thanon Chang Klan ☎053 818498, ⓦletsrelaxspa.com. Part of a nationwide chain, this reasonably priced spa lays on a few more frills, longer opening hours and a wider range of treatments than the basic massage centres (from B400 for a 1hr Thai massage).

The Peak Spa & Beauty Salon Twin Peaks Condo, 187/13 Thanon Chang Klan ☎053 818869, ⓦpeak -spa.com. Excellent choice, offering a wide range of treatments at moderate prices, but with service and facilities comparable to a luxury hotel (from B800 for 90min Thai massage). Free transfers included.

Thai Massage Conservation Club 99 Thanon Ratchamankha, near Wat Chedi Luang ☎053 904452. Basic setup with traditional massages by extremely competent, blind masseurs (B150/hr), who focus on acupressure rather than stretching.

ESSENTIALS

Availability and reservations Usually there are plenty of beds to go around, but many places fill up from December to February and at festival time, particularly during Songkhran (April) and Loy Krathong (Nov). At these times, you'll need to book to stay at one of the expensive hotels, and for guesthouses it's a good idea to phone ahead – even if you can't book a place, you can save yourself a journey if the place is full.

Scams Beware of tuk-tuk and songthaew drivers at the bus and train stations offering a free ride if you stay at a particular guesthouse – perhaps adding, falsely, that the place you had planned to stay is full or closed – as you'll probably find that the price of a room is bumped up to pay for your ride. To get around this, some guesthouses send their own staff to the stations, who will genuinely give you a free ride; and many places will offer a free pick-up when you book.

Trekking hassles Many of the least expensive places in Chiang Mai make their money from trekking and tours, which can be convenient as a trek often needs a lot of organizing beforehand, but can equally be annoying if you're in Chiang Mai for other reasons and are put under pressure to trek; most of the guesthouses we've listed can arrange trekking, but at none of them should you get this kind of undue hassle.

THA PAE GATE AREA

GUESTHOUSES

Awana House 7 Soi 1, Thanon Ratchdamnoen ☎053 419005, ⓦawanahouse.com. This helpful, Thai–Dutch guesthouse has a tiny pool and large, nicely furnished rooms (some with balconies), complete with colourful trompe l'oeil paintings, a/c, hot water, cable TV, fridge and safety boxes. There are also two rooftop fan rooms, which have good single rates and share a hot-water bathroom. Internet access and free wi-fi. Fan B350, a/c B500

Chiang Mai Thai House 5/1 Soi 5, Thanon Tha Pae ☎053 904110, ⓦchiangmaithaihouse.com. There's a choice of smallish but well-furnished rooms with fan or bigger ones with a/c in this centrally located place which also has a tiny pool. Wi-fi and internet. Fan B400, a/c B950

★ **Eagle House 1** 16 Soi 3, Thanon Chang Moi Kao ☎053 235387 and **Eagle House 2** 26 Soi 2, Thanon Ratchawithi ☎053 418494, ⓦeaglehouse.com. Run by an Irishwoman and her Thai husband who are keen to promote ethical ecotourism, these two guesthouses offer spacious garden terrace areas with good cafés and well-organized treks, as well as Thai cookery courses at *EH2*. Friendly, well-maintained *EH1* is preferable to *EH2*. The former has a wide variety of en-suite rooms of different sizes, some with hot water, some with a/c; the latter's rooms have hot showers and either fans or a/c, and include dorms (B100). Phone for a free pick-up. Fan and cold shower B170, fan and hot shower B200, a/c B320

Gap's House 3 Soi 4, Thanon Ratchdamnoen ☎053 278140, ⓦgaps-house.com. Set around a relaxing, leafy compound strewn with antiques is a wide range of plush a/c rooms with hot showers. The room price includes a simple cooked breakfast, there's free internet access and wi-fi, and a vegetarian buffet is served in the evening (not Sun); one- or two-day cookery courses available. No reservations are taken, though you can call on your proposed arrival date to check availability. Decent rates for singles. B470

3

Giant Guesthouse Soi 6, Thanon Moonmuang ☎ 053 227338, ⓦ giantguesthouse.com. This popular option is right next to the market and has its own kitchen; ideal if you fancy practising your Thai cooking. The staff are helpful and offer free bicycles and free internet, and also put on films in their comfortable lounge. Rooms with wi-fi come with fan (shared or en-suite bathrooms) or a/c. There's

another branch at the bottom of Thanon Ratchaphakinai with dorm beds (B120). Fan B180, a/c B400

Jonadda Guest House 23/1 Soi 2, Thanon Ratchawithi ☎ 053 227281, ⓦ jonadda.com. Friendly Thai–Australian place with a variety of bright, clean, comfortable fan rooms (including triples) with strong hot showers, in a modern, multistorey building. Good prices for singles. B300

THA PAE GATE AREA

● SHOPS
Backstreet Books	3
Boots	5
Fair Trade Shop	7
Gecko Books	4
Ginger	1
The Lost Bookshop	8
Neramit	2
Nova Collection	6

● RESTAURANTS & CAFÉS
Aroon Rai	7
Blue Diamond	2
Jerusalem Falafel	6
La Fontana	9
Miguel's	1
Mit Mai	8
Pho Vieng Chane	5
Ratana's Kitchen	3
Ruen Tamarind	4

■ ACCOMMODATION
Awana House	12
Chiang Mai Thai House	15
Eagle House 1	6
Eagle House 2	8
Gap's House	14
Giant Guesthouse	4, 21
Jonadda Guest House	5
Karinthip Village	9
Kavil Guest House	10
Libra House	3
Mini Cost	11
Pha Thai House	19
Portico 21	17
Raming Lodge	18
Sabai Garden	20
SK House	1
Supreme Guest House	2
Tamarind Village	13
Three Sis	16
Your House	7

■ BARS & CLUBS
Jack Van Bar	1
Second Floor Gallery & Bar	3
THC (The Hemp Collective)	4
UN Irish Pub	2

Map labels: Thai Farm Cooking School, Wat Chiang Man, SOI 9, SOI 8, SOI 7, Somphet Market, SOI 6, SOI 5, SOI 2, THANON RATCHAWITHI, Mr. Mechanic, North Wheels, THANON CHAIYAPOOM, THANON SITHIWONG, THANON CHANG MOI, N, RATCHAWONG, Wanrot Market, THANON RATCHAPHAKINAI, Baan Thai Cooking School, SOI 1, SOI 5, THANON MOONMUANG, CHANG MOI KAO, Moat, Air Asia, Tha Pae Gate, Journey, AUA, THANON RATCHADAMNOEN, Chiang Mai Thai Cookery School, SOI 4, SOI 3, THANON THA PAE, Wat Bupparam, SOI 6, SOI 15, SOI 4, SOI 3, THANON RATCHAMANKA, Queen Bee Travel Service, Chiang Mai Rock Climbing Adventures, THANON LOI KHRO, THANON KOTCHASARN, SOI 2, SOI 1, Wat Phra Singh, Wat Chedi Luang, Night Bazaar, 0 50 metres

Kavil Guest House 10/1 Soi 5, Thanon Ratchdamnoen ☎053 224740 or ☎089 852 1875. Friendly place in a modern four-storey building on a quiet soi with free wi-fi throughout. All twelve rooms have en-suite hot-water bathrooms; the rooms with fans are small, plain and clean, while those with a/c are pleasantly decorated and more spacious (the a/c can be switched off to turn these into fan rooms). The downstairs café is at the front, which means there's no noisy courtyard effect. Fan B200, a/c B350

Libra House 28 Soi 9, Thanon Moonmuang ☎053 210687, ⓦlibrahousechiangmai.com. Excellent, family-run, trekking-oriented guesthouse with keen, helpful service and 24hr check-in. Forty large, plain but well-maintained rooms, spread across five buildings with some quiet sitting areas, are en suite and wi-fi enabled, some with hot water. Internet access. Call for free pick-up. Fan with cold shower B250, fan with hot shower B350, a/c with hot shower B500

Mini Cost 19–19/4 Soi 1, Thanon Ratchdamnoen ☎053 418787–8, ⓦminicostcm.com. Smart ochre-painted block offering comfortable rooms with some colourful modern Thai decorative touches, as well as a/c, hot water, fridges, wi-fi and cable TV. Staff are eager to please and there's internet access. B600

Pha Thai House 48/1 Thanon Ratchaphakinai ☎053 278013 or ☎081 998 6933, ⓦphathaihouse.com. Wide variety of rooms, all with en-suite hot showers and wi-fi, in a leafy garden setting: some boast balconies, colourful decor, fridges and antique-style furniture, while plainer rooms at the front of the compound by the road are much cheaper. Family rooms also available. Fan B400, a/c B500

Sabai Garden 36 Thanon Ratchaphakinai ☎053 208921, ✉sabaigarden_vicky@yahoo.com. Homestay-style accommodation in an airy, traditional wooden house on stilts, set in a large, pretty garden where Thai food is served. Rooms sport lovely teak floorboards, old wooden furniture and cable TVs (some with DVDs); hot showers are shared. Massages and cookery classes are available, as well as free bicycles and free wi-fi. Breakfast included. B600

SK House 30 Soi 9, Thanon Moonmuang ☎053 210690, ⓦtheskhouse.com. Efficient, brick-built high-rise with a ground-floor café and internet access, a small, shaded swimming pool and a slightly institutional feel. Fan rooms come with hot-water bathrooms, while the a/c rooms are much more colourful and attractive, with cable TV. Free pick-ups from the train station. Fan B250, a/c B600

Supreme Guest House 44/1 Soi 9, Thanon Moonmuang ☎053 222480. Friendly Scottish-run guest-house in a modern concrete block with a pleasant roof veranda. The rooms are comfortable and have fans and solar-heated showers. B250

Three Sis 1 Soi 8, Thanon Phra Pokklao ☎053 273243, ⓦ3sisbedandbreakfast.com. Genteel B&B opposite Wat Chedi Luang with lots of attractive open-plan public areas

to loll about in. Rooms in the new building have wooden floors and tasteful furnishings that also feature a lot of dark wood, while those in the original building are equally spacious but less stylish; all have a/c, hot water, cable TV and fridges. Free internet and wi-fi. Breakfast included. B1800

★ **Your House** 8 Soi 2, Thanon Ratchawithi ☎053 217492, ⓦyourhouseguesthouse.com. Very welcoming, old-town atmosphere (though some rooms get a bit of noise from nearby bars) and a wide choice of accommo-dation: in the attractive, original teak house, six airy rooms share three bathrooms with hot showers; the two modern annexes across the lane, both with hot water en suite, include lovely, big, new rooms with polished teak floors, small balconies, well-equipped bathrooms and internet access. Optional a/c in most rooms. The restaurant serves good Thai and French food, with buffalo steak and chips a speciality. Good for treks, day-trips and train, plane and bus tickets. Call for free pick-up. Discounts for singles. Fan B250, a/c B450

HOTELS

Karinthip Village 50/2 Thanon Chang Moi Kao ☎053 235414–8, ⓦkarinthipvillage.com. Peaceful compound located just east of the old city, with 62 rooms set around a decent-sized swimming pool, all nicely decorated in Lanna style and some with four-poster beds. Breakfast included. Discounts often available on their website. B4000

Portico 21 7 Soi 1, Thanon Kotchasarn ☎053 278378, ⓦportico21.com. Sleek, contemporary digs, with a/c, hot showers, TVs and fridges, centrally located behind *Aroon Rai* restaurant, but set well back from the busy roads. Free wi-fi and continental breakfast. B1600

Raming Lodge 17–19 Thanon Loi Kroh ☎053 271777, ⓦraminglodge.com. Right in the heart of the downtown action, this red-brick, six-storey place offers tasteful, well-equipped a/c rooms with desks, cable TV, hot showers, fridges and wi-fi (payable). Facilities include a small massage spa and swimming pool. B1800

Tamarind Village 50/1 Thanon Ratchdamnoen ☎053 418896–9, ⓦtamarindvillage.com. Named for a huge, 200-year-old tamarind tree that shades the compound, this small, tranquil boutique resort in the heart of Chiang Mai's old city is designed in Lanna style, though the extremely comfortable rooms, which all enjoy lovely garden views, have modern touches. Good-sized pool, attractive spa and excellent restaurant (see p.296) too. B4900

REST OF CHIANG MAI
GUESTHOUSES

Baan Kaew Guest House 142 Thanon Charoen Prathet ☎053 271606, ⓦbaankaew-guesthouse.com. Set back from the road in a quiet, pretty garden, this attractive modern building has twenty large, simple but well-equipped and well-maintained rooms with hot water, free wi-fi and a/c. **B800**

★ **Baan Orapin** 150 Thanon Charoenrat ☎053 243677, ⓦ baanorapin.com. Delightful compound overshadowed by tall longan trees, offering big, comfy and characterful rooms with teak and rattan furnishings and wooden floors. Some rooms come with four-poster beds and balconies. Breakfast included; minimum stay two nights. **B2100**

Eco Resort 109 Thanon Bamrungrat ☎053 247111, ⓦ ecoresortchiangmai.com. This former school in huge, lush, quiet gardens has been tastefully transformed into a modern hostel-cum-hotel, with a/c and hot water through-out. Choose between well-equipped dorms (some with only 2 beds) with smart, white bedding, and attractive rooms with large bathrooms in a subtle contemporary style. Lovely, 25m pool surrounded by hanging plants, stylish common rooms, internet access and free wi-fi throughout. Simple breakfast included. Dorm **B400**, double **B1200**

★ **Elliebum** 114/3–4 Thanon Ratchamanka ☎053 814723 or ☎085 018 7400, ⓦ elliebum.com. Sociable and very helpful home-from-home in the centre of town, with huge, fresh, modern rooms (big enough for a family) with a/c, hot water, TV and DVD, above a café (see p.298); plus some very spruce and comfortable rooms at an affiliated guesthouse (ⓦ rachamankhaflorahouse.com) 100m away. Free wi-fi and internet, and free cooking classes if you stay seven days. Tasty à la carte breakfasts included, plus a wide choice of activities, including culinary walking tours (see opposite) and shopping tours. **B1400**

Galare Guest House 7 Soi 2, Thanon Charoen Prathet ☎053 818887 or ☎053 821011, ⓦ galare.com. Near Narawat Bridge, this long-standing, well-run upmarket guesthouse is justly popular. Plain a/c rooms, each with hot-water bathroom, TV and fridge, overlook a shady lawn that gives way to a riverside terrace restaurant. Wi-fi available. **B1150**

Green Tulip 18 Thanon Samlarn ☎053 278367, ⓦ greentuliphouse.com. In a good location opposite the post office near Wat Phra Singh, with a bar-restaurant offering good food downstairs and a pleasant roof garden. Has eighteen clean, bright, basic rooms with fan or a/c and with shared or en-suite hot showers, featuring a lot of green in the decor. Internet access. Dorm **B150**, double **B400**

★ **Hollanda Montri** 365 Thanon Charoenrat ☎053 242450, ⓦ hollandamontri.com. North of the centre by the busy Rama IX Bridge, in a modern building by the river, this Dutch–Thai guesthouse has large, comfortable and attractive fan or a/c rooms with TVs and hot-water bathrooms, and cheerful staff. A very pleasant, terraced riverside bar-restaurant offers a long menu of Thai and European dishes. Free internet and wi-fi, and free daytime bicycles. Fan **B450**, a/c **B550**

The Pub 189 Thanon Huai Kaeo ☎053 211550, ⓦ thepubchiangmai.com. In the garden of this long-running watering hole sit some good-value clapboard or brick bungalows with small terraces. They're quite tightly packed but spacious and very comfy, with a/c, fridges, cable TV, free wi-fi and big, sparkling, well-equipped bathrooms with hot water. **B800**

Riverside House 101 Thanon Chiang Mai–Lamphun ☎053 241860, ⓦ riversidehousechiangmai.com. Welcoming place with a lush garden on the east bank of the river, though just a short walk from the night bazaar, with plain but clean and cosy a/c rooms with cable TV, hot showers and free wi-fi, plus a small swimming pool. **B500**

River View Lodge 25 Soi 4, Thanon Charoen Prathet ☎053 271109–10, ⓦ riverviewlodgch.com. Tasteful, well-run and good-value alternative to international-class hotels, with a beautiful riverside garden, a small swimming pool and neat decorative touches in the rooms; the most expensive have balconies overlooking the river. Breakfast included. **B1800**

HOTELS

Centara Duangtawan 132 Thanon Loi Khro ☎053 905000, ⓦ centarahotelsresorts.com. This five-hundred-room, international-standard hotel by the night bazaar pulls in package groups with attractive rates and an impressive range of facilities: spacious pool, well-equipped gym, spa and highly regarded 24th-floor Chinese restaurant with fine views of Doi Suthep. **B1900**

The Chedi 123 Thanon Charoen Prathet ☎053 253333, ⓦ ghmhotels.com. Occupying a prime riverside site, though hemmed in by noisy Charoen Prathet, this luxury place offers high-concept minimalist design in its spacious rooms, along with balconies, river views and free wi-fi. There's a good-looking spa and swimming pool, while the renovated teak bar-restaurant – formerly the British Consulate, built in 1905 – dishes up excellent Indian, Thai and Western food. Breakfast included. **B7400**

Chiang Mai Gate Hotel 11/10 Thanon Suriyawong ☎053 203895–9, ⓦ chiangmaigatehotel.com. Located just to the south of the old city, this place has 120 well-equipped rooms with Lanna touches in the design, a/c and hot water, plus a swimming pool and helpful staff. Breakfast included. **B1750**

D2 Hotel 100 Chang Klan ☎053 999999, ⓦ dusit.com. With its muted orange theme, flat-screen TVs and helpful staff in street fashions, plus stunning lighting and minimalist furnishings, this place in the heart of the night bazaar, run by the Dusit Group, is one of the city's hippest places to stay. A beer garden, spa, fitness centre and rooftop pool are among the amenities. **B4600**

Dhara Devi 51/4 Thanon Chiang Mai–Sankamphaeng ☎053 888888, ⓦ mandarinoriental.com. Occupying huge grounds a few kilometres east of the city centre, the

Dhara Devi transports its guests into another era – the heyday of the Lanna Kingdom, with traditional Lanna architecture complemented by modern touches such as a/c, dimmer switches and cable TV. The villas, suites and residences are equipped with every conceivable comfort and look out over rice fields and vegetable gardens. With its own breathtaking spa (modelled on the royal palace of Mandalay), cooking school, craft village, shopping centre, library of books and DVDs, two swimming pools, tennis courts and four restaurants, guests need never leave the premises. B24,900

★ **Four Seasons** About 15km north of Chiang Mai on Mae Rim–Samoeng Old Road, at the start of the Mae Sa valley ☎053 298181, ⓦfourseasons.com. The last word in Lanna luxury, with superbly appointed rooms and apartments, a swimming pool and a gorgeous spa, all set around a picturesque lake and rice paddies (where you can learn to plant rice) with fine views of Doi Suthep behind. On a long menu of activities, the highlight is a top-quality cooking school. B18,700

People Place 9 Soi 8, Thanon Charoen Prathet ☎053 274652 or ☎053 282487, ⓦpeople-place.com. Two compact modern buildings, just a few steps from the night bazaar, whose spacious, comfy rooms come with en-suite hot-water bathrooms, a/c, cable TV and mini-bars. B800

★ **Rachamankha** 6 Soi 9, Thanon Ratchamanka ☎053 904111, ⓦrachamankha.com. Looking more like a temple than a hotel, this spacious, architect-owned

property with just 24 elegant rooms is hidden in the quiet backstreets of the old city. There's a lovely, large pool, a spa, an excellent restaurant (see p.298), a well-stocked library with sherry laid out for browsers, and even a small museum of lacquerware and silver. Free wi-fi and internet; breakfast included. B8000

Royal Princess 111 Thanon Chang Klan ☎053 253900, ⓦdusit.com. Tidy, centrally located hotel close to the night bazaar, with two hundred elegant rooms, an attractive swimming pool and fitness centre, fine restaurants and impeccable service. B2800

Tri Yaan Na Ros 156 Thanon Wualai ☎053 273174, ⓦtriyaannaros.com. Snuggled away to the south of the old city centre, this renovated colonial building oozes atmosphere, from the four-poster beds to the photos of ancient Lanna on the walls. A small library, swimming pool, internet access and free bicycle use for guests. Breakfast included. B4075

U Chiang Mai 70 Thanon Ratchdamnoen ☎053 327000, ⓦuhotelsresorts.com. Recently built hotel with lots of innovative ideas: 24hr use of room (no matter what time you check in), heritage talks and walks, breakfast (included) available in your bedroom all day, free bikes and wi-fi. The reading room and spa occupy the hundred-year-old former governor's residence, while some of the rooms – decorated in contemporary Thai style, with daybeds on the balconies, rain showers and iPods – give straight onto the small, black swimming pool. B4400

EATING

The main difficulty with **eating** in Chiang Mai is knowing when to stop. All over town there are inexpensive and enticing restaurants serving typically northern food, which has been strongly influenced by Burmese cuisine, especially in curries such as *kaeng hang lay* (usually translated on menus as "Northern Thai curry"), made with pork, ginger, garlic and tamarind. At **lunchtime** the thing to do is to join the local workers in one of the simple, inexpensive cafés that put all their efforts into producing just one or two special dishes – the traditional meal at this time of day is *khao soi*, a thick broth of curry and coconut cream, with egg noodles and a choice of meat. The main **night markets** are at the back and front entrances to Chiang Mai University on Thanon Suthep and Thanon Huai Kaeo; along Thanon Bamrungburi by Chiang Mai Gate; along Thanon Manee Noparat by Chang Puak Gate; plus a few stalls in front of Somphet market on Thanon Moonmuang. Also in the evening you'll find restaurants which lay on touristy **cultural shows** with *khan toke* dinners, a selection of northern dishes traditionally eaten on the floor off short-legged lacquer trays. Of these, the Old Chiangmai Cultural Centre, 185/3 Thanon Wualai (B650; ☎053 275097, ⓦoldchiangmai.com), with its show of northern Thai and hill-tribe dancing, has the best reputation. Many of the **bars** listed in "Drinking and nightlife" (see p.299) have good reputations for their food, especially *The Riverside* and *The UN Irish Pub*.

FOOD WALKS AND DINNER CRUISES

In the mornings, *Elliebum Guesthouse* (see opposite) offers fascinating guided **food walks** around the old town (4hr; B750/person). With plenty of insights about Thai cuisine and culture along the way, they take in Chiang Mai Gate Market and the city's best street restaurants and dessert stalls. Every evening.

The Riverside (see p.300) runs a **dinner cruise**, charging B110 per person on top of whatever you order from their very good menu; get there by 7.15pm to put your orders in (boat departs at 8pm). Mae Ping River Cruises (see p.281) also runs dinner cruises at 7.30pm for B550 per person for a Thai set menu.

THA PAE GATE AREA

THAI

Aroon Rai Thanon Kotchasarn ☎053 276947. Sample all the classic Lanna dishes, such as tasty *kaeng hang lay muu* (B50) and *khao soi*, at this basic, long-standing restaurant by Tha Pae Gate, then buy their curry pastes to take home with you. Daily 11am–9pm.

★ **Ratana's Kitchen** 320–322 Thanon Tha Pae ☎053 874173. A good-value favourite among locals and visitors both for northern specialities (B50–100) like *kaeng hang lay*, *khao soi* and mixed hors d'oeuvres, and for tasty Western breakfasts, sandwiches, cottage pie and steaks. Extensive vegetarian menu, wine and cocktails too. Daily 7.30am–11.30pm.

Ruen Tamarind 50/1 Thanon Ratchdamnoen ☎053 418896–9. Overlooking the pool at the *Tamarind Village* hotel (see p.293), this elegant restaurant serves up excellent Thai cuisine such as *tom kha thaleh* (coconut soup with seafood) and *kaeng phet linchee* (roast duck with lychees in red curry sauce) for around B200–300 a dish. Also offers a long vegetarian menu and a few Western dishes. Daily 7am–11pm.

INTERNATIONAL

Blue Diamond Soi 9, Thanon Moonmuang. Popular, mostly vegetarian restaurant in a quiet neighbourhood of guesthouses, serving very good Thai dishes, Western breakfasts (from B65), home-made bread, shakes, herbal teas and hill-tribe coffee. Mon–Sat 7am–8.30pm.

Jerusalem Falafel 35/3 Thanon Moonmuang ☎053 270208. Small and friendly a/c café serving all manner of Middle Eastern food, including tasty hummus (B100), home-made cheeses and yoghurt, and baklava; if the choices overwhelm you, go for a meze set menu (B500 for two people). Daily except Fri 9am–10pm.

★ **La Fontana** 39/7–8 Thanon Ratchamanka ☎053 207091. Chiang Mai's best Italian, dishing up great home-made pastas (B150–200), risottos, pizzas, meat and fish dishes, as well as tempting antipasti and panna cotta, ice cream and other desserts, all washed down by reasonably priced house wine. Daily 11.30am–11.30pm; often closes Tues and at lunchtimes in low season.

Miguel's Thanon Chaiyapoom ☎053 874148, ⟨w⟩miguels-café.com. A warm welcome, a relaxing terrace and good Mexican food: feast on the nachos grande for B150, perhaps with a side order of guacamole (in season). There's a smaller branch at 43 Thanon Nimmanhaemin, open till midnight. Daily 9am–11pm.

Mit Mai 42/2 Thanon Ratchamanka ☎053 275033. It looks like a simple Thai eatery from the street, but in fact *Mit Mai* serves up excellent food from Yunnan province in China, including a zesty chicken salad (B55) and Yunnanese ham stir-fried with ginger and chilli, as well as more exotic dishes such as *fong nom thawt* (fried cheese) and white bamboo grubs. Daily 10am–10pm.

Pho Vieng Chane Kad Klang Wieng, Thanon Ratchdamnoen, corner of Ratchaphakinai. Specializes in *pho* (pronounced "fur"; from B30), a tasty noodle soup, but serves all manner of excellent, cheap Vietnamese food. At the shared outside tables in the grassy courtyard, you can also order good Italian dishes from the neighbouring restaurant. Daily 10am–9pm.

REST OF CHIANG MAI

THAI

Café de Nimman Rooms Shopping Centre, 61 Thanon Nimmanhemin (south of Soi 17) ☎053 218405. Excellent food such as squid stuffed with pork in green curry (B120) and creative Thai salads, at this stylish, reasonably priced bar-restaurant and terrace. Daily 11am–10pm.

Hong Tauw Inn 95/17–18 Nantawan Arcade, Thanon Nimmanhemin ☎053 400039. Comfortable a/c restaurant done out in "country inn" style, with antiques, plants and old clocks, making for a relaxing environment. The creative menu ranges from rice and noodle dishes such as *khanom jiin*, to delicious central and northern Thai main dishes, such as a *phanaeng* curry for B90, and includes a wide range of *nam phrik*, spicy relishes, and Thai desserts. Daily 11am–10pm.

★ **Huan Soontaree** 208 Thanon Patan, 3km north of the Superhighway ☎053 872707–8. A convivial riverfront restaurant owned by the famous northern Thai folk-singer Soontaree Vechanont, who entertains diners from her balcony-level stage (she performs Mon–Sat, but is augmented by other good local musicians nightly). Delicious, very reasonably priced northern specialities such as fried Chiang Mai sausage with whole baby garlic. Split levels allow a choice of seating, including on a leafy riverside terrace hung with paper lanterns, or on a balcony near the stage. Daily 4pm–midnight.

Huen Phen 112 Thanon Ratchamanka. Probably Chiang Mai's most authentic northern restaurant. Try local specialities such as *sai oua* (sausage), *kaeng hang lay* (pork curry) and *khao soi* (noodle curry; B40). The restaurant around the back with the same name that opens in the evening is pricier and disappointing. Daily 8am–4pm, or until the food runs out.

Khao Soi Samoe Jai Thanon Faham. Thick, tasty and very cheap *khao soi* (spiced to order) and other northern specialities, plus delicious satay, *som tam*. No English sign – it's a wooden house with a red, white and blue awning. Daily except Wed 8am–5pm.

Khun Churn 4 Soi 17, Thanon Nimmanhemin ☎053 224124. Sophisticated vegetarian restaurant in a cool garden setting, most famous for its B129 lunchtime buffet

WAT PHRA THAI DOI SUTHEP, CHIANG MAI (P.305) >

(11am–2.30pm); also does breakfasts and vegan options. Daily 8am–10pm.

Kiat Ocha 41–43 Thanon Inthrawarorot, off Thanon Phra Pokklao (no English sign). Delicious and very popular satay and *khao man kai* – boiled chicken breast served with dipping sauces, broth and rice – from around B30 a dish. This and the surrounding cafés are especially handy if you're looking round the old town. Daily 5am–2.30pm, or until the food runs out.

Lamduon Faharm Khao Soi 352/22 Thanon Charoenrat. Excellent, very cheap *khao soi* prepared to a secret recipe, which can be spiced according to your taste; delicious crackling with the pork version. Also satay, *khanom jiin*, *som tam* and an assortment of juices. Daily 8am–4pm.

Palaad Tawanron Above Chiang Mai Zoo ☎053 216039. Go to the end of Thanon Suthep, then turn right and follow the signs to one of Chiang Mai's most attractive restaurants, set beside a small waterfall with panoramic views of the city. Dishes like *tom yam kung* (B280) and fried sea bass in fish sauce keep the customers coming, and there's usually live music in the evening. Daily 11.30am–midnight.

Rachamankha 6 Soi 9, Thanon Ratchamanka ☎053 904111. In the courtyard of the boutique hotel of the same name (see p.295), this is one of Chiang Mai's classiest places to eat, with starched linen tablecloths and elegant cutlery and often with live traditional music in the evening. From an unusual menu of Thai, Shan, Burmese and fusion dishes (mostly B300–400), try the Burmese-style beef curry and finish off with the mango flambé in a papaya bowl. Daily 7am–11pm.

★ **Samsen Villa** Rimping Condominium, 201 Thanon Charoenrat ☎053 306588, ⓦsamsenvilla.com. The best of several restaurants on the east bank of the Ping River, serving excellent, creative Thai food in the charming waterfront garden of this prominent condo by Nakhon Ping Bridge. Don't miss the grilled beef with elephant garlic (B100), but avoid the signature "jelly beer" – unless you like your beer flat and frozen like a Slurpie. Daily 11am–11pm.

Wan Lamun Thanon Inthrawarorot (no English sign, but look for the pink flower on their Thai sign). Delightful spot purveying excellent, cheap lunches such as *khanom jiin*, and delicious Thai and Western desserts. One or two tables but mostly takeaway – to the square in front of the City Arts and Cultural Centre, for example. Alternatively, try its full-blown café-restaurant on Soi 2, Thanon Chang Moi (☎053 232328, ⓦwanlamun.com; Tues–Sun 11.30am–10pm), if you'd rather have a sit-down meal. Daily 7am–5pm.

INTERNATIONAL

Amazing Sandwich 20/2 Thanon Huai Kaeo ⓦamazingsandwich.com. The place to go if you hanker for a sandwich, bagel or baguette made up to order; also serves breakfasts and home-made yoghurts, juices and lassis. Mon–Sat 8am–8pm, Sun 8.30am–4pm.

Arcobaleno 60 Thanon Wat Ket ☎053 306254, ⓦarcobaleno-cm.com. Tasty Italian food (main dishes from around B200) served in and around a spacious house on a quiet lane near Nakhon Ping Bridge. Try the *spaghetti arcobaleno* (with smoked bacon, mushrooms and tomato sauce) and the delicious panna cotta for dessert. Daily 11am–2pm & 5.30–10pm.

The Duke's 49/4–5 Thanon Chiang Mai–Lamphun ☎053 249231. If you're looking for a decent steakhouse while in northern Thailand, head on down to *The Duke's*, which rustles up imported steaks, ribs, seafood, pizzas, American desserts and the rest. Burgers cost B95, but most other dishes are B200 and up. Everything's big here, from the portions to the chairs. Also has a (more expensive) branch in the Night Bazaar Pavilion on Thanon Chang Klan. Daily 11am–10.30pm.

Elliebum 114/3–4 Thanon Ratchamanka ☎053 814723. Probably the best coffee in town, delicious fruit smoothies, top-notch breakfasts such as blueberry pancakes with maple syrup and fresh fruit, plus great sandwiches and Thai dishes for lunch. Free wi-fi. Mon–Sat 7.30am–6pm, Sun 7.30am–1pm.

Hinlay 8/1 Thanon Na Wat Ket ☎053 242621. Appealing garden restaurant dishing up very good Indian as well as Burmese and Thai curries (*kaeng matsaman* for B68), accompanied by roti bread and raita. Worth calling ahead as hours are sometimes erratic. Usually Mon–Sat 10am–9pm.

iberry Off the south side of Soi 17, Thanon Nimmanhemin. Chiang Mai's best and most famous ice-cream shop, owned by comedian "Nose" Udom – who is portrayed as a yellow dog in a huge statue in the quirky garden. Also does home-made sorbets and cakes and good coffee. Daily 10.30am–10pm.

Love at First Bite 28 Soi 1, Thanon Chiang Mai–Lamphun ☎053 242731, ⓦloveatfirstbite-cm.com. Head south from the east side of Nawarat Bridge, then turn into the first lane on the left to discover this relaxing haven of home-baked cakes and pies, plus delicious coffee, served in a tiny café or on a neat lawn surrounded by flower beds. Tues–Sun 10.30am–6pm.

★ **Su Casa** Soi 11, Thanon Nimmanhemin ☎080 033 2825, ⓦmicasachiangmai.com. Top-notch traditional and contemporary tapas (around B450 for six dishes) by a Spanish chef in pleasant surroundings, whether indoors (with a/c) or out on the patio. The menu also features pastas and desserts, while their *Next Door* grill bar serves meats and pizzas. Mon–Sat 11am–10pm.

★ **Tengoku de Cuisine** Opposite the Dhara Devi hotel, south off the San Kamphaeng road ☎053 851133. Superb Japanese cuisine makes this stylish little restaurant to the east of town well worth the trip. The sushi (starting from B400) and the tartare (tataki) of New Zealand beef with spring onion (B350) are both very good, while the aubergine with miso sauce (B120) is not to be missed. Daily 10.30am–2pm & 5–10pm.

West Fahtani Square, Thanon Huai Kaeo ☎080 122 7136, ⓦ west-restaurant.com. In a large square-cum-car park lined with bars off Thanon Sirimuangkarajan, this open-fronted restaurant serves very good, modern, bistro-style comfort food that's carefully prepared and presented. Spaghetti with meatballs in tomato cream sauce (B180) and fish and chips are popular, washed down by good Aussie wine. The set menus of three courses, including excellent desserts, are very good value at B220 (B190 at lunchtime). Daily 11.30am–2.30pm & 5.30–10.30pm.

DRINKING AND NIGHTLIFE

Although there's a clutch of hostess bars bordering the east moat and along Loi Khro, and several gay bars offering sex shows, Chiang Mai's **nightlife** generally avoids Bangkok's sexual excesses, but offers plenty of opportunities for a good night out. The main concentrations of **bars** are on the east bank of the Ping River, around Tha Pae Gate and to the west of town along Thanon Nimmanhemin, which swarms with students from nearby Chiang Mai University. It's also well worth checking out the strip of good-time bars at **JJ Market** on Thanon Assadatorn on the north side of town, which sport aspirational Bangkok names like *Tha Chang* and *Hualamphong* and which heave at weekends with the youth of Chiang Mai, drinking and watching the live bands. One place to avoid is the makeshift, illegal complex of bars at the northeast corner of the Ratchawithi/Ratchaphakinai junction, where theft is rife.

THA PAE GATE AREA

Jack Van Bar Thanon Chaiyapoom. Favourite late-late hangout, where you can sit at outdoor tables on a large forecourt (with a brazier for the cool season) and order up mean cocktails from a Jack Daniels-sponsored camper van. Hours are temperamental: usually around 10pm–very late.

Second Floor Gallery & Bar Thanon Ratchawithi, corner of Thanon Ratchaphakinai. Chilled, happening bar – "leave your ego at the door" – with a mellow soundtrack most nights, but live bands on Saturdays, plus regular salsa and dance nights. Tues–Sun 6pm–midnight.

THC (The Hemp Collective) 19/4–5 Thanon Kotchasarn, opposite Tha Pae Gate. Laidback crusty place, decorated with paper lanterns and floor cushions in the rooftop bar, where DJs play an eclectic music choice. Daily roughly 6pm–late.

★ **UN Irish Pub** 24/1 Thanon Ratchawithi. Though it hasn't had an Irish owner for a few years now, this is a cordial, well-run pub that serves Guinness on tap and reasonably priced wine, as well as good food, including home-made bread for satisfying breakfasts and sandwiches, home-made pies and pizzas. Quiz night Thurs, and all manner of sports on TV. Daily 8am–1am.

REST OF CHIANG MAI

Brasserie 37 Thanon Charoenrat ☎053 241665. Decent restaurant with pretty riverside terraces, but more famous as the venue for some of the city's best live blues and rock. Warms up around 10/11pm. Daily 4pm–1am.

★ **Drunken Flower (Mao Dok Mai)** Soi 17, Thanon Nimmanhemin ☎053 894210, ⓦ thedrunkenflower .com. Laidback and very congenial, this quirky venue is a favourite among university students and twenty-somethings, both Thai and farang. Reasonable prices for drinks and an eclectic range of background music. Tues–Sun 6pm–midnight.

Good View 13 Thanon Charoenrat ☎053 241866, ⓦ goodview.co.th. An upmarket clone of the neighbouring *Riverside*, this large venue appeals to fashionable Thais with its smart staff, extensive menu of Thai, Chinese and Western food, free wi-fi and slick, competent musicians, who play anything middle of the road from country to jazz. Daily 10am–1am.

Infinity Soi 6, Thanon Nimmanhemin ☎053 400085, ⓦ facebook.com/infinity.chiangmai. At the end of Soi 6 in what's known as Prasertland or Kad Cherng Doi (a huge car park and loosely designated entertainment zone), this stylish and spacious venue, with live bands, DJs and lots of outdoor tables, is the club of the moment in Chiang Mai. Daily 6pm–1am.

Monkey Club 7 Soi 9, Thanon Nimmanhemin ☎053 226997–8, ⓦ monkeyclub2000.com. More sophisticated than your average Chiang Mai bar-restaurant, with stylish white outdoor seating around a small pond, though none of that matters later in the evening when the crowd of

GAY NIGHTLIFE IN CHIANG MAI

For an introduction to the city's **gay scene**, check out the small bars on Soi 1, Thanon Tha Pae, behind *D2 Hotel*, or the roads off the west side of Thanon Chotana, where there's a clutch of bars around the gay-owned *Lotus Hotel*. In the latter area, the long-running *Adam's Apple*, 1/21–22 Soi Viengbua (daily 8.30pm–12.30am; ⓦ adamsappleclub.com), has go-go dancers all evening and a popular show at 10pm.

twenty-something Thais starts dancing round their tables to Thai pop bands and DJs. Daily 6pm–2am.

North Gate Jazz Co-op Thanon Si Phum. Chilled, open-fronted bar with pavement tables overlooking Chang Phuak Gate, featuring high-quality live jazz nightly; Tuesday is open-mike night. Open most nights 9pm–midnight.

The Pub 189 Thanon Huai Kaeo ⓦthepubchiangmai .com. Homely, relaxing expat hangout that's been around for forty years, with the nearest thing to an English pub atmosphere to be found in Chiang Mai. Draught and imported beers, Sunday roasts, darts and TV sports. Daily 7am–midnight.

★ **The Riverside** Thanon Charoenrat ☎053 243239, ⓦtheriversidechiangmai.com. On one side of the road candlelit terraces by the water (best to book if you want a table here) and an often heaving, lively bar for gigs, on the other a spacious complex of rooms, terraces and a stage. Various soloists and bands perform nightly on the two stages, with the tempo increasing as the night wears on. Long, high-quality menu of Western and Thai food and drinks also on offer, as well as dinner cruises (see p.295). Daily 10am–1am.

Warm Up 40 Thanon Nimmanhemin ☎053 400677, ⓦwarmupcafe1999.com. Hugely popular venue with students and young locals, offering both live bands and local and international DJs spinning the latest sounds in different indoor and outdoor zones. Daily 6pm–2am.

Writer's Club and Wine Bar 141/3 Thanon Ratchdamnoen ☎053 814187. Welcoming bar near the centre of the old city, run by an English writer and popular among farang residents and visitors, serving a range of beers and wines, plus good Thai and Western food. Daily except Sat noon–midnight.

ENTERTAINMENT

Cinemas Go to ⓦmovieseer.com for details of which English-soundtrack or English-subtitled films are showing at the various cineplexes around town. French-language films with English subtitles are screened at the Alliance Française, 138 Thanon Charoen Prathet, on Fridays at 8pm (☎053 275277), while popular, mostly recent, art-house films are shown at the Faculty of Media Art and Design, behind CMU Art Museum, every Saturday at 7pm (see p.287; ☎053 944846); monthly schedules for both are given in the free *Guidelines* magazine.

SHOPPING

Shopping is an almost irresistible pastime in Chiang Mai, whether it be for traditional silver bracelets, chic contemporary lacquerware or even secondhand books. Serious shoppers should get hold of a copy of *Nancy Chandler's Map of Chiang Mai* (see p.290), and of the free, quarterly booklet, *Art and Culture Lanna* (ⓦartandcultureasia.com), which carries adverts for some of the town's leading boutiques and galleries, with maps.

MARKETS AND THE SAN KAMPHAENG ROAD

Two main tourist shopping areas, the San Kamphaeng road and the night bazaar, conveniently operating at different times of the day, sell the full range of local handicrafts, backed up by markets, shopping malls and the weekend walking streets (see box below).

THE SAN KAMPHAENG ROAD

The road to San Kamphaeng, which extends due east from the end of Thanon Charoen Muang for 13km, is the main daytime strip, lined with every sort of handicrafts shop and factory, where you can usually watch the craftsmen at work. The biggest concentrations are at Bo Sang, the "umbrella village", 9km from town, and at San Kamphaeng itself, once important for its kilns but now dedicated chiefly to silk weaving.

Getting there Frequent white songthaews to San Kamphaeng leave Chiang Mai from the central Lamyai market, but it's difficult to decide when to get off if you don't know the area. You could sign up for a tour or hire a tuk-tuk for a few hundred baht, but the catch here is that the drivers will want to take you to the shops where they'll pick up a commission. The best way to go is by bicycle or

---

CHIANG MAI'S WALKING STREETS

If you're in Chiang Mai at the weekend it's worth heading down to **Thanon Wualai**, just south of the old city, on a Saturday between about 5pm and 11pm, or to the larger affair on **Thanon Ratchdamnoen** and part of **Thanon Phra Pokklao** in the old city on a Sunday at the same time. Closed to traffic for the duration, these "**walking streets**" become crowded with vendors selling typical northern Thai items such as clothes, musical instruments and snacks, as musicians busk to the throngs of people. The walking streets have become almost as popular as the night bazaar, as they are ideal places to pick up a souvenir and mingle with a very mixed crowd of Thais and farangs.

motorbike, which allows you to stop where and when you please, but take care with the fast-moving traffic on the narrow road.

THE NIGHT BAZAAR

The other main shopper's playground is the night bazaar, sprawling around the junction of Thanon Loi Khro and Thanon Chang Klan (and into the adjacent, quieter Anusarn market). Here bumper-to-bumper street stalls and several indoor areas (including the original Chiang Mai Night Bazaar shopping centre on the west side of Thanon Chang Klan) sell just about anything produced in Chiang Mai, plus crafts from other parts of Thailand and Southeast Asia, as well as counterfeit designer goods; the action starts up at around 5pm, and there are plenty of real bargains.

WAROROT MARKET

During the day, bustling Warorot market on Thanon Chang Moi has lots of cheap and cheerful cotton, linen and ceramics for sale on the upper floors. In the heart of the market, you can watch locals buying chilli paste, sausage and sticky rice from their favourite stalls, and maybe even join the queue. There's also a pungent and colourful flower market just east of here, on Thanon Praisani by the river, while the atmospheric warren of narrow lanes to the south and west of the market is well worth a browse, for everything from silk and hill-tribe crafts to stationery and plastic.

THE NORTHERN VILLAGE

The Northern Village in the Airport Plaza shopping centre (Mon–Fri 11am–9pm, Sat & Sun 10am–9pm), at the corner of the Superhighway and Highway 108, is like a market of stalls moved into an a/c mall. It has all manner of handicrafts and contemporary decorative products, including a shop selling work from the Pa-Da Cotton Textile Museum (see p.334) and a branch of Classic Model (see below). Free hourly songthaew shuttle shoppers from eight downtown hotels, including the *D2* on the hour.

FABRICS, CLOTHES AND CONTEMPORARY INTERIOR DESIGN

Few visitors leave Chiang Mai without some new item of clothing and, to tempt you to dig deeper into your purse, upmarket silks and cottons often share shelf-space with bold examples of modern interior design.

Silk The silk produced out towards San Kamphaeng, to the east of Chiang Mai, is richly coloured and hard-wearing, with various attractive textures. Bought off a roll, the material is generally cheaper than in Bangkok, and can cost as little as B300/metre for top-quality four-ply (suitable for shirts and suits), for example at Kritiya (see below). Ready-made silk clothes, though inexpensive, are generally staid and more suited to formal wear.

Cotton In Chiang Mai you'll also see plenty of traditional,

pastel-coloured cotton, which is nice for furnishings, most of it from the village of Pa Sang southwest of Lamphun. Outlets in the basement of the main Chiang Mai night bazaar shopping centre on Thanon Chang Klan have good, cheap selections of this sort of cloth at around B200–300/metre, plus hand-painted and batik-printed lengths, and ready-made tablecloths and the like.

Interior design You'll find some stunning contemporary interior design in Chiang Mai, fusing local crafts with modern, often minimalist elements. A fruitful place for this kind of shopping is Thanon Nimmanhemin, on the west side of the city, which savvy locals sometimes tag Chiang Mai's Sukhumvit for its services to well-to-do expats. Its northern end towards Thanon Huai Kaeo, particularly on and around Soi 1, has a concentration of interesting fashion and decor boutiques. Thanon Charoenrat, on the east side of the river, also hosts several stylish outlets for clothes and interior design between Nawarat and Nakhon Ping bridges.

Classic Model 95/22 Thanon Nimmanhemin, opposite Soi 1 ☎053 279031, ⌨cmdfashion.com. Striking and classy ready-to-wear clothes for women, made from local fabrics by traditional northern methods. Daily 9am–7.30pm.

Doi Tung Lifestyle Thanon Nimmanhemin, opposite Soi 1 ☎053 217981, ⌨doitung.org. Part of the late Princess Mother's development project based at Doi Tung, selling very striking and attractive cotton and linen in warm colours, made up into clothes, cushion covers, rugs and so on. Daily 8am–8pm.

Ginger 199 Thanon Moonmuang ☎053 419014; 6/21 Thanon Nimmanhemin; ⌨thehousethailand.com. Chi-chi boutiques selling striking and original women's and men's wear, accessories and contemporary home decor, especially cushion covers. Thanon Moonmuang daily 10am–10.30pm; Thanon Nimmanhemin daily 9am–9pm.

Gong Dee Soi 1, Thanon Nimmanhemin ☎053 225032, ⌨gongdeegallery.com. Stunning, contemporary wood and lacquer vases, boxes, lamps and bowls, much of it gleaming with gold and silver leaf, plus jewellery and furniture. Daily 8am–8pm.

Kritiya 46 Thanon Khwang Men, the lane that runs south from the west side of Warorot Market ☎053 234478. This small, atmospheric shop is probably the best place in town to buy bolts of high-quality local silk at competitive prices. Mon–Sat 9/10am–4.30/5pm.

Nandakwang 6/1–5 Thanon Nimmanhemin ☎053 222261. Outlet of the most famous cotton company from Lamphun province's Pa Sang, whose main draws are cushion covers (including axe cushions) and bags in rich colours, often featuring floral motifs. Daily 9am–5pm.

Neramit Off Thanon Chang Moi at 91/2 Thanon Ratchawong ☎053 234353, ⌨neramit-custom -tailoring.com. Has a good reputation for men's tailoring. Mon–Sat 9am–7pm, Sun 4–7pm.

CHIANG MAI'S TRADITIONAL CRAFTS

Chiang Mai is the best place in Thailand to buy handicrafts, a hotbed of traditional cottage industries offering generally high standards of workmanship at low prices.

WOODCARVING

The city has a long tradition of **woodcarving**, which expresses itself in everything from salad bowls to half-size elephants. In the past the industry relied on the cutting of Thailand's precious teak, but manufacturers are now beginning to use other imported hardwoods, while bemoaning their inferior quality.

Wooden objects are sold all over the city, but the most famous place for carving is **Ban Tawai**, a large village of shops and factories where prices are low and where you can watch the woodworkers in action. One of Thailand's most important woodcarving centres, Ban Tawai relied on rice farming until thirty years ago, but today virtually every home here has carvings for sale outside and each backyard hosts its own cottage industry. To get there, you'll need your own transport: follow Highway 108 south from Chiang Mai 13km to Hang Dong, then head east for 2km. A regularly updated, free **map** of Ban Tawai's outlets, which now include all manner of antiques and interior decor shops, is available around town (or go to ⓦ ban-tawai.com).

LACQUERWARE

Lacquerware can be seen in nearly every museum in Thailand, most commonly in the form of **betel sets**, which used to be carried ceremonially by the slaves of grandees as an insignia of rank and wealth (see box, p.285). Betel sets are still produced in Chiang Mai according to the traditional technique, whereby a woven bamboo frame is covered with layers of rich red lacquer and decorated with black details. A variety of other objects, such as trays and jewellery boxes, are also produced, some decorated with gold leaf on black gloss. Lacquerware makes an ideal choice for gifts, as it is both light to carry, and at the same time typically Thai, and is available in just about every other shop in town.

CELADON

Celadon, sometimes known as greenware, is a delicate variety of stoneware which was first made in China over two thousand years ago, and later produced in Thailand, most famously at Sukhothai and Sawankhalok.

Mengrai Kilns at 79/2 Soi 6, Thanon Samlarn (☎ 053 272063, ⓦ mengraikilns.com; daily 8am–5pm), is the best of several kilns in Chiang Mai that have revived the art of celadon. Sticking to the traditional methods, Mengrai produces beautiful and reasonably priced vases, crockery and larger items, thrown in elegant shapes and covered with transparent green, blue and purple glazes.

UMBRELLAS AND PAPER

The village of **Bo Sang** bases its fame on souvenir **umbrellas** – made of silk, cotton or mulberry (*sa*) paper and decorated with bold, painted colours – and celebrates its craft with a colourful **umbrella fair** every January. The artists who work here can paint a small motif on your bag or camera in two minutes flat.

The grainy **mulberry paper**, which makes beautiful writing or sketching pads, is sold almost as an afterthought in many of Bo Sang's shops. The best place to buy it is **HQ**, down a small soi opposite Wat Phra Singh at 3/31 Thanon Samlarn (☎ 053 814717, ⓦ hqpapermaker.com; daily 8.30am–5.30pm), which sells sheets of beautifully coloured mulberry paper, along with a huge range of other specialist papers.

SILVER AND JEWELLERY

Chiang Mai's traditional **silversmiths**' area is on **Thanon Wualai**, on the south side of the old town, though the actual smithing is now done elsewhere. If you're serious about buying silver, however, this is still the place to come, with dozens of small shops on Wualai itself and on Soi 3 selling repoussé plates, bowls and cups, and attractive, chunky jewellery. For sterling silver, check the stamp that shows the item is 92.5 percent pure; some items on sale in Chiang Mai are only eighty percent pure and sell much more cheaply.

A good general **jewellery** store is **Nova Collection** at 179 Thanon Tha Pae (☎ 053 273058, ⓦ nova-collection.com; Mon–Sat 9am–8.30pm & Sun 12.30–8.30pm), which has some lovely rings and necklaces blending gold, silver and precious stones in striking and original designs.

Pa Ker Yaw 180 Thanon Loi Khro, near the Downtown Inn ☎053 275491. Weather-beaten wooden shophouse stuffed with a selection of rich fabrics from Thailand, Laos and Burma, as well as hill-tribe jewellery and basketware and other crafts. Hours variable, but always closed Sun.

Shinawatra 7km out on the San Kamphaeng road ☎053 338053, ⓦthaisilk.co.th (with a shop at 18/1 Thanon Huai Kaeo ☎053 221096). Century-old silk factory and showroom, owned by the prime minister's family, that's a good place to follow the silk-making process right from the cocoon. Daily 9am–6pm.

Sop Moei Arts 150/10 Thanon Charoenrat ☎053 306123, ⓦsopmoeiarts.com. Gorgeous fabrics – scarves, wall-hangings, bags and cushion covers – and stylish basketware, with part of the profits going back to the eponymous Karen village and nearby refugee camp near Mae Sariang, where they're made. Mon–Fri & Sun 10am–6pm, Sat noon–4pm.

Studio Naenna 138/8 Soi Changkhian, Thanon Huai Kaeo, & **Adorn by Studio Naenna** 22 Soi 1, Thanon Nimmanhemin ☎053 895136, ⓦstudio-naenna.com. If you're interested in the whole process of traditional fabric production, particularly the use of natural dyes, this is an excellent place to begin. If you phone for an appointment, you can see a demonstration of dyeing, including the plants from which the dyes are extracted, and watch the weavers in action at the main studio on Soi Changkhian. Adorn is the main outlet for their products, which consist of top-quality, ready-made silk and cotton garments and accessories. Studio Naenna April–Sept Mon–Fri 8.30am–5pm, Oct–March Mon–Sat 8.30am–5pm; Adorn daily 10am–6pm.

Vila Cini 30–34 Thanon Charoenrat ☎053 246246; OP Place, Le Meridien Hotel, corner of Thanon Chang Klan and Thanon Loi Khro; ⓦvilacini.com. Lacquerware and sumptuously coloured silk scarves and cushion covers. Next door to the main shop on Charoenrat is Oriental Style, under the same ownership, for cotton and basketware.

Thanon Charoenrat daily 8.30am–10.30pm; OP Place daily 11am–11pm.

HILL-TRIBE CRAFTS

Thai Tribal Crafts 208 Thanon Bamrungrat ☎053 241043; 25/9 Thanon Moonmuang, near Thanon Ratchamanka (Fair Trade Shop); Northern Village, Airport Plaza; ⓦttcrafts.co.th. Long-running, non-profit, fair-trade shops, sponsored by a Christian charity, with a huge range of products made by seven of the region's hill tribes, from bags, scarves, home furnishings and silverware to musical instruments and bamboo basketry. Bamrungrat Mon–Sat 9am–5pm; Moonmuang Mon–Sat 10am–7pm; Northern Village daily 10am–8pm.

BOOKS

3

Backstreet Books 2/8 Thanon Chang Moi Kao ☎053 874143, ⓦbackstreetsiam.com. Large, well-organized secondhand bookshop near Tha Pae Gate, where you can buy or exchange books, with a smaller branch, The Lost Bookshop, at 34/3 Thanon Ratchamanka (☎053 206656). Daily 9am–9pm.

Gecko Books 2/6 Thanon Chang Moi Kao ☎053 874066, ⓦgeckobooks.net. Very similar to Backstreet Books, with a long-standing rivalry – and, very conveniently for book-buyers, they're located right next door to each other. Also has several other branches around town. Daily 8am–9pm.

Suriwong 54/1 Thanon Sri Dornchai ☎053 281052. The best place for new English-language publications, stocking a wide selection of novels, books about Thailand and maps in an organized display; it also features newspaper and stationery sections. Mon–Sat 9am–7pm, Sun 9am–12.30pm.

COMPUTERS

For sales and repairs, either Panthip Plaza, corner of Chang Klan and Sri Dornchai roads, or Computer Plaza, Thanon Manee Nopparat on the north side of the moat.

DIRECTORY

Banks, ATMs and exchange Dozens of banks with ATMs are dotted around Thanon Tha Pae and Thanon Chang Klan, and many exchange booths here stay open for evening shoppers.

Consulates China, 111 Thanon Chang Lo ☎053 280380; India, 33/1 Thanon Thung Hotel ☎053 243066; UK, 198 Thanon Bamrungrat ☎053 263015; US, 387 Thanon Witchayanon ☎053 107700.

Hospitals Lanna, at 103 Superhighway (☎053 999777, ⓦlanna-hospital.com), east of Thanon Chotana, has a 24hr emergency service and dentistry department; McCormick (☎053 921777) is cheaper, used to farangs and is nearer, on Thanon Kaeo Nawarat; Chiang Mai Ram, at 8 Thanon Boonruangrit (☎053 920300), also has a very good reputation.

Immigration office On the southern leg of the Superhighway, 300m before the airport, on the left (Mon–Fri 8.30am–4.30pm; ☎053 201755–6).

Internet and wi-fi Most guesthouses and hotels have internet access, and every second shop in town appears to be an internet café. Rates vary from as little as B20/hr in locations near Chiang Mai University to as much as B120 in downtown areas. Nearly all accommodation in Chiang Mai now has access to wi-fi, and an increasing number of cafés and restaurants are now offering it free.

Pharmacies Boots branches include Thanon Tha Pae, opposite the Tha Pae Gate, and Thanon Chang Klan, in front of the Chiang Inn Plaza.

Post offices The GPO is way out of the centre on Thanon Charoen Muang near the train station, but there's a far more convenient post office at 43 Thanon Samlarn (Phra Singh PO), near Wat Phra Singh (Mon–Fri 8.30am–4pm, Sat 9am–noon), which offers a packing service and sells cheap phonecards, amulets, you name it. There are also post offices on Thanon Phra Pokklao at the junction with Thanon Ratchawithi (Sri Phum PO), plus a small branch office on Thanon Ratchdamnoen by Tha Pae Gate, both in the old town, as well as on Thanon Wichayanon near Nawarat Bridge (Mae Ping PO), and at the airport.

Thai language courses AUA (American University Alumni), 24 Thanon Ratchdamnoen (☎053 277991 or ☎053 278407, ⍟learnthaiinchiangmai.com), is the longest-established and best place to learn Thai, certified by the Ministry of Education. Several levels of classes are offered, starting with spoken Thai for beginners (60hr over about 6 weeks; B4200), with class sizes limited to 5–12 students. Individual and small-group instruction can also be arranged.

Tourist police Rimping Plaza, Thanon Charoenrat, near the Superhighway ☎053 247318 or ☎155.

Around Chiang Mai

You'll never feel cooped up in Chiang Mai, as the surrounding countryside is dotted with day-trip options in all directions. Dominating the skyline to the west, **Doi Suthep** and its eagle's-nest temple are hard to ignore, and a wander around the pastoral ruins of **Wiang Kum Kam** on the southern periphery has the feel of fresh exploration. Much further south, the quiet town of **Lamphun** offers classic sightseeing in the form of historically and religiously significant temples and a museum. To the north, the **Mae Sa valley** may be full of tour buses, but its highlight, the **Queen Sirikit Botanic Gardens**, as well as the nearby lake of **Huay Tung Tao** and **Darapirom Palace**, merit an independent jaunt. Distinctly missable, however, is the recently opened Chiang Mai **Night Safari** to the southwest of the city, which has encroached on land belonging to Doi Suthep National Park, and even announced as an opening promotion that the meat of all the animals on display would also be available in its restaurant (though the offer has now been withdrawn) – much better to spend your money at Chiang Mai Zoo (see p.286). All the excursions described here can be done in half a day; not all of them are covered by public **transport**, but a car with driver arranged through a Chiang Mai guesthouse should cost you around B600 for a half-day local trip. There are also some good options for longer jaunts, notably to Doi Inthanon National Park (see p.331), to Lampang and the Thai Elephant Conservation Centre (see p.311) and to the Elephant Nature Park (see p.353).

Doi Suthep

A jaunt up **DOI SUTHEP**, the mountain which rises steeply at the city's western edge, is the most satisfying brief trip you can make from Chiang Mai, chiefly on account of beautiful **Wat Phra That Doi Suthep**, which dominates the hillside and gives a towering view over the goings-on in town. This is the north's holiest shrine, its pre-eminence deriving from a magic relic enshrined in its chedi and the miraculous legend of its founding. The original chedi was built by King Ku Na at the end of the fourteenth century, after the glowing relic of Wat Suan Dork had self-multiplied just before being enshrined. A place had to be found for the clone, so Ku Na put it in a travelling shrine on the back of a white elephant and waited to see where the sacred animal would lead: it eventually climbed Doi Suthep, trumpeted three times, turned round three times, knelt down and died, thereby indicating that this was the spot. Ever since, it's been northern Thailand's most important place of pilgrimage, especially for the candlelit processions on **Makha Puja**, the anniversary of the sermon to the disciples, and **Visakha Puja**, the anniversary of the Buddha's birth, enlightenment and death, when thousands of people walk up to the temple through the night from Chiang Mai.

Doi Suthep-Pui National Park

Park headquarters are about 1km beyond the wat; B200; ☏ 053 210244, ⊛ dnp.go.th

A signpost halfway up the road to the temple is about the only indication that you're in **Doi Suthep-Pui National Park**, which also encompasses the 1685m peak of Doi Pui to the northwest of Doi Suthep; however, an entry fee is not levied if you are only visiting the wat, Phuping Palace and Ban Doi Pui, a highly commercialized Hmong village near the palace that's worth avoiding. Despite the nearness of the city, its rich mixed forests support 330 species of bird, and the area is a favoured site for nature study, second in the north only to the larger and less-disturbed Doi Inthanon National Park. At the park headquarters you can get information about the park's trails, including a track up to Doi Pui summit beyond Phuping Palace.

About 5km from the base of the mountain road, a road on the right leads 3km to **Mon Tha Than Falls**, a beautiful spot, believed by some to be home to evil spirits. The higher fall is an idyllic 5m drop into a small bathing pool, completely overhung by thick, humming jungle.

Wat Phra That Doi Suthep

B30, or B50 including the cable car; ⊛ doisuthep.com; see p.288 for information about meditation courses

Opposite a car park and souvenir village, a flight of three hundred naga-flanked steps – or the adjacent cable car – is the last leg on the way to **Wat Phra That Doi Suthep**. From the temple's **lower terrace**, the magnificent views of Chiang Mai and the surrounding plain, 300m below, are best in the early morning or late afternoon in the cool season, though peaceful contemplation of the view is frequently shattered by people sounding the heavy, dissonant bells around the terrace – they're supposed to

---

KHRUBA SRIVIJAYA

Khruba Srivijaya, widely regarded as the "patron saint" of northern Thailand, was born in 1878 in a small village 100km south of Chiang Mai. His birth coincided with a supernatural thunderstorm and earthquake, after which he was given the auspicious nickname Faa Rawng (Thunder) until he joined the monkhood. Appointed abbot of his local temple by the age of 24, he came to be regarded as something of a rebel – though a hugely popular one among the people of Lanna. Despite the suspicions of the Sangha, both locally and in Bangkok, he became abbot of Lamphun's Wat Chama Thevi, which he set about restoring with gusto. This was the beginning of a tireless campaign to breathe life into Buddhist worship in the north by renovating its religious sites: over a hundred temples got the Khruba treatment, including Chiang Mai's Wat Phra Singh, Wat Phra That Haripunjaya in Lamphun and Wat Phra That Doi Tung near Mae Sai, as well as bridges, schools and government buildings. His greatest work, however, was the construction in 1935 of the paved road up to Wat Phra That Doi Suthep, which beforehand could only be reached after a climb of at least five hours. The road was constructed entirely by the voluntary labour of people from all over the north, using the most primitive tools. The project gained such fame that it attracted donations of B20 million, and on any one day as many as four thousand people were working on it. So that people didn't get in each other's way, Khruba Srivijaya declared that each village should contribute 15m of road, but as more volunteers flocked to Chiang Mai, this figure had to be reduced to 3m. The road was completed after just six months, and Khruba Srivijaya took the first ride to the temple in a donated car.

When Khruba Srivijaya died back in his native village in 1938, Rama VIII was so moved that he sponsored a royal cremation ceremony, held in 1946 (a long wait until the auspicious day for a cremation signifies high respect for the deceased). The monk's relics were divided up and are now enshrined at Wat Suan Dork in Chiang Mai, Wat Phra Kaeo Don Tao in Lampang and at many other holy places throughout the north. There's a statue of him at the end of Thanon Huai Kaeo, where the road to Wat Phra That Doi Suthep starts, and you'll see photos of him in temples, shops and restaurants all over the north, where Khruba amulets are still hugely popular, over seventy years after his death.

bring good luck. At the northwestern corner is a 2m-high statue of the elephant which, so the story goes, expired on this spot.

Before going to the **upper terrace** you have to remove your shoes – and if you're showing a bit of knee or shoulder, the temple provides wraps to cover your impoliteness. This terrace is possibly the most harmonious piece of temple architecture in Thailand, a dazzling combination of red, green and gold in the textures of carved wood, filigree and gleaming metal – even the tinkling of the miniature bells and the rattling of fortune sticks seem to keep the rhythm. A cloister, decorated with gaudy murals, tightly encloses the terrace, leaving room only for a couple of small minor viharns and the altars and ceremonial gold umbrellas which surround the central focus of attention, the **chedi**. This dazzling gold-plated beacon, a sixteenth-century extension of Ku Na's original, was modelled on the chedi at Wat Phra That Haripunjaya in Lamphun – which previously had been the region's most significant shrine – and has now become a venerated emblem of northern Thailand.

A small *hong*, or swan, on a wire stretching to the pinnacle is used to bless the chedi during major Buddhist festivals: a cup in the swan's beak is filled with water, and a pulley draws the swan to the spire where the water is tipped out over the sides of the chedi. Look out also for an old photograph opposite the northeastern corner of the chedi, showing a cockerel which used to peck the feet of visitors who entered with their shoes on.

Phuping Palace

4km up the paved road from the wat • Daily 8.30am–4.30pm, tickets on sale 8.30–11.30am & 1–3.30pm; usually closed between Jan and early March when the royals are in residence • B50 • ⓦ bhubingpalace.org • Dress politely – no shorts or bare shoulders (clothes rental available)

Phuping Palace is the residence for the royals when they come to visit their village development projects in the north. There's a viewpoint over the hills to the south, rose and fern gardens and some pleasant trails through the grounds, but the buildings themselves are off-limits.

ARRIVAL AND DEPARTURE DOI SUTHEP

The best way to get up the mountain is in a rented vehicle, allowing you to stop along the way to admire the views. The road, although steep in places, is paved and well suited for motorbikes.

By shared songthaew Songthaews leave from Thanon Huai Kaeo in front of the zoo or Chiang Mai University for the 16km trip up to Wat Phra That (B40 to the wat, B80 return; B180 return to include Phuping Palace and Doi Pui village), but will only set off once they have a complement of six passengers.

By chartered vehicle It costs around B500 and up to charter a whole songthaew, about the same price it'll cost you to arrange a car and driver through your guesthouse.

ACCOMMODATION

On the higher slopes near the national park headquarters, there are national park **bungalows** with hot-water bathrooms (from B400 for two people) and **campsites**, for which tents can be rented (from B150 for two people). There's a campsite and bungalows with hot-water bathrooms (B1500 for six people) beside Mon Tha Than Falls.

Wiang Kum Kam

5km south of Chiang Mai city centre, beyond the Superhighway, on the east bank of the Ping River

The well-preserved and little-visited ruins of the ancient city of **WIANG KUM KAM** – traditionally regarded as the prototype for Chiang Mai – are hidden away in the picturesque, rural fringe of town. According to folklore, Wiang Kum Kam was built by King Mengrai as his new capital of the north, but was soon abandoned because of inundation by the Ping River. Recent excavations, however, have put paid to that theory: Wiang Kum Kam was in fact established much earlier, as one of a cluster of fortified satellite towns that surrounded the Mon capital at Lamphun. After Mengrai had conquered Lamphun in 1281, he resided at Kum Kam for a while, raising a chedi, a viharn and several Buddha statues before moving on to build Chiang Mai. Wiang Kum Kam was abandoned some time before 1750, probably as a result of a Burmese invasion.

About half of Wiang Kum Kam's 22 known temple sites have now been uncovered, along with a stone slab (now housed in the Chiang Mai National Museum) inscribed in a unique forerunner of the Thai script. A recently opened **museum** (daily 8.30am–5pm; B10) gives a dry, basic introduction to the temples, but it's inconveniently located on the far southern edge of Wiang Kum Kam: if you head east on Chiang Mai's second ring road, it's on the left, just after the first permissible left turn after the river bridge.

Chedi Si Liam

1km south of the Superhighway on the east bank of the river

Head first for **Chedi Si Liam**, which provides a useful landmark: this Mon chedi, in the shape of a tall, squared-off pyramid with niched Buddha images, was built by Mengrai in memory of his dead wife. Modelled on Wat Kukut in Lamphun, it was restored in 1908 by a wealthy Mon resident of Chiang Mai using Burmese artisans and is still part of a working temple.

Wat Kan Thom

About 2km from Chedi Si Liam: backtrack along the road you've travelled down from Chiang Mai, take the first right turn, turn right again and keep left through a scattered farming settlement

Wat Kan Thom (aka Wat Chang Kham) lay at the centre of the old city and is still an important place of worship. Archeologists were only able to get at the site after much of it had been levelled by bulldozers building a playground for the adjacent school, but they have managed to uncover the brick foundations of Mengrai's viharn. The modern shrine next to it is where Mengrai's soul is said to reside. Also in the grounds are a white chedi and a small viharn, both much restored, and a large new viharn displaying fine craftsmanship.

If you have your own transport, from here you can head off along the trails through the thick foliage of the longan plantations to the northwest of Wat Kan Thom, back towards Chedi Si Liam. On this route, you come across surprisingly well-preserved chedis and the red-brick walls of Wiang Kum Kam's temples in a handful of shady clearings set between rural dwellings.

| ARRIVAL AND DEPARTURE | WIANG KUM KAM |

By boat and horse carriage The best way of seeing Wiang Kum Kam is on a trip with Mae Ping River Cruises (2–4 daily; 2hr altogether; B700/person including pick-up from your accommodation), which involves a 20min cruise down the river followed by a carriage ride to the museum and six temples (see p.281).

By motorbike or bicycle About 3km square, the ancient city can be explored on a bicycle or a motorbike, though it's easy to get lost in the maze of lanes connecting the ruins. If you're happy to look around under your own steam, the best way to approach Wiang Kum Kam is by heading down Thanon Chiang Mai–Lamphun, then forking right at Nong Hoi market (a short way after the *Holiday Inn*) onto Thanon Koh Klang, which will bring you under the Superhighway to Chedi Si Liam.

Lamphun

Though capital of its own province, **LAMPHUN** lives in the shadow of the tourist attention (and baht) showered on Chiang Mai, 26km to the north. Yet for anyone interested in history, a visit to this former royal city is a must and, if you have your own transport, combines very well with a trip to Wiang Kum Kam. The town's largely plain architecture is given some character by the surrounding waterways, beyond which stretch lush rice-fields and plantations of *lamyai* (longan); the sweetness of the local variety is celebrated every year in early August at the **Ngan Lamyai** (Longan Festival), when the town comes alive with processions of fruity floats, a drum-beating competition and a Miss Lamyai beauty contest. Lamphun also offers a less frantic alternative to Chiang Mai during the Songkhran and Loy Krathong festivals, the Khuang River being a far less congested place to float your *krathong* than Chiang Mai's Ping River. Though the streets of the town are usually sleepy, the ancient working **temples** of Wat Phra That Haripunjaya and Wat Kukut are lively and worth aiming for on a half-day trip from Chiang Mai.

Lamphun claims to be the oldest continuously inhabited town in Thailand, and has a history dating back to the late eighth or early ninth century when the ruler of the major Dvaravati centre at Lopburi sent his daughter, Chama Thevi, to found the Theravada Buddhist city-state of **Haripunjaya** here. Under the dynasty she established, Haripunjaya flourished as a link in the trade route to Yunnan in southwest China and managed to resist coming under the suzerainty of the Khmers at Angkor, who absorbed Lopburi and the other Dvaravati cities in central Thailand in the eleventh century. In 1281, after a decade of scheming, King Mengrai conquered Lamphun and brought it under Chiang Mai's control.

Chama Thevi's planners are said to have based the **layout** of the town on the shape of an auspicious conch shell. The rough outcome is a rectangle, narrower at the north end than the south, with the Khuang River running down its kilometre-long east side, and moats around the north, west and south sides. The main street, Thanon Inthayongyot, bisects the conch from north to south, while the road to Wat Kukut (Thanon Chama Thevi) heads out from the middle of the west moat.

Wat Phra That Haripunjaya

Easiest access through the rear entrance on Thanon Inthayongyot

One of the north's grandest and most important temples, **Wat Phra That Haripunjaya** has its bot and ornamental front entrance facing the Khuang River. Its main festival is Visakha Puja, the anniversary of the Buddha's birth, enlightenment and death, which is said to coincide with the anniversary of the temple's establishment. However, the date of its founding is actually hard to fathom: the earliest guess is 897, when the king of Haripunjaya is said to have built a chedi to enshrine a hair of the Buddha. More certain is the date of the main rebuilding of the temple, under King Tilok of Chiang Mai in 1443, when the present ringed chedi was erected in the then-fashionable Sri Lankan style (later copied at Doi Suthep and Lampang). Clad in brilliant copper plates, it has since been raised to a height of about 50m, crowned by a gold umbrella.

The plain open courtyards around the chedi contain a compendium of religious structures in a wild mix of styles and colours. On the north side, the tiered Haripunjaya-style pyramid of **Chedi Suwanna** was built in 1418 as a replica of the chedi at nearby Wat Kukut. You get a whiff of southern Thailand in the open space beyond the Suwanna chedi, where the **Chedi Chiang Yan** owes its resemblance to a pile of flattened pumpkins to the Srivijayan style. On either side of the viharn (to the east of the main chedi) stand a dark red **bell tower**, containing what's claimed to be the world's largest bronze gong, and a weather-beaten **library** on a raised base. Just to add to the temple's mystique, an open pavilion at the southwest corner of the chedi shelters a stone indented with four overlapping **footprints**, believed by fervent worshippers to confirm an ancient legend that the Buddha once passed this way. Next to the pavilion is a small **museum** which houses bequests to the temple, including some beautiful Buddha images in the Lanna style. Finally, beside the back entrance, is the **Phra Chao Tan Jai**, a graceful standing Buddha, surrounded by graphic murals that depict a horrific version of Buddhist hell.

Hariphunchai National Museum

Thanon Inthayongyot, across the road from the wat's back entrance • Wed–Sun 9am–4pm • B100

The **Hariphunchai National Museum** contains a well-organized but not quite compelling collection of religious finds, and occasionally stages some interesting temporary exhibitions. The terracotta and bronze Buddha images here give the best overview of the distinctive features of the Haripunjaya style: large curls above a wide, flat forehead, bulging eyes, incised moustache and enigmatic smile.

Wat Chama Thevi

Thanon Chama Thevi

Art-history buffs will get a thrill out of **Wat Chama Thevi** (also known as Wat Kukut), where the main brick chedi, Suwan Chang Kot, which was built around 1150 and repaired in 1218, is the only complete example of Haripunjaya architecture. Queen Chama Thevi is supposed to have chosen the site by ordering an archer to fire an arrow from the city's western gate – to retrace his epic shot, follow the road along the National Museum's southern wall to the west gate at the city moat, and keep going for nearly 1km along Thanon Chama Thevi. Chedi Suwan Chang Kot is five-tiered and rectangular, inset with niches sheltering beautiful, wide-browed Buddha images in stucco, typical of the Haripunjaya style. Believed to enshrine Chama Thevi's ashes, it lost its pinnacle at some stage, giving rise to the name Wat Kukut, the temple with the "topless" chedi. On your way back to the town centre from Wat Chama Thevi, you might like to pop in at **Wat Mahawan**, famous for the Buddha image amulets on sale here.

ARRIVAL AND DEPARTURE

LAMPHUN

It's not worth considering catching the train to Lamphun from Chiang Mai as schedules are unreliable and the station there is way out to the northeast of the town centre.

By songthaew or bus Blue songthaews from Thanon Chiang Mai–Lamphun in Chiang Mai, just south of Nawarat Bridge and opposite the TAT office, or buses from Chang Puak bus station, via Lamyai market on Thanon Praisani, will put you off outside the back entrance of Wat Haripunjaya.

By motorbike The direct (and scenic) route from Chiang Mai to Lamphun is Thanon Chiang Mai–Lamphun, which becomes Highway 106, for much of the way a stately avenue lined by 30m-tall *yang* trees that makes for a pleasant motorbike ride.

ACCOMMODATION

Lamphun Will Hotel Thanon Chama Thevi opposite Wat Kukut ☎ 053 534865–6, ✆ lamphunwillhotel.com. It's unlikely you'll want to stay overnight in Lamphun, but this stylish, contemporary hotel is a decent choice.

There's a swimming pool, a restaurant, an internet corner and en-suite, hot-water bathrooms, a/c and wi-fi in all the bedrooms. **B1200**

EATING AND DRINKING

Lamphun Ice 6 Thanon Chaimongkol ☎ 053 511452. Among the few restaurants in Lamphun with an English-language menu, this place serves tasty Thai food at

reasonable prices; it's conveniently situated on the road that runs along the south wall of Wat Haripunjaya. Daily 10am–midnight.

Huay Tung Tao

Signed off Highway 107 (the continuation of Thanon Chotana) about 10km north of Chiang Mai; it's then 2km west from the turn-off to the paved road around the lake

With your own transport, **Huay Tung Tao**, a large man-made lake at the base of Doi Suthep, is a great place to cool off during the hot season; it's safe to swim in, with canoes and inner tubes to rent, and is also used by anglers and windsurfers. Floating bamboo shelters along the water's edge provide shade from the sun, and you can order simple food such as sticky rice, grilled chicken and *som tam*.

Darapirom Palace

16km north of Chiang Mai in Mae Rim: look out for a sign on the left of Highway 107 just before Mae Rim police station • Tues–Sun 9am–5pm • B50 • ☎ 053 299175

In **Mae Rim**, a small market town that's now almost a suburb of Chiang Mai, the **Darapirom Palace** is a gorgeous colonial-style building from the early twentieth century. The palace was once the home of Princess Dara Rasamee (1873–1933), daughter of Chao Inthanon, the lord of Chiang Mai, who became the favourite concubine of King Chulalongkorn (Rama V) in the days before Chiang Mai was fully integrated into the Siamese state. Extremely proud of her northern heritage – and now something of a heroine to lovers of Lanna culture – the princess had this residence built in 1914, a few years after Chulalongkorn's death, when she returned from Bangkok to live out her later years in her homeland. Bangkok's Chulalongkorn University has recently opened the palace as a museum, featuring period furnishings and many items that once belonged to the princess. Photographs of her show her knee-length hair – which contrasted strongly with the fashion among Siamese women of the time to sport short-cropped hair – and the various rooms of the museum display her wardrobe and personal effects including musical instruments.

The Mae Sa valley

About 1km north of central Mae Rim on Highway 107, Route 1096, a good sealed road, heads west up the valley

Running west from Mae Rim, the **Mae Sa valley** has the atmosphere of a theme park, sheltering a menagerie of snake farms, monkey shows, elephant camps, "adventure sports" venues, and orchid and butterfly farms, but its highlight, the lovely botanic gardens, is well worth the trip. The main Route 1096 through the valley also passes the unspectacular **Mae Sa Waterfall** (part of Doi Suthep-Pui National Park; B200), where you can walk up a peaceful trail passing lots of little cascades along the way. Once you've seen all you want to in the valley, you have the option of continuing west for a scenic drive in the country: turn left on to Route 1269 before Samoeng, and follow this road as it swoops up and down over hills, skirting all the way round Doi Suthep to join Highway 108 8km south of Chiang Mai, a two-hour drive in all.

Queen Sirikit Botanic Gardens

12km up Route 1096 from the Mae Rim turn-off • Daily 8.30am–5pm, Natural Science Museum daily 9.30am–3.45pm • B100, plus B100 per car • Shuttle buses B3 (unlimited rides) • ⓦ qsbg.org

The magnificent **Queen Sirikit Botanic Gardens**, which offer fine views across the mountain valley, are the main reason for coming to Mae Sa. If you are at all botanically inclined, you could easily spend half a day here, exploring the four nature trails that link its arboretum, ornamental beds, rock garden, orchid nursery, areas of climbers and medicinal plants and a complex of a dozen glasshouses. There's also an interesting and attractive Natural Science Museum, with English labels, to put things in context, and a café. Hop-on, hop-off shuttle buses run around the steep, extensive grounds, if the heat gets too much; cars are also allowed to drive round, but motorbikes must park at the entrance.

ACCOMMODATION AND EATING   MAE SA VALLEY

Pong Yang Angdoi Resort 2km beyond the botanic gardens on the south side of the road ☎ 053 879151–3, ⓦ pongyangangdoi.com. Set in a steep, tree-covered valley with a view of an attractive waterfall, this resort might tempt you to spend a night out of Chiang Mai. It boasts cosy, well-equipped bungalows, all with a/c, hot water and balconies, as well as a very good, scenic restaurant. B2500

Doi Khun Tan National Park

Around 50km southeast of Chiang Mai · B100 · ☎ 053 546335, ⓦ dnp.go.th

One of three major national parks close to Chiang Mai, along with Suthep and Inthanon, **DOI KHUN TAN NATIONAL PARK** is easily accessible by train from Chiang Mai: a 1352m-long rail tunnel, the longest in Thailand, built between 1907 and 1918 by German engineers and Thai workers (of whom over a thousand died due to accidents, malaria and tigers), cuts through the mountain that gives the park its name. Despite this, and the fact that the king has famously holidayed here, the park remains unspoiled, but has enough infrastructure to encourage overnighting. The park is most popular on weekends, when groups of Thai schoolchildren visit, and during the cool season.

Covering 255 square kilometres, the park's vegetation varies from bamboo forest at an altitude of 350m to tropical evergreen forest between 600m and 1000m; the 1373m summit of Doi Khun Tan is known for its wild flowers, including orchids, gingers and lilies. Most of the small mammal species in the park are squirrels, but you're more likely to see some birds, with over 182 species found here.

Trails through the park

The park's **trails** are clearly marked, running from short nature trails around the park headquarters (where maps are available) to three major trails that all eventually lead to the summit of **Doi Khun Tan** – with impressive views of the surrounding countryside, it's clear how it fulfilled its role as a World War II military lookout. The main 8.3km trail from the train station to the Doi Khun Tan summit, though steep, is very easy, divided into four quarters of approximately 2km each, with each quarter ending at a resting place. While you shouldn't have a problem getting to the summit and back in a day, a more rewarding option is to do the walk in two days, staying overnight in the bungalows or at one of the campsites along the trail. Alternatively, you can take a circular route to the summit and back, forsaking a large chunk of the main trail for the two subsidiary trails which curve around either side, taking in two **waterfalls**.

ARRIVAL AND DEPARTURE   DOI KHUN TAN NATIONAL PARK

By train There are currently two morning and three afternoon trains daily from Chiang Mai to Khun Tan station on their way to Lampang and beyond, but there's no longer an evening train back (the last one's at 1.35pm), ruling out a day-trip by rail from the city (though it might be worth checking the latest timetables, just in case the evening service is reinstated). The park headquarters is a 1300m walk up the summit trail from the train station.

Destinations Bangkok (4 daily; 11–13hr); Chiang Mai (5 daily; 1hr 30min); Lampang (5 daily; 50min).

By car or motorbike A car or motorbike can take you to the park headquarters, though no further: from Chiang Mai follow Highway 11 to the turn-off to Mae Tha and head northeast for 18km, following signs for the park.

ACCOMMODATION AND EATING

If you want to stay in the park, consider booking in advance through the Department of National Parks website (ⓦ dnp.go.th). There's a basic **restaurant** at the headquarters and beside the bungalows.

Bungalows The park's bungalows, just up the main trail from the headquarters, are mostly spacious and well-appointed log cabins with hot-water bathrooms, sleeping up to six people. Some have outside seating areas with great views over the rolling hills. B1500

Camping There's a well-equipped (and often very busy) campsite at the park headquarters; if you don't have your own tent you can hire one here. B150

Lampang and around

A high road pass and a train tunnel breach the narrow, steep belt of mountains between Chiang Mai and **LAMPANG**, the north's second-largest town, 100km to the southeast.

Lampang is an important transport hub – Highway 11, Highway 1 and the Northern Rail Line all converge here – and given its undeniably low-key attractions, nearly all travellers sail through it on their way to the more trumpeted sights further north. But unlike most other provincial capitals, Lampang has the look of a place where history has not been completely wiped out: houses, shops and temples survive in the traditional style, and the town makes few concessions to tourism. Out of town, the beautiful complex of **Wat Phra That Lampang Luang** is the main attraction in these parts, but while you're in the neighbourhood you could also stop by to watch a show at the **Elephant Conservation Centre**, on the road from Chiang Mai.

The modern centre of Lampang sprawls along the south side of the Wang River, with its most frenetic commercial activity taking place along Thanon Boonyawat and Thanon Robwiang near Ratchada Bridge. Here, you'll find stalls and shops selling the famous local **pottery**, a kitsch combination of whites, blues and browns, made from the area's rich and durable kaolin clay. On all street signs around town, and in larger-than-life statues at key

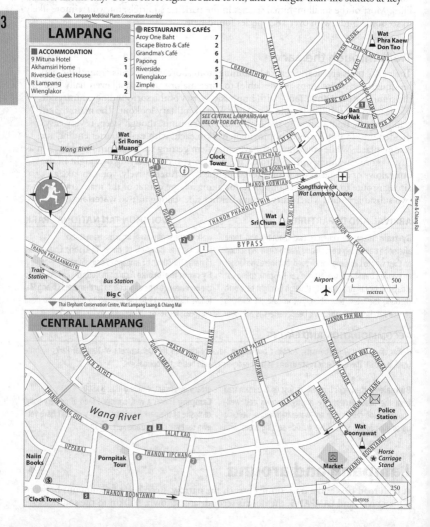

intersections, is a **white chicken**. This symbol of Lampang relates to a legend concerning the Buddha, who sent down angels from Heaven in the form of chickens to wake up the local inhabitants in time to offer alms to the monks at the end of Buddhist Lent. Perhaps the town's image as a laidback, sleepy place is justified in the light of this tale.

Brief history

Founded as Kelang Nakhon by the ninth-century Haripunjaya queen Chama Thevi, Lampang became important enough for one of her two sons to rule here after her death. After King Mengrai's conquest of Haripunjaya in 1281, Lampang suffered much the same ups and downs as the rest of Lanna, enjoying a burst of prosperity as a **timber** town at the end of the nineteenth century, when it supported a population of twenty thousand people and four thousand working elephants. Many of its temples were financially endowed by the waves of outsiders who had settled in Lampang: refugees from Chiang Saen (who were forcibly resettled here by Rama I at the beginning of the nineteenth century), Burmese teak-loggers and, more recently, rich Thai pensioners attracted by the town's sedate charm.

Wat Phra Kaew Don Tao

Thanon Phra Kaeo, 1km northeast of the Ratchada Bridge • Daily 7am–6pm • B40

Lampang's few sights are well scattered; the best place to start is on the north side of the river (the site of the original Haripunjaya settlement), whose leafy suburbs today contain the town's most important and interesting temple, **Wat Phra Kaew Don Tao**. An imposing, rather forbidding complex, the temple was founded in the fifteenth century to enshrine the Phra Kaew Don Tao image, now residing at Wat Phra That Lampang Luang (see p.314). For 32 years it also housed the Emerald Buddha (local stories aver this to be a copy of Phra Kaew Don Tao), a situation that came about when an elephant carrying the holy image from Chiang Rai to Chiang Mai made an unscheduled and therefore auspicious halt here in 1436. The small **museum** at the back of the compound displays some dainty china among its exhibits, but its main focus is woodcarving, a craft at which Burmese artisans excel.

The chedi and mondop

The clean, simple lines of the white, gold-capped **chedi**, which is reputed to contain a hair of the Buddha, form a shining backdrop to the wat's most interesting building, a Burmese **mondop** stacked up in extravagantly carved tiers; it was built in 1909 by craftsmen from the local Burmese community, employed for the task by a Thai prince (whose British-style coat of arms can be seen on the ceiling inside). All gilt and gaudy coloured glass, the interior decoration is a real fright, mixing Oriental and European influences, with some incongruously cute little cherubs on the ceiling. The mondop's boyish bronze centrepiece has the typical features of a Mandalay Buddha, with its jewelled headband, inset black and white eyes, and exaggerated, dangling ears, which denote the Buddha's supernatural ability to hear everything in the universe. In front of the Buddha is an image of Khruba Srivijaya, the north's most venerated monk (see box, p.305).

Ban Sao Nak

6 Thanon Ratwattana • Daily 10am–5pm • B50

Not far from Wat Phra Kaew Don Tao can be found **Ban Sao Nak** ("house of many pillars"), a private museum containing a fine display of ceramics, lacquerware and teak furnishings. Built in 1895 in a mixture of Burmese and Lanna styles, this sprawling wooden mansion is supported by a maze of 116 teak pillars and contains some interesting fading photographs of its former occupants, who were local notables. Here and outside, in the carefully landscaped grounds, you'll get a sense of how life would have been for the north's wealthier residents at the turn of the twentieth century.

Wat Sri Chum

Thanon Sri Chum, a 5min walk south of Thanon Robwiang

The Burmese who worked on Wat Phra Kaew Don Tao were brought to Lampang in the late nineteenth century when, after the British conquest of Upper Burma, timber companies expanded their operations as far as northern Thailand. Fearing that the homeless spirits of fallen trees would seek vengeance, the Burmese loggers often sponsored the building of temples, most of which still stand, to try to appease the tree spirits and gain merit. Though the spirits had to wait nearly a century, they seem to have got their revenge: due to a short circuit in some dodgy wiring, the viharn of **Wat Sri Chum**, which is the biggest Burmese temple in Thailand as well as the most important and beautiful Burmese temple in town, was damaged by fire in 1992. Now restored to its former glory, with fresh carvings and murals by Burmese craftsmen, it's sited in a small grove of bodhi trees.

Wat Sri Rong Muang

Towards the west end of Thanon Takrao Noi

To get more of a flavour of Burma, head for hundred-year-old **Wat Sri Rong Muang**, which presents a dazzling ensemble: the crazy angles of its red-and-yellow roof shelter Mandalay Buddhas and several extravagantly carved gilt sermon-thrones, swimming in a glittering sea of coloured-glass wall tiles.

Thanon Talat Kao

Behind the south bank of the river • Walking street Sat & Sun roughly 5–10pm

When you've had your fill of temples, **Thanon Talat Kao**, the "Old Market Street", is good for a quiet stroll in the early morning. It has some very old shophouses and mansions, showing a mixture of European, Burmese and Chinese influences (it used to be known as Talat Jiin, "Chinese market"), with intricate balconies, carved gables and unusual sunburst designs carved over some of the doors. On Saturday and Sunday evenings, Talat Kao comes to life as a "**walking street**", similar to those in Chiang Mai, with food, silk and other crafts for sale and musicians playing.

Lampang Medicinal Plants Conservation Assembly

3km northwest of the town centre on Thanon Kunmuang • Daily 8am–9pm • ☏ 054 350787, ⊛ herblpg.com • Traditonal massage from B200/hr • A songthaew from the centre of Lampang costs around B60; if driving yourself, follow Thanon Chammathewi towards Haeng Chat for about 2km, then turn right and left, following signs for Lampang Herbs Conservation

Though the **Lampang Medicinal Plants Conservation Assembly** (Rak Samoonprai) sounds like the kind of place where botanists might hold seminars, it is in fact a traditional health centre set in a shady compound. If you feel like pampering your body, head out here for a strong traditional massage, herbal sauna, face scrub, mud skin treatment or even a bare-footed health walk over a path of rounded pebbles designed to provide a natural foot massage. The facilities are spotless, the grounds are full of labelled herbs, and a huge range of medicinal plant products is on sale.

Wat Phra That Lampang Luang

18km southwest of Lampang • Blue songthaews from Thanon Robwiang charge around B40 • If driving yourself, head south from Lampang on Highway 1, then cross the bridge over the Wang River at Kor Kha and turn right, heading north for about 3km on Route 1034; if you're coming from Chiang Mai or the elephant centre, just after Hang Chat (before you reach Lampang) turn right off Highway 11 onto Route 1034

A grand and well-preserved capsule of Lanna art and design, **Wat Phra That Lampang Luang** is one of the architectural highlights of northern Thailand. The wat was built

early in the Haripunjaya era as a *wiang* (fortress), one of a satellite group around Lampang – you can still see remains of the threefold ramparts in the farming village around the temple. Outside the wat, simple snacks, handicrafts and antiques can be bought from market stalls.

The main viharn

At the main entrance, a naga staircase leads you up to a wedding cake of a gatehouse, richly decorated with stucco, which is set in the original brick boundary walls. Just inside, the oversized fifteenth-century **viharn** is open on all sides in classic Lanna fashion, and shelters a spectacular centrepiece: known as a *ku*, a feature found only in the viharns of northern Thailand, this gilded brick tower looks like a bonfire for the main Buddha image sitting inside, the Phra Chao Lan Thong. Tall visitors need to mind their heads on the panels hanging from the low eaves, which are decorated with attractive, though fading, early nineteenth-century paintings of battles, palaces and nobles in traditional Burmese gear.

The rest of the main compound

The temple's main walled compound is home to no less than four other viharns. In front of the murky, beautifully decorated viharn to the left, look out for a wooden *tung chai* carved with flaming, coiled nagas, used as a heraldic banner for northern princes. The battered, cosy **Viharn Nam Tame**, second back on the right, dates to the early sixteenth century. Its drooping roof configuration is archetypal: divided into three tiers, each of which is divided again into two layers, it ends up almost scraping the ground. Under the eaves you can just make out fragments of panel paintings, as old as the viharn, illustrating a story of one of the exploits of the Hindu god Indra.

The wat's huge central **chedi** enshrines a hair of the Buddha and ashes from the right side of his forehead and neck. By its northwest corner, a sign points to a drainage hole in the wat's boundary wall, once the scene of an unlikely act of derring-do: in 1736, local hero Thip Chang managed to wriggle through the tiny hole and free the *wiang* from the occupying Burmese, before going on to liberate the whole of Lampang.

At the chedi's southwest corner, the **Haw Phra Phuttabhat** (no entry for women) is a small chamber that acts as a camera obscura. If you close the door behind you, an image of the chedi is projected through a small hole in the door onto a sheet hung from the ceiling.

Phra Kaew Don Tao

A gate in the south side of the main compound's boundary wall leads first to a spreading **bodhi tree** on crutches: merit-makers have donated hundreds of supports to prop up its drooping branches. The tree, with its own small shrine standing underneath, is believed to be inhabited by spirits, and the sick are sometimes brought here in search of a cure.

The path beyond the bodhi tree will bring you to a small, unimpressive viharn to the west of the main compound, which is the home of **Phra Kaew Don Tao**, the much-revered companion image to Bangkok's Emerald Buddha, and the wat's main focus of pilgrimage. Legend has it that the statuette first appeared in the form of an emerald found in a watermelon presented by a local woman to a venerated monk. The two of them tried to carve a Buddha out of the emerald, without much success, until the god Indra appeared and fashioned the marvellous image, at which point the ungrateful townsfolk accused the monk of having an affair with the woman and put her to death, thus bringing down upon the town a series of disasters which confirmed the image's awesome power. In all probability, the image was carved at the beginning of the fifteenth century, when its namesake wat in Lampang was founded. Peering through the rows of protective bars inside the viharn, you can just make out the tiny meditating Buddha, which is actually made of jasper, not emerald. Like the Emerald Buddha in Bangkok, Phra Kaew Don Tao has three costumes, one for each season of the year (see p.86).

Thung Kwian market

21km from Lampang on Highway 11, en route to the Thai Elephant Conservation Centre

If you have your own vehicle, the **Thung Kwian market** (open daily) offers not only a useful stop for refreshments near the elephant centre, but also a chance to view the panoply of products on sale – rabbits and birds, honeycombs, bugs and creepy crawlies of every description. This is a favourite spot for city Thais to pick up some exotic taste to take back home with them.

The Thai Elephant Conservation Centre

34km west of Lampang on Highway 11 • Shows daily at 10am, 11am & 1.30pm, with the chance to see the elephants bathing at 9.40am & 1.10pm • B170 • ☎ 054 247875 or ☎ 08 9755 4917, ⊕ thailandelephant.org • The centre is on the bus route between Chiang Mai and Lampang; from the gates, there are regular shuttle buses into the elephant showground 2km away

The **Thai Elephant Conservation Centre** (aka the National Elephant Institute) is the most authentic and worthwhile place in Thailand to see elephants displaying their skills. Entertaining **shows** put the elephants through their paces, with plenty of loud trumpeting for their audience. After some photogenic bathing, they walk together in formation and go through a routine of pushing and dragging logs, then proceed to paint pictures and play custom-made instruments. You can feed them bananas and sugarcane after the show, and even take a **ride** on one (available daily 8am–3.30pm) – B200 gets you ten minutes, while B1000 gives you an hour's ride, with a chance to get out into the nearby forest (overnight treks and mahout training programmes are also on offer – see the website). Visitors are also free to look around the hospital, but not the royal stables, where six of Rama IX's eleven white elephants are kept.

Run by the Thai government, the conservation centre was originally set up in 1969 in another nearby location as a young elephant-training centre, the earliest of its kind in Thailand. However, since the ban on logging, the new centre, opened in 1992, emphasizes the preservation of the elephant in Thailand (see box, p.318). By promoting ecotourism the centre is providing employment for the elephants and enabling Thai people to continue their historically fond relationship with these animals. Money raised from entrance fees and donations helps to finance the **elephant hospital** here, which cares for sick, abused, ageing and abandoned elephants. The centre has three simple **restaurants** on site, and offers the possibility of homestay **accommodation** (from B1000 including meals; see the website for more details).

ARRIVAL AND DEPARTURE   LAMPANG

By plane Bangkok Airways runs flights from Sukhothai roughly twice a week (30min), and from Bangkok (1hr) at least five times a week. The airport is just south of town, and songthaews are on hand for the short ride to the centre.
By train The train station lies less than 1km southwest of the town centre. A songthaew from here to the guesthouses costs B20.
Destinations Bangkok (6 daily; 10–12hr); Chiang Mai (7 daily; 2hr–2hr 30min).
By bus The bus station is southwest of the town centre,

just off the bypass. Most buses pull in here (Chiang Rai buses also make a stop on Thanon Phaholyothin in the centre). Yellow-and-green songthaews wait at the edge of the terminal, departing when full up (B20 to guesthouses and hotels within the city).
Destinations Bangkok (at least hourly; 8hr); Chiang Mai via Lamphun (every 30min; 1hr 30min); Chiang Rai (every 30min; 4–5hr); Mae Sai (3 daily; 5hr); Mae Sot (2 daily; 4–5hr); Nan (8 daily; 4hr); Phrae (hourly; 2hr–2hr 30min); Tak (2 daily; 3–4hr).

GETTING AROUND

Most of the town can be covered on foot, but there are alternatives, including the town's horse-drawn carriages (see box, p.319).

By songthaew There are plenty of yellow-and-green songthaews that cruise the streets looking for custom (B20/person within the city).
By bicycle or motorbike Bicycles (B50–60/day) can be

rented at *Akhamsiri Home* and *Riverside Guest House*; motorbikes at *Riverside Guest House* (B200/day, or B150/4hr) and Pornpitak Tour, 363/1 Thanon Tipchang (☎ 081 950 1543, ⊕ pornpitaktour.com; B250/day).

THE ELEPHANT IN THAILAND

To Thais the **elephant** has profound **spiritual significance**, derived from both Hindu and Buddhist mythologies. Carvings and statues of **Ganesh**, the Hindu god with an elephant's head, feature on ancient temples all over the country and, as the god of knowledge and remover of obstacles, Ganesh has been adopted as the symbol of the Fine Arts Department – and is thus depicted on all entrance tickets to historical sights. The Hindu deity Indra rarely appears without his three-headed elephant mount **Erawan**, and miniature devotional elephant effigies are sold at major Brahmin shrines, such as Bangkok's Erawan Shrine. In Buddhist legend, the future **Buddha's mother** was able to conceive only after she dreamt that a white elephant had entered her womb: that is why elephant balustrades encircle many of the Buddhist temples of Sukhothai, and why the rare white elephant is accorded royal status (see p.116) and featured on the national flag until 1917.

The **practical** role of the elephant in Thailand was once almost as great as its symbolic importance. The kings of Ayutthaya relied on elephants to take them into battle against the Burmese – one king assembled a trained elephant army of three hundred – and during the nineteenth century King Rama IV offered Abraham Lincoln a male and a female to "multiply in the forests of America" and to use in the Civil War. In times of peace, the phenomenal strength of the elephant has made it invaluable as a beast of burden: elephants hauled the stone from which the gargantuan Khmer temple complexes of the northeast were built, and for centuries they have been used to clear forests and carry timber.

The traditional cycle for domestic elephants born in captivity is to spend the first three years of their lives with their mothers (who are pregnant for 18–22 months and get five years' maternity leave), before being separated and raised with other calves in training schools. Each elephant is then looked after by a **mahout** (*kwan chang*), a trainer, keeper and driver rolled into one. Traditionally the mahout would have stayed with the elephant for the rest of its life, but nowadays this rarely happens, as being a mahout is seen as a low-status job.

Training begins gently, with mahouts taking months to earn the trust of their charge; over the next thirteen years the elephant is taught about forty different commands, from simple "stop" and "go" orders to complex instructions for hooking and passing manoeuvres with the trunk. By the age of 16, elephants are ready to be put to work and are expected to carry on working until they reach 50 or 60, after which they are retired and may live for another twenty years.

Ironically, the **timber industry** was the animal's undoing. Mechanized logging destroyed the wild elephant's preferred river-valley grassland and forest habitats, forcing them into isolated upland pockets. As a result, Thailand's population of wild elephants is now thought to be under two thousand, while there are around 2500 domesticated animals – down from a roughly estimated total population of a hundred thousand in 1900 (the Asian elephant is now officially classified as an endangered species). With the 1989 **ban on commercial logging** within Thai borders – after the 1988 catastrophe when the effects of deforestation killed a hundred people and wiped out villages in Surat Thani province, as mudslides swept down deforested slopes carrying cut timber with them – elephants and their mahouts were faced with the further problem of **unemployment**. Though a small number of elephants continue to work in the illegal teak-logging trade along the Burmese border, most mahouts struggle to find the vast amount of food needed to sustain their charges – about 125kg per beast per day.

Tourism has stepped into the breach, mostly in the form of elephant shows and trekking, though it's been a mixed blessing to say the least, as the elephants are often poorly treated, overworked or downright abused. In town streets and on beaches, you'll often see mahouts charging both tourists for the experience of handfeeding their elephants bananas or sugar cane, and Thais for the chance to stoop under their trunks for good luck. At any one time, there may be up to two hundred elephants effectively begging in this way in Bangkok, which is simply not the right environment for them – they're regularly involved in road accidents, for example, despite the red reflectors that many sport on their tails; overall, it's best not to feed city elephants in this way. Demand from the tourism industry is now outstripping supply, and it's feared that captive beasts – which have a lower birth rate than elephants in the wild – may disappear in the next ten years or so, which in turn will mean that wild elephants will again be under threat (see p.763). According to recent reports, the number of baby elephants being registered exceeds the number of births, suggesting many are being taken from the wild.

LAMPANG'S HORSE-DRAWN CARRIAGES

If you want to get out to Wat Phra Kaew Don Tao you might want to employ the services of a **horse-drawn carriage**, which, along with white chickens (see p.312), is a prevalent symbol of Lampang (in fact, Thais often refer to the city as *muang rot mah*, or "horse-cart city"). These colourfully decked-out carriages, complete with Stetson-wearing driver, can be hired towards the east end of Thanon Boonyawat or opposite the tourist office. There are two "standard routes" around town; the shorter one (3km) costs B150, while the longer one (4km) costs B200. An alternative is the B300 city tour, which includes a stop at Wat Phra Kaew Don Tao, plus a handful of other city sights.

INFORMATION AND TOURS

Tourist information The small, municipal tourist information centre (Mon–Fri 8.30am–noon & 1–4.30pm, Sat & Sun roughly 9am–noon & 1–5pm; ☎054 237229, ⓦ lampangcity.go.th), just west of the clocktower and next to the fire station on Thanon Takrao Noi, can provide a map of the town, which shows horse-drawn carriage routes.
Tours Staff at the tourist information centre can book local

excursions for you. A popular day-trip calls at the Thai Elephant Conservation Centre in the morning, and then continues on to Wat Phra That Lampang Luang in the afternoon, returning to Lampang at 3pm (B700 for two people). Another good bet is Pornpitak Tour, 363/1 Thanon Tipchang (☎081 950 1543, ⓦ pornpitaktour.com), where staff can organize local sightseeing tours.

ACCOMMODATION

9 Mituna Hotel 285 Thanon Boonyawat ☎054 222261; map p.312. No-frills fan and a/c rooms in a huge concrete block in the middle of town. It feels a little musty around the edges, but the sheets are clean and fresh, and there are few places in the region quite this cheap. Fan **B143**, a/c **B286**

Akhamsiri Home 54/1 Thanon Pamaiket ☎054 228791, ⓦ akhamsirihome.com; map p.312. In a quiet part of town, attractive, slightly cutesy rooms in modern Thai style, with balconies upstairs and small gardens downstairs; all have a/c, hot water and fridges. There's also a café with internet access. **B450**

★ **Riverside Guest House** 286 Thanon Talat Kao ☎054 227005, ⓦ theriverside-lampang.com; map p.312. This peaceful, traditional compound of two teak houses with a small, attractive garden offers tasteful en-suite rooms, all with hot-water bathrooms and a few with a/c. Rooms are more elegant in the main house, simpler in the second house; some boast balconies or terraces overlooking the river. Varied breakfasts are served in the relaxing riverside café (not to be confused with the

Riverside restaurant, further west). Tours available, including trips to local ceramics markets and pineapple plantations (from B900/person). Internet access available. Fan **B400**, a/c **B600**

R Lampang Talat Kao, just east of Riverside Guest House ☎054 225278, ⓦ r-lampang.com; map p.312. Part guesthouse, part doll's house, *R Lampang* occupies a prime spot on the riverfront, with shades of pastel green and soft pink providing the backdrop for a weird and wonderful collection of corridor curios – from white-painted samlors to clapped-out old TV sets. The fan rooms are too small, with mattresses on the floor, but the a/c rooms with TV and fridge are worth the investment. Fan **B350**, a/c **B650**

Wienglakor 138/35 Thanon Phaholyothin ☎054 316430–5, ⓦ wienglakor.com; map p.312. Of several big and expensive hotels in town, this one has the cosiest rooms and the most tasteful decor, with coffered ceilings, parquet floors and ornamental ponds in traditional Thai style. Breakfast included. **B1400**

EATING AND DRINKING

Along with the riverfront, the stretch of **Thanon Takrao Noi** between the clocktower and Thanon Wienglakon is a lively part of town after dark, featuring many simple restaurants and the Atsawin **night market** running off its side streets to the south, as well as **pubs** and **karaoke bars**.

★ **Aroy One Baht** Thanon Tipchang ☎089 700 9444; map p.312. Cheap eats in a friendly roadside restaurant staffed by happy young Thais. The spicy snakehead fish soup, served in coconut milk, is a bargain at B40. Highly recommended. Daily 4pm–midnight.

Escape Bistro & Café 357/37 Thanon Duangrat

☎054 322622; map p.312. The most refined snack-stop on broad and busy Thanon Duangrat, this chilly a/c café is spread over two floors and a sunny outdoor terrace area. Try the blueberry smoothie (B70) as you flick through the huge selection of magazines. Daily 9am–7pm.

Grandma's Café Thanon Tipchang ☎054 322792; map p.312. Conveniently located coffee hangout that's popular with artsy young Lampangers, especially in the early evening. Serves good espressos and lots of noodle and rice dishes. Daily 10am–6pm.

Papong Thanon Tipchang; map p.312. Offering what the owners describe as "unseen home food", this cool little restaurant is brimming with clutter and bursting with authentic style. It's famous locally for its delicious northern-style curries, which start from B35. Daily 10am–midnight, with a limited menu on Sat & Sun.

Riverside 328 Thanon Tipchang ☎054 221861; map p.312. Cosy, relaxing spot on rustic wooden terraces overlooking the water, serving a wide variety of excellent Thai dishes, including northern specialities, and Western food, to the sounds of live music (quality variable) in the evenings. A wood-fired pizza oven is stoked up Tues, Thurs, Sat & Sun (evenings only; from B120); during the daytime, *Riverside* operates as a bakery-café. Daily 11am–midnight.

Wienglakor 138/35 Thanon Phaholyothin ☎054 316430–5; map p.312. The best hotel restaurant in town with a wide choice of well-prepared, good-value northern dishes and an inviting ambience, overlooking the landscaped gardens. Dinner on Fri and Sat nights is accompanied by live Thai music (6–8pm). Daily 10am–midnight.

Zimple On the corner of Thanon Wienglakon and Thanon Takrao Noi; map p.312. Enormous indoor-outdoor venue for drinking, dancing and dining. The big terrace out front gets packed on busy nights. Mon–Fri 5.30pm–midnight; Sat & Sun 5.30pm–1am.

DIRECTORY

ATM There's an ATM across from Naiin Books, near the clocktower.

Cinema The complex that houses the Big C hypermarket, just west of the bus station, shows films in Thai and English (B70).

Phrae

Heading east out of Lampang on your way to the small city of **PHRAE**, you'll pass through the tobacco-rich Yom valley, dotted with distinctive brick curing-houses. Phrae province is famous for woodcarving and the quality of its *seua maw hawm*, the

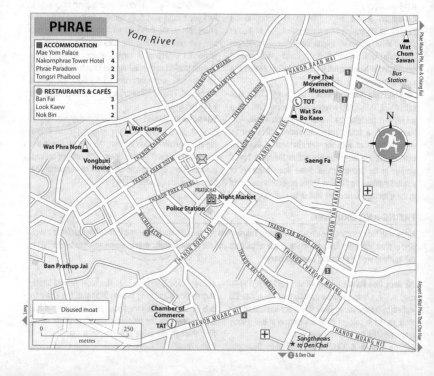

PHRAE

ACCOMMODATION
Mae Yom Palace	1
Nakornphrae Tower Hotel	4
Phrae Paradorn	2
Tongsri Phaibool	3

RESTAURANTS & CAFÉS
Ban Fai	3
Look Kaew	1
Nok Bin	2

deep-blue, collarless working shirt seen all over Thailand (produced in the village of Ban Thung Hong, 4km north of Phrae on Highway 101). The main reason to stop here, however, is to explore Phrae's old town, with its peaceful lanes filled with temples and traditional teak houses – as in Lampang, the former logging industry attracted Burmese workers and the influence is evident – and to enjoy the old-fashioned and friendly nature of a place still virtually untouched by tourism.

Sited on the southeast bank of the Yom River, Phrae is clearly divided into old and new towns; an earthen wall surrounds the roughly oval-shaped old town, with a moat on its southeastern side and the new town centre beyond that. At the centre of the **old town**, a large roundabout is the main orientation point; running northwest–southeast through the roundabout, through Pratuchai (the main gate on the southeastern side of the old town), and into the **new town** is Thanon Charoen Muang, where several shops sell the trademark deep-indigo shirts. The main street in the new town, Thanon Yantarakitkoson, intersects Thanon Charoen Muang about 300m southeast of the old town.

Vongburi House

Thanon Khamlue • Daily 9am–5pm • B30

The white-and-pink **Vongburi House** (Baan Wongburi) is a good place to begin an exploration of the old town. Built of teak between 1897 and 1907 in Thai–European style for the wife of the last lord of Phrae, it's smothered in elaborate, lace-like woodcarving on all the eaves, gables and balconies, and around doors and windows. Inside the house, exhibits include fine silverware, antique furniture, undershirts with magic spells written on them to ward off danger, and various documents such as elephant identity papers and artefacts that shed light on the history of the family, who still live in part of the complex.

Wat Luang

Just south of Thanon Rob Muang, around 100m from Vongburi House

Phrae's oldest temple complex, **Wat Luang**, dates from the town's foundation around the twelfth century; it contains the only intact original brick entrance gate to the city, though unfortunately it has been closed up and turned into an ugly shrine to Chao Pu, an early Lanna ruler. Apart from the gate, the oldest component of the wat is the crumbling early Lanna-style **chedi** called Chang Kham after the four elephants – now mostly trunkless – which sit at its octagonal base; these alternate with four niches containing Buddha images and some haphazardly leaning, gilded bronze parasols. Architectural experts have been called in from Bangkok to plan the restoration of the chedi and the overall complex: unfortunately, over the years, Wat Luang has been added to and parts of it have been quite spoiled in a gaudy modernization process. Until recently, a dishonest monk was even taking down parts of the temple to sell.

Apart from the ruined entrance gate, this meddling is most evident in the **viharn**, opposite, where an ugly and very out-of-place laterite brick facade has been placed in front of the original Lanna-style sixteenth-century entrance. Opposite the chedi on the north side of the compound, a **museum** (weekends only; free) on two floors houses some real treasures, the most important being a collection of sixteenth-century bronze Buddhas and several glass cases containing old manuscripts with beautifully gilded covers, which are located upstairs.

Wat Phra Non

About a block west of Wat Luang along Thanon Rob Muang

In the far northwestern corner of the old city is **Wat Phra Non**, established three centuries ago, whose name comes from the 9m-long reclining Buddha housed in a small viharn; look out for the Lanna-style bot's finely carved wooden pediment showing scenes from the *Ramayana*.

Ban Prathup Jai

Beyond the old town's west gate • Daily 8am–5pm • B40

Signposted among the tranquil lanes out beyond the old town's west gate lies the massive two-storey teak house of **Ban Prathup Jai**, constructed out of nine old houses in the mid-1980s. A visit here allows you to appreciate the beauty and strength of the wood, even if the overall effect is a bit over the top. The lower floor has an impressive interior of 130 pillars of solid teak carved with jungle scenes; huge wooden elephants wander among the columns, and solid teak walls provide a backdrop for ornately carved furniture. There's also a souvenir shop where you can buy all things wooden. Upstairs has the feel of a traditional house, and the furniture and objects are those that you might find in a well-to-do Thai home: ornately carved cabinets crammed with bowls and other ordinary household objects, tables displaying framed family portraits, wall carvings and even a teak bar.

Wat Chom Sawan

Around 200m north of the bus station on Thanon Yantarakitkoson

Built in 1894 under the reign of King Rama V, **Wat Chom Sawan** is a fine example of Burmese-style architecture. Recently restored, the main teak structure (notable for its impressive multi-tiered roof) houses the ordination hall and the monks' residence. Inside, the ceiling and columns are beautifully carved and dotted with glittering stained glass. Treasures include an ivory image of the Buddha in Burmese style, scripture slabs and Luang Pho San, a seated Buddha figure made of woven bamboo.

Free Thai Movement Museum

Tucked behind the Phrae Paradorn hotel • Daily dawn–dusk • Free • Enter via the hotel's reception area (ask at reception if doors are locked)

This fascinating little museum tells the story of Thailand's struggle to maintain its long-held independence, which looked severely compromised during World War II, when the country came under increasing pressure from Japanese occupation on one side and British and American interests on the other. Among the exhibits on show are photos and newspaper articles from the era, plus weapons used by **Seri Thai** (the Free Thai Movement) during their clandestine resistance against Japanese forces.

Wat Phra That Cho Hae

9km east of town (1km beyond the village of Padang) • Without your own transport, you'll need to charter a songthaew (about B300) from the bus station

Wat Phra That Cho Hae is an important pilgrimage centre sited on a low hill, approached by two naga stairways through a grove of teak trees. One staircase leads to a shrine where a revered Buddha image, Phra Chao Tan Chai, is said to increase women's fertility. The small grounds also house a gilded 33m-high **chedi**, traditionally wrapped in the yellow satin-like cloth, *cho hae* (which gives the wat its name), in March or April, and a brightly decorated viharn with an unusual cruciform layout. To the north of the main compound, a new viharn houses a shiny Buddha and some well-crafted murals and window carvings.

Phae Muang Phi

18km northeast of Phrae off Highway 101

Out of town are the so-called ghost pillars at **Phae Muang Phi**, a geological quirk of soil and wind erosion. Overzealous reports describe this as Thailand's Grand Canyon, but it's not a fair comparison, and it's probably only worth visiting if you're going on through to Nan with your own transport. Some locals believe the place is haunted, which may explain the lack of development in the area.

ARRIVAL AND DEPARTURE
PHRAE

By plane Nok Air runs two to three flights a week from Bangkok to Phrae's airport, 3km southeast of town. From the airport, motorbike taxis can run you into the centre.

By bus or minibus Buses stop at the main bus station off Thanon Yantarakitkoson, towards the northeast of town, as do fast a/c minibuses from Lampang. Samlors and motorbike taxis usually congregate here for journeys to the guesthouses.

Destinations Bangkok (11 daily; 8hr); Chiang Mai (hourly; 4hr); Chiang Rai (hourly; 4hr); Den Chai (hourly; 30min);

Lampang (hourly; 2hr–2hr 30min); Nan (hourly; 2hr); Phitsanulok (hourly; 4hr).

By train Den Chai train station, just 20km to the southwest, is on the main Bangkok–Chiang Mai line. Frequent songthaews run from Den Chai (30–40min) to a stand south of Phrae's old town, returning from the same spot.

By car If you're driving here from Lampang, turn left from Highway 11 at Mae Khaem onto Route 1023 and approach the town via Long and some lovely scenery.

GETTING AROUND

By motorbike taxi or samlor Short, one-way journeys around town cost B20–40 with a samlor or motorbike taxi.

By bicycle, motorbike or car The Mae Yom Palace Hotel (see below) rents out bicycles (B100/day) and four-wheel

drives (B1200/day). Motorbikes can be rented for B200 per day at Saeng Fa (no English sign; ☏ 054 521598), next to the Bank of Ayudhaya on Thanon Yantarakitkoson.

INFORMATION AND TOURS

Tourist information For information about the town and a clutch of handy maps, try the new, helpful and well-staffed TAT office at 34/130 Thanon Muang Hit (daily 8.30am–4.30pm; ☏ 054 521118, ✉ tatphrae@tat.or.th), next to the Chamber of Commerce. Alternatively, head to

Nok Bin coffee shop on Thanon Wichairacha (see below), where owner Khun Apinya can provide a wealth of information on the old town and the surrounding area.

Samlor tours The TAT office can arrange guided samlor trips around town (from B250/person for a 2hr trip).

ACCOMMODATION

Mae Yom Palace Hotel 181/6 Thanon Yantarakitkoson ☏ 054 521028–35, ✉ wccphrae@hotmail.com. The best hotel in town, with a handy central location near the bus station. Facilities include a large, attractive swimming pool, a restaurant with a pleasant outdoor terrace, bicycle rental and internet access (B50/hr). Rooms are carpeted and air-conditioned. B1400

Nakornphrae Tower Hotel 3 Thanon Muang Hit ☏ 054 521321, ✉ nakornphrae@yahoo.com. The smart, spacious rooms here have their own private balconies, large double beds and showers over the clean bathtubs. The location is good (near the old town and the TAT office) but it's too far to walk from the bus station with heavy bags. B550

Phrae Paradorn 177 Thanon Yantarakitkoson ☏ 054 511177. Not as "absolutely clean" as the sign outside proclaims, but still a very good budget choice, with a simple breakfast of coffee and noodle soup thrown in with the a/c and fan rooms, all of which have hot water. Wi-fi is available in the lobby. Fan B480, a/c B800

Tongsri Phaibool 84 Thanon Yantarakitkoson, near the junction with Thanon Charoen Muang ☏ 054 511011. A reasonable budget choice with fairly grubby, very simply furnished rooms and attached (cold-water) bathrooms, set around a courtyard car park. TVs are available at B30 extra per room. Fan B130, a/c B310

EATING AND DRINKING

For eating in the town centre, your best bet is the lively **night market** by the Pratuchai gate on Thanon Charoen Muang.

Ban Fai A couple of kilometres south out of town at the junction of the Nan and Den Chai roads. This open-sided barn-like place is the best restaurant around, serving very good Thai food including northern specialities such as nem (spiced pork sausages) and the typical Lanna pork curry, kaeng hang lay. A motorbike taxi here will cost around B30. Daily 8am–5pm.

Look Kaew Opposite Phrae Paradorn on Thanon Yantarakitkoson. Very popular by night (it's one of the few places open late), this friendly restaurant has a good range of cheap eats, including big plates of fresh vegetables served in oyster sauce (B80). English menus available on request. Daily 5pm–late.

Nok Bin 24 Thanon Wichairacha ☏ 089 433 3285. A

3

pretty little garden café run by a pair of helpful journalists, who are more than happy to share their knowledge of

Phrae with visitors. B30 for a decent cup of coffee. Daily 10am–6pm.

DIRECTORY

ATMs There are several ATMs on Thanon Charoen Muang, east of the old town.

Internet access You can access the internet at *Mae Yom*

Palace Hotel (B50/hr), or there's wi-fi in the lobby of the *Phrae Paradorn Hotel* (see p.323).

Nan

After leaving the Yom River, Highway 101 gently climbs through rolling hills of cotton fields and teak plantations to its highest point, framed by limestone cliffs, before descending into the high, isolated valley of the **Nan River**, the longest in Thailand (740km) and one of the tributaries of the Chao Phraya. Ringed by high mountains, the small but prosperous provincial capital of **NAN**, 225km northeast of Lampang, rests on the grassy west bank of the river. Few visitors make it out this far, but it's a likeable place with a thriving handicrafts tradition, a good museum and some superb temple murals at **Wat Phumin**, as well as at Wat Nong Bua out in the countryside (see p.328). Nan's centre comprises a disorientating grid of crooked streets, around a small core of shops and businesses where Thanon Mahawong and Thanon Anantaworarichides meet Thanon Sumondhevaraj.

The town comes alive for the **Lanna boat races**, usually held in late October or early November, when villages from around the province send teams of up to fifty oarsmen to race in long, colourfully decorated canoes with dragon prows. The lush surrounding valley is noted for its cotton-weaving, sweet oranges and the attractive grainy paper made from the bark of local *sa* (mulberry) trees.

Brief history

Although it has been kicked around by Burma, Laos and Thailand, Nan province has a history of being on the fringes, distanced by the encircling barrier of mountains.

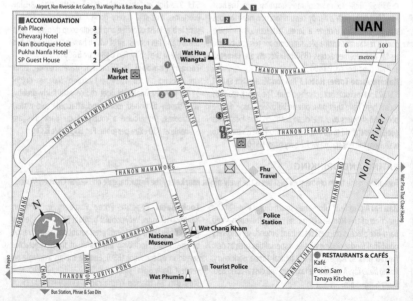

NAN

ACCOMMODATION
Fah Place	3
Dhevaraj Hotel	5
Nan Boutique Hotel	1
Pukha Nanfa Hotel	4
SP Guest House	2

RESTAURANTS & CAFÉS
Kafé	1
Poom Sam	2
Tanaya Kitchen	3

Airport, Nan Riverside Art Gallery, Tha Wang Pha & Ban Nong Bua

Night Market

Pha Nan

Wat Hua Wiangtai

THANON NOKHAM

THANON MAHAYOI
THANON SUMONDHEVARAJ
THANON PHA LUANG

THANON JETABOOT

Nan River

THANON ANANTAWORARICHIDES

THANON MAHAWONG

Fhu Travel

ROBMUANG

THANON PHAKONG

Police Station

THANON MANO

Wat Pha That Chae Haeng

THANON MAHAPHOM

National Museum

Wat Chang Kham

Phapo

ARIYAWONG

THANON SURIYA PONG

THANON THAII

Tourist Police

Wat Phumin

Bus Station, Phrae & Sao Din

0   100
metres

Rama V brought Nan into his centralization programme at the start of the twentieth century, but left the traditional ruling house in place, making it the last province in Thailand to be administered by a local ruler (it remained so until 1931). During the troubled 1970s, Communist insurgents holed up in this twilight region and proclaimed Nan the future capital of the liberated zone, which only succeeded in bringing the full might of the Thai Army down on them; the insurgency faded after the government's 1982 offer of amnesty. Today, energies are focused on development, and the province has become less isolated with the building of several new roads.

The National Museum

Just off Thanon Phakong in the southwest part of town • Daily 9am–4pm • B100

The best place to start an exploration is at the **National Museum**, located in a tidy, century-old palace with superb teak floors, which used to be home to the rulers of Nan. Its informative, user-friendly displays give you a bite-sized introduction to Nan, its history and its peoples, the prize exhibit being a talismanic elephant tusk with a bad case of brown tooth decay, which is claimed to be magic black ivory. The tusk was discovered over three hundred years ago and now sits on a colourful wooden *khut*, a mythological eagle. The museum also houses elegant pottery and woodcarving, gorgeously wrought silverware and some rare Lao Buddhas.

Wat Phumin

Thanon Phakong

Wat Phumin will grab even the most over-templed traveller. Its five-hundred-year-old centrepiece is an unusual cruciform building, combining both the bot and the viharn, which balances some quirky features in a perfect symmetry. Two giant nagas pass through the base of the building, with their tails along the balustrades at the south entrance and their heads at the north, representing the sacred oceans at the base of the central mountain of the universe. The doors at the four entrances, which have been beautifully carved with a complex pattern of animals and flowers, lead straight to the four Buddha images arranged around a tall altar in the centre of the building – note the Buddhas' piercing onyx eyes and pointed ears, showing the influence of Laos, 50km away. What really sets the bot apart are the **murals**, whose bright, simple colours seem to jump off the walls. Executed in the late nineteenth century – though occasionally retouched – the paintings take you on a whirlwind tour of heaven, hell, the Buddha's previous incarnations, local legends and incidents from Nan's history, and include stacks of vivacious, sometimes bawdy, detail, which provides a valuable pictorial record of that era.

Wat Chang Kham

Thanon Phakong

Like Wat Phumin, **Wat Chang Kham** is over five hundred years old, though the two viharns that stand side by side are unexceptional in design. The main feature here is a gorgeous, gold-capped chedi, supported by elephants on all sides; those on the corners are adorned with gold helmets and straps. The temple is attached to a school, a reminder that temples were once the only source of education in the country.

Wat Phra That Chae Haeng

2km southeast of town, just off Highway 1168

Wat Phra That Chae Haeng is a must, as much for its setting on a hill overlooking the Nan valley as anything else. The wat was founded in 1300, at a spot determined by the

Buddha himself when he passed through this way – or so local legend would have it. The nagas here outdo even Wat Phumin's: the first you see of the wat across the fields is a wide driveway flanked by monumental serpents gliding down the slope from the temple. A magnificent gnarled bodhi tree with hundreds of spreading branches and roots guards the main gate, set in high boundary walls. Inside the walls, the highlight is a slender, 55m-high golden chedi, surrounded by four smaller chedis and four carved and gilded umbrellas, as well as small belfries and stucco lions. Close competition comes from the viharn roof, which has no fewer than fifteen Lao-style tiers, stacked up like a house of cards and supported on finely carved *kan tuei* (wood supports) under the eaves.

ARRIVAL AND DEPARTURE NAN

BY PLANE
Nok Air runs regular flights (at least daily; 1hr 40min) between Bangkok and Nan. The airport is 2km northwest of town, and is served by a/c minibuses to and from the *Dhevaraj Hotel* (see below).

BY BUS
The bus station is in the southwest corner of town, off the main road to Phrae; songthaews to the centre cost B20.
From/to Chiang Mai The bus journey to Nan from Chiang

Mai takes around six hours, so it might be worth catching one of the first-class a/c or VIP vehicles that serve this route, shaving an hour off the journey time.
From/to Chiang Rai One bus a day winds its tortuous way over the mountains from Chiang Rai, via Chiang Kham; if you're prone to motion sickness and want to avoid the worst of the twisting roads, change buses in Phrae instead.
Destinations Bangkok (10 daily; 12hr); Chiang Mai (8 daily; 6hr); Chiang Rai (1 daily; 6–7hr); Den Chai (hourly; 2hr 30min); Phitsanulok (6 daily; 8hr); Phrae (hourly; 2hr).

INFORMATION, TOURS AND GETTING AROUND

Tourist information For tourist information about the town and the province, or to find out about local tours, visit helpful Fhu Travel at 453/4 Thanon Sumondhevaraj (☎054 710636 or ☎081 287 7209, ☜fhutravel.com).
National parks information There's a national parks

information booth opposite Wat Phumin (Mon–Sat 8.30am–4.30pm; ☎054 710216).
Bicycle and motorbike rental If you want to explore the area on two wheels, *SP Guest House* (see below) rents out decent bicycles (B50/day) and motorbikes (B200–250/day).

ACCOMMODATION

Despite being a small town with few visitors, Nan has some attractive accommodation options, ranging from family-run guesthouses to clean, reasonably priced hotels. The only time of year when finding somewhere to stay might be a problem is during the Lanna boat races (late Oct or early Nov).

Dhevaraj 466 Thanon Sumondhevaraj ☎054 751577, ☜dhevarajhotel.com. Large, centrally positioned hotel, popular with tour groups, that has a slightly institutional feel but is a hub of Nan social life. There's a pool, gym and a wide range of well-maintained accommodation, all with hot water and nice cosy beds. Internet access. **B800**
Fah Place Soi Kha Luang 1, 237/8 Thanon Sumondhevaraj ☎054 710222, ☜fahplace.com. Just down a small soi off the main road, this striking, modern, cream block (no English sign) contains spacious, very good-value a/c rooms, done out with attractive tiles, tasteful wooden furniture and large hot-water bathrooms. Wi-fi available. **B400**
Nan Boutique Hotel North of the centre at 1/11 Thanon Kha Luang ☎054 775 532, ☜nanboutiquehotel .com. Set rather bizarrely around a car park, the handsome and well-equipped bedrooms here are good value for money, with lots of extras like bathrobes, slippers and herbal toiletries to help you unwind. On-site facilties

include a restaurant and a small gift shop, and guests are given free access to bikes. There's even a free daily bike tour of the old town (ask at reception). **B1600**
Pukha Nanfa Hotel 369 Thanon Sumondhevaraj ☎054 771111, ☜pukhananfahotel.co.th. An eye-catching wooden building on the city's main street, with an imposing facade that sparkles with fairy lights. Inside, ornate carvings and wall hangings lead the way to a massive wooden staircase, which twists up towards the elegant, panelled bedrooms. There's a wonderful first-floor terrace with views over the street, and a restaurant downstairs. **B2500**
★ **SP Guest House** 233 Thanon Sumondhevaraj ☎054 774897. Actually on Trok Hua Wiangtai, a narrow alley off the main road, this well-maintained, friendly guesthouse offers spacious rooms, all with hot-water bathrooms. The owners are extremely helpful, and there are big family rooms available. Internet and wi-fi. Fan **B450**, a/c **B500**

EATING AND DRINKING

Plenty of restaurants cluster around Thanon Anantaworarichides, while the **night market** is just around the corner on Thanon Phakong.

★ **Kafé** Thanon Mahayot. Sit inside this quirky restaurant's homely, terracotta-coloured dining area, or outside on the streetside terrace. The reasonably priced food here, a curious mix of Italian spaghetti dishes and Thai staples, is tasty enough to make it worth heading over for dinner. But even if you're not hungry, you can learn a lot by chatting to the young owners over an ice-cold beer. Daily 10am–10pm.

★ **Poom Sam (Poom 3)** Thanon Anantaworarichides, next to the Sukkasem Hotel ☏ 054 772 100. It may look like any other streetside restaurant, but *Poom Sam* prepares excellent Thai and Chinese food with great service at rock-bottom prices, and there's a comfy a/c room as well. Try the *tom yam kung* (B120) or the delicious green aubergines with minced pork and sweet basil. Daily 5pm–late.

Tanaya Kitchen Thanon Anantaworarichides ☏ 054 710930. Right next door to *Poom Sam*, this tiny, homely café serves good vegetarian food and is very popular with locals – though in high season it attracts a good number of tourists, too. Mon–Sat 10am–3.30pm & 5–8pm.

SHOPPING

Loyalty to local traditions ensures the survival of several good **handicrafts shops** in Nan, most of which are found on Thanon Sumondhevaraj north of the junction with Anantaworarichides.

Chom Phu Phuka About 2km west of Wat Phumin along the road to Phayao (Route 1091), on the right and opposite a petrol station. A large silverware showroom and workshop (no English sign) stocking a wide range of bracelets, necklaces, bowls and trays, priced according to design and weight. Staff are happy for visitors to look around the workshop at the back. A small selection of local hand-woven cloth is also on sale here. Daily 8.30am–5pm.

Pha Nan 21/2 Thanon Sumondhevaraj, between Wat Hua Wiangtai and the Chinese temple ☏ 054 774439 or ☏ 086 923 2046. Sells traditional lengths of superb cotton (much of it *pha sin*, used as wraparound skirts) woven in local villages; as the owner is a teacher, the shop has sporadic hours – best to try in the evenings.

DIRECTORY

ATMs Scattered across town, with the most central on Thanon Sumondhevaraj.

Internet access Places open and close frequently, but the *Dhevaraj Hotel* (see opposite) is a safe bet.

Massage You can get a good, hour-long massage at the *Dhevaraj Hotel* (B250; see opposite).

Tourist police There's a tourist police booth (☏ 054 710216 or ☏ 1155) opposite Wat Phumin.

Around Nan

The remote, mountainous countryside **around Nan** runs a close scenic second to the precipitous landscape of Mae Hong Son province, but its remoteness means that Nan has even worse transport and is even more poorly mapped. This does, of course, make it an exciting region to explore, where you may encounter the province's ethnic minorities: the Thai Lue (see p.328); the **Htin**, an upland Mon-Khmer people, most of whom have migrated since the Communist takeover of Laos in 1975; the **Khamu**, skilled metalworkers who have moved to Nan over the last 150 years from southwest China and Laos; and the little-known Mrabri (see box, p.328) – a good place to organize excursions is Fhu Travel (see box, p.329). More straightforward targets include the temple at **Nong Bua**, with it superb murals, and beautiful **Doi Phukha National Park**.

Nan Riverside Art Gallery

20km north of Nan up Route 1080 • Daily except Wed 9am–5pm • B20 • ☏ 054 798046 • Served by buses (roughly hourly) from Nan bus station en route to Tha Wang Pha

The impressive **Nan Riverside Art Gallery** was founded by local artist, Winai Prabripu, in a lovely setting by the banks of the Nan River. His work – mostly local landscapes

3

SPIRITS OF THE YELLOW LEAVES

Inhabiting the remote hill country west of Nan, the population of about three hundred **Mrabri** represent the last remnants of nomadic hunter-gatherers in Thailand, though their way of life is rapidly passing. Believing that spirits would be angered if the tribe settled in one place, grew crops or kept animals, the Mrabri traditionally built only temporary shelters of branches and wild banana leaves, moving on to another spot in the jungle as soon as the leaves turned yellow; thus they earned their poetic Thai name, **Phi Tong Luang** – "Spirits of the Yellow Leaves". They eked out a hard livelihood from the forest, hunting with spears, trapping birds and small mammals, digging roots and collecting nuts, seeds and honey.

In recent decades, however, deforestation by logging and slash-and-burn farming has eaten into the tribe's territory, and the Mrabri were forced to sell their labour to Hmong and Mien farmers, often under slave-like conditions. But in the last few years, salvation for many Mrabri has come in the form of weaving **hammocks**: foreign visitors noticed their skill at making string bags out of jungle vines and helped them to set up a small-scale hammock industry. The hammocks are now exported to countries around the world, and the Mrabri weavers have the benefits of education, free healthcare and an unemployment fund. For more information, go to ⓦjumbohammock.com.

focusing on details of plants in season and paintings inspired by the Wat Phumin murals – is displayed upstairs, while the ground floor and the studio gallery host rotating exhibitions by other contemporary Thai artists. A visit to the gallery combines well with Ban Nong Bua (see below).

Ban Nong Bua

About 40km north of Nan off the west side of Route 1080 • Hourly services from Nan bus station to Tha Wang Pha, from whose southern outskirts signs in English point you left across the Nan River to Wat Nong Bua, 3km away (coming by bus, either hire a motorbike taxi in the centre of Tha Wang Pha, or walk the last 3km)

BAN NONG BUA, site of a famous muralled **temple** of the same name, makes a rewarding day-trip from Nan. The village and surrounding area are largely inhabited by **Thai Lue** people, distant cousins of the Thais, who've migrated from China in the past 150 years. They produce beautiful cotton garments in richly coloured geometric patterns; walk 200m behind the wat towards the west side of the village and you'll find **weavers** at work at the house of Khun Chansom Prompanya, who sells the opulent fabrics in her on-site shop. The quality of design and workmanship is very high here, and prices, though not cheap, are reasonable for the quality.

Wat Nong Bua

Built in 1862 in typical Lanna style, **Wat Nong Bua**'s beautifully gnarled viharn has low, drooping roof tiers surmounted by stucco finials – here you'll find horned nagas and tusked makaras (elephantine monsters), instead of the garuda finial which invariably crops up in central Thai temples. The viharn enshrines a pointy-eared Lao Buddha, but its most outstanding features are the **murals** that cover all four walls. Executed between 1867 and 1888, probably by the Wat Phumin painters, they depict with much humour and vivid detail scenes from the *Chanthakhat Jataka* (the story of one of the Buddha's previous incarnations, as a hero called Chanthakhat). This is a particularly long and complex *Jataka* (although a leaflet outlining the story in English is sometimes available, in return for a small donation to temple funds), wherein our hero gets into all kinds of scrapes, involving several wives, other sundry liaisons, some formidably nasty enemies and the god Indra transforming himself into a snake. The crux of the tale comes on the east wall (opposite the Buddha image): in the bottom left-hand corner, Chanthakhat and the love of his life, Thewathisangka, are shipwrecked and separated; distraught, Thewathisangka wanders through the jungle, diagonally up the wall, to the hermitage

TOURS AROUND NAN

Nan is a pleasant spot to spend a day or two, but if you fancy doing something a bit more energetic, it's worth heading out to the countryside. With or without your own vehicle, your best option is to head for the reliable ★ Fhu Travel at 453/4 Thanon Sumondhevaraj (☎054 710636 or ☎081 287 7209, ☻fhutravel.com). As well as dispensing advice about the region, Fhu and Ung, his wife, organize popular and enjoyable guided **tours** and **trekking** trips. One-day tours to Wat Nong Bua, including a visit to the local weavers, cost B3200 for two people or B900 per person for five people, including lunch. Two- to three-day treks (around B3700/person, based on two sharing) head west, through tough terrain of thick jungle and high mountains, visiting Mrabri, Htin, Hmong and Mien villages. As well as offering **cycling** tours around town, one- to three-day **whitewater-rafting** excursions on the Wa River near Mae Charim to the east of town, and **kayaking**, whether overnight or just paddling for half a day on the Nan River near town, Fhu can also arrange trips to Luang Prabang in Laos, via the border crossing at Huai Kon in the extreme north of Nan province, which is open to foreigners.

of an old woman, where she shaves her head and becomes a nun; Chanthakhat travels through the wilderness along the bottom of the wall, curing a wounded naga-king on the way, who out of gratitude gives him a magic crystal ball, which enables our hero to face another series of perils along the south wall, before finally rediscovering and embracing Thewathisangka in front of the old woman's hut, at the top right-hand corner of the east wall.

Doi Phukha National Park

Around 80km northeast of Nan off Route 1256 • B200 • ☎054 701000, ☻dnp.go.th

East of Tha Wang Pha, Route 1080 curves towards the town of **Pua**, on whose southern outskirts Route 1256, the spectacular access road for **Doi Phukha National Park**, begins its journey eastwards and upwards; you can pick up a brochure with map from the national parks information booth in Nan town (see p.326). The paved road climbs up a sharp ridge, through occasional stands of elephant grass and bamboo, towards Doi Dong Ya Wai (1939m), providing one of the most jaw-droppingly scenic drives in Thailand. Across the valleys to the north and south stand rows of improbably steep mountains (including the 1980m Doi Phukha itself, far to the south), covered in lush vegetation with scarcely a sign of human habitation.

From the park headquarters, 24km up the road from Pua, there's a self-guided, 4km **trail**, but to hike up any of the park's many peaks, you'll need to hire a guide (about B200/day) from the headquarters.

ARRIVAL AND DEPARTURE   DOI PHUKHA NATIONAL PARK

It's difficult to get into the park on public transport, and you'll usually have to stay the night. The trip is most exciting if tackled on a motorbike (though watch out for loose chippings on the bends).

By bus and songthaew Hourly buses from Nan's main station run to Pua (2hr), from where irregular songthaews (best in the mornings, though you may find school songthaews in the late afternoon) serve the handful of villages along Route 1256 towards Bo Kleua.

ACCOMMODATION AND EATING

Food is available at the park's simple **restaurant**, and there are also several food stalls serving basic snacks. The following places are listed in order of distance from the park headquarters.

National park bungalows Park headquarters, 24km up the road from Pua ☎054 701000, ☻dnp.go.th. Accommodation ranges from large bungalows sleeping six or seven through rooms for four, to small, basic bungalows for two. Small bungalows B300, rooms B800, large bungalows B2000

National park camping There's a large, open campsite near the park headquarters.
Bo Klua View About 20km beyond the park headquarters towards Bo Kleua ☏054 778140 or

☏081 809 6392, ⊛bokluaview.com. This mid-range resort has a dozen stylish a/c bungalows with large verandas set around a terraced rice field. B1650

Sao Din

60km south of Nan; head south on Highway 101 to Wiang Sa, then turn left and follow Route 1026 to Na No, just after which a turning on the right leads into the site

One of several brief excursions from Nan possible with your own transport, **Sao Din** ("earth pillars") provides a more intriguing example of soil erosion than the better-known site at Phae Muang Phi near Phrae. Here the earth pillars cover a huge area and appear in fantastic shapes, the result of centuries of erosion by wind and rain. There's little in the surrounding area, which makes wandering among the formations a peaceful experience. If you come here, be sure to wear long trousers and boots, especially in the cool season, as a thorny plant that grows in the region can cause discomfort.

The Mae Hong Son loop

Two main roads head in opposite directions from Chiang Mai over the western mountains, meeting each other in Mae Hong Son, at the heart of Thailand's most remote province – and offering the irresistible prospect of tying the highways together into a 600km **loop**. The towns en route give a taste of Burma to the west, but the journey itself, winding over implausibly steep forested mountains and through tightly hemmed farming valleys, is what will stick in the mind.

The **southern** leg of the route, **Highway 108**, first passes **Doi Inthanon National Park**, with its twisting curves, lofty views over half of northern Thailand and enough waterfalls to last a lifetime; from here, with your own vehicle you could shortcut the southernmost part of the loop by taking the paved but very winding Routes 1088 and 1263 from Mae Chaem to Khun Yuam. Sticking to the main loop, however, you'll next reach **Mae Sariang**, an important town for trade across the Burmese border and a gentle, low-key base for trekking and trips on the Salween River. The provincial capital, **Mae Hong Son**, roughly at the midpoint of the loop, is a more developed hub for exploring the area's mountains, rivers and waterfalls, though it can become frantic with tour groups in the cool season, especially on November and December weekends when the sunflowers are out.

The **northern** leg follows **Route 1095**, much of which was established by the Japanese army to move troops and supplies into Burma after its invasion of Thailand during World War II. The road heads northeast out of Mae Hong Son towards the market town of **Soppong**, whose surroundings feature beautiful caves (notably **Tham Lot**), appealing accommodation and stunning scenery to trek, cycle or kayak through. Halfway back towards Chiang Mai from Mae Hong Son is **Pai**, a cosy, cosmopolitan and hugely popular tourist hangout with plenty of activities and some gentle walking trails in the surrounding valley.

GETTING THERE AND AROUND   MAE HONG SON LOOP

We've covered the loop in a **clockwise** direction here, in part because Doi Inthanon is best reached direct from Chiang Mai, but you could just as easily go the other way round. Travelling the loop is straightforward, although the mountainous roads go through plenty of bends and jolts. The labour-intensive job of **paving** every hairpin bend was completed in the 1990s, but ongoing repair work can still give you a nasty surprise if you're riding a motorbike.

By plane From Chiang Mai, there are Nok Air flights to Mae Hong Son and Kan Air flights to Pai.

By bus Mae Hong Son is about eight hours' travelling time from Chiang Mai by a/c or ordinary bus, although services along the shorter but even more winding northern route are now augmented by faster, hourly a/c minibuses, which cover the ground via Pai in about six hours.

By motorbike or jeep Above all the loop is made for motorbikes and jeeps: the roads are generally quiet (but watch out for huge, speeding trucks) and you can satisfy the inevitable craving to stop every five minutes and admire the mountain scenery. A useful piece of equipment for this journey is the 1:375,000 map of the Mae Hong Son loop, with useful insets of Pai's and Mae Hong Son's environs, published by Golden Triangle Rider (ⓦ gt-rider.com) and available in local bookshops, or online for US$7.50.

Doi Inthanon National Park

Traversed by Route 1009 to the west of Chom Thong and Highway 108 • A checkpoint by Mae Klang Falls collects the B200 entrance fee plus B20 per motorbike and B30 per car • ⓣ 053 286728, ⓦ dnp.go.th

Covering a huge area to the southwest of Chiang Mai, **DOI INTHANON NATIONAL PARK**, with its Karen and Hmong hill-tribe villages, dramatic waterfalls and panoramas over rows of wild, green peaks to the west, gives a pleasant, if slightly sanitized, whiff of northern countryside, its attractions and concrete access roads kept in good order by the national parks department. The park, named after the highest mountain in the country and so dubbed the "Roof of Thailand", is geared mainly to wildlife conservation but also contains a hill-tribe agricultural project producing strawberries, apples and flowers for sale. Often shrouded in mist, Doi Inthanon's temperate forests shelter a huge variety of flora and fauna, which make this one of the major destinations for naturalists in Southeast Asia. The park supports about 380 **bird species**, the largest number of any site in Thailand – among them the ashy-throated warbler and a species of the green-tailed sunbird, both unique to Doi Inthanon – as well as, near the summit, the only red rhododendrons in Thailand and a wide variety of ground and epiphytic orchids. The waterfalls, birds and flowers are at their best in the cool season, but night-time temperatures sometimes drop below freezing, making warm clothing a must.

Wat Phra That Si Chom Thong

Chom Thong, 58km southwest of Chiang Mai on Highway 108

The gateway to the park is **CHOM THONG**, a market town with little to offer apart from the attractive **Wat Phra That Si Chom Thong**, whose impressive brass-plated chedi dates from the fifteenth century. The nearby bo tree has become an equally noteworthy architectural feature: dozens of Dalí-esque supports for its sagging branches have been

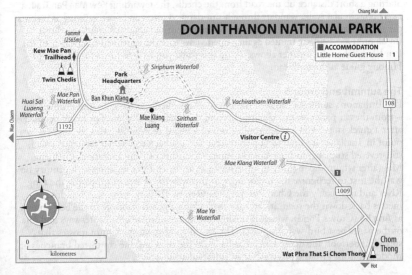

DOI INTHANON NATIONAL PARK

■ ACCOMMODATION
Little Home Guest House ┃ 1

Summit (2565m)
Kew Mae Pan Trailhead
Twin Chedis
Huai Sai Luaeng Waterfall
Mae Pan Waterfall
Park Headquarters
Ban Khun Klang
Siriphum Waterfall
Vachiratharn Waterfall
Mae Chaem
1192
Mae Klang Luang
Sirithan Waterfall
Visitor Centre ⓘ
Mae Klang Waterfall
108
N
1009
Mae Ya Waterfall
0   5 kilometres
Chom Thong
Wat Phra That Si Chom Thong
Chiang Mai
Hot

sponsored by the devoted in the hope of earning merit. Inside the renovated sixteenth-century viharn, a towering, gilded *ku* housing a Buddha relic (supposedly from the right side of his skull) just squeezes in beneath the ceiling, from which hangs a huge, sumptuous red-and-green umbrella. Weaponry, gongs, umbrellas, thrones and an elephant-tusk arch carved with delicate Buddha images all add to the welcoming clutter. The temple is also famous for its meditation retreats (see p.50).

The main waterfalls and Mae Klang Luang

Four sets of waterfalls provide the main roadside attractions along Route 1009 from Chom Thong to the park headquarters: overrated **Mae Klang Falls**, 8km in, which with its picnic areas and food vendors gets overbearingly crowded at weekends; **Vachiratharn Falls**, the park's most dramatic, with a long, misty drop down a granite escarpment 11km beyond; **Sirithan Falls**, which looks like a smaller version of Vachiratharn and is just a couple of kilometres further up the hill; and finally the twin cascades of **Siriphum Falls**, backing the park headquarters a further 9km on. With your own wheels you could reach a fifth and much more beautiful cataract, **Mae Ya**, which is believed to be the highest in Thailand – the winding, 14km paved track to it heads west off Route 1009, 2km north of Highway 108. At the Karen village of **Mae Klang Luang**, 5km east of the headquarters on the south side of Route 1009, you can hire an English-speaking **guide** to walk with you to **Pha Dok Siew** waterfall (2hr return; B300) or up **Doi Huea Sua** (1881m; 6hr; B500).

The chedis

11km beyond the headquarters

For the most spectacular views in the park, continue 11km beyond the headquarters along the summit road to the sleek, twin chedis looming incongruously over the misty green hillside: on a clear day you can see the mountains of Burma to the west from here. Built by the Royal Thai Air Force, the chedis commemorate the sixtieth birthdays of the Thai king and queen; the king's monument, **Napamaytanidol Chedi** (1987), is brown to the more feminine lilac of the queen's **Napapolphumsiri Chedi** (1992).

Kew Mae Pan Trail

Trailhead a short way up the summit road from the chedis • 2hr; open Nov–May • B200 for compulsory guide

Starting a short distance up the road from the chedis, the rewarding **Kew Mae Pan Trail**, a two-hour circular walk, wanders through sun-dappled forest and open savanna as it skirts the steep western edge of Doi Inthanon, where violent-red epiphytic rhododendrons (in bloom Dec–Feb) are framed against open views over the canyoned headwaters of the Pan River, when the weather allows. To do this walk, you have to hire a local Karen or Hmong guide at the trailhead.

The summit and around

Doi Inthanon's **summit** (2565m), 6km beyond the chedis, is a big disappointment – from the car park you can see little beyond the radar installation. For many people, after a quick shiver and a snapshot in front of a board proclaiming this the highest point in Thailand, it's time to hop in the car and get back to warmer climes. A small, still-revered stupa behind this board contains the ashes of King Inthanon of Chiang Mai (after whom the mountain was renamed): at the end of the nineteenth century he was the first to recognize the importance of this watershed area in supplying the Ping River and ultimately the Chao Phraya, the queen of Thailand's rivers. A hundred metres back down the road, it's an easy stroll along a raised walkway to the bog known as **Ang Ka** (Crow's Pond), which is the highest source of these great waterways and one of the park's best bird-watching sites. The cream and brown sphagnum mosses that spread underfoot, the dense ferns that hang off the trees and the contorted branches of rhododendrons give the place a creepy, primeval atmosphere.

The Mae Chaem road

Around 7km after it turns off the main summit road, the paved **Mae Chaem road** skirts yet another set of waterfalls: look for a steep road to the right, leading down to a ranger station and, just to the east, the dramatic long drop of **Huai Sai Luaeng Falls**. A 2.5km circular walking trail from the ranger station takes in **Mae Pan Falls**, a series of short cascades in a peaceful, shady setting.

ARRIVAL AND DEPARTURE   DOI INTHANON NATIONAL PARK

The main road through the park, Route 1009, turns west off Highway 108, 1km north of the gateway town of Chom Thong, winding generally northwestwards for 48km to the top of Doi Inthanon, passing the park headquarters about 30km in. A second paved road forks left 10km before the summit, affording breathtaking views as it helter-skelters down for 20km to the sleepy, riverside weaving village of Mae Chaem, southwest of the park.

By bus Frequent blue buses to Chom Thong from Chiang Mai's Chang Puak bus station can be picked up at the southern end of Thanon Phra Pokklao (Chiang Mai Gate). At Chiang Mai Gate, it should also be possible to pick up a yellow songthaew (slower and only slightly cheaper) for the journey to Chom Thong. Once there, you can charter a whole songthaew or a/c minibus to explore the park for around B1000–1500 for the day.

By motorbike or jeep You could do the park justice in a day with an early start from Chiang Mai, or treat it as the

first stage of a longer trip to Mae Hong Son: from Mae Chaem, either follow Route 1088 south to pick up Highway 108 again towards Mae Sariang, 25km west of Hot; or take Route 1088 north then Route 1263 west through remote countryside, joining Highway 108 just north of Khun Yuam.

With a tour Most tour operators in Chiang Mai (see p.289) offer day-trips to the national park (around B1500–3000/ person, depending on group size) – if you don't have your own transport, this is the easiest way to visit.

INFORMATION

Park information For information on the park, stop at the visitor centre 1km beyond the Mae Klang checkpoint, or at the park headquarters, a further 22km on.

Birding information Two hundred metres beyond the headquarters on the left-hand side of Route 1009, at Mr

Daeng's Birds Visitor Centre (☎053 286731–2 or ☎081 884 8108, ⓦmrdeang.com), bird-watchers can consult a useful logbook, pick up a simple, photocopied map of birding sites, or hire a guide for B1000–3000/day for up to five people.

ACCOMMODATION AND EATING

In the daytime, **foodstalls** operate at Mae Klang, Vachiratharn and Mae Ya falls, and there's a popular canteen with a reasonable variety of food by the twin chedis. The **restaurants** beside the park headquarters and at the Birds Visitor Centre are open daytime and evening. The following places are listed in order of distance from the park's headquarters.

National park bungalows Bookings at the park on ☎053 286730, or in Bangkok ☎02 561 0077, ⓦdnp .go.th. Inside the park, accommodation comes in standard log-cabin or concrete varieties, with electricity, mattresses or beds and bedding. Three- to 23-berth bungalows, set among dense stands of pine near the headquarters, have hot-water bathrooms, while simpler, fifteen-person bungalows at Huai Sai Luaeng Falls cost B1500/night. Accommodation is often fully booked at weekends and national holidays, but at other times you should be OK to turn up on the day. Headquarters bungalows B800–8000

Birds Visitor Centre 200m west of the headquarters on Route 1009 ☎053 286731–2 or ☎081 884 8108, ⓦmrdeang.com. Uncle Daeng offers pleasant, colourful, tile-floored rooms with hot water and TV at his Birds Visitor Centre (see above). B500

National park camping Camping, an often chilly alternative, is permitted on a site about 500m from the park headquarters and another site at Huai Sai Luaeng Falls. Two- to three-person tents can be rented at headquarters for B225/night (bedding extra).

Homestay Mae Klang Luang ☎081 960 8856 or ☎087 178 0231, ⓦcbtnetwork.org. Simple homestay accommodation is available at this Karen coffee-growing village 5km east of the park headquarters on the south side of the main road. Rates include breakfast and dinner. B400

Little Home Guest House & Restaurant 7km from Chom Thong along the main park road ☎053 267382, ⓦlittlehomeinthanonresort.com. This cutesy place has clean, well-maintained, fan or a/c bungalows and rooms with hot-water bathrooms. Fan B700, a/c B1000

West towards Mae Sariang

Heading south from Chom Thong, the road flattens out a little, passing dusty and seldom-visited weaving villages as it follows the Ping River downstream. Just after Hot the road bends west, climbing up once again towards the **Ob Luang Gorge National Park**, where attractions include whitewater rafting down the Chaem River.

Pa-Da Cotton Textile Museum

On the east side of Highway 108 between kilometre-stones 68 and 69, in Ban Rai Pai Ngarm • Daily except Thurs 8.30am–4.30pm • Free • All buses between Chiang Mai and Hot or Mae Sariang pass Ban Rai Pai Ngarm

Among several weaving villages to the south of Chom Thong, the **Pa-Da Cotton Textile Museum** at Ban Rai Pai Ngarm is well worth a look; it's reached down a beautiful avenue of bamboo trees. The museum is dedicated to the work of Saeng-da Bansiddhi, a local woman who started a cooperative practising traditional dyeing and weaving techniques using only natural products. Saeng-da died in the late 1980s, and the museum, which displays some of her personal effects as well as looms, fabrics and plants used in dyeing, was established to honour her efforts to revive these disappearing skills. It's situated on the upper floor of a large wooden building, while on the ground floor weavers can be seen busy at work. Lovely bolts of cloth and a small range of clothes and scarves in earthy and pastel colours are on sale at reasonable prices.

Ob Luang Gorge National Park

17km west of Hot on Highway 108 • B200 • ☎ 053 315302, ⓦ dnp.go.th

Weaving through pretty wooded hills up the valley of the Chaem River for 17km from Hot will bring you to **Ob Luang Gorge National Park**, which is billed with wild hyperbole as "Thailand's Grand Canyon". A wooden bridge over the short, narrow channel lets you look down on the Chaem River bubbling along between sheer walls 50m below. The park is also tagged "Land of Prehistoric Human" because of the discovery of Bronze Age graves here, containing seashell bracelets and other decorative items, as well as rock paintings of elephants and human figures. Upstream from the bridge near the park headquarters, you can relax at the roadside foodstalls and swim in the river when it's not too fast. At the headquarters you can arrange hour-long 5km **whitewater-rafting** trips on the river's class II–III rapids (from B1400 for four people up to B1800 for eight, including guides, transport, life jackets and helmets).

West of Ob Luang, the highway gradually climbs through pine forests, the road surface bad in patches and the countryside becoming steeper and wilder.

ARRIVAL AND DEPARTURE OB LUANG GORGE NATIONAL PARK

Buses travelling between Chiang Mai and Mae Sariang pass by the park headquarters, as do buses travelling between Bangkok and Mae Hong Son.

ACCOMMODATION

National park bungalows ☎ 053 315302, ⓦ dnp .go.th. There are a few large bungalows with three bedrooms and two bathrooms with hot water, sleeping ten people, in which you can usually rent a room for two.

Bungalow B2100, room B700
Campsite The shady riverbank shelters a campsite; you can rent a two- to three-person tent for B225.

Mae Sariang and around

After its descent into the broad, smoky valley of the Yuam River, Highway 108's westward progress ends at **MAE SARIANG**, 191km from Chiang Mai, a quietly industrious market town showing a marked Burmese influence in its temples and rows of low wooden shophouses. Halfway along the southern route between Chiang Mai and Mae Hong Son, this is an obvious place for a stopover. From here you can make

MAE SARIANG

▲ Khun Yuam & Mae Hong Son

108

■ ACCOMMODATION
Mae Sariang Guest House	5
Northwest Guest House	3
River Bank Guest House	1
River House Hotel	2
River House Resort	4

● RESTAURANT
Sawatdee	1

■ BAR
Mae Sariang Bar	1

Yuam River

Bus Terminal

Wat Utthayarom

Wat Si Boonruang

THANON WIANG MAI

Chiang Mai

THANON LAENG PHANIT

THANON MAE SARIANG

Mae Sam Laeb

1194

THANON WAI SEUKSA

Police Station

105

N

Mae Sariang River

0 250
metres

▼ Mae Sot

an intriguing day-trip to the trading post of **Mae Sam Laeb** on the border with Burma and out onto the Salween River.

Soaking up the atmosphere is the main activity in this border outpost, which is regularly visited by local hill tribes and dodgy traders from Burma. If you want something more concrete to do, stroll around a couple of temples off the north side of the main street, whose Burmese features provide a glaring contrast to most Thai temples. The first, **Wat Si Boonruang**, sports a fairy-tale bot with an intricate, tiered roof piled high above. Topped with lotus buds, the unusual *sema* stones, which delineate the bot's consecrated area, look like old-fashioned street bollards. The open viharns here and next door at **Wat Utthayarom** (aka Wat Jong Sung) are mounted on stilts, with broad teak floors that are a pleasure to get your feet onto. Both wats enshrine Burmese-style Buddhas, white and hard-faced.

Mae Sam Laeb

46km southwest of Mae Sariang and accessible by hourly songthaews from the market in the morning (1hr 30min)

MAE SAM LAEB lies on the mighty Salween (or Salawin) River, which, having descended from Tibet through Burma, forms the Thai–Burmese border for 120km here, before emptying into the Andaman Sea. The village is no more than a row of bamboo stores and restaurants, but with its Thai, Chinese, Karen and Burmese inhabitants, it has a classic frontier feel about it. The best way to get a feel for Mae Sam Laeb's relaxed vibe is to sign up for one of the highly recommended **boat trips** organized by Tuk Ta at *Northwest Guest House* in Mae Sariang (B1000/person, based on a group of four). The boat cruises down the Salween through idyllic countryside for an hour to the small unspoilt Karen village of Sop Moei, right on the confluence of the Moei River with the Salween, where lunch is taken before sailing back to Mae Sam Laeb.

ARRIVAL AND DEPARTURE

MAE SARIANG

By bus Mae Sariang is on the Chiang Mai–Mae Hong Son bus route, with a/c and non-a/c buses departing from Chiang Mai's Arcade bus station, as well as one a/c minibus a day from Wat Ubokut on Chiang Mai's Thanon Tha Pae (on the corner of Thanon Chang Klan). Buses from Bangkok's Northern Mo Chit terminal also pass through on the way to

Mae Hong Son.
Destinations Bangkok (3 daily; 12hr); Chiang Mai (8 daily; 4hr); Mae Hong Son (8 daily; 4hr).
By songthaew Scenic Highway 105 up from Mae Sot (see p.260) is covered by songthaews (5–7 daily; 6hr), though the journey's really too long to make on a rattling bench seat.

GETTING AROUND

By bicycle or motorbike Bicycles (B50–100/day) and motorbikes (B150–200/day), handy for exploring temples

and Karen weaving villages in the surrounding Yuam valley, can be rented from *Northwest Guest House*.

TREKS AND TOURS FROM MAE SARIANG

Mae Sariang's location close to the Burmese border makes it an ideal base for exploring some lesser-travelled areas. The centrally located *Northwest Guest House* organizes local **tours**, such as **boat trips** on the Salween River (see opposite) and three-day **treks** into the wild countryside along the Burmese border near Mae Sam Laeb, including the Salween boat trip (around B2500/person based on a group of two; cheaper in a larger group). The friendly and helpful owner, Tuk Ta, can arrange trips to suit your needs, and is open to offering discounts.

ACCOMMODATION

For such a tiny town, Mae Sariang has a good range of accommodation. In addition, **homestays** in a Lawa village near Mae La Noi to the north of town, where you can learn to make jewellery, cook hill-tribe cuisine and weave, among many other activities, can be arranged through Thailand Hilltribe Holidays (☎085 548 0884; ⓦthailand hilltribeholidays.com).

Mae Sariang Guest House On the corner of Thanon Laeng Phanit and the road leading east towards the bus station, opposite River House Resort ☎053 681203. The cheapest option of all, with a choice between tatty en-suite fan rooms in the main house, with its brightly painted wooden shutters, or slightly quieter box rooms (also en suite, with fan) in a ramshackle block at the back. B200

Northwest Guest House 81 Thanon Laeng Phanit ☎089 700 9928, ⓦnorthwestgh.blogspot.com. Clean, friendly spot with plenty of local information and tidy, polished-wood rooms, some with their own computers with internet access; hot-water bathrooms are either shared or en suite. Reductions for singles. Fan B200, a/c B350

River Bank Guest House Thanon Laeng Phanit ☎053 682787. A new riverside place with classy, all-wooden

rooms that have cable TV, spotless bathrooms, decent showers and crisp white linen. No English spoken, but the fan rooms are great value. Fan B450, a/c B800

River House Hotel Thanon Laeng Phanit ☎053 621201, ⓦriverhousehotels.com. Modern timber-built hotel in traditional open-plan style, where the rooms have simple, tasteful furnishings, fine river views, verandas, a/c and en-suite hot-water bathrooms. Wi-fi. B1000

River House Resort Thanon Laeng Phanit ☎053 683066, ⓦriverhousehotels.com. Run by the owner of *River House Hotel*, this is Mae Sariang's fanciest place to stay. All rooms come with a/c, hot water and smart teak furnishings; some have river-view balconies, while the more expensive ones boast bathtubs, and there's also an attractive garden overlooking the river. Wi-fi. Breakfast included. B1800

EATING AND DRINKING

Mae Sariang Bar Thanon Laeng Phanit. Incongruously modern-looking sports bar/drinking den just back from the riverside and fronted by large tracts of slatted timber. Popular with locals and visitors after dark, who come for the ice-cold beer. Daily 8am–midnight.

Sawatdee Thanon Laeng Phanit. Popular with local NGO

workers, *Sawatdee* bar-restaurant offers mostly Thai food, as well as good coffees and breakfasts, on a terrace overlooking the river, with some low tables, hammocks and axe cushions for chilling out. The view is superb. For something cheap and filling, try the tasty fried rice (B40). Daily 8am–11pm.

DIRECTORY

ATM There's an ATM on Thanon Mae Sariang, just west of Wat Utthayarom.

Internet access As well as at the guesthouses and hotels

mentioned above, internet access is available at Computer House, on Thanon Laeng Phanit, immediately south of *River House Hotel*.

Khun Yuam

North of Mae Sariang, wide, lush valleys alternate with tiny, steep-sided glens – some too narrow for more than a single rice paddy – turning Highway 108 into a winding rollercoaster. The market town of **KHUN YUAM**, 95km from Mae Sariang, is a popular resting spot, especially for those who've taken the direct route here (Route 1263) over the mountains from Mae Chaem.

World War II Museum

Daily 8am–5pm • B50

In the Thai–Japan Friendship Memorial Hall, on the left of the main thoroughfare, Thanon Rajaburana, at the north end of town, the **World War II Museum** has a curious collection of rusting relics from the Japanese World War II occupation – old trucks, rifles, water canisters and uniforms. Lining the walls, hundreds of black-and-white photos document this period, when after their retreat from Burma in 1944, some of the Japanese rested here with the sick and wounded for two years and longer.

ACCOMMODATION AND EATING
KHUN YUAM

Ban Farang Just off Thanon Rajaburana, north of the museum and well signposted ☎053 622086, ⓦbanfarang-guesthouse.com. Each of the smart, very clean rooms here has duvets and a hot-water bathroom; there are cheap dorm beds, too (B150). The restaurant serves up good Thai and Western food, at reasonable prices. Fan **B500**, a/c **B600**

The Buatong fields

Just north of Khun Yuam, Route 1263 branches off to the east over the hills towards Mae Chaem; after about 20km, a side road leads north towards Ban Mae U-Khor and the **Buatong fields** on the slopes of Doi Mae U-Khor, where Mexican sunflowers make the hillsides glow butter-yellow in November and early December. You'll often see the same flowers by the roadside at this time of year, but the sheer concentration of blooms at Mae U-Khor, combined with sweeping views over endless ridges to the west, draws dozens of tour groups in air-conditioned minibuses.

Mae Surin Waterfall

On a spur road branching north from Route 1263, around 15km beyond Ban Mae U-Khor • B200 • ☎053 061073, ⓦdnp.go.th

Mae Surin Waterfall in Nam Tok Mae Surin National Park is arguably the most spectacular waterfall in the whole country, the waters hurtling over a cliff and plunging almost 100m before crashing on huge boulders and foaming down a steep gorge. The kind topography of the region allows a great view of the falls from directly in front, but the best view, from below, requires a steep and at times precarious three-hour hike down and back from the park's well-appointed campsite.

Mae Ko Vafe and Ban Pha Bong

Back on Highway 108, 35km north of Khun Yuam, a right turn leads up to **Mae Ko Vafe** – a Thai rendition of "microwave", referring to the transmitters that grace the mountain's peak; the paved road climbs for 10km to a Hmong village, where the fantastic view west stretches far into Burma. Around 15km beyond this turn-off, Highway 108 climbs to a roadside **viewing area**, with fine vistas, this time to the east, of the sheer, wooded slopes and the Pha Bong Dam in the valley far below. Subsequently the road makes a dramatic, headlong descent towards Mae Hong Son, passing the **Ban Pha Bong** hot springs, 7km north of the viewing area (11km before Mae Hong Son). These have been turned into a small spa complex with hot spring-water baths, traditional masseurs, private treatment rooms and a restaurant.

Mae Hong Son and around

MAE HONG SON, capital of Thailand's northwestern-most province, sports more nicknames than a town of ten thousand people seems to deserve. In Thai, it's Muang Sam Mok, the "City of Three Mists": set deep in a mountain valley, Mae Hong Son is often swathed in mist, the quality of which differs according to the three seasons

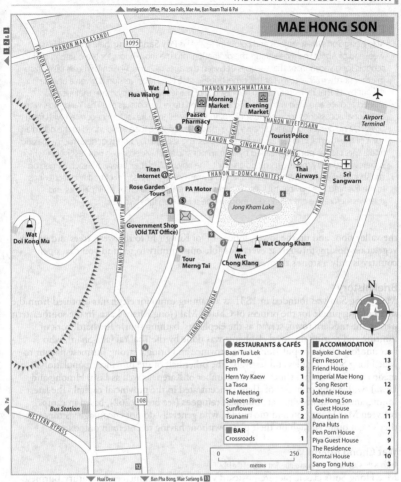

▲ Immigration Office, Pha Sua Falls, Mae Aw, Ban Ruam Thai & Pai

MAE HONG SON

THANON MAKKASANDI
1095
THANON SIRIMONGKOL
Wat Hua Wiang
THANON PANISHWATTANA
Morning Market
Evening Market
THANON NIVETPISARN
Airport Terminal
Paaset Pharmacy
THANON KHUNLUMPRAPAS
THANON PRADIT JONGKHAM
THANON SINGHANAT BAMRUNG
Tourist Police
Titan Internet @
THANON U-DOMCHAONITESH
Thai Airways
Sri Sangwarn
THANON CHAMNANSATHI
Rose Garden Tours
PA Motor
Jong Kham Lake
Wat Doi Kong Mu
THANON PADUNGMUAYTAW
Government Shop (Old TAT Office)
Wat Chong Kham
Tour Merng Tai
Wat Chong Klang
THANON KHUHPHUAK
N
Pai
Bus Station
108
WESTERN BYPASS

RESTAURANTS & CAFÉS
Baan Tua Lek	7
Ban Pleng	9
Fern	8
Hern Yay Kaew	1
La Tasca	4
The Meeting	6
Salween River	3
Sunflower	5
Tsunami	2

BAR
Crossroads	1

ACCOMMODATION
Baiyoke Chalet	8
Fern Resort	13
Friend House	5
Imperial Mae Hong Song Resort	12
Johnnie House	6
Mae Hong Son Guest House	2
Mountain Inn	11
Pana Huts	1
Pen Porn House	7
Piya Guest House	9
The Residence	4
Romtai House	10
Sang Tong Huts	3

0   250
metres

▼ Huai Deua   ▼ Ban Pha Bong, Mae Sariang & 13

3

(in the hot season it's mostly composed of unpleasant smoke from burning fields). In former times, the town, which wasn't connected to the outside world by a paved road until 1968, was known as "Siberia" to the troublesome politicians and government officials who were exiled here from Bangkok. Nowadays, thanks to its mountainous surroundings, it's increasingly billed as the "Switzerland of Thailand": eighty percent of Mae Hong Son province is on a slope of more than 45 degrees.

To match the hype, Mae Hong Son has become a hugely popular destination, sporting, alongside dozens of backpacker guesthouses, several upmarket hotels and resorts for Thai and farang tourists. Many visitors come here for **trekking** in the beautiful countryside (see box, p.341), others just for the cool climate and lazy upcountry atmosphere. The town is still small enough and sleepy enough to hole up in for a quiet week, though in the high season (Nov–Feb) swarms of minibuses disgorge tour groups who hunt in packs through the souvenir stalls and fill up the restaurants.

Running north to south, Mae Hong Son's main drag, **Thanon Khunlumprapas**, is intersected by Thanon Singhanat Bamrung at the traffic lights in the centre of town. Beyond the typical concrete boxes in the centre, Mae Hong Son sprawls lazily across

POY SANG LONG

Mae Hong Son's most famous and colourful festival is **Poy Sang Long**, held over the first weekend of April, which celebrates the ordination into the monkhood, for the duration of the schools' long vacation, of Thai Yai boys between the ages of 7 and 14. Similar rituals take place in other northern Thai towns at this time, but the Mae Hong Son version is given a unique flavour by its Thai Yai elements. On the first day of the festival, the boys have their heads shaved and are anointed with turmeric and dressed up in the colours of a Thai Yai prince, with traditional accessories: long white socks, plenty of jewellery, a headcloth decorated with fresh flowers, a golden umbrella and heavy face make-up. They are then announced to the guardian spirit of the town and taken around the temples. The second day brings general merry-making and a spectacular **parade**, headed by a drummer and a richly decorated riderless horse, which is believed to carry the town's guardian spirit. The boys, still in their finery, are each carried on the shoulders of a chaperone, accompanied by musicians and bearers of traditional offerings. In the evening, the novices tuck into a sumptuous meal, waited on by their parents and relatives, before the ordination ceremony in the temple on the third day.

the valley floor and up the lower slopes of Doi Kong Mu to the west, trees and untidy vegetation poking through at every possible opportunity to remind you that open country is only a stone's throw away.

Brief history

Mae Hong Son was founded in 1831 as a training camp for elephants captured from the surrounding jungle for the princes of Chiang Mai (Jong Kham Lake, in the southeastern part of the modern town, served as the elephants' bathing spot). The hard work of hunting and rearing the royal elephants was done by the **Thai Yai** (aka Shan), who account for half the population of the province and bring a strong Burmese flavour to Mae Hong Son's temples and festivals. The other half of the province's population is made up of various hill tribes (a large number of Karen, as well as Lisu, Hmong and Lawa), with a tiny minority of Thais concentrated in the provincial capital. The latest immigrants to the province are **Burmese refugees** (see box, p.262), based in camps between Mae Hong Son and the border, who generally do not encourage visitors as they've got quite enough on their plates without having to entertain onlookers.

Wat Chong Kham

Towards the southeast of the town centre, just south of the lake

Mae Hong Son's classic picture-postcard view is its twin nineteenth-century Burmese-style temples, Wat Chong Kham and Wat Chong Klang, from the opposite, north shore of Jong Kham Lake (Nong Jong Kham), their gleaming white and gold chedis and the multi-tiered roofs and spires of their viharns reflected in the water. In the viharn of **Wat Chong Kham** is a huge, intricately carved sermon throne, decorated with the *dharmachakra* (Wheel of Law) in coloured glass on gold; the building on the left has been built around the temple's most revered Buddha image, the benign, inscrutable Luang Pho To.

Wat Chong Klang

Next to Wat Chong Kham, just south of the lake

Wat Chong Klang, the other of the two lakeside temples, is famous for its paintings on glass, which are said to have been painted by artists from Mandalay over a hundred years ago; they're displayed over three walls on the left-hand side of the viharn. The first two walls behind the monks' dais (on which women are not allowed to stand) depict *Jataka* stories from the Buddha's previous incarnations in their lower sections, and the life of the Buddha himself in their upper, while the third wall is devoted entirely to the Buddha's life. A room to the left houses an unforgettable collection of **teak statues**, brought over from Burma in the middle of the nineteenth century. The dynamically expressive, often humorous figures are characters from the *Vessantara Jataka*, but the woodcarvers have taken as their models people from all levels of traditional Burmese society, including toothless emaciated peasants, butch tattooed warriors and elegant upper-class ladies.

The morning market

Between Thanon Nivetpisarn and Thanon Panishwattana • Daily from dawn until around 9am

The town's vibrant, smelly **morning market** is worth dragging your bones up at dawn to see. People from the local hill tribes often come down to buy and sell, and the range of produce is particularly weird and wonderful, including, in season, porcupine meat, displayed with quills to prove its authenticity.

Wat Hua Wiang

Thanon Panishwattana

The many-gabled viharn of **Wat Hua Wiang** shelters, under a lace canopy, one of the most beautiful Buddha images in northern Thailand, the **Chao Palakeng**. Copied from a famous statue in Mandalay, the strong, serene bronze has the regal clothing and dangling ears typical of Burmese Buddhas.

3

TOURS AND TREKKING AROUND MAE HONG SON

Once you've exhausted the few obvious sights in town, the first decision you'll have to grapple with is whether to visit one of the three villages of "long-neck" women around Mae Hong Son (see p.343). Our advice is don't: they're effectively human zoos for snap-happy tourists, offering no opportunity to discover anything about Kayan culture. Less controversially, **boat and raft trips** on the babbling Pai River are fun (see box, p.342), while the roaring **Pha Sua Falls** and the villages of **Mae Aw** and **Ruam Thai** to the north of town make a satisfying day out. Other feasible targets include the hot springs at **Ban Pha Bong** (see p.338) and, further out, **Mae Surin Waterfall** (see p.338) and **Tham Lot** (see p.346). A reliable company for guided **tours** around the area is Rose Garden Tours at 86/4 Thanon Khunlumprapas (☎053 611577, ⊛rosegarden-tours.com), with day-long excursions starting from B900. It's also worth dropping by Mae Hong Son Discovery Tours (based at *Sunflower* bar-restaurant; ☎080 124 4056), which runs one-day community-based trips, including a tour that calls at a White Karen village, a waterfall and a working farm (B1250/person, based on two sharing); bespoke bird-watching trips are also possible. If all that sounds too easy, Mae Hong Son is Thailand's third-largest centre for **trekking**.

There's no getting away from the fact that trekking up and down Mae Hong Son's steep inclines is tough, though the scenery is magnificent. Most of the hill-tribe villages here are Karen, interspersed with indigenous Thai Yai (Shan) settlements in the valleys. Heading east, where many villages are very unspoilt, having little contact with the outside world, is preferable to the more populous, less traditional west; to the southeast, you'll be able to visit Hmong and Karen, to the northeast, Lisu also. In the latter direction, if you're very hardy, you might want to consider the five- to six-day routes to Soppong or Pai, which have the best scenery of the lot.

About a dozen guesthouses and travel agencies in Mae Hong Son run **multi-day treks**, on which guides can often build a camp of natural materials while overnighting in the forest. Worth recommending is the currently independent guide, Chakaphan (Chan) Prowinchaikul (☎053 611040 or ☎081 951 5880, ✉natural_walks@yahoo.com), who speaks good English and specializes in flowers and insects (one-day treks from B1500/person). Among a wide variety of trips, Tour Merng Tai at 89 Thanon Khunlumprapas (☎053 611979, ⊛tourmerngtai.com) offers several community-based tourism programmes, employing village guides and cooks and contributing part of the profits to local communities. They're mostly one-day treks, involving four or five hours' walking to Lahu, Thai Yai and Karen villages (B1100–2400/person, including 4WD transport where necessary, English-speaking guide and lunch), though longer treks and homestays are possible.

TRIPS ON THE PAI RIVER FROM MAE HONG SON

Scenic **boat trips** on the Pai River start from Huai Deua, 7km southwest of town near the Mae Hong Son Resort. Any travel agent can fix up an organized tour, but the cheapest way to do it is to rent a motorbike and approach the owners at Huai Deua boat station yourself. Twenty minutes downriver from Huai Deua (B600) will get you to the "long-neck" village of **Ban Nam Phiang Din**, but you're better off enjoying the river for its own sake, as it scythes its way between cliffs and forests towards the nearby Burmese border.

A small stretch of the Pai River to the northwest of Mae Hong Son is clear enough of rocks to allow safe clearance for **bamboo rafts**. The journey takes between one and one-and-a-half hours, as the rafts glide down the gentle river, partly hemmed in by steep wooded hills, and it can be combined with an hour-long elephant ride through the jungle and a relatively easy three- to four-hour trek. Rose Garden Travel (see p.341) can fix this combined trip up for you, including all transfers, for B1450 per person (cheaper if you have a big group).

Wat Doi Kong Mu

On the hill to the west of town

For a godlike overview of the area, drive or climb up to **Wat Doi Kong Mu** on the steep hill to the west. From the temple's two chedis, which enshrine the ashes of respected nineteenth-century Thai Yai monks, you can look down on the town and out across the sleepy farming valley north and south. Behind the chedis, the viharn contains an unusual and highly venerated white marble image of the Buddha, surrounded in gold flames. If you've got the energy, trek up to the bot on the summit, where the view extends over the Burmese mountains to the west.

Pha Sua Falls, Mae Aw and Ban Ruam Thai

North of Mae Hong Son: if driving yourself, turn left off Route 1095 10km north of town, following signposts for Pha Sua

North of Mae Hong Son, a trip to **Pha Sua Falls** and the border villages of **Mae Aw** and **Ruam Thai** takes in some spectacular and varied countryside. Your best options are to rent a vehicle or join a tour (B900–1200/person for a one-day excursion, including a visit to the highly overrated Fish Cave). With your own wheels, you can stop off en route at the Phu Klon Country Club, not far north of the turning off Route 1095 (⚆053 282579, ⚆phuklon.co.th), more commonly known as the **mud spa**, where you can get a face or body mask or bathe in the hot spring water.

Pha Sua Falls

About 20km from the turn-off from Route 1095 you'll reach **Pha Sua Falls**, a wild, untidy affair, which crashes down in several cataracts through a dark overhang cut in the limestone. The waterfall is in full roar in October after the rainy season, but has plenty of water all year round. Take care when swimming, as several people have been swept to their deaths here.

Mae Aw

Above the falls the paved road climbs precipitously, giving glorious, broad vistas of both Thai and Burmese mountains, before reaching the unspectacular half-Hmong, half-Thai Yai village of **Naphapak** after 11km. From here, a largely flat stretch of tarmac (built by the Thai military to help the fight against the opium trade) heads north for 7km to **MAE AW** (aka Ban Rak Thai), a settlement of Kuomintang anti-Communist Chinese refugees (see p.364), right on the Burmese border. The tight ring of hills around the village heightens the feeling of being in another country: delicate, bright-green tea bushes line the slopes, while Chinese ponies wander the streets of long, unstilted bamboo houses. In the central marketplace on the north side of the village reservoir, shops sell great bags of Oolong and Chian Chian teas, as well as dried mushrooms.

Ban Ruam Thai

Heading 6km west from Naphapak along a fairly rough paved road, you'll come to **BAN RUAM THAI**, a Thai Yai settlement where a royal project has had a lot of success in substituting coffee for opium. At the western end of the village lies **Pang Oung**, a large reservoir surrounded by pine-clad slopes that's very popular with Thai tourists and has been dubbed "Switzerland in Mae Hong Son" – the locals have even put bells on their cows.

ARRIVAL AND DEPARTURE   MAE HONG SON

By plane Mae Hong Son airport is close to the centre, towards the northeast of town. Nok Air runs direct flights here from and to Chiang Mai twice a day (35min). From the airport terminal motorbike taxis (B30–40) and tuk-tuks (B50) run into the centre.

By bus Buses to Mae Hong Son (about half of which are a/c) depart from Chiang Mai's Arcade bus station, travelling via Mae Sariang or Pai. Daily buses also run from Mae

Sariang and, to meet tourist demand, there are also regular a/c minibuses from and to Pai. Minibuses coming into Mae Hong Son go past the *Crossroads* bar, so ask the driver to drop you there if you're staying in town. From the new bus station, south of the centre, motorbike taxis (B30–40) and tuk-tuks (B50) run into the centre.

Destinations Bangkok (2 daily; 16hr); Chiang Mai (8 daily; 8–9hr); Mae Sariang (8 daily; 4hr); Pai (10 daily; 3hr).

GETTING AROUND

Local transport, in the form of songthaews from the north side of the morning market, is thinly spread and unreliable, so for all excursions it's best to rent your own vehicle or join an organized tour through your guesthouse or one of the many travel agents in town.

"LONG-NECK" WOMEN

The most famous – and notorious – of the Mae Hong Son area's spectacles is its contingent of **"long-neck" women**, members of the tiny **Kayan Lahwi** tribe of Burma (sometimes called Padaung) who have come across to Thailand to escape Burmese repression. Though the women's necks appear to be stretched to 30cm and more by a column of brass rings, the "long-neck" tag is a technical misnomer: a *National Geographic* team once X-rayed one of the women and found that instead of stretching out her neck, the pressure of eleven pounds of brass had simply squashed her collarbones and ribs. Girls of the tribe start wearing the rings from about the age of 6, adding one or two each year up to the age of 16 or so. Once fastened, the rings are for life, for to remove a full stack may eventually cause the collapse of the neck and suffocation – in the past, removal was a punishment for adultery.

The **origin** of the ring-wearing ritual remains unclear, despite an embarrassment of plausible explanations. Kayan Lahwi legend says that the mother of their tribe was a dragon with a long, beautiful neck, and that their unique custom is an imitation of her. Tour guides will tell you the practice is intended to enhance the women's beauty. In Burma, where it is now outlawed as barbaric, it's variously claimed that ring-wearing arose out of a need to protect women from tiger attacks or to deform the wearers so that the Burmese court would not kidnap them for concubines.

In spite of their handicap (they have to use straws to drink, for example), the women are able to carry out some kind of an ordinary life: they can marry and have children, and they're able to weave and sew, although these days they spend most of their time posing like circus freaks for photographs. Only half of the Kayan Lahwi women now lengthen their necks; left to follow its own course, the custom would probably die out, but the influence of **tourism** may well keep it alive for some time yet. The villages in Mae Hong Son, and now also in Chiang Mai and Chiang Rai provinces, where they live, are set up by Thai entrepreneurs as a money-making venture (visitors are charged B500 to enter these villages). At least, contrary to many reports, the "long necks" are not held as slaves – they are each paid a living wage of about B1500 per month – though their plight as refugees is certainly precarious and vulnerable. Since 2005, the United Nations High Commission for Refugees has been offering permanent resettlement in third countries for about twenty Kayan Lahwi. However, the authorities in Thailand, where the "long necks" bring in a huge amount of tourist dollars every year, have refused to sign the necessary paperwork on a technicality. Our advice (see p.341) is not to visit the villages.

By motorbike or 4WD PA Motor on Thanon Pradit Jongkham opposite *Friend House* (see below) rents out motorbikes for B150–200/day and four-wheel drives for B1500.

By bicycle Titan Internet, on Thanon Khunlumprapas, has good mountain bikes for B80/day.

INFORMATION

Tourist information At the time of writing, the TAT office on Thanon Khunlumprapas was being moved to a new location on Thanon Ratchathumpitak, towards the northeast of the city centre (daily 8.30am–4.30pm; ☎053 612982–3, ⱳ travelmaehongson.org).

ACCOMMODATION

Mae Hong Son has a healthy roster of **guesthouses**, most of them being good-value, rustic affairs built of bamboo or wood and set in their own quiet gardens; many are sited around Jong Kham Lake or on the northern slopes of Doi Kong Mu on the northwestern edge of town, which greatly adds to their scenic appeal. If you've got a little more money to spend, you can get out into the countryside to one of several self-contained **resorts**, though staying at one of these is not exactly a wilderness experience – they're really designed for weekending Thais travelling by car. Finally, several **luxury hotels** have latched onto the area's meteoric development, offering all the usual international-standard facilities.

Baiyoke Chalet Thanon Khunlumprapas, just across from the post office ☎053 613132–9. The standard rooms here are small and simple, with plain white walls, bedside lamps, a desk and TV. Upgrading to a superior room buys you much more space, plus a balcony overlooking a topiary-filled courtyard, a mini-bar and fluffy towels folded into the shape of swans. The restaurant is open for breakfast (included in rate) and lunch. Wi-fi. B1280

★ **Fern Resort** 6km south of town on Highway 108, then signposted 2km east on a paved minor road ☎053 686110–1, ⱳ fernresort.info. The best resort around Mae Hong Son, this eco-friendly place employs local villagers as much as possible. In a peaceful, shady valley, a brook runs through the beautiful grounds, past stylish cottages with hot water, a/c and verandas (no phones or TV). There's an attractive swimming pool and nature trails in the surrounding Mae Surin National Park; regular free shuttle bus to the *Fern Restaurant* in town. Breakfast included. B2500

Friend House 20 Thanon Pradit Jongkham ☎053 620119. Decent, clean, modern teak-and-concrete house with upstairs balcony giving views of the lake. Larger rooms have hot-water bathrooms, smaller ones share hot showers. Free wi-fi. B200

Imperial Mae Hong Son Resort 149 Moo 8, Tambon Pang Moo ☎053 684444–5, ⱳ imperialhotels.com. On the south side of the town by the turn-off for Huai Deua, this grand building is set in pretty landscaped gardens, overlooked by spacious rooms featuring satellite TV and mini-bar; there's a swimming pool, sauna and fitness centre, too. Good discounts available online. B1300

Johnnie House Thanon U-Domchaonitesh ☎053 611667. In a small compound near the lake, this clean, friendly place has airy rooms, sharing hot showers, in a nice, old, wooden house, as well as bright, concrete affairs with en-suite hot-water bathrooms. B200

Mae Hong Son Guest House 295 Thanon Makkasandi ☎053 612510, ⱳ maehongsonguesthouse.com. Relaxing old-timer in a big, shady garden on the western outskirts of town, with a restaurant and friendly staff. Choose between large, attractive, en-suite bungalows and simpler, shared or en-suite rooms, all with hot water. Rooms B350, bungalows B500

Mountain Inn 112 Thanon Khunlumprapas ☎053 611802–3, ⱳ mhsmountaininn.com. Large, neat and tasteful rooms with a/c, hot-water bathrooms, carpeting, mini-bars and TVs, set round a flower-strewn garden and swimming pool. Look out for the stencilled wall art and quirky smiling statues in the lobby. B1400

Pana Huts Signposted 300m south off Thanon Makkasandi ☎053 614331 or ☎086 772 8502, ⱳ panahuts.com. Congenial spot in a quiet, lush valley in the shadow of Doi Kong Mu that feels a lot further from town than it actually is. Made from woven bamboo, the six rooms have well-equipped bathrooms, mosquito nets and nice touches like pot plants and bedside lights. B600

Pen Porn House 16/1 Thanon Padungmuaytaw ☎053 611577 or ☎089 635 9588. The smart, clean and well-maintained rooms at this motel-like place come with hot showers, and are set around a small, shady garden. Fan B300, a/c B400

★ **Piya Guest House** 1/1 Soi 3, Thanon Khunlumprapas ☎053 611260, ✉ piyaguesthouse @hotmail.com. Friendly, well-run, hotel-like guesthouse, boasting large, brightly painted bungalows with spacious, hot-water bathrooms and a/c in a lush garden beside the lake. B600

The Residence 41/4 Thanon Nivetpisarn ☎053 614100, ⱳ theresidence-mhs.com. Tasteful three-storey guesthouse furnished throughout with golden teak. The a/c rooms boast smart, hot-water bathrooms, crisp, white linen and duvets on the beds and even proper desks with reading lamps. Wi-fi and bicycles available to guests. B1300

Romtai House 22 Thanon Chamnansathit ☎053 612437, ⓦmaehongson-romtai.com. There's a wide choice of spacious, well-kept rooms and bungalows with hot water at this tranquil place that's set around a rambling, colourful garden and a big lotus pond. **B600**

Sang Tong Huts Down a small lane across from Mae Hong Son Guest House off Thanon Makkasandi ☎053 620680, ⓦsangtonghuts.com. Upmarket, German-run

guesthouse with a cute swimming pool, offering rustic chic on a steep, jungly slope on the edge of town. Roofed with traditional, thatched *tong teung* leaves, and decorated with rugs and tapestries, the "huts" have verandas, mosquito nets on the beds and large, attractively tiled bathrooms with hot water. Home-baked bread and cakes for breakfast, and Thai dinners, are served in a simple, open-sided seating area around an open fire. **B900**

EATING AND DRINKING

Eating options are limited, although a few good tourist-oriented restaurants have sprung up in town. In addition, there's a small, popular, takeaway-only **evening market** on Thanon Panishwattana, along from the day market, that closes around 8pm.

Baan Tua Lek South side of Jong Kham Lake, across from Wat Chong Klang ☎053 620688. Stylish bakery with a small garden patio, serving good coffees, cakes, croissants, bagels and pies. The tasty flavoured teas cost B25. Daily 9am–7pm.

Ban Pleng 108/5 Thanon Khunlumprapas ☎053 612522. Divided in two by the main road, this restaurant, with its traditional roofs of *tong teung* leaves, specializes in northern Thai and Local Thai Yai dishes, many of which are available in small B30 portions; try the crunchy fern salad with sesame seeds and oil or the very tasty *pla lung*, minced fish balls with tomato, garlic and ginger. Daily 10.30am–10pm.

Crossroads 16 Thanon Singhanat Bamrung. This welcoming, aptly named bar – located at the junction of the town's two main roads – serves up Thai and Western food, including American breakfasts (B120), great shakes, good coffee and draught Singha beer, and is a cool place to chill out in the evenings. Daily 8am–midnight.

Fern 87 Thanon Khunlumprapas ☎053 611374. Large, justly popular eating place, with a nice terrace and a good reputation for its Thai food, such as spicy coconut shoot salad (B85) and river fish with spicy mango salad (B180). It also serves a few Thai Yai, northern Thai and Western dishes, and there's a coffee shop at the front with a computer that's hooked up to the internet (10min free). Daily 10.30am–10pm.

Hern Yay Kaew Thanon Singhanat Bamrung ☎084 614 9428. Chilled, contemporary dining in a beautiful wooden building that faces the street. The menu is limited to a handful of Western dishes like pasta and T-bone steaks (served in a uniquely Thai way), but it's competently put together. Daily 8am–10pm.

La Tasca 88/4 Thanon Khunlumprapas ☎053 611344. Reasonably authentic Italian restaurant right in the middle of town, with home-made pizzas and a long menu of pasta dishes, including home-made gnocchi, lasagne and fettuccini (B170). Daily 10am–10pm.

The Meeting 3/2 Thanon Pradit Jongkham, next to Sunflower Café ☎053 620726. A good-value if slightly disorganized jewellery shop, watering hole and travellers' café all rolled into one. The food, including standards such as fried rice with vegetables and basil leaves (B45), is tasty and honestly priced. Open daily for breakfast, lunch and dinner.

★ **Salween River** 23 Thanon Pradit Jongkham ☎053 613421, ⓦsalweenriver.com. English- and Thai-run restaurant and bar with wi-fi and a book exchange. The kitchen serves up a wide variety of Western favourites (B70 and up), as well as northern Thai, Thai Yai and Burmese food (mostly B50–80), including a delicious green tea salad. Sells good maps of Mae Hong Son province. Daily 8am–10pm.

Sunflower Thanon Pradit Jongkham. A good place for breakfast, lunch, dinner or just a drink, on a terrace overlooking the lake and the temples behind; on high-season evenings you can relax to the sounds of a live band playing Western and Thai pop and folk music. Home-made bread, cakes, pizzas and pastas, espresso coffees, and some tasty Thai dishes, including Lanna and Thai Yai specialities. Wi-fi available. Daily 7.30am–11pm.

Tsunami On the corner of Thanon Singhanat Bamrung and Thanon Pradit Jongkham. Clean, fan-cooled restaurant serving a great range of fresh sushi and tempura. Sushi sets from B79. Open daily for lunch and dinner.

SHOPPING

Though the town is generally quiet during the day while visitors are out exploring the hills, the main streets come alive in the evening as **handicraft stalls** display colourful bolts of cloth, lacquerware, Burmese puppets, ceramics and jewellery.

Government-sponsored shop In the old TAT building, opposite the post office on Thanon Khunlumprapas.

Sells some attractive fabrics (including bags and clothes), local teas and other foodstuffs. Daily 8am–4pm.

DIRECTORY

ATM and exchange You'll find an ATM just across from *Baiyoke Chalet* in the heart of town, plus several banks and exchange booths along Thanon Khunlumprapas. The airport has a bank currency exchange.

Hospital Sri Sangwarn, Thanon Singhanat Bamrung ☎ 053 611378 or ☎ 053 611907.

Immigration office Thanon Khunlumprapas, north of the town centre (Mon–Fri 8.30am–4.30pm, although senior staff don't usually arrive until about 9am; ☎ 053 612106).

Internet access Titan Internet on Thanon Khunlumprapas has good, reliable internet access (B30/hr).

Post office On Thanon Khunlumprapas.

Pharmacy Paaset, Thanon Singhanat Bamrung.

Tourist police The tourist police are on Thanon Singhanat Bamrung (☎ 053 611812 or ☎ 1155).

Soppong and Tham Lot

The small market town of **SOPPONG**, 68km from Mae Hong Son on Route 1095 in the district of Pang Ma Pha (which is sometimes used on signposts), gives access to the most famous of over two hundred known caves in the area, **Tham Lot**, 9km north in **BAN THAM**. Due to its proximity to Pai, Soppong has become popular for day-trippers, and now even supports an ATM at its far west end in front of the police station.

Tham Lot

Ban Tham, 9km north of Soppong; Thai Yai guide with lantern B150 per group, bamboo raft B400 return for up to three people

Turn right in Ban Tham to find the entrance to the **Tham Lot Nature Education Station** set up to look after the cave. A short walk through the forest brings you to the entrance of Tham Lot, where the Lang River begins a 600m subterranean journey through the cave. Access to the various parts of the cave depends on the time of year and how much rain there has been, and may involve hiring a bamboo raft for some or all of your journey: for most of the year you'll need to raft from Doll to Coffin Cave, while at the driest times it may be possible to wade, and at the highest water levels it may be necessary to walk around to the exit and get to the last part, Coffin Cave, from there. Normally two hours should allow you enough time for travelling through the broad, airy tunnel, and for the main attraction, climbing up into the sweaty caverns in the roof – be sure not to touch any of the cave formations.

The first of these, **Column Cavern**, 100m from the entrance on the right, is dominated by a 20m-high cave stalagmite snaking up towards the ceiling. Another 50m on the left, bamboo ladders lead up into **Doll Cave**, which has a glistening, pure white wall and a weird red and white formation shaped like a Wurlitzer organ; deep inside, stalagmites look like dolls. Just before the vast exit from the cave, wooden ladders on the left lead up into **Coffin Cave**, named after the remains of a dozen crude log coffins discovered here, one of them preserved to its full length of 5m. Hollowed out from teak trunks about 1700 years ago, they are similar to those found in many of the region's caves: some are raised 2m off the ground by wooden supporting poles, and some still contained bones, pottery and personal effects when they were discovered. It's worth hanging round the cave's exit at sunset, when hundreds of thousands of tiny black chirruping swifts pour into the cave in an almost solid column, to find their beds for the night.

TOURS FROM CAVE LODGE

The owners of *Cave Lodge* can provide plenty of useful information about Tham Lot and other **caves** in the region, and organize robust, active **guided trips** (from B600/person, including equipment and lunch). They also offer **kayaking**, including trips through Tham Lot, plus 6km of fun rapids (in the rainy and cool seasons; from B650). Maps for self-guided walking from the lodge to local Thai Yai, Karen, Lahu and Lisu villages are available, as well as local, English-speaking guides for full-on **trekking** (typically B2500 for 3 days). Other activities include learning to weave or cook, mountain-biking and bird-watching.

ARRIVAL AND DEPARTURE

By bus All buses connecting Mae Hong Son with Pai and Chiang Mai pass through Soppong. From the bus stop in the centre of Soppong, it's possible to pick up a motorbike taxi

SOPPONG AND BAN THAM

(B70) or pick-up truck (B300) for the gentle run along the paved forest road to Ban Tham.

ACCOMMODATION AND EATING

SOPPONG

Little Eden Guest House A short walk east of Soppong's bus stop ☎053 617054, ⓦlittleeden -guesthouse.com. This tranquil spot has a variety of neat, attractive bungalows and plush rooms, each with a private hot-water bathroom. The pretty garden has a decent-sized swimming pool, and slopes down towards the Lang River and a relaxing riverside pavilion. Services here include motorbike rental and free internet access, and there are plenty of tours and treks on offer. Bungalows **B450**, doubles **B700**

Soppong River Inn At the west end of town ☎053 617107, ⓦsoppong.com. Here on a densely foliated plot you'll find a handful of cottage-style rooms, tastefully decorated and thoughtfully designed, many with outdoor bathrooms and all with hot showers. As well as free wi-fi, there's a lovely, partly thatched deck over the Pai River, which here runs swiftly through a craggy, jungly defile. **B700**

BAN THAM

★ **Cave Lodge** On the other side of Ban Tham from the cave ☎053 617203, ⓦcavelodge.com. This long-established guesthouse makes an excellent, friendly base for exploring the area. The owners can arrange local sightseeing trips and activities (see box opposite) and there's a good range of accommodation, from dorms (B120) to wooden rooms and bungalows, some with shared hot showers and others with their own bathrooms. There's also a relaxing communal area around an open fire for hanging out and eating Thai, Thai Yai and Western food, including home-baked bread. Rooms **B300**, bungalows **B500**

BAN NONG TONG

Lisu Homestay In the village of Ban Nong Tong, a 10min motorbike ride from Soppong ☎089 998 4886, ⓦlisuhilltribe.com. A genuine Lisu homestay where you can go trekking and learn the hill tribe's crafts, music, dance and cooking (courses extra at around B1000/day). **B300**

Pai

Set in a broad, gentle valley 43km beyond Soppong, **PAI** was once just a small-town stopover on the tiring journey to Mae Hong Son, but in recent years has established itself as a major tourist destination in its own right. There's nothing special to see here, but you can partake of all manner of outdoor activities, courses and holistic therapies – even retail therapy at the art studios, bookshops and jewellery shops – and the

HOT SPRINGS, SPAS AND TRADITIONAL MASSAGE

Just because you're hundreds of kilometres from the nearest beach, that doesn't mean you can't enjoy a good soak. The Pai area is home to some natural hot springs and a clutch of decent spas, all of which offer massages.

Accessible from the minor road south from Wat Mae Yen, 2km beyond Joy Elephant Camp (or by turning left off the main Chiang Mai road straight after the bridge over the Pai River), are some **hot springs** (B200), part of Huai Nam Dang National Park, which have one or two very hot, rough pools that aren't really up to much. Much better than the pools, however, are the nearby **spas**, which put the piped hot water from the springs to more productive use. *Pai Hotsprings Spa Resort* (☎053 065748–9, ⓦpaihotspringssparesort.com), down a side road about 1km north of the springs, has two shady mineral pools (B50) and provides various **massages** (B300/hr), plus accommodation with spa-water bathrooms.

Massages are also available at several spots in town, including *Mr Jan's* guesthouse (see p.350), famous for its Thai (B150/hr) and Burmese/Shan massages (B200/hr) and saunas (B60). Having trained at the Old Medicine Hospital in Chiang Mai, the staff at Pai Traditional Thai Massage (PTTM) on Thanon Tessaban 1 (☎053 699121, ⓦpttm1989.com) have a good reputation for traditional massages (B180/hr), as well as foot, herbal and oil massages (B250–300/hr) and saunas (B100), and run government-approved, three-day **massage courses** (B2500).

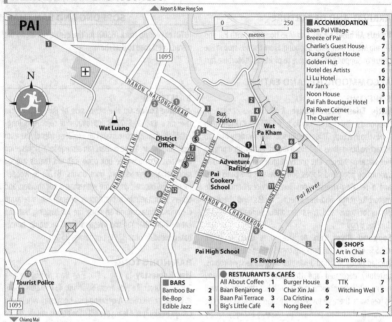

PAI

ACCOMMODATION

Baan Pai Village	9
Breeze of Pai	4
Charlie's Guest House	7
Duang Guest House	5
Golden Hut	2
Hotel des Artists	6
Li Lu Hotel	12
Mr Jan's	10
Noon House	3
Pai Fah Boutique Hotel	11
Pai River Corner	8
The Quarter	1

● SHOPS

Art in Chai	2
Siam Books	1

■ BARS

Bamboo Bar	2
Be-Bop	3
Edible Jazz	1

● RESTAURANTS & CAFÉS

All About Coffee	1	Burger House	8	TTK	7
Baan Benjarong	10	Char Xin Jai	6	Witching Well	5
Baan Pai Terrace	3	Da Cristina	9		
Big's Little Café	4	Nong Beer	2		

guesthouses, out-of-town resorts and restaurants have tailored themselves to the flood of visitors who make the journey out from Chiang Mai. Westerners settle into the town's full-on traveller culture and laidback, New-Agey feel for weeks or even months – the local tourist maps even give handy lists of tattoo studios and non-MSG restaurants. Meanwhile, Pai is now firmly on the radar of Thai tourists, so in high season, especially on weekends when the sunflowers near Mae Hong Son are out (see p.338), the narrow through-streets get clogged with a/c minibuses. It can be an odd mix, but an evening promenade along the "walking street" of Thanon Chaisongkhram, with its Thai-style galleries and gift shops in the traditional buildings at the western end and more traveller-oriented outlets to the east – plus a sprinkling of local hill-tribe people and shrouded Thai Muslims – is undoubtedly pleasant and *sanuk*.

ARRIVAL AND DEPARTURE   PAI

Aya Service, a travel agency on Thanon Chaisongkhram (☎ 053 699940 or ☎ 053 699888, ⓦ ayaservice.com), sells air, bus, boat and train tickets and organizes overnight minibuses directly to Chiang Khong (B750; via Tha Ton), arriving in time to take the morning boat to Luang Prabang and including accommodation for the short stopover.

By plane Domestic airline Kan Air (ⓦ kanairlines.com) flies to Pai from Chiang Mai (25min) four times a week, landing at the airstrip on the north side of town.

By bus As well as public buses, faster, more comfortable, hourly a/c minibuses run to Pai from both Chiang Mai and Mae Hong Son: Prempracha (☎ 053 064307) covers both routes, using the respective bus stations, while Aya Service

(☎ 053 699940 or ☎ 053 699888 in Pai, ☎ 053 247663 in Chiang Mai) runs from Chiang Mai only, but offers pick-ups from your accommodation.

Destinations Chiang Mai (hourly; 3–4hr); Mae Hong Son (hourly; 3–4hr); Mae Malai (4 daily; 2hr 30min); Soppong (4 daily; 1hr 30min).

GETTING AROUND

If you're driving yourself, note that the eastern part of Thanon Chaisongkhram, the north end of Rungsiyanon and Thanon Tessaban 1 are pedestrianized, at least in the tourist season.

By motorbike taxi Motorbike taxis sometimes wait on Thanon Chaisongkhram opposite the bus station, but if you're staying in one of the more central guesthouses it's easy enough to walk.

By rented motorbike Aya Service, on Thanon Chaisongkhram, is the best place to rent motorbikes,

charging from B80 a day, not including insurance, which is an extra B40–80.

By mountain bike Several places in town rent out mountain bikes, including *Noon House* (B50/day) down the continuation of Thanon Rungsiyanon behind the bus station.

ACTIVITIES AROUND PAI

Away from the main hubbub of central Pai, there's plenty to keep you occupied. Several undemanding **walks** can be made around Pai's broad, gently sloping valley. The easiest – a round-trip of about an hour – takes you across the river bridge on the east side of town and up the hill to **Wat Mae Yen**, which commands a great view over the whole district. On the way to the wat, you'll pass Fluid, the town's large open-air **swimming pool** (daily 9am–6.30pm; B60), with food and drink available, as well as fitness equipment, a steam room and yoga classes.

To the west of town, beyond Pai Hospital, the continuation of Thanon Chaisongkhram passes, after 3km, **Wat Nam Hu**, whose Buddha image has an unusual hinged topknot containing holy water. As you continue, the road gradually climbs through comparatively developed Thai Yai, Kuomintang (with a Chinese Cultural Centre where you can taste tea), Lisu and Lahu villages to **Mo Pang Falls**, with a pool for swimming, about 10km west of Pai.

Among several **elephant camps** on the minor road from Mae Yen towards the hot springs, Joy, 5km from town (☎081 881 3923), charges B300 per hour per person for an elephant ride (minimum two people), which includes going into the river with the elephant and feeding it, as well as a free bathe in a hot spring pool.

The Pai Cookery School, Thanon Wan Chalerm, holds Thai **cooking courses** (☎081 706 3799; from B750/day) of one to three days, including a trip to the market to learn about ingredients, making six dishes, eating them and getting a free recipe book; vegetarians are catered for.

As befits a town that's popular with spiritual types, there are several places offering **yoga classes** to beginners and experienced practitioners. At Xhale Yoga (based at *PS Riverside*, due south of *Da Cristina*; ☎089 758 3635, ⓦxhaleyogapai.com) certified tutor Bhud runs daily drop-in classes at 10am (B200). Alternatively you can join one of her highly recommended five-night yoga retreats (starting every Mon in high season; from B10,500 including meals, accommodation and tuition).

Pai makes a good base for **trekking**, which can be arranged through the guesthouses or trekking agents, among which *Duang Guest House*, Thai Adventure Rafting (see below) and Back Trax at 17 Thanon Chaisongkhram (☎053 699739, ⓔbacktraxinpai@yahoo.com) are reliable.

Thai Adventure Rafting head off to friendly, hassle-free Karen, Lisu and Lahu villages to the north of Soppong near the border, taking in Tham Lot (see p.346), some beautiful scenery and, in the rainy season, waterfalls; two days cost B1600 per person (minimum four people), three days B2300, the latter including one night in a camp you build with the guide, with a bit of jungle cooking and survival training thrown in. Their one-day treks head north of Pai (B800/person, minimum three people). *Duang* charge B750–800 for one day (two to three people), B750 per day for two or three days (minimum four people). Both of these places can add bamboo rafting and can arrange one-way treks to Mae Hong Son (5–7 days), while *Duang* also offer sightseeing tours.

If you just fancy a bit of **bamboo-rafting** without the trekking, *Duang* and plenty of other agents can arrange transport and a two-hour trip down the Pai River for around B500 per person.

With a little more cash to spare, you could strike up with the reliable and experienced, French-run Thai Adventure Rafting for a **rubber-raft trip** (☎053 699111, ⓦthairafting.com; main branch at 39 Thanon Chaisongkhram, with a second branch on Thanon Rungsiyanon; not to be confused with the imitative Pai Adventure Rafting). Heading down the Pai River to Mae Hong Son, you'll pass through gorges and sixty rapids (up to class IV) and take in waterfalls and hot springs. The full journey lasts two days, including a night at a comfortable jungle camp by the river, and costs B2700 per person, though one-day trips (B1500) are also available; the season normally runs from mid-June to the middle of February, with the highest water from August to early September, and participants must be able to swim.

3

INFORMATION

Events listings and maps The free, bimonthly, English-language *Pai Events Planner*, widely available in restaurants and guesthouses, has news about what's on. Aya Service,

on Thanon Chaisongkhram, can also provide you with an excellent map of the area.

ACCOMMODATION

The streets in the centre of town teem with places to stay, and there are dozens of hotels, resorts and "treehouse retreats" in the countryside around Pai, useful for escaping the growing bustle downtown. You might notice that guesthouse owners have a penchant for Pai-based puns: think *Pai in the Sky*, *Pai Chart* and so on.

CENTRAL PAI

Baan Pai Village South off Thanon Chaisongkhram, by the river ☎053 698152, ⓦbaanpaivillage.com. In the heart of Pai, rural simplicity – bamboo huts with roofs of *tong teung* leaves and mattresses on the floor – made palatable by a few home comforts, including large bathrooms with hot showers and Western loos. A few baht more gets you a bed, a wooden floor and French windows. Clustered rather closely together in a lush garden strewn with ponds. Nearby Riverside and Mountain View annexes cater for any overspill. Fan B1000, a/c B1700

Breeze of Pai Just off Thanon Chaisongkhram near Wat Pa Kham ☎081 998 4597, ⓦbreezeofpai.com. Congenial, well-maintained place with large, simple but chic, ochre bungalows and single-storey rooms with nice parquet floors and hot showers. The compound's little

crowded but lent privacy by plenty of foliage. Book exchange and free wi-fi. Fan room B500, fan bungalow B800, a/c bungalow B1000

Charlie's Guest House 9 Thanon Rungsiyanon ☎053 699039. A variety of clean rooms, with en-suite or shared hot showers, set around a lush garden; decent rates for singles. Fan B200, a/c B600

Duang Guest House 5 Thanon Rungsiyanon ☎053 699101, ⓦduangguesthousepai.com. Opposite the bus station, this is a clean and reliable place to stay, with hot showers throughout, whether shared or en suite, and a good restaurant, though it all feels a little cramped; the best rooms have a fridge and TV. Good rates for singles. B200

Golden Hut 107 Moo 3, north of Breeze of Pai ☎053 699949. The cheap fan rooms here, in a mishmash of wooden buildings and bungalows by the water (or in a peaceful garden at the rear), are nothing special, but offer good value all the same. B250

Hotel des Artists (Rose of Pai) Thanon Chaisongkhram, across from Pai River Corner ☎053 699539, ⓦhotelartists.com. On a corner plot near the river and centred around an attractive glass-sided living room, this stylish new hotel has just fourteen bedrooms, the best of which have fantastic terraces that face out across the water. In the spacious rooms, bell-shaped lanterns illuminate the beds (which are raised off the ground on platforms made from local wood) while facilities include a/c, TVs, DVD players, and artfully tiled en-suite bathrooms. B3600

Li Lu Hotel Thanon Rungsiyanon, close to the junction with Thanon Ratchadamrong ☎053 064351, ⓦliluhotel.com. With a sister property in Chiang Mai, this is a comfortable if slightly stark hotel in a central part of town. The plain a/c rooms have an almost industrial feel, with swathes of distressed concrete and white paint, but there are comforting touches like woven bamboo slippers, and the en-suite bathrooms are always sparkly clean. Facilities include a library and internet access. B1900

Mr Jan's Thanon Sukhaphibun 3 (Tessaban) ☎053 699554. On one of a mess of small streets behind and to the east of *Charlie's*, these quiet, comfy concrete rooms with hot showers are set in a delightfully overgrown and fragrant medicinal herb garden. Also

AROUND PAI

■ ACCOMMODATION
Belle Villa	1
Mountain View	2
Spicy Pai	3

Soppong & Mae Hong Son

Pai Airport

1095

PAI

SEE PAI MAP FOR DETAIL

BYPASS

Tourist Police

Fluid Swimming Pool

Wat Mae Yen

MAE YEN

Pai River

1095

4024

N

Joy Elephant Camp

Hot Springs

Pai Hot Springs Resort

1095

WWII Bridge

0 — 1 kilometre

Wat Nam Hu & Mo Pang Falls

Huai Nam Dang National Park & Chiang Mai

offers on-site sauna and massages (see p.347). **B200**

Noon House Down the continuation of Thanon Rungsiyanon behind the bus station ☎053 699383. Clean and quiet little houses brightly painted in shades of yellow and green. Each has a veranda overlooking a shady driveway cluttered with the owner's considerable collection of pushbikes, which are available to rent (see p.349). Fan **B600**, a/c **B700**

Pai Fah Boutique House Thanon Tessaban 1 ☎088 409 1151, ⓦpaifahhotel.com. Terracotta-coloured walls wrapped by foliage separate this good-looking hotel from the road, creating a surprisingly quiet little enclave. Inside, the a/c rooms are small but tastefully pieced together, with spacious private bathrooms, and there are plenty of shady public areas to relax in on sunny afternoons. **B900**

Pai River Corner Eastern end of Thanon Chaisongkhram, by the river ☎053 699049, ⓦpairivercorner.com. Elegant, Mediterranean-style resort with beautifully furnished, balconied rooms, some of which have their own jacuzzis, set around an attractive garden and swimming pool. Overshadowed slightly by the much newer *Hotel des Artists*. Wi-fi and breakfast included. **B3270**

★ **The Quarter** Thanon Chaisongkhram, just west of Pai Hospital ☎053 699423, ⓦthequarterhotel.com. Chic and welcoming luxury hotel, in a central but quiet location, with an attractive spa. Set in two-storey houses around a lovely contemporary Thai garden and a smart pool with jacuzzi, the modern minimalist rooms feature distressed concrete, dark wood and splashes of dark silk.

Free internet, wi-fi and mountain bikes. Breakfast included. **B4800**

OUT OF TOWN

Belle Villa About 1km north of town, signposted to the right off the Mae Hong Son road ☎053 698226–7, ⓦbellevillaresort.com. Elegant luxury rooms and villas on stilts, all with balconies, mini-bars and safes. Traversed by a stream and decorated with rice fields, the grounds sport a stylish pool. Wi-fi, mountain bikes for rent and free transfers to town. Breakfast included. **B3850**

Mountain View 500m up a side road by the tourist police at the south end of town ☎086 180 5998, ⓦthemountainviewpai.com. Laidback, old-style resort of wood and woven bamboo bungalows, some with private bathrooms and some with shared facilities, set in ten acres of land among a small arboretum of flowering trees. Free access to Fluid swimming pool (see p.349). **B200**

★ **Spicypai** Around 700m east of the Thanon Ratchadamrong bridge; keep right at the junctions you pass along the way and then follow the signs to the hostel ☎085 715 9627, ⓦspicyhostels.com. Ultra-cheap and ultra-sociable dorm rooms in a series of lofty thatched huts surrounded by vivid green paddy fields. The main, mixed dorm (known as the Spicy Hall) sleeps twenty people, with the best and most desirable beds right up in the rafters. There are also single-sex dorms. Facilities include mozzie nets, shared toilets, a self-catering kitchen and lockers for your valuables. Breakfast and wi-fi included. Dorm **B150**

EATING

As with the accommodation scene, new cafés and restaurants are opening practically every week, ever more sophisticated and cosmopolitan. To save cash and reduce plastic waste, check in at *Art In Chai*, opposite Pai High School on Thanon Ratchadamrong, where you can refill bottles with fresh drinking water for B3 per litre.

All About Coffee Thanon Chaisongkhram ☎053 699429. Superb coffee in any variety you might want, in an atmospheric wooden shophouse. Also does great breakfasts with home-made bread, a daily selection of home-made cakes, sandwiches and teas, hot chocolate, shakes and juices. Daily 8.30am–5.30pm.

Baan Benjarong South end of town, near Be-Bop Bar ☎053 698010. In a town where you can get everything from sushi to falafel, this place offers a wide variety of authentic and tasty Thai dishes – the salted crab in coconut milk is the house speciality. Small and often full on busy nights (no reservations). Daily approximately 11am–2pm & 5–10pm.

Baan Pai Terrace Thanon Rungsiyanon, opposite Pai Country House. Fresh farang food served on the streetside terrace of a wooden house built in the traditional Pai style more than ninety years ago. Continental breakfasts from B80 and reasonable pizzas from B180. Daily 8am–11pm.

Big's Little Café Thanon Chaisongkhram. Run by Big, who has worked as a chef in England, this tiny streetside burger bar is renowned for its tasty and keenly priced Western breakfasts. Customers sit around on bar stools while their food is prepared right in front of them. A good spot for meeting other travellers. Open for breakfast and lunch.

Burger House Thanon Rungsiyanon ☎053 699093. Surprisingly tasty burgers in various forms using imported beef (mostly B80–135), plus breakfasts, baguettes and other Western dishes, in a good central location. For something different, try the tasty chicken and avocado burger (B95). Daily except Mon 8.30am–9pm.

Char Xin Jai Thanon Ratchadamrong. Chinese vegetarian and vegan garden restaurant, offering tasty buffet food such as green curry with tofu on brown rice (B25) and pricier made-to-order dishes like tempura. Daily 8am–8pm.

Da Cristina Thanon Ratchadamrong, just west of the bridge over the river. Currently the best and most authentic of Pai's few Italian restaurants, offering large, crispy pizzas (B110–370), great salads, home-made pasta and Italian wines. Daily noon–10pm.

Nong Beer Corner of Chaisongkhram and Khetkalang ☎053 699103. One of Pai's longest-standing and most popular places for cheap eats – now self-service but with loads of tables – dishing up great *khao soi*, pork satay and a wide range of buffet stir-fries and curries. Daily 8am–9pm.

TTK Thanon Ratchadamrong, next to TTK Guesthouse

☎053 698093. Famous for its falafel, this large indoor-outdoor restaurant has a good range of international dishes to supplement its mostly Middle Eastern menu. Open for breakfast, lunch and dinner.

★ **Witching Well** Thanon Tessaban 1, just over from Pai River Corner ⓦwitchingwellpai.com. Pretty, peaceful and popular, this cosy little café attracts free-thinking backpackers from around the world. There's a distinctly witchy theme – from the drinkable potions (healthy teas, B50) to the magical home-made cakes. Daily except Tues 9am–7pm.

DRINKING AND NIGHTLIFE

Several **bars** around town offer live music: as well as those listed below, look out for posters around town, which sometimes also announce one-off parties.

Bamboo Bar Just east of the Thanon Ratchadamrong. bridge. A ramshackle late-night party place on the water's edge that's made entirely of logs and bamboo. Currently the most heavily promoted venue in town, so keep an eye out for flyers advertising free drinks promos. Daily 6pm–5am.

Be-Bop South end of town, beyond the junction of Khetkalang and Rungsiyanon. Among a clutch of nightspots, this large, well-designed bar hosts live music

every evening and is a popular spot for travellers to congregate. Daily 8pm–1am.

★ **Edible Jazz** Just off Thanon Chaisongkhram near Wat Pa Kham ☎087 177 7455. This garden café and bar on a quiet, leafy lane is a mellow spot for a cheap drink, currently offering an acoustic set 8.30–10pm. The owner, Tom, takes great pride in introducing travellers to one another. Daily 9am–midnight.

SHOPPING

You can buy Lisu handicrafts and handmade jewellery on Pai's "**walking street**", Thanon Chaisongkhram, which hits its stride at around 6pm in the evening.

Art in Chai Opposite Pai High School on Thanon Ratchadamrong ⓔartinchai@hotmail.se. This art-strewn café towards the south of town sells an effective natural mosquito repellent. Daily 10am–10pm.

Siam Books Thanon Chaisongkhram ☎053 699075. There's a good selection of used paperbacks at this bookshop, handily located on the main walking street. Daily 9.30am–9pm.

DIRECTORY

ATMs You'll find ATMs in the centre, on Thanon Chaisongkhram and Thanon Rungsiyanon.
Hospital Thanon Chaisongkhram ☎053 699211.
Internet access Several shops near the intersection of Thanon Rungsiyanon and Thanon Ratchadamrong.

Laundry There are several places to get clothes washed on Thanon Chaisongkhram, each charging B20/kg (B50 for express 2hr service).
Tourist police South end of town, on the road to Chiang Mai ☎053 611812–3 or ☎1155.

From Pai to Chiang Mai

Once out of the Pai valley, Route 1095 climbs for 35km of hairpin bends, with beautiful views north to 2175m Doi Chiang Dao near the top. In the cool season, with your own transport, you can witness – if you get started from Pai an hour before dawn – one of the country's most famous views of the sun rising over a sea of mist at **Huai Nam Dang National Park** (B200). The viewpoint is signposted on the left 30km out of Pai; take this turning and go on 6km to the park headquarters. Back on Route 1095, once over the 1300m pass, the road steeply descends the south-facing slopes in the shadow of Doi Mae Ya (2005m), before working its way along the narrow, more populous lower valleys. After 55km (at kilometre-stone 42), a left turn leads 6.5km over some stomach-churning hills to **Pong Duet hot springs** (also part of Huai Nam Dang National Park), where scalding water leaps up to 4m into the air, generating copious quantities of steam in the cool season. A few hundred metres downstream of the springs, a series of pools allows you to soak in the temperature of your choice. The last appealing detour of the route is to **Mokfa Falls** (part of Doi Suthep-Pui National Park; B100), where a cascade tumbles about 30m into a sand-fringed pool that is ideal for **swimming**, making an attractive setting for a break – it's 2km south of the main road, 76km from Pai. Finally, at **Mae Malai**, turn right onto the busy Highway 107 and join the mad, speeding traffic for the last 34km across the wide plains to Chiang Mai.

To Chiang Rai via Tha Ton

If you're coming up from Chiang Mai, the quickest and most obvious **route to Chiang Rai** is Highway 118, a fast, 185km road that swoops through rolling hill country. A much more scenic approach, however, is to follow Highway 107 and Highway 1089; a two-day trip along this route will leave you enough time for a longtail boat trip along the **Kok River** and an overnight stay in **Tha Ton**, which boasts several appealing riverside resorts and a wide variety of outdoor activities. There are other diversions en route, including the admirable **Elephant Nature Park** and a couple of good guesthouses that can arrange trekking in the countryside near **Chiang Dao**.

The Elephant Nature Park

12km beyond Mae Taeng • Full-day trip costs B2500/person • Book your visit online, at 209/2 Thanon Sridornchai in Chiang Mai, or at one of their other offices in Chiang Mai • ☎ 053 818754, ⓦ elephantnaturepark.org

From Chiang Mai the route towards Tha Ton heads north along Highway 107, retracing the Mae Hong Son Loop as far as Mae Malai. About 3km after Mae Taeng, a signposted left turn leads 9km to the **Elephant Nature Park**, which is essentially a rescue centre and hospital for sick, orphaned and neglected elephants, but hands-on educational – and recreational – visits by the public are encouraged. On a daytime visit, you'll get to feed, bathe and learn about the elephants close up, but it's also possible to stay for two days or sign up as a paying volunteer for a week or longer. The park's owner, Sangduan ("Lek") Chailert, has become something of a celebrity in recent years, being featured on the BBC and in *Time* magazine for her conservation efforts. Visits must be booked in advance.

Chiang Dao

Around kilometre-stone 72, **CHIANG DAO**, an oversized market village, stretches on and on along the old main road as the dramatic limestone crags and forests of Thailand's third-highest peak, Doi Luang Chiang Dao (or Doi Luang, "Great Mountain"; 2240m), loom up on the left. A new bypass sweeps round to the west of town, carrying traffic heading straight for Tha Ton.

Tham Chiang Dao

5km northwest of Chiang Dao, across the bypass • Daily 8am–4pm • Admission to the caves is B20 and guides ask around B100 to take a group of up to five people on a 30min tour • Access from Chiang Dao by yellow songthaews and motorbike taxis

An extensive complex of interconnected caverns, **Tham Chiang Dao** has an attached monastery (the caves were given religious significance by the local legend of a hermit sage who is said to have dwelt in them for a millennium). Several of the caverns can be visited; a couple have electric light but others need the services of a guide with a lantern; guides will point out unusual rock formations and keep you on the right track – it's said the deepest parts of the cave are 12km underground, and just a few of the caverns are considered safe to visit.

> ### TREKS UP DOI CHIANG DAO
>
> Guided treks to the **summit of Doi Chiang Dao**, famous for its many rare alpine plants and birds, can be arranged by both *Malee's* and *Chiang Dao Nest* (see below) during the cool season, roughly from November to March. It takes two to three days to go up and down and costs around B3400 per person in a large group.

ARRIVAL AND GETTING AROUND
CHIANG DAO

By bus Take one of the buses from Chiang Mai's Chang Phuak bus station bound for Fang or Tha Ton. You'll need to tell the driver or ticket seller that you want to stop in Chiang Dao otherwise they might plough straight past.

By motorbike taxi or songthaew From the junction at the southern end of town, where bus drivers are most likely to make a stop, you can take a motorbike taxi (B50) or songthaew (B120) to the guesthouses.

ACCOMMODATION AND EATING

Chiang Dao Nest About 1500m further north along the road from the caves ☎053 456242, ⓦchiangdao.com. There are two branches of this farang favourite, one on each side of *Malee's*, with around twenty bungalows in total – all with attached hot-water bathrooms and balconies. The one nearer to the caves serves Thai food, while the further one – which has a small swimming pool – turns out gourmet Western dishes (mains at around B325). B895

Malee's Nature Lovers Bungalows About 1500m further north along the road from the caves ☎053

456426 or ☎081 961 8387, ⓦmaleenature.com. In this cosy compound, delightfully set in the shadow of the mountain, you'll find comfy rooms and bungalows of varying size, some with shared hot showers and others with en-suite bathrooms, as well as camping facilities (B80/person), two-person tents to rent (B200) and good food. They can arrange treks, elephant trekking and bird-watching trips, or just point birders in the right direction; bicycle and motorbike rental is available. Rooms B350, bungalows B850

Doi Angkhang

Back on Highway 107, the road shimmies over a rocky ridge marking the watershed between the catchment areas of the Chao Phraya River to the south and the Mekong River ahead, before descending into the flat plain around Fang and the Kok River. Branching off to the left some 60km from Chiang Dao, a steep and winding 25km road, Route 1249, leads up to the mountain known as **Doi Angkhang** (1928m; map of the mountain available from Chiang Mai TAT office). Besides a royal agricultural project that produces peaches, raspberries and kiwis in the cool season, the mountain is home to a luxurious resort (see below), where you can stop for food and spend a couple of hours soaking up the scenery.

ARRIVAL AND DEPARTURE
DOI ANGKHANG

The best way to get here is using your own transport. Otherwise, you could take a bus bound for Fang or Tha Ton from Chiang Mai's Chang Puak bus station and hop off at kilometre-stone 137 on Highway 107, then try to pick up a motorbike taxi for the remaining 20km – but there's no guarantee you'll find one.

ACCOMMODATION

★ **Angkhang Nature Resort** 1/1 Moo 5 Baan Khum ☎053 450110, ⓦoamhotels.com/angkhang. At this gorgeous hillside resort, the luxurious teak pavilions have balconies with great views, the restaurant uses organic

produce from the royal project, and bird-watching, trekking, mule riding or mountain biking to nearby hill-tribe villages are the main activities. B1900

Tha Ton and around

The tidy, leafy settlement of **THA TON**, nearly 180km north of Chiang Mai, huddles each side of a bridge over the Kok River, which flows out of Burma 4km to the north upstream. Life in Tha Ton revolves around the bridge – buses and boats pull up here, and most of the accommodation is clustered nearby. The main attractions here are longtail-boat and bamboo-raft rides downstream to Chiang Rai.

Wat Tha Ton

On the west side of the bridge • W wat-thaton.org

The over-the-top ornamental gardens of **Wat Tha Ton**, endowed with colossal golden and white Buddha images and an equally huge statue of Kuan Im, the Chinese *bodhisattva* of mercy, are well worth the short climb. From any of the statues, the views up the narrow green valley towards Burma and downstream across the sun-glazed plain are heady stuff.

ARRIVAL AND DEPARTURE   THA TON

By bus or songthaew Regular services run between Chiang Mai's Chang Phuak bus station and Tha Ton (4hr). Otherwise, you could take one of the half-hourly buses to the ugly frontier outpost of Fang, 153km from Chiang Mai, then change onto a half-hourly songthaew to Tha Ton. From Tha Ton, it's also possible to move on to Mae Salong by songthaew (see p.366) or Mae Sai by bus (1 daily; 1hr 40min).

BOAT AND RAFT TRIPS ALONG THE KOK RIVER

Travelling down the 100km stretch of the **Kok River** to Chiang Rai gives you a chance to soak up a rich diversity of typical northern landscapes, which you never get on a speeding bus. Heading out of Tha Ton, the river traverses a flat valley of rice fields and orchards, where it's flanked by high reeds inhabited by flitting swallows. After half an hour, you pass the 900-year-old **Wat Phra That Sop Fang**, with its small hilltop chedi and a slithering naga staircase leading up from the river bank. Beyond the large village of **Mae Salak**, 20km from Tha Ton, the river starts to meander between thickly forested slopes. From among the banana trees and giant wispy ferns, kids come out to play, adults to bathe and wash clothes, and water buffalo emerge simply to enjoy the river. About two hours out of Tha Ton the hills get steeper and the banks rockier, leading up to a half-hour stretch of small but feisty rapids, where you might well get a soaking. Beyond the rapids, crowds of boats suddenly appear, ferrying tour groups from Chiang Rai to the Karen village of **Ruammid**, 20km upstream, for elephant-riding. From here on, the landscape deteriorates as the bare valley around Chiang Rai opens up.

The best time of year to make this trip is in the cool season (roughly Nov–Feb), when you'll get both lush vegetation and exciting rapids. Canopied **longtail boats** (B450/person) leave from the south side of the bridge in Tha Ton every day at 12.30pm for the trip to Chiang Rai, which takes around four rather noisy hours. The slower, less crowded journey upriver gives an even better chance of appreciating the scenery – the longtails leave Chiang Rai at 10.30am. If you can get a group of up to six people together (up to twelve when the river's deeper in the rainy season), it's better to charter a longtail from the boat landing in Tha Ton (around B2200; ☎053 459427), which will allow you to stop at the hill-tribe villages and hot springs en route. A round-trip to Chiang Rai and back costs B3800 per boat.

If you have more time, the peaceful **bamboo rafts** which glide downriver to Chiang Rai in three days almost make you part of the scenery. Each party is accompanied by two steersmen who dismantle the rafts in Chiang Rai and bring the bamboo back to be recycled in Tha Ton. *Garden Home Nature Resort*, for example (see p.356), charge B8000–12,000 per boat for two to six passengers, including soft drinks and food, staying at a Lahu village and the hot springs along the way. They also offer two-day versions, starting at Ban Pa Tai, east of Tha Ton (B6000 for two people), as well as half- and full-day trips downriver from Tha Ton, by either raft or kayak, returning by car.

Passengers departing from Tha Ton boat landing are required to sign the log book at the adjacent **tourist police** booth. A peaceful **guesthouse** between Mae Salak and Ruammid, from which you can go trekking (guided or self-guided), might tempt you to break your river journey. *Akha Hill House* (☎089 997 5505 or ☎081 460 7450, W akhahill.com; fan B250, a/c B1000), on the south bank of the Kok, 3km on foot from the riverside hot springs near Huai Kaeo waterfall, offers lofty views, comfortable rooms and bungalows, some with en-suite hot showers (with decent rates for singles), and free transport daily to and from Chiang Rai.

By car or motorbike If you're coming up Highway 107 with your own transport, you can give Fang a miss altogether by branching west on a bypass signposted to Mae Ai.

ACCOMMODATION AND EATING

There are several simple **restaurants** opposite the boat landing; in addition, all of the following resorts have good restaurants open to non-guests.

Garden Home Nature Resort On the east bank of the river, 300m north of the bridge ☎053 373015, ⓦ thatonaccommodation.com. A very appealing riverside option, with friendly, clued-up staff, internet access and attractive en-suite rooms and bungalows (all with hot showers) sheltering in plenty of space under an orchard of lychees. The restaurant serves Western breakfasts, coffee and a good choice of Thai food – at lovely, thatched *salas* on stilts over the river if you like – and they offer motorbike rental, off-road motorbike day-trips and trekking (from B950/person), as well as various journeys down the Kok River (they can even arrange for the 12.30pm boat to Chiang Rai to pick you up from the resort). Rooms B400, fan bungalows B500, a/c bungalows B1200

★ **Mae Kok River Village Resort** About 1km east of

the bridge on the right-hand side of Highway 1089 ☎053 459328, ⓦ maekok-river-village-resort.com. An excellent upmarket choice, set in extensive gardens, with well-designed, stylish, a/c rooms set around a swimming pool (which includes a pool for toddlers). A huge range of activities – from Thai cooking to rock climbing – is on offer, and the Thai guides speak superb English. Breakfast included. B3250

River View Resort About 200m beyond Garden Home ☎053 373173–5, ⓦ thaton-riverview-resort.chiangmai -chiangrai.com. With an even better location than *Garden Home* on a bend in the river that's hemmed in by densely forested hillside. You can enjoy great views of it all from the well-equipped a/c rooms and bungalows and the excellent Thai terrace restaurant. Rates include breakfast. B1400

DIRECTORY

ATM About 200m before the bridge on the Fang road, at *Hotel Alilak*.

Internet access *Coffee Mug*, opposite the boat landing area, has internet access.

Ban Lorcha

Beyond Tha Ton, Route 1089 heads east towards Mae Chan and Highway 1; about 20km out of town, at Ban Kew Satai, a dramatic side road leads north for 16km to Mae Salong (see p.364). On the way, it's worth breaking your journey (about 1km west of Kew Satai on Route 1089, and accessible by songthaews from Tha Ton and Mae Salong) at **BAN LORCHA**. As part of a community-based tourism development project, owned and managed by the villagers, with technical assistance from the PDA in Chiang Rai (see p.360), this Akha settlement has been opened to visitors, who pay an entrance fee of B100 (income goes into a village development fund). A guide leads you on 1km walk through the village, which is strategically dotted with interesting display boards in English, and you'll get a chance to have a go on an Akha swing (not the ceremonial one), see a welcome dance and watch people weaving and tool-making, for example.

Chiang Rai

Sprawled untidily over the south bank of the Kok River, **CHIANG RAI** continues to live in the shadow of the local capital, Chiang Mai, but in the last few years has acquired several genuine sights of interest, notably **Rai Mae Fah Luang**, a beautiful storehouse of Lanna art. There's now also a good choice of guesthouses and upmarket riverside hotels to lay your head down in, and from here you can set up a wide range of trekking, day-trips and other outdoor activities in the surrounding countryside. The town quietly gets on with its own business during the day, when most of its package tourists are out on manoeuvres, but at night the neon lights flash on and souvenir stalls and ersatz Western restaurants are thronged. Meanwhile, Chiang Rai keeps up its reputation as a dirty-weekend destination

CHIANG RAI

N

ACCOMMODATION

Baan Bua Guest House	11	Jitaree Guest House	4
Baan Bua Homestay	13	The Legend	2
Baan Rub Aroon		Le Meridien	7
Guest House	9	Mae Hong Son	
Chat House	6	Guest House	5
Dusit Island Resort Hotel	3	Moon & Sun	8
Golden Triangle Inn	10	Tourist Inn	14
Imperial		Wiang Inn	12
River House Resort	1		

RESTAURANTS & CAFÉS

Aye's	4
Baan Chivit Mai	5
Cabbages & Condoms	2
Kaffee Hub	3
Muang Thong	6
Salungkham	1

New Bus Station, Wat Rong Khun & Chiang Mai ▼

for Thais, a game given away by just a few motels with carports – where you drive into the garage and pay for a discreet screen to be pulled across behind you.

Brief history

Chiang Rai is most famous for the things it had and lost. It was founded in 1263 by King Mengrai of Ngon Yang who, having recaptured a prize elephant he'd been chasing around the foot of Doi Tong, took this as an auspicious omen for a new city. Tradition has it that Chiang Rai then prevailed as the capital of the north for thirty years, but historians now believe Mengrai moved his court directly from Ngon Yang to the Chiang Mai area in the 1290s. Thailand's two holiest images, the Emerald Buddha (now in Bangkok) and the Phra Singh Buddha (now either in Bangkok's National Museum, Chiang Mai or Nakhon Si Thammarat, depending on which story you believe), also once resided here before moving on – at least replicas of these can be seen at Wat Phra Kaeo and Wat Phra Singh.

Doi Tong

Northwest of the centre

A walk up to **Doi Tong**, the hummock to the northwest of the centre, is the best way to get your bearings in Chiang Rai and, especially at sunset, offers a fine view up the Kok

3

TOURS AND TREKKING FROM CHIANG RAI

Communities from all the hill tribes have settled around **Chiang Rai**, and the region offers the full range of terrain for **trekking**, from reasonably gentle walking trails near the Kok River to tough mountain slopes further north towards the Burmese border; elephant riding is included in most treks. However, this natural suitability has attracted too many tour and trekking agencies, and many of the hill-tribe villages, especially between Chiang Rai and Mae Salong, have become weary of the constant toing and froing; the south side of the river to the west of town is generally a better bet. Sizes of group treks from Chiang Rai tend to be smaller than those from Chiang Mai, often with just two or three people, with a maximum of about seven in a group. Nearly all guesthouses in Chiang Rai can fit you up with a trek – *Chat House* and *Mae Hong Son Guest House* are responsible and reliable, typically charging B2500–3500 per person for three days and two nights in a group of between two and six people. One place to avoid is the Union of Hilltribe Villages, just north of Chiang Rai's airport, where people from various ethnic groups, including "long-neck" women (see p.343), are brought to live together in an artificial village for the convenience of tourists.

More expensive treks are offered by several nonprofit foundations promoting **community-based tourism** that are based in and around Chiang Rai. The Hill Area and Community Development Foundation has set up Natural Focus (☎053 758658 or ☎085 888 6869, ⓦnaturalfocus-cbt.com), which offers one- to fifteen-day tours to learn about mountain life, as well as youth, workstay and volunteer skills programmes. Hilltribe Tour, part of the Mirror Art Group (ⓦthemirrorfoundation.org; see p.59), runs tours, one- to three-day treks and longer village **homestays**, on which you can learn a hill-tribe skill such as weaving or playing an instrument. The development agency PDA at the Hilltribe Museum (☎053 719167, ⓦpda.or .th/chiangrai; see p.360) offers one- or multi-day jungle treks to non-touristy areas, usually including elephant riding and a longtail-boat trip. They also lay on a wide range of **guided tours**, to their Akha project at Ban Lorcha (see p.356), Mae Salong and other places of interest. Most of the guesthouses can also arrange sightseeing tours, as well as boat trips, elephant rides and motorbike trekking.

River as it emerges from the mountains to the west. On the highest part of the hill stands a kind of phallic Stonehenge centred on the town's new **lak muang** (city pillar) representing the Buddhist layout of the universe. Historically, the erection of a *lak muang* marks the official founding of a Thai city, precisely dated to January 26, 1263 in the case of Chiang Rai; the new *lak muang* and the elaborate stone model around it were erected 725 years later to the day, as part of the celebrations of King Bhumibol's sixtieth birthday. The *lak muang* itself represents Mount Sineru (or Meru), the axis of the universe, while the series of concentric terraces, moats and pillars represent the heavens and the earth, the great oceans and rivers, and the major features of the universe. Sprinkling water onto the garlanded *lak muang* and then dabbing your head with the water after it has flowed into the basin below brings good luck. The old wooden *lak muang* can be seen in the viharn of **Wat Phra That Doi Tong**, the city's first temple, which sprawls shambolically over the eastern side of the hill.

Wat Phra Kaeo

Thanon Trairat • Temple daily 7am–6pm • Sangkaew Hall daily 9am–5pm • Free • ⓦ watphrakaew-chiangrai.com

Thailand's most important image, the Emerald Buddha, which had supposedly been sculpted by the gods in Patna, India, in 234 BC, was placed in the chedi at **Wat Phra Kaeo** by King Mahaprom of Chiang Rai in 1390. However, lightning destroyed the chedi 44 years later, allowing the image to continue its perambulations around Southeast Asia, finally settling down in Bangkok. A beautiful replica can now be seen here in a tiny, Lanna-style pavilion, the **Hor Phra Yok**. Carved in China from milky green Canadian jade, the replica was presented by a Chinese millionaire to mark the ninetieth

birthday of the Princess Mother, Mae Fah Luang, in 1990, and consecrated by King Bhumibol himself. At 47.9cm wide and 65.9cm tall, it's millimetres smaller than the actual Emerald Buddha, as religious protocol dictated that it could not be an exact copy of the original. There's much else of interest in the temple complex, which has recently been renovated to a high standard, notably the **Sangkaew Hall**. Distinguished by its informative labels on Thai religious practice in English, this museum houses all sorts of Buddhist paraphernalia, including the belongings of famous monks from Chiang Rai.

The Hill Tribe Museum and Handicrafts Shop

620/25 Thanon Tanalai • Mon–Fri 9am–6pm, Sat & Sun 10am–6pm • Museum B50

The **Hill Tribe Museum and Handicrafts Shop** stocks an authentic selection of tasteful and well-made hill-tribe handicrafts. The shop, on the second floor, was started by the country's leading development campaigner, Meechai Viravaidya, under the auspices of the PDA (Population and Community Development Association), and all proceeds go to village projects. The museum is a great place to learn about the hill tribes before going on a trek, and includes a slick, informative slide show (20min). You can donate old clothes or money for jumpers and blankets, and they also organize treks and tours themselves (see p.358).

Rai Mae Fah Luang

5km west of the city centre in Ban Pa Ngio • Tues–Sun 8.30am–5.30pm • B200 • ⓦ maefahluang.org • To get here, charter a songthaew for B100 one way, or B200 return; with your own transport, head west on Thanon Tanalai for 1.7km from Thanon Trairat, turn right at the traffic lights onto Thanon Hong Lee and follow the road for 2–3km until you see the entrance on the left-hand side

By far Chiang Rai's most compelling attraction is **Rai Mae Fah Luang**, a beautiful showcase of Lanna art and architecture, and its influences from Burma, Laos and China. In particular, the museum displays the consummate skills of local woodcarvers, with a focus on teak, which in Thailand is associated with concepts of dignity. It's set in lovely parkland, including a young teak garden that holds 43 varieties from northern Thailand.

The main reason for coming here is to see the **Haw Khum**, an amazing, multi-tiered barn of a building on massive stilts. It took five years to construct in the 1980s, in honour of the Princess Mother, Mae Fah Luang, using materials from 32 old houses in Chiang Rai province. Look out especially for the *ben grit* (fish scales) roof tiles, which inevitably are also made of teak. Lit by candles, the interior's dramatic centrepiece is a huge, slender, wooden prasat, representing the centre of the universe, Mount Meru, set in a sunken white sandpit – which not only symbolizes the Ocean of Milk, but also soaks up moisture to protect the teak. Dozens of very fine wooden artefacts surround the prasat, including a beautifully serene Burmese Buddha in a delicate, many-frilled robe that looks as if it's moving. Standouts among the displays in the nearby **Haw Kaew** – which is also made entirely of teak – are some ornate *oop*, or ceremonial alms bowls, and a bed headboard and footboard that sport scary carvings of Rahoo: the monster eating the moon connotes not only eclipses, but also a good night's sleep.

Wat Rong Khun

13km south of Chiang Rai on the west side of Highway 1 • Daily 8am–5.30pm • Catch a Phayao-bound bus from the old bus station

Wat Rong Khun almost defies description. Begun in 1997, it's the life's work of local contemporary artist, **Chalermchai Kositpipat** (see p.759), who has rediscovered Buddhism in a big way since spending time as a monk in 1992; he is also training dozens of "disciples", as he calls them, to finish the temple long after his death. Taking traditional Buddhist elements such as nagas and lotus flowers, and Lanna features such as long, slender *tung kradan* banners, Ajarn Chalermchai has enlarged and elaborated them, adding all sort of frills, layers and tiers. Surrounded by ponds, fountains and bridges, and done all in white (to stand for the Buddha's purity), inlaid with clear glass tiles (to represent his wisdom), the end result is like a frosted wedding cake. Inside the bot, which houses an eerily lifelike waxwork of the wat's former abbot, you can watch Chalermchai's disciples at work on the golden-toned murals, to the sound of loud, piped-in Thai pop music. In the adjacent Hall of Masterwork, some of the artist's original paintings are on display, while reproductions are on sale (to raise money for the project) in the souvenir shop, along with a useful B50 booklet on the temple in English, which explains the meaning of the complex design.

If you're a fan of Chalermchai's work, you'll want to check out his new **clocktower**, back in Chiang Rai at the junction of Banphaprakan and Jet Yot roads, which hosts a mini *son et lumière* for ten minutes every night at 7, 8 and 9pm.

ARRIVAL AND DEPARTURE | CHIANG RAI

By plane Thai Airways (☎ 053 798200) and Air Asia (☎ 02 515 9999) fly between Bangkok and Chiang Rai (3–5 daily; 1hr 15min), whose airport is 8km north of town – about a B300 taxi ride.

By bus Chiang Rai's new bus station is about 6km south of the centre on Highway 1. It handles inter-provincial routes (including a/c and some non-a/c services from/to Lampang), while the old bus station on Thanon Phaholyothin serves Chiang Rai province (Mae Sai, Chiang Saen, Chiang Khong), plus Nan and most non-a/c buses to Lampang; some services will stop at both, however, and the division of labour may change. Fares on shared shuttles between the two bus stations are low: B10 by songthaew, B20 by tuk-tuk.

Destinations Bangkok (22 daily; 11–12hr); Chiang Khong (every 20min; 2–3hr); Chiang Mai (every 30min; 3–4hr); Chiang Saen (every 20min; 1hr 30min); Khon Kaen (6 daily; 12hr 30min); Khorat (6 daily; 13hr); Lampang (every 30min; 4hr–5hr 30min); Mae Sai (every 20min; 1hr 30min); Mae Sot (2 daily; 10hr); Nakhon Phanom (3 daily; 19hr); Nan (1 daily; 6–7hr); Phitsanulok (1 daily; 7hr); Phrae (hourly; 4hr); Rayong (4 daily; 19hr); Sukhothai (4 daily; 7hr 30min); Udon Thani (3 daily; 13hr).

By boat Longtails from/to Tha Ton dock at the boat station, northwest of the centre on the north side of the Mae Fah Luang Bridge.

GETTING AROUND

By songthaew or tuk-tuk Shared blue songthaews, which have no set routes, cost B15 for short hops, while tuk-tuks start at around B50.

By bicycle Mountain bikes (B100/day) can be rented at *Tourist Inn*, while ordinary bicycles (B70/day, or B50 for guests) are available at *Mae Hong Son Guest House*.

By car or motorbike Car rental is available through North Wheels – who also have motorbikes with insurance – at 591 Thanon Phaholyothin, next to the tourist police office (☎ 053 740585, ⓦ northwheels.com), or through Avis at the airport (☎ 053 793827, ⓦ avisthailand.com). Motorbikes can also be rented at *Tourist Inn*.

INFORMATION AND MAPS

Tourist information TAT has a helpful office at 448/16 Thanon Singhaklai (daily 8.30am–4.30pm; ☎ 053 717433 or ☎ 053 744674–5, ✉ tatchrai@tat.or.th) with some useful free maps and brochures.

Chiang Rai Treasure Map Keep an eye out for the *Chiang Rai Treasure Map*, a free flyer published several times a year with loads of local information. You'll find it at the airport and around town in restaurants and hotels.

ACCOMMODATION

A wide choice of good **guesthouses** is within walking distance of central Chiang Rai, while several very appealing **hotels** hug the tranquil banks of the Kok River on the town's fringes.

Baan Bua Guest House 879/2 Thanon Jet Yot ☎ 053 718880. Congenial and well-run establishment arrayed around a surprisingly large, quiet and shady garden, set back off the road. The very clean and attractive concrete, single-storey rooms all come with hot showers. Free wi-fi. Fan B250, a/c B400

Baan Bua Homestay 1047/2 Thanon Jet Yot ☎ 053 717952, ⓦ baanbuahomestay.com. Despite being painted in lurid shades of pink and green, this wooden

house is hard to spot, as it's nestled in a quiet side street, tucked away behind *Tourist Inn*. The a/c rooms are quiet and fresh; some have private bathrooms outside the room while others are en suite. There's also a fan-cooled dorm (B180/bed) on the ground floor sleeping three people. B600

★ **Baan Rub Aroon Guest House** 65 Thanon Ngam Muang ☎ 053 711827, ⓦ baanrubaroon.net. In a pretty, quiet garden, this lovely early twentieth-century mansion

3

has polished teak floors, lots of houseplants and immaculate hotel-style rooms with a/c, wi-fi and clean white sheets. The downside is that rooms share hot-water bathrooms, but there's also a very well-equipped kitchen and a nice terrace for eating breakfast (included). There's also a six-bed dorm (B300/bed). **B550**

Chat House 3/2 Soi Sangkaew, Thanon Trairat ☎053 711481, ⓦchatguesthouse.com. Located behind its own garden café on a quiet soi, this is Chiang Rai's longest-running travellers' hangout, with a laidback, friendly atmosphere. The cheaper rooms (including a dorm and three singles for B100) are in an old, mostly wooden house with shared hot showers, while a concrete row of garden rooms have en-suite hot water, some with a/c. In the garden you can use the free wi-fi while tucking into tasty treats like home-made banana cake (B30). Fan **B180**, a/c **B350**

Dusit Island Resort Hotel 1129 Thanon Kaisornrasit ☎053 607999, ⓦdusit.com. Set on an expansive island in the Kok River offering unbeatable views of the valley, this is one of the swankiest places to stay in town, with high standards of service. The huge rooms are lavishly furnished, with fancy bathrooms, mini-bars and big TVs. Hotel facilities include a rooftop restaurant and bar, fitness centre, tennis courts and swimming pool. Good discounts online. **B2700**

Golden Triangle Inn 590 Thanon Phaholyothin ☎053 713918 or ☎053 740478. Large, comfortable, tastefully decorated rooms with a/c and hot water in a garden compound in the heart of town. **B500**

Imperial River House Resort 482 Moo 4, Thanon Mae Kok ☎053 750830–4, ⓦimperialriverhouse.com. Opposite *The Legend* on the north bank of the Kok, this four-storey boutique resort has elegantly designed and sumptuously furnished rooms with lovely wooden floors, all overlooking the large swimming pool and landscaped riverside gardens. Extremely relaxing location and excellent service. **B2700**

Jitaree Guest House 246/3 Soi Santirat Singhaklai ☎053 719348, ⓦjitaree.house.tripod.com. A more clinical atmosphere than *Mae Hong Son Guest House* next door, but for the same money you get newer, tiled rooms set around a large courtyard. **B200**

The Legend 124/15 Thanon Kohloy ☎053 910400, ⓦthelegend-chiangrai.com. Describing itself as a "boutique river resort", this place offers large luxury rooms

decorated in contemporary Lanna style with verandas and outdoor bathrooms. Hugging the south bank of the Kok, the compound also features a huge infinity pool and a top-class spa. **B3900**

★ **Le Meridien** South bank of the river, 1km east of the Highway 1 bridge ☎053 603333, ⓦlemeridien .com. Artfully built around an infinity-edge lake, which in turn is fed by a lovely infinity-edge swimming pool, this luxury hotel offers huge, balconied rooms in a crisp contemporary style, and attentive service. Overlooking the river are an attractive spa, a good Italian restaurant, a chill-out bar (with a bonfire in the cool season) and a boat landing for trips on the Kok. Free shuttles to town and Rai Mae Fah Luang. **B4400**

Mae Hong Son Guest House 126 Thanon Singhaklai, next door to Jitaree Guest House ☎053 715367, ⓦmaehongsonguesthouse.com. This family-run establishment in a quiet street comprises wooden buildings with very pleasant rooms (they have wall-mounted fans, but it can still be very warm), arranged around a shady courtyard with a neat bar and café. Hot showers throughout, whether shared (with cheap rates for singles) or en suite, and internet access. **B200**

Moon & Sun 632 Thanon Singhaklai ☎053 719279, ⓦmoonandsun-hotel.com. Good-value small hotel, with decent-sized a/c rooms with fridges and hot showers, plus attractive furnishings and fittings in cream and light brown; a B300 upgrade to a suite with a separate sitting room is tempting. Internet and wi-fi at reception. Breakfast included. **B500**

Tourist Inn 1004/4–6 Thanon Jet Yot ☎053 752094, ⓔtouristinn1@hotmail.com. Clean guesthouse in a modern four-storey building run by a Japanese–Thai team. The reception area downstairs has a European-style bakery, serving good breakfasts, while bright, light rooms come with hot-water bathrooms. There are cheaper, older rooms in attached buildings at the back, with shared or en-suite hot showers. There's a bookcase in the lobby, a shared fridge on the landing and free wi-fi in the main building. Fan **B150**, a/c **B350**

Wiang Inn 893 Thanon Phaholyothin ☎053 711533, ⓦwianginn.com. Set back off the main road, this 260-room hotel has a bright and spacious lobby, an attractive pool and comfortably furnished rooms equipped with all facilities and decorated with Thai murals. Breakfast included. **B1600**

EATING AND DRINKING

Chiang Rai's **restaurants**, including a growing number of Western places, congregate mostly along Phaholyothin road near the night bazaar. There's a huge **food centre** – with lots of delicious Thai snacks, as well as some more substantial dishes and Japanese food – at the night bazaar itself, where you can catch a free performance of transvestite cabaret, local folk-singers or traditional dancers. You need never go without a good **coffee** fix in Chiang Rai: the stuff grown on the nearby mountains of Doi Wawee, Doi Chaang and Doi Mae Salong is served up at several cafés around the main Rattanakhet–Phaholyothin junction.

Aye's 479 Thanon Phaholyothin ☎053 752534. A spacious, popular restaurant with a relaxing atmosphere and a wide menu of international and Thai dishes – try the *kaeng hang lay* (B225), a delicious, northern pork and ginger curry. Has wi-fi. Mon–Sat 8am–11pm.

Baan Chivit Mai 172 Thanon Prasobsuk, opposite the old bus station ☎053 712357. Scandinavian bakery run by a Swedish charity that helps children in Chiang Rai and Bangkok slums (see ⓦ baanchivitmai.com). Very clean, a/c café with internet access serving excellent sandwiches, cakes and coffees, plus pastas and simple Thai dishes. Mon–Sat 8am–9pm.

Cabbages and Condoms At the Hill Tribe Museum (see p.360). Proudly proclaiming "our food is guaranteed not to cause pregnancy", this restaurant covers its walls with paraphernalia devoted to family planning and HIV/AIDS prevention. The Thai food, including some traditional northern dishes and a few dishes suitable for vegetarians, is a bit hit-and-miss but it's for a good cause. Live band every night. Daily 11am–10pm.

Kaffee Hub Near the clock tower on Thanon Banphaprakan ☎089 544 4599, ⓦ kaffeehub.com. Stylish, three-storey café-bar catering to young Thais and the odd tourist lured in by the smell of freshly brewed coffee. There's a good selection of teas and Thai mains, plus wine (expensive at around B700 a bottle). Daily 8am–midnight.

Muang Thong 889/1–2 Thanon Phaholyothin, just south of the Wiang Inn Hotel. This no-frills and inexpensive place does a wide range of Thai and Chinese dishes and displays a huge selection of ingredients outside its open-sided eating area. Popular with Thais and foreigners alike. Daily 24hr.

★ **Salungkham** 834/3 Thanon Phaholyothin, between King Mengrai's statue and the river ☎053 717192, ⓦ salungkham.com. Justifiably rated by locals as serving the best Thai food in town (main dishes from B80), with a garden for evening dining; try the superb banana-flower salad with fresh prawns. There's no sign in English, but look out for the Cosmo petrol station on the opposite side of the road. Daily 10.30am–10pm.

SHOPPING

Night bazaar Off Thanon Phaholyothin next to the old bus station. Sells cheap DVDs and all sorts of handicrafts, some of good quality and competitively priced – though it's usually crowded with tour groups. Daily 4pm–midnight.

Walking street Thanon Tanalai, around the junction with Wisetwiang. Chiang Rai's "walking street", similar to those in Chiang Mai, comes alive with musicians and all

manner of stalls, including lots of food and local crafts and products such as coffee and macadamias. Sat late afternoon to around 10.30pm.

Wet market Thanon Wisetwiang. During the afternoons an excellent wet market sets up along Thanon Wisetwiang, selling flowers, fruits and vegetables. Daily around 1–4pm.

DIRECTORY

ATMs and exchange ATMs and exchange booths are concentrated around the old bus station.

Cookery classes *Chat House* runs one-day cookery classes including transfers from your accommodation and a trip to the local market (B950/person).

Internet access You can access the internet over coffee and snacks at *Connect Café* on Thanon Prasobsuk, just south

of the bus station (Mon–Fri 9am–9pm; Sat & Sun 8am–9pm).

Massage Tevari Spa & Beauty Salon at 869/21–22 Thanon Phaholyothin (☎053 717814; ⓦ chiangrai-spa.com) offers a huge menu of massage treatments from B400/30min.

Tourist police The tourist police (☎1155) are on Thanon Phaholyothin, next to the *Golden Triangle Inn*.

North of Chiang Rai

The northernmost tip of Thailand, stretching from the Kok River and Chiang Rai to the border, is split in two by Highway 1, Thailand's main north–south road. In the western half, rows of wild, shark's-tooth mountains jut into Burma, while to the east, low-lying rivers flow through Thailand's richest rice-farming land to the Mekong River, which forms the border with Laos here.

At a push, any one of the places described in this section could be visited in a day from Chiang Rai, while hardly anyone visits **Mae Sai** on the Burmese border except on a visa-run day-trip. If you can devote two or three days, however, you'd be better off moving camp to **Mae Salong**, a mountain-top Chinese enclave, or **Chiang Saen**, whose atmospheric ruins by the banks of the Mekong contrast sharply with the ugly commercialism of nearby **Sop Ruak**. Given more time and patience, you could also stop over at the palace, temple and arboretum of **Doi Tung** to look down over Thailand, Laos and Burma, and continue beyond Chiang Saen to **Chiang Khong** on the banks of the Mekong, which is now a popular crossing point to Laos.

For hopping around the main towns here by **public transport**, the setup is straightforward enough: frequent buses to Mae Sai run due north up Highway 1; to Chiang Saen, they start off on the same road before forking right onto Highway 1016; for most other places, you have to make one change off these routes onto a songthaew.

Hill Tribe Culture Centre and Ban Therd Thai

Route 1130, a dizzying rollercoaster of a road, ploughs its way westwards up to Mae Salong for 36km from **Ban Pasang**, 32km north of Chiang Rai on Highway 1. If you have your own transport, a few marginally interesting attractions might tempt you to stop en route, notably the **Hill Tribe Culture Centre**, 12km from Ban Pasang, where there's a handicrafts shop, and a couple of Mien and Akha souvenir villages. At Sam Yaek, 24km from Ban Pasang, a paved side-road heads north for 13km to **Ban Therd Thai**. In its former incarnation as Ban Hin Taek, this mixed village was the opium capital of the notorious Khun Sa (see box opposite): the Thai army drove Khun Sa out after a pitched battle in 1983, and the village has now been renamed and "pacified" with the establishment of a market, school and hospital.

Mae Salong (Santikhiri)

Perched 1300m up on a ridge, commanding fine views of sawtoothed hills, stands the Chinese Nationalist outpost of **MAE SALONG** – the focal point for the area's fourteen thousand **Kuomintang**, who for two generations now have held fast to their cultural identity, if not their political cause. Though it has temples, a church and a mosque, it's the details of Chinese life in the backstreets – the low-slung bamboo houses, the pictures of Chiang Kai-shek, ping-pong tables, the sounds of Yunnanese conversation – that make the village absorbing.

Mae Salong straggles for several kilometres along a roughly east–west road, with a central junction near the morning market and the steps for the Princess Mother Pagoda. It gets plenty of Thai visitors, especially at weekends, when they throng the main street's souvenir shops to buy such delicacies as sorghum whisky (pickled with ginseng, deer antler and centipedes) and locally grown Chinese tea, coffee, mushrooms and herbs. Free cups of tea are offered nearly everywhere, and it's possible to visit, for example, **Mae Salong Villa**'s own estate and factory – ask at the resort for directions and tea-processing times. It might also be worth braving the dawn chill to get to the **morning market**, held in the middle of town near *Shin Sane Guest House* from around 5am to 7am, which pulls shoppers in from the surrounding Akha, Lisu and Mien villages.

Brief history

The ruling party of China for 21 years, the **Kuomintang** (Nationalists) were swept from power by the Communist revolution of 1949 and fled in two directions: one group, under party leader Chiang Kai-shek, made for Taiwan, where it founded the Republic of China; the other, led by General Li Zongren, settled in northern Thailand and Burma. The Nationalists' original plan to retake China from Mao Zedong in a two-pronged attack never came to fruition, and the remnants of the army in Thailand became major players in the **heroin trade** and, with the backing of the Thai government, minor protagonists in the war against Communism.

In the 1980s, the Thai government began to work hard to "pacify" the Kuomintang by a mixture of force and more peaceful methods, such as **crop programmes** to replace opium. Around Mae Salong at least, its work seems to have been successful, as evidenced by the slopes to the south of the settlement, which are covered with a carpet

DRUGS AND THE GOLDEN TRIANGLE

Opium will always be associated with the Far East in the popular imagination, but the opium poppy actually originated in the Mediterranean. It arrived in the East, however, over twelve centuries ago, and was later brought to Thailand from China with the hill tribes who migrated from Yunnan province. Opium growing was made illegal in Thailand in 1959, but during the 1960s and 1970s rampant production and refining of the crop in the lawless region on the borders of Thailand, Burma and Laos earned the area the nickname **the Golden Triangle**. Two main "armies" operated most of the trade within this area. The ten-thousand-strong **Shan United Army** (SUA), set up to fight the Burmese government for an independent state for the Shan (Thai Yai) people, funded itself from the production of heroin (a more refined form of opium). Led by the notorious warlord Khun Sa, the SUA attempted to extend their influence inside Thailand during the 1960s, where they came up against the troops of the **Kuomintang** (KMT). These refugees from China, who fled after the Communist takeover there, were at first befriended by the Thai and Western governments, who were pleased to have a fiercely anti-Communist force patrolling this border area. The Kuomintang were thus able to develop the heroin trade, while the authorities turned a blind eye.

By the 1980s, the danger of Communist incursion into Thailand had largely disappeared, and the government was able to concentrate on the elimination of the crop, putting the Kuomintang in the area around Mae Salong on a determined "**pacification**" programme. In 1983 the Shan United Army was pushed out of its stronghold at nearby Ban Hin Taek (now Ban Therd Thai), over the border into Burma, and in 1996, Khun Sa cut a deal with the corrupt Burmese military dictatorship. The man once dubbed the "Prince of Death", who had a US$2 million bounty on his head from the United States, was able to live under Burmese army protection in a comfortable villa in Rangoon until his death in 2007.

The Thai government has succeeded in reducing the size of the opium crop within its borders to an insignificant amount, but Thailand still has a vital role to play as a conduit for heroin; most of the production and refinement of opium has simply moved over the borders into Burma and Laos. And in the last few years, opium growing within northern Thailand, although still at a very low level, has apparently started to increase again, based on small patches in remote mountains and using a high-yield, weather-resistant breed supplied by the Burmese drug barons.

The destruction of huge areas of poppy fields has had far-reaching repercussions on the **hill tribes**. In many cases, with the raw product not available, opium addicts have turned to injecting heroin from shared needles, leading to a devastating outbreak of AIDS. The Thai government has sought to give the hill tribes an alternative livelihood through the introduction of legitimate cash crops, yet these often demand the heavy use of pesticides, which later get washed down into the lowland valleys, incurring the wrath of Thai farmers.

The dangers of the heroin trade have in recent years been eclipsed by the flood of **methamphetamines** – either *yaa baa* (literally "crazy medicine") or Ice (crystal meth) – that is infiltrating all areas of Thai society, but most worryingly the schools. Produced in vast quantities in factories just across the Burmese border, mostly by former insurgents, the United Wa State Army, *yaa baa* and Ice are the main objective of vehicle searches in border areas, with perhaps a billion tablets smuggled into Thailand each year. It's estimated that three million Thais are methamphetamine users, prompting the Thaksin government into a fierce crackdown in the first half of 2003 which, much to the consternation of human rights watchers, led to two thousand extra-judicial deaths and 51,000 arrests. Things have quietened down since then, but the frequent busts of methamphetamine dealers show that the problem has not gone away.

of rich green tea bushes. Since its rehabilitation, Mae Salong is now officially known as **Santikhiri** (Hill of Peace).

The Princess Mother Pagoda

Towering above the village on top of a hill, the **Princess Mother Pagoda**, a huge, gilt-topped chedi, is so distinctive that it has quickly become Mae Salong's proud symbol. It's a long and steep climb up 718 steps from near the morning market to get

---

HORSE TREKS AND HIKES FROM MAE SALONG

The Kuomintang live up to their Thai nickname – *jiin haw*, meaning "galloping Chinese" – by offering **treks on horses**, a rare sight in Thailand. Trips to Akha, Lahu and other Chinese villages can be arranged at the *Shin Sane Guest House* from B500 for four hours, but it's worth meeting your guide and checking out the itinerary and the horses before you hand over any money.

Armed with a sketch map from one of the guesthouses, it would be possible to **walk** to some of the same villages yourself – or better still, hire a **guide** from *Little Home Guest House* for B200 per day.

---

there, but with a rented vehicle you can follow the road to the western end of the village and branch right opposite the evening market on a road that carries you heavenward, revealing some breathtaking views on the way.

Chinese Martyrs Memorial Museum

At the western edge of the village • Daily 8am–5pm • B30

The **Chinese Martyrs Memorial Museum** recounts the origins of the Kuomintang in Thailand, giving details of battles such as the famous one fought against Thai and Lao Communists and Hmong at Phu Chi Fa near Chiang Khong, and depicting the Kuomintang as heroic protectors of the Kingdom of Thailand. The huge building encompasses a shrine to the KMT martyrs who fell in the fighting.

ARRIVAL AND DEPARTURE
MAE SALONG

When it's time to leave Mae Salong, you'll find local songthaews for Tha Ton and Ban Pasang by the 7-Eleven, just east of the central junction.

From/to Chiang Rai Buses (every 20min; 45min) leave Chiang Rai's old bus station for Pasang, 32km to the north on Highway 1. You'll then need to change to a blue songthaew for the 1hr 30min chug up to Mae Salong, so leave early for the best chance of making the connection.
From/to Tha Thon There are four direct yellow songthaews a day between Tha Ton and Mae Salong, via the interesting Akha village of Ban Lorcha (see p.356). Alternatively, accommodation in Tha Ton can arrange private transport to take you directly to Mae Salong, a far quicker option. *Mae Kok River Village Resort,* for example, offers one-way trips by private songthaew (B600) or a/c minibus (B1500).

GETTING AROUND

By motorbike *Shin Sane Guest House* rents out motorbikes for B200/day.

ACCOMMODATION

You'll appreciate Mae Salong best if you spend the night here, after the day-trippers have left. Fortunately, there's a wide range of **accommodation**, including half a dozen budget guesthouses clustered around the central junction. Rates are significantly lower out of season, when the village feels wonderfully peaceful.

★ **Little Home Guest House** Central junction ☏ 053 765389, ⓦ maesalonglittlehome.com. This friendly hillside spot gives you the option of rooms in the main wooden house (with a touch of style and shared hot showers), or smart bungalows in a pretty garden, with nice views from their verandas and hot-water en-suite bathrooms. The staff bend over backwards to help guests and make them feel at home. Detailed local maps available, free Chinese tea and free wi-fi. Rooms **B300**, bungalows **B800**
Mae Salong Villa On the main road towards the eastern end of the village ☏ 053 765114–9, ⓦ maesalong-villa.com. Choose between large, comfortable rooms in a two-storey block and Chinese-style bungalows with fridges and better views from their picture windows, all with hot showers. In a pretty, sloping garden facing the Princess Mother Pagoda and Burmese mountains. Rates negotiable for longer stays. Rooms **B800**, bungalows **B2000**
Saeng Aroon Central junction, across from Little Home Guesthouse ☏ 053 765029. Large, bright rooms with tiled floors and hot showers, run by a sweet old couple who have a tea shop below. Wi-fi available. **B500**

Shin Sane Guest House Central junction ☎053 765026, ⓦmaesalong-shinsane.blogspot.com. Friendly place with plenty of local information, offering small bedrooms with shared hot-water bathrooms in a funky wooden building and well-kept bungalows (with hot showers) in the garden behind. Free use of washing machine, and in-room massage for B120/hr. Particularly good rates for singles. Doubles **B200**, bungalows **B300**

EATING AND DRINKING

The choice of restaurants in Mae Salong is narrower than its hotel selection, but there are some excellent places to sample Yunnanese dishes.

Little Home At Little Home Guest House ☎053 765389, ⓦmaesalonglittlehome.com. Set on a balcony, the popular Yunnanese restaurant here serves a good range of hot and spicy dishes, plus a tasty pork leg stew. Daily 7–10am & 5–10pm.

Mae Salong Villa On the main road towards the eastern end of the village ☎053 765114–9. Has great views and cooks up some of the best food in town, including delicious but expensive Chinese specialities like roast pork, *het hawm* (wild mushrooms) and *kai dam* (black chicken), which is usually served in soup with Chinese herbs (B200–250). Open for breakfast, lunch and dinner.
★ **Sweet Mae Salong** 41/3 Moo 1, between the central junction and Mae Salong Villa ☎083 096 7777. This place hits the spot with delicious, home-baked banana cake, excellent espresso, mellow sounds, internet access and lovely views from the rear terraces; they'll also rustle up a green curry with *roti*, if you're more peckish. Daily 8am–8pm.

DIRECTORY

ATM There's an ATM towards the west end of town, on the way out towards Tha Ton.

Internet access All the guesthouses provide internet access.

Doi Tung

Steep, wooded hills rise abruptly from the plains west of Highway 1 as it approaches the Burmese border. Crowned both by a thousand-year-old wat and by the country retreat of the Princess Mother (the present king's late mother), the central peak here, 1322m **DOI TUNG**, makes a worthwhile outing just for the journey. A broad, new road, Route 1149, runs up the mountainside, beginning 43km north of Chiang Rai on Highway 1, just before the centre of **Ban Huai Khrai**.

Cottage Industry Centre and Outlet

Around 1km from Ban Huai Khrai • Daily 7am–6pm

The old road to the mountain from the centre of Ban Huai Khrai passes after 1km or so the **Cottage Industry Centre and Outlet**, set up by the Princess Mother, where you can watch crafts such as paper-making from the bark of the *sa* (mulberry) tree in progress and buy the finished products in the on-site shop (daily 8am–5pm).

The Royal Villa and Mae Fah Luang Garden

12km up the main summit road, then left up a side road • Daily 7am–5/6pm; villa closed if royals in residence • Villa B90; Hall of Inspiration B50; garden B90; all three (plus access to the arboretum; see p.368) B220

The largely Swiss-style **Royal Villa** on Doi Tung was built for the Princess Mother (the mother of the present king, she was never queen herself, but was affectionately known as *Mae Fah Luang*, literally "royal sky mother"). She took up residence here on several occasions before her death in 1995, often staying for months at a time to work on development projects in the area.

Detailed English-language leaflets are available to help visitors guide themselves around. In the Grand Reception Hall, which also features some beautiful floral wall panels made of embroidered silk, the positions of the planets and stars at the time of the Princess Mother's birth in 1900 have been carved into the ceiling. You can also visit her living room, bedroom and study, all left as when she lived here.

The Hall of Inspiration and the gardens

On the access road to the Royal Villa, a few hundred metres back down the hill, the **Hall of Inspiration** contains hagiographical displays on the Princess Mother and her family and is strictly for royal watchers. Next door, the immaculate ornamental **Mae Fah Luang Garden** throngs with snap-happy day-trippers at weekends. The Princess Mother's hill-tribe project has helped to develop local villages by introducing new agricultural methods: the slopes which were formerly blackened by the fires of slash-and-burn farming and sown with opium poppies are now used to grow teak and pine, and crops such as strawberries, macadamia nuts and coffee, which, along with pottery, *sa* paper, rugs and clothes, are sold in the shops and stalls near the entrance to the gardens. There's also an information booth that has simple maps of the mountain here.

Wat Phra That Doi Tung

Beyond the turn-off for the Royal Villa, a paved road heads northeast, climbing over a precarious saddle with some minor temple buildings and passing through a tuft of thick woods, before reaching **Wat Phra That Doi Tung** on top of the mountain. Pilgrims to the wat earn themselves good fortune by clanging the rows of dissonant bells around the temple compound and by throwing coins into a well, which are collected for temple funds. For non-Buddhist travellers, the reward for getting this far is the stunning view out over the cultivated slopes and half of northern Thailand. The wat's most important structures are its twin **chedis**, erected to enshrine relics of the Buddha's collarbone in 911. When the building of the chedis was complete, King Achutaraj of Ngon Yang ordered a giant flag (*tung*), reputedly 2km long, to be flown from the peak, which gave the mountain its name.

Doi Chang Moob Arboretum

Daily 8am–5pm • B50

A very steep, sometimes rough, paved **back road** runs right along the border with Burma to Mae Sai (22km), via two army checkpoints and the Akha village of Ban Pha Mee, beginning near the saddle beneath the peak of Doi Tung. After about 4km of asphalt, you reach the delightful **arboretum** at the pinnacle of **Doi Chang Moob** (1509m), a landscaped garden planted with rhododendrons, azaleas, orchids and ferns and furnished with fantastic terrace viewpoints looking east to Chiang Saen, the Mekong and the hills of Laos beyond, and west to the mountains around Mae Salong. For the most awesome view, however, continue a short way up the Mae Sai road to the Thai military checkpoint, to gaze at the opposing Burmese camp and seemingly endless layers of Burmese mountain stacked up to the north.

ARRIVAL AND DEPARTURE   DOI TUNG

The easiest and most reliable way to visit Doi Tung is with your own vehicle or on a tour from Chiang Rai.

By bus and songthaew Any bus between Chiang Rai and Mae Sai can put you off in Ban Huai Khrai, and you'll then find infrequent lilac songthaews (B70) just west of the junction of highways 1 and 1149 ferrying villagers up the mountain.

ACCOMMODATION AND EATING

There's a Doi Tung coffee shop, an excellent restaurant and a self-service café on the access road to the Royal Villa, in the complex of shops near Mae Fah Luang Garden.

Doi Tung Lodge In the woods below the Royal Villa ☎ 053 767015–7, ⊛ doitung.org. The spacious, simply furnished rooms at this upmarket tourist lodge are rather institutional and overpriced, but all come with a/c, hot water, balcony, TV and fridge. **B2500**

Mae Sai

With its bustling border crossing into Burma and kilometres of tacky souvenir stalls, **MAE SAI** can be an interesting place to watch the world go by, though most foreigners only come here on a quick visa run. Thailand's most northerly town lies 61km from Chiang Rai at the dead end of Highway 1, which forms the town's single north–south street. Wide enough for an armoured battalion, this ugly boulevard still has the same name – **Thanon Phaholyothin** – as at the start of its journey north in the suburbs of Bangkok. The road ends at the Mae Sai River, which here serves as the Thailand–Burma border.

For a lofty perspective on the comings and goings, climb up through the market stalls to the chedi of **Wat Phra That Doi Wao**, five minutes' walk from the bridge on the west side of Phaholyothin, behind the *Top North Hotel*. As well as Doi Tung to the south and the hills of Laos in the east, you get a good view up the steep-sided valley and across the river to Thachileik.

ARRIVAL AND DEPARTURE

MAE SAI

By bus From Chiang Rai, frequent green buses to Mae Sai run due north up Highway 1. They stop 4km short of the frontier at the bus station, from where red songthaews shuttle into town. Returning to the bus station, you should be able to flag down a songthaew.

Destinations Bangkok (13 daily; 13hr); Chiang Mai (6 daily; 4–5hr); Chiang Rai (every 20min; 1hr 30min); Fang (1 daily; 2hr 30min); Khorat (6 daily; 14hr); Lampang (3 daily; 5hr); Mae Sot (2 daily; 12hr); Phitsanulok (1 daily; 10hr); Sukhothai (1 daily; 8hr); Tha Ton (1 daily; 1hr 40min).

GETTING AROUND

By motorbike Motorbikes can be rented from Pornchai, a few doors south of *Piyaporn Place* (see "Accommodation", below) on the west side of Thanon Phaholyothin, for B150/day.

ACCOMMODATION AND EATING

A handful of **guesthouses** are strung out along the river bank west of the bridge.

Mae Sai Guest House A 15min walk west of the bridge on the river bank ☎053 732021, ✉neng_xfour@hotmail.com. A relaxing place to stay, with a pretty lawn, small, well-maintained rooms sharing hot showers and cute A-frame log cabins with riverside verandas and hot water en suite. Rooms B200, bungalows B500

Piyaporn Place On the west side of the main road about 500m south of the bridge ☎053 734511–3. Mae Sai's best hotel is this seven-storey block, with well-equipped rooms in a smart, contemporary style, plus a/c, hot-water bathtubs and fridges. Breakfast included. B1000

Rim Nam (Riverside) Right under the western side of the bridge, down a slip road to the left of the border checkpoint. A popular, reasonably priced restaurant with a riverside terrace, which gets crowded during the day with tourists watching the border action and serves cheap one-dish meals as well as its speciality, Burmese crab with curry powder. Daily for breakfast, lunch and dinner.

Yeesun West of the bridge along the river bank at 816/13 Thanon Sailomjai ☎053 733455. This is a good mid-range option, with neat, carpeted rooms with a/c, hot water and fridge. B600

DIRECTORY

Banks and ATMs There's a branch of the Thanachart Bank, with an ATM, on Thanon Phahonyothin, south of the border checkpoint.

Internet access For internet access, head to Empower,

CROSSING THE BURMESE BORDER TO THACHILEIK

Thanon Phaholyothin ends at a short pedestrianized **bridge** over the Mae Sai River, which forms the border with Burma. Here, during daylight hours, you can have the dubious pleasure of crossing over to **Thachileik**, the Burmese town opposite, for yet more tacky shopping. You'll first be stamped out by **Thai immigration** at the entrance to the bridge, then on the other side of the bridge, you pay US$10, or an exorbitant B500, to Burmese immigration for a one-day stay. Coming back across the bridge, you'll be given a new fifteen-day entry stamp – unless you have a multiple-entry visa or re-entry permit – by Thai immigration.

a charity that helps Thai sex workers (W empower foundation.org), about 150m west of the bridge on the riverside road, Thanon Sailomjai.

Tourist police There's a tourist police booth (1155) by the frontier bridge.

Sop Ruak

The "**Golden Triangle**", a term coined to denote a huge opium-producing area spreading across Burma, Laos and Thailand (see p.365), has, for the benefit of tourists, been artificially concentrated into the precise spot where the borders meet, 70km northeast of Chiang Rai. Don't come to the village of **SOP RUAK**, at the confluence of the Ruak (Mae Sai) and Mekong rivers, expecting to come across sinister drug-runners or poppy fields – instead you'll find souvenir stalls, pay-toilets, a huge, supremely tacky golden Buddha shrine, two opium museums and lots of signs saying "Golden Triangle" which pop up in a million photo albums around the world.

Hall of Opium

At the Mae Sai end of the village • Tues–Sun 8.30am–5.30pm, last ticket sale 4pm • B200 • W maefahluang.org

Under the auspices of the Mae Fah Luang Foundation based at Doi Tung (see p.367), the ambitious **Hall of Opium** took B400 million and nine years to research and build, with technical assistance from the People's Republic of China. It provides a well-presented, largely balanced picture, in Thai and English, of the use and abuse of opium, and its history over five thousand years, including its spread from Europe to Asia and focusing on the nineteenth-century **Opium Wars** between Britain and China. Dioramas, games and audiovisuals are put to imaginative use, notably in a reconstruction of a nineteenth-century Siamese opium den, playing the interactive "Find the Hidden Drugs", and, most movingly, watching the personal testimonies of former addicts and their families.

House of Opium

Towards the north of the village, near Wat Phra That Phu Khao • Daily 7am–8pm • B50 • W houseofopium.com

The **House of Opium** is smaller and cheaper than the similarly named Hall of Opium, which it imitates, and it tends more to glorify opium use. All the paraphernalia of opium growing and smoking is housed in several display cases, including beautifully carved teak storage boxes, weights cast from bronze and brass in animal shapes and opium pipes.

The meeting of the waters

At Sop Ruak you can witness the confluence of the Ruak (Mae Sai) and Mekong rivers – a monumental sight, poetically referred to as "**the meeting of the waters**" – but to get an unobstructed view of it you'll need to climb up to **Wat Phra That Phu Khao**, a 1200-year-old temple perched on a small hill above the village. To the north, beyond the puny Ruak River, you'll see the mountains of Burma marching off into infinity, while eastwards across the mighty Mekong are the hills and villages of Laos. This pastoral scene has now been marred, however, by the appearance of a Thai luxury hotel, which is actually over on an uninhabited strip of Burmese land immediately upstream of the confluence. The attached casino bypasses Thai laws against gambling, and the usually strict border formalities are waived for visitors coming from Thailand.

A QUICK TRIP TO LAOS

Sop Ruak puts you tantalizingly close to Laos and, even if you don't have time to spend exploring the country properly, you can still have the thrill of stepping on Lao soil. A **longtail boat** from next to *Sriwan Restaurant*, for example, will give you a kiss-me-quick tour of the "Golden Triangle" (B400), including a stop at a souvenir market on the Lao island of Done Xao (B20 admission).

ARRIVAL AND DEPARTURE	**SOP RUAK**

By songthaew from Mae Sai Frequent blue songthaews make the 45min trip to Sop Ruak's main river road from the Kasikorn Bank on the east side of Thanon Phaholyothin, about 300m south of the bridge in Mae Sai (they leave when they're full).

By songthaew or bicycle from Chiang Saen You can take a regular blue songthaew from (and back to) Thanon Rim Khong in Chiang Saen (roughly every 20min; 15min) or rent a bike and cycle there (it's an easy 10km ride on a paved road, though not much of it runs along the river bank).

ACCOMMODATION

There's nowhere decent to stay in Sop Ruak for budget travellers, but for those willing to splurge, there are some excellent options.

Anantara Entrance off the main road, at the Mae Sai end of the village ✆053 784084, ⍵goldentriangle .anantara.com. Tastefully designed in a blend of traditional and contemporary styles and set in extensive grounds, this palatial luxury hotel is one of the finest in northern Thailand. The balconies of all its rooms and its swimming pool offer breathtaking views over the countryside to the Mekong, Burma and Laos. Among many amenities available to guests are a spectacular spa, a northern-Thai cookery school, yoga classes and a well-run elephant camp that rescues street elephants (⍵helpingelephants.org). Rates include round-trip transfers from Chiang Rai airport, full-board meals and a range of activities. B38,000

Greater Mekong Lodge In the Golden Triangle Park,

next to the Hall of Opium ✆053 784450. Decent-value if slightly institutional rooms, all with a balcony, fridge, hot water and a/c. You can choose between rooms in the main hotel building or stilted chalets (where the views are better). Includes breakfast. B1200

Serene at Chiang Rai About 500m south of the House of Opium, on the riverside ✆053 784500, ⍵sereneatchiangrai.com. With good service, a handy location and an elegant poolside terrace right by the river, this place merits the high prices. The a/c rooms are big, clean and contemporary, and the attached bathrooms impress with freestanding tubs. There's a café on site serving breakfasts, lunches and dinners, and guests can use bikes free of charge. B4000

EATING

As well as the places listed below, there's a row of ramshackle **restaurants** by the waterfront, serving up basic Thai food and some decent fruit shakes.

Baan Dahlia At the Anantara ✆053 784084, ⍵goldentriangle.anantara.com. This magnificent but pricey Italian restaurant has a menu that includes decadent delights like spaghetti served in a wheel of parmesan, and tiger prawns with pine nuts and pesto. The wine list is excellent. Daily, evenings only.

Sriwan In front of the Imperial Golden Triangle Hotel, along the main river road. The best of the riverfront restaurants, *Sriwan* specializes in *tom yam pla buk* (giant catfish), but also offers cheaper dishes such as chicken fried rice (B40), as well as great views of the Mekong. Daily for lunch and dinner.

Chiang Saen

Combining dozens of tumbledown temple ruins with sweeping Mekong River scenery, **CHIANG SAEN**, 60km northeast of Chiang Rai, is a rustic haven and a good base camp for the border region east of Mae Sai. The town's focal point, where the Chiang Rai road (Thanon Phaholyothin) meets Thanon Rim Khong (the main road along the banks of the Mekong), is a lively junction thronged by buses, songthaews and longtails. Turning left at this T-junction soon brings you to Sop Ruak, and you may well share the road with the tour buses that sporadically thunder through (though most of them miss out the town itself by taking its western bypass). Very few tourists turn right in Chiang Saen, passing the port for cargo boats from Laos and China, along the road to Chiang Khong, even though this is the best way to appreciate the slow charms of the Mekong valley.

The layout of the old, ruined city is defined by the Mekong River running along its east flank; a tall rectangle, 2.5km from north to south, is formed by the addition of the ancient ramparts, now fetchingly overgrown, on the other three sides. The grid of leafy streets inside the ramparts is now too big for the modern town, which is generously scattered along the river road and across the middle on Thanon Phaholyothin.

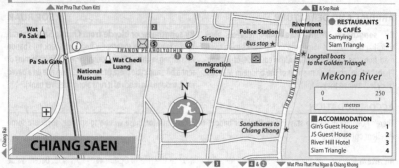

Brief history

Originally known as Yonok, the region around Chiang Saen seems to have been an important Thai trading crossroads from some time after the seventh century. The city of Chiang Saen itself was founded around 1328 by the successor to the renowned King Mengrai of Chiang Mai, Saen Phu, who gave up his throne to retire here. Coveted for its strategic location guarding the Mekong, Chiang Saen had multiple allegiances, paying tribute to Chiang Mai, Kengtung in Burma and Luang Prabang in Laos, until Rama I razed the place in 1804. The present village was established only in 1881, when Rama V ordered a northern prince to resettle the site with descendants of the old townspeople mustered from Lamphun, Chiang Mai and Lampang.

National Museum

Thanon Phaholyothin, just inside the old city walls • Wed–Sun 8.30am–4.30pm • B100 • ⓦ thailandmuseum.com

The **National Museum** makes an informative starting point for a visit, housing some impressive architectural features rescued from the surrounding ruins, with good labelling in English, as well as a plethora of Buddha images – the two typical northern Thai styles of Buddha are sometimes referred to jointly as the "Chiang Saen style", though most academics instead use the more helpful term "Lanna style" (see p.285). As in many of Thailand's museums, the back end is given over to exhibits on folk culture, one of many highlights being the beautiful wooden lintel carved with *hum yon* (floral swirls representing testicles), which would have been placed above the front door of a house to ward off evil and for ventilation.

Wat Phra That Chedi Luang

Thanon Phaholyothin, next door to the museum

Wat Phra That Chedi Luang, originally the city's main temple, is worth looking in on for its imposing octagonal chedi, said to house a relic of the Buddha's breastbone and now decorated with weeds and a huge yellow ribbon, while handicraft stalls in the grounds sell Thai Lue cloths among their wares. In March 2011, a 6.8-magnitude earthquake rocked Burma, and the aftershocks (felt strongly in Chiang Saen) caused the top of the spire to break off. Other buildings around the chedi, including Wat Pa Sak (see below), also suffered damage.

Wat Pa Sak

Beyond the ramparts to the west • Daily 8.30am–4.30pm • B30

Wat Pa Sak's brick buildings and laterite columns have been excavated and restored by the Fine Arts Department, making it the most accessible and impressive of Chiang Saen's many temples. The wat's name is an allusion to the hundreds of teak trees that Saen Phu planted in the grounds when he built the chedi in 1340 to house relics of the Buddha's right ankle from India. The chedi's square base is inset with niches housing alternating Buddhas and *deva* (angels) with flowing skirts, and above rises the tower for the Buddha relic, topped by a circular spire. Beautiful carved stucco covers much of the structure, showing intricate floral scrolls and stylized lotus patterns as well as a whole zoo of mythical beasts.

Wat Phra That Chom Kitti

Outside the northwest corner of the ramparts • Daily 8.30am–5pm

The open space around modern Chiang Saen, which is dotted with trees and another 140 overgrown ruins (both inside and outside the ramparts), is great for a carefree wander. A spot worth aiming for is the gold-topped, crooked chedi of **Wat Phra That Chom Kitti**, which gives a good view of the town and the river from a small hill outside the ramparts.

Wat Phra That Pha Ngao

3km southeast along the river road – look out for the tall brick gate on the right

Wat Phra That Pha Ngao, well worth the short detour from the centre, is thought to have been built originally in the sixth century. The temple contains a supposedly miraculous chedi perched on top of a large boulder, but the real attraction is the **new chedi** on the hillside above: take the 1km track which starts at the back of the temple and you can't miss the gleaming, white-tiled Phra Borom That Nimit, designed by an American, with attractive modern murals and built over and around a ruined brick chedi. From here, though you have to peer through the trees, the views take in Chiang Saen, the wide plain and the slow curve of the river. To the east, the Kok River, which looks so impressive at Chiang Rai, seems like a stream as it pours into the mighty Mekong. On the way down from the chedi, have a look at the new Lao-style bot, which was inaugurated by Princess Sirindhorn in 1999 and is covered from tip to toe in beautiful woodcarving.

3

ARRIVAL AND DEPARTURE   CHIANG SAEN

By bus or songthaew Buses from Chiang Rai (every 20min; 1hr 30min) and regular blue songthaews from Sop Ruak (15min) and Mae Sai (1hr) stop by the market on Thanon Phaholyothin, while green songthaews from Chiang Khong (2hr; usually involving a change at Ban Hat Bai) stop on the river road to the south of the T-junction; motorized samlors wait to ferry people around town.

GETTING AROUND

By longtail boat Longtail boats congregate around the riverside near the central T-junction, offering local tours of the "Golden Triangle" lasting a couple of hours (B500/boat one way, B600 return), including the Lao souvenir market on Done Xao island (B20 admission), and trips to Chiang Khong (approximately 1hr 30min downriver; B2000 one way, B2500 return).

By bicycle or motorbike To get around the ruins and the surrounding countryside, bicycles (B80/day) and motorbikes (B250/day) can be rented at *Gin's Guest House*. Motorbikes are also available for B200 from Siriporn on Thanon Phaholyothin.

TROUBLE ON THE MEKONG

Armed with a **Chinese visa** from Bangkok or Chiang Mai, it was until recently possible to catch a passenger boat from Chiang Saen up the Mekong to **Jing Hong** in China. However, in October 2011, close to Sop Ruak, two Chinese cargo ships were subjected to a brutal **armed attack** by a group of men from the Thai army. The motive wasn't immediately clear, but thirteen Chinese sailors died in the incident, and at the time of writing all passenger services between the two countries had been suspended. Cargo shipments from China were also stopped temporarily.

This is a crucial trade route for countries that are linked by the Mekong, and in a bid to get cargo services running again, officials from China, Thailand, Laos and Burma sanctioned coordinated **patrols** along stretches of the river. But in December 2011, after less than a fortnight of patrols, three Burmese soldiers were killed in a clash with suspected drug traffickers, suggesting that the situation is still some way from being resolved.

INFORMATION

Tourist information There's a municipal tourist office (daily 8.30am–4.30pm; ☎053 777084) on Thanon Phaholyothin, opposite the National Museum, which houses exhibits on the architecture and conservation of the city.

ACCOMMODATION

Gin's Guest House Outside the ramparts, 2km north of the T-junction ☎053 650847. At this attractive guesthouse – which also serves good food – there's a choice between basic A-frame bungalows in a lychee orchard, or pricier spacious, well-furnished rooms in the main house, with polished wood floors, all en suite, most with hot showers. The owner organizes local trekking and tours, and there's internet access too. Fan **B300**, a/c **B900**

JS Guest House In a lane leading north from the post office ☎053 777060, ✉sureegreutmann@bluewin.ch. A cheap, reasonably clean option offering simple, box-like concrete rooms in rows in the back garden, some with en-suite hot showers. Breakfast included. **B250**

River Hill About 500m south of the T-junction and a block back from the river road ☎053 650826–7, ✇chiangsaenriverhillhotel.com. This hotel sets a high standard in a modern four-storey building with some traditional touches. Friendly and well run, it's in a quiet rustic street; the rooms, all of which have a/c, fridges and hot-water bathrooms, are very nicely kitted out, right down to the axe cushion seats on the floor. Breakfast included. **B990**

Siam Triangle By the river, 1km south of the T-junction on the continuation of Thanon Rim Khong (Route 1129) ☎053 651115–7, ✇siamtriangle.com. A swanky, high-end place that has polished a/c rooms, some with their own balconies overlooking Laos, plus a swimming pool, sauna and gym. Executive suites and "Grand Deluxe" rooms come with iPod docks and jacuzzis. **B3000**

EATING AND DRINKING

Food in Chiang Saen is nothing special; you could do worse than try the **street-food stalls** on the riverfront promenade just north of the T-junction, where you can sprawl on mats at low tables in the evening, followed by a drink at one of the small, lively bars opposite.

Samying On Thanon Phaholyothin, beside the bank. Popular with locals, this is a cheap, clean, well-run restaurant serving river fish in various preparations and a good *tom yam*. Daily 8am–7pm.

Siam Triangle By the river, 1km south of the T-junction on the continuation of Thanon Rim Khong (Route 1129) ☎053 651115–7, ✇siamtriangle.com. There's a good range of Thai and international dishes at the *Siam Triangle*'s riverside restaurant, which has gorgeous views across the river. An expensive choice. Daily 6am–midnight.

DIRECTORY

ATM Across from the post office on the south side of Thanon Phaholyothin.

Internet There's an internet shop two doors west from Siriporn on Thanon Phaholyothin.

Chiang Khong and around

As one of the few places in Thailand where it's possible for foreigners to cross to Laos, **CHIANG KHONG** is constantly bustling with travellers waiting to go over the river to the Lao town of Houayxai and embark on the lovely Mekong boat journey down to Luang

---

GIANT CATFISH

The **Mekong giant catfish** (*pla buk*) is the largest scaleless freshwater fish in the world, measuring up to 3m in length and weighing in at 300kg. Chiang Khong has traditionally been the catfish capital of the north, attracting fish merchants and restaurateurs from Chiang Rai, Chiang Mai and Bangkok – the mild, tasty meat of the *pla buk* is prized for its fine, soft texture, and one fish can fetch B60,000–80,000. The **catfish season** is officially opened at the port of Ban Hat Khrai on April 18 with much pomp, including an elaborate ceremony to appease Chao Por Pla Buk, the giant catfish god. The season's haul used to be between thirty and sixty fish all told, but recent years have been so disappointing (only two were caught in 2008, for example) that Thailand's Fishery Department has begun an artificial spawning programme.

Prabang. On a high, steep bank above the water, Chiang Khong is strung out along a single, north–south street, Thanon Sai Klang, between the cross-river pier at Hua Wiang and the fishing port of Ban Hat Khrai. Once you've admired the elevated view of the traffic on the Mekong and glimpsed the ruined, red-brick turrets of the French-built Fort Carnot in Houayxai, there's little to do in the town itself, though several local excursions might tempt you to stay a little longer. On Fridays, there's a bustling **market** around the bridge to the south of central Chiang Khong, while Saturdays see a night market, mostly for food, on the main street.

Village excursions

If you'd like to explore the area around Chiang Khong more fully, the best option is to put yourself up at *Baan Tam-Mi-La* guesthouse (see p.376), where Khun Wat has simple local maps and lots of information. **Thung Na Noi**, a Hmong village 8km west, with a market every Friday, makes a good cycling trip, with the possibility of returning by a more circuitous, 12km route through the forest. There's a guesthouse in the village and an attractive waterfall, Huai Tong, 3km away. At the Thai Lue village of

Hua Wiang Boat Pier (for boats to Laos) & Chiang Saen

CHIANG KHONG

■ **ACCOMMODATION**
Baan Fai	5
Baan Tam-Mi-La	3
Chiang Khong Hotel	1
Nam Khong Riverside Hotel	6
Ruanthai Sopaphan Resort	4
Sopaphan Guest House	2

● **RESTAURANTS & CAFÉS**
Bamboo	2
Baan Tam-Mi-La	3
Fai Nguan	5
Lomtawan	1
Naka	4

Wat Phra Kaew

Songthaews to Chiang Saen

Wat Luang

Mekong River

Police Station

Sob Som River

Buses to Bangkok
Buses to Chiang Rai
Buses to Chiang Mai

1020

0   250
metres

Chiang Rai (137km), Si Dornchai & Phu Chi Fa

Ban Hat Khrai

Si Dornchai, 14km south of Chiang Khong on Route 1020, you can watch weavers at work at three shops near the bridge – this would also make a good trip by bike, returning via back roads along the river. With your own car or motorbike, you could push on from Si Dornchai for 50km to the interesting Kuomintang village of **Ban Pha Tang** and the precipitous mountain viewpoint at **Phu Chi Fa**, 25km beyond.

ARRIVAL AND DEPARTURE
CHIANG KHONG

By bus or minibus Direct buses between Chiang Khong and Chiang Rai follow three different routes taking 2hr, 2hr 30min or 3hr (hourly, from the left side of the toilet in Chiang Rai's old bus station); be sure to ask for the quickest time, *sawng chua mohng*. All buses arriving in Chiang Khong stop on the main road at the south end of town. Because of the popularity of the border crossing here, there are now direct a/c minibuses from and to Chiang Mai and Pai; you can arrange tickets through guesthouses and travel agents such as Queen Bee (see p.289) and Aya Service (see p.348).

BOAT TRIPS ON THE MEKONG

If you're twiddling your thumbs in Chiang Khong while waiting to cross to Laos, or simply want to spend some time out on the water, ask at your guesthouse about one-hour **boat trips** on the Mekong (B400) or full-day voyages up to Chiang Saen and back (B2400). As you leave Chiang Khong itself and chug past sandy outcrops, it's likely you'll catch glimpses of villagers fishing, playing or washing in the river (usually met with big smiles and lots of frantic waving).

3

CROSSING TO LAOS

Foreigners can get thirty-day Lao **visas** on arrival in Houayxai (US$30 or B1500 and up, depending on nationality) – for information about other means of getting a Lao visa, see Basics (p.27). As paying in baht is so unfavourable, gold shops (where the rates are often best), guesthouses and banks in Chiang Khong sell dollars. Hua Wiang pier, at the north end of town, is the departure point for frequent passenger **ferries to Houayxai** (B40, plus B10 for a big bag, plus US$1 – or an inflated B40 – "overtime" payment to Lao immigration after 4pm and on Sat or Sun). These cross-river ferries are likely to be phased out when the new Mekong bridge, 8km downstream from Chiang Khong, is constructed. However, the project has experienced serious delays, so completion may still be some way off by the time you read this.

From Houayxai, there are buses to Luang Prabang, Vientiane, Luang Namtha and Oudomxai, but by far the most popular option is to catch a **passenger boat to Luang Prabang**. Usually departing between 10am and noon every morning, these glide down the scenic Mekong in two days, with an overnight and a change of boat at Pakbeng (200,000 Lao kip per person). The alternative is to take one of the cramped, noisy and dangerous **speedboats**, on which passengers should be provided with helmets and life jackets. These cover the same stretch in six to seven hours for 375,000 kip (minimum six people; best to be at the speedboat pier by 9–10am). From Houayxai's cross-river pier, **tuk-tuks** will take you to the regular passenger-boat pier or the speedboat pier.

It's easy to sort all of this out yourself and there's really no need to pay commission to a Thai or Lao travel agent to book in advance.

Destinations Bangkok (10 daily; 13–14hr); Chiang Mai (3 daily; 5–6hr); Chiang Rai (every 20min; 2–3hr).

By songthaew from/to Chiang Saen The town is served by songthaews from and to Chiang Saen; the 2hr journey is best done in the early morning and usually involves a change of vehicle at Ban Hat Bai. In Chiang Khong, songthaews drop off and leave from the roadside next to Wat Luang.

By car from/to Chiang Saen If you're driving yourself between Chiang Saen and Chiang Khong, it's best to branch off the direct Route 1129 onto the winding, scenic, paved roads that hug the northward kink in the Mekong River.

GETTING AROUND

By tuk-tuk If you need to get from the bus to the ferry (or anywhere else about town), the local version of a tuk-tuk, a converted motorbike, should take you there for B30–40.

By mountain bike Good mountain bikes (B150/day) can be rented from Khun Wat at *Baan Tam-Mi-La*, who sometimes leads afternoon cycling tours around Chiang Khong.

By motorbike *Baan Fai* and other guesthouses rent motorbikes for around B200/day.

ACCOMMODATION

Baan Fai 27 Thanon Sai Klang ☏053 791394. A variety of basic rooms, some with shared hot showers and others with attached bathrooms, in a funky old wooden house on a small plot of land in front of *Nam Khong Riverside Hotel* – B100 for a single is hard to argue with. Internet access. **B200**

★ **Baan Tam-Mi-La** Soi 1, Thanon Sai Klang (signposted down a lane in the middle of town among a cluster of shops) ☏053 791234. With helpful, clued-up staff and a scenic, easy-going riverfront location, this place has tasteful, well-designed rooms and wooden bungalows on a leafy slope, with en-suite hot showers, and sells good hammocks. Fan rooms **B350**, a/c bungalows **B650**

Chiang Khong Hotel 68/1 Thanon Sai Klang ☏053 791182, ⓦchiangkhong-hotel.com. Motel-like place with cheap, if slightly murky, rooms set back off the street with hot showers. The rooms furthest back from the street are more expensive but worth the upgrade.

Fan **B200**, a/c **B300**

Nam Khong Riverside Hotel Thanon Sai Klang ☏053 791796 ⓦnamkhongriverside.com. The town's top spot to stay, a huge, low-rise hotel set around a pretty riverside garden with smartly furnished rooms, all with a/c, hot water, fridges, balconies and Mekong views. Accordingly, ground-floor rooms tend to be cheapest. Breakfast included. **B1000**

Ruanthai Sopaphan Resort Right next to Ban Tam-Mi-La ☏053 791023, ✉sukatungka@gmail.com. The smart rooms in this large teak house, hung with textiles and sporting lovely polished floors, have en-suite hot showers, and the best have good views of the river. Internet access. **B450**

Sopaphan Guest House Thanon Sai Klang ☏053 792022, ✉sukatungka@gmail.com. Under the same ownership as *Ruanthai Sopaphan*, opposite, this is a slightly more basic guesthouse, though also sporting a small forest's worth of highly polished teak. The warren-like premises contain a huge variety of rooms (including three very cheap singles), with hot showers, either shared or en suite. Internet access. B200

EATING AND DRINKING

Baan Tam-Mi-La 113 Thanon Sai Klang ☎053 791234. Excellent guesthouse terrace restaurant with a sweeping view of the river, making it an ideal spot to while away the time. Very good Thai food, lots of vegetarian options and a few Western dishes, plus espressos, home-baked cakes and bread, and hearty breakfasts. Daily from breakfast until 6.30pm.

Bamboo Thanon Sai Klang ☎053 791621. Small, eclectic bakery, juice bar and restaurant that turns out home-baked pies, good espressos, a wide choice of breakfasts and small selections of Thai and Mexican food. Daily 7am–9pm.

Fai Nguan Nam Khong Riverside Hotel, Thanon Sai Klang ☎053 791796. Well-appointed restaurant overlooking the river, with a wide range of Thai dishes, notably salads (B80–100), burgers (B70) and a few pizzas. Daily 7am–midnight.

Lomtawan 354 Thanon Sai Klang ☎053 655740. Popular bar/restaurant serving Thai dishes such as spicy salads (around B80) and Western fast food on a candlelit terrace overlooking the canal, as well as drinks at the bar inside, plus live music every night. Open daily from mid-afternoon to late.

Naka Thanon Sai Klang. Lively, evening-only bar-restaurant, with good music, serving well-priced Lanna dishes such as the pork curry *kaeng hang lay*, as well as steak and spaghetti. Daily, usually from about 5pm until late.

DIRECTORY

Internet access Opposite *Bamboo* restaurant, and at many guesthouses in town.

The east
coast

LONELY BEACH, KO CHANG

The east coast

Just a few hours' drive from the capital, the east-coast resorts attract a mixed crowd of weekending Bangkokians and sybaritic tourists. Transport connections are good and, for overlanders, there are several Cambodian border crossings within reach. Beautiful beaches aren't the whole picture, however, as the east coast is also crucial to Thailand's industrial economy, its natural gas fields and deep-sea ports having spawned massive development along the first 200km of coastline, an area dubbed the Eastern Seaboard. The initial landscape of refineries and depots shouldn't deter you though, as offshore it's an entirely different story, with beaches as glorious as more celebrated southern retreats and enough peaceful havens to make it worth packing your hammock.

The first worthwhile stop comes 100km east of Bangkok at the town of **Si Racha**, which is the point of access for tiny **Ko Si Chang**, whose dramatically rugged coastlines and low-key atmosphere make it a restful retreat. In complete contrast, nearby **Pattaya** is Thailand's number one package-tour destination, its customers predominantly middle-aged European men enticed by the resort's sex-market reputation and undeterred by its lacklustre beach. Things soon look up, though, as the coast veers sharply eastwards towards Ban Phe, revealing the island of **Ko Samet**, the prettiest of the beach resorts within comfortable bus-ride range of Bangkok.

East of Ban Phe, the landscape becomes lusher and hillier around **Chanthaburi**, the dynamo of Thailand's gem trade and one of only two eastern provincial capitals worth visiting. The other is **Trat**, 68km further along the highway, and an important hub both for transport into **Cambodia** via Hat Lek – one of this region's two main border points, the other being Aranyaprathet (see box, p.383) – and for the forty islands of the Ko Chang archipelago. The most popular of this island group is large, forested **Ko Chang** itself, whose long, fine beaches have made it Thailand's latest resort destination. A host of smaller, less-developed islands fill the sea between Ko Chang and the Cambodian coast, most notably temptingly diverse **Ko Mak** and **Ko Kood**.

Highway 3 extends almost the entire length of the east coast, beginning in Bangkok as Thanon Sukhumvit, and known as such when it cuts through towns, and hundreds of **buses** ply the route, connecting all major mainland destinations. It's also possible to travel between the east coast and the northeast and north without doubling back through the capital: the most direct routes into **Isaan** start from Pattaya, Rayong and Chanthaburi. Bangkok's Suvarnabhumi Airport is less than 50km from Si Racha, and there are two domestic **airports** along the east coast itself: at U-Tapao naval base,

Highlights

①Ko Samet This pretty little island, fringed with a dozen or so beaches of fine, dazzlingly white sand, is easy to get to and offers a wide choice of accommodation, though it's suffering a little for its popularity these days. **See p.396**

②Trat Welcoming guesthouses and restaurants and an atmospheric old quarter make for a worthwhile stopover on the way to the islands or Cambodia. **See p.406**

③Ko Chang Head for Lonely Beach if you're in the mood to party, or to Hat Khlong Phrao,

Ao Bang Bao or Hat Khlong Gloi for progressively more tranquil scenes. **See p.410**

④Ko Mak Lovely, lazy, palm-filled island with peaceful white-sand beaches, a welcoming atmosphere and some stylish accommodation. **See p.424**

⑤Ko Kood The real beauty of the east, with some great beaches, Thailand's fourth-largest island is untamed and as yet largely undeveloped. **See p.428**

HIGHLIGHTS ARE MARKED ON THE MAP ON P.382

southeast of Pattaya, and just west of Trat. Though a rail line connects Bangkok with Si Racha and Pattaya, it is served by just one slow **train** a day in each direction; a branch line makes two journeys a day to Aranyaprathet near the Cambodian border.

Si Racha

The eastbound journey out of Bangkok is not at all scenic, dominated initially by traffic-choked suburban sprawl and then by the industrial landscape of the

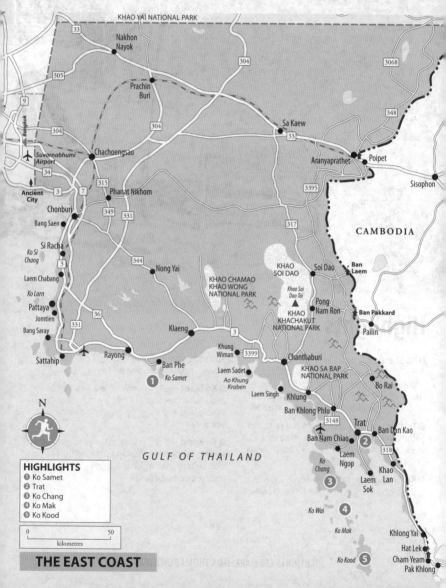

HIGHLIGHTS
1. Ko Samet
2. Trat
3. Ko Chang
4. Ko Mak
5. Ko Kood

0 ____ 50
kilometres

THE EAST COAST

CROSSING THE CAMBODIAN BORDER VIA ARANYAPRATHET

The most commonly used overland crossing into **Cambodia** from Thailand is at **Poipet**, which lies just across the border from the Thai town of **Aranyaprathet**, 210km due east of Bangkok. It's best to arm yourself in advance with an e-visa for Cambodia (see p.27) and to make the journey by regular public transport, but it's also possible to buy a package all the way through to Siem Reap and to get a thirty-day visa on arrival at the border, though both of the latter options are more likely to open you up to possible **scams**, including a fake "Cambodian Consulate" in Aranyaprathet and rip-off currency exchange (it's not compulsory to buy riel before entering Cambodia, despite what some touts may say). For further details, see ⓦ thaivisa.com for its visa-run forum; and ⓦ talesofasia.com/cambodia-overland.htm for a very detailed description of the crossing and for advice on onward transport into Cambodia. Once you've walked across the border and entered Cambodia, it's about two hours in a taxi or bus to reach Siem Reap, 150km away. If you have the deep misfortune of getting stuck in dusty, dirty Aranyaprathet, where local transport comes in the form of tuk-tuks, try the comfortable fan and a/c rooms at *Inter Hotel* at 108/7 Thanon Chatasingh (☎037 231291, ⓦ ourweb.info/interhotel; fan B300, a/c B550).

From **Bangkok**, you can travel to Aranyaprathet Station, 4km from the border post, by **train** (2 daily; 6hr); you'll need to catch the 5.55am if you want to get across the border the same day. Return trains depart Aranyaprathet at 6.35am and 1.35pm (5hr 25min–6hr). Alternatively, take a **bus** from Bangkok's Northern (Mo Chit) Bus Terminal to Aranyaprathet (at least hourly; 4hr 30min), or a faster, more expensive a/c minibus from Victory Monument. To reach Aranyaprathet from east-coast towns, the easiest route is to take a bus from **Chanthaburi** to the town of **Sa Kaew**, 130km to the northeast, and then change to one of the frequent buses for the 55km ride east to Aranyaprathet.

It's also possible to buy a **through ticket to Siem Reap** from Trat and Ko Chang, or from Thanon Khao San in Bangkok (B200–600), but this option is dogged by scams (including a visa "service charge", described in detail at ⓦ talesofasia.com/cambodia-overland-bkksr-package.htm and on the forum at ⓦ thaivisa.com), takes much longer than doing it independently, and nearly always uses clapped-out buses or even pick-ups on the Cambodian side, despite the promised "luxury bus".

petrochemical and shipping industries that power Thailand's Eastern Seaboard. The first major population centre is the provincial capital of **Chonburi**, whose only notable attraction is its annual October bout of buffalo-racing. Twenty kilometres on, you reach the fast-growing town of **SI RACHA**, a prosperous residential and administrative hub for the Eastern Seaboard's industries and home to a sizeable population of expat families. The town is best known though as the source of *nam phrik Si Racha*, the chilli-laced ketchup found on every kitchen table in Thailand, and as the departure point for the island of **Ko Si Chang** (see p.384). Si Racha's only sight is the Sino–Thai "island temple" of **Wat Ko Loy**, a gaudy hexagon presided over by a statue of the Chinese Goddess of Mercy, Kuan Im, and located on an islet at the end of a 1500m causeway, adjacent to the pier for boats to Ko Si Chang.

ARRIVAL AND DEPARTURE — SI RACHA

BY BUS

Frequent buses pass through Si Racha on their journeys between Bangkok's Eastern (Ekamai) and Northern (Mo Chit) bus terminals, and Pattaya and Trat further east. They all drop off and pick up passengers near the huge Robinsons/Pacific Park shopping centre on Thanon Sukhumvit in Si Racha's town centre.

First-class terminal Fast, first-class, dedicated Si Racha–Bangkok buses have their own small terminal a couple of hundred metres south of Robinsons, on the east side of

Thanon Sukhumvit, set back slightly from the road next to Tops supermarket; from here, there are also a/c minibuses to Suvarnabhumi Airport.

Destinations Bangkok (Eastern/Northern bus terminals; every 30min; 1hr 30min–2hr 30min); Chanthaburi (6 daily; 3hr 30min); Pattaya (every 20min; 30min); Trat (6 daily; 5hr).

BY TRAIN

Though a rail line connects Bangkok with Pattaya and Sattahip via Si Racha, it is served by just one slow, third-class, often late, train a day in each direction. The train station is on the far eastern edge of town, a tuk-tuk ride from the pier for Ko Si Chang.

Destinations Bangkok (daily; 3hr 30min); Pattaya (daily; 30min).

BY BOAT

Ko Si Chang pier, known as Tha Wat Ko Loy, is 2.5km from

Robinsons shopping centre; a motorbike taxi or tuk-tuk will drive you there for B30–50 or, if walking, take any road west towards the sea as far as Thanon Chermchompon (also spelt Jermjompol), then head north up Chermchompon until you reach the junction for the Ko Si Chang pier and Wat Ko Loy. Boats run to Ko Si Chang between 7am and 8pm.

Destinations Ko Si Chang (hourly; 40–50min).

ACCOMMODATION AND EATING

For **eating**, Thanon Si Racha Nakhon 3 is a good place to browse, lined with restaurants and night-time foodstalls, or there's an official night market by the day market and clocktower further south down Thanon Chermchompon.

City Hotel 6/126 Thanon Sukhumvit ☎038 322700, ⓦcitysriracha.com. This high-rise, 200-room hotel, 300m south of Pacific Place, offers smart a/c digs with wi-fi throughout, as well as a gym, a spa, a tennis court, Japanese and international restaurants and a pool. B2825

Sri Wattana Soi Sri Wattana, directly across Thanon

Chermchompon from Thanon Si Racha Nakhon 3, about 500m south of the pier junction ☎038 311037. Very simple, cabin-like en-suite fan rooms, built on a jetty jutting out over the atmospheric but sometimes smelly waterfront, with a pleasant sea-view terrace. B200

Ko Si Chang

The unhurried pace and absence of consumer pressures make small, dry, rocky **KO SI CHANG** an engaging place to get away from it all for a day or two. Unlike most other east-coast destinations, it offers no real beach life – it's a populous, working island with a deep-sea port, rather than a tropical idyll – and there's little to do here but explore the craggy coastline by kayak or ramble up and down its steep, scrubby contours on foot or by motorbike. The island is famous as the location of one of Rama V's summer palaces, a few parts of which have been restored, and of a popular Chinese pilgrimage temple, as well as for its rare white squirrels, which live in the wooded patches inland.

Rama V's Palace

Hat Tha Wang • Tues–Sun 9am–5pm • Free

The most famous sight on the island is **Rama V's Palace**, which occupies a large chunk of gently sloping land midway down the east coast, behind pebbly **Hat Tha Wang**. It's an enjoyable place to explore and can be reached on foot from *Tiew Pai Park Resort* in about half an hour. Shortly before reaching the palace ruins, you'll pass the small and less than riveting **Cholatassathan Museum**, established by the resident Aquatic Resources Research Institute to provide an introduction to the coral and marine life around Ko Si Chang.

Built in the 1890s as a sort of health resort for sickly royals, the palace (also known as **Phra Judhadhut Ratchathan**) formed the heart of an extensive complex comprising

---

KO SI CHANG FESTIVALS

Ko Si Chang celebrates three particularly interesting festivals. **Songkhran** is marked from April 17 to 19 with sandcastle-building, greasy-pole-climbing and an exorcism ritual for any islanders who have suffered unpleasant deaths over the previous year. At **Visakha Puja**, the full-moon day in May when Buddha's birth, death and enlightenment are honoured, islanders process to the old palace with hand-crafted Chinese lanterns. And on September 20, Ko Si Chang honours its royal patron **King Chulalongkorn**'s birthday with a *son et lumière* in the palace grounds and a beauty contest staged entirely in costumes from the Chulalongkorn era.

homes for royal advisers, chalets for convalescents, quarters for royal concubines and administrative buildings. By the turn of the twentieth century, however, Rama V (King Chulalongkorn) had lost interest in his island project and so in 1901 his golden teak palace was moved piece by piece to Bangkok, and reconstructed there as Vimanmek Palace; its foundations are still visible just south of the palace's Saphan Asadang pier. Following recent renovations, the elegant design of the palace grounds is apparent once more. They fan out around an elaborate labyrinth of fifty interlinked ponds and a maze of stone steps and balustrades that still cling to the shallow hillside. Close to the shore, four of the original Western-style **villas** have been reconstructed to house displays, of varying interest, on Chulalongkorn's relationship with Ko Si Chang; one of them also doubles as a weekend coffee shop. Inland, signs direct you up the hillside to the palace's unusual whitewashed shrine, **Wat Asadang**, whose circular walls are punctuated with Gothic stained-glass windows and surmounted by a chedi.

Hat Tham Pang and Ko Khang Khao

The main beach on the west coast, and the most popular one on the island, is **Hat Tham Pang**. It's a tiny patch of sand, backed by shoulder-to-shoulder umbrellas and deckchairs belonging to the basic beach restaurants; you can rent snorkels and kayaks here too. The best **snorkelling** spots are further south, around the tiny islands off Ko Si Chang's southern tip, particularly off the north coast of **Ko Khang Khao**, forty minutes by kayak from Hat Tham Pang.

Wat Tham Yai Prik

Accessible via a fork off Thanon Asadang opposite *Tiew Pai* (10min walk)

The **Wat Tham Yai Prik** temple and meditation centre is open to interested visitors and meditators. Unusually, nuns as well as monks here wear brown (rather than white) and everyone participates in the upkeep of the monastery: you can see some of the fruits of their labour in the extensive roadside orchard. Just west of the wat lies the pretty, rocky cove known as **Hat Tham** or **Hat Sai**, which is only really swimmable at low tide.

Khao Khat

On the northwest trajectory of the ring road, you'll pass beneath the gaze of a huge yellow Buddha before reaching the rocky northwest headland of **Khao Khat**, a few hundred metres further on. The uninterrupted panorama of open sea makes this a classic sunset spot, and there's a path along the cliffside.

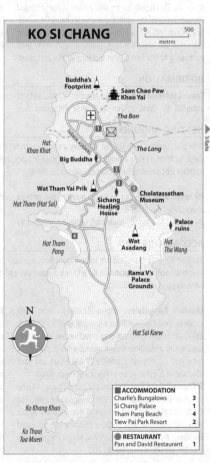

KO SI CHANG

0 — 500 metres

Buddha's Footprint

Saan Chao Paw Khao Yai

Tha Bon

THANON ASADANG

Hat Khao Khat

Big Buddha

Tha Lang

Wat Tham Yai Prik

Hat Tham (Hat Sai)

Sichang Healing House

Cholatassathan Museum

Palace ruins

Hat Tham Pang

Wat Asadang

Hat Tha Wang

Rama V's Palace Grounds

N

Hat Sai Kaew

Ko Khang Khao

Ko Thaai Taa Muen

Si Racha

■ ACCOMMODATION
Charlie's Bungalows	3
Si Chang Palace	1
Tham Pang Beach	4
Tiew Pai Park Resort	2

● RESTAURANT
Pan and David Restaurant	1

4

Saan Chao Paw Khao Yai

The showy, multi-tiered Chinese temple of **Saan Chao Paw Khao Yai** (Shrine of the Father Spirit of the Great Hill) is stationed at the top of a steep flight of steps and commands a good view of the harbour and the mainland coast. Established here long before Rama V arrived on the island, the shrine was dedicated by Chinese seamen who saw a strange light coming out of one of the **caves** behind the modern-day temple. The caves, now full of religious statues and related paraphernalia, are visited by boatloads of Chinese pilgrims, particularly over Chinese New Year. Continue on up the cliffside to reach the small pagoda built for Rama V and enshrining a **Buddha's Footprint**. Two very long, very steep flights of stairs give access to the footprint: the easternmost one starts at the main waterfront entrance to the Chinese temple and takes you past a cluster of monks' meditation cells, while the westerly one rises further west along the ring road and offers the finest lookouts.

ARRIVAL AND DEPARTURE
KO SI CHANG

By boat Ferries to Ko Si Chang leave from Tha Wat Ko Loy in Si Racha (see p.384) from 7am to 8pm (B40), wending their way past the congestion of international cargo boats and Thai supply barges that anchor in the protected channel between the mainland and Ko Si Chang. On arrival, boats dock first at Tha Lang (also signed as Tateawavong Bridge) in the island's main settlement, with many then continuing to Tha Bon a short distance up the east coast.

Motorized samlor drivers meet the boats and charge B40 to most accommodation, or B80 to Hat Tham Pang; as they are paid commission by some hotels and restaurants, be wary of any opinionated remarks. Boats to the mainland leave Tha Lang between 6am and 7pm; the same boats depart Tha Bon 15min earlier.

Destinations Si Racha (hourly; 40–50min).

INFORMATION

Tourist information ⓦ ko-sichang.com, a useful website compiled by David at *Pan and David Restaurant* (see opposite), offers detailed coverage of the island.

GETTING AROUND

Both piers connect with Thanon Asadang, a small, concrete ring road on which you'll find the market, a bank and many shops. In town it's easy enough to walk from place to place, but to really enjoy what Ko Si Chang has to offer you'll need to either rent a motorbike or charter a samlor for the day.

By motorbike Bikes can be rented from the pier or from *Tiew Pai Park Resort* for B250.

By samlor The island's trademark samlors are driven by distinctive, elongated 1200cc motorbikes and virtually monopolize the roads, as there are barely any private cars; a tour of the island will set you back around B250.

ACCOMMODATION

Because water on the island has to be bought from a private desalination company at six times the price it costs on the mainland, **accommodation** on Ko Si Chang is expensive and disappointingly poor value. Booking ahead is advisable for weekends and public holidays.

Charlie's Bungalows Thanon Asadang, 2min walk south of Tiew Pai Park Resort in town ☎ 085 191 3863, ⓦ kohsichang.net. A dozen or so attractive new bungalows, done out in a maritime theme around a small garden; all come with a/c, hot water, satellite TV and fridge, and most have free wi-fi. Prices go up a little at weekends. **B900**

Si Chang Palace Thanon Asadang, across from Tha Bon in town ☎ 038 216276–9, ⓦ sichangpalace.com. The most upmarket place on the island has good a/c rooms with balconies, the best of them enjoying fine eastward sea views; all have hot water, TV and fridge. There's a pool here too. Breakfast included. **B1200**

Tham Pang Beach Hat Tham Pang ☎ 038 216179, ⓦ tampangbeachresort.com. The busiest west-coast accommodation, whose twenty fairly rudimentary concrete bungalows – all with bathroom, fans and TVs, some with sea views – are stacked in tiers up the cliffside behind Ko Si Chang's only beach. There's a restaurant plus beach equipment for rent. Reservations essential for weekends. **B550**

Tiew Pai Park Resort Thanon Asadang, in town near Tha Lang ☎ 038 216084, ⓦ tiewpai.net. Very central and cheaper than the competition, this is most backpackers' first choice. Bungalows and rooms are crammed around a scruffy garden across the road from the restaurant and many are pretty basic; the best value are the en-suite fan bungalows, some of which have TV and fridge, and there are also some cheap single rooms with shared bathrooms. Fan B400, a/c B700

EATING

★ **Pan and David Restaurant** Thanon Asadang, 200m before the entrance to the old palace grounds ☎ 038 216075, ⓦ ko-sichang.com. The only restaurant of note on the island, run by a sociable and well-informed American expat and his Thai wife. The long and delicious menu includes authentically fiery Thai salads, tasty home-made fettuccine (B235 with bolognese sauce), fillet steak, Thai curries (around B160), and home-made fresh strawberry ice cream. Daily except Wed roughly 10am–9.30pm, opens earlier Sat & Sun.

DIRECTORY

Massage The charming little Sichang Healing House (☎ 038 216467; daily except Wed 9am–6pm), west off Thanon Asadang on the way to the old palace, offers Thai massage (B500 for 90min) and herbal treatments, as well as five-day massage courses (B6000), at its cute little garden retreat. There's a small branch on Hat Tham Pang too.

Pattaya

With its streets full of high-rise hotels and hustlers on every corner, **PATTAYA** is the epitome of exploitative tourism gone mad, but most of Pattaya's two million annual visitors don't mind that the place looks like the Costa del Sol bathed in smog because what they are here for is sex. The city swarms with male and female **prostitutes**, spiced up by Thailand's largest population of transvestites (*katoey*), and plane-loads of Western men flock here to enjoy their services in the rash of hostess bar-beers, go-go clubs and massage parlours for which "Patpong-on-Sea" is notorious. The signs trumpeting "Viagra for Sale" say it all. Pattaya also has the largest **gay scene** in Thailand, with several exclusively gay hotels and an entire zone devoted to gay sex bars.

Pattaya's evolution into sin city began with the Vietnam War, when it got fat on selling sex to American servicemen. When the soldiers and sailors left in the mid-1970s, Western tourists were lured in to fill their places, and ex-servicemen soon returned to run the sort of joints they had once blown their dollars in. These days, at least half the bars and restaurants in Pattaya are Western-run. More recently, there has been an influx of criminal gangs from Germany, Russia and Japan, who reportedly find Pattaya a convenient centre for running their rackets in passport and credit-card fraud, as well as child pornography and prostitution; expat murders are a regular news item in the *Pattaya Mail*.

Local tourism authorities are trying hard to improve Pattaya's **image**, and with surprising success have begun enticing families and older couples with a catalogue of more wholesome entertainments such as theme parks, golf courses, shopping plazas and year-round diving. Russian holidaymakers seem particularly keen and Cyrillic script is now much in evidence around the resort. A recent flush of more sophisticated boutique hotels and restaurants is also starting to bring in a younger Thai crowd, which has brightened the picture a little. But in truth the beach here is far from pristine – way outshone by Ko Samet just along the coast – so after-hours "entertainment" is still the primary inducement.

Pattaya Beach

At the heart of this ever-expanding adult playground is 4km-long **Pattaya Beach**, the noisiest, most unsightly zone of the resort, crowded with yachts and tour boats and fringed by a sliver of sand and a paved beachfront walkway. The densest glut of hotels, restaurants, bars, fast-food joints, souvenir shops and tour operators is halfway down Pattaya Beach Road (also signed as Pattaya Saineung), in **Central Pattaya** (Pattaya Klang), between sois 6 and 13, but after dark the action moves to the neon zone south of Soi 13/2. Here, in **South Pattaya**, and specifically along ultra-sleazy **Walking Street**, sex is peddled in hundreds of go-go bars, discos, massage parlours and open-sided bar-beers. The gay district is also here, in the lanes

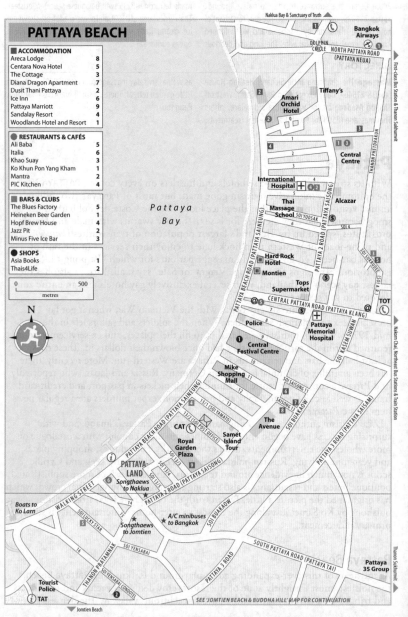

Naklua Bay & Sanctuary of Truth ▲

PATTAYA BEACH

■ ACCOMMODATION
Areca Lodge	8
Centara Nova Hotel	5
The Cottage	3
Diana Dragon Apartment	7
Dusit Thani Pattaya	2
Ice Inn	6
Pattaya Marriott	9
Sandalay Resort	4
Woodlands Hotel and Resort	1

● RESTAURANTS & CAFÉS
Ali Baba	5
Italia	6
Khao Suay	3
Ko Khun Pon Yang Kham	1
Mantra	2
PIC Kitchen	4

■ BARS & CLUBS
The Blues Factory	5
Heineken Beer Garden	1
Hopf Brew House	4
Jazz Pit	2
Minus Five Ice Bar	3

● SHOPS
Asia Books	1
Thais4Life	2

0 — 500
metres

N

Bangkok Airways

DOLPHIN CIRCLE — NORTH PATTAYA ROAD (PATTAYA NEUA)

Tiffany's

Amari Orchid Hotel

Central Centre

International Hospital

Thai Massage School — SOI YODSAK

Alcazar

SOI 4

Pattaya Bay

Hard Rock Hotel

Montien

Tops Supermarket

CENTRAL PATTAYA ROAD (PATTAYA KLANG)

Police

Pattaya Memorial Hospital

Central Festival Centre

Mike Shopping Mall

SOI SAISONG 11

The Avenue

SOI BUA KAOW

13/1 (SOI YAMATO)

13/2 (SOI POST OFFICE)

CAT

Royal Garden Plaza

Samét Island Tour

PATTAYALAND

Songthaews to Naklua

PATTAYA 2 ROAD (PATTAYA SAISONG)

Boats to Ko Larn

WALKING STREET

SOI LUCKY STAR

Songthaews to Jomtien

A/C minibuses to Bangkok

SOI YENSABAI

SOI BUA KAOW

PATTAYA 3 ROAD

SOUTH PATTAYA ROAD (PATTAYA TAI)

Pattaya 35 Group

THANON PRATAMNAK

SOI YENSABAI CONDOTEL

Tourist Police

TAT

SEE 'JOMTIEN BEACH & BUDDHA HILL' MAP FOR CONTINUATION

▼ Jomtien Beach

PATTAYA BEACH ROAD (PATTAYA SAINEUNG)

PATTAYA 2 ROAD (PATTAYA SAISONG)

THANON PHETRAKUN

SOI KASEM SUWAN

SOI BUAKAOW

SOI SAISONG 11

SAISONE 7

8

PATTAYA 3 ROAD (PATTAYA SAISAM)

First-class Bus Station & Thanon Sukhumvit ▶

Nakorn Chai, Northeast Bus Stations & Train Station ▶

Thanon Sukhumvit ▶

TOT

SOI 4

SOI 6

ACTIVITIES IN PATTAYA

DIVING AND SNORKELLING

Though Pattaya's reefs are far less spectacular than those along the Andaman Coast, they can be dived year-round, and underwater visibility is consistent. Most **dive trips** focus on the group of "outer islands" about 25km from shore, which include Ko Rin, Ko Man Wichai and Ko Klung Badaan, where you have a reasonable chance of seeing barracuda, moray eels and blue-spotted stingrays. There are also three rewarding wreck dives in the Samae San/Sattahip area. Be careful when choosing a dive operator as there are plenty of charlatans around. All tour agents sell **snorkelling** trips to nearby islands, the majority of them going to the reefs and beaches of **Ko Larn**. You can also make your own way to Ko Larn by public boat from the Bali Hai pier at the far southern end of Walking Street (roughly hourly; 45min; B30).

Mermaid's Dive Centre Thanon Tabphaya in Jomtien, plus 3 branches around the resort ☎ 038 303333, ⊛ mermaiddive.com. One of the most reputable dive shops in Pattaya, a PADI Five-Star Career Development Centre. It charges B3000 for two dives, with accompanying snorkellers paying B1000, and B14,000 for the four-day Openwater course.

WATERSPORTS

Beachfront stalls in Pattaya and Jomtien offer **waterskiing**, **parasailing** and **jet-skiing**, but you should avoid the last-mentioned: the jet-ski jockeys are notorious for finding scratches on the machine at the end of the rental and trying to charge an exorbitant amount in damages.

Amara Watersports Blue Lagoon Watersports Club, Soi 14 Naa Jomtien, at the far south end of Jomtien Beach ☎ 038 233276, ⊛ amarawatersports .com. Windsurfing courses, rental and sales, as well as paddleboards, catamarans and kayaks.

Kiteboarding Asia Blue Lagoon Watersports Club, Soi 14 Naa Jomtien, at the far south end of Jomtien Beach ☎ 085 134 9588, ⊛ kiteboardingasia.com. Kitesurfing courses, rental and sales.

MASSAGE

Thai Massage Development School Soi Yodsak, Central Pattaya ☎ 038 414115–6, ⊛ tmdmassage .com. In among the full-body soaps and "full-service" massage joints, you'll find this traditional place, where you can have a proper Thai massage (B300/60min), or a herbal compress, oil or foot massage; it also offers two-week massage training courses.

COOKING CLASSES

Happy Home Soi 14, off the north side of Central Pattaya Rd, out towards Pattaya 3 Rd ☎ 084 417 5258, ⊛ happyhome-thaicookingschool.com. Morning (including a market visit) and afternoon classes, with vegetarian versions of all dishes available, and including a weekly dessert class. B1000 including a recipe booklet.

known as **Pattayaland** sois 1, 2 and 3 (or **Boyz Town**), but actually signed as sois 13/3, 13/4 and 13/5.

Jomtien Beach and Buddha Hill

South around the headland from South Pattaya, **Jomtien Beach** (sometimes spelt Chom Tian) is also fronted by enormous high-rises, many of them condominiums. Though the atmosphere here is not as frantic as in Pattaya, Jomtien also flounders under an excess of bar-beers and shops flogging tacky souvenirs and, like its neighbour, is forever under construction. The nicest stretch of sand is shady **Dongtan Beach**, beyond the northern end of Jomtien Beach Road, which is also Pattaya's main gay beach, though used by all. The bulge of land behind Dongtan Beach, separating Jomtien from South Pattaya, is Khao Phra Tamnak, variously translated as **Buddha Hill** or **Pattaya Hill**, site of several posh hotels and the Pattaya Park waterpark and funfair.

Underwater World

Thanon Sukhumvit, just south of the Thep Prasit junction near Tesco Lotus, behind Jomtien Beach • Daily 9am–6pm • B500 •
ⓦ underwaterworldpattaya.com

If you've been disappointed with local reef life, the small and expensive but rather beautiful aquarium at **Underwater World** might make up for it, with its trio of long fibreglass tunnels that transport you through shallow rockpools to the ocean floor. There are touch pools and masses of reef fish, as well as a long roster of feeding times, detailed on the website.

Sanctuary of Truth (Wang Boran)

Off the west end of Soi 12, Thanon Naklua, close to the Garden Sea View hotel, beyond the north end of Pattaya Beach • Daily 8am–8pm •
B500 • ⓦ sanctuaryoftruth.com • From Central Pattaya take a Naklua-bound songthaew as far as Soi 12, then a motorbike taxi

The hugely ambitious **Sanctuary of Truth**, or **Wang Boran**, stands in a dramatic seaside spot behind imposing crenellated walls. Conceived by the man behind the Muang Boran Ancient City complex near Bangkok, it's a majestic 105m-high temple-palace built entirely of wood and designed to evoke the great ancient Khmer sanctuaries of Angkor. Though begun in 1981, it is still a work-in-progress, its external walls covered in a growing gallery of beautiful, symbolic woodcarvings inspired by Cambodian, Chinese, Thai and Indian mythologies.

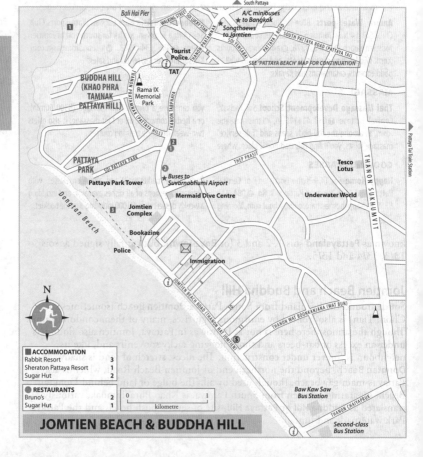

ACCOMMODATION	
Rabbit Resort	3
Sheraton Pattaya Resort	1
Sugar Hut	2

RESTAURANTS	
Bruno's	2
Sugar Hut	1

JOMTIEN BEACH & BUDDHA HILL

ARRIVAL AND DEPARTURE

PATTAYA

BY PLANE

Pattaya's **U-Tapao Airport** (☎038 245599) is inconveniently located at the naval base near Sattahip, about 25km south of the resort, from where a taxi will cost you about B800, so you're probably better off using Bangkok's Suvarnabhumi Airport (see p.133). The Bangkok Airways office is at Fairtex Arcade, North Pattaya Rd (☎038 412382).

Destinations Ko Samui (1–2 daily; 1hr); Phuket (1 daily; 1hr 35min).

BY BUS

All first-class and VIP Bangkok buses, and some airport buses, arrive at and depart from the bus station on North Pattaya Rd. Slower second-class buses and some airport buses use the station on Thanon Chaiyapruk in Jomtien, and there are also airport buses from a terminal on Thanon Tabphaya in Jomtien. It's also possible to get to Pattaya direct from Isaan and the north: Nakorn Chai buses to and from Chiang Mai, Chiang Rai, Khorat and Ubon use a terminus on Thanon Sukhumvit, across from the Central Pattaya Rd intersection (☎038 424871); other Isaan buses can be found at two terminals on the opposite side of Thanon Sukhumvit and at the first-class bus station on North Pattaya Rd. Coming by bus from Si Racha, Rayong or Trat you'll probably get dropped on Thanon Sukhumvit, the resort's eastern limit, from where songthaews will ferry you into town. If heading on to these towns, you need to pick up your bus from one of the drops on Thanon Sukhumvit (easiest at the junctions with North, Central and South Pattaya roads).

Destinations Bangkok (Eastern/Northern bus terminals; every 30min; 2hr 30min–4hr); Bangkok (Southern Bus Terminal; roughly hourly; 3hr 30min); Bangkok (Suvarnabhumi Airport, Floor 1 of the terminal; 7 daily; 2hr); Chanthaburi (6 daily; 3hr); Chiang Mai (8 daily; 12–14hr); Chiang Rai (2 daily; 15–17hr); Khorat (4 daily; 5hr); Rayong (every 30min; 1hr 30min); Si Racha (every 20min; 30min); Trat (6 daily; 4hr 30min); Ubon Ratchathani (6 daily; 10–12hr).

BY AIR-CONDITIONED MINIBUS

You can catch an a/c minibus to Bangkok's Victory Monument for B100 from several spots, including the east end of Central Pattaya Rd near Foodland and South Pattaya Rd in front of the Family Mart near Krung Thai Bank. Any hotel can arrange a ticket on a shared a/c minibus to Suvarnabhumi Airport for around B250/person (or about B800/car for a metered taxi). There are also tourist minibus services to Ko Samet and Ko Chang (tickets can also be booked through most tour agents): Samet Island Tour on Soi Yamato (☎038 427277, ⓦmalibu-samet.com) to the Ban Phe pier (for Ko Samet; B250); and Pattaya 35 Group opposite Big C on South Pattaya Rd (☎038 423447) to Ko Chang (B400 including ferry), via Ban Phe and Chanthaburi.

BY TRAIN

Pattaya is on a branch of the eastern rail line, and there's one slow train a day in each direction between the resort and Bangkok. Pattaya has two stations, both off the east side of Thanon Sukhumvit: the main one is about 500m north of the Central Pattaya Rd intersection, while Pattaya Tai Station is in South Pattaya near the Thanon Thep Prasit junction.

Destinations Bangkok (daily; 4hr); Si Racha (daily; 30min).

INFORMATION

Tourist information There are municipal tourist service booths (daily roughly 8.30am–4pm) on the beach at the mouth of Walking Street, at City Hall on North Pattaya Rd, at the north end of Jomtien Beach Rd and opposite Thanon Chaiyapruk on Jomtien Beach. The TAT office is inconveniently located at 609 Thanon Pratamnak between South Pattaya and Jomtien (daily 8.30am–4.30pm; ☎038 428750, ⓔtatchon@tat.or.th).

Newspapers The weekly *Pattaya Mail* (ⓦpattayamail .com) is one of several local newspapers that fills readers in on the often lurid goings-on.

GETTING AROUND

By songthaew Public songthaews – known locally as baht buses, and also available to charter – circulate continuously around the resort from dawn until at least 11pm. Most follow a standard anticlockwise route up Pattaya 2 Rd as far as North Pattaya Rd and back down Pattaya Beach Rd, for a fixed fee of B10/person; others run along the main east–west arteries of North, Central and South Pattaya roads. Songthaews to Jomtien start from next to the school on the south side of the junction of Pattaya 2 Rd and South Pattaya Rd and cost B10–20. Songthaews to Naklua, beyond north Pattaya, start from the north side of the same junction and head up Pattaya 2 Rd (also B10–20).

By motorbike Motorbike rental is available everywhere from B200/day, but beware of faulty vehicles, and of scams – sometimes rented bikes get stolen by touts keen to keep the customer's deposit, so you may want to use your own lock.

By car Avis car rental (ⓦavisthailand.com) has an office inside the *Dusit Resort* (☎038 361627); many of the motorbike touts also rent out jeeps for about B1200/day.

ACCOMMODATION

The quietest and least sleazy end of town to stay in is **North Pattaya**, between Central Pattaya Road and North Pattaya Road (Thanon Hat Pattaya Neua). There's no travellers' scene in Pattaya and hotels offering doubles under B450 outside low season are almost impossible to find; the cheapest alternatives are often rooms above the bars on sois 6, 13/2, 13/3 and 13/4.

PATTAYA BEACH

Areca Lodge 198/21 Soi Saisong 13 (aka Soi Diana Inn), Central Pattaya ☎038 410123, ⦿arecalodge .com; map p.388. An unusually stylish place for Pattaya, with pleasantly furnished a/c rooms in three wings built around two swimming pools, most of them with balconies, all with hot showers, mini-bars, TV and wi-fi. Buffet breakfast included. B1850

Centara Nova Hotel Soi 12 (aka Soi A.R. or Soi Sukrudee), Central Pattaya Rd ☎038 725999, ⦿centarahotelsresorts.com; map p.388. Central, quiet and welcoming boutique hotel, done out in a plush contemporary style that features a lot of burnished gold. There's a large, attractive pool fed by an artificial waterfall, a spa that uses Dead Sea mud and salt, a fitness centre and free computers and wi-fi. Breakfast included. B4500

The Cottage Off Pattaya 2 Rd, North Pattaya ☎038 425650, ⦿thecottagepattaya.com; map p.388. Good-value, simply furnished semi-detached brick bungalows, all with a/c, hot water, TV and fridge, pleasantly set among tall trees within a mature tropical garden away from the main road but opposite the Central Centre. Facilities include two small swimming pools and wi-fi in most rooms. B1000

Diana Dragon Apartment 198/16 Soi Saisong 13 (aka Soi Diana Inn), Central Pattaya ☎038 423928, ⦿dianapattaya.co.th; map p.388. This long-running Pattaya institution has some of the cheapest doubles in town, and they're good value considering the competition: huge and quite light, with wi-fi available, plus use of the pool at *Diana Inn*, 100m away. Fan B450, a/c B750

Dusit Thani Pattaya 240/2 Pattaya Beach Rd, North Pattaya ☎038 425611, ⦿dusit.com; map p.388. In the less sleazy part of town, this luxury Thai chain hotel is one of only a few Beach Rd hotels to be actually on the beach (the others are at the southern end). Sea-view rooms are worth paying extra for as the impressive panoramas take in the whole bay. Also on offer are two swimming pools, a spa and tennis courts, as well as good-value transfers from their hotel on Thanon Silom in Bangkok. B5300

Ice Inn Corner of Saisong 12 and Pattaya 2 Rd, Central Pattaya ☎038 720671, ⦿iceinnpattaya.com; map p.388. Cheap fan-cooled singles and reasonably priced a/c doubles in this small thirty-room hotel behind a handicrafts shop a few metres from the busier bar-beer sois. Rooms are simple but are all en suite. B790

Pattaya Marriott 218 Pattaya Beach Rd, Central Pattaya ☎038 412120, ⦿marriotthotels.com; map p.388. Located in the heart of the resort (attached to the Royal Garden Plaza shopping centre), and across the road from the beach, this international chain hotel is both very central and refreshingly calm, not least because it's designed around a huge swimming pool and tropical garden full of palms. Not surprisingly it's the first choice for anyone in Pattaya on business, with wi-fi available (at a price) throughout. Rooms are capacious and comfortable and have either pool- or sea view. Facilities include two restaurants, a fitness centre and kids' yoga. B6900

Sandalay Resort Between sois 1 and 2, Pattaya Beach Rd, North Pattaya ☎038 422660, ⦿sandalayresort .com; map p.388. This hundred-room hotel with swimming pool is in the quieter northern part of town just across the road from the beach. It has contemporary-styled, well-designed, though quite small, standard a/c rooms plus impressively large deluxe versions. Both options are available with sea view and tiny balcony at extra cost, but all have free wi-fi. Good discounts often available. Breakfast included. B2900

Woodlands Hotel and Resort 164 Thanon Pattaya-Naklua, North Pattaya ☎038 421707, ⦿woodland -resort.com; map p.388. A quiet, unpretentious and welcoming family-friendly garden resort 100m north of the Dolphin Circle roundabout, 400m from a scruffy but quiet thread of beach. The elegant, a/c rooms are in two storeys set round the pools and garden; the most expensive have direct access to the pool from ground-floor balconies. Broadband throughout. B2100

JOMTIEN AND BUDDHA HILL

★ **Rabbit Resort** Dongtan beachfront, Jomtien ☎038 303303, ⦿rabbitresort.com; map p.390. Beautiful place that's the most appealing option in Jomtien, and located on the nicest stretch of beach, the predominantly but not exclusively gay Dongtan Beach. Most accommodation is in teakwood cottages that are elegantly furnished with Thai fabrics and antiques and have garden-style bathrooms; there are also some "forest rooms" in a two-storey block. All are set around a tropical garden and pool just metres off the beach. Breakfast included. Rooms B4900, cottages B5900

Sheraton Pattaya Resort 437 Thanon Pratamnak (Cliff Rd), South Pattaya ☎038 259888, ⦿starwood hotels.com; map p.390. Pattaya's best hotel is smaller and more intimate than most in its class and offers five-star rooms and private pavilions, all with balconies, rain showers, DVD players and wi-fi, for which you pay extra. The beautiful series of freeform swimming pools and the spa are set within lush gardens – compensating for the minuscule private beach – though it's built on a hill so be prepared for lots of steps. You'll need transport to get to the shops and restaurants of downtown Pattaya. B6800

Sugar Hut 391/18 Thanon Tabphaya, midway between South Pattaya and Jomtien ☎038 251686, ⓦsugar-hut .com; map p.390. The most characterful accommodation in Pattaya comprises a charming collection of Ayutthaya-style

traditional wooden bungalows set in a fabulously profuse garden with three swimming pools. The bungalows are in tropical-chic style, with low beds, open-roofed shower rooms, mosquito nets and private verandas. You'll need your own transport as it's nowhere near the restaurants, shops or sea. B4000

EATING

In among the innumerable low-grade Western cafés that dominate Pattaya's **restaurant scene** are a few much classier joints serving good, sophisticated cuisine – at top-end prices. For the cheapest, most authentic Thai food, just head for the nearest of Pattaya's myriad building sites and you'll find street stalls catering to the construction-site workers.

PATTAYA BEACH

Ali Baba 1/13–14 Central Pattaya Rd ☎038 361620; map p.388. Look beyond the name and the wonderfully kitsch decor and waiters' uniforms, and you'll find some very good Indian food, which keeps many of Pattaya's visitors from the subcontinent happy. There's an authentically long menu of vegetarian dishes, featuring plenty of cheese, some interesting starters with okra, and the butter chicken's a real winner (B215). Daily 11am–midnight.

Italia Walking St, South Pattaya; map p.388. This very Italian café is an incongruously swish little haven with outdoor tables for watching the sleazy cabaret show that is Walking Street. Delicious home-made ice creams (B95 for 2 scoops), espressos, Sambuca and the like. Daily 9am–4am.

Khao Suay Ground Floor, Central Centre, Pattaya 2 Rd, North Pattaya; map p.388. A long menu of good modern Thai food (most mains about B110) draws Thai families to this tiny café inside the shopping centre. The varied options include *kaeng tai pla* (southern Thai fish stomach curry) and *nam prik pla thuu* (chilli relish with mackerel). Daily 11am–9.45pm.

★ **Ko Khun Pon Yang Kham** North Pattaya Rd, at Soi 6 ☎038 420571, ⓦko-khun.com; map p.388. This garden restaurant offers Thailand's equivalent of wagyu beef, from pampered Pon Yang Kham cows that are bred (from French, Swiss and Thai breeds) and reared in Isaan. It's served northeastern-style too, so no chips or mustard, but it goes well with *som tam*, and the red wine is decent (B90/glass). B135 for a small but delicious portion of sirloin on a sizzling hot plate. Daily 5.30pm–midnight.

★ **Mantra** Amari Orchid Hotel, Beach Rd, North Pattaya ☎038 429591, ⓦmantra-pattaya.com; map p.388. Setting the standard unexpectedly high for Pattaya, this large, beautifully designed bar-restaurant creates an

ambience somewhere between a contemporary Shanghai hotel and a maharaja's palace. Downstairs there's an open-plan view of the seven different, equally eclectic kitchens specializing in Japanese, Chinese, Indian, Mediterranean and Western food, grills and seafood. A meal might begin with avocado sushi (B410), supplemented with bite-sized Peking duck (B240), continue with coq au vin (B380), and end with lemon grass and pandanus crème brûlée. The walk-in wine cellar keeps over 160 imported wines. Daily 5pm–1am, Sun brunch 11am–3pm.

PIC Kitchen Soi 5, North Pattaya ☎038 428374, ⓦpic-kitchen.com; map p.388. One of Pattaya's top traditional Thai restaurants, set in a stylish series of teak buildings with the option of Thai-style cushion seating. Elegantly presented curries, lots of different seafood platters, spicy salads and some vegetarian dishes. Mains from B160. Daily 11am–2pm & 5–10.30pm.

JOMTIEN BEACH

Bruno's 306/63 Chateau Dale Plaza, Thanon Tabphaya, Jomtien ☎038 364600–1, ⓦbrunos-pattaya.com; map p.390. A local institution that's a favourite with expats celebrating special occasions. The food is upmarket, expensive, European – Provençal-style rack of lamb, sirloin steak, dark-chocolate mousse – and there's a cellar of some 150 wines. Main dishes from B250. Daily noon–2.30pm & 6pm–late.

Sugar Hut 391/18 Thanon Tabphaya, Jomtien; map p.390. Attached to the charming hotel of the same name (see above), this restaurant gives you the chance to soak up the ambience and enjoy the tropical gardens without shelling out for a bungalow (though the food's not cheap either). Meals are served in an open-sided *sala* and the menu is mainly classy Thai; recommendations include roast duck in red curry. Daily 7am–midnight.

DRINKING AND NIGHTLIFE

Pattaya's **nightlife** revolves around sex (see box, p.394). It is, however, just about possible to have a night out without getting entangled in sleaze, at one of the growing number of hostess-free **bars** listed below, a few of which are surprisingly style-conscious. However you choose to spend your evening, be warned that Pattaya is notorious for transvestite **pickpockets**, who target drunk men walking home in the early hours: while one "distracts" the victim from the front, the other extracts the wallet from behind.

PATTAYA'S SEX INDUSTRY

Of the thousand-plus bars in Pattaya, the vast majority are staffed by women and men whose aim is to get bought for the night – depending on whom you believe, there are between six thousand and twenty thousand Thais (and quite a few Russians) working in Pattaya's **sex industry**; most depressing of all is that this workforce includes children as young as 10, despite fairly frequent high-profile paedophile arrests. The vast majority of Pattaya's bars are open-air "**bar-beers**", which group themselves in neon clusters all over North, Central and South Pattaya so that there's barely a 500m stretch of road without its rowdy enclave. The setup is the same in all of them: from mid-afternoon the punters – usually lone males – sit on stools around a brashly lit circular bar, behind which the hostesses keep the drinks, bawdy chat and well-worn jokes flowing.

Drinks are a lot more expensive in the bouncer-guarded **go-go bars** on Walking Street in South Pattaya, where near-naked hostesses serve the beer and live sex shows keep the boozers hooked through the night. The scene follows much the same pattern as in Patpong, Nana and Soi Cowboy in Bangkok, with the women dancing on a small stage in the hope they might be bought for the night – or the week. Go-go dancers, shower shows and striptease are also the mainstays of the **gay scene**, centred on Pattayaland Soi 3 (Soi 13/5), South Pattaya.

The Blues Factory Soi Lucky Star, Walking St, South Pattaya ⓦthebluesfactorypattaya.com; map p.388. Considered to be the best live-music venue in Pattaya, with sets most nights (Tues–Sat) from the famously charismatic rock guitarist Lam Morrison and his band, and (except on Tues & Wed) from the house blues band as well. Daily 8.30pm–late.

Heineken Beer Garden Central Centre, Pattaya 2 Rd, North Pattaya; map p.388. Outdoor tables, draught Heineken and live music nightly (from about 8pm) from Thai singers and bands, doing mostly Thai pop and country. Also serves a full menu of Thai food (dishes from about B120), with Isaan and seafood specialities. Daily 5pm–2am.

Hopf Brew House Pattaya Beach Rd, between sois 13/1 (Yamato) and 13/2 (Post Office), Central Pattaya; map p.388. Cavernous and very popular a/c beer hall that brews its own Pilsener and wheat beer, serves generous wood-fired pizzas and other Italian dishes, and stages live music nightly. Attracts a youngish crowd, including vacationing couples. Daily 2pm–1/2am.

Jazz Pit Soi 5, North Pattaya ⓦjazzpitpub.com; map p.388. Nightly live jazz (from 8pm) in the cosy lounge-bar adjacent to the *PIC Kitchen* restaurant, and occasional high-profile celeb jamming sessions. Daily 7pm–midnight.

Minus Five Ice Bar Amari Nova Suites, Soi 12 (Soi Sukrudee), Central Pattaya Rd ☏038 426768, ⓦminus5pattaya.com; map p.388. Your chance to literally chill out at this cube of a bar sculpted entirely from ice, right down to the draught beer kegs on the ice-cold counter. For B500 you get lent a winter coat and mittens and are given 20min to down as many vodka shots as you can, then it's back out into the warmth of the trendy Bangkok-style bar adjacent. Daily 6pm–late.

ENTERTAINMENT

CINEMAS

There are several English-language screenings a day at the multiplexes.

Major Cineplex The Avenue shopping centre, Pattaya 2 Rd, Central Pattaya ⓦmajorcineplex.com.

SF Cinema City Central Festival Centre, Pattaya Beach Rd, Central Pattaya ⓦsfcinemacity.com.

TRANSVESTITE CABARETS

Tour groups – and families – constitute the main audience at Pattaya's *katoey* **cabarets**. Glamorous and highly professional, each theatre has a troupe of sixty or more transvestites who run through twenty musical-style numbers in fishnets and crinolines, ball gowns and leathers, against ever more lavish stage sets. Any tour agent can organize tickets.

Alcazar Opposite Soi 4 on Pattaya 2 Rd in North Pattaya ⓦalcazarpattaya.com. Daily 6.30pm, 8pm & 9.30pm. B600

Tiffany's North of Soi 1 on Pattaya 2 Rd in North Pattaya ⓦtiffany-show.co.th. Daily 6pm, 7.30pm & 9pm. B500. Also hosts an annual international *katoey* beauty pageant over 5 days in early Nov, Miss International Queen (ⓦmissinternationalqueen.com).

SHOPPING

Asia Books Floor 3, Central Festival Centre, between Pattaya Beach and Pattaya 2 roads. Good selection of English-language books. Daily 11am–11pm.

Thais4Life 504 Soi Yensabai Condotel, off Soi 17 (Soi

VC), South Pattaya ⓦthais4life.com. One of Pattaya's best secondhand bookshops, this charity sells all its books for B80 and donates profits to medical and other needy

projects including Baan Jing Jai orphanage. Mon–Sat noon–6pm.

DIRECTORY

Emergencies For all emergencies, call the tourist police on ⓣ1155 (free, 24hr) or contact them at their office beside TAT on Buddha Hill, between South Pattaya and Jomtien; in the evenings, they also set up a post at the north end of Walking Street.

Hospitals and dentists The best-equipped hospital is

the private Bangkok-Pattaya Hospital (ⓣ1719 or ⓣ038 259999, ⓦbangkokpattayahospital.com) on Thanon Sukhumvit, about 400m north of the intersection with North Pattaya Rd, which also has dental services.

Immigration office Soi 5, off Jomtien Beach Rd, Jomtien (Mon–Fri 8.30am–4.30pm; ⓣ038 252750).

Ban Phe

The small coastal town of **BAN PHE**, which lies 17km east of Rayong, its provincial capital, and about 200km from Bangkok, is the port for Ko Samet. Several piers for Samet boats compete for attention here, along with minimarkets, internet centres and tour desks selling onward bus tickets and private transfers. Ban Phe's main street runs from west to east behind the seafront, passing in turn the Chok Krisda pier and the nearby Taruaphe pier, before petering out a few hundred metres later at the municipal pier, Tha Reua Tessaban.

ARRIVAL AND DEPARTURE
BAN PHE

4

When the time comes to leave Ko Samet, you can book tickets for any of the followng direct buses and minibuses from Ban Phe at tour agencies on the island.

BY BUS
There are direct a/c buses operated by Cherdchai between Bangkok's Eastern (Ekamai) Bus Terminal and Ban Phe; on departure from Ban Phe, you can easily find them near the municipal pier. Coming by bus from Chanthaburi or Trat, you'll be dropped at a T-junction on Highway 3, from where a songthaew or motorbike taxi will take you the remaining 5km to the Ban Phe piers. Rayong has a wider choice of buses, including services to Chiang Mai and Isaan; the Ban Phe piers are served by frequent songthaews (about 30min) from Rayong bus station.

Destinations Bangkok (14 daily; 3hr); Chanthaburi (from Highway 3; 6 daily; 1hr 30min); Trat (from Highway 3; 6 daily; 3hr).

BY AIR-CONDITIONED MINIBUS
A/c minibuses run between many locations in Bangkok,

including Thanon Khao San (about 4hr; B250), Victory Monument (about 3hr 30min; B200) and Suvarnabhumi Airport (about 3hr; B500), and Ban Phe. There are also services from Pattaya (see p.391) and Ko Chang (see p.412). On departure, you'll find numerous a/c minibus companies in Ban Phe, including some at the municipal pier and in the two sois opposite Taruaphe (including Pattaya and Ko Chang services); a frequent Victory Monument service 200m west of the municipal pier; and the helpful RMT at the front of the Chok Krisda pier (ⓣ086 344 4026), which serves all three bus terminals in Bangkok, as well as Victory Monument.

BY BOAT
Frequent boats run from Ban Phe to Ko Samet, leaving from various piers – Tha Reua Tessaban has the widest choice. Details are given in our Ko Samet coverage (see p.399).

ACCOMMODATION

Christie's Prominent green building opposite the Taruaphe pier ⓣ089 834 9103, ⓦchristiesbanphe .com. If you get stuck in Ban Phe, this is a good choice for accommodation, offering homely, attractive rooms, some on the back away from the main road, all with a/c,

hot water, TV, fridge and free wi-fi. Downstairs is a restaurant and Irish bar, which organizes visa runs to Cambodia and trips to Siam Reap, and next door is a secondhand bookshop. **B600**

DIRECTORY

Tourist police At the municipal pier ⓣ038 651669 or ⓣ1155.

Ko Samet

B200 national park admission fee

Blessed with the softest, squeakiest sand within weekending distance of Bangkok, the tiny island of **KO SAMET**, which measures just 6km from top to toe, is a favourite escape for Thais, expats and tourists. Its fourteen small but dazzlingly white beaches are breathtakingly beautiful, lapped by pale blue water and in places still shaded by coconut palms and occasional white-flowered cajeput (*samet*) trees, which gave the

4

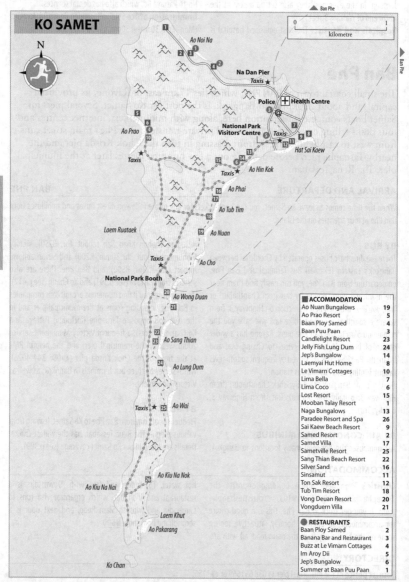

KO SAMET

N

▲ Ban Phe

0 _____ 1
kilometre

Ao Noi Na

Na Dan Pier
Taxis ★

Police ✚ Health Centre

**National Park
Visitors' Centre**
Taxis ★

Ao Prao

Hat Sai Kaew

Taxis ★

Ao Hin Kok

Ao Phai

Ao Tub Tim

Laem Ruataek

Ao Nuan

Taxis ★

Ao Cho

National Park Booth

Ao Wong Duan

Ao Sang Thian

Ao Lung Dum

Taxis ★ Ao Wai

Ao Kiu Na Nok

Ao Kiu Na Nai

Laem Khut

Ao Pakarang

Ko Chan

▲ Ban Phe

■ ACCOMMODATION	
Ao Nuan Bungalows	19
Ao Prao Resort	5
Baan Ploy Samed	4
Baan Puu Paan	3
Candlelight Resort	23
Jelly Fish Lung Dum	24
Jep's Bungalow	14
Laemyai Hut Home	8
Le Vimarn Cottages	10
Lima Bella	7
Lima Coco	6
Lost Resort	15
Mooban Talay Resort	1
Naga Bungalows	13
Paradee Resort and Spa	26
Sai Kaew Beach Resort	9
Samed Resort	2
Samed Villa	17
Sametville Resort	25
Sang Thian Beach Resort	22
Silver Sand	16
Sinsamut	11
Ton Sak Resort	12
Tub Tim Resort	18
Vong Deuan Resort	20
Vongduern Villa	21

● RESTAURANTS	
Baan Ploy Samed	2
Banana Bar and Restaurant	3
Buzz at Le Vimarn Cottages	4
Im Aroy Dii	5
Jep's Bungalow	6
Summer at Baan Puu Paan	1

WATERSPORTS AND BOAT TRIPS ON SAMET

Samet has no decent coral reefs of its own, so you'll have to take a boat trip to the islands of Ko Kudi and Ko Thalu, off the northeast coast, to get good **snorkelling** (around B700 from most beaches) or **diving**. From the main beaches you can also organize **boat trips** around Samet itself (around B500), rent kayaks and jet skis and arrange banana boat rides and parasailing.

Samed Resorts Diving Centre Ao Prao ☎038   and B17,000 for the four-day PADI Openwater course.
644100–3, ⓦ samedresorts.com. B3500 for two dives

---

island its name and which are used to build boats. But they are also crowded – although on weekdays there's a lot more room to breathe and relax – and developed to full capacity with over fifty sprawling, albeit low-rise, bungalow developments, a disfiguring number of which pay scant attention to landscaping and rubbish disposal. It's a sobering state of affairs considering that much of the island's coastline has been protected as part of the Khao Laem Ya – Mu Ko Samet **national park** since 1981; all visitors to Ko Samet are required to pay the standard national park fee on arrival, and most hoteliers also pay rent to park authorities, but there's little evidence that this income has been used to improve the island's infrastructure.

Samet's best **beaches** are along the **east coast**, where you'll find nearly all the bungalow resorts, though there's one rather exclusive beach on the otherwise largely inaccessible west coast, and the north-coast shoreline retains a pleasingly village ambience. Most islanders and many resort staff live in the northeast, near the island's main pier, in the ramshackle, badly drained village of **Na Dan**, which has small shops and cheap foodstalls as well as Samet's only school, health centre and wat. Na Dan's high street, which runs from the pier down to Hat Sai Kaew, and its other small roads, are paved, as is the road along the north coast to Ao Noi Na. However, from Hat Sai Kaew south, there's only one poorly maintained dirt road (with a branch west to Ao Prao) that runs down the island's forested central ridge, and much of the **interior** is dense jungle, home to hornbills, gibbons and spectacular butterflies. The evergreen vegetation belies the fact that there are no rivers on this unusually dry island, which gets only scant rainfall in an average year. Lack of rain is another plus point for tourists, though it means water is a precious and expensive commodity as it has to be trucked in from the mainland.

The most backpacker-oriented beaches are east-coast **Ao Hin Kok**, **Ao Phai** and **Ao Tub Tim**, with Ao Hin Kok and Ao Phai both quite lively in the evenings; the travellers' vibe at nearby **Ao Nuan** is more alternative, with **Ao Sang Thian** and north-coast **Ao Noi Na** also worth investigating. **Hat Sai Kaew** and **Ao Wong Duan** are the biggest centres on the east coast, dominated by upper-scale accommodation aimed at families, package tourists and Bangkok trendies. Samet's super-deluxe accommodation is on west-coast **Ao Phrao** and southern beauty **Ao Kiu**.

Shops and stalls in Na Dan (which has a pharmacy) and on all the main beaches sell basic travellers' necessities. Many bungalows have **safety deposits** and it's worth making use of them: theft is an issue on Samet and there are occasional instances of drinks being spiked by freelance bar-girls and punters waking next day without their valuables.

Hat Sai Kaew and Na Dan

From **NA DAN** pier, a ten-minute walk south along the paved high street brings you to **HAT SAI KAEW**, or Diamond Beach, named for its long and extraordinarily beautiful stretch of luxuriant sand, so soft and clean it squeaks underfoot – a result, apparently, of its unusually high silicon content. Unsurprisingly, it's the busiest beach on Samet, its shorefront packed with bungalows, restaurants, beachwear stalls, deckchairs and parasols, though the northern end is slightly more peaceful.

Ao Hin Kok

Separated from Hat Sai Kaew by a low promontory on which sits a mermaid statue (a reference to the early nineteenth-century poem, *Phra Abhai Mani*, by famous local poet Sunthorn Phu), **AO HIN KOK** is much smaller than its neighbour, and has more of a travellers' vibe. Just three sets of bungalows overlook the petite white-sand beach from the slope on the far side of the dirt road, and you can walk here from Na Dan in about fifteen minutes.

Ao Phai

Narrow but sparkling little **AO PHAI**, around the next headland from Ao Hin Kok, is Samet's party beach, where the shoreside *Silver Sand* bar and disco is known for its late-night dance music (with a strong gay presence at weekends). Not everyone has to join in though, as the bungalows on the fringes of the bay are far enough away for a good night's sleep. There's a minimarket and travel agent on the beach, and you can walk to Na Dan pier in twenty minutes.

Ao Tub Tim

Also known as Ao Pudsa, **AO TUB TIM** is another cute white-sand bay sandwiched between rocky points, partly shaded with palms and backed by a wooded slope. It has just two bungalow operations and is only a short stroll from Ao Phai and the other beaches further north, and a half-hour hike from Na Dan pier.

Ao Nuan

Clamber up over the headland from Ao Tub Tim (which gives you a fine panorama over Hat Sai Kaew) to reach Samet's smallest and most laidback beach, the secluded **AO NUAN**, effectively the private domain of *Ao Nuan Bungalows* (see p.401). Because it's some way off the main track, the beach gets hardly any through-traffic and feels quiet and private. Although not brilliant for swimming, the rocky shore reveals a good patch of sand when the tide withdraws; the more consistent beach at Ao Tub Tim is only five minutes' walk to the north, and **Ao Cho**, which has some coral, is a five-minute walk south along the footpath.

Ao Wong Duan

The horseshoe bay of **AO WONG DUAN**, a ten-minute walk round the next-but-one point from Ao Nuan, is Samet's second most popular beach after Hat Sai Kaew. Though it's not as pretty and suffers even more from hordes of day-trippers, it does offer some attractive upmarket accommodation; most guests are either package tourists, Pattaya overnighters, or weekending Bangkokians so shoestring travellers aren't well catered for. Although the beach is fairly long and broad, the central shorefront is almost lost under a knot of tiny bars (many with irresistibly comfy armchairs) and tourist shops, and the main stretch of beach all but disappears at high tide. Facilities include minimarkets, ATMs and internet access.

Ao Sang Thian (Candlelight Beach) and Ao Lung Dum

A favourite with Thai students, who relish the beauty of its slightly wild setting, **AO SANG THIAN** ("Candlelight Beach") and contiguous Ao Lung Dum display almost none of the commerce of Wong Duan, a couple of minutes' walk over the hill, though the scenic shorefront is fronted by an unbroken line of bungalows. The narrow, white-sand coastline is dotted with wave-smoothed rocks and partitioned by larger outcrops that create several distinct bays; as it curves outwards to the south you get a great view of the island's east coast. At its southern end, Ao Sang Thian becomes **AO LUNG DUM**, and the various little bungalow outfits fringing the shore here are pretty similar.

Ao Wai

A fifteen-minute walk along the coast path from Lung Dum brings you to **AO WAI**, a very pretty white-sand bay, partially shaded and a good size considering it supports just one (large) **bungalow** operation, *Sametville Resort*, which also spills across on to neighbouring little Ao Hin Kleang.

Ao Kiu

Over an hour's walk south of Ao Sang Thian, via a track that begins behind *Vong Deuan Resort* on Ao Wong Duan and can be joined at the southern end of Ao Thian, the gorgeous little twin bays of **AO KIU** – Ao Kiu Na Nok on the east coast and Ao Kiu Na Nai on the west – are separated by just a few hundred metres of land. Both beaches are the domain of Samet's most exclusive hotel, the *Paradee Resort and Spa* (see p.402).

Ao Prao (Paradise Bay)

Across on the upper west coast, the rugged, rocky coastline only softens into beach once, at **AO PRAO**, also known as Paradise Bay, on the northwestern stretch, some 4km north of Ao Kiu Na Nai. This is Samet's most upmarket beach, dominated by two expensively elegant resorts, plus one slightly more affordable option, and nothing else to lower the tone. If you're only visiting for the day, the most direct route from the east-coast beaches is via the inland track from behind *Sea Breeze* on Ao Phai, which takes about twenty minutes on foot. If staying on Ao Prao, your hotel will arrange boat transfers.

Ao Noi Na

West of Na Dan, the island's north coast – known simply as **AO NOI NA** even though it's not strictly a single bay – has a refreshingly normal village feel compared to the rest of Samet. There are an increasing number of places to stay along the narrow coastal road here, offering serene views across the water to the mainland hills behind Ban Phe, and just one white-sand beach of note at the far western end. Though this beach has been hogged by the luxurious *Mooban Talay Resort*, it's not private and you can walk there from Na Dan pier in about twenty-five minutes, passing a couple of good **restaurants** (see p.403) en route.

ARRIVAL AND DEPARTURE   **KO SAMET**

The port of departure for Ko Samet is **Ban Phe** (see p.395). If you want to book your onward travel while on Ko Samet, CP Travel on Hat Sai Kaew (☎ 038 644136), in the beach-access arcade near the National Park office, sells **bus** and **minibus** as well as domestic and international **air tickets**; it also has a few new and secondhand books.

BY BOAT
RESORT BOATS
If you're staying in any of Samet's mid-range or expensive accommodation, ask the resort about boats when you book: many establishments have their own big boats or speedboats to ferry you direct from Ban Phe on reasonably

priced shared transfers (usually at set times). Such transfers may be free, but a few resorts make their paid transfers compulsory. You might also want to look into the packages offered by many resorts, which is how most Thais travel to Ko Samet: as well as boats and accommodation, these might include things like dinners and massages.

PUBLIC BOATS

There are half a dozen competing piers in Ban Phe, offering a bewildering variety of speedboats and bigger, slower but much cheaper wooden boats; prices on the latter to Samet's main pier, Na Dan, are fixed (B50 one way; 40min). Watch out for rip-off touts in Ban Phe who try to sell boat tickets at inflated prices or falsely claim that visitors to Ko Samet have to buy a return boat ticket. The first boat from Ko Samet back to Ban Phe leaves Na Dan pier at 7am, and in theory there's then an hourly service across to Ban Phe until 6pm, but if you have a plane to catch you should allow for boat no-shows and delays.

Tha Reua Tessaban The municipal pier at the east end of Ban Phe has a rather chaotic market hall of a dozen or so private booths which offer the widest choice of speedboats, as well as wooden boats (in high season, hourly to Na Dan, plus three daily to Ao Wong Duan for B80).

Chok Krisda About 500m west of Tha Reua Tessaban, this helpful pier (☎ 081 862 4067, ⓦ ck-pier.com) offers speedboats (B1300/boat to Na Dan) as well as wooden boats hourly to Na Dan (8am–6pm), Ao Noi Na (2 daily; about 40min; B60) and Ao Wong Duan (2 daily, 3 daily in the opposite direction; about 1hr 15min; B70).

GETTING AROUND

The best way to get up and down the island is by walking along the east-coast beaches and the mostly well-marked paths that connect them. Samet's principal inland road is a rough, deeply rutted and alternately dusty/muddy dirt track that runs north–south and gives access to all the main beaches.

By songthaew Fleets of green songthaews wait for fares at the Na Dan pier and half-a-dozen other stands around the island, as marked on our map; they will also pick up from accommodation if you get staff to phone them. Rates are fixed and high. You'll generally be charged for chartering the whole vehicle (potentially up to B350 to go from Na Dan pier to Ao Sang Thian). Only if there's a large group of people travelling, for example

when boats dock at Na Dan, will you get the "shared" rates (B20–40/person).

By motorbike or ATV You need to be very confident to negotiate the mud and potholes on a motorbike (from B300/day), which is why it's become fashionable to rent a lumbering four-wheeled ATV instead (from B1200/day); both are available for rent at Na Dan pier and on most beaches.

ACCOMMODATION

The trend across the island is upmarket and in high season you'll be hard pressed to secure an en-suite **bungalow** for under B800, though a few no-frills B300 huts do remain. All beaches get packed on weekends and national holidays, when booking ahead is advisable, though, unusually for Thailand, walk-in guests are often offered the best rates. Many bungalow managers raise their **prices** by sixty percent during peak periods and sometimes on weekends as well: the rates quoted here are typical weekday high-season rates.

HAT SAI KAEW AND NA DAN

Much of the accommodation on Hat Sai Kaew is crammed uncomfortably close together and prices are high. Cheap rooms are sometimes available above the shops and restaurants on the Na Dan road.

Laemyai Hut Home North end of Hat Sai Kaew ☎ 038 644282, ⓦ laemyai.com. The fan bungalows here are the best of the cheapest options on this beach, not least because they're dotted widely around a shaded, sandy, plant-filled garden in one of the prettiest spots, under the Laem Yai headland at the quieter northern end. Fan bungalows are simple but en suite and colourfully painted; a/c versions, some with hot showers, are also available. Fan B800, a/c B1200

Lima Bella Na Dan ☎ 038 644222, ⓦ limasamed.com. This little garden haven occupies a quiet heliconia-filled plot with its own pretty swimming pool, on the semicircular road that arcs round behind and to the east of Na Dan high street. Its 26 design-conscious a/c rooms all have hot water, fridges, TVs and daybeds; some have separate mezzanine

bedrooms or living areas and many have bathtubs. The ambience is more intimate and private than most hotels on Samet and it's popular with families. Free wi-fi in the lobby; breakfast included. B3730

Sai Kaew Beach Resort Hat Sai Kaew ☎ 038 644197, ⓦ samedresorts.com. This popular and highly efficient resort has over 150 a/c rooms with hot water, TV and fridge, most of them in distinctive and thoughtfully designed bungalows in bright primary colours. The cheaper "deluxe" cottages and rooms occupy their own grassy area with a separate swimming pool, in front of a pretty but minute little patch of sandy shoreline; they have garden bathrooms and the cottages have private decks. "Premier" rooms are more urban and hotel-like. B6200

Sinsamut Hat Sai Kaew ☎ 038 644134, ⓦ sinsamut-kohsamed.com. Initial appearances aren't encouraging here, with various types of rooms stuffed into cheek-by-jowl little blocks behind the restaurant midway down the beach, but most are pleasant inside, with bright, colourful, contemporary decor, and some have outdoor space. The quirky fan-cooled "*katom*" bungalows, set around a grassy little roof garden, enjoy the best outlook. Free wi-fi throughout. Fan B800, a/c B1500

Ton Sak Resort Hat Sai Kaew ☎ 038 644314, ⊛ tonsak .com. The timbered cabins here are packed very close together, but the surrounding borders of shrubs add a little privacy, and few are more than 100m from the water. Interiors are comfortable if a little old-fashioned, and have a/c and modern hot-water bathrooms. Breakfast included. B3300

AO HIN KOK

Jep's Bungalow Ao Hin Kok ☎ 038 644112–3. A spread of options in unremarkable wooden chalets and concrete bungalows, ranged up the shady, terraced, sandy-soiled garden: fan-cooled with shared or en-suite bathrooms, or a/c with hot water, TV and breakfast included. It has internet access (computers and wi-fi, both payable), a tour desk and a good restaurant (see p.403). Fan and shared bathroom B300, fan en-suite B500, a/c B1200

Naga Bungalows Ao Hin Kok ☎ 087 958 6206. Long-running, somewhat jaded resort, with a beachfront bar, a Thai boxing ring, a secondhand bookshop, a bakery, currency exchange, internet access and some of the cheapest accommodation on Ko Samet: simple bamboo and wood huts stacked in tiers up the slope, with decks, mosquito nets and shared bathrooms, as well as pricier concrete a/c rooms with their own adjacent cold-water bathroom. The compound's a bit scrappy, but the rooms are reasonably well maintained. Fan B400, a/c B600

AO PHAI

Lost Resort Ao Phai, on the main track to Wong Duan and Ao Prao ☎ 038 644041–2, ⊛ thelostresort.net. A short way inland from *Sea Breeze*, this two-storey block sits peacefully among the hornbills and fruit bats in a grove of tall trees. The ten rooms here can be fan or a/c and are of a good standard and well priced. Fan B600, a/c B800

Samed Villa South end of Ao Phai ☎ 038 644094, ⊛ samedvilla.com. The huge rooms and villa-style bungalows at this Swiss-owned resort are packed into a fairly small area along the rocks at the southern end of the bay (good views from the front row) and up the slope behind the restaurant. Interiors are luxurious and well furnished and especially good for families; they all have a/c, hot water, TV, free wi-fi and fridges. Buffet breakfast included. B1600

Silver Sand Middle of Ao Phai ☎ 038 644300–1, ⊛ silversandresort.samet.i8.com. This party hub has a spread of well-turned-out rooms, including whitewashed, a/c chalets ranged around a pretty garden; they all come with safety boxes, verandas and good modern hot-water bathrooms, and some have polished wooden floors. Fan B800, a/c B1200

AO TUB TIM

★ **Tub Tim Resort** Ao Tub Tim ☎ 038 644025–9, ⊛ tubtimresort.com. The most popular place to stay here is a sprawling, well-run resort with over a hundred handsome chalet-style wooden bungalows of various sizes and designs, all with classy modern furnishings and outdoor space, plus a good restaurant. Fan B600, fan and hot shower B1000, a/c (breakfast included) B1500

AO NUAN

Ao Nuan Bungalows Ao Nuan ☎ 087 142 7512. The octagonal restaurant and simple, idiosyncratic huts here hark back to a mellower, old-school island vibe, entirely removed from the commercialism of the other beaches (though room rates are definitely modern-day). The nine sturdy timber huts are each built to a slightly different design and dotted across the tree-covered slope that drops down to the bay, with a few hanging right over the beach. Sharing bathrooms, the cheapest are large but spartan, with just a platform bed and a mosquito net; the most expensive now boast a/c and hot water. Fan B800, a/c B1500

AO WONG DUAN

Vong Deuan Resort Middle of Ao Wong Duan ☎ 038 651777, ⊛ vongdeuan.com. Ideally located in the middle of the beach, with attractive a/c bungalows in various designs set around a pretty tropical garden, including nice white cottages with thatched roofs, contemporary styled interiors and garden bathrooms (with hot showers). Service is efficient, attentive and hotel-like, which makes it a favourite with older guests. Breakfast included. B2000

Vongduern Villa Southern Ao Wong Duan ☎ 038 652300, ⊛ vongduernvilla.com. Occupying a big, shady chunk of the bay's southern end, this resort features over fifty rooms of various types and standards, all of them design-conscious and a/c. "Standard" rooms are whitewashed timber huts built on stilts, with picture windows, decks and modern furnishings; while "Deluxe" means more minimalist versions kitted out with dark-wood floors, Japanese-style platform beds and DVD players. There's also an attractive restaurant deck jutting out over the water, a coffee bar and kayaks and snorkelling equipment for rent. Standard B1200, deluxe B1800

AO SANG THIAN

Candlelight Resort Ao Sang Thian ☎ 089 247 9597. Very nice wooden bungalows with lots of light and air strung out in a long line, each one facing the water. Most are fan-cooled, with hot showers and TVs; the resort's a/c options are either in these wooden bungalows or in large, very clean concrete rooms with small bathrooms behind the restaurant. Fan B800, a/c B1200

4

Sang Thian Beach Resort Towards Ao Sang Thian's northern end ☎038 644255, ⓦsangthianbeachresort .com. This complex comprising a minimart, an ATM, a massage centre and expansive, waterfront restaurant areas (with free wi-fi) is somewhat institutional, and the welcome lacks the human touch, too. However, the resort boasts tasteful a/c timber chalets built up the cliffside on a series of decks and steps – the decor is navy-and-white maritime chic. There's hot water, TVs and fridges, and views, mostly encompassing the sea, are pretty. It also has much less interesting compact brick bungalows and concrete rooms up the eastern slope. B2000

AO LUNG DUM

Jelly Fish Lung Dum Ao Lung Dum ☎081 458 8430 or ☎081 652 8056. Friendly spot under the bougainvillaea with a decent waterside restaurant. Most of the twenty bungalows with hot showers are right on the rocky shore, practically overhanging the water; a few cheaper rooms and bungalows at the back are also available. Fan B800, a/c B1000

AO WAI

Sametville Resort Ao Wai ☎038 651681–2, ⓦsametvilleresort.com. At this sizeable resort with a large pool, bungalows in all categories vary in quality, but you've plenty to choose from – including some cute converted boats – unless you come at the weekend, when it tends to fill up with Thai groups. Also on offer are rental motorbikes, snorkelling equipment and Thai massage. Fan B1100, a/c B1700

AO KIU

Paradee Resort and Spa Ao Kiu ☎038 644104–7, ⓦsamedresorts.com. Top of the range on Samet, a very luxurious five-star resort where each of the forty villas stretches over more than 100 square metres and most have their own small private pools. There's also an infinity-edged main pool, a spa and fitness centre, plus lots of nice little extras like DVD players, free wi-fi, free kayaks and snorkelling equipment. B17,000

AO PRAO (PARADISE BAY)

Ao Prao Resort Ao Prao ☎038 644101, ⓦsamedresorts .com. Fifty luxurious wooden chalets and rooms set in a mature tropical garden that slopes down to the beach, all with a/c, TVs and mini-bars. There's an infinity pool, a dive centre, windsurfing and kayaking, among lots of watersports, and a picturesquely sited restaurant with a live band most evenings in high season. The resort runs a shuttle boat from Ban Phe three times a day (B250). B7700

Le Vimarn Cottages Ao Prao ☎038 644104, ⓦsamedresorts.com. The most indulgent resort on this beach comprises charming, gorgeously furnished cottages, a delightful spa and an infinity pool. Its *Buzz* restaurant (see opposite) is highly regarded. B10,700

Lima Coco Ao Prao ☎038 644068, ⓦlimasamed.com. The youngest, trendiest and cheapest choice on the beach, with a Bangkok contemporary chic look and lots of white walls, brightly coloured cushions, day beds and decks. Rooms are built close together in layers up the side of the hill, so that most have some kind of a sea view. Free wi-fi; kayaks, snorkels and sunbeds for rent. Breakfast included. B4400

AO NOI NA

Baan Ploy Samed (Ploy Sea) Ao Noi Na ☎02 438 9771–2, ⓦsamedresorts.com. Striking, brown contemporary building with an orange infinity pool, where bedrooms done out in dark wood and orange come with a/c, rain showers, TV and fridge. Pricier options come with a sea-view deck, while the most expensive rooms are in stilted wooden houses, 50m out in the sea. Breakfast and boat transfers included. B5500

★ **Baan Puu Paan** Ao Noi Na ☎081 172 4486, ⓔlizziecj@hotmail.com or ⓔbaanpuupaan@hotmail .com. Less than 15min walk from Na Dan, this chilled-out boutique guesthouse offers three beautiful en-suite bungalows built on stilts in the sea. They're all furnished with cushions and lamps, and prices stay the same year-round and at weekends; the pick of them is large and fan-cooled, with cheery maritime decor and a huge deck offering unparalleled views. Guests can either swim off the jetty or from the tiny beaches to either side, and there's a pool table and free wi-fi throughout. Fan B1200, a/c B1500

Mooban Talay Resort Northwestern Ao Noi Na ☎081 838 8682, ⓦmoobantalay.com. At the far northwest end of the beach is one of the classiest resorts on the island, a secluded haven at the end of the road, set under the trees on a gorgeous, quiet white-sand beach. Accommodation is in large, attractive a/c bungalows, all with platform beds, garden bathrooms, wi-fi and outdoor seating: the priciest, seafront ones have enormous decks, and there's a beachside pool and a spa. Boat transfers and breakfast included. B6800

Samed Resort Ao Noi Na ☎038 644334 or ☎081 427 9571, ⓦsamed-resort.net. British-managed set of a dozen bungalows, occupying a wide sandy grove just across the road from a tiny, almost private beach; though the beach is a bit scruffy it has shade, with hammocks and good swimming. Bungalows range from small, en-suite concrete affairs with hammocks to large cottages with nice mezzanine beds, a/c, TV and hot showers; interiors in all are modern and cheery. In busy periods, you can also rent tents here (B300 for two including bedding). The shoreside restaurant, and its lively bar, has a pool table and table tennis. Free wi-fi throughout. Discounts for longer stays. Fan B500, a/c B1000

EATING AND DRINKING

Most visitors to Ko Samet just eat at their resorts, and in truth there are few restaurants worth making an effort to get to.

HAT SAI KAEW AND NA DAN

Banana Bar and Restaurant Na Dan high street, not far from the police station. Tiny establishment serving tastily authentic yellow, green and red curries (B80), as well as *tom yam* and spicy salads. Daily 9am–11.30pm.

Im Aroy Dii Na Dan high street, 10m from the National Park box on Hat Sai Kaew, on the left-hand side of the road (no English sign). There's not much to this basic but clean and bright restaurant, but its name, meaning "Full, Delicious, Good", says it all: tasty, cheap dishes on rice (from B50), as well as more interesting options such as squid with salted egg and chicken with cashew nuts (both B120). Fruit shakes and a cheery chef-owner, too. Daily early–9pm.

AO HIN KOK

★ **Jep's Bungalow** Ao Hin Kok ⊙ 038 644112, ⓦ jepbungalow.com. Popular all-rounder serving a great menu of authentic Thai dishes (including popular *som tam* sets for B150), seafood, Indian (with chicken tikka for B120 and plenty of veggie dishes), Japanese, Italian and Mexican food at its tables on the sand, set under trees strung with fairylights and given extra atmosphere by mellow music.

Also does cappuccino and cakes. Daily 7am–12.30am.

AO PRAO (PARADISE BAY)

Buzz at Le Vimarn Cottages Ao Prao ⊙ 038 644104, ⓦ samedresorts.com. Very refined restaurant serving highly regarded, highly priced Thai food, including a wide choice of salads, dips and curries (from B260), in its chic modern dining room and upstairs terrace. The attached Italian restaurant, *O*, is just overpriced.

AO NOI NA

Baan Ploy Samed Ao Noi Na ⊙ 038 644188–9. Seafood restaurant in a group of wooden houses on stilts, 50m out in the sea – a boatman will come over and pick you up. Rock lobster is a speciality (B1500/kg), but there are also more manageable dishes such as shrimp green curry (B200). Daily 10am–10pm.

Summer at Baan Puu Paan Ao Noi Na ⊙ 081 172 4486. Stunningly sited eating area at the end of a jetty, where you can tuck into all kinds of tasty global dishes, from fish tikka (B320) to pasta and risotto. There's also a Moroccan-styled roadside bar-restaurant. Daily 8am–10pm or later.

DIRECTORY

Banks There are ATMs at the Na Dan pier-head, beside the Hat Sai Kaew national park office, on Ao Wong Duan and Ao Sang Thian; the bigger bungalows also change money.

Emergencies Ko Samet's health centre and police station (⊙ 038 644111) are on Na Dan high street, but for anything serious you should go to the Bangkok-Rayong hospital in Rayong (⊙ 038 921999, ⓦ rayonghospital.com).

Internet There are internet centres around the National Park office on the Na Dan high street, a couple of which have wi-fi, and on almost every beach.

Post office At *Naga Bungalows* on Ao Hin Kok.

Chanthaburi

For over five hundred years, the seams of rock rich in sapphires and rubies that streak the hills of eastern Thailand have drawn prospectors and traders of all nationalities to the provincial capital of **CHANTHABURI**, 80km east of Ban Phe. Many of these hopefuls established permanent homes in the town, particularly the Shans from Burma, the Chinese and the Cambodians. Though the veins of precious stones have now been all but exhausted, Chanthaburi's reputation as a gem centre has continued to thrive and this is still one of the most famous places in Thailand to trade in gems (most of them now imported from Sri Lanka and elsewhere), not least because Chanthaburi is as respected a cutting centre as Bangkok, and Thai lapidaries are considered among the most skilled – and affordable – in the world. Chanthaburi is also an exceptionally fertile province, renowned for its abundance of orchards, particularly durian, rambutan and mangosteen, which are celebrated with an annual **fruit festival** in the town, held in May or June.

The town is made for low-key exploration, without being particularly compelling. Similarly, the Chanthaburi coastline is barely developed for tourism, though it's popular with Thai visitors for its quiet, shady beaches. However, even if you're not planning a visit to Chanthaburi, you may find yourself stranded here for a couple

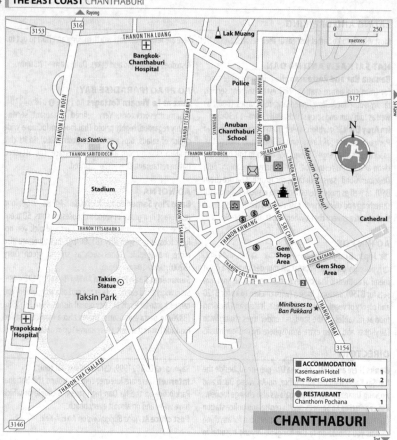

CHANTHABURI

Rayong

3153
316

THANON THA LUANG

Lak Muang

Bangkok-
Chanthaburi
Hospital

Police

THANON LEAP NOEN

Bus Station

THANON SARITDIDECH

THANON SARITDIDECH

THANON BENCHAMA-RACHUTIT

Anuban
Chanthaburi
School

SOI RAT MAITRI

THANON RIM NAM

317

Sa Kaew

Maenam Chanthaburi

Stadium

THANON TETSABARN 3

THANON TETSABARN 2

THANON KHWANG

THANON SRI CHAN

Cathedral

THANON SRI CHAN

Gem
Shop
Area

TROK KACHANG

Gem Shop
Area

Taksin
Statue

Taksin Park

Prapokkao
Hospital

THANON THA CHALAEB

Minibuses to
Ban Pakkard

THANON TRIRAT

2

3154

3146

0   250
metres

N

Trat

---

of hours between **buses**, as this is a major transit point for east-coast services (including most Rayong–Trat buses) and a handy terminus for buses to and from the northeast.

Thanon Rim Nam

Chanthaburi's most interesting neighbourhoods are close to the **river**, particularly along **Thanon Rim Nam**, with its mix of pastel-painted, colonial-style housefronts and traditional wooden shophouses, many displaying finely carved latticework. This district is home to a large Catholic Vietnamese community, most of whom fled here in waves following religious persecution between the eighteenth century and the late 1970s. The earliest refugees constructed what is now, following several revamps, Thailand's largest cathedral, the **Church of the Immaculate Conception**, located across the footbridge from the southern end of Thanon Rim Nam.

The gem dealers' quarter

West of the bridge, the **gem dealers' quarter** begins, centred around Trok Kachang and Thanon Sri Chan (the latter signed in English as "Gem Street") and packed with dozens of gem shops. Most lie empty during the week, but on Fridays, Saturdays and

CROSSING TO CAMBODIA VIA CHANTHABURI PROVINCE

Most foreigners use the Aranyaprathet–Poipet crossing to get into **Cambodia** (see p.383), with access possible by bus via Chanthaburi. There are also two less used crossings in Chanthaburi province, giving access to the Cambodian town of Pailin, just east of the border. Daung Lem Border Crossing at **Ban Laem** is 88km northeast of Chanthaburi (not served by public transport) and the Phsa Prom border crossing is at **Ban Pakkard** (aka Chong Phakkat), 72km northeast of Chanthaburi. There's a minibus service in the morning from Chanthaburi (just south across the bridge from *The River Guest House*) to Ban Pakkard (1hr; B150). It's best to arm yourself in advance with an e-visa for Cambodia, but it's also possible to get a thirty-day visa on arrival at the border; if entering Thailand via this route you'll probably be obliged to show proof of onward travel from Thailand.

Sunday mornings they come alive as local dealers arrive to sift through mounds of tiny coloured stones and classify them for resale to the hundreds of buyers who drive down from Bangkok.

Taksin Park

West of the gem quarter and market, the landscaped **Taksin Park** is the town's recreation area and memorial to King Taksin of Thonburi, the general who reunited Thailand between 1767 and 1782 after the sacking of Ayutthaya by the Burmese. Chanthaburi was the last Burmese bastion on the east coast – when Taksin took the town he effectively regained control of the whole country. The park's heroic bronze statue of Taksin is featured on the back of the B20 note.

ARRIVAL AND DEPARTURE   CHANTHABURI TOWN

By bus Chanthaburi bus station (☎039 311299) is on Thanon Saritdidech, about 750m northwest of the town centre and market. Seven daily buses make the scenic Chanthaburi–Sa Kaew–Khorat journey in both directions – Sa Kaew is a useful interchange for buses to Aranyaprathet and Cambodia (see box on p.383).

Destinations Bangkok (Eastern Bus Terminal; at least hourly; 4–5hr); Bangkok (Northern Bus Terminal; 13 daily; 3–4hr); Bangkok (Suvarnabhumi Airport; 5 daily; 3hr); Khorat (7 daily; 6hr); Laem Ngop (for Ko Chang; 3 daily; 1hr); Phitsanulok (daily; 11hr); Rayong (8 daily; 2hr); Sa Kaew (for Aranyaprathet; 10 daily; 3hr); Trat (hourly; 1hr 30min).

ACCOMMODATION

Kasemsarn Hotel 98/1 Thanon Benchama-Rachutit ☎039 312340, ⓦkasemsarnhotel.net. Unexpectedly contemporary hotel, whose comfortable a/c rooms, with hot showers, fridges and TVs, are built round a central atrium and done out in whitewash and dark wood; they all have free wi-fi and there are free computers and a smart coffee shop downstairs. B800
The River Guesthouse 3/5–8 Thanon Sri Chan ☎039

328211. Traveller-oriented outfit on the edge of the gems quarter, with a riverside terrace next to the road bridge where breakfast is served. Its cheapest rooms are tiny and windowless and share cold-water bathrooms; the better fan and a/c en-suite rooms have narrow beds and TVs, and some boast river-view balconies and hot showers. Computers and free wi-fi throughout. Fan B150, en-suite fan B250, a/c B400

EATING

Foodstalls in the market and along the riverside sois sell Vietnamese spring rolls (*cha gio*) with sweet sauce. Locally made Chanthaburi rice noodles (*sen Chan*) are popularly used in *phat thai* throughout Thailand, but in Chanthaburi they're also crucial to the local beef noodle soup, *kway tiaw neua liang*, whose dark broth is flavoured with pungent herbs and spices, including the cardamom that the Chanthaburi mountains are famous for.
Chanthorn Phochana 102/5–8 Thanon Benchama-

Rachutit. By far the best of the town's restaurants is this spot a few metres up the road from the *Kasemsarn Hotel*, for which Thai foodies make a beeline. As well as selling Chanthaburi delicacies as souvenirs, it serves regional dishes such as *lon puu* (a kind of salad dip with crab; B100) and *kway tiaw neua liang,* and a delicious range of spicy *yam* salads, Thai curries and stir-fries, many of them using local herbs and vegetables. Daily 8.30am–9pm.

Coastal Chanthaburi

The barely developed **coastline** to the west of Chanthaburi is very pretty, popular with Thai visitors for its empty beaches and shady casuarina trees and worth exploring if you have your own transport.

Hat Khung Wiman and Ao Khung Kraben

Just off Route 3399, about 30km southwest of Chanthaburi, or 80km east of Ban Phe, **HAT KHUNG WIMAN** is a quiet, shady, bronze-sand beach and has two nice places to stay. A couple of kilometres southeast of here and you're at the lip of **AO KHUNG KRABEN**, a deep, lagoon-like scoop of a bay that's occasionally visited by dugongs and is edged by dense mangrove forest. A wide swathe of this mangrove swamp is protected under a royal conservation project and crossed by a km-long boardwalk; you can also rent kayaks in the cool season to follow a signed riverine trail. Access is via Laem Sadet on the southern curve of the bay.

KKB (Khung Kraben Bay) Aquarium

Across the road from the mangrove project on Laem Sadet's beach road • Tues–Fri 8.30am–4.30pm, Sat & Sun 8.30am–5.30pm • Free • ⓦ aquariumthailand.com

The impressively stocked **KKB Aquarium** is a royal initiative and displays a multicoloured variety of reef fish, some sea horses and a few larger marine creatures, with informative English signage.

ACCOMMODATION   **KHUNG WIMAN**

Al Medina Beach House Hat Khung Wiman ☎039 417105, ⓦalmedinabeach.com. Nine very chic, Moroccan-inspired rooms, all with a/c, hot water and DVD players, some with rain showers and bathtubs. Bicycles, kayaks and wi-fi available. Breakfast included. B4550

★ **Faasai Resort** Khung Wiman ☎039 417404, ⓦfaasai.com. This New Zealand–Thai owned, environmentally conscious resort is an ideal base from which to explore the coast. Its comfortable, family-friendly, a/c bungalows sit in a tropical garden with views of the Cardamom mountains on the Cambodian border and there's a swimming pool, wi-fi and Wat Pho-trained massage therapists on site. Very unusually, the resort also has its own private little wetland conservation area, where you can sit bird-watching, swim in the natural spring pool or kayak along the rivulet. Hat Khung Wiman is 10min walk away and *Faasai* rents bicycles, motorbikes and cars and organizes interesting local tours. B1700

Trat

The small and pleasantly unhurried provincial capital of **TRAT**, 68km southeast of Chanthaburi, is the perfect place to stock up on essentials, extend your visa, or simply take a break before striking out again. Most travellers who find themselves here are heading either for Ko Chang, via the nearby port at **Laem Ngop**, for the outer islands, or for Cambodia, via the border at **Hat Lek**, 91km southeast of town. But Trat itself has its own distinctive, if understated, old-Thailand charm and there are lots of welcoming guesthouses to tempt you into staying longer.

YELLOW OIL

Trat is famous across Thailand for the **yellow herbal oil** mixture, *yaa luang*, invented by one of its residents, Mae Ang Ki, and used by Thais to treat many ailments: sniff it for travel sickness and blocked sinuses, or rub it on to relieve mosquito and sandfly bites, ease stomach cramps, or sterilize wounds. Ingredients include camphor and aloe vera. It's well worth investing in a lip-gloss-sized bottle of the stuff before heading off to the sandfly-plagued islands; you can buy it for about B70 and upwards at Trat market and at nearby Tratosphere bookshop. There are now several imitations, but Mae Ang Ki's original product (ⓦ somthawinyellowoil.com) has a tree logo to signify that it's made by royal appointment.

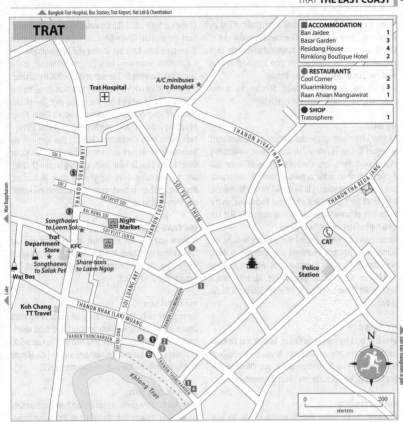

TRAT

ACCOMMODATION
Ban Jaidee	1
Basar Garden	3
Residang House	4
Rimklong Boutique Hotel	2

RESTAURANTS
Cool Corner	2
Kluarimklong	3
Raan Ahaan Mangsawirat	1

SHOP
Tratosphere	1

Though there are no real sights in Trat, the historic neighbourhood down by Khlong Trat, where you'll find most of the guesthouses and traveller-oriented restaurants, is full of old wooden shophouses and narrow, atmospheric sois. The covered market in the heart of town is another fun place to wander. Out-of-town attractions that make enjoyable focuses for a leisurely cycle ride (ask at *Cool Corner* restaurant for detailed directions and other recommended routes) include the mangrove forest to the southeast near Dan Khao, and the ornate seventeenth-century **Wat Buppharam**, 2km west of Trat Department Store, and the nearby lake.

Mangrove forest

Slightly further afield, in the **mangrove forest** near Dan Khao, 5.5km southeast of town, a boardwalk with informative English signs takes you through the swamp; after dark it's a good place to see twinkling fireflies too. The boardwalk access is currently unsigned in English, but head for Dan Kao and after about 5.4km you'll pass dolphin statues on your left; the track to the mangroves is about 100m further on, on the right (if you get to the estuary and road's end you've gone about 500m too far).

ARRIVAL AND DEPARTURE
TRAT

BY PLANE

Tiny **Trat airport** (☏039 525767–8), served by Bangkok

Airways, is about 16km from the Ko Chang piers at Laem Ngop. There's an airport shuttle minibus direct to Ko Chang hotels for B470/person, including ferry ticket (B700 by speedboat). However, Bangkok Airways keeps the cost of shared a/c minibuses to Trat town extortionately high at B500/person, for a ride of less than 30min (though at least you'll be dropped off at your hotel).

Destinations Bangkok (3 daily; 50min); Ko Samui (4 weekly; 1hr 15min); Phuket (4 weekly; 3hr).

BY BUS

All buses terminate at the bus station, 1.5km northeast of central Trat on Highway 318, from where songthaews shuttle passengers into the town centre (B20, or B60 if chartered) or on to the departure points for the islands (see below). A/c minibuses to Bangkok's Victory Monument leave from the 7-Eleven just off Thanon Vivatthana, on the north side of town; there are also minibuses to Hat Lek from the bus station (see box below).

Destinations Bangkok (Eastern Bus Terminal; 6 daily; 4hr 30min–6hr); Bangkok (Northern Bus Terminal; 6 daily; 4hr 30min); Bangkok (Suvarnabhumi Airport; 6 daily; 4hr 10min); Chanthaburi (hourly; 1hr 30min); Pattaya (6 daily; 4hr 30min); Rayong (6 daily; 3hr 30min); Si Racha (6 daily; 5hr).

BY BOAT

Details of boat services to Ko Chang, Ko Mak and Ko Kood are given in the relevant accounts. If you book your boat ticket through your guesthouse in Trat, you should be able to arrange pick-up (usually free) from the guesthouse.

VIA LAEM NGOP

All ferries to Ko Chang and some services to Ko Mak leave from one of three piers to the west of the small port town of Laem Ngop, 17km southwest of Trat (see map, p.412): Tha Thammachat and Tha Centrepoint for the Ko

Chang car ferries, and Tha Kromaluang (Naval Monument Pier) for Ko Mak. These piers are served by songthaew share-taxis from Trat's bus station and by songthaew and a/c minibus share-taxis from Thanon Sukhumvit in the town centre, costing B50/person or B250–300 if chartered; if sharing, allow 60–90min before your boat leaves for the share-taxi to fill up and get you to the pier. There's also plenty of long-distance transport direct to Laem Ngop, bypassing Trat town: a/c buses from Bangkok (5hr 15min–6hr), either from the Eastern (Ekamai) Bus Terminal, via Suvarnabhumi Airport and Chanthaburi (3–4 daily), or from Thanon Khao San and Hualamphong Station (2 daily); and a/c minibuses from Bangkok's Victory Monument, Northern and Eastern bus terminals, Suvarnabhumi Airport and Thanon Khao San.

VIA TRAT–SALAK PET SONGTHAEW

If you're going to the east coast of Ko Chang you can take a direct songthaew to Salak Pet (B150, including car ferry) from the temple compound behind *KFC* and Trat Department Store in Trat.

VIA LAEM SOK

Some boats to Ko Mak and nearly all boats to Ko Kood depart from Laem Sok, 30km south of Trat; boat tickets bought in Trat should include free transfers to Laem Sok, but there's also a Laem Sok songthaew service (30–60min) that leaves from the town centre (see map, p.407).

VIA BAN DAN KAO

A few boats to the outer islands depart from Ban Dan Kao, on the river estuary 6km northeast of Trat town; again, your boat ticket should include free transfers to Dan Kao, but otherwise you'll have to charter a songthaew from Trat market.

CROSSING THE CAMBODIAN BORDER VIA HAT LEK

Many travellers use the **Hat Lek–Koh Kong border crossing** for overland travel into Cambodia. It's best to arm yourself in advance with an **e-visa** for Cambodia (see p.27) and to make the journey by regular public transport, but it's also possible to buy a package all the way through to Sihanoukville and Phnom Penh (B750–1000 through travel agents in Trat) and to get a thirty-day visa on arrival at the border, though both of the latter options are more likely to open you up to possible **scams** (see p.383). For a comprehensive guide to the crossing and to the various transport options – and scams – on both sides of the border, see ⓦ talesofasia.com/cambodia-overland.htm and the ⓦ thaivisa.com forum.

The only way to get to **Hat Lek** under your own steam is by minibus from Trat bus station, 91km northwest (roughly every 45min; 1hr–1hr 30min; B120). Hat Lek (on the Thai side) and Koh Kong (in Cambodia) are on opposite sides of the Dong Tong River estuary, but a bridge connects the two banks. Once through immigration, taxis ferry you into **Koh Kong** town for onward transport to Sihanoukville and Phnom Penh or for guesthouses should you arrive too late for connections (mid-afternoon onwards). **Vans, buses and share-taxis** to Phnom Penh and Sihanoukville take around 4–5hr.

INFORMATION

Tourist information The Trat and Ko Chang TAT office (daily 8.30am–4.30pm; ☎039 597259, ✉tattrat@tat .or.th) is out in Laem Ngop, but any guesthouse will help you out with information on transport to the islands or into Cambodia. Alternatively, drop by the Tratosphere bookshop at 23 Soi Kluarimklong (☎039 523200) for tips on Trat and the islands from the knowledgeable French owner, have a look at his website, ⓦtratmap.com, or visit *Cool Corner* restaurant for a browse through the travellers' comment books.

ACCOMMODATION

Most **guesthouses** in Trat are small and friendly and are well used to fielding travellers' queries about the islands and Cambodia. All those listed here are within 10min walk of the covered market.

★**Ban Jaidee** 67 Thanon Chaimongkon ☎039 520678 or ☎083 589 0839, ✉maneesita@hotmail .com. Very calm, inviting and rather stylish guesthouse with a pleasant seating area downstairs and just nine simple bedrooms. The nicest rooms are in the original building and have polished wood floors, though those in the modern extension are further from the traffic noise. All rooms share hot-water bathrooms. Free wi-fi. B200

Basar Garden 87 Thanon Thoncharoen ☎039 523247 or ☎087 402 4620. Decent-sized en-suite rooms in a lovely, atmospheric old wooden house at the greener end of town. Curtains and drapes made from faded batik sarongs add to the faintly bohemian ambience and all rooms have fans and mosquito nets. Free wi-fi and free bicycles. B250

Residang House 87/1–2 Thanon Thoncharoen ☎039 530103, ⓦtrat-guesthouse.com. Comfortably appointed, good-value three-storey German–Thai-managed guesthouse. Rooms are large, light and clean and all have windows, thick mattresses, hot-water bathrooms and wi-fi; there are family rooms too. Internet access downstairs. Fan B300, a/c B500

★**Rimklong Boutique Hotel** 194 Thanon Lak Muang ☎039 523388, ✉soirimklong@hotmail.co.th. The four ground-floor rooms (plus one apartment) at this friendly, popular hotel are done out in a crisp contemporary style and well-equipped: a/c, hot water, cable TV, fridge and free wi-fi. Those on the side offer a bit more privacy than the two whose doors open right onto Thanon Lak Muang. The café in reception boasts a serious espresso machine, but you'll have to bring in your own food from outside for breakfast. B800

EATING

Two of the best and cheapest **places to eat** in Trat are at the covered day market on Thanon Sukhumvit, and the night market (roughly 5–10pm), between Soi Vichidanya and Soi Kasemsan, east of Thanon Sukhumvit.

★**Cool Corner** 49–51 Thanon Thoncharoen. Run single-handedly by a local writer/artist, this place has lots of personality, both in its cute hand-painted decor and in its traveller-oriented menu of real coffee, Indian chai, veggie specials, quality breakfasts and great Thai food (including chicken and cashew nuts for B90). A good place to while away an hour or three, listening to the mellow music and perusing the travellers' comment books. Daily roughly 7am–10pm, sometimes closing in the afternoon.

Kluarimklong Soi Kluarimklong. More Bangkok than Trat in its style and menu, this unexpectedly classy little place, under the same ownership as the nearby *Rimklong Boutique Hotel*, has both an indoor and a courtyard dining area. It serves delicious, upmarket Thai food, including steamed *haw mok thalay* seafood curry with coconut (B80) and lots of spicy *yam* salads and *tom yam* soups. Daily 11am–10pm.

Raan Ahaan Mangsawirat No English sign, but follow the soi near Ban Jaidee, off Thanon Chaimongkon. Typical no-frills, very cheap Thai vegetarian place, where you choose two portions of veggie curry, stir-fry or stew from the trays laid out in the display cabinet, and pay about B30 including rice. Open early morning until about 1/2pm.

SHOPPING

Tratosphere 23 Soi Kluarimklong ☎039 523200. This French–Thai place is a cut above most secondhand bookshops and a very good source of local information; you can also buy curios from all over Thailand here, as well as Mae Ang Ki yellow oil. Daily, variable hours.

DIRECTORY

Emergencies Call the tourist police, who have a base at Laem Ngop, on ☎1155 (free, 24hr).

Hospital The best hospital is the private Bangkok–Trat

Hospital (☎039 532735 or freephone ☎1719, ⓦbangkok trathospital.com), part of the Bangkok Hospital group, which has emergency facilities; it's on the Sukhumvit

Highway, 1km north of Trat Department Store.
Immigration office Located in Laem Ngop, 100m west of the TAT office (Mon–Fri 8.30am–4.30pm; ☎039 597261).
Travel agencies Book international and domestic flights

at Koh Chang TT Travel on Thanon Sukhumvit (☎039 531420; closed Sun); they also book accommodation on the islands, arrange taxis to Trat airport and transport to Cambodia, and provide local information.

Ko Chang

Edged with a chain of long, mostly white-sand beaches and dominated by a broad central spine of jungle-clad hills that rises sharply to over 700m, **KO CHANG** is developing fast but still feels green. It's Thailand's second-largest island, after Phuket, but unlike its bigger sister has no villages or tourist facilities within its steeply contoured and densely forested **interior**, just a few rivers, waterfalls and hiking trails that come under the auspices of the Mu Ko Chang National Park. Some of its marine environment is also protected, as the national park extends to over forty other islands in the Ko Chang archipelago. Ko Chang's own coast, however, has seen major development over the past decade, and the island is now well established as a mainstream destination, crowded with package tourists and the overspill from Pattaya, and suffering the inevitable inflated prices and inappropriate architecture. That said, it's still possible to find accommodation to suit most budgets and though the beaches may be busy they're undeniably handsome, with plenty of inviting places to swim, stroll, or snooze under a palm tree.

At 30km north to south, Ko Chang has plenty of coast to explore. The western **beaches** are the prettiest and the most congested, with **White Sand Beach** (Hat Sai Khao) drawing the biggest crowds to its mainly upmarket and increasingly overpriced mid-range accommodation; smaller **Hat Kai Bae** is also busy. Most backpackers opt for so-called **Lonely Beach** (officially **Hat Tha Nam**), with its roadside village of travellers' accommodation and famous beachfront party scene; those in search of quiet choose the more laidback **Hat Khlong Phrao**, a long and lovely sweep of sand that caters to most pockets, or **Bang Bao**, which has a village on a jetty with fine views, and its quiet neighbouring beach, **Hat Khlong Gloi**. Every beach has **currency exchange** and most have **ATMs**, along with minimarkets, tour agents, dive shops, internet access, clothes stalls and souvenir shops. White Sand Beach and Hat Kai Bae have the densest concentrations of facilities.

During **peak season**, accommodation on every beach tends to fill up very quickly, so it's worth booking ahead. The island gets a lot quieter (and cheaper) from June to October, when heavy downpours and fierce storms can make life miserable, though sunny days are common too; be especially careful of riptides on all the beaches during the monsoon season.

Sandflies can be a problem on the southern beaches (see p.67); watch out also for **jellyfish**, which plague the west coast in April and May, and for **snakes**, including surprisingly common cobras, sunbathing on the overgrown paths into the interior. The other hazard is **theft** from rooms and bungalows: use your own padlock on bags (and doors where possible) or, better still, make use of hotel safety boxes. After a local eradication programme, Ko Chang is no longer considered to be a malaria-risk area by health authorities in the US and the UK.

ARRIVAL AND DEPARTURE   KO CHANG

Access to Ko Chang from the **mainland** is by boat from the Laem Ngop coast, 17km southwest of Trat; details of transport to and from Laem Ngop are given on p.408. On arrival, tickets on tourist buses and minibuses to Ko Chang will often include the ferry crossing and transport to your hotel. During high season there are also boats to Ko Chang from Ko Mak and Ko Kood. On Ko Chang, **songthaew share-taxis** meet boats at the Tha Dan Kao and Ao Saparot ferry piers and transport passengers to west-coast beaches (B50 to White Sand Beach, 25min; B100 to Lonely Beach, 1hr; B150 to Bang Bao, 1hr 15min). On departure, either wait for a songthaew on the main road or ask your accommodation to book one for you (for a small extra fee, usually B20). If you're heading to Ko Chang's east coast, you can make use of the songthaew through-service from central Trat (see p.408).

CLOCKWISE FROM TOP KO MAK (P.424); LANTERN, SAAN CHAO PAW KHAO YAI, KO SI CHANG (P.386); WAT ASADANG, KO SI CHANG (P.385) >

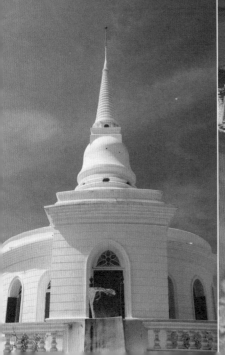

福如東海
壽比南山

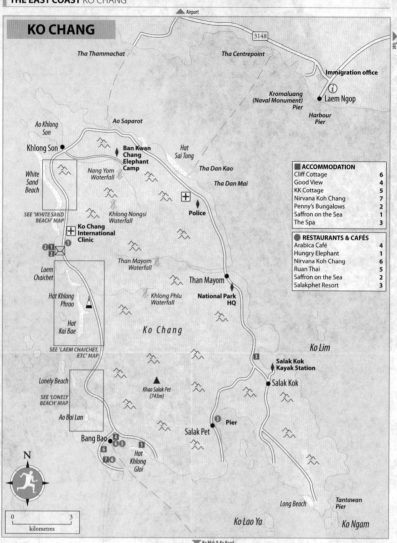

KO CHANG

ACCOMMODATION

Cliff Cottage	6
Good View	4
KK Cottage	5
Nirvana Koh Chang	7
Penny's Bungalows	2
Saffron on the Sea	1
The Spa	3

RESTAURANTS & CAFÉS

Arabica Café	4
Hungry Elephant	1
Nirvana Koh Chang	6
Ruan Thai	5
Saffron on the Sea	2
Salakphet Resort	3

BY BOAT AND PLANE

Bangkok Airways runs a shuttle bus service from Ko Chang beaches via the ferry and on to Trat Airport (B470/person, or B700 by speedboat; see p.407); contact the office in central Hat Sai Khao on ☏ 039 551654.

BY BOAT VIA LAEM NGOP

The main Laem Ngop–Ko Chang boat services are operated by two different car ferry companies from two different piers. Fares are competitive and change frequently: expect to pay B80–120/person one way, and about B200 for a vehicle, though deals on the latter vary considerably.

Centrepoint Ferry (☏ 039 538196) runs from Tha Centrepoint, 3km west of Laem Ngop, to Tha Dan Kao; and the more popular Ferry Ko Chang (☏ 039 518588 or ☏ 039 555188) runs from Tha Thammachat, 9km west of Laem Ngop, to Ao Saparot.

Destinations Tha Thammachat–Ao Saparot (25min); Tha Centrepoint–Tha Dan Kao (45min). Departures 6/6.30am–6/7pm, hourly in high season, every 2hr rest of year.

BY BOAT AND BUS FROM KO CHANG

Every tour agency on Ko Chang offers all manner of bus and a/c minibus packages (including ferries) from the island to other popular tourist destinations – we've listed the key ones. Most (it's worth checking) will include pick-up from your hotel either by songthaew, if you're going by big bus from the mainland ports, or by the minibus itself, which will then board the ferry and take you all the way through.

Destinations Bangkok (big bus to Khao San Rd B300, not including songthaew to the ferry; minibus to Khao San Rd B650; minibus to Sukhumvit Rd hotels B800; about 5hr); Bangkok Suvarnabhumi Airport (big bus B450; minibus B800; about 5hr); Ban Phe (for Ko Samet, minibus B600; about 3hr 30min); Pattaya (minibus B600; about 4hr 30min); Cambodia (minibus to Siem Reap, changing at the border, B600; about 10hr).

BY BOAT VIA KO MAK AND KO KOOD

In high season, Bang Bao Boat (☎087 054 4300, ⦿bangbaoboat.com) runs wooden boats from Bang Bao on Ko Chang to *Koh Mak Resort* on Ao Suan Yai on Koh Mak, as well as speedboats to *Koh Mak Resort* and on to the west coast of Ko Kood. Prices include transfers to or from the west coast of Ko Chang. Several other companies run similar high-season inter-island speedboats (for the same prices), including Kai Bae and Leelawadee, who sail from Hat Kai Bae on Ko Chang, via *Makathanee Resort* on Ao Kao on Ko Mak, to the west coast of Ko Kood. Tour agencies on Ko Chang, as well as guesthouses on Ko Mak and Ko Kood, will have current details.

Bang Bao Boat destinations Wooden boat Ko Chang–Ko Mak (roughly Sept–June daily; 1hr 30min–2hr; B400); speedboat Ko Chang–Ko Mak (roughly Sept–June 2 daily; 1hr; B550), then Ko Mak–Ko Kood (about 1hr; B400 – Ko Chang to Ko Kood B900).

GETTING AROUND

By songthaew A paved road runs nearly all the way round the island connecting all the beaches, served by plentiful, white songthaew share-taxis. They tend to charge according to how many passengers they have as well as the distance travelled (usually B50–150/person), but sometimes, especially on more remote beaches, you might have to wait until they fill up with enough passengers or the driver will ask you to charter the whole vehicle.

By motorbike or car You can rent motorbikes (from B250) and cars (from B1000) on every beach, but the road is notoriously dangerous, with precipitously steep hills punctuated by sharp, unexpected hairpins, and many reckless, often drunk drivers, so think twice if you're an inexperienced motorcyclist – accidents happen every day and fatalities are frequent.

By mountain bike Available opposite Ko Chang Gym in the VJ Plaza complex in Laem Chaichet (B250/day).

INFORMATION

Tourist information The widely distributed detailed free maps and quarterly Ko Chang guides published by Whitesands Publications (⦿koh-chang-guide.com) are a handy source of information, and the website provides an accommodation-booking service, but for more intelligent insights and opinionated advice, check out ⦿iamkoh chang.com, compiled by a Ko Chang resident.

DIRECTORY

Clinic The private 24hr Ko Chang International Clinic (☎1719 or ☎039 532735, ⦿bangkoktrathospital.com) is located beyond the south end of White Sand Beach, 1km south of *Plaloma Resort*; it has emergency ambulances and a dental service, and will transfer seriously ill patients to its parent Bangkok–Trat Hospital in Trat.

Post office On the main road beyond the southern end of White Sand Beach (Mon–Fri 10am–noon & 1–6pm, Sat 10am–1pm).

Tourist police At the north end of Hat Khlong Phrao (☎1155).

Travel agent A good, helpful agent – for flights, hotel bookings, day-trips, onward transport, car and bike rental, as well as overseas calls and internet access – is Koh Chang Adventure Travel on Hat Sai Khao, between Bangkok Airways and Soi Kert Manee (☎039 551389 or ☎089 247 6834).

White Sand Beach (Hat Sai Khao)

Framed by a band of fine white sand at low tide, a fringe of casuarinas and palm trees and a backdrop of forested hills, **Hat Sai Khao**, more commonly referred to as **White Sand Beach**, is, at 2.5km long, the island's longest beach and its most commercial, with scores of mid-range and upmarket hotel and bungalow operations packed together along the shore, plus dozens of shops, travel agents, bars and restaurants lining the inland side of the road. The vibe is much more laidback and traveller-oriented at the far quieter

KO CHANG ACTIVITIES

Tour agents on every beach or at your accommodation should be able to sell you tickets for most of the **activities** described below. There are **spas** at Ao Bai Lan (see p.422) and Ao Salak Kok (see p.423); you can also **snorkel** and **dive** in the archipelago (see p.416).

ELEPHANT CAMPS

Ko Chang or "Elephant Island" is named for its hilly profile rather than its indigenous pachyderms, but there are several **elephant camps** on the island that have brought in their own lumbering forest dwellers so that tourists can ride and help bathe them.

Ban Kwan Chang (Khlong Son) Elephant Camp East of Khlong Son village ☎ 081 919 3995 (not to be confused with Baan Chang Thai in Khlong Phrao). Based in a quiet, forested area in the north of the island, this is the camp with the best reputation. It was set up by the man behind the Asian Elephant Foundation and is staffed by Suay mahouts and their elephants from Ban Ta Klang village in northeast Thailand, which has for centuries been a centre for working elephants (see p.459). In the morning, visitors can either do a 40min elephant ride through adjacent plantations (B500) or extend the ride to an hour and bathe and feed the animals as well (B900); in the afternoon, 35min rides cost B450. Return transport from your accommodation is included. You could extend your trip to this part of the island by making the easy 300m walk to tiny Nang Yom falls, 500m beyond the camp, though Khlong Phlu falls in Khlong Phrao are more satisfying (see p.417).

KAYAKING

Kayak Chang At Amari Emerald Cove Resort, Hat Khlong Phrao ☎ 087 673 1923, ⓦ kayakchang.com. Well-organized, safety-conscious, British-run company offering half- (B1500) and full-day (B2100) local trips and expeditions around the archipelago of up to 7 days, as well as kayaking lessons and rental. Return transport from your accommodation is included.

YOGA

Baan Zen Hat Khlong Phrao ☎ 086 530 9354, ⓦ baanzen.com. Private, 90min yoga classes (B900) and short courses (from B5500 for 3 days), as well as reiki courses.

COOKING CLASSES

KaTi Culinary Cooking School Hat Khlong Phrao ☎ 039 557252, ⓦ kati-culinary.com. The amiable chef who runs the recommended *KaTi* restaurant teaches well-regarded cooking classes (Mon–Sat; B1200, including recipe book and transfers as far as White Sand Beach and Hat Kai Bae).

northern end of the beach, however, beyond *KC Grande*, and this is where the most budget-priced accommodation squeezes in, some of it pleasingly characterful and nearly all of it enjoying its own sea view. An extra bonus is that the road is well out of earshot up here, and there's hardly any passing pedestrian traffic. There are some low-key beach **bars** up there too, and more along the shorefront in the central beach area – all of them quite different in feel from the rash of brash, Pattaya-style bar-beers inland from *Plaloma Cliff Resort* in southern Hat Sai Khao. Wherever you stay on Hat Sai Khao, be careful when swimming as the **currents** are very strong and there's no lifeguard service.

ACCOMMODATION
WHITE SAND BEACH

Arunee Resort Just across the road from White Sand Beach ☎ 039 551075, ⓔ aruneeresorttour@hotmail .com; map opposite. Built in a partitioned wooden row-house, the sixteen small, very simple terraced rooms here all have a small veranda, mattress, fan and tiny en-suite bathroom and are a good price for central Hat Sai Khao. The friendly owner has a tour desk and internet shop out front. B500

Cookies Hotel White Sand Beach ☎ 081 861 4227, ⓦ cookieskohchang.com; map opposite. If you want hotel-style facilities at affordable prices this is a good option, right in the middle of the beach. Rooms are in two locations, with the far less interesting site being across the road, with only shops and traffic to look at through the picture windows. Better to pay B500 extra and go for a ground-floor, sea-view "superior" room, set round the shorefront swimming pool. Rooms are large and comfortable and all have a/c, hot water, TV, fridge and a veranda. B2000

KC Grande Resort White Sand Beach ☎039 551199, ⓦkckohchang.com; map, right. The largest and priciest hotel on the beach is able to charge top dollar because it spreads over a huge area of the northern shorefront. Accommodation ranges from rows of a/c bungalows set in landscaped gardens fronting the beach to more expensive rooms, some with sea views, in the three-storey hotel block. Facilities are good and include a pool, a spa, free wi-fi and a bar with live bands in the evening. Breakfast included. B4500

Maylamean Bungalows White Sand Beach ☎082 257 6271; map, right. In the cluster of funky, north-beach cliffside shanty bungalows, this stands out both for its colourful paintwork and because its en-suite rooms and wooden huts, while also built on stilts steeply up the cliffside, are larger and a bit more private than many of its neighbours. B450, with hot shower B800

Penny's Bungalows Beyond the south end of White Sand Beach, down a lane behind the post office ☎039 551122, ⓦpenny-thailand.com; map p.412. Welcoming, helpful, German-run place on what's sometimes called Pearl Beach (Hat Khai Mook), though it's just a rocky extension of Hat Sai Kaew. On a compact, flowery plot around a lovely little pool with a kids' pool and jacuzzi, the well-maintained bungalows and hotel-style rooms all have a/c, hot water, TV, fridge and a few decorative touches; the smaller, cheaper ones are near the sea. The free wi-fi in the restaurant reaches some of the rooms. B1200

★ **Saffron on the Sea** Beyond the south end of White Sand Beach, three doors north of Penny's (see above) ☎039 551253, ⓔkochangsaffron onthesea@yahoo.com; map p.412. In a lovely, lush garden behind a very good restaurant (see p.417) are seven attractive, homely rooms with a/c, hot water, TV and fridge; cheaper rooms have no sea view. Management is friendly and there's free wi-fi in the restaurant, free kayaks and snorkels. B1600

Star Beach White Sand Beach ☎087 558 4085; map, right. Basic, cheerily painted plywood huts cling limpet-like to the rock-face here, just above the sand on the quiet, northern stretch of the beach. Rooms are very simple but are all en suite (some with hot showers) and enjoy high-level sea views and breezes. B500

White Sand Beach Resort White Sand Beach ☎081 863 7737, ⓦwhitesandbeachresort.net; map, right. Spread across a long, attractive stretch of uncommercialized beach at the far north end of the beach, *White Sand* offers a big range of nicely spaced bungalows, many of them lapping up uninterrupted sea views. Interiors are fairly

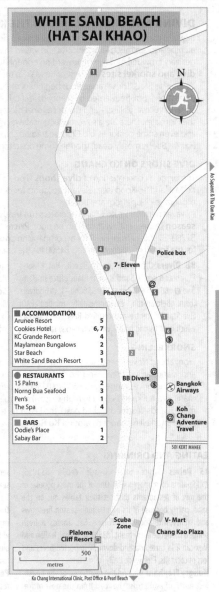

**WHITE SAND BEACH
(HAT SAI KHAO)**

N

Ao Sapparot & Tha Dan Kao

Police box

7- Eleven

Pharmacy

■ **ACCOMMODATION**
Arunee Resort	5
Cookies Hotel	6, 7
KC Grande Resort	4
Maylamean Bungalows	2
Star Beach	3
White Sand Beach Resort	1

● **RESTAURANTS**
15 Palms	2
Norng Bua Seafood	3
Pen's	1
The Spa	4

■ **BARS**
Oodie's Place	1
Sabay Bar	2

BB Divers

Bangkok Airways

Koh Chang Adventure Travel

SOI KERT MANEE

Scuba Zone

V-Mart

Chang Kao Plaza

Ploma Cliff Resort ■

0 — 500
metres

Ko Chang International Clinic, Post Office & Pearl Beach ▼

simple, but have a/c, wooden floors, hot showers, TVs, fridges and a faintly contemporary style. For a proper peaceful beach vibe and a little bit of affordable comfort, within 10min walk of resort facilities, this is a good option considering the competition. If arriving by songthaew, get off at the 7-Eleven beside *KC Grande* and phone for transport. B1500

DIVING AND SNORKELLING IN THE KO CHANG ARCHIPELAGO

Because there's just one main tide a day in the inner Gulf, the **reefs** of the Ko Chang archipelago are much less colourful and varied than Andaman coast dive sites, and they can get very crowded, but they're rewarding enough to make a day-trip worthwhile. The main **dive and snorkel sites** are west of Ko Mak, in the national marine park around **Ko Rang** and its satellite islets. These range from beginners' reefs with lots of hard corals and anemones at depths of 4–6m, frequented by plenty of reef fish – including a resident ten-thousand-strong shoal of yellow fusiliers – and the occasional moray eel, to the more challenging 25m dive at the Pinnacles. There are also some technical wreck dives of Japanese boats from World War II and even some centuries-old Chinese trading ships. The coral around Ko Yuak, off Ko Chang's Hat Kai Bae, is mostly dead, though some operators still sell trips there.

DIVE SHOPS ON KO CHANG

The biggest concentration of **dive shops** is on Ko Chang, though there are also some on Ko Mak and Ko Kood (see relevant accounts for details). All dive shops on Ko Chang will organize pick-ups from any beach.

Waves permitting, Ko Chang operators run trips year-round, though during the **monsoon season** (June–Sept), visibility can be poor. **Prices** for local dive trips, with two tanks, are about B2700–B2900, or from B850 for accompanying **snorkellers**. Dive courses cost about B14,500 for the four-day Openwater, and B4500 for the one-day Discover Scuba introduction.

BB Divers Offices at Lonely Beach, Hat Khlong Phrao and White Sand Beach, main office in Bang Bao ☏ 086 155 6212 or ☏ 039 558040–1, ⓦ bbdivers .com. Belgian-run, environmentally minded PADI Five-Star IDC centre and certified Reef Check Facility which uses fishing boats (with sun decks) rather than speedboats. Accommodation is available at *Barrio Bonito* on Lonely Beach (see p.420).

Scuba Zone Offices at White Sand Beach, Hat Kai Bae and Lonely Beach ☏ 039 619035, ⓦ scuba -kohchang.com. British-run PADI Five-Star centre, which also offers technical and wreck diving.

SNORKELLING

From about November to May, several companies run dedicated **snorkelling trips** to reefs and islands around Ko Chang, Ko Wai and Ko Rang. Tickets are sold by tour agents on every beach and prices range from B600 to B1500, depending on the size of the boat (some take as many as a hundred people in high season) and the number of islands visited. In general the more islands "featured" (sailed past), the less time there is for snorkelling, though nearly all the actual snorkelling happens around **Ko Rang**.

EATING AND DRINKING

15 Palms White Sand Beach ☏ 039 551095, ⓦ 15palms.com; map p.415. One of the most popular of the row of restaurants that set their tables out on the sand, partly because of its nightly high-season fireshows and transvestite shows on Tues & Sat. There's a fresh seafood barbecue every night (B350), plus Thai, Italian and Mexican à la carte, washed down by imported beers and lots of cocktails. Free wi-fi. Daily 8am–1am.

Hungry Elephant Beyond the south end of the beach, just north of and across the road from the post office; map p.412. The French and Thai food at this unassuming roadside place has a good reputation with local expats. The Thai chef trained at the French Embassy in Bangkok and does toothsome steaks – au poivre, chateaubriand and crème cognac – mostly for about B300. Daily roughly 10/11am–10pm.

Norng Bua Seafood On the main road, White Sand Beach; map p.415. Popular, bustling basic restaurant, serving noodle soups, fried noodles and fried rice with seafood (B45); other seafood dishes start at B100. Daily 7am–10pm.

Oodie's Place On the main road, White Sand Beach; map p.415. Ko Chang's most famous live-music venue, with live blues, rock, reggae and r'n'b played most nights, plus Thai food (from B80), pizzas (from B200) and French food (from B300). Daily 4pm–1am.

Pen's White Sand Beach; map p.415. Tiny beach restaurant in the northern bungalow cluster that serves exceptionally good home-style Thai food at fairly cheap prices (B80–100 for curries), as well as Western breakfasts. Daily 8.30am–9.30pm.

Sabay Bar White Sand Beach ⓦ sabaybarkohchang .com; map p.415. One of Ko Chang's longest-running institutions, where you can choose to sit in the chic a/c bar and watch the nightly live sets from the in-house cover band, or lounge on mats and cushions on the sand and listen in via the outdoor speakers. You pay for the pleasure, however, as drinks are pricey. Also stages fire-juggling shows on the beach and full-moon parties. Daily 6pm–2am.

Saffron on the Sea Beyond the south end of the beach, behind the post office three doors north of Penny's (see p.415) ☎039 551253; map p.412. On a pretty seafront deck, this restaurant is highly recommended for its Thai food, which doesn't stray too far from the usual suspects, such as green curry (B180) and

nam tok pork salad (B150); also serves baguettes and pastas. Daily roughly 7.30am–9.30pm.

The Spa On the main road, White Sand Beach; map p.415. Welcoming, environmentally friendly outreach restaurant of *The Spa Resort* (see p.424). Food is mostly vegetarian, and organic where possible, and includes a delicious "ginger nuts" stir-fry (B140), very good omelettes, seafood, breakfasts and Mexican dishes. There are lots of health drinks and good espressos. Daily 10am–10pm.

Laem Chaichet and Hat Khlong Phrao

Four kilometres south of Hat Sai Khao, the scenic, rocky cape at **LAEM CHAICHET** curves round into sweeping, casuarina-fringed **HAT KHLONG PHRAO**, one of Ko Chang's nicest beaches, not least because it has yet to see the clutter and claustrophobic development of its neighbours. For the moment at least, most of the restaurants, bars and shops are way off the beach, along the roadside, with the shorefront left mainly to a decent spread of accommodation. Laem Chaichet protects an inlet and tiny harbour and offers beautiful views south across the bay and inland to the densely forested mountains. To the south, Hat Khlong Phrao begins with a nice 1km-long run of beach that's interrupted by a wide khlong, whose estuary is the site of some characterful stilt homes and seafood restaurants. You can rent a kayak from almost anywhere along the beach to explore the estuary, and after dark you could paddle upriver to see the fireflies twinkling in the khlongside *lamphu* trees. Beyond the estuary, the long southern beach is partly shaded by casuarinas and backed in places by a huge coconut grove that screens the shore from the road; it's quite a hike to the roadside shops and restaurants from here though, at least 1km along a rutted track.

4

Both Chaichet and Khlong Phrao have roadside tourist villages with **ATMs**, minimarkets, tour agents, dive centres, internet access, shops and restaurants. The **tourist police** have a post here, and from the southern end of Khlong Phrao it's only a few hundred metres south to the start of the Kai Bae tourist village amenities.

Khlong Phlu Falls

2km east off the main road • B200

Upstream from Hat Khlong Phrao, the khlong that divides the beach in two tumbles into Ko Chang's most famous cascade, **Khlong Phlu Falls** (Nam Tok Khlong Phlu). Signs lead you inland to a car park and some hot-food stalls, where you pay your national park entry fee and walk the last five minutes to the 25m-high waterfall (best in the rainy season) that plunges into an invitingly clear pool defined by a ring of smooth rocks.

ACCOMMODATION	**LAEM CHAICHET AND HAT KHLONG PHRAO**

Amari Emerald Cove Resort Hat Khlong Phrao ☎039 552000, ⓦamari.com; map p.418. Top-of-the-scale hotel from the reliable Thai chain, occupying a lovely, tranquil spot on the southern beach, complete with its own palm-shaded sandy terrace, spa and huge seafront swimming pool with a palatial jacuzzi. The rooms, in low-rise three-storey blocks set around the pool, tropical garden and lagoons, are in luxurious style, with wooden floors and balconies. **B4980**

Baan Rim Nam Hat Khlong Phrao ☎087 005 8575, ⓦiamkohchang.com; map p.418. Peaceful, scenic and unusual, this converted fishing family's house is built on stilts over the wide, attractive khlong at the end of a

walkway through the mangroves. Run by the British author of the best Ko Chang website, it has just five comfortable a/c rooms with good hot-water bathrooms and free wi-fi, plus decks for soaking up views of the khlongside village, but no restaurant. You can borrow kayaks and it's a couple of minutes' walk to the beach, or 20min to the main Khlong Phrao facilities. **B800**

Barali Beach Resort Hat Khlong Phrao ☎039 557238, ⓦbaralikohchang.com; map p.418. One of the more elegant spots on the southern beach, with tastefully designed, Balinese-style rooms (some with their own plunge pools), furnished with four-poster beds, sunken

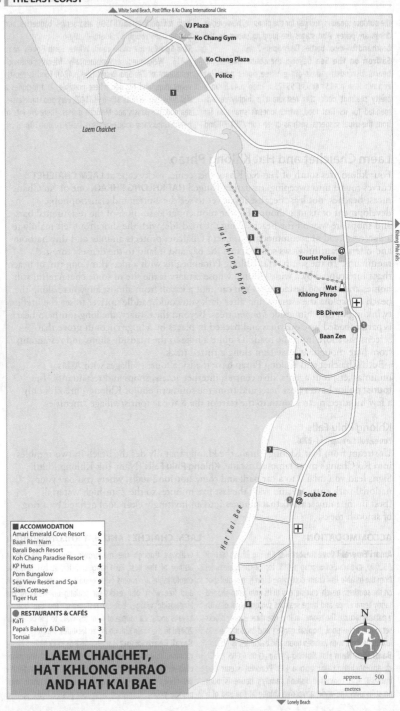

White Sand Beach, Post Office & Ko Chang International Clinic

VJ Plaza

Ko Chang Gym

Ko Chang Plaza

Police

Laem Chaichet

Khlong Phu Falls

Hat Khlong Phrao

Tourist Police

Wat
Khlong Phrao

BB Divers

Baan Zen

Scuba Zone

Hat Kai Bae

ACCOMMODATION

Amari Emerald Cove Resort	6
Baan Rim Nam	2
Barali Beach Resort	5
Koh Chang Paradise Resort	1
KP Huts	4
Porn Bungalow	8
Sea View Resort and Spa	9
Siam Cottage	7
Tiger Hut	3

RESTAURANTS & CAFÉS

KaTi	1
Papa's Bakery & Deli	3
Tonsai	2

**LAEM CHAICHET,
HAT KHLONG PHRAO
AND HAT KAI BAE**

N

0   approx.   500
metres

Lonely Beach

baths and lots of polished wood, and set around a beachfront infinity-edge swimming pool and a spa. B4330 **Koh Chang Paradise Resort** Laem Chaichet ☎039 551100–1, ⓦkohchangparadise.com; map opposite. The biggest and most popular place to stay on the Chaichet end of the beach occupies a huge area between the road and the shore so offers easy access to the beach as well as shops and restaurants. Its generously designed concrete bungalows have French windows and comfortable, hotel-style, a/c interiors. Some have private plunge pools and there's also a central swimming pool and a spa. B4425 **KP Huts** Hat Khlong Phrao ☎084 077 5995, Ⓔkp_huts 2599@hotmail.com; map opposite. Though the fifty timber huts here are very simple for the price, they are attractively scattered through the broad, grassy shoreside coconut grove (about 1.5km from roadside amenities) with

plenty of sea views. Even some of the cheapest options (with shared bathrooms) are right on the shore, and a few are raised high on stilts for an extra-seductive panorama; all of the en-suite huts have hot showers and some are designed for families. Internet access. Shared bathroom B400, en suite B700
Tiger Hut Hat Khlong Phrao ☎084 109 9660; map opposite. One of the few budget-minded, old-school travellers' beach bungalows left on Ko Chang, occupying a sandy beachfront garden just south of the khlong and about 2km down a track from the main road. The woven-bamboo and clapboard huts have simple interiors with mosquito nets over the beds and decent-sized bathrooms, and there's a restaurant deck and bar with pool table. Shared bathroom B300, en suite B600

EATING AND DRINKING

KaTi On the main road, Hat Khlong Phrao ☎039 557252; map opposite. Restaurant and cookery school (see p.414) serving very tasty Thai food, slightly adapted for Western tastes, including lots of seafood, *matsaman* chicken curry (B150) and *laap* beef salad (B120), plus delicious home-made ice creams and Thai desserts. Mon–Sat 11am–3pm & 6–10pm, Sun 6–10pm.

Tonsai On the main road, Hat Khlong Phrao; map opposite. The atmosphere at this welcoming, civilized restaurant is pleasingly mellow, and the menu includes *matsaman* curries (B150), some interesting Thai dips and relishes, pastas, lots of vegetarian options and at least fifty cocktails. Mon 5–10pm, Tues–Sun 11.30am–10pm.

Hat Kai Bae

Narrow, pretty little **HAT KAI BAE** presents a classic picture of white sand, pale blue water and overhanging palms, but in places the shorefront is very slender indeed – and filled with bungalows – and the beach can disappear entirely at high tide. The beach is bisected by a khlong and rocky point, with most of the accommodation to the south. Seaward views from the southernmost end take in the tiny island of Ko Man Nai, whose sandy shores are easily reached by kayak, half an hour offshore from *Porn's Bungalows*. Kai Bae's roadside tourist village is busy and stretches a couple of kilometres. It's got plenty of shops, bars and restaurants, as well as ATMs, currency exchange, dive shops and internet access.

ACCOMMODATION HAT KAI BAE

Porn Bungalow Off the access road to Sea View, Hat Kai Bae ☎080 613 9266 or ☎089 099 8757, ⓦpornsbungalows-kochchang.com; map opposite. The most famous of the dwindling number of budget accommodation options on Hat Kai Bae has scores of fan bungalows in various styles, well spaced out under the trees along a huge expanse of the shorefront. The cheapest are concrete huts at the back at the south end; the most luxurious are spacious wooden cabins with hot showers and wraparound decks. Porn's has two reception areas, at its northernmost and southernmost ends, and a two-storey restaurant, with a bar, wi-fi and pool table, in the middle. Also has kayaks for paddling to offshore Ko Man Nai. Fan and cold shower B600, fan and hot shower B800
Sea View Resort and Spa Hat Kai Bae ☎081 830

7529, ⓦseaviewkochchang.com; map opposite. Swanky and huge beachfront hotel set in lawns and tropical flower gardens, which stretch around the steep headland at the south end of the beach and up to a lighthouse by the main road, which shelters view-filled tables belonging to their *Lighthouse Restaurant*. A cable car joins up the resort's two swimming pools, pretty spa and its large, light and airy a/c rooms and cottages. B3000
Siam Cottage Hat Kai Bae ☎089 153 6664; map opposite. With cheerily painted interiors, fans, partly outdoor bathrooms and decks, the 36 wooden bungalows here face each other across a narrow but well-watered, flowery lot that runs down to the sea. There's a cute restaurant and internet access, as well as kayaks for rent. Fan B500, a/c B800

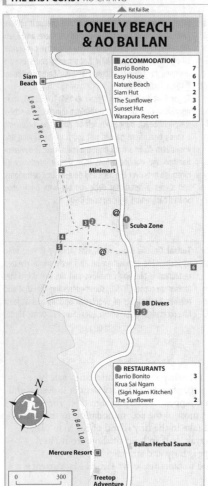

LONELY BEACH & AO BAI LAN

ACCOMMODATION	
Barrio Bonito	7
Easy House	6
Nature Beach	1
Siam Hut	2
The Sunflower	3
Sunset Hut	4
Warapura Resort	5

Siam Beach

Lonely Beach

Minimart

Scuba Zone

BB Divers

RESTAURANTS	
Barrio Bonito	3
Krua Sai Ngam (Sign Ngam Kitchen)	1
The Sunflower	2

N

Ao Bai Lan

Bailan Herbal Sauna

Mercure Resort

0 — 300 metres

Treetop Adventure Park

Bang Bao

Hat Kai Bae

EATING AND DRINKING

Papa's Bakery & Deli On the main road, Hat Kai Bae; map p.418. Hot pretzels, pizzas, croissants, baguettes and cakes emerge from this friendly German bakery, as well as the bread for some very tasty sandwiches (around B100). If you're sitting in, you can also tuck into pastas and good espressos; to take away, there are imported cheeses and salamis, too. Internet access. Daily 8am–7pm.

Lonely Beach (Hat Tha Nam)

Hat Tha Nam – dubbed **LONELY BEACH** before it became Ko Chang's top place to party – is small and lively, with a shorefront that's occupied by increasingly expensive accommodation and a hinterland village, ten minutes' walk away, that's the most traveller-oriented on the island. It's at Lonely Beach, overlooking the rocks immediately south of the strand, and along the sandy sois that run inland to the main road, that backpackers feel most at home, in little bungalows and guesthouses squashed any old how beneath the remaining trees, with every other shop-shack offering tattoos or internet access. Despite the creeping concrete, creatively designed little wood and bamboo bar-restaurants abound, some of them offering chilled, low-key escapes from the loud dance music, all-night parties and buckets of vodka Red Bull that the beachfront places are notorious for.

Day and (especially) night, you should be extremely careful when swimming off Lonely Beach, particularly around *Siam Beach* at the northern end, as the steep shelf and dangerous current result in a sobering number of **drownings** every year, particularly during the monsoon season; do your swimming further south and don't go out at all when the waves are high. Also be careful with your belongings – many a drunken night sees cameras, phones and wallets pilfered unnoticed.

Among the roadside shops you'll find an **ATM**, dive centres, tour agents and motorbike rental and repair.

ACCOMMODATION

LONELY BEACH

Barrio Bonito On the main road, towards the south end of Lonely Beach ☎080 092 8208, ⓦbarrio bonitokohchang.com; map above. Behind this excellent bar-restaurant (see opposite), the garden shelters some cute, colourful, single-storey rooms, all with bathrooms and armchairs, though they're quite small and tightly packed. There's wi-fi in the restaurant, where good breakfasts are served, and a tiny swimming pool at the front. Fan and cold shower **B350**, fan and hot shower **B500**

Easy House Inland, up a side road opposite Kachapura Resort, Lonely Beach ☎089 116 8191, ☻hippeehappy @yahoo.com; map opposite. Laidback place built around polished, dark-wood platforms, with free wi-fi. The old-style bungalows, decorated with murals and equipped with mosquito nets, fans and en-suite bathrooms, are quite crowded together, but quiet and cheap. B500

Nature Beach Central Lonely Beach ☎039 558027 or ☎081 803 8933; map opposite. Responsible for Lonely Beach's party reputation, this place's rooms, bar-restaurant (with built-in DJ station) and the beach out front are all hugely popular. It occupies a prime location in the middle of the strand and is at the heart of the action (so if you prefer a quiet night's sleep head elsewhere). All 65 of its shady, closely set bungalows have been recently upgraded, ranging from attractive, polished-concrete en-suite abodes with verandas at the back by the road, through fan-cooled log cabins, some with hot showers, further forward, to large a/c bungalows at the front with hot water and a bit of chic. There's a tour desk, internet access and wi-fi (both payable). Fan B500, fan and hot shower B700, a/c B1500

Siam Hut Central Lonely Beach ☎086 609 7772, ☻siamhutkohchang.com; map opposite. The cheapest place to stay right on the beach, this classic traveller's rest has evening barbecues and movies, a dive school, a tattoo parlour, recycling bins, kayaks for rent and a 24hr kitchen (with wi-fi). Accommodation consists of rows and rows of primitive, split-bamboo huts – eighty in total – all en suite (some with hot showers) and with little else but plank floors, mattresses and mozzie nets. Fan B380, a/c B520

The Sunflower Lonely Beach, inland on Soi Sunset ☎084 017 9960, ☻the-sunflower.com; map opposite.

Run by a genial German and his Thai family, the two-dozen bungalows here are set under palm and banana trees 200m or so from the roadside village and equidistant from the rocky coast at *Sunset Hut*, a 5min walk south of the sandy beach. Choose between bamboo or wooden fan bungalows with mosquito nets and open-roofed bathrooms, and concrete bungalows with a/c and hot showers; all have good thick mattresses and are kept very clean. The restaurant is good (see below) and has wi-fi. Fan B300, a/c B700

Sunset Hut Lonely Beach, 5min walk south beyond Siam Hut, on the rocks ☎089 245 4626; map opposite. The concrete en-suite bungalows here have hot showers, proper beds and big windows; some have perfect, private, over-sea decks too. There are also some big a/c bungalows, but all are tightly packed together in rows running parallel to the shore. The seafront deck-restaurant and bar holds occasional parties. Though you can only swim here at high tide, it's a short walk to the sandy beach and just 400m inland to roadside shops and restaurants. The builders were in for refurbishment at the time of research, so prices will probably go up once they've finished. Fan B300, a/c B500

Warapura Resort Lonely Beach, 2min walk south beyond Sunset Hut, on the rocks ☎083 987 4777, ☻warapuraresort.com; map opposite. Welcoming place with a good dose of Bangkok chic in its twenty gleaming-white, balconied rooms and villas, a few of which are on the seafront; all have large bathrooms with hot rain showers, a/c, mini-bars, TVs and DVD players. "Cozy Seaview" rooms are especially stylish, with dark-wood furniture and a large indoor sitting area (B2200 including breakfast). Good-sized, attractive pool and free wi-fi throughout. B1400

EATING AND DRINKING

The most intense **partying** on Ko Chang happens down on the beach here, usually at *Nature Beach*, which kicks off most high-season nights with seafood barbecues, live music and fire-juggling shows; there's also a big beach party at *Siam Hut* on Friday nights.

★ **Barrio Bonito** On the main road, towards the south end of Lonely Beach ☎080 092 8208, ☻barriobonitokohchang.com; map opposite. Mexican-run bar-restaurant serving excellent, authentic food such as nachos with minced beef (B200) as well as some more unusual dishes, washed down with Corona and lots of tequila cocktails. It's a very congenial haven, with lots of places to chill in the landscaped garden, free wi-fi and Latin sounds all the way. Daily 8am–10pm.

Krua Sai Ngam (Sign Ngam Kitchen) On the main road, central Lonely Beach; map opposite. Popular, basic, authentic Isaan restaurant, which even does *som tam* with crab and *pla ra* (fermented fish sauce) – an acquired taste but very northeastern (on the menu as "Som Tam

E-sarn"; B40). Also offers catfish and snakehead fish in various soups, curries and salads (try the *yam plaa duk foo*; B120), grilled chicken and simple dishes on rice (B40). No English sign, but look for the corrugated-iron roof and the seafood displayed on ice at the front, directly opposite Soi Sunset. Daily noon–11.30pm.

The Sunflower Lonely Beach, inland on Soi Sunset ☎084 017 9960, ☻the-sunflower.com; map opposite. Friendly, laidback guesthouse restaurant dishing up very generous set breakfasts (B150), authentically spicy Thai curries (B50), a wide choice of pricier Western food and German beer. Flop on to the axe cushions and soak up the cool sounds or watch a movie. Free wi-fi. Daily 8am–3pm & 5–10pm.

Ao Bai Lan

A fifteen-minute walk along the road and over the hill from the southern end of Lonely Beach village will bring you to **AO BAI LAN**, which hasn't got much of a beach to speak of, but is the site of two of Ko Chang's most interesting attractions, the **Treetop Adventure Park** and the **Bailan Herbal Sauna**.

Treetop Adventure Park

South end of Ao Bai Lan • Daily 9am–5pm • B950/half-day, including transport from the west coast • ☎ 084 310 7600, ⊛ treetopadventurepark.com

If you're happy with heights and like a physical challenge, make an afternoon of it at **Treetop Adventure Park**, an enjoyable and professionally managed jungle activity centre where you get to swing through the trees on a series of trapezes, flying foxes, aerial skateboards, rope ladders and webs. Everyone gets a full safety harness and gloves and starts off with a training session before tackling the two adventure courses (or the special kids' one), which take around two hours in all, though there's no limit to repeat attempts.

Bailan Herbal Sauna

On the main road, Ao Bai Lan • Daily 3–9pm • Sauna B200, treatments from B50, massages B300/hr • ☎ 039 558077, ⊛ bailan-kohchang.com

Bailan Herbal Sauna is the perfect place to tease out any sore muscles. This charming, creatively designed US–Thai-run herbal steam sauna is an alternative little sanctuary of adobe buildings with glass-bottle windows, secluded within a patch of roadside forest. There's a sociable communal sauna, home-made DIY herbal treatments using fresh herbs from their own garden (kaffir lime for hair, white-mud for face and turmeric for skin), and massages are also available, along with fresh juices and herbal teas.

Bang Bao

Almost at the end of the west-coast road, the southern harbour village of **BANG BAO**, much of it built on stilts off a 1km-long central jetty, is the departure point for boat trips and transfers to the outer islands and is also an increasingly popular place to stay. Though it has no beach of its own, you're within a short motorbike ride of both little-developed Hat Khlong Gloi, 2km to the east, and Lonely Beach, 5km up the coast. It's possible to stay on the jetty itself and tuck into seafood at one of its famous restaurants, but you'll probably have to fight your way through vanloads of day-trippers, who clog the narrow path along the jetty as they linger over the trinket shops, clothes stalls and dive shops.

ACCOMMODATION
BANG BAO

Cliff Cottage West side of Ao Bang Bao, next to Nirvana ☎ 085 904 6706, ⊛ cliff-cottage.com; map p.412. British-run resort with a nice deck restaurant on the west-facing cove, and kayaks and snorkels for rent. Basic, thatched, bare-wood huts with decent mattresses, mosquito nets and good sunset views sit up on a small, dusty, shady rise; there's also a rowhouse of fan and a/c rooms, all with hot showers, facing in on Bang Bao bay. Smarter wooden bungalows for families are planned. Fan hut **B400**, fan room **B700**, a/c **B900**

Good View Bang Bao jetty ☎ 087 927 1357 or ☎ 089 108 0429, ⊛ goodviewbangbao.wordpress.com; map p.412. As the name says, the views from this guesthouse, built over the water halfway down the east side of the jetty, are good, though not great, taking in the shoreline opposite. Lovely, clean, bright, large, wooden-floored bedrooms come with huge hot-water bathrooms, big balconies and a/c – it's worth paying B200 extra for an upstairs room. There's a very large, attractive ground-floor deck with a book corner, and free wi-fi throughout. **B800**

★ **Nirvana Koh Chang** West side of Ao Bang Bao ☎ 039 558061–4, ⊛ nirvanakohchang.com; map p.412. Secluded on a narrow neck of land across the bay to the west of the village, this boutique resort is a relaxed and lushly landscaped retreat with two pools and access to good snorkelling in the bay behind (free equipment available); there's no real beach but Nirvana runs free boats over to Hat Khlong Goi twice a day. Also on offer are cooking classes, free kayaks and free wi-fi throughout. Accommodation is in a wide range of chic, Balinese-accented rooms and villas, some with direct sea views, and there's an attractive restaurant too (see opposite). Good à la carte breakfast included. **B2000**

EATING AND DRINKING

Arabica Café Opposite 7-Eleven, just before the start of Bang Bao jetty; map p.412. Good espressos (B40), pancakes, sandwiches and Western breakfasts, in a leafy little café with cute fountains. Daily 8am–9pm.

Nirvana Koh Chang West side of Ao Bang Bao ☎039 558061–4, ⓦ nirvanakohchang.com; map p.412. Even if you're not staying you can come and eat at the dramatically sited *Tantra* restaurant, built on stilts in the bay, or drink at the panoramic, sunset-facing *Sun Deck*, which is reached by a cliffside boardwalk and hosts soothing live music most days – or both. Creatively furnished with woodcarvings from the Indonesian archipelago, the restaurant serves a menu of contemporary Thai and French food (including imported artisan cheeses), as well as tasty fusion dishes created by the French chef, such as beef tournedos in panaeng sauce (B350). Very good wine list. Free transfers from anywhere on the west coast of Ko Chang. Sun Deck daily 5–7pm; Tantra daily 6–10pm.

Ruan Thai Bang Bao jetty ☎089 833 5117; map p.412. The best of several neighbouring restaurants, with a deck built on stilts off the west side of the jetty and fresh seafood awaiting its fate in tanks at the front. The fried rice stuffed with prawns is very good (B50), or you could upgrade to salads, curries and squid dishes (B100); most other seafood dishes are B200. Daily 9am–10pm.

Hat Khlong Gloi

The nearest swimmable beach to Bang Bao is long, sandy **Hat Khlong Gloi**, 2km east of the village and not far short of the end of the tarmac. It's backed by a lagoon and a long stretch of beach-scrub, but has great views from its small beach cafés and deckchairs. If you're coming by motorcycle, park up at the west end of the beach and walk, as the paved access road then takes a steep, tortuous route around the back of the beach.

ACCOMMODATION   HAT KHLONG GLOI

KK Cottage 100m from the west end of Hat Khlong Gloi ☎039 558169, ⓦ facebook.com/klongkloicottage; map p.412. Friendly, popular spot on a nice stretch of beach, with deckchairs and umbrellas and great views of the bay and the offshore islands. The rather scruffy compound has small, thatched, fan-cooled, en-suite bungalows at the back, concrete ones at the front. B500

The east coast

The beaches along the mangrove-fringed **east coast** are less inviting than those in the west, but this side of Ko Chang is much less developed and makes for a fun day-trip; it's about 35km from Khlong Son in the north to Salak Pet in the south.

Than Mayom

South of the piers at Ao Saparot and Tha Dan Kao, the east-coast road runs through long swathes of rubber and palm plantations, with jungle-clad hills to the west and bronze-coloured beaches to the east, passing the national park office and bungalows at **Than Mayom**, where signs direct you inland to Than Mayom falls, a 45-minute uphill hike away.

Salak Kok

On the western side of Ao Salak Kok, *The Spa* (see p.424) is a wellness and detox retreat that's open to day visitors for food or treatments. Fork left at the junction just south of *The Spa* to reach the southern edge of the bay and its small fishing settlement, **SALAK KOK**, site of the award-winning Salak Kok Kayak Station run by the Koh Chang Discovery Club, a community tourism venture that offers **kayak rental** along a marked route through the mangroves (B100/hr). From Salak Kok, continue down to the tip of the southeastern headland to reach **Hat Sai Yao**, or **LONG BEACH**, the prettiest white-sand beach on this coast, which is good for swimming and has some coral close to shore.

Salak Pet

Most day-trippers turn right not left just after *The Spa* and head instead for the little fishing port of **SALAK PET** on the south coast, which is served by daily songthaews all the way from Trat town (see p.408). Still a fairly quiet spot, Salak Pet is best known for its excellent **seafood restaurant**, *Salakphet Resort*.

ACCOMMODATION AND EATING THE EAST COAST

★**Salakphet Resort** Salak Pet ☏081 429 9983, ⓦkohchangsalakphet.com; map p.412. The bayside dining deck here offers fine views and seafood so good that people travel all the way from Trat just for lunch; crabs are a speciality – particularly stir-fried with black pepper, or with curry powder – but it's all fresh so the possibilities are infinite. Daily 8am–8pm.

The Spa Ao Salak Kok ☏039 553091, ⓦthespakohchang

.com; map p.412. Beautifully designed wellness and detox retreat that's upmarket but reasonably priced; it also has branches on Ko Samui and in Chiang Mai. Its a/c accommodation is set in a lovely mature tropical garden that runs down to the mangrove-ringed bay of western Ao Salak Kok and has a good restaurant. Breakfast included. Day visitors are welcome for massage (B500/1hr, B700/90min), herbal saunas and facials and to eat at its restaurant. B1800

Ko Mak

Small, slow-paced, peaceful **KO MAK** (sometimes spelt "Maak") makes an idyllic, low-key alternative to Ko Chang, 20km to the northwest. Measuring just sixteen square kilometres, it's home to little more than four hundred people, divided into five main clans, who work together to keep the island free of hostess bars, jet skis, banana boats and the like, and on initiatives such as mountain-bike trails. A couple of narrow concrete roads traverse the island, which is dominated by coconut and rubber plantations; elsewhere a network of red-earth tracks cuts through the trees. Ko Mak is shaped like a star, with fine white-sand beaches along the northwest coast at **Ao Suan Yai** and the southwest coast at **Ao Kao**, where most of the island's (predominantly mid-range and upper-bracket) tourist accommodation is concentrated; the principal village, **Ban Ao Nid**, is on the southeast coast and there's another village at **Ban Laem Son** on the east coast. The main beaches are just about within walking distance of each other, and other parts of the island are also fairly

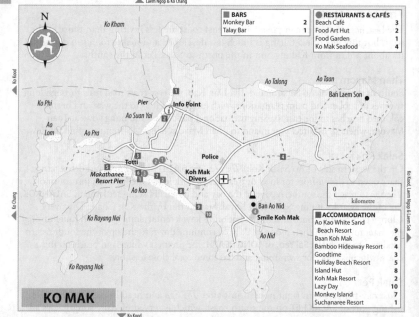

■ BARS	
Monkey Bar	2
Talay Bar	1

● RESTAURANTS & CAFÉS	
Beach Café	3
Food Art Hut	2
Food Garden	1
Ko Mak Seafood	4

■ ACCOMMODATION	
Ao Kao White Sand Beach Resort	9
Baan Koh Mak	6
Bamboo Hideaway Resort	4
Goodtime	3
Holiday Beach Resort	5
Island Hut	8
Koh Mak Resort	2
Lazy Day	10
Monkey Island	7
Suchanaree Resort	1

KO MAK

ACTIVITIES ON KO MAK

The mediocre reefs of Ko Rang (see p.416), part of the Ko Chang National Marine Park, are less than an hour's boat ride west of Ko Mak and are the island's main **diving and snorkelling** destination; they're the main focus of Ko Chang dive and snorkel boats too, so you won't be alone. You can also join a **cookery class**.

Koh Mak Divers On the Ao Kao road just east of Island Hut ⓣ083 297 7724, ⓦkohmakdivers.com. British-run PADI centre that charges B2400 for two fun dives, B3500 for the beginners' one-day Discover Scuba Diving course and B750 for snorkellers; transfers from your accommodation included.

Smile Koh Mak Next to Koh Mak Seafood restaurant at Ban Ao Nid ⓣ081 901 9972, ⓦsmilekohmak.com. 4hr cookery classes (B1200, including a recipe book), with vegetarian options available. Also offers fruit and vegetable carving courses over 2 days (6hr). Transfers from your accommodation included.

Totti On the Ao Kao road opposite the Makathanee Resort ⓣ081 916 6536 or book through your accommodation. Snorkelling day-trips in a wooden boat to the national marine park. B750, including transfers from your accommodation and lunch box.

easy to explore on foot, or by mountain bike, motorbike or kayak – the best way to discover the empty undeveloped beaches hidden along the north and eastern coasts. The **reefs** of Ko Rang are also less than an hour's boat ride away so snorkelling and diving trips are quite popular. There is as yet no major commercial development on the island and **no bank or ATM**, but bungalows on both beaches will change money. There's a small clinic off the Ao Nid road, though for anything serious a speedboat will whisk you back to the mainland.

During the **rainy season** (early June–Sept), choppy seas mean that boat services to Ko Mak are much reduced. Most Ko Mak accommodation stays open – and offers tempting discounts – but the smaller places often don't bother to staff their restaurants. Islanders say that it can be very pleasant during this "green season", though you may be unlucky and hit a relentlessly wet few days.

4

Ao Kao

Ko Mak's longest and nicest beach is **AO KAO** on the southwest coast, a pretty arc of sand overhung with stooping palm trees and backed in places by mangroves. The beach is divided towards its southern end by a low rocky outcrop that's straddled by *Ao Kao White Sand Beach Resort*, with *Lazy Day Resort* occupying the strand beyond, while the long western beach is shared by a dozen other sets of bungalows, most of them around the pier at the *Makathanee Resort*. The roadside inland from the main accommodation area is where you'll find most of the restaurants and bars: if you're walking from the southern end, by far the easiest access is via the beach, tides permitting.

Ao Suan Yai and around

Long, curvy **AO SUAN YAI** is not quite as pretty a beach as Ao Kao and only has a couple of resorts, but the sand is fine and the outlook is beautiful, with Ko Chang's hilly profile filling the horizon and Ko Kham and other islets in between. You'll need a bicycle or motorbike to access the variety of restaurants on the Ao Kao road.

ARRIVAL AND DEPARTURE — KO MAK

As the island gets more popular, **boat services** from the mainland and the other islands are increasing: check ⓦkohmak.com for current routes and schedules. Boats arrive at one of Ko Mak's three **piers** – at *Koh Mak Resort* on Ao Suan Yai, at the *Makathanee Resort* on Ao Kao or at Ao Nid – and are always met by a modest welcoming committee of accommodation staff offering free transport; similarly, if you book a room in advance, ask your resort for a free pick-up. When it comes to moving on, all hotels keep current boat schedules and can sell you a ticket.

VIA LAEM SOK

A new catamaran service sails to Ao Nid on Ko Mak from Laem Sok pier, 30km south of Trat (☎086 972 4918, ⓦkohmakcatamaran.com; daily, 1hr 30min; B350 including transfer to/from Trat bus station or downtown market); it's likely that this service will run in the off-season, too. Some of the Laem Sok–Ko Kood high-season speedboats will call in at Ao Nid if they have enough customers (see p.431).

VIA LAEM NGOP

A year-round slow boat runs from the Kromaluang (Naval Monument) pier in Laem Ngop, some 20km southwest of Trat (3 weekly, 3hr; B300). From approximately October to

May, Panan's speedboats also operate from this pier to Ko Mak Resort on Ao Suan Yai (2 daily, 45min–1hr; B450); the second of these is at 4pm, handy if you're arriving from Bangkok. A/c minibuses to Laem Ngop from Bangkok, for example, will sometimes only go as far as the Thammachat or Centrepoint Ko Chang piers, however – check exactly which piers are served when you buy your minibus ticket, or you may be able to pay the driver a little extra to go on to Kromaluang.

VIA KO CHANG OR KO KOOD

Boats run between Ko Chang, Ko Mak and Ko Kood in high season (see p.413).

INFORMATION

Tourist information The best one-stop shop for information about Ko Mak, accommodation bookings and all kinds of transport is the helpful, farang-run Info Point at Koh Mak Resort on Ao Suan Yai (Oct–March daily 8.30am–8pm; ☎085 665 3794, ⓔkohmakinfopoint @yahoo.com). As well as boat and bus tickets, it offers currency exchange, Visa cash advances, internet access, motorbike, mountain bike and kayak rental, activities bookings and postal services. There's also a travel agent at Makathanee Resort (☎081 870 6287), by the pier on Ao Kao, which offers internet access. ⓦkohmak.com is a useful, fairly comprehensive website about the island.

GETTING AROUND

The island has hardly any traffic, and most visitors rent a mountain bike or motorbike. Apparently it's possible to walk, wade and swim around the entire perimeter in 10hr.

By taxi ☎089 752 5292 or ☎089 833 4474. B50/person, minimum charge/vehicle B100; B100/person after 10pm.
By mountain bike or motorbike These (respectively B150/day and B300–350/day) can be rented through accommodation or from Ko Mak Resort's Info Point; otherwise, Food Art Hut on Ao Kao (see opposite) has a particularly wide choice of bicycles, including kids' bikes.

The island has some long and potentially interesting signed mountain-bike routes – discreet concrete posts enigmatically carved with route numbers A1–C7 – but the explanatory map for navigating them is currently out of print: you should be able to pick them up if you simply go exploring.

ACCOMMODATION

AO KAO

Ao Kao White Sand Beach Resort Ao Kao ☎039 501005, ⓦaokaoresort.com. This welcoming, efficiently managed and lively set of upmarket bungalows occupies an attractive garden fronting the prettiest part of the beach. Its twenty large, comfortable, attractive timber bungalows come with a/c, hot showers and DVD players and most have direct sea views. There are lots of activities, including live bands on Saturday nights, giant chess in the bar, a kids' trampoline, massage, free internet and wi-fi and kayaks and motorbikes for rent. Breakfast included. **B2500**
★ **Baan Koh Mak** Near the pier on Ao Kao ☎089 895 7592, ⓦbaan-koh-mak.com. Arrayed around a clipped lawn, the eighteen bungalows at this chic and welcoming resort are modern, bright and comfortable, cutely done out in white, green and polished concrete, with a/c, hot water, small bedrooms and decent-sized bathrooms; verandas sport either swings or bamboo hammocks. There's a very good restaurant here too (with computers and free wi-fi). **B1400**
Goodtime Ao Kao ☎039 501000, ⓦgoodtime-resort .com. Luxurious, tasteful, Thai-style rooms and villas, all with a/c, hot water, TV, fridge, DVD player, wi-fi and use of a pool. They're located on higher ground inland from Ao Kao's Makathanee Resort, around 15min walk from the beach. Room **B2600**, villa **B4400**
Holiday Beach Resort Ao Kao ☎086 751 7668, ⓦholidaykohmak.com. Friendly, well-maintained place, strewn with flowers, facing a large, beachside lawn with deckchairs and tables. White clapboard is the architectural style of choice here, either in cute cottages with cold showers and mosquito nets in the second row, or in large, attractive, hot-water bungalows at the front. Computers and free wi-fi in the restaurant, and kayaks, mountain bikes and motorbikes for rent. Breakfast included. Fan **B800**, a/c **B1300**

Island Hut Ao Kao ☎087 139 5537. This family-run little place has the best-value and most idyllically sited accommodation on the beach, though not always the friendliest welcome. The two-dozen en-suite rough-hewn timber huts are more artfully designed than they might appear: most have cheery stripey doors and idiosyncratic driftwood artwork; all have fans, hanging space and their own deckchairs on decks or on private sandy porches. Price depends on proximity to the narrow but pretty shore: the most expensive are at the water's edge. B250

Lazy Day Ao Kao ☎081 882 4002, ⓦkohmaklazyday .com. Civilized spot on a huge beachside lawn strewn with flowers and trees. As well as a/c, hot showers and mini-bars (but no TVs, to preserve the quiet), the spacious, bright, mostly beachfront bungalows sport polished concrete floors, shining white walls and French windows out onto their balconies. Free wi-fi and kayaks; bikes and motorbikes to rent. Breakfast included. B2250

★ **Monkey Island** Ao Kao ☎081 447 8448, ⓦmonkeyislandkohmak.com. There's a big range of quality, contemporary-styled bungalows here, all in timber and thatch, and a laidback, hippy-ish vibe. Top-end "Gorilla" seafront villas are huge, with a/c, hot water and the possibility of connecting villas; the large a/c "Chimpanzee" bungalows are also good, while some of the small "Ape" and "Baboon" options share bathrooms. There's a kids' swimming pool, plus free wi-fi and internet access. Fan and shared bathroom B350, fan en-suite B600, a/c (including breakfast) B1300

AO SUAN YAI AND AROUND

Bamboo Hideaway Resort A couple of kilometres southeast of Ao Suan Yai, accessed via tracks through the rubber plantations ☎039 501085, ⓦbamboo hideaway.com. An idiosyncratic haven, built almost entirely from lengths of polished bamboo. Its comfortable a/c rooms all have mosquito nets on the beds, hammocks and hot showers, and are connected by a raised bamboo walkway. Although the south coast is just a couple of minutes' walk downhill, Ao Suan Yai has the nearest decent beach. There's an attractive swimming pool on site, as well as a good restaurant. Breakfast included. B2200

★ **Koh Mak Resort** Ao Suan Yai ☎039 501013, ⓦkohmakresort.com. With no less than 1km of shoreline to play with, nearly all of the bungalows here are beachfront (including the "Standard" fan options with hot showers) and enjoy lovely panoramas from their verandas. Among a huge range of accommodation, the most interesting are the very modern, design-conscious rooms and villas – all polished concrete, stacked slate walls, huge picture windows and rain showers, some with private little walled gardens, some with jacuzzis on their rooftop verandas. There's an infinity-edged swimming pool and similarly chic pool bar here too, two restaurants and the jack-of-all-trades Info Point (see opposite). Free wi-fi in all rooms. Breakfast included. Fan B1500, a/c B1800

Suchanaree Resort Ao Suan Yai ☎081 983 2629, ⓔSuchanaree_Tour @hotmail.com. Right next door to *Koh Mak Resort*, but couldn't be more different: it's an intimate, friendly little place in a lush garden, set by a khlong with tables and deckchairs on the shady, beachfront lawn. The small, basic but good-quality, shaggy-thatched wooden bungalows all have fan, mozzie nets and bathrooms. B550

EATING AND DRINKING

AO KAO

★ **Beach Café** At Baan Ko Mak, Ao Kao. Coolly done out in black, white and orange with some nice sofas, this restaurant serves exceptionally delicious Thai food, including good *tom kha* soups and great *phanaeng* curries (both B90). Daily 8am–10pm.

Food Art Hut Opposite Monkey Island, Ao Kao. Idiosyncratic all-rounder, offering ice cream, desserts, cakes and espressos, as well as Thai dishes and simple, passable Western food such as spaghetti bolognese (B99), breakfasts, pizzas and sandwiches, washed down with German wheat beer. Daily 8am–3pm & 5–9pm.

Food Garden Opposite Monkey Island, Ao Kao. This popular, cheap and enjoyable garden restaurant serves *phat thai*, various spicy salads and *matsaman* curries (B80), as well as breakfasts and seafood barbecues in the evening. Daily 8am–10pm.

Monkey Bar Monkey Island, Ao Kao. Live music nightly, including jamming sessions, at this bar built around the beachfront trees. Daily 8pm–midnight.

Talay Bar On the beach in front of Beach Café at Baan Ko Mak, Ao Kao. Tables on the sand – with a fire show at 8pm – and great margaritas (B150) plus a long list of other cocktails. Mellow music and evening barbecues. Evenings till late.

BAN AO NID

Ko Mak Seafood Just north of Ao Nid pier ☎089 833 4474. Built out into the sea on stilts, with views of the bay and, apparently, of Cambodia on a clear day, this restaurant is mostly true to its name, serving *phat thai* with fresh prawns (B90) and more complex dishes such as tasty squid with salted eggs (B200). (Don't get your hopes up about the advertised Ko Mak Museum next door, though – it's just a collection of old things in an old house.) Free transfers, free wi-fi. Daily 10.30am–9.30pm.

4

Ko Kood

The fourth-largest island in Thailand, forested **KO KOOD** (also spelt Ko Kut and Ko Kud) is still a wild and largely uncommercialized island. Though it's known for its sparkling white sand and exceptionally clear turquoise water, particularly along the west coast, Ko Kood is as much a nature-lover's destination as a beach-bum's. Swathes of its shoreline are fringed by scrub and mangrove rather than broad sandy beaches and those parts of the island not still covered in virgin tropical rainforest are filled with palm groves and rubber plantations. Most of the 25km-long island is penetrated only by sandy tracks and, in places, by navigable khlongs, if at all. All of this makes Ko Kood a surprisingly pleasant place to explore on foot (or kayak), especially as the cool season brings refreshing breezes most days. The interior is also graced with several waterfalls, the most famous of which is Nam Tok Khlong Chao, inland from Ao Khlong Chao and the focus of occasional day-trips from Ko Chang and Ko Mak.

Because of its lack of roads, Ko Kood has to date been the almost exclusive province of package-tourists, but things are becoming much easier for independent travellers, with a choice of scheduled boat services from the mainland, as well as from Ko Chang and Ko Mak, and the emergence of some budget-minded guesthouses. The island is still pretty much a **one-season destination**, though, as rough seas mean that nearly all the boat services only operate from November through May. An increasing number of places are staying open year-round, however, and offer tempting discounts to those willing to chance the rains and the off-season quiet. There is some **malaria** on the island so be especially assiduous with repellent and nets if you are not taking prophylactics; there's a malaria-testing station in Ban Khlong Hin Dam.

Most of Ko Kood's fifteen hundred residents make their living from fishing and growing coconut palms and rubber trees. Many have Khmer blood in them, as the island population mushroomed at the turn of the twentieth century when Thais and Cambodians resident in nearby Cambodian territory fled French control.

The main settlements are **Ban Khlong Hin Dam**, just inland from the main Nam Leuk (Hin Dam) pier, **Ban Khlong Mat**, a natural harbour-inlet a few kilometres further north up the coast, the stilted fishing village of **Ban Ao Salat** across on the northeast coast and the fishing community of **Ban Ao Yai** on the southeast coast. On the southwest coast, several of the main beaches also have small villages. Of these, the obvious choices for budget travellers are **Ao Khlong Chao** and **Ao Ngamkho**, which both have a choice of accommodation and eating options and are within walking distance of each other; **Ao Bang Bao** also has cheapish bungalows and is the longer and arguably better beach but has no village and is more isolated. Seclusion is the thing on all the other west-coast beaches, most of which are the province of just one or two upmarket resorts.

DIVING AND SNORKELLING OFF KO KOOD

Ko Kood's three **dive operators** charge around B3000 for two dives, with **snorkellers** paying B1000, and B14,500 for the four-day Openwater Diver course. You might prefer to opt for a local Ko Kood dive as the usual sites around Ko Rang (see p.416) are always packed with dive boats from Ko Chang and Ko Mak.

BB Divers Opposite Away Resort at the north end of Ao Khlong Chao ☎ 082 220 6002, ⓦ bbdivers.com.

Koh Kood Divers Next to Siam Beach Resort at Ao Bang Bao ☎ 085 698 4122, ⓦ kohkooddivers.com.

Paradise Divers Headquarters at Ko Kood Beach Resort at Ao Khlong Mat, with another desk at Happy Days on Ao Ngamkho ☎ 087 144 5945, ⓦ kohkood -paradisedivers.com.

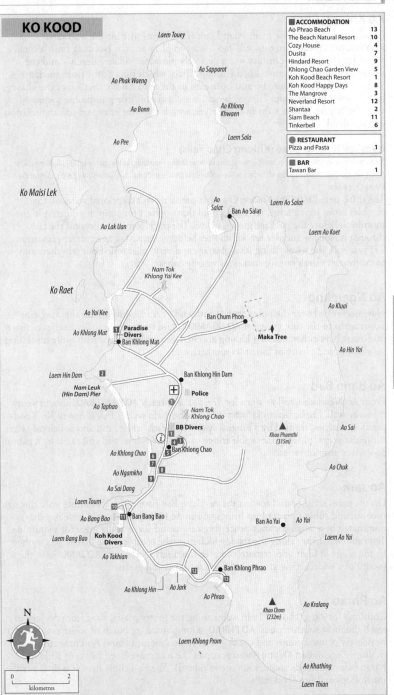

KO KOOD

Laem Touey

Ao Sapparot

Ao Phak Waeng

Ao Bonn

Ao Khlong
Khwaen

Ao Pee

Laem Sala

Ko Maisi Lek

Ao
Salat   Laem Ao Salat

Ban Ao Salat

Ao Lak Uan   Laem Ao Koet

Ko Raet

Nam Tok
Khlong Yai Kee

Ao Kluai

Ao Yai Kee

Ao Khlong Mat

Paradise
Divers
Ban Khlong Mat

Ban Chum Phon

Maka Tree

Ao Hin Yai

Laem Hin Dam

Ban Khlong Hin Dam

Nam Leuk
(Hin Dam) Pier

Police

Ao Taphao

Nam Tok
Khlong Chao

BB Divers   Khao Phaenthi
(315m)   Ao Sai

Ao Khlong Chao

Ban Khlong Chao

Ao Ngamkho

Ao Chuk

Ao Sai Dang

Laem Toum

Ban Bang Bao

Ao Bang Bao

Ban Ao Yai   Ao Yai

Koh Kood
Divers

Laem Bang Bao

Laem Ao Yai

Ao Takhian

Ban Khlong Phrao

Ao Khlong Hin   Ao Jark

Ao Phrao

Khao Chom
(232m)   Ao Kralang

Laem Khlong Prom

Ao Khathing

N

0   2
kilometres

Laem Thian

■ ACCOMMODATION	
Ao Phrao Beach	13
The Beach Natural Resort	10
Cozy House	4
Dusita	7
Hindard Resort	9
Khlong Chao Garden View	5
Koh Kood Beach Resort	1
Koh Kood Happy Days	8
The Mangrove	3
Neverland Resort	12
Shantaa	2
Siam Beach	11
Tinkerbell	6

● RESTAURANT	
Pizza and Pasta	1

■ BAR	
Tawan Bar	1

4

Ao Khlong Chao

About 5km south of the main Nam Leuk (Hin Dam) pier on the west coast, **AO KHLONG CHAO** (pronounced "Jao") is a fun place to stay, boasting both a small sandy beach – no great beauty but a perfectly pleasant "village" beach – and the pretty 2km-long mangrove-lined Khlong Chao, which runs down from the famous Khlong Chao Falls. Close by and upstream of the road-bridge that spans the khlong, just 300m from the palm-fringed beach, is a cluster of little guesthouses, some of them built partially on stilts over the river, which offer the cheapest accommodation on the island.

Nam Tok Khlong Chao (Khlong Chao Falls)

30min walk from Ao Khlong Chao, or kayak 20min upriver from the Khlong Chao bridge to the jetty near the falls, then walk for 10min; you can drive to within 500m of the falls, following the signs from near Khlong Chao Garden View Resort, south of the Khlong Chao bridge

The three-tiered **Nam Tok Khlong Chao** is a pretty if not exceptional waterfall that tumbles down into a large, refreshing pool that's perfect for a dip; it's quietest in the mornings, before the package groups arrive. The track continues beyond the falls through jungle for another few kilometres before terminating at a rubber plantation – if you walk the whole thing it's a pleasant and very quiet four-hour trip there and back, though watch out for snakes, especially cobras.

Ao Ngamkho

Having climbed over the point at the south end of Ao Khlong Chao, the road dips down again to the tiny village at **AO NGAMKHO** and its beach, actually a series of pretty, miniature bays either side of a khlong and between rocky points, with quite rewarding snorkelling and plenty of fish at its southern end.

Ao Bang Bao

From Ao Ngamkho, follow signs for *The Beach* to reach **AO BANG BAO**, about twenty minutes' walk further south (15min west off the main road). This is one of Ko Kood's prettiest beaches, fronted by a longish sweep of bleach-white sand and deliciously clear turquoise water, plus the inevitable fringe of coconut palms, and embraced by a pair of protective promontories.

Ao Jark

On the main southbound road at the Ao Bang Bao turn-off, a 35-minute walk through coconut and rubber plantations brings you to **Ao Khlong Hin**, a wild little bay that's dominated by a small coconut-processing centre and is not really great for swimming. Ten minutes further along the road, which hugs the coast so close here it gets washed by the waves at high tide, remote and breathtakingly lovely little **AO JARK** sits at the mouth of a wide, serene khlong and feels secluded and private.

Ao Phrao

Continue for 2km (about 20min walk) along the pretty coastal road from Ao Jark to reach the most southerly bay, **AO PHRAO**, a long, stunning beach of white sand backed by densely planted palms and the slopes of Khao Chom. Behind Ao Phrao, the tiny fishing village of **Ban Khlong Phrao** occupies the mangrove-lined banks of Khlong Phrao (which extends another kilometre inland). There's a clinic here as well as a few small shops and hot-food stalls.

Ao Yai

A 5km track that's very steep and rough in places connects Ban Khlong Phrao with **Ban Ao Yai**, the southeast coast's main if rather lacklustre fishing village, built entirely on stilts and jetties around the shoreline of a natural harbour. Its main visitors are the crews of anchored fishing boats from Thailand and Cambodia, who come here for drink, supplies, karaoke and the rest.

Ban Khlong Hin Dam and around

The bays of northern Ko Kood, beyond Ao Khlong Chao, are even more thinly populated than the southwest coast, with just a few resorts. Inland is the island's administrative centre, **Ban Khlong Hin Dam**, 3.5km north of Ao Khlong Chao, site of a few shops, the hospital, police station, school and principal island temple. Ko Kood's main west-coast pier is a couple of kilometres to the west, at **Nam Leuk (Laem Hin Dam)**.

About 5km north of Ban Khlong Hin Dam, the small but appealing three-tiered waterfall **Nam Tok Khlong Yai Kee** is basically a miniature version of the famous Nam Tok Khlong Chao and rushes down into a good-sized pool that's ideal for swimming. It's accessible via a five-minute path that's very steep in places, but there are ropes at the crucial points.

Ban Ao Salat and around

The road northeast from Ban Khlong Hin Dam ends after 9km at the tiny stilt village, fishing community and port of **Ban Ao Salat**. Several of the wooden houses strung out along the jetty-promenade serve food and this is a great place for a fresh-seafood lunch, especially crab.

East off this road, in the mature rainforest near Ban Chum Phon, is a locally famous **five-hundred-year-old maka tree** (*Bridelia insulana*), known to islanders as the *ton maai yai*, that's an impressive 35m or more in height and drips with lianas and epiphytes. A kilometre-long path through rubber trees and rainforest will get you there, but you'll need to go with a local to stay on the right track.

ARRIVAL AND DEPARTURE

KO KOOD

BY BOAT

All boat tickets to Ko Kood from the mainland should include transfers to the pier from Trat, though it's worth double-checking. Mainland and Ko Chang speedboats will drop off at and pick up from most of the west-coast accommodation. All Ko Kood hotels keep current timetables and sell tickets.

FERRIES FROM THE MAINLAND

In all but the worst weather, Ninmungkorn (☎ 086 126 7860) runs a year-round boat service to Ko Kood from the Trat mainland, departing from Laem Sok, about 30km south of Trat, occasionally calling at Ao Nid on Ko Mak, and terminating at Ao Salat on the island's northeast coast (1–2 daily; about 1hr 30min; B350 including transfers on Ko Kood). Ninmungkorn now has high-season competition from the recently inaugurated Ko Kood Express, which sails from Laem Sok to Nam Leuk pier on Ko Kood's west coast (☎ 039 501150; 1 daily, though this may increase to 2; 1hr 30min–2hr; B350).

SPEEDBOATS FROM THE MAINLAND

There are also several different companies offering high-season speedboat services between the Trat mainland and Ko Kood's western piers and beaches; these are faster and more expensive (up to 4 daily; about 1hr; B600) but can be wet and uncomfortable in all but the flattest seas. Schedules and mainland departure points vary – the usual piers are Laem Sok and Dan Kao, 6km northeast of central Trat – and are best checked with Trat guesthouses or travel agents, the TAT office in Laem Ngop, or guesthouses on Ko Kood.

VIA KO CHANG AND KO MAK

Boats run between Ko Chang, Ko Mak and Ko Kood in high season (see p.413). Speedboats from the mainland to Ko Kood will go via Ao Nid on Ko Mak if there are enough takers (B350, either from Laem Sok or Ko Kood).

INFORMATION

Tourist information There's a municipal tourist information office on Ao Khlong Chao, just north of the bridge on the west side of the road (daily 8.30am–6pm).

GETTING AROUND

Exploring the island on foot is both feasible and fun, and south of Ao Khlong Chao much of the route is shady. From Ao Khlong Chao to Ao Bang Bao takes about 40min; from Ao Bang Bao to Ao Jark is about 1hr, then another 20min to Ao Phrao.

By songthaew These can be chartered for around B1000/ day.

By motorbike You can rent motorbikes through most guesthouses and resorts (from B250/day), but be warned that the mostly concrete west-coast road is narrow and steep, and badly rutted in places.

By mountain bike The number of hills may also deter you from getting around by mountain bike – they're available at *Happy Days* on Ao Ngamkho (B150/day) and through some other resorts.

ACCOMMODATION

Ko Kood now offers the whole spectrum of accommodation, from cheap crashpads to swanky villas, though nearly all of the budget resorts are inland from the beaches.

AO KHLONG CHAO

Cozy House On the south bank of the khlong, Ao Khlong Chao ☎089 094 3650, ⓦkohkoodcozy.com. Has the cheapest rooms in Khlong Chao (with shared bathrooms), in an extended stilt house centred round a lovely breezy communal khlong-side deck. The pricier rooms and bungalows are not such good value but the home-cooked food is exceptional, especially the fish. Lots of facilities for backpackers, including computers, rental kayaks and motorbikes, petanque and volleyball. B250

Khlong Chao Garden View Ao Khlong Chao ☎087 908 3593. Away from the khlong, this friendly place is set on a lawn dotted with ornamental trees beside the road 50m south of the bridge, and about 100m inland from the sea. Choose between basic, fan-cooled huts with small bathrooms, and larger a/c bungalows with TVs. There's good food at the popular garden restaurant too, especially the *phanaeng* curries. Fan B400, a/c B1000

★ **The Mangrove** On the south bank of the khlong, Ao Khlong Chao ☎085 279 0278, ⓦkohkood -mangrove.com. The best of the khlong-side options, with nice views of the water and sturdy wooden bungalows spaced around a well-tended lawn, dotted with pretty plants and trees. Interiors are modern and well furnished with TV and hot water. Free kayaks and motorbikes for rent. Fan B800, a/c B1500

Tinkerbell Ao Khlong Chao ☎081 813 0058, ⓦtinkerbellresort.com. Stylishly designed and land-scaped resort at the south end of the beach, which offers a difficult choice. For the same price (including breakfast), you can plump for either a bright, pastel-coloured villa with a/c, hot rain shower, fridge, TV, DVD player and large balcony hard on the beach, or an equally attractive two-storey house in the second row, with a plunge pool and a separate large living room and toilet upstairs. There's a small swimming pool fed by an artificial waterfall, and free wi-fi throughout. B6900

AO NGAMKHO

Dusita Ao Ngamkho ☎081 420 4861, ⓦdusitakohkood .com. Directly on the shore, just south of the khlong, this small, friendly outfit offers plainly outfitted fan and a/c wooden cabins, some with nice pebbledash outdoor bathrooms, that all enjoy beautiful sea views and some shade among the sparse coconut grove hung with hammocks. Fan B900, a/c B1400

Hindard Resort Ao Ngamkho ☎081 762 9519, ⓔrungdech@hotmail.com. The large, comfortable, hot-water wooden chalets here, some with outdoor bath-rooms, sit on a flower-strewn slope atop the little rocky point at the southern end of the bay, with panoramic sea views and easy access to swimming and snorkelling among the coral off the point. Massage and free wi-fi, snorkels and kayaks. Fan B1200, a/c B1500

Koh Kood Happy Days Ao Ngamkho ☎087 144 5945 or ☎086 018 6012; ⓦkohkood-happydays.com. This backpacker-oriented resort, beside the road, 200m from the northern section of the beach, offers ten en-suite fan and a/c rooms in a little guesthouse block, all with wooden floors, pretty furnishings and a shared veranda. There's also motorbike and mountain-bike rental and internet access, plus a dive shop, a sociable bar and restaurant and a general store next door. Fan B450, a/c B800

AO BANG BAO

The Beach Natural Resort Ao Bang Bao ☎086 009 9420, ⓦthebeachkohkood.com. Though it doesn't actually sit on the nicest part of the beach, but behind a rocky area towards the northern end, this resort's diverse, thatched Balinese-style bungalows are tastefully furnished and have garden bathrooms; they're grouped quite closely together so most only offer sea glimpses. All have hot showers and some have a/c (6pm–7.30am only). Facilities include computers and free wi-fi, kayaks, bicycles and motorbikes. Breakfast included. Fan B1400, a/c B2200

Siam Beach Ao Bang Bao ☎081 899 6200, ⓦsiam beachkohkood.net. This resort occupies almost all of the best part of the beach, sprawling across an extensive area, and is popular with budget travellers, though it's more isolated than similarly priced options on Ao Ngamkho and Ao Khlong Chao. Its big, no-frills huts and bungalows on the seafront nearly all enjoy uninterrupted bay views. Some of the newer a/c rooms are in a less idyllic spot close to a khlong and back from the shore a bit, but they're cheaper than the beachside a/c options and have hot showers. The restaurant cooks up regular seafood barbecues and there's internet access, motorbike and kayak rental. Breakfast included. Fan B1200, a/c and hot showers B1500, a/c and cold showers B1800

AO JARK

Neverland Resort Ao Jark ☎081 762 6254, ⓦneverlandresort.com. The only accommodation on this beach is set among the palms between the limpid blue sea and the calm green khlong. It offers comfortable, balconied, log-clad a/c bungalows, some with hot showers, in a pretty garden, as well as fully equipped two-person tents (B500), kayaks and snorkels. Breakfast included. B1600

AO PHRAO

Ao Phrao Beach Ao Phrao ☎081 429 7145, ⓦkokut .com. Mainly but not exclusively package-oriented clusters of thatched and more expensive concrete a/c bungalows, all with hot showers and TVs; facilities include internet, free wi-fi, free kayaks and a karaoke room. Breakfast included. B3600

AROUND BAN KHLONG HIN DAM

★ **Koh Kood Beach Resort** Ao Khlong Mat, about 2km northwest of Ban Khlong Hin Dam ☎081 908 8966, ⓦvisitbeyond.com. This excellent Danish-run resort is set in loads of space on a sweeping, grassy slope above a lovely pool and a nice stretch of sandy beach. Rooms are of two types, all with a/c, outdoor hot showers, mini-bars, TVs, DVD players and sea views from their generous decks: high-roofed, thatched Balinese-style bungalows and slightly more expensive "Thai Twin Houses", very suitable for families, in which two rooms share a jacuzzi. Motorbikes, mountain bikes, snorkels and kayaks are available, as well as computers and wi-fi in the restaurant. Breakfast included. B3500

Shantaa North end of Ao Taphao, about 2km west of Ban Khlong Hin Dam ☎081 817 9648, ⓦshantaa kohkood.com. On a landscaped grassy rise, these nicely decorated villas have a/c and hot rain showers in attractive indoor-outdoor bathrooms. There's not much of a beach but plenty of decks with sunloungers. Computers and wi-fi available in the restaurant. Breakfast included. B4500

EATING AND DRINKING

There are very few eating and drinking options away from the resorts, but a couple might tempt you to make a detour.

Pizza and Pasta South side of Ban Khlong Hin Dam ☎083 297 2860, ⓦpizzanpasta.info. Genial Italian–Thai roadside restaurant serving a mean bolognese with home-made tagliatelle (B250), pizzas (B220), a few salads, espressos and pastries for breakfast. Also does a delivery service. Daily 8.30am–9pm.

Tawan Bar Ao Khlong Chao. Small roadside bar run by a friendly musician, with live music every night. Daily 3pm–2am.

DIRECTORY

Exchange There's no bank on Ko Kood, but you can change money at the bigger resorts.

Hospital Ban Khlong Hin Dam (☎039 521852).

Internet access In the tourist information centre on Ao Khlong Chao and at most resorts.

Pharmacy The shop across from the hospital in Ban Khlong Hin Dam has a small pharmacy section and sells antihistamine tablets for bites from sandflies (see p.67), which can be legion on Ko Kood.

Police Ban Khlong Hin Dam (☎039 521745).

Postal agent In the shop next to *Happy Days* on Ao Ngamkho.

4

The northeast: Isaan

MAIN PRANG, PRASAT PHANOM RUNG

5

The northeast: Isaan

Bordered by Laos and Cambodia on three sides, the scorching-hot tableland of northeast Thailand – known as Isaan, after the Hindu god of death and the northeast – comprises a third of the country's land area and is home to nearly a third of its population. This is the least-visited region of the kingdom, and the poorest: almost three-quarters of Isaan residents are in debt, and it's thought that the majority still earn less than the regional minimum wage of B164–183 a day. Farming is the traditional livelihood here, despite appallingly infertile soil (the friable sandstone contains few nutrients and retains little water) and long periods of drought punctuated by downpours and intermittent bouts of flooding. As you'd expect, the landscape is mostly flat, but there are plenty of lively festivals and ancient temples to make a visit worth the effort.

In the 1960s, government schemes to introduce hardier crops set in motion a debt cycle that has forced farmers into monocultural cash-cropping to repay their loans for fertilizers, seeds and machinery. For many families, there's only one way off the treadmill: of the twenty-one million people who live in Isaan, an average of two million economic refugees leave the area every year, most of them heading for Bangkok, where northeasterners now make up the majority of the capital's lowest-paid workforce. Children and elderly parents remain in the villages, increasingly dependent on the money sent back every month from the metropolis and awaiting the annual visit in May, when migrant family members often return for a couple of months to help with the rice planting.

Rather than the cities – which are chaotic, exhausting places, with little going for them apart from accommodation and onward transport – Isaan's prime destinations are its **Khmer ruins** and **Khao Yai National Park**. Five huge northeastern **festivals** also

HAEW SUWAT FALLS, KHAO YAI NATIONAL PARK

Highlights

❶ Khao Yai National Park Easy and tough trails, lots of birds, gibbons and elephants, several waterfalls and night safaris. **See p.440**

❷ Khmer ruins Exquisite Angkor Wat-style temples at Phimai, Phanom Rung and Khao Phra Viharn. **See p.449, p.453 & p.463**

❸ Silk A northeastern speciality, available all over the region but particularly in Khon Kaen. See p.462

❹ Yasothon rocket festival Bawdy rainmaking ritual involving ornate home-made rockets. See p.472

❺ Phu Kradung Teeming table mountain, the most dramatic of the region's national parks. See p.486

❻ The Mekong The best stretch in Thailand for gentle exploration of the mighty riverscape is between Chiang Khan and Nong Khai. See p.489

❼ Wat Phu Tok Extraordinary meditation temple on a steep sandstone outcrop. **See p.501**

❽ Wat Phra That Phanom Isaan's most fascinating holy site, especially during the February pilgrimage. **See p.504**

HIGHLIGHTS ARE MARKED ON THE MAP ON P.438

5

draw massive crowds: in May, Yasothon is the focus for the bawdy rocket festival; the end of June or beginning of July sees the equally raucous rainmaking festival of Phi Ta Kon in Dan Sai near Loei; in July, Ubon Ratchathani hosts the extravagant candle festival; in October, strange, pink fireballs float out of the Mekong near Nong Khai; while the flamboyant, though inevitably touristy, "elephant round-up" is staged in Surin in November.

It's rural life that really defines Isaan though, and you can learn a lot about the local residents by staying at one of the family-run **guesthouses** and **homestays** in the southern part of the region. If you make it this far you should endeavour to see at least one set of Isaan's Khmer ruins: those at **Phimai** are the most accessible, but it's well worth making the effort to visit either **Phanom Rung** or **Khao Phra Viharn** as well, both of which occupy spectacular hilltop locations, though the latter was closed at the time of writing. Relics of an even earlier age, prehistoric cliff-paintings also draw a few tourists eastwards to the little town of **Khong Chiam**, which is prettily set between the Mekong and Mun rivers.

Isaan's only mountain range of any significance divides the uninspiring town of **Loei** from the central plains and offers some stiff walking, awesome scenery and the possibility of spotting unusual birds and flowers in the **national parks** that spread across its heights. Due north of Loei at **Chiang Khan**, the **Mekong River** begins its leisurely course around Isaan with a lush stretch where a sprinkling of guesthouses has opened up the river countryside to travellers. The powerful waterway acts as a natural boundary between Thailand and Laos, but it's no longer the forbidding barrier it once was; with

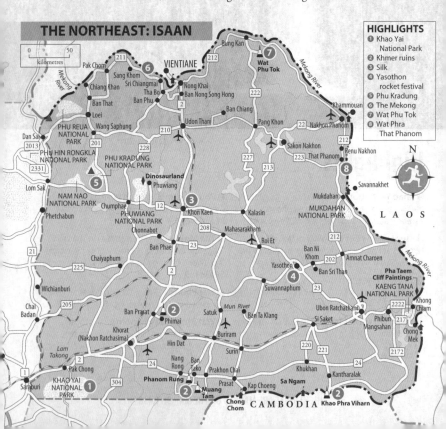

THE NORTHEAST: ISAAN

HIGHLIGHTS
1. Khao Yai National Park
2. Khmer ruins
3. Silk
4. Yasothon rocket festival
5. Phu Kradung
6. The Mekong
7. Wat Phu Tok
8. Wat Phra That Phanom

Laos opening further border crossings to visitors, the river is becoming an increasingly important transport link.

At the eastern end of this upper stretch, the border town of **Nong Khai** is surrounded by wonderfully ornate temples, some of which are used by the significant population of Chinese and Vietnamese migrants. The grandest and most important religious site in the northeast, however, is **Wat Phra That Phanom**, way downstream beyond **Nakhon Phanom**, a town that affords some of the finest Isaan vistas.

GETTING THERE AND AROUND   ISAAN

All towns and cities in Isaan are connected by public transport, as are many of the larger villages, but compared to many other regions of the country, northeastern roads are fairly traffic-free, so renting your own vehicle is also a good option.

By bus Many travellers approach Isaan from the north, either travelling directly from Chiang Mai to Loei, or going via Phitsanulok, in the northern reaches of the central plains, to Khon Kaen, but you can also take direct buses to Khorat from the east-coast towns of Pattaya, Rayong and Chanthaburi. All major northeastern centres have direct bus services from Bangkok.

By train Two rail lines cut through Isaan, providing useful connections with Bangkok and Ayutthaya.

By plane There are flights between Bangkok and several northeastern cities.

Brief history

Most northeasterners speak a dialect that's more comprehensible to residents of Vientiane than Bangkok, and Isaan's historic allegiances have tied it more closely to Laos and Cambodia than to Thailand. Between the eleventh and thirteenth centuries, the all-powerful **Khmers** covered the northeast in magnificent stone temple complexes, the remains of which constitute the region's most satisfying tourist attractions. During subsequent centuries the territories along the Mekong River changed hands numerous times, until the present border with Laos was set at the end of World War II. In the 1950s and 1960s, **Communist insurgents** played on the northeast's traditional ties with Laos; a movement to align Isaan with the Marxists of Laos gathered some force, and the Communist Party of Thailand, gaining sympathy among poverty-stricken northeastern farmers, established bases in the region. At about the same time, major US air bases for the **Vietnam War** were set up in Khorat, Ubon Ratchathani and Udon Thani, fuelling a sex industry that has plagued the region ever since. When the American military moved out, northeastern women turned to the tourist-oriented Bangkok flesh-trade instead, and today the majority of prostitutes in the capital come from Isaan.

ISAAN'S BORDER CROSSINGS

Isaan has four major **border crossings into Laos** (see p.27), all of which issue Lao visas. The most popular of these is at Nong Khai, a route that provides easy road access to the Lao capital, Vientiane; the others are Nakhon Phanom, Mukdahan and Chong Mek. If you want to avoid possible queues at the border, you can get a Lao visa in advance from the consulate in the central Isaan town of Khon Kaen. Here you'll also find a Vietnamese consulate issuing visas for Vietnam.

It's also possible to travel **overland between Isaan and Cambodia** (see p.27) through two different border crossings: via the Thai town of Kap Choeng, in Surin province, to O'Smach, which has transport to Anlong Veng and then on to Siem Reap; and via Sa Ngam in the Phusing district of Si Saket province to Choam in Anlong Veng.

5

Khao Yai National Park

B400 (B50 extra/vehicle)

About 120km northeast of Bangkok, the cultivated lushness of the central plains gives way to the thickly forested Phanom Dangkrek mountains. A 2166-square-kilometre chunk of this sculpted limestone range has been conserved as **KHAO YAI NATIONAL PARK**, the country's first national park to be established (in 1962) and one of its most popular. Spanning five distinct forest types and rising to a height of 1341m, the park sustains over three hundred bird and twenty large land-mammal species – hence its UNESCO accreditation as a World Heritage Site – and offers a plethora of waterfalls and several undemanding walking trails.

Rangers discourage visitors from exploring the outer, non-waymarked reaches unguided, partly for environmental reasons, but also because of trigger-happy **sandalwood poachers**. The highly prized sandalwood oil is extracted by making cuts in a mature aloewood tree and collecting chunks of oil-saturated wood – which sells for B20,000–40,000/kg – several months later. Sandalwood trees are indigenous to Khao Yai, and though oil-collection does not usually kill the tree, it does weaken it. Guides can point out trees that have been cut in this way along the trails.

For many Thais, however, especially Bangkokians, Khao Yai is not so much a place for wildlife spotting as an easy weekend escape from the fumes. Some have second homes in the area, while others come for the golf and the soft-adventure activities, especially horseriding and off-road driving in ATVs, offered by the increasingly popular "dude-ranch" resorts. The cooler climate here has also made Khao Yai one of Thailand's most productive areas for viticulture and dairy farming.

There's camping and basic accommodation in the park itself, and plenty more comfortable options just beyond the perimeter and in the nearby town of **Pak Chong**. It's quite easy to trek the park trails by yourself, but as some of Khao Yai's best waterfalls, caves and viewpoints are as much as 20km apart, a tour is worth considering. Try to avoid visiting at weekends and holidays, when it's busy; that said, even at peak times,

---

KHAO YAI'S WILDLIFE

During the daytime you're bound to hear some of the local wildlife, even if you don't catch sight of it. Noisiest of all are the **white-handed (lar) gibbons**, which hoot and whoop from the tops of the tallest trees, and the bubbling trills of the **pileated (capped) gibbons**. Gibbons generally avoid contact with the ground, unlike the hard-to-miss **pig-tailed macaques**, many of which gather at favoured spots on the road through the park. **Hornbills** also create quite a racket, calling and flapping their enormous wings; Khao Yai harbours large flocks of four different hornbill species, which makes it one of the best observation sites in Southeast Asia. The great hornbill is particularly beautiful, with brilliant yellow and black undersides and a 2m wingspan; the magnificent oriental pied hornbill boasts less striking black and white colouring, but is more commonly seen at close range because it swoops down to catch fish, rats and reptiles. You might also see red-headed trogons, orange-breasted trogons, woodpeckers and Asian fairy-bluebirds, and, if you're very lucky, silver pheasants or Siamese firebacks, endemic only to Thailand and western Cambodia. From November to March Khao Yai hosts several species of **migrant birds**, including the dramatically coloured Siberian thrush and the orange-headed thrush.

A herd of between 200 and 250 Asian **elephants** lives in the park, and its members are often seen at night – it's the only place in Thailand where you have much chance of spotting wild elephants. Khao Yai is also home to a very small number of **tigers**, sightings of which are extremely rare. You're almost certain to spot **civets**, and you might come across a **slow loris**, while barking and sambar **deer** are less nervous after dark. **Wrinkle-lipped bats** assemble en masse at sunset, especially at the cave entrance next to Wat Tham Silathong, just outside the north (main) gate into the park, which every evening disgorges millions of them on their nightly forage.

LEECHES

If hiking during or just after the rainy season you will almost certainly have some unsolicited encounters with **leeches**; mosquito repellent helps deter them, as do leech socks (canvas gaiters), available from the cafeteria complex opposite the visitor centre, or in the nearby accommodation office (B70/pair, although unless you want to keep them as a souvenir, you should insist on borrowing a pair from your tour guide). To get leeches off your skin, burn them with a cigarette or lighter, or douse them in salt; oily suntan lotion or insect repellent can make them lose their grip and fall off.

don't expect it to be like a safari park. Bring binoculars if you have them and some warm clothes, as it gets cool at the higher altitudes, especially at night.

The park

Visitor centre daily 7am–6pm

Several well-worn **trails** radiate from the area around the visitor centre and park headquarters at kilometre-stone 37, and a few more branch off from the roads that traverse the park; a few are signposted en route and some are colour-coded. The **visitor centre** provides brochures showing the more popular trails. Wear good boots, be prepared for some wading through rivers, and take a hat and plenty of water.

You won't spot much wildlife unless you know where to look, which is one reason to join a tour of the park (see p.442), since the guides know which trees the hornbills perch on and where gibbons go to feed. However, if you prefer to go it alone, the following trails are the most popular options.

Kong Kaew Nature Trail

The shortest and least taxing trail is the kilometre-long **Kong Kaew Nature Trail**, which starts just behind the visitor centre. It's paved all the way and takes just thirty minutes in each direction; if it's not too crowded, you could see gibbons, woodpeckers and kingfishers en route.

To Nong Pak Chee observation tower

Of the more adventurous hikes that begin from the park headquarters, the most popular runs from just uphill of the visitor centre restaurant to **Nong Pak Chee observation tower** in the west of the park. This is a fairly easy walk through forest and grassland that culminates at an observation tower built next to a lake. En route you'll hear white-handed gibbons in the tallest trees, and might spot barking deer in the savanna. If you stay at the tower long enough you could see eagles soaring or needletails dive-bombing the lake; elephants and gaurs sometimes come to drink here, too. The walk takes about two and a half hours to the observation tower (4.5km), from where it's another 900m down a dirt track that meets the main road between kilometre-stones 35 and 36. From the road, you can walk or hitch back either to the headquarters (2km) or down to the checkpoint (12km) and then travel on to Pak Chong. If you just want to spend a few hours at the observation tower and forget the main part of the walk, stop beside the main road between kilometre-stones 35 and 36 (before reaching the park headquarters) and walk the kilometre down the access track to the tower.

Haew Suwat Falls and trail

Another good focus for walks is the area around **Haew Suwat Falls**, east of the visitor centre. These 25m-high falls are a great place for an invigorating shower, and featured in the 1999 film *The Beach*. To get to the falls from the park headquarters, either follow the 8km trail (allow 3–4 hours each way), or walk, drive or hitch the 6km road beyond the headquarters to Haew Suwat – it's a popular spot, so there

5

should be plenty of cars. The **trail** begins on the Nature Trail behind the visitor centre, then veers off it, along a path marked with red flashes. En route to Haew Suwat you'll pass a turn-off to *Pha Kluai/Orchid* campsite and waterfall, 6.1km from the park headquarters (see below). Due to a series of deaths, swimming at Haew Suwat is only allowed in the dry season, when the falls lose some of their power. Even then, it's wise to exercise caution.

To Pha Kluai/Orchid campsite

Day-trippers often do the shorter walk from Haew Suwat waterfall to **Pha Kluai/Orchid campsite**, which is paved most of the way and takes two hours at most (3.1km). You've a good chance of spotting gibbons and macaques along this route, as well as kingfishers and hornbills. The area around nearby Pha Kluai Falls is famous for its impressive variety of orchids.

ARRIVAL AND DEPARTURE   KHAO YAI NATIONAL PARK

There are two access roads to the park – one from the south and another from the north – with checkpoints on both. Everyone travelling by public transport approaches the park from **Pak Chong** (see p.444), about 25km north of the northern entrance.

By shared songthaew The cheapest way to get to Khao Yai from Pak Chong is to take a public songthaew from outside the 7-Eleven shop, 200m west of the footbridge on the north side of the main road near Soi 21 (every 30min 6.30am–4pm, less frequently on Sun; 30min; B35). Public songthaews are not allowed to enter the park itself, so you'll be dropped at the park checkpoint, about 14km short of the Khao Yai visitor centre, park headquarters and most popular trailheads. At the checkpoint (where you pay the national-park entrance fee), park rangers will flag down passing cars and get them to give you a ride up to the visitor centre; this is common practice here. The whole journey from Pak Chong to the visitor centre takes about 1hr.

Chartering a songthaew A quicker but pricier option is to charter a songthaew from Pak Chong: these count as private vehicles and are allowed inside the park. They can be chartered from the corner of Soi 19 in Pak Chong, and cost around B1000 for the ride from Pak Chong to Haew Suwat Falls, or about B1500 for a return trip, including several hours in the park.

Getting back Coming back from the park is often easier, as day-trippers will usually give lifts all the way back to Pak Chong. Otherwise, hitch a ride as far as the checkpoint, or walk to it from the visitor centre – it's a pleasant 3–4hr walk along the fairly shaded park road, and you'll probably spot lots of birds and some macaques, gibbons and deer as well. At the checkpoint you can pick up a songthaew to Pak Chong: the last one usually leaves here at about 5pm. To get back to Pak Chong from one of the resorts on the road to the park, simply ask the owner to call one of the public songthaews. You may have to wait a while, and pay a little extra for them coming to get you, but it still shouldn't be more than B50/person.

GETTING AROUND

By mountain bike You can rent mountain bikes from outside the visitor centre (B50/hr) when available.

INFORMATION AND TOURS

The **visitor centre**, by the park office and main trailheads, offers maps and brochures. Khao Yai's **tours** are reasonably priced and cater primarily for independent tourists rather than big groups. But be warned: in recent years, the park has been plagued with unscrupulous operators who charge exorbitant up-front fees for tours and then later ask customers to pay the park entry fee separately (including fees for the car, driver and/or guide). As a result, we recommend only reputable outfits, all offering customized trips as well as their own version of the popular, undemanding **one-and-a-half-day programme** (around B1500/person, including the B400 park entry fee) which typically features a trip to a bat cave just outside the park at dusk, walks along one or two easy trails, a swim in Haew Suwat Falls (dry season only) and some after-dark wildlife spotting; it's usual, though not compulsory, to stay in the tour operator's own **accommodation** overnight. It's worth booking ahead, especially for overnight expeditions. Prices quoted are for a minimum of two trekkers. Note that it's also possible to hire a **park ranger** as your personal guide for the more remote trails, though their command of English is limited; you can arrange this at the park headquarters the night before, but will have to sort out your own transport. There's no set fee, but a fair rate would be B500 for a few hours, or around B1000 for the whole day.

TOUR OPERATORS

Green Leaf Guest House and Tour ☎ 044 365073 or ☎ 089 424 8809, ⓦ greenleaftour.com. At this family-run outfit treks are mostly led by owner Nine, who gets good reviews, particularly as a bird-spotter. It's based at kilometre-stone 7.5 on the park road (B20 by songthaew from Pak Chong). Accommodation is available at the family guesthouse (see p.444).

Khao Yai Nature Life & Tours ☎ 081 827 8391, ⓦ khaoyainaturelifetours.com. What used to be *Khao Yai Garden Lodge* has moved to a new resort 10km south of Pak Chong's train station on Route 2090 (the road that runs into the park). Along with spacious rooms and poolside villas, it offers a variety of programmes, including half-day visits (B500), one-day photography-focused tours (B2000–3500, depending on group size), and tailor-made

treks. Their knowledgeable guides can lead you to some exciting wildlife sightings. For details of their accommodation, see p.444.

Spice Roads ☎ 02 712 5305, ⓦ spiceroads.com /thailand/khao_yai. Upmarket bicycle tour of Khao Yai and its wineries, departing from Bangkok (2 days, 1 night B7750/person all-inclusive).

Wildlife Safari ☎ 044 312922 or ☎ 089 628 8224, ⓔ jayjungletrek@gmail.com. A good range of bespoke tours, including half-day trips (B300) for those on a tight schedule. They are based about 2km north of Pak Chong train station at 39 Thanon Pak Chong Subsanun, Nong Kaja (call to arrange free transport from Pak Chong); accommodation here is in comfortable rooms (fan B200, a/c B500) in the garden of the family home. Very kind and welcoming owners.

ACCOMMODATION

You have several options when it comes to **accommodation** in Khao Yai, either in the park, or the road that leads up to it. Alternatively you could stay in Pak Chong (see p.444), 37km from the park's centre. If you decide to do a tour, it's usual to stay in the lodgings run by your tour guide. But be wary of places not listed here; plenty of people have been ripped off by unscrupulous outfits, and we've even had reports of resorts offering to pick visitors up from the bus station and then adding huge transfer charges to the bill on departure. In Pak Chong, food options are plentiful, and most out-of-town guesthouses and hotels serve meals, although you will be at the mercy of their prices so check before you order.

IN THE PARK

If you're intending to do several days' independent exploring in the park, the most obvious places to stay are the national park lodges, dorms and tents in the heart of Khao Yai. In high season, the lodges usually have to be booked in advance at the Royal Forestry Department office in Bangkok (☎ 02 562 0760) or online (see p.37). However, you could also contact the Khao Yai accommodation office direct (daily 8am–9pm; ☎ 08 1877 3127), as accommodation is often available to walk-ins Sun–Thurs. Advance booking is not usually necessary if camping, but is advisable at weekends.

Dorms Behind the visitor centre. The 35–50 beds in the basic wooden dorms are only available to individuals if there are no groups booked in. B50

Lodges Spread across the park, these sleep two to thirty people. If you book in advance, you'll need to bring the receipt to the accommodation office. B800

Tents Two-person tents can be rented at *Lam Takong* campsite, about 5km from the headquarters, and at *Pha Kluai Mai* campsite (aka *Orchid Camp*, very good for bird-spotting), about 4km east of the park headquarters, on the road to Haew Suwat falls. Equipment such as sleeping bags (B50) and pillows (B20) is available as well.

NIGHT SAFARIS

A much-touted park attraction is the hour-long **night safaris**, or "night-lightings", which take truckloads of tourists round Khao Yai's main roads in the hope of catching some interesting wildlife in the glare of the specially fitted searchlights.

Night-time **sightings** often include deer and civets, and if you're very lucky you might see elephants too. Opinions differ on the quality of the experience: some find it thrilling to be out on the edges of the jungle after dark, others see it as rather a crass method of wildlife observation, especially at weekends, when the park can feel like a town centre, with four or five trucks following each other round and round the main roads.

All night-lightings are run by the **park rangers**, so tour operators sometimes join forces to hire a truck with ranger and searchlights. If you're on your own, you'll probably need to accompany one of these groups.

The safaris depart the park headquarters **every night** at 7pm and 8pm (they can pick you up from the campsite if requested); trucks cost B500 to rent and can take up to ten people: book your place at the national park accommodation office, next to the visitor centre.

5

You can pitch your own tent at either site for B30/person. B150

THE PARK ROAD

The 23km road that runs from Pak Chong up to the park checkpoint is dotted with luxurious hotels and resorts; most guests arrive by car, but Pak Chong transfers are usually available and the Pak Chong songthaew will also bring you here. Addresses are determined by the nearest kilometre-stone on Thanon Thanarat.

Green Leaf Guest House and Tour 12.5km from Pak Chong, at kilometre-stone 7.5 ☏044 365073, ⊚green leaftour.com. One of the cheapest places to stay on the park road, this friendly, family-run outfit has 21 en-suite fan rooms behind the good, cheap restaurant; it also does guided treks into the national park (see p.443). B200

Khao Yai Nature Life & Tours 10km from Pak Chong, just before kilometre-stone 5 ☏081 827 8391, ⊚khao yainaturelifetours.com. Family owned, this new resort has a good selection of a/c rooms and villas set around two excellent outdoor pools. The best rooms have wooden floors and beds covers made from fine Thai silk. Breakfast included. B2500

Juldis Khao Yai Resort At kilometre-stone 17 ☏044 297272, ⊚juldiskhaoyai.com. Offers good-value upmarket accommodation in its large a/c rooms and has a swimming pool, tennis courts, mountain-bike rental, a restaurant and a pub. Includes breakfast. Discounts at weekends. B1900

Pak Chong

Whether you decide to see Khao Yai National Park on your own or as part of a tour, your first port of call is likely to be the town of **PAK CHONG**, 37km north of Khao Yai's visitor centre and major trailheads, and served by trains and buses. One of the three recommended Khao Yai tour leaders operates from Pak Chong, and there are a couple of places to stay in town too. The obvious drawback to basing yourself here is that it's about an hour's journey from the Khao Yai trailheads, but if you make an early start you can make use of the cheap public songthaew service.

Thanon Tesaban cuts through central Pak Chong, and numerous small sois shoot off it: sois to the north are odd-numbered in ascending order from west to east (Soi 13–Soi 25) while those on the south side of the road have even numbers, from west to east (from Soi 8–Soi 18). The heart of the town is on the north side, between the train station on Soi 15 and the footbridge a few hundred metres further east at Soi 21.

ARRIVAL AND DEPARTURE

By train Pak Chong train station (☏044 311534) is on Soi 15, one short block north of Thanon Tesaban.

Destinations Ayutthaya (12 daily; 1hr 45min–2hr 45min); Bangkok (12 daily; 3hr 30min–4hr 45min); Khorat (13 daily; 1hr 15min–1hr 30min); Si Saket (8 daily; 4hr 20min–7hr 30min); Surin (10 daily; 3hr 10min–5hr 30min); Ubon Ratchathani (7 daily; 6hr 50min–8hr 40min); Udon Thani (2 daily; 6hr 30min–7hr 15min).

By bus and minibus The bus station is towards the west end of town, one block south off the main road between sois 8 and 10. Some long-distance buses also stop in the town centre, beside the footbridge, while a/c minibuses to Bangkok and Khorat leave from offices on opposite sides of the road near the Beautiful Optical shop on Thanon Tesaban, just west of Soi 18.

Destinations Bangkok (hourly; 2–3hr); Khorat (every 20min; 1hr).

ACCOMMODATION

Pak Chong Hotel About 600m southeast of the railway station at 650/1 Thanon Mittraphap ☏044 279082, ⊚hotelpakchong.com. This big white block just back from the main road isn't the most peaceful place in town, but its clean and spartan rooms are reasonable value. Rates include breakfast and free wi-fi. Fan B460, a/c B520

Phubade Hotel 50m south of the train station down Tesaban Soi 15 ☏044 314964. Pak Chong's cheapest

hotel with clean-ish, very basic rooms. A safe bet if you arrive late in the evening and need somewhere central to stay. Also offers a laundry service. Fan B250, a/c B400

Rim Tarn Inn 300m west of the bus station at 430 Thanon Mittraphap ☏044 313364, ⊚rimtarninn.com. Smarter and more appealing than *Phubade*, this tall multi-coloured building has large, fairly comfortable a/c rooms, plus a pool, restaurant and beer garden. B1500

EATING

There's a **day market** selling fresh fruit and vegetables in the centre of town, between the train station on Soi 15 and the footbridge a few hundred metres further east at Soi 21. You'll find a **supermarket** near here on the south side of the main road.

★ **Ban Mai Chay Nam** 21 Thanon Mittraphap ⊙081 660 2826, ⓦbanmaichaynam.com. Awesome old-style Thai restaurant stuffed with retro curios – from giant Spiderman figures to American gas pumps from the 1950s. It's far more popular with Thais than it is with tourists, and the food is fresh and authentic. Dishes include a mean catfish salad. Most dishes B80–150. Daily 10am–10pm.

Night Market The cheapest and most popular place to eat after dark, the night market sets up along the main road between Tesaban sois 17 and 19. Daily 6–10/11pm.

DIRECTORY

ATMs There are several ATMs near the train station.
Hospital There's a branch of the Bangkok Hospital (⊙044 316611) at 51 Thanon Mittraphap.

Internet access There are several internet centres near the train station.
Post office On the corner of Soi 25 and Thanon Tesaban.

Khorat (Nakhon Ratchasima)

Beyond Pak Chong, Highway 2 and the rail line diverge to run either side of picturesque Lam Takong Reservoir, offering a last taste of undulating, forested terrain before reaching the largely barren Khorat plateau. They rejoin at **KHORAT** (officially known as **Nakhon Ratchasima**) – literally "Frontier Country" – which is considered the gateway to the northeast.

If this is your first stop in Isaan, it's not a pleasant introduction: Khorat is one of Thailand's most populous cities, its streets teem with traffic, and there's nothing here you could call a genuine tourist attraction. On the plus side, Khorat is at the centre of a good transport network and is within striking distance of the **Khmer ruins** at Phimai, Phanom Rung and Muang Tam, as well as the archeological remains of **Ban Prasat** and the pottery village at **Dan Kwian**. Aside from serving Bangkok and all the main centres within Isaan, Khorat's bus network extends south along Highway 304 to the east coast, enabling you to travel directly to Pattaya, Rayong and Chanthaburi without going through the capital.

Thao Suranari Monument

Sights are thin on the ground in Khorat, but if you spend more than a couple of hours in the city you're bound to come across the landmark statue at the western gate of the old city walls. This is the much-revered **Thao Suranari Monument**, erected to commemorate the heroic actions of the wife of the deputy governor of Khorat, during an attack by the kingdom of Vientiane – capital of modern-day Laos – in 1826. Some chronicles say she organized a feast for the Lao army and enticed them into bed, where they were then slaughtered by the Thais; another tells how she and the other women of Khorat were carted off as prisoners to Vientiane, whereupon they attacked their guards with such ferocity that the Lao retreated out of fear that the whole Thai army had arrived. At any rate, Thao Suranari saved the day and is still feted by the citizens of Khorat, who lay flowers at her feet, light incense at her shrine and even dance around it. From March 23 to April 3, the town holds a week-long **festival** in her honour, with parades through the streets and the usual colourful trappings of Thai merry-making.

Maha Veeravong Museum

In the grounds of Wat Suthachinda, Thanon Ratchadamnoen · Wed–Sun 9am–4pm · B100 · ⓦthailandmuseum.com

The **Maha Veeravong Museum** houses a small and unexceptional collection of predominantly Dvaravati- and Lopburi-style Buddha statues that belonged to a monk

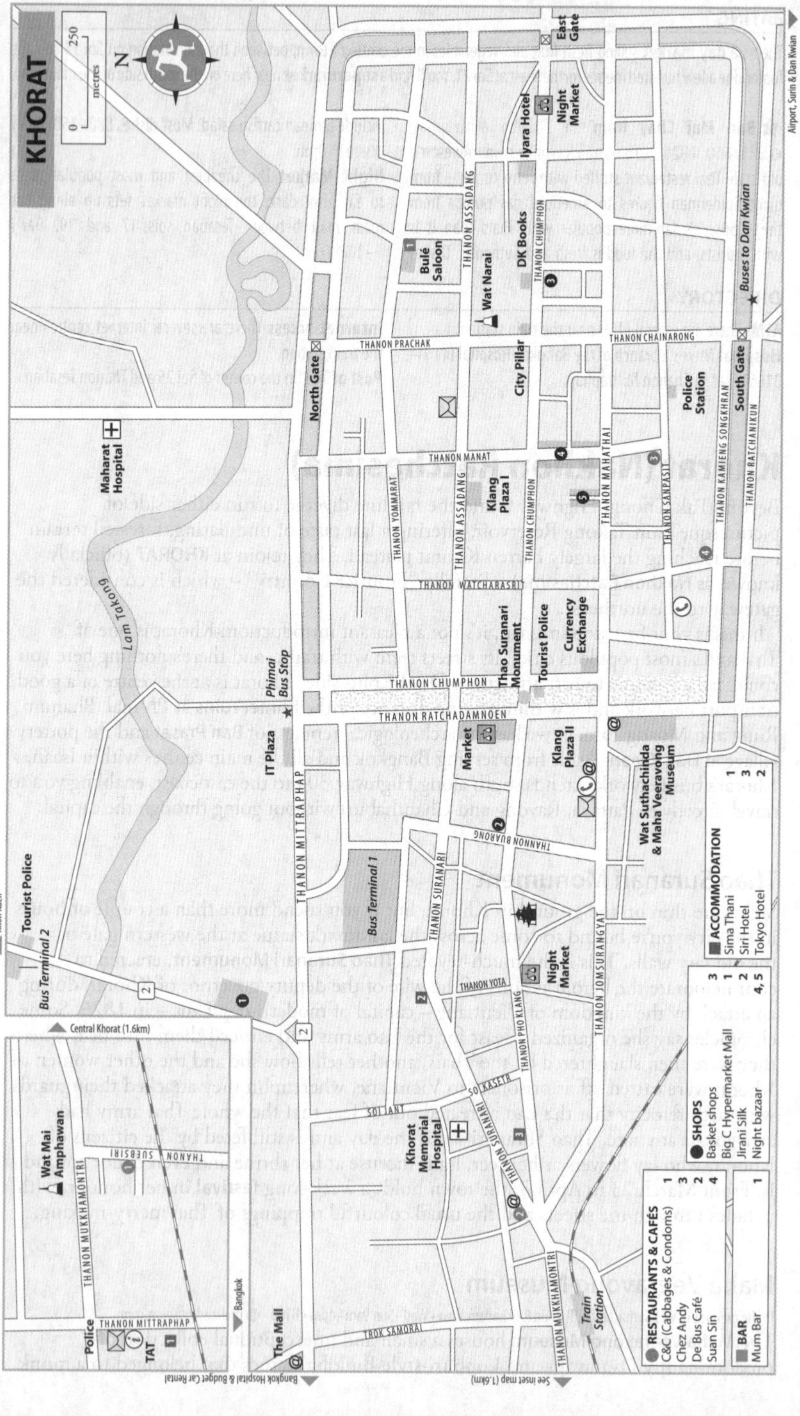
KHORAT
0
250
metres
N
East Gate
Night Market
Iyara Hotel
THANON ASSADANG
Bulé Saloon
Wat Narai
DK Books
THANON CHUMPHON
Buses to Dan Kwian
Airport, Surin & Dan Kwian
THANON PRACHAK
North Gate
City Pillar
THANON CHAINARONG
Police Station
South Gate
THANON KAMIENG SONGKHRAN
THANON RATCHANIKUN
Maharat Hospital
THANON MANAT
THANON MAHATHAI
THANON YOMMARAT
THANON ASSADANG
THANON CHUMPHON
Klang Plaza I
THANON SANPASIT
THANON WATCHARASRIT
Lam Takong
Thao Suranari Monument
Tourist Police
Currency Exchange
Phimai Bus Stop
THANON CHUMPHON
THANON RATCHADAMNOEN
IT Plaza
Market
Klang Plaza II
Wat Suthachinda & Maha Veeravong Museum
THANON MITTRAPHAP
THANNON BUARONG
Bus Terminal 1
THANON SURANARI
Tourist Police
Khon Kaen
Bus Terminal 2
Night Market
THANON YOTA
THANON JOMSURANGYAT
THANON PHO KLANG
Central Khorat (1.6km)
SOI KASETR
Khorat Memorial Hospital
THANON SURANARI
Wat Mai Amphawan
THANON SUEBSIRI
THANON MUKKHAMONTRI
Bangkok
Police
TAT
THANON MITTRAPHAP
The Mall
TROK SAMORAI
THANON MUKKHAMONTRI
Train Station
Bangkok Hospital & Budget Car Rental
See inset map (1.6km)
ACCOMMODATION
Sima Thani 1
Siri Hotel 3
Tokyo Hotel 2
SHOPS
Basket shops 3
Big C Hypermarket Mall 1
Jirani Silk 2
Night bazaar 4, 5
RESTAURANTS & CAFÉS
C&C (Cabbages & Condoms) 1
Chez Andy 3
De Bus Café 2
Suan Sin 4
BAR
Mum Bar 1

who was once the abbot of Wat Suthachinda. The single-storey museum was built by Thailand's Fine Arts Department in 1954, and makes for a pleasant diversion from the chaos of the city.

Dan Kwian

15km south of Khorat on Route 224 • Local bus #1307 (destination Chok Chai; every 30min; 30min) from Bus Terminal 2, or at Khorat's South Gate; get off as soon as you see the roadside pottery stalls

Some of the most popular household pottery in Thailand is produced by the potters of **DAN KWIAN**, a tiny village 15km south of Khorat. The local clay, dug from the banks of the Mun River, has a high iron content, which when fired in wood-burning kilns combines with ash to create the unglazed metallic finish that is characteristic of **Dan Kwian pottery**. The geometrical latticework pattern is also typical, and is incorporated into everything from incense burners and ashtrays to vases and storage jars. Dan Kwian potters also produce ceramic tiles and large-scale religious and secular murals, a favourite in modern wats and city homes.

ARRIVAL AND DEPARTURE
KHORAT (NAKHON RATCHASIMA)

BY TRAIN

The train station, on Thanon Mukkhamontri (☎044 242044), is served by city bus routes #2 and #3.

Destinations Ayutthaya (12 daily; 3hr 30min); Bangkok (12 daily; 4–6hr 40min); Khon Kaen (5 daily; 3hr 20min); Pak Chong (13 daily; 1–2hr); Si Saket (11 daily; 4hr–5hr 30min); Surin (13 daily; 2hr–3hr 20min); Ubon Ratchathani (10 daily; 4hr–6hr 10min); Udon Thani (4 daily; 5hr–5hr 40min).

BY BUS

Bus Terminal 2 (☎044 256006–9), the main terminal, is situated on the far northern edge of the city on Highway 2. It's the arrival and departure point for regular and a/c buses serving regional towns such as Pak Chong (for Khao Yai) and Phimai, as well as long-distance destinations such as Bangkok, Ban Tako (for Phanom Rung), Chiang Mai, Khon Kaen, Nong Khai, Pattaya, Rayong (for Ko Samet) and Surin. Traffic is chaotic in the city, so avoid choking in a

tuk-tuk and take a cheaper a/c taxi instead (B35 to train station or nearby hotels).

Bus Terminal 1 (☎044 268899) is more centrally located just off Thanon Suranari, and also operates both fan and a/c buses to Bangkok, via Pak Tong Chai and Pak Chong. However, departures from Terminal 2 are more frequent.

Destinations Bangkok (every 20min; 4–5hr); Ban Tako (for Phanom Rung; every 30min; 2hr); Buriram (every 30min; 3hr); Chanthaburi (more than 20 daily; 6–8hr); Chiang Mai (9 daily; 12–14hr); Chiang Rai (5 daily; 14–16hr); Dan Kwian (every 30min; 30min); Khon Kaen (at least hourly; 2hr 30min–3hr); Lopburi (12 daily; 3hr 30min); Nakhon Phanom (3 daily; 8hr); Nong Khai (11 daily; 6–8hr); Pattaya (8 daily; 6–8hr); Phimai (every 30min; 1hr–1hr 30min); Phitsanulok (9 daily; 7–9hr); Rayong (for Ko Samet; at least 8 daily; 6–8hr); Si Racha (7 daily; 5hr); Surin (every 30min; 4–5hr); Ubon Ratchathani (every 30min; 5–7hr); Udon Thani (at least hourly; 3hr 30min–5hr).

GETTING AROUND

By songthaew and city bus Flat-fare songthaews (B8) and city buses (B8) travel most main roads within town. Expect to pay up to B15 for longer journeys to the city limits. The most useful routes – served by both songthaews and buses – are #2, which runs between the main TAT office in the west, via the train station, along Thanon Suranari and Thanon Assadang to beyond the *lak muang* (city pillar) in the east, and #3, which also runs right across the city, via Mahathai and Jomsurangyat roads, past the train station, to the TAT office in the west.

By tuk-tuk Easily flagged down off the main routes around town. Expect to pay B50 for journeys of 1–2km (from the Thao Suranari Monument to the Big C hypermarket, for example).

By taxi Metered taxis cruise the streets but are not yet as ubiquitous as tuk-tuks. Expect to pay a minimum fee of B30.

Car rental Cars with insurance are available from Budget at 719/5 Thanon Mittraphap, outside Tesco Lotus (daily 8am–6pm; ☎0662 2030250 ⓦ budget.co.th).

INFORMATION

Tourist information The TAT office (daily 8.30am–4.30pm; ☎044 213666, ⓔ tatsima@tat.or.th) is 1.6km west of the train station on Thanon Mittraphap. It's only

really worth making the trip for one of their free maps of the city. To reach it from the city centre, take city bus #2 or #3 (see above).

5

ACCOMMODATION

Another reason not to stay in Khorat is that its budget **hotels** are noisy and not that cheap (if visiting Phimai, consider staying there instead). There are, however, some reasonable a/c options.

Sima Thani 2112/2 Thanon Mittraphap, near the TAT office ☎ 044 213100, ⓦ simathani.com. One of the city's best hotels, with smart a/c rooms, a swimming pool, three restaurants and a babysitting service. There's a relaxed feel to the place despite its popularity with businesspeople, and the rooms are good value. It's located beside Highway 2 (the Bangkok–Nong Khai road), and buses from Bangkok or Khao Yai can drop you at the door en route to Bus Terminal 2, but it's too far to walk from the hotel to the town centre. B1400

Siri Hotel 688–690 Thanon Pho Klang ☎ 044 242831, ⓦ sirihotelkorat.com. Less than a 10min walk from the train station, the *Siri* has a/c throughout, and is ideal for budget travellers. Rooms are surprisingly quiet and spacious (though don't expect a view). B520

Tokyo Hotel 256–258 Thanon Suranari ☎ 044 242788, ✉ tokyo-hotel@windowslive.com. A 5min walk from Bus Terminal 1, or #15 from the train station. Conveniently located option with large, reasonably clean rooms. Fan B350, a/c B500

EATING AND DRINKING

The night bazaar on and around Thanon Manat includes a few hot-food stalls, but there's a bigger selection of **night-market**-style foodstalls, with some streetside tables, about 800m further east near the *Iyara Hotel* on Thanon Chumphon. A smaller, more convenient grouping sets up about 400m east of *Sri Hotel* on the corner of Thanon Yota. Because of its sizeable contingent of (mostly retired) expats, Khorat also offers the chance to satisfy foreign-food cravings. For big international-brand **restaurants**, head for the huge shopping mall that houses the Big C hypermarket.

★ **C&C (Cabbages & Condoms)** 86/1 Thanon Suebsiri. Excellent Thai food at this cosy, mid-priced restaurant (most dishes B60–B100), managed along the same lines as its sister operation in Bangkok, with all proceeds going to the Population and Community Development Association of Thailand (PDA). Daily 10am–10pm.

Chez Andy 5–7 Thanon Manat ⓦ chezandy.com. Swiss-run restaurant famous for its Australian steaks (around B250), but which also does some Swiss and Thai dishes. There's a Mediterranean buffet every Friday night (B250) and a happy hour on spirits (daily 3–7pm; B80 a drink). Mon–Sat 11am–midnight.

De Bus Café Thanon Suranari, near the junction with Thanon Mukkhamontri ☎ 044 277464. Bright and peaceful a/c café off one of Khorat's biggest and busiest streets. Lattes, mochas and cappuccinos for B35, plus an interesting range of breakfast choices, from hot dogs to toast with mayonnaise and pork floss. Delivery available. Mon–Fri 7am–10pm, Sat–Sun 8am–10pm.

★ **Mum Bar** Thanon Yommarat, just east of *Bulé Saloon* ☎ 085 779890. Friendly late-night bar tucked away on the ground floor of a stilted house that's cluttered with old Pepsi merchandise. Popular among the city's young rockers, who turn up in their rebuilt classic cars. Daily until 2am.

Suan Sin 163 Thanon Watcharasrit. Cheap place that's highly rated by locals for its tasty Isaan favourites, especially *som tam* and *kai yang* (from B50). Daily 10am–10pm.

SHOPPING

Basket shops Thanon Chumphon. Across the road from DK Books is a cluster of authentic basketware shops whose sticky-rice baskets, fish traps and rice winnowers make attractive souvenirs.

Big C Hypermarket Mall Just off Thanon Mittraphap. Your best bet for cheap music, DVDs and trainers.

Jiranai Silk On the corner of Thanon Buarong and Pho Klang. If you're not going further east to Surin, Khorat is not a bad place to buy silk, much of which is produced in Pak Tong Chai, an uninteresting and overexploited town 32km south of Khorat on Highway 304. This city-centre place has the best and most exclusive selection, while the specialist shops along Thanon Chumphon sell lengths of silk at reasonable prices.

Night bazaar Thanon Manat and Thanon Mahathai. This sets up at dusk every evening and deals mainly in bargain-priced fashions.

DIRECTORY

Hospitals Expats favour the private Bangkok Hospital (☎ 044 429999), 1308/9 Thanon Mittraphap (Highway 2), near Tesco Lotus; the government Maharat Hospital (☎ 044 235000) is on the northeast edge of town.

Internet access Internet cafés are dotted all over town, with a big cluster in the area around the post office and Klang Plaza II on Thanon Jomsurangyat. Most places charge B15/hr.

Tourist police For all emergencies, call the tourist police (☎ 1155; free, 24hr), or contact them at one of their booths in town: their main office (☎044 341777–9) is opposite Bus Terminal 2 on Highway 2, and there's a more central booth beside the Thao Suranari Monument on Thanon Chumphon.

Tours Korat Travel Service at 1936/9 Thanon Mittraphap (☎044 262158, ⓦkorat-travelservice.com) runs guided day-trips to Phanom Rung and Phimai.

Ban Prasat

The quintessentially northeastern village of **BAN PRASAT**, north of Khorat, became a source of great interest to archeologists following the 1990s discovery of a series of **burial grounds** within its boundaries, some of which date back three thousand years. The skeletons and attendant artefacts have been well preserved in the mud, and many are now on display; the village has made extra efforts to entice tourists with low-key craft demonstrations and a homestay programme. It's also a pleasant village in its own right, a traditional community of stilt houses set beside the Tarn Prasat River.

There are currently three **excavation pits** open to the public, each clearly signed from the centre of the village and informatively labelled. From these pits, archeologists have surmised that Ban Prasat was first inhabited in around 1000 BC and that its resident rice farmers traded with coastal people. Each pit contains bones and objects from different eras, buried at different depths but also with the head pointing in different directions, suggesting a change in religious or superstitious precepts.

Signs in the village direct you to local family-run projects, such as the household of **silk-weavers**, where you should be able to see several stages of the sericulture process (see box, p.462) and buy some cloth. Other village crafts include the weaving of floor mats from locally grown bulrushes, and the making of household brooms.

ARRIVAL AND DEPARTURE | BAN PRASAT

By bus Ban Prasat is 2km off Highway 2, 46km north of Khorat and 17km southwest of Phimai. Any Khorat–Phimai bus (#1305 from Khorat's Bus Terminal 2; every 30min; about 1hr from Khorat or 20min from Phimai) will drop you at the Highway 2 junction, from where motorbike taxis will ferry you to the village.

ACCOMMODATION

There are no hotels or restaurants in the village, but there is a **homestay programme** (B400/person half-board) giving visitors a chance to learn more about Isaan life; stays should be arranged a week in advance by contacting the village headman, Khun Thiam Laongkarn, of the Eco-tourism Society, 282 Mu 7, Tambon Tarn Prasat, Amphoe Non Sung, Nakhon Ratchasima 30420 (☎044 367075). Alternatively, staff at the Khorat TAT office may be able to help (☎044 213666, ⓔtatsima@tat.or.th).

Phimai

Hemmed in by its old city walls and encircled by tributaries of the Mun River, the small modern town of **PHIMAI**, 60km northeast of Khorat, is dominated by the charmingly restored Khmer temple complex of **Prasat Hin Phimai**. No one knows for sure when the temple was built or for whom, but as a religious site it probably dates back to the reign of the Khmer king Suriyavarman I (1002–49), and parts of the complex are said to be older than Cambodia's Angkor Wat. The complex was connected by a direct road to Angkor and oriented southeast, towards the Khmer capital. Over the next couple of centuries Khmer rulers made substantial modifications, and by the end of Jayavarman VII's reign in 1220, Phimai had been officially dedicated to Mahayana Buddhism. Phimai's other claim to fame is **Sai Ngam** (Beautiful Banyan), reputedly the largest banyan tree in Thailand. Otherwise there's plenty to like about its peaceful, small-town feel. Most visitors arrive here on day-trips, but with an excellent guesthouse and plenty of opportunities for early-morning bike rides, it's worth staying overnight.

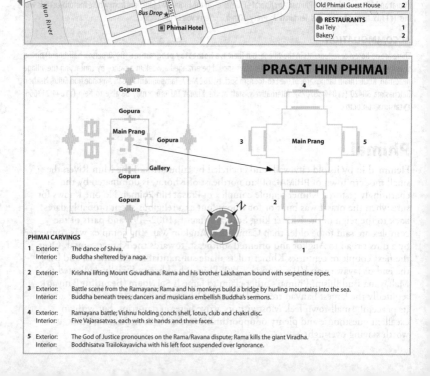

PHIMAI

Khorat, Ban Prasat & Route 208

Mun River

Restaurants

Sai Ngam
Banyan Tree

Phimai
National
Museum

Prasat
Hin Phimai

Night
Market

Clocktower
★ Bus Drop

THANON ANANTAJINDA

THANON CHOMSUDASADI

Buses to
Khorat

Bus Drop

Bus Station

Mun River

Phimai Hotel

N

0   300
metres

■ ACCOMMODATION
Boonsiri Guest House   1
Old Phimai Guest House   2

● RESTAURANTS
Bai Teiy   1
Bakery   2

PRASAT HIN PHIMAI

Gopura

Gopura

Main Prang   Gopura

Gallery

Gopura

Gopura

4

3   Main Prang   5

2

1

PHIMAI CARVINGS

1 Exterior: The dance of Shiva.
   Interior: Buddha sheltered by a naga.

2 Exterior: Krishna lifting Mount Govadhana. Rama and his brother Lakshaman bound with serpentine ropes.

3 Exterior: Battle scene from the Ramayana; Rama and his monkeys build a bridge by hurling mountains into the sea.
   Interior: Buddha beneath trees; dancers and musicians embellish Buddha's sermons.

4 Exterior: Ramayana battle; Vishnu holding conch shell, lotus, club and chakri disc.
   Interior: Five Vajarasatvas, each with six hands and three faces.

5 Exterior: The God of Justice pronounces on the Rama/Ravana dispute; Rama kills the giant Viradha.
   Interior: Boddhisatva Trailokayavicha with his left foot suspended over Ignorance.

PHIMAI BOAT RACES

Phimai's biggest event of the year is its festival of **boat races**, held on the Mun's tributaries over a weekend in early November, in a tradition that's endured for over a century. In common with many other riverside towns, Phimai marks the end of the rainy season by holding fiercely competitive longboat competitions and putting on lavish parades of ornate barges done up to emulate the Royal Barges of Bangkok. During the festival, a **son et lumière** show is staged at the temple ruins for five nights in a row; check with the Khorat TAT office for details (☏044 213666, ✉tatsima@tat.or.th).

Prasat Hin Phimai

Ruins Daily 7.30am–6pm · B100 · **Visitors' centre** Daily 8.30am–4.30pm · Free

Built mainly of dusky pink and greyish white sandstone, **Prasat Hin Phimai** is a seductive sight from a distance; closer inspection reveals a mass of intricate carvings. Entering the complex from the main southeastern gate, it's worth checking out the visitors' centre on the right-hand side after the ticket office, which uses simple wall-hung exhibits to explain the history of the site.

Outer areas

Heading into the complex from the southeastern gate, a staircase ornamented with classic naga (serpent) balustrades leads to a gopura in the **outer walls**, which are punctuated on either side by false balustraded windows – a bit of sculptural sleight-of-hand to jazz up the solid stonework without piercing the defences. A raised pathway bridges the space between these walls and the inner gallery that protects the prangs of the **inner sanctuary**. The minor prang to the right, made of laterite, is attributed to the twelfth-century Buddhist king Jayavarman VII, who engaged in a massive temple-building campaign. His statue is enshrined within; it's a copy of the much more impressive original, now housed in the Phimai National Museum. The pink sandstone prang to the left, connected to a Brahmin shrine where seven stone linga were found, was probably built around the same time.

The main prang

After more than twenty years of archeological detective work and painstaking reassembly, the towering white-sandstone **main prang** has now been restored to its original cruciform groundplan and conical shape, complete with an almost full set of carved lintels, pediments and antefixes, and capped with a stone lotus-bud. The impressively detailed **carvings** around the outside of the prang depict predominantly Hindu themes. Shiva the Destroyer dances above the main entrance to the southeast antechamber: his destruction dance heralds the end of the world and the creation of a new order, a supremely potent image that warranted this position over the most important doorway. Most of the other external carvings pick out momentous episodes from the *Ramayana* (see box, p.88), starring heroic Rama, his brother Lakshaman and their band of faithful monkeys in endless battles of strength, wits and magical powers against Ravana, the embodiment of evil. Inside, more sedate Buddhist scenes give evidence of the conversion from Hindu to Buddhist faith, and the prasat's most important image, the Buddha sheltered by a seven-headed naga, sits atop a base that once supported a Hindu Shiva lingam.

Phimai National Museum

Just northeast of Prasat Hin Phimai between one of the old Khmer reservoirs and the Mun River · Daily 9am–4pm · B100 · ⊛ thailandmuseum.com · Walking distance from the ruins, though the Khorat–Phimai bus will stop outside the museum if requested

Much of the ancient carved stonework discovered at Phimai but not fitted back into the renovated structure can be seen at the **Phimai National Museum**, where it's easier to

5

appreciate, being at eye-level, well labelled and put in context. The museum's *pièce de résistance* is the exceptionally fine sandstone statue of Jayavarman VII that was found in Phimai's laterite prang; seated and leaning slightly forward, he's lost his arms and part of his nose, but none of his grace and serenity. Elsewhere in the galleries, displays take you through the religious and cultural history of the Phimai region, featuring prehistoric items from Ban Prasat as well as some exquisite Buddha statues from more recent times.

Sai Ngam

2km northeast of the museum • Walk or rent a bicycle from one of the guesthouses (B80/day) – locals will be able to point you in the right direction if you get lost en route

Sai Ngam is a banyan tree so enormous that it's reputed to cover an area about half the size of a soccer pitch (approximately 2300 square metres). It might look like a grove of small banyans, but Sai Ngam is in fact a single *Ficus bengalensis* whose branches have dropped vertically into the ground, taken root and spawned other branches, so growing further and further out from its central trunk. Banyan trees are believed to harbour animist spirits, and you can make merit here by releasing fish or turtles into the artificial lake that surrounds Sai Ngam (B15–30, depending on which creature you choose to set free). The tree is a popular recreation spot, and several restaurants have sprung up alongside it.

ARRIVAL AND DEPARTURE   PHIMAI

By train It is feasible, if a bit of an effort, to visit Phimai en route to points east or west without having to pass through Khorat. You can do this by taking a train to the tiny station of Hin Dat (about 1hr 40min west of Surin, 55min east of Khorat). Hin Dat is 25km south of Phimai, so from here you should either wait for one of the infrequent songthaews to Phimai, splash out on an expensive motorbike taxi or try hitching. Either way it's best to start early. Songthaews back to Hin Dat from Phimai are generally timed to link up with east-bound trains; check ⍵ railway.co.th for up-to-date timetables.
Destinations Bangkok (2 daily; 7hr); Khorat (5 daily; 1hr); Surin (5 daily; roughly 2hr).
By bus Phimai's bus station is inconveniently located 1.5km

southwest of the ruins, on the bypass, but nearly everybody gets on and off in the town centre, either by the clock tower in the night market area or in front of the *Phimai Hotel*. Regular bus #1305 runs direct to Phimai from Khorat's Bus Terminal 2, with a pick-up point near the Thanon Mittraphap/ Ratchadamnoen junction (every 30min until 5.30pm, then sporadically until 10pm; 1hr 30min); the last return bus departs for Khorat at 7pm. The bus passes the turn-off to Ban Prasat, so if you get up early you can combine the two places on a day-trip from Khorat. If travelling from Khon Kaen, Udon Thani or Nong Khai, take any Khorat-bound bus along Highway 2 as far as the Phimai turn-off (Highway 206), then change onto the Khorat–Phimai service for the last 10km; the same strategy works in reverse.

GETTING AROUND

By bicycle The best way to get about, although cycling isn't permitted inside the ruins. *Boonsiri Guest House* and *Old Phimai Guest House* both have bicycles for rent (B80/ day). Aside from the ride out to Sai Ngam, the area just

west of the ruins, beyond the post office, is especially atmospheric: many of the traditional wooden houses here double as workshops, and you'll often see householders weaving cane chairs in the shade beneath the buildings.

INFORMATION AND TOURS

Tourist information Both the *Boonsiri* and *Old Phimai* guesthouses are excellent sources of local information.
Tours The *Old Phimai* runs day-trips to Phanom Rung

(see opposite) at around B2500–2800/vehicle (depends on petrol prices and the number of people travelling), excluding park entry fees.

ACCOMMODATION

★ **Boonsiri Guest House** Above a duck restaurant on Thanon Chomsudadet ☏ 044 471159, ⍵ boonsiri .net. Central, family-run place offering clean dorms and en-suite rooms that are stylishly put together. The owners' cheery and knowledgeable son speaks great

English, can provide you with a map and tips for getting around Phimai, and may even be able to offer lifts to Bai Teiy (see opposite; offer to cover at least the cost of his petrol). Wi-fi and internet available. Dorm **B150**, fan double **B400**, a/c double **B500**

EATING

If you fancy a meal with a view, head out to the string of basic **restaurants** just across from Sai Ngam. The **night market** sets up at dusk on the eastern stretch of Thanon Anantajinda, just southeast of the ruins.

★ **Bai Teiy** On the main road, about 4km north of the town centre ☎044 481191, ⊕baiteiy.com. This huge indoor restaurant is a big hit with Thais from across the region, and has a worthy reputation for duck dishes, spicy salads and fresh fish. The spring rolls (B70) are excellent. Staff speak

English and can organize a taxi for you. Daily 9am–10pm.
Bakery At the southern end of the ruins. A nice shady place to cool off with a banana split or a cold frappe after wandering around the ruins, but don't expect to get any hearty evening meals. Daily 8am–8pm.

DIRECTORY

Internet access You can access the internet at *Boonsiri Guest House* (B170 for two days' wi-fi access).

Post office There's a post office just west of Prasat Hin Phimai.

Phanom Rung and Muang Tam

East of Khorat the bleached plains roll on, broken only by the occasional small town and, if you're travelling along Highway 24, the odd tantalizing glimpse of the smoky Phanom Dangkrek mountain range above the southern horizon. That said, it's well worth jumping off the Surin-bound bus for a detour to the fine Khmer ruins of **Prasat Hin Khao Phanom Rung** and **Prasat Muang Tam**. Built during the same period as Phimai, and for the same purpose, the temple complexes form two more links in the chain that once connected the Khmer capital of Angkor with the limits of its empire. Sited dramatically atop an extinct volcano, Phanom Rung has been beautifully restored, and the more recently renovated Muang Tam lies on the plains below. Most people visit in the morning, so if you're staying in nearby **Buriram** or **Nang Rong**, consider visiting in the afternoon when the sites are less crowded.

Prasat Hin Khao Phanom Rung

Main complex Daily 6am–6pm • B100, joint ticket with Muang Tam B150 **Tourist Information Centre** Daily 9am–4.30pm

Prasat Hin Khao Phanom Rung is the finest example of Khmer architecture in Thailand, graced with innumerable exquisite carvings, its sandstone and laterite buildings designed to align with the sun at certain times of the year (see box below). As at most Khmer prasats, **building** here spanned several reigns, probably from the beginning of the tenth century to the early thirteenth. The heart of the temple was constructed in the mid-twelfth century, in early Angkorian style, and is attributed to local ruler Narendraditya and his son Hiranya. Narendraditya was a follower of the Shivaite cult, a sect which practised yoga and fire worship and used alcohol and sex in its rituals; carved depictions of all these practices decorate the temple. There are cheap foodstalls outside the Gate 1 entrance and in its car park area, where the museum-like tourist information centre provides an outstanding introduction to the temple's construction, iconography and restoration.

SPIRITUAL ALIGNMENT

Prasat Hin Khao Phanom Rung is so perfectly built that on the morning of the fifteenth day of the waxing moon in the fifth month of the lunar calendar you can stand at the westernmost gopura and see the rising sun through all fifteen doors. This day (usually in April: check dates at ⊕thailandgrandfestival.com or contact Buriram municipality on ☎044 613315) is celebrated with a day-long **festival** of huge parades all the way up the hill to the prasat – a tradition believed to go back eight hundred years.

5

The approach

The **approach** to the temple is one of the most dramatic of its kind. Symbolic of the journey from earth to the heavenly palace of the gods, the ascent to the inner compound is imbued with metaphorical import: by following the 200m-long avenue, paved in laterite and sandstone and flanked with lotus-bud pillars, you are walking to the ends of the earth. Ahead, the main prang, representing Mount Meru, home of the gods, looms large above the gallery walls, and is accessible only via the first of three **naga bridges**, a raised cruciform structure with sixteen five-headed naga balustrades. Once across the bridge you have traversed the abyss between earth and heaven. A series of stairways ascends to the eastern entrance of the celestial home, first passing four small ponds, thought to have been used for ritual purification.

A second naga bridge crosses to the **east gopura**, entrance to the inner sanctuary, which is topped by a lintel carved with Indra (god of the east) sitting on a lion throne. The gopura is the main gateway through the **gallery**, which runs right round the inner compound and has been restored in part, with arched stone roofs, small chambers inside and false windows; real windows wouldn't have been strong enough to support such a heavy stone roof, so false ones, which retained the delicate pilasters but backed them with stone blocks, were an aesthetically acceptable compromise.

The main prang

Phanom Rung is surprisingly compact, the east gopura leading almost directly into the **main prang**, separated from it only by a final naga bridge. A dancing Shiva, nine of his ten arms intact, and a lintel carved with a relief of a **reclining Vishnu** preside over the eastern entrance to the prang. This depicts a common Hindu creation myth, known as "Reclining Vishnu Asleep on the Milky Sea of Eternity", in which Vishnu dreams up a new universe, and Brahma (the four-faced god perched on the lotus blossom that springs from Vishnu's navel) puts the dream into practice.

On the pediment above this famous relief is a lively carving of **Shiva Nataraja**, or Shiva's Dance of Destruction, which shows him dancing on Mount Kailash in front of several other gods, including Ganesh, Brahma and Vishnu. The dance brings about the total destruction of the world and replaces it with a new epoch. Of the other figures decorating the prang, one of the most important is the lion head of Kala, also known as Kirtimukha, symbolic of both the lunar and the solar eclipse and – because he's able to "swallow" the sun – considered far superior to other planetary gods. Inside the prang kneels an almost life-size statue of Shiva's vehicle, the bull Nandi, behind which stands the all-powerful **Shiva lingam**, for which the prang was originally built; the stone channel that runs off the lingam and out of the north side of the prang was designed to catch the lustral water with which the sacred stone was bathed.

Two rough-hewn laterite libraries stand alongside the main prang, in the northeast and southeast corners, and there are also remains of two early tenth-century brick prangs just northeast of the main prang. The unfinished **prang noi** ("Little Prang") in the southwest corner now contains a stone Buddha footprint, which has become the focus of the merit-making at the annual April festivities, neatly linking ancient and modern religious practices.

Prasat Muang Tam

Main complex Daily 6am–6pm • B100, joint ticket with Phanom Rung B150 **Tourist Information Centre and Film** Daily 9am–4.30pm • Free

Down on the plains 8km southeast of Phanom Rung, and accessed via a scenic minor road that cuts through a swathe of rice fields, the small but elegant temple complex of **Prasat Muang Tam** is sited behind a huge kilometre-long *baray* (Khmer reservoir), which was probably constructed at the same time as the main part of the temple, in the early eleventh century. Like Phanom Rung, Muang Tam was probably built in stages

FROM TOP PRASAT HIN PHIMAI (P.451); NIGHT MARKET, KHORAT (P.448) >

5

between the tenth and thirteenth centuries, and is based on the classic Khmer design of a central prang flanked by minor prangs and encircled by a gallery and four gopura. The history of Muang Tam is presented in brief at the Tourist Information Centre in the temple car park.

The ruins

The approach to Muang Tam is nothing like as grand as at Phanom Rung but, once through the main, eastern, gopura in the outside wall, it's a pretty scene, with the central gallery encircled by four **L-shaped ponds** – such important features that they are referred to in a contemporary inscription that states "this sanctuary is preserved by sacred water". The shape of the ponds gives the impression that the prasat is set within a moat that's been severed by the four entrance pathways at the cardinal points. Each pond is lined with laterite brick steps designed to enable easy access for priests drawing sacred water, and possibly also for devotees to cleanse themselves before entering the central sanctuary. The rims are constructed from sandstone blocks that form naga, the sacred water serpents.

The rectangular central **gallery** was probably roofed with timber (long since rotted away) and so could be punctuated with real windows, rather than the more load-bearing false versions that had to be used at Phanom Rung. Inside, the **five red-brick towers** of the inner sanctuary are arranged on a laterite platform, with three prangs in the front (eastern) row, and two behind. The main, central, prang has collapsed, leaving only its base, but the four other towers are merely decapitated and some have carved **lintels** intact. The lintel above the doorway of the front right tower is particularly lively in its depiction of the popular scene known as Ume Mahesvara (Uma and her consort Shiva riding the bull Nandi). There are interesting details in the temple complex, including recurrent motifs of foliage designs and Kala lion-faces, and figures of ascetics carved into the base of the doorway pillars on the eastern gopura of the outer wall.

ARRIVAL AND DEPARTURE   **PHANOM RUNG AND MUANG TAM**

Most people check out the ruins of Phanom Rung and Muang Tam on a **day-trip** from Khorat or Surin, though it's also possible to stay closer to the sights, in **Nang Rong** or **Buriram** (see opposite). There's public transport from Khorat, Surin, Nang Rong and Buriram as far as the little town of **Ban Tako**, from where you'll need to take a motorbike taxi for the final few kilometres to the ruins. Alternatively, rent your own motorbike from Nang Rong, or join a day-tour from Phimai or Khorat. There are three car parks and three entrances to the Phanom Rung complex: if you have your own transport, ignore the Gates 2 and 3 (west) entrances, signed off the access road, and carry on to the main, Gate 1 (east), entrance and car park – the drama of the site is lost if you explore it back-to-front; motorbike taxis should take you to the main entrance.

GETTING TO BAN TAKO

By bus Served by frequent buses from Khorat (via Nang Rong) and Surin, the town of Ban Tako is located on Highway 24 about 115km southeast of Khorat or 83km southwest of Surin. Bus #274 travels between the two provincial capitals roughly every 30min. Buses connect Buriram with Ban Tako (about 1hr).

BAN TAKO TO THE RUINS

By taxi or hitching From Ban Tako it's 12km south to Phanom Rung and another 8km southeast along a side road to Muang Tam. There's no public transport to the ruins, so most people take a motorbike taxi here (B300–400/person for the round trip to Phanom Rung, Muang Tam and back to Ban Tako). Alternatively, you could hitch – a time-consuming option during the week (so you should take

a very early bus from Khorat or Surin), but a lot easier at weekends. The best place to hitch from is a small village south of Ban Tako called Ban Don Nong Nae, which you can reach from Ban Tako by taking a 10min ride on bus #523.

BURIRAM

By train Buriram is served by all Bangkok–Ubon trains.
Destinations Ayutthaya (10 daily; 4hr 30min–7hr 45min); Bangkok (10 daily; 6hr–9hr 30min); Khorat (13 daily; 1hr 15min–2hr 15min); Pak Chong (10 daily; 2hr 30min–4hr); Si Saket (11 daily; 1hr 50min–3hr 10min); Surin (13 daily; 35–55min); Ubon Ratchathani (10 daily; 2hr 40min–4hr 15min).
By air Nok Air (ⓦnokair.com; Mon & Thurs) and Thai Regional Airlines (ⓦthairegionalairlines.com; 5 weekly) fly to Buriram from Bangkok's Don Muang Airport. The airport is

35km northeast of town off Highway 219 – taxis are available for the ride into town (B600) or across to Surin (B1500).
By bus Ban Tako (1hr).

NANG RONG
By bus Nang Rong is 14km west of Ban Tako on Highway 24 and served by the #274 and #523 bus routes. For

transport to the ruins at Phanom Rung and Muang Tam, either take the #274 bus to Ban Tako, then a motorbike taxi (see opposite); hire a motorbike taxi all the way from Nang Rong (slightly pricier than from Ban Tako), or rent a car or motorbike from *Honey Inn* or *P. Inter California Hostel*. At *Honey Inn* you can also hire a pick-up with driver to take you around both sets of ruins (B600 for a 6hr tour).

ACCOMMODATION

The nearest accommodation to Phanom Rung is in **Nang Rong**, 14km west of Ban Tako on Highway 24. There's little to see here, but there are few tourists and its quaint guesthouses are handy bases for a bit of temple exploring. Much larger is the provincial capital of **Buriram**, 40km north of Ban Tako, which has slightly more upmarket accommodation options, but little else worth recommending.

BURIRAM
Buriram Siri Resort 7km south west of Buriram train station, just off highway 218 at 555 Moo 7, Baan Huay ☎ 044 690055, ☒ siriresort.com. More upmarket than *Thai Hotel*, with good-sized chalet-style rooms (all with a/c, private bathrooms and patio areas). There's wi-fi, too, and an outdoor pool, but without your own transport it's a bit too far from town. **B550**

Thai Hotel About 200m south of Buriram train station along the main drag, Thanon Romburi ☎ 044 611112. A reasonable budget choice, if only for its central location and half-decent a/c rooms. **B200**

NANG RONG
Honey Inn 8/1 Soi Sri Koon ☎ 044 622825, ☒ honeyinn

.com. A welcoming and homely guesthouse run by a couple of school teachers. Offers motorbike rental (B250/day), meals with the family (from B30) and free internet access. To get to *Honey Inn* from the Nang Rong bus terminal, either take a B30 samlor ride or walk north about 100m onto Highway 24, cross the highway, turn right and walk east along the highway for about 300m, passing a PTT petrol station after about 200m. Turn left at the *Honey Inn* sign and it's about 100m further on. **B200**

P. Inter California Hostel East of the bus station at 59/11 Thanon Sangkhakrit (B40 by samlor) ☎ 044 622214. The comfortable rooms at this family-owned guesthouse have views across the surrounding countryside. Motorbikes for rent at B250/day. Fan **B200**, a/c **B350**

Surin and around

Best known for its much-hyped annual elephant round-up, the provincial capital of **SURIN**, around 150km east of Khorat, is an otherwise typical northeastern town, a reasonably comfortable place to absorb the easy-going pace of Isaan life. There's a handful of good, mid-range hotels in the centre and, as a bonus, there are some fantastic Khmer ruins nearby. Many pass through the city on their way to the village of Ban Tha Sawang, 7km away, where Thailand's most exclusive silk is produced.

SURIN ELEPHANT ROUND-UP

Surin's **elephant round-up**, held every year on the third weekend of November, draws some forty thousand spectators to watch four hundred elephants play football, engage in tugs of war and parade in full battle garb. These shows last about three hours and give both trainers and animals the chance to practise their skills, but if you arrive early (about 7.30am) you can watch the preliminary street processions when locals set out long trestle tables filled with pineapples, bananas and sugar cane so the elephants can munch their way into town. Note that however well controlled the elephants appear, you should always approach them with caution – in the past, frightened and taunted elephants have killed tourists. Tickets cost B500–800 and can be booked through TAT, the provincial government website (☒ surin.go.th) or Saren Travel (see p.460), who can also arrange accommodation and transport if you contact them three months ahead; alternatively, you could join one of the overnight packages organized by Bangkok travel agencies.

5

Surin's elephant tie-in comes from the local Suay people, whose prowess with pachyderms is well known and can sometimes be seen first-hand in the nearby village of **Ban Ta Klang**. Thais, Lao and Khmers make up the remainder of the population of Surin province; the Khmers have lived and worked in the region for over a thousand years, and their architectural legacy is still in evidence at the ruined temples of Ta Muean and Ban Pluang. For the twenty-first-century traveller, there's **overland access between Thailand and Cambodia** via Surin province's Chong Chom checkpoint near Kap Choeng.

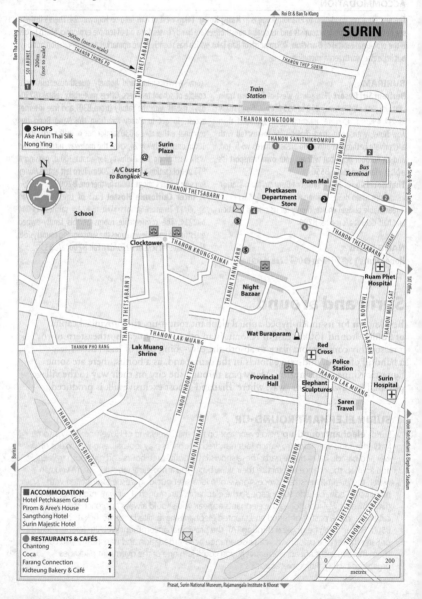

SURIN

▲ Roi Et & Ban Ta Klang

THANON THETSABARN 3
THANON THUNG PO
900m (nor to scale)
THANON THEP SURIN
Ban Tha Sawang ▶
SOI ARUNEE
200m (nor to scale)

Train Station

THANON NONGTOOM

SHOPS
Ake Anun Thai Silk 1
Nong Ying 2

Surin Plaza

@

THANON SANITNIKHOMRUT

THANON JITBUMRUNG

Bus Terminal

The Strip & Thong Tarin ▶

N

A/C buses to Bangkok ★

Ruen Mai

THANON THETSABARN 1

Phetkasem Department Store

THANON THETSABARN 1

SIRIRAT

School

Clocktower

THANON KRUNGSRINAI

THANON TANNASARN

THANON THETSABARN 3

Night Bazaar

Ruam Phet Hospital

THANON MULASAT

TAT Office ▶

THANON LAK MUANG

Wat Buraparam

THANON THETSABARN 2

Lak Muang Shrine

THANON PHO RANG

Red Cross

Police Station

Surin Hospital

Ubon Ratchathani & Elephant Stadium ▶

THANON PHROM THEP

Provincial Hall

Elephant Sculptures

THANON LAK MUANG

Saren Travel

Buriram ◀

THANON KRUNG SRINOK

THANON TANNASARN

THANON KRUNG SRINOK

THANON THETSABARN 2

THANON THETSABARN 4

ACCOMMODATION
Hotel Petchkasem Grand ... 3
Pirom & Aree's House 1
Sangthong Hotel 4
Surin Majestic Hotel 2

RESTAURANTS & CAFÉS
Chantong 2
Coca 4
Farang Connection 3
Kidteung Bakery & Café ... 1

0 _____ 200
metres

Prasat, Surin National Museum, Rajamangala Institute & Khorat ▼

SURIN VILLAGE TOURS

One of the best reasons for coming to Surin, other than November's elephant round-up (see box, p.457), is to take one of the excellent **local tours** (from B1400/person, depending on the group size) organized from *Pirom & Aree's House*. Pirom is a highly informed former social worker whose trips give tourists an unusual chance to catch glimpses of rural northeastern life as it's really lived. His village tours feature visits to local silk-weavers and basket-makers, as well as to Ban Ta Klang elephant trainers' village, and it's also possible to do overnight village trips, including one that takes in Khao Phra Viharn (when open), Khong Chiam and Pha Taem.

Ban Tha Sawang

7km west of Surin • Flag down any bus from the corner of Thanon Thung Po, just north of the railway tracks in Surin, get off at the sign "Wat Sameka 300m", then follow the side road on the opposite side of the road from the wat sign for 1km

Some of Thailand's most exclusive silk is produced in the village of **BAN THA SAWANG**. Though it is possible to visit by yourself, there is no English information and going with a guide will offer some behind-the-scenes insight (see box, p.462); you can arrange a guide through *Pirom & Aree's House* or Saren Travel. The best months to visit are between November and June, when the women aren't required to work all day in the fields.

The **Tha Sawang fabric** is gold-brocade silk whose ancient designs are so intricate that it takes four weavers working simultaneously on a single loom a whole day to produce just 6cm. And while a standard everyday *mut mee* sarong might use five heddles (vertical frames of threads that determine the pattern) in its design, a Ban Tha Sawang sarong will use more than eight hundred; not surprisingly, Ban Tha Sawang sarongs cost B30,000 and must be ordered several months in advance. The Ban Tha Sawang weaving centre houses around twenty looms and visitors are welcome to observe the weavers at close quarters. There's a display area across the road, down the asphalt chipping path, where you can see some fine examples of brocade cloth. Several stalls in the village sell local silk, but not the Ban Tha Sawang brocades.

Ban Ta Klang

58km north of Surin • Local bus from Surin (hourly; 2hr); if driving, head north along Highway 214 for 36km, turn left at the village of Ban Nong Tad and continue for 22km

The quiet, ramshackle "elephant village" of **BAN TA KLANG** is the main settlement of the Suay people and the training centre for their elephants. One out of every two Ta Klang families owns its own elephant, occasionally using it as a Western farmer would a tractor, but otherwise treating it as a much-loved pet (see box, p.460).

Ban Ta Klang's busy time, elephant-wise, is November, when the creatures and their mahouts help with the rice harvest and to prepare for the annual elephant show in Surin. In addition, every year on the first weekend of November, the elephants compete in **swimming races**, held further up the Mun River in the town of Satuk, 30km west of Ta Klang. A more authentic local spectacle is the annual **monks' ordination ceremony**, which usually takes place in May in Ban Ta Klang as part of the preparations for the beginning of Buddhist Lent, when young men ride to the temple on ceremonially clad elephants.

ARRIVAL AND DEPARTURE   **SURIN**

By train Several services a day make the Bangkok–Surin connection, stopping at the train station (☎044 511295) on the northern edge of town.

Destinations Ayutthaya (10 daily; 5hr–7hr 30min); Bangkok (10 daily; 6hr 30min–9hr 30min); Buriram (13 daily; 40–50min); Khorat (13 daily; 1hr 50min–3hr 10min); Pak Chong (10 daily; 3hr 10min–5hr); Si Saket (12 daily; 1hr 15min–1hr 50min); Ubon Ratchathani (11 daily; 2hr 15min–3hr 20min).

By bus The bus terminal (☎044 511756) off Thanon

5

THE SUAY AND THE SURIN PROJECT

Traditionally regarded as the most expert hunters and trainers of elephants in Thailand, the **Suay tribe** (also known as the Kui people) migrated to Isaan from Central Asia before the rise of the Khmers in the ninth century. It was the Suay who masterminded the use of elephants in the construction of the great Khmer temples, and a Suay chief who in 1760 helped recapture a runaway white elephant belonging to the king of Ayutthaya, earning the hereditary title "Lord of Surin". Surin was governed by members of the Suay tribe until Rama V's administrative reforms of 1907.

Now that elephants have been replaced almost entirely by modern machinery in the agricultural and logging industries, there's little demand for the Suay mahouts' skills as captors and trainers of wild elephants, or their traditional pre-hunting rituals involving sacred ropes, magic clothing and the keeping of certain taboos. The traditions are, however, documented, along with other elephant-related subjects, at the rather desultory **Centre for Elephant Studies** in the southern part of Ban Ta Klang village (daily 8.30am–4.30pm; free). To satisfy tourist curiosity, the centre also puts on elephant shows (B100) to coincide with the arrival of tour groups.

There are currently around two hundred elephants registered as living in Ban Ta Klang, and their mahouts are given subsidies for keeping them there. This discourages them from taking the elephants to Bangkok, where curious urbanites would have been charged for the pleasure of feeding the elephants or even walking under their trunk or belly for good luck (pregnant women who do this are supposedly guaranteed an easy birth). The downside is that there's very little for the elephants to do at the study centre, and they spend much of their time shackled up.

In a bid to give Surin's elephants a better life, the not-for-profit Elephant Nature Foundation has set up the **Surin Project** (ⓦsurinproject.org), which provides open spaces for elephants to roam in and teaches mahouts the benefits of ecotourism. At the time of writing, just twelve of the study centre's elephants were being cared for full-time at the project, with five more elephants at the centre on a part-time basis, but the aim is for more to join them soon. It's possible to volunteer at the camp, and for B12,000 a week you can help to dig irrigation channels, build shelters and plant food for the animals. The rate includes food, accommodation and transport from Buriram, Bangkok or Chiang Mai (pick-ups every Mon).

Jitbumrung runs frequent services to and from Bangkok, to major northeastern towns, and to Pattaya, Rayong and Chiang Mai. Buses and minivans also run from Surin to Cambodia (see box opposite).

Destinations Bangkok (at least hourly; 8–11hr); Ban Ta Klang (hourly; 2hr); Buriram (13 daily; 35–55min); Chiang Mai (5 daily; 15–18hr); Khorat (at least hourly; 4–5hr); Khon Kaen (11 daily; 4hr–5hr 30min); Pattaya (9 daily; 8–10hr); Rayong (9 daily; 10–12hr); Roi Et (13 daily; 2–3hr); Si Saket (hourly; 3hr–3hr 30min).

INFORMATION, TOURS AND GETTING AROUND

Tourist information There's a helpful TAT office (daily 8.30am–4.30pm; ☎044 514447–8, ⓔtatsurin@tat.or.th) at 355/3-6 Thanon Thetsabarn 1, just east of the town centre, and the provincial government has a quite useful, though outdated, website (ⓦsurin.go.th), which includes booking forms for the elephant round-up.

Farang Connection This farang-friendly restaurant at 257/11 Thanon Jitbumrung (☎044 511509, ⓦfarang connection.com), offers car, 4x4 and motorcycle rental (see website for latest prices and models).

Saren Travel 202/1-4 Thanon Thetsabarn 2 (Mon–Sat 8am–6pm; ☎044 713828, ⓔsarentour@yahoo.com; outside office hours ☎089 949 1185) sells air and train tickets and offers cars with/without driver (from B1600/day, excluding fuel). Can also arrange day-trips to Phanom Rung, Muang Tam and Ban Ta Klang (B2800 for four people sharing a car, excluding entry fees). Transfers to Siem Reap (Cambodia) via Chong Chom and Sa Ngam (B4500 for up to six people) are also available, as are elephant-show tickets. Elephant rides in Ban Ta Klang can be arranged too, from B200–400/person.

Surin village tours At Pirom & Aree's House, at the far end of Soi Arunee off Thanon Thung Po ☎089 355 4140. Great opportunities to explore the villages around Surin with a friendly and very knowledgable guide (see box, p.459).

ACCOMMODATION

Except during the elephant round-up – when room rates in Surin rocket and **accommodation** is booked out weeks in advance – you'll have no trouble finding a place to stay.

Hotel Petchkasem Grand 104 Thanon Jitbumrung ☎044 511274, ✉pkhotel@yahoo.com. A reasonable mid-range choice (if only for its proximity to the bus station) with sizeable a/c rooms with cable TV. There's a swimming pool, nightclub and karaoke bar. Breakfast is included, but it's not worth rushing out of bed for. B850

★ **Pirom & Aree's House** At the far end of Soi Arunee off Thanon Thung Po ☎089 355 4140. Surin's famously long-running guesthouse occupies a tranquil spot overlooking rice fields about 1.5km northwest of the train station. The super-clean rooms in this modern take on a traditional home are large and simply furnished with fans and shared bathrooms, plus there are garden seating areas.

The owners are incredibly friendly and welcoming, and can tell you everything you need to know about the local area. Good rates for singles. B200

Sangthong Hotel 279–281 Thanon Tannasarn ☎044 512099. The best of the budget hotels, this place is friendly, good value and well run. All rooms are large and en suite, and some have a/c and TV. Fan B250, a/c B400

Surin Majestic Hotel At the back of the bus station, 99 Thanon Jitbumrung ☎044 713980, ⊛surinmajestic hotel.com. Still the nicest hotel in town, with smartly furnished rooms. All have a/c and TV plus a balcony overlooking the attractive, good-sized ground-floor swimming pool. B900

EATING AND DRINKING

Aside from a reasonable range of local **restaurants**, Surin boasts a good-sized **night bazaar**, which occupies the eastern end of Thanon Krungsrinai and offers a tasty selection of local food (including roasted crickets and barbecued locusts in season), as well as stalls selling fashions and toys. Surin also has a surprisingly wild **nightlife** for a provincial town, with a clutch of seedy bars and discos catering to young Thais and Western sex tourists around the neon-lit "Strip" east of the centre at the northern end of Thanon Sirirath and along Soi Kola, just north of the *Thong Tharin Hotel*.

Chantong At the back of the bus terminal, off Thanon Sirirat (no English sign, but it's next to Oasis Café). Despite its unprepossessing location, this is a rather classy a/c restaurant, serving good Thai food, including *tom yam* and various sea bass dishes, from B80. Daily 10am–midnight.

Coca 128 Thanon Thetsabarn 1 (no English sign but it's easy to spot opposite Phetkasem Department Store). A good range of Chinese and Thai dishes such as fluffy catfish salad with mango and stewed duck feet with noodles (both B80), served in a clean and welcoming setting. Daily 11am–9pm.

Farang Connection 257/11 Thanon Jitbumrung, at the back of the bus terminal, off Thanon Sirirat. The place to come for imported beer, TV sports, internet access and the chance to meet local expats. It serves great Western breakfasts and roast dinners, as well as a good range of Thai dishes, with prices around B80–350. Daily 9am–late.

Kidteung Bakery & Café Thanon Sanitnikhomrut, close to the junction with Thanon Tannasarn. Breezy alfresco seating area draped in foliage and lined with pretty elephant statues. Serves delicious cakes and ice vanilla lattes (B50) to a mixed crowd. Popular with the local police officers. Daily 8.30am–8.30pm.

CROSSING THE CAMBODIAN BORDER VIA CHONG CHOM

There are a/c minivans (every 30min 5am–5.30pm; 1hr 30min; B80) and non-a/c buses (every 30min 8am–3pm; B60; 2hr) via Prasat to the **Chong Chom border pass**, 70km south of Surin; or you can arrange a taxi through *Farang Connection*, located behind Surin bus station (☎044 511509, ⊛farangconnection.com). Cambodian visas are issued on arrival at the Chong Chom–O'Smach checkpoint (daily 7am–8pm; US$20, although you may be asked for B1000), from where you can get transport to Anlong Veng and then on to Siem Reap, which is 150km from the border crossing (start negotiations for a taxi transfer to Siem Reap at B350/car, but expect to pay slightly more). There have been reports of people on visa runs being asked for more money by officials on the Cambodian side, especially if they try to return to Thailand on the same day. There's a casino on the Cambodian side, making this crossing popular with Thai gamblers.

Arriving **from Cambodia**, songthaews and motorbike taxis ferry travellers from the border checkpoint to the bus stop for Prasat and Surin. For details on other overland routes into Cambodia, see p.27.

5

SILK PRODUCTION

Most hand-woven **Thai silk** is produced by Isaan village women, some of whom oversee every aspect of sericulture, from the breeding of the silkworm to the dyeing of the fabric. Isaan's pre-eminence is partly due to its soils, which are particularly suitable for the growth of mulberry trees, the leaves of which are the **silkworms'** favoured diet. The cycle of production begins with the female silk-moth, which lives just a few days but lays around 300–500 microscopic eggs in that time. The eggs take about nine days to hatch into tiny silkworms, which are then kept in covered rattan trays and fed on mulberry leaves three or four times a day. The silkworms are such enthusiastic eaters that after three or four weeks they will have grown to about 6cm in length (around ten thousand times their original size), ready for the cocoon-building **pupal** stage.

The silkworm constructs its **cocoon** from a single white or yellow fibre that it secretes from its mouth at a rate of 12cm a minute, sealing the filaments with a gummy substance called sericin. The metamorphosis of the pupa into a moth can take anything from two to seven days, but the sericulturist must anticipate the moment when the new moth is about to break out in order to prevent the destruction of the precious fibre, which at this stage is often 900m long. At the crucial point the cocoon is dropped into boiling water, killing the moth (which is often eaten as a snack) and softening the sericin, so that the unbroken filament can be unravelled. The fibres from several cocoons are "reeled" into a single thread, and two or three threads are subsequently twisted or "thrown" into the yarn known as **raw silk** (broken threads from damaged cocoons are worked into a second-rate yarn called "spun silk"). In most cases, the next stage is the "de-gumming process", in which the raw silk is soaked to dissolve away the sericin, leaving it soft and semi-transparent. Extremely absorbent and finely textured, reeled silk is the perfect material for **dyeing**; most silk producers now use chemical dyes, though traditional vegetable dyes are making a bit of a comeback.

These days, it's not worth the bother for women who live near town to raise their own silkworms and spin their own thread as they can easily buy Japanese ready-to-weave silk in the market. **Japanese silk** is smoother than Thai silk but lasts only about seven years when woven into a sarong; hand-raised, raw Thai silk is rougher but lasts around forty years, and so is still favoured by women living in remote villages.

Once dyed (or bought), the silk is ready for **weaving**. This is generally done during slack agricultural periods, for example just after the rice is planted and again just after it's harvested. Looms are usually set up in the space under the house, in the sheltered area between the piles, and most are designed to produce a sarong of around 1m by 2m. Isaan weavers have many different weaving techniques and can create countless patterns, ranging from the simplest single-coloured plain weave for work shirts to exquisitely complex wedding sarongs that may take up to six weeks to complete. The most exclusive and intricate designs are those produced in Ban Tha Sawang (see p.459), costing tens of thousands of baht for a single sarong.

SHOPPING

Surin is famous for the variety of **silk weaves** produced here: there are seven hundred designs in Surin province alone, many of them of Cambodian origin, including the locally popular rhomboid pattern. In high season, there are usually several women selling their cloth around the Tannasarn–Krungsrinai intersection, and you can also visit local silk-weaving villages (see p.459).

Nong Ying 52 Thanon Jitbumrung. A superb selection of silks as well as ready-made silk jackets, bags and accessories, silver jewellery and axe pillows.

DIRECTORY

Hospitals Ruam Phet Hospital, on the eastern arm of Thanon Thetsabarn 1 ☎ 044 513638 & ☎ 044 513192; and the government-run Surin Hospital on Thanon Lak Muang ☎ 044 511006 & ☎ 044 511757.

Internet access At *Farang Connection* at the back of the bus station; and at Focus Comnet next to Surin Plaza off the north end of Thanon Thetsabarn 3.

Khao Phra Viharn (Preah Vihear)

140km southwest of Ubon Ratchathani and 220km southeast of Surin • Daily 8.30am–3.30pm (when open) • B405 (in a combination of entry fees)

Perched atop a 547m-high spur of the Dangkrek mountains right on the Thai–Cambodian border, the ninth-to-twelfth-century Khmer ruins of **KHAO PHRA VIHARN** (or **Preah Vihear**) surpass even the spectacularly set Phanom Rung. A magnificent avenue over 500m long rises to the clifftop sanctuary, from where you get breathtaking views over the jungle-clad hills of Cambodia.

Unfortunately, the sanctuary has been closed on and off since 2008 due to a **territorial dispute** between Thailand and Cambodia over who owns the site. In July 2011, following a fresh series of skirmishes, the International Court of Justice ruled that both countries should remove their forces from the area. But in November 2011 the stalemate continued, with significant numbers of soldiers still stationed along the border, and, at the time of writing, the complex remained closed.

In fact, the complex was only opened to visitors in 1998, following almost a century of squabbling between the two governments. During Cambodia's civil war, the Khmer Rouge laid mines around the temple, and while the ruins have been de-mined, there are skull-and-crossbones signs in the vicinity, which should be heeded if and when the temple reopens to visitors.

The ruins

The temple buildings themselves, built of grey and yellow sandstone, retain some fine original carvings and have been sufficiently restored to give a good idea of their original structure. Constructed over a three-hundred-year period, Khao Phra Viharn was dedicated to the Hindu god Shiva and is thought to have served both as a retreat for Hindu priests – hence the isolated site – and an object of pilgrimage, with the difficulty of getting there an extra challenge. The large complex would have also been inhabited by a big cast of supporting villagers who took care of the priests and the pilgrims, which explains the presence of several large reservoirs on the site.

The approach to the **temple complex** begins with a steep stairway and continues up the cliff face via a series of pillared causeways, small terraces with naga balustrades and four cruciform-shaped **gopura** (pavilions), each built with doorways at the cardinal points, and decorated with carved reliefs of tales from Hindu mythology. Beyond the first gopura, you'll see to the left (east) one of the temple's biggest **reservoirs**, a large stone-lined tank sunk into the cliff and guarded by statues of lions.

The Churning of the Sea of Milk

As you pass through the last, southernmost, doorway of the second gopura, look back at the door to admire the pediment carving, which depicts the Hindu creation myth, the **Churning of the Sea of Milk**, in which Vishnu appears in his tortoise incarnation and, along with a naga and a sacred mountain (here symbolized by the churning stick), helps stir the cosmic ocean and thereby create the universes, as well as the sacred nectar of immortality.

The central sanctuary

The ascent of the cliff face finally reaches its climax at the **central sanctuary**, built on the summit and enclosed within a courtyard whose impressive colonnaded galleries are punctuated by windows to the east and west. The pediment above the northern entrance to this shrine depicts the multi-armed **dancing Shiva**, whose ecstatic dance brings about the destruction of the existing world and the beginning of a new epoch. Climb through one of the gallery windows to walk across to the cliff edge, from where you get far-reaching views of Cambodia and can appreciate just how isolated the temple must have been. A look back at the temple complex shows that though the

5

sanctuary's southernmost wall is punctuated by a couple of beautifully carved false doors, there are no genuine south-facing doors or windows; experts assume that this was to stop priests being distracted by the clifftop panorama.

ARRIVAL AND DEPARTURE   KHAO PHRA VIHARN

Even when open, Khao Phra Viharn is not served by **public transport**, so by far the easiest way of getting to the ruins is to join a **tour** or rent a vehicle from Ubon Ratchathani, Surin or Si Saket. Alternatively, you could take a combination of motorbike taxi and songthaew to the temple from the nearby town of **Kantharalak**. From the temple car park it's about 1km to the base of the temple steps.

KANTHARALAK

By bus There's an hourly bus service to Kantharalak, 36km north of the temple, from Ubon Ratchathani's Warinchamrab suburb (1hr 30min), and a half-hourly bus service from Si Saket; buses arrive at the bus station (☎ 045 661486), 50m from the market on the main street, Thanon Sinpradit.

By songthaew and motorbike taxi There is no songthaew service from Kantharalak to Khao Phra Viharn, but occasional songthaews do connect Kantharalak with Ban Phum Saron, the junction near the national-park barrier 12km north of Khao Phra Viharn, from where you can get a motorbike taxi to the temple; you can also get a motorbike taxi all the way from Kantharalak to Khao Phra Viharn (about B120 each way, depending on petrol prices).

ACCOMMODATION

The two-street town of **Kantharalak** is just off the Khao Phra Viharn–Si Saket road (Highway 221). Unless you're planning a quick overnight stay on the way to or from the temple, there's not much reason to visit.

Kantharalak Hotel 131/35–36 Thanon Sinpradit, about 1km off Highway 221 ☎ 045 661085. This budget hotel's scruffy but serviceable rooms (the better ones are upstairs) are set back off Kantharalak's main street, all with en-suite bathrooms. Fan B250, a/c B350

Si Saket

Though it is 98km from Khao Phra Viharn, the quiet provincial capital of **SI SAKET** is a more enjoyable place to base yourself than Kantharalak if you're visiting Khao Phra Viharn, with a better choice of hotels, a good night market and decent transport connections. It's also a handy place to stop over if you're heading to the Cambodian border crossing at Sa Ngam.

ARRIVAL AND DEPARTURE   SI SAKET

By train Si Saket train station (☎ 045 611525) is in the centre of the town.
Destinations: Bangkok (8 daily; 8–11hr); Khorat (10 daily; 3–4hr 30min); Surin (12 daily; 1hr 10min–2hr); Ubon Ratchatani (11 daily; 50min–1hr 10min).

By bus The bus station (☎ 045 612500) is in the southern part of town and connects Si Saket with Ubon Ratchathani, Surin and Bangkok. There are no buses from here to Khao Phra Viharn, so you have to get the orange bus to Kantharalak (hourly; 2hr) and make onward arrangements

from there. You should also be able to get buses from here to Sa Ngam for access to the Cambodian border crossing to Choam (for Anlong Veng and Siem Reap). Buses don't run all the way, so you'll need to get dropped off on Highway 24 and flag down a songthaew for the rest of the (very bumpy) journey to the border.
Destinations: Bangkok (3 daily; 7hr); Kantharalak (hourly; 2hr); Surin (hourly; 3hr–3hr 30min); Ubon Ratchathani (every 45min; 45min–1hr).

ACCOMMODATION

Kessiri Hotel 1102–5 Thanon Khukan ☎ 045 614007, ⊛ kessiri.com. Slightly more luxurious than *Prompiman*, with a/c rooms and similar amenities, plus a coffee shop and swimming pool. Thanon Khukan runs south from the rail line from a point some 150m east of the train station. B500

Prompiman Hotel 849/1 Thanon Lak Muang ☎ 045 612677, ⊛ prompimanhotel.com. Better for its location near the train station (it's about 200m west of the station on the road that parallels the rail line to the south) than its rather characterless a/c rooms, which are big, clean and bright nevertheless. B400

EATING

The best place to **eat** in town is the lip-smackingly diverse night market, which sets up around a small plaza along the southern edge of the rail line. There are half-a-dozen small Thai-Chinese **restaurants** on Thanon Khukan, between the *Kessiri Hotel* and the rail line.

SHOPPING

On Thanon Khukan, between the *Kessiri Hotel* and the rail line, you'll find several **handicraft** shops selling locally produced lengths of silk and triangular axe pillows.

Ubon Ratchathani

East of Si Saket, the sprawling provincial capital of **UBON RATCHATHANI** (almost always referred to simply as Ubon – not to be confused with Udon, aka Udon Thani, to the north) holds little in the way of attractions beyond a couple of wats and a decent museum. Still, it's more sedate than many northeastern cities, with plenty of opportunities for getting to grips with Isaan culture. The best bet is to visit at festival time (see box below), but Ubon also makes a handy base for trips east to Khong Chiam beside the Mekong River and the Lao border market at Chong Mek, or southwest to the Khmer ruins of Khao Phra Viharn, astride the Cambodian border, when they are open.

Thung Si Muang Park

Just south of Thanon Phalorangrit

Ubon's centrepiece is **Thung Si Muang Park** and its unmissable 22m-high **Candle Sculpture**, an enormous yellow-painted replica of the wax sculptures that star in the annual Candle Festival. This particular sculpture was inspired by a story written by the king and features a boat with an enormous garuda figurehead that's ploughing past various figures who are apparently being devoured by sea monsters.

In the northeast corner of the park stands a far more unassuming memorial in the shape of a 3m-high obelisk. Known as the **Monument of Merit**, it was erected by a group of Allied POWs who wanted to show their gratitude to the people of Ubon for their support during World War II. Despite the real threat of punishment by the Japanese occupiers, between 1941 and 1943 Ubon citizens secretly donated food and clothes to the POWs imprisoned in a nearby camp.

UBON FESTIVALS

If you're near Ubon in early July, you should definitely consider coming into town for the local **Asanha Puja** festivities, an auspicious Buddhist holiday celebrated all over Thailand to mark the beginning of Khao Pansa, the annual three-month Buddhist retreat. Ubon's version is the most spectacular in the country, famous for the majestic orange beeswax sculptures created by each of its temples, which are mounted on floats around enormous candles and paraded through the town – hence the tourist name for the celebrations, the **Ubon Candle Festival**. The sculptures are judged and then returned to the temple, where the candle is usually kept burning throughout the retreat period. The end of the retreat, **Awk Pansa** (early to mid-Oct), is also exuberantly celebrated with a procession of illuminated boats, each representing one of the city's temples, along the Mun River between Wat Suphat and the night market, as well as beauty contests, parades and lots of fireworks throughout the city, and *likay* theatre shows in Thung Si Muang Park. Traditional longboat races are staged on the river in the days following Awk Pansa.

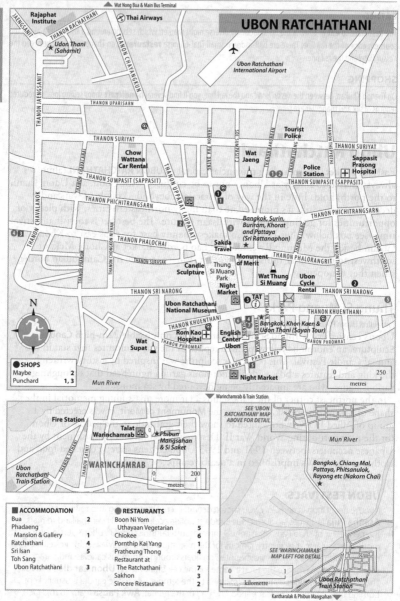

UBON RATCHATHANI

SHOPS

Maybe	2
Punchard	1, 3

■ ACCOMMODATION		● RESTAURANTS	
Bua	2	Boon Ni Yom	
Phadaeng		Uthayaan Vegetarian	5
Mansion & Gallery	1	Chiokee	6
Ratchathani	4	Pornthip Kai Yang	1
Sri Isan	5	Pratheung Thong	4
Toh Sang		Restaurant at	
Ubon Ratchathani	3	The Ratchathani	7
		Sakhon	3
		Sincere Restaurant	2

Ubon Ratchathani National Museum

South from Thung Si Muang Park across Thanon Sri Narong and also accessible from Thanon Khuenthani • Wed–Sun 9am–4pm • B100 • ⓦ thailandmuseum.com/thaimuseum_eng/ubon/main.html

Ubon Ratchathani National Museum is airily designed around a central courtyard and offers a good overview of the history, geology and culture of southern Isaan, with well-labelled displays on everything from rock formations to folk crafts, plus a couple of very fine Khmer sculptures and examples of the star-embroidered fabric that is a speciality of Ubon.

5

Wat Thung Si Muang

200m east of Thung Si Muang Park, along Thanon Sri Narong

Of the city's eight main wats, **Wat Thung Si Muang** is the most noteworthy, mainly for its unusually well-preserved teak library (*ho trai*) which is raised on stilts over a pond to keep book-devouring insects at bay. The murals in the bot, to the left of the library, have also survived remarkably well; their lively scenes of everyday life in the nineteenth century include local merit-making dances and musicians playing *khaen* pipes, as well as conventional portraits of city activities in Bangkok.

Wat Nong Bua

Off Thanon Chayangkun near the main bus terminal at the northern edge of town • City songthaew #2 or #3 via Thanon Khuenthani

The modern **Wat Nong Bua** is modelled on the stupa at Bodh Gaya in India, scene of the Buddha's enlightenment; the whitewashed replica is carved with scenes from the *Jataka* and contains a scaled-down version of the stupa covered in gold leaf. Of more interest, especially if you don't happen to be here during the Candle Festival, is the wax float kept in a small building behind the chedi.

ARRIVAL AND DEPARTURE   UBON RATCHATHANI

BY PLANE

Thai Airways (w thaiairways.com) operates at least two flights a day between Ubon and Bangkok (1hr 5min), as does budget airline Air Asia (w airasia.com). Also cheap is Nok Air (w nokair.com), which runs a further three flights a day. Air Asia has two flights a week to Chiang Mai. The airport (ⓣ 045 263916) is just north of the town centre; a metered taxi to the town-centre hotels costs B50–60 (ⓣ 045 256111; call to ask for a pick-up).

BY TRAIN

Ubon's train station (ⓣ 045 321001) is in the suburb of Warinchamrab (Warin Chamrap), about 2km south across the Mun River from central Ubon. White city songthaew #2 meets all trains at Warinchamrab and takes passengers into central Ubon (B12), passing along Thanon Khuenthani, where several hotels and the TAT office are located.
Destinations Ayutthaya (7 daily; 7hr–10hr 40min); Bangkok (7 daily; 8hr 30min–12hr 15min); Buriram (9 daily; 2hr 30min–3hr 30min); Khorat (9 daily; 3hr 45min–6hr); Si Saket (11 daily; 40min–1hr); Surin (11 daily; 1hr 50min–2hr 40min).

BY BUS

Confusingly, several different companies run long-distance bus services in and out of Ubon, each with their own drop-off and pick-up points. Note that if you're travelling between Ubon and Khong Chiam you'll need to change

buses at the town of Phibun Mangsahan (known locally as Phibun), 45km east of Ubon. Bus company depots are shown on our map (see opposite).

Main bus terminal Nearly all services pass through the main terminal on Thanon Chayangkun, on the northwest edge of town, which is served by city songthaews #2 and #3 from Warinchamrab via Thanon Khuenthani in central Ubon. The government Baw Khaw Saw bus company (ⓣ 045 312773) is based here and runs regular and a/c services to Pakse in Laos, Bangkok, Buriram, Chiang Mai, Khorat, Si Saket, Surin and Yasothon.

Nakhon Chai Air This nationwide private company (ⓣ 045 269777, w nca.co.th) runs a/c services from its terminal just south of the Mun River, on the road to Warinchamrab, served by city buses #1, #2, #3 and #6. There's a non-stop service to Bangkok as well as routes to and from Buriram, Chiang Mai, Khorat, Pattaya, Phitsanulok, Rayong, Si Saket and Surin.

Sahamit A/c services (ⓣ 045 241319) to Udon Thani. It's located in the northwest of town off Thanon Ratchathani.

Talat Warinchamrab Most local buses and songthaews to Phibun Mangsahan, as well as those to Si Saket, use this terminal near the marketplace in Warinchamrab, southeast of the river and served by city songthaews #1 (grey), #3 (pink) and #6 (pink) from Ubon. Buses to Phibun Mangsahan leave several times an hour until 4.30pm and terminate at Phibun's town-centre bus station behind the

---

BRUSH UP ON YOUR THAI IN UBON

If you find yourself in Ubon for more than a few days, and want to learn some **Thai**, check out English Center Ubon, where teacher Ooh offers a range of useful one-to-one courses.

English Center Ubon 100 Thanon Ratchabut ⓣ 086 2460754, ⓔ oohkha@yahoo.com. Rates start at B350/ hr, but it's possible to get a discount for longer courses – 10hr course for B2900 or a 50hr course costs B13,500.

5

market, where you can change onto the songthaews that run to Chong Mek (only useful if you decide not to get a direct connection). Khong Chiam songthaews leave from Kaeng Saphue bridge in Phibun Mangsahan, a short tuk-tuk ride or 10min walk from Phibun's bus station: exit the bus station through the market to the main road, turn right and walk the few hundred metres to the main highway (passing currency exchange and internet facilities), then turn left to reach the river and the songthaew stop.

Destinations Bangkok (hourly; 10–12hr); Buriram (8 daily; 6–8hr); Chiang Mai (6 daily; 17–18hr); Chong Mek (17 daily; 1hr); Kantharalak (every 15min; 1hr 30min); Khon Kaen (19 daily; 4–6hr); Khorat (hourly; 5–7hr); Mukdahan (every 30min; 2–3hr); Pakse (Laos) (2 daily; 2–3hr); Pattaya (10 daily; 12hr–13hr 30min); Phibun Mangsahan (every 25min; 1hr); Rayong (11 daily; 14hr); Si Saket (every 45min; 45min–1hr); Surin (at least 7 daily; 2hr 30min–3hr); Udon Thani (19 daily; 5–7hr); Yasothon (19 daily; 1hr 30min–2hr).

GETTING AROUND

By bike Try Ubon Cycle Rental, 115 Thanon Sri Narong, east of the post office (📞 045 242813; B100/24hr).

By motorbike or car Motorbikes (B200–500/day) and cars (B1200/day) can be rented from Chow Wattana (📞 045

242202) at 269 Thanon Suriyat, opposite Nikko Massage, and at the airport. Avis (📞 090 197 2262–3, 🌐 avisthailand .com) and Budget (📞 045 240507, 🌐 budget.co.th) car rental are at the airport.

INFORMATION AND TOURS

Tourist information Staff at the TAT office (daily 8.30am–4.30pm; 📞 045 243770, 📧 tatubon@tat.or.th) at 264/1 Thanon Khuenthani can provide a helpful map of the city with songthaew routes marked, and should be able to give information about the latest situation at Khao

Phra Viharn.

Tours Sakda Travel World, 234 Thanon Phalorangrit, central Ubon (📞 045 254333, 🌐 sakdatour.com), offers guided tours around Isaan and into Laos, sells air tickets and offers car plus driver from B1500/day.

ACCOMMODATION

Ubon's choice of hotels is broad enough, but as there's not much of a travellers' scene in the city, there are none of the cosy, great-value guesthouses you'll find elsewhere in Thailand. Prices shoot up during the Candle Festival, when you'll need to book a room as far ahead as possible.

Bua 179 Thanon Upparat 📞 045 261748. A 5min walk north of the museum, this is Ubon's answer to the new breed of big, funky city hangouts masquerading as "boutique hotels". The place has its own karaoke bar, massage room, and there's wi-fi in some areas. Skip the cheaper double rooms, which seem to have been forgotten in the renovations, and go for one of the classy B650-a-night rooms instead. **B500**

Phadaeng Mansion & Gallery 126 Thanon Pha Daeng, near Punchard crafts shop 📞 045 254600, 🌐 thephadaeng.blogspot.com. Clean, good-sized rooms in a quiet part of town, all with TV and a/c. Some have their own private balconies – although don't expect a great view. There's a rather bizarre "fine art gallery" on the ground floor, featuring prints of works by the likes of Da Vinci and Michelangelo, but it gives a splash of colour to the place. Free wi-fi. **B500**

★ **Ratchathani** 297 Thanon Khuenthani 📞 045 244388. A recent renovation has brought a sophisticated

air to this centrally located a/c place. Rooms are bright with attractive furnishings and fittings; those at the back are quieter. The rooms aren't huge, but they are good value. Free wi-fi. Breakfast included. **B650**

Sri Isan 62 Thanon Ratchabut 📞 045 261011, 🌐 sriisan hotel.com. This small, quite classy hotel enjoys a good location in Ubon's old quarter, just across from the market and night market, and a mere 100m from the river. Its 33 small rooms are set around an open-roofed atrium and all have a/c and cable TV. Breakfast included. **B500**

Toh Sang Ubon Ratchathani 251 Thanon Phalochai 📞 045 245531, 🌐 tohsang.com. The poshest hotel in town, with comfortable a/c rooms and gorgeous suites in a peaceful but rather inconvenient location 1km west of Thanon Chayangkun or about 2km from TAT. It also houses the city's smartest restaurant, the *Pratheung Thong* (see opposite). City songthaews #4 and #8 pass the door. Breakfast included. Look online for best rates. **B1000**

EATING

Ubon is a good place for sampling local Isaan specialities, either in a/c comfort at some of the **restaurants** listed below, or at one of the city's **night markets**: try behind the day market on the north bank of the Mun River, or on Thanon Ratchabut (north off Thanon Khuenthani).

5

Boon Ni Yom Uthayaan Vegetarian Restaurant and Centre Thanon Sri Narong; no English sign but its barn-like, open-sided wooden structure is unmistakeable. Famous, canteen-style veggie place that's run by members of a Buddhist organization who grow, sell and cook their own produce. All sorts of meat substitutes and tasty veg and tofu dishes are on offer here at very cheap per-plate prices (B20–30). Tues–Sun 6am–2pm.

Chiokee 307–317 Thanon Khuenthani. Café-style place serving a large menu of Thai and Western staples (B30–100). Especially popular at breakfast time, when Westerners come for the ham and eggs, local office workers for rice gruel. Daily 6am–8pm.

Pornthip Kai Yang 136 Thanon Sumpasit, just east of Wat Jaeng. This simple streetside restaurant, which also has an a/c room, is famous across town for its signature barbecued chicken (*kai yang*) and papaya salad (*som tam*), for B20–60. Daily 8am–6pm.

Pratheung Thong Toh Sang Hotel, 251 Thanon Phalochai. With its starched tablecloths and wide-ranging

menu of Thai and Chinese dishes (B80–220), this restaurant oozes sophistication, and a pianist serenades diners in the evening. Daily 6am–midnight.

★ **Restaurant at The Ratchathani** 297 Thanon Khuenthani ☎045 244388. Classy, upscale restaurant at the side of the hotel, offering fresh, good-value meals from menus in English and Thai. Like *Pratheung Thong*, there's often a pianist tinkling away on the keys, but here the diners seem keen to get up and croon along. The *tom kha kai* (spicy and sour chicken soup; B100) is excellent. Daily until late.

Sakhon 66–70 Thanon Pha Daeng. One of Ubon's top northeastern restaurants, particularly recommended for its more unusual seasonal dishes, like *tom yam* with fish eggs and red-ant eggs. Most dishes around B60. Daily 10am–10pm.

Sincere Restaurant 126/1 Thanon Sumpasit ☎045 245061. High-quality American steaks (B365) and baby clams (B175) served in an intimate little a/c restaurant just back from the main road. Mon–Sat 11am–10pm.

SHOPPING

Silk, cotton and silverware are all good buys in Ubon. Both shops listed here specialize in fine-quality regional goods, like triangular axe pillows (*mawn khwaan*) and lengths of silk, and also deal in antique farm and household implements.

Maybe On the eastern end of Thanon Sri Narong. This shop has the biggest selection of clothes made from the stripey rough cotton weaves peculiar to the Ubon area. Daily 9am–7pm.

Punchard 128–130 Thanon Ratchabut, 50m east of

the museum, and on Thanon Pha Daeng. You'll find cotton tableware and clothes made to local designs, as well as Ubon's best collection of northeastern crafts, at Punchard's two branches. Daily 8am–8pm.

DIRECTORY

Hospitals Sappasit Prasong Hospital (☎045 244973), to the northeast of the town centre, has a 24hr emergency clinic.

Immigration office In the town of Phibun Mangsahan, 45km east of Ubon (Mon–Fri 8.30am–4.30pm;

☎045 441108). Phibun Mangsahan is best accessed by bus (see p.467).

Tourist police For all emergencies, call the tourist police on ☎1155 (free) or contact them at their office on Thanon Suriyat ☎045 244941.

Around Ubon

The area **around Ubon** is a good deal more interesting than the metropolitan hub, particularly if you venture eastwards towards the appealing Mekong riverside town of **Khong Chiam** and the prehistoric paintings at **Pha Taem**. There is also a crossing into Laos, and a border market, southeast of Ubon at **Chong Mek**.

Khong Chiam

The riverside village of **KHONG CHIAM** (pronounced Kong Jiem) is a popular destination for day-tripping Thais, who drive here from across Isaan to see the somewhat fancifully named "two-coloured river" for which the village is nationally renowned. Created by the merging of the muddy brown Mun with the muddy brown Mekong at "the easternmost point of Thailand", the water is hardly an irresistible attraction (come in April to see the colour contrast at its most vivid), but the village itself has plenty of tranquil appeal.

5

TRIPS FROM KHONG CHIAM

Khong Chiam doesn't have many sights, but you can rent motorbikes (B200/day) or bicycles (B100/day) from *Apple Guest House* and explore the quiet streets around the riverfront, or charter a **longtail boat** for a trip up the Mekong River to see the Pha Taem cliff-paintings (B1500/boat; ask at your hotel). Otherwise you could charter a songthaew to **Pha Taem** from Khong Chiam (round trip about B500); ask at the bus station.

Even though **Laos** is just a few hundred metres away from Khong Chiam, on the other bank of the Mekong, foreigners are not supposed to cross the border here, though you may be able to persuade boatmen to take you there and back for B350/boat, with a quick stop at the bankside village of Ban Mai; the official border crossing is further downstream at Chong Mek.

If you have your own transport, Khong Chiam combines well with visits to Chong Mek (just 27km away) and Kaeng Tana National Park.

Comprising little more than a collection of wooden houses and a few resorts, Khong Chiam feels like an island, with the Mun defining its southern limit and the Mekong its northern one. A cracked concrete walkway runs several hundred metres along the banks of the Mekong, lined by predictable souvenir stalls and leading to the large *sala* that's built right over the confluence and affords uninterrupted views. Behind the *sala*, **Wat Khong Chiam** is a typically charming rural Thai temple and has an old wooden bell tower in its compound. Khong Chiam's other temple, the cliffside **Wat Tham Khu Ha Sawan**, located near the point where Route 2222 turns into Khong Chiam, is a striking white colour, with natural wood sculptures festooned with orchids in its grounds, and a huge Buddha image staring down on the villagers below.

ARRIVAL AND DEPARTURE
KHONG CHIAM

Khong Chiam is 30km northeast of **Phibun Mangsahan**, along Route 2222, and 75km from Ubon. Songthaews and buses terminate at the Khong Chiam bus station at the west end of Thanon Kaewpradit, Khong Chiam's main drag.

From Ubon via Phibun Mangsahan From Ubon, take one of the regular buses and songthaews from Talat Warinchamrab terminal (every 25min until 4.30pm; 1hr) to Phibun. Khong Chiam songthaews leave from Kaeng Saphue bridge, a short tuk-tuk ride or 10min walk from Phibun's bus station: exit the bus station through the market to the main road, turn right and walk the few hundred metres to the main highway (passing currency exchange and internet facilities), then turn left to reach the river and the songthaew stop. Khong Chiam-bound songthaews leave Kaeng Saphue bridge every 30min

throughout the morning and then hourly until 4.30pm (1hr 30min). Returning to Phibun is more difficult; one songthaew a day leaves from the market near the bus station (at the time of writing this was scheduled for 11am; more may leave later in the day if there are enough people to make the journey worthwhile). Miss these and you should be able to find a private driver – ask around at the bus station.

From Bangkok Four daily buses run between Khong Chiam and Bangkok in both directions, with the last one leaving at 4.30pm (travelling via Yasothon).

ACCOMMODATION

Khong Chiam's **accommodation** options are relatively limited, and apart from a couple of exceptions, most places feel poor value compared to other parts of the northeast.

Apple Guest House Opposite the post office on Thanon Kaewpradit, also accessible from Thanon Phukamchai, about a 5min walk from the bus station and the Mekong ☎ 045 351160. The most traveller-oriented place in Khong Chiam, connected to an old electrical shop, with decent en-suite rooms set around a yard. Fan <u>B150</u>, a/c <u>B300</u>

Ban Kiang Nam 89 Thanon Kaewpradit ☎ 045 351374 or ☎ 045 351375. Small, cosy and good-quality bungalows

set away from the road down a quiet private driveway. TV & a/c in every room, but little English spoken. <u>B600</u>

Ban Rim Khong Resort 37 Thanon Kaewpradit ☎ 045 351101. Also has another entrance one block north on the road in front of the Mekong River, between the district office and the wat. Great-looking little resort with half-a-dozen timbered a/c chalets wreathed in bougainvillea and ranged round a lawn, plus a couple of fabulous riverside ones (#1 and #2, worth phoning ahead to reserve) with huge verandas overlooking the Mekong. The interiors are nothing special but all are spacious and have a/c, TVs and fridges, and there are discounts for stays of more than one night. **B800**

Sibae Guest House Just north of the immigration checkpoint, one street back from the river and close to the junction ☎045 351068, ✉watasinsibae@hotmail .com. Beautiful wooden house that has very clean (but very plain) rooms, the most luxurious of which have a/c, TVs and fridges. Friendly owner. Fan **B200**, a/c **B350**

Toh Sang Khongjiam Resort On the south bank of the Mun ☎045 351174, ✉tohsang.com. Romantically located, upmarket resort where all rooms have balconies overlooking the river and are very comfortably, if a little kitschly, furnished. There's a swimming pool, table-tennis room, spa, internet access, bicycle and kayak rental, plus a couple of restaurants and boat trips to Pha Taem and other riverside sights. Check out their website for spa/ resort package offers. It's about 3km from Khong Chiam; with your own wheels, follow Highway 2134 south past Khong Chiam bus station, cross the river, take the first left and follow the signs. **B2500**

EATING

There's not much happening in Khong Chiam after dark: the restaurants listed here only stay open until around 8 or 9pm, depending on when the last couple of farangs decide to leave. For late-night snacks, there's a small minimarket on Thanon Kaewpradit.

Araya On the Mekong in front of the district office. Two floating restaurants – *Araya* and nearby *Chonlada* – are the most popular places to eat at lunch and dinner. Neither is signed in English, and there's little to choose between them; both serve fairly pricey menus of Thai-Chinese dishes (around B60 for basics) and, of course, plenty of fish.

Rim Khong Next to the riverside bungalows at Ban Rim Khong Resort. Cheaper and less flashy than the other riverside restaurants (fried rice from B40), and a good deal friendlier too. A good spot for a sunset beer.

Tuk Tik Tham Mua 10m east of the bus station on Thanon Kaewpradit (no English sign). Good local dishes at good cheap prices: spicy *som tam*, green bean salads (*yam thua fak yao*), grilled fish (*ping plaa*) and chicken (*ping kai*), all served with individual baskets of sticky rice. Dishes from B35.

DIRECTORY

Bank The bank on Thanon Kaewpradit has an exchange facility and an ATM.

Pharmacy The small pharmacy on Thanon Kaewpradit sells basic supplies.

The Pha Taem cliff-paintings

18km up the Mekong from Khong Chiam (clearly signposted) • Daily 5am–6pm • B200

Contained within craggy Pha Taem National Park, which overlooks Laos, the **Pha Taem cliff-paintings** cover a 170m stretch of cliff face 18km up the Mekong from Khong Chiam. Clear proof of the antiquity of the fertile Mekong valley, these bold, childlike paintings are believed to be between three thousand and four thousand years old, the work of rice-cultivating settlers who lived in huts rather than caves. Protected from the elements by an overhang, the clearly discernible red-painted images (daubed from a mixture of soil, tree gum and fat) include alien-like forms, handprints and geometric designs as well as massive depictions of animals and enormous fish – possibly the prized catfish still occasionally caught in the Mekong. Try to avoid coming here on a weekend when the place gets swamped with tour buses. It's an especially popular spot at sunrise, this being the first place in Thailand to see the sun in the morning – a full eighteen minutes ahead of Phuket, the westernmost point.

Just after the checkpoint, the road passes a group of weird, mushroom-shaped sandstone rock formations known as **Sao Chaliang** before reaching the Pha Taem car park, site of a restaurant and the visitor centre, on top of the cliff. From the car park, follow the path to the left of the visitor centre, which runs down the cliff face and along the shelf in the rock to the paintings. If you continue along the path past the paintings, you'll eventually climb back up to the top of the cliff again, via the **viewpoint** at Pha Mon, taking in fine views of the fertile Mekong valley floor and glimpses of hilly western Laos. It's just under 2km from Pha Mon back to the car park, along a signed trail across the rocky scrub.

CROSSING THE LAO BORDER VIA CHONG MEK

It is possible to get a Lao **visa** on arrival at Chong Mek **border crossing**; you'll be charged US$30–42, depending on your nationality, and will receive a thirty-day visa; you'll also need two passport photos (expect to pay an extra dollar if you turn up without photos). If you get an advance visa from Khon Kaen or elsewhere, it must specify Chong Mek as the entry point (see p.27).

Whichever option you choose, once at Chong Mek you first need to get the **Thai exit stamp** from the office hidden behind the market on the Thai side (daily 8.30am–4.30pm; ☎ 045 485107); once you cross to the Lao side of the border, you pass via the Lao immigration office (official hours Mon–Fri 8am–4pm; "surcharge" hours Mon–Fri 4–6pm, Sat, Sun & hols 8.30am–6pm), where you need to pay US$1 if you arrive during **"surcharge" hours** and an extra B20 (B50 during "surcharge" hours) for an entry stamp. A songthaew service runs from Vangtao to the city of Pakse, 40km away (until about 5pm), and more expensive minivans are often available too. In reverse, you simply pay the Lao exit tax (B20/50) and get your Thai visa on arrival for free (but note the shorter hours on the Thai side).

ARRIVAL AND DEPARTURE — PHA TAEM

By songthaew Aside from using your own wheels, the most practical way to reach the national park is by chartering a songthaew from Khong Chiam, 18km away (see p.470).

ACCOMMODATION

National park bungalows Sao Chaliang, book in advance through the Pha Taem office (☎ 045 246332, ✉ phataem_3@hotmail.com) or via ⓦ dnp.go.th. If you want to stay and catch the sunrise, you can rent bungalows and large two-person tents (B150) near the national park checkpoint at Sao Chaliang, about 2km before the car park. Fan B1200, a/c B2000

Chong Mek and the Lao border

The village of **CHONG MEK**, 44km east of Phibun Mangsahan at the Thai–Lao border, hosts a busy Thai–Lao market and is one of the legal border crossings for foreigners, with onward transport to Pakse.

Even if you're not planning to cross into Laos, the **border market** is good for a browse, especially at weekends when it's at its liveliest. The market on the Thai side of the border is full of Bangkok fashions, jeans and sarongs, but you'll also find traditional herbalists flogging bits of dried vegetable and animal matter, lots of basketware sellers and plenty of restaurant shacks serving Thai and Lao dishes.

ARRIVAL AND DEPARTURE — CHONG MEK

By bus There's a daily bus between Chong Mek and Bangkok that departs Chong Mek market at 4pm and arrives at Mo Chit Northern Bus Terminal about 11hr later. Buses run twice a day (9.30am & 3.30pm; B200) from Ubon Ratchathani's main bus station to Pakse in Laos, the smoothest way to do the trip.

By songthaew Large pale-blue songthaews run to Chong Mek from Phibun Mangsahan bus station (approximately hourly 7am–3.30pm; 1hr 30min). From Phibun you can transfer to another songthaew for the ride to Khong Chiam.

Yasothon and around

By the beginning of May, Isaan is desperate for rain; there may not have been a significant downpour for six months and the rice crops need to be planted. In northeastern folklore, rain is the fruit of sexual encounters between the gods, so at this time villagers all over Isaan hold the bawdy, merit-making **Bun Bang Fai rocket festival** to encourage the gods to get on with it. The largest and most public of these festivals takes place in the provincial capital of **YASOTHON**, 98km northwest of Ubon, on a weekend in mid-May (check with TAT for dates). Not only are the fireworks spectacular, but the rockets built to launch them are superbly crafted machines in themselves, beautifully decorated and carried proudly through the streets before blast-off. Up to 25kg of gunpowder may be packed into the 9m-long rockets and, in keeping with the fertility theme, performance is everything. Sexual innuendo, general flirtation and dirty jokes are essential components of Bun Bang Fai; rocket-builders compete to shoot their rockets the highest, and anyone whose missile fails to leave the ground gets coated in mud as a punishment.

At other times of the year, Yasothon has little to tempt tourists other than a handful of unremarkable wats and a few evocative old colonial-style shopfronts near **Wat Singh Tha** at the west end of Thanon Srisonthoon.

Ban Sri Than

21km east of Yasothon • Follow Route 202 northeast towards Amnat Charoen as far as kilometre-stone 18.5km, then turn south (right) off the highway for 3km; or take a songthaew (every 30min until noon) or bus (hourly throughout the day) to Ban Ni Khom on Route 202, then a motorbike taxi for the last 3km

The most interesting attraction in the surrounding area is the village of **BAN SRI THAN**, where nearly every household is employed in the making of the famous *mawn khwaan* triangular **axe pillows**. However, the scenes of sewing machines surrounded by heaps of cloth are not exactly photo contest winners, so it's really only worth a visit if you plan to buy the product. These pillows (*mawn*), so named because their shape supposedly resembles an axe-head (*khwaan*), have been used in traditional Thai homes for centuries, where it's normal to sit on the floor and lean against a densely stuffed *mawn khwaan*. It's possible to buy the cushions unstuffed so you can actually fit them in your luggage. The price depends on the number of triangular pods that make up the pillow: in Ban Sri Than, a stand-alone ten-triangle pillow costs B120, or B370 with three attached cushions – about half of what it'll cost in Bangkok or Chiang Mai.

ARRIVAL AND DEPARTURE   YASOTHON

By plane The nearest airports are in Roi Et (85km northwest) and in Ubon Ratchathani (see p.467). The travel agent inside the *JP Emerald* hotel sells domestic and international air tickets.

By bus Buses between Ubon and Khon Kaen stop at the bus station on Thanon Rattanakhet (19 daily; 3hr–3hr 30min from Khon Kaen, 1hr 30min–2hr from Ubon).

ACCOMMODATION

If you want to stay here during festival time, book your **hotel** well in advance and be prepared to pay double the normal prices quoted here.

Orchid Garden Hotel 219 Thanon Prachasamphan, just east of the town centre ☏045 721000, ⓦorchid -garden-hotel.com. This smart yet simple hotel has big, clean, a/c rooms and friendly, helpful staff. B400

JP Emerald 36 Thanon Pha Pa ☏045 724848. The fanciest hotel in town, with large, attractive a/c rooms close to the provincial hall. B820

EATING

The most lively place to **eat** is at the covered night bazaar, which runs east off the central section of Thanon Chaeng Sanit; some of the stalls here also open during the day, including a vegetarian one that serves tasty curries (daily 6am–2pm).

DIRECTORY

Bank Thanon Chaeng Sanit is where you'll find all the main banks, with ATMs and currency exchange facilities.

Post office Thanon Chaeng Sani, a couple of blocks west of the night bazaar.

5

Khon Kaen

At Isaan's centre, **KHON KAEN** is the wealthiest and most sophisticated city in the northeast, seat of a highly respected university as well as Channel 5 and Channel 11 television studios. There's a noticeably upbeat feel to the place, underlined by its apparently harmonious combination of traditional Isaan culture – huge markets and hordes of street vendors – with flashy shopping plazas and a world-class hotel. Its location, 188km northeast of Khorat on the Bangkok–Nong Khai rail line and Highway 2, makes it a convenient resting point, even though a startling modern temple and the provincial museum are the only real sights in town. However, the wider

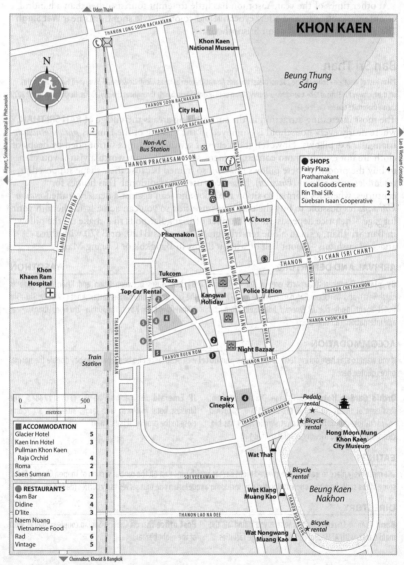

KHON KAEN

● **SHOPS**
Fairy Plaza	4
Prathamakant Local Goods Centre	3
Rin Thai Silk	2
Suebsan Isaan Cooperative	1

■ **ACCOMMODATION**
Glacier Hotel	5
Kaen Inn Hotel	3
Pullman Khon Kaen Raja Orchid	4
Roma	2
Saen Sumran	1

● **RESTAURANTS**
4am Bar	2
Didine	4
D'lite	3
Naem Nuang Vietnamese Food	1
Rad	6
Vintage	5

province has some impressive prehistoric credentials, which you can get to grips with at Phuwiang's **dinosaur graveyard**, within day-tripping distance of the city. Local silk is another draw; available year-round at outlets across the city, it gets special focus during the annual **Silk and Phuk Siao Festival** (usually Nov 29–Dec 10; check with TAT) when weavers from across the province congregate at the City Hall on Thanon Na Soon Rachakarn to display and sell their fabrics; this is also the chance to witness the moving *phuk siao* ceremony, a traditional friendship-deepening ritual involving the exchange of symbolic wrist strings. During the rest of the year, the foreigners staying in the city tend to be expat husbands of local women, businesspeople or university teachers rather than tourists, though an increasing number of travellers are stopping here for **Lao and Vietnamese visas**, now that both nations have consulates in Khon Kaen.

Wat Nongwang Muang Kao

Far southern end of Thanon Klang

Khon Kaen's most arresting sight is the enormous nine-tiered pagoda at **Wat Nongwang Muang Kao**. Unmissable in its glittering livery of red, white and gold, this breath-takingly grand structure was the brainchild of the temple's famously charismatic and well-travelled abbot, Phra Wisuttikittisan. The nine-tiered design is said to have been inspired by Burma's most sacred stupa, Shwedagon, but the gallery running around each tier is more Lao in style, and the crowning *that* (tower) is typically Thai. Nine is an auspicious number in Thailand, triply so in this case as the current king is Rama IX and the current abbot of the temple is the ninth since the wat's foundation in 1789. Inside the pagoda, the walls of the first tier are painted with modern murals that depict the founding of Khon Kaen. Each tier has its different purpose, with the first used for assemblies, the second for monks' residences, the third for a scripture library and so on. If you arrive before 4pm, you can climb the staircase all the way up to the ninth tier for views north across the city and east to the lake, Beung Kaen Nakhon.

Beung Kaen Nakhon

In the southeast of town, 500m from the Fairy Plaza • Bike rental B20/hr, pedalo rental B40/hr

A walk or cycle round the rippling waters of **Beung Kaen Nakhon** and its perimeter park is a pleasant way to spend a few hours. You can rent bicycles at three different spots, close to each of the lakeside temples, there are table-tennis tables near the Wat Klang Muang Kao entrance, several kids' playparks, and foodstalls all over, as well as restaurants. It's also possible to rent pedalos from the northern shore of the lake.

Hong Moon Mung Khon Kaen City Museum

On the eastern shore of Beung Kaen Nakhon, across from the ornate Chinese temple in the utilitarian building beneath the outdoor amphitheatre • Mon–Sat 9am–5pm • B90

The **Hong Moon Mung Khon Kaen City Museum**, sometimes referred to as the "treasure hall", presents the history of Khon Kaen province in a series of tableaux. It showcases the region's rich cultural heritage, from the first signs of settlement right up to the present day. The museum is organized into five chronological sections, making it easy to find your way around, and there's a fair amount of explanation in English.

Khon Kaen National Museum

North of the centre at Thanon Lung Soon Rachakarn • Wed–Sun 9am–4pm • B100 • ⓦ thailandmuseum.com/thaimuseum_eng /khonkaen/main.htm

Khon Kaen National Museum presents a digestible introduction to the region through an assortment of locally found artefacts, some of which date back to the Bronze Age. The star **exhibit** on the ground floor of the museum is a ninth-century Dvaravati-era

5

sema (boundary stone) carved with a sensuous depiction of Princess Bhimba wiping the Buddha's feet with her hair. Also on this floor is an interesting reconstruction of a local musical ensemble centred around the *pong lang*, a wooden xylophone that's particular to the region. The highlights of the upstairs gallery are some exquisite little Khmer-influenced Lopburi-style bronze Buddha images.

ARRIVAL AND DEPARTURE   KHON KAEN

By plane Khon Kaen airport (☎043 227708), 10km northwest of the city centre, runs Thai Airways flights to and from Bangkok. Hotel minibuses meet all flights – some hotels provide this service for free, others charge B70–90. Alternatively, pick up a metered taxi (around B60 to central hotels) from the road approaching the airport. The Thai Airways office (☎043 227701; Mon–Fri 8am–5pm) is inside the *Pullman Hotel* on Thanon Prachasamran.
Destinations Bangkok (3 daily; 55min).

By train The train station (☎043 221112) is on the southwestern edge of town, a short walk from downtown hotels and bars. If you're staying near the TAT office, you can walk from the station in 15min, although it's worth picking up a tuk-tuk if you have bags (B50–60).
Destinations Ayutthaya (4 daily; 7hr–7hr 30min); Bangkok

(4 daily; 8hr 30min–9hr 45min); Khorat (5 daily; 3hr–3hr 30min); Nong Khai (3 daily; 2hr 25min–3hr 30min); Udon Thani (6 daily; 1hr 50min–2hr 30min).

By bus Khon Kaen has two bus terminals: one serving normal, fan-cooled buses (☎043 237472, 5min walk northwest of the Thanon Klang Muang hotels), and one serving a/c buses (☎043 239910, right in the town centre).
Destinations Bangkok (every 30min; 6–7hr); Chiang Mai (12 daily; 10–12hr); Khorat (every 30min; 3hr); Loei (every 30min; 4hr); Nong Khai (5 daily; 3hr 30min); Pattaya (1 daily; 11hr); Phitsanulok (12 daily; 6–7hr); Rayong (6 daily; 10–12hr); Sukhothai (2 daily; 7hr); Surin (every 30min; 5hr 30min); Ubon Ratchathani (19 daily; 4hr–4hr 30min); Udon Thani (every 30min; 2hr–2hr 30min).

GETTING AROUND

By songthaew Local songthaews ply the streets 5am–8pm, charging a fixed fare of B10–15. Route numbers change regularly – ask staff at your hotel for advice.

By tuk-tuk or samlor A short tuk-tuk ride within the city should cost you B50–60, while the minimum fare in a samlor is B20.

By taxi Taxis tend to congregate near the *Pullman Hotel*. Ask for the meter to be switched on; short journeys within the city should cost B30–50.

Car rental Avis (☎043 344313, ⓦavisthailand.com) and

Budget (☎043 345460, ⓦbudget.co.th) both have desks at the airport. Cars with a driver (B1700/day, excluding fuel) are available at Top Car Rent (☎043 227448), just opposite the *Pullman Hotel* on Thanon Prachasamran. The service here is reliable, and the owners are able to plan customized trips around the northeast.

Motorbike rental Malida, on the approach road to the airport (☎089 5757398), rents automatic bikes (from B200/day) and can deliver them to downtown guesthouses for you if you book in advance.

INFORMATION AND TOURS

Tourist information The TAT office (daily 8.30am–4.30pm; ☎043 244498, ⓔtatkhkn@tat.or.th) is at 15/5 Thanon Prachasamoson, about a 5min walk east of the non-a/c bus station. For information about the city and attractions in the surrounding area, ⓦkhonkaen.com is a useful resource,

but it's not especially up to date.

Tours and trips Kangwal Holiday (☎043 227777, ⓦkangwal.com), on the *Charoen Thani* approach road on Thanon Si Chan, can arrange trips across Thailand, as well as flights and organized tours to destinations across the region.

ACCOMMODATION

Khon Kaen has some of the best **accommodation** anywhere in the northeast, from all-out luxury to quirky and clean city hotels.

Glacier Hotel 141 Thanon Prachasamran ☎043 334999, ⓦglacier-hotel.com. A cool, crisply styled hotel that's vaguely themed around ice and snow (yes, there's a/c throughout). There are white pod chairs in the lobby, and the carpeted rooms have unusual touches like see-through glass walls separating the bathroom from the bedroom. **B2450**

Kaen Inn Hotel 56 Thanon Klang Muang ☎043 245420. Clean and well-looked-after rooms with a/c and fresh white walls, plus a host of other on-site facilities including a snooker room and barber shop. The only downside is that it can be a little noisy. **B500**

★ **Pullman Khon Kaen Raja Orchid** 9/9 Thanon Prachasamran ☎043 322155, ⓦpullmanhotels.com.

CLOCKWISE FROM TOP MAKING A CEREMONIAL CHAIR, KHORAT (P.445); HOUSEBOATS ON THE MEKONG (P.493); KHON KAEN SILK (P.478) >

5

Quite simply the nicest hotel in the northeast, this gorgeously appointed, luxury high-rise hotel has extremely comfortable rooms, a swimming pool and spa, and plenty of bars and restaurants. It's shaped in the form of a giant *khaen*, the bamboo pan-pipes played in northeastern folk music. Significant discounts are often available, which makes it well worth splashing out on. B2000

⭐ **Roma** 50/2 Thanon Klang Muang ☎043 334444. Don't be fooled by the grim-looking lobby; this newly renovated place has some of the cheeriest mid-range rooms in town. Some feature Warhol-style pop-art prints, while others have funky bird-shaped stickers on the walls. Other unexpected quirks include pine-coloured floors and shocking pink chairs. Not all of the rooms had been renovated when we visited, and the ones that had varied quite a lot, so ask to see a few before settling in. Free wi-fi. Fan B500, a/c B600

Saen Sumran 55 Thanon Klang Muang ☎043 239611, ✉saensamran@gmail.com. One of the oldest hotels in Khon Kaen, this is also the most traveller-friendly place in town (though most of its customers are Thai salesmen), with genial, clued-up managers. All the (fan) rooms are basic but en suite: the price depends on the size of the room and thickness of the mattress. The large, wooden-floored rooms upstairs are nicest. B250

EATING, DRINKING AND ENTERTAINMENT

Khon Kaen has a reputation for very **spicy food**, particularly sausages, *sai krog isaan*, which are occasionally available with cubes of raw ginger, onion, lime and plenty of chilli sauce at stalls along Thanon Klang Muang to the north of the *Roma Hotel*. In high season, these and other local favourites – such as pigs' trotters, roast duck and shellfish – can also be sampled at the stalls along the northern edge of lake Bueng Kaen Nakhon. Food stalls pop up across town at dusk, with a particular concentration at the **night bazaar** on the eastern end of Thanon Ruen Rom. **Nightlife** is mainly focused along Thanon Prachasamran, behind the *Pullman Hotel*.

4am Bar Across from the Pullman Hotel driveway, off Thanon Prachasamran. Popular little roadside hut serving strong drinks late into the night; one of several in the area. A large Sangsom and cola will set you back B70. Daily 6pm–4am.

Cinema Fairy Cineplex inside Fairy Plaza, between southern Thanon Nah Muang and Klang Muang. Tickets B80–120.

Didine Thanon Prachasamran. Run by a Franco-Thai couple, this welcoming place attracts an eclectic crowd with 150 European dishes, seventy Thai dishes, well-priced drinks and a free pool table. Daily 4pm–late.

⭐ **D'lite** On the lane immediately east of the Pullman Hotel. The place to come for stylishly presented Isaan dishes like long bean salad with crispy pork (B95). You can sit outside in the dimly lit garden, which has soothing water features and an old English phonebox, or in the small a/c area, which is all wonky picture frames and floral wallpapers. Get 10 percent off everything (except alcohol) on Wed. Daily 6pm–late.

Naem Nuang Vietnamese Food Next door but one to the Saen Sumran hotel at 87/14–15 Thanon Klang Muang. Very popular a/c place that serves mainly Vietnamese food plus some northeastern standards. Their eponymous speciality is *naem nuang*, Vietnamese spring rolls made with barbecued fermented pork sausage, which you assemble yourself from half a dozen or more ingredients of your choice, including lots of fresh coriander, mint, ginger, lemon rind, thin noodles and beansprouts. Build-your-own spring rolls from B10/item and all-you-can-eat lunch buffets from B129. Daily 6am–9.30pm.

Rad Thanon Prachasamran. This one-stop entertainment complex has it all – restaurant and coffee shop, raucous rock and easy-listening live music venues, plus girls dancing on the bar. Daily 6pm–late.

Vintage Thanon Prachasamran, ⓦvintagepubkhonkaen .com. Cool, alfresco restaurant in front of a rather grand-looking building that regularly hosts club nights. Wildly popular with wealthy young Thais (especially couples). The *tom yam* soup (B140) is especially good, if pricey. Daily 10pm–4am.

SHOPPING

Khon Kaen's shops carry a wide range of regional **arts and crafts**, particularly high-quality Isaan **silk** of all designs and weaves. Vendors, who you'll sometimes see wandering the main streets with panniers stuffed full of silk and cotton lengths, also offer competitive prices. Usually they're gathered around the *Roma Hotel* and along the stretch of Thanon Klang Muang just north of the hotel.

Fairy Plaza Between Nah Muang and Klang Muang. A huge modern mall with all the usual clothes, accessories and mobiles concessions, plus *Pizza Co*, *McDonald's*, *Swensen's* and a cinema. Mon–Fri 10.30am–9.30pm, Sat–Sun 10am–9.30pm.

Prathamakant Local Goods Centre 81 Thanon Ruen Rom. One of the best outlets in Khon Kaen, with a phenomenal selection of gorgeous *mut mee* cotton and silk weaves, as well as clothes, furnishings, triangular axe pillows (B400 for an unstuffed three-seater), *khaen* pipes and silver jewellery. It's much better than the disappointing government-sanctioned OTOP (One Tambon One Product) shop beside the *Kosa Hotel* on Soi Kosa, and though it feels touristy, locals buy their home furnishings and dress fabrics here too. Mon–Sat 9am–8pm.

Rin Thai Silk 410–412 Thanon Nah Muang. Stocks a smaller range of Isaan silk, but will tailor clothes too.

Mon–Sat 8am–6.30pm.

Suebsan Isaan Cooperative 16 Thanon Klang Muang. Another fair-trade outlet for local craftspeople, which sells textiles fabricated from bamboo fibre and water hyacinth, as well as more usual *mut mee* silks, cottons, basketware, herbal cosmetics and other traditional products. Daily 8am–6.30pm.

DIRECTORY

Consulates The Lao consulate (Mon–Fri 8am–noon & 1–4pm; ☎043 242856–8) is located some way east of TAT at 171/102–3 Thanon Prachasamoson. Thirty-day tourist visas for the trip over the border (see p.497) can be processed here on the spot; fees vary according to the applicant's nationality. There's also a Vietnamese consulate (Mon–Fri 8–11.30am & 1.30–4.30pm; ☎043 242190 and ☎043 241586, ⓦ vietnamconsulate-khonkaen.org) south of the Lao consulate and about 1.5km from the TAT office, off Thanon Prachasamoson at 65/6 Thanon Chataphadung.

Hospitals Khon Kaen Ram Hospital (☎043 333800,

ⓦ khonkaenram.com), on the far western end of Thanon Si Chan, is the main private hospital. The government Srinakarin Hospital (☎043 242331) is attached to Khon Kaen University, north of town on Highway 2.

Internet access There are several internet/computer games centres around the *Roma Hotel* on Thanon Klang Muang.

Pharmacy Pharmakon (daily 8am–6.30pm), on Thanon Nah Muang, one block west of the *Kaen Inn Hotel*.

Tourist police For all emergencies, call the tourist police 24hr on ☎1155 (free), or contact them at the TAT office on Thanon Prachasamoson ☎043 236937.

Around Khon Kaen

The outer reaches of Khon Kaen province hold a couple of places that are worth exploring on **day-trips**. If you're looking for other things to occupy yourself, don't be duped by the TAT brochure on the "tortoise village" in the village of Ban Kok, about 5km west of Chonnabot, which is both duller and more depressing than the tourist literature implies. Chonnabot itself is a good place to see silk weavers at work, while Phuwiang National Park is most famous for Dinosaurland, a paleontological attraction with nine dig sites and its own museum.

Chonnabot

54km southwest of Khon Kaen • Any ordinary Khorat-bound bus to Ban Phae (every 30min), then a songthaew for the final 10km

Khon Kaen makes a reasonable base from which to explore the local silk-weaving centre of **CHONNABOT**. Traditionally a cottage industry, this small town's **silk production** (see box, p.462) has become centralized over the last few years, and weavers now gather in small workshops in town, each specializing in just one aspect of the process. You can walk in and watch the women (it's still exclusively women's work) at their wheels, looms or dye vats, and then buy from the vendors in the street out front.

Dinosaurland at Phuwiang National Park

☎085 852 1771, ⓦ dnp.go.th **Park** Daily 8.30am–6pm • B200 • **Museum** Daily except Wed 9am–5pm • Free

Khon Kaen hit the international headlines in 1996 when the oldest-ever fossil of a tyrannosaur **dinosaur** was unearthed in Phuwiang, about 90km northwest of Khon Kaen, which has since been made into a national park. Estimated to be 120 million years old, the fossil measures just 6m from nose to tail and has been named *Siamotyrannus isanensis* – Siam for Thailand, and Isaan after the northeastern region of Thailand. Before this find at Phuwiang, the oldest tyrannosaur fossils were the 65-million- to 80-million-year-old specimens from China, Mongolia and North America. These younger fossils are twice the size of the *Siamotyrannus*; the latter's age

5

and size have therefore established the *Siamotyrannus* as the ancestor of the *Tyrannosaurus rex*, and confirmed Asia as the place of origin of the tyrannosaur genus, which later evolved into various different species.

The fossil of this extraordinary dinosaur – together with eight moderately interesting paleontological finds – is on show to the public at Dinosaurland in **Phuwiang National Park**. The main attractions here, apart from waterfalls and nature trails, are nine dig sites and a **museum**, which is located just before the park entrance.

The *Siamotyrannus isanensis* is displayed at **Site 9**, which is accessible via the 1.5km track that starts across the road from the visitor centre; from the car park at the end of the track, it's a 500m climb to the quarry. The fossil is an impressive sight for paleontologists, with large sections of the rib cage almost completely intact, but many visitors will wonder what all the fuss is about. **Site 1**, 900m south along a track from Site 9, contains the cream of the other finds, including two previously undiscovered species. The theropod *Siamosaurus suteethorni* (named after the paleontologist Warawut Suteethorn) is set apart from the other, carnivorous, theropods by its teeth, which seem as if they are unable to tear flesh; the 15–20m-long *Phuwiangosaurus sirindhornae* (named in honour of Thailand's Princess Royal) is thought to be a new species of sauropod.

ARRIVAL AND DEPARTURE   DINOSAURLAND

By bus Non-a/c buses run from Khon Kaen to Phuwiang town (every 30min; about 1hr) – you then need to hire a motorbike taxi to Dinosaurland and back (about B150 return).

By car It's easier to rent your own wheels in Khon Kaen (see p.476). To get to the park, head west out of Khon Kaen on Highway 12, following the signs for Chumpae as far as

kilometre-stone 48, marked by a dinosaur statue. Turn right off the main road here, and continue for another 38km along Highway 2038, passing through the small town of Phuwiang, and follow signs for the national park. About halfway between Phuwiang and the national park, there is a park to the left of the road containing life-size statues of many species of dinosaur.

ACCOMMODATION AND EATING

In addition to the options listed below, two-bedroom tents are also available to rent (B250). There's a **food** and drink stall at the car park in front of Quarry #3, about 1km north of the visitor centre.

Bungalows ⓦ web3.dnp.go.th/parkreserve/reservations .asp?lg=2. There are three basic bungalows in the area around the park headquarters, each sleeping six people (fan and bedding included). **B1200**

Hostel ⓦ web3.dnp.go.th/parkreserve/reservations.asp? lg=2. Nearer to Tat Fa Waterfall, there's a hostel-style room sleeping thirty people (shared bathroom) but it is not possible to book individual beds online. Whole hostel **B3000**

Udon Thani

The capital of an arid sugar-cane and rice-growing province, 137km north of Khon Kaen, **UDON THANI** was given an economic boost during the Vietnam War with the siting of a huge American military base nearby, and despite the American withdrawal in 1976, the town has maintained its rapid industrial and commercial development. Seen as charmless but economically important for many years, Udon has now started to attract more casual visitors, with the city's new entertainment plaza and the relaxing Nong Prajak park providing the main focus for a couple of lazy days in the city. By night the area known as UD Town springs into life, with tourists and locals thronging the pedestrianized streets to eat, chatter and watch local dance troupes. Apart from these places, and the excavated Bronze Age settlement of **Ban Chiang** (see p.482), 50km to the east, there aren't many tourist attractions in the area.

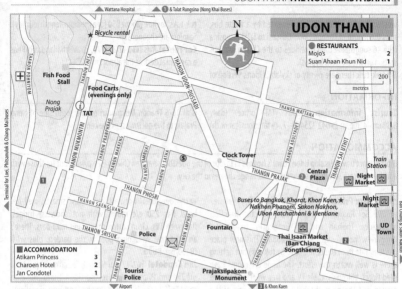

UDON THANI

● RESTAURANTS
Mojo's 2
Suan Ahaan Khun Nid 1

0   200
metres

Map labels: Wattana Hospital • & Talat Rungsina (Nong Khai Buses) • Bicycle rental • THANON PHOINVAN • THANON THESA • THANON UDON-DUSSADI • THANON WATTANA • Fish Food Stall • Food Carts (evenings only) • Nong Prajak • TAT • THANON MUKMONTRI • THANON PHANPHRAO • THANON MAKKENG • THANON SI SATHA • THANON TAMRUT • Clock Tower • THANON ADULYADET • THANON SAI UTHIT • Train Station • THANON PRAJAK • Central Plaza • Night Market • Terminal for Loei, Phitsanulok & Chiang Mai buses • THANON SAENGLUANG • THANON PHOSRI • $ • Buses to Bangkok, Khorat, Khon Kaen, Nakhon Phanom, Sakon Nakhon, Ubon Ratchathani & Vientiane • Night Market • Ban Chiang & Sakon Nakhon • THANON SRISUK • THANON AMPHOE • Police • Fountain • UD Town • THANON MARSUAN • Thai Isaan Market (Ban Chiang Songthaews) • THANON SURAON • ■ ACCOMMODATION • Atikarn Princess ... 3 • Charoen Hotel ... 2 • Jan Condotel ... 1 • Tourist Police • Prajaksilpakom Monument • Airport • & Khon Kaen

Nong Prajak Park

Just west of the TAT office • Bike rental B20/hr

Away from the racket of Udon's busier streets is **Nong Prajak Park**, a surprisingly quiet space set around a tranquil, fish-filled lake. Approaching from Thanon Thesa, on the eastern shore of the lake, it's possible to walk across a bridge to the central island, where you'll find bushes chopped lovingly into the shape of rabbits. An alternative to feeding the fish (local women sell bags of food) is cycling around the lake's perimeter; bikes can be rented from its northeastern edge.

ARRIVAL AND DEPARTURE
UDON THANI

By plane Thai Airways and Air Asia operate several flights a day from Bangkok to Udon Thani, while Nok Air currently runs a twice-daily service from Chiang Mai and Air Asia flies daily from Phuket; a/c minibuses meet incoming flights at the airport, 3km southwest of the centre (B80/person), dropping off anywhere in town. There are also direct a/c minibuses (B150–200) from the airport that head north to the Friendship Bridge and downtown Nong Khai.
Destinations Bangkok (7 daily; 1hr); Chiang Mai (2 daily; 1hr); Phuket (1 daily; 1hr 50min).
By train Udon's train station is on the east side of the centre, close to the night market.
Destinations Ayutthaya (4 daily; 7hr 30min–9hr 30min); Bangkok (4 daily; 10–12hr); Khon Kaen (6 daily; 1hr 35min–2hr 15min); Khorat (3 daily; 4hr 30min–5hr 30min); Nong Khai (4 daily; 40min–1hr).
By bus Buses pull in at a variety of locations, depending on where they've come from: Loei, Phitsanulok and

Chiang Mai services use the terminal on the town's western bypass; Nong Khai buses are stationed at Talat Rungsina (Rungsina market, also used by Ban Phu buses) on the north side of town; and Bangkok, Khorat, Khon Kaen, Nakhon Phanom and Ubon Ratchathani services use the other main terminal on Thanon Sai Uthit, which also has a service direct to Vientiane (B100), across the border in Laos, for those who have arranged their visa in advance.
Destinations Bangkok (every 30min; 9hr); Chiang Mai (4 daily; 11–13hr); Chiang Rai (4 daily; 12–14hr); Khon Kaen (every 30min; 1hr 30min–2hr); Khorat (hourly; 3hr 30min–5hr); Loei (every 30min; 3–4hr); Mukdahan (5 daily; 4hr–4hr 30min); Nakhon Phanom (14 daily; 5hr); Nong Khai (every 30min; 1–2hr); Phitsanulok (5 daily; 7hr); Rayong (7 daily; 12hr); Sakon Nakhon (every 20min; 3hr); That Phanom (4 daily; 4–5hr); Ubon Ratchathani (9 daily; 6hr); Vientiane (Laos; 8 daily; 1hr 30min).

GETTING AROUND

By songthaew Numbered songthaews ply set routes around town for B10/person (a rough map is available

from TAT); among the more useful routes, #7 connects the Thanon Sai Uthit bus terminal with the terminal on the

5

western bypass, while #6, supplemented by a white bus, runs the length of Thanon Udon-Dussadi to Talat Rungsina (the #6 songthaew then continues to the Chiang Mai bus station on the western bypass).

By tuk-tuk There are plenty of skylabs, Udon's version of

tuk-tuks, for hire (about B50 for a medium-length journey). Samlors are cheaper still.

Car rental Avis (☎ 042 244770, ⓦ avisthailand.com) has a car-rental desk at the airport.

INFORMATION

Tourist information Udon's TAT office (daily 8.30am–4.30pm; ☎ 042 325406–7, ⓔ tatudon@tat.or.th) is at 16/5 Thanon Mukmontri on the south side of Nong Prajak, to the northwest of the centre.

ACCOMMODATION

Most budget travellers skip Udon Thani's **hotels** in favour of the guesthouse at Ban Chiang (see p.484), but for those with a little extra cash, there are some great mid-range choices in the city.

★ **Atikarn Princess** South of the university complex at 297 Soi Rakmit – when you reach the junction of Thanon Thahan and Soi Jintakarm, follow the burgundy "hotel" signs ☎ 042 340888. This new place is a long ride from the centre (B50 by tuk-tuk) but getting there is well worth the effort. The huge a/c rooms have tiled floors, balconies, cable TV and free wi-fi, and they're around half the price of what you'd pay for one of the drab central business hotels. Pay an extra B100 for an even bigger "VIP" room with funky chairs, a huge bed and a quirky yellow-and-white colour scheme. **B450**

Charoen Hotel 549 Thanon Phosri ☎ 042 248155,

ⓔ charoenhotel@hotmail.com. This smart, well-run hotel has 250 a/c rooms with hot showers, fridges, flatscreen TVs, clean cotton sheets and mini-bars. There's an attractive swimming pool in the garden, plus wi-fi (B100/hr). **B890**

Jan Condotel 102/17 Soi Sansuk, a narrow, quiet soi off Thanon Phosri opposite the Udon Thani Museum ☎ 042 329223–7, ⓦ janhotelthailand.com. Excellent-value rooms in a well-appointed condo, with a/c, hot water, cable TV, fridges and duvets; some also have broadband, or there's internet access downstairs. **B500**

EATING, DRINKING AND ENTERTAINMENT

In Udon the main **night market**, on the west side of the train station, is the place to come for food and cut-price clothing. Just south of here is **UD Town**, a massive new entertainment complex that is *the* commercial face of modern Udon Thani. After dark you'll find street entertainers, dance shows and stalls selling everything from indulgent perfumes to fruit shakes and spicy sausages. Thais and tourists pour into the restaurants, which range from Western fast-food joints to high-end noodle bars, giving the place a real buzz in the evenings. For cheaper eats, head to Thanon Thesa, where several simple bar-restaurants set out low-slung tables in the evening, alongside paint-your-own-pottery and massage stalls.

Mojo's 254/24 Thanon Prajak ☎ 042 343409. Pizzas (from B150), cocktails, free pool, free wi-fi and a huge menu of Western breakfasts – the food varies in quality, but is always stylishly presented. The place runs fundraising buffets for the *Friends of Udon Foundation* (B110/head, with proceeds going to help local kids with disabilities). Daily 8am–12.30am.

★ **Suan Ahaan Khun Nid** Soi 9 (Soi Nonniwate), Thanon Udon-Dussadi ☎ 042 246128. For an authentic culinary treat, head out into the northern suburbs to this

clean and friendly restaurant, which is famous among Thai gourmets for its carefully prepared Isaan food, such as spiced, salted and grilled snakehead fish, deep-fried land crab, deep-fried sun-dried beef and a wide variety of northeastern salads. Take a skylab or catch songthaew #6 or the white bus up Thanon Udon-Dussadi as far as Soi 9, then walk 10min west along the soi, passing the temple. The restaurant is on the left at the end of a short alley. Daily 10am–1pm.

DIRECTORY

Hospital Wattana Hospital, 70/7–8 Thanon Supakitjunya (☎ 042 325999, ⓦ wattanahospital.net), on the north shore of Nong Prajak towards the north of town, has international-standard facilities.

Internet access There are dozens of internet places in and around the Charoensi Complex shopping centre on Thanon Prajak.

Ban Chiang

The excavated Bronze Age settlement of **BAN CHIANG**, 50km east of Udon Thani in sleepy farming country, was listed as a UNESCO World Heritage Site in 1992. It achieved worldwide fame in 1966, when a rich seam of archeological remains was accidentally discovered: clay pots, uncovered in human graves alongside sophisticated **bronze** objects, were eventually dated to around 2000 BC, implying the same date for the bronze pieces. Ban Chiang has been hailed as the Southeast Asian vanguard of the Bronze Age, about three hundred years after Mesopotamia's discovery of the metal.

The village of Ban Chiang is unremarkable nowadays, although its fertile setting is attractive and the villagers, who still weave (and sell) especially rich and intricate lengths of silk and cotton *mut mee*, are noticeably friendly to visitors. The museum here, which focuses on the Bronze Age finds, is one of the region's most interesting. There's also a bird and animal sanctuary 6km away, and a couple of interesting forest wats closer to the village.

Some travellers base themselves in Udon Thani (see p.480) but others visit Ban Chiang on a day-trip from Nong Khai (see p.493).

National Museum

Towards the north of the village • Tues–Sun 8.30am–4pm • B150

The village's fine **National Museum** has managed to retain some of the choicest Bronze Age finds, which it fleshes out with a fascinating and thoughtful rundown of Ban Chiang culture, including its agriculture, pathology and burial rites. It also houses the country's best collection of characteristic late-period Ban Chiang clay pots, with their red whorled patterns on a buff background, which were used as funeral offerings – although not of prime historical significance, these pots have become an attractive emblem of Ban Chiang, and are freely adapted by local souvenir producers.

Excavation Site

In the grounds of Wat Pho Si Nai, on the east side of the village • Daily 8.30am–6pm • Same ticket as the museum

In the grounds of **Wat Pho Si Nai**, on the east side of the village, part of an early dig has been covered over and opened to the public. A large burial pit has been left exposed to show how and where artefacts were found, providing an interesting insight into the work of archeologists here.

ARRIVAL AND DEPARTURE   BAN CHIANG

From Udon, you can either take a direct songthaew (here a big, multicoloured truck) or take a bus then a samlor. Heading back to Udon the same day by songthaew is not possible as the return service stops around 9am, so you'll have to make do with a samlor-and-bus combination.

By songthaew Irregular songthaews (Mon–Fri until about noon, sometimes on Sat & Sun also; roughly 1hr) run from Udon's morning market, Isaan Talat Thai.
By bus and samlor Catch a Sakon Nakhon-bound bus

from the Thanon Sai Uthit terminal (1hr) to Ban Palu and then a motorized samlor (B50/person) for the last 5km or so from the main road to the village.

GETTING AROUND

By bicycle or motorbike Bicycles are available from *Lakeside Sunrise* (who may also be able to arrange motorbike rental) for exploring the surrounding countryside – there's

a bird and animal sanctuary 6km away, and a couple of interesting forest wats closer to the village, all marked on a useful hand-drawn map of the area.

5

ACCOMMODATION

Lakeside Sunrise A few mins' walk from the museum ☏ 087 220 7769 or ☏ 042 208167. Guests at this excellent guesthouse sleep in clean first-floor rooms with fans, mosquito screens and shared hot showers and can relax on a huge balcony, equipped with a small library, and access the internet; the friendly owner, Tong, will cook Thai meals if you order in advance (otherwise, there are half-a-dozen simple restaurants in the village). Facing the museum, head left then turn right at the first intersection and look for a large Western-style wooden two-storey house overlooking an artificial lake. **B300**

Loei

Most visitors carry on from Udon Thani due north to Nong Khai, but making a detour via **LOEI**, 147km to the west, takes you within range of several towering national parks and sets you up for a lazy tour along the Mekong River. The capital of a province renowned for the unusual shapes of its stark, craggy mountains, Loei is also the crossroads of one of Thailand's least-tamed border regions, with all manner of illegal goods coming across from Laos. This trade may have been reined in – or perhaps spurred on – by the opening in 2008 of a 3km-long bridge across the Heuang River, 80km northwest of Loei, to Xainyabouli province in Laos (the crossing is open to foreigners, but there's no public transport on either side). Despite its frontier feel, the town, lying along the west bank of the small Loei River, is friendly and offers legitimate products of its own, such as sweet tamarind paste and pork sausages, which are for sale along Thanon Charoenrat, Loei's main street, and the adjacent Thanon Oua Aree. But Loei is really only useful as a transport hub and a base for the nearby national parks. The most popular are Phu Kradung National Park, which has some excellent walking trails, Nam Nao National Park, home to around a hundred different

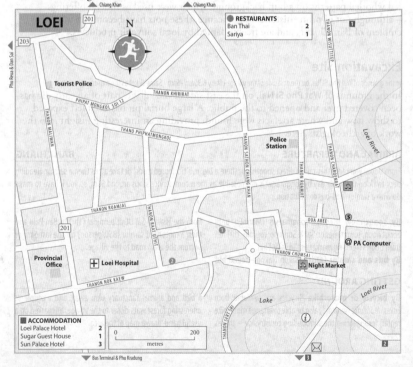

PHI TA KON

One reason to make a special trip to Loei province is to attend the unique rainmaking **festival of Phi Ta Kon**, or Bun Phra Wet, held over three days either at the end of June or the beginning of July in the small town of **Dan Sai**, 80km to the southwest of the provincial capital. In order to encourage the heavens to open, townsfolk dress up as spirits in colourful patchwork rags and fierce, brightly painted masks (made from coconut palm fronds and the baskets used for steaming sticky rice), then rowdily parade the town's most sacred Buddha image round the streets while making fun of as many onlookers as they can, waving wooden phalluses about and generally having themselves a whale of a time. Top folk and country musicians from around Isaan are attracted to perform in the evenings during Phi Ta Kon; the afternoon of the second day of the festival sees the firing off of dozens of bamboo rockets, while the third day is a much more solemn affair, with Buddhist sermons and a purification ceremony at Wat Phon Chai. The carnival can be visited in a day from Loei (ask at Loei's TAT office for transport details), though rooms are hard to come by at this time. The town's main permanent attraction is the **Dan Sai Folk Museum** on Thanon Kaew Asa, the town's high street (daily 9am–5pm; free), which explains some of the traditions surrounding Phi Ta Kon and has an impressive collection of vivid costumes and masks.

INFORMATION AND ACCOMMODATION   DAN SAI

Tourist information You can find out more about the event, and other local happenings, at the information centre, inside the "city hall" on Thanon Kaew Asa, the town's high street (☎ 042 891231, ⓦ tessabandansai .com).

Homestay If you fancy immersing yourself in a local homestay, contact Dan Sai's library (*hawng samut*; ☎ 042 891094), about 1km up Thanon Kaew Asa from the main through-road (R2013).

species of mammals, and Phu Reua National Park, which affords magnificent views over Laos.

ARRIVAL AND DEPARTURE   LOEI

By bus The terminal is on Thanon Maliwan, the main through north–south road (Highway 201), about 2.5km south of the centre.
Destinations Bangkok (20 daily; 10hr); Chiang Khan (hourly, plus frequent songthaews; 1hr); Chiang Mai

(6 daily; 9–11hr); Chiang Rai (4 daily; 9–12hr); Khon Kaen (every 30min; 4hr); Lom Sak (3 daily; 3hr); Nong Khai (2–3 daily via Pak Chom; 6–7hr); Phitsanulok (3 daily; 4hr); Sang Khom (2–3 daily; 3hr); Udon Thani (every 30min; 3–4hr).

INFORMATION

Tourist information The TAT office (daily 8.30am–4.30pm; ☎ 042 812812, ⓔ tatloei@tat.or.th), in the old district office on Thanon Charoenrat, has information about the region's

many national parks, including Phu Luang Wildlife Sanctuary to the west.

ACCOMMODATION

Unless it's festival time, finding a decent place to stay in Loei shouldn't be a problem.

Loei Palace Hotel 167/4 Thanon Charoenrat ☎ 042 815668–74, ⓦ oamhotels.com. A shining white landmark in the landscaped city park on the southeast side of the centre, and the best hotel in Loei. The attractive, international-standard rooms are ranged around an echoing, full-height atrium. They all enjoy fine views and wi-fi, and there's a large swimming pool, a hot tub, a fitness centre and internet access. B1200

★ **Sugar Guest House** 4/1 Soi 2, Thanon Wisuttitep ☎ 042 812982. Set in a quiet residential area a 5min walk

from the top of Thanon Charoenrat on the north side of the centre, the bright, colourful rooms here are either fan-cooled with shared hot-water bathrooms, or a/c with cable TV and en-suite hot-water bathrooms. Bicycles (B50) and motorbikes (B250) can be rented, and the owners can arrange day-trips in a car with driver to, for example, Phu Reua (B1600) or the relaxing Huay Krating (B500), where bamboo rafts are towed out onto the reservoir and you can eat lunch delivered to you by longtail boat. Good rates (B180) for singles. Fan B250, a/c B380

5

Sun Palace Hotel 191/5 Thanon Charoenrat ✆042 815714. This hotel south of the centre offers a/c, hot water, TVs and fridges throughout, and some of the rooms on the higher floors offer good mountain views. **B350**

EATING

During the evening your best bet for Isaan and Thai food is the pleasant **night market** on a broad, pedestrianized street off Thanon Chumsai, which wears its "Clean Food, Good Taste" signs with pride.

Ban Thai Thanon Nok Kaew ✆042 833472. The food here includes pizzas and tasty German breakfasts, plus decent Thai dishes (from B60), while good espressos and German beer further enhance its popularity with Loei's smattering of expats. Daily 10am–11pm.

Sariya 1/41 Thanon Sathon Chiang Khan ✆042 861888. A smart little place at the front of the *Loei Orchid Hotel* serving Thai dishes (including the house speciality – Thai-style steak). There are tables inside and out. Daily 6–11pm.

DIRECTORY

Internet access PA Computer is near the centre at 139 Thanon Charoenrat.

Police The tourist police have an office on Thanon Maliwan (✆042 861164 or ✆1155).

Phu Kradung National Park

Closed during the rainy season (June–Sept) • B400 • ✆042 871333 or ✆042 871458, ⓦ dnp.go.th

The most accessible and popular of the parks in Loei province, **PHU KRADUNG NATIONAL PARK** protects a grassy 1300m plateau 80km south of Loei whose temperate climate supports a number of tree, flower and bird species not normally found in Thailand. Walking trails crisscross much of sixty-square-kilometre Phu Kradung (Bell Mountain), and you could spend three days here exploring them fully – you'll need one night as a minimum, as the trip from Loei to the top of the plateau and back can't be done comfortably in a day. The park is at its busiest during weekends in December and January, when the main headquarters up on the plateau is surrounded by a sea of tents.

The attractions of the mountain come and go with the **seasons**. October is muddy after the rains, but the waterfalls that tumble off the northwestern edge of the plateau are in full cascade and the main trail is green and shady. December brings out the maple leaves; by February the waterfalls have disappeared and the vegetation on the lower slopes has been burnt away. April is good for rhododendrons and wild roses, which in Thailand are only found at such high altitudes as this.

Among the park's **wildlife**, mammals such as elephants, sambar deer and gibbons can be seen very occasionally, but they generally confine themselves to the evergreen forest on the northern part of the plateau, which is out of bounds to visitors. In the temperate pines, oaks and beeches that dot the rest of the plateau you're more likely to spot resident **birds** such as jays, sultan tits and snowy-browed flycatchers if you're out walking in the early morning and evening.

The trails

The challenging main **trail** leads from the Sri Taan visitor centre, at the base of the mountain, 5.5km up the eastern side of Phu Kradung, passing occasional refreshment stalls, and becoming steeper and rockier on the last 1km, with wooden steps over the most difficult parts; most people take at least three hours, including rest stops. The main trail is occasionally closed for maintenance, when a parallel 4.5km trail is opened up in its place. At the end of the actual climb, the unbelievable view as your head peeps over the rim more than rewards the effort: flat as a playing field, the broad plateau is dotted with odd clumps of pine trees thinned by periodic lightning fires, which give it the appearance of a country park.

Several feeder trails fan out from here, including a 9.5km path along the precipitous southern edge that offers sweeping views of Dong Phaya Yen, the untidy range of mountains to the southwest that forms the unofficial border between the northeast and the central plains. Another trail heads along the eastern rim for 2.5km to Pha Nok An – also reached by a 2km path east from the main visitor centre – which looks down on neat rice fields and matchbox-like houses in the valley below, an outlook that's especially breathtaking at sunrise.

ARRIVAL AND DEPARTURE — PHU KRADUNG NATIONAL PARK

To get to the park, take any **bus** from Loei to Khon Kaen (every 30min; 1hr 30min) or Khon Kaen to Loei (every 30min; 2hr 30min) and get off at the village of Phu Kradung, then hop on a **songthaew** for the remaining 5km to the Sri Taan visitor centre.

INFORMATION

Tourist information The well-organized Sri Taan visitor centre (daily Oct–May 8.30am–4.30pm) at the base of the plateau has a trail map. You can leave your gear at the visitor centre, or hire a porter to carry it to the top for you. The main visitor centre, which also gives out maps, is up on the plateau at Wang Kwang, 8km from the Sri Taan visitor centre.

ACCOMMODATION AND EATING

It's best to avoid going up and back down the mountain in one day, so try to stay here if you can. Simple **restaurants** at Wang Kwang rustle up inexpensive, tasty food from limited ingredients, so there's no need to bring your own provisions.

Sri Taan There are four national park bungalows at Sri Taan, with the added bonus of hot water. Each sleeps four people. These tend to take the overflow when accommodation on the mountain itself is full. B1200

Wang Kwang Up on the plateau at the main visitor centre, 8km from the Sri Taan visitor centre. There are over twenty bungalows and rooms sleeping four to twelve people, most with hot-water bathrooms; at busy times it's best to reserve in advance through ⓦ dnp.go.th. There are also fully equipped tents for rent (B270), sleeping two people each. Room B900, bungalow with fan and hot water B2400

Nam Nao National Park

B200 • ☎ 056 810724 or ☎ 081 9626236, ⓦ dnp.go.th

With its tallest peak reaching 1271m, **Nam Nao National Park** is easily visible among the undulating sandstone hills of the Phetchabun range. However, it remains a seldom-visited place, at least as far as tourists go, with plenty of wildlife and some good, challenging hikes.

At just under a thousand square kilometres, Nam Nao, which is 160km south of Loei by road, is home to a healthy wildlife population: around a hundred mammal species, including large animals such as forest elephant and banteng and a handful of tigers, and more-often-seen barking deer, gibbons and leaf monkeys, as well as over two hundred bird species. These creatures thrive in habitats ranging from tropical bamboo and banana stands to the dominant features of dry evergreen forest, grasslands, open forest and pine stands that look almost European.

Though the park was established in 1972, it remained a stronghold for guerillas of the Communist Party of Thailand until the early 1980s and was regarded as unsafe for visitors. Still much less visited than Phu Kradung, it can provide a sense of real solitude. The range of wildlife here also benefited from a physical isolation that stopped abruptly in 1975, when Highway 12 was cut through the park and poachers could gain access more easily. However, as the park adjoins the Phu Khieo Wildlife Sanctuary, there is beneficial movement by some species between the two areas.

The trails

A good network of clearly marked circular forest **trails** begins near the **park headquarters**, ranging from a 1km nature trail teeming with butterflies to a 6km track known for

5

occasional elephant sightings; another 3.5km trail climbs through mixed deciduous forest to the Phu Kor outlook, with its sweeping views across to Phu Phajit.

Other trails can be accessed directly from **Highway 12**, most of them clearly signposted from the road: at kilometre-stone 39, a steep climb up 260 roughly hewn steps leads to the Tham Pha Hong viewpoint, a rocky outcrop offering stunning panoramas of the park; at kilometre-stone 49, there's a 4km nature trail taking in Suan Son Dang Bak viewpoint; and at kilometre-stone 67, a 700m trail leads to the beautiful Haew Sai waterfall, best seen during or immediately after the rainy season. Experienced hikers can reach the top of Phu Phajit along a rugged trail which begins from kilometre-stone 69; you need to hire a guide from the visitor centre (best booked in advance) for the steep six-hour climb.

ARRIVAL AND DEPARTURE   NAM NAO NATIONAL PARK

By bus Several buses a day run through at irregular times from the bus stations in Khon Kaen, Phitsanulok and Loei – all about 2–3hr journeys.

By car The turn-off to the park headquarters is on Highway

12; look out for the sign at kilometre-stone 50, 147km west of Khon Kaen and 160km by road from Loei. The park entrance, where you'll be asked to pay, is 2km from the main road.

INFORMATION

Tourist information Once you've paid the admission fee, walk or hitch the 2km down the potholed road past the park HQ to the visitor centre, where you can pick up an

English-language brochure that contains a rough sketch map of the park.

ACCOMMODATION AND EATING

Visitor centre There are a dozen or so bungalows and a campsite (B30/person) near the visitor centre. Stalls near

the headquarters sell simple meals. Four-person unit **B1000**

Phu Reua National Park

B200 · ☎ 042 801716 or ☎ 042 807625, ⌚ dnp.go.th

The 120-square-kilometre **PHU REUA NATIONAL PARK**, 50km west of Loei, gets the name "Boat Mountain" from its resemblance to an upturned sampan, with the sharp ridge of its hull running southeast to northwest. The highest point of the ridge, Yod Phu Reua (1365m), offers one of the most spectacular panoramas in Thailand: the land drops away sharply on the Laos side, allowing views over toy-town villages and the Heuang and Mekong rivers to countless green-ridged mountains spreading towards Louang Phabang. To the northwest rises Phu Soai Dao (2102m) on Laos' western border; to the south are the Phetchabun mountains.

In the park itself, a day's worth of well-marked trails fans out over the mountain's meadows and pine and broad-leaved evergreen forests, taking in gardens of strange rock formations, orchids that flower year-round, the best sunrise viewpoint, Loan Noi, and, during and just after the rainy season, several waterfalls. The most spectacular **viewpoint**, Yod Phu Reua (Phu Reua Peak), is an easy 1km stroll from the top of the summit road. The park's population of barking deer, wild pigs and pheasants has

---

CHÂTEAU DE LOEI VINEYARD

If you happen to be driving yourself here from the west along Highway 203, it might be worth breaking your journey 10km from the Phu Reua turn-off at the **Château de Loei vineyard**, for the novelty value if nothing else: you can drive for 6km around the vast, incongruous fields of vines and taste a variety of wines and brandy, as well as getting something to eat at the simple restaurant and perusing a dizzying array of local foodstuffs in the attached shop.

5

declined over recent years, but you may be lucky enough to spot one of 26 bird species, which include the crested serpent-eagle, green-billed malkoha, greater coucal, Asian fairy-bluebird, rufescent prinia and white-rumped munia, as well as several species of babbler, barbet, bulbul and drongo.

Warm clothes are essential on cool-season nights – the lowest temperature in Thailand (-4°C) was recorded here in 1981 – and even by day the mountain is usually cool and breezy.

ARRIVAL AND DEPARTURE	PHU REUA NATIONAL PARK

The 9km paved road north from the village of Ban Phu Reua on Highway 203 to the summit means the park can get crowded at weekends, though during the week you'll probably have the place to yourself. On the summit road, you have to pay B200 admission at a checkpoint, before reaching the headquarters and Visitor Centre One after 4km.

By bus and songthaew There's no organized public transport up the steep summit road – regular Lom Sak and Phitsanulok buses (3 daily; 1hr 30min) from Loei can drop you at the turn-off to the park on Highway 203, but then you'll have to walk/hitch or charter a songthaew (B400–700, depending on how far up the mountain you want to be taken).

By bike The easiest way of accessing Phu Reua is probably to rent a motorbike at the *Sugar Guest House* in Loei (see p.485).

INFORMATION

Tourist information Visitor Centre One is 4km after the entrance checkpoint, and has a trail map and a simple restaurant. Visitor Centre Two (Phuson), a 3km walk or 5.5km drive further up the mountain near Hin Sam Chan waterfall, boasts several restaurants and is at the heart of the mountain's network of paths.

ACCOMMODATION

You can sleep in government-owned **bungalows** inside the park, which offer easy access to the trails. There are also plenty of private accommodation options, both on Highway 203 around Ban Phu Reua and on the summit road itself.

Chatchada Grand Resort At the eastern end of Ban Phu Reua, 1km towards Loei from the turn-off to the national park ☎ 042 899399 or ☎ 081 841 4111. Offers decent, spacious chalets that are set around a spacious lawn. All with hot water. Fan B500, a/c B2000

Phupet Hill Resort 800m up the summit road at 369 Moo 7 ☎ 042 899157 or ☎ 081 320 2874. A small and friendly place with large, attractive rooms and chalets with hot water, a/c and TV. B500

Visitor Centre One There are six four- to six-berth national park bungalows with hot showers at Visitor Centre One. Bungalows B2000–3000

Chiang Khan

A road runs parallel to the Mekong for 630km, linking the fast-growing border town of Mukdahan with **CHIANG KHAN**, a friendly town 55km north of Loei, which happily hasn't been entirely converted to concrete yet. Rows of shuttered wooden shophouses

---

THE MAGNIFICENT MEKONG

The **Mekong** is one of the great rivers of the world and the third longest in Asia, after the Yangtse and the Yellow rivers. From its source 4920m up on the east Tibetan plateau it roars down through China's Yunnan province – where it's known as Lancang Jiang, the "Turbulent River" – before snaking its way a little more peaceably between Burma and Laos, and then, by way of the so-called "Golden Triangle", as the border between Thailand and Laos. After a brief shimmy into rural Laos via Luang Prabang, the river reappears in Isaan to form 750km of the border between Thailand and Laos. From Laos it crosses Cambodia and continues south to Vietnam, where it splinters into the many arms of the Mekong Delta before flowing into the South China Sea, 4184km from where its journey began.

5

stretch out in a 2km ribbon parallel to the river, which for much of the year runs red with what locals call "the blood of the trees": rampant deforestation on the Lao side causes the rust-coloured topsoil to erode into the river. The town has only two streets – the main through-route (Highway 211), also known as **Thanon Sri Chiang Khan**, and the quieter **Thanon Chai Khong** on the waterfront – with a line of sois connecting them, numbered from west to east. There's a cool vibe to the place, with entrepreneurial young Thais setting up quirky new gift shops and guesthouses all the time and, away from all the kitsch, there are a few interesting sights to see. Arguably the most enjoyable thing you can do here is to join up with other travellers for a **boat trip** on the river.

Wat Tha Khaek

About 2km east of town along the main highway, turn left back towards the river

Wat Tha Khaek, a formerly ramshackle forest temple, has, on the back of millions of bahts' worth of donations from Thai tourists, embarked on an ambitious but slow-moving building programme in a bizarre mix of traditional and modern styles. The result is a temple that looks half finished, but if you grow weary of looking at the retro memorabilia that seems to clutter the main hotel street, it makes for a refreshing change.

Kaeng Kut Khu

East of town, about 1km along a side road from Wat Tha Khaek • Boats B400/30min

A kilometre from Wat Tha Khaek, the river runs over rocks at a wide bend to form the modest rapids of **Kaeng Kut Khu**. Set against the forested hillside of imaginatively named Phu Yai (Big Mountain), it's a pretty enough spot, with small restaurants and souvenir shops shaded by trees on the river bank. If you're feeling brave, try the local speciality *kung ten*, or "dancing shrimp" – fresh shrimp served live with a lime juice and chilli sauce. Boats can be rented here for a pootle around the rapids – you can also get a boat here from Chiang Khan.

Phu Thok

On Highway 211 just east of the turn-off to Wat Tha Khaek and Kaeng Kut Khu, follow the signpost down 3km of rough paved road, before forking right and climbing steeply for nearly 2km to the summit

With your own transport you could continue your explorations to **Phu Thok**, an isolated hill topped by a communications mast to the south of here. From there,

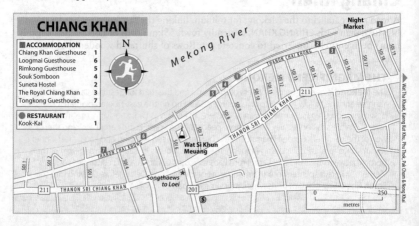

5

BOAT TRIPS FROM CHIANG KHAN

Most guesthouses can arrange these tours, or variations of them, charging per boat.

Downstream The journey to Pak Chom and back takes you through some of the most beautiful scenery on the Thai Mekong: hills and cliffs of all shapes and sizes advance and recede around the winding flow, and outside the rainy season, the rapids are dramatic without being dangerous (best Dec–April), and the shores and islands are enlivened by neat grids of market gardens. B3000/boat, around 6hr.

Kaeng Kut Khu (See opposite). B1000/boat.

Sunset on the Mekong The most basic of the boat trips, giving you the chance to see Chiang Khan from the water when the sunlight is at its best. B750/boat,

lasts around 1hr.

Upstream Upstream trips head west towards the lofty mountains of Khao Laem and Khao Ngu on the Thai side and Phu Lane and Phu Hat Song in Laos, gliding round a long, slow bend in the Mekong to the mouth of the Heuang River tributary, 20km from Chiang Khan. Stops can be arranged to share the fine views with Phra Yai, a 20m-tall golden Buddha standing on a hilltop at the confluence, and at Hat Sai Kaew, a sandy beach for swimming, fishing and picnicking. Best undertaken in the afternoon, returning at sunset. B1500/boat, around 3hr.

you'll be rewarded with splendid views of Chiang Khan, the Mekong and the striking patchwork of fields in the broad valley to the south, especially at sunset.

ARRIVAL AND DEPARTURE
CHIANG KHAN

By bus and songthaew Big, slow songthaews (roughly every 30min) and buses from Loei (roughly hourly) stop at the west end of town near the main junction of Highway

201 (the road from Loei) and Highway 211.

Destinations Bangkok (2 daily; 9–11hr); Khorat (hourly; 7hr); Loei (hourly, plus frequent songthaews; 45min–1hr).

GETTING AROUND

By bicycle and motorbike Most of Chiang Khan's guesthouses rent out bicycles (B50–100/day) and

motorbikes (B200–250/day).

ACCOMMODATION

Truly budget accommodation is getting harder to find in Chiang Khan as wealthy Thais tend to holiday here, which pushes prices up. Most guesthouses and hotels and can arrange herbal steam baths and traditional massages.

Chiang Khan Guesthouse Thanon Chai Khong, near Soi 19 ☎ 042 821691, ⓦ thailandunplugged.com. Fan rooms in a friendly, well-kept old wooden house with a riverside balcony upstairs. There are mosquito nets and shared hot-water bathrooms, and the owner, Pim, knows a lot about the area. Small discounts for solo travellers. B350

★ **Loogmai Guesthouse** 112 Thanon Chai Khong, near Soi 5 ☎ 042 822334 or ☎ 086 234 0011. Spacious, colonial-style white mansion, adorned with green shutters and hung with modern art. Most of the lovely, airy, fan rooms where one large room is en suite), and there's a pretty garden terrace overlooking the river. B400

Rimkong Guesthouse 294 Thanon Chai Khong, opposite Soi 8 ☎ 042 821125, ⓦ rimkhong.free.fr. There's a wide variety of recently refurbished wooden rooms here (some riverside), with mosquito screens and hot-water bathrooms, as well as French bread and filter coffee for breakfast. The helpful Thai-French owners, who have lived in Chiang Khan for years, are a good source of information on the area. B200

The Royal Chiang Khan 195 Thanon Chai Khong, between Soi 15 and 16 ☎ 089 900 9788, ⓦ royal

chiangkhan.9f.com. *The Royal* has to be given credit for its lavish and frankly bizarre styling, with exposed bricks and gleaming plastic panels all over the place. The a/c rooms here are individually themed and, as a general rule, the most expensive ones are on the top floors; our pick are the private rooms "Sunshine 2" and "Sunshine 4". The roof terrace has magnificent views. Wi-fi. B1800

Souk Somboon 243/3 Thanon Chai Khong, near Soi 9 ☎ 042 822334, ⓦ souksomboon.com. One of the bigger hotels on the street, with a/c, buffed wooden floors and a restaurant with sweeping views of the Mekong. Very popular with French tour groups. Wi-fi, plus a chauffeur service to and from the hotel. B800

Suneta Hostel Opposite Soi 15 on the river side of Thanon Chai Khong, at no. 187/1 ☎ 086 999 9218, ⓦ suneta.net. Fun, a/c and youthful-feeling wooden house with posters all over the walls and clean, hotel-style rooms that share bathrooms. A big hit with arty young Thais on holiday. B1200

Tonkong Guest House 62/1 Thanon Chai Khong, between sois 3 & 4 ☎ 042 821879, ⓔ ben_jama

5

@hotmail.com. A good variety of bright, clean and spacious rooms, including an en-suite family room that sleeps six and three simple rooms with fan and a shared

bathroom. Owner Ben (female) runs a cooking course (2–3hr; B500) which includes a trip to the local market. Wi-fi. Fan B450, a/c B650, family room B1200

EATING

Most visitors eat at their guesthouses or at the **night market**, which sets up along Thanon Chiang Khan, between sois 17 and 18, every night with everything from chicken on a stick to sweet, freshly made pancakes.

Kook-kai Between sois 9 and 10, on the river side of Thanon Chai Khong. As kooky as the name suggests, with a small riverside terrace that's strewn with fairy lights and hanging lanterns. No English, but French is

spoken, and there's a good selection of healthy noodles and vegetarian dishes available at bargain prices (from B40). Daily 4–10pm.

Sang Khom and around

The scenery downstream from Chiang Khan is still relatively wild, with just a couple of small towns dotted between the stretches of lush vegetation. Unfortunately there's no direct public transport along the river road between Chiang Khan and the otherwise forgettable town of Pak Chom, 41km downriver, so having your own wheels in this area is handy, if not vital. With the flexibility of a car or bike, a pleasant stopover on the much longer journey to Nong Khai is the peaceful town of Sang Khom, about 60km east of Pak Chom, which has some basic amenities and a smile-inducing location by the water.

Than Tip Falls

Beyond Pak Chom, the road through the Mekong valley becomes a little flatter and straighter. After 50km (10km from Sang Khom), a sign in English points down a side road to **Than Tip Falls**, 3km south, which is well worth seeking out. The 10m-high waterfall splashes down into a rock pool overhung by jungle on three sides; higher up, a bigger waterfall has a good pool for swimming, and if you can face the climb you can explore three higher levels.

Sang Khom

Staying in **SANG KHOM**, which straggles along the tree-shaded south bank of the Mekong about 60km east of Pak Chom, puts you in the heart of an especially lush stretch of the river within easy striking distance of several backroad villages and temples – a lovely guesthouse here offers bike rental and boat trips (see opposite).

Wat Hin Maak Peng

Another 19km east on Route 211, overlooking a narrow section of the Mekong, **Wat Hin Maak Peng** is a famous meditation temple, popular with Thai pilgrims and rich donors. The long white boundary wall, huge modern buildings and immaculate riverside gardens are evidence of the temple's prosperity, but its reputation is in fact based on the asceticism of the monks of the Thammayut sect, who keep themselves in strict poverty and allow only one meal a day to interrupt their meditation. The flood of merit-makers, however, proved too distracting for the founder of the wat, Luang Phu Thet, who before his death in 1994 decamped to the peace and quiet of Wat Tham Kham near Sakon Nakhon. Further east, between Tha Bo and Ban Nong Song Hong, the main route to Nong Khai passes Wat Phra That Bang Phuan (see p.499).

GETTING AROUND

By bus Buses run between Sang Khom and Bangkok (2 daily; 10hr), Loei (2–3 daily via Pak Chom; 3hr) and Nong Khai (2–3 daily; 3–4hr). From Loei, two or three small, green buses run daily to Pak Chom, Sang Khom and Nong Khai (as long as there are enough takers, and sometimes terminating at Pak Chom in the afternoon). To continue eastwards from Chiang Khan, you need to take a bus or songthaew

SANG KHOM AND AROUND

20km south down Highway 201 to Ban That, where you can pick up one of these buses towards Nong Khai.
By boat Trips up the Mekong (B200/person for groups of 2–4) can be booked with *Bouy Guest House* in Sang Khom.
By motorbike or bicycle You can rent motorbikes (B200/day) and bicycles (B50/day) at *Bouy Guest House* in Sang Khom.

ACCOMMODATION

★ **Bouy Guest House** By the river at 87/4 Thanon Ming Mueng ☎ 042 441065 ✉ toy_bgh@hotmail.com. The best of the accommodation in Sang Khom, enjoying a particularly choice location: decent bamboo huts, with beautiful views out over the river, are set in a spacious, flower-strewn compound on a spit of land that's reached by a wooden bridge over a small tributary. The welcoming owners can arrange day-trips to Ban Phu (see p.500), or if that sounds too strenuous, you can settle for a massage (B250) or just relax in the hammocks strung from the

veranda of each hut. Good Thai and Western food is available on a deck overlooking the stream (most of it also in vegetarian versions). B200
Bungalow Cake Resort On the Pak Chom side of town, just west of the bridge ☎ 042 441440 or ☎ 087 219 9184. The tidy, concrete bungalows here are set in a small, shady garden, with a large, attractive riverside terrace; some have a/c, hot water and TVs, but the best of them, with fans and cold-water bathrooms, overlook the Mekong. Fan B250, a/c B500

DIRECTORY

Bank Sang Khom has a bank and two ATMs.
Internet access Available at *Bouy Guest House* in Sang

Khom (B30/hr).

Nong Khai

The major border town in this corner of Isaan is **NONG KHAI**, an ethnically diverse town that's thrived since the construction of the **Thai-Australian Friendship Bridge** over the Mekong on the west side of town in 1994. Occupying a strategic position at the end of Highway 2 and the northeastern rail line, and just 24km from Vientiane, Nong Khai acts as a conduit for goods bought and sold by Thais and Lao, who are allowed to pass between the two cities freely for day-trips. Consequently, the covered souvenir market that sprawls to the east of the main pier, **Tha Sadet**, carries Lao silver, wood and cane items, as well as goods from as far afield as China, Korea and Russia, plus local basketware and silk.

5

As with most of the towns along this part of the Mekong, the thing to do in Nong Khai is just to take it easy, enjoying the **riverside atmosphere** and the peaceful settings of its guesthouses, which offer good value. Before you lapse into a relaxation-induced coma, though, try joining an evening **river-tour**, or make a **day-trip** out to see the impressive sculptures and rock formations in the surrounding countryside (see p.498).

Thanon Meechai

Nong Khai is laid out for 4km along the south bank of the Mekong. Running from east to west, Thanon Meechai dominates activity; the main shops and businesses are plumb in the middle around the post office and Tha Sadet. Although most of the old buildings have been replaced by concrete boxes, one or two weather-beaten wooden houses remain, their attractive balconies, porticoes and slatted shutters showing the influence of colonial architecture, which was imported from across the river before the French were forced out of Laos in 1954.

The riverside

The most pleasant place for a stroll is the riverside area. There's a pedestrianized promenade in the centre to the east of Tha Sadet, while things become more rustic and leafy around the fringes, which are often busy with people bathing, washing their clothes and fishing, especially in the early morning and evening.

Phra That Nong Khai

At the far eastern end of town

If you're lucky, you might catch sight of a sunken chedi at the far eastern end of town. **Phra That Nong Khai** slipped into the river during floods in 1847 and has since subsided so far that it's only visible in the dry season (though a replica has been constructed on the adjacent bank); this is thought to be a good spot to see naga fireballs (see p.496), said to be produced by the serpent that guards the relic of the Buddha's right foot in the chedi.

Hat Jommani

2km west of the centre beyond the Friendship Bridge

If you're toiling around Nong Khai in the dog days of the hot season, you might want to cool off at **Hat Jommani**, the so-called "Pattaya of Isaan": this sunny riverine beach can stretch for up to 200m when the river is at its lowest in April.

Wat Po Chai

Off the east end of Thanon Prajak

The main temple of the region is **Wat Po Chai**. The cruciform viharn, with its complex and elegant array of Lao tiers, shelters a venerated golden image, the Phra Sai Buddha, which is paraded around town and blessed with water during Songkhran. Prince

---

BOAT TRIPS FROM NONG KHAI

To catch the best of life on the river, take a **boat trip** on the *Nagarina*, which sets out from the *Mut Mee Guest House* every evening at around 5pm (B100) and runs up and down the length of Nong Khai for ninety minutes or so, sticking to the Thai side. Drinks are available and food (see p.498) can be ordered before the boat leaves. There's no stunning scenery, but plenty of activity on both river banks as the sun sets behind the Friendship Bridge.

SALA KAEO KOU, NONG KHAI (P.499) >

5

NAGA FIREBALLS

Nong Khai celebrates the generic Thai and Isaan **festivals** with due gusto, but in recent years a peculiarity of this stretch of the Mekong River has been attracting thousands of celebrants from Bangkok and beyond. Every year on the full-moon night in October, silent and vapourless **naga fireballs** appear from the river, small, pink spheres that float vertically up to heights of as much as 300m, then disappear; in some years, several thousand appear, in others, just a handful. A tentative scientific theory proposes that the balls are a combination of methane and nitrogen from decomposed matter on the bottom of the river, which reach a certain temperature at that time of the year and are released, combusting in the presence of oxygen when they break the water's surface; romantics will prefer the local belief that the nagas or naks (serpents) of the river breathe out the fireballs to call the Buddha to return to earth at the end of Buddhist Lent.

This strange occurrence has now been consolidated into the two-day festival of **Bang Fai Phaya Nak**, which coincides with Awk Phansa and the end of the longboat-racing season on the river. The fireballs have appeared as far afield as Sang Khom and Bung Kan, but are generally most numerous at Phon Phisai, 40km east of Nong Khai; if you make the trek out there, take great care on the way back, when the road is thronged with drunk drivers.

Chakri, the future Rama I, is said to have looted the image from Vientiane, along with the Emerald Buddha, but the boat which was bringing back the Phra Sai overturned and sank in the Mekong. Later, the statue miraculously rose to the surface and the grateful people of Nong Khai built this great hangar of a viharn to house it, decorating the walls with murals of its miraculous journey; the present king, Chakri's descendant, still comes every year to pay his respects. It's worth a visit for the Buddha's stagy setting, in front of a steep, flame-covered altar, dazzlingly lit from above and below. The solid gold head is so highly polished that you have to peer carefully to make out the Sukhothai influence in its haughty expression and beaked nose.

ARRIVAL AND DEPARTURE   NONG KHAI

By plane A/c minibuses (B150–200) from Udon Thani airport (see p.481) meet incoming flights from Bangkok and drop passengers at the Friendship Bridge or at their downtown hotels.

By train From Bangkok, you'll most likely be coming to Nong Khai by night train, arriving just after dawn at the station 3km southwest of the centre near the Friendship Bridge.

Destinations Ayutthaya (3 daily; 9hr 30min–11hr); Bangkok (3 daily; 11–13hr); Khon Kaen (4 daily; 2hr 45min); Khorat (1 daily; 6hr); Tha Naleng (Laos; 2 daily; 15min); Udon Thani (4 daily; 1hr).

By bus Day buses from all points in Isaan and night buses from further afield pull in at the bus station on the east side of town off Thanon Prajak; Udon Thani buses make an extra stop at the corner of highways 2 and 212.

Destinations Bangkok (20 daily; 11hr); Bung Kan (hourly; 2hr); Khon Kaen (20 daily; 3hr 30min); Khorat (20 daily; 6hr 30min); Loei (2–3 daily via Pak Chom; 7hr); Nakhon Phanom (7 daily; 6hr); Rayong (19 daily; 12hr); Sang Khom (2–3 daily; 3–4hr); Udon Thani (every 30min; 1hr); Vientiane (Laos; 6 daily; 1hr).

GETTING AROUND

As everything in Nong Khai is so spread out, you might want to consider hopping on a **tuk-tuk** for getting around, or renting a bicycle or motorbike.

By tuk-tuk Around B30–40 for a short journey such as bus station–Tha Sadet, up to B60 for bus station–train station. The rates for these and other journeys are posted up in the bus station.

By bicycle and motorbike Bicycles (B30/day) and

motorbikes (around B200/day) can be rented on Thanon Keawworut in front of the *Mut Mee Guest House*; bicycles are also available at *Mut Mee* itself (B69/day) and *Ruan Thai*, *Khiang Khong* and *Sawasdee* guesthouses.

INFORMATION

Tourist office The TAT office, 1.5km south of the centre on the west side of Highway 2 (daily 8.30am–4.30pm; ☏042

421326, ✉tat_nongkhai@yahoo.com), has information about local homestays.

CROSSING THE LAO BORDER VIA NONG KHAI

The crossing at Nong Khai is popular with tourists and relatively easy to use. Thais and Laos can cross the border via the ferry at Tha Sadet, but everyone else must use Nong Khai's **Thai-Australian Friendship Bridge** (daily 6am–10pm, although the buses across the bridge stop at 9pm, and we've had reports of it sometimes closing as early as 6pm).

GETTING A VISA ON ARRIVAL

To get a **visa at the border**, take a tuk-tuk to the foot of the bridge (about B30–40 from the railway station), where you'll be stamped out of Thailand. You'll then need to take a bus (B20) across the span itself to the Laos immigration post, where you can get a thirty-day tourist visa (see p.27) for US$30–42 (depending on nationality; pay $1 extra if you arrive after 6pm), plus one photo. It's possible to pay in baht at the bridge, though it's over the odds at B1500 and upwards; *Mut Mee Guest House* sells dollars at a decent rate, but if not, try the Porntip jewellery shop (☎081 6619988) within the covered market. From the Laos immigration post, you can catch a shared air-conditioned minibus (B100–150 per person), tuk-tuk (about B300/vehicle) or infrequent bus (B20) to Vientiane, 24km away.

WITH A VISA

If you have already arranged a visa through a Lao embassy or consulate, you can head straight from Nong Khai into Laos. Six daily **buses** run all the way through to Vientiane from the bus station (B55, plus B5 to Thai immigration). **Trains** also run from Nong Khai to Tha Naleng in Laos (2 daily; B20–50), but as the tracks stop here (around 20km from downtown Vientiane) you'll need to charter a tuk-tuk, car or minibus for the rest of the journey. The border is also accessible from further afield – there are direct buses from Udon Thani and Khon Kaen to Vientiane.

ACCOMMODATION

Grand Paradise Hotel 589 Moo 5, Nongkhai–Phonpisai road ☎042 420033, ⓦnongkhaigrand.com. On the southern bypass but handy for the centre, this mid-range hotel has high standards of service and a small swimming pool, but the blue-and-pink interiors take a bit of getting used to. There's also a rooftop terrace restaurant offering panoramic views over Nong Khai and Laos. Breakfast included. B1000

Janhom Apartment 479 Soi Srichumchuen, Thanon Prajak ☎042 460293. A modern, lime-green block on a quiet soi, set against the wall of Wat Sri Chum Chuen and with a pleasant, shady sitting area at the front. Not really apartments, though they are available by the month, with substantial discounts, but large, clean, a/c rooms with armchairs, fridges, TVs and hot-water bathrooms. Internet access. B350

Khiang Khong Guest House 541 Thanon Rimkhong ☎042 422870 or ☎081 832 3925. In a spruce, cream, modern block next door to *Ruan Thai*, spacious rooms with TVs and tiled, hot-water bathrooms that are on the small side. Laundry facilities and a nice first-floor terrace overlooking the water. Fan B300, a/c B400

Mut Mee Guest House 1111 Thanon Keawworut ☎042 460717, ⓦmutmee.com. A huge range of well-kept rooms sprawls around an attractive riverside restaurant at this magnet for travellers. Choose between ultra-basic single rooms (B150), clean twin rooms (both types share bathrooms) or top-notch en-suite doubles with

their own verandas. With helpful, well-informed staff, it also offers yoga, meditation and massage sessions (high season only), as well as local information about bicycle and motorbike tours and homestays. Julian, the English owner, has added loads of useful information about the area to the guesthouse's website. Fan B200, a/c B600

Pantawee Hotel 1049 Thanon Haisoke ☎042 411568, ⓦpantawee.com. A comfortable, efficiently run, though rather brash mid-range choice, festooned with neon and filled with muzak – often of the Christmas variety. The clean a/c rooms come with hot-water bathrooms, TVs, DVD players, fridges, computers and free wi-fi. There's also a small jacuzzi pool, a beer garden and a 24hr restaurant. Breakfast included, and enormous suites available. B700

Ruan Thai Guest House 1126 Thanon Rimkhong ☎042 412519. Renovated wooden houses in a quiet compound with attractive, well-maintained rooms, which range from keenly priced singles with shared hot-water bathrooms, through standard rooms with hot-water en suites to family rooms. Internet access available. Fan B300, a/c B400

★ **Sawasdee Guest House** 402 Thanon Meechai ☎042 412502, ⓔsawasdee_gh@hotmail.com. A grand old wooden shophouse set around a pleasant courtyard, with helpful and meticulous management: free luggage storage and showers available for those catching a night train or bus. Rooms are either fan-cooled (try to avoid those overlooking the noisy main road) with shared bathrooms

5

and hot showers available, or a/c with en-suite hot-water bathrooms. Facilities include massages, internet access and wi-fi. Fan B220, a/c B400

Siri Guest House 187/1–3 Thanon Hai Sok, just east of Mut Mee, close to the riverfront ☏ No phone. Rooms

at this friendly place run by two teachers come in two different sizes, although both types are very clean with good, strong a/c. The more expensive rooms are in a newer block, and come with in-room TVs. B500

EATING AND DRINKING

Nong Khai is a great place to sample Isaan cuisine, as well as Vietnamese at *Daeng Namnuang*, the town's most famous **restaurant**. If you're counting the baht, head for the night-time **stalls** on Thanon Prajak, near the corner of Soi Watnark, which include a good *phat thai* place on the north side of the road, and great fruit and vegetable smoothies on the south side.

★ **Daeng Namnuang** Thanon Rimkong ☻daeng namnuang.net. Delicious, inexpensive Vietnamese food at this immaculately clean and popular place, with an a/c room and a lovely riverside terrace. Specialities include *nam nuang* (Vietnamese sausages), fresh spring rolls and deep-fried prawns on sugar-cane skewers. Set meals from B160 per person. Mon–Wed noon–8pm, Thurs 8am–11pm, Fri–Sun 10am–9pm.

★ **Mut Mee Guest House** 1111 Thanon Keawworut. You're spoilt for choice at this traveller's favourite. The *Nagarina* floating restaurant specializes in seafood and Isaan dishes – try the squid with preserved eggs and the *som tam* with Chinese crispy bacon; the cosy, attached *Gaia* bar hosts singer-songwriters on Sunday night. Under bamboo shelters back on dry land, the main guesthouse

restaurant is inexpensive and relaxing: good Thai and Isaan dishes, particularly vegetarian versions, vie with tasty Western efforts including home-made apple pie. Small beer B60. Daily 10am–9pm.

Nam Tok Rim Khong Thanon Rimkhong (no English sign). Simple but popular and cheap restaurant in an old wooden building with an attractive terrace overlooking the river, specializing in *nam tok*, spicy hot beef salad (B50), as well as other Isaan delicacies such as *som tam*, dried beef and sausages. Daily lunchtime–8.30pm.

Tem-Im Soi Watnark, Thanon Meechai ☻tem-im.com. Cheap, tasty veggie buffet, plus *phat thai*, *som tam*, fresh juices and plenty of Western additions. Daily around 8am–6pm.

SHOPPING

Woven handicrafts are the main attraction here, shopping-wise. The northeastern method **mut mee** (literally "tied strings") involves tie-dyeing bundles of cotton thread before hand-weaving, which produces geometrical patterns on a coloured base. Tha Sadet market usually has a selection of ready-made clothes, wall hangings, bags and axe pillows.

Hornbill bookshop On the narrow lane leading down to *Mut Mee Guest House*. Stocks an excellent

selection of new and secondhand books in English. Mon–Sat 10am–7pm.

DIRECTORY

Internet access Available at plenty of places, including Oxynet, 569/2 Thanon Meechai (daily 9am–10pm).
Massages Good, strong body and foot massages can be had at Suan Sukapab, 623 Thanon Banterngjit

(☏042 423323).
Police The tourist police are based on Thanon Prajak (☏042 460186 or ☏1155).

Around Nong Khai

If you're not heading straight across the bridge to Laos, consider making a trip to **Sala Kaeo Kou**, also known as Wat Khaek, where you'll find dozens of curious stone sculptures. To the southwest of Nong Khai is **Wat Phra That Bang Phuan**, which offers some classic temple sightseeing, while the natural rock formations at **Ban Phu** and the spectacular temple **Wat Phu Tok** require much more effort and a full day out. The scenic riverside route upstream to Chiang Khan (see p.492) is also within day-tripping distance, and it's quite possible to get to **Ban Chiang** (see p.483) and back in a day, changing buses at Udon Thani.

Sala Kaeo Kou (Wat Khaek)

5km east of Nong Khai • Daily 6am–6pm • B20 • About B150 return in a tuk-tuk

By far the easiest and most popular day-trip out of Nong Khai takes in **Sala Kaeo Kou**, a short hop to the east. The temple is best known for its bizarre sculpture garden, which looks like the work of a giant artist on acid. Also known as Wat Khaek, it was founded by the late **Luang Phu Boonlua Surirat**, an unconventional Thai holy man who studied under a Hindu guru in Vietnam and preached in Laos until he was thrown out by the Communists in the 1970s. His charisma – those who drank water offered by him would, it was rumoured, give up all they owned to the temple – and heavy emphasis on morality attracted many followers among the farmers of Nong Khai. Luang Phu's popularity suffered, however, after his eleven-month spell in prison for insulting King Bhumibol, a crime alleged by jealous neighbours and probably without foundation; he died aged 72 in August 1996, a year after his release.

If you're heading over to Laos, the **Xiang Khouan** sculpture garden – Sala Kaeo Kou's precursor, 25km from downtown Vientiane on the Mekong River – shouldn't be missed; Luang Phu spent twenty years working on the sculptures there before his expulsion.

The sculpture garden

Arrayed with pretty flowers and plants, the **sculpture garden** bristles with Buddhist, Hindu and secular figures, all executed in concrete with imaginative abandon by unskilled followers under Luang Phu's direction. The religious statues, in particular, are radically modern. Characteristics that marked the Buddha out as a supernatural being – tight curls and a bump on the crown of the head called the *ushnisha* – are here transformed into beehives, and the *rashmis* on top (flames depicting the Buddha's fiery intellect) are depicted as long, sharp spikes. The largest statue in the garden shows the familiar story of the kindly naga king, Muchalinda, sheltering the Buddha, who is lost in meditation, from the heavy rain and floods: here the Buddha has shrunk in significance and the seven-headed snake has grown to 25m, with fierce, gaping fangs and long tongues.

Many of the statues illustrate **Thai proverbs**. Near the entrance, an elephant surrounded by a pack of dogs symbolizes integrity, "as the elephant is indifferent to the barking dogs". The nearby serpent-tailed monster with the moon in his mouth – Rahoo, the cause of eclipses – serves as an injunction to oppose all obstacles, just as the people of Isaan and Laos used to ward off eclipses by banging drums and firing guns. In the corner furthest from the entrance, you enter the complex Circle of Life through a huge mouth representing the womb, inside which a hermit, a policeman, a monk, a rich man and a beggar, among others, represent different paths in life (for a detailed map of the Circle of Life sculpture, go to ⓦmutmee.com). A man with two wives is shown beating the older one because he is ensnared by the wishes of the younger one, and an old couple who have made the mistake of not having children now find they have only each other for comfort.

The disturbingly vacant, smiling faces of the garden Buddhas bear more than a passing resemblance to Luang Phu himself, photos of whom adorn the **temple building**, a huge white edifice with mosque-like domes. On the second floor, his corpse is preserved on a domed palanquin, which is decorated with fairy lights and a virtual fish-tank.

Wat Phra That Bang Phuan

Ban Bang Phuan hamlet, around 22km southwest of Nong Khai on Highway 211 • Buses from Nong Khai to Pak Chom and Loei pass this way; depending on departure times it may be quicker to take an Udon-bound service 12km down Highway 2 to Ban Nong Song Hong, then change onto an Udon–Sri Chiangmai bus

More famous as the site of a now-concealed two-thousand-year-old Indian chedi than for its modern replacement, rural **Wat Phra That Bang Phuan** remains a highly revered place of pilgrimage.

5

The original **chedi** is supposed to have been built by disciples of the Buddha to hold 29 relics – pieces of breastbone – brought from India. A sixteenth-century king of Vientiane earned himself merit by building a tall Lao-style chedi over the top of the previous stupa; rain damage toppled this in 1970, but it was restored in 1977 to the fine, gleaming white edifice seen today. The unkempt compound also contains a small museum, crumbling brick chedis and some large open-air Buddhas.

Ban Phu

61km southwest of Nong Khai **Phu Phra Bat Historical Park** daily dawn–dusk • B30 **Information Centre** daily 8.30am–4.30pm

Deep in the countryside, the wooded slopes around the village of **BAN PHU** are dotted with strangely eroded sandstone formations, which have long exerted a mystical hold over people in the surrounding area. Local wisdom has it that the outcrops, many of which were converted into small temples from around the ninth century onwards, are either meteorites – believed to account for their burnt appearance – or, more likely, were caused by glacial erosion. Together with a stupa enshrining a Buddha footprint that is now an important pilgrimage site, especially during its annual festival in March, the rock formations have been linked up under the auspices of fifty-square-kilometre **Phu Phra Bat Historical Park**.

The **information centre** by the park entrance contains fairly interesting displays on the red prehistoric paintings of animals, humans, hands and geometric patterns that are found on the rock formations, and on the tale of Ussa and Barot. Around the information centre, a well-signposted network of **paths** has been cleared from the thin forest to connect 25 of the outcrops, each of which has a helpful English-language information board attached. It would take a good five hours to explore the whole park, but the most popular circuit, covering all the sights listed below, can be completed in an ambling two hours.

The outcrops

Among the most interesting of the outcrops are **Tham Wua** and **Tham Khon**, two natural shelters whose paintings of oxen and human stick figures suggest that the area was first settled by hunter-gatherers two to three thousand years ago. A legend that's well known in this part of Thailand and Laos accounts for the name of nearby **Kok Ma Thao Barot** (Prince Barot's Stable), a broad platform overhung by a huge slab of sandstone. A certain Princess Ussa, banished by her father to these slopes to be educated by a hermit, sent out an SOS that was answered by a dashing prince, Barot. The two fell in love and were married against the wishes of Ussa's father, prompting the king to challenge Barot to a distinctly oriental sort of duel: each would build a temple, and the last to finish would be beheaded. The king lost. Kok Ma Thao Barot is celebrated as the place where Barot kept his horse when he visited Ussa.

The furthest point of the circuit is the viewpoint at **Pha Sadej**, where the cliff drops away to give a lovely view across the green fields and forests of the Mekong valley to the distant mountains. More spectacular is **Hor Nang Ussa** (Ussa's Tower), a mushroom formed by a flat slab capping a 5m-high rock pillar. Under the cap of the mushroom, a shelter has been carved out and walled in on two sides. The *sema* found scattered around the site, and the square holes in which others would have been embedded, indicate that this was a shrine, probably during the ninth to eleventh centuries in the Dvaravati period. Nearby, a huge rock on a flimsy pivot miraculously balances itself against a tree at **Wat Por Ta** (the Father-in-Law's Temple); the walls and floor have been evenly carved out to form a vaguely rectangular shrine, with Dvaravati Buddha images dotted around.

5

Wat Phra Bat Bua Bok

The left fork shortly before the park entrance leads to **Wat Phra Bat Bua Bok**: a crude *that* built in imitation of Wat Phra That Phanom (see p.504), it's decorated with naive bas-reliefs of divinities and boggle-eyed monsters, which add to the atmosphere of simple, rustic piety. In a gloomy chamber in the tower's base, the only visible markings on the sandstone **Buddha footprint** show the Wheel of Law. Legend has it that the Buddha made the footprint here for a serpent that had asked to be ordained as a monk, but had been refused because it was not human. Higher up the slope, a smaller *that* perches on a hanging rock that seems to defy gravity.

ARRIVAL AND DEPARTURE   BAN PHU

By bus From Nong Khai, take the 7.15am bus to Ban Phu; if you leave any later you won't have time to see the park properly, as the whole journey takes at least a couple of hours and the last bus back leaves at around 3.15pm. From Ban Phu, it's another 14km west to the historical park; take a songthaew for the first 10km to the Ban Tiu intersection; from here a motorbike taxi will bring you the final 4km up to the main park entrance. If you are coming from Udon Thani, catch a bus from Talat Rungsina towards either Nam Som or Na Yung, which will drop you off at Ban Tiu.

Wat Phu Tok

The most compelling destination in the area to the east of Nong Khai is the extraordinary hilltop retreat of **Wat Phu Tok**. One of two sandstone outcrops that jut steeply out of the plain 35km southeast of Bung Kan, Phu Tok has been transformed into a meditation wat, its fifty or so monks building their scattered huts on perches high above breathtaking cliffs. The outcrop comes into sight long before you get there, its sheer red face sandwiched between green vegetation on the lower slopes and tufts of trees on the narrow plateau above. As you get closer, the horizontal white lines across the cliffs reveal themselves to be painted wooden walkways, built to give the temple seven levels to represent the seven stages of enlightenment.

The ornamental garden

In an ornamental garden at the base, reflected in a small lake, an elegant, modern marble chedi commemorates **Phra Ajaan Juen**, the famous meditation master who founded the wat in 1968 and died in a plane crash ten years later while on his way to Bangkok to celebrate the queen's birthday. Within the chedi, the monk's books and other belongings, and diamond-like fragments of his bones, are preserved in a small shrine.

HOMESTAYS IN THE NORTHEAST

The lazy **villages** just downstream from Nong Khai and close to Mukdahan can be a welcome breath of fresh air after traipsing around Isaan's dusty cities. There's a good selection of welcoming **homestays** to bed down in, providing an opportunity to unwind and enjoy the slow pace of rural Isaan – and many rent out bikes and motorbikes for local exploration.

Homestay Ban Kham Pia Off Highway 212 between Bung Kan and Nakhon Phanom, 3km southwest of Bung Khla, on the road running towards Phu Wua Wildlife Reserve ☎ 081 3059343, ⓦ homestaybkp .moonfruit.com. Close to a reserve that's packed with wildlife, this German-Thai run homestay offers simple wooden bungalows with a/c and TV. There's also an outdoor pool to splash about in, and you can rent motorbikes for B200/day. Internet available. Pick-up from Nong Khai can be arranged. B500

Thai House Isaan Around 60km southwest of Mukdahan, just off Highway 2042 ☎ 087 0654635, ⓦ thaihouse-isaan.com. Set around an attractive northeastern-style building in a peaceful Phu Thai village, with a handful of a/c bungalows and an apartment that has its own living room and karaoke machine. The owners can arrange tours of the local area, including a day-trip to Dinosaurland at Phuwiang National Park (B900/person, including lunch). Pick-ups available from Khon Kaen. B700

5

The ascent

The first part of the **ascent** of the outcrop takes you to the third level up a series of long, sometimes slippery, wooden staircases, the first of many for which you'll need something more sturdy than flip-flops on your feet. A choice of two routes – the left fork is more interesting – leads to the fifth and most important level, where the **Sala Yai** houses the temple's main Buddha image in an airy, dimly lit cavern. The artificial ledges that cut across the northeast face are not for the fainthearted, but they are one way of getting to the dramatic northwest tip here on level five: on the other side of a deep crevice spanned by a wooden bridge, the monks have built an open-sided Buddha viharn under a huge anvil rock (though the gate to the viharn is usually locked). This spot affords stunning **views** over a broad sweep of countryside and across to the second, uninhabited outcrop. The flat top of the hill forms the seventh level, where you can wander along overgrown paths through thick forest.

ARRIVAL AND DEPARTURE   WAT PHU TOK

Getting to Wat Phu Tok isn't easy – the location was chosen for its isolation, after all – but the journey out gives you a slice of life in remote countryside. The attached village sports a collection of simple **restaurants** and foodstalls.

By motorbike or tuk-tuk The best option is to rent a motorbike or charter a car or large tuk-tuk in Nong Khai (B1500–2000) – leave early to make it there and back in a day, allowing two hours to explore the temple.

By bus Going via public transport is a slog. Catch a bus from Nong Khai to Bung Kan (hourly; 2hr); once there, you might be lucky enough to coincide with one of the occasional songthaews to Phu Tok via Ban Siwilai, 25km south on Route 222; otherwise, take one of the hourly buses to Siwilai and charter a motorized samlor (B200–250) for the last 20km east to Phu Tok.

Nakhon Phanom

Beyond Bung Kan, the river road rounds the hilly northeastern tip of Thailand before heading south through remote country where you're apt to find yourself stopping for water buffalo as often as for vehicles. The Mekong can only be glimpsed occasionally until you reach **NAKHON PHANOM** ("City of Mountains"), 313km from Nong Khai, a clean and prosperous town which affords the finest view of the river in northern Isaan, framed against the giant ant hills of the Lao mountains opposite.

The town makes a pleasant place to hang out, its quiet, broad streets lined with some grand old public buildings, colonial-style houses and creaking wooden shophouses. But most importantly for those with their sights set on Laos, the town is home to the third Thai-Lao Friendship Bridge, which opened to much fanfare in November 2011.

Walking around town, you'll see several lit-up boat shapes around the place, a reminder of Nakhon Phanom's best-known festival, the **illuminated boat procession**, which is held on the river every year at the end of the rainy season, usually in late October. Around fifty boats of up to 10m in length, adorned with elaborate lights and carrying offerings of food and flowers, are launched on the river in a spectacular display. The week-long celebrations – marking the end of the annual three-month

---

BOAT TRIPS FROM NAKHON PHANOM

Even if you're not crossing the border, you can still appreciate the beautiful riverscape by joining one of the daily **boat trips** that depart from just south of the main pier at 5pm (B50; drinks available). Setting out as the sun begins to sink, they motor along between the banks nice and slowly, usually returning just before dark.

5

CROSSING VIA THE THIRD THAI-LAO FRIENDSHIP BRIDGE

Almost two-and-a-half years after foundation stones were laid on both sides of the Mekong, the third **Thai-Lao friendship bridge** finally opened in late 2011, at a site 8km north of Nakhon Phanom's town centre. At the time of writing, private cars were being allowed to cross for B50. It's not yet clear what the opening of the bridge means for the passenger **ferry** that leaves from the main pier across to **Khammouan** (Thakhek) in Laos (daily 8.30am–noon & 1–6pm; around 15 daily, mostly in the mornings and evenings; B60 one way). However you cross, thirty-day Lao **visas** will be available on arrival for US$30–42 (see p.27).

Buddhist Rains Retreat – also feature colourful dragon-boat races along the Mekong, pitting Thai and Lao teams against each other.

Ho Chi Minh's House

5km away on the southwestern edge of Nakhon Phanom at Ban Na Joke (ask for directions at TAT) • Daily 8am–5pm

The Vietnamese national hero, Ho Chi Minh, lived here in the late 1920s, when he was forced to go underground during the struggle for independence from France. The Vietnamese-style wooden house – terracotta roof tiles and no stilts – has recently been reconstructed, but is really only for Uncle Ho devotees; homestays at Ban Na Joke can be arranged through TAT.

ARRIVAL AND DEPARTURE

NAKHON PHANOM

By plane You can fly to Nakhon Phanom from Bangkok with Air Asia (1 daily; 1hr 15min); taxis from the airport 15km west of town cost B100 per person.

By bus The main bus station is about 1km west of the centre off the north side of Highway 22.

Destinations Bangkok (17 daily; 12hr); Khon Kaen (5 daily; 5hr 30min); Mukdahan (hourly; 2hr); Nong Khai (7 daily; 6hr); That Phanom (hourly; 1hr); Ubon Ratchathani (roughly hourly; 5hr); Udon Thani (14 daily; 5hr).

INFORMATION

Tourist information TAT has an office in an impressive old mansion at 184/1 Thanon Suntorn Vichit, corner of Thanon Salaklang (daily 8.30am–4.30pm; ☎042 513490–1, ☎ tatphnom@tat.or.th), 500m north of the pier for Laos; they also cover Mukdahan province.

ACCOMMODATION

Grand Hotel 210 Thanon Sri Thep, a block back from the river just south of the passenger ferry ☎042 511526. This echoey four-storey block has reasonably bright rooms, all with hot-water bathrooms. Fan B200, a/c B350

Nakhonphanom River View On Highway 212 towards the southern edge of town ☎042 522333–40, ☎ nakhonphanomriverviewhotel.com. This is the best place in town, with an outdoor swimming pool, internet access and smart, tasteful riverside rooms that boast wi-fi and bathtubs. B1050

Sri Thep Hotel 150m south of the Grand Hotel, on the opposite side of the road ☎042 512395. By far the friendliest budget choice, this Chinese-style hotel is a definite step up from the *Grand Hotel*, with red carpets and solid wooden furniture in its clean, airy rooms. Fan B300, a/c B400

EATING AND DRINKING

Thanon Fueng Nakhon, which runs west from the clocktower just north of the pier, has a choice of several simple places to **eat** and is a lively spot at night.

Satang A few hundred metres north of the Nakhonphanom River View Hotel. Among several riverside restaurants, friendly *Satang* stands out, though it has no English menu. You can sit at the pleasant tables out front or on an open balcony, tucking into specialities such as *thawt man kung* (deep-fried prawn cakes), *hor mok* (seafood curry soufflé) and *gataa rawn* (a sizzling hot plate of seafood). Daily roughly 11am–late.

DIRECTORY

Internet access Crab Technology, opposite the *Grand Hotel* on Thanon Sri Thep. Daily 8am–10pm.

Police There's a tourist police office on the riverfront just north of the *Nakhonphanom River View Hotel* (☎ 1155).

That Phanom

Fifty kilometres south of Nakhon Phanom, **THAT PHANOM**, a riverside village of weather-beaten wooden buildings, sprawls around Isaan's most important shrine, **Wat Phra That Phanom**. This far-northeastern corner of Thailand may seem like a strange location for one of the country's holiest sites, but the wat was built to serve both Thais and Lao, as evidenced by the ample boat-landing in the village. Plenty of Lao still come across the river for the fascinating Monday and Thursday morning waterfront **market**, bringing for sale such items as wild animal skins, black pigs and herbal medicines, alongside the usual fruit and veg.

Wat Phra That Phanom

Just off Highway 212, five blocks west from the Mekong

Popularly held to be one of the four sacred pillars of Thai religion (the other three are Chiang Mai's Wat Phra That Doi Suthep, Wat Mahathat in Nakhon Si Thammarat, and Wat Phra Phutthabat near Lopburi), **Wat Phra That Phanom** is a fascinating place of pilgrimage, especially at the time of the ten-day Phra That Phanom festival, usually in February, when thousands of people come to pay homage and enjoy themselves in the traditional holiday between harvesting and sowing; pilgrims believe that they must make the trip seven times during a full moon before they die.

The temple reputedly dates back to the eighth year after the death of the Buddha, when five local princes built a simple brick chedi to house bits of his breastbone. It's been restored or rebuilt seven times, most recently after it collapsed during a rainstorm in 1975; the latest incarnation is in the form of a Lao *that*, 57m high, modelled on the That Luang in Vientiane. From the river pier, a short ceremonial way leads under a Disneyesque **victory arch** erected by the Lao, past a stubby, brick replica of the original chedi on an island in a pond, then through the temple gates to the present chedi, which, as is the custom, faces water and the rising sun.

The chedi

A brick-and-plaster structure covered with white paint and gold floral decorations, the **chedi** looks like nothing so much as a giant, ornate table-leg turned upside down. From each of the four sides, an eye forming part of the traditional flame pattern stares down, and the whole thing is surmounted by an umbrella made of 16kg of gold, with precious gems and gold rings embedded in each tier. The chedi sits on a gleaming white marble platform, on which pilgrims say their prayers and leave every imaginable kind of offering to the relics. Look out for the **brick reliefs** in the shape of four-leaf clovers above three of the doorways in the base: on the northern side, Vishnu mounted on a garuda; on the western side, the four guardians of the earth putting offerings in the Buddha's alms bowl; and above the south door, a carving of the Buddha entering nirvana. At the corners of the chedi, brick plaques, carved in the tenth century but now heavily restored, tell the stories of the wat's princely founders.

ARRIVAL AND DEPARTURE

By bus The bus station is out on the western bypass, but all services from Nakhon Phanom and Mukdahan also stop in front of the temple; the Nakhon Phanom route is also covered by frequent songthaews, which gather to the north of the wat.

Destinations Bangkok (4 daily; 12hr); Mukdahan (hourly; 1hr 20min); Nakhon Phanom (hourly; 1hr); Ubon Ratchathani (hourly; 3–4hr); Udon Thani (4 daily; 4–5hr).

ACCOMMODATION

Kritsada Rimkhong Hotel & Resort 90 Moo 2, Thanon Rim Khong, 800m northeast of Wat Phra That Phanom ☎ 042 540038. A fairly safe bet (although don't expect a Phuket-style resort) with bright, well-kept rooms with a/c and hot water, some with fridges and small kitchen areas. Free wi-fi. B400

Saeng Thong Rim Khong 57 Moo 1, Thanon Rim Khong, southeast of the wat ☎ 042 555614. Probably the best truly cheap choice, but the rooms are far from inspiring. B250

EATING

That Phanom Pochana On the north side of the victory arch. Simple, clean, airy place that's good for a *phat thai* or a choice of Isaan, Thai and Chinese dishes.

There are also several riverside restaurants to the north of the pier and a night market just north of the temple.

DIRECTORY

Banks There are several banks with ATMs on Thanon Chayangkun near the wat.

Internet access There are places scattered around town, including one by the victory arch.

Mukdahan

Fifty kilometres downriver of That Phanom, **MUKDAHAN** is the last stop on the Mekong trail before Highway 212 heads off inland to Ubon Ratchathani, 170km to the south. You may feel a long way from the comforts of Bangkok out here, but this is one of the fastest-developing Thai provinces, owing to increasing friendship between Laos and Thailand and the proximity of **Savannakhet**, the second-biggest Lao city, just across the water. Few farang visitors make it this far, though Mukdahan–Savannakhet is an officially sanctioned crossing to Laos, via the new bridge 7km north of town, and as the cranes dominating the skyline show, new hotels are springing up all the time.

Indochina Market

The promenade overlooking Savannakhet is swamped by the daily **Indochina Market**, which is especially busy at weekends. On sale here are household goods and inexpensive ornaments, such as Vietnamese mother-of-pearl and Chinese ceramics, brought over from Laos; the market is also good for local fabrics like lengths of coarsely woven cotton in lovely muted colours, and expensive but very classy silks.

Mukdahan Tower

Daily 8am–6pm • B20

At the southern edge of town rises the 65m-high **Mukdahan Tower** (*Ho Kaeo Mukdahan*), a modern white edifice that looks somewhat out of place in the low-rise outskirts. Built in 1996 to commemorate the fiftieth anniversary of the king's accession to the throne, the tower houses an interesting array of historic artefacts from the Mukdahan area, including traditional Isaan costumes, pottery, coins, amulets, vicious-looking weaponry and fossils. The highlight, however, is the expansive view from the sixth floor – 50m high to reflect

---

CROSSING THE LAO BORDER VIA MUKDAHAN

Mukdahan–Savannakhet is an officially sanctioned **crossing** to Laos, via the second **Thai-Lao Friendship Bridge**, 7km north of town. Buses (12 daily 8.30am–7pm; B45–50) cross the bridge to **Savannakhet**, and it's possible to get a visa on arrival (US$30–42; see p.27 for further details). When being stamped out of the country, you may be charged B20 by the officials.

5

fifty years of Rama IX – over Mukdahan and the Mekong into Laos. On the smaller floor above is a much-revered, Sukhothai-style silver Buddha image, the Phra Phuttha Nawaming Mongkhon Mukdahan, fronted by the bone relics of famous monks in small glass containers.

ARRIVAL AND DEPARTURE   MUKDAHAN

By bus Hourly buses from That Phanom and Ubon Ratchathani stop at the bus terminal about 2km northwest of the centre on Highway 212.
Destinations Bangkok (20 daily; 11hr); Khon Kaen (every

30min; 4hr); Khorat (20 daily; 6hr); Nakhon Phanom (hourly; 2hr); That Phanom (hourly; 1hr 20min); Ubon Ratchathani (roughly hourly; 2–3hr); Udon Thani (5 daily; 4hr–4hr 30min).

GETTING AROUND

By bicycle and motorbike *Huanum* hotel has mountain bike (B100/day) and motorbike rental (B250/day).
By songthaew Songthaews shuttle between the bus station and Mukdahan Tower via the corner of Thanon

Pitakpanomkhet, the main east–west street, and Thanon Samut Sakdarak, the main north–south street (B10–15/person).

ACCOMMODATION

Huanum 36 Thanon Samut Sakdarak at the corner of Thanon Song Nang Sathit, a block back from the pier ☎ 042 611137, ✉ pueeainbkk@hotmail.com. Fresh, good-value rooms – choose between simple ones with shared cold-water bathrooms and smarter, quieter affairs overlooking the internal courtyard with a/c, en-suite hot showers and TVs. The brown blankets aren't particularly appealing, but for the money, it's hard to complain. There's a surprisingly modern café in the lobby serving Western breakfasts and great coffees. Fan B150, a/c B300
Ploy Palace Hotel West of the centre at 40 Thanon Pitakpanomkhet ☎ 042 631111, ⓦ ploypalace.com.

A grand pink edifice with a marbled lobby and tasteful bedrooms, this is probably the best of Mukdahan's big business hotels, with good service, a rooftop restaurant with fine views and an outdoor swimming pool on the third floor. B1250
Riverfront 22 Thanon Somranchaikhong, opposite the Indochina Market ☎ 042 633348, ⓦ riverfront mukdahan.com. The wood-fronted lobby of this place is right by the main river road. The best rooms have balconies that face Laos, and inside there are TVs, a/c and microwaves. All are en suite, and there's a smart new coffee shop attached to the lobby downstairs. B750

EATING AND DRINKING

There's a lively, popular **night market** selling deep-fried insects and plenty of other Isaan specialities, four blocks back from the pier along Thanon Song Nang Sathit.

Kingdom Country Club Opposite Mukdahan Tower. Good-time country-and-western-style bar with live Thai pop and folk music. Daily until late.
Riverside 1km south of the pier on Thanon Somranchaikhong. Of the handful of restaurants that dot

the riverfront promenade, the best – and priciest – is the popular *Riverside*, which serves excellent food on a pretty bougainvillea-covered terrace built out over the Mekong. Daily noon–late.

Mukdahan National Park

15km southeast of town • B100 • ☎ 042 601753, ⓦ dnp.go.th • Accessed via R2034 along the Mekong – regular songthaews from Mukdahan's bus terminal to Don Tan pass the turning for the park 14km out of town, then it's 1km walk uphill to the park headquarters

If you're tired of concrete Isaan towns, stretch your legs exploring the strange rock formations and beautiful waterfalls of **Mukdahan National Park** (aka Phu Pha Terp). Just above the headquarters is a hillside of bizarre rocks, eroded into the shapes of toadstools, camels and crocodiles, which is great for scrambling around. The hillside also bears two remnants of the area's prehistory: the red finger-painting under one of the sandstone slabs is reckoned to be four thousand years old, while a small cage on the ground protects a 75-million-year-old fossil. Further up, the bare sandstone ridge seems to have been cut out of the surrounding forest by a giant lawnmower, but from

October to December it's brought to life with a covering of grasses and wildflowers. A series of ladders leads up a cliff to the highest point, on a ridge at the western end of the park (a 2km walk from the headquarters), which affords a sweeping view over the rocks to the forests and paddies of Laos. Nearby, at least from July to November, is the park's most spectacular waterfall, a 30m drop through thick vegetation, and a cave in which villagers have enshrined scores of Buddha images.

ACCOMMODATION AND EATING   MUKDAHAN NATIONAL PARK

The simple **foodstalls** near headquarters will keep you going with fried rice and noodles.

Bungalow Near the headquarters. The park has just one standard-issue bungalow, sleeping six. It's also possible to camp here, but you will need to bring your own gear. B1800

Southern Thailand: the Gulf coast

FULL MOON PARTY ON KO PHA NGAN AT SUNRISE

Southern Thailand: the Gulf coast

Southern Thailand's gently undulating Gulf coast is famed above all for the Samui archipelago, three small, idyllic islands lying off the most prominent hump of the coastline. This is the country's most popular seaside venue for independent travellers, and a lazy stay in a beachfront bungalow is so seductive a prospect that most people overlook the attractions of the mainland, where the sheltered sandy beaches and warm clear water rival the top sunspots in most countries. Added to that you'll find scenery dominated by forested mountains that rise abruptly behind the coastal strip, and a sprinkling of fascinating historic sights.

The crumbling temples of ancient **Phetchaburi** are the first historic sight you'll meet heading south out of Bangkok and fully justify a break in your journey. Beyond, the stretch of coast around **Cha-am** and **Hua Hin** is popular with weekending Thais escaping the capital and is crammed with condos, high-rise hotels and bars, not to mention a large population of foreign tourists. Far quieter and preferable are the beaches further south: the sophisticated little resort of **Pak Nam Pran**; golden-sand **Hat Phu Noi**, which is also the best base for exploring the karsts and caves of **Khao Sam Roi Yot National Park**; the welcoming town of **Prachuap Khiri Khan**, fronted by a lovely bay and flanked by an equally appealing beach; and laidback, lightly developed **Ban Krud**.

Of the islands, **Ko Samui** is by far the most naturally beautiful, with its long white-sand beaches and arching fringes of palm trees. The island's beauty has not gone unnoticed by tourist developers of course, and its varied spread of accommodation these days draws as many package tourists and second-homers as backpackers. In recent years the next island out, **Ko Pha Ngan**, has drawn increasing numbers of independent travellers away from its neighbour: its accommodation is generally simpler and cheaper than Ko Samui's, and it offers a few stunning beaches with a more laidback atmosphere. The island's southeastern headland, **Hat Rin**, has no fewer than three white-sand beaches to choose from, but now provides all the amenities the demanding backpacker could want, not to mention its notorious full moon parties. The furthest inhabited island of the archipelago, **Ko Tao**, has taken off as a **scuba-diving** centre, but despite a growing nightlife and restaurant scene, still has the feel of a small, rugged and isolated outcrop.

Tucked away beneath the islands, **Nakhon Si Thammarat**, the cultural capital of the south, is well worth a short detour from the main routes through the centre of the peninsula – it's a sophisticated city of grand old temples, delicious cuisine and distinctive handicrafts. With its small but significant Muslim population, and machine-gun dialect, Nakhon begins the transition into Thailand's deep south.

Highlights

❶ Phetchaburi Charming historic town, boasting several fine old working temples, as well as delicious traditional desserts. **See p.513**

❷ Pak Nam Pran Chic, artfully designed boutique hotels on a long, sandy beach, a popular weekend escape for design-conscious Bangkokians. **See p.526**

❸ Ang Thong National Marine Park A dramatic, unspoilt group of over forty remote islands, accessible on boat-trips from Ko Samui or Ko Pha Ngan. **See p.557**

❹ Full moon at Hat Rin, Ko Pha Ngan Party on, and on… **See p.564**

❺ Ao Thong Nai Pan on Ko Pha Ngan Beautiful, secluded bay with good accommodation. **See p.568**

❻ A boat-trip round Ko Tao Satisfying exploration and great snorkelling, especially off the unique causeway beaches of Ko Nang Yuan. **See p.571**

❼ Nakhon Si Thammarat Historic holy sites, intriguing shadow puppets, great-value accommodation and excellent cuisine. **See p.580**

❽ Krung Ching waterfall Walk past giant ferns and screeching monkeys to reach this spectacular drop. **See p.587**

HIGHLIGHTS ARE MARKED ON THE MAP ON P.512

SOUTHERN THAILAND: THE GULF COAST

BANGKOK

Ratchaburi

Samut Songkhram

Phetchaburi ❶

Cha-am

KAENG KRACHAN NATIONAL PARK

Pala-u Falls

Hua Hin ❷

Pranburi

Pak Nam Pran
Hat Phu Noi

Kuiburi

KHAO SAM ROI YOT NATIONAL PARK

Prachuap Khiri Khan

BURMA

Wang Duan

Ban Krud

Bang Saphan Yai
Suan Luang

GULF OF THAILAND

Thung Wua Laen

Chumphon

Hat Sai Ri
Ao Thung Makham

Ranong

Lang Suan

❻ Ko Tao

ANDAMAN SEA

Wat Suan Mokkh

Chaiya

ANG THONG NATIONAL MARINE PARK

❺ Ko Pha Ngan

❸

❹

Don Sak

Khanom

Surat Thani

Phunphin

Sichon

KHAO SOK NATIONAL PARK

❽ Krung Ching

Phang Nga

Khao Luang (1835m)

❼ Nakhon Si Thammarat

Thung Song

Ron Phibun

Krabi

Phuket

Trang

Phatthalung

Pattaya

HIGHLIGHTS

❶ Phetchaburi
❷ Pak Nam Pran
❸ Ang Thong National Marine Park
❹ Full moon at Hat Rin, Ko Pha Ngan
❺ Ao Thong Nai Pan on Ko Pha Ngan
❻ A boat-trip round Ko Tao
❼ Nakhon Si Thammarat
❽ Krung Ching waterfall

Ko Samui

0	50

kilometres

N

The Gulf coast has a slightly different **climate** from the Andaman coast and much of the rest of Thailand, being hit heavily by the northeast monsoon's rains, especially in November, when it's best to avoid this part of the country altogether. Most times during the rest of the year should see pleasant, if changeable, weather, with some effects of the southwest monsoon felt between May and October. Late December to April is the driest period, and is therefore the region's high season, which also includes July and August.

ARRIVAL AND GETTING AROUND   THE GULF COAST   6

The main arteries through this region are highways 4 (also known as the Phetkasem Highway, or usually Thanon Phetkasem when passing through towns) and 41, served by plentiful buses.

By plane The main airports in this region are on Ko Samui, at Surat Thani and Nakhon Si Thammarat, the latter two providing, in combination with buses and boats, cheaper but slower competition for getting to the islands.

By train The railway from Bangkok connects all the mainland towns, including a branch line to Nakhon; nearly all services depart from Hualamphong Station, but a few slow trains use Thonburi Station. You can also head south from Kanchanaburi by train, changing at Ban Pong or Nakhon Pathom.

By boat Daily boats run to all three main islands from two jumping-off points: Surat Thani, 650km from Bangkok, is close to Ko Samui and is generally more convenient for Ko Pha Ngan too, but if you're heading from Bangkok to Pha Ngan you might want to consider Chumphon, which is certainly the main port for Ko Tao.

Phetchaburi

Straddling the Phet River about 120km south of Bangkok, the provincial capital of **PHETCHABURI** (sometimes "Phetburi") has been settled ever since the eleventh century, when the Khmers ruled the region, but only really got going six hundred years later, when it flourished as a trading post between the Andaman Sea ports and Ayutthaya. Despite periodic incursions from the Burmese, the town gained a reputation as a cultural centre – as the ornamentation of its older temples testifies – and after the new capital was established in Bangkok it became a favourite country retreat of Rama IV, who had a hilltop palace, **Phra Nakhon Khiri**, built here in the 1850s. Modern Phetchaburi is known for its limes and rose apples but its main claim to fame is as one of Thailand's finest sweet-making centres, the essential ingredient for its assortment of *khanom* being the sugar extracted from the sweet-sapped palms that cover the province. This being very much a cottage industry, today's downtown Phetchaburi has lost relatively little of the ambience that so attracted Rama IV: the central riverside area is hemmed in by historic wats in varying states of disrepair, along with plenty of traditional wooden shophouses. The town's top three temples, described below, can be seen on a leisurely two-hour circular walk beginning from Chomrut Bridge, while Phetchaburi's other significant sight, the palace-museum at Phra Nakhon Khiri, is on a hill about 1km west of the bridge.

Despite the attractions of its old quarter, Phetchaburi gets few overnight visitors as most people see it on a day-trip from Bangkok, Hua Hin or Cha-am. It's also possible to combine a day in Phetchaburi with an early-morning expedition from Bangkok to the floating markets of Damnoen Saduak, 40km north; budget tour operators in Bangkok's Thanon Khao San area offer this option as a day-trip package for about B600 per person. The town sees more overnighters during the **Phra Nakhon Khiri Fair**, spread over at least five days in February, which features parades in historic costumes, cooking demonstrations and traditional entertainments such as *likay* and *lakhon*.

Wat Yai Suwannaram

Thanon Phongsuriya, about 700m east of Chomrut Bridge

Of all Phetchaburi's temples, the most attractive is the still-functioning seventeenth-century **Wat Yai Suwannaram**. The temple's fine old teak **sala** has elaborately carved doors, bearing a gash reputedly inflicted by the Burmese in 1760 as they plundered their way towards Ayutthaya. Across from the *sala* and hidden behind high, whitewashed walls stands the windowless Ayutthaya-style bot. The bot compound overlooks a pond, in the middle of which stands a small but well-preserved scripture library, or **ho trai**: such structures were built on stilts over water to prevent ants and other insects destroying the precious documents. Enter the walled compound from the south and make a clockwise tour of the cloisters filled with Buddha statues before entering the bot itself via the eastern doorway (if the door is locked, one of the monks will get the key for you). The **bot** is supported by intricately patterned red and gold pillars and contains a remarkable, if rather faded, set of murals, depicting Indra, Brahma and other lower-ranking divinities ranged in five rows of ascending importance. Once you've admired the interior, walk to the back of the bot, passing behind the central cluster of Buddha images, to find another Buddha image seated against the back wall: climb the steps in front of this statue to get a close-up of the left foot, which for some reason was cast with six toes.

Wat Kamphaeng Laeng

Thanon Phra Song, a 15min walk east and then south of Wat Yai

The five tumbledown prangs of **Wat Kamphaeng Laeng** mark out Phetchaburi as the likely southernmost outpost of the Khmer empire. Built probably in the thirteenth century to honour the Hindu deity Shiva and set out in a cruciform arrangement facing east, the laterite corncob-style prangs were later adapted for Buddhist use, as can be seen from the two that now house Buddha images. There has been some attempt to restore a few of the carvings and false balustraded windows, but these days

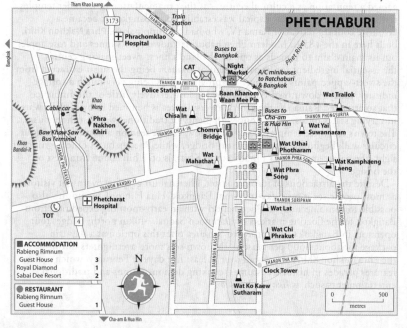

PHETCHABURI

ACCOMMODATION
Rabieng Rimnum	
Guest House	3
Royal Diamond	1
Sabai Dee Resort	2

RESTAURANT
| Rabieng Rimnum | |
| Guest House | 1 |

0 — 500 metres

worshippers congregate in the modern whitewashed wat behind these shrines, leaving the atmospheric and appealingly quaint collection of decaying prangs and casuarina topiary to chickens, stray dogs and the occasional tourist.

Wat Mahathat

Thanon Damnoen Kasem

Heading west along Thanon Phra Song from Wat Kamphaeng Laeng, across the river you can see the prangs of Phetchaburi's most fully restored and important temple, **Wat Mahathat**, long before you reach them. Boasting the "Mahathat" title only since 1954 – when the requisite Buddha relics were donated by the king – it was probably founded in the fourteenth century, but suffered badly at the hands of the Burmese. The five landmark prangs at its heart are adorned with stucco figures of mythical creatures, though these are nothing compared with those on the roofs of the main viharn and the bot. Instead of tapering off into the usual serpentine *chofa*, the gables are studded with miniature *thep* and *deva* figures (angels and gods), which add an almost mischievous vitality to the place. In a similar vein, a couple of gold-embossed crocodiles snarl above the entrance to the bot, and a caricature carving of a bespectacled man rubs shoulders with mythical giants in a relief around the base of the gold Buddha, housed in a separate mondop nearby.

Khao Wang

Dominating Phetchaburi's western outskirts stands Rama IV's palace, a stew of mid-nineteenth-century Thai and European styles scattered over the crest of the hill known as **Khao Wang** ("Palace Hill"). During his day, the royal entourage would struggle its way up the steep brick path to the summit, but now there's a **cable car** (daily 8.30am–4.30pm; B40 return) which starts from the western flank of the hill off Highway 4; there's also a path up the eastern flank, starting near Thanon Rajwithi. If you do walk up the hill, be warned that hundreds of quite aggressive monkeys hang out at its base and on the path to the top.

Up top, the wooded hill is littered with wats, prangs, chedis, whitewashed gazebos and lots more, in an ill-assorted combination of architectural idioms – the prang-topped viharn, washed all over in burnt sienna, is particularly ungainly. Whenever the king came on an excursion here, he stayed in the airy summer house, **Phra Nakhon Khiri** (daily 9am–4pm; B150), with its Mediterranean-style shutters and verandas. Now a museum, it houses a moderately interesting collection of ceramics, furniture and other artefacts given to the royal family by foreign friends. Besides being cool and breezy, Khao Wang also proved to be a good stargazing spot, so Rama IV, a keen astronomer (see p.530), had an open-sided, glass-domed observatory built close to his sleeping quarters.

ARRIVAL AND DEPARTURE | PHETCHABURI

BY TRAIN

Phetchaburi station is on the north side of the town centre.

Destinations Bangkok (Hualamphong Station 10 daily, Thonburi Station 3 daily; 2hr 45min–3hr 45min); Chumphon (10 daily; 4hr–6hr 30min); Hat Yai (4 daily; 11hr 30min–13hr 30min); Hua Hin (12 daily; 1hr); Nakhon Pathom (13 daily; 1hr 30min–2hr); Nakhon Si Thammarat (2 daily; 12–13hr); Prachuap Khiri Khan (11 daily; 2–3hr); Ratchaburi (13 daily; 40min–1hr); Surat Thani (8 daily; 6hr 45min–9hr); Trang (2 daily; 13hr).

BY BUS

Phetchaburi is served mostly by through-buses on their way to or from Bangkok – all services between the capital and southern Thailand have to pass through the town on Highway 4.

Through-buses There's a small Baw Khaw Saw terminal on the east side of Highway 4 (Thanon Phetkasem), which is where southbound through-buses will set you down or pick you up. Northbound through-buses on their way to Bangkok stop on the opposite side of the highway: ask to get off at "Sii Yaek Phetcharat", the crossroads of Highway 4 and Thanon Bandai-It by Phetcharat Hospital – otherwise you might be put off at the Big C Department Store about 5km south of town. Songthaews and motorbike taxis run between Highway 4 and the town centre.

From/to Cha-am and Hua Hin Non-a/c buses from and to Cha-am and Hua Hin use the small terminal in the town centre, less than a 10min walk from Chomrut Bridge.

From/to Bangkok The terminal for dedicated Phetchaburi–Bangkok a/c buses is about a 10min walk from Chomrut Bridge, just off Thanon Rajwithi. Note that if you're coming here from Kanchanaburi, you can avoid

Bangkok by heading for Ratchaburi, where you can catch a bus, a/c minibus or train to Phetchaburi.

Destinations Bangkok (4–7 daily; 2hr 15min); Cha-am (every 30min; 1hr 20min); Hua Hin (every 30min; 1hr 50min).

BY MINIBUS

Several companies offer licensed a/c minibuses to Victory Monument in Bangkok, including one just east of the night market and the river (marked on our map) that also covers Ratchaburi.

GETTING AROUND

By samlor or songthaew Shared songthaews circulate round the town, but to see the major temples in a day and have sufficient energy left for climbing Khao Wang, you might want to hire a samlor or a songthaew for a

couple of hours, at about B100/hr.

By bicycle or motorbike You can rent bicycles (B120/day) and motorbikes (B250–350/day) from *Rabieng Rimnum Guest House*.

INFORMATION AND TOURS

Rabieng Rimnum Guest House There's no TAT office in town, but *Rabieng Rimnum Guest House* (see below) is a good source of local information. It also offers internet

access and organizes day-trips and overnight visits to Kaeng Krachan National Park for bird-watching and hiking from November to July.

ACCOMMODATION

Rabieng Rimnum (Rim Nam) Guest House 1 Thanon Chisa-in, on the southwest corner of Chomrut Bridge ☎032 425707 or ☎089 919 7446, ⚲rabiengrimnum .com. Occupying a century-old house next to the Phet River and, less appealingly, a noisy main road, this popular, central guesthouse offers nine simple rooms with shared, cold-water bathrooms, lots of local information and the best restaurant in town. Excellent rates for singles. **B240**

Royal Diamond Soi Sam Chao Phet, in a grid of small streets just off the Phetkasem Highway ☎032 411061–70, ⚲royaldiamondhotel.com. On the northwest side of Khao Wang, this welcoming place is

Phetchaburi's best upmarket option. The large, comfortable a/c rooms with hot water, TVs, fridges and free wi-fi are fairly well insulated from the noise of the highway (though not necessarily from the live bands in the hotel's own beer garden). Very modest breakfast included. **B800**

Sabai Dee Resort Thanon Khong Kacheng ☎086 344 4418. Your best budget option if *Rabieng Rimnum* across the street is full. All sharing cold-water bathrooms, accommodation is either in very simple bamboo bunga-lows with mosquito nets in a small garden by the river, or in slightly more expensive, large, white rooms with polished wooden floors in the main building. **B250**

EATING

As well as for *khanom*, Phetchaburi is famous for savoury **khao jae**: originally a Mon dish designed to cool you down in the hot season, it consists of rice in chilled, flower-scented water served with delicate, fried side dishes, such as shredded Chinese radish and balls of shrimp paste, dried fish and palm sugar. It's available at the day market until sold out, usually around 3pm.

PHETCHABURI'S KHANOM

Almost half the shops in Phetchaburi stock the town's famous **khanom** (sweet snacks), as do many of the souvenir stalls crowding the base of Khao Wang and vendors at the day market on Thanon Matayawong. The most well-known local speciality is *maw kaeng* (best sampled from Raan Khanom Waan Mee Pin on the west side of Thanon Matayawong, just north of Phongsuriya), a baked sweet egg custard made with mung beans and coconut and sometimes flavoured with lotus seeds, durian or taro. Other Phetchaburi classics to look out for include *khanom taan*, small, steamed, saffron-coloured cakes made with local palm sugar, coconut and rice flour, and wrapped in banana-leaf cases; and *thong yot*, orange balls of palm sugar and baked egg yolk.

Rabieng Rimnum Guest House 1 Thanon Chisa-in, on the southwest corner of Chomrut Bridge ☎032 425707 or ☎089 919 7446, ⦿rabiengrimnum.com. The town's best restaurant, an airy, wooden house with riverside tables attached to the guesthouse of the same name. It offers a long and interesting menu of inexpensive Thai dishes, from banana-blossom salad (B70) to the tasty Phetchaburi speciality, sugar-palm fruit curry with prawns (B75), and is deservedly popular with local diners. Daily 7.30am–midnight.

Cha-am and around

6

Forever in the shadow of its more famous neighbour, Hua Hin, 25km to the south, the resort of **CHA-AM** is nevertheless very popular with Thais on short breaks, and it sports one or two package-holiday high-rises and Western-style restaurants for Europeans, too. Mostly, though, it's weekending families and partying student groups from Bangkok who eat and drink at the rows of umbrella-shaded tables and deckchairs on the sand, or brave the sea on banana boats or rubber tyres, the women clad modestly in T-shirts and shorts rather than bikinis. The long, straight beach here is pleasantly shaded, though rather gritty and very narrow at high tide, and the water is perfectly swimmable, if not pristine. During the week the pace of life in Cha-am is slow, and it's easy to find a solitary spot under the thick canopy of casuarinas, particularly at the northerly end of the beach, but that's rarely possible at weekends, when prices shoot up and traffic thickens considerably.

Cha-am has a functional pocket of development around Thanon Phetkasem (Highway 4), close to the junction with Thanon Narathip, the main access road to the beach, 1km to the east. However, the 3km seaside promenade of Thanon Ruamchit is where you'll find most of the hotels, restaurants, a small police station (corner of Thanon Narathip), several internet shops and a few other tourist-oriented businesses; Thanon Ruamchit's sois are numbered according to whether they're north or south of Thanon Narathip.

Phra Ratchaniwet Marukhathaiyawan

10km south of Cha-am, off the road to Hua Hin, Highway 4 • Daily except Wed 8.30am–4.30pm • Grounds B30, palace B30; English guidebook B80 • Best accessed by private transport, but Cha-am–Hua Hin buses (roughly every 30min) stop within 2km of the palace at the sign for Rama VI Camp – just follow the road through the army compound

Set in beautiful grounds, the lustrous seaside palace of Rama VI, **Phra Ratchaniwet Marukhathaiyawan** (aka Mrigadayavan Palace), is rarely visited by foreigners, though it sees plenty of Thai visitors. Designed by an Italian architect, Ercole Manfredi, in a Westernized Thai style, and completed in 1924, the entire, 400m-long complex of sixteen golden teak pavilions and connecting walkways is raised off the ground on over a thousand concrete columns, with a niche for water at the base of each to keep out ants. It's often referred to as "the palace of love and hope" as Rama VI first visited with his pregnant queen, who later miscarried (and was subsequently demoted to royal consort), but it was abandoned to the corrosive sea air after the king's death in 1925. Restoration work began in the 1970s, and today most of the structure looks as it once did, a stylish composition of verandas and latticework painted in shades of cream and light blue, with an emphasis on cool simplicity. The spacious open hall in the north wing, hung with chandeliers and encircled by a first-floor balcony, was used as a meeting room and as a theatre for the king to perform in his own plays. The king stayed in the central group of buildings, with the best sea view and a 50m-long elevated walkway to his private bathing pavilion, while the south wing contained the apartments of the royal consorts, with its own bathing pavilion connected by a walkway.

ARRIVAL AND DEPARTURE

By train The station, a few blocks west of the main Phetkasem–Narathip junction, is served by a handful of trains a day, from either Hualamphong or Thonburi stations in Bangkok.

Destinations Bangkok (5 daily; 3hr 30min–4hr 30min); Chumphon (3 daily; 5–7hr); Hat Yai (1 daily; 13hr 30min); Hua Hin (5 daily; 30min); Prachuap Khiri Khan (4 daily; 2hr).

By bus Through-buses and local services from and to Hua Hin and Phetchaburi stop on Highway 4, close to the junction with Thanon Narathip, the main road running east to the beach. Bangkok–Cha-am a/c buses use the depot at the little plaza off the beachfront Thanon Ruamchit, just south of Thanon Narathip.

Destinations Bangkok (roughly hourly; 2hr 45min–3hr 15min); Hua Hin (roughly every 30min; 35min); Phetchaburi (every 20–30min; 50min–1hr 20min).

By minibus If you're heading for Bangkok, you could catch one of the frequent Hua Hin–Victory Monument a/c minibuses, operated by several companies: either go to one of the companies' pavement desks at the Phetchaburi–Narathip junction, or phone ahead to book (see p.521).

GETTING AROUND

By bicycle or motorbike A number of shops along the beachfront rent motorbikes as well as bicycles, tandems and even three- and four-person bikes.

INFORMATION

Tourist information The local TAT office (daily 8.30am–4.30pm; ☎032 471005–6, ✉tatphet@tat.or.th), which provides information about the whole of Phetchaburi province, is on Highway 4 (west side), about 1km south of Thanon Narathip.

ACCOMMODATION

There are no obvious backpacker-oriented places in Cha-am; instead you'll find mainly small, mid-range hotels and guesthouses, concentrated on Thanon Ruamchit and the adjoining sois, and upmarket, out-of-town resorts, many on the road down to Hua Hin (covered on p.522). Many Cha-am hotels put their prices up on Saturdays, over bank-holiday weekends and during school holidays (mid-March to mid-May and Oct).

Golden Beach Cha-am Hotel Just south of Soi Cha-am North 8 at 208/14 Thanon Ruamchit ☎032 433833, ⊚goldenbeachchaam.com. Good-value twenty-storey hotel with a full-height atrium, a swimming pool, gym and internet access, set back from the promenade. The nicely appointed rooms have a/c, hot water, mini-bars and TVs, as well as balconies, most with sea views. **B2000**

Hôtel de la Paix 6km north of central Cha-am ☎032 709555, ⊚hoteldelapaixhh.com. Sleek designer hideaway featuring a triumphal, white-marble staircase up to the lobby and a huge reflective pool as its centrepiece. The accommodation blocks have a striking cubic look but are very comfortable for all that, while creative, beautifully presented food is served at the breezy restaurant, *Clouds Loft*. There are two swimming pools (plus seven villas with private pools), a spa and an events centre offering cooking classes, kayaking and mountain-biking. **B9700**

Nana House North of Soi Cha-am North 10 towards the canal ☎032 433632, ⊚nanahouse.net. Wide range of well-kept accommodation with a/c, hot water and wi-fi, including two-bedroom houses (B4000). The bright, pretty, tiled rooms in the purple building down the quieter side alley are better value than the swankier affairs in the main building on the front. Breakfast included. **B900**

Nirandorn 3 Just south of the Narathip junction on Thanon Ruamchit ☎032 470300. Clean, well-maintained hotel rooms and a few tightly packed, motel-style bunga-lows, decorated in crisp, modern whites and browns, with sofas, safes, a/c, TVs, fridges and hot water; all rooms in the hotel block are sea-facing, sporting balconies and deckchairs. There's also a small, attractive swimming pool. Rooms **B700**, bungalows **B800**

EATING AND DRINKING

The choice of **restaurants** in Cha-am is not a patch on the range you get in Hua Hin, but there should be enough Thai-style seafood to keep you satisfied, including at the dozens of deckchair-and-umbrella places on the beach.

Krua Medsai North end of the beach, just after the canal ☎032 430196. A very Thai institution, this huge, open-sided, thatched pavilion sits on the beach, with *luk thung* on the sound system, views down to Hua Hin and nice breezes off the sea. People flock here for the very good seafood, simply grilled or in dishes such as delicious *hoy jor*, crabmeat, minced pork and water chestnuts wrapped in tofu skin (B80). Daily 10am–10pm.

O-Zone Thanon Ruamchit, north of Soi Cha-am North 7 ☎032 470897. Popular bar-restaurant whose attractions include mellow live folk music early evening (about 7–8.15pm), followed by bands playing Thai and Western pop (about 9.15pm–12.30am), and a menu that encompasses a few Western dishes such as pizza and steak, one-plate Thai dishes and more complex offerings such as crispy fried catfish salad (B150). Daily 5/6pm–12.30/1am.

Poom North of Soi Cha-am North 6 at 274/1 Thanon Ruamchit ☏ 032 471036. Welcoming, no-frills restaurant which serves a good selection of seafood dishes on its sea-view terrace – try the shrimps with garlic (B250) or crab with black pepper (B300–400, according to weight). Daily 10am–midnight.

Hua Hin

Thailand's oldest beach resort, **HUA HIN** used to be little more than an overgrown fishing village with one exceptionally grand hotel, but the arrival of mass tourism, high-rise hotels and farang-managed hostess bars has made a serious dent in its once idiosyncratic charm. With the far superior beaches of Ko Samui, Krabi and Ko Samet so close at hand, there's little to draw the dedicated sunseeker here. The town's most distinctive attractions are its squid-pier restaurants and guesthouses on Thanon Naretdamri, characterful spots to stay or enjoy fine seafood, while at the other end of the scale the former *Railway Hotel* (now the *Centara Grand*) provides all the atmosphere you can afford. In addition, the town makes a convenient base for day-trips to Khao Sam Roi Yot National Park to the south and Pala-u Falls in Kaeng Krachan National Park to the west. If none of that appeals, you might consider stopping by for Hua Hin's well-respected **jazz festival** in August (ⓦhuahinjazz.com) or for the rather more unusual **elephant polo tournament**, held every September (ⓦanantaraelephantpolo.com).

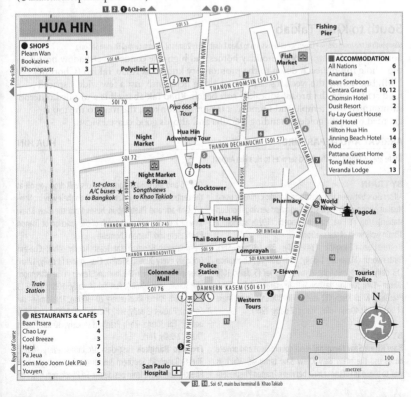

Brief history

The **royal family** were Hua Hin's main visitors at the start of the twentieth century, but the place became more widely popular in the 1920s, when the opening of the Bangkok–Malaysia rail line made short excursions to the beach much more viable. The Victorian-style *Railway Hotel* was opened in 1922, originally as a necessary overnight stop on the three-day journey to Malaysia. At the same time Rama VI commissioned the nine-hole Royal Hua Hin Golf Course (now 18 holes; ☎032 512475) to the west of the station, and in 1926 Rama VII had his own summer palace, Klai Klangwon ("Far from Worries"), erected at the northern end of the beach. It was here, ironically, that Rama VII was staying in 1932 when the coup was launched in Bangkok against the system of absolute monarchy. The current king has made many visits here too, which means that the navy is on constant guard duty in the resort and the police are also on their best behaviour; consequently both Thais and expats consider Hua Hin an especially safe place to live and do business – hence the number of farang-oriented real-estate agencies in the area.

The central shorefront

The prettiest part of Hua Hin's 5km-long **beach** is the patch in front of and to the south of the *Centara Grand*, where the sand is at its softest and whitest. North of here the shore is crowded with tables and chairs belonging to a string of small restaurant shacks, beyond which the beach ends at a Chinese temple atop a flight of steps running down to Thanon Naretdamri. The coast to the north of the pagoda is dominated by the jetties and terraces of the squid-pier guesthouses and seafood restaurants, the hub of the original fishing village, which dates back to the early nineteenth century.

South to Khao Takiab

6km south of the town centre • Green songthaews run to Khao Takiab every 20min or so from central Thanon Sa Song

South of the *Centara Grand*, holiday homes and high-rise condos overshadow nearly the whole run of beach down to the promontory known as Khao Takiab (Chopstick Hill), but during the week it's fairly quiet along here, with just a few widely spaced food stalls along the broad, squeakily soft beach. **Khao Takiab** itself is a wooded outcrop surmounted by a temple and home to a troupe of monkeys; the road to the top is guarded by a tall, golden, standing Buddha and affords good coastal views.

ARRIVAL AND DEPARTURE   HUA HIN

There are currently no scheduled services to Hua Hin Airport.

BY TRAIN
All services between the south and Bangkok (mostly using Hualamphong, with a few stopping trains serving Thonburi station) stop at Hua Hin's photogenic 1920s station, a 10min walk west of the seafront.

Destinations Bangkok (14 daily; 3hr 30min–5hr); Butterworth (Malaysia; 1 daily; 17hr 30min); Chumphon (13 daily; 3hr 30min–5hr 20min); Hat Yai (5 daily; 10hr 30min–12hr 30min); Nakhon Si Thammarat (2 daily; 12hr); Prachuap Khiri Khan (11 daily; 1hr 30min); Surat Thani (11 daily; 5hr 40min–8hr); Trang (2 daily; 12hr).

BY BUS
Baw Khaw Saw terminal Most government and private buses use the main Baw Khaw Saw terminal, which is well to the south of the centre, between Thanon Phetkasem

sois 96 and 98, though some services will drop you off at the central clocktower (Wat Hua Hin) on their way in. Non-a/c Cha-am and Phetchaburi buses from the Baw Khaw Saw pick up at a spot just north of the junction of Thanon Phetkasem and Thanon Chomsin.

Destinations Bangkok (at least hourly; 4hr); Cha-am (roughly every 30min; 35min); Chiang Mai (3 daily; 12hr); Chumphon (hourly in the morning, fewer in the afternoon; 3hr 30min–4hr 30min); Hat Yai (4 daily; 10hr); Krabi (3 daily; 9hr); Phetchaburi (every 20–30min; 1hr 15min–1hr 50min); Phuket (3 daily; 9hr); Prachuap Khiri Khan (roughly hourly; 1hr 30min–2hr); Pranburi (hourly; 30min); Surat Thani (2 daily; 7hr).

From/to Bangkok First-class a/c buses (every 40min; 3hr) to Bangkok's Southern Bus Terminal, stopping only at Phetchaburi, leave from beside the *Sri Phetkasem* hotel on

EXCURSIONS AND ACTIVITIES AROUND HUA HIN

A popular day-trip from Hua Hin is 63km west to the fifteen-tiered **Pala-u Waterfall**, situated close to the Burmese border and within **Kaeng Krachan National Park** (B200; ⓦ dnp.go.th). Though the falls themselves are hardly exceptional, the route there takes you through lush, hilly landscape and past innumerable pineapple plantations. There's no public transport to the falls, but every tour operator features them in its programme. To get there under your own steam, follow the signs from the west end of Thanon Chomsin along Highway 3218. Once inside the park you'll see hundreds of butterflies and may also catch sight of monitor lizards and six species of hornbills. A slippery and occasionally steep path follows the river through the fairly dense jungle up to the falls, passing the (numbered) tiers en route to the remote fifteenth level, though most people opt to stop at the third level, which has the first pool of any decent depth (full of fish but not that clear) and is a half-hour walk from the car park.

Hua Hin also offers excursions to Khao Sam Roi Yot National Park, Phetchaburi and Amphawa floating market, not to mention the old summer palace of Phra Ratchaniwet Marukhathaiyawan just to the north (see p.517). In addition, a number of **activities** are available, such as cycling and kiteboarding.

TOUR OPERATORS

Hua Hin Adventure Tour 69/8 Thanon Naebkehat ⓣ032 530314, ⓦ huahinadventuretour.com. A huge range of tours, including Pala-u Falls (from B1800/person), a boat trip in Kaeng Krachan National Park (from B2200) and Khao Sam Roi Yot National Park (from B1700, kayaking on Khao Daeng canal B400 extra), plus Thai cooking classes.

Hua Hin Bike Tours 4/34 Soi 96/1, Thanon Phetkasem ⓣ081 173 4469, ⓦ huahinbiketours .com. A variety of guided half-day (B1500) and day rides (from B2500 including lunch), including transfers, as well as rental from B375/day.

Kiteboarding Asia ⓣ081 591 4593, ⓦ kiteboarding asia.com. Kiteboarding courses and rental from three shops, including a spot off the end of Soi 75/1, about 2.5km south of the *Sofitel* (B4000 for a one-day course, B11,000 for three days; best conditions from Feb to mid-May).

Mermaid Cruises ⓣ032 632223 or ⓣ084 800 7400, ⓦ huahincruises.com. Eco-friendly trips on the Pran River to the south of Hua Hin (B1950/person, including lunch and transfers), using quiet electric-powered longtails that allow you to get close to the wildlife, including 3m-long monitor lizards, egrets, ospreys, wild peacocks and six species of kingfisher. Kayaking day-trips on the river are also offered (B1150, including packed lunch). Among several sea cruises, Mermaid also run full-day trips on a big boat down to Khao Sam Roi Yot (B1950, including lunch; park admission fee B200 extra).

Western Tours 11 Thanon Damnern Kasem ⓣ032 533304, ⓦ westerntourshuahin.com. Weekly roster of day-trips to Khao Sam Roi Yot National Park (B1700/person, kayaking on Khao Daeng canal B500 extra), Pala-u Falls (B1700, elephant riding B500 extra), Phetchaburi (B1500), Amphawa Floating Market (B2400) and a snorkelling tour (B2700).

Thanon Sa Song – these are much faster than the second-class a/c services from the Baw Khaw Saw and clocktower.
To the islands Lomprayah (ⓣ032 533739, ⓦ lomprayah .com; book at their office on Soi Kanjanomai) runs a twice-daily bus and catamaran service, beginning in Bangkok and picking up at Hua Hin's clocktower (daily at 8.30am and 11.30pm) to Ko Tao (B1000), Ko Pha Ngan (B1300) and Ko Samui (B1400), via Chumphon.

BY MINIBUS

Several private companies run a/c minibuses to and from Bangkok's Victory Monument (departing when full, usually around every 30min; 2hr 30min), including Piya 666 Tour on Thanon Naebkehat, south of Thanon Chomsin (ⓣ081 571 0071; in Cha-am ⓣ082 249 2882; in Bangkok ⓣ084 464 6586), who have their base in Bangkok at Century Plaza, on the corner of Thanon Phrayathai and Thanon Rangnam, on the south side of the monument.

GETTING AROUND

By taxi service Hua Hin's taxi services include plentiful motorcycle taxis, samlors and pricy tuk-tuks.

By songthaew Green songthaews operate a fixed route from the airport, 6km north of town, via Thanon Sa Song to Khao Takiab in the south.

By car or motorbike Car rental outlets include Avis, on the north side of town at 15/112 Thanon Phetkasem, near Soi 29 (ⓣ032 547523, ⓦ avisthailand.com). Among the transport touts who rent out mopeds for B200/day (B150/day for two days or more) on Thanon Damnern

Kasem, try Khun Dennapa (☎081 942 5615, ⓦden -carrental.com), who hangs out on the pavement in front

of the *Sirin Hotel*, near 7-Eleven.

INFORMATION

Tourist information The TAT office is on Thanon Phetkasem, just north of Thanon Chomsin (daily 8.30am–4.30pm; ☎032 513885). There's also a municipal tourist information office (Mon–Fri 8.30am–4.30pm; ☎032 511047, ext 100) in the local government buildings on the corner of Thanon Damnern Kasem and Thanon Phetkasem,

with a satellite office just up Phetkasem at the clocktower (Mon–Fri 8.30am–4.30pm, Sat & Sun 9am–5pm).

Publications and websites Among Hua Hin's many English-language publications and maps, the *Hua Hin Pocket Guide*, a free, monthly booklet, is worth looking out for, while ⓦ huahinafterdark.com is a useful website.

ACCOMMODATION

A night or two at the former *Railway Hotel* (now the *Centara Grand*) is reason in itself to visit Hua Hin, but there are plenty of other **places to stay**. The most unusual **guesthouses** are those built on the **squid piers** on Thanon Naretdamri, north of the pagoda, with rooms strung out along wooden jetties so you can hear, feel – and smell, especially at low tide – the sea beneath you, even if you can't afford a room with an actual sea view. Room rates at many places can drop significantly from Mondays to Thursdays, so don't be afraid to ask for a discount.

All Nations 10 Thanon Dechanuchit ☎032 512747, ⓦ allnationshuahin.com. A range of comfortable rooms in varying sizes with free wi-fi and balconies, a few with distant sea views. A/c rooms have hot showers, TVs and fridges and are priced according to size; bathrooms with hot water are shared between two fan rooms. Also has a roof terrace. Fan B350, a/c B600

Anantara 5km north of central Hua Hin on Thanon Phetkasem ☎032 520250, ⓦ anantara.com. Set in effusive, beautifully designed tropical gardens, this is a lovely resort-style idyll, just out of town (with a regular shuttle service). Accommodation is in eight-room Thai-style pavilions, whose stylishly appointed rooms use plenty of red wood. The hotel has very good Italian, Thai and grill restaurants, two pools, a gorgeous spa, a kids' club, two tennis courts and its own stretch of beach, with kayaks available. B8200

Baan Somboon 13/4 Thanon Damnern Kasem ☎032 511538 or ☎032 533638, ⓔ baansomboon@gmail .com. Down a quiet but very central soi, this guesthouse divides between a lovely, old-fashioned house with polished teak floors, decorated with a melange of Thai antiques, woodcarvings and Western "old master" prints, and a small annexe. Spruce, homely rooms come with small, hot-water bathrooms, fridges, TVs and either fan or a/c, and there's a small garden crammed with plants, songbirds and a fish

tank. Continental breakfast included. B950

★ **Centara Grand** 1 Thanon Damnern Kasem ☎032 512021–38, ⓦ centarahotelsresorts.com. The original Thai "destination hotel", the main building is a classic of colonial-style architecture, boasting high ceilings, polished wood panelling, period furniture, wide sea-view balconies and a huge, landscaped garden full of topiary animals. Across the road, lush gardens shelter gorgeous, all-white clapboard villas, most with their own small marble pools, some with large outdoor jacuzzis. With a total of four swimming pools, a spa, tennis courts, a kids' club, snooker and a giant chessboard, you need never leave the grounds. You can even tuck into afternoon tea at *The Museum*, the original lobby, which now displays hotel memorabilia. Rooms B7600, villas B11,700

Chomsin Hotel 130/4 Thanon Chomsin ☎032 515348–9, ⓦ chomsinhuahin.com. Handsome, cream-coloured small hotel with a pleasant welcome, offering smart, bright, compact rooms in neutral colours with a few decorative touches and plenty of amenities: a/c, hot showers, cable TV, mini-bars, safes and free wi-fi (plus computers in the lobby). B1000

Dusit Resort Hua Hin 9km north of Hua Hin on Thanon Phetkasem ☎032 520009, ⓦ dusit.com. One of the most luxurious spots on this stretch of coast, with large, elegant rooms set around a tropical garden and

SOI 67 GUESTHOUSES

About fifteen minutes' walk south down the beach from the *Centara Grand*, or 2km by road down Thanon Phetkasem, there's a little knot of accommodation on Soi 67. Here, facing each other across the short, narrow soi about 100m back from the beach, are a dozen little guesthouses, mainly Scandinavian–Thai run, which share a swimming pool; none comprises more than twenty rooms and most charge about B900. They're very popular with older European couples, many of whom return for several months every winter, so booking is essential.

6

lotus-filled lagoon. Facilities include four restaurants, a huge swimming pool with children's pool and a separate saltwater pool, a spa, fitness centre, watersports, horse-riding, tennis and squash courts and an Avis car rental desk. B7000

Fu-Lay Guest House and Hotel 110/1 Thanon Naretdamri, guesthouse ☎ 032 513145, ⍈ fulayhuahin .net; hotel ☎ 032 513670, ⍈ fulayhuahin.com. Fu-Lay is in two halves, with guesthouse rooms strung along a jetty and balconied, a/c hotel accommodation in a low-rise block across the street. The jetty guesthouse is the most stylish of its kind in Hua Hin, offering attractively appointed a/c rooms with nice hot-water bathrooms, plus some cheap en-suite fan rooms (some with hot water) and a breezy seating area set right over the water. Fan B430, a/c B980

Hilton Hua Hin 33 Thanon Naretdamri ☎ 032 538999, ⍈ huahin.hilton.com. Set bang in the centre of Hua Hin's beachfront, the Hilton's high-rise profile disfigures the local skyline, but the facilities are extensive and the views excellent. There's a large, inviting lagoon-like swimming pool right on the seafront, a spa, a kids' club, a panoramic rooftop Chinese restaurant and an impressive indoor-outdoor water garden in the lobby. All three hundred rooms are large and comfortable and have sea-view balconies. B7300

Jinning Beach Hotel East end of Soi 67, off Thanon Phetkasem ☎ 032 532597, ⍈ jinningbeachhotel.com. Typical Soi 67 guesthouse under welcoming Danish–Thai management, with seventeen a/c rooms in seven different sizes, some with verandas, and all with hot water, TV and fridge. B800

Mod 116 Thanon Naretdamri ☎ 032 512296. A friendly little jetty guesthouse that's recently been renovated. Rooms are all shining white, with small but attractive bathrooms, and come with either fan and cold water or a/c and hot; all have cable TV and free wi-fi. There's a nice, breezy, covered sea-view terrace at the end. Fan B600, a/c B800

Pattana Guest Home 52 Thanon Naretdamri ☎ 032 513393, ✉ huahinpattana@hotmail.com. Small, comfortable rooms with character, in an appealingly traditional, teak former fisherman's house, with a flower-strewn courtyard, quietly located at the end of a small soi. Some rooms have private, cold-water bathrooms, some have balconies. Shared bathroom B300, en-suite B400

Tong Mee House 1 Soi Raumpown, Thanon Naebkehat ☎ 032 530725, ✉ tongmeehuahin@hotmail.com. In a modern, five-storey block on a quiet soi, this friendly guesthouse offers great value: small but neat rooms come with a/c, hot water, wi-fi, fridges, TVs and small balconies, and there's a computer and books to borrow in the lobby. B550

Veranda Lodge Soi 67, Thanon Phetkasem ☎ 032 533678, ⍈ verandalodge.com. Chic boutique hotel set in its own beachfront garden. Deluxe rooms have a contemporary look (lime green, pink or china-blue walls) and petite balconies; most of the various suites and bungalows have separate living rooms and small kitchen areas, and all have balconies. A/c, wi-fi, cable TV, DVD players and mini-bars throughout, and there's a small pool fed by a waterfall and a seafront terrace restaurant. Breakfast included. B2900

EATING AND DRINKING

Hua Hin is renowned for its **seafood**, and some of the best places to enjoy the local catch are the seafront and squid-pier restaurants along Thanon Naretdamri. Fish also features heavily at the large and lively **night market**, which sets up at sunset along Soi 72 (the western end of Thanon Dechanuchit). The biggest concentration of **bars** is in the network of sois between the Hilton Hotel and Wat Hua Hin, particularly along Soi Bintabat, Soi Kanjanomai and Thanon Poonsuk; most of these places are so-called "bar-beers", with lots of seating round the bar and hostesses dispensing beer and flirtation through the night.

★ **Baan Itsara** 7 Thanon Naebkehat, north of Soi 51 ☎ 032 530574. Excellent seafood in a traditional lime-green wooden house with simple tables on a seaside terrace. The speciality here is sweet basil sauce – which comes out something like pesto – with, for example, squid (B180) or king prawns (B420), but the grilled mackerel and the seafood laap with land-lotus leaves are also very good. Daily 10.30am–10pm.

Chao Lay 15 Thanon Naretdamri. Hua Hin's most famous jetty restaurant is deservedly popular, serving up high-quality seafood, including rock lobster, blue crab, scallops, cottonfish, mixed seafood hot plates and specialities such as mackerel curry soufflé (haw mok). Most main dishes cost B150–200. Daily 10am–10pm.

Cool Breeze 62 Thanon Naretdamri ☎ 032 531062. Either in the nice little garden at the back or amid the fresh, leafy decor inside, you can tuck into some very tasty tapas (including plenty of vegetarian options) at this new bar-café, which imports many of its ingredients from Spain. Interesting weekly specials might include scallops with Serrano ham (B225), or you can get a set of twelve tapas for B425. Also does baguettes, paella and other seafood and meat mains. Happy hour till 7pm includes 3-for-2 tapas and 2-for-1 sangria. Daily 11am–11pm.

Hagi Centara Grand, corner of Damnern Kasem and Naretdamri rds ☎ 032 512021–38. Tasty, authentic sushi (sets from B480), including delicious, hand-rolled temaki with crispy salmon skin and cucumber, tempura and *teppanyaki* grills at this elegant and welcoming Japanese restaurant. Pick your spot in the Zen-style garden, adorned with black slate, bamboo plants and a rocky pond, or in the a/c section with its sushi counter. Daily 5–11pm.

Pa Jeua Thanon Naretdamri, opposite the Hilton Hua Hin. Famous roadside stall that sells Thailand's favourite dessert, delicious *khao niaw mamuang* (fresh mango with sticky rice and coconut milk), for B60. Daily 9am–3pm.

Som Moo Joom (Jek Pia) 51/6 Thanon Dechanuchit (corner of Thanon Naebkehat); no English sign. Exceptionally good seafood at very cheap prices has made this bare-bones evening restaurant extremely popular with

Thai holiday-makers. The trademark dish, *moo joom*, is a clear soup in which you cook your own pork (or shrimp/squid), but the menu also covers the range of standard seafood dishes. From 6am to 1pm, several popular stalls take over the space, offering coffee, seafood, satay and noodle soup with seafood. Daily 5–8pm.

Youyen (Hua Hin Balcony) Thanon Naebkehat, near Soi 51 ☎032 531191–2. At the lovely terrace seating by the sea here, you can enjoy an excellent variety of authentic Thai food – try the delicious stir-fried shrimp with green sauce, green peppercorns, crispy garlic and sweet basil (B280). Daily 11am to roughly 9pm.

ENTERTAINMENT

Sasi Dinner Theatre Near the Hyatt Regency, about 4km south of the Centara Grand ☎032 512488 or ☎081 880 4004, ⓦsasi-restaurant.com. The Sasi Dinner Theatre was closed for renovation at the time of writing, but usually stages a performance of classical Thai dance, plus traditional fighting and contemporary ballet, every night (about B750 including set dinner and transfer).

Thai Boxing Garden Off Thanon Poonsuk ☎032 515269. Tuesdays and Saturdays are fight nights at the *Thai Boxing Garden* with programmes starting at 9pm and featuring five different fights (B400–600); it's owned by local *muay thai* champion Khun Chop, who also runs Thai boxing classes every day by appointment (B400/hr).

SHOPPING

Bookazine Near the corner of Damnern Kasem and Naretdamri rds ☎032 516512. Small outlet in a supermarket for English books, magazines and newspapers. Daily 8am–11pm.

Cicada Market Suan Sri, Thanon Takiab (near the Hyatt Regency, about 4km south of the Centara Grand), ⓦcicadamarket.net. Modelled on Chiang Mai's walking streets, this weekend market features jewellery, cute accessories, lots of T-shirts and other clothes, art galleries and, of course, plenty of food, plus regular performances of all kinds in the amphitheatre. Fri & Sat 4–11pm, Sun 4–10pm.

Hua Hin International Colonnade Mall, corner of Phetkasem and Damnern Kasem rds. Decent selection of secondhand books. Daily 10am–9pm.

Khomapastr 218 Thanon Phetkasem ☎032 511250, ⓦkhomapastrfabrics.com. Famous outlet for *pha kiaw* (or

pha khomapastr), brightly coloured, hand-printed cotton with lovely, swirling *kannok* patterns, usually with strong elements of gold – Khomapastr's founder, himself a prince, was inspired to start the business when rummaging through trunks of nineteenth-century royal clothing at Bangkok's National Museum in the 1940s. You can buy the cloth by the piece or metre, or made up into skirts, shirts, cushion covers and bags. Mon–Sat 9am–7pm, Sun 9am–5pm.

Plearn Wan Thanon Phetkasem, between sois 38 and 40 ⓦplearnwan.com. Curious exercise in nostalgia and commercialism – the name "Enjoy the Past" says it all – that's been a raging success with Thais from all over the country. It's essentially a shopping mall, but in vintage wooden style, selling retro everything: *luk krung* CDs, old-fashioned toys, traditional coffee and desserts, ukuleles… Mon–Thurs 10am–10pm, Fri 10am–midnight, Sat 9am–midnight, Sun 9am–10pm.

DIRECTORY

Banks and exchange There are currency-exchange counters all over the resort, especially on Thanon Damnern Kasem and Thanon Naretdamri; most of the main bank branches with ATMs are on Thanon Phetkasem.

Hospital Bangkok Hospital, 888 Thanon Phetkasem, south of the centre near Soi 94 (☎032 616800).

Immigration office On the canal road, left off Soi 10, Thanon Phetkasem, about 5km northwest of the town centre (Mon–Fri 8.30am–4.30pm; ☎032 526556).

Internet access Dozens of outlets, including the pricy but comfortable *World News*, owned by the *Hilton* on Thanon Naretdamri (daily 8am–10.30pm), where the good coffees,

juices and snacks might tempt you to part with more of your baht.

Meditation English-medium classes in sitting and walking meditation, with talks on Buddhism, at Wat Khao Santi, just off Soi 91, Thanon Phetkasem (Wed 8.30–11.30am; free, donations welcome; ⓦmeditationinhuahin.org).

Pharmacy Several in the resort, including the helpful and well-stocked Medihouse (daily 9.30am–11pm), opposite the *Hilton* on Thanon Naretdamri.

Thai language Classes and private lessons at TLC, 83/14 Wongchomsin Building, Thanon Phetkasem (near Soi 63/1; ☎032 533428, ⓦthailanguagecentre.org).

Tourist police For all emergencies, call the tourist police on the free, 24hr phoneline (☎1155), or contact them at their office opposite the *Centara Grand* at the beachfront end of Thanon Damnern Kasem (☎032 516219).

Travel agency Reliable Western Tours (see p.521) sells international and domestic air tickets, as well as bus tickets to southern Thailand.

Pak Nam Pran

6

The stretch of coast between Hua Hin and Chumphon barely registers on most foreign tourists' radar, but many better-off Bangkokians have favourite beaches in this area, the nicest of which is sophisticated **PAK NAM PRAN** (aka Pranburi). Just 30km or so south of Hua Hin, Pak Nam Pran used to cater only for families who owned beach villas here, but in the past few years the shorefront homes have been joined by a growing number of enticing, if pricey, boutique hotels, and signs are there's more development to come. For now, facilities consist of just a few minimarkets, car-rental outlets and independent bars and restaurants, especially around the *Evason* hotel towards the northern end of the beach, plus the possibility of organizing day-trips to nearby Khao Sam Roi Yot National Park through hotel staff; there's also kiteboarding through Kiteboarding Asia, about 1km south of the *Evason* (☎089 743 5564, ⓦkiteboardingasia.com).

As along much of the Gulf coast, the **beach** itself, also known as Hat Naresuan, is not exceptional (it has hardly any shade and is suffering from erosion in parts), but it is long, with fine sand, and nearly always empty, and you're quite likely to see dolphins playing within sight of the shore. The strand stretches south from Pak Nam Pran town at the mouth of the Pran River – which is known for its colourful fishing boats, specializing in squid – for around 7km to Khao Kalok headland and the tiny Thao Kosa Forest Park.

ARRIVAL AND DEPARTURE
PAK NAM PRAN

Easiest access is via the town of **Pranburi**, which straddles Highway 4 some 23km south of Hua Hin. There's no public transport from Pranburi to Pak Nam Pran beach, 10km or so away, but hotels can arrange transfers and any Pranburi songthaew driver will taxi you there. Pranburi's main crossroads (Highway 4 and Thanon Ratbamrung) is 2km south of Tesco Lotus at Talat Chaikaew – if making your own way, the easiest route is to turn east off Highway 4 here and take minor road 3168 down to the sea, picking up the relevant sign for your hotel.

FROM/TO PRANBURI
By train Pranburi's quaint old station is 4km east of the Highway 4 crossroads (Talat Chaikaew) towards the beach, off the north side of Route 3168.

Destinations Bangkok (Hualamphong 1 daily, Thonburi 2 daily; 5hr–5hr 30min); Chumphon (2 daily; 4hr 30min); Hat Yai (1 daily; 12hr 30min); Prachuap Khiri Khan (3 daily; 1hr).

By bus As well as many through services to and from the south, Pranburi is served by a/c buses from Bangkok's

Southern Bus Terminal, which drop passengers close by the main Highway 4 crossroads at Talat Chaikaew.

Destinations Bangkok (first-class: hourly, 3hr; second-class, stopping at Hua Hin: every 30min, 4hr); Hua Hin (every 30min; 30min).

By minibus A/c minibuses from Bangkok's Victory Monument (☎085 403 6113) generally stop at the Tesco Lotus supermarket on Highway 4 opposite Pranburi's City Hall, but you could ask the driver to take you to your beach hotel for a little extra money.

ACCOMMODATION

Pak Nam Pran's charming **accommodation** is its biggest draw: for once, "boutique" is the appropriate term, as many of the hotels here offer a dozen or fewer rooms. With influences ranging from Greece to the South Pacific, from Morocco to Scandinavia, the style tends to be more arty than five-star, though you will certainly be comfortable. Some hotels aren't suitable for kids owing to their multiple levels and unfenced flights of steps. Breakfast is generally included in the price of the room. During weekends in high season (Nov–May), hoteliers routinely put their prices up and you'll need to book ahead. The following are spread over a 2km stretch of the beachfront road, starting about 4km south of Pak Nam Pran town.

★ **Aleenta** Central Pak Nam Pran beach ☎ 032 618333, ⊛ aleenta.com. This stunningly designed hotel, divided between the Main Wing and the Frangipani Wing, 500m down the beach, offers gorgeous circular, thatched bungalows and very tasteful villa-style rooms, most with uninterrupted sea views, decks and plunge pools. The feel is modernist chic, with elegantly understated local furnishings and huge windows, and iPods and wi-fi capability rather than TVs. There's a small rooftop pool and spa; yoga, t'ai chi and cooking classes are available. B7100

Baan Panali Southern Pak Nam Pran beach, 200m south of Huaplee ☎ 086 051 2333 or ☎ 081 844 2484, ⊛ baan-panali.com. Not as striking as some of the beach's other offerings, but much cheaper and stylish enough: a cream-painted, adobe-style block with large, colourful, tiled rooms and a cute little swimming pool on its beachfront terrace. All but one room face the sea with a terrace or balcony, and all have a/c, hot showers, TVs and fridges. B2000

Evason Northern Pak Nam Pran beach ☎ 032 632111, ⊛ sixsenses.com/evason. The biggest and best-known hotel in Pak Nam Pran, but as accommodation is screened by graceful gardens, the feel is quite private and small-scale. Rooms are attractively cool and contemporary, with big

balconies and DVD players; for extra privacy, you could check into a super-luxe private-pool villa, a favourite choice of Thai film stars. Facilities include a huge pool, a spa, two restaurants, tennis courts and a kids' club with its own pool. B5700

★ **Huaplee Lazy Beach** Central Pak Nam Pran beach ☎ 032 630554–5, ⊛ huapleelazybeach.com. This exceptionally cute collection of seven idiosyncratic white-cube beachfront rooms and one suite around a pretty lawn is the work of the architect-interior designer owners. It's a characterful place of whimsical, marine-themed interiors done out with white-painted wood floors, blue-and-white colour schemes and funky shell and driftwood decor. The rooms are airy and bright but all have a/c, as well as fridges and TVs (no hot water); some have fantastic sea-view terraces. B3300

Jamsawang Resort Northern Pak Nam Pran beach ☎ 032 570050, ⊛ jamsawang.com. One of the cheapest places to stay in the area, run by a friendly family. Dotted around a neatly trimmed garden across the road from the beach, all bungalows have a/c, hot water, fridge and TV; a few ("Thai-style") are comfortable if not especially sophisticated pale-blue concrete affairs, but most are pricier (from B2000), more stylishly furnished, yellow-painted "Bali-style" bungalows, with garden bathrooms. B1400

EATING

Krua Jaew On the edge of Pak Nam Pran town, about 2km north of the Evason ☎ 032 631302. The best of several neighbouring seafront restaurants, offering an enormous, mid-priced menu of 120 mostly fish and seafood dishes, including excellent crab curry (B300), seafood curry soufflé (*haw mok thalay*; on the menu as "steamed seafood with spicy and coconut milk"; B120) and the local speciality, deep-fried dried squid (*pla meuk det diaw*; B150). Unsigned in English, but it's the first restaurant you'll come to heading up the beach road into Pak Nam Pran, with its kitchen and most of its tables on the

left-hand side, and a few tables towards the beach on the right. Daily 9am–9pm.

Krua Sawatdikan Khao Kalok On the south side of Khao Kalok's rocky outcrop at the far southern end of Pak Nam Pran beach, about 1km from Baan Panali ☎ 086 701 8597 (unsigned in English). This simple shorefront restaurant has an extensive menu of very good seafood dishes (mostly B80–150) and great views of Khao Sam Roi Yot from its beach tables under the casuarinas; mosquitoes are a problem here though, so take repellent. Daily 10am–8pm.

Khao Sam Roi Yot National Park

National park entry fee B200 • ☎ 032 821568, ⊛ dnp.go.th

With a name that translates as "The Mountain with Three Hundred Peaks", **KHAO SAM ROI YOT NATIONAL PARK**, with its northern entrance 28km south of Pak Nam Pran beach or 63km from Hua Hin, encompasses a small but varied, mosquito-ridden coastal zone of just 98 square kilometres. The dramatic limestone crags after which it is named are the dominant feature, looming 600m above the Gulf waters and the forested interior, but perhaps more significant are the mud flats and freshwater marsh which attract and provide a breeding ground for thousands of migratory birds. **Bird-watching** at Thung Khao Sam Roi Yot swamp is a major draw, but the famously photogenic Phraya Nakhon Khiri cave is the focus of most day-trips, while a few decent trails and a couple of secluded beaches provide added interest.

6

Orientation in the park is fairly straightforward. One main inland road runs roughly north–south through it from the R3168 (the road from Pranburi's main junction to Pak Nam Pran), passing, in order: the 2km side road to **Hat Phu Noi**, a quiet, golden-sand beach that offers several resort alternatives to the park's accommodation and the chance to see dolphins in the cool season; the northern park checkpoint, 4km further on; the turn-offs for Ban Bang Pu (the jumping-off point for Tham Phraya Nakhon), Ban Khung Tanot (for Tham Sai) and Hat Sam Phraya (all to the east); then going over Khao Daeng canal, before looping westwards around the main massif, past the **park headquarters** (where park brochures and maps are available) and the southern checkpoint (14km from the northern checkpoint), to Highway 4 at kilometre-stone 286.5.

Tham Phraya Nakhon

B300 return per boat from Wat Bang Pu

Khao Sam Roi Yot's most visited attraction is the **Tham Phraya Nakhon** cave system, hidden high up on a cliffside above **Hat Laem Sala**, an unremarkable sandy bay with a national park visitor centre that's inaccessible to vehicles. The usual way to get to Hat Laem Sala is by a five-minute boat ride from the knot of food stalls behind Wat Bang Pu on the edge of **Ban Bang Pu** fishing village (6km from the northern checkpoint). It's also possible to walk over the headland from behind Wat Bang Pu to Hat Laem Sala, along a signed, but at times steep, 500m trail. From Hat Laem Sala, another taxing though shaded trail runs up the hillside to Tham Phraya Nakhon in around thirty minutes.

The huge twin **caves** are filled with stalactites and stalagmites and wreathed in lianas and gnarly trees, but their most dramatic features are the partially collapsed roofs, which allow the sunlight to stream in and illuminate the interiors, in particular beaming down on the famous royal pavilion, Phra Thi Nang Khua Kharunhad, which was built in the second cave in 1890 in honour of Rama V.

Tham Sai

A three-hour trek south from Tham Phraya Nakhon brings you to **Tham Sai**, a thoroughly dark and dank limestone cave, complete with stalactites, stalagmites and petrified waterfalls; lamps and torches are available here for B60. The trek offers some fine coastal views, but a shorter alternative is the twenty-minute trail from **Ban Khung Tanot** village (accessible by road, 8km on from the Ban Bang Pu turn-off).

Khao Daeng and around

Canal cruise B400 for up to 6 people, kayaks B500 • ☎ 089 903 1619

The next turning off the main road will take you down to **Hat Sam Phraya**, a quiet, kilometre-long beach with a national park visitor centre, while a little further on the road crosses mangrove-fringed **Khao Daeng canal**. From beside Wat Khao Daeng, on the west side of the main road here, you can charter a boat for a one-hour cruise that's best in the early morning or the late afternoon; kayaks are available at the same spot.

A couple of kilometres on, you can scramble up **Khao Daeng** itself, a 157m-high outcrop that offers good summit views over the coast, via a thirty-minute trail that begins near the park headquarters. The park's two official **nature trails** also begin close to the headquarters – the thirty-minute "Horseshoe Trail" takes in the forest habitats of monkeys, squirrels and songbirds, while the 45-minute "Mangrove Trail" leads through the swampy domiciles of monitor lizards and egrets, with the chance of encountering long-tailed (crab-eating) macaques.

Thung Khao Sam Roi Yot

Accessed not from the main park road, but by turning east off Highway 4, 200m north of kilometre-stone 276, and continuing for 9km • Punts B150 per person • ☎ 081 486 1842

The park hosts up to three hundred species of **birds** and between September and November the mud flats are thick with migratory flocks from Siberia, China and northern Europe. To the west of Khao Sam Roi Yot lies Thailand's largest freshwater marsh, **Thung Khao Sam Roi Yot** (aka Beung Bua), near the village of Rong Jai (Rong Che). This is an excellent place for observing waders and songbirds, and is one of only two places in the country where the **purple heron** breeds; punts are available here for one- to two-hour bird-watching excursions.

ARRIVAL AND GETTING AROUND KHAO SAM ROI YOT

Like most of Thailand's national parks, Khao Sam Roi Yot is hard to explore without your own **transport**, and its sights are spread too far apart to walk between.

By motorbike or car Motorbikes can be rented in Hua Hin (which also has car rental), as well as at *Dolphin Bay Resort* or Prachuap Khiri Khan.

With a tour The park can be visited on a one-day tour from Hua Hin, including cycling tours with Hua Hin Bike Tours (see p.521), Pak Nam Pran or *Dolphin Bay Resort*.

ACCOMMODATION AND EATING

Given the limitations of the park accommodation, many people prefer to stay a few kilometres to the north at the long, pleasingly shaded beach of Hat Phu Noi.

IN THE PARK

National Park accommodation ☎ 032 821568, ⓦ dnp.go.th. Accommodation is at headquarters, at Hat Sam Phraya, a beach between Khao Daeng canal and Ban Khung Tanot, at Hat Laem Sala and at Thung Khao Sam Roi Yot; all four sites have restaurants. At Hat Laem Sala it's a choice between camping, at B150–225 per tent, or staying in one of the national park bungalows with hot showers (for 6–9 people); at Sam Phraya and Thung Khao Sam Roi Yot it's camping only; and at the headquarters it's bungalows only (for 5–6 people). Bungalows must be booked ahead through the National Parks office in Bangkok (see p.37). Hat Laem Sala B1600, HQ B1200

HAT PHU NOI

Brassiere Beach Bottom end of Hat Phu Noi ☎ 032 630555, ⓦ brassierebeach.com. Under the same architect owners as *Huaplee* at Pak Nam Pran (see p.527), *Brassiere Beach* gets its name from the two conical Nom Sao ("Breast") islands offshore and the mainland spirit house where fishermen leave bras for good luck, and contains rooms with playful monikers like "La Perla". That may sound a bit naff to some, but the hotel itself is the height of quirky chic, airy and light-filled, with a mostly white-and-blue colour scheme. Some rooms have their own small jacuzzi and pool or an outdoor bathroom, and kayaks and bicycles are available. Breakfast included. B3800

Dolphin Bay Northern end of the beach ☎ 032 559333, ⓦ dolphinbayresort.com. Eco-conscious, family-friendly resort offering comfortable a/c rooms, bungalows, apartments and villas with fridges, hot water and TVs, large children's and adults' pools set in an attractive, palm-fringed lawn, plus a kids' playground and internet access and wi-fi. Pick-ups from Pranburi (B250) can be arranged and there's plenty of things to do once you're here: half-day tours of the park (B700 for a car with driver), boat trips to local islands, plus kayak, motorbike and bicycle rental. B1590

Prachuap Khiri Khan and around

Despite lacking any must-see attractions, the tiny, unfrequented provincial capital of **PRACHUAP KHIRI KHAN**, 67km south of Pranburi, makes a pleasant place to break any journey up or down the coast. Its greatest asset is its setting: a huge, palm-fringed, half-moon bay, dotted with colourful fishing boats and tipped by a rocky outcrop at the north end and by a small group of jungly islands to the south – the waterfront promenade in the town centre is great for a seafood lunch with a view. There's a lovely **beach** in the next bay to the south, Ao Manao, and generally Prachuap is a fine spot to settle into small-town Thai life.

6

6

The town is contained in a small grid of streets that runs just 250m east to west, between the sea and the train station – with Highway 4 beyond the railway tracks – and around 1km north to south, from the Khao Chong Krajok hill at the northern end to the Wing 5 air-force base in the south. **Orientation** couldn't be simpler: the major road across from the station to the pier is Thanon Kongkiat, and there are four main north–south roads: Thanon Phitak Chat near the station, Thanon Salacheep, Thanon Susuek and the seafront road, Thanon Chai Thalay.

Khao Chong Krajok

The monkey-infested hill of **Khao Chong Krajok** is Prachuap's main sight: if you climb the 417 steps from Thanon Salacheep to the golden-spired chedi at the summit you get a great perspective on the scalloped coast below and west to the mountainous Burmese border, just 12km away.

Ao Manao

Inside Wing 5 air-force base (you usually need to sign in at the base checkpoint) • Head south down Thanon Salacheep (or down the promenade and turn right) to reach the checkpoint and continue for 2km through the base to the beach • Tuk-tuk to the beach around B60

At the far southern end of town, the long sandy beach at **Ao Manao** is the best place in the area for swimming and sunbathing. On weekdays you're likely to have the sand almost to yourself, but it's a very popular spot with Thai families on weekends when the stalls at the beachfront food centre do a roaring trade in the locally famous *som tam puu* (spicy papaya salad with fresh crab), which you can eat at the deckchairs and tables under the trees on the beach. You can walk to the north end of the bay to the base of an outcrop known as Khao Lommuak, where a memorial commemorates the skirmish that took place here between Thai and Japanese forces in World War II.

King Mongkut Memorial Park of Science and Technology

12km south of town, on the beach at Wa Ko (Waghor) • Daily 9am–4pm, fish-feeding at 11am & 2pm (subject to change) • Aquarium B20 • ☎ 032 661104 • To get there, turn east off Highway 4 at kilometre-stone 335, or go through Ao Manao air-force base, bearing left along the coast all the way

The main feature of the **King Mongkut Memorial Park of Science and Technology** (also signed as Phra Chomklao Science Park) is the extensive and well-stocked **Waghor Aquarium**. Highlights include an underwater tunnel, touch pools and fish-feeding, and there are display boards and labels for most of the fish in English. It's nothing like as slick as Siam Ocean World in Bangkok, but then again it's less than a tenth of the price. About 500m south along the beach road, the park also contains an astronomy museum that's decidedly low-tech but with enough labels in English to maintain interest.

The park is thought to mark the spot where **Rama IV**, known as the father of Thai science, came to observe a solar eclipse on August 18, 1868. Having predicted the eclipse's exact course, King Mongkut decided to publicize science among his subjects by mounting a large expedition, aiming specifically to quash their centuries-old fear that the sun was periodically swallowed by the dragon Rahoo, and more generally to rattle traditional notions of astrology and cosmology. To this end, he invited scientists all the way from France and the British governor of Singapore, and himself turned up with fifty elephants and all his court, including the astrologers – who, as the leader of the French expedition noted, "could hardly be blamed if they did not display much enthusiasm for the whole project". Unfortunately, both the king and his 15-year-old son contracted malaria at Waghor; Mongkut passed away in Bangkok on October 1, but Chulalongkorn survived to become Thailand's most venerated king, Rama V.

ARRIVAL AND DEPARTURE

PRACHUAP KHIRI KHAN

BY TRAIN

Nearly all services on the Southern Line from Bangkok stop at the train station, which is just on the west side of the centre, at the western end of Thanon Kongkiat.

Destinations Bangkok (11 daily; 5–7hr); Chumphon (11 daily; 2hr–3hr 30min); Hat Yai (4 daily; 9–11hr); Nakhon Si Thammarat (2 daily; 10hr 30min); Surat Thani (8 daily; 4hr 30min–6hr); Trang (1 daily; 11hr).

BY BUS OR MINIBUS

Prachuap doesn't have a proper bus station, and the number of dedicated services to and from the town centre is dwindling, with many people either heading out to Highway 4 to flag down a through-bus, or catching an a/c minibus.

Buses from/to Bangkok Pudtan Tour, on Thanon Phitak Chat just south of Thanon Kongkiat, runs a "first-class" a/c service to Bangkok's Southern Terminal, which stops at Pranburi and Phetchaburi, but takes the Hua Hin bypass, Highway 37. Further north just off Thanon Phitak Chat, there's a sometimes unreliable, "second-class" a/c service

to Bangkok, which stops frequently, including in central Hua Hin.

A/c minibuses from/to Bangkok Several companies offer a/c minibuses to Bangkok, including Monsiri Travel on Thanon Phitak Chat north of Thanon Kongkiat (☎089 005 5139), whose services run either to Victory Monument or to the Southern and Northern Bus Terminals, stopping at Pranburi and Phetchaburi on the way.

Buses to the south There's a daily non-a/c bus to Chumphon from Thanon Phitak Chat but for the fastest services to the south you need to wait on Highway 4 at the Highway Police office, about 1km north of the access road into town, for the a/c buses that whizz down from Bangkok; several southbound services pick up passengers here between 8.30am and 11.30am (and many more around midnight).

Destinations Bangkok (roughly hourly; 4–5hr); Chumphon (1 daily; 3hr); Hua Hin (2–3 daily; 1hr 30min–2hr); Phetchaburi (roughly hourly; 3hr–3hr 30min); Pranburi (roughly hourly; 1hr–1hr 30min).

INFORMATION AND GETTING AROUND

Tourist information There's a small tourist information office (daily 8.30am–4.30pm, occasionally closing noon–1pm for lunch; ☎032 611491), where town maps are available, at the far northern end of town in a compound of provincial offices; it's on the ground floor of a modern, white building facing the beachfront road.

Bicycle and motorbike rental Bicycles (B70/day) and motorbikes (B250/day) can be rented from *Sun Beach Guesthouse*.

Kayak rental You can rent a kayak from Kayak Adventures, on the seafront next to the *Hadthong Hotel*.

ACCOMMODATION

Faa Chom Khleun Ao Manao ☎032 661088–9, ✆aomanao.com. If you don't mind cosying up to the Thai military, this spruce, wi-fi-enabled air-force hotel on the Wing 5 base puts you right on the beach. All rooms have sea-view balconies, a/c, hot water, TV and fridge, and there's a large swimming pool. No English sign. B900

Hadthong Hotel 21 Thanon Susuek, but also with an entrance just south of the pier on the beachfront road ☎032 601050–5, ✆hadthong.com. Well-run spot with comfortable rooms, many sporting balconies and great sea views, all with wi-fi, fridges, a/c, hot water and TVs – plus a 15m swimming pool, internet room and snooker club. Breakfast included. B950

Maggie's Home-stay 5 Soi Tampramuk 4, between Salacheep and Susuek rds, just south of Thanon Kongkiat ☎032 604216 or ☎087 597 9720, ✉maggies.homestay@gmail.com. Welcoming spot behind a pretty front garden, with hammocks and salas for chilling out

under the trees. The diverse rooms are either in a bright and airy, traditional wooden house with polished floors and shared hot-water bathrooms or, less attractively, in outhouses at the back, though some of these are en-suite (cold showers). There's wi-fi throughout, and bikes and motorbikes for rent. Good rates for singles. Fan B260, a/c B500

★ **Sun Beach Guesthouse** 160 Thanon Chai Thalay, 500m or so down the promenade from the pier ☎032 604770, ✆sunbeach-guesthouse.com. Run by a welcoming and helpful Thai–German couple, this palatial guesthouse is done out like a Mediterranean villa, with Corinthian columns and smart tiling everywhere. The bright, comfortable, sky-blue rooms come with a/c, hot water, fridges, TVs, free wi-fi and balconies, with prices varying according to the quality of the sea view. There's a seductive pool and whirlpool, and internet access. B700

EATING AND DRINKING

Prachuap's famously good seafood is most cheaply sampled at the town's lively and varied main **night market**, which sets up shop in the empty lot around the junction of Thanon Kongkiat and Thanon Phitak Chat.

6

Ma-prow Thanon Chai Thalay, south of the Hadthong Hotel. Mellow, rustic, airy restaurant, which serves tasty squid with salted eggs (B150) and deep-fried sea bass fillet with tamarind and peanut sauce (B180), as well as a few Western dishes such as fish'n'chips. Daily 11am–11pm.

★ **Plern Smud** South of the pier at 44 Thanon Chai Thalay, alongside the Hadthong Hotel ☎032 611115 (English-language sign at the Thanon Susuek entrance only, not on the beachfront road). The town's best

restaurant has a pleasant, spacious courtyard facing the sea, and serves delicious pan-fried oysters, tasty crab claws (B150) and excellent *kaeng pa pla say* (fish jungle curry; B100) on its seafood-dominated menu. Daily 10am–9.30pm.

Rome Beer (MC Club House) Thanon Chai Thalay, just south of Ma-prow. Excellent spot for a waterside drink, hung with motorcycle memorabilia and home to some of the friendliest bikers you're ever likely to meet. Daily 4.30pm–late.

DIRECTORY

ATMs and exchange On Thanon Salacheep and Thanon Phitak Chat, including on the latter at Krung Thai Bank, which opens daily.

Internet access Many places on Thanon Salacheep.

Post office Directly behind the *Hadthong Hotel* on Thanon Susuek (Mon–Fri 8.30am–4.30pm, Sat & Sun 9am–noon).

Ban Krud

Graced with a tranquil, 5km sweep of white sand, pale-blue sea and swaying casuarinas, **BAN KRUD**, 70km south of Prachuap, supports a dozen or so fairly upmarket bungalow outfits and seafood restaurants along the central stretch of its shorefront road. About 1km inland from the main T-junction at the beach, the small, traditional village, which now includes several ATMs, clusters around the train station. At the beach's northern end are a colourful fishing village, which hosts a Thursday afternoon market, and a panoramic headland beyond, **Khao Thongchai**, that's dominated by the 14m-high Phra Phut Kitti Sirichai Buddha image and its sparkling modern temple, **Wat Phra Mahathat Phraphat**. Crowned with nine golden chedis, the temple displays an impressive fusion of traditional and contemporary features, including a series of charming modern stained-glass windows depicting Buddhist stories; reach it via a 1.5km-long road that spirals up from the beachfront. Other than a visit to the temple and possibly a snorkelling trip to Ko Thalu (B350/person through, for example, *Sala Thai Resort*), the main pastime in Ban Krud is sitting under the trees and enjoying a long seafood lunch or dinner.

ARRIVAL AND DEPARTURE
BAN KRUD

By train Most services on the Southern Line from Bangkok stop at Ban Krud's tiny train station, where you should be able to find a motorbike taxi (with sidecar).
Destinations Bangkok (3 daily; 5hr 30min–7hr 30min); Chumphon (6 daily; 2hr); Hat Yai (2 daily; 8hr 30min–10hr 30min); Nakhon Si Thammarat (1 daily; 10hr); Surat Thani

(5 daily; 4hr–5hr 30min); Trang (1 daily; 10hr).

By bus Most southbound buses drop passengers on Highway 4, from where motorbike-and-sidecar taxis cover the 8km down to the beach; just two Bangkok–Bang Saphan a/c buses a day stop at Ban Krud itself.

ACCOMMODATION

★ **Bayview** North of the headland and the ramshackle youth hostel, 4km from Sala Thai on Hat Tangsai ☎032 695566–7, ⊛bayviewbeachresort.com. Very welcoming and relaxed spot with a swimming pool, a kids' pool and a lovely area for deckchairs under the beachside casuarinas. All the well-spaced, diverse bungalows boast a/c, fridges, TVs and hot water, and there's an excellent restaurant, internet access and wi-fi, free bicycles, and kayaks, cars and motorbikes to rent. Prices rise a little at weekends. Breakfast included. **B1300**

Sala Thai About 1km north of the central beachfront T-junction ☎032 695181, ⊛salathaibeachresort.com. Friendly resort, whose cutesy wooden bungalows with a/c, hot water and TV are spread around a spacious, pretty garden with lots of shady trees, just across the road from the beach; it also has a few very basic bamboo bungalows with fans, mosquito nets and shared bathrooms, as well as a popular burger bar. Bikes and motorbikes for rent. Fan **B250**, a/c from **B600**

Chumphon

South Thailand officially starts at **CHUMPHON**, where the main highway splits into west- and east-coast branches, and inevitably the provincial capital saddles itself with the title "gateway to the south". Most tourists take this tag literally and use the town as nothing more than a transport interchange between the Bangkok train and boats to **Ko Tao, Pha Ngan and Samui**, so the town is well equipped to serve these passers-through, offering clued-up travel agents, efficient transport links and plenty of internet cafés. In truth, there's little call for exploring the fairly average beaches, islands and reefs around town when the varied and attractive strands of Ko Tao are just a short hop away, while the Chumphon National Museum is little short of pitiful.

6

ARRIVAL AND DEPARTURE   CHUMPHON

BY PLANE

Solar Air (☎ 02 535 2455–6, in Chumphon ☎ 081 902 9466, ⓦ solarair.co.th) has recently launched a daily service from Bangkok, with discounted through-tickets with Lomprayah to Ko Tao and Pha Ngan available. If you haven't got a through-ticket, a taxi to town from Chumphon airport, which is 40km to the north, will cost around B700.

BY TRAIN

Chumphon train station is on the northwest edge of town, less than ten minutes' walk from most guesthouses and hotels.
Destinations Bangkok (12 daily; 7hr–9hr 30min); Butterworth (Malaysia; 1 daily; 14hr); Hat Yai (6 daily; 7hr–8hr 30min); Nakhon Si Thammarat (2 daily; 7hr); Surat Thani (11 daily; 2hr 5min–4hr); Trang (2 daily; 7hr).

BY BUS OR MINIBUS

Government bus station The government bus station is 11km south of town on Highway 4, connected to the centre by songthaews (B50/person) and motorbike taxis (B100), though long-distance services will sometimes drop in town; two Bangkok a/c buses a day drop off and pick up on Thanon Tawee Sinka, west of TAT.

Private bus and minibus services There are several private a/c bus and minibus services that depart from various locations (see map below), including minibuses to Ranong and Surat Thani; Suwanathep buses to Bangkok; and Chokeanan Tour buses to Bangkok and Hat Yai – some Rungkit buses to Phuket, via Ranong and Khao Lak, start from the same spot, though some use the government bus station. Agents such as *Suda* and *Fame* (see p.534) can

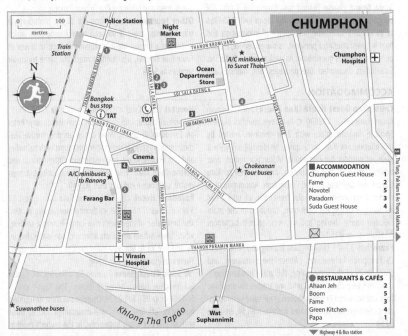

CHUMPHON

ACCOMMODATION
Chumphon Guest House	1
Fame	2
Novotel	5
Paradorn	3
Suda Guest House	4

RESTAURANTS & CAFÉS
Ahaan Jeh	2
Boom	5
Fame	3
Green Kitchen	4
Papa	1

Highway 4 & Bus station

also fix you up with minibuses to Krabi, Ko Lanta and Phetchaburi.

Destinations Bangkok (roughly hourly; 7–9hr); Hat Yai (4 daily; 7hr 30min); Hua Hin (hourly; 3hr 30min–4hr 30min); Khao Lak (4 daily; 5hr); Phuket (4 daily; 7hr); Prachuap Khiri Khan (6 daily; 2–3hr); Ranong (4 daily; 2–3hr); Surat Thani (roughly hourly; 3hr 30min).

BY BOAT

There are several different boat services from Chumphon to Ko Tao, Pha Ngan and Samui, tickets for all of which are sold by travel agents and guesthouses in town. Of these, the Songserm Express is the most likely to be cancelled if the weather is very bad. The fast Seatran service between Chumphon and Ko Tao has recently been suspended, but may resurface.

GETTING TO THE PIER

Lomprayah and Songserm tickets include transport to the pier from town, with pick-ups available even from guest-houses and from the station, including off the overnight train from Bangkok that arrives around 4am. The car ferry and the less comfortable midnight boat do pick-ups from town guesthouses at around 10pm (B50/person); however, these boats (and their pick-ups) sometimes leave an hour or two early, because of tides and the weather.

BOATS AND SERVICES

Lomprayah Catamaran Office at the train station ☎ 077 558212–3, ⊛ lomprayah.com. Daily 7am & 1pm, from Ao Thung Makham Noi, 27km south of Chumphon; 1hr 45min to Ko Tao (B600); around 3hr 30min to Ko Pha Ngan (B1000); around 4hr to Maenam, Ko Samui (B1100).

Songserm Express Office at the train station ☎ 077 506205, ⊛ songserm-expressboat.com. Daily 7am, from Pak Nam, about 20km south of Chumphon; 2hr 30min to Ko Tao (B450); around 4hr 30min to Ko Pha Ngan (B750).

Car ferry ☎ 077 580030. Mon–Sat 11pm, from Tha Yang, about 15km south of Chumphon; 6hr; B300, including blankets and pillows in an a/c room (the Ko Jaroen 2 that runs from Tha Yang on Mon, Wed & Fri also has dorm-style bunk beds for B400).

Midnight boat ☎ 077 553052. Daily midnight, from Tha Yang, about 15km south of Chumphon; 6hr; B200.

INFORMATION AND TOURS

Tourist information The TAT office is down a short soi at 111 Thanon Tawee Sinka (daily 8.30am–4.30pm; ☎ 077 501831, ⊜ tatchumphon@tat.or.th), offering free internet access.

Suda Guest House Thanon Sala Daeng Soi 3 (aka Soi Bangkok Bank), 30m off Thanon Tha Tapao ☎ 077 504366 or ☎ 085 571 2229. The best source of information and fixer in town, offering a personal, unbiased service, is Suda at her eponymous guesthouse. As well as tickets to Ko Tao, Suda offers discounted dive packages; bus, minibus and train tickets; twice-daily visa runs via Ranong to Burma (from B650, excluding B500 for Burmese visa); motorbike (B150–200/day) and car (B1000–1300/day) rental; internet access; packages to Ko Chang (Ranong) and Ko Phayam; and jungle treks and rafting at Pha To near Ranong.

Other tour agencies Among the bigger multipurpose travel agents, avoid if you can busy *Farang Bar*, which resembles a human meat-processing factory, in favour of *Fame* (see below), which offers much the same transport services as Suda.

ACCOMMODATION

Chumphon Guest House (Kae House) Soi 1, Thanon Kromluang ☎ 077 502900, ⊛ facebook.com/Sunisa Jet. Sociable, laidback place with 24hr check-in, hosted by the effervescent Kae, on a quiet, residential soi with a pleasant outdoor bar-restaurant. Motorcycle rental, boat tickets, free wi-fi and computers, and informal cooking classes and day-trips around Chumphon. Accommodation ranges from small rooms out front, one of which has an en-suite cold-water bathroom, to rooms in the main wooden house sharing hot showers. Shared bathroom **B150**, en-suite **B250**

Fame 188/20–21 Thanon Sala Daeng ☎ 077 571077, ⊛ chumphon-kohtao.com. Above the restaurant and tour agency of the same name, this place has ten good-sized and very clean rooms with mattresses on the floor, fans and hot water in either shared or en-suite bathrooms; computers and free wi-fi. Shared bathroom **B150**, en-suite **B250**

Novotel 15km southeast near Pak Nam ☎ 077 529529, ⊛ novotel-chumphon.com. This low-rise luxury hotel on Paradornpab beach, done out in an unobtrusive Thai contemporary style, features spacious rooms with balconies and lots of dark wood, two restaurants (international and northeastern Thai), two swimming pools, a spa, fitness centre, golf course and kids' club. **B2240**

Paradorn Hotel 180/12 Thanon Sala Daeng ☎ 077 511598 or ☎ 077 511500, ⊛ chumphon-paradorn.com. The best value of the town's mid-range hotels, a shining, white block where all rooms have a/c, hot water, fridge, TV and free wi-fi. Not on a main road, so should be quiet. There's an espresso bar too. **B360**

★ **Suda Guest House** Thanon Sala Daeng Soi 3 (aka Soi Bangkok Bank), 30m off Thanon Tha Tapao ☎ 077 504366 or ☎ 085 571 2229. Chumphon's most welcoming homestay, offering clean, well-maintained rooms, most with shared hot-water bathrooms, in the owner's modern house. Plenty of information available, B20 showers for passers-through and much more (see opposite). Phone for free transport from train or bus station. Suda plans to install wi-fi and to open an all-en-suite extension. Good reductions for singles. Fan and shared bathroom B200, en-suite B400, a/c and shared bathroom B350, en-suite B500

EATING AND DRINKING

The cheapest place to eat is the **night market**, which sets up along both sides of Thanon Kromluang and is an enjoyable place to munch your way through a selection of fried noodles, barbecued chicken and sticky, coconut-laced sweets.

Ahaan Jeh Right next to Fame on Thanon Sala Daeng. Tiny place offering a ready-cooked buffet of Thai–Chinese vegetarian food at B20 per serving – get there early, as most dishes are finished before closing time. Daily 7am to about 3pm.

Boom (The Bakery Café) Thanon Tha Tapao ☎ 077 511523. A bakery with a few pavement tables for watching the world go by, serving good espressos, tasty brownies and other Western and Thai cakes. Mon–Sat 8am–7pm.

Fame 188/20–21 Thanon Sala Daeng ☎ 077 571077. Travellers' restaurant specializing in Italian food, including pizzas, as well as Indian dhal, loads of sandwiches using home-baked bread, and huge American (B140) and veggie

(B110–120) breakfasts; free wi-fi. Daily 5am–9.30pm.
Green Kitchen Off Thanon Suksumer ☎ 077 571731. Good, authentic Vietnamese cuisine such as grilled beef in betel leaves (B50) and fresh spring rolls (B60), plus Thai food and some European dishes. Daily 10am–10pm.

Papa Across from the train station on Thanon Kromluang ☎ 077 504504. One of the liveliest places to eat dinner, this huge restaurant – mostly open-air, but with an a/c room – has an extensive menu of fresh seafood, Thai salads such as wingbean salad (B80) and Chinese dishes, plus a few Western standards. Also puts on live music every evening, and has as an attached nightclub, Papa 2000. Daily noon–2/3am.

Chaiya

About 140km south of Chumphon, **CHAIYA** is thought to have been the capital of southern Thailand under the Srivijayan civilization, which fanned out from Sumatra between the eighth and thirteenth centuries. Today there's little to mark the passing of Srivijaya, but this small, sleepy town has gained new fame as the site of **Wat Suan Mokkh**, a progressively minded temple whose meditation retreats account for the bulk of Chaiya's foreign visitors (most Thais only stop to buy the famous local salted eggs). Unless you're interested in one of the retreats, the town is best visited on a day-trip, either as a break in the journey south, or as an excursion from Surat Thani.

Wat Phra Boromathat

Western side of town, on the access road from Highway 41

The main sight in Chaiya is **Wat Phra Boromathat**, where the ninth-century chedi – one of very few surviving examples of Srivijayan architecture – is said to contain relics of the Buddha himself. Hidden away behind the viharn in a pretty, red-tiled cloister, the chedi looks like an oversized wedding cake surrounded by an ornamental moat. Its unusual square tiers are spiked with smaller chedis and decorated with gilt, in a style similar to the temples of central Java.

National Museum

On the eastern side of the temple • Wed–Sun 9am–4pm • B30 • ⓦ thailandmuseum.com

The **National Museum** is a bit of a disappointment. Although the Srivijaya period produced some of Thailand's finest sculpture, much of it discovered at Chaiya, the best pieces have been carted off to the National Museum in Bangkok. Replicas have been left in their stead, which are shown alongside fragments of some original statues, two intricately worked 2000-year-old bronze drums, found at Chaiya and Ko Samui, and various examples of Thai handicrafts. The best remaining pieces are a calm and elegant sixth- to seventh-century stone image of the Buddha meditating from

Wat Phra Boromathat, and an equally serene head of a Buddha image, Ayutthayan-style in pink sandstone, from Wat Kaeo.

Wat Kaeo

On the south side of town

Heading towards the centre of Chaiya from Wat Phra Boromathat, you can reach this imposing ninth- or tenth-century brick chedi by taking the first paved road on the right, which brings you first to the restored base of the chedi at Wat Long, and then after 1km to **Wat Kaeo**, enclosed by a thick ring of trees. Here you can poke around the murky antechambers of the chedi, three of which house images of the Buddha subduing Mara.

Wat Suan Mokkh

6km south of Chaiya on Highway 41 • ⓦ suanmokkh.org • All buses between Surat Thani and Chumphon stop near the wat

The forest temple of **Wat Suan Mokkh** (Garden of Liberation) was founded by the abbot of Wat Phra Boromathat, **Buddhadasa Bhikkhu**, southern Thailand's most revered monk until his death in 1993 at the age of 87. His radical, back-to-basics philosophy, encompassing Christian, Zen and Taoist influences, lives on and continues to draw Thais from all over the country to the temple, as well as hundreds of foreigners. It's not necessary to sign up for one of the wat's **retreats** to enjoy the temple, however – you can simply drop by for a quiet stroll through the wooded grounds.

The unusual layout of the wat is centred on the Golden Hill: scrambling up between trees and monks' huts, past the cremation site of Buddhadasa Bhikkhu, you'll reach a hushed clearing on top of the hill, which is the temple's holiest meeting place, a simple open-air platform decorated with images of the Buddha and the Wheel of Law. At the base of the hill, the outer walls of the Spiritual Theatre are lined with bas-reliefs, replicas of originals in India, which depict scenes from the life of the Buddha. Inside, every centimetre is covered with colourful didactic painting, executed by resident monks and visitors in a jumble of realistic and surrealistic styles.

MEDITATION RETREATS AT SUAN MOKKH

Meditation retreats are led by Western and Thai teachers over the first ten days of every month at the International Dharma Heritage (ⓦ suanmokkh-idh.org), a purpose-built compound 1km from the main temple at Wat Suan Mokkh. Large numbers of foreign travellers, both novices and experienced meditators, turn up for the retreats, which are intended as a challenging exercise in mental development – it's not an opportunity to relax and live at low cost for a few days. Conditions imitate the rigorous lifestyle of a *bhikkhu* (monk) as far as possible, each day beginning before dawn with meditation according to the Anapanasati method, which aims to achieve mindfulness by focusing on the breathing process. Although talks are given on Dharma (the doctrines of the Buddha – as interpreted by Buddhadasa Bhikkhu) and meditation technique, most of each day is spent practising Anapanasati in solitude. To aid concentration, participants maintain a rule of silence, broken only by daily chanting sessions, although supervisors are sometimes available for individual interviews if there are any questions or problems. Men and women are segregated into separate dormitory blocks and, like monks, are expected to help out with chores.

PRACTICALITIES

Turn up at Wat Suan Mokkh as early as possible (by 3pm at the latest) on the last day of the month to register (you can stay in Suan Mokkh the night before registration for free). The busiest period for the retreats is December–April, especially February and March. The fee is B2000 per person, which includes two vegetarian meals a day and accommodation in simple cells. Participants are required to hand in their mobile phones and are not allowed to leave the premises during the retreat – bring any supplies you think you might need (though there is a small, basic shop on site).

ARRIVAL AND DEPARTURE
CHAIYA

By train The town lies on the main Southern Rail Line, served by trains (mostly overnight) from and to Bangkok (9 daily; 8–11hr).

By bus Chaiya is 3km east of Highway 41, the main road down this section of the Gulf coast: buses running between Chumphon and Surat Thani will drop off (or pick up) on the

highway, from where you can catch a motorbike taxi or blue songthaew into town.

By minibus or songthaew From Surat Thani's Talat Kaset II bus station, hourly a/c minibuses and more frequent but slower songthaews take around an hour to reach Chaiya town centre.

6

Surat Thani

Uninspiring **SURAT THANI** ("City of the Good People"), 60km south of Chaiya, is generally worth visiting only as a jumping-off point for the Samui archipelago. Strung along the south bank of the Tapi River, with a busy port for rubber and coconuts near the river mouth, the town is experiencing rapid economic growth and paralyzing traffic jams. It might be worth a stay, however, when the Chak Phra Festival (see box, p.538) is on, or as a base for seeing the nearby historic town of Chaiya.

ARRIVAL AND DEPARTURE
SURAT THANI

Surat's best **travel agency** is the reliable Phantip, in front of Talat Kaset I at 293/6–8 Thanon Taladmai (☎077 272230 or ☎077 272906), where among many other things you can book train and plane tickets. Be aware that there have been many reports of overcharging and **scams** by unregistered agents and touts selling tickets for minibus and bus services out of Surat, especially involving any kind of combination ticket, including those heading for Khao Sok National Park, Phuket, Krabi and Malaysia. To avoid this, either go direct to the relevant a/c minibus office at Talat Kaset II bus station (local offices are generally on the west side of the station, long-distance ones on the east side, and they all have to be authorized by the provincial office), or buy a bus ticket direct from the station, or walk the short distance to Phantip Travel.

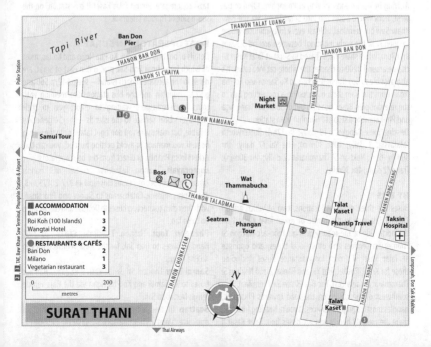

6

THE CHAK PHRA FESTIVAL

At the start of the eleventh lunar month (usually in October) the people of Surat Thani celebrate the end of Buddhist Lent with the **Chak Phra Festival** (Pulling the Buddha), which symbolizes the Buddha's return to earth after a monsoon season spent preaching to his mother in heaven. On the Tapi River, tugboats pull the town's principal Buddha image on a raft decorated with huge nagas, while on land sleigh-like floats bearing Buddha images and colourful flags and parasols are hauled across the countryside and through the streets. As the monks have been confined to their monasteries for three months, the end of Lent is also the time to give them generous offerings in the *kathin* ceremony, of which Surat Thani has its own version, called Thot Pha Pa, when the offerings are hung on tree branches planted in front of the houses before dawn. Longboat races, between teams from all over the south, are also held during the festival.

BY PLANE

Arriving by air from Bangkok (currently Air Asia 2 daily, Nok Air 3 daily, Thai Airways 2 daily; 1hr 15min) or Kuala Lumpur (Air Asia 3 weekly; 1hr 35min), you can take a B100 minibus through Phantip or from the *Wangtai Hotel* for the 27km journey south from the airport (☎ 077 441230–1) into Surat Thani, or a combination ticket to Ko Samui (B350) or Ko Pha Ngan (B550). Budget (☎ 077 441166) has an outlet at the airport for car rental. If you're flying out of Surat, you can most easily catch the airport minibus from town at the Phantip office. Thai Airways have an office in town at 3/27–28 Thanon Karoonrat, off Thanon Chonkasem (☎ 077 272610).

BY TRAIN

Arriving by train means arriving at Phunphin, 13km to the west, from where buses run into Surat Thani, via the Baw Khaw Saw bus terminal, at least every forty minutes (more frequently in the early morning) between around 5.30am and 7pm, while share-taxis (based in Surat at Talat Kaset II) charge around B200 to charter the whole car into town. It's also possible to buy through-tickets to Ko Samui and Ko Pha Ngan from the train station, including a connecting bus to the relevant pier. Buses heading out of Surat to Phang Nga and Phuket make a stop at Phunphin train station.
Destinations Bangkok (10 daily; 9–12hr); Butterworth (Malaysia; 1 daily; 10hr 30min); Hat Yai (7 daily; 4hr 30min–6hr); Nakhon Si Thammarat (2 daily; 4hr 30min); Trang (2 daily; 4hr 30min).

BY BUS

Buses use three different locations, two of which are on Thanon Taladmai in the centre of town: Talat Kaset I on the north side of the road (Phunphin, non-a/c Nakhon Si Thammarat services and other local buses) and opposite at Talat Kaset II (most long-distance buses, including those for Krabi, Phuket, Hat Yai and Ranong, and Nakhon Si Thammarat a/c services). The Baw Khaw Saw terminal, 2km southwest of the centre on the road towards Phunphin, handles mostly Bangkok services. If you're heading for Krabi, there are roughly hourly non-a/c buses from Talat Kaset II

and faster hourly a/c buses through Phantip (as well as a/c minibuses).
Destinations Bangkok (Southern Terminal; 10 daily; 10–12hr); Chumphon (roughly hourly; 3hr 30min); Hat Yai (10 daily; 5hr–5hr 30min); Khao Sok (10 daily; 2hr 30min); Krabi (hourly; 3–4hr); Nakhon Si Thammarat (21 daily; 2hr 10min–2hr 40min); Phang Nga (5 daily; 3hr 30min); Phuket (8 daily; 5hr); Phunphin (at least every 40min; 40min); Ranong (10 daily; 4–5hr).

BY MINIBUS OR SHARE-TAXI

A/c minibuses (to Chumphon, Ranong, Ratchabrapa Dam, Khao Sok, Phang Nga, Phuket, Krabi, Trang, Hat Yai and Nakhon Si Thammarat) and a dwindling number of share-taxis congregate around Talat Kaset II bus station, on the south side of Thanon Taladmai.

BOAT OPERATORS IN SURAT

Details of boats to Ko Samui, Ko Pha Ngan and Ko Tao, most of which leave from Don Sak pier, 68km east of Surat, are given in the account of each island – see p.542, p.560 and p.572. Phunphin and the bus stations are teeming with touts, with transport waiting to escort you to their employer's boat service to the islands – they're generally reliable, but make sure you don't get talked onto the wrong boat. If you manage to avoid getting hustled, you can buy tickets from Phantip or direct from the boat operators.
Lomprayah Thanon Taladmai, corner of Thanon Amphoe, just east of Taksin Hospital ☎ 077 288732–3, ⓦ lomprayah.com. Catamarans to Samui and Pha Ngan, with their own connecting buses to Don Sak and connections on to Ko Tao.
Phangan Tour Thanon Taladmai ☎ 077 205799. Handles buses to Don Sak for the Raja vehicle ferries to Ko Pha Ngan.
Samui Tour Thanon Sri Surat ☎ 077 282352. Handles buses to Ko Samui and Ko Pha Ngan via the Raja vehicle ferries from Don Sak.
Seatran In the petrol station on Thanon Taladmai opposite Wat Thammabucha ☎ 077 275060–2,

Ⓦ seatranferry.com. Vehicle ferries to Samui (with their own connecting buses), from Don Sak.
Night boats The night boats to Samui, Pha Ngan and Tao, which are barely glorified cargo boats, line up during the day at Ban Don Pier in the centre of Surat; it's just a question of turning up and buying a ticket.

GETTING AROUND

By share-songthaew Small share-songthaews buzz around town, charging around B15–20/person.

INFORMATION

Tourist information TAT's office is at the western end of town at 5 Thanon Taladmai (daily 8.30am–noon & 1–4.30pm; ☎077 288817–9 or ☎077 282352, Ⓔ tatsurat @tat.or.th).

6

ACCOMMODATION

A lot of **accommodation** in Surat Thani is noisy, grotty and overpriced, but there are a few notable exceptions.

Ban Don Hotel Above a restaurant at 268/2 Thanon Namuang ☎077 272167. Most of the very clean rooms here, with en-suite cold-water bathrooms, TV and fans or a/c, are set back from the noise of the main road. Fan B̲3̲0̲0̲, a/c B̲4̲5̲0̲
Roi Koh (100 Islands) On the southern bypass near the tourist police and opposite Tesco Lotus ☎077 201150–8, Ⓦ roikoh.com. Though out of the centre, this place offers attractive, comfortable rooms with a/c, hot

water, TVs and mini-bars, a small spa and a decent-sized pool set in a lush garden with a waterfall. Breakfast included. B̲7̲7̲0̲
Wangtai Hotel 1 Thanon Taladmai, on the western side of the centre by the TAT office ☎077 283020–5, Ⓦ wangtaisurat.com. Surat Thani's best upmarket option, and surprisingly good value, with over two hundred large, smart rooms with wi-fi around a good-sized swimming pool. B̲7̲9̲0̲

EATING

Besides the restaurants listed below, there's a large **night market** between Thanon Si Chaiya and Thanon Ban Don, which displays an eye-catching range of dishes; a smaller offshoot by Ban Don pier offers less choice but is handy if you're taking a night boat.

Ban Don Restaurant 268/2 Thanon Namuang. Basic, bustling restaurant with plain, marble-topped tables, which serves large portions of tasty, inexpensive Thai and Chinese food – mostly noodle and rice dishes, such as *khao man kai* (B35), but also green curry and *tom yam*. Daily 6am–11pm.
Milano Near the night-boat piers on Thanon Ban Don. This place has an authentic oven turning out very tasty and reasonably priced pizzas, though its home-made pasta is

not so successful. Also serves other Western main courses, Mexican dishes, sandwiches, breakfasts and espresso coffee. Daily 10am–11pm.
Vegetarian restaurant One block east of Talat Kaset II bus station on Thanon Tha Thong. Wide selection of cheap and delicious curries and other tray food for B25/ plate. Look for the yellow flags outside and a sign saying "vegetarian food". Daily 7am till about 3.30pm.

DIRECTORY

Internet access Boss, just west of the post office on Thanon Taladmai (daily 9am–midnight).
Tourist police On the southern bypass near the junction with Thanon Srivichai, the westward continuation of Thanon Taladmai (☎1155 or ☎077 405575).

Ko Samui

A million visitors a year, ranging from globetrotting backpackers to suitcase-toting fortnighters, come to southern Thailand just for the beautiful beaches of **KO SAMUI**, 80km from Surat. At 15km across and down, Samui is generally large enough to cope with this diversity – except during the rush at Christmas and New Year – and the paradisal sands and clear blue seas have to a surprising extent kept their good looks, enhanced by a thick fringe of palm trees that gives a harvest of more than two million coconuts each month. However, development behind the beaches – which has brought the islanders far greater prosperity than the crop could ever provide – speeds along in a messy, haphazard fashion with little concern for the environment. At least there's a local bylaw limiting new construction to the height of a coconut palm (usually about three storeys), though this has not deterred either the luxury hotel groups or the real-estate developers who have recently been throwing up estates of second homes for Thais and foreigners.

For most visitors, the days are spent indulging in a few watersports or just lying on the beach waiting for the next drinks-seller, hair-braider or masseur to come along. For something more active, you should not miss the almost supernatural beauty of the **Ang Thong National Marine Park** (see p.557), which comprises many of the eighty islands in the Samui archipelago. Otherwise, a day-trip by rented car or motorbike on the 50km round-island road, perhaps making time for a meal at the excellent *Ban Hua Thanon Seafood* on the south coast, will throw up plenty more fine beaches.

The island's most appealing strand, **Chaweng**, has seen the heaviest, most crowded development and is now the most expensive place to stay, though it does offer by far the best range of amenities and nightlife, ranging from tawdry bar-beers to hip nightclubs. Its slightly smaller neighbour, **Lamai**, lags a little behind in terms of looks and top-end development, but retains large pockets of backpacker bungalow resorts. The other favourite for backpackers is **Maenam**, which, though less attractive again, is markedly quiet, with plenty of room to breathe between the beach and the round-island road. Adjacent **Bophut** is similar in appearance, but generally more sophisticated, with a cluster of boutique resorts, fine restaurants and a distinct Mediterranean feel in

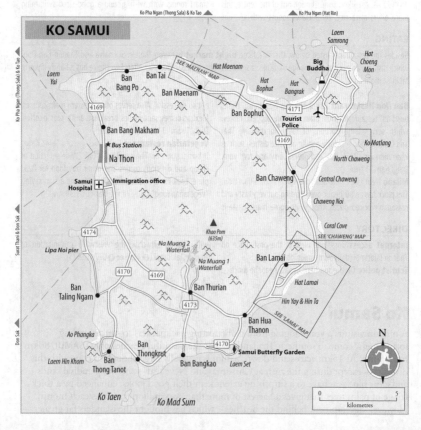

KO SAMUI ACTIVITIES

Samui has around a dozen scuba-diving companies, offering trips for divers and snorkellers and courses throughout the year, and there's a recompression chamber at Bangrak (**☎** 077 427427, **ⓦ** sssnetwork.com). Most trips for experienced divers, however, head for the waters around Ko Tao (see p.574) as their diving costs around B4000–5500, but of course if you can make your own way to Ko Tao, you'll save money. Also on offer are plenty of spas, as well as meditation retreats, island tours, ziplines, go-karting, kiteboarding and cooking classes.

6

DIVE OPERATORS

Easy Divers Head office opposite Sandsea Resort, Lamai **☎** 077 413373, **ⓦ** easydivers-thailand.com. PADI Five-Star dive centre, with several branches around the island.

Planet Scuba Head office next to the Seatran pier on Bangrak **☎** 077 413050, **ⓦ** planetscuba.net. PADI Five-Star dive centre, with several branches.

SPAS

Eranda Far north end of Chaweng **☎** 077 422666, **ⓦ** erandaspa.com. Set on a waterfall- and flower-splashed hillside with a plunge pool, offering plenty of style (2hr Thai massage B1900).

Peace Tropical Spa On Route 4169 near the centre of Bophut beach **☎** 077 430199, **ⓦ** peacetropicalspa.com. Half a dozen types of massage, including a 1hr 30min Thai massage for B1500, as well as body and facial treatments.

The Spa Resort Lamai **☎** 077 230855, **ⓦ** thespa resorts.net. Everything from Thai massage (B447/hr) for non-guests, to residential fasting programmes

(from B21,000 for 8 days). Also on offer are body and facial wraps, and yoga, meditation and raw-food culinary classes, as well as in-house accommodation, either on the beach or in the hills above Lamai.

Tamarind Springs Lamai **☎** 077 230571, **ⓦ** tamarindsprings.com. Set in a beautiful, secluded coconut grove just off the main road. A session in their herbal steam room, set between boulders by a waterfall-fed plunge pool, and a 2hr 30min Thai massage, for example, costs B5500; massage training courses are also available.

OTHER ACTIVITIES

Canopy Adventures **☎** 077 414150–1 or **☎** 087 046 7307, **ⓦ** canopyadventuresthailand.com. A series of ziplines between treehouses and past waterfalls in the hills 4km above Maenam (2–3hr; B1750, including transfers).

Kiteboarding Asia **☎** 081 591 4592, **ⓦ** kiteboarding asia.com. Instruction in kiteboarding (B4000 for one day), either from the beach south of Ban Hua Thanon or from Nathon, depending on the time of year, as well as rentals.

Mr Ung's Magical Safari Tours **☎** 077 230114, **ⓦ** ungsafari.com. Day-trips that traverse the rough tracks of the mountainous interior to some spectacular viewpoints, as well as taking in Hin Yay Hin Ta, the Big Buddha and monkey and elephant shows (from B1400, including lunch).

Samui Go-kart Route 4169 1km west of Bophut

village **☎** 077 425097. Offers everyone the chance to let off steam without becoming another accident statistic on the roads of Samui (daily 9am–8/9pm; from B600/10min, including free transfers).

Samui Institute of Thai Culinary Arts (SITCA) Soi Colibri, opposite Centara Grand Resort in Chaweng **☎** 077 413172, **ⓦ** sitca.net. This highly recommended outfit runs 3hr cookery classes in the morning and afternoon (B1950), plus six- and twelve-day courses and fruit-carving classes. Closed Sun.

Wat Suan Mokkh meditation retreats **ⓦ** dipa bhavan.org. Wat Suan Mokkh (see p.536) offers retreats from the 20th to the 27th of each month at Dipabhavan, a hermitage in the hills above Lamai (full details on the website); pick-ups are laid on from *Utopia Resort*, north of the central crossroads in Lamai.

its congenial beachfront village. **Choeng Mon**, set apart in Samui's northeast corner, offers something different again: the small, part-sandy, part-rocky bay is tranquil and pretty, the seafront between the handful of upmarket hotels is comparatively undeveloped, and Chaweng's nightlife is within easy striking distance.

No particular **season** is best for coming to Ko Samui (see also p.59). The northeast monsoon blows heaviest in November, but can bring rain at any time between October and January, and sometimes causes high waves and strong currents, especially on the east coast. January is often breezy, March and April are very hot, and between

May and October the southwest monsoon blows onto Samui's west coast and causes some rain. **Festivals** include a week-long jazz festival in September (ⓦsamuijazzfestival .com) and a six-day sailing regatta in May/June, with lots of attendant parties and festivities (ⓦsamuiregatta.com). At the lower end of Samui's **accommodation** scale, there are very few bungalows left for under B400, while at the most upmarket places you can pay well over B4000 for the highest international standards. The prices listed are based on high-season rates, but out of season (roughly April–June, Oct & Nov) dramatic reductions are possible.

ARRIVAL AND DEPARTURE   KO SAMUI

BY PLANE

Flights to Samui Airport, in the northeastern tip of the island, are among the most expensive in Thailand, so you might want to consider flying from Bangkok to Surat Thani (see p.538) or Nakhon Si Thammarat (see p.583), nearby on the mainland; Nok Air, for example, offers good-value through-tickets via either of these airports, including flight, bus and boat to Samui.

Airlines You can get to Ko Samui direct from Suvarnabhumi Airport with Thai Airways (2 daily; in Bangkok ☎02 356 1111), or with Bangkok Airways (about 20 daily; in Bangkok ☎02 265 5555, at Samui airport ☎077 428555), which also operates flights from Chiang Mai, Hong Kong, Krabi, Pattaya, Phuket, Singapore and Trat. Berjaya Airlines currently operates a twice-weekly service from Kuala Lumpur, while Firefly runs daily from KL.

Airport facilities As well as bars and restaurants, the terminals have currency-exchange facilities and ATMs, a post office with international telephones and several car rental outlets including Avis (☎084 700 8161, ⓦavisthailand.com).

Minibus transfers A/c minibuses meet incoming flights (and connect with departures, bookable through your accommodation), charging B120 to Chaweng for example. Destinations Bangkok (20 daily; 1hr–1hr 30min); Chiang Mai (2 weekly; 2hr 30min–3hr 30min); Hong Kong (1 daily; 3hr 30min); Krabi (1 daily; 50min); Kuala Lumpur, Malaysia (1–2 daily; 2hr); Pattaya (U-Tapao; 1–2 daily; 1hr); Phuket (2–5 daily; 50min); Singapore (1 daily; 2hr); Trat (4 weekly; 1hr 20min).

BY BOAT AND BUS

The most obvious route for getting to Ko Samui by boat (45min–1hr 30min) is from Don Sak, 68km east of Surat Thani (see p.538); catching a boat from Chumphon is generally more expensive and leaves you a long time on the sometimes choppy sea. There are also boats from Ko Samui to Ko Pha Ngan (see p.560) and to Ko Tao (see p.573); all offer the same service in the return direction.

FROM SURAT THANI

Don Sak to Na Thon From Don Sak, hourly Seatran vehicle ferries (on Ko Samui ☎077 426000–2) and

twice-daily Lomprayah catamarans (on Samui ☎077 950028) run to the island capital, Na Thon, all with their own connecting buses from Surat.

Don Sak to Lipa Noi and Na Thon Raja vehicle ferries run hourly between Don Sak and Lipa Noi, 8km south of Na Thon (on Samui ☎077 415230–3); every two hours to coincide with alternate boats, Samui Tour (on Samui ☎077 421092) runs buses from Surat or Phunphin via the ferry, and on to Na Thon.

Surat Thani to Na Thon The night boat leaves Ban Don pier in Surat Thani itself for Na Thon at 11pm every night; tickets are sold at the pier on the day of departure.

Fares and journey times Seatran and Samui Tour charge B250 to get to Samui from Surat, B280 from Phunphin train station, including a connecting bus; total journey time from Surat is around 3hr. Lomprayah charge B450 from Surat (special offers sometimes available; total journey time 2hr 15min), B500 from Phunphin, including a connecting bus. The night boat takes 6hr and costs B250.

LONG-DISTANCE SERVICES

Ko Samui's government bus terminal (Baw Khaw Saw) is on Thanon Taweeratpakdee towards the north end of Na Thon (☎077 421125 or ☎077 420765). It handles bus-and-boat services (via Don Sak and Lipa Noi), for example from Bangkok's Southern Terminal (mostly overnight; some also stopping at Mo Chit bus terminal), which cost from B540 on a basic a/c bus to B940 on a VIP bus – these are far preferable to the cheap deals offered by dodgy travel agents on Thanon Khao San, as the vehicles used on the latter service are often substandard and many thefts have been reported. The Baw Khaw Saw also sells through-tickets to Nakhon Si Thammarat, which involve catching the ferry to Don Sak, then changing on to an a/c minibus. Destinations Bangkok (8 daily; 13hr); Hat Yai (2 daily; 7hr); Krabi (1 daily; 7hr); Phuket (1 daily; 8hr).

BY BOAT AND TRAIN FROM BANGKOK

At Hualamphong Station, you can buy a discounted through-ticket to Samui with the State Railway – B698, for example, in a second-class a/c bunk, upper tier, to Phunphin station, plus B350 for your bus and Lomprayah catamaran to Na Thon from there.

ANG THONG NATIONAL MARINE PARK (P.557) >

6

GETTING AROUND

BY SONGTHAEW

Songthaews, which congregate at the car park near the southerly pier in Na Thon, cover a variety of set routes during the daytime, either heading off clockwise or anticlockwise on Route 4169, to serve all the beaches; destinations are marked in English and fares range from B50 to Maenam to B60 to Chaweng or Lamai. In the evening, they tend to operate more like taxis and you'll have to negotiate a fare to get them to take you exactly where you want to go.

BY TAXI

Ko Samui sports dozens of a/c taxis. Although they all have meters, you'd be wasting your breath trying to persuade any driver to use his; instead, you're looking at a flat fare of

around B300 from Na Thon to Maenam, B500 to Chaweng, for example. You'll also see one or two motorbike taxis buzzing about the island, which charge from B30 for a local drop, up to B250 from Na Thon to Chaweng.

BY MOTORBIKE OR CAR

You can rent a motorbike for around B200 in Na Thon and on the main beaches. Dozens are killed on Samui's roads each year, so proceed with great caution, and wear a helmet – apart from any other consideration you can be landed with an on-the-spot B500 fine by police for not wearing one. In addition, thieves have been snatching bags from the front baskets of moving motorbikes on Samui, so keep yours on your person – or think about upgrading to a four-wheel drive, from around B800 a day.

INFORMATION

Tourist information TAT runs a small but helpful office (daily 8.30am–noon & 1–4.30pm; ☎077 420504 or ☎077 420720, ✉tatsamui@tat.or.th), tucked away on an unnamed side road in Na Thon (north of the pier and inland from the post office). Here, and at many other places around Samui, you can pick up Siam Map Company's

detailed map of the island.
Tourist police The tourist police are on the Route 4169 ring road between Bophut and Chaweng, north of Big C supermarket on the same side of the road (☎1155 or ☎077 430016).

Na Thon

The island capital, **NA THON**, at the top of the long western coast, is a frenetic half-built town which most travellers use only as a service station before hitting the sand: although most of the main beaches now have post offices, currency-exchange facilities, ATMs, supermarkets, travel agents and clinics, the biggest concentration of amenities is here. The town's layout is simple: the three piers come to land at the promenade, Thanon Chonvithi, which is paralleled first by narrow Thanon Ang Thong, then by Thanon Taweeratpakdee, aka Route 4169, the round-island road; the main cross-street is Thanon Na Amphoe, by the central pier. If you're driving yourself, note that there's a one-way system in the centre of town: south on Taweeratpakdee, north on Chonvithi.

ACCOMMODATION   NA THON

Nathon Residence Thanon Taweeratpakdee next to Siam City (Thanachart) Bank ☎077 236081, ✉nathon -res@windowslive.com. If you really need a place to stay in Na Thon, this is your best bet, a friendly, well-run

establishment with plain but spotless tiled rooms with a/c, cable TV, free wi-fi, fridges and en-suite bathrooms, some with hot water – ask for a quiet room at the back. Computers available for guest use. **B500**

EATING AND DRINKING

Several stalls and small cafés purvey inexpensive Thai food around the market on Thanon Taweeratpakdee and on Thanon Chonvithi (including a lively night market by the piers).

About Art & Craft Thanon Chonvithi, opposite the southerly pier, a few doors up from Siam Commercial Bank. The tiny frontage here reveals a dim crafts shop and café, serving good, mostly vegetarian food and dozens of juices and smoothies. There are some interesting veggie versions of Thai dishes, such as *laap* with tofu, or try the

burritos with avocado (B160). Mon–Sat 8am–5pm.
Coffee Island Corner of Thanon Chonvithi and Thanon Na Amphoe ☎077 420153. Inexpensive and justifiably popular, especially for breakfast; also serves sandwiches (tuna B80), pancakes and pizzas, as well as Thai food and a wide variety of coffees. Free wi-fi. Daily 6.30am–late.

DIRECTORY

Bookshop Nathon Book Store on Thanon Na Amphoe (Mon–Sat 9am–6pm or later; ☎077 420332) is a good, helpful secondhand place, with some new titles.

Hospital The state hospital (☎077 421230–2) is 3km south of town off Route 4169.

Immigration office Located 2km south of town down Route 4169 (Mon–Fri 8.30am–4.30pm; ☎077 421069).

Post office Towards the northern end of the promenade, just north of the central pier (Mon–Fri 8.30am–4.30pm, Sat & Sun 9am–noon), with poste restante and packing services. International telephones upstairs (Mon–Fri 8.30am–4pm).

Travel agent The reliable Phantip, for everything from international flight tickets to local bus and train tickets, is on Thanon Taweeratpakdee, north of Thanon Na Amphoe (☎077 421221–2).

6

Maenam

MAENAM, 13km from Na Thon in the middle of the north coast, is Samui's most popular beach for budget travellers. Its exposed 4km-long bay is not the island's prettiest, being more of a broad dent in the coastline, and the sloping, white-sand beach is relatively narrow and slightly coarse by Samui's high standards. But Maenam features many of the cheapest bungalows on the island, unspoilt views of fishing boats and Ko Pha Ngan, and good swimming. Despite the recent opening of some upmarket developments on the shoreline and a golf course in the hills behind, this is still the quietest and most laidback of the major beaches. Though now heavily built up with multistorey concrete shophouses (including several banks) and rows of small bars, the main road is set back far from the sea, connected to the beachside bungalows by an intricate maze of minor roads through the trees. At the midpoint of the bay, **Ban Maenam** is centred on a low-key road down to the fishing pier, which is flanked by cafés, internet shops, travel agents, dive shops, secondhand bookshops and small boutiques. On Thursday evenings this becomes a pleasant **walking street** (modelled on Chiang Mai's walking streets), with performances of traditional music and dance. On offer are lots of cheap clothes and some souvenirs, everything from bras to ukeleles, but what's most tempting is the panoply of food, both savoury and sweet, that locals cook up to sell.

ACCOMMODATION   MAENAM

As well as several luxury resorts, Maenam has around thirty inexpensive and moderately priced bungalow complexes, most offering a spread of accommodation; the cheapest of these are at the far eastern end of the bay and offer the possibility of walking round to Bophut beach if you fancy a change of scene.

★ **Four Seasons Resort** About 5km west of Maenam near Laem Yai ☎077 243000, ⓦfourseasons.com. The top hotel in the Maenam area, this ultra-luxury spot has its own small beach and enjoys lovely views of Ko Pha Ngan and the setting sun. Each of the large, beautiful villas, designed for indoor-outdoor living in a subtle, modern but natural style, using brown and marine colours, has its own infinity-edge swimming pool; the resort lays on a wide range of other activities, from spa treatments to sailing and Thai cooking classes. B24,500

Harry's At the far western end, near Wat Na Phra Larn ☎077 425447, ⓦharrys-samui.com. Popular, well-run place, set back about 100m from the beach amid a secluded and shady tropical garden. The public areas feature strong elements of traditional Thai architecture, though not the bungalows, which are nevertheless clean and spacious, with a/c, hot water, TV, fridge and safe. Free internet access and a decent-sized swimming pool and jacuzzi. B1000

Lolita On the east side of Santiburi Resort ☎077 425134, ⓔlolitakohsamui@yahoo.com. Quiet, friendly and efficiently run resort in a beautiful, grassy garden on a long stretch of beach. A wide variety of large, wood and concrete bungalows, all with hot showers, cluster around a kitsch, circular bar-restaurant adorned with pink Corinthian columns, and come in just two price categories: at the back, with fans, or with a/c and fridges on the beach. Fan B800, a/c B1700

Maenam Resort 500m west of the village, just beyond Santiburi Resort ☎077 247287, ⓦmaenamresort.com. A welcoming, tranquil resort (no TVs) in tidy, shady grounds, with an especially long stretch of beach. The large bungalows, with verandas, hot water, fridges, wi-fi and a/c, offer good-value comfort. B1600

Maenam Villa At the far eastern end of the bay, next to SR (see p.546 for directions) ☎077 425501, ⓔmaenamvilla@hotmail.com. Friendly spot on a spacious triangular plot with kayaks available. Choose between clean, bright, older bungalows with verandas and cold showers, and large, concrete, open-plan villas with a/c, hot water and small terraces. Fan B500, a/c B1200

Moonhut On the east side of the village ☎ 077 425247, ⓦ moonhutsamui.com. Welcoming English-run place on a large, sandy, shady plot, with a lively restaurant and beach bar, wi-fi and colourful, substantial and very clean bungalows; all have verandas, mosquito screens, wall fans and en-suite bathrooms, and some have hot water and a/c. Kayaking, waterskiing and wakeboarding available. Fan B550, a/c B1100

Santiburi Resort 500m west of the village ☎ 077 425031, ⓦ santiburi.com. German-run, top-end hotel in beautifully landscaped grounds spread around a huge freshwater swimming pool and stream. Accommodation is mostly in Thai-style villas, inspired by Rama IV's summer palace at Phetchaburi, each with a large bathroom and separate sitting area, furnished in luxurious traditional style; some also have a private outdoor plunge pool. Facilities include watersports on the private stretch of beach, tennis courts, squash court, gym and golf course,

a kids' club and a spa. B23,900

Shangrilah West of Maenam Resort, served by the same access road ☎ 077 425189. In this huge compound that sprawls onto the nicest, widest stretch of sand along Maenam, the main area of shoulder-to-shoulder bungalows sports beautiful flowers, trees and carefully tended topiary. All rooms are well maintained and en-suite, with verandas, ceiling fans and sturdy furniture; some fan rooms at the front boast hot showers, which are also provided in all of the large, a/c rooms. The restaurant serves good Thai food. Fan B400, with hot water B800, a/c B1200

SR At the far eastern end of the bay ☎ 077 427529–30, ⓔ sr_bungalow@hotmail.com. A quiet, welcoming, good-value place, set in a narrow flower garden, with a very good restaurant and wi-fi. Accommodation is in large, smart, concrete bungalows with verandas and chairs, a/c, hot showers, TVs and fridges. To get there, either walk along the beach, or turn off Route 4169 at Family Mart and continue through the grounds of W Hotel. B700

EATING AND DRINKING

Angela's Bakery Opposite the police station on the main through-road to the east of the pier ☎ 077 427396. American-style, a/c diner, with a few shady tables out front, offering great breakfasts (French toast B80) and a wide choice of sandwiches, salads, soups and Western main courses, as well as cakes and apple pie. Mon–Sat 8.30am–4pm, Sun 8.30am–2pm.

Ko Seng On the road parallel to and just east of the pier road ☎ 077 425365. This locally famous seafood restaurant, simply decorated apart from the chunky wooden tables and chairs, has featured on national TV.

Buy your fish and seafood according to weight, or plump for dishes such as *kaeng som plaa* (B150), a thin fish curry with tamarind paste. Daily 10am–10pm.

Sunshine Gourmet At the west end of the bay, signposted on a lane that runs east from Wat Na Phra Larn. Popular, clean and friendly spot that does a bit of everything, from cappuccino, through own-baked pies (B150 for steak and kidney), sandwiches and cakes, to international, especially German, main courses, seafood and other Thai dishes. Daily noon–9pm.

Bophut

The next bay east is **BOPHUT**, which has a similar look to Maenam but shows a marked difference in atmosphere and facilities, with a noticeable Mediterranean influence. The

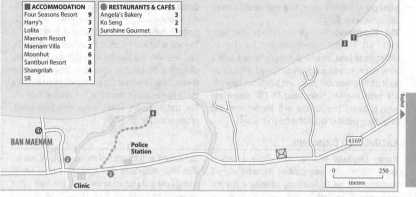

■ ACCOMMODATION	
Four Seasons Resort	9
Harry's	3
Lolita	7
Maenam Resort	5
Maenam Villa	2
Moonhut	6
Santiburi Resort	8
Shangrilah	4
SR	1

● RESTAURANTS & CAFÉS	
Angela's Bakery	3
Ko Seng	2
Sunshine Gourmet	1

BAN MAENAM

Police Station

Clinic

4169

0 — 250 metres

quiet, 2km-long beach attracts a mix of young and old travellers, as well as families, and **Ban Bophut**, now tagged "**Fisherman's Village**", at the east end of the bay, is well geared to meet their needs, with a sprinkling of boutique hotels and banks, ATMs, scuba-diving outlets, travel agents, internet cafés and minimarts. While through traffic sticks to Route 4169 to Chaweng and Route 4171 towards the airport, development of the village has been reasonably sensitive, preserving many of its old wooden shophouses on the two narrow, largely car-free streets that meet at a T-junction by the pier. At night, in sharp contrast to Chaweng's frenetic beach road, it's a fine place for a promenade, with a concentration of good upmarket restaurants and low-key farang-run bars; on Friday evenings, the village hosts a **walking street**, very similar to Maenam's Thursday affair (see p.545). The nicest part of the beach itself is at the west end of the bay, towards *Zazen* resort, but again the sand is slightly coarse by Samui's standards. Kayaks, sailing and windsurfing are available, for example, near the centre of the beach at *Bandara Resort*, next to *Anantara*.

ACCOMMODATION   BOPHUT

There's very little inexpensive accommodation left among Bophut's twenty or so resorts. Most establishments are well spaced out along the length of the beach, though a handful of small, comfortable hotels cluster together in Ban Bophut.

Anantara West of the village on the main road ☏ 077 428300, ⓦ anantara.com. Luxury hotel with attentive service in the style of an opulent oriental palace. Blocks of balconied rooms are arrayed round lush gardens, ponds, an attractive swimming pool and a central bar and restaurant, offering contemporary Italian cuisine with Asian influences. There's also a very attractive spa, a kids' club and a huge range of activities, from yoga and Thai cooking classes to tennis and watersports. B9100

Hansar At the west end of the village ☏ 077 245511, ⓦ hansarsamui.com. You'll be surprised how spacious this hotel feels, with its long beachfront and just 74 low-rise rooms (all with huge shower areas and sea views from their big balconies), set around gardens and a pool. The stylish decor is a riot of geometry in brown and beige – unvarnished wood, bamboo, marble and granite – and there's a spa, gym and luxury restaurant, *H Bistro*, with ingredients flown in from around the world. B9500

Juzz'a Pizza 2 East of the village T-junction ☏ 077

245663. Above a good restaurant (see p.548), four small but smart rooms, well equipped with comfy beds, a/c, hot showers, fridges and cable TV. Two rooms look onto the road, while the other two have beachside terraces with great views. B800

The Lodge Towards the western end of the village ☏ 077 425337, ⓦ lodgesamui.com. Small, two-storey, beachfront hotel with immaculately clean and tastefully decorated modern rooms, all with balconies looking over the water, and boasting a/c, ceiling fan, mini-bar, satellite TV, plus spacious bathrooms with tubs to soak in. There's a seafront bar downstairs where you can get breakfast. B1930

Samui Ley West of the village T-junction ☏ 077 245647, ⓦ samuiley.com. Kitsch and very cute small hotel, with a strong Thai pop aesthetic, sporting floral prints, retro posters and bright pastel colours everywhere. The large rooms have free wi-fi and antique TVs that actually work, as well as a/c, hot showers, sofas and beachfront balconies. Downstairs are a boutique with free computers for guests' use and a terrace café on the beach. B2700

The Waterfront East of the village T-junction ☎077 427165, ⓦthewaterfrontbophut.com. English-run boutique hotel, sociable and family-friendly, with a small swimming pool in a grassy garden. All of the simply but tastefully decorated rooms and bungalows have a/c, hot water, mini-bars, safes, cable TV, DVD players and views of the sea. Free pick-ups, wi-fi, internet access and babysitting; breakfast included in the price. B3045

Zazen At the far west end of the beach ☎077 425085, ⓦsamuizazen.com. Stylish bungalows and villas clustered round a cute pool and kids' pool, furnished with Thai and other Asian objets d'art, as well as satellite TV, DVD, free wi-fi and mini-bar (plus iPod docks in some); all sport a tropical-style open-air bathroom with rain shower. Other facilities at this eco-friendly resort include a spa, a fine restaurant that hosts Thai dancing Thurs and Sun, cooking classes, kayaks, windsurfers, table tennis, pétanque and the like. B7150

EATING AND DRINKING

Happy Elephant West of the village T-junction ☎077 245347. This long-standing restaurant offers a good choice of mostly Thai food, including a few less mainstream dishes such as pork *nam tok* (B220) and lots of seafood, which is displayed out front and priced by weight. Service is friendly and there's an attractive beachside terrace. Daily 11am–10pm.

Juzz'a Pizza 2 East of the village T-junction ☎077 245663. Friendly, small, elegant restaurant with a beachside terrace, serving excellent, authentic pizzas (around B250), with vegetarian and seafood options, as well as pastas, sandwiches and Thai and Western main courses. Daily noon–10pm.

Ristorante alla Baia Just west of the village T-junction ☎077 245566. Run by an Italian who is passionate about his food and has come up with a well-designed menu of standard but authentic dishes, such as *scaloppine al vino bianco* (pork or chicken fillets in white wine; B290). Also on offer are pizzas, home-made pasta

and seafood, with the catch of the day displayed outside. With white tablecloths, flowers on every table, lots of wrought iron and a terrace on the beach, you could almost be overlooking the Adriatic. Daily 11am–10.30pm.

Samui French Bakery 200m south of the village T-junction, towards Route 4169. The real deal: delicious croissants, breads, quiches (B70) and patisserie such as *tarte aux pommes* (B70), to go with espresso coffee. Also offers sandwiches and salads. Daily 7.30am–5pm.

The Shack Grill West of the village T-junction ☎077 246041 or ☎087 264 6994, ⓦtheshackgrillsamui.com. Small, pricey spot, run by an ebullient New Yorker, and focused on the large, open grill at the front of the restaurant: here all manner of local seafood and imported meats, such as Wagyu beef and New Zealand lamb, are cooked to your liking. Good cold meat platters with mozzarella (B465), delicious apple pie and decent house wine. Daily 6–11pm.

Bangrak

Beyond the sharp headland with its sweep of coral reefs lies **BANGRAK**, sometimes called **Big Buddha Beach** after the colossus that gazes sternly down on the sun worshippers from its island in the bay. The beach is no great shakes, especially during the northeast monsoon, when the sea retreats and leaves a slippery mud flat, and generally it's hard to recommend staying here, as the resorts are squeezed together in a narrow, noisy strip between busy Route 4171 and the shore, underneath the airport flight path.

The **Big Buddha** (*Phra Yai*) is certainly big and works hard at being a tourist attraction, but is no beauty. A short causeway at the eastern end of the bay leads across to a messy clump of souvenir shops and foodstalls in front of the temple, catering to day-tripping Thais as well as foreigners. Ceremonial dragon-steps then bring you up to the covered terrace around the Big Buddha, from where there's a fine view of the sweeping north coast. Look out for the B10 rice-dispensing machine, which allows you symbolically to give alms to the monks at any time of the day.

Choeng Mon

After Bangrak comes the high-kicking boot of Samui's **northeastern cape**, with its small, rocky coves overlooking Ko Pha Ngan and connected by sandy lanes. Songthaews run along Route 4171 to the largest and most beautiful bay, **Choeng Mon**, whose white sandy beach is lined with casuarina trees that provide shade for the bungalows and upmarket resorts. Choeng Mon is now popular enough to support small supermarkets, travel agents and a bank, but on the whole it remains relatively uncommercialized and laidback.

ACCOMMODATION CHOENG MON

Boat House Hotel Central Choeng Mon ☎077 425041–52, ⓦimperialhotels.com. Named after the two-storey rice barges that have been converted into suites in the grounds, the *Boat House* also offers good-value luxury rooms with balconies in more prosaic modern buildings, often filled by package tours. As well as a beachside boat-shaped pool, there's a garden pool, a spa, a fitness room, a kids' club, free wi-fi, kayaks and windsurfers. B4000
Island View Tucked in on the east side of the Boat House Hotel ☎077 245031, ⓦislandviewsamui.com. Smart, good-value rooms and chalets with a/c, hot water, TV and fridge, in a lively compound that crams in a supermarket, a small bookshop and a beachfront bar, as well as a massage *sala* and kayaks on the beach. Rooms B1000, bungalows B1200
Kirati Resort 100m east of Island View ☎081 881 2703, ⓦkiratisamui.com. All the accommodation here has a/c, hot water, free wi-fi, a balcony and a fridge. Choose between a variety of spacious chalets with nice decorative touches in the jungly garden, and bright, new rooms in a hotel-style block, with granite-tiled floors, dark-wood

sofas and smart, modern bathrooms. Bungalows B1000, rooms B2200
Ô Soleil West of the Boat House Hotel ☎077 425232, ⓔbuisseretjean@yahoo.fr Lovely, orderly, Belgian-run place in a pretty, tranquil garden dotted with ponds. Among the well-built, clean bungalows, the cheapest are fan-cooled, with cold showers, at the back, while the a/c offerings, all with hot showers, fridges and TVs, are priced according to size. New, more luxurious bungalows are being built and prices may go up. Fan B400, a/c B600
★ **Tongsai Bay** North side of Choeng Mon ☎077 245480, ⓦtongsaibay.co.th. Easy-going, environmentally aware establishment with excellent service. The luxurious rooms, red-tiled cottages and palatial villas (some with their own pool) command beautiful views over the huge, picturesque grounds, the private beach and two swimming pools. In addition they all sport second bathtubs on their secluded open-air terraces, and some also have outdoor, four-poster beds with mosquito nets if you want to sleep under the stars. There's also an array of very fine restaurants and a delightful spa. B9300

Chaweng

For looks alone, none of the other beaches can match **CHAWENG**, with its broad, gently sloping strip of white sand sandwiched between the limpid blue sea and a line of palm trees. Such beauty has not escaped attention of course, which means, on the plus side, that Chaweng can provide just about anything the active beach bum demands, from thumping nightlife to ubiquitous and diverse watersports. The negative angle is that the new developments are ever more cramped and expensive, while building work behind the palm trees and repairs to the over-commercialized main beach road are always in progress.

North Chaweng

The 6km bay is framed between the small island of Ko Matlang at the north end and the 300m-high headland above Coral Cove in the south. From **Ko Matlang**, where the waters provide some decent snorkelling, an often exposed coral reef slices southwest across to the mainland, marking out a shallow lagoon and **North Chaweng**. This S-shaped part of the beach is comparatively peaceful, though it has some ugly pockets of development; at low tide it becomes a wide, inviting playground, and from October to January the reef shelters it from the northeast winds. Here, on the beach by the *Chaweng Regent*, Samui Ocean Sports (☎081 940 1999, ⓦsailing-in-samui.com) rents windsurfers and kayaks, as well as offering sailing lessons, trips and charters.

Central Chaweng and Chaweng Noi

South of the reef, the idyllic shoreline of **Central Chaweng** stretches for 2km in a dead-straight line, the ugly, traffic-clogged and seemingly endless strip of amenities on the parallel main drag largely concealed behind the tree line and the resorts. Around a low promontory is **Chaweng Noi**, a little curving beach in a rocky bay, which is comparatively quiet in its northern part, away from the road. Well inland of Central Chaweng, the round-island road, Route 4169, passes through the original village of **Ban Chaweng**.

Coral Cove

South of Chaweng, the road climbs past **Coral Cove**, a tiny, isolated beach of coarse sand hemmed in by high rocks, with some good coral for snorkelling. It's well worth making the trip to the *Beverly Hills Café*, at the tip of the headland dividing Chaweng from Lamai, for a jaw-dropping view over Chaweng and Choeng Mon to the peaks of Ko Pha Ngan (and for some good, moderately priced food, notably seafood).

6

ACCOMMODATION   CHAWENG

Over fifty **bungalow resorts** and **hotels** at Chaweng are squeezed into thin strips running back from the beachfront at right angles. The cheapest digs here are generally little more than functional, while more and more expensive places are sprouting up all the time, offering sumptuous accommodation at top-whack prices.

NORTH CHAWENG

Amari Palm Reef North Chaweng ⊙077 422015–8, ⊚amari.com. Congenial, eco-friendly luxury hotel that's unpretentious and good value. Spacious accommodation,

stretching back across the road from the beach and all with DVD players, includes family-friendly duplexes, and there are two elegant restaurants, including *Prego* (see p.552), a full-service spa, a gym, two free-form swimming pools

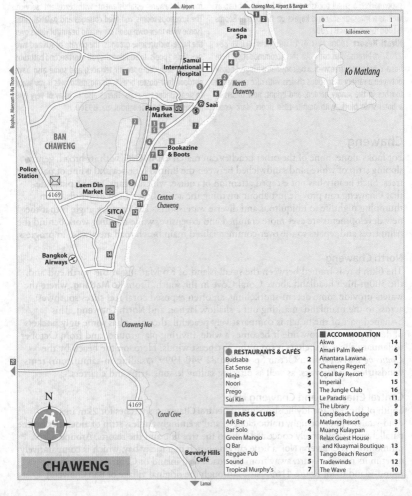

CHAWENG

Ko Matlang

BAN CHAWENG

North Chaweng

Eranda Spa

Samui International Hospital

Pang Bua Market

@ Saai

Bookazine & Boots

Police Station

Laem Din Market

Central Chaweng

SITCA

Bangkok Airways

Chaweng Noi

Chaweng

Coral Cove

Beverly Hills Café

Airport

Choeng Mon, Airport & Bangkok

Bophut, Maenam & Na Thon

4169

4169

Lamai

N

0   1
kilometre

● RESTAURANTS & CAFÉS

Budsaba	2
Eat Sense	6
Ninja	4
Noori	4
Prego	3
Sui Kin	1

■ BARS & CLUBS

Ark Bar	6
Bar Solo	4
Green Mango	3
Q Bar	1
Reggae Pub	2
Sound	5
Tropical Murphy's	7

■ ACCOMMODATION

Akwa	14
Amari Palm Reef	1
Anantara Lawana	6
Chaweng Regent	7
Coral Bay Resort	2
Imperial	15
The Jungle Club	16
Le Paradis	11
The Library	9
Long Beach Lodge	8
Matlang Resort	3
Muang Kulaypan	5
Relax Guest House and Kluaymai Boutique	13
Tango Beach Resort	4
Tradewinds	12
The Wave	10

and a kids' pool. Various discounts and packages available on their website. B5320

Anantara Lawana North Chaweng ☎077 960333, ⊛anantara.com. The design of this luxury hotel was inspired by Chinese merchants' houses in Thailand in the last century, which gives a pleasing retro feel to the rooms, most of which have outdoor bathrooms. Much of the accommodation is in two-storey houses, in which the ground-floor room has a plunge pool and the first-floor room a terrace; other villas either have their own pools or share semi-private ones. There's also a main, semicircular pool, of course, down by the beach, as well as an excellent spa and a very good restaurant, *Tree Tops*, where you eat in romantic, open-sided treehouses. B9500

Chaweng Regent At the bottom end of North Chaweng ☎077 230391–400, ⊛chawengregent.com. Reliable, well-run, luxury place offering elegant bungalows and low-rise rooms with private terraces and all mod cons, around lotus ponds, two pools, a fitness centre, sauna and spa. B6100

★ **Coral Bay Resort** At the far north end of North Chaweng ☎077 234555, ⊛coralbay.net. A charming, eco-friendly vision of how Chaweng might have developed – if only there'd been more space. In quiet, delightful, ten-acre gardens with over 500 species of plants, the huge, thatched villas have been thoughtfully and tastefully designed with local woods, bamboo and coconut; all have extensive verandas, waterfall showers, free broadband and DVD/CD/MP3 players (movies available from the library). There's an attractive pool, a spa and a good beachside bar-restaurant; kayaks and snorkels available. B6850

Matlang Resort At the far north end of North Chaweng ☎077 230468–9. Tranquil, friendly place on the beach with nice views of Ko Matlang, though getting ever more tightly squeezed by the surrounding luxury resorts. Choose between old-style thatched, wooden bungalows with verandas, mosquito screens and hot showers, and brightly painted, new rooms with a/c. Fan B500, a/c B1000

Muang Kulaypan North Chaweng ☎077 230849–50, ⊛kulaypan.com. Chaweng's original boutique hotel is arrayed around a large, immaculate garden with a black-tiled swimming pool and an excellent beachside restaurant (see p.552). Stylish rooms – each with their own private balcony or garden – combine contemporary design with traditional Thai-style comforts. Breakfast included. B4500

Tango Beach Resort North Chaweng ☎077 422470, ⊛tangobeachsamui.com. This helpful and welcoming place has a modern Thai style that sets it apart from most of Samui's farang-oriented hotels: a variety of cutesy, colourful, well-equipped rooms are separated by a small, shady pool (and kids' pool) and a wooden boardwalk that runs down to the beach, where kayaks are available. Breakfast included. B2650

CENTRAL CHAWENG

★ **Akwa** Towards the south end of Central Chaweng ☎084 660 0551, ⊛akwaguesthouse.com. Cute, homely, brightly coloured rooms all decorated with cartoon murals and well equipped with a/c, hot water, mini-bars, TVs, DVD players (with DVDs to borrow) and free wi-fi. "Deluxe" are bigger than "Standard", and there are penthouses and a garden apartment. Not on the beach but close to it, guests get free access to the pool at *Seascape Resort*, opposite. B500

Le Paradis Central Chaweng ☎077 239041–3, ⊛leparadisresort.com. Set in lush gardens, this place was partly under renovation at the time of writing but offers very stylish contemporary villas hung with large, colourful paintings and equipped with open-air bathrooms with large baths, large balconies, a/c, cable TV, DVD players, safes and free wi-fi. Attractive beachside swimming pool and health spa. B6300

The Library Central Chaweng ☎077 422767–8, ⊛thelibrary.name. High-concept design hotel, based around a library of books, DVDs and CDs with computer terminals. The idea is continued in the rooms, which all sport iMacs (with free wi-fi) and DVD players, and have a sleek, cubic theme; they're divided into suites (downstairs) and studios with balconies (upstairs). There's a blood-red swimming pool, a fitness centre and a beachfront terrace restaurant, *The Page*. Studios B15,800, suites B18,000

Long Beach Lodge Towards the north end of Central Chaweng ☎077 422162, ⊛longbeachsamui.com. An unusually spacious and shady, sandy compound. All the orderly, clean bungalows and rooms are a decent size and have hot water, fridge, TV and a/c. Service is friendly, and breakfast is included in the price. From B1200

Relax Guest House and Kluaymai Boutique Soi Colibri, a small lane at the south end of Central Chaweng, opposite the landmark Centara Grand Beach Resort ☎077 413836, ✉sombatsamui@hotmail.com. Functional crashpads, but well maintained and good value for the facilities: either fan and hot water or a/c, hot water, fridge and TV (wi-fi available in the office). Or you could upgrade to the "boutique" rooms next door, under the same management, with DVD players, in-room wi-fi and a touch of decor. Fan B300, a/c B500, "boutique" B800

Tradewinds Central Chaweng ☎077 414294, ⊛tradewinds-samui.com. A cheerful, well-run place of characterful bungalows and rooms (all with a/c, hot water, mini-bar, cable TV, wi-fi and balcony) with plenty of room to breathe in colourful tropical gardens. The resort specializes in sailing, with its own catamarans (instruction available), as well as offering kayaking, snorkelling and croquet. Breakfast included. B2500

The Wave Central Chaweng ☎077 230803, ⊛thewavesamui.com. One of the cheapest guesthouses on Chaweng, this helpful, English-run place is not on the

6

beach, but above a popular bar-restaurant on the main road. Most of the rooms have fans and share cold-water bathrooms, while the a/c offerings, including a top-floor duplex with a rooftop terrace, feature hot showers, TVs, fridges and free wi-fi. All kinds of advice and tours available, as well as a huge library. Fan B400, a/c B850

CHAWENG NOI

Imperial Chaweng Noi ☎ 077 422020–36, ⊛ imperial hotels.com. The longest-established luxury hotel on Samui is a grand but lively establishment with a Mediterranean feel, set in sloping, landscaped gardens; features include two pools (one sea water, one fresh with a jacuzzi),

a spa, a tennis court and classes such as Thai cookery and fruit carving. B7800

★ **The Jungle Club** 2km up a steep, partly paved road from Chaweng Noi ☎ 081 894 2327, ⊛ jungleclub samui.com. Breezy, French–Thai antidote to Chaweng's commercial clutter: a huge, grassy, shady plot with a small pool on the edge of the slope to catch the towering views of Ko Pha Ngan and beyond. A chic bar-restaurant has been built into the rocks, while the accommodation – all thatched, with mosquito nets and fans – includes wooden huts with cold showers and concrete bungalows with hot water and DVD players. Free pick-ups twice a day. B800, with hot shower from B1800

EATING

Chaweng offers all manner of foreign **cuisines**, from French to Russian, much of it of dubious quality. Among all this, it's quite hard to find good, reasonably priced Thai food – as well as the places recommended below, it's worth exploring the cheap and cheerful foodstalls, popular with local workers, at either **Laem Din night market**, on the middle road between Central Chaweng and Highway 4169, or Pang Bua market (roughly 6am–midnight) on the Ban Chaweng road, which includes a famous stall for *khao niaw mamuang* (mango with sticky rice).

Budsaba Restaurant At the Muang Kulaypan Hotel ☎ 077 230849–50. This charming, upmarket beachfront restaurant fully justifies the journey up to North Chaweng: you get to recline in your own seaside *sala* or open-sided hut on stilts while tucking into excellent Thai dishes such as pomelo salad (B180). Daily 7am–10.30pm.

Eat Sense Central Chaweng, next to Charlie's Huts ☎ 077 414242, ⊛ eatsensesamui.com. Spacious, relaxing, mostly open-air restaurant on the beachfront, serving expensive but delicious Thai and international food, using only organic vegetables – try the deep-fried prawns with cashew nuts and tamarind sauce. Daily 11am–midnight.

Ninja Opposite Burirasa Resort in Central Chaweng. Popular, well-run, very basic and cheap restaurant, serving simple Thai favourites such as *tom yam* (B55), *som tam* and *phat thai*, as well as crêpes, breakfasts and other Western food. Open 24hr.

Noori Opposite Chaweng Buri Resort towards the north end of Central Chaweng ☎ 077 413108, ⊛ noori indiasamui.com. Superior Indian food in relatively basic

surroundings, including all the old favourites such as chicken tikka masala (B210), as well as plenty of seafood and vegetarian options. Also has a branch further south on Central Chaweng, past the *Centara Grand Resort*, and offers Indian cooking classes. Daily 11.30am–11.30pm.

★ **Prego** Amari Palm Reef, North Chaweng ☎ 077 422015–8. Excellent, chic, open-sided restaurant that would stand on its own two feet in Milan, the head chef's home town. The varied menu of contemporary Italian dishes includes good *antipasti*, pizzas, handmade pastas and top-notch risottos, and there's a very good selection of wines. Booking advised in high season. Daily 11.30am–midnight.

Sui Kin The Akyra, North Chaweng ☎ 077 915100, ⊛ theakyra.com. Very good, open-air restaurant overlooking this Japanese-style resort that features a lot of dark wood in its attractive decor. The *unagi* sushi (eel; B280) and the tuna and scallop tartare (B250) are both very tasty, or you could opt for teppanyaki, tempura, grilled fish or contemporary sushi (mostly California rolls). Daily noon–10.30pm.

DRINKING AND NIGHTLIFE

Avoiding the raucous hostess bars and English theme pubs on the main through road, the best place to **drink** is on the beach: at night dozens of resorts and dedicated bars lay out candlelit tables with axe cushions for reclining on the sand, especially towards the north end of Central Chaweng and on North Chaweng.

Ark Bar North end of Central Chaweng ☎ 077 961333, ⊛ ark-bar.com. Hosts very popular beach parties, with international and Thai house DJs, live music, fire shows and a free barbecue. Parties Wed & Fri from 2pm until well into the night.

Bar Solo North end of Central Chaweng, on the main road just north of Green Mango ⊛ barsolosamui.com.

One of the bars of the moment, whose black-and-white industrial look is matched by the hardcore techno on the sound system. Diversions include a pool table and shisha pipes, and there's a happy hour till 8pm. Look out for its regular beach parties at Hat Plai Laem, in the northeast corner of the island. Daily 2pm–3am.

Green Mango North end of Central Chaweng.

Long-standing dance venue, in a huge shed that combines an industrial look with that of a tropical greenhouse. Now with its own alley, Soi Green Mango, lined with other vibrant bars and clubs. Daily 10pm–3am.

Q Bar North off the Ban Chaweng road ☎077 962420, ⊛qbarsamui.com. Sleek, futuristic decor, great views over the lake from high on its north shore and cutting-edge music from local and international DJs, at this branch of the famous Bangkok bar-club. Daily 6pm–late.

Reggae Pub Inland from Central Chaweng across the lake ⊛reggaepubsamui.com. Chaweng's oldest nightclub is a venerable Samui institution – with a memorabilia shop to prove it. It does time now as an unpretentious, good-time,

party venue, with plenty of drinking games, pool tables, big-screen sports and live reggae bands every night, plus occacional big-name concerts. Daily 6pm–3am.

Sound Next soi south of Green Mango. With its smart front bar and large garden club at the back, this is where people stagger on to when other places close. Daily 11pm–6am.

Tropical Murphy's Opposite McDonald's in Central Chaweng. One theme pub that is worth singling out: with draught Guinness, Magners and Kilkenny, a huge range of big-screen sports, quiz nights, live music, free wi-fi and decent food, *Murphy's* has turned itself into a popular landmark and meeting place. Daily 8am–2am.

DIRECTORY

Airlines Bangkok Airways, south end of Ban Chaweng on Route 4169 ☎077 601300.

Bookshops There are several branches of Bookazine, most conveniently next to *Tropical Murphy's* on the beach road in Central Chaweng (daily 10am–10pm), selling English-language books, newspapers and magazines. In North Chaweng, on the east side of the beach road at the T-junction with the Ban Chaweng road, Saai is good for secondhand books (daily 9am–11pm).

Hospital The private Samui International Hospital in North Chaweng (☎077 230781–2, ⊛sih.co.th) provides

24hr ambulance and emergency services, house calls, a dental clinic and travel inoculations.

Internet access Dozens of outlets, including at Saai bookshop (see above).

Pharmacy Boots has a convenient branch in the middle of Central Chaweng, just up the road from *Tropical Murphy's* pub.

Walking street Very similar to Maenam's (see p.545), on Wed evenings near the beach, between *Long Beach Lodge* and *Ninja*.

Lamai

LAMAI is like a second city to Chaweng's capital, not quite as developed and much less frenetic, while lacking the latter's wide range of chic hotels, restaurants and nightclubs. Development is concentrated into a farang toytown of tawdry open-air hostess bars and Western restaurants that has grown up behind the centre of the beach, interspersed with supermarkets, clinics, banks, ATMs, internet cafés, dive shops and travel agents. Running roughly north to south for 4km, the white, palm-fringed beach itself is still a picture, and generally quieter than Chaweng, with far less in the way of watersports – it's quite easy to get away from it all by staying at the peaceful extremities of the bay, where the backpackers' resorts are preferable to Chaweng's functional guesthouses. At the northern end, the spur of land that hooks eastward into the sea is perhaps the prettiest spot and is beginning to attract some upmarket development: it has more rocks than sand, but the shallow sea behind the coral reef is protected from the high seas of November, December and January.

The original village of **Ban Lamai**, set well back on Route 4169, remains surprisingly aloof, and its wat contains a small museum of ceramics, agricultural tools and other everyday objects. Most visitors get more of a buzz from **Hin Yay** (Grandmother Rock) and **Hin Ta** (Grandfather Rock), small rock formations on the bay's southern promontory, which never fail to raise a giggle with their resemblance to the male and female sexual organs.

ACCOMMODATION   LAMAI

Lamai's **accommodation** is generally less cramped and slightly better value than Chaweng's, though it presents far fewer choices at the top end of the market. The far southern end of the bay towards the Grandparent Rocks has the tightest concentration of budget bungalows.

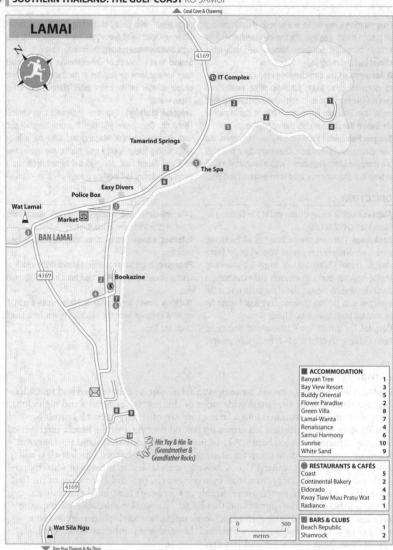

LAMAI

Coral Cove & Chaweng

4169

@ IT Complex

Tamarind Springs

The Spa

Easy Divers

Police Box

Wat Lamai

Market

BAN LAMAI

4169

Bookazine

Hin Yay & Hin Ta
(Grandmother &
Grandfather Rocks)

4169

Wat Sila Ngu

Ban Hua Thanon & Na Thon

0   500
metres

■ **ACCOMMODATION**

Banyan Tree	1
Bay View Resort	3
Buddy Oriental	5
Flower Paradise	2
Green Villa	8
Lamai-Wanta	7
Renaissance	4
Samui Harmony	6
Sunrise	10
White Sand	9

● **RESTAURANTS & CAFÉS**

Coast	5
Continental Bakery	2
Eldorado	4
Kway Tiaw Muu Pratu Wat	3
Radiance	1

■ **BARS & CLUBS**

| Beach Republic | 1 |
| Shamrock | 2 |

Banyan Tree On the bay's northern headland ☎077 915333, ⊛banyantree.com. Occupying a steep-sided, landscaped valley, with towering views of Chaweng from the lobby bar, *Banyan Tree* provides the height of luxury in its beautiful, stilted pool villas: lofty living rooms, walk-in wardrobes, possibly the biggest big-head showers in Thailand and lots of extra touches such as iPod docks. Electric buggies will ferry you down to the spa, the main swimming pool, kids' pool and private cove with a good stretch of beach, where plenty of watersports are on offer. B34,800

Bay View Resort On the bay's northern headland ☎077 458778–9, ⊛bayviewsamui.com. Neat, stylish bungalows with verandas, mini-bars, wi-fi and hot-water bathrooms in an extensive, flower-bedecked compound; the poshest come with a/c and cable TV. Offers a friendly, German–Thai welcome, kayaking, internet access and great sunset views of the beach from the attractive restaurant. Fan B1500, a/c B1900

Buddy Oriental East of Ban Lamai ☎077 458560–5, ⊛buddysamui.com. Welcoming branch of the Khao San Rd hotel, in "colonial" style: four-poster beds with mosquito nets, wooden blinds and bathrooms tiled with black and white marble. The bedrooms and one swimming pool are set well back from the road beyond an avenue of shops, while on the beach side of the road are another pool, a restaurant and bar. Other facilities include a spa, a large kids' club, free wi-fi and computers for guest use. B6000

Flower Paradise On the bay's northern headland ☎ 077 418059 or ☎ 089 288 8362, ⊕ samuiroestiland.com. Just a short walk from the beach, a friendly, well-run German-Swiss place in a small but beautiful garden. All the attractive, well-tended bungalows of varying sizes have verandas and hot water, and there's a good restaurant, *Röstiland* (closed Mon) – specializing in the eponymous hash browns – which also offers free wi-fi. Fan B350, a/c B650

Green Villa On the access road to White Sand, at the far southern end of the bay ☎ 077 424296, ⊕ greenvilla@hotmail.com. Though set back from the beach towards the main road, this resort enjoys a spacious garden among palm trees, and a small swimming pool. Clean, simple, en-suite, wooden bungalows with fans (some with hot water) or grand, a/c villas with TVs, fridges, hot-water bathtubs and open-air showers. Fan B450, with hot water B550, a/c B2000

Lamai-Wanta East of the central crossroads ☎ 077 424550, ⊕ lamaiwanta.com. Welcoming, well-placed hotel with a seductive beachfront swimming pool and a good restaurant (see below). Set around trim lawns, the large, plain rooms are decorated in white, beige and dark wood in a minimalist Thai style, while the bungalows (which feature DVD players) are a little more elegant; all have a/c, TVs, mini-bars, safes, wi-fi and hot water. Discounts for longer stays. Breakfast included. Rooms B2650, villas B4100

Renaissance On the bay's northern headland ☎ 077 429300, ⊕ marriott.com. In a fine position with access to

two beaches, this luxury Marriott resort presents a stark choice: long, lofty villas, each with its own plunge pool, in lush, frog-filled gardens, or far cheaper rooms at the back with balconies and outdoor jacuzzis. There's an enticing, many-tiered beachside pool, a spa, tapas bar, and a roster of activities including Thai massage and towel-folding classes. Rooms B8850, villas B16,500

Samui Harmony South of Buddy ☎ 077 458120, ⊕ samuiharmony@hotmail.com. Tightly packed between the road, canal and beach, but friendly, well tended and shaded by lush vegetation, with a café, travel agency (with computers for guest use) and free wi-fi throughout. You've got three choices: small, neat, en-suite, wooden huts, with either fan and cold shower (though these may be upgraded to hot soon), or a/c, hot water, TV and fridge, or larger a/c affairs on the beach. Fan B500, a/c B800

Sunrise On the Hin Yay Hin Ta access road ☎ 077 424433, ⊕ sunrisebungalow.com. Welcoming and clued-up establishment on the far southern end of the beach. In a quiet, shady garden amid coconut palms, choose between clean fan rooms with cold or hot showers and larger a/c bungalows with hot water, some with cable TV and fridge. Free wi-fi, a decent restaurant, books to borrow, a gym and, in high season, a small spa. Fan B550, with hot water B800, a/c B1200

White Sand At the far southern end of the bay ☎ 077 424298. Long-established and laidback place in a large, shady, sandy compound, which attracts plenty of long-term travellers. It offers simple, old-style, fan-cooled huts, either with mosquito nets and shared bathrooms or en suite with mosquito screens on the windows, as well as concrete bungalows with hot water, TV and a/c, and three attractive bamboo cottages on the beach that get the best of the sea breezes (cold showers and no a/c). Fan B150, en-suite B300, a/c B600

EATING AND DRINKING

There are far fewer eating options on Lamai than on Chaweng to tempt you away from your guesthouse kitchen. Besides the **restaurants** recommended below, there's a **market** of cheap takeaway foodstalls and simple restaurants inland just off Highway 4169 (east of Tesco Lotus supermarket) that's popular with locals for lunch and dinner (closes around 8 or 9pm). Apart from a few bar-restaurants on the beach near *Lamai-Wanta*, Lamai's **nightlife** is all within spitting distance of the central crossroads.

Beach Republic On the bay's northern headland ☎ 077 458100, ⊕ beachrepublic.com. Although it features accommodation and a spa, this hip beach club is best known for its restaurant and bar, arrayed around two pools and a jacuzzi, with plenty of loungers and day-beds and fine views of the bay. Among sandwiches, global tapas, pasta and pizza, the very good beer-battered fish and chips (B380) stand out. Weekly events currently include "Soulful Saturdays" with a DJ (1–6pm) and Sunday brunch (11.30am–3.30pm), with a DJ until 6pm. Restaurant daily 10.30am–10.30pm.

Coast Lamai-Wanta, east of the central crossroads ☎ 077 424550. Hip, open-sided restaurant by the hotel pool and beach, minimalist but mellow, with a menu that's half Thai, including tasty *kaeng matsaman kai* (B160), and half international, with some touches of Asian fusion. Daily 6.30am–9pm.

Continental Bakery North of the central crossroads, near Highway 4169. Friendly, Swiss-run place serving good breads, cakes, sandwiches and espressos, as well as all-day breakfasts ranging from French and American to Belgian (with pork steak, apparently). Daily 6am–3pm,

6

possibly later in high season.

Eldorado Just west of the central crossroads. Highly recommended friendly, good-value Swedish restaurant, serving a few Thai favourites, salads, steaks, pizzas and other international main courses, plus one or two indigenous specialities such as Swedish meatballs (B190). Daily 8am–10.30pm.

Kway Tiaw Muu Pratu Wat Highway 4169, Ban Lamai. A locals' favourite, this basic restaurant serves very tasty noodle soup with pork, spare ribs or seafood, or a combination of all three (B35–65). There's no English sign, but it's right beside the entrance to Wat Lamai, with a white-on-red Thai sign. Daily 9am–7pm.

Radiance The Spa Resort, at the far north end of the beach. Excellent, casual beachside restaurant, serving a huge range of vegetarian Thai and international (including Mexican) dishes, plus raw and vegan food, as well as plenty of meat and marine offerings. The veggie "ginger nuts" stir-fry (B100) and *som tam* with spicy Thai sausage (B70) are excellent. A long menu of juices, smoothies and shakes includes a delicious lime juice with honey. Daily 7am–10pm.

Shamrock North of the central crossroads. Popular, friendly Irish bar with pool tables and TV sports, which hosts lively cover bands every evening and keeps Guinness, Magners cider and Kilkenny bitter on draught. Happy hour till 8pm. Daily 10am–2am.

The south and west coasts

Lacking the long, attractive beaches of the more famous resorts, the **south and west coasts** have much less to offer in the way of accommodation, though there are one or two interesting spots that are worth heading for on a round-island tour. If you happen to be here in November, the west coast's flat, unexceptional beaches might make a calm alternative when the northeast winds buffet the other side of the island.

Samui Butterfly Garden

Off Route 4170, about 3km south of Ban Hua Thanon, opposite Centara Villas • Daily 8.30am–5.30pm • B200

On a net-covered, rocky hillside with fine views of the sea, the **Samui Butterfly Garden** is opposite (and owned by) *Centara Villas*. The entrance fee is a bit steep, but it allows you to wander among artificial waterfalls and lush vegetation, surrounded by dozens of brilliantly coloured lepidopterans.

Ko Taen and Ko Mad Sum

The two small islands of **Ko Taen** and **Ko Mad Sum**, a short way off the south coast, offer some of Samui's best snorkelling. TK Tour in Ban Thongkrut (☎077 334052–3, ⓦtktoursamui.com) covers both on a five-hour boat trip, costing B1100 per person (B1300 with kayaking), including pick-up from your accommodation, snorkelling equipment and lunch on the long beach of Ko Mad Sum.

Na Muang Falls

About 5km inland of **Ban Hua Thanon**, near **Ban Thurian**, the **Na Muang Falls** make a popular outing as they're not far off the round-island road (each of the two main falls has its own signposted kilometre-long paved access road off Route 4169). The lower fall splashes and sprays down a 20m wall of rock into a large pool, while Na Muang 2, upstream, is a more spectacular, shaded cascade that requires a bit of foot-slogging from the car park (about 15min uphill).

Ko Si Ko Ha

At **Ban Taling Ngam**, on the west coast, the *Five Islands Gallery Café* (☎077 415359, ⓦthefiveislands.com) lays on half-day **boat trips** in luxury longtails to see the caves of **Ko Si Ko Ha**, the heavily guarded islands just offshore where sea gypsies gather swifts' nests for bird's-nest soup (see p.680). With time for snorkelling and swimming, the trip is rounded off by a varied Thai lunch or dinner at *Five Islands* beachside restaurant; the package costs from B6600 for two people including transfers from your accommodation.

★ **Ban Hua Thanon Seafood** Highway 4169, Ban Hua Thanon ☎077 418355. Justly famous restaurant, recommended in all the Thai food guides, in a Muslim fishing village just south of Lamai. A world away from Samui's slick resort restaurants, this rustic wooden shophouse with lovely outdoor tables on the water keeps its reasonably priced fish (about B100/100g) in tanks at the front. Recommended dishes include baked green mussels with lemon grass and excellent crispy, shredded prawn with mango salad. Daily 10am–10pm.

Ang Thong National Marine Park

6

Closed Nov • Park entry fee B200 (usually included in price of tour) • Park headquarters ☎077 280222 or ☎077 286025, ⊛ dnp.go.th

Even if you don't get your buns off the beach for the rest of your stay on Samui or Pha Ngan, it's worth taking at least a day out to visit the beautiful **Ang Thong National Marine Park**, a lush, dense group of 42 small islands strewn like a dragon's teeth over the deep-blue Gulf of Thailand, 30km or so west of Samui. Once a haven for pirate junks, then a Royal Thai Navy training base, the islands and their coral reefs, white-sand beaches and virgin rainforest are now preserved under the aegis of the National Parks Department. Erosion of the soft limestone has dug caves and chiselled out fantastic shapes that are variously said to resemble seals, a rhinoceros, a Buddha image and even the temple complex at Angkor.

The surrounding waters are home to dolphins, wary of humans because local fishermen catch them for their meat, and *pla thu* (short-bodied mackerel), part of the national staple diet, which gather in huge numbers between February and April to spawn around the islands. On land, long-tailed macaques, leopard cats, wild pigs, sea otters, squirrels, monitor lizards and pythons are found, as well as dusky langurs, which, because they have no natural enemies here, are unusually friendly and easy to spot. Around forty bird species have had confirmed sightings, including the white-rumped shama, noted for its singing, the brahminy kite, black baza, little heron, Eurasian woodcock, several species of pigeon, kingfisher and wagtail, as well as common and hill mynah; in addition, island caves shelter swiftlets, whose homes are stolen for bird's nest soup (see p.680).

Ko Wua Talab

The largest landmass in the group is **Ko Wua Talab** (Sleeping Cow Island) where the park headquarters shelter in a hollow behind the small beach. From there it's a steep 430m **climb** (about 1hr return; bring walking sandals or shoes) to the island's peak to gawp at the panorama, which is especially fine at sunrise and sunset: in the distance, Ko Samui, Ko Pha Ngan and the mainland; nearer at hand, the jagged edges of the surrounding archipelago; and below the peak, a secret cove on the western side and an almost sheer drop to the clear blue sea to the east. Another climb from the beach, only 200m but even harder going (allow 40min return), leads to **Tham Buabok**, a cave set high in the cliff-face. Some of the stalactites and stalagmites are said to resemble lotuses, hence the cave's appellation, "Waving Lotus". If you're visiting in September, look out for the white, violet-dotted petals of **lady's slipper orchids**, which grow on the rocks and cliffs.

Ko Mae Ko

The park's name, Ang Thong ("Golden Bowl"), comes from a landlocked saltwater lake, 250m in diameter, on **Ko Mae Ko** to the north of Ko Wua Talab, which was the inspiration for the setting of the bestselling novel and film, *The Beach*. A well-made path (allow 30min return) leads from the beach through natural rock tunnels to the rim of the cliff wall that encircles the lake, affording another stunning view of the archipelago and the shallow, blue-green water far below, which is connected to the sea by a natural underground tunnel.

6

ARRIVAL AND DEPARTURE   ANG THONG

There are no scheduled boats to Ang Thong, only organized **day-trips**, which can be booked through your accommodation or a travel agent. If you do want to stay, you can go over on a boat-trip ticket – it's valid for a return on a later day.

FROM KO SAMUI

Blue Stars North end of Central Chaweng, next soi south of Soi Green Mango ☏077 413231, ⓦbluestars .info. If you want to make the most of the park's beautiful scenery of strange rock formations and hidden caves, take a dedicated kayaking trip with Blue Stars. For a one-day trip, taking in the lake at Ko Mae Ko and kayaking and snorkelling among the islands in the northern part of the park, they charge B2200, including pick-up from your accommodation and boat over to the park, buffet lunch and snorkelling gear.

Highway Opposite the southerly pier, near Siam Commercial Bank, on Thanon Chonwithi, Na Thon ☏077 421290 or ☏081 843 1533, ⓦhighseatour.com. The main operator, whose big boats leave Na Thon every day at 8.30am, returning at 4.30–5pm. In between, there's a two-hour stop to explore Ko Wua Talab (just enough time to visit the viewpoint, the cave and have a quick swim, so don't dally), lunch on the boat, some cruising through the archipelago, a visit to the viewpoint over the lake on Ko Mae Ko and a snorkelling stop. Tickets cost B1300/person (or B1850 with kayaking), including pick-up from your accommodation.

Lomprayah Maenam ☏077 427765–6, ⓦlomprayah .com One of several companies in Maenam, Bangrak and Bophut offering speedboat day-trips to Ang Thong (B2200).

FROM KO PHA NGAN

Similar day-trips to those from Samui are available on Pha Ngan, costing B1800 or B2000 with kayaking.

Orion ☏081 999 2000, ⓦwww.phanganboattrips .com. Day-trips in a wooden cruiser.

Safari Boat ☏077 238232, ⓦsafariboat.info. Day-trips to Ang Thong by speedboat.

Seaflower Bungalows Ao Chaophao (see p.570). Organizes occasional two-day, one-night boat treks into the park, which involve snorkelling, caving, catching your own seafood, and sleeping in tents or hammocks on the beach (B3500/person, including food and soft drinks; minimum eight people).

FROM KO TAO

Davy Jones' Locker ☏077 456604, ⓦdavyjoneslocker .asia. This dive company attached to *Silver Sands Resort* (see p.577) occasionally runs overnight trips to Ang Thong (B4500/person, B6000 including diving).

INFORMATION AND GETTING AROUND

Tourist information In the past, the marine park has operated a satellite information office near the middle pier in Na Thon, Samui, which may reopen.

Boat rental For getting around the archipelago from Ko Wua Talab, it's possible to charter a motorboat from marine park staff; the best snorkelling is off Ko Thai Plao.

ACCOMMODATION AND EATING

National park bungalows At park headquarters on Ko Wua Talab ☏077 280222 or ☏077 286025, ⓦdnp .go.th. Simple two- to eight-berth bungalows and a restaurant. B500

Camping At park headquarters on Ko Wua Talab and on Ko Samsao. Two-person tents can be rented for around B200 a night from headquarters.

Ko Pha Ngan

In recent years, backpackers have tended to move over to Ko Samui's fun-loving little sibling, **KO PHA NGAN**, 20km to the north, which still has a comparatively simple atmosphere, mostly because the poor road system is an impediment to the developers. With a dense jungle covering its inland mountains and rugged granite outcrops along the coast, Pha Ngan lacks the huge, gently sweeping beaches for which Samui is famous, but it does have plenty of coral to explore and some beautiful, sheltered bays. If you're seeking total isolation, trek out to **Hat Khuat (Bottle Beach)** on the north coast or the half-dozen pristine beaches on the east coast; **Thong Nai Pan**, at the top of the east coast, is not quite as remote, and offers a decent range of amenities and accommodation; while on the long neck of land at the southeast corner, **Hat Rin**, a pilgrimage site for ravers, is a thoroughly commercialized backpackers' resort in a gorgeous setting.

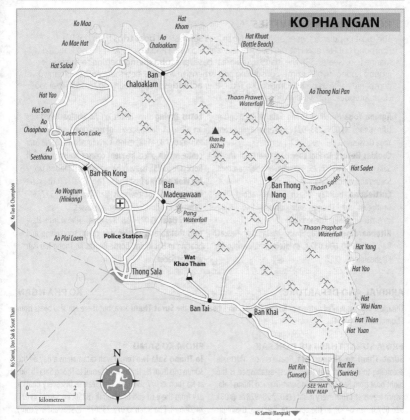

KO PHA NGAN

Ko Maa
Ko Mae Hat
Ao Mae Hat
Hat Khom
Ao Chaloaklam
Hat Khuat (Bottle Beach)
Hat Salad
Ban Chaloaklam
Ao Thong Nai Pan
Hat Yao
Thaan Prawet Waterfall
Hat Son
Ao Chaophao
Laem Son Lake
Khao Ra (627m)
Ao Seethanu
Ban Hin Kong
Ao Wogtum (Hinkong)
Ban Madeuawaan
Ban Thong Nang
Thaan Sadet
Hat Sadet
Pang Waterfall
Ao Plai Laem
Police Station
Thaan Praphat Waterfall
Wat Khao Tham
Thong Sala
Hat Yang
Hat Yao
Ban Tai
Ban Khai
Hat Wai Nam
Hat Thian
Hat Yuan
N
Hat Rin (Sunset)
Hat Rin (Sunrise)
SEE 'HAT RIN' MAP
0   2
kilometres
Ko Samui (Bangrak)

Ko Tao & Chumphon

Ko Samui, Don Sak & Surat Thani

6

Much of Pha Ngan's development has plonked itself on the south and west sides along the only coastal roads on the island, which fan out from **Thong Sala**, the capital. The long, straight south coast is lined with bungalows, especially around **Ban Tai** and **Ban Khai**, to take the overspill from nearby Hat Rin, but it's hard to recommend staying here, as the beaches are mediocre by Thai standards, and the coral reef that hugs the length of the shoreline gets in the way of swimming. The west coast, however, offers several handsome sandy bays with great sunset views, notably **Hat Yao** and **Hat Salad**.

Pha Ngan's **bungalows** all now have running water and electricity, and plenty of places offer air conditioning, though there are only a handful of real luxury hotels. The three hundred-plus resorts generally have more space to spread out than on Ko Samui, and the cost of living is lower. The **prices** given on the following pages are standard for most of the year (though on Hat Rin they vary with the phases of the moon), but in slack periods you'll be offered discounts (possible, roughly, in May, June, Oct & Nov), and at the very busiest times (especially Dec & Jan) Pha Ngan's bungalow owners are canny enough to raise the stakes. **Nightlife** is concentrated at Hat Rin, climaxing every month in a wild **full moon party** on the beach; a couple of smaller outdoor parties have now got in on the act: the **Half Moon Festival** (twice monthly, about a week before and after the full moon; ⊛halfmoonfestival.com) and the monthly **Black Moon Party** (⊛blackmoon-culture.com), both at Ban Tai on the south coast.

KO PHA NGAN ACTIVITIES

The most popular activities on Ko Pha Ngan are round-island **boat trips** from Hat Rin, Ao Thong Nai Pan and Hat Yao (see the relevant accounts) and trips to Ang Thong National Marine Park (see p.558). The island isn't a great base for **scuba diving**: getting to the best sites around Ko Tao involves time-consuming and expensive voyages, and there aren't as many dive companies here as on Ko Samui or Ko Tao. Other **activities** include learning to cook Thai food, yoga, kiteboarding, windsurfing and sailing.

Agama Yoga North of Thong Sala at Ao Wogtum (Hin Kong) ☎089 233 0217, ⓦagamayoga.com. Yoga classes.

Cookies Resort Ao Plai Laem, just north of Thong Sala ☎083 181 7125, ⓦcookies-phangan.com. Sailing and windsurfing.

Cuttlebone Holiday Beach Resort, about 2km southeast of Thong Sala ☎081 940 1902, ⓦcuttlebone.net. Kiteboarding.

Kiteboarding Asia Opposite Milky Bay Resort, Ban Tai ☎080 600 0573, ⓦkiteboardingasia.com. Kiteboarding.

Lotus Diving Dive resort on Ao Chaloaklam (plus an office at Backpackers Information Centre in Hat Rin) ☎077 374142, ⓦlotusdiving.net. PADI Five-Star centre, which offers frequent courses and trips to Sail Rock (see p.575), halfway between Pha Ngan and Tao.

My Wok and Me East end of Thong Sala, at the start of the road out towards Ban Tai ☎077 377846, ⓦmywokandme.com. Cooking classes.

Safari Boat ☎077 238232, ⓦsafariboat.info. Day-trips that take in an elephant camp, snorkelling and boating to Hat Khom, Bottle Beach, Ao Thong Nai Pan and Hat Sadet.

ARRIVAL AND DEPARTURE   KO PHA NGAN

The most obvious way of getting to Ko Pha Ngan is on a boat from the **Surat Thani** area, but there are also boats from Chumphon (see p.534).

FROM SURAT THANI OR DON SAK

Surat Thani to Thong Sala Boat services fluctuate according to demand, but the longest-established is the night boat from Ban Don pier in Surat Thani to Thong Sala, which leaves at 11pm every night (☎077 284928 or ☎081 326 8973; 7hr; B450); in the opposite direction, the night boat departs from Thong Sala at 10pm. Tickets are available from the pier on the day of departure, but note that occasionally these boats don't depart, if they haven't got enough takers to make it worth their while.

Don Sak to Thong Sala There are five Raja vehicle ferries a day (on Pha Ngan ☎077 377452–3), which charge B400, including bus transport to the pier from Surat Thani, with a total journey time of around 4–5hr. In addition, there are two Lomprayah catamarans a day (on Pha Ngan ☎077 238411–2, ⓦlomprayah.com), charging B550, with a total journey time from Surat of about 3hr.

FROM BANGKOK

Bus and train packages From Bangkok bus and train packages similar to those for getting to Ko Samui are available (see p.542), notably government buses from the Southern Terminal (first-class a/c 1 daily B800; VIP 1 daily B1100; 12–14hr). Leaving Pha Ngan, you can catch these buses from the Raja Ferry pier in Thong Sala (☎077 238507 or ☎077 238762).

FROM KO SAMUI

To Thong Sala Two Lomprayah catamarans a day do the 30min trip from Na Thon on Ko Samui to Thong Sala (B300; at Na Thon ☎077 950028). Two Seatran Discovery boats a day from the east end of Bangrak (B250; on Samui ☎077 246086–8, Pha Ngan ☎077 238679; ⓦseatranferry.com) and two Lomprayah catamarans from Maenam (B300; at Maenam ☎077 427765–6) call in at Thong Sala after 30min, on their way to Ko Tao.

To Hat Rin and the east coast From the centre of Bangrak, the *Haad Rin Queen* crosses four times a day to Hat Rin in under an hour (times have remained fairly constant over the years: from Bangrak 10.30am, 1pm, 4pm & 6.30pm, from Hat Rin 9.30am, 11.40am, 2.30pm & 5.30pm; B200; on Samui ☎077 484668, on Pha Ngan ☎077 375113). If there are enough takers and the weather's good enough – generally reliable between roughly mid-Jan and late Oct – one small boat a day crosses from the pier in Ban Maenam at noon to Hat Rin (B250), before sailing up Ko Pha Ngan's east coast, via Hat Sadet and anywhere else upon demand, to Thong Nai Pan (B350).

FROM KO TAO

There are boats from Ko Tao to Ko Pha Ngan (see p.573); all offer the same service in the return direction.

CLOCKWISE FROM TOP KO SAMSAO, ANG THONG NATIONAL MARINE PARK (P.557); THAM PHRAYA NAKHON KHAO SAM ROI YOT (P.528); LONGTAIL BOATS ON KO TAO (P.571) >

6

MEDITATION RETREATS AT WAT KHAO THAM

On a quiet hillside above Ban Tai, 4km from Thong Sala on the south coast, **Wat Khao Tham** holds ten-day **meditation retreats** most months of the year (B5000/person to cover food; ⓦ watkowtahm.org). The American and Australian teachers emphasize compassionate understanding as the basis of mental development. Space is limited (retreats are especially heavily subscribed Dec–March), so it's best to pre-register either in person or in writing; go to the website for full details of rules and requirements and the schedule of retreats.

INFORMATION

Tourist information There's no TAT office on Ko Pha Ngan, but a free, widely available booklet, *Phangan Info*, provides regularly updated information about the island, and has a good website, ⓦ phangan.info, on which you can book accommodation. Affiliated to this is the website of Hat Rin's travel agency, ⓦ backpackersthailand.com, which is also a good source of information.

Maps The best map for serious exploration of the island is Visid Hongsombud's *Guide Map of Koh Pha-ngan and Koh Tao* (B120), though it's hard to find.

Thong Sala

Like the capital of Samui, **THONG SALA** is a port of entrance and little more, where the incoming ferries, especially around noon, are met by touts sent to escort travellers to bungalows elsewhere on the island. Songthaews and jeeps to the rest of the island congregate by the pier heads, while the main street that runs inland from the Raja Ferry pier shelters a dusty row of banks, supermarkets, travel agents and scuba-diving outfits, with a popular night market on the north side of the road.

GETTING AROUND   THONG SALA

By motorbike or jeep Motorbikes (B150–200/day) and jeeps (B800–1000/day) can be rented from many places on the main road to the piers.

ACCOMMODATION AND EATING

Nira's South along the waterfront from the main street, opposite the Seatran pier. Very pleasant branch of the famous Hat Rin café (see p.566) offering "quick meals to catch the boat": all-day breakfasts, espressos, bakery goods such as quiche lorraine (B65), deli sandwiches and Thai and Western main courses. Free computer for customers' use. Daily 7am–7pm.

Pha Ngan Chai Hotel By the piers, Thong Sala ⓣ 077 238109. If you really need to stay in Thong Sala, head for this incongruous white high-rise overshadowing the piers, which makes a fair stab at international-standard features for visiting businesspeople and government officials, with a/c, hot water, TVs, fridges and, in some rooms, sea-view balconies, as well as a pool, free wi-fi and internet access. Breakfast included. B1000

DIRECTORY

Hospital The island's basic main hospital (ⓣ 077 377034 or ⓣ 077 375103) lies 3km north of town, on the inland road towards Mae Hat. There's also a 24hr emergency rescue service, staffed by volunteers (ⓣ 077 377500).

Police The main station is 2km up the Ban Chaloaklam road (ⓣ 077 377114), and there's a tourist police office at the main pier in Thong Sala (ⓣ 1155).

Post office About 500m southeast of the piers on the old main street (Mon–Fri 8.30am–noon & 1–4.30pm, Sat 9am–noon).

Pang (Phaeng) Waterfall

Than Sadet–Ko Pha Ngan National Park, 4km northeast of Thong Sala off the road to Chaloaklam • Free admission • Take a Chaloaklam-bound songthaew as far as Ban Madeuawaan, from where it's a 1km signposted walk east

From most places on the island, it's fairly easy to get to the grandiosely termed Than Sadet–Ko Pha Ngan National Park, which contains **Pang (Phaeng) Waterfall**, Pha Ngan's biggest drop. The park headquarters and a simple canteen are northeast of Thong Sala off the main road to Chaloaklam. From here, the main fall – bouncing down in stages over the hard, grey stone – is a steep 250m walk up a forest path. The trail then continues for 300m to a stunning viewpoint overlooking the south and west of the island.

Hat Rin

HAT RIN is firmly established as the major party venue in Southeast Asia, especially in the peak seasons of August, December and January, but it's most famous for its year-round **full moon parties** – something like *Apocalypse Now* without the war. Hat Rin's compact geography is ideally suited to an intense party town: it occupies the flat neck of Pha Ngan's southeast headland, which is so narrow that the resort comprises two back-to-back beaches, joined by transverse roads at the north and south ends. The eastern beach, usually referred to as **Sunrise**, or Hat Rin Nok (Outer Hat Rin), is what originally drew visitors here, a classic curve of fine white sand between two rocky

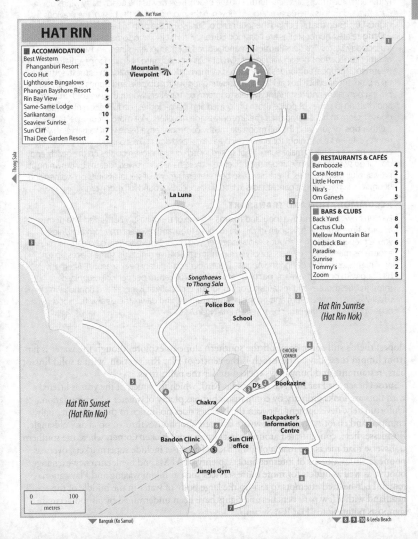

HAT RIN

ACCOMMODATION

Best Western Phanganburi Resort	3
Coco Hut	8
Lighthouse Bungalows	9
Phangan Bayshore Resort	4
Rin Bay View	5
Same-Same Lodge	6
Sarikantang	10
Seaview Sunrise	1
Sun Cliff	7
Thai Dee Garden Resort	2

RESTAURANTS & CAFÉS

Bamboozle	4
Casa Nostra	2
Little Home	3
Nira's	1
Om Ganesh	5

BARS & CLUBS

Back Yard	8
Cactus Club	4
Mellow Mountain Bar	1
Outback Bar	6
Paradise	7
Sunrise	3
Tommy's	2
Zoom	5

Hat Yuan

Mountain Viewpoint

N

Thong Sala

La Luna

Songthaews to Thong Sala

Police Box

School

Hat Rin Sunrise (Hat Rin Nok)

CHICKEN CORNER

D's

Bookazine

Chakra

Hat Rin Sunset (Hat Rin Nai)

Backpacker's Information Centre

Bandon Clinic

Sun Cliff office

Jungle Gym

0   100
metres

Bangrak (Ko Samui)

8, 9, 10 & Leela Beach

6

FULL MOON PARTIES: A SURVIVOR'S GUIDE

Even if you're not the type to coat yourself in day-glo and dance till dawn, a **full moon party** at Hat Rin is certainly a sight to see, and the atmosphere created by thousands of folk mashing it up on a beautiful, moon-bathed beach, lit up by fireworks and fire-jugglers, is quite a buzz. If you're planning to get in on the action, first of all you'll need to check exactly when the party is: when the full moon coincides with an important **Buddhist festival**, the party is moved one night away to avoid a clash; check out ⓦfullmoon.phangan.info for details. There's also a big party at Hat Rin on Christmas Day, and a massive one on New Year's Eve. An **admission fee** to the parties of B100 is now charged.

On full moon night, *Paradise*, at the very southern end of Sunrise, styles itself as the main party **venue**, sometimes bringing in big-name international DJs. However, the mayhem spreads along most of Sunrise, fuelled by hastily erected drinks stalls and around a dozen major **sound systems** – listen out for psy-trance and driving techno at *Zoom*, and tech house at *Tommy's* and funky house and drum'n'bass at *Sunrise* further up the beach. Next day, as the beach party winds down, *Back Yard* kicks off its afterparty at around eleven in the morning, with the best of the previous night's DJs; it's up the hill behind the south end of Sunrise off the path to Leela Beach.

Drug-related horror stories are common currency in Hat Rin, and some of them are even true: dodgy Ecstasy, *ya baa* (Burmese-manufactured methamphetamines) and all manner of other concoctions put an average of two farangs a month into hospital for psychiatric treatment. The local authorities have started clamping down on the trade in earnest, setting up a permanent police box at Hat Rin, instigating regular roadblocks and bungalow searches, paying bungalow and restaurant owners to inform on travellers whom they've sold drugs to, and drafting in scores of police (both uniformed and plain-clothes) on full moon nights. It doesn't seem to have dampened the fun, only made travellers a lot more circumspect.

Other **tips** for surviving the full moon are mostly common sense: leave your valuables in your resort's safe – it's a bad night for bungalow break-ins – and don't take a bag out with you; keep an eye on your drink to make sure it's not spiked; watch out for broken bottles on the beach; and do not go swimming while under the influence – there have been several deaths by drowning at previous full moon parties. There have also been several reports of sexual assaults on women and of unprovoked, late-night gang attacks in Hat Rin, especially around full moon night.

ACCOMMODATION AND TRANSPORT

Hat Rin now has around five thousand **rooms** – some of them hastily converted into dorms at party time – but on full moon nights up to thirty thousand revellers may turn up. Unless you're prepared to forget about sleep altogether, you should arrive several days early to bag a room, as many resort owners specify a minimum stay of five nights (in some places up to nine nights, especially during the August, December and January peak seasons). Alternatively, hitch up with one of the many **party boats** (about B700 return per person) organized through guesthouses and restaurants on Ko Samui, especially at Bangrak and Bophut, which usually leave between 9pm and midnight and return around dawn; there's also transport by boat or car from all the other beaches on Pha Ngan.

slopes; there's still some coral off the southern slope to explore, though the water is far from limpid these days. This beach is the centre of Hat Rin's action, with a solid line of bars, restaurants and bungalows tucked under the palm trees.

Sunset beach, or Hat Rin Nai (Inner Hat Rin), which for much of the year is littered with flotsam, looks ordinary by comparison but has plenty of quieter accommodation. Unfortunately, development between the beaches does no justice to the setting: it's ugly, cramped and chaotic, with new low-rise concrete shophouses thrown up at any old angle. Businesses here, concentrated around what's known as **Chicken Corner**, where the southern transverse road meets the road along the back of Sunrise, include supermarkets, overseas phone facilities, dozens of internet outlets, plenty of ATMs and bank currency-exchange booths, as well as outlets for more outré services such as bikini waxing and Playstation rental. Half-hearted attempts to tart up the large body of water in the middle of the headland with a few park benches and lights have been undermined by all-too-accurate signposts pointing to "Hat Rin Swamp".

HAT RIN ACTIVITIES

Many places on Hat Rin, including the Backpackers Information Centre (see below), book one-day **boat trips** up the east coast and back, typically charging B800 (including simple lunch and snorkelling equipment) and taking in Mae Hat, Thong Nai Pan, Bottle Beach and Thaan Sadet. Back on dry land, Chakra, in an alley off the southern transverse (☎087 283 4365), does good **massages** and runs massage courses, while Jungle Gym near the pier (☎077 375115) offers **Thai boxing** classes, a steam room and **yoga**.

ARRIVAL AND DEPARTURE

By songthaew or minibus Songthaews (B100 during the day, more at night) and a/c minibuses (B150) run between Thong Sala and Hat Rin.

By boat The easiest approach to Hat Rin, if you're coming

from Ko Samui, or even Surat Thani, is on the boat from Bangrak on Samui's north coast (see p.560): four boats a day cross to the pier on Sunset beach in under an hour.

GETTING AROUND

By jeep or motorbike Plenty of places on Hat Rin rent jeeps (about B1000/day) and motorbikes (from B150/day). There have been lots of reports, however, of travellers being charged exorbitant amounts if they bring the vehicle back with even the most minor damage – at the very least, check the vehicle over very carefully before renting. *Sun*

Cliff (see p.566), who have an office just off the southern transverse, is a reliable place for motorbikes, and won't try this scam. The section of road between Hat Rin and Ban Khai is paved but winding and precipitous – take care if you're driving yourself.

INFORMATION AND TOURS

★ **Backpackers Information Centre** The excellent, English-Thai Backpackers Information Centre, based to the south of Chicken Corner (daily 10am–10pm; ☎077 375535, ⓦbackpackersthailand.com), is a reliable, helpful and clued-up full-service travel agency, with a website that's very useful not just for Pha Ngan but for the whole of Thailand, including lots of advice and mini-package tours.

They can book tours and other activities on Ko Pha Ngan and through-tickets from Hat Rin to all the tourist centres in southern Thailand, as well as to Kuala Lumpur and Singapore. They also act as agents for Ko Pha Ngan's Lotus Diving and Ko Tao's Crystal Diving (with discounted deals available for advance bookings).

ACCOMMODATION

Staying on **Sunrise** is often expensive and noisy, though you should have more luck towards the north end of the beach. On **Sunset**, the twenty or more resorts are squeezed together in orderly rows, and are especially quiet and inexpensive between April and June and in October. Many visitors choose to stay on the **headland** to the south of the main beaches, especially at white-sand, palm-fringed **Leela Beach** on the west side of the promontory, which is a twenty-minute walk along a well-signposted route from Chicken Corner. At any of the places out here your bungalow is likely to have more peace and space and better views, leaving you a torchlit walk to the night-time action.

Best Western Phanganburi Resort Towards the north end of Sunset beach ☎077 375481, ⓦbest westernphanganburi.com. Welcoming, luxury complex that encompasses three hotel blocks, dozens of bungalows, a spa, a gym and two very attractive pools in its extensive, beachside grounds. Decorated in a simple but smart Thai style, all the rooms have a/c, hot water, fridge, safety box, free wi-fi and satellite TV. Breakfast included. B2400

Coco Hut Leela Beach ☎077 375369, ⓦcocohut.com. On a clean, quiet stretch of beach, this lively, efficiently run place is smart and attractive, with some traditional southern Thai elements in the architecture. On offer is a wide variety of upscale accommodation, from wooden bungalows with a/c, hot showers, fridges, TVs and DVDs,

to beachfront villas with outdoor jacuzzis, as well as an attractive pool, an adobe-style spa and free wi-fi at the restaurant. Breakfast included. B2600

Lighthouse Bungalows On the far southwestern tip of the headland ☎077 375075, ⓦlighthouse bungalows.com. At this friendly haven, fan-cooled wooden and concrete en-suite bungalows, sturdily built to withstand the wind and backed by trail-filled jungle, are priced according to size and comfort; all have good-sized balconies with hammocks. The restaurant food is varied and tasty. Phone for a boat pick-up from Sunset pier or Thong Sala, or do the 30min walk from Chicken Corner, the last section along a wooden walkway over the rocky shoreline. B600

6

Phangan Bayshore Resort In the middle of Sunrise ☎077 375227, ⓦphanganbayshore.com. Hat Rin's first upmarket resort, a well-ordered, slightly institutional place, boasting 80m of beachfront. There's a large, kidney-shaped pool and a wide variety of close-knit bungalows and rooms with a/c, hot water, TV and fridge, on a green lawn shaded with palms. Minimum stay 3 nights. B1680

Rin Bay View Near the pier on Sunset ☎077 375188. A good-value, friendly option in a tightly squeezed central location, occupying a narrow strip of land by the beach, ornamented with flowers and trees. The a/c bungalows and rooms with mosquito screens, hot showers, TVs, fridges and balconies are a decent size and generally well maintained and clean. B1000

Same-Same Lodge Above Sunrise at the start of the road to Leela Beach ☎077 375200, ⓦsame-same.com. Sociable Danish-run spot with free wi-fi set above a popular, often raucous, bar-restaurant. The clean, colourful and decent-sized rooms come with fan and cold showers or a/c and hot water. Fan B550, a/c B850

Sarikantang Leela Beach ☎077 375055–6, ⓦsarikantang.com. Boutique resort with two swimming pools, a beachside spa and a good measure of style. Accommodation ranges from bungalows with a/c, TVs, fridges, verandas and hot-water bathrooms to villas with DVD players, separate living rooms and outdoor jacuzzis. Internet room, free wi-fi and free kayaks. Breakfast included. B1700

Seaview Sunrise Northern end of Sunrise ☎077 375160, ⓦseaviewsunrise.com. On a big plot of shady, flower-strewn land at the quieter end of the beach, this clean, friendly, orderly old-timer with a good restaurant offers a total of forty bungalows and rooms. Those on the beachfront are all fan-cooled, with cheaper versions available further back, with or without hot showers. The a/c offerings all have hot water, TV and fridge. Fan B400, fan and hot shower B600, a/c B1000

Sun Cliff High up on the tree-lined slope above the south end of Sunset ☎077 375134 or ☎077 375463, ⓔrsvnsuncliff@hotmail.com. Friendly, spacious place with great views of the south coast and Ko Samui, especially from its heart-shaped pool by the restaurant. Among a wide range of bungalows that are a bit rough around the edges, you'll find some quirky architectural features such as rock-built bathrooms and fountains; some have huge decks for partying. A/c rooms all have hot showers, fridges and TVs. Fan B300, fan and hot shower B500, a/c B600

Thai Dee Garden Resort Northern transverse ☎089 770 2290, ⓔthaidee-@hotmail.com. Pleasant staff and a range of smart concrete and white clapboard bungalows, on a broad, grassy slope strewn with trees and plants and set back from the road. Choose either fan and cold water or a/c and hot. One of the last places to fill at full moon; discounts for stays of two nights or more possible at other times. Free wi-fi at reception. Fan B300, a/c B890

EATING

Bamboozle Off the southern transverse, near Sunset pier ☎085 471 4211. Among a wide variety of tasty Mexican food here, the chicken fajitas with all the trimmings (B250) are especially good. Also offers pizzas and a short menu of tapas. Daily 10am–late.

★ **Casa Nostra** On the southern transverse ☎086 267 8445. Excellent, tiny Italian café-restaurant which prepares great pastas – try the spaghetti bolognese (B180) – pizzas, espresso coffee, salads and plenty of other dishes for vegetarians, such as home-made cannelloni with ricotta and spinach, and a chocolate mousse to die for. Daily 1–11.30pm.

Little Home On the southern transverse. This well-organized, basic restaurant is your best bet for cheap

Thai food in Hat Rin, serving staples such as chicken and cashew nuts (B80) and green, red and yellow curries, plus Western breakfasts. Daily 11am–11pm.

Nira's Near Chicken Corner. Justly popular restaurant and bakery. Around the clock it offers great croissants – sweet and savoury – cakes, sandwiches and coffees; during the busy part of the day, it operates as a restaurant, serving up good breakfasts, burgers and other basic hot meals. Free wi-fi. Bakery 24hr; restaurant daily 8am–8pm.

Om Ganesh On the southern transverse near the pier ☎086 063 2903. Relaxing Indian restaurant with good thalis (from B150), biryanis, plenty of veggie dishes and breads, and cheerful service. Free deliveries. Daily 8am–11pm.

NIGHTLIFE

Cactus Club South end of Sunrise. Open-air dance hall that pumps out mostly radio-friendly dance music onto low-slung candlelit tables and mats on the beach. Evenings till late.

Mellow Mountain Bar North end of Sunrise. Made for chilling, this trippy hangout occupies a great position

up in the rocks, with peerless views of the beach. Evenings till late.

Outback Bar On the southern transverse. Lively, British-run meeting place with free pool tables, big-screen sports, free wi-fi, draught Carlsberg and well-received steak pies and the like. Daily 10am–late.

DIRECTORY

Bookshops Bookazine (daily 11am–8pm), on the southern transverse, carries a decent line of new fiction and travel books, as well as magazines and newspapers, while D's (daily 9am–10pm), on a new, little-used road that runs parallel to and north of the southern transverse, is good for secondhand books and has a café.

Clinic Bandon International Hospital, a large private hospital on Ko Samui, runs a clinic on the southern transverse near the pier (☎077 375471–2).

Hat Yuan, Hat Thian and Hat Sadet

North of Hat Rin, there are no roads along the rocky, exposed east coast, which stretches as far as **Ao Thong Nai Pan**, the only substantial centre of development. First up are the adjoining small, sandy bays of **HAT YUAN** and **HAT THIAN**, which have established a reputation as a quieter alternative to Hat Rin. A rough track has recently been bulldozed from Ban Khai, and the bays now sport about a dozen bungalow outfits between them.

Steep, remote **HAT SADET**, about 8km as the crow flies from Hat Rin, has a handful of bungalow operations, sited here because of their proximity to **Thaan Sadet**, a boulder-strewn brook that runs out into the sea. The spot was popularized by various kings of Thailand – Rama V visited no less than fourteen times – who came here to walk, swim and vandalize the huge boulders by carving their initials on them; the river water is now considered sacred and is transported to Bangkok for important royal ceremonies. A rough track runs through the woods above and parallel to Thaan Sadet to connect with the road from Thong Sala to Ao Thong Nai Pan.

If you're feeling intrepid, you could try hiking along this stretch of coast, which in theory is paralleled by a steep, 15km trail (as marked on Visid Hongsombud's map – see p.562), though it's reported to be overgrown in many places. With decent navigational skills, the leg between Hat Rin, starting from near *Laluna Bungalows*, and Hat Yuan should certainly be manageable (about 2hr), aided by green dot and white arrow markers.

ARRIVAL AND DEPARTURE   HAT YUAN, HAT THIAN, HAT SADET

By boat A daily, seasonal boat runs via the east coast beaches from Hat Rin to Thong Nai Pan, having started its voyage across at Maenam on Ko Samui (see p.560).

Otherwise there are ample longtails at Hat Rin that will take you up the coast – around B150/person to Hat Yuan, for example.

ACCOMMODATION

HAT YUAN

Barcelona ☎077 375113. Good, relaxing budget choice, with great views and well-built accommodation, mostly in white, stilted bungalows running up the hillside from the beach, the best of them (B700) with large verandas and hot showers. Shared bathrooms B200, en-suite B300

Centara Pariya Resort ☎081 737 3883, ⊚centara hotelsresorts.com. The most luxurious resort in the vicinity of Hat Rin comprises forty spacious villas, some with their own private jacuzzi pool, all with rain showers, bathtubs and large verandas; a/c and hot water are available from 6pm to 10am. There's a free-form pool and kids' pool and a spa, as well as plenty of watersports and wi-fi. Access is by speed boat, either from Hat Rin or from Bophut on Samui. B4600

HAT THIAN

The Sanctuary ☎081 271 3614, ⊚thesanctuary thailand.com. The main operation on Hat Thian offers a huge range of basic and luxury en-suite bungalows and family houses, as well as dorm accommodation (B200–300), kayaking and good vegetarian meals, seafood and home-made bread and cakes. It also hosts courses in yoga, meditation and many new-age subjects, and provides two kinds of treatment: the spa does massage, facials and beauty treatments, while the wellness centre goes in for fasting and cleansing. B450

HAT SADET

Mai Pen Rai ☎081 999 2000, ⊚thansadet.com. Best of the bungalows on Hat Sadet, this welcoming spot has a wide variety of attractive accommodation with airy bathrooms, fans and hammocks (some with big upstairs terraces), either on the beach at the stream mouth or scattered around the rocks for good views. A jeep taxi leaves Thong Sala pier for the resort every day at 1pm (B200). B500

Ao Thong Nai Pan

AO THONG NAI PAN is a beautiful, semicircular bay backed by steep, green hills, which looks as if it's been bitten out of the island's northeast corner by a gap-toothed giant, leaving a tall hump of land (occupied by *Panviman Resort*) dividing the bay into two parts: **Thong Nai Pan Noi** to the north, **Thong Nai Pan Yai** to the south. With lovely, fine, white sand, the longer, more indented Thong Nai Pan Yai has marginally the better beach, but both halves of the bay are sheltered and deep enough for swimming. A bumpy road, only partly paved, winds its way for 13km over the steep mountains from Ban Tai on the south coast to Thong Nai Pan, but once you get here you'll find most of the basic amenities you'll need: internet shops, travel agents, dive outfits, ATMs and a tiny post office (on Thong Nai Pan Yai).

ARRIVAL AND DEPARTURE | AO THONG NAI PAN

By jeep Jeeps connect with incoming and outgoing boats at Thong Sala every day (B200/person).

By boat One seasonal boat a day runs via the east coast beaches from Hat Rin to Thong Nai Pan, having started its voyage across at Maenam on Ko Samui (see p.560).

TOURS

Boat tours Day-trips taking in Ao Mae Hat, Hat Khuat and Thaan Sadet can be arranged through *Baan Panburi Village*, for example (B600/person, minimum 8 people).

ACCOMMODATION

★ **Anantara Rasananda** Thong Nai Pan Noi ☎077 239555, ⓦanantara.com. Congenial and chic luxury hideaway, with speedboat transfers from Samui. Accommodation is in 60 spacious, contemporary villas and suites, all with their own plunge pool, most with outdoor bathrooms. There's also a main, infinity-edge swimming pool, which forms the central hub of the resort, along with the sociable bar and excellent restaurant. The very good spa stretches up the hillside behind, with a steam room built into the rocks. Other activities include kayaking, cooking and massage classes. B16,500

Baan Panburi Village Southern end of Thong Nai Pan Yai ☎077 238599 or ☎077 445075, ⓦbaanpanburi village.com. Two rows of well-designed bungalows with verandas and deckchairs run down a slope dotted with wicker hammocks, either side of a small, artificial waterfall.

Choose between old-style, thatched, wood-and-bamboo huts with mosquito nets, fans and cold showers, and large, wooden, a/c affairs with hot water and tiled floors. Free kayaks. Fan B600, a/c B1300

★ **Dolphin** Southern end of Thong Nai Pan Yai ⓔkimgiet@hotmail.com (no phone bookings). Popular, tranquil spot, overgrown with lush vegetation and with lots of comfortable *salas* and hammocks to recline in. The 26 large, very clean, en-suite bungalows come with either fans (some with hot water for B800) or a/c and hot showers; the latter include big family affairs and luxury rooms (both B2500) with silk cushions and other nice decorative touches. Also has an appealing clothes and crafts boutique, Karma, on the main road in Thong Nai Pan Yai. Fan B600, a/c B1500

EATING

Dolphin Southern end of Thong Nai Pan Yai. Good, mellow beachfront restaurant serving Western breakfasts, great coffee, lasagne (B220) and other pastas, salads, sandwiches and Thai food, plus tapas in the evening. Daily 8.30am–4.30pm & 6.30pm–late.

The north coast

The largest indent on the **north coast**, Ao Chaloaklam, has long been a famous R&R spot for fishermen from all over the Gulf of Thailand, with sometimes as many as a hundred trawlers littering the broad and sheltered bay. As a tourist destination, it has little to recommend it – save that its village, **Ban Chaloaklam**, can easily be reached from Thong Sala, 10km away, by songthaew (B150) along a paved road – but the small, quiet beaches to the east, Hat Khom and Hat Khuat, have much more to offer.

Hat Khom

Dramatically tucked in under Ao Chaloaklam's eastern headland is the tiny cove of **HAT KHOM**. Linked to the outside world by a partly paved road, it offers a handful of simple bungalows, a secluded strip of white sand and good coral for snorkelling.

Hat Khuat (Bottle Beach)

If the sea is not too rough, longtail boats run several times a day for most of the year from Ban Chaloaklam (east of the fishing pier; B100/person or about B600/boat) to isolated **HAT KHUAT** (**BOTTLE BEACH**), the best of the beaches on the north coast, sitting between steep, jungle-clad hills in a perfect cup of a bay that's good for swimming. You could also walk there along a testing trail from Hat Khom in around ninety minutes.

6

ACCOMMODATION   THE NORTH COAST

Coral Bay Hat Khom ☎077 374245. Friendly, laidback outfit with plenty of space and great views on the grassy, flower-strewn promontory dividing Hat Khom from Ao Chaloaklam. The sturdy bungalows range from simple affairs with shared bathrooms and no fans to large pads with a/c and hot showers, some with funky bathrooms built into the rock; snorkelling equipment can be rented to make the most of Hat Khom's reef. Phone ahead to ask about their daily transfers from Thong Sala. Fan B200, a/c B1200

Haad Khuad Resort Hat Khuat ☎077 445153–4, ⓦhaadkhuadresort.com. Well-organized spot in the middle of the bay, offering deluxe rooms in a two-storey hotel block with view-filled French windows, a/c, hot water, TV, DVD-players, mini-bars and breakfast included. Also has a choice of wooden or concrete fan bungalows with cold showers on the beachfront and in the garden. Kayaks available. Four daily transfers from Thong Sala (B400/person). Closed mid-Oct to mid-Dec. Fan B250, a/c B1500

EATING

L'Oasi 1km south of Ban Chaloaklam on the main road ☎086 470 4253. A handy, congenial spot for lunch on a round-island tour. As well as burgers and barbecues, it serves up tasty Italian specialities such as pizza, panini and

spaghetti with pesto (B250) and decent wine by the glass, in a pretty garden setting with a small kids' playground. Daily 11am–9.30pm.

The west coast

Pha Ngan's **west coast** has attracted about the same amount of development as the forgettable south coast, but the landscape here is more attractive and varied, broken up into a series of long sandy inlets with good sunset views over the islands of the Ang Thong National Marine Park to the west. Most of the bays, however, are sheltered by reefs which can keep the sea too shallow for a decent swim, especially between May and October.

Laem Son Lake and Ao Chaophao

About halfway up the west coast from Thong Sala, there's a surprise in store in the shape of **Laem Son Lake**, a tranquil stretch of clear water cordoned by pines; however, you should avoid swimming here, as the lake, site of a former tin mine, is apparently considered toxic. Beyond, on the small, pretty bay of **AO CHAOPHAO**, there's good accommodation and food at *Seaflower*.

Hat Yao

North of Chaophao, the long, gently curved, fine-sand beach of **HAT YAO** is gradually and justifiably becoming busier and more popular, with several stand-alone bars, diving outfits, a 7-Eleven supermarket, a currency-exchange booth, ATMs and jeep and bike rental, as well as a nonstop line of bungalows. **Boat trips** from here to Hat Salad, Ao Mae Hat, Hat Khom, Bottle Beach and either Thong Nai Pan or Than Sadet waterfall (B750/person, including snorkels) can be arranged, for example, through *Ibiza Bungalows* or directly with Khun Tonan (☎086 279 0166 or ☎077 349139).

Hat Salad

To the north of Hat Yao, **HAT SALAD** is another pretty bay, sheltered and sandy, with good snorkelling off the northern tip. On the access road behind the beach is a rather untidy service village of shops, travel agents, bike and jeep rental outlets and internet offices. Take your pick from a dozen or so bungalow outfits.

Ao Mae Hat

On the island's northwest corner, **AO MAE HAT** is good for swimming and snorkelling among the coral that lines the sandy causeway to the tiny islet of Ko Maa. The broad, coarse-sand bay supports several bungalow resorts.

ARRIVAL AND GETTING AROUND
THE WEST COAST

There's a paved coastal road up as far as Hat Salad, where it loops inland to meet the main inland road from Thong Sala via the hospital to Ao Mae Hat.

By songthaew Songthaews from Thong Sala serve all of the beaches on the west coast, charging B150/ person to go as far as Hat Yao, for example.

ACCOMMODATION

AO SEETHANU

Loy Fa ☎077 377319, ⓦloyfanaturalresort.com. Well-run, flower-strewn place that commands good views from its perch on the steep southern cape of otherwise nondescript Ao Seethanu. There's good snorkelling and swimming from its private beach below, as well as a decent-sized pool. Bungalows are scattered around the hilltop and the slope down on the beach, and come with fan and hot showers (one with an outdoor bathroom) or a/c, hot water and mini-bar (some with TV); villas with private pools are planned. Internet access, free wi-fi, kayaks and bicycles are available. Fan B1000, a/c B1800

AO CHAOPHAO

Seaflower ☎077 349090, ⓦseaflowerbungalows.com. Quiet spot, set in a lush garden, with good veggie and non-veggie food. En-suite bungalows with their own hot-water bathrooms vary in price according to their size and age: the newer ones – more like cottages – have marble open-air bathrooms and big balcony seating areas. Wi-fi and snorkels available, as well as fishing and snorkelling day-trips and occasional overnighters to Ang Thong National Marine Park (see p.558). Fan B650, a/c B1700

HAT YAO

Ibiza Bungalows ☎077 349121, ⓦibizabungalow .com. Lively, central spot on a spacious lawn with mature trees for shade. The 34 airy bungalows run the full gamut, from fan and cold-water offerings near the beach (pay B100 extra to be right on the beach) to a/c, hot-shower affairs. There's also internet access, snorkelling equipment, a branch of Lotus Diving (see p.560) and an ATM. Fan B500, a/c B800

Long Bay Resort ☎077 349057, ⓦphangan.info /longbay. Hat Yao's nicest upmarket spot boasts a long stretch of beach and spacious gardens towards the north end of the bay. Choose between small but smart bungalows and a range of large cottages, all with a/c and hot water. There's an attractive swimming pool and kayaks and snorkels to rent. Breakfast included. B2000

Shiralea ☎080 719 9256 or ☎077 349217, ⓦshiralea .net. On a broad, grassy bank beneath coconut trees behind the north end of the beach, the spacious, very attractive thatched bungalows here all come with hot water, and there's a seductive pool, a dive school and free wi-fi. Fan B600, a/c B1200

HAT SALAD

★ **Salad Hut** ☎077 349246, ⓦsaladhut.com. Among the dozen or so bungalow outfits here, this congenial, family-friendly and well-run old-timer stands out. Parallel to the beachfront behind a swimming pool, in a shady, colourful garden, are twelve stylish bungalows done out in dark woods, red and white, with day beds with axe cushions and large verandas. All come with hot water, mini-bar and TV, and a cooked breakfast at the chic bar-restaurant is included. Computers, wi-fi and snorkel and kayak rental. Fan B1900, a/c B2200

AO MAE HAT

Wang Sai Resort ☎077 374238, ⓔwangsaikohma @live.com. Popular, friendly spot by a shady creek at the south end of the bay. On a huge plot of land, most of the en-suite bungalows are set back from the beach, with fans and cold showers – pay B200 extra for those that are up the slope, with great sunset views. The best and most expensive are across the creek on the beach, all with a/c, some with hot water. Free wi-fi in the restaurant, on-site dive school and kayaks and snorkels for rent. Fan B600, a/c B1000

EATING AND DRINKING

Most people staying on the west coast eat and drink at their resort, but one bar here is worth a detour.

AO CHAOPHAO

Pirates Bar ⓣ 084 728 6064. On its own tiny beach cove (reached by a short wooden walkway at the south end of Ao Chaophao), with a stonking sound system right on the sand, this is a great place for regular parties, especially its popular Moon Set party, three nights before the full moon. Evenings till late.

Ko Tao

KO TAO (Turtle Island) is so named because its outline resembles a turtle nose-diving towards Ko Pha Ngan, 40km to the south. The rugged shell of the turtle, to the east, is crenellated with secluded coves where one or two bungalows hide among the rocks. On the western side, the turtle's underbelly is a long curve of classic beach, **Hat Sai Ree**, facing **Ko Nang Yuan**, a beautiful Y-shaped group of islands offshore, also known as Ko Hang Tao (Turtle's Tail Island). The 21 square kilometres of granite in between is topped by dense forest on the higher slopes and dotted with huge boulders that look as if they await some Easter Island sculptor. It's fun to spend a couple of days exploring the network of rough trails, after which you'll probably know all 1700 of the island's inhabitants. Ko Tao is now best known as a venue for **scuba-diving courses**, with a wide variety of dive sites in close proximity (see p.574).

The island is the last and most remote of the archipelago that continues the line of Surat Thani's mountains into the sea. It served as a jail for political prisoners from 1933 to 1947, then was settled by a family from Ko Pha Ngan. Now, there are around 150 sets of **bungalows** for visitors, just about enough to cope during the peak seasons of December to March and August, concentrated along the west and south sides; they include a rapidly growing number of upscale resorts with such luxuries as air conditioning, hot water and swimming pools. There's a limited government supply of electricity, so some of it still comes from private generators on the remotest beaches, usually evenings only.

If you're just arriving and want to stay on one of the less accessible beaches, it might be a good idea to go with one of the touts who meet the ferries at **Mae Hat**, the island's main village, with pick-up or boat on hand, since at least you'll know their bungalows aren't full; otherwise call ahead, as even the remotest bungalows now have landlines or mobile phones and most owners come to market once a day (pick-ups are either free or B50–150/person). Some resorts with attached scuba-diving operations have been known to refuse guests who don't sign up for diving trips or courses; on the other hand, most of the dive companies now have their own lodgings, available free or at a discounted price to divers. With a year-round customer base of divers – and resident dive instructors – a growing number of sophisticated Western **restaurants** and **bars** are springing up all the time, notably in Mae Hat and on Hat Sai Ree. For nightlife, your best bet is to watch out for posters advertising weekly and monthly parties around the island, which keep the crowds rotating.

BOAT TOURS AND SNORKELLING ON KO TAO

Round-island **boat tours** are available at Mae Hat or through your bungalow, with stops for snorkelling and swimming (B650/person, including lunch and pick-ups, or around B2000 to hire your own longtail boat for the day); these take in snorkelling in the Japanese Gardens off Ko Nang Yuan, but you'll have to pay the B100 entrance fee if you set foot on the island to climb up to the viewpoint. Some dive companies will take along **snorkellers**, usually on their afternoon trips, when they visit the shallower sites; Davy Jones' Locker (ⓣ 077 456604, ⓦ davyjoneslockerasia.com) at *Silver Sands Resort* in Ban Hat Sai Ree, for example, charges B650.

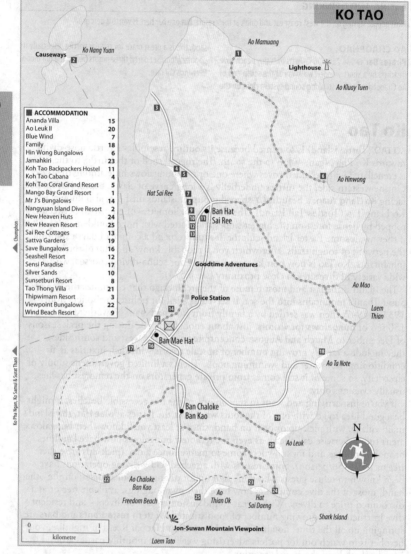

KO TAO

ACCOMMODATION

Ananda Villa	15
Ao Leuk II	20
Blue Wind	7
Family	18
Hin Wong Bungalows	6
Jamahkiri	23
Koh Tao Backpackers Hostel	4
Koh Tao Cabana	11
Koh Tao Coral Grand Resort	5
Mango Bay Grand Resort	1
Mr J's Bungalows	14
Nangyuan Island Dive Resort	2
New Heaven Huts	24
New Heaven Resort	25
Sai Ree Cottages	13
Sattva Gardens	19
Save Bungalows	16
Seashell Resort	12
Sensi Paradise	17
Silver Sands	10
Sunsetburi Resort	8
Tao Thong Villa	21
Thipwimarn Resort	3
Viewpoint Bungalows	22
Wind Beach Resort	9

The **weather** is much the same as on Pha Ngan and Samui (see p.59), but being that bit further off the mainland, Ko Tao feels the effect of the southwest monsoon more: June to October can have strong winds and rain, with a lot of debris blown onto the windward coasts.

ARRIVAL AND DEPARTURE
KO TAO

All boats to Ko Tao dock at Mae Hat. Boat services and prices fluctuate according to demand, and in high season extra boats may appear. Voyages to and from Ko Tao may also be affected by the weather at any time between June and January.

FROM CHUMPHON AND BANGKOK

The main jumping-off point for boats to Ko Tao is Chumphon (see p.534), which is connected to Bangkok by train and bus. The two main Chumphon–Ko Tao boat companies both offer through-tickets from Bangkok; with Lomprayah (on Ko Tao ☎ 077 456176, ⓦ lomprayah .com), for example, this costs B950–1050, including a VIP bus from their office on Thanon Ram Bhuttri (☎ 02 629 2569–70), via Hua Hin (see p.521). It's better to buy a Bangkok–Tao through-ticket direct from the boat company's office in the capital rather than from a travel agency, otherwise you're unlikely to get your money back if the boat turns out to be full, which is possible in high season, or is cancelled because of very bad weather.

FROM KO PHA NGAN AND KO SAMUI

Three companies currently operate daily scheduled boats between Thong Sala on Ko Pha Ngan and Ko Tao. Songserm (on Ko Tao ☎ 086 273 0389 or ☎ 077 456274, ⓦ songserm-expressboat.com) does the voyage in around 2hr (1 daily; B300). Lomprayah (see above) and Seatran (on Ko Tao ☎ 077 456907–8, ⓦ seatrandiscovery.com) cover the ground in about 1hr 15min (both 2 daily; B400). The Lomprayah catamaran originates at Maenam, Seatran at Bangrak, on Ko Samui (total journey time to Ko Tao on either about 2hr; B600).

FROM SURAT THANI

With Lomprayah If you're coming from Surat Thani, you could take Lomprayah's Don Sak–Na Thon (Samui)–Thong Sala catamaran all the way to Ko Pha Ngan, then change onto its Maenam (Samui)–Thong Sala–Ko Tao service (total journey time from Surat about 6hr; B700).

With the night boat There's a night boat from Ban Don pier in Surat Thani town, departing at 11pm (☎ 077 284928 or ☎ 081 326 8973; 8hr; B550); in the opposite direction, this leaves Ko Tao at 9pm.

GETTING AROUND

You can **get around** easily enough on foot, but there are roads of sorts now to most of the resorts, though many are still very rough tracks, suitable for four-wheel drive only.

By motorbike taxi or pick-up Motorbike taxis (B100 to Chaloke Ban Kao, for example) and pick-ups (B100/person to Chaloke Ban Kao, for example, minimum 2 people; rates are higher at night, or for a 4WD to somewhere more remote) are available in Mae Hat.

By moped Rental mopeds are available from B150/day. If you can, resist the temptation to rent a quad bike, or ATV – not only do they have a disproportionate number of accidents, but they're also very polluting. As on Ko Phangan, there have been lots of reports of travellers being charged exorbitant amounts if they bring the vehicle back with even the most minor damage – avoid the outfits in front of the main pier in Mae Hat, and rent from your bungalow or someone reliable like Mr J (see p.576) or Save

---

ECO TAO

With so many divers and other visitors coming to this tiny island, the pressures on the environment, both above and below the waterline, are immense. To minimize your impact, look out for the work of a community group, **Save Koh Tao** (ⓦ savekohtao.com), which has been formed among concerned locals and resident Westerners, with a sub-group devoted to marine conservation (ⓦ marineconservationkohtao.com, which features a list of the dive schools that are involved in the various conservation projects). Activities include a turtle-release programme, erosion control, a campaign for septic tanks to stop waste water being run straight into the sea, coral nurseries and more than half a dozen artificial reefs around Ko Tao, which allow divers to practise their skills without damaging coral. Their monthly land and underwater clean-ups are given a big splash once a year, during the two-day **Underwater Festival** in March, which involves mass beach-cleaning, fundraising, live bands and turtle releasing. Look out also for **Sabai Jai**, a free quarterly eco-travel magazine produced by the owner of Yakuzen Japanese Bath Village.

Much of what visitors can do to help is common sense: avoiding littering, recycling where possible and turning down plastic bags when you're shopping. The island suffers from a scarcity of water, with occasional droughts during the hot season after a poor rainy season, so conserve water whenever possible. In the sea, the main rule is not to touch the coral, which may mean avoiding snorkelling when the water is low from April to September – if in doubt, ask locally for advice, be careful and go out at high tide. Don't take away dead shells, and don't buy coral or shell jewellery. If you're feeling really keen, check whether your bungalow resort has a septic tank. And some dive schools have a Save Koh Tao donation box.

6

DIVING OFF KO TAO

Some of the best **dive sites** in Thailand are found off Ko Tao, which is blessed with outstandingly clear (visibility up to 35m), safe and relatively deep water close in to shore. On top of that, there's a kaleidoscopic array of coral species and other marine life, and you may be lucky enough to encounter whale sharks, barracudas, leatherback turtles and pilot whales. Diving is possible at any time of year, with sheltered sites on one or other side of the island in any **season** – the changeover from southwest to northeast monsoon in November is the worst time, while **visibility** is best from April to July, in September (usually best of all) and October. Ko Tao supports several evacuation centres, clinics that specialize in diving medicine, while the nearest recompression chamber is on Ko Samui, ninety minutes away by speedboat (see p.541).

DIVE COMPANIES, COURSES AND TRIPS

Ko Tao has about fifty **dive companies**, making this the largest dive-training centre in Southeast Asia; most of them are staffed by Westerners and based at Mae Hat, Hat Sai Ree or Ao Chaloke Ban Kao. You'll generally be offered discounted or free accommodation while you're diving, but ask exactly how long it's for (three or four nights for an Openwater course), where it is and what it's like. **Operators** on Ko Tao include Crystal (☎077 456106–7, ⓦcrystaldive.com), a large, lively, sociable PADI 5-Star Career Development Centre, with two swimming pools, three big boats and a speedboat, offering courses in fifteen languages and the chance to buy videos of your dives plus a wide choice of good accommodation in two resorts on the north side of Mae Hat. At the other end of the scale are schools that are small, personal and laidback (though with no compromising on safety) such as New Heaven on Chaloke Ban Kao (☎077 457045, ⓦnewheavendiveschool.com), which boasts of later starts and a maximum of four people on each course, and will take snorkellers along on their dive trips. Both of these companies have a strong commitment to marine conservation (also check out the website of Crystal's marine conservation department, ⓦecokohtao.com, which features internships in various specialities) and run reef conservation and research programmes for qualified divers among many other activities. You'll find further advice on choosing a dive company in Basics (see p.52).

By far the most popular **course**, PADI's four-day "Openwater" for beginners, costs around B9800 in high season with a reputable dive centre. One-day introductions to diving are also available for B2000, as is the full menu of PADI courses, up to "Instructor".

For **qualified divers**, one dive typically costs B1000, a ten-dive package B7000, with fifteen-percent discounts if you bring your own gear. Among specialities, Crystal (see above) offers nitrox and underwater photography and videography courses, while Tech Thailand (ⓦtechthailand.com), affiliated to Master Divers in Mae Hat, covers technical and wreck diving.

Shop, on the front street, just south of the piers (☎077 456347).

By mountain bike Mountain bikes can be rented from in front of the mini-golf course, on the southern edge of Mae Hat on the Chaloke Ban Kao road (☎089 675 5798; B100/day, or B80/day for rentals of two days or more).

INFORMATION

Koh Tao Info There isn't a TAT office on Ko Tao, but the regularly updated and widely available free booklet, *Koh Tao Info*, is a useful source of information, along with its associated website, ⓦkohtaoonline.com, which allows online accommodation booking.

Mae Hat and around

MAE HAT, a small, lively village and port in a pleasant, beachfront setting, boasts the lion's share of the island's amenities. A paved high street heads straight up the hill from the main pier (eventually ending up in Ao Chaloke Ban Kao), with a narrower front street running at right angles, parallel to the seafront. Three of the ferry companies each have their own pier, Lomprayah and Songserm to the south of the main one, Seatran to the north.

MAIN DIVE SITES

Ko Nang Yuan Surrounded by a variety of sites, with assorted hard and soft corals and an abundance of fish: the Nang Yuan Pinnacle, a granite pinnacle with boulder swim-throughs, morays and reef sharks; Green Rock, a maze of boulder swim-throughs, caves and canyons, featuring stingrays and occasional reef sharks; Twins, two rock formations covered in corals and sponges, with a colourful coral garden as a backdrop; and the Japanese Gardens, on the east side of the sand causeway, which get their name from the hundreds of hard and soft coral formations here and are good for beginners and popular among snorkellers.

White Rock (**Hin Khao**) Between Hat Sai Ree and Ko Nang Yuan, where sarcophyton leather coral turns the granite boulders white when seen from the surface; also wire, antipatharian and colourful soft corals, and gorgonian sea fans. Plenty of fish, including titan triggerfish, butterfly fish, angelfish, clown fish and morays.

Shark Island Large granite boulders with acropora, wire and bushy antipatharian corals, sea whips, gorgonian sea fans and barrel sponges. Reef fish include angelfish, triggerfish and barracuda; there's a resident turtle, and leopard and reef sharks may be found as well as occasional whale sharks.

Hinwong Pinnacle At Ao Hinwong; generally for experienced divers, often with strong currents. Similar scenery to White Rock, over a larger area, with beautiful soft coral at 30m depth. A wide range of fish, including blue-spotted fantail stingrays, sweetlips pufferfish and boxfish, as well as hawksbill turtles.

Chumphon or **Northwest Pinnacle** A granite pinnacle for experienced divers, starting 14m underwater and dropping off to over 36m, its top covered in anemones; surrounded by several smaller formations and offering the possibility of exceptional visibility. Barrel sponges, tree and antipatharian corals at deeper levels; a wide variety of fish, in large numbers, attract local fishermen; barracudas, batfish, whale sharks (seasonal) and huge groupers.

Southwest Pinnacle One of the top sites in terms of visibility, scenery and marine life for experienced divers. A huge pyramid-like pinnacle rising to 6m below the surface, its upper part covered in anemones, with smaller pinnacles around; at lower levels, granite boulders, barrel sponges, sea whips, bushy antipatharian and tree corals. Big groupers, snappers and barracudas; occasionally, large rays, leopard and sand sharks, swordfish, finback whales and whale sharks.

Sail Rock (**Hin Bai**) Midway between Ko Tao and Ko Pha Ngan, emerging from the sand at a depth of 40m and rising 15m above the sea's surface. Visibility of up to 30m, and an amazing 10m underwater chimney (vertical swim-through). Antipatharian corals, both bushes and whips, and carpets of anemones. Large groupers, snappers and fusiliers, blue-ringed angelfish, batfish, kingfish, juvenile clown sweetlips and barracuda; a possible spot for sighting whale sharks and mantas.

Yakuzen Japanese Bath Village

Up a small hill on the southeast side of the village, inland from the Songserm pier • B500 per person, minimum 5 people • Visits by appointment on ☎ 084 837 3385

The delightful, eco-friendly **Yakuzen Japanese Bath Village** is highly recommended. Under the stars and the coconut palms here, you can relax in five landscaped bathing pools among the boulders, each set at a different temperature and made with different textures of rock and wood, and massage yourself with herbal compresses. There's also a daytime café (closed Wed) serving drinks, snacks and desserts, and a very good restaurant, *Kakureya* (see p.576).

ACCOMMODATION

MAE HAT AND AROUND

Ananda Villa North end of the village, on the beach ☎ 077 456478, ⍟ anandavilla.com. Cute, well-designed and maintained a/c rooms in a two-storey block, sporting French windows that give onto balconies with wooden balustrades. Inside, silks and other decorative touches set off the dark-wood furniture; facilities include large,

hot-water bathrooms, TVs, DVD-players and fridges. Also has some fan rooms that are tiny but boast hot showers. Fan B500, a/c B1800

Mr J's Bungalows Behind Mr J's supermarket (see p.576), a 5min walk north of Mae Hat ☎ 077 456066–7. If you just want functional, reliable, good-value accommodation, come to this place, which offers large, clean rooms, with hot showers in some of the a/c offerings. Fan with shared bathroom B250, a/c B800

Save Bungalows At the Save Shop supermarket on the front street, just south of the piers ☎077 456347. Owned by the same family as *Mr J's*, with a similar ethos: clean, good-value, functional bungalows, most with en-suite cold or hot showers. Fan with shared bathroom B250, fan en-suite B500, a/c B1000

Sensi Paradise On the lower slopes of the headland just south of the village ☎077 456244, ⊛kohtao paradise.com. Charming resort in flower-covered grounds, offering a pretty beachside restaurant, an attractive free-form pool, free snorkelling equipment and some of the best upmarket accommodation on the island: well-designed wooden Thai-style cottages and villas with mini-bars, some with a/c and hot showers and some with large terraces and open-air bathrooms. Breakfast included. B2900

Tao Thong Villa 50min walk south of Mae Hat (about B150/person in a taxi-boat) ☎077 456078. Sturdy, en-suite bungalows dotted around a rocky outcrop and the slope behind, with a breezy restaurant on the tiny, grassy isthmus with two small beaches in between. Plenty of shady seclusion, great views and good snorkelling and swimming. B500

EATING AND DRINKING

Cappuccino 100m from the pier, up the high street on the left ☎077 456870. French-run café and bakery that does a mean pain au chocolat, plus gourmet sandwiches and burgers and salads. Daily 6.30am–6pm.

★ **Kakureya** Yakuzen Japanese Bath Village (see p.575) ☎087 936 2160 or ☎086 059 0408. Small, relaxing and thoroughly authentic Japanese restaurant, serving the best food on the island. Don't miss the excellent tasting set (B140) as a starter, which you might follow with grilled salmon (B180), sashimi (from B340 for a set) or hot or cold noodles. Asahi beer on draught and a good choice of sake. Closed June & Nov. Daily except Wed 5–9.30pm.

Moov On the southeast side of the village, inland from the Songserm pier. Chilled-out bar-restaurant with a Belgian chef and plenty of sofas to recline on in the house and on the big lawn at the back. Tasty global tapas (under B100) include wonton and sweet potato falafels. Fleamarket first Sun of every month. Daily 3pm–late.

Tukta About 2km out on the Chaloke Ban Kao road. Relaxing, cheap restaurant – open-sided with a few garden tables – serving a wide choice of tasty Thai food, including a good *kaeng matsaman* with chicken. Daily 8am–10pm.

★ **Whitening** 200m south of the main pier down the front street ☎077 456199. Congenial, mellow and chic bar-restaurant with a great deck and relaxing beach tables overlooking the bay. It dishes up some very tasty Thai food, such as green curries (B130), and more creative, pricier Western food, as well as good cocktails. Daily 1pm–midnight (kitchen closes 11pm).

Zest 100m from the pier up the high street ☎077 456178. Very good coffees, pastries, salads and a huge range of sandwiches (roast beef and horseradish sauce B75). Delivery service available. Daily 6am–6pm.

SHOPPING

Little Book and Old Dog Just off the high street on the south side, in front of the main pier. Sells second-hand books and newspapers and magazines. Daily 9.30am–4.30pm & 6.30–9.30pm.

Mr J 5min walk north of Mae Hat. At the top of a small rise opposite the primary school you'll find the head office of Ko Tao's all-purpose fixer and all-round character, Mr J. Here you can rent motorbikes, recycle batteries and buy and sell secondhand books.

DIRECTORY

Banks Thanachat (Siam City Bank), up the high street on the left, with an ATM.

Health Mae Hat has a small government health centre (halfway up the high street, turn right) plus several private clinics and pharmacies.

Police station A 5min walk north of Mat Hat, on the narrow road towards Hat Sai Ree (☎077 456631).

Post office At the top of the village (turn left and left again at the top of the high street), near the start of the main paved road to Ban Hat Sai Ree (Mon–Fri 9am–5pm, Sat 9am–noon).

Hat Sai Ree

To the north of Mae Hat, beyond a small promontory, you'll find **Hat Sai Ree**, Ko Tao's only long beach. The strip of white sand stretches for 2km in a gentle curve, backed by a smattering of coconut palms and scores of bungalow resorts. Around the northerly end of the beach spreads **BAN HAT SAI REE**, a burgeoning village of supermarkets,

HAT SAI REE ACTIVITIES

The main organizers of activities on Hat Sai Ree are the folk at Goodtime Adventures, towards the southern end of the beach (☎087 275 3604, ⊛gtadventures.com), who specialize in **rock-climbing** and **bouldering**, including courses for beginners. They also organize **abseiling**, **hiking** and a **zipline** adventure on Ko Nang Yuan, as well as pub crawls. **Yoga** classes are held at Blue Wind Bungalows (see below; 1–2 daily, not Sun; B300; ☎084 440 6755, ⊕shambhalayoga@yahoo.co.nz).

6

clinics, pharmacies, travel agents, internet outlets, a Thanachat (Siam City Bank) currency-exchange booth with an ATM, restaurants and bars. A narrow, mostly paved track runs along the back of the beach between Mae Hat and Ban Hat Sai Ree, paralleled by the main road further inland.

ACCOMMODATION

HAT SAI REE

★ **Blue Wind** Two doors north of Sunsetburi Resort ☎077 456116, ⊕bluewindkohtao@hotmail.com. This popular old-timer offers a variety of well-kept, en-suite rooms and bungalows scattered about a shady compound, including some very smart new constructions with clapboard walls, four-poster beds with mosquito nets and nice balcony furniture. It also has a good restaurant with free wi-fi (see p.578). Fan and cold water B350, fan and hot water B800, a/c and hot water B1400

Koh Tao Backpackers Hostel Ban Hat Sai Ree, inland from Silver Sands Resort ☎077 601828, ⊛kohtao backpackers.com. Functional, eight-bed dorms with a/c and hot showers in a small, concrete building set back from the beach. Free use of Davy Jones' Locker's pool, discounts on their dive courses and at their bar-restaurant. Dorm B300

Koh Tao Cabana Far north end of beach ☎077 456504–5, ⊛kohtaocabana.com. Welcoming, rustic-chic luxury resort and spa on a long beach frontage, backed by pleasant lawns that are dotted with elegant day beds. All the thatched, a/c rooms feature open-air bathrooms with hot water: choose between round, adobe-style villas up the slope behind the beach and stilted cottages on the headland, some with fantastic views and some with private pools. Breakfast included. B3700

Koh Tao Coral Grand Resort North of Ban Hat Sai Ree ☎077 456432, ⊛kohtaocoral.com. Welcoming luxury beachfront development with a dive school, where the sandstone-pink octagonal cottages with polished coconut-wood floors and large, attractive bathrooms gather – some a little tightly – around a pretty, Y-shaped pool; all have hot water, TV, free wi-fi and a/c. Breakfast included. B4050

Sai Ree Cottages Towards the midpoint of the beach, a 20min walk from Mae Hat ☎077 456374, ⊛sairee cottagediving.com. In a large, beautiful, flower-strewn garden, the full spectrum of digs, all en suite and well maintained, from basic rooms and bungalows with cold showers, all the way up to Thai-style villas on the beach with TV, fridge and breakfast included (fan B2000, a/c B2500). Also offers dorm beds with access to hot shower,

TV and fridge (fan B250, a/c B350). Kayaks and snorkels for rent, dive school and excellent grub. Fan and cold shower B350, fan and hot shower B800, a/c and hot shower B1300

Seashell Resort Near the midpoint of the beach, next door to Sai Ree Cottages ☎077 456299–300, ⊛seashell-resort.com. In a spacious, tidy compound, a friendly, well-run place with a dive school that's been very successfully upgraded. Facilities now include two pools, one with a jacuzzi, a spa, a popular seafood restaurant and computers and free wi-fi in the lobby (paid wi-fi available in the rooms). Among the a/c, hot-water rooms, it's well worth paying a little extra for the new "Superior Garden View" offerings (B2420), which have a very attractive, contemporary look with dark wood furniture; those on the first floor have nice big balconies. Breakfast included. B2130

Silver Sands Ban Hat Sai Ree ☎077 456603–6, ⊛silver-sands-resort.com. Clean, well-kept bungalows and rooms, nearly all of them with hot water, on a narrow but lush and shady plot. Among its bungalows, the cheapest are simple wooden affairs well off the beach, while the priciest are beachside, a/c and cottage-like. New, distressed-concrete rooms, however, in a two-storey hotel block at the back of the compound are more industrial than chic and probably not worth the money. Guests can use the adjacent pool at the affiliated dive company, Davy Jones' Locker. Computers and free wi-fi at reception and snorkels to rent. Fan B800, a/c bungalow B1800, a/c room B2500

Sunsetburi Resort Ban Hat Sai Ree ☎077 457101, ☎077 456101. On a narrow but flower-strewn strip of land with a beachside swimming pool, modern, concrete cottages with TVs and mini-bars, many with a/c and some with the luxury of hot water, as well as a hotel block of a/c, hot-water rooms right at the back on the main road. Fan B700, a/c B1200

Thipwimarn Resort North of Hat Sai Ree, opposite Ko Nang Yuan ☎077 456409, ⊛thipwimarnresort .com. Stylish, eco-friendly, upscale spot with a spa, which tumbles down a steep slope, past an elevated, infinity-edge swimming pool, to its own small beach. Dotted around the hillside, smart, thatched, whitewashed, a/c villas, most with hot water, enjoy a fair measure of seclusion, satellite TV, DVD-players, mini-bars and fine sunset views. Breakfast included. **B3800**

Wind Beach Resort Ban Hat Sai Ree ☎ 077 456082, ⓦ windbeach-resort.com. Welcoming, recently renovated resort lined with mature trees and offering lots of facilities: free wi-fi in the restaurant and nearby rooms, a travel agency, a dive school, massage, and kayaks and snorkels for rent. The choice of rooms and bungalows is also wide-ranging, including some large, very stylish, a/c hotel rooms in two-storey buildings with hot showers, TVs, fridges and breakfast included (B2000). Fan and cold water **B500**, fan and hot water **B700**, a/c and hot water **B1300**

EATING AND DRINKING

★ **Blue Wind** Two doors north of Sunsetburi Resort ☎ 077 456116. Very good beachside restaurant serving home-made breads, cakes, croissants and fruit shakes, as well as Indian and Thai food (B70 for a green curry), home-made pasta, pizzas and other Western meals. Daily 8am–10pm.

Choppers On the main transverse road down to the beach. Popular, well-run, full-service bar, with good food, plenty of imported bottled and draught beers and no fewer than sixteen screens for TV sports. Plenty of offers on drink, including happy hours 4–8pm. Live music from 9pm. Daily 9am–late.

Fizz On the beach at Silver Sands Resort. Chic bar-restaurant, where you can sink into the green beanbags and soak up some mellow sounds over a drink, or sit up for some very good food: there's a long menu of Thai dishes (most under B100) and Western food, with veggie options, pasta, salads and very tasty grilled tuna with mango salsa (B260). Evenings till late.

Lotus Bar On the beach near New Heaven Deli & Bakery. Raucous, very popular late-night haunt for drinking and dancing, with fire shows and regular parties. Happy hour 4–7pm. Evenings till very late.

New Heaven Deli & Bakery On the beach road on the south side of the village. Stylish spot offering great home-baked breads and cakes, as well as sandwiches, salads, pizzas, ice cream, espressos and booster juices, plus free wi-fi. Daily 7am–8pm.

Ko Nang Yuan

One kilometre off the northwest of Ko Tao, **KO NANG YUAN**, a close-knit group of three tiny islands, provides the most spectacular beach scenery in these parts, thanks to the causeway of fine white sand that joins up the islands. You can easily swim off the east side of the causeway to snorkel over the Japanese Gardens, which feature hundreds of hard and soft coral formations.

ARRIVAL AND DEPARTURE
KO NANG YUAN

By boat Boats from the Lomprayah pier in Mae Hat, just south of the main pier, run back and forth twice a day (B200 return), and there are other, irregular services from Hat Sai Ree. Note that rules to protect the environment here include banning all visitors from bringing cans, plastic bottles and fins with them, and day-trippers are charged B100 to land on the island. Lomprayah charge B550 for an all-in day-trip, including boat transfers, snorkelling, buffet lunch and island fee.

ACCOMMODATION AND EATING

Nangyuan Island Dive Resort ☎ 077 456088–93, ⓦ nangyuan.com. The decor at this resort is not much to write home about but it makes the most of its beautiful location, its bungalows, all with en-suite bathrooms, TVs and fridges, most with hot water and some with a/c, spreading over all three islands. There's also a restaurant, a coffee shop and an on-site dive shop. Transfers from and to Mae Hat are free for guests. Breakfast included. Fan **B1500**, a/c **B2000**

The north and east coasts

Ao Mamuang (Mango Bay), the lone bay on the **north coast**, is a beautiful, tree-clad bowl, whose shallow reef is a popular stop on snorkelling day-trips, though there's little in the way of a beach. The attractive bar-restaurant of *Mango Bay Grand Resort* spreads its large deck over the rocks here.

The sheltered inlets of the **east coast**, most of them containing one or two sets of bungalows, can be reached by boat, pick-up or four-wheel-drive. The most northerly habitation here is at **Ao Hinwong**, a deeply recessed, limpid bay strewn with large boulders and great coral reefs, which has a particularly remote, almost desolate air.

In the middle of the coast, the dramatic tiered promontory of Laem Thian shelters on its south side a tiny beach and a colourful reef, which stretches down towards the east coast's most developed bay, **Ao Ta Note**, with half a dozen resorts; the paved road from Mae Hat was about to be completed at the time of writing. Ta Note's horseshoe inlet is sprinkled with boulders and plenty of coarse sand, with excellent snorkelling just north of the bay's mouth.

The last bay carved out of the turtle's shell, **Ao Leuk**, has a well-recessed beach and water that's deep enough for good swimming and snorkelling, featuring hard and soft coral gardens. Snorkels and kayaks are available to rent at the beachfront bar.

6

ACCOMMODATION

AO MAMUANG

Mango Bay Grand Resort ☎ 077 456948–9, ⊛ kohtao mangobay.com. At this remote resort, the well-appointed, colourful, heavily varnished wooden bungalows on stilts all come with hot water, and some have a/c and TV. Transfers from Mae Hat included. Fan B1500, a/c B2800

AO HINWONG

Hin Wong Bungalows ☎ 077 456006 or ☎ 081 229 4810. The most spacious of this bay's small handful of resorts is welcoming and provides good en-suite accommodation on a steep, grassy slope above the rocks, in wooden bungalows with mosquito nets and large bathrooms. It has a nice waterside deck in front of its restaurant and rents out kayaks and snorkels. B400

AO TA NOTE

Family (Ta Note Bay Resort) ☎ 077 456757–8, ✉ tanotebay@hotmail.com. The pick of the half-dozen resorts here, with a dive centre and plenty of well-designed en-suite wooden bungalows, set among thick bougainvillea, some enjoying large verandas and views out towards Ko Pha

THE NORTH AND EAST COASTS

Ngan and Ko Samui. Snorkelling equipment is available, as are computers and wi-fi. Breakfast included with the more expensive rooms. Fan B600, fan and hot shower B1000, a/c and hot shower B1800

AO LEUK

Ao Leuk II ☎ 077 456779, ⊛ aowleuk2.com. Large bungalows and family rooms, with big balconies, fans and hot showers, on the bay's southern cape. Discounts for longer stays. If there happens to be no room here, don't worry – the same friendly family own the bay's other two resorts (including some cheaper, cold-shower bungalows), its taxis and the beachfront bar. B1000

Sattva Gardens (Baan Talay) ☎ 077 457045, ⊛ newheavendiveschool.com. Sustainable, secluded retreat with great views from the hillside above the north side of the bay, owned by New Heaven Dive School (see p.574). Stylish bungalows on stilts sport big verandas, mosquito nets on the beds and indoor-outdoor bathrooms. Big discounts for divers. Fan B1200, fan and hot shower B1800, a/c and hot shower B2500

The south coast

The southeast corner of the island sticks out in a long, thin mole of land, which points towards Shark Island, a colourful diving and snorkelling site just offshore; the headland shelters the sandy beach of **Hat Sai Daeng** on one side if the wind's coming from the northeast, or the rocky cove on the other side if it's blowing from the southwest. Beyond quiet, sandy **Ao Thian Ok**, the next bay along on the south coast, the deep indent of **Ao Chaloke Ban Kao** is protected from the worst of both monsoons, and consequently has seen a fair amount of development, with several dive resorts taking advantage of the large, sheltered, shallow bay, which sometimes gets muddy at low tide. Behind the beach are clinics, ATMs, bike rental shops, bars and restaurants. At New Heaven dive school (see p.574), **yoga** classes are held daily between 5 and 7pm on a veranda overlooking the bay (B300).

On the east side of Ao Chaloke Ban Kao, carved out of the Laem Tato headland, the idyllic white sand of **Freedom Beach** is a secluded palm-lined spot with a beach bar; it's reached by walking through *Taatoh Freedom Beach Bungalows*. A fifteen-minute walk above the bungalows, the last stretch up a steep hillside, will bring you to **Jon-Suwan Mountain Viewpoint**, which affords fantastic views, especially at sunset, over the neighbouring bays of Chaloke Ban Kao and Thian Ok and across to Ko Pha Ngan and Ko Samui.

ACCOMMODATION AND EATING

THE SOUTH COAST

HAT SAI DAENG AND AO THIAN OK

Jamahkiri ☎077 456400, ⍟jamahkiri.com. The remote, rocky coastline between Sai Daeng and Thian Ok provides the spectacular location for this luxurious spa resort. There's a panoramic bar-restaurant, a dive centre and a tiered swimming pool, as well as opulent, secluded rooms and bungalows, in a chic mix of Thai and Western design, with great sea views. Their spa offers saunas, body wraps and massages to guests and non-guests (call for reservation and information about the free, thrice-daily transfers from their Mae Hat office, just north of the main pier). Breakfast included. B6900

New Heaven Huts ☎087 933 1329, ⍟newheaven kohtao.com. Straddling the headland on the east side of Hat Sai Daeng, a laidback, well-equipped place with a good kitchen and snorkelling equipment, whose fourteen pleasantly idiosyncratic, en-suite bungalows – some with hot showers and some big enough for a family – enjoy plenty of elbow room and good views. B600

New Heaven Resort ☎077 456462, ⍟newheaven kohtao.com. A scenic restaurant and attractive bungalows that are easily reached by paved road from Ao Chaloke Ban Kao. On a beautiful deck perched on the eastern flank of Laem Tato, the kitchen (daily 7.30am–9.30pm) specializes in seafood in the evenings (B180 for prawns stir-fried with cashew nuts), as well as offering plenty of vegetarian

options. During the day, you can tuck into sandwiches (such as chicken pesto for B110), pasta and simple Thai fare. The bungalows, set on a tree-covered slope running down to a private sandy beach, feature large bathrooms and verandas with great views, and include a/c rooms with hot showers. Wi-fi. Snorkels for rent. Fan B1700, a/c B2700

AO CHALOKE BAN KAO

Koppee On the main road near the centre of the beach. Lovely little bakery-café with books and magazines to browse and free wi-fi. It offers tasty gourmet sandwiches on a choice of breads, salads such as tuna niçoise (B100), all-day breakfasts and a good choice of drinks and sweet treats. Daily 7.30am–6.30pm (low season) or 8/9pm (high season).

Viewpoint Bungalows ☎077 456444, ⍟kohtao viewpoint.com. Run by a friendly bunch, these distinctive bungalows sprawl along the western side of the bay and around the headland beyond, with great sunset views; architect-designed in chic Balinese style, they boast rock bathrooms, lovely polished hardwood floors, mosquito nets and attractive verandas. There are also half a dozen tasty a/c villas with their own infinity-edge pools (from B8000), as well as kayaks and snorkels to explore the reef just offshore. B1000

Nakhon Si Thammarat

NAKHON SI THAMMARAT, the south's second-largest town, occupies a blind spot in the eyes of most tourists, whose focus is fixed on Ko Samui, 100km to the north. Nakhon's neglect is unfortunate, for it's an absorbing place: the south's major pilgrimage site and home to a huge military base, it's relaxed, self-confident and sophisticated, well known for its excellent cuisine and traditional **handicrafts**. The stores on Thanon Thachang are especially good for local nielloware (*kruang tom*), household items and jewellery, elegantly patterned in gold or silver, often on black, and *yan lipao*, sturdy basketware made from intricately woven ferns stems of different colours. Nakhon is also the best place in the country to see how Thai **shadow plays** work, at Suchart Subsin's workshop, and the main jumping-off point for towering **Khao Luang National Park** and its beautiful waterfall, **Krung Ching** (see p.586).

The town is recorded under the name of Ligor (or Lakhon), the capital of the kingdom of Lankasuka, as early as the second century, and classical dance-drama, *lakhon*, is supposed to have been developed here. Well placed for trade with China and southern India (via an overland route from the port of Trang, on the Andaman Sea), Nakhon was the point through which the Theravada form of Buddhism was imported from Sri Lanka and spread to Sukhothai, the capital of the new Thai state, in the thirteenth century.

Orientation in Nakhon is simple, though the layout of the town is puzzling at first sight: it runs in a straight line for 7km from north to south and is rarely more than a few hundred metres wide, a layout originally dictated by the availability of fresh water. The

FESTIVALS IN NAKHON

Known as *muang phra*, the "city of monks", Nakhon is still the religious capital of the south, and the main centre for **festivals**. The most important of these are the **Tamboon Deuan Sip**, held during the waning of the moon in the tenth lunar month (either Sept or Oct), and the **Hae Pha Khun That**, which is held several times a year, but most importantly on Makha Puja, the February full moon, and on Visakha Puja, the May full moon (see p.46). The purpose of Tamboon Deuan Sip is to pay homage to dead relatives and friends; it is believed that during this fifteen-day period all *pret* – ancestors who have been damned to hell – are allowed out to visit the world, and so their relatives perform a merit-making ceremony in the temples, presenting offerings from the first harvest to ease their suffering. A huge ten-day fair takes place at Thung Talaat park on the north side of town at this time, as well as processions, shadow plays and other theatrical performances. The Hae Pha Khun That also attracts people from all over the south, to pay homage to the relics of the Buddha at Wat Mahathat. The centrepiece of this ceremony is the Pha Phra Bot, a strip of yellow cloth many hundreds of metres long, which is carried in a spectacular procession around the chedi.

6

modern centre for businesses and shops sits at the north end around the landmark **Tha Wang intersection**, where Thanon Neramit meets Thanon Ratchadamnoen. To the south, centred on the elegant, traditional mosque on Thanon Karom, lies the old Muslim quarter; south again is the start of the old city walls, of which few remains can be seen, and the historic centre, with the town's main places of interest now set in a leafy residential area.

Wat Mahathat

Main entrance faces Thanon Ratchadamnoen, about 2km south of the modern centre

Missing out **Wat Mahathat** would be like going to Rome and not visiting St Peter's, for the Buddha relics in the vast chedi make this the south's most important shrine. In the courtyard inside the temple cloisters, row upon row of smaller chedis, spiked like bayonets, surround the main chedi, the 60m-tall **Phra Boromathat**. This huge, stubby Sri Lankan bell supports a slender, ringed spire, which is in turn topped by a shiny pinnacle said to be covered in 600kg of gold leaf. According to the chronicles, relics of the Buddha were brought here from Sri Lanka two thousand years ago by an Indian prince and princess and enshrined in a chedi. It's undergone plenty of face-lifts since then: an earlier Srivijayan version, a model of which stands at one corner, is encased in the present twelfth-century chedi. The most recent restoration work, funded by donations from all over Thailand, rescued it from collapse, although it still seems to be leaning dangerously to the southeast. Worshippers head for the north side's vast enclosed stairway, framed by lions and giants, which they liberally decorate with gold leaf to add to the shrine's radiance and gain some merit.

Viharn Phra Kien Museum

Extends north from the chedi • Hours irregular, but usually daily 9am–4pm • Free

An Aladdin's cave of bric-a-brac, the **Viharn Phra Kien Museum** is said to house fifty thousand artefacts donated by worshippers, ranging from ships made out of seashells to gold and silver models of the Bodhi Tree. At the entrance to the museum, you'll pass the Phra Puay, an image of the Buddha giving a gesture of reassurance. Women pray to the image when they want to have children, and the lucky ones return to give thanks and leave photos of their chubby progeny.

Viharn Luang

Outside the cloister to the south

The eighteenth-century **Viharn Luang**, raised on elegant slanting columns, is a beautiful example of Ayutthayan architecture. The interior is austere at ground level, but the red

6

National Museum & ⬛2

◀

NAKHON SI THAMMARAT

coffered ceiling shines with carved and gilded stars and lotus blooms. In the spacious grounds on the viharn's south side, cheerful, inexpensive stalls peddle local handicrafts such as shadow puppets, bronzeware and basketware.

The National Museum

Thanon Ratchadamnoen, a 10min walk south from Wat Mahathat • Wed–Sun 9am–noon & 1–4pm • B150 • ⓦ thailandmuseum.com

The **National Museum** houses a small but diverse collection, mostly of artefacts from southern Thailand. In the prehistory room **downstairs**, look out for the two impressive ceremonial bronze kettledrums dating from the fifth century BC; they were beaten in rainmaking rituals and one of them is topped with chunky frogs (the local frogs are said to be the biggest in Thailand and a prized delicacy). Also on the ground floor are some interesting Hindu finds, including several stone lingams from the seventh to ninth centuries AD and later bronze statues of Ganesh, the elephant-headed god of wisdom and the arts. Look out especially for a vivacious, well-preserved bronze of Shiva here, dancing within a ring of fire on the body of a dwarf demon, who holds a cobra symbolizing stupidity. Among the collections of ceramics **upstairs**, you can't miss the seat panel from Rama V's barge, a dazzling example of the nielloware for which Nakhon is famous – the delicate animals and landscapes have been etched onto a layer of gold which covers the silver base, and then picked out by inlaying a black alloy into the background. The nearby exhibition on local wisdom includes interesting displays on Buddhist ordinations and weddings, and on *manohra*, the southern Thai dramatic dance form.

The shadow puppet workshop

Ban Nang Thalung Suchart Subsin, 110/18 Soi 3, Thanon Si Thammasok, a 10min walk east of Wat Mahathat • Free • ☎ 075 346394

The best possible introduction to *nang thalung*, southern Thailand's **shadow puppet theatre** (see box, p.584), is to head for the atmospheric compound of Suchart Subsin, a designated National Artist and one of the south's leading exponents of *nang thalung*. He and his sons have opened up their workshop to the public, including a small museum of puppets dating back as far as the eighteenth century, and, especially if you

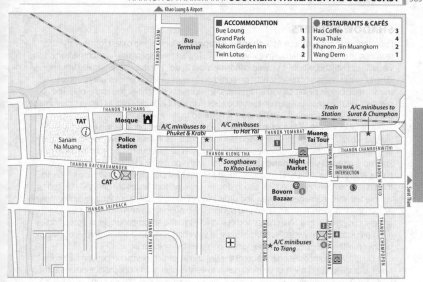

■ ACCOMMODATION		● RESTAURANTS & CAFÉS	
Bue Loung	1	Hao Coffee	3
Grand Park	3	Krua Thale	4
Nakorn Garden Inn	4	Khanom Jiin Muangkorn	2
Twin Lotus	2	Wang Derm	1

phone in advance, they'll usually be able to show you a few scenes from a shadow play in the small open-air theatre, for which you might want to leave a tip or donation. You can also see the intricate process of making the leather puppets and can buy the finished products as souvenirs: puppets sold here are of much better quality and design than those usually found on southern Thailand's souvenir stalls.

The Phra Buddha Sihing shrine

In the provincial administration complex on Thanon Ratchadamnoen • Mon–Fri 8.30am–noon & 1–4.30pm • Free

Magically created in Sri Lanka in the second century, the **Phra Buddha Sihing** statue was, according to legend, sent by ship to the king of Sukhothai in the thirteenth century, but the vessel sank and the image miraculously floated on a plank to Nakhon. Two other images, one in the National Museum in Bangkok, one in Wat Phra Singh in Chiang Mai, claim to be the authentic Phra Buddha Sihing, but none of the three is in the Sri Lankan style, so they are all probably derived from a lost original. Although similar to the other two in size and shape, the image in Nakhon has a style unique to this area, distinguished by the heavily pleated flap of its robe over the left shoulder, a beaky nose and harsh features, which sit uneasily on the short, corpulent body. The image's plumpness has given the style the name *khanom tom* – "banana and rice pudding".

ARRIVAL AND DEPARTURE   **NAKHON SI THAMMARAT**

BY PLANE

The airport (☏ 075 369540–2), served daily by Nok Air and Air Asia, is about 20km northwest of the city off the Surat Thani road. From here, taxis charge around B300 to take you into Nakhon while big hotels such as the *Twin Lotus* and *Grand Park* offer airport shuttle buses. Nok Air offer flight-and-boat through-tickets to Ko Samui and Ko Pha Ngan.

Destinations Bangkok (7 daily; 1hr 10min).

BY TRAIN

The train station is very central.

Destinations Bangkok (2 daily; 15–16hr); Hat Yai (2 daily; 4–5hr).

BY BUS

All buses (including a/c vehicles to Surat Thani) use the terminal on the west side of the centre, except for a local, non-a/c service to Surat Thani, which starts about 1km north of the centre on the left-hand side of Thanon

6

SHADOW PUPPETS

Found throughout southern Asia, **shadow puppets** are one of the oldest forms of theatre, featuring in Buddhist literature as early as 400 BC. The art form seems to have come from India, via Java, to Thailand, where it's called *nang*, meaning "hide": the puppets are made from the skins of water buffalo or cows, which are softened in water, then pounded until almost transparent, before being carved and painted to represent the characters of the play. The puppets are then manipulated on bamboo rods in front of a bright light, to project their image onto a large white screen, while the story is narrated to the audience.

The grander version of the art, **nang yai** – "big hide", so called because the figures are life-size – deals only with the *Ramayana* story (see p.88). It's known to have been part of the entertainment at official ceremonies in the Ayutthayan period, but has now almost died out. The more populist version, **nang thalung** – *thalung* is probably a shortening of the town name, Phatthalung (which is just down the road from Nakhon), where this version of the art form is said to have originated – is also in decline now: performances are generally limited to temple festivals, marriages, funerals and ordinations, lasting usually from 9pm to dawn. As well as working the 60cm-high *nang thalung* puppets, the puppet master narrates the story, impersonates the characters, chants and cracks jokes to the accompaniment of flutes, fiddles and percussion instruments. Not surprisingly, in view of this virtuoso semi-improvised display, puppet masters are esteemed as possessed geniuses by their public.

At big festivals, companies often perform the *Ramayana*, sometimes in competition with each other; at smaller events they put on more down-to-earth stories, with stock characters such as the jokers Yor Thong, an angry man with a pot belly and a sword, and Kaew Kop, a man with a frog's head. Yogi, a wizard and teacher, is thought to protect the puppet master and his company from evil spirits with his magic, so he is always the first puppet on at the beginning of every performance.

In an attempt to halt their decline as a form of popular entertainment, the puppet companies are now incorporating modern instruments and characters in modern dress into their shows, and are boosting the love element in their stories. They're fighting a battle they can't win against television and cinemas, although at least the debt owed to shadow puppets has been acknowledged – *nang* has become the Thai word for "movie".

Ratchadamnoen near Wat Pradu.
Destinations Bangkok (Southern Terminal; 19 daily; 12hr); Hat Yai (14 daily; 3hr 30min); Krabi (7 daily; 4hr); Phuket (7 daily; 6hr); Ranong (1 daily; 6hr); Surat Thani (21 daily; 2hr 30min).

BY MINIBUS
A/c minibus offices around town include one for Ko Samui (via the Don Sak ferry), 1km north of the centre on the right-hand side of Thanon Ratchadamnoen opposite the stop for Surat Thani buses; others are marked on our map.

GETTING AROUND

By share-songthaew Small blue share-songthaews ply up and down Thanon Ratchadamnoen for B10

a ride.

INFORMATION

Tourist information TAT has an office in a restored 1920s government officers' club on Sanam Na Muang (daily 8.30am–4.30pm; ☏ 075 346515–6, ✉ tatnksri@tat.or.th).

Internet access Klickzone, Bovorn Bazaar, Thanon Ratchadamnoen (daily 9am–6pm).

ACCOMMODATION

Nakhon has no guesthouses or traveller-oriented accommodation, but the best of its hotels offer very good value in all price ranges.

Bue Loung (Bua Luang) Hotel 1487/19 Soi Luang Muang, Thanon Chamroenwithi ☏ 075 341518, ☏ 075 343418. Friendly and central but reasonably quiet; gets

the thumbs-up from visiting sales reps, with a choice of fan and cold water or a/c, cable TV and hot water in basic double or twin rooms. Fan B180, a/c B340

CLOCKWISE FROM TOP LEFT WAT MAHATHAT, NAKHON SI THAMMARAT (P.581); SEAFOOD IN HUA HIN (P.524); LONGTAIL BOAT NEAR KO PHA NGAN (P.558) >

6

Grand Park Hotel 1204/79 Thanon Pak Nakhon ☎075 317666–75, ⓦgrandparknakhon.com. If you're looking for an upmarket option in the centre of town, this place, set back a little from the busy road, is worth considering – it's large, smart and bright, with a/c, hot water, TV and mini-bar in every room, free wi-fi in the lobby and cheery and attentive staff. B600

★ **Nakorn Garden Inn** 1/4 Thanon Pak Nakhon ☎075 313333, ☎075 342926. A rustic but sophisticated haven in two three-storey, red-brick buildings overlooking a tree-shaded courtyard. Large, attractive rooms come with a/c, hot water, cable TV and mini-bars. Free wi-fi in the lobby and some rooms. B445

Twin Lotus About 3km southeast of the centre at 97/8 Thanon Patanakarn Kukwang ☎075 323777, ⓦtwinlotushotel.net. Gets pride of place in Nakhon – though not for its location; sports five bars and restaurants, a large, attractive outdoor swimming pool, a sauna and a fitness centre. B1600

EATING AND DRINKING

Nakhon is a great place for inexpensive food, not least at the busy, colourful **night market** on Thanon Chamroenwithi near the *Bue Loung Hotel*.

Hao Coffee In the Bovorn Bazaar, Thanon Ratchadamnoen. Popular place in a quiet courtyard, modelled on an old Chinese-style coffee shop and packed full of ageing lamps, clocks and other antiques. Offers a wide selection of inexpensive Thai dishes, Western breakfasts, cakes, teas, juices and coffees, including Thai filter coffee and delicious iced cappuccinos. Daily 7am–5pm.

Khanom Jiin Muangkorn Thanon Panyom, near Wat Mahathat. Justly famous, inexpensive outdoor restaurant dishing up one of the local specialities, *khanom jiin*, noodles topped with hot, sweet or fishy sauce served with *pak ruam*, a platter of crispy raw vegetables. Daily 8am–3pm.

★ **Krua Thale** Thanon Pak Nakhon, opposite the Nakorn Garden Inn (no English sign – look for the Coke sign). The town's best restaurant, renowned among locals for its excellent, varied and inexpensive seafood. Plain and very clean, with an open kitchen and the day's catch displayed out front, and relaxing patio tables and an a/c room at the back. Recommended dishes include a very good *yam plaa duk foo*, shredded and deep-fried catfish with a mango salad dip (B80), whole baked fish and king prawns, and *hoy maleang poo op mordin*, large green mussels in a delicious herb soup containing lemon grass, basil and mint (B60). Daily 4–10pm.

Wang Derm Thanon Nang Ngam (no English sign). A great place to sample southern food, buffet-style in a big, open-air pavilion in an interesting complex of coffee shops and bakeries, with good *khanom jiin* and other very cheap local dishes (from B15): *kaeng som*, a mild yellow curry; *kaeng tai plaa*, fish stomach curry; *khao yam*, a delicious southern salad of rice and vegetables; and various *khanom wan*, coconut milk puddings. Daily 7am–5pm.

Khao Luang National Park

Headquarters to the south of the summit near Karom Waterfall • National park admission fee B200 • ☎075 391240 or ☎075 391218, ⓦdnp.go.th

Rising to the west of Nakhon Si Thammarat and temptingly visible from all over town is 1835m-high **Khao Luang**, southern Thailand's highest mountain. A huge **national park** encompasses Khao Luang's jagged green peaks, beautiful streams with numerous waterfalls, tropical rainforest and fruit orchards. The mountain is also the source of the Tapi River, one of the peninsula's main waterways, which flows into the Gulf of Thailand at Surat Thani. **Fauna** here include macaques, musk deer, civets and binturongs, as well as more difficult-to-see Malayan tapirs, serows, tigers, panthers and clouded leopards, plus over two hundred bird species. There's an astonishing diversity of **flora** too, notably rhododendrons and begonias, dense mosses, ferns and lichens, plus more than three hundred species of both ground-growing and epiphytic orchids, some of which are unique to the park.

The best **time to visit** is after the rainy season, from January onwards, when there should still be a decent flow in the waterfalls, but the trails will be dry and the leeches not so bad. However, the park's most distinguishing feature for visitors is probably its difficulty of **access**: main roads run around the 570-square-kilometre park with spurs into some of the waterfalls, but there are no roads across the park and very sparse public transport along the spur roads. The Ban Khiriwong Ecotourism Club

(☎075 533113) can arrange **treks** to the peak between January and June, beginning at Ban Khiriwong on the southeast side of the park and including two nights camping on the mountain, meals and guides, as well as homestays in the village. Otherwise only **Krung Ching Waterfall**, one of Thailand's most spectacular, really justifies the hassle of getting to the park.

Krung Ching Waterfall

A trip to **Krung Ching**, a nine-tier waterfall on the north side of the park, makes for a highly satisfying day out with a **nature trail** taking you through dense, steamy jungle to the most beautiful, third tier. Starting at the Krung Ching park office, which lies 13km south of Ban Huai Phan, this shady, mostly paved, 4km trail is very steep in parts, so you should allow four hours at least there and back. On the way you'll pass giant ferns, including a variety known as *maha sadam*, the largest fern in the world, gnarled banyan trees, forests of mangosteen and beautiful, thick stands of bamboo. You're bound to see colourful birds and insects, but you may well only hear macaques and other mammals. At the end, a long, stepped descent brings you to a perfectly positioned wooden platform with fantastic views of the 40m fall, which used to appear on the back of thousand-baht notes; here you can see how, shrouded in thick spray, it earns its Thai name, Fon Saen Ha, meaning "thousands of rainfalls".

ARRIVAL AND DEPARTURE | KHAO LUANG

By songthaew Irregular songthaews on the main roads around the park and to Ban Khiriwong congregate on Thanon Klong Tha south of the *Bue Luang Hotel* in Nakhon. None of them is scheduled to go to Krung Ching – you'd have to catch one to Ban Huai Phan (about 1hr) and then do a deal with the driver to take you the extra 13km to the Krung Ching park office.

By car Rental cars, with or without driver, are available from Muang Tai Tour on Thanon Yomarat in Nakhon (☎075 343996 or ☎075 342768; around B1500/day plus petrol. The easiest way to get to Krung Ching from Nakhon with your own transport is to head north on Highway 401 towards Surat Thani, turning west at Tha Sala on to Highway 4140, then north again at Ban Nopphitam on to Highway 4186, before heading south from Ban Huai Phan on Highway 4188, the spur road to the Krung Ching park office, a total journey of about 70km.

ACCOMMODATION AND EATING

National park accommodation ☎075 391240 or ☎075 391218, ☻dnp.go.th. Two- to twenty-person bungalows, most with hot water, are available at the Krung Ching park office. There's also a campsite. Bungalows B600 **National park canteen** There's a basic canteen near the park office, where food needs to be ordered in advance.

Southern Thailand: the Andaman coast

AO MAYA, KO PHI PHI

Southern Thailand: the Andaman coast

As Highway 4 switches from the east flank of the Thailand peninsula to the Andaman coast it enters a markedly different country: nourished by rain nearly all the year round, the vegetation down here is lushly tropical, with forests reaching up to 80m in height, and massive rubber, palm-oil and coconut plantations replacing the rice and sugar-cane fields of central Thailand. Sheer limestone crags spike every horizon and the translucent Andaman Sea laps the most dazzlingly beautiful islands in the country, not to mention its finest coral reefs. This is of course the same sea whose terrifyingly powerful tsunami waves battered the coastline in December 2004, killing thousands and changing countless lives and communities forever. The legacies of that horrific day are widespread (see p.616), but all the affected holiday resorts have been rebuilt, with the tourist dollar now arguably more crucial to the region's well-being than ever before.

The **cultural mix** along the Andaman coast is also different from central Thailand. Many southern Thais are Muslim, with a heritage that connects them to Malaysia and beyond. This is also the traditional province of nomadic *chao ley*, or sea gypsies, many of whom have now settled but still work as boat captains and fishermen. The commercial fishing industry, on the other hand, is mostly staffed by immigrants – legal and not – from neighbouring Burma, just a few kilometres away along the northern Andaman coast.

The attractions of the northern Andaman coast are often ignored in the race down to the high-profile honeypots around Phuket and Krabi, but there are many quiet gems up here, beginning with the low-key little sister islands of **Ko Chang** (quite different from

KAYAKERS EXPLORING A HONG IN AO PHANG NGA

Highlights

❶ Island idylls Tranquillity rules on the uncommercial islands of Ko Phayam, Ko Ra, Ko Yao Noi and Ko Jum. **See p.601, p.605, p.649 & p.684**

❷ Khao Sok National Park Sleep in a jungle treehouse or on a lake amid spectacular karst scenery, and wake to the sound of hooting gibbons. **See p.610**

❸ Ko Similan Remote island chain offering the finest snorkelling and diving, and easily accessible on day-trips and live-aboards. **See p.620**

❹ Phuket Town Handsome Sino-Portuguese architecture and some of the most interesting

sleeping, eating and drinking options on the island. **See p.627**

❺ Sea-canoeing in Ao Phang Nga The perfect way to explore the limestone karsts and hidden lagoons of this spectacular bay. **See p.656**

❻ Rock-climbing Even novices can get a bird's-eye view of the Railay peninsula's fabulous coastal scenery. **See p.672**

❼ Ko Lanta Yai The "island of long beaches", with an atmospheric old town, offers an appealing choice of relaxing mid-range facilities. **See p.688**

HIGHLIGHTS ARE MARKED ON THE MAP ON P.592

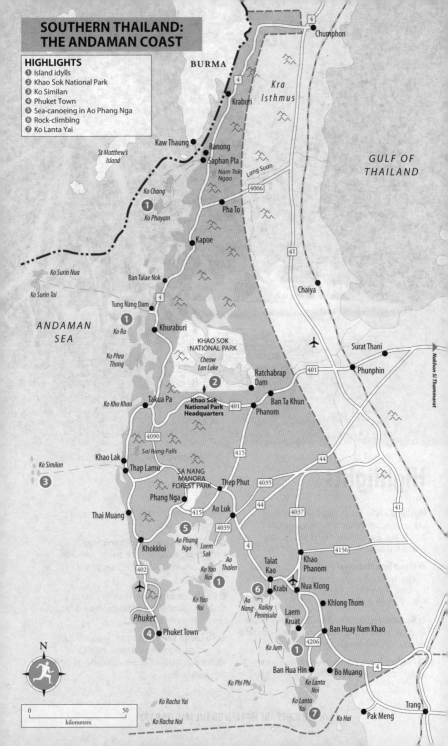

SOUTHERN THAILAND: THE ANDAMAN COAST

HIGHLIGHTS
1. Island idylls
2. Khao Sok National Park
3. Ko Similan
4. Phuket Town
5. Sea-canoeing in Ao Phang Nga
6. Rock-climbing
7. Ko Lanta Yai

BURMA

Chumphon

Kra Isthmus

Kraburi

Kaw Thaung

Ranong
Saphan Pla

Nam Tok Ngao

Long Suan

4006

Pha To

GULF OF THAILAND

St Matthew's Island

Ko Chang

Ko Phayam

Kapoe

Ban Talae Nok

Ko Surin Nua

Ko Surin Tai

Tung Nang Dam

Khuraburi

41

Chaiya

ANDAMAN SEA

Ko Ra

Ko Phra Thong

KHAO SOK NATIONAL PARK

Cheow Lan Lake

Ratchabrap Dam

Surat Thani

Phunphin

401

Ko Kho Khao

Takua Pa

Khao Sok National Park Headquarters

401

Ban Ta Khun

Phanom

Ko Similan

Khao Lak

4090

Sai Rung Falls

Thap Lamu

SA NANG MANORA FOREST PARK

415

Thep Phut

4035

44

Phang Nga

Ao Luk

44

4037

4156

Thai Muang

415

4039

Laem Sak

Ao Thalen

4

Talat Kao

Khao Phanom

Khokkloi

Ao Phang Nga

Ko Yao Noi

Krabi

Nua Klong

Khlong Thom

402

Ko Yao Yai

Ao Nang

Railay Peninsula

Laem Kruat

Ban Huay Nam Khao

Phuket

Phuket Town

Ko Jum

4206

Ban Hua Hin

Bo Muang

4

Ko Phi Phi

Ko Lanta Noi

Trang

Ko Racha Yai

Ko Lanta Yai

Ko Hai

Pak Meng

Ko Racha Noi

Nakhon Si Thammarat

N

0   50
kilometres

> ## THE KRA ISTHMUS
>
> Thailand's Andaman coast begins at **Kraburi**, where, at kilometre-stone 545 (the distance from Bangkok), a signpost welcomes you to the **Kra Isthmus**, the narrowest part of peninsular Thailand. Just 44km separates the Gulf of Thailand from the Andaman Sea's Chan River estuary, and Burmese border, here. Though a seemingly obvious short cut for shipping traffic between the Indian Ocean and the South China Sea, avoiding the 1500km detour via the Strait of Malacca, the much-discussed **Kra Canal** project has yet to be realized, despite being on the table for over three hundred years.

its larger, more famous East Coast namesake) and **Ko Phayam**, where the hammocks and paraffin lamps offer an old-style travellers' vibe that's harder to find further south. Snorkellers and divers are drawn in their hundreds to the reefs of the remote National Park island chains of **Ko Surin** and **Ko Similan**, with many choosing to base themselves at the mainland beach resort of **Khao Lak**, though homestay programmes around **Khuraburi** offer an interesting alternative. Inland, it's all about the jungle – with twenty-first-century amenities – at the enjoyable **Khao Sok National Park**, where accommodation is on rafts on the lake and treehouses beneath the limestone crags.

Phuket, Thailand's largest island, is the region's major resort destination for families, package tourists and novice divers; its dining, shopping and entertainment facilities are second to none, but the high-rises and hectic consumerism dilute the Thai-ness of the experience. There's Thai life in spades across on the quiet rural island of **Ko Yao Noi**, scenically located within the spectacular bay of **Ao Phang Nga**, whose scattered karst islets are one of the country's top natural wonders, best appreciated from a sea-canoe. The Andaman coast's second hub is **Krabi** province, rightly famous for its turquoise seas and dramatic islands. Flashiest of these is the flawed but still handsome **Ko Phi Phi**, with its great diving, gorgeous beaches and high-octane nightlife. Mainland and mainstream **Ao Nang** can't really compete, but is at least close to the majestic cliffs and superb rock-climbing of the **Railay** peninsula at **Laem Phra Nang**. Offshore again, there's horizon-gazing aplenty at mellow, barely developed **Ko Jum** and the choice of half a dozen luxuriously long beaches, and plentiful resort facilities, at **Ko Lanta Yai**.

Unlike the Gulf coast, the Andaman coast is hit by the **southwest monsoon**, which usually generally lasts from the end of May until at least the middle of October. During this period, heavy rain and high seas render some of the outer islands inaccessible, but conditions aren't usually severe enough to ruin a holiday on the other islands, or on the mainland, and you'll get tempting discounts on accommodation. Some bungalows at the smaller resorts shut down entirely during low season (highlighted in the text), but most beaches keep at least one place open, and some dive shops lead expeditions year-round.

ARRIVAL AND DEPARTURE   THE ANDAMAN COAST

There is no rail line down the Andaman coast, but many travellers take the **train** from Bangkok to the Gulf coast and then nip across by bus; most direct **buses** from the capital travel south overnight. The fastest option is to arrive by plane: both Phuket and Krabi have international **airports**, and there's a domestic airport at Trang, not far from Ko Lanta in the deep south.

Ranong

Despite being the soggiest town in the country, with over 5000mm of rain a year, **RANONG** has a pleasing buzz about it, fuelled by the mix of Burmese, Thai, Chinese and Malay inhabitants. It's a prosperous town, the lucrative nineteenth-century tin-mining concessions now replaced by a thriving fishing industry centred around the port of Saphan Pla, 5km southwest of town, and its scores of fishing boats and fish-processing factories staffed mainly by notoriously poorly treated Burmese workers. As with most border areas, there's also said to be a flourishing illegal trade in amphetamines, guns and labour, not to mention the inevitable tensions over international fishing rights, which sometimes end in shoot-outs, though the closest encounter you're likely to have will be in the pages of the *Bangkok Post*. Thai tourists have been coming here for years, to savour the health-giving properties of the local spring water, but foreign travellers have only quite recently discovered it as a useful departure point for the alluring nearby little islands of **Ko Chang** and **Ko Phayam**. The other reason to stop off in Ranong is to make a visa run to the Burmese town of **Kaw Thaung**.

A stroll along the town centre's main road, **Thanon Ruangrat**, brings its history and geography to mind. The handsome, if faded, shopfront architecture bears many of the hallmarks of nineteenth-century Sino-Portuguese design (see p.628), with its arched "five-foot" walkways shading pedestrians, pastel paintwork and shuttered windows. Chinese goods fill many of the shops – this is a good place to stock up on cheap clothes too – and many signs are written in the town's three main languages: Thai, Chinese and curly Burmese script.

7

The geothermal springs

Raksawarin Park, about 3km east of the Thanon Ruangrat market • **Raksawarin Hot Springs** daily 7am–9pm • B40 or B60 including transfer from Tinidee Hotel (see p.597) • **Siam Hot Spa Ranong** daily noon–9pm • treatments from B200 ☎ 077 813551–4, ⓦ siamhotsparanong.com • Accessible on red songthaew #2 from the market or by motorbike taxi

Though there's little in Ranong to warrant a sightseeing tour, it can be fun to follow the crowds of domestic tourists in their quest for the medicinal and stress-relieving

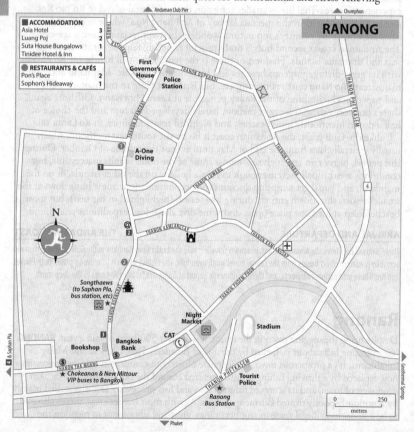

RANONG

▲ Andaman Club Pier

▲ Chumphon

■ **ACCOMMODATION**
Asia Hotel	3
Luang Poj	5
Suta House Bungalows	2
Tinidee Hotel & Inn	4

● **RESTAURANTS & CAFÉS**
| Pon's Place | 2 |
| Sophon's Hideaway | 1 |

THANON RATCHAT

THANON DUPKHADI

First Governor's House

Police Station

THANON RUANGRAT

THANON PHETKASEM

A-One Diving

THANON CHONRAU

THANON LUANG

4

THANON KAMLANGSAP

THANON KAMLANGSAP

Songthaews (to Saphan Pla, bus station, etc)

THANON RUANGRAT

THANON PHOEM PHON

Night Market

CAT

Stadium

Bookshop

Bangkok Bank

★ *Chokeanan & New Mittour VIP buses to Bangkok*

THANON THA MUANG

THANON PHETKASEM

Tourist Police

★ *Ranong Bus Station*

◀ & Saphan Pla

N

Geothermal Springs ▶

| 0 | | 250 |
| metres |

▼ Phuket

properties of Ranong's famously pure **geothermal springs**. They're the focus of forested Raksawarin Park, which is set in a narrow, lush river valley, surrounded by restaurants and souvenir shops. At the park, you can bathe or paddle in either the open-access, public mineral spa pools or the better-appointed and deeper, jacuzzi-type spa pools of Raksawarin Hot Springs, which are run by the *Tinidee Hotel*. Alternatively, you can opt for a more leisurely soak at the indoor Siam Hot Spa Ranong across the road, which offers public and private jacuzzi pools, private bathrooms and inexpensive massage and steam treatments.

First Governor's House

West off Thanon Ruangrat on the northern edge of town • Daily 9am–4.30pm • Free

Ranong's history is closely associated with its most famous son, Khaw Soo Cheang, a poor Hokkien Chinese emigrant turned tin baron who became the first governor of Ranong province in 1854; he is still so esteemed that politicians continue to pay public homage at his grave, and his descendants bear the respected aristocratic surname "na Ranong" ("of Ranong"). Little now remains of Khaw Soo Cheang's house, but in its grounds stands a Khaw clan house and small museum, the **First Governor's House** (Nai Khai Ranong).

ARRIVAL AND DEPARTURE

RANONG

There are currently no services to Ranong airport, 20km south of town on Highway 4.

By bus or minibus Most Andaman-coast buses travelling between Bangkok or Chumphon and Khuraburi, Takua Pa or Phuket stop briefly at Ranong's bus station on Highway 4 (Thanon Phetkasem), 1500m southeast of the central market. If coming from Khao Sok or Surat Thani, you'll usually need to change buses at Takua Pa, though there is also an a/c minibus service from and to Surat Thani (hourly 7am–3pm; 3hr; B190). There are direct buses operated by Rungkit from Chumphon (4 daily; 2–3hr), as well as faster a/c minibuses (hourly 7am–5pm; 2hr; B120), so from Bangkok it's often more comfortable to take a night train to Chumphon and then change on to a bus or minibus. Alternatively, Chokeanan and New Mittour run VIP buses from opposite Wat Bowoniwes and the Siam Commercial Bank in Banglamphu, via the Southern Bus Terminal, to Chumphon's Thanon Tha Muang. Rungkit buses to Chumphon and Phuket and the a/c minibuses operate out of Ranong Bus Station; a/c minibuses to Phuket may be in

the pipeline – check at *Pon's Place* (see below) or Phuket Town bus station.

Destinations: Bangkok (15 daily; 9hr); Chumphon (4 daily; 2–3hr); Khao Lak (7 daily; 3hr 45min); Khuraburi (7 daily; 2hr); Krabi (1–2 daily; 5hr); Phang Nga (1–2 daily; 4hr); Phuket (7 daily; 5hr 30min); Surat Thani (10 daily; 4–5hr); Takua Pa (7 daily; 3hr).

By boat to the islands via Saphan Pla Boats to Ko Chang (see p.600) and Ko Phayam (see p.603) leave from Ranong's port at Saphan Pla, 5km southwest of the town centre and served by songthaews (see below) or by share-taxi from *Pon's Place* (B50). Songthaews drop passengers on the main road through Saphan Pla, from where it's a 500m walk south to the Islands Pier, while share-taxis take you to the pier itself; phone *Pon's Place* if you want to arrange a pick-up from the pier on your return from the islands.

Destinations: Ko Chang (1–5 daily; 1hr–1hr 30min); Ko Phayam (1–5 daily; 45min–2hr).

GETTING AROUND

By songthaew Songthaews shuttle across and around Ranong, starting from the Thanon Ruangrat market, close to the town-centre hotels. Many have their destinations written in English on the side, and most charge around B15 per ride. Several songthaews pass Ranong bus station, including the #2 (red), which runs to the Thanon Ruangrat hotels and day market, and the #6 (blue), which starts at the

day market and heads on to the port area at Saphan Pla, 5km to the southwest (for boats to Ko Chang, Ko Phayam and Kaw Thaung); red #3 songthaew runs direct from the market on Thanon Ruangrat to the Saphan Pla port area.

Car and bike rental *Pon's Place*, 129 Thanon Ruangrat (daily 7.30am–9pm; 081 597 4549, ponplace-ranong .com), rents bicycles, motorbikes and cars.

INFORMATION AND TOURS

Tourist information The best source of tourist information in town is the ever helpful Pon at *Pon's Place*

restaurant and tour agency, 129 Thanon Ruangrat (daily 7.30am–9pm; 081 597 4549, ponplace-ranong.com), where you can also organize a visa run to Burma and back, arrange tours of the local area, book accommodation on Ko Chang and Ko Phayam, and buy air, bus and minibus tickets, as well as train tickets from Chumphon or Surat Thani. There's a branch of A-One Diving (see p.603) at 256 Thanon Ruangrat (☎077 832984).

ACCOMMODATION

Asia Hotel 39/9 Thanon Ruangrat ☎077 811113. Typical, basic Chinese–Thai hotel just south of the market, a bit battered but reasonably clean, with most rooms set back from the road. Airy en-suite fan rooms or large a/c versions with hot water, TV and two big beds (B500). B160
Luang Poj 225 Thanon Ruangrat ☎077 833377, ✉ luangpoj@gmail.com. Appealing conversion of a Sino-Portuguese shophouse, maintaining its polished wooden floors, which styles itself as a "boutique hostel" though there are no dorms. The smart, modern bedrooms come with attractive murals: heavy sleepers who like to be in the thick of the action will like the two fan rooms with wooden shutters facing the street; others will want to plump for the windowless a/c options. Hot showers are shared, though en-suite a/c rooms with TV and fridge are planned in the building at the back (as well as a coffee shop and bar with garden seating). Wi-fi throughout. B400
Suta House Bungalows Thanon Ruangrat ☎077 832707–8. Set back 50m from the road, this is an unusual find in a city, with its row of small but well-maintained a/c bungalows, all of them with clean tiled floors, built-in beds, hot showers, fridges, cable TV and free wi-fi. They're set round a small yard, with car parking, a little bar-coffee shop and a restaurant. Open 24hr. B350
TCDF Eco-Logic Pak Song, near Pha To, 45km southeast of Ranong ⌨tcdf-ecologic.jimdo.com. Thai–Dutch eco-tourism guesthouse on a farm in the mountains (and on the Ranong–Surat Thani bus route), with artistically decorated en-suite rooms and bungalows set in lovely grounds, some with garden bathrooms. Lots of activities for adults and kids,

---

INTO BURMA: VISA RUNS AND KAW THAUNG (KO SONG)

The southernmost tip of Burma – known as **Kaw Thaung** in Burmese, Ko Song in Thai, and Victoria Point when it was a British colony – lies just a few kilometres west of Ranong across the gaping Chan River estuary, and is easily reached by longtail boat from Saphan Pla fishing port just outside Ranong town centre. It's quite straightforward for foreign tourists to hop across to **Burma** at this point, and hop back for a new fifteen-day stay in Thailand (the "tourist visa exemption"). You can either do it independently, as described below, or you can make use of one of the all-inclusive **"visa run" services** advertised all over town, including at *Pon's Place* (B850 including visa). Most visa-run operators use the Saphan Pla route, but they can also book you on the faster, more luxurious **Andaman Club boat** (6 daily 7am–4pm, later boats available for those staying overnight; 20min each way; B1000 including visa), which departs from the Andaman Club pier 5km north of Ranong's town centre and travels to and from the swanky *Andaman Club* hotel (⌨andamanclub.com), casino and duty-free complex, located on a tiny island in Burmese waters just south of Kaw Thaung.

Boats to Kaw Thaung leave from the so-called Burmese Pier (go through the PTT petrol station on the main road) in the port of Saphan Pla, 5km southwest of town and served by songthaews from Ranong market (B15) – the blue #6 goes via the bus station but the red #3 is more direct. Thai exit formalities are done at the pier (daily 8am–6pm), after which longtail boats take you to Kaw Thaung (B300–400 return per boat – pay at the end; 30min each way) and **Burmese immigration**. Here you pay US$10 (or B500) for a pass that should entitle you to stay in Kaw Thaung for a week but forbids travel further than 8km inland. Note that Burma time is thirty minutes behind Thailand time, and that to get back into Thailand you'll have to be at the immigration office in Saphan Pla before it closes at 6pm. The photocopy shop at the pier in Saphan Pla often keeps US dollars, and you should be able to haggle them down to B400 for a $10 bill. Thai money is perfectly acceptable in Kaw Thaung.

There's nothing much to do in **Kaw Thaung** itself, but it has quite a different vibe to Thai towns. As you arrive at the quay, the market, immigration office and tiny town centre lie before you, while over to your right, about twenty minutes' walk away, you can't miss the hilltop **Pyi Taw Aye Pagoda**, surmounted by a huge reclining Buddha and a ring of smaller ones. Once you've explored the covered market behind the quay and picked your way through the piles of tin trunks and sacks of rice that crowd the surrounding streets, all that remains is to take a coffee break in one of the quayside pastry shops.

including bamboo rafting, hiking and Thai cooking classes. In support of the Thai Child Development Foundation (see p.59). Dorm B200, double B750

★ **Tinidee Hotel** 41/144 Thanon Tha Muang ☎077 835240, ⓦtinidee-ranong.com. The top digs in town are at this welcoming, good-value high-rise hotel, a 10min walk from the market, which fully lives up to its name ("It's good here"). The large, bright a/c rooms are tastefully furnished and all come with mini-bars, TVs and bathtubs

fed by the local mineral water; there's also a spa and an attractive swimming pool and jacuzzi. B1100

Tinidee Inn 41/144 Thanon Tha Muang ☎077 834112, ⓦtinidee-ranong.com. A wing of the *Tinidee Hotel* has been converted into this low-cost inn, offering less style and smaller rooms, but all with a/c, hot showers, TV and fridge. Guests get access to the hotel's pool and jacuzzi; wi-fi is payable, or you can go across to the hotel's lobby to use it for free. B550

EATING AND DRINKING

Ranong's ethnic diversity ensures a tasty range of eating options, and a stroll up Thanon Ruangrat takes you past Muslim foodstalls and Chinese pastry shops as well as a small but typically Thai night market. A bigger night market convenes at dusk just east of the CAT phone office off Thanon Phoem Phon. The stretch of Thanon Ruangrat between the Thanon Luwang junction and *Sophon's Hideaway* is also abuzz after dark, especially at weekends, with urbane little local bars that keep reinventing themselves.

Pon's Place 129 Thanon Ruangrat ☎081 597 4549. This nice little restaurant hung with orchids is the obvious place for farang-style breakfast (French toast B55) with traditional Thai coffee, free wi-fi and as much local information as you care to gather. It also offers sandwiches and standard Thai dishes, including plenty of seafood and some veggie options. Daily 7.30am–9pm.

Sophon's Hideaway Thanon Ruangrat. Lively, enjoyable bar and rustic-style restaurant, where Thai families and expats congregate for the wide-ranging menu, which includes chicken with cashew nuts (B85), T-bone steaks (B350), pizzas, pastas, ice cream and breakfast. The cheapish beer and friendly staff are a plus and there's international sports on the TV, a free pool table and free wi-fi. Daily 10am–12.30am.

Ko Chang

Not to be confused with the much larger Ko Chang off Thailand's east coast (see p.410), Ranong's **KO CHANG** is a forested little island about 5km offshore, whose car-free, ultra laidback, roll-your-own vibe more than compensates for the less than perfect beaches. The pace of life here is very slow, encouraging long stays, and for the relatively small number of tourists who make it to the island the emphasis is strongly on kicking back and chilling out – bring your own hammock and you'll fit right in. Those in search of (slightly) livelier scenes head across the water to sister-island Ko Phayam (see p.601). Most islanders make their living from fishing and from the rubber, palm and cashew nut plantations that dominate the flatter patches of the interior. The beaches are connected by tracks through the trees and there are only sporadic, self-generated supplies of electricity for a few hours each evening.

The best of Ko Chang's beaches are on the west coast, and of these the longest, nicest and most popular is **Ao Yai**. The tiny bays to the north and south mostly hold just one set of bungalows each and are good for getting away from it all, though access to Ao Yai is easy enough if you don't mind the hike. About halfway between the west and east coasts, a crossroads bisects Ko Chang's only **village**, a tiny settlement that is home to most of the islanders and holds just a few shops, restaurants and a clinic.

Nearly all the bungalows on Ko Chang **close** down from about late April or early May until mid- or late October, when the island is subjected to very heavy rain, the beaches fill with flotsam, paths become dangerously slippery and food supplies dwindle with no ice available to keep things fresh. Many bungalow staff relocate to the mainland for this period, so you should phone ahead to check first.

7

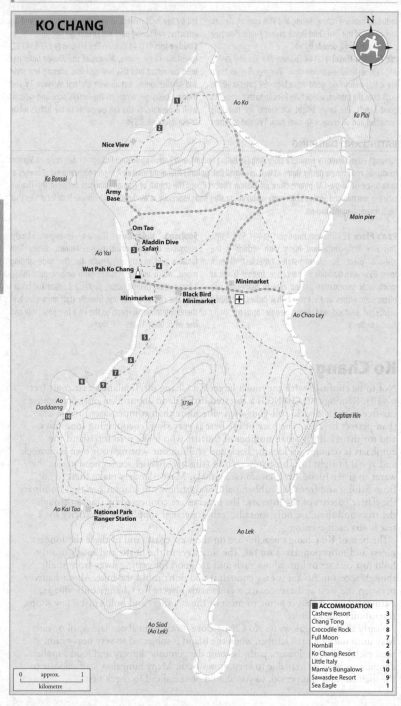

KO CHANG

N

Ao Ko

Ko Plai

Nice View

Ko Bonsai

Army
Base

Om Tao

Aladdin Dive
Safari

Ao Yai

Wat Pah Ko Chang

Main pier

Minimarket

Minimarket

Black Bird
Minimarket

Ao Chao Ley

5

6

8

7

9

Ao
Daddaeng

10

373m

Saphan Hin

Ao Kai Tao

National Park
Ranger Station

Ao Lek

Ao Siad
(Ao Lek)

0	approx.	1
	kilometre	

■ **ACCOMMODATION**

Cashew Resort	3
Chang Tong	5
Crocodile Rock	8
Full Moon	7
Hornbill	2
Ko Chang Resort	6
Little Italy	4
Mama's Bungalows	10
Sawasdee Resort	9
Sea Eagle	1

ACTIVITIES ON KO CHANG

Going for walks (and not minding getting lost) is the most popular activity on this large, traffic-free island, but several resorts, including *Ko Chang Resort*, run **fishing, snorkelling and camping trips** to Ko Kham, which is famed for its beautiful beaches and reefs, and to Ko Phayam. For **divers**, Ko Chang is particularly well placed for the sites in the Mergui Archipelago across the border in Burma, while the top local dive sites in Thailand are Ko Surin, Ko Bon, Ko Tachai, Ko Similan and Richelieu Rock.

Aladdin Dive Safari Cashew Resort, Ao Yai, and at the Islands Pier in Saphan Pla ☏087 278 6908, ⓦ aladdindivesafari.com. This German–Dutch-run dive shop teaches PADI dive courses and runs a huge selection of live-aboards that take in all the local dive sites (from

B14,900 for three days excluding equipment and national park fees).

Om Tao North of Cashew Resort, Ao Yai. Morning yoga classes and t'ai chi in season.

Ao Yai (Long Beach) and Ao Daddaeng

Effectively divided in two by a khlong (canal) and the stumps of a long wooden pier, **Ao Yai**, or **Long Beach**, enjoys a fine view of the brooding silhouette of Burma's St Matthew's Island, which dominates the western horizon. The 800m-long stretch of Ao Yai that runs north from the khlong is the most attractive on the island, nice and wide even at high tide, and especially good for kids. South of the khlong, the beach is very narrow at high tide, but when the water goes out you have to walk a longish distance to find any depth. Further south still, around a rocky headland, tiny secluded gold-sand **Ao Daddaeng** (Tadang) is sandwiched between massive boulders and holds just a few bungalows: reach it via a five-minute footpath from behind *Tadang Bay Bungalows*.

A narrow concrete road connects central Ao Yai with the mangrove-filled little harbour on the east coast, a distance of around 1700m that can be walked in under half an hour. The western end of the road begins beside the island's only temple, **Wat Pah Ko Chang**, whose bot and monks' quarters are partially hidden among the trees beside the beach, with a sign that asks tourists to dress modestly when in the area and not to swim or sunbathe in front of it.

Northern Ko Chang

North of Ao Yai, the crenellated coast reveals a series of tiny bays occupied by just one set of bungalows apiece. The gritty gold-sand beaches are secluded and feel quite remote, accessible only via a track through forest and rubber plantations. Even if you don't want to base yourself up here, you can do an enjoyable **loop** around the northern bays in well under three hours from Ao Yai. Alternatively, you could make use of the Ranong boats, which charge about B50 for any hop up or down the west coast.

Following **the track** inland from just north of Om Tao, a ten-minute walk north brings you to the top of the first of several hills and the barbed-wire perimeters of a military camp, established here to monitor activity along the (maritime) Thai–Burma border. Ten minutes further on, *Nice View* restaurant and bungalows are aptly named: perched atop an outcrop with glorious panoramas over the unfolding little bays and islets beyond, it's a perfect spot to break for lunch or a drink. It's another twenty minutes to *Sea Eagle* (you need to go via the beach at *Hornbill* before returning inland), the last of the northern bay bungalows, beyond which a ten-minute walk up and over the next hill takes you to the edge of the northeast-facing fishing village, an unprepossessing place complete with incongruous Christian church. This is **Ao Ko**, which is linked by road to the east coast's rainy season pier, and also to Ao Yai.

Southern Ko Chang

Ao Siad, at the southern end of the island, is even more isolated than the north coast and makes a good focus for a day-walk. It's sometimes known as Ao Lek, though the real **Ao Lek** is the mangrove-lined bay fifteen minutes' walk to the northeast, on the other coast. From Ao Daddaeng, a clear path takes you south, in about an hour, to **Ao Kai Tao**, a pretty beach and site of the national park ranger station. From Ao Kai Tao, the route then follows an indistinct path across the saddle between two hills and along a creek bed to reach east-coast Ao Lek (this takes another hour), after which it's fifteen minutes south to Ao Siad. Retracing your steps to Ao Lek to start with, it's then about 5km (2hr) to the crossroads in the village.

ARRIVAL AND DEPARTURE

Cashew Resort (see below) can arrange bus tickets.

BY BOAT
To/from Ranong The island's main link with the outside world is the daily boat service from the Islands Pier in Saphan Pla (see p.595) to the pier on the east coast (currently 2pm; 1hr; B100; sometimes cancelled in the rainy season). You should be able to arrange some kind of a pick-up from the pier through your resort; otherwise it's a 3km walk to Ao Yai. From about early November to late April, there are also three or four daily boat departures to

Ko Chang's west coast, stopping at most resorts, from Saphan Pla's Islands Pier (1hr 30min; B150); ask your resort or at *Pon's Place* in Ranong for the latest schedules.
To/from Ko Phayam The easiest and cheapest option for getting to or from Ko Phayam is to use the day-trippers' boat run by *Ko Chang Resort* several times a week in high season (B150); a charter between the two islands costs about B1500 per boat.

INFORMATION
Tourist information For general information on the island see ⓦ kohchang-ranong.com.

ACCOMMODATION
Most of the bungalows on Ko Chang are simple, old-school wooden-plank or woven bamboo constructions with mosquito nets on the beds; you shouldn't necessarily expect flush toilets (buckets and dippers are provided), curtains or a door on your bathroom. Though the bungalow resorts nearly all have their own generators (which usually only operate in the evenings), some stick to candles and paraffin lamps in the bungalows so it's best to bring a torch; very few bungalows have fans. There are no stand-alone restaurants, and as the distances between resorts are long and there's no transport, most visitors dine at their own resort's restaurant.

AO YAI (LONG BEACH)
Cashew Resort ⓣ 077 820226 or ⓣ 084 538 5385, ⓔ cashew_resort@hotmail.com. The longest-running accommodation on the island, and also the largest, *Cashew* feels like a tiny village, with its forty en-suite bungalows spread among the cashew trees along 700m of prime beachfront, and returnees personalizing their bungalows like mini homes. All the wood or brick bungalows enjoy both a sea view and some privacy, and some have big glass windows. The resort offers the most facilities on the island, including internet access, foreign exchange, Visa and MasterCard capability, an overseas phone service, transport bookings, massage and books to borrow. Its restaurant bakes bread and serves Thai and a few German dishes. May open year-round in the future. B300
Chang Tong ⓣ 080 526 8422 or ⓣ 089 875 3353, ⓔ aoy_changthong@hotmail.com. The cheapest wood and bamboo bungalows at this friendly spot are very basic, though they're all en suite and are well spaced

beneath the shoreside trees; pay a bit more for newer, better appointed ones on the beachfront. B150
★ **Crocodile Rock** ⓣ 081 370 1434 or ⓣ 087 040 8087, ⓔ tonn1970@yahoo.com. In a shady, secluded, elevated position at the start of Ao Yai's southern headland, with great views of the whole bay, on which the friendly owners have capitalized, with attractive decks at the restaurant and picture windows in some of the bathrooms. Bungalows, some of which have nice pebbledash bathrooms, have a touch more style than the Ko Chang average. The restaurant bakes its own bread, cookies and banana muffins, and serves fresh juices and espresso coffee. Internet access. B300
Full Moon ⓣ 084 850 3809, ⓔ familymoon99 @hotmail.com. Though simple, the attractive wooden en-suite bungalows here are well designed and a cut above many others on Ao Yai. The cheaper ones are prettily painted, with cute stencil work in the bathrooms, and there are larger, pastel-painted, clapboard versions with

big decks. Beach bar and massage *sala*. B300

Ko Chang Resort ☎ 081 896 1839, ⓦ kohchang andaman.com. Occupying a fabulous spot high on the rocks right over the water, the best of the en-suite wooden bungalows here have fine sea views from their balconies; the cheaper bamboo ones are set further back beside the path. Interiors are very rudimentary but the decks are huge, and there's also a large, more luxurious family bungalow, and two concrete bungalows with fans (all B1000). You can swim below the rocks at low tide, or the more reliable beach is just a couple of minutes' scramble to south or north. There's internet on site, plus the very chilled, fairy-lit *Air Bar*. May open year-round in the future. B300

Little Italy ☎ 084 851 2760, ⓔ daniel060863@yahoo .it. This tiny Italian–Thai-run outfit has just two attractive bungalows set in a shady, secluded garden of paperbark trees 100m inland from *Cashew Resort*. Bungalows are two-storey, with exceptionally clean, smartly tiled papaya-coloured bathrooms downstairs and Thai-style bamboo-walled sleeping quarters upstairs, with varnished wood floors and big decks. The garden restaurant serves deliciously authentic pastas. Wi-fi available. B250

Sawasdee Resort ☎ 084 846 5828, ⓦ sawasdee kohchang.com. This welcoming place by a khlong at the far southern end of Ao Yai is a little pricier than many but more style-conscious too and tends to attract slightly older, less hammock-bound guests. The eleven thoughtfully designed wooden bungalows have big decks and good bathrooms, and a couple of them, by the beach, are especially large and well equipped, including fans (B800). There's a good, attractive restaurant, serving a wide variety of Thai dishes and plenty of vegetarian options, with decks and terraces under the shady trees. B350

AO DADDAENG

★ **Mama's Bungalows** 5min walk south over the headland from Ao Yai, on Ao Daddaeng ☎ 077 820180 or ☎ 088 476 7144, ⓔ mamas-bungalows@hotmail .com. At this congenial spot, the fourteen attractive, well-maintained wooden and bamboo bungalows with colourfully decorated bathrooms come in several sizes, some of them with big decks. They're built in a pretty flower garden staggered up the hillside; several are on the beach and the uppermost ones overlook the bay from the edge of a rubber plantation. The restaurant serves espresso coffee and generous portions of carefully prepared food, including tasty tzatziki and many German specialities. Very popular, so book ahead. B250

NORTHERN BAYS

Hornbill North around two headlands from Ao Yai, about a 35min walk ☎ 077 870240, ⓔ 66_hornbill @hotmail.com. Set among the trees fronting their own little gold-sand bay, the unobtrusive en-suite bungalows here are constructed to different designs, some of them extremely comfortable, and all enjoy sea views. The food here has a good reputation and the owner is very welcoming. It lives up to its name, as majestic black-and-white hornbills are a common sight. Internet access, kayaks and boat trips on offer. B200

Sea Eagle About 40min walk from Ao Yai ☎ 082 289 0683, ⓦ seaeaglebangkalow.com. The sole occupants of the longest and widest of the northern bays, which is graced by an attractive band of gold sand, the en-suite bamboo and wooden bungalows here are set among trees just back from the shore. They have comfy deck furniture for soaking up the sea views and there are kayaks and windsurfers for rent and a beach volleyball net. The restaurant serves Thai and European food and has internet access. B300

Ko Phayam

The diminutive kangaroo-shaped island of **KO PHAYAM** offers fine white-sand beaches and coral reefs and is home to around five hundred people, most of whom either make their living from prawn, squid and crab fishing, or from growing cashew nuts, *sator* beans, coconut palms and rubber trees. Many islanders live in Ko Phayam's only **village**, behind the pier on the northeast coast, which connects to other corners of the island by a network of concrete roads and rutted tracks. The bays either side of the village have a couple of nice places to stay, but the main beaches and accommodation centres are on the west coast, at **Ao Yai** and **Ao Kao Kwai**. A motorbike taxi service covers all routes, but no journey is very great as the island measures just five by eight kilometres at its widest points.

Ko Phayam has a livelier, younger and slightly more developed feel than neighbouring Ko Chang (see p.597), underlined by a low-key beach-bar scene – all hand-painted signs and driftwood sculptures – and the presence of a significant number of foreigners who choose to spend six or more months here every year. Some expats even take up the rainy-season challenge, staying on through the downpours and rough seas that lash the island from June to October, but a number of bungalows close down during this time and staff take refuge in Ranong. As the island gets more popular, residents and expats are beginning to try and forestall the inevitable negative impact on the island's **environment**. In particular, they are urging visitors not to accept plastic bags from the few shops on the island, to take non-degradable rubbish such as batteries and plastic items back to the mainland, and to minimize plastic water-bottle usage by buying the biggest possible bottles and by asking to refill them from the water coolers that all bungalow resorts have.

The village and around

The tiny cluster of homes and shops that constitute Ko Phayam's only **village** is within a few minutes' walk of the pier. There are a few little general stores here, plus several restaurants and a **clinic**. North a little way up the shoreline stands the island **temple**, with its circular viharn resting on a huge concrete lotus flower at the end of its own pier.

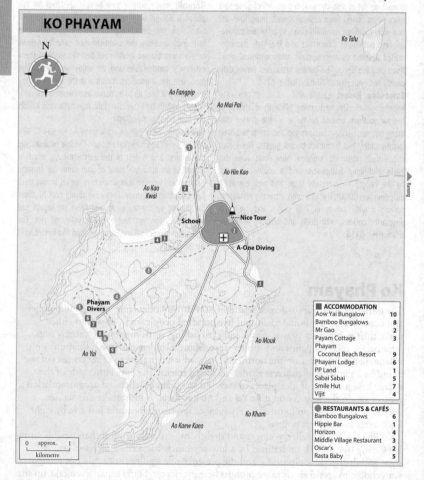

KO PHAYAM

■ ACCOMMODATION	
Aow Yai Bungalow	10
Bamboo Bungalows	8
Mr Gao	2
Payam Cottage	3
Phayam Coconut Beach Resort	9
Phayam Lodge	6
PP Land	1
Sabai Sabai	5
Smile Hut	7
Vijit	4

● RESTAURANTS & CAFÉS	
Bamboo Bungalows	6
Hippie Bar	1
Horizon	4
Middle Village Restaurant	3
Oscar's	2
Rasta Baby	5

ACTIVITIES ON KO PHAYAM

Most bungalows can arrange fishing and snorkelling day-trips, while *Oscar's* in the village takes people wakeboarding in the bay. The dive companies teach PADI courses and run liveaboards to Ko Surin, Richelieu Rock, Ko Tachai, Ko Bon and Ko Similan (from about B16,000 for three days, not including equipment).

A-One Diving In the village ☎081 891 5510, ⓦa-one-diving.com. Also does live-aboards to Burma Banks and the Mergui archipelago across the Burmese border.

Mr Gao Ao Kao Kwai ☎077 870222, ⓦmr-trip -phayam.com. Runs occasional two-day snorkelling

trips to Ko Surin at B4000 per person, including accommodation in national park tents.

Phayam Divers Phayam Lodge, Ao Yai ☎086 995 2598, ⓦphayamlodge.com. Also does one-day trips to Ko Surin or Richelieu Rock for B4900 (plus equipment rental and national park fee).

Ao Yai

Ko Phayam's main beach is the 3km-long **AO YAI** on the southwest coast, a wide and handsome sweep of powdery white sand backed by an unbroken line of casuarina trees, which curves quite deeply at its northern and southern ends into rocky outcrops that offer some snorkelling possibilities. The shore is pounded by decent waves that are fun for boogie-boarding and pretty safe; the sunsets are quite spectacular too. For the moment Ao Yai's bungalow operations are mostly widely spaced along the shoreline, and much of the forest behind the beach is still intact. You're more than likely to see – and hear – some of the resident black-and-white hornbills at dawn and dusk, along with many white-bellied sea eagles, and sightings of crab-eating macaques are also common.

Ao Kao Kwai and around

The northwest coast is scalloped into **AO KAO KWAI**, a name that's pronounced locally as **Ao Kao Fai** and translates as **Buffalo Horn Bay**; from the cliffside midway along the bay you can see the two halves of the beach curve out into buffalo-like horns. The southern half of Ao Kao Kwai is subject to both very low and very high tides, which makes it unreliable for swimming, but the northern stretch, from *Mr Gao* bungalows onwards, is exceptionally pretty, secluded between outcrops with decent swimming at any tide, and none of the big waves that characterize Ao Yai.

From the northern end of Ao Kao Kwai, a thirty-minute walk brings you to the pretty little sandy beach at **Ao Fangpip** (also spelt Ao Kwang Pib), which is the best spot on the island for snorkelling. There's also some snorkellable reef at **Ao Hin Kao** on the northeast coast.

ARRIVAL AND DEPARTURE   KO PHAYAM

Nice Tour and Travel, north of the pier-head in the village (☎089 651 5177, ✉nicetour40@hotmail.com), sells bus, train, airline and boat tickets. Nearby *Oscar's* (☎084 842 5070) also sells transport tickets and charters speedboats to other islands. Most bungalows also sell boat tickets, and some sell bus tickets, too.

BY BOAT

To/from Ranong From November to May there are two daily slow boats to Ko Phayam from the Islands Pier in Saphan Pla (see p.595), 5km south of Ranong town centre (currently 9.30am & 2pm, returning from the island at 8am & 2pm; 2hr; B150), as well as up to three speedboat services (45min; B350). During the rainy season only the

2pm slow boat runs, returning from the island at 8am; *Pon's Place* in Ranong keeps the latest timetables.

To/from Ko Chang The easiest and cheapest way of travelling between Ko Phayam and Ko Chang is on the day-trippers' boat organized by *Ko Chang Resort* several times a week in high season (see p.600).

7

GETTING AROUND

Many travellers heading into the village from one of the beaches opt to walk at least one way: from Ao Yai's *Smile Hut* it's an enjoyable 7km stroll along the narrow concrete road that cuts through the cashew plantations, with the possibility of stopping for a breather at the aptly named *Middle Village Restaurant*. From southern Ao Kao Kwai to the village takes less than an hour.

Motorbike taxis Motorbikes meet incoming boats at the pier and can be booked through any bungalow; a ride between the village and the beaches costs about B80 (there are no cars on the island).

Motorbike rental You can rent your own motorbike through resorts on the beaches and outlets in the village, including *Oscar's* and *Nice Tour and Travel*.
Bike rental *Nice Tour and Travel* in the village.

INFORMATION

Nice Tour and Travel In the village ☎089 651 5177. Changes money and does Visa cash advances, can arrange boat hire and fishing tours, has a book exchange, and offers internet access and an international phone service.

Oscar's Bar In the village ☎084 842 5070. A good source of island information and tickets; also changes money at good rates.

ACCOMMODATION

Most bungalows only provide electricity from around 6 to 11pm and the cheapest rooms often don't have a fan. There's internet access at many, and wi-fi at an increasing number. Unless otherwise stated, all bungalows open year-round.

THE VILLAGE AREA

Most people choose to stay at the west-coast beach centres, but there are a couple of nice little hideaways within easy reach of the village and its facilities.

PP Land ☎081 678 4310, ⓦpayampplandbeach.com. Fronting a small beach about a 10min walk north from the village, this Belgian–Thai place with an organic garden is a cut above many places to stay on the island. Its tasteful, green-painted shaggy thatched bungalows and family rooms line the beach and boast pretty furnishings, polished wood floors inside and out, nice bathrooms, and big comfy decks. There's an attractive swimming pool, plus internet, wi-fi and 24-hour electricity. B800

Sabai Sabai ☎087 895 4653, ⓦsabai-bungalows .com. On their own little beach, a 5min walk south of the pier, are these seven wooden bungalows, some with 24-hour electricity and all but one en suite; cute, stylish touches give them a modern look. Tents are also available, and there's a cool shisha lounge, regular movie nights, TV sports and other events, including live music. Internet access, motorbikes, bicycles, kayaks and snorkels available. B200

AO YAI

Aow Yai Bungalow ☎083 389 8688 or ☎084 061 3283, ⓦaowyai.com. Established by a French–Thai couple, this was the first set of bungalows on the island and remains one of the most popular, especially with return guests. The 26 good-quality en-suite bungalows are dotted around an extensive garden of flowers, fruit trees and palms and come in various styles: the cheapest wooden or thatched bamboo affairs come with mosquito nets but no fans, while the most expensive are built with

concrete and have hot showers. There's wi-fi and internet access, plus snorkels and kayaks. B300

Bamboo Bungalows ☎077 820012, ⓦbamboo -bungalows.com. Ao Yai's liveliest accommodation is Israeli–Thai managed and very traveller-savvy, with free wi-fi, plus snorkels, kayaks, surf- and boogie-boards, currency exchange and overseas phone services. Its en-suite bungalows are set under the trees in a well-tended flower garden and range from luxuriously large chalets with pretty furnishings to shell-studded concrete bungalows and a choice of bamboo and wood huts with mosquito nets. Electricity is 24hr in high season, but with more limited hours in low season. B500

Phayam Coconut Beach Resort ☎089 920 8145 or ☎083 389 6408, ⓦkoh-phayam.com. Occupying a great spot in the centre of the bay and run by a Ko Phayam family, the 27 good-value bungalows here are of a high standard, each set in its own tiny garden. Accommodation ranges from small bamboo en-suite huts through larger wood or bamboo versions to big concrete or clapboard bungalows at the top end (up to B1200). Wi-fi planned. Closed during the worst of the rainy season. B300

Phayam Lodge ☎086 995 2598, ⓦphayamlodge .com. Not quite finished at the time of writing – and with not much shade – but this welcoming place is probably a sign of things to come on Ko Phayam: rows of large, smart concrete villas with attractive teak fittings, proper bathrooms, a/c and hot showers (though electricity is not 24hr). Wi-fi available. B2200

Smile Hut ☎077 820335 or ☎081 515 0856, ⓦsmilehutthai.com. Like *Bamboo*, this is very popular with travellers. The 35 split-bamboo and wooden huts with mosquito nets are simple but en suite and are spread among the shorefront trees, with the slightly cheaper versions set one row behind. Has internet access and kayaks. **B400**

AO KAO KWAI

Ao Kao Kwai is particularly popular both with long-stay guests and returnees, so you might want to book your accommodation in advance. *PP Land* (see opposite) have recently opened a branch over here, *Heaven Beach* (ⓦpayamheavenbeach.com).

★ **Mr Gao** ☎077 870222, ⓦmr-gao-phayam.com. Located on the best stretch of the beach, this is one of the most famous and popular spots, a well-established operation comprising a good restaurant and just nine well-designed bungalows, in assorted sizes and luxury, set in a spacious, lovingly tended garden of shrubs and bamboos. All have good bathrooms and generous decks and most have polished wood floors, screened windows and thoughtfully furnished interiors. Internet access. **B500**

Payam Cottage ☎085 222 1847, ⓦpayamcottage .com. More resort-like in style and facilities than others on Ko Phayam, with 24hr electricity, the option of a/c, a kids' play area and a good-sized swimming pool. Bungalows are tastefully furnished and built in angled rows across a central garden to give each one some sort of sea view. Internet access and free wi-fi. **B1600**

Vijit ☎077 834082, ⓦohpayam-vijit.com. This long-running outfit in a lush garden is very popular. Some of the en-suite, clapboard bungalows are designed for families and they're all reasonably spacious and have fans. Free wi-fi. **B400**

EATING AND DRINKING

Several laidback little beach-bars, including the long-running *Rasta Baby* on Ao Yai and *Hippie Bar* on Ao Kao Khwai, put on fireshows and occasional parties.

THE VILLAGE

★ **Oscar's** Just north of the pier-head ☎084 842 5070. Offers breakfasts, including home-baked bread, Thai standards such as *tom yam kung* (B90), pizzas, Indian curries, shepherd's pie (B180) and other English favourites, but is most famous for its partially open-air bar, which is the focal point of the expat social scene. Wi-fi planned. Daily 7am–late.

AO YAI

Bamboo Bungalows Tasty spaghetti with pesto (B150), schnitzels, sandwiches and Western breakfasts at this beachfront restaurant, as well as lots of Thai standards, including seafood priced by weight. Also does wine by the glass and Middle Eastern coffee. Daily 7.45am–10pm.

Horizon Just inland on the Ao Yai road. Congenial outdoor restaurant for very tasty Thai food, all of it offered vegetarian, with the option of adding meat: a toothsome *matsaman* curry with carrot, pumpkin and potatoes costs B60, and you can add chicken for B20. Also does a few Western main courses, sandwiches, a wide choice of breakfasts, Thai desserts, and all kinds of teas, juices and lassis. High season daily 7/8am–8/9pm, closed evenings in shoulder season, closed in low season.

Khuraburi

The small town of **KHURABURI**, 110km south of Ranong on Highway 4, is the main departure point for the magnificent national park island chain of Ko Surin. Much closer to Khuraburi are the islands of **Ko Ra** and **Ko Phra Thong**, which offer empty beaches and decent snorkelling and bird-watching, or there's the chance to participate in typical village life at **homestays** in mainland coastal communities.

Khuraburi's commercial heart is a 500m strip of shops and businesses either side of Highway 4. Most travellers use the town just as a staging post en route to or from the Surin islands: the main pier for boats to the islands is just 7.5km away, and Khuraburi's tour agents sell boat tickets and offer transport to the pier. Though lacking in famous attractions, the local area is nonetheless scenic, both offshore and inland: with an afternoon or more to spare, you could either rent a motorbike, mountain bike or kayak to explore it independently, or charter a motorbike taxi or longtail boat.

Ko Ra

Hilly, forested **Ko Ra** (measuring about 10km north to south and 3km across) sits just off Khuraburi pier's mangrove-lined estuary and is graced with intact rainforest full of towering trees, hornbills and wild, empty beaches. The island is home to some two

7

ANDAMAN DISCOVERIES HOMESTAY PROGRAMME

Khuraburi is the headquarters of the community-based tourism initiative Andaman Discoveries (☎087 917 7165, ⑩andamandiscoveries.com), which runs a recommended **day-trip and homestay programme** in several local villages, as well as interesting trips to Ko Surin (see p.609). It was established after the tsunami to help the area's many devastated fishing communities get back on their feet and has since developed a range of stimulating one- to five-day packages (from B1600 per person per day) featuring all sort of village jobs and activities, from soap-making and batik design to cashew nut-farming and roof-thatching. The office is just east off the highway (south of the bus station), up the soi beside the police box, across from the post office.

---

dozen *chao ley* people (see p.608), plus just one place to stay, the rather special American–Thai *Ko Ra Ecolodge*. On offer are half-day guided tours to the nearby Moken village on Ko Ra; kayak rental and guided day and multi-day sea-kayaking trips; guided and self-guided hiking and bird-watching; yoga classes and retreats; snorkelling trips to nearby Ko Surin (B2900 per person, all-inclusive), as well as to the little-visited islands of Laem Son National Park; and diving to the Surin islands (B6900 for two dives, not including national park entrance fee and equipment rental) and Reef Check courses to monitor the local coral.

Ko Phra Thong

Immediately to the south of Ko Ra, just 1km or so off the Khuraburi coast, **Ko Phra Thong** (Golden Buddha Island) also has some lovely beaches, the nicest of which, on the west coast, is 10km long and blessed with fine gold sand. This is the site of the *Golden Buddha Beach Resort* and of the British-run Blue Guru Dive Centre (☎080 144 0551, ⑩blue-guru.org). The resort offers kayaking, trekking and yoga, while Blue Guru runs all manner of snorkelling tours, PADI courses and dive trips and live-aboards to Ko Tachai, Ko Surin, Richelieu Rock and into Burma, including unique one-day dive trips to Richelieu and overnighters on Ko Surin (diving Richelieu). Blue Guru's owners also organize longtail tours of the island's mangroves and maintain a website to promote the island, ⑩kohphrathong.com, which includes information about homestays and budget bungalows.

ARRIVAL AND DEPARTURE · KHURABURI, KO RA AND KO PHRA THONG

KHURABURI

By bus The bus station is just off the east side of Highway 4 in the centre of town, but some long-distance through buses stop only on the highway.

Destinations: Bangkok (6 daily to Southern Bus Terminal, of which 2 continue to Mo Chit; 10hr); Khao Lak (6 daily; 1hr 45min); Phuket (6 daily; 3hr 30min–4hr); Ranong (6 daily; 2hr); Takua Pa (6 daily; 1hr).

KO RA

By boat A longtail transfer to the *Ecolodge* from the pier at Khuraburi costs B600 (20min).

KO PHRA THONG

By boat A longtail transfer to *Golden Buddha Beach Resort* from the pier at Khuraburi costs B1800 (90min).

GETTING AROUND

KHURABURI

Bike and motorbike rental Tom & Am Tour, who have their office on the west side of the main road in the town centre and maintain a desk in the bus station in high season (☎086 272 0588, ✉tom_am01@hotmail.com), rent bicycles, motorbikes and cars. *Boon Piya Resort* also rent motorbikes.

ACCOMMODATION

KHURABURI

Boon Piya Resort 100m north of the bus station, on the same side of the main road ☎081 752 5457. Well-appointed, if rather tightly packed, motel-style concrete bungalows in a tree-strewn courtyard set just back off the road. All have a/c and powerful hot showers; they're the usual choice of sales reps and NGOs. Wi-fi available. B650

Mr Tom's Bungalows On the north bank of the river, east of the bridge ☎086 272 0588, ✉tom_am01 @hotmail.com. Decent bungalows in a pleasant setting on the north bank of the river, with wi-fi and breakfast included, and kayaks for rent; call in at Tom & Am Tour (see opposite) first. B290

Tararin On the south bank of the river towards the northern end of town, about 200m north of the bus station ☎076 491789. This cute, rustic-style place has just a handful of simple but appealing en-suite wooden and concrete bungalows, some of them on stilts with balconies right over the water, plus an attractive riverside restaurant and eating deck. All rooms have TVs; a/c (B500) have hot showers. B300

KO RA

★ **Ko Ra Ecolodge** ☎089 867 5288, ⊕thaiecolodge .com. This ecotourism venture fronts a curve of bronze sand on the north coast, with magnificent views to the Khuraburi hills, but its star feature is its wild, forty-acre, forest garden. Filled with screw palms, red-barked *samet daeng* trees, dipterocarps and over seventeen epiphytic orchids, the private forest is crossed by trails and home both to a rich bird life, especially sunbirds and oriental pied hornbills, and to monitor lizards, crab-eating macaques and dusky langurs. Accommodation is in eighteen plain but spacious rooms in split-bamboo longhouses just back from the shore, communal meals are taken in the beach-side *sala* (full board B75/day) and there's a genuine focus on community and environmental projects (volunteer placements and internships are offered). Closed May–Oct. B1100

KO PHRA THONG

Golden Buddha Beach Resort ☎081 892 2208, ⊕goldenbuddharesort.com. Tasteful complex of 25 individually styled wooden Thai-style homes, sleeping two to six, with a spa and clubhouse. B4000

EATING AND DRINKING

KHURABURI

At night, many people eat at the night market south of the bus station, where the roti stall is a particular favourite, flipping out a constant pile of sizzling *roti mataba* (chicken) and *roti kluay* (banana). The morning market (daily from 5am) across from *Boon Piya* is the place to stock up on food for the Surin islands.

Tararin Bungalows On the south bank of the river towards the northern end of town, about 200m north of the bus station. Popular with visiting Thais, this riverside deck restaurant hits the spot with specialities such as *nam phrik kapi*, a southern relish made with shrimp paste, and *kaeng liang*, peppery vegetable soup, as well as loads of salads, fish and seafood. Mon–Sat 10am–9pm.

Ko Surin

Mu Ko Surin National Park, about 60km offshore • Nov 1–April 30 • B400 entry fee, valid for 5 days • ⊕dnp.go.th

Unusually shallow reefs, a palette of awesomely clear turquoise waters and dazzling white sands, and dense forests of lofty dipterocarps combine to make the islands of **Ko Surin** one of the most popular destinations in south Thailand. However, Ko Surin's most famous feature, its spectacular and diverse coral lying in fields just below the surface at the perfect depth for snorkelling, was severely bleached by a sudden rise in sea temperature in early 2010. Four of the most popular reefs are now closed to visitors, though half a dozen other sites that were less severely affected by the bleaching remain open; the national park is still a good spot for snorkellers, with plenty of fish to see, but it will take many years for the reefs to recover.

   Ko Surin is very much an outdoors experience, with the bulk of accommodation in national park tents, no commerce on the islands at all, and twice-daily snorkelling the main activity. Several tour operators run snorkelling day-trips from Khuraburi, and there are diving trips too, most of which also take in nearby Richelieu Rock, considered to be Thailand's top dive site (see p.642), but independent travel is also recommended. Because the islands are so far out at sea, Ko Surin is closed to visitors from roughly May to October, when monsoon weather renders the 60km trip a potentially suicidal undertaking.

THE CHAO LEY: MOKEN AND URAK LAWOY

Sometimes called sea gypsies, the **chao ley** or *chao nam* ("people of the sea" or "water people") have been living off the seas around the west coast of the Malay peninsula for hundreds of years. Some still pursue a traditional nomadic existence, living in self-contained houseboats known as **kabang**, but many have now made permanent homes in Andaman coast settlements in Thailand, Burma and Malaysia. Dark-skinned and sometimes with an auburn tinge to their hair, the *chao ley* of the Andaman Sea are thought to number around five thousand, divided into five groups, with distinct lifestyles and dialects.

Of the different groups, the **Urak Lawoy**, who have settled on the islands of Ko Lanta, Ko Jum, Ko Phi Phi, Phuket and Ko Lipe, are the most integrated into Thai society. They came north to Thailand from Malaysia around two hundred years ago (having possibly migrated from the Nicobar Islands in the Indian Ocean some two centuries prior) and are known as *Thai Mai*, or "New Thai". Thailand's Urak Lawoy have been recognized as Thai citizens since the 1960s, when the late Queen Mother granted them five family names, thereby enabling them to possess ID cards and go to school. Many work on coconut plantations or as fishermen, while others continue in the more traditional *chao ley* **occupations** of hunting for pearls and seashells on the ocean floor, attaching stones to their waists to dive to depths of 60m with only an air-hose connecting them to the surface; sometimes they fish in this way too, taking down enormous nets into which they herd the fish as they walk along the sea bed. Their agility and courage make them good bird's-nesters as well (see box, p.680).

The **Moken** of Thailand's Ko Surin islands and Burma's Mergui archipelago probably came originally from Burma and are the most traditional of the *chao ley* communities. Some still lead remote, itinerant lives, and most are unregistered as Thai citizens, owning no land or property, but dependent on fresh water and beaches to collect shells and sea slugs to sell to Thai traders. They have extensive knowledge of the plants that grow in the remaining jungles on Thailand's west-coast islands, using eighty different species for food alone, and thirty for medicinal purposes.

The *chao ley* are **animists**, with a strong connection both to the natural spirits of island and sea and to their own ancestral spirits. On some beaches they set up totem poles as a contact point between the spirits, their ancestors and their shaman. The sea gypsies have a rich **musical heritage** too. The Moken do not use any instruments as such, making do with found objects for percussion; the Urak Lawoy, on the other hand, due to their closer proximity to the Thai and Malay cultures, are excellent violin- and drum-players. During community entertainments, such as the Urak Lawoy's twice-yearly full-moon **festivals** on Ko Lanta (see p.694), the male musicians form a semicircle around the old women, who dance and sing about the sea, the jungle and their families.

Building a new boat is the ultimate expression of what it is to be a *chao ley*, and tradition holds that every newly married couple has a *kabang* built for them. But the complex art of constructing a seaworthy home from a single tree trunk, and the way of life it represents, is disappearing. In Thailand, where **assimilation** is actively promoted by the government, the truly nomadic flotillas have become increasingly marginalized, and the number of undeveloped islands they can visit unhindered gets smaller year by year. The 2004 tsunami further threatened their cultural integrity: when the waves destroyed the Moken's boats and homes on Ko Surin, they were obliged to take refuge on the mainland, where some were encouraged by missionaries to convert from their animist religion. Though the Moken have since returned to the Surin islands, inappropriate donations and the merging of two villages have exacerbated family rivalries and caused divisions that may prove lethal to their traditional way of life.

Surin Nua and Surin Tai

The most easily explored of the reefs are those off the two main islands in the group, Ko Surin Nua (north) and Ko Surin Tai (south), which are separated only by a narrow channel. **Surin Nua**, slightly the larger at about 5km across, holds the national park headquarters, visitor centre and park accommodation.

Across the channel, **Surin Tai** is the long-established home of a community of **Moken** *chao ley*, who are no longer allowed to fish in national park waters but make their living mostly as longtail boatmen for snorkellers staying on Surin Nua. Their recent history has been an unhappy one: not only were their settlements destroyed in the 2004 tsunami, but the aid and outside intervention that followed has changed the community forever, amalgamating two villages, building new homes too close together and introducing various modern-day vices; on top of that, tourist numbers are down since the coral bleaching in 2010. In **Ao Bon** village, Bangkok's Chulalongkorn University has recently built a visitor centre with English display boards, where you can hire a Moken guide to lead you on a nature trail around the village; don't go just in your swimwear, but take a sarong for modesty's sake. You can also make a positive contribution by buying one of the woven pandanus-leaf souvenirs or wooden model boats the villagers make; donations of toothpaste and clothes would also be appreciated. One of the Moken traditions that does persist is the new year celebration that's held every April, during Songkhran, when *chao ley* from nearby islands (including those in Burmese waters) congregate here and, among other rites, release several hundred turtles into the sea, a symbol of longevity.

ARRIVAL AND DEPARTURE   KO SURIN

By boat There are no public boats to Ko Surin, but if you want to stay on the islands, it's perfectly possible to come over on one of the tour boats from Khuraburi and return on another day.

GETTING AROUND

By longtail Once on the islands, there's an efficient system of boat hire: Moken longtails depart twice a day from the national park campsites to the different reefs and Ao Bon village and charge B100/person for about two hours (snorkel sets cost B80/day). You can also charter your own longtail for B2500/day.

TOURS

Most visitors either do **snorkelling day-trips** to the islands from Khuraburi or opt for **dive trips** or live-aboards out of Ko Ra, Ko Phra Thong, Khao Lak, Phuket, Ranong, Ko Chang or Ko Phayam. For snorkellers, there are also day-trips from Ko Ra and Ko Phra Thong, and two-day trips run by *Mr Gao* on Ko Phayam. During the season, speedboat snorkelling trips to Ko Surin depart from Khuraburi pier, 7.5km northwest of Khuraburi town, most days; big, slow, wooden boats (2–3hr; B1300 return) only run at weekends and on national holidays for large groups of Thai tourists.

Andaman Discoveries Khuraburi (see p.606). Four-day trips, with two nights on Ko Surin, focusing on learning about Moken life, including guided forest, village and snorkelling tours and cooking classes (B14,500).
Blue Guru Dive Centre Ko Phra Thong (see p.606). Upmarket day-trips on a dive cruiser or speedboat, including "gourmet lunch", for snorkelling (from B3500) or diving (two dives; from B4900); transfers from Khuraburi hotels included. Also offers multi-day trips to Surin; and transfers from Khao Lak.
Boon Piya Resort Khuraburi (see p.606). Sells boat tickets and packages, including discounts on national park bungalows on weekdays.
Tom & Am Tour Office on the west side of the main road in Khuraburi town centre, but they also maintain a desk in the bus station in high season ✆086 272 0588, ✉tom_am01@yahoo.co.th. Speedboats to Ko Surin (1hr 15min–2hr), departing the pier at 8.30am, leaving the islands at about 2pm; B1600 including transfers. They also rent tents (B50–100/day), bedding sets (B20/day), snorkel sets (B50/day) and fins (B50/day) for Ko Surin (all cheaper than national park prices).

ACCOMMODATION

All island accommodation is on Surin Nua and is provided by the national park. Both campsites have bathrooms, lockers (B100/day) and dining rooms where meals are served at fixed times three times a day (B80–220); many people take their own supplies from Khuraburi instead. Bungalows need to be booked in advance either through the national parks websites (Ⓦdnp.go.th or Ⓦthaiforestbooking.com) or at the Khuraburi pier office (✆076 472145–6), but tents should be available on spec except during public holidays and long weekends.

Ao Chong Khad On the beach here, near the park headquarters and pier, you have the choice between en-suite national park bungalows (for 2 people) and either renting a national park tent (B300–450/day) or pitching your own (available for rent in Khuraburi) for B80/day; bedding sets cost B60/day. Bungalow B2000
Ao Mai Ngam Home to the nicer campsite, with tents (B300–450/day) and pitches (B80/day) but no bungalows, and reached via a 2km trail from headquarters or by longtail.

Khao Sok National Park

☎ 077 395154, ⓦ dnp.go.th • B200, payable at the checkpoint at headquarters and valid for 24hr; you'll have to pay again at Cheow Lan Lake if you arrive more than 24hr later

Most of the Andaman coast's highlights are, unsurprisingly, along the shoreline, but the stunning jungle-clad karsts of **KHAO SOK NATIONAL PARK** are well worth heading inland for. Located about halfway between the southern peninsula's two coasts and easily accessible from Khao Lak, Phuket and Surat Thani, the park has become a popular stop on the travellers' route, offering a number of easy trails, a bit of amateur spelunking and some scenic rafthouse accommodation on Cheow Lan Lake. Much of the park, which protects the watershed of the Sok River and rises to a peak of nearly

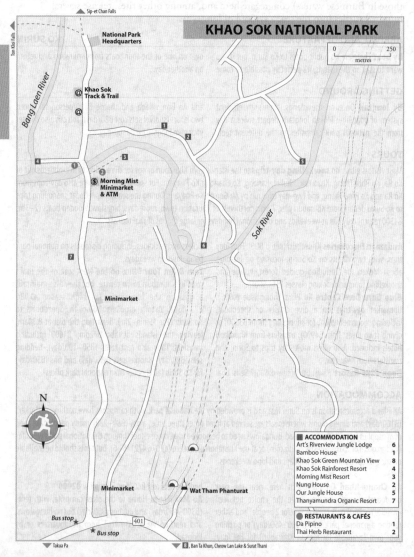

KHAO SOK NATIONAL PARK

National Park Headquarters

Khao Sok Track & Trail

Morning Mist Minimarket & ATM

Minimarket

Minimarket

Wat Tham Phanturat

Bus stop

Bus stop

Takua Pa

Ban Ta Khun, Cheow Lan Lake & Surat Thani

0 — 250 metres

■ ACCOMMODATION	
Art's Riverview Jungle Lodge	6
Bamboo House	1
Khao Sok Green Mountain View	8
Khao Sok Rainforest Resort	4
Morning Mist Resort	3
Nung House	2
Our Jungle House	5
Thanyamundra Organic Resort	7

● RESTAURANTS & CAFÉS	
Da Pipino	1
Thai Herb Restaurant	2

GUIDED TREKS AND TOURS OF KHAO SOK

PARK TREKS AND NIGHT SAFARIS

The vast majority of visitors choose to join a **guided trek** at some point during their stay in the park. Though the trails are waymarked and easy to navigate alone, the guided experience alerts you to details you'd certainly miss on your own – the claw marks left by a sun-bear scaling a tree in search of honey, for example, or the medicinal plants used for malarial fevers and stomach upsets – and is both fun and inexpensive; prices are fixed but exclude the national park entrance fee.

The usual **day trek** (B700–900) goes to Ton Kloi waterfall, and from about December to March there's also a special route that takes in the blooming of the world's second-biggest flower, the **rafflesia kerrii meier**, a rather unprepossessing brown, cabbage-like plant whose enormous russet-coloured petals unfurl to a diameter of up to 80cm; it's also known as "stinking corpse lily" because it gives off a stink like rotting flesh.

After-dinner **night safaris** along the main park trails (B600–800 for 2–4hr) are also popular, not least because they're good for spotting civets, mouse deer and slow loris and, if you're exceptionally lucky, elephants and clouded leopards as well – more likely on darker nights away from the full moon.

You get to stay out in the jungle on the **overnight camping trips** (about B2300), usually around Tan Sawan falls.

Reputable and long-serving **guides** include those booked through *Bamboo House*, *Nung House* and *Khao Sok Rainforest Resort* and at Khao Sok Track & Trail (☎081 958 0629, ⓦkhaosoktrackandtrail.info).

Any guesthouse can also arrange **elephant-rides** (B800–900) and fix you up with equipment and transfers for **tubing** and **canoeing** trips along the Sok River (from B300/B600).

CHEOW LAN LAKE TOURS

The Australian–Thai-run Limestone Lake Rainforest Tours (☎087 268 8017, ⓦlimestonelaketours .com) offers a big range of **lake-based tours**, including a two-hour trip (B1800/boat) and a full-day trip with optional overnight in a rafthouse (from B2500/3700 per person for up to three people, including park entry fee, or cheaper with larger groups).

Khao Sok guesthouses charge B1500 for a day-trip to the lake and around B2500 for two-day, one-night trips. It's also possible to simply turn up at the dam and hire a boat for around B2000.

1000m, is carpeted in impenetrable rainforest, home to gaurs, leopard cats and tigers among others – and up to 155 species of bird. The limestone crags that dominate almost every vista both on and away from the lake are breathtaking, never more so than in the early morning: waking up to the sound of hooting gibbons and the sight of thick white mist curling around the karst formations is an experience not quickly forgotten.

The park has two centres: the **tourist village** that has grown up around the park headquarters and trailheads, which offers all essential services, including an **ATM** at Morning Mist Minimarket and currency exchange and overseas phone services at Khao Sok Track & Trail; and the dam, 65km further east, at the head of **Cheow Lan Lake**. Most visitors stay in the tourist village and organize their lake trips from there, but it's also feasible to do one or more nights at the lake first. Take plenty of water when hiking as Khao Sok is notoriously humid.

The trails

Seven of the park's nine attractions (waterfalls, pools, gorges and viewpoints) branch off the clearly signed main **trail** that runs west of the park headquarters and visitor centre, along the Sok River. The first 3.5km constitute the **interpretative trail** described in *Waterfalls and Gibbon Calls* (see p.613), an unexceptional ninety-minute one-way trail along a broad, road-like track. Most people continue along the river to **Ton Kloi waterfall**, 7km from headquarters (allow 3hr each way), which flows year-round and tumbles into a pool that's good for swimming. En route, signs point to **Bang Liap Nam waterfall** (4.5km from headquarters), which is a straightforward hike; and **Tan Sawan waterfall** (6km from headquarters), which involves wading along a river bed for the final kilometre and should not be attempted during the rainy season. The trail to the rather spectacular eleven-tiered **Sip-et Chan waterfall**, which shoots off north from the park headquarters and follows the course of the Bang Laen River, is no longer much used and can be quite indistinct. Though the falls are only 4km from headquarters, there's a fair bit of climbing on the way, plus half a dozen river crossings, so you should allow three hours each way.

Cheow Lan Lake

65km from national park headquarters

Dubbed Thailand's Guilin because of its photogenic karst islands, forested inlets and mist-clad mountains encircling jade-coloured waters, the vast 28km-long **Cheow Lan Lake** (also known as **Ratchaprapa Dam** reservoir) is Khao Sok's most famous feature and the most popular destination for guided tours. It was created in the 1980s when the Khlong Saeng River was dammed to power a new hydroelectricity plant, and its forested shores and hundred-plus islands now harbour abundant bird life, as well as some primates, most easily spotted in the very early morning. Tours generally combine a trip on the lake with a wade through the nearby flooded cave system and a night on a floating rafthouse. The lake can only be explored by longtail boat tour, arranged either from Khao Sok or from Ratchaprapa Dam.

For many people, the highlight of their lake excursion is the adventurous three-hour trek to and through the 800m-long horseshoe-shaped **Nam Talu cave**, a five-minute boat ride from the national park rafthouses, or about an hour's boat ride from the dam. The **trek** is not for everyone, however, as the cave section entails an hour-long wade through the river that hollowed out this tunnel: it's slippery underfoot and pitch black and there will be at least one 20m section where you have to swim. When the river level is high there will be longer swims. Never attempt the cave without an authorized park guide and heed any closure signs posted because of high water levels and strong currents; in October 2007 a flash flood caused nine fatalities here and the park authorities are now stricter. Wear sandals with decent grip and request (or take) your own torch.

Part of the appeal of a night in a rafthouse on Cheow Lan Lake is the **dawn safari** the next morning, when you've a good chance of seeing langurs, macaques and gibbons on the lakeshore; some tours include this option, or you can usually borrow a kayak from your accommodation and paddle around the shore yourself.

ARRIVAL AND DEPARTURE — KHAO SOK NATIONAL PARK

Khao Sok National Park headquarters, its tourist village and Cheow Lan Lake are all north off Highway 401, which is served by frequent **buses**: all services between the junction town of **Takua Pa**, 40km south of Khuraburi, and Surat Thani come this way, including some Surat Thani services to and from Khao Lak and Phuket. Coming from Bangkok, Hua Hin or Chumphon, take a Surat Thani-bound bus as far as the Highway 401 junction, about 20km before Surat Thani, and change onto one for Takua Pa.

PARK HEADQUARTERS

The access road to the tourist village and trailheads is at kilometre-stone 109 on Highway 401, where guesthouse staff meet bus passengers and offer free lifts to their accommodation, the furthest of which is about 3km from the main road.

Khao Sok Track & Trail in the tourist village (☎ 081 958 0629, ⓦ khaosoktrackandtrail.info) sells bus (including a VIP bus to Bangkok), boat, plane and train tickets, as well as tickets for a/c minibuses to destinations that include Krabi (2hr), Surat Thani's Talat Kaset II via the train station at Phunphin (1hr 45min), Ko Samui (3hr) and Trang (4hr 30min).

Bus destinations: Bangkok (1 daily; 11hr); Khao Lak (9 daily; 1hr 30min); Surat Thani (every 90min; 2hr); Takua Pa (every 90min; 50min).

CHEOW LAN LAKE

Access to the lake is via the town of **Ban Ta Khun**, 50km east of Khao Sok on Route 401, from where it's 12km north to the dam. Many travellers book their tour of the lake from their Khao Sok accommodation, in which case all transport is included, but if coming from Surat Thani or Phang Nga, you could do the lake first. There's a regular **minibus service** from Talat Kaset II in Surat Thani, via Phunphin train station, to Cheow Lan Lake (about every 2hr; 1hr), or you could take a Surat Thani–Takua Pa bus, alight at Ban Ta Khun and get a motorbike taxi to the dam.

INFORMATION

Map The checkpoint office at headquarters supplies a small sketch map of the park and trails.

Guidebooks The best introduction to Khao Sok is the guidebook *Waterfalls and Gibbon Calls* by Thom Henley (see p.789), which is available at some Khao Sok minimarkets and bungalows.

ACCOMMODATION

PARK HEADQUARTERS

The bulk of the budget accommodation is scenically sited beneath the karsts near the park headquarters, but despite the edge-of-the rainforest location, it can get noisy of an evening, with the sound systems at some backpacker bars pitched against the chattering of the cicadas. Some guesthouses (not listed here) can make life difficult for guests who choose not to book park trips through them. "Treehouses" round here means bungalows built on very tall stilts among the trees, rather than actually in the trees.

★ **Art's Riverview Jungle Lodge** ✆086 479 3234 or ✆087 885 6185. Popular place nicely located away from the main fray next to a good swimming hole, surrounded by jungle and enjoying pretty river views from its terrace restaurant (though the food's no great shakes). The cheaper bungalows are spacious, tastefully designed wooden affairs, with shutters and a deck, while the deluxe versions are bigger still and attractively furnished, some with red-brick outdoor bathrooms and waterfall-style showers; there are also treehouse-style bungalows and family cottages. All rooms have fans and mosquito nets. **B650**

Bamboo House ✆081 787 7484, ⊕krabidir.com /bamboohouse/index.htm. Set in a grassy orchard, this was one of the first guesthouses in the park and is run by welcoming members of the park warden's family. The simple, stilted, en-suite, wooden huts with mosquito nets here are the cheapest in this part of the park and there are also pebble-dashed concrete versions, a couple of treehouse-style bungalows and large, wooden affairs with hot showers and balconies on stilts right over the river (B800). **B200**

Khao Sok Green Mountain View 1500m north up a mostly paved road from Highway 401, just east of the km 106 marker ✆087 263 2481, ⊕khaosok -greenmountainview.com. In a very quiet spot far from almost everyone else, this is a great budget option if you want a remote location. The seven good-quality bamboo and wood bungalows of varying sizes are all en suite and have some nice touches, with pretty open-roofed bath-rooms, fans, mosquito nets, decks and hammocks. They sit on the edge of a rubber plantation on the other side of the karsts from the main accommodation area. There's free transport to the park village or you can walk to *Our Jungle House* across the river in 15min and on to the park headquarters in another 25. **B300**

Khao Sok Rainforest Resort ✆077 395135, ⊕khaosokrainforest.com. This welcoming place has some spectacularly sited "mountain view" bungalows – set high on a jungle slope and affording unsurpassed karst views – plus a/c treehouses and fan or a/c riverside bungalows. The a/c options have hot showers, TVs and mini-bars, and include breakfast in the price. Interiors are decent enough though lacking style. Fan **B500**, a/c **B1650**

★ **Morning Mist Resort** ✆089 971 8794, ⊕khaosok morningmistresort.com. Built within a profuse riverside garden that's filled with carefully tended tropical blooms and a big herb garden that supplies the excellent restaurant, this well-run place offers large, immaculate rooms in variously styled wooden and concrete bungalows, all with hot water and either river, mountain or garden view. It's nicely set up for families, with some rooms sleeping up to four, plus lots of space for kids to play in and a small swimming pool. Good rates for singles. **B550**

Nung House ✆077 395147, ⊕nunghouse.com. Friendly place run by the park warden's son and his family, with eighteen very good huts set around an attractive grassy garden full of rambutan trees. Choose between simple but sturdy bamboo and wood constructions with en-suite facilities, brick and concrete bungalows, and treehouses; some have hot showers and large verandas. **B300**

Our Jungle House ✆081 417 0546, ⊕khaosok accommodation.com. Peaceful, riverside option, a 20min walk from park headquarters, secluded in lush rainforest where you might spot hornbills and several species of monkey. Choose between airy, well-designed, wood and bamboo bungalows and treehouses; all have fans and mosquito nets and most are on the river bank, which has a small beach. Free internet access and wi-fi. Bungalows **B800**, treehouses **B1300**

Thanyamundra Organic Resort ✆077 336000, ⊕thanyamundra.com. Quiet and charming luxury

7

retreat set amid extensive sloping lawns, with a lovely 50m pool and spectacular views over its own organic farm and rice paddies to the karst mountains. Across two buildings, arranged in southern Thai-style compounds, there are just nine rooms and suites, constructed mostly of golden teak wood, with Chinese antique furniture, brass rain showers, free wi-fi, iPod docks and espresso machines. Full-service spa planned. B6290

CHEOW LAN LAKE
On overnight tours to the lake (see p.611), accommodation is either in tents in the jungle or at rafthouses on the lake.

There are both private and national park rafthouses moored at various scenic spots around the lake shore, mostly around an hour's boat ride from the dam. All rafthouse huts are rudimentary bamboo structures with nets and mattresses, offering fabulous lake views from your pillow. If you've arranged your own boat transport, you can fix accommodation at any of the lake's rafthouses for B600 per person including three meals. Jungle Yoga runs yoga, meditation and massage retreats at the remote *Praiwan* rafthouses from December to April (ⓦjungleyoga.com).

EATING AND DRINKING

In the tourist village near park headquarters, there are just a couple of places that might tempt you away from your guesthouse restaurant.

PARK HEADQUARTERS
Da Pipino Homely, rustic, not to say scruffy, Italian restaurant, strewn with lovely plants in a scenic spot by the river. The menu runs to seafood antipasti, decent fettuccine bolognese (B195), a few Italian main courses and a wide range of tasty handmade pizzas. Daily noon–10pm.

Thai Herb Restaurant Morning Mist Resort. Exceptionally tasty and inventive spicy *yam* salads (B70) and other Thai classics, plus a wide choice for vegetarians and breakfasting Westerners; staff grow much of their own produce. Also does Thai desserts and lassis, shakes and herb juices such as roselle. Daily 8am–9pm.

Khao Lak

Handily located just an hour north of Phuket International Airport, and some 30km south of Takua Pa, **KHAO LAK** has established itself as a thriving, mid-market beach resort with plentiful opportunities for diving and snorkelling, easy access to the supreme national park reefs of Ko Similan, and a style that is determinedly unseedy. It lacks sophistication, and is mostly a bit pricey for backpackers, but is ideal for families and extremely popular with northern European tourists. High season here runs from November to April, when the weather and the swimming are at their best and the Similan Islands are open to the public; during the rest of the year, Khao Lak quietens down a lot – and becomes much cheaper too.

The area usually referred to as Khao Lak is in fact a string of beaches west off Highway 4. **Khao Lak** proper is the southernmost and least developed, 5km from the most commercial part of the resort, **Nang Thong** (aka Bang La On), which throngs with shops, restaurants, dive centres and countless places to stay, both on the beachfront and inland from Highway 4. North again about 3km (5min by taxi or a 45min walk up the beach) is lower-key, slightly more youthful **Bang Niang**, a lovely long stretch of golden sand that's backed by a developing tourist village whose network of sois is away from the highway and feels more enticing than its neighbour. Removed from all this commerce, **Laem Pakarang**, 12km further up the coast, a headland and popular sunset-watching spot that gives onto 11km Hat Pakweeb (Hat Bang Sak), is where you find the area's most exclusive accommodation.

There is, thankfully, little obvious evidence these days of the area's devastating experience during the December 2004 **tsunami**, when the undersea earthquake off Sumatra sent a series of murderous waves on to Khao Lak's shores (and the rest of the Andaman coast), vaporizing almost every shorefront home and hotel here and killing thousands. Nang Thong quickly became the centre of a huge reconstruction effort, with thousands of volunteers arriving to help, and rebuilding was mostly

▲ **1** Laem Pakarang, Bang Sak, Ban Nam Khem, Takua Pa & Surat Thani

KHAO LAK, NANG THONG & BANG NIANG

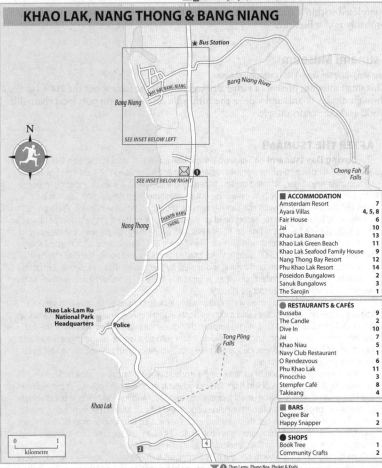

★ Bus Station

Bang Niang

CHAI HAT BANG NIANG

Bang Niang River

N

SEE INSET BELOW LEFT

✉ ❶

SEE INSET BELOW RIGHT

THANON NANG THONG

Nang Thong

Chong Fah Falls

Khao Lak-Lam Ru National Park Headquarters

Police

Tong Pling Falls

Khao Lak

0	1
kilometre	

② ④

▼ **1** Thap Lamu, Phang Nga, Phuket & Krabi

■ ACCOMMODATION

Amsterdam Resort	7
Ayara Villas	4, 5, 8
Fair House	6
Jai	10
Khao Lak Banana	13
Khao Lak Green Beach	11
Khao Lak Seafood Family House	9
Nang Thong Bay Resort	12
Phu Khao Lak Resort	14
Poseidon Bungalows	2
Sanuk Bungalows	3
The Sarojin	1

● RESTAURANTS & CAFÉS

Bussaba	9
The Candle	2
Dive In	10
Jai	7
Khao Niau	5
Navy Club Restaurant	1
O Rendezvous	6
Phu Khao Lak	11
Pinocchio	3
Stempfer Café	8
Takieang	4

■ BARS

Degree Bar	1
Happy Snapper	2

● SHOPS

Book Tree	1
Community Crafts	2

7

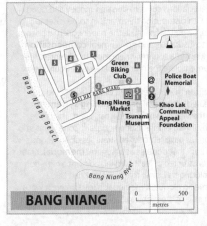

Green Biking Club

CHAI HAT BANG NIANG

Bang Niang Market

Tsunami Museum

@

Police Boat Memorial

Khao Lak Community Appeal Foundation

Bang Niang Beach

Bang Niang River

0	500
metres	

BANG NIANG

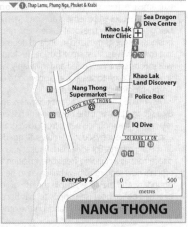

Sea Dragon Dive Centre

Khao Lak Inter Clinic

Khao Lak Land Discovery

Nang Thong Supermarket

THANON NANG THONG

Police Box

@

IQ Dive

SOI BANG LA ON

Everyday 2

0	500
metres	

NANG THONG

completed within a couple of years, though for many survivors recovery will probably take a lifetime.

Tsunami Museum

Bang Niang • Daily 9am–7pm • B100 • ⓦ tsunamimuseum.net

This small museum presents a rather dry summary of the facts about the 2004 tsunami, through display boards and videos; the admission fee helps to support local charitable work, as do the crafts on sale.

AFTER THE TSUNAMI

The **Boxing Day tsunami** hit Thailand's Andaman coast just after 9.30am on December 26 2004. The first place to suffer significant damage was Phuket, and the next two hours saw village after resort get battered or decimated by the towering waves thundering in from the Sumatra fault line, 1000km away. The entire coastline from Ranong to Satun was affected, but not all of it with the same intensity: the worst-hit province was Phang Nga, where 4200 people were recorded dead or missing, many of them in the resort of Khao Lak; over 2000 suffered a similar fate on Ko Phi Phi; and more than 900 died on the beaches of Phuket, especially on Patong and Kamala. There were 8212 fatalities in all, a third of them holidaymakers. Another 6000 people were made homeless and some 150,000 lost their jobs, mostly in the tourism and fishing industries. By the end of that day, nearly a quarter of a million people in a dozen countries around the Indian Ocean had lost their lives in the worst natural disaster in recorded history.

Many homes, shops and hotels were quite swiftly rebuilt, but the emotional and social **legacy** of the tsunami endures and most residents along the Andaman coast have a story of terror and bereavement to tell. It's no surprise that many survivors are now afraid of the sea: fearing ghosts, some longtail boatmen won't motor solo past where villages once stood, and hundreds of hotel staff have since sought new jobs in the northern city of Chiang Mai, as far from the sea as they could go.

Immediately after the tsunami, many were surprised when then prime minister Thaksin Shinawatra declined offers of **aid** from foreign governments. But help poured in instead from the Thai government and from royal foundations and local and foreign NGOs and individuals. Of the many **projects** established to help support and rebuild affected communities, the majority have now completed their task; others have evolved into longer-term NGO ventures, including an English-teaching programme in Khao Lak (see p.69), and the community-based tourism company Andaman Discoveries in Khuraburi (see p.606).

Generosity and altruism were not the only responses to the disaster, however. Almost every tsunami-affected community talks of **dishonourable practice** and **corruption**, experiences which have caused bitterness and rifts. Many allegations concern donated money and goods being held back by the local leaders charged with distributing them, and in some cases big business interests muscled in on land deemed "ownerless" because the paperwork had been lost to the waves. Most small businesses had no insurance, and government **compensation** was inconsistently awarded and invariably lacking. In a country where most family enterprises scrape by season to season, it's sobering to contemplate the number of tsunami victims who simply picked up and started over.

Determined not to be caught unawares again, in the unlikely event of Thailand being struck by a second tsunami, the government has created a **tsunami early-warning system** that relays public announcements from towers all the way down the Andaman coast. They have also mapped out evacuation routes, flagged by innumerable "Tsunami Hazard Zone" signs in all the big resorts. For their part, Phuket authorities have remodelled stretches of Ao Patong's beachfront as a building-free zone, creating a park that doubles as a tsunami **memorial**. Krabi officials now require all new buildings to be constructed at least 30m inland from a high-tide boundary, and they even forbid the use of sunloungers below that point. In Khao Lak, a beached police boat (see opposite) has become an eloquent memorial: it rests where it was hurtled by the wave, 2km inland, on the other side of the highway.

Police Boat Memorial

Bang Niang

Inland from the highway – and accessible from it across a field and a bridge – a **beached police boat** has become a memorial to the extraordinary power of the tsunami waves. It was propelled up here, 2km inland, while patrolling the waters in front of *La Flora* resort, where Princess Ubolrat and her children, one of whom perished in the disaster, were staying.

Ban Nam Khem Memorial

13km north of Laem Pakarang up Highway 4, then left for a signposted 3km

The main local tsunami memorial is on the beach at **Ban Nam Khem**, the worst-hit village in Thailand, where half of the four thousand inhabitants died in the waves, as described in Erich Krauss' *Wave of Destruction* (see p.786). Built by the Thai army, it's an evocative installation: you walk down a path between a curling, 4m-high, concrete "wave" and a grassy bank, representing the land, on which plaques commemorate individual victims. Through a window in the concrete wave, a fishing boat looms over you – this "miracle boat" was swept inland but stopped just short of devastating a house and its occupants.

While you're out here, it's worth popping in on the **Saori weaving factory and shop** (not Sun), on the left about 1km further up Highway 4 from the Ban Nam Khem turn-off, towards the northern end of Ban Bang Muang village. It's a regeneration and occupational therapy project, where you can watch the women weaving and buy some lovely scarves.

ARRIVAL AND DEPARTURE   KHAO LAK

Boats to the Similans depart from the pier at Thap Lamu, which is 6km south of Nang Thong, then 5km west off Highway 4 (see p.622).

By plane Khao Lak is just 70km north of Phuket airport (1hr; B1700–2200 by taxi; see p.625).

By bus and minibus All buses running from Phuket to Takua Pa and Ranong (and vice versa) pass through Khao Lak and can drop you anywhere along Highway 4; coming from Krabi or Phang Nga you'll generally need to change buses in Khokkloi, from Khao Sok, in Takua Pa. On departure, you can flag down most buses on the main road, but the Bangkok services use a bus station at the far north end of Bang Niang. There are also a/c tourist minibuses that

run at least daily to Surat Thani (via Khokkloi, not Khao Sok; 4hr), Krabi/Ao Nang (3hr/3hr 30min) and Trang (change in Krabi; 5hr 30min). Bus and a/c minibus tickets can be booked through, for example, Khao Lak Land Discovery in Nang Thong (☎076 485411, ⊕khaolaklanddiscovery.com), who also offer transfers to and from Phuket Airport (B600/person or B1500/minibus).

Destinations: Bangkok (3 daily; 12hr); Phuket (20 daily; 2hr 30min); Ranong (8 daily; 2hr 30min–3hr); Takua Pa (18 daily; 30min).

GETTING AROUND

By songthaew In the Khao Lak area, a few public songthaews shuttle between Nang Thong and Bang Niang (where they have a base in front of the market), charging B10–20 but mostly they act as private taxis instead and charge B100 or more.

Motorbike and car rental Many hotels can rent motorbikes, and rental cars are available through tour operators; Budget also has an agent on the soi down to *Nang Thong Resort* (☎076 443454, ⊕budget.co.th).

ACCOMMODATION

LAEM PAKARANG

★ **The Sarojin** 12km north of Khao Lak ☎076 427905, ⊕thesarojin.com. With a staff-to-guest ratio of two to one and a style and attitude that exudes understated, unpretentious class, this is the top place to stay around Khao Lak. The 56 sleek, tastefully simple rooms are discreetly sited around the wide beachfront garden and

stunning square turquoise swimming pool. It's an obvious honeymoon choice, with a policy of no under-10s, a range of excursions designed for two, and private candlelit tables for dinner on the beach or at a nearby waterfall. There are complimentary non-motorized watersports and mountain bikes, free wi-fi and a spa. All-day breakfast with sparkling wine included. Special promotions often available. B13,500

BANG NIANG

Amsterdam Resort Soi 3 ☎081 857 5881, Ⓦamsterdamresortkhaolak.com. Just 200m inland from the beach, this helpful Dutch-run little complex offers some of the cheapest accommodation in Bang Niang and serves good food. The rooms and red-brick bungalows of varying size have either fans or a/c; most have hot water. Also has internet and free wi-fi, cycle and motorbike rental and a tour desk. Fan B600, a/c B900

Ayara Villas ☎076 486478–9, Ⓦayara-villas.com. An attractive upper-mid-range option, spread over three different compounds with two swimming pools. At the top end are beachfront villas right on the sand; many others are terraced bungalows just a few metres from the sea, and the rest are in a three-storey building, with ground-floor rooms enjoying direct pool access. Interiors are a/c and nicely furnished with dark wood in contemporary style and all have kitchenettes. Breakfast included. B4500

Fair House ☎089 473 7985. Currently one of the cheapest places to stay in Bang Niang, with its handful of large, neat, fan-cooled concrete bungalows and rooms with fridges and hot showers, widely spaced around a pretty little garden set back about 50m from the highway, about 1km walk from the beach. B600

Sanuk Bungalows ☎081 979 0308, Ⓦsanukresort .com. Dinky little Swiss-managed group of five comfortable and spacious brick bungalows in a small garden with a heart-shaped whirlpool, just 100m from the beach. Bungalows come with a/c, hot showers, fridges, kitchenettes and wi-fi. B1000

NANG THONG

Jai ☎076 485390, ✉jai_bungalow@hotmail.com. A busy, family-run place that offers some of the cheapest accommodation in Khao Lak. The good-quality, decent-sized, en-suite concrete bungalows are set around a lawn dotted with trees behind the popular restaurant, quite close to the highway and about 600m from the beach; a/c options have hot showers and fridges. Fan B400, a/c B600

Khao Lak Banana Soi Bang La On ☎076 485889, Ⓦkhaolakbanana.com. Dozens of thoughtfully designed fan and a/c bungalows packed into a garden of banana trees and tropical flowers. All have a safety box, hot shower, wi-fi and fridge and there's a tiny swimming pool. Fan B700, a/c B900

★**Khao Lak Green Beach** ☎076 485845, Ⓦgreenbeach.de. The attractive design and shorefront location of the bungalows here make this a good-value option, and the staff are great too. Arrayed around a pond, the cream-painted chalet-style bungalows have a/c, hot showers, polished wood floors, pretty furnishings and nice bathrooms and most have a fridge. Price mainly depends on location: some are right on the shore and none is more than a few metres away. Discounts for singles. B1400

DIVING AND SNORKELLING AROUND KHAO LAK

Khao Lak is the closest and most convenient departure point for **diving and snorkelling trips** to the awesome national park islands of **Ko Similan** (see p.620), which can be reached in three to four hours on a live-aboard or other large boat or in two hours in a much less comfortable speedboat. The islands are currently only open from approximately November to April and all divers have to pay a one-off national park fee of B400 plus a B200-a-day diving fee, usually on top of dive-trip prices. **Local Khao Lak dives** are generally possible year-round, especially the highly rated **wreck** of a tin-mining boat near Bang Sak, which is especially rich in marine life such as ghost pipefish, moray eels, scorpion fish, nudibranchs and yellow-tail barracuda. All Khao Lak dive shops also teach PADI **dive courses**, with the last two days of the Openwater course often done on location in the Similans; for advice on choosing a dive shop see "Basics" (see p.52).

IQ Dive Nang Thong, opposite McDonald's ☎076 485614, Ⓦiq-dive.com. Swiss–Thai-run PADI Five-Star Centre that specializes in one-day dive trips to the Similans, on a big dive boat (B4700 plus equipment; B2800 for snorkellers). Their Openwater courses cost B17,000 with two days spent diving the Similans.

Sea Dragon Dive Center Nang Thong ☎076 485420, Ⓦseadragondivecenter.com. Highly recommended PADI Five-Star Instructor Development Centre which has three live-aboard boats – including budget and deluxe options – running frequent three-day trips to the Similans and Ko Bon (from B11,900 including equipment), and four-day trips to the Similans, Surin islands, Ko Bon, Ko Tachai and Richelieu Rock (from B17,900). Snorkellers get about one-third off. Also offers local wreck and other dives (starting from B1000, not including equipment) for a two-tank dive) and PADI dive courses: the four-day Openwater is B9800, or B15,900 (plus B1200 national park fees) with two day-trips diving the Similans.

Similan Tour At Poseidon Bungalows, 7km south of central Nang Thong, in Khao Lak ☎076 443258, Ⓦsimilantour.com. Highly recommended three-day live-aboard snorkelling trips to the Similans (B8200). Current departures are twice weekly on Tuesdays and Fridays, from roughly the end of October to May.

KHAO LAK DAY-TRIPS AND OTHER ACTIVITIES

Aside from diving and snorkelling trips (see opposite), there are several other attractions within day-tripping distance of Khao Lak, including a number of local **waterfalls**. Of these, Sai Rung (Rainbow Falls), about 16km north of Nang Thong in Bang Sak, is the most satisfying. Others include Tong Pling, across from the *Merlin* resort in Khao Lak; Nam Tok Lumphi, about 20km south of Khao Lak; and Chong Fah Falls, located less than 5km east of Bang Niang, but subject to a B100 entry fee because it's part of Khao Lak–Lam Ru National Park (@dnp.go.th). The national park's headquarters is on the headland between Nang Thong and Khao Lak beaches, and about 1km south of it, you can easily walk down to a quiet, pretty sandy cove – look for a sign saying "small sandy beach" on the west side of the main road, opposite a layby.

Everyday 2 Restaurant South end of Nang Thong @085 299 0410. Morning Thai cooking courses for B1200, including pick-ups.

The Green Biking Club Bang Niang @076 443211, @greenbikingclub.com. Runs interesting guided mountain-bike trips around rural and coastal Khao Lak (from B1850 for half a day).

Khao Lak Land Discovery Nang Thong @076 485411, @khaolaklanddiscovery.com. One of the best and most reputable, though not the cheapest, local tour operators, whose day-trips include elephant-riding (from B1600), kayaking around Ao Phang Nga (B3200) and trekking, canoeing and elephant-riding in Khao Sok National Park (B2800).

The Yoga Studio Khao Lak Community Appeal Foundation, Bang Niang @089 710 5770, @yoga khaolak.com. High-season yoga classes (B500 for one class) – see the website for the schedule.

Khao Lak Seafood Family House Soi Noen Thong @076 485318, @khaolakseafood.com. The large, good-quality bungalows here are set well back from the road in a garden behind the eponymous restaurant. The fan ones are especially good value for Khao Lak: roomy and nicely designed with good, hot-water bathrooms; a/c rooms in a couple of two-storey blocks are also available. It's a family business and very popular with returning guests and long stayers. Wi-fi available. Fan B600, a/c B1200

Nang Thong Bay Resort @076 485088–9, @nangthong.com. Well priced considering its on-the-beach location, this popular, long-established place offers smartly maintained a/c bungalows that are well spaced around the shorefront garden and mostly enjoy sea views, plus some hotel-style rooms. There's a sea-view swimming pool and restaurant as well. B2000

★ **Phu Khao Lak Resort** @076 485141, @phukhaolak.com. There is a luxurious amount of space at this well-run place, where the thirty large, spotlessly clean bungalows sit prettily amid a grassy park-style

coconut plantation. Fan rooms have tiled floors and most have hot-water bathrooms; a/c ones have picture windows and quite stylish interiors. There's a swimming pool, good restaurant and wi-fi in the lounge-library. About 500m walk from the beach. Fan B500, a/c B1500

KHAO LAK

Poseidon Bungalows @076 443258, @similantour .com. Seven kilometres south of central Nang Thong, surrounded by rubber plantations and set above a sandy shore of wave-smoothed rocks just north of the Thai navy's private beach, this Swedish–Thai-run guesthouse is both a quiet place to hang out for a few days and a long-established organizer of snorkelling expeditions to the Similan islands (see opposite). All fifteen bungalows are en suite and fan cooled, with generous amounts of space, hot showers and balconies, some enjoying sea views; there's also internet access, free wi-fi and motorbike rental. Get off the bus at the *Poseidon* sign between kilometre-stones 53 and 54, then phone for a pick-up or walk 1km. B900

EATING AND DRINKING

BANG NIANG

The Candle @076 486123, @thecandlerestaurant .com. White-tablecloth bistro, with an a/c room and outdoor tables, serving tasty Thai traditional and fusion dishes, such as green curry with deep-fried crispy chicken and sweet peppers (B215), and Thai desserts. Daily 11.30am–10.30pm.

Degree Bar With its wooden tables, water-buffalo skulls and folksy, Thai-country vibe, this cheap, welcoming and enjoyably local bar-restaurant is a fun place to listen to live

bands, from 10pm every night, playing Thai and Western pop, *luk thung* and "Songs for Life". Daily 9pm–2am.

Khao Niau Rustic, open-sided restaurant dishing up very good northeastern Thai food, including loads of salads such as *som tam* (from B60), *laap* and *nam tok*. Daily 1–10pm; closed 9th and 23rd of each month.

Pinocchio @076 443079. Home-made pastas, decent pizzas made in a wood-fired oven (around B300), a few Italian meat main courses and lots of seafood, topped off with tiramisu and other home-made desserts. Look for the

7

white picket fence and fairy lights. Daily noon–11pm.

Takieang Wooden roadside restaurant that's gone slightly upmarket, offering authentic Thai food, including good *tom yum kung* (B150), banana-flower salad (B120) and exceptional seafood hotplates (B250). Daily noon–10pm.

NANG THONG

Bussaba Welcoming bistro with a long menu of Thai food, including seafood and fish priced by weight and some slightly more unusual dishes such as shrimp green curry with roti bread (B189). Also does sandwiches and a few other Western choices, and good espressos. Daily 1.30–11pm.

★ **Dive In** Khao Lak Banana Resort, Soi Bang La On. Owner and chef Sunny cooks up a storm here and is a favourite with expats, locals and returning tourists. High-lights include a deliciously aromatic *matsaman* curry (B90), *khanom jiin* Phuket-style noodles with fish and red curry, and deep-fried fish topped with mango. The Western menu runs to home-made cakes and bread, breakfasts and espressos. Free wi-fi. Daily 6.30am–11pm.

Happy Snapper ⓦ happysnapperbar.com. Khao Lak's most famous dive-staff hangout is chilled and pleasant, with a folksy lounge ambience and a drinks menu that runs to over a hundred cocktails. There's live music, including punk, Mon–Sat from around 10.30pm, and a chill-out DJ on Sun – plus the occasional open-mike session. Daily 8.30pm–1am.

Jai This lofty, open-sided, roadside restaurant is deservedly popular for its hearty, often fiery curries in good-sized portions (B80), including *kaeng phanaeng* and *matsaman*, seafood and *tom yum kung*. Also does a few Thai desserts

and Western breakfasts. Daily 8.30am–10pm.

O Rendezvous ⓣ 076 485108, ⓦ orendezvouskhaolak .com. Thatched, indoor-outdoor, French–Thai bar-restau-rant, very popular with local expats, where you can feast on duck in orange and wine sauce (B420) or Thai specialities like shrimp and banana-flower salad, as well as cheaper standard dishes such as chicken *matsaman* curry (B110). Daily 4–11pm.

Phu Khao Lak Well-known and good-value restaurant attached to the bungalows of the same name serving exceptionally good Thai food from a picture menu that stretches to over a hundred dishes. Everything from red, yellow and green curries (B120–150) to seafood platters. Daily 7am–10pm.

Stempfer Café Genteel, German-style café serving good breakfasts, espresso coffees, hot chocolate and all kinds of teas, lots of bread and cakes including apple tart (B100), plus salads and sandwiches. Free wi-fi. Daily 8.30am–9.30pm.

THAP LAMU

Navy Club Restaurant On the right by the pier, 11km southwest of Nang Thong ⓣ 081 648 8656. It's worth the trip out here for some authentic Thai food and the freshest seafood, at prices lower than in Khao Lak itself. Specialities include soft-shell crab, white snapper, pomfret (B35/100g), king prawns and squid, and there are dozens of Thai salads (B80). The restaurant is unprepossessing, but you could phone ahead to book a table on the terrace overlooking the harbour. Daily 10am–10pm.

SHOPPING

Nang Thong offers plenty of shopping, mainly for clothes, souvenirs and handicrafts, with countless tailors and opticians too.

Book Tree Far north end of Nang Thong. New and secondhand books plus magazines, newspapers and art cards, and also serves coffee. Daily 9am–9pm.

Community Crafts Khao Lak Community Appeal Foundation, on the east side of the main road in Bang

Niang ⓦ khaolakappeal.com. Non-profit shop selling bead jewellery, batiks, bags and lanterns, made by Thai, Moken and immigrant Burmese groups. Mon–Sat 1–6pm, sometimes open Mon–Fri mornings.

Ko Similan

Mu Ko Similan National Park • B400, valid for 5 days if staying within the national park • Closed May to Oct

Rated as one of the world's best spots for both above-water and underwater beauty, the eleven islands at the heart of the Mu **Ko Similan** National Park are among the most exciting **diving** destinations in Thailand. Massive granite boulders set magnificently against turquoise waters give the islands their distinctive character, but it's the 30m visibility that draws the divers. The 5000-year-old reefs are said to be the oldest in Thailand, so there's an enormous diversity of species, and the underwater scenery is nothing short of overwhelming: the reefs teem with coral fish, and you'll also see turtles, manta rays, moray eels, jacks, reef sharks, sea snakes, red grouper and quite possibly white-tip sharks, barracuda, giant lobster and enormous tuna.

KHAO SOK TREEHOUSE (P.613) >

The **islands** lie 64km off the mainland and include the eponymous Ko Similan chain of nine islands as well as two more northerly islands, Ko Bon and Ko Tachai, which are both favoured haunts of manta rays and whale sharks and are halfway between the Similan chain and the islands of Ko Surin. The Similans are numbered north–south from nine to one and are often referred to by number: Ko Ba Ngu (9), Ko Similan (8), Ko Payoo (7), Ko Hin Posar (aka Ko Hok; 6), Ko Ha (5), Ko Miang (4), Ko Pahyan (3), Ko Pahyang (2) and Ko Hu Yong (1). The national park headquarters and accommodation is on Ko Miang and there's also a campsite and restaurant on Ko Similan. Ko Similan is the largest island in the chain, blessed with a beautiful, fine white-sand bay and impressive boulders and traversed by two nature trails; Ko Miang has two pretty beaches, twenty minutes' walk apart, and three nature trails; Ko Hu Yong has an exceptionally long white-sand bay but access is restricted by the Thai navy as **turtles** lay their eggs there from November to February.

Such beauty has not gone unnoticed and the islands are extremely popular with day-trippers from Phuket and Khao Lak, as well as with divers and snorkellers on longer live-aboard trips. This has caused the inevitable congestion and environmental problems and the Similan reefs have been damaged in places by anchors and by the local practice of using dynamite in fishing. National parks authorities have responded by banning fishermen and enforcing strict regulations for tourist boats, including **closing the islands** during the monsoon season, from May to October.

ARRIVAL AND DEPARTURE   KO SIMILAN

Independent travellers wanting to stay on the island for a few days can usually use the snorkelling tour boats for transfers. There are also plenty of live-aboard diving or snorkelling trips to the islands, the best and cheapest of which run out of Khao Lak (see p.618).

Snorkelling tours Most travel agents in Khao Lak, Phuket and Phang Nga sell snorkelling packages to Ko Similan, usually as day-trips featuring at least four island stops (from B3100 including national park fees); two-day, one-night (B5800 staying in tents); and three-day, two-night (B7200) packages, staying on Ko Miang, are also available. The majority of these trips carry quite large groups and use fast boats that depart from Thap Lamu pier, about 11km southwest of Khao Lak's Nang Thong, 90km north of Phuket town, at about 8.30am and get to the islands in under two hours. They depart the islands at around 3pm. Companies offering this service, all of which offer pick-ups in Khao Lak and Phuket, include Medsye Travel and Tours, who also do pick-ups in Krabi (☎076 443276, ⓦmedsye.com), and Jack Similan (☎081 648 8656, ⓦjacksimilan.com), both of which have offices at the Thap Lamu pier; and Khao Lak Land Discovery in Nang Thong (☎076 485411, ⓦkhaolaklanddiscovery.com).

GETTING AROUND

If travelling independently, you'll need to use Ko Similan longtail boats to travel **between the islands** and to explore different reefs: prices are fixed and cost around B200 per person for a half-day trip.

ACCOMMODATION AND EATING

Limited accommodation is available on **Ko Miang**, in the shape of national park rooms and bungalows (fan B1000, a/c B2000) and tents (B300–450), and there's a campsite on **Ko Similan** too; both islands also have a restaurant. Accommodation should be booked ahead, either at the national parks office 500m east of Thap Lamu pier (☎076 453272) or online (ⓦdnp.go.th or ⓦthaiforestbooking.com), as facilities can get crowded with tour groups, especially on weekends and holidays.

Phuket

Thailand's largest island and a province in its own right, **PHUKET** (pronounced "Poo-ket") has been a prosperous region since the nineteenth century, when Chinese merchants got in on its tin-mining and sea-borne trade, before turning to the rubber industry. It remains the wealthiest province in Thailand, with the highest per-capita income, but what mints the

PHUKET DAY-TRIPS AND OTHER ACTIVITIES

Bookings for most of the following **Phuket day-trips and activities** can be made through any tour agent and should include return transport from your hotel (though not for the cooking classes). In addition to the trips listed below, diving is also available (see p.642). Other **sights** worth checking out, especially for kids, include the Phuket Butterfly Garden and Insect World in Phuket town (see p.629), the Aquarium on Laem Panwa (p.646), the Shell Museum in Rawai (p.646), the Big Buddha near Chalong (p.646) and the Gibbon Rehabilitation Project near Thalang (p.649). Avoid any tour that features Ko Siray (Ko Sireh), the island across the narrow channel from Phuket town, which merely encourages tour-bus passengers to gawp at Phuket's largest and longest-established indigenous *chao ley* community (see p.608).

Bicycle touring Full- and half-day guided mountain-bike rides into Phuket's rural hinterlands and to Ko Yao Noi, as well as multi-day rides around Phang Nga Bay, with Action Holidays Phuket (☎076 263575, ⓦbike toursthailand.com; full day from B2400).

Elephant trekking Award-winning, conservation-conscious Siam Safari (☎076 280116, ⓦsiamsafari .com) runs Four-in-One tours featuring their hillside elephant camp plus rubber tapping, buffalo-cart riding and a sail on a Burmese junk (B2350); tours to Khao Sok National Park are also on offer.

Kiteboarding One- (B4000) and three-day courses (B11,000) at Hat Nai Yang and Ao Chalong (depending on the season) are offered by Kiteboarding Asia (☎081 591 4594, ⓦkiteboardingasia.com).

Mini-golf If you just need a little time off from the beach, head for the eighteen-hole Dino Park mini-golf (daily 10am–midnight; B240; ⓦdinopark.com), next to *Marina Phuket Resort* on the headland between Ao Karon and Ao Kata, which is part of a pseudo-prehistoric theme park comprising a dinosaur restaurant and an erupting "volcano" (evenings only).

Sea-canoeing There are dozens of companies offering canoeing and kayaking in Phuket, but the two with the best reputations are John Gray's Sea Canoe (☎076 254505–7, ⓦjohngray-seacanoe.com), who offer "Starlight" afternoon and evening trips around the

spectacular limestone karsts of Ao Phang Nga (B3900), as well as multi-day and self-paddle trips; and Paddle Asia (☎076 241519, ⓦpaddleasia.com), who run day-trips to Ao Phang Nga (B4200) and multi-day trips, which can include Khao Sok National Park and other adventure activities.

Surfing The rainy season (roughly May–Oct) is the best time for surfing off Phuket's west coast; courses (B1500 for a 90min private lesson) and board rental are available from Phuket Surf on Ao Kata Yai (☎087 889 7308, ⓦphuketsurf.com).

Thai cookery courses Most famously, every Sat and Sun morning at *The Boathouse* hotel on Ao Kata Yai (B2200; ☎076 330015, ⓦboathousephuket.com); but also at the *Holiday Inn Phuket*, 86/11 Thanon Thavee Wong, Patong (Mon–Sat afternoons; B1800; ☎076 340608, ⓦphuket.holiday-inn.com); and the *Blue Elephant Restaurant*, 96 Thanon Krabi, Phuket town (B3300 for a half-day class; ☎076 354355, ⓦblueelephant.com).

Thai culture and wildlife tours Plan to Phuket (☎081 691 1955, ⓦplantophuket.com; B1500) run a number of tours, including full-day "Culture Tours" that include market and temple visits, batik-making and rubber production; and "Jungle Tours" to Ton Sai water-fall and the Gibbon Rehabilitation project (see p.649); or a combination of both.

money nowadays is **tourism**: with an annual influx of visitors that tops five million, Phuket ranks second in popularity only to Pattaya, and the package-tour traffic has wrought its usual transformations. Thoughtless tourist developments have scarred much of the island, and the trend is upmarket, with very few budget possibilities (expect to shell out up to twice what you'd pay on the mainland for accommodation and food, and sometimes more than double for transport, which is a particular headache on Phuket). However, many of the beaches are still strikingly handsome, resort facilities are second to none, and the offshore snorkelling and diving is exceptional. Away from the tourist hubs, many inland neighbourhoods are clustered round the local mosque – 35 percent of Phuketians are **Muslim**, and there are said to be more mosques on the island than Buddhist temples; though the atmosphere is generally as easy-going as elsewhere in Thailand, it's especially important to dress with some modesty outside the main resorts, and not to sunbathe topless on any of the beaches.

Phuket's capital, Muang Phuket or **Phuket town**, is on the southeast coast, 42km south of the Sarasin Bridge causeway to the mainland. Though it's the most

PHUKET

Ranong & Krabi

Sarasin Bridge

Hat Sai Kaew

Ban Soun Maprao

Hat Mai Khao

3016

402

Ko Wa

Laem Sai

Sirinath
National
Park HQ

4031

4026

Hat Nai Yang

402

4027

Hat Nai Thon

4031

Wat
Phra Thong

Bang Pae
Waterfall

Ao Por

Ko Nakha Yai

4018

Thalang

PHRA TAEW
NATIONAL PARK

Gibbon
Project

Bang Rong

Ko Nakha Noi

4030

Ton Tai
Waterfall

402

4027

Ao Bang Tao

Ban Cherngtalay

4025

Thalang Museum

Royal
Phuket
Marina

Ao Pansea
Hat Surin

Heroines'
Monument

Laem Singh

Phuket
Fantasea

Hat Kamala

Ko Rang

402

402

Ko Maphrao

Kathu

Phuket
Butterfly
Garden

Mission
Hospital

4020

SEE 'AO PATONG MAP'

4029

Phuket
International
Hospital

SEE 'PHUKET TOWN' MAP

Ao
Patong

Central
Festival

Bangkok
Phuket
Hospital

Phuket
Town

Ko Siray

Freedom Beach

Ao Karon Noi

Rassada
Harbour

Big
Buddha

4022

4021

4023

Ao Phuket

SEE 'AO KARON,
AO KATA YAI &
AO KATA NOI' MAP

Wat Chalong

Deep Sea
Port

Ao Karon

CHALONG
CIRCLE

4028

Ao Makham

Laem Panwa

Ao Kata Yai

4024

Ao Chalong

Aquarium

Ao Kata Noi

Phuket
Seashell
Museum

Ko Lone

4233

Hat Nai Harn
Ko Man
Hat Ya Nui
Laem Promthep

Ko Aew

Ko Maiton

Hat Rawai

Ko Bon

Ko Kaeo Pitsadan

Ko Hai
(Coral Island)

Ko Kaeo Noi

N

Ko Tao Tai & Ko Tao Noi

Ko Phi Phi, Ko Nang & Ko Lanta

0   5
kilometres

culturally stimulating place on Phuket, most visitors pass straight through the town on their way to the **west coast**, where three resorts corner the bulk of the trade: high-rise **Ao Patong**, the most developed and expensive, with an increasingly seedy nightlife; the slightly nicer, if unexceptional, **Ao Karon**; and adjacent **Ao Kata**, the smallest of the trio. If you're after a more peaceful spot, aim for the 17km-long national park beach of **Hat Mai Khao**, its more developed neighbour **Hat Nai Yang**, or one of the smaller alternatives at **Hat Nai Thon** or **Hat Kamala**. Most of the other west-coast beaches are dominated by just a few upmarket hotels, specifically **Hat Nai Harn**, **Ao Pansea** and **Ao Bang Tao**; the southern and eastern beaches are better for seafood than swimming.

As with the rest of the Andaman coast, the sea around Phuket is at its least inviting during the **monsoon**, from June to October, when the west-coast beaches in particular become quite rough and windswept. At any time of year, beware the strong **undertow** and heed any red warning flags; there are dozens of fatalities in the water each year, but there is currently no official lifeguard service on the island. Some stretches of Phuket's coast were very badly damaged by the December 2004 **tsunami** (see box, p.616), which caused significant loss of life and destroyed a lot of property. Reconstruction was swift, however, and a first-time visitor to the island is now unlikely to notice any major post-tsunami effect.

ARRIVAL AND DEPARTURE

PHUKET

BY PLANE
Phuket International Airport (☎076 327230–79) is near the northern tip of the island, between Hat Mai Khao and Hat Nai Yang, 32km northwest of Phuket town. It has ATMs, currency exchange, a post office, a Bangkok Hospital clinic, hotel booking and travel agency counters plus a left-luggage service (daily 6am–10pm; B80 per item per day). There are scores of international flights into Phuket, including several direct services from Australia and dozens of mostly seasonal flights from northern Europe. Between them, Thai Airways, Air Asia, Bangkok Airways, Orient Thai and Nok Air run around thirty domestic flights a day between Bangkok and Phuket, while Thai Airways and Air Asia fly direct from Chiang Mai and Bangkok Airways connects Phuket with Pattaya and Ko Samui.

Onward transport The airport bus (☎076 232371, ⊚airportbusphuket.com; B85; 1hr 20min) runs approximately hourly to the bus station in Phuket town, via Thalang; as it doesn't serve the beaches, you'll need to change on to the songthaews in town to reach those. Travel agents in the arrivals hall organize a/c minibuses, which leave when they have ten passengers, to Phuket town (B100), Rassada pier (B150), Patong (B150) and Kata (B180). Outside the arrivals hall at the south end of the building, you'll find a booth for metered taxis (though even here the drivers often need a lot of persuading to turn their meters on): to get to Patong, for instance, will set you back around B450, including a B100 airport charge. On departure from the beaches, most people use taxis organized by their hotel – about B500 for the hour's ride from Patong or Karon. If you're landing at the airport and want to catch a bus north, you can save going into Phuket town by getting a taxi or the airport bus to Ban Muang Mai,

about 6km southeast of the airport on Highway 402, where you can pick up your northbound bus.

Destinations: Bangkok (30 daily; 1hr 20min); Chiang Mai (3 daily; 2hr); Ko Samui (2–5 daily; 50min); Pattaya/U-Tapao (daily; 1hr 35min).

BY BUS AND MINIBUS
Nearly all buses to and from Phuket use the Baw Khaw Saw bus station off the eastern end of Thanon Phang Nga in Phuket town (though there is talk of a possible move to a more spacious location to the north of town). From there it's a 10min walk or a short tuk-tuk ride to the town's central hotel area, and slightly further to the Thanon Ranong departure point for songthaews to the beaches. On the west side of the bus station, licensed private companies offer a/c minibuses to Krabi, Ko Lanta, Surat Thani, Nakhon Si Thammarat, Trang and Hat Yai (a service to Ranong may be granted a licence soon).

From Bangkok Most a/c buses from Bangkok's Southern Bus Terminal to Phuket make the journey overnight, departing from mid-afternoon onwards. There's no train service to Phuket, but you could book an overnight sleeper train to Surat Thani, about 290km east of Phuket, and take one of the regular buses from there to Phuket (about 5hr).

Bus destinations: Bangkok (30 daily; 10–14hr); Chumphon (17 daily; 6hr 30min); Hat Yai (roughly hourly; 7hr); Khao Lak (20 daily; 2hr 30min); Khao Sok (4 daily; 3–4hr); Khuraburi (20 daily; 3hr 30min–4hr); Ko Samui (daily; 8hr); Krabi (at least hourly; 3hr 30min); Nakhon Si Thammarat (8 daily; 7hr); Phang Nga (at least hourly; 2hr 30min); Ranong (20 daily; 5hr); Satun (4 daily; 7hr); Surat Thani (13 daily; 4hr 30min–5hr 30min); Takua Pa (20 daily; 2hr 30min–3hr); Trang (roughly hourly; 5–6hr).

7

BY BOAT

If you're coming to Phuket from Ko Lanta or Ao Nang in Krabi province, the quickest and most scenic option is to take the boat.

To/from Ko Phi Phi During peak season, up to three ferries a day, plus a speedboat or two, make the trip to and from Ko Phi Phi, docking at Rassada Harbour on Phuket's east coast; during low season, there's at least one ferry a day in both directions.

To/from Ko Yao Noi Boats from Ko Yao Noi and the high-season speedboat service from Ao Nang via Ko Yao Noi terminate at Bang Rong on Phuket's northeast coast.

To/from Ko Lanta Travellers from Sala Dan on Ko Lanta (Nov–May only) may have to change boats at Ao Nang or Ko Phi Phi to get to Phuket's Rassada Harbour.

To/from Ao Nang Ferries go to Rassada Harbour; the speedboat service from Ao Nang via Ko Yao Noi terminates at Bang Rong.

Onward transport from Rassada Harbour Shared a/c minibuses meet the ferries at Rassada Harbour and charge B50 per person for transfers to Phuket town hotels, B150 to Patong and B200 to the airport; taxis charge B500–600 per car to the major west-coast beaches or the airport (leave plenty of extra time if you have a flight to catch as boats are notoriously tardy).

Onward transport from Bang Rong Infrequent songthaews shuttle between Bang Rong and Phuket town (about 1hr; B40), while taxis charge B500–800 to the airport or the west-coast beaches.

Destinations: Ao Nang (Nov–May 2 daily; 2hr); Ko Lanta Yai (Nov–May 2 daily; 4hr 30min); Ko Phi Phi Don (1–3 daily; 2hr); Ko Yao Noi (roughly hourly; 40min–1hr 10min).

GETTING AROUND

Getting around the island is a nightmare: on one hand, tuk-tuks and taxis know that they have a captive audience and charge through the nose; on the other, Phuket has probably the worst, most dangerous drivers in Thailand, driving on roads that are often steep and winding, with quite a few hairpin bends – which all discourages renting a vehicle. If you do decide to drive yourself, stay alert and be defensive. There is a system of public songthaews (supplemented by buses) radiating out from Phuket town, but to get from one beach to another by this method you nearly always have to go back into town. For transport within resorts, the cheapest option is to make use of the public songthaews where possible, or to hail a motorbike taxi where available (B30–100).

By songthaew Songthaews run regularly throughout the day (when they have a full complement of passengers) from Thanon Ranong in the centre of Phuket town to the coast and cost B25–45.

By tuk-tuk or taxi Tuk-tuks and taxis do travel directly between major beaches, but are notoriously overpriced (there are almost no metered taxis on the island), charging at least B100 from Kata to Karon or B250 between Patong and Karon and often doubling their prices after dark – they have been known to ask for B1000 to go from Patong to Karon at night. Phuket TAT (see p.630) issues a list of price guidelines but you'll have to bargain hard to get near the quoted prices.

Motorbike rental Many tourists rent their own motorbike or moped, which are widely available (from B250/day), but be warned that there is a very sobering average of 10,000 motorbike injuries a year on Phuket, and about a hundred fatalities; it makes sense to obey the compulsory helmet law, which is anyway strictly enforced in most areas of Phuket, with flouters subject to a B500 fine.

Car rental At the airport, there are offices of Avis (☎076 351244, ⓦ avisthailand.com) and Budget (☎076 327744, ⓦ budget.co.th), who also have a branch on Patong (see p.637); both charge from around B1200/day.

INFORMATION

On the web There's a wide-ranging website about Phuket, ⓦ phuket.com, which is particularly good for discounted accommodation.

Guidebooks For a detailed historical and cultural guide to the island, it's hard to better Oliver Hargreave's impressive *Exploring Phuket & Phi Phi* (Within Books).

Tourist office Phuket's TAT office is in Phuket Town (see p.630), though it's not worth going out of your way to visit.

DIRECTORY

Dentists At Phuket International Hospital and Bangkok Hospital Phuket (see below).

Hospitals Phuket International Hospital (☎076 249400, emergencies ☎076 210935, ⓦ phuketinternationalhospital .com), north of Central Festival shopping centre on Highway 402, just west of Phuket town, is considered to have Phuket's best facilities, including an emergency department and an ambulance service. Reputable alternatives include Bangkok

Hospital Phuket, on the northwestern edge of Phuket town just off Thanon Yaowarat at 2/1 Thanon Hongyok Uthis (☎076 254425, ⓦ phukethospital.com), and the Mission Hospital (aka Phuket Adventist Hospital), on the northern outskirts at 4/1 Thanon Thepkasatri (☎076 237220–6, emergencies ☎076 237227, ⓦ missionhospitalphuket.com).

Immigration office At the southern end of Thanon Phuket, in the suburb of Saphan Hin, Phuket town (☎076

221905, ⓦphuketimmigration.go.th; Mon–Fri 8.30am–
noon & 1–4.30pm), plus an information centre in Patong
(see p.639).

Tourist police For all emergencies, contact the tourist

police, either on the free, 24hr phone line (☎1155), at
their main office at 327 Thanon Yaowarat in Phuket town
(☎076 223891, ⓦphukettouristpolice.go.th), or at their
branch in Patong (see p.639).

Phuket town

Though it has plenty of hotels and restaurants, **PHUKET TOWN** (Muang Phuket) stands
distinct from the tailor-made tourist settlements along the beaches as a place of tangible
history and culture. Most visitors hang about just long enough to jump on a beach-
bound songthaew, but you may find yourself returning for a welcome dose of real life;
there's plenty to engage you in a stroll through the small but atmospherically restored
heart of the Old Town, along with many idiosyncratic cafés and art shops, several
notable restaurants and some good handicraft shops. The town works well as an
overnight transit point between the islands and the bus station or airport, but is also

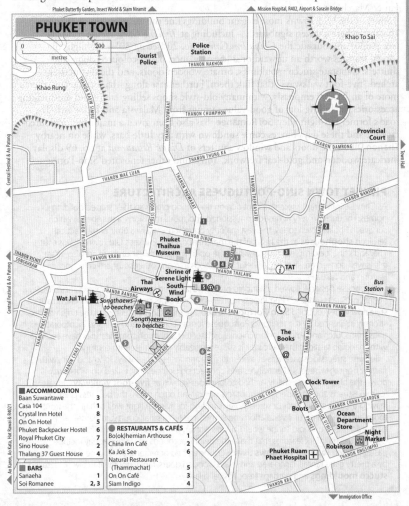

◼ ACCOMMODATION	
Baan Suwantawe	3
Casa 104	1
Crystal Inn Hotel	8
On On Hotel	5
Phuket Backpacker Hostel	6
Royal Phuket City	7
Sino House	2
Thalang 37 Guest House	4

◼ BARS	
Sanaeha	1
Soi Romanee	2, 3

● RESTAURANTS & CAFÉS	
Bo(ok)hemian Arthouse	1
China Inn Café	2
Ka Jok See	6
Natural Restaurant	
(Thammachat)	5
On On Café	3
Siam Indigo	4

worth considering as a base for exploring the island, with more interesting and affordable accommodation, eating and drinking options than the beaches, but linked to them by regular songthaews.

The Old Town
Between Thanon Dibuk and Thanon Rat Sada; ⓦ lestariheritage.net/Phuket

Phuket town's most interesting features are clustered together in the **Old Town** conservation zone, a grid of streets between Thanon Dibuk and Thanon Rat Sada whose colonial-style **Sino-Portuguese shophouses** (see below) date back to the nineteenth century, the former homes of emigrant Chinese merchants from Penang, Singapore and Melaka. Modern-day residents have put a lot of effort into restoring these handsome old neighbourhoods and there's an engagingly bohemian style to a number of the businesses here. The Phuket Old Town Foundation helps to publish the excellent free **Phuket Town Treasure Map**, available all over the Old Town, and also stages the **Old Town Festival** just before Chinese New Year (sometime between Jan & March).

Some of the Old Town's most elegant buildings line the western arm of **Thanon Thalang**, where a dozen signboards – including at *Thalang Guest House* at no. 37 (see p.630) and outside the *China Inn Café* at no. 20 (see p.630) – highlight the special features worth an upward or sideways glance: pastel-coloured doors and shutters, elaborate stucco mouldings, ornate wooden doors, and the distinctively arched "five-foot walkways" that link them. Further east along Thanon Thalang there's more of an Islamic emphasis, with many old-style shops selling fabric and dressmaking accessories, including lots of good-value sarongs from Malaysia and Indonesia. The road's former red-light alley, **Soi Romanee**, has also been given a major multicoloured face-lift and these days buzzes come sundown with arty little bars, while on nearby **Thanon Dibuk** the doors and window shutters of *Dibuk Restaurant* at no. 69 display intricate wooden and gold-leaf fretwork. You'll find other renovated Sino-Portuguese

---

PHUKET TOWN SINO-PORTUGUESE ARCHITECTURE

As Chinese immigrant merchants got rich on tin-mining profits so they started building homes. Though the very richest commissioned enormous mansions, a number of which survive in Phuket town today, the vast majority bought themselves eminently practical terraced **shophouses** at the heart of the merchant district. Phuket's Old Town retains south Thailand's finest examples, some of which are open to the public, but there are also intact, if less well-conserved, shophouse neighbourhoods in many other southern cities, including Ranong and Takua Pa.

Shophouse design followed a standard prototype favoured by the mixed-race Chinese–Malay ("Baba", or "Straits Chinese") immigrants from Melaka and other parts of the Malay Peninsula. It's a style now widely dubbed **Sino-Portuguese** because Melakan architecture of the time was itself strongly influenced by the territory's Portuguese former colonists, though it also incorporates traits from Dutch and Anglo-Indian colonial architecture. Although some features have evolved with changing fashions the basic look is still recognizably mid-nineteenth century.

Because streetside space was at a premium, shophouses were always long and thin, with narrow frontages, recessed entrances and connecting porches that linked up all the way down the block to make shady, arched colonnades known as **five-foot walkways**, ideal for pedestrians and shoppers. The front room was (and often still is) the business premises, leaving the rest of the two- or three-storey building for living. A light well behind the front room encouraged natural ventilation and sometimes fed a small courtyard garden at its base, and the household shrine would always occupy a prominent and auspicious position. Outside, the hallmark features that make the neighbourhoods so striking today include pastel-painted **louvred windows** that might be arched or rectangular and perhaps topped by a pretty glass fantail, lacquered and inlaid wooden doors, fancy gold-leaf fretwork, detailed **stucco mouldings** and perhaps Neoclassical pilasters.

NGAN KIN JEH: THE VEGETARIAN FESTIVAL

For nine days, usually in October or November, at the start of the ninth lunar month (see ⓦ phuketvegetarian.com for exact dates), the celebrations for **Ngan Kin Jeh** – the Vegetarian Festival – set the streets of Phuket buzzing with processions, theatre shows and food stalls, culminating in the unnerving spectacle of men and women parading about with steel rods through their cheeks and tongues. The festival marks the beginning of **Taoist Lent**, a month-long period of purification observed by devout Chinese all over the world, but celebrated most ostentatiously in Phuket, by devotees of the island's five Chinese temples. After six days' abstention from meat (hence the festival's name), alcohol and sex, the white-clad worshippers flock to their local temple, where drum rhythms help induce a trance state in which they become possessed by spirits. As proof of their new-found transcendence of the physical world they skewer themselves with any available sharp instrument – fishing rods and car wing-mirrors have done service in the past – before walking over red-hot coals or up ladders of swords as further testament to their otherworldliness. In the meantime there's singing and dancing and almost continuous firework displays, with the grandest festivities held at Wat Jui Tui on Thanon Ranong in Phuket town.

The ceremony dates back to the mid-nineteenth century, when a travelling Chinese opera company turned up on the island to entertain emigrant Chinese working in the tin mines. They had been there almost a year when suddenly the whole troupe – together with a number of the miners – came down with a life-endangering fever. Realizing that they'd neglected their gods, the actors performed elaborate rites and kept to a vegetarian diet, and most were soon cured. The festival has been held ever since, though the self-mortification rites are a later modification, possibly of Hindu origin.

buildings on **Thanon Yaowarat**, and on **Thanon Ranong** (where the Thai Airways office occupies a fine old mansion), **Thanon Phang Nga** (especially the *On On Hotel*) and **Thanon Damrong**, whose town hall, just east of the Provincial Court, stood in for Phnom Penh's US embassy in the film *The Killing Fields*.

Phuket Thaihua Museum

28 Thanon Krabi • Daily 9am–5pm • B200 • ⓦ thaihuamuseum.com

This 1930s Neoclassical former school – complete with grand columns, stucco decoration, shuttered windows and central light well – has been turned into the **Phuket Thaihua Museum**. Some of the old school desks are still *in situ*, but the focus of the museum's excellent displays, videos and historic photos is on the role and traditions of Phuket's main immigrant groups, namely the Chinese and mixed-race Baba (Malay–Chinese) communities who arrived to work in the island's burgeoning tin-mining industry.

San Jao Saeng Tham (Shrine of Serene Light)

Accessed via a soi through the narrow archway next to South Wind Books on Thanon Phang Nga • Daily 8.30am–noon & 1.30–5.30pm

The spiritual heritage of Phuket's Chinese immigrants is kept very much alive by their descendants, notably in the extraordinary spectacle of the annual Vegetarian Festival (see above). They also maintain many shrines around town, including **San Jao Saeng Tham**, the tiny **Shrine of Serene Light**, whose roof is decorated with intensely coloured ceramic figurines of dragons, carp and sages in bright blues, greens and reds.

Phuket Butterfly Garden

2km beyond the northern end of Thanon Yaowarat at 71/6 Soi Paneang in Ban Sam Kong • Daily 9am–5pm • B300 • ☎ 076 210861, ⓦ phuketbutterfly.com • A tuk-tuk from the town centre should cost around B150 return

Kids usually enjoy the **Phuket Butterfly Garden and Insect World**, whose thousands of butterflies of some twenty indigenous species flit around the prettily landscaped grounds; there's also a silk museum documenting the amazingly industrious short life of the silkworm, plus scorpions, tarantulas and other notorious creepy-crawlies.

ARRIVAL AND DEPARTURE

Songthaews (supplemented by buses) run regularly throughout the day from the market on Thanon Ranong in the town centre to all the main beaches and cost B25–45.

INFORMATION

Tourist information The TAT office is at 191 Thanon Thalang (daily 8.30am–4.30pm; ☎076 212213, ✉ tatphket@tat.or.th), though it's not worth going out of your way to visit.

ACCOMMODATION

★ **Baan Suwantawe** 1/10 Thanon Dibuk ☎076 212879, ⓦ baansuwantawe.com. Offering four-star rooms at two-star prices, this apartment-style hotel is designed with long-stay residents in mind but is also exceptionally comfortable for tourists. The huge, pleasantly decorated a/c rooms all have a balcony overlooking the small swimming pool and come with TV, broadband, fridge and kettle. There's no restaurant or hotel services but the front desk is helpful and the location very handy for the Old Town. **B1500**

Casa 104 104 Thanon Yaowarat ☎076 221268, ✉ casa 104phuket@gmail.com. Friendly, popular establishment offering four chic but windowless rooms away from the street noise, behind a French bistro, with access to a lovely, shady garden at the back; all have a/c, flat-screen TVs and attractive, hot-water bathrooms. Substantial Continental breakfast with home-baked bread included. **B1200**

Crystal Inn Hotel 2/1–10 Soi Surin, Thanon Montri ☎076 256789, ⓦ phuketcrystalinn.com. Surprisingly stylish and contemporary cream- and dark-wood decor makes this small, 54-room downtown hotel an inviting and good-value option. All rooms have a/c and there's internet downstairs. Breakfast included. **B950**

On On Hotel 19 Thanon Phang Nga ☎076 211154. This attractive, colonial-style 1920s building is a long-running travellers' favourite, mainly because the rooms are so cheap. They're pretty basic, with very thin walls, holes in the floorboards and ancient plumbing, but they're adequate and there are lots of them; the cheapest share bathrooms, the most expensive have a/c. There's wi-fi, an internet café and a tour agent in the lobby. Shared bathroom **B180**, en suite **B250**, a/c **B400**

Phuket Backpacker Hostel 167 Thanon Ranong ☎076 256680, ⓦ phuketbackpacker.com. Popular, sociable and well-organized hostel, with lots of tours and information available and a lively bar downstairs. Dorms squeeze in up to ten guests, but there are some nice, clean and small fan rooms with TVs and hot showers overlooking the quiet garden at the back. Internet access, free wi-fi, bicycle rental and a common room for showing movies. Fan dorm **B250**, a/c dorm **B300**, fan double **B550**, a/c double **B650**

Royal Phuket City 154 Thanon Phang Nga ☎076 233333, ⓦ royalphuketcity.com. Large, high-rise business hotel, with large swimming pool, gym, business centre and light, bright, comfortable a/c rooms, most of them with fine views over the city and all with broadband. **B2200**

Sino House 1 Thanon Montri ☎076 232494–5, ⓦ sino housephuket.com. Beautifully styled with Chinoiserie artefacts and elegant flourishes, the apartment-style rooms in this striking Art Deco building are huge and light and all come with a/c, fridge, DVD player, complimentary wi-fi, coffee-making facilities and Continental breakfast. There's a restaurant and the Raintree Spa on site, plus some tour services, but no pool. **B2000**

Thalang 37 Guest House 37 Thanon Thalang ☎076 214225, ⓦ thalangguesthouse.com. Housed in a 1940s, Sino-Portuguese, wood-floored shophouse in one of the Old Town's most attractive streets, this place is fairly simple but full of character, traveller-friendly and good value. The twelve fan and a/c rooms are large and en suite – the best of them are up on the rooftop, affording unusual panoramic views. It's very popular, so it's best to book ahead; rates include a simple breakfast. Fan **B400**, a/c **B500**

EATING AND DRINKING

Phuket town has much the largest concentration of good Thai food on the island, well worth making the trip for. Unlike Thais in most other parts of the country, Phuketians like to breakfast on noodles rather than rice; spindly white *khanom jiin* noodles, made with rice-flour and ladled over with one of several different fiery, soupy curry sauces, are a local speciality and served at some of the restaurants listed below.

Bo(ok)hemian Arthouse 61 Thanon Thalang. Artsy little hangout for cappuccinos (B60), free wi-fi, DVD rental and occasional film screenings. Daily 10am–9pm.

China Inn Café 20 Thanon Thalang ☎076 356239. This beautifully renovated heritage house and courtyard garden would be reason enough to stop by for a meal, but the menu is also enticing, proffering Thai dishes such as *phat thai* (B190) and spicy salads, as well as a few Western, mostly Italian, dishes including delicious mozzarella salad (B290). Streetside, the gallery shop displays Asian antiques, textiles and lacquerware. High season Mon–Wed 11am–6pm, Thurs–Sat 11am–10pm, low season

Mon–Sat 11am–6pm.

Ka Jok See 26 Thanon Takuapa ☎076 217903. A Phuket institution, housed in a charmingly restored traditional shophouse (unsigned), this place serves fabulous Thai food on a pricey set menu (B1500) and fosters a fun, sociable atmosphere. Mains are sophisticated and beautifully presented – their *goong sarong*, individual shrimps bound in a crisp-noodle wrap, is famous island-wide. Reservations are essential. Tues–Sun 7.30–10.30pm.

★ **Natural Restaurant (Thammachat)** 62/5 Soi Putorn ☎076 214037. There are plenty of reasons to linger over dinner at this rambling, informal, hugely popular, plant-wreathed restaurant, not least the two hundred different choices on the menu, and the affordable prices (main dishes around B100). Highlights include fried sea bass with chilli paste, fried chicken with Muslim herbs, soft-shelled crab with garlic and pepper, and spicy Phuket bean salad. Daily 10.30am–11.30pm.

On On Café Thanon Phang Nga. Sociable spot for cheap, mostly Thai–Chinese meals, as well as breakfasts, including fry-ups (B120 for an "American" set breakfast) and espresso coffee. Mon–Sat 7am–7pm, Sun 7am–noon.

Sanaeha Thanon Yaowarat. Lively, hip bar in an old mansion, all done out in blue and white with chandeliers and mirror balls, with live bands playing jazz and other stuff on the central stage from 9pm. Daily 6/7pm–12.30am.

Siam Indigo 8 Thanon Phang Nga ☎076 256697, ⓦ siamindigo.com. In a hundred-year-old house with an attractive rear patio, this stylish bar-restaurant and clothes boutique is festooned with chandeliers, red velvet curtains and striking mosaic portraits of film stars. The menu features tapas and lots of local dishes such as *nam prik kung siab* (a spicy relish with dried shrimps; B120); happy hour 5–7pm. Daily 2pm till late.

Soi Romanee This artfully restored, plant-strewn soi connecting Dibuk and Thalang roads shows off its handsome new pastel paintwork and stuccoed Old Town facades with half a dozen little café-bars whose seating spills out on to the pavement for ultimate architectural appreciation.

ENTERTAINMENT

Siam Niramit Phuket North of town off Thanon Chalerm Prakiat ☎076 335000, ⓦ siamniramit.com. Recently opened offshoot of the Siam Niramit Bangkok extravaganza, this 70min show presents a tourist-oriented rendering of traditional Thai theatre, in a high-tech spectacular of fantastic costumes and huge chorus numbers, enlivened by acrobatics and flashy special effects. Tickets from B1300. Daily except Tues 8.30pm.

SHOPPING

The two most fruitful shopping roads for handicrafts and antiques are Thanon Yaowarat and Thanon Rat Sada, while the shops on eastern Thanon Thalang keep a phenomenal range of well-priced sarongs, mostly of Burmese, Malaysian and Indonesian designs. *Art and Culture South*, a useful, free, quarterly booklet that's available at TAT and other outlets, details shops and galleries in the town and around.

The Books Thanon Phuket. Decent selection of new English-language books and magazines, with a coffee corner and internet access. Daily 8.30am–9.30pm.

South Wind Books Thanon Phang Nga. Big, sprawling range of secondhand books. Mon–Sat 9am–6pm, Sun 10am–3pm.

DIRECTORY

Travel agent Mark Travel, in the lobby of the *On On Hotel* on Thanon Phang Nga (☎076 225741 or ☎081 693 6207), is a helpful agent, good for all kinds of transport tickets, including cheap boat tickets, as well as activities and day-trips.

Hat Mai Khao

Phuket's longest and quietest beach, the 17km **HAT MAI KHAO**, unfurls along the island's upper northwest coast, beginning some 3km south of the Sarasin Bridge causeway and ending just north of the airport (34km from Phuket town). It's a beautiful piece of casuarina- and palm-shaded coastline, minimally developed and protected in part as **Sirinath National Park** because of the few giant marine turtles that lay their eggs here between October and February.

ACCOMMODATION   HAT MAI KHAO

Accommodation on Hat Mai Khao is predominantly five-star: an enclave of half a dozen luxury hotels is elegantly spaced behind the sloping shoreline towards the north end of the beach, accessed by an all-but-private road that is not served by any public transport. Most of the resorts have a swimming pool but the undertow here can be fierce and unpredictable.

★ **Anantara Phuket Villas** ☎076 336100–9, ⓦ anantara.com. Set amid stylishly landscaped grounds and lagoons, all the secluded villas here have their own plunge pool, outdoor bath and garden *sala*, while the luxurious interiors feature antique furniture, lots of dark wood, dressing rooms, espresso machines and free wi-fi. There's an impressive selection of free activities, including sailing and yoga, a kids' club, a beautiful spa and excellent seafood at the stylish restaurant, *Sea Fire Salt*. Rates are sometimes reduced by more than half in low season. B18,000

JW Marriott Phuket Resort and Spa ☎076 338000, ⓦ marriott.com. Complemented by high standards of service, this luxury resort offers well-appointed rooms, a spa, two tennis courts and no less than seven restaurants. Two swimming pools, a well-equipped children's pavilion, good sports facilities and extensive landscaped lawns all help make it a favourite with families. B6960

Mai Khao Beach Bungalows ☎081 895 1233, ⓦ maikhaobeach.wordpress.com. Six simple en-suite bungalows sit in spacious, grassy grounds just behind the shore beneath coconut palms hung with hammocks, next door to the *Holiday Inn*. There's a restaurant and motorbike rental here too, but not much else. Easiest access to *Mai Khao Beach Bungalows* is by bus to or from Phuket town: ask to be dropped at Thachatchai police box, 4km away on Highway 402, from where you can phone the bungalows for a pick-up. Closed Aug, sometimes longer, during the rainy season. Fan B900, a/c B1300, with hot water B1800

Sala Phuket ☎076 338888, ⓦ salaphuket.com. The sharp, Sino-modern architecture of the villa compounds here – all done out in cool creams and silver, with colour-coordinated planting and the occasional lacquered screen – attract mainly couples, especially honeymooners, who enjoy the style and privacy, especially of the pool villas. There's an enticing open-air seafront lounging area here too, with deliciously squishy sofas, plus a rooftop terrace, a spa and three swimming pools. Breakfast and wi-fi included. B10,100

Hat Nai Yang

The long curved sweep of **HAT NAI YANG**, 5km south of Hat Mai Khao and 30km north of Phuket town, is partly under the protection of Sirinath National Park and has only fairly low-key development. In the plentiful shade cast by the feathery casuarinas and cajeput trees that run most of the length of the bay stand more than a dozen small seafood restaurants, and a small, low-rise tourist village of travel agents, a few accommodation options, ATMs, a massage pavilion, internet and dive shops. The beach is clean and good for swimming at the southern end, and there's a reasonable, shallow **reef** about 1km offshore (10min by longtail boat) from the Sirinath National Park headquarters, which is a fifteen-minute walk north of the tourist village (if you're driving yourself to Hat Nai Yang, when the main access road hits the beach, turn left for the tourist village, right for the national park).

ARRIVAL AND DEPARTURE

HAT NAI YANG

By taxi Hat Nai Yang is just 2km south of the airport, about B150 by taxi.

By songthaew An infrequent songthaew service (B35; 1hr 45min) runs between Phuket town and Hat Nai Yang.

ACCOMMODATION

Indigo Pearl ☎076 327006, ⓦ indigo-pearl.com. Luxurious rooms and villas look on to attractively land-scaped plantation-style gardens that run down to the southern end of the beachfront road; facilities include a meandering lagoon-like salt-water swimming pool, a dive shop, an inventively programmed activities centre, a spa and kids' club. Interiors are designed to evoke Phuket's tin-mining history, with metallic colour schemes, polished cement floors and a penchant for industrial art, but the look is softened by very comfortable furniture, generous balconies and plenty of greenery. B11,700

Nai Yang Beach Resort ☎076 328300, ⓦ naiyang beachresort.com. Good upper-mid-range option at the south end of the beach, its cosy, modern, whitewashed a/c rooms fitted with attractive dark-wood furniture and ranged in two- and three-storey wings around pretty tropical gardens; there are three swimming pools, a dive centre and wi-fi throughout. Breakfast included. B2700

EATING AND DRINKING

The tourist village in Nai Yang is locally famous for its small shorefront restaurants that serve mostly barbecued seafood (and the odd wood-fired pizza), on mats under the trees and at tables on the sand, which are candlelit and exceptionally tranquil at night.

The Beach Club One of several little beach bars in the tourist village, a cool, relaxed place for a drink in its low-slung track-side chairs or on one of its day beds with triangular cushions on the beach. Happy hour 3–5pm & 10–11pm. Daily noon–1am.

Black Ginger Indigo Pearl ☎076 327006. For a really top-notch romantic dinner, you can't top the intimate,

black-painted *sala* here. Highlights from the very classy menu here (from B300) include the Phuket lobster with red coconut curry, fresh Vietnamese-style rice-flour pancakes stuffed with shrimps, coriander and herbs and local *kaeng leuang*, yellow curry with fish fillet. Reservations advisable. Daily 6.30–11pm.

Hat Nai Thon

The next bay south down the coast from Hat Nai Yang is the small but perfectly formed 500m-long gold-sand **HAT NAI THON**, with good snorkelling at reefs a brief longtail ride offshore. Shops, hotels and restaurants line the inland side of its narrow little shorefront road, but there's still a low-key, village-like atmosphere here.

ARRIVAL AND DEPARTURE

HAT NAI THON

Most visitors rent their own transport as songthaews don't make the detour from the highway and taxis are thin on the ground.

ACCOMMODATION

Andaman White Beach Resort ☎076 316300, ⓦandamanwhitebeach.com. About 2km south over the southern headland, occupying secluded cliffside land that runs down to a gorgeous little private bay of white sand and turquoise water (sometimes known as Hat Nai Thon Noia), this resort offers luxurious rooms and villas with unsurpassed views, including some designed

for families, plus a 40m swimming pool, a spa and wi-fi. B7750

Naithonburi Beach Resort ☎076 318700, ⓦnaithonburi.com. Huge resort, with over two hundred posh a/c rooms in a U-shaped complex enclosing an enormous pool, some of them with direct pool access, though it doesn't dominate the bay. B2800

Ao Bang Tao

Re-landscaped from a former tin-mining concession to encompass lagoons, parkland and Phuket's best eighteen-hole golf course, **AO BANG TAO** is dominated by the vast, upscale *Laguna Phuket*, a gated "integrated resort" of seven luxury hotels on an impressive 8km shorefront. It's a world away from the thrust and hustle of Patong and a popular choice for families, with no need to leave the *Laguna* village, though beware of the undertow off the coast here, which confines many guests to the hotel pools. There's free transport between the seven hotels, which between them offer a huge range of leisure and sports facilities, as well as a shopping centre.

ARRIVAL AND DEPARTURE

AO BANG TAO

Half-hourly **songthaews** (B25; 1hr 15min) cover the 24km from Phuket town to Ao Bang Tao during the day, or there are resort shuttle **buses** and on-site car rental.

ACCOMMODATION

Laguna Phuket ☎076 362300, ⓦlagunaphuket.com. The main website sometimes has discounted rates at *Laguna*'s seven hotels, while the family-oriented *Best Western Allamanda Laguna* (☎076 362700, ⓦallamanda .com), comprising 150 apartment-style suites with kitchenette and separate living area, has the cheapest rates

in the complex (B5000). Haunt of high society and sports stars, the exclusive *Banyan Tree Phuket* (☎076 324374, ⓦbanyantree.com) offers lavish villas in private gardens, many with private pools, and the gloriously indulgent, award-winning, Banyan Tree spa (B20,000).

Hat Surin and Ao Pansea

South around Laem Son headland from Ao Bang Tao, handsome little **HAT SURIN** is a favourite weekend getaway for sophisticated Phuketians and a big draw for expats, who inhabit the ever-expanding forest of condo developments inland from the small, pretty beach. The shorefront gets very crowded, however, packed with sunloungers and beach restaurants, so it can be hard to appreciate the setting. Eating and shopping facilities cater to the upmarket clientele, and beachfront dining and drinking is the main pastime. Things are much quieter on Hat Surin's northern bay, **AO PANSEA**, which is divided from the main beach by a rocky promontory.

ARRIVAL AND DEPARTURE

HAT SURIN AND AO PANSEA

By songthaew Songthaews travel the 24km between Phuket town and Hat Surin approximately every half-hour

during the day and cost B30.

ACCOMMODATION

Amanpuri ✆076 324333, ⊛amanresorts.com. Secluded from the riffraff on Ao Pansea, this is a favourite haunt of royalty and Hollywood stars, who stay in the butler-staffed pavilions, some with their own pools, relax in the spa and charter the hotel's yachts. B31,500

Benyada Lodge 103 Thanon Hat Surin ✆076 271261, ⊛benyadalodge-phuket.com. Just across the small park from the beach, this thirty-room lodge with high standards

of service has had a recent makeover in a crisp, bright contemporary style, with the addition of a rooftop pool and bar-restaurant. The spacious a/c rooms all have wi-fi, hot showers, TV and fridge. Breakfast included. B2800

Surin Bay Inn 106 Thanon Hat Surin ✆076 271601, ⊛surinbayinn.com. Large, attractive rooms above a restaurant and bar near *Benyada Lodge*, with in-room a/c, hot showers, free wi-fi, TV and fridge. Breakfast included. B1800

EATING AND DRINKING

Opus One ✆076 386562, ⊛opusonephuket.com. Chic, atmospherically lit lounge-bar and bistro done out in black and red, serving very tasty dishes, such as risotto with mushrooms and truffles, in large portions (B450); live soul band Fri from 9.30pm. Daily 6pm–midnight/1am, kitchen closes 10pm.

Taste ✆076 270090, ⊛tastesurinbeach.com. This sophisticated seafront restaurant and art gallery is especially known for its great seafood, such as steamed red snapper fillet with a lemon and butter sauce (B390) and wild ginger and green pepper shrimp (B390). Tues–Sun 2pm–midnight.

Hat Kamala and Laem Singh

With its cheerfully painted houses and absence of high-rises, the small, village-like tourist development at **HAT KAMALA** is low-key and mid-market, sandwiched between the beach and the predominantly Muslim town of Ban Kamala, about 300m west of the main Patong–Surin road, 6km north of Patong and 26km northwest of Phuket town. Accommodation, shops, restaurants and other tourist services are mostly clustered either side of shoreside Thanon Rim Had (also spelt Rim Hat) which, despite its limited choice, is a much pleasanter place to browse than the big resorts. The beach gets prettier and quieter the further north you go, away from Thanon Rim Had, with restaurant shacks renting sunloungers along most of its course. A stretch of this area is backed by the Muslim cemetery, so it's particularly important to respect local sensibilities and avoid going topless.

Kamala was very badly hit by the 2004 **tsunami**, which killed many residents and wiped out the beachfront school, the temple and countless homes and businesses. Though extensive rebuilding has extinguished most of the physical scars, a copper sculpture in the park opposite *Print Kamala* bears witness to the devastation, and a volunteer English-teaching programme at the school, Phuket Has Been Good to Us (see p.69), aims to help rebuild some of the young lives affected.

About 1km northeast of Hat Kamala, a couple of steep paths lead west off the main Patong–Surin road down to **Laem Singh** cape, a pretty little sandy cove whose picturesque combination of turquoise water and smooth granite boulders makes it one of Phuket's finest. It's good for swimming and very secluded, plus there's a decent patch of shade throughout the day.

| **ARRIVAL AND DEPARTURE** | **HAT KAMALA AND LAEM SINGH** |

By songthaew The cheapest way to get to Hat Kamala is by songthaew from Phuket town (about every 30min during the day, 1hr 15min; B35).

ACCOMMODATION

Hat Kamala is popular with long-stay tourists, and several hotels offer rooms with kitchenettes; there's also a preponderance of small-scale places.

Benjamin Resort 83 Thanon Rim Had, opposite the school at the southerly end of the beachfront road ☎076 385146–7, ⍵phuketdir.com/benjaminresort. Set right on the beach and about the best and friendliest deal in Kamala, this block of 37 a/c rooms lacks character but couldn't be closer to the sea. Although views are obstructed from all but the most expensive rooms, the spacious interiors are almost identical and all have balcony, fridge, TV, hot water and breakfast included, plus use of sunloungers out front. B500

Coconut Garden Soi Police Station ☎081 477 3331, ⍵coconutgarden.se. The best thing about the dozen good-sized but unexceptional concrete a/c bungalows, two- and three-bedroom houses here is their location on the nicer northerly stretch of the central beach; all have a/c, hot shower, fridge, TV and DVD. B2000

Kamala Dreams 74/1 Thanon Rim Had ☎076 279131, ⍵kamaladreams.net. Epitomizing all the best things about Kamala, this is a really nice, small hotel set right on the shore, in the middle of the tourist village. Its eighteen rooms are large and furnished in contemporary style, and all have a/c, TVs, a kitchenette and a large balcony overlooking the pool and the sea. B2300

Malinee House 75/4 Thanon Rim Had ☎081 691 7879, ⍵malineehouse.com. Very friendly, traveller-oriented guesthouse in the middle of the tourist village, with internet access and the Jackie Lee travel agency downstairs, and large, comfortably furnished and cheerfully painted a/c rooms upstairs, all of them with balconies, hot showers and fridges. B1000

Print Kamala Resort 74/8 Thanon Rim Had ☎076 385396–8, ⍵printkamalaresort.net. The best accommodation here is in a village-like complex of very generously sized bungalows, connected via stilted walkways around a tropical Bali-style garden. The bungalows all have prettily furnished a/c bedrooms plus separate living rooms, and capacious, shaded decks. The hotel also has some less interesting, but more expensive, rooms in a hotel wing, and a large pool. Breakfast included. B3500

EATING AND DRINKING

Most people eat and drink on the beach, especially at the restaurant shacks and bars that pretty much line the shore all the way north from opposite *Print Kamala*; seafood is the big seller here, and you can bury your feet in the sand.

Rockfish Kamala Beach Estate Hotel ☎076 279732, ⍵rockfishrestaurant.com. This Australian-run restaurant enjoys lovely views from its southern headland location and an island-wide reputation for great food, mostly Asian fusion and seafood dishes such as tiger prawns in tamarind sauce (B600) or a blue crab and mango salad starter (B350); simpler, cheaper dishes available for breakfast and lunch. Daily 8am–10pm.

ENTERTAINMENT

Phuket FantaSea About 1km northeast of Hat Kamala off the main Patong–Surin road ☎076 385111, ⍵phuket-fantasea.com. The enjoyable, hi-tech megaspectacular, "Fantasy of a Kingdom, Cultural Illusion Show", is staged at the enormous FantaSea entertainments complex, featuring high-wire trapeze acts, acrobatics, pyrotechnics, illusionists, comedy and traditional dance – plus a depressing baby elephant circus. B1500 or B1900 including the unexciting pre-show dinner. Daily except Thurs 9pm.

Ao Patong

The busiest and most popular of all Phuket's beaches, **AO PATONG** – 5km south of Ao Kamala and 15km west of Phuket town – is vastly overdeveloped and hard to recommend. A congestion of high-rise hotels, tour agents and souvenir shops disfigures the beachfront road, tireless and tiresome touts are everywhere, and hostess bars and strip joints dominate the nightlife, attracting an increasing number of single Western men to the most active scene between Bangkok and Hat Yai. On the plus side, the broad, 3km-long beach offers good sand and plenty of shade beneath the parasols and there are hundreds of shops and bars plus a surprising number of good restaurants to keep you busy after dark.

ARRIVAL AND DEPARTURE
AO PATONG

Songthaews from Phuket town (approx every 15min, 6am–6pm; 30min; B25) approach Patong from the northeast, driving south along one-way Thanon Raja Uthit Song Roi Phi (Thanon Raja Uthit 200 Phi) then circling

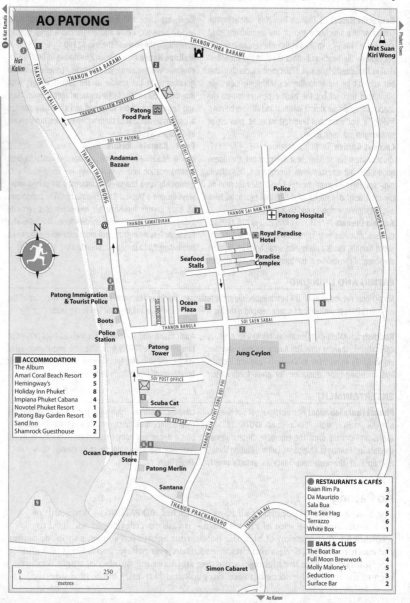

AO PATONG

ACCOMMODATION

The Album	3
Amari Coral Beach Resort	9
Hemingway's	5
Holiday Inn Phuket	8
Impiana Phuket Cabana	4
Novotel Phuket Resort	1
Patong Bay Garden Resort	6
Sand Inn	7
Shamrock Guesthouse	2

RESTAURANTS & CAFÉS

Baan Rim Pa	3
Da Maurizio	2
Sala Bua	4
The Sea Hag	5
Terrazzo	6
White Box	1

BARS & CLUBS

The Boat Bar	1
Full Moon Brewwork	4
Molly Malone's	5
Seduction	3
Surface Bar	2

back north along beachfront Thanon Thavee Wong (also one-way) via the *Patong Merlin*, where they wait to pick up passengers for the return trip.

GETTING AROUND

National **car rental** (☎076 340608, ⓦ nationalcarthailand.com) has a desk inside the *Holiday Inn*, the local Budget agent is at the nearby *Patong Merlin* (☎076 292389, ⓦ budget.co.th), or you can rent jeeps and motorbikes from any transport tout on Thanon Thavee Wong. Otherwise, aim to stroll – tuk-tuks ask for as much as B200 for short trips within the resort.

INFORMATION AND TOURS

Most of the **tour agents** have offices on the southern stretch of Thanon Thavee Wong, offering a number of day-trips and activities (see box, p.623); this is also where you'll find many of the **dive operators** (see box, pp.642–643).

ACCOMMODATION

It's hard to find much accommodation under B900 in Patong, and there are no backpacker places, but upper-end hotels are reasonable value and all have excellent facilities.

The Album 29 Thanon Sawatdirak ☎076 297023, ⓦ thealbumhotel.com. Tiny urban-chic boutique inn, where the 22 carefully designed a/c rooms all have a flatscreen TV, DVD player, free wi-fi, and a petite balcony. There's a small jacuzzi pool on the fourth-floor roof terrace and rates include continental breakfast and high tea. B2900

Amari Coral Beach Resort 104 Thanon Traitrang ☎076 340106, ⓦ amari.com. Occupying its own secluded little beach on a headland at the southernmost end of the bay, this upmarket Thai chain hotel offers contemporary-chic rooms with generous sea-view balconies, plus two swimming pools, romantic spa facilities, tennis courts and several restaurants. The views are exceptional and the location peaceful but convenient; as it's ranged up a slope it's not ideal for guests with mobility problems. B5700

Hemingway's 179/95–8 Soi Saen Sabai ☎076 343264–5, ⓦ patonghemingways.com. Smart, modern, a/c rooms done out in dark wood, black and red, with small, hot-water bathrooms, TVs, fridges and free wi-fi. Wicker chairs and old-fashioned ceiling fans downstairs are all that conjure up the ghost of Papa Hemingway, but the big plus-point of this place is the small rooftop pool, jacuzzi and bar with views of the surrounding hills. B2500

★ **Holiday Inn Phuket** 86/11 Thanon Thavee Wong ☎076 340608, ⓦ phuket.holiday-inn.com. Well-run, innovative, upmarket chain hotel that offers smart, contemporary rooms just across the road from the beach, in two differently styled wings, and fosters an informal, unpretentious atmosphere. The poshest Busakorn villa rooms have their own interconnected pools and there are also large, attractive pools for each wing, plus several restaurants and an interesting programme of daily activities. The hotel makes a big effort to be family-friendly, with special "kidsuites" for children, an all-day kids' club and a teens' club and two children's pools. Also offers wheelchair-accessible rooms. Breakfast and wi-fi included. B6300

Impiana Phuket Cabana 94 Thanon Thavee Wong ☎076 340138, ⓦ impiana.com. Located right on the beach and in the heart of the resort, the very tastefully designed a/c cabanas here are set around a garden and smallish swimming pool; also has a kids' pool and a spa. B7600

Novotel Phuket Resort Thanon Phra Barami/Thanon Hat Kalim ☎076 342777, ⓦ novotelphuket.com. Luxurious and relaxing chain hotel built on the hillside above Kalim Bay, the quieter, northern end of the resort, a 10min walk or a free shuttle ride to Patong's main beach and shops, but very close to some of the best restaurants. Occupying sloping landscaped tropical gardens and offering exceptional high-level sea views, it's especially popular with families as it offers heaps of activities plus a multi-level swimming pool. B4500

Patong Bay Garden Resort 33/1 Thanon Thavee Wong ☎076 340297–8, ⓦ patongbaygarden.com. Lively, mid-sized 71-room hotel set right on the beach, with the top "studio" rooms having uninterrupted sea views, quite unusual in central Patong. Other rooms look out on the small shorefront pool or have no view at all. Rooms are quite elegantly furnished and all have a/c, free wi-fi and TV. Breakfast included. B3200

Sand Inn 171 Soi Saen Sabai ☎076 340275, ⓦ sandinnphuket.com. Thirty well-appointed a/c rooms, a little on the compact side, but maintained to a good standard and in the ideal location for nightlife, just east off bar-packed Thanon Bangla. There's TV, hot showers and fridges in all rooms, a *Euro Deli* restaurant downstairs, and use of a small swimming pool just a few metres up the soi. B1600

Shamrock Guesthouse Above The Deli supermarket, 31 Thanon Raja Uthit Song Roi Phi ☎076 340991, ⓦ deliguesthouse.com. Friendly, good-value three-storey hotel at the northern end of the resort with large, pleasant, well-maintained and cheerily painted a/c rooms, all with TVs, fridges, and safety boxes. Ask for a room on the north side of the building: they're cooler, have balconies and are away from the noise of the adjacent Irish bar. B800

7

EATING

Much of the food on Patong is dire, but in among the disastrous little cafés advertising everything from Hungarian to Swedish "home cooking" you'll find a few genuinely reputable, long-running, upmarket favourites; reservations are recommended at all the places listed here. For well-priced Thai fast food, there are the regional speciality stalls at the *Food Haven* food centre in Jung Ceylon, the *Patong Food Park* night market that sets up around 5pm towards the northern end of Thanon Raja Uthit Song Roi Phi, and the row of seafood stall-restaurants further south, opposite the *Royal Paradise Hotel* complex.

★ **Baan Rim Pa** Across from the Novotel on Thanon Hat Kalim ☎076 340789, ⊛baanrimpa.com. One of Phuket's most famous fine-dining restaurants, this is an elegant spot that's beautifully set in a teak building on a clifftop overlooking the bay, with tables also on its sea-view terrace. Known for its classic "Royal Thai" cuisine (mains from about B400), including banana blossom salad, creamy duck curry and fried tiger prawns with tamarind sauce, as well as for its wine cellar. Live jazz every night in the *Piano Bar*. Daily 1pm–midnight.

Da Maurizio Across from the Novotel on Thanon Hat Kalim ☎076 344079, ⊛damaurizio.com. Superior Italian restaurant in a stunning location set over the rocks beside the sea. Serves authentic antipasti and home-made pasta such as pappardelle with scallops and crab in a spicy tomato sauce, Phuket lobsters and other great seafood, and a good wine list. Main dishes from B450. Daily noon–11pm.

Sala Bua 41 Thanon Thavee Wong ☎076 340138, ⊛sala-bua.com. Fabulously stylish, breezy, beach-view restaurant attached to the *Impiana Phuket Cabana* hotel. The innovative, pricey, Pacific Rim and Thai menus include Cajun-style red snapper with fermented black bean sauce (B485) and desserts such as sticky-rice sushi rolls with green mango shake (B250). Daily 6am–midnight.

★ **The Sea Hag** Soi Dr Wattana (Soi Permpong 3) ☎076 341111, ⊛kenyaphuket.com. The same chef has been cooking great seafood here for two decades and this is where expat hoteliers come for a good Patong feed. Fish and seafood cooked any number of Thai-style ways for B200–400. Daily noon–4pm & 6pm–midnight.

Terrazzo Holiday Inn Phuket, 86/11 Thanon Thavee Wong ☎076 340608, ⊛phuket.holiday-inn.com. Good, crispy, thin pizzas (around B300) and tasty pastas including home-made ravioli and gnocchi, in a very pleasant, open-plan garden setting, with a popular oval bar, on the main beachfront drag. Daily 6–11.15pm.

White Box Thanon Hat Kalim, 1.5km north of the Novotel ☎076 346271, ⊛whiteboxphuket.com. This chic, sophisticated waterside restaurant and bar, strikingly designed as a modernist cube with panoramic picture windows, is a magnet for visiting celebs and style-conscious expats. The very expensive menu (mains from B480) mixes Thai and Mediterranean flavours – grilled Phuket lobster with mint and ginger, beef carpaccio, red curry with roasted duck – and the rooftop sofas are ideal for a pre- or post-dinner drink. Daily 11am–11.30pm.

NIGHTLIFE AND ENTERTAINMENT

After dark, everyone heads to pedestrianized Thanon Bangla for their own taste of Patong's notorious **nightlife** and the road teems with a cross section of Phuket tourists, from elderly couples and young parents with strollers, to glammed-up girlfriends and groups of lads. The big draw for the more innocent onlookers is Thanon Bangla's Soi Crocodile, better known as Soi Katoey, or "Trannie Alley", where pouting, barely clad transvestites jiggle their implants on podiums at the mouth of the soi and charge for photos with giggling tourists. But the real action happens further down the many bar-filled sois shooting off Thanon Bangla, where open-air bar-beers and neon-lit go-go clubs packed with strippers and goggle-eyed punters pulsate through the night. The pick-up trade pervades most bars in Patong, and though many of these joints are welcoming enough to couples and female tourists, there are a few alternatives, listed below, for anyone not in that kind of mood. The **gay** entertainment district is concentrated around the Paradise Complex, a network of small sois and dozens of bar-beers in front of *Royal Paradise Hotel* on Thanon Raja Uthit Song Roi Phi: see ⊛gaypatong.com for events listings, including dates for the annual Gay Pride festival, which has recently been held in late April. If you're looking for something else to do with yourself (or your kids) in the evening, check out the transvestite Simon Cabaret, or the spectacular show at nearby Phuket FantaSea (see p.635). The Jung Ceylon shopping centre has a seven-screen **cinema**, SF Cinema City.

The Boat Bar Soi 5, Paradise Complex, off Thanon Raja Uthit Song Roi Phi ⊛boatbar.com. Long-running, very popular gay bar and disco, with two cabaret shows nightly, at around midnight and 1.30am. Daily 9pm–late.

Full Moon Brewwork Port Zone (next to the replica junk), Jung Ceylon shopping centre, Thanon Raja Uthit Song Roi Phi ⊛facebook.com/fullmoonbrewwork. The best of this microbrewery's offerings is their dark ale, a decent bitter that might appease homesick Brits, and there's good food, too, including tom yam kung (B145). Live music upstairs (daily except Tues & Thurs 7.30–10pm). Daily 11am–midnight.

Molly Malone's 94/1 Thanon Thavee Wong ⓦmolly malonesphuket.com. Genial Thai–Irish pub chain that serves draught Guinness and Kilkenny, shows international sports TV, stages live bands playing pub rock from 9.30pm and has pool tables, a small beer garden and no overt hostess presence. Daily 10am–2am.

Seduction Soi Happy, off Thanon Bangla ⓦseduction disco.com. Currently the favourite dance venue for partying couples and others not looking for freelance company, this three-storey bar and club has fairly classy lounge areas, hi-tech lighting and a catholic music policy, and occasionally brings in big-name international DJs. Free

until midnight, B200 thereafter. Daily 10pm–4am.

Simon Cabaret Thanon Prachanukho, south end of Patong ⓣ076 342011–5, ⓦphuket-simoncabaret .com. Famously flamboyant extravaganza starring a troupe of transvestites. It's all very Hollywood – a little bit risqué but not at all sleazy – and popular with tour groups and families. B700. Nightly 6pm, 7.45pm & 9.30pm.

Surface Bar Top floor, La Flora Resort Patong, 39 Thanon Thavee Wong ⓣ076 344241. The perfect place for a sophisticated sundowner, enjoyed from the comfort of enormous sofas on the hotel's wide rooftop terrace. Expansive ocean views and a sea breeze as well. Daily 5pm–midnight.

SHOPPING

Jung Ceylon Thanon Raja Uthit Song Roi Phi ⓦjungceylon.com. Though you can't move for shops in downtown Patong, by far the best, and least hectic, place to browse is this enormous shopping centre, whose refreshingly tasteful and spacious design includes fountains and plaza seating plus countless shops and restaurants.

There are branches of Robinsons Department Store and, on the ground floor at the front end, Boots the Chemist and Asia Books (for English-language books, magazines and newspapers), plus the That's Siam Thai handicrafts emporium in the basement. Daily 11am–10pm.

DIRECTORY

Immigration The tiny Patong branch (information only) of Phuket's Immigration office is next to *Sala Bua* restaurant on Thanon Thavee Wong (ⓣ076 340477; Mon–Fri 10am–noon & 1–3pm).

Post office Thanon Thavee Wong (daily 9am–7pm).
Tourist police In front of the Immigration office on Thanon Thavee Wong (ⓣ076 340244 or ⓣ1155).

Ao Karon

AO KARON, Phuket's second resort, after Patong, is very much a middle-of-the-road destination. Far less lively, or congested, than Patong, but more commercial and less individual than the smaller beaches, it's the domain of affordable guesthouses and package-tour hotels and appeals chiefly to mid-budget tourists, many of them from Scandinavia. The 2.5km-long **beach** is graced with squeaky soft golden sand and is completely free of developments, though there's very little natural shade; an embankment screens most of the southern half of the beach from the road running alongside, but north of the *Hilton* the road is more often in view and parts of the shore back on to lagoons and wasteland. Karon's main **shopping and eating areas**, with all the usual resort facilities, are grouped around the *Centara Karon Resort* on the northern curve of Thanon Patak; along and around Thanon Luang Pho Chuain, location of the Kata Plaza enclave of accommodation, restaurants and bars; and along Thanon Taina (sometimes referred to as Kata Centre).

The **undertow** off Ao Karon is treacherously strong during the monsoon season from June to October, so you should heed the warning signs and flags and ask for local advice – fatalities are not uncommon. The tiny bay just north of Ao Karon – known as **Karon Noi** or Relax Bay – is almost exclusively patronized by guests of the *Le Meridien* hotel, but non-guests are quite welcome to swim and sunbathe here.

ARRIVAL AND DEPARTURE   AO KARON

Ao Karon is 5km south of Patong and 20km southwest of Phuket town. Most **songthaews** from Phuket town (approx every 20min; 30min; B30) arrive in Karon via Thanon Patak, hitting the beach at the northern end of Ao Karon and then driving south along beachfront Thanon Karon, continuing over the headland as far as *Kata Beach Resort* on Ao Kata Yai. To catch a songthaew back into town, just stand on the other side of the road and flag one down. Transport touts throughout the resort rent motorbikes and jeeps.

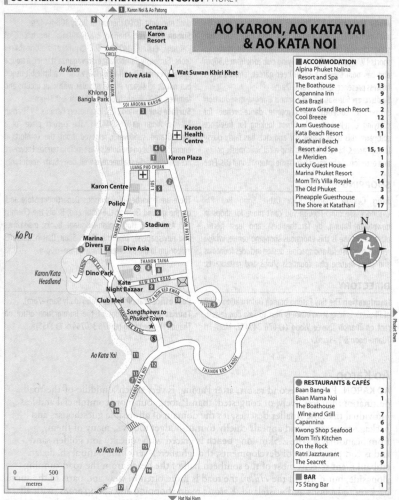

AO KARON, AO KATA YAI & AO KATA NOI

■ ACCOMMODATION	
Alpina Phuket Nalina Resort and Spa	10
The Boathouse	13
Capannina Inn	9
Casa Brazil	5
Centara Grand Beach Resort	2
Cool Breeze	12
Jum Guesthouse	6
Kata Beach Resort	11
Katathani Beach Resort and Spa	15, 16
Le Meridien	1
Lucky Guest House	8
Marina Phuket Resort	7
Mom Tri's Villa Royale	14
The Old Phuket	3
Pineapple Guesthouse	4
The Shore at Katathani	17

● RESTAURANTS & CAFÉS	
Baan Bang-la	2
Baan Mama Noi	1
The Boathouse Wine and Grill	7
Capannina	6
Kwong Shop Seafood	4
Mom Tri's Kitchen	8
On the Rock	3
Ratri Jazztaurant	5
The Seacret	9

■ BAR	
75 Stang Bar	1

ACCOMMODATION

★**Casa Brazil** 9 Soi 1, Thanon Luang Pho Chuain ☎076 396317, ⓦphukethomestay.com. Appealingly arty little hotel, designed in Santa Fe style, with adobe-look walls, earth-toned paintwork, and funky decor and furnishings. The 21 rooms are comfortable, with hot showers, fridges and TVs, and nearly all have a/c. Choose rooms at the back for a rare green and peaceful view of Karon's hilly backdrop, best enjoyed from the French windows and private balconies. Rates include breakfast and there's wi-fi. Fan B1200, a/c B1400

Centara Grand Beach Resort 683 Thanon Patak ☎076 201234, ⓦcentarahotelsresorts.com. Huge, low-rise, beachfront luxury hotel, which very loosely echoes Phuket's Sino-Portuguese architecture, all in different shades of pink. It's particularly good for children, with two kids' clubs, a kids' pool, a free-form main pool and a "Lazy River", an artificial river that runs under bridges and under tunnels for exploration on inner tubes. There's an adults-only pool too, and grown-ups can also enjoy kayaking, windsurfing, tennis, the spa and a long menu of other activities. B10,500

Jum Guesthouse Off Thanon Kata, about 100m from the beach, directly behind and accessible through Andaman Seaview Hotel ☎076 396570. Friendly place in a lush, shady garden with just five large, concrete bungalows, all with fridges, TVs, wardrobes, free wi-fi and a few decorative touches; the big, well-equipped bathrooms have hot showers. Fan B1000, a/c B1200

Le Meridien Ao Karon Noi (also known as Relax Bay), north of Ao Karon ☎076 370100, ⓦlemeridien.com. This huge hotel complex has the tiny bay all to itself and boasts an amazing breadth of facilities, including ten restaurants and bars, two lagoon-style swimming pools (with islands), a spa, squash and tennis courts, free non-motorized watersports and private woods. It's a good choice for kids, with reliable babysitting services and a kids' club. Breakfast included. B9200

Lucky Guest House 110/44–45 Thanon Taina, Kata Centre ☎076 330572, ⓔluckyguesthousekata @hotmail.com. Good-value place offering unusually large, bright en-suite rooms in a low-rise block (the best have balconies) and some rather plain but very clean semi-detached bungalows on land further back; set back a bit down a small soi, this guesthouse has a refreshing sense of space that's at a premium on this road packed with shops, bars and restaurants. Fan B450, a/c B650

Marina Phuket Resort 47 Thanon Karon, far southern end of Ao Karon, on the Karon/Kata headland ☎076 330625, ⓦmarinaphuket.com. Enjoying both a very central location, backing on to the beach and just steps from restaurants and shops, and a luxuriously spacious and secluded tropical garden in a former coconut plantation, this is a good upper-end choice. Accommodation is in a/c cottages – Garden View options are old-fashioned and plain, but Jungle View versions are very appealing – and there's a pool, wi-fi and the prettily located *On the Rock* restaurant. Breakfast included. B6000

The Old Phuket Soi Aroona Karon, 192/36 Thanon Karon ☎076 396353–6, ⓦtheoldphuket.com. The Sino Wing at this attractive, peacefully secluded, heritage-conscious hotel is designed to evoke Sino-Portuguese shophouse architecture. Its rooms are both pretty and modern, with coloured glass window panels and East Indies-style wooden doors. Furnishings in the more expensive Serene Wing are much more contemporary and minimalist and many of its rooms have direct access to the lagoon-like pool. B8200

Pineapple Guesthouse Karon Plaza, off Patak and Luang Pho Chuain rds ☎076 396223, ⓦpineapple phuket.com. Good-value British–Thai guesthouse offering 21 sprucely kept, tiled-floor rooms, all with fridges, TV and hot water, most with a/c, plus a ten-bed mixed dorm, with lockers and several fans. The downstairs restaurant serves full English breakfasts and the guesthouse is surrounded by other expat bars and restaurants in the enclave known as Karon Plaza (not to be confused with the Karon Plaza market stalls at the north end of Karon beachfront). Free internet access and free wi-fi throughout. Dorm B200, fan B500, a/c B900

EATING AND DRINKING

Karon's choice of restaurants is underwhelming, lacking either the big-name restaurants of Patong or Kata, or the authenticity of Phuket town. Though go-go bars haven't arrived yet, clusters of outdoor bar-beers with hostess service are popping up at a depressing rate.

75 Stang Bar Karon Plaza, up a lane off Thanon Luang Pho Chuain, near Thanon Patak. In among the sports bars and rooms for rent in Karon Plaza are a couple of "art bars" run by cool local creative types, including this invitingly bohemian little outdoor place. It's a mess of driftwood and found objects, where the only things that seem to have been designed are the red, gold and green stools, which match the wall-to-wall reggae on the sound system. Daily 6pm–2am.

Baan Bang-la 6 Soi Patak, off Thanon Patak. The seafood here has a good reputation and there are also pasta dishes and pizzas – made in a brick oven by an Italian *pizzaiolo* – on the menu too. Dining is mostly alfresco in Thai *salas* set around a pretty little garden. Mains B180–300. Daily 6pm–late.

Baan Mama Noi Karon Plaza, next door but one to Pineapple Guesthouse on a lane off Thanon Patak. Expats, dive staff and Italian tourists fill this place at lunch and dinnertime, savouring the home-from-home taste of the excellent, mid-priced, Italian food, such as spaghetti bolognese (B130). Daily 7am–10pm.

Kwong Shop Seafood 114 Thanon Taina. Unassuming but very popular, friendly family-run institution sporting gingham tablecloths that's famous for its well-priced fresh fish (all B40 per 100 grammes) and seafood cooked to order. Daily 8am–midnight.

On the Rock In the grounds of Marina Phuket Resort, Kata/Karon headland ☎076 330625, ⓦmarinaphuket .com. Occupying a fine spot above the rocks at the southern end of Ao Karon, this open-air restaurant serves especially good baskets of grilled and deep-fried seafood, baked mussels and mixed seafood satay. Especially romantic at night. Main dishes from B350. Daily 11am–10.30pm.

Ao Kata Yai and Ao Kata Noi

Broad, curving **AO KATA YAI** (Big Kata Bay) is only a few minutes' drive around the headland from Karon (17km from Phuket town), but both prettier and safer

DIVING AND SNORKELLING OFF PHUKET

The reefs and islands within sailing distance of Phuket rate among the most spectacular in the world, and **diving and snorkelling** trips are both good value and hugely popular. Many trips operate year-round, though some of the more remote islands and reefs become too dangerous to reach during part or all of the monsoon season, roughly June to October.

DIVE SHOPS AND TRIPS

All the dive **shops** listed below are established and accredited PADI Five-Star Instructor or Career Development Centres; they teach courses, organize dive trips and rent equipment. Advice on choosing a dive shop and other general diving information can be found in "Basics" (see p.52). Expect to pay around B4500 for a one-day introductory **diving course**, and B14,500 for the four-day Openwater course, including equipment. **Day-trips** to the closest of the dive sites listed below, including at least two dives, cost around B3800, while multi-day **live-aboard** cruises to the more distant top-rated reefs of Ko Similan and Ko Surin, Hin Daeng and Hin Muang, and the Mergui archipelago can cost as much as B33,000 for four days, including sixteen dives and full board but excluding equipment and national park fees.

There are **recompression chambers** at Phuket International Hospital in Phuket town (see p.626), and at Vachira Hospital, Soi Wachira, Thanon Yaowarat, Phuket town (☎076 211114, ⓦvachiraphuket.go.th).

Dive Asia 24 Thanon Karon, Kata/Karon headland, Ao Karon, and 623 Thanon Patak, Karon Circle, Ao Karon ☎076 330598, ⓦdiveasia.com.

Marina Divers Next to *Marina Phuket Resort* at 45 Thanon Karon, Ao Karon ☎076 330272, ⓦmarinadivers.com.

Santana 240 Thanon Raja Uthit Song Roi Phi, Ao Patong ☎076 294220, ⓦsantanaphuket.com.

Scuba Cat 94 Thanon Thavee Wong, Ao Patong ☎076 293120, ⓦscubacat.com.

SNORKELLING TRIPS

The most popular snorkelling destination from Phuket is **Ko Phi Phi** (see p.676). All travel agents sell mass-market day-trips there, on huge ferries with capacities of a hundred plus; prices average B1600 and include snorkelling stops at Phi Phi Leh and Phi Phi Don, snorkel rental and a seafood lunch. Smaller speedboat trips to Ko Phi Phi are usually worth the extra money to avoid the big groups; those run by Offspray Leisure (B3200; ☎076 281375, ⓦoffsprayleisure.com) get good reviews, and they also run speedboat snorkel trips to **Ko Racha Yai** (B3200). Day-trips to the remote but beautiful **Ko Similan** islands start from B2600 (see p.620). Many of the dive companies listed welcome snorkellers

for swimming, thanks to the protective rocky promontories at either end. It's also a good distance from the main road. The northern stretch of Kata Yai is overlooked by the unobtrusive buildings of the *Club Med* resort, and the southern by *Kata Beach Resort*: in between the soft sand is busy with sunloungers and the occasional drink and fruit stall. The rest of the accommodation, and the bulk of the tourist village, with its restaurants, bars, tour operators and many shops, fans out eastwards from the walled *Club Med* compound, up to the main road, Thanon Patak.

Beyond the southern headland, **AO KATA NOI**'s (Little Kata Bay) smaller white-sand bay feels secluded, being at the end of a no-through road, but is very popular and filled with loungers and parasols. Kata Noi has its own low-key but rather charmless cluster of businesses, including an ATM and minimarket, though it's dominated by the various sections of the enormous *Katathani* hotel; public access to the beach is down to the right just beyond the hotel's Thani wing.

ARRIVAL AND DEPARTURE   AO KATA YAI AND AO KATA NOI

Most **songthaews** from Phuket go first to Karon, then drive south past *Club Med* and terminate beside *Kata Beach Resort* on the headland between Kata Yai and Kata Noi (B30; returning songthaews depart approx every 20min 5am–4.30pm). To get to Kata Noi, continue walking over the hill for about ten minutes, or take a tuk-tuk for about B100.

on board their day-trips, and sometimes on the live-aboards too, for a discount of about thirty percent.

ANDAMAN COAST DIVE AND SNORKEL SITES

Anemone Reef About 22km east of Phuket. Submerged reef of soft coral and sea anemones starting about 5m deep. Lots of fish, including leopard sharks, tuna and barracuda. Usually combined with a dive at nearby Shark Point. Unsuitable for snorkellers.

Burma Banks About 250km northwest of Phuket; only accessible on live-aboards. A series of submerged "banks", well away from any landmass and very close to the Burmese border. Only worth the trip for its sharks. Visibility up to 25m.

Hin Daeng and **Hin Muang** 56km southwest of Ko Lanta. Hin Daeng is an exceptional reef wall, named after the red soft corals that cover the rocks, with visibility up to 30m. One hundred metres away, Hin Muang also drops to 50m and is good for stingrays, manta rays, whale sharks and silvertip sharks. Visibility up to 50m. Because of the depth and the current, both places are considered too risky for novice divers who have logged fewer than twenty dives. Unsuitable for snorkellers.

King Cruiser Near Shark Point, between Phuket and Ko Phi Phi. Dubbed the *Thai Tanic*, this became a wreck dive in May 1997, when a tourist ferry sank on its way to Ko Phi Phi. Visibility up to 20m, but hopeless for snorkellers because of the depth, and collapsed sections make it dangerous for any but the most experienced divers.

Ko Phi Phi 48km east of Phuket's Ao Chalong (see p.676). Visibility up to 30m. The most popular destination

for Phuket divers and snorkellers. Spectacular drop-offs; good chance of seeing whale sharks.

Ko Racha Noi and **Ko Racha Yai** About 33km and 28km south of Phuket's Ao Chalong respectively. Visibility up to 40m. Racha Yai (aka Raya Yai) is good for beginners and for snorkellers; at the more challenging Racha Noi there's a good chance of seeing manta rays, eagle rays and whale sharks.

Ko Rok Nok and **Ko Rok Nai** 100km southeast of Phuket, south of Ko Lanta (see box, p.691). Visibility up to 18m. Shallow reefs that are excellent for snorkelling.

Ko Similan 96km northwest of Phuket; easiest access from Khao Lak (see p.620). One of the world's top diving spots. Visibility up to 30m. Leopard sharks, whale sharks and manta rays, plus caves and gorges.

Ko Surin 174km northwest of Phuket; easiest access from Khuraburi (see p.607). Shallow reefs of soft and hard corals that are good for snorkelling.

Richelieu Rock Just east of Ko Surin, close to Burmese waters. A sunken pinnacle that's famous for its whale sharks. Considered by many to be Thailand's top dive spot.

Shark Point (Hin Mu Sang) 24km east of Phuket's Laem Panwa. Protected as a marine sanctuary. Visibility up to 10m. Notable for soft corals, sea fans and leopard sharks. Often combined with the *King Cruiser* dive and/or Anemone Reef; unrewarding for snorkellers.

ACCOMMODATION

Alpina Phuket Nalina Resort and Spa 7/1 Thanon Ked Kwan, Kata Yai ☎076 370999, ⓦphuketnalina.com. Very pleasant hotel with comfortable, tastefully Thai-style rooms and a surprisingly quiet location that's close to shops and restaurants and about 10min walk from the beach. A free shuttle also runs guests to the hotel's private beach club in front of *Club Med*. Rooms have generous balconies overlooking the free-form pool and the hills beyond, with some enjoying direct pool access; suites and private pool villas are enormous. Also has a spa, several restaurants and wi-fi throughout. Breakfast included. B6150

The Boathouse Thanon Kok Tanode, Kata Yai ☎076 330015–7, ⓦboathousephuket.com. Exclusive beach-front boutique hotel in a graceful, contemporary style, with just 38 elegantly furnished sea-front rooms, a reputation for classy service, and a famously top-notch restaurant. All rooms have free wi-fi, there's a pool, a spa and weekend cooking classes. Advance booking essential. B9600

Capannina Inn The Beach Centre, "New Kata Road",

Kata Yai ☎076 284450, ⓦphuket-capannina-inn .com. Smart, modern, large bedrooms and well-equipped bathrooms, with a/c, cable TV, hot water, fridges and espresso machines. Guests have the use of an attractive, shared, garden pool in front. It's set in a new development of shops and hotels, a 5min walk from the beach — or there's a free tuk-tuk to the beach or the restaurant (see p.644). Continental breakfast included. B2000

Cool Breeze 225 Thanon Kok Tanode, Kata Yai ☎076 330484 or ☎085 900 3681, ⓦphuketindex.com /coolbreezebungalows. Though one of the cheapest places in Kata, for your money you get a spacious private bungalow, plus a view of sorts from the terrace (either of the distant sea or of the hilltop Big Buddha in profile), the bungalows being ranged steeply up the hillside, in a grassy palm- and shrub-filled garden. Interiors are nothing fancy but good value, with hot shower (in most), TV and fridge, and are sufficiently far above the narrow, noisy road. Fan B800, a/c B1000

7

Kata Beach Resort Thanon Kata, Kata Yai ☎076 330530–4, ⍟katagroup.com. This huge 275-room, four-storey hotel occupies a great spot right on the edge of the southern end of Kata Yai's white-sand beach. It has a shorefront restaurant and two swimming pools, a palm-shaded seaside garden, a spa and a dive shop. Some of the attractive, balconied, wooden-floored rooms have direct pool access, and some have sea views. B9300

Katathani Beach Resort and Spa 14 Thanon Kata Noi, Kata Noi ☎076 330124–6, ⍟katathani.com. The various wings and offshoots of the enormous and luxurious *Katathani* now occupy almost the entire shoreline of small, secluded Kata Noi. The beachfront all-suite Thani wing has the prime position, with the narrow lawn dropping seamlessly onto the white sand; all rooms here have sea-view balconies. Across the effectively private, no-through road, the cheaper, garden-view Bhuri wing has a distinctively contemporary, pastel-coloured look and its rooms too are very deluxe. There's broadband throughout (free in the lobby) and a daily shuttle service to town and to

Patong. The hotel has six restaurants, six swimming pools and a spa, plus an arm-long menu of activities and a kids' club. Breakfast included. B8750

Mom Tri's Villa Royale 12 Thanon Kata Noi, Kata Noi ☎076 333569, ⍟villaroyalephuket.com. Luxurious suites, richly decorated with fine textiles and teak, a renowned restaurant (see below), an excellent spa and two saltwater and one freshwater pools, set in landscaped tropical gardens with fine views above Kata Noi. Free wi-fi throughout. B12,900

The Shore at Katathani 18 Thanon Kata Noi, Kata Noi ☎076 330124, ⍟theshore.katathani.com. The sister hotel of the *Katathani* has its own spa, restaurant and infinity pool, and targets couples (no under-12s allowed). Stacked up the hillside at the south end of the beach, the relaxing, 130-square metre pool villas sport a fresh, breezy modern design and ample space to lounge inside and out, as well as thoughtful extras such as espresso machines and iPod docks. B25,000

EATING AND DRINKING

The Boathouse Wine and Grill Thanon Kok Tanode, Kata Yai ☎076 330015–7, ⍟boathousephuket.com. One of the best-known restaurants on Phuket – not least for its famously extensive, award-winning wine list – where the skills of the French chef are best sampled on four-course Thai or French tasting menus (B1500, or just over B3000 with paired wines). The beachside terrace and dining room, decorated with nautical touches and attached to the boutique hotel of the same name, enjoy fine sunset views, and there are cooking classes here every weekend. Reservations recommended. Daily 6.30am–11pm.

Capannina Down a short alley of shops off Kata Road, Kata Yai ☎076 284318, ⍟capannina-phuket.com. Done out in cool red and black, this Italian-run, open-sided restaurant (with an a/c room) prepares good, home-made pastas (tagliatelle bolognese B230), pizzas from a wood-fired oven and a wide range of seafood and meat main courses; finish off with your choice of grappas and an Illy espresso. Daily 11am–late.

Mom Tri's Kitchen Mom Tri's Villa Royale, 12 Thanon Kata Noi, Kata Noi ☎076 333569, ⍟villaroyalephuket .com. Highly regarded luxury restaurant, offering Thai and European fine dining, in dishes such as veal parmigiana

and jumbo prawns in red curry. Mains from B460. Reservations recommended. Daily 6.30am–11.30pm.

Ratri Jazztaurant Reached by a vertiginous but short climb (or by road) east off Thanon Patak ☎076 333538, ⍟ratrijazztaurant.com. This rather sophisticated eyrie makes a panoramic spot for cocktails at sundown, with high-level views across Kata, plenty of squishy sofas to sink into and a good if pricey menu of Thai food (B220–850), including *matsaman* and Indian–Thai curries. The enthusiastic in-house jazz band plays from about 8.30pm late into the night and is worth lingering for. Daily 3pm–late.

★ **The Seacret** Katathani Beach Resort and Spa, 14 Thanon Kata Noi, Kata Noi ☎076 330124–6, ⍟katathani.com. Excellent Phuket and southern Thai cuisine, such as the classic dried-shrimp relish, *nam prik kung siap* (B220), *pla thawt khamin* (deep-fried fish with turmeric and pineapple relish) and *muu hong* (stewed pork belly with cinnamon). All this and an attractive, open-air setting by the swimming pool, with the best tables on a deck under fairy-lit trees by the beach. Daily 11am–5pm & 6–10.30pm.

Hat Nai Harn

The favourite beach of the many expats who live in nearby Rawai, **HAT NAI HARN**, 18km southwest of Phuket town, is an exceptionally beautiful curved bay of white sand backed by a stand of casuarinas and plenty of foodstalls but only minimal development. It does get crowded with parasols and loungers, however, and during the monsoon the waves here are huge.

ARRIVAL AND DEPARTURE	HAT NAI HARN

Songthaews from Phuket town (approx every 30min; 45min; B40) go to Nai Harn, via Rawai, with the last one returning at about 5pm.

ACCOMMODATION

All Seasons Naiharn Phuket ☎076 289327, ⓦallseasons-naiharn-phuket.com. Run by the French Accor group, this well-sited, though architecturally unexciting, hotel offers contemporary-styled concrete row rooms with ocean or garden view, five restaurants and bars, a spa, a kids' club and a decent-sized pool, just over the narrow road from the shore, next door to *The Royal Phuket Yacht Club*. B3470

The Royal Phuket Yacht Club ☎076 380200, ⓦpura-varna.com. The beach's northern headland is dominated by this long-standing luxurious hotel, whose rooms are raked up the hill amid terraced gardens of bougainvillaea; all have huge bathrooms and living-room sized balconies to make the most of the fine sea views. A spa, a swimming pool, tennis courts and lots of watersports complete the picture. B6000

EATING AND DRINKING

★**Trattoria del Buongustaio** ☎087 467 2554, ⓦtrattoriabuongustaio.ilmiosito.net. From a lovely balcony above the rocks on the northern headland, this Italian-run restaurant offers gorgeous views of the bay; reach it via the paved road through *The Royal Phuket Yacht Club* (the road may appear to be private, but persevere).

The full menu covers a wide choice of starters and meat and especially seafood main courses, plus risottos and pastas such as delicious seafood ravioli with sage and butter (B350). Daily noon–12.30am; the kitchen closes at 11pm, while the downstairs lounge bar closes at 2am.

Hat Ya Nui and Laem Promthep

Follow the coastal road 2km south around the lumpy headland from Hat Nai Harn and you reach the tiny roadside beach of **Hat Ya Nui**, which gets a surprising number of visitors despite being so small and right next to the admittedly quiet road. There are coral reefs very close to shore, though the currents are strong, and kayaks and sunloungers for rent.

The rugged, wind-blasted, grassy flanked headland of **Laem Promthep**, 1km beyond Hat Ya Nui, marks Phuket's southernmost tip, jutting dramatically – and photogenically – into the deep blue of the Andaman Sea. The cape is one of the island's top beauty spots, and at sunset busloads of tour groups get shipped in to admire the spectacle; Thais pay their respects at the Hindu shrine here, offering elephant figurines in honour of the enshrined four-headed god Brahma and his elephant mount, Erawan. You can escape the crowds by following the trail along the ridge and down to the rocks just above the water.

ARRIVAL AND DEPARTURE — HAT YA NUI AND LAEM PROMTHEP

You could catch a **songthaew** from Phuket town to Nai Harn, then walk up and around the promontory in a couple of hours, to pick up another songthaew back to town from Rawai.

ACCOMMODATION

Nai Ya Beach Bungalow ☎076 238179 or ☎076 288817. Two hundred metres uphill from Ya Nui beach towards the cape, this friendly and very pleasant place has attractive, sturdy, thatch-roofed bamboo bungalows with fans, en-suite cold showers and verandas. They're set in a flowery garden that's nicely shaded by cashew nut trees and bougainvillaea and enjoys high-level sea views. Closed May–Oct. B950

Hat Rawai

Phuket's southernmost beach, **HAT RAWAI**, was the first to be exploited for tourist purposes, but, half a century on, the hoteliers have moved to the far more appealing sands of Kata and Karon, leaving Rawai to its former inhabitants, the Urak Lawoy *chao ley* (see p.608), and to an expanding expat population. Most visitors are here for the many alfresco **seafood restaurants** along Thanon Viset's beachside promenade.

7

Phuket Seashell Museum

1500m north of the beach on Highway 4024 • Daily 8am–5.30pm • B200

Aside from its seafront restaurants, Rawai's chief attraction is the **Phuket Seashell Museum**, which displays some two thousand species of shell, including 380-million-year-old fossils, giant clams, and a 140-carat gold pearl.

ARRIVAL AND DEPARTURE — HAT RAWAI

Songthaews from Phuket town pass through Rawai (35min; B30) on their way to and from Nai Harn.

EATING AND DRINKING

Nikita's Towards the northern end of the promenade ⓣ076 288703, ⓦnikitas-phuket.com. A standout among the many expat-favoured bar-restaurants in the area, not least for the horizon-gazing potential from its peaceful tables on the sand (candle-lit at night). Pizzas from a wood-fired oven (from B200) feature on its Thai and Western menu, alongside well-priced cocktails, wines by the glass and espresso coffees. Daily 10am–2am at the latest, kitchen closes 11pm.

7

Salaloy Opposite Nikita's, towards the northern end of the promenade ⓣ076 613740. The best and most famous of Rawai's restaurants, whose highlights include *pla thawt khamin* (fried fish with turmeric) and omelette topped with baby oysters (B90); it has some lovely outdoor tables right on the shorefront under the casuarinas. Daily 10am–9.30pm.

Ao Chalong, Laem Panwa and around

North of Rawai, the sizeable offshore island of Ko Lone protects the broad sweep of **AO CHALONG**, where many a Chinese fortune was made from the huge quantities of tin mined in the bay. These days, Ao Chalong is the main departure point for dive excursions and snorkelling and fishing trips, which mostly leave from Chalong Pier, east of the bottle-neck roundabout known as Chalong Circle, or Chalong Ha Yaek.

Wat Chalong

8km southwest of Phuket town, on Thanon Chao Fa Nok, aka Route 4022 • Phuket–Karon songthaews pass the entrance

For islanders, Chalong is important as the site of **Wat Chalong**, Phuket's loveliest and most famous temple, which enshrines the statue of revered monk Luang Pho Saem, who helped resolve a violent rebellion by migrant Chinese tin-miners in 1876. Elsewhere in the temple compound, the Phra Mahathat chedi is believed to contain a relic of the Buddha.

Big Buddha of Phuket

Access is via the very steep and winding 6km Soi Jao Fa 51, signed west off Thanon Chao Fa Nok (Route 422), 2km south of Wat Chalong, or 1km north of Chalong Circle • ⓦmingmongkolphuket.com

With your own transport, a visit to Wat Chalong combines well with a pilgrimage to the newly erected **Big Buddha of Phuket** (officially Phra Phuttha Mingmongkol Eaknakakeeree), a towering 45m statue atop the aptly named Khao Nakkerd hill, which dominates many island vistas, including from Kata Yai to the southwest, and is easily spotted from aeroplane windows. Made of concrete but faced with glistening white-marble tiles, the eastward-looking Buddha boasts enormous proportions: he sits on a lotus flower that's nearly 25m across and even his individual hair curls measure almost 1m each. Views from the base of the statue extend east over Ao Chalong to hilly Ko Lone beyond, while western panoramas take in Kata Noi; it's a popular sunset-viewing spot.

Phuket Aquarium

Laem Panwa, 10km south of Phuket town • Daily 8.30am–4.30pm, feeding show Sat & Sun 11am • B100 • ⓦphuketaquarium.org • Songthaews from the market in Phuket town (B25), the last one returning at about 3.30pm

Ao Chalong tapers off eastwards into **Laem Panwa**, at the tip of which you'll find the **Phuket Aquarium**. Run by the island's Marine Biological Centre, it's not a bad primer

CLOCKWISE FROM TOP LEFT PHUKET SEAFOOD (P.41); MONK BOARDING A BUS IN AO PATONG (P.635); SINO-PORTUGUESE ARCHITECTURE IN PHUKET OLD TOWN (P.628) >

for what you might see on a reef and has walk-through tunnels, a sea-turtle pool and a shark-feeding show.

ARRIVAL AND DEPARTURE   AO CHALONG

Songthaews to Ao Chalong from Phuket town charge B25.

ACCOMMODATION

Shanti Lodge Soi Bangrae, 1500m south down Thanon Chao Fa Nok from Wat Chalong (the Phuket–Karon songthaew can drop you close by) ☏076 280233, ⓦshantilodge.com. Though there's no special reason to stay in this part of the island, you might make an exception for this alternative, traveller-oriented place. It's set in a relaxing garden, with salt-water swimming pool, book exchange and predominantly vegetarian restaurant, and has fan and a/c doubles with or without private hot-water bathrooms, some of them wheelchair accessible, and family rooms. Fan B750, a/c B850

EATING AND DRINKING

Kan Eang @ Pier Ao Chalong ☏076 381212, ⓦkaneang-pier.com. Classy, long-running restaurant, which is handily, and scenically, sited on a 200m frontage at the mouth of Chalong Pier. The big draw here is the seafood, the best of it barbecued old-style on burning coconut husks (from B1200/kg); deep-fried seaweed with shrimps and chilli sauce is also good and the *haw mok* (fish curry steamed in a banana leaf) is exceptional. Sister restaurant *Kan Eang Seafood*, north up the beach (☏076 381323, ⓦphuket-seafood.com), enjoys a similarly good reputation and offers free pick-ups. Daily 10.30am–11pm.

Thalang and around

There's not a great deal for tourists in the northeast of Phuket island around the district town of **THALANG**, but you're quite likely to pass the landmark **Heroines' Monument**, which stands in the centre of the Tha Rua junction, 12km north of Phuket town on Highway 402. The monument commemorates the repulse of the Burmese army by the widow of the governor of Phuket and her sister in 1785; together they rallied the island's womenfolk who, legend has it, frightened the Burmese away by cutting their hair short and rolling up banana leaves to look like musket barrels – a victory that's celebrated every March 13 to 15 with a monks' ordination ceremony and processions.

Thalang National Museum

On Route 4027, 200m east of the Heroines' Monument • Daily 8.30am–4pm • B30 • ⓦthailandmuseum.com • All mainland-bound traffic and all songthaews between Phuket and Hat Surin and Hat Nai Yang pass the monument

As the only official introduction to Phuket's rich and intriguing history, **Thalang National Museum** doesn't really match up to the task, but taken in conjunction with the privately funded Thaihua Museum in Phuket town (see p.629), the picture starts to flesh out. Displays include some interesting exhibits on the local tin and rubber industries, accounts of some of the more colourful folkloric traditions and photos of the masochistic feats of the Vegetarian Festival (see box, p.629).

Wat Phra Thong

Just beyond the crossroads in Thalang town, 8km north of the Heroines' Monument

Wat Phra Thong is one of Phuket's most revered temples on account of the power of the Buddha statue it enshrines. The solid gold image is half-buried and no one dares dig it up for fear of a curse that has struck down excavators in the past. After the wat was built around the statue, the image was encased in plaster to deter would-be robbers.

Khao Phra Taew Forest Reserve

Visitor centre 3km east of the crossroads in Thalang town

Several paths cross the small hilly enclave of **Khao Phra Taew Wildlife Park and Forest Reserve**, leading you through the forest habitat of macaques and wild boar, but the most popular features of the park are the Gibbon Rehabilitation Project and the Ton Sai and Bang Pae waterfalls, which combine well as a day-trip or on a tour (see p.623). You can get drinks and snacks at the foodstall next to the Rehabilitation Centre, and the route to the waterfalls is signed from here.

The Gibbon Rehabilitation Project

10km northeast of the Heroines' Monument, off Route 4027 • Daily 9am–4.30pm • National park admission fee B200 • ✆ gibbonproject.org • Songthaews from Phuket town, more frequent in the morning, will take you most of the way: ask to be dropped off at Bang Pae (a 40min drive from town) and then follow the signed track for about 1km to get to the project centre

Phuket's forests used to resound with the whooping calls of indigenous white-handed lar gibbons (see p.763), but they make such charismatic pets that they were poached to extinction on the island by the mid-1980s. The lar is now an endangered species, and in 1992 it became illegal in Thailand to keep them as pets, to sell them or to kill them. Despite this, you'll come across a depressing number of pet gibbons on Phuket, kept in chains by bar and hotel owners as entertainment for their customers. The **Gibbon Rehabilitation Centre** aims to reverse this state of affairs, first by rescuing as many pet gibbons as they can, and then by resocializing and re-educating them for the wild before finally releasing them back into the forests. It is apparently not unusual for gibbons to be severely traumatized by their experience as pets: not only will they have been taken forcibly from their mothers, but they may also have been abused by their owners.

Visitors are welcome at the project, which is centred in the forests of Khao Phra Taew Reserve, protected as a "non-hunting area", close to Bang Pae waterfall, but because the whole point of the rehab project is to minimize the gibbons' contact with humans, you can only admire the creatures from afar. There's a small exhibition here on the aims of the project, and the well-informed volunteer guides will fill you in on the details of each case and on the idiosyncratic habits of the lar gibbon. Should you want to become a **project volunteer** yourself, adopt a gibbon, or make a donation, email the project centre.

Bang Pae and Ton Sai waterfalls

If you follow the track along the river from the Gibbon Project, you'll soon arrive at **Bang Pae Falls**, a popular picnic and bathing spot, ten to fifteen minutes' walk away. Continue on the track for another 2.8km (about 1hr 30min on foot) and you should reach **Ton Sai Falls**: though not a difficult climb, the route is unsigned and indistinct, is steep in places and rough underfoot. There are plenty of opportunities for cool dips in the river en route. Once at Ton Sai you can either walk back down to the access road to the Khao Phra Taew Reserve visitor centre and try to hitch a ride back home, or return the way you came.

Ko Yao Noi

Located in an idyllic spot in Phang Nga bay, almost equidistant from Phuket, Phang Nga and Krabi, the island of **KO YAO NOI** enjoys magnificent maritime views from almost every angle and makes a refreshingly tranquil getaway. Measuring about 12km at its longest point, it's home to some four thousand islanders, the vast majority of them Muslim, who earn their living from rubber and coconut plantations, fishing and shrimp-farming. Tourism here is low-key, not least because the beaches lack the wow factor of more sparkling nearby sands, and visitors are drawn instead by the rural ambience and lack of commercial pressures. Nonetheless, there's decent swimming off the east coast at high tide, and at low tide too in a few places, and plenty of potential for kayaking, rock-climbing and other activities.

Most tourists stay on the east side, which has the bulk of the accommodation, at **Hat Tha Khao**, **Hat Khlong Jaak (Long Beach)**, **Hat Pasai** and **Laem Sai**. Exploring the interior is a particular pleasure, either via the barely trafficked round-island road as it runs through tiny villages and the island's diminutive town, **Ban Tha Khai**, or via the trails that crisscross the forested interior, where you've a good chance of encountering monkeys as well as cobras and even pythons, not to mention plenty of birds, including majestic oriental pied hornbills.

Hat Tha Kao and Hat Sai Taew

The most northerly of the main eastern beaches is **HAT THA KAO**, site of a small village, **BAN THA KAO**, with a couple of shops and restaurants, the pier for boats to

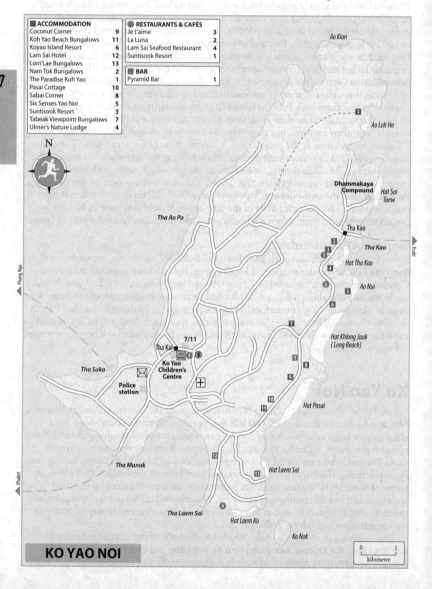

■ ACCOMMODATION	
Coconut Corner	9
Koh Yao Beach Bungalows	11
Koyao Island Resort	6
Lam Sai Hotel	12
Lom'Lae Bungalows	13
Nam Tok Bungalows	2
The Paradise Koh Yao	1
Pasai Cottage	10
Sabai Corner	8
Six Senses Yao Noi	5
Suntisook Resort	3
Tabeak Viewpoint Bungalows	7
Ulmer's Nature Lodge	4

● RESTAURANTS & CAFÉS	
Je t'aime	3
La Luna	2
Lam Sai Seafood Restaurant	4
Suntisook Resort	1

■ BAR	
Pyramid Bar	1

KO YAO NOI

0   1
kilometre

and from Krabi, and the cheapest and most backpacker-oriented bungalows on the island. It's not an attractive beach itself, barely swimmable, but is the closest point to Ko Yao's nicest beach, so-called **Temple Beach** or **Hat Sai Taew**, 2km away, whose pretty, gold-sand shore is great for swimming at any tide. However, it's backed by private land that belongs to the Dhammakaya Foundation, a populist Buddhist sect, and is unsigned and a bit tricky to find. From Tha Kao pier, head inland and take the first right behind the shops, walk alongside the khlong and its sheltered marina, over the bridge, then via the faint trail over the hill to the beach. Or just kayak there from the pier.

Hat Khlong Jaak (Long Beach)

A couple of kilometres south of Hat Tha Kao, **HAT KHLONG JAAK**, more commonly referred to as **Long Beach**, is the site of the longest-running and best-known tourist accommodation and the liveliest places to eat and drink. The beach is indeed long, around 1500m from the northern end to *Sabai Corner* on the southern headland. Much of it is rocky and all but unswimmable at low tide, except in front of *Koyao Island Resort*, the smoothest stretch. The seaward views are glorious from every angle, however, taking in the many lovely islets of eastern Ao Phang Nga.

Hat Pasai

A minute's walk south from *Sabai Corner* on Hat Khlong Jaak and you're on **HAT PASAI**, a rather pretty little beach, with some shade, several resorts and a few simple beach restaurants with tables under the casuarinas at the south end.

Laem Sai

Beyond Hat Pasai, tiny **HAT LAEM SAI** is often known simply as **Hat Lom'Lae**, after the appealing Thai–Canadian *Lom'Lae Bungalows*, which sits on the shore (see p.654).

A few hundred metres west from the *Lom'Lae* turn-off, about 3km from Tha Kai, another side-road takes you down towards **Laem Sai pier**, along a coast that has no real beach but is scenically dotted with houses on stilts, fishing platforms, dozens of longtails and some inviting views of Ko Yao Noi's larger twin, Ko Yao Yai, just across the channel. At the tip of the peninsula stands a good seafood restaurant (see p.654), and there's a nice little beach 300m east further around the rocks.

Ban Tha Kai and north

The island's commercial and administrative centre is **BAN THA KAI**, inland from the main piers on the southwest coast. This is where you'll find the post office, banks, hospital, police station, obligatory 7-Eleven shop with ATM, as well as several internet centres, the main market and several roti stalls.

Visitors are very much encouraged to drop by the **Ko Yao Children's Community Centre** (☎087 929 4320, ⓦkoyao-ccc.com), at the western end of town, an NGO that aims to help improve the English-language, arts, handicraft and computer skills of island children and adults, as well as organizing regular beach clean-ups.

The road running **north from Tha Kai**'s 7-Eleven is particularly scenic, taking you through several hamlets with their mosques and latex-pressing mangles, and past rice fields and their resident buffaloes, framed by mangroves in the middle distance, sea eagles hovering overhead, and the rounded hills of nearby islands in the background. At a junction about 3km from Tha Khai, the northbound road soon turns into a rough track leading to the beautiful beach at **AO LOH HA**, while veering right will take you over the hill and down to Tha Kao on the east coast, about 4km away.

KO YAO NOI ACTIVITIES

KAYAKING AND SNORKELLING

Kayaking around the coast is a very enjoyable pastime, and the dozens of tiny islands visible from eastern shorelines make enticing destinations for experienced paddlers; kayaks can be rented through Ko Yao Noi hotels for about B300 per day. Just about every hotel and travel agent sells kayaking and snorkelling trips to Ko Hong and other islands in Ao Phang Nga.

Koh Kayak Expeditions Just south of Coconut Corner on Hat Pasai ⓣ 087 929 4320. Good-quality kayaks, fully equipped for self-guided overnight expeditions that can last anything from 24 hours to a month, for rent (B1500 per single or B2000 per tandem per 24hr, including camping equipment plus an itinerary and maps).

Ko Yao Islander Tour Next to Pasai Cottage on Hat Pasai ⓣ 084 744 3686. Friendly place offering local snorkelling trips from B600 per person (minimum 4 people) or B1700 per boat, and kayaking and snorkelling day-trips in Phang Nga bay from B1400 per person (minimum 4 people).

DIVING

7

Koh Yao Diver Lom'Lae Resort, Laem Sai ⓣ 076 597406, ⓦ kohyaodiver.com. Diving trips and courses on the island are the speciality of Koh Yao Diver, where two local dives cost B3600, two dives at the reefs around Phi Phi in a longtail B5520, and the Openwater course is B16,680.

ROCK-CLIMBING

Ko Yao Noi is fast becoming a respected destination for **rock-climbers**, who appreciate the fresh sites and uncrowded routes compared to the hectic scene at nearby Ton Sai and Railay. There are over 150 bolted routes on the island, from beginner level to advanced (5 to 8A), established by the American and Thai climbers who run The Mountain Shop in Ban Tha Kao. Many routes are over water and accessible only by boat, or at the least via a hike off the dirt track to *Paradise* hotel.

The Mountain Shop At Sea Gypsy Restaurant in Ban Tha Kao ⓣ 083 969 2023, ⓦ themountainshop.org. For beginners, prices start from B2500 for a half-day's course, with multi-day courses also available; there are guides and rental gear for experienced climbers.

OTHER CLASSES AND ACTIVITIES

Lam Sai Hotel Laem Sai ⓦ phuket-krabi-muaythai.com. B300 for a two-hour Thai boxing class or B2500 for a week of classes.

Tappi Thai Cookery School Ban Tha Kai ⓣ 087 887 3161. Three-hour classes, morning or afternoon, for B1600, including transfers.

Ulmer's Nature Lodge Hat Tha Kao ⓣ 084 690 3731, ⓦ thailandyogaretreats.com. Daily drop-in yoga classes (B300), plus diverse workshops and retreats.

ARRIVAL AND DEPARTURE — KO YAO NOI

There are three mainland departure points for **boats** to Ko Yao Noi – from Phuket, Krabi's Ao Thalen, and Phang Nga – plus services from Ao Nang. On Ko Yao Noi, shared songthaew **taxis** meet all arriving boats and charge up to B100 per person (depending on distance) for transfers to accommodation, or up to B150 if chartered for a single traveller.

To/from Phuket The most common route is from Bang Rong on Phuket's northeast coast to Tha Manok on Ko Yao Noi's southwest coast, which is covered by five longtail boats a day (1hr 10min; B120) and seven speedboats a day (40min; B200), with the last service at around 5pm. Returning to Bang Rong, boats depart Tha Manok every hour or so until 4.40pm. Infrequent songthaews run between Phuket town's Thanon Ranong market and the pier at Bang Rong, via the Heroines' Monument (about 1hr; B40). A taxi to Bang Rong from town or the main beaches costs about B500, from Phuket airport B350, or about B260 if you can cajole the driver into turning his meter on; the taxi service at Bang Rong pier charges B500 to the airport, B800 to Patong.

To/from Ao Thalen Most of the Krabi province boats leave from Ao Thalen, 33km northwest of Krabi town, and arrive at the Tha Kao pier on Ko Yao Noi's northeast coast: three longtail boats a day (1hr; B120) and four speedboats (30min; B200), with the last service at 5pm. Songthaews from Krabi town connect with most boats, leaving about an hour before from the morning market on Maharat Soi 7, passing the 7-Eleven on Thanon Maharat and Talat Kao bus terminal.

To/from Ao Nang In high season, the Green Planet speedboat service connects Ao Nang's Hat Nopparat Thara with Ko Yao Noi once a day (30min; B550, including pick-ups in the Krabi area), and continues to Bang Rong in Phuket; there's also a daily big boat from Ao Nang (about 1hr; B350).

To/from Phang Nga The most scenic journey to Ko Yao Noi is the daily (Mon–Sat) service from Phang Nga, which takes you through the heart of Ao Phang Nga, passing close by the stilt-house island of Ko Panyi (see p.655). It departs the Phang Nga bay pier at Tha Dan, 9km south of Phang Nga town, at 1pm and returns from Tha Suka on Ko Yao Noi at 7.30am (90min; B200); songthaews connect Phang Nga town with the pier.

GETTING AROUND

Songthaew taxis are easily arranged and many hotels can organize **motorbike** (B200–350/day) and **bicycle** (B200) rental.

INFORMATION

A good, free, regularly updated **map** of the island and its tourist businesses, produced by Pakorn Photo Classic, is available on the island. There's an **ATM** at the 7-Eleven in Ban Tha Kai and in front of *Six Senses* on Hat Khlong Jaak.

ACCOMMODATION

HAT THA KAO

Nam Tok Bungalows ☎087 292 1102. Set back from the beach around a khlong, a 5min walk south from the Tha Kao ferry pier, this ultra laidback set of bungalows is one of the cheapest places to stay on the island. The budget options are comfortable bamboo and wood huts, with cute bathrooms and hammocks on the deck, encircling a small garden full of flowers and a fishpond; the more luxurious ones have hot water. *Nam Tok*'s manager, Danny, occasionally takes guests on camping trips to Ko Pak Bia (from B4000 per boat). B400

★ **Suntisook Resort** ☎089 781 6456, ⌨suntisook kohyao.com. Genial, well-organized place where the bungalows are nicely spaced around a garden and come with TVs, fridges and good, hot-water bathrooms. They're all a bit different but each has a deck and a hammock and some have a/c and three beds. Internet access and free wi-fi, as well as motorbikes, mountain bikes and kayaks for rent. Fan B900, a/c B1500

Ulmer's Nature Lodge ☎084 848 5112, ⌨almar_k @hotmail.com. Occupying a peaceful spot by a mangrove swamp, down a track at the far southern end of the bay, *Ulmer's Nature Lodge* is establishing itself as a centre for yoga, though of course anyone is welcome to stay at its en-suite shoreside bungalows, which are either small and thatched or large and smart, with lots of polished wood. Fan B600, a/c B1500

HAT KHLONG JAAK (LONG BEACH)

Koyao Island Resort ☎076 597474, ⌨koyao.com. This lovely, stylish resort occupies the best part of the beach and comprises just eighteen chic, thatched, mostly fan-cooled cottage compounds, all of them with separate living areas, huge bathrooms with open-air showers, and sliding doors that give access to the spacious garden and its fine bay views. There's a swimming pool and spa, internet access, wi-fi, mountain bikes and kayaks. Breakfast included. B7000

Sabai Corner ☎081 892 1827, ⌨sabaicorner bungalows.com. Occupying Long Beach's rocky southern headland, this long-established, Italian–Thai, laidback little outfit has eleven thoughtfully designed wooden bungalows, all with fans, nets and rustic bathrooms, plus decks and hammocks. They're dotted along a rise between the road and the beach, under cashew and jackfruit trees. There's a good restaurant, serving home-made bread and yoghurt, plus Italian and Thai food, and kayak hire on site. B1000

Six Senses Yao Noi ☎076 418500, ⌨sixsenses.com. Extraordinarily luxurious and expensive retreat, hidden in its own little bay and accessed by a private road. The huge villas are designed in natural-chic style, mostly wood and thatch, but all come with private pool, expansive sun deck and personal staff. B28,000

Tabeak Viewpoint Bungalows ☎089 590 4182, ⌨kohyaotravel.com. Two hundred metres inland, on a cross-island track, this Japanese–Thai place has large, well-outfitted, fan-cooled, wood and bamboo bungalows, all with hot showers, polished wood floors and French windows and balconies that give commanding views of the islands. The Thai owner is a community policeman and enthusiastic fisherman, and an excellent source of island information. B900

HAT PASAI

Coconut Corner ☎076 454221, ⌨kohyaotravel.com. Offering some of the cheapest and most traveller-friendly accommodation on the island, in simple en-suite bungalows set around a small garden just across the road from the northern end of Hat Pasai beach. It's just a few minutes' walk from *Pyramid Bar* on Long Beach and has internet access, bicycle and motorbike rental. B500

Koh Yao Beach Bungalows ☎076 454213, ⌨kohyao beach.com. Clean, well-kept bungalows around a pretty, well-tended lawn, across the main road from the south end of the beach. The smaller fan bungalows – thatched, with mosquito nets and small, cold-water bathrooms – are better value than the larger ones with TVs (B800); there are

7

also some big, smart, a/c options with hot showers, TVs and fridges. Free wi-fi. Fan B500, a/c B1500

Pasai Cottage ☎076 454235, ✉pasaicottage @hotmail.com. The ten bamboo cottages here, just across from Pasai's beach but set back from the road, have unexpectedly tasteful interiors, folding glass doors and prettily tiled bathrooms. B800

LAEM SAI

Lam Sai Hotel ☎084 746 3861, �🌐lamsaihotel.com. British-run hotel and *muay thai* training camp (see p.652) on the less appealing western side of the peninsula, with a two-storey block of good-quality tiled rooms and a few bungalows, all with TVs, hot showers, wi-fi and balconies and use of the small swimming pool. Kayaks and motorbikes for rent, free bicycles. Fan B1000, a/c B1700

Lom'Lae Bungalows ☎076 597486, 🌐lomlae.com. Beautiful, secluded haven, backed by rice fields and rubber plantations and enjoying stunning bay views from its palm-fringed beach and grassy garden. The attractive, airy, wooden, fan-cooled bungalows are thatched and widely spaced, and have sliding doors, decks and hammocks to capitalize on the vistas. Some have additional upstairs loft beds, and there are two-bedroom family houses as well; all have free wi-fi. Kayaks, bikes and motorbikes are available for rent and there's a dive shop. Twenty percent discount for stays of five nights or more. B2500

AO LOH HA

The Paradise Koh Yao ☎076 584450, 🌐theparadise .biz. Set on a lovely but isolated beach, these large, deluxe, thatched, a/c rooms and villas all have plenty of outdoor space and semi-outdoor bathrooms, some with private jacuzzis. There's a huge pool, a spa, wi-fi throughout, kayaks and yoga classes. Breakfast included. B8500

EATING AND DRINKING

HAT THA KAO

Suntisook Resort Charming restaurant serving a long menu of Thai food, including fish (according to market price) and a good, generous chicken *matsaman* curry, as well as spaghetti, mashed potato and Western breakfasts. Daily 7.30am–9pm.

HAT KHLONG JAAK (LONG BEACH)

★ **La Luna** ☎084 629 1550, 🌐lalunakohyao.com. Congenial, Italian-owned bar-restaurant in a garden setting with hammocks. On offer are home-made pastas, including very tasty tagliatelle with cream and prosciutto (B230), proper pizzas (around B200), Italian desserts and lots of cocktails. Daily from roughly 2pm till late (kitchen closes 9.30/10pm).

Pyramid Bar Famous island meeting place, with a pool table, sports TV and extensive menu of cocktails, wine and Thai and Western food, including sandwiches (from B120), breakfasts and seafood; it's at its liveliest on Friday nights when half the island turns up for the very enjoyable weekly sets by island musicians. Daily 9/10am till late (kitchen closes 10pm).

LAEM SAI

Lam Sai Seafood Restaurant ☎081 446 0689. About 1.5km further down the road from the *Lam Sai Hotel*, just beyond where the paving stops, this is a great place for seafood, which is pulled up fresh from nets off a pontoon according to your order (priced according to weight). Tables are set on a deck over the water with good views across to Ko Yao Yai. Daily 10am–10pm.

BAN THA KAI

Je t'aime ☎076 597495. At the T-junction at the heart of the village, this welcoming French- and Danish-owned restaurant is especially good for locally caught fish and seafood – try the green curry for B180 – but also does a bit of Western food, including breakfasts. Daily 9am–10pm.

Ao Phang Nga

National Park admission B200 • 🌐dnp.go.th

Protected from the ravages of the Andaman Sea by Phuket, **AO PHANG NGA** has a seascape both bizarre and beautiful. Covering some four hundred square kilometres of coast between Phuket and Krabi, the mangrove-edged bay is spiked with limestone karst formations up to 300m in height, jungle-clad and craggily profiled. This is Thailand's own version of Vietnam's world-famous Ha Long Bay, reminiscent too of Guilin's scenery in China, and much of it is now preserved as **national park**. The bay is thought to have been formed about twelve thousand years ago when a dramatic rise in sea level flooded the summits of mountain ranges, which over millions of years had been eroded by an acidic mixture of atmospheric carbon dioxide and rainwater. Some of these karst islands have been further eroded in such a way that they are now hollow, hiding secret lagoons or *hongs* that can only be accessed at certain tides and only by kayak. The main *hong* islands are in the **western** and **eastern** bay areas – to the west or east of Ko Yao Noi, which sits roughly midway between Phuket and Krabi. But the most famous scenery is in the **central bay** area, which boasts the biggest concentration of karst islands, and the weirdest rock formations.

The central bay

On tours of the **central bay**, the standard itinerary follows a circular or figure-of-eight route, passing extraordinary karst silhouettes that change character with the shifting light – in the eerie glow of an early morning mist it can be a breathtaking experience. Some of the formations have nicknames suggested by their weird outlines – like **Khao Machu (Marju)**, which translates as "Pekinese Rock". Others have titles derived from other attributes – **Tham Nak** (or Nark, meaning Naga Cave) gets its name from the serpentine stalagmites inside; **Ko Thalu** (Pierced Cave) has a tunnel through it; and a close inspection of **Khao Kien** (Painting Rock) reveals a cliff wall decorated with paintings of elephants, monkeys, fish, crabs and hunting weapons, believed to be between three thousand and five thousand years old.

Ao Phang Nga's most celebrated features, however, earned their tag from a movie: the cleft **Khao Ping Gan** (Leaning Rock) and its tapered outcrop **Khao Tapu** (Nail Rock) are better known as **James Bond Island**, having starred as Scaramanga's hideaway in *The Man with the Golden Gun*. Every boat stops off here so tourists can pose in front of the iconic rock – whose narrowing base is a good example of how wave action is shaping the bay – and the island crawls with seashell and trinket vendors.

The central bay's other major attraction is **Ko Panyi**, a Muslim village built almost entirely on stilts around the rock that supports the mosque. Nearly all boat tours stop here for lunch, so you're best off avoiding the pricey seafood restaurants around the jetty, and heading instead towards the islanders' foodstalls near the mosque. You can enjoy a more tranquil Ko Panyi experience by joining one of the overnight tours from Phang Nga town (see p.657), which include an evening meal and guesthouse accommodation on the island – and the chance to watch the sun set and rise over the bay; you can also rent a kayak from the jetty and go exploring yourself.

At some point on your central-bay tour you should pass several small brick **kilns** on the edge of a mangrove swamp, which were once used for producing charcoal from mangrove wood. You'll also be ferried beneath **Tham Lod**, a photogenic archway roofed with stalactites that opens onto spectacular limestone and mangrove vistas.

7

THE HONGS

Hongs are the *pièce de résistance* of Ao Phang Nga: invisible to any passing vessel, these secret tidal lagoons are enclosed within the core of seemingly impenetrable limestone outcrops, accessible via murky tunnels that can only be navigated at certain tides in kayaks small enough to slip beneath and between low-lying rocky overhangs. Like the karsts themselves, the *hongs* have taken millions of years to form, with the softer limestone hollowed out from above by the wind and the rain, and from the side by the pounding waves. Eventually, when the two hollows met, the heart of the karst was able to fill with water via the wave-eroded passageway at sea level, creating a lagoon. The world inside these roofless hollows is an extraordinary one, protected from the open bay by a ring of cliff faces hung with vertiginous prehistoric-looking gardens of upside-down cycads, twisted bonsai palms and tangled ferns. And as the tide withdraws, the *hong's* resident creatures emerge to forage on the muddy floor, among them fiddler crabs, mudskippers, dusky langurs and crab-eating macaques, with white-bellied sea eagles often hovering overhead.

The western bay: Ko Panak and Ko Hong

The main attraction of **the western bay** is **Ko Panak**, whose limestone cliffs hide secret tunnels to no less than five different **hongs** within its hollowed heart. These are probably Ao Phang Nga's most spectacular hidden worlds, the pitch-black tunnel approaches infested by bats and the bright, roofless *hongs* an entire other world, draped in hanging gardens of lianas and miniature screw pines and busy with cicadas and the occasional family of crab-eating macaques. Western-bay tours also usually take in nearby **Ko Hong** (different from the Ko Hong in the eastern bay), whose exterior walls are coated with red, yellow and orange encrusting sponges, oyster shells and chitons (560-million-year-old slipper-shaped shells), which all make good camouflage for the scuttling red, blue and black crabs. Ko Hong's interior passageways light up with bioluminescent plankton in the dark and lead to a series of cave-lagoons.

The eastern bay: Ko Hong, Ao Thalen and Ao Luk

The principal *hong* island in the **eastern bay**, known both as **Ko Hong** and **Ko Lao Bileh**, lies about midway between Krabi's Hat Klong Muang beach and the southeast coast of Ko Yao Noi. The island is fringed by white-sand beaches and exceptionally clear aquamarine waters that make it a popular snorkelling destination. The island's actual *hong* lacks the drama of Ao Phang Nga's best *hongs* because it's not fully enclosed or accessed via dark tunnels as at Ko Panak, but it is pretty, full of starfish, and tidal, so can only be explored at certain times.

The eastern bay's other big attractions are the mangrove-fringed inlets along the mainland coast between Krabi and Phang Nga, particularly around **Ao Luk** and **Ao Thalen** (sometimes Ao Talin or Talane), though the latter can get very crowded with tour groups. Trips around here take you through complex networks of channels that weave through the mangrove swamps, between fissures in the limestone cliffs, beneath karst outcrops and into the occasional cave. Many of these passageways are *hongs*, isolated havens that might be up to 2km long, all but cut off from the main bay and accessible only at certain tides. The **Ban Bor Tor** (or Ban Bho Tho) area of Ao Luk bay is especially known for **Tham Lod**, a long tunnel hung with stalactites whose entrance is obscured by vines, and for nearby **Tham Phi Hua Toe**, whose walls display around a hundred prehistoric cave-paintings, as well as some interestingly twisted stalactite formations.

TOURS OF THE BAY   AO PHANG NGA

By sea canoe The most rewarding, and generally the most expensive option is to join a sea-canoeing trip (either guided or self-paddle), which enables you both to explore inside the *hongs* and to see at close quarters the extraordinary ecosystems around and inside the karst islands. Most sea-canoeing tours use large support boats carrying groups of up to thirty people. They can be arranged from any resort in Phuket, or through the specialist operators John Gray's Sea Canoe and Paddle Asia (see p.623); at Khao Lak, for example through Khao Lak Land Discovery (see p.619); at all Krabi beaches and islands and in Krabi town (see p.668), and on Ko Yao Noi (see p.652). The itinerary is usually determined by your departure point, with Phuket trips focusing on the western bay and Krabi tours concentrating on the eastern half.

By tour boat Most tours of the central bay are either in large tour boats booked out of Phuket or Krabi, which generally feature snorkelling and beach stops rather than kayaking, or in inexpensive, small-group longtail boats that depart from Phang Nga town (see opposite), as well as from Phuket and Ko Yao Noi. All the main areas of the bay are extremely popular so don't expect a solitary experience.

Phang Nga town

Friendly if unexciting little **PHANG NGA TOWN**, beautifully located under looming limestone cliffs edged with palm groves midway between Phuket and Krabi, serves mainly as a point from which to organize budget longtail trips around the spectacular

TOURS FROM PHANG NGA TOWN

AO PHANG NGA

The most popular budget tours of Ao Phang Nga (see p.654) are the **longtail-boat trips** run by tour operators based inside Phang Nga bus station. Competition between these outfits is fierce and the itineraries they offer are almost identical, so it's best to get recommendations from other tourists fresh from a bay trip, especially as reputations fluctuate with every change of staff. To date the one that's remained most constant is Mr Kean Tour (☎076 430619 or ☎089 871 6092); next door but one is Sayan Tour (☎076 430348, ⊛sayantour .com). Both offer half-day tours of the bay (daily at about 8.30am & 2pm; 3–4hr) costing B500 per person (including national park fee; minimum four people), as well as full-day trips, which cost B800, including lunch and national park fee; take the 8.30am tour to avoid seeing the bay at its most crowded. All tours include a chance to swim in the bay, and most offer the option of an hour's canoeing around Ko Thalu as well, for an extra B350.

All tour operators also offer the chance to **stay** overnight at their own guesthouse on **Ko Panyi**. This can be tacked onto the half- or full-day tour for an extra B250–300; dinner, accommodation, and breakfast are included in the price. Mr Kean can also sometimes offer (dependent on the tides) an interesting alternative overnight programme on his home island of **Ban Mai Phai**, a much less commercial version of Ko Panyi, with the chance to trek, cycle and kayak.

LOCAL SIGHTS AROUND PHANG NGA TOWN

Mr Kean can arrange trips (B500) to **Tham Phung Chang**, or **Elephant Belly Cave**, a natural 1200m-long tunnel through the massive 800m-high wooded cliff that towers over the Provincial Hall, about 4km west of the town centre. With a bit of imagination, the cliff's outline resembles a kneeling elephant, and the hollow interior is, of course, its belly. You can travel through the elephant's belly to the other side of the cliff and back on a two-hour excursion that involves wading, rafting and canoeing along the freshwater stream, Khlong Tham, that has eroded the channel.

Mr Kean also offers tours (B450) that take in several other local caves, plus **Sa Nang Manora Forest Park**, which has hiking trails through thick, impressive rainforest and several waterfalls with swimmable pools, 9km north of the town centre.

karst islands of Ao Phang Nga (see above). But there are also several caves and waterfalls nearby, accessible on cheap tours run by Phang Nga tour operators.

ARRIVAL AND DEPARTURE	PHANG NGA TOWN

Tour operators inside the bus station compound sell bus and boat tickets and will store your baggage for a few hours.

By bus Phang Nga has good bus connections: during the day, all services between Krabi and Phuket detour off Highway 415 to make a stop at the bus station (☎076 412014) on Thanon Phetkasem, located towards the northern end of this long, thin town; evening services don't make the detour, but Mr Kean (see above) will give you a free lift to the junction of Highway 415 and Highway 4, 4km west of town, if you buy your bus ticket from him. If you're heading to Khao Sok National Park headquarters (see p.610), it's usually fastest to take a Surat Thani bus and change in Phanom. Some of the services to Bangkok's Southern Bus Terminal continue to Mo Chit station on the north side of the city.

Destinations: Bangkok (8 daily; 11hr); Ko Samui (daily; 6hr); Krabi (every 30min; 1hr 30min–2hr); Phuket (at least hourly; 1hr 30min–2hr 30min); Ranong (1–2 daily; 4hr); Satun (4 daily; 5hr 30min); Surat Thani (5 daily; 4hr); Takua Pa (hourly; 1hr); Trang (every 30min; 3hr).

By boat The pier for boats around Ao Phang Nga, and to Ko Yao Noi, is at Tha Dan, 9km south of town and served by songthaews that pass the bus station (B25).

Destinations: Ko Yao Noi (daily; 90min).

INFORMATION

Tourist information The TAT information office for Phang Nga is inconveniently located 2km south of the town on Highway 4 (daily 8.30am–4.30pm; ☎076 411586). You may find the tour operators inside the bus station compound (see above) more helpful.

ACCOMMODATION

Phang Nga's best hotels are all within 250m of the bus station, heading northeast (right) up Thanon Phetkasem (Highway 4).

Baan Phang Nga 100/2 Thanon Phetkasem (on the left-hand side) ☎076 413276, ⱳbaanphangnga.com. Friendly, new, upmarket guesthouse above a café, offering a/c rooms with TVs, small, hot-water bathrooms and a few touches of kitsch contemporary decor. There's also internet access and free wi-fi. **B650**

Phang Nga Guest House 99/1 Thanon Phetkasem (on the right-hand side, next to Krung Thai Bank) ☎076 411358. The public areas here have been recently redecorated with some colourful touches, but the clean and comfortable rooms with small, mostly cold-water, en-suite bathrooms and TVs remain much the same; few have anything but a brick-wall view. Fan **B380**, a/c **B480**

Thawisuk Hotel 77 Thanon Phetkasem (just beyond Phang Nga Guest House on the right-hand side) ☎076 412100. The choice of local civil servants, this is an old-style, well-maintained hotel with very clean and bright fan rooms, a couple of huge a/c options, and a rooftop terrace. Fan **B180**, a/c **B500**

EATING

Duang Thanon Phetkasem, a couple of doors away from Baan Phang Nga Guesthouse (a tiny sticker shows the name in English). Locals rate this simple but friendly restaurant with a few outdoor tables as the best in town; it's been going 30 years and serves a good squid salad (*yam pla meuk*; B150), as well as rice and noodle dishes for about B70. Daily 10.30am–10pm.

Kafeh Thanon Phetkasem (no English sign). For a great Thai breakfast, go left down Phetkasem about 100m from the bus station to find this hugely popular dessert shop on the left. Fill your tray with assorted Thai *khanom* – banana-leaf parcels of sticky rice laced with sweet coconut milk and stuffed with banana, mango or other delights – at about B5 apiece, then order from the selection of hot and cold coffees and watch Thai breakfast TV with everyone else. Daily 6am–6pm.

Krabi town

The estuarine town of **KRABI** is both provincial capital and major hub for onward travel to some of the region's most popular islands and beaches, including Ko Phi Phi, Ko Lanta, Ao Nang, Klong Muang and Laem Phra Nang (Railay). So efficient are the transport links that you don't really need to stop here, but it also makes an appealing base, strung out along the west bank of the Krabi estuary, with mangrove-lined shorelines to the east, craggy limestone outcrops on every horizon, and plenty of guesthouses. The beaches of **Ao Nang** (see p.664) and **Railay** (see p.670) are both within 45 minutes of town, and other nearby attractions include the **mangrove swamps** and **Ko Klang** peninsula across the estuary, the dramatically sited Tiger Cave Temple at **Wat Tham Seua** and **Khao Phanom Bencha National Park**. A number of

---

MANGROVE TOURS

A boat trip through the eerily scenic **mangrove**-lined channels of the Krabi estuary is a fun way to gain a different perspective on the area. As well as a close-up view of the weird creatures that inhabit the swamps (see box, p.660), you'll get to visit a riverside cave or two. **Tours** are best organized directly with the longtail boatmen who hang around Krabi's two piers and the surrounding streets (B300–500/boat/hr), but can also be arranged through most tour agents.

The estuary's most famous features are the twin limestone outcrops known as **Khao Kanab Nam**, which rise a hundred metres above the water from opposite sides of the Krabi River near the *Maritime Park and Spa Resort* and are so distinctive that they've become the symbol of Krabi. One of the twin karsts hides caves, which can be explored – many skeletons have been found here over the centuries, thought to be those of immigrants who got stranded by a flood before reaching the mainland. You can also choose to visit the Muslim island of Ko Klang (see p.660).

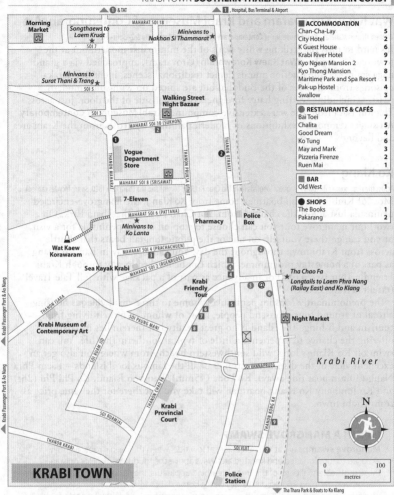

KRABI TOWN

ACCOMMODATION	
Chan-Cha-Lay	5
City Hotel	2
K Guest House	6
Krabi River Hotel	9
Kyo Ngean Mansion 2	7
Kyo Thong Mansion	8
Maritime Park and Spa Resort	1
Pak-up Hostel	4
Swallow	3

RESTAURANTS & CAFÉS	
Bai Toei	7
Chalita	5
Good Dream	4
Ko Tung	6
May and Mark	3
Pizzeria Firenze	2
Ruen Mai	1

BAR	
Old West	1

SHOPS	
The Books	1
Pakarang	2

organized **day-trips in the Krabi area**, including snorkelling and kayaking excursions, are available (see box, p.668).

Krabi town has no unmissable sights, but is small enough for a pleasant stroll around its main landmarks. Its chief attraction is its setting, and a good way to appreciate this is to follow the paved **riverside walkway** down to the fishing port, about 800m south of Tha Chao Fa; several hotels capitalize on the views here, across to mangrove-ringed Ko Klang, and towards the southern end the walkway borders the municipal Thara Park.

Inland, in the centre of town, you can't fail to notice the bizarre sculptures of hulking **anthropoid apes** clutching two sets of traffic lights apiece at the Thanon Maharat/Soi 10 crossroads. They are meant to represent Krabi's most famous ancestors, the tailless *Siamopithecus oceanus*, whose forty-million-year-old remains were found in a lignite mine in the south of the province and are believed by scientists to be among the earliest examples worldwide of the ape-to-human evolutionary process.

Wat Kaew Korawaram and Krabi Museum of Contemporary Art

West off Thanon Maharat · **Krabi Museum of Contemporary Art** Tues–Sun 10am–1pm & 2–5pm · Free

It's hard to miss the striking white walls of the minimalist modern bot at the town-centre temple, **Wat Kaew Korawaram** (Grovaram), approached via a grand naga staircase. The interior murals depict traditional scenes, including Jataka episodes from the lives of the Buddha, but are spiced up with some modern twists – including warring hairy foreigners on either side of the door. Just across Thanon Isara from the wat's extensive compound, **Krabi Museum of Contemporary Art** stages temporary exhibitions of modern paintings by artists from the Krabi area and beyond.

Ko Klang

Across the river from Krabi town · Frequent longtails from Tha Chao Fa (B20; 10min) and Tha Thara Park (B20; 3min; bicycles carried)

Most of Krabi's longtail boatmen come from **Ko Klang**, the mangrove-encircled peninsula just across the channel from Tha Chao Fa and Tha Thara Park. On a two-hour mangrove tour you can choose to stop off on the peninsula for a visit, or you can go there yourself, on one of the public longtail **boats** that shuttle across from Krabi town throughout the day. You can also stay in Ban Ko Klang as part of a **homestay** programme, which can be booked locally through Krabi Friendly Tour (see p.662) or in advance as part of a package with Tell Tale Travel (ⓦ telltaletravel.co.uk).

The predominantly Muslim peninsula is home to three small **villages** housing a total of around four thousand people, most of whom earn their living from tourism and fishing. The island is no great beauty but therein lies its charm, offering the chance to experience a little of typical southern Thai life. You can swim off Ko Klang's long, wild southwestern **beach**, from where you also get an excellent view of the distinctive profiles of all the famous local **islands** – Laem Phra Nang (30min boat ride away), Ko Poda (45min), Bamboo Island, Ko Phi Phi (2hr) and Ko Jum; any Ko Klang boatman will take you out there for the same price as from Krabi town.

> ### LIFE IN A MANGROVE SWAMP
>
> **Mangrove swamps** are at their creepiest at low tide, when their aerial roots are fully exposed to form gnarled and knotted archways above the muddy banks. Not only are these roots essential parts of the tree's breathing apparatus, they also reclaim land for future mangroves, trapping and accumulating water-borne debris into which the metre-long mangrove seedlings can fall. In this way, mangrove swamps also fulfil a vital ecological function: stabilizing shifting mud and protecting coastlines from erosion and the impact of tropical storms.
>
> Mangrove swamp mud harbours some interesting creatures too, like the instantly recognizable **fiddler crab**, named after the male's single outsized reddish claw, which it brandishes for communication and defence purposes; the claw is so powerful it could open a can of baked beans. If you keep your eyes peeled you should be able to make out a few **mudskippers**. These specially adapted fish can absorb atmospheric oxygen through their skins as long as they keep their outsides damp, which is why they spend so much time slithering around in the sludge; they move in tiny hops by flicking their tails, aided by their extra-strong pectoral fins. You might well also come across **kingfishers** and white-bellied **sea eagles**, or even a **crab-eating macaque**.
>
> Though the Krabi mangroves have not escaped the **environmentally damaging** attentions of invasive industry, or the cutting down of the bigger trees to make commercial charcoal, around fifteen percent of the Andaman coastline is still fringed with mangrove forest, the healthiest concentration of this rich, complex ecosystem in Thailand.

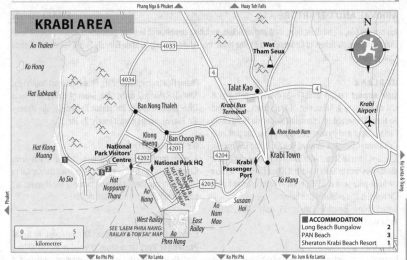

Wat Tham Seua

10km northeast of Krabi town, about 2km north of Highway 4 • Red songthaews from Krabi town, heading for the Tesco Lotus supermarket (about B20), pass the T-junction on Highway 4, from where you could take a motorbike taxi (about B30); you might be able to persuade the songthaew driver to detour to the temple for an extra fee (about B50) or you could walk the last 2km

Spectacularly situated amid limestone cliffs within a tropical forest, **Wat Tham Seua** (Tiger Cave Temple) is a famous meditation temple of caves, wooded trails and panoramic viewpoints. As it's a working monastery, visitors are required to wear respectable dress (no shorts or sleeveless tops for men or women).

Wat Tham Seua's abbot is a renowned teacher of Vipassana meditation, and some of his educational tools are displayed in the main **bot**, on the left under the cliff overhang, in the main temple compound. Though these close-up photos of human entrails and internal organs may seem shockingly unorthodox, they are there as reminders of the impermanence of the body, a fundamental tenet of Buddhist philosophy; the human skulls and skeletons dotted around the rest of the compound serve the same purpose. Beyond the bot, follow the path past the nuns' quarters to reach the pair of steep **staircases** that scale the 600m-high cliffside. The first staircase is long (1272 steps) and very steep, and takes about an hour to climb, but the vista from the summit is quite spectacular, affording fabulous views over the limestone outcrops and out to the islands beyond. There's a large seated Buddha image and chedi at the top, and a few monks' cells hidden among the trees. The second staircase, next to the large statue of the Chinese Goddess of Mercy, Kuan Im, takes you on a less arduous route down into a deep dell encircled by high limestone walls. Here the monks have built themselves self-sufficient meditation cells (*kuti*) in and around the rocky crannies, linked by paths through the lush ravine: if you continue along the main path you'll eventually find yourself back where you began, at the foot of the staircase. The valley is home to squirrels and monkeys as well as a pair of remarkable trees with overground **buttress roots** over 10m high.

Khao Phanom Bencha National Park

25km north of Krabi • B200 • ⓦ dnp.go.th

With your own transport, you could combine a visit to Wat Tham Seua with a meander around the scenic backroads and a plunge into **Huay Toh Falls**, a five-tiered cascade that lies within **Khao Phanom Bencha National Park**.

ARRIVAL AND DEPARTURE   KRABI TOWN

You can buy bus, a/c minibus, boat, train and air tickets, including combination bus and train tickets, to Bangkok via Surat Thani and through-tickets to Ko Samui and Ko Pha Ngan, from clued-up, helpful Krabi Friendly Tour & Travel, 9/3 Thanon Chao Fa (☎075 612558).

BY PLANE

Krabi **airport** (☎075 636541–2, ⊛krabiairport.org) is just off Highway 4, 18km east of Krabi town, 35km from Ao Nang. It's served by international Air Asia flights from Kuala Lumpur and by domestic flights from Bangkok with Thai Airways, Bangkok Airways, Nok Air, Orient Thai and Air Asia, and from Ko Samui with Bangkok Airways. An airport shuttle bus runs to Krabi town at B100 per person, or there are fixed-price taxis at B350 per car to Krabi town and port. Car rental is also available (see below).

Destinations: Bangkok (up to 15 daily; 1hr 20min); Ko Samui (1 daily; 50min).

BY BUS

Numerous long-distance buses run to Krabi's bus terminal, which is 5km north of the town centre in the suburb of Talat Kao, beside Highway 4. Frequent red songthaews (B20) shuttle between the town centre (where they do a little circuit to pick up passengers, starting from the 7-Eleven on Thanon Maharat or *Pak-up Hostel* on Thanon Utrakit) and the bus station.

To/from Bangkok A/c and VIP buses between Bangkok's Southern Bus Terminal and Krabi depart mainly in the late afternoon or evening, arriving at the other end in the early morning. Think twice before taking a private bus direct from Thanon Khao San (see p.136).

By a/c minibus Private a/c minibus services (all roughly hourly) run from Krabi to Surat Thani, Nakhon Si Thammarat, Trang and Ko Lanta (see map, p.659). Aimed specifically at tourists, in competition with the boats, the Lanta service will pick up from hotels in Krabi and charges B250–350, depending on which beach you want to be dropped off at on Ko Lanta Yai. From the Talat Kao bus terminal, you can also catch an a/c minibus that originates on Lanta to Phuket airport and town (roughly every 2hr; bookable through Krabi hotels and travel agents).

Bus destinations: Bangkok (12 daily; 12hr); Hat Yai (13 daily; 4–5hr); Nakhon Si Thammarat (at least hourly; 3hr);

Phang Nga (every 30min; 2hr); Phuket (at least hourly; 3hr 30min); Ranong (2 daily; 5hr); Satun (4 daily; 5hr); Surat Thani (at least hourly; 2hr); Takua Pa (4 daily; 3hr 30min–4hr 30min); Trang (at least hourly; 2–3hr).

BY TRAIN AND BUS

A more comfortable alternative to taking a bus from Bangkok is to catch an overnight train from the capital to Surat Thani and then change on to one of the frequent a/c buses or minibuses to Krabi (hourly; 2hr).

BY BOAT

Ferries to Ko Phi Phi, Ko Lanta and Ko Jum leave from **Krabi Passenger Port** (sometimes referred to as Tha Khlong Jilad; ☎075 620052), a couple of kilometres southwest of Krabi town centre. Ferry tickets bought from tour operators in town should include a free transfer to Krabi Passenger Port, but there are also red songthaews that do a circuit of the town centre before heading out to the port.

Ko Phi Phi Ferries to Ko Phi Phi from Krabi Passenger Port depart four times daily in high season and at least twice daily in low season (2hr; B350–400).

Ko Lanta Yai Going by a/c minibus to Ko Lanta is more popular these days, but there's still one ferry a day from Krabi Passenger Port, via Ko Jum, in peak season (roughly mid-Nov to mid-April 11.30am; 2hr 30min; B400).

Laem Phra Nang (East Railay) Longtail boats for East Railay on Laem Phra Nang (45min; B1500 per boat or B150 per person if there are 8–10 passengers) leave on demand from the town-centre pier at Tha Chao Fa on Thanon Kong Ka.

Ko Yao Noi As well as boats from Ao Nang, there are services from the pier at Ao Thalen, 33km northwest of Krabi town, to Ko Yao Noi (see p.652).

Destinations: Ko Jum (roughly mid-Nov to mid-April daily; 1hr 30min–2hr); Ko Lanta Yai (roughly mid-Nov to mid-April daily; 2hr 30min); Ko Phi Phi Don (2–4 daily; 2hr); Ko Yao Noi (from Ao Thalen; 6–7 daily; 1hr).

GETTING AROUND

By songthaew Most of the public songthaew services to local beaches, towns and attractions circulate around town before heading out, making stops outside the 7-Eleven just south of the Soi 8 intersection on Thanon Maharat and along Thanon Utrakit; most run at least twice an hour from dawn till noon, and then less frequently until dusk. For getting around town, the most useful are probably the red songthaews that run between Tesco Lotus, out on Highway 4 beyond the Wat Tham Seua turn-off, and Krabi Passenger

Port. White songthaews start at Talat Kao bus terminal and do a spin around town before heading out to Ao Nang (B50 daytime, B60 after 6pm).

By car or motorbike Budget (☎075 636171, ⊛budget.co.th) and Avis (☎089 969 8676, ⊛avisthailand.com) have desks at the airport, or try Krabi Friendly Tour in town at 9/3 Thanon Chao Fa (☎075 612558).

By bicycle *Pak-up Hostel* (see opposite) rents mountain bikes for B150/day.

INFORMATION AND TOURS

Tourist information Krabi's unhelpful TAT office (daily 8.30am–4.30pm; ☎075 612812, ✉tatkrabi@tat.or.th) is inconveniently located 2km north of the centre on Thanon Maharat.

Books If you're spending some time in this region, it's worth buying a copy of *Krabi: Caught in the Spell – A Guide to Thailand's Enchanted Province*, expat environmentalist Thom Henley's lively and opinionated book about Krabi

people, islands and traditions (see p.789).

Tour agents Any of the town's numerous tour agents will fill you in on the many organized day-trip options (see p.668), and fix you up with a room on one of the beaches – a service that's worth considering for your first night or two, particularly during the notoriously oversubscribed Christmas–New Year period. Recommended agents include Krabi Friendly Tour & Travel, 9/3 Thanon Chao Fa (☎075 612558).

ACCOMMODATION

★ **Chan-Cha-Lay** 55 Thanon Utrakit ☎075 620952, chanchalay.com. With its stylish blue-and-white theme throughout, funky bathrooms, white-painted wooden furniture and blue shutters, this is the most charming and arty place to stay in Krabi. The en suites in the garden come with fan or a/c and are by far the nicest option; rooms in the main building share bathrooms and some don't have windows. Internet access. Shared bathroom `B250`, en suite fan `B450`, a/c `B700`

City Hotel 15/2–4 Soi 10, Thanon Maharat ☎075 611961, ⊛citykrabi.com. Comfortable, friendly, modern hotel where most of the rooms are set well back from the road; choose between fan with cold shower and a/c with hot shower (all come with TVs). Wi-fi in the lobby and the most expensive rooms. Fan `B450`, a/c `B650`

K Guest House 15–25 Thanon Chao Fa ☎075 623166, ✉kguesthouse@yahoo.com. Deservedly popular and well run, in a peaceful but central spot, this long, timber-clad row house has bedrooms with wooden floors, panelled walls, streetside balconies and hot showers – ask for a more attractive upstairs room. Also offers some cheaper rooms with shared bathroom downstairs and at the back. Internet access and free wi-fi. Shared bathroom `B200`, en suite `B350`, a/c `B500`

Krabi River Hotel 73/1 Thanon Kong Ka ☎075 612321, ⊛krabiriverhotel.com. Occupying a scenic spot beside the estuary on the southern edge of Krabi town, a few minutes' walk south of Tha Chao Fa pier, this place offers high-standard a/c rooms, the best of which have big river-view balconies; the smaller, cheaper ones look onto the wall of the adjacent hotel. There's a riverside eating area too. Standard `B800`, river view `B1200`

Kyo Ngean (Ngoen) Mansion 2 25/1 Thanon Chao Fa, ☎075 621111, ✉kyo-ngean@hotmail.com. Good-value

little hotel in a modern block, popular with long-stay guests, with very clean and well-appointed rooms, all of them with a/c, TV, free wi-fi, fridge, hot water and balconies; some on the upper floors have long-range river views. Staff are friendly but don't speak much English. `B600`

Kyo Thong Mansion 31 Thanon Chao Fa ☎075 613001, ✉baankyothong@hotmail.com. Very similar setup to *Kyo Ngean*, three doors away, with large, well-appointed, modern rooms with small, hot-water bathrooms, a/c, TV, free wi-fi, fridge and balconies. `B600`

Maritime Park and Spa Resort 2km north of town off Thanon Utrakit ☎075 620028–35, ⊛maritimepark andspa.com. Beautifully located upper-end hotel, set beside the limestone karsts and mangroves of the Krabi River. Rooms are a little old-fashioned but large and comfortable, and have fine views over the extensive landscaped grounds and lake. There's a big pool and a spa, and shuttles into Krabi town and Ao Nang. Good-value packages sometimes available on their website. Breakfast included. `B3200`

Pak-up Hostel 87 Thanon Utrakit ☎075 611955, ⊛facebook.com/pakuphostel. Colourful, modern hostel in a short tower block on probably Krabi's busiest corner, with smart ten-bed dorms. Lots of tours available, as well as free wi-fi throughout and pay computers. There are plenty of guesthouses in town with cheaper private rooms for groups of two or more, but this is the place to come to be sociable, with lots of common areas, a rooftop bar and an adjacent garden bar. Fan dorm `B180`, a/c dorm `B200`

Swallow 31 Soi 4, Thanon Maharat ☎075 612464. Tiny six-roomed guesthouse that's kept spotlessly clean and is a good budget option. All rooms have windows and fans; the cheapest share bathrooms. No advance booking. Shared bathroom `B250`, en suite `B350`

EATING AND DRINKING

Krabi offers plenty of traveller-oriented restaurants – and Krabi Friendly Tour has a good juice bar if you need a healthy shot-in-the-arm – but there's also inexpensive local-style dining at the night markets on riverside Thanon Kong Ka and on Maharat Soi 10. The Walking Street **night bazaar** on Soi 8 (Fri, Sat & Sun 5–10pm) also brims with excellent food stalls, as well as an entertainments stage and trinket and craft stalls.

Bai Toei Just south of Thara Guesthouse on Thanon Kong Ka ☎075 611509 (English sign on the riverside

only; look for a Pepsi sign on the roadside). A good place for a sundowner, with pleasing views over the promenade

7

to the river and Ko Klang, and great seafood: try the local *nam prik kung siap* (on the menu as "smoke-shrimp paste"; B120) or the fried squid with salted eggs; fried rice and noodles start as low as B60. Mon–Sat 10am–10pm, Sun 4–10pm.

Chalita Thanon Chao Fa. Congenial, Italian–Thai restaurant that serves mostly Thai food, but also steaks, burgers, pastas and one or two fusion dishes such as spaghetti with chicken green curry (B110), which works surprisingly well. Daily 4–10.30pm.

Good Dream 83 Thanon Utrakit ☎ 075 622993. A great, farang-run place for breakfast – very good French toast (B70), mega fry-ups (B170), Continental sets, muesli and fruit, all served with fresh coffee – plus plenty more Western and Thai dishes and cocktails later in the day. There's free wi-fi and internet access for customers too. Daily 8am–11pm.

★ **Ko Tung** 36 Thanon Kong Ka ☎ 075 611522. Though it looks nothing much, this little Thai restaurant is always packed with locals savouring the excellent, good-value, southern-style seafood. Special highlights include the sweet mussels (*hawy wan*), baked crab, and mushroom, long bean and shrimp *yam* salads. Most dishes around B80.

Mon–Sat 11am–10pm.

May and Mark Soi 2, Thanon Maharat. Early hours, home-baked bread, fresh coffee and full-English fry-ups make this a popular spot for breakfast. Also does tacos, sandwiches, cheese and tuna melts (B160), pizzas and Thai, German and vegetarian food. Daily 6.30am–9pm.

Old West Thanon Utrakit. All bare wood and Wild West photos, with racks of imported spirits behind the long bar that get mixed into some serious cocktails. The top-notch sound system churns out wall-to-wall rock and there are a couple of pool tables. Daily 4pm–4am.

Pizzeria Firenze Thanon Kong Ka. Authentic Italian dishes, including twenty different thin-crust pizzas (from B175), home-made pasta, ice cream, tiramisu, espresso coffee and Italian wines. Daily 9am–9.30pm.

Ruen Mai About 2km north of the town centre at 315/5 Thanon Maharat. Popular with locals and well regarded, this inviting, artfully planted garden restaurant is well worth making the effort to get to. Among the many highlights of its mostly Thai menu (B60–180), standouts include the perfectly spiced *tom yam kung* with satisfyingly large prawns, juicy deep-fried ribs, and fried butterfish with tamarind and ginger. Daily 11am–9pm.

SHOPPING

Bookshops The Books, next to Vogue Department Store on Thanon Maharat (daily 8am–9.30pm), has a decent selection of new English-language books, and the well-stocked Pakarang on Thanon Utrakit (daily 8am–9pm) buys and sells secondhand books, as well as selling handicrafts and espresso coffees.

DIRECTORY

Hospitals Krabi Hospital is about 1km north of the town centre at 325 Thanon Utrakit (☎ 075 611202) and also has dental facilities, but the better hospital is considered to be the private Muslim hospital, Jariyatham Ruam Phet Hospital (☎ 075 611223), which is about 3km north of town at 514 Thanon Utrakit and has English-speaking staff.

Immigration office In the compound of government offices on the way to Krabi Passenger Port (Mon–Fri 8.30am–4.30pm; ☎ 075 611097).

Police For all emergencies, call the tourist police on the free, 24hr phone line ☎ 1155, or contact the local branch of the tourist police in Ao Nang on ☎ 075 637208.

Ao Nang

AO NANG (sometimes confusingly signed as Ao Phra Nang), 22km west of Krabi town, is a busy, continually expanding, rather faceless mainland resort that mainly caters for mid-budget and package-holiday tourists. Although it lacks the fine beaches of the nearby Railay peninsula (an easy 10min boat-ride away), it is less claustrophobic, and has a much greater choice of restaurants and bars, masses of shopping (mostly beachwear, DVDs and souvenirs), plus a wealth of dive shops, day-tripping and snorkelling possibilities and other typical resort facilities. Adjacent **Hat Nopparat Thara**, part of which comes under the protection of a national marine park, is prettier, and divided into two separate beaches by a khlong. The uncrowded, 2km-long **eastern beach** is effectively linked to Ao Nang by a conurbation of accommodation and shops, but the **western beach**, sometimes known as **Hat Ton Son**, across the khlong, is an altogether quieter and more beautiful little enclave, accessible only via longtail or a circuitous back road. Fifteen kilometres' drive west of Ao Nang, **Hat Klong Muang** is no great shakes as a beach but does have some attractive four- and five-star accommodation.

Central Ao Nang and Ao Phai Plong

Ao Nang's central beach is unexceptional and busy with longtail traffic, though it's backed by a pleasantly landscaped promenade. The nicer stretch is east beyond *Ao Nang Villa Resort*, accessed by the pavement that takes you all the way along the shore to the appropriately named *Last Café*, a very pleasant spot for a shady drink. Follow the wooden walkway from beyond *The Last Café* and scale the steps up and over the headland to reach, in about ten minutes, the beach at diminutive **Ao Phai Plong**, which is the sole province of the luxurious *Centara Grand* hotel.

Hat Nopparat Thara east

Immediately west of Ao Nang, beyond the headland occupied by *Krabi Resort* but reached by simply following the road (on foot or in one of the frequent Krabi-bound songthaews), **Hat Nopparat Thara east** is long and pretty, with the road running along a landscaped promenade behind it. Its eastern hinterland is developing fast with hotels and restaurants, but the other end, close to the T-junction with Route 4202, is the site of the Hat Nopparat Thara–Mu Ko Phi Phi **national park headquarters** and accommodation. Here too is the **tsunami memorial**, *Hold Me Close* by Louise Bourgeois (2005), a broken, roofless, wood-slatted corncob structure enclosing two pairs of hands, joined, prayer like and pleading, extending from a lumpy sea.

At low tide it's almost impossible to swim on this beach, but the sands come alive with thousands of starfish and hermit crabs, and the view out towards the islands is glorious; you can walk to the nearest outcrop at low water.

The **national park visitor centre** is at the end of the beach, beside the khlong and its sheltered marina and jetty, Tha Nopparat Thara, which is the departure point for Ao Nang ferry services to Phuket, Phi Phi and Ko Lanta, as well as for longtails to the western beach. The visitor centre's car park is famous for its **seafood restaurants**, and Krabi residents also like to picnic under the shorefront casuarina trees here.

Hat Nopparat Thara west

Hat Nopparat Thara west has a quite different atmosphere from its eastern counterpart: just a handful of small bungalow hotels and a few private residences share its long swathe of peaceful casuarina- and palm-shaded shoreline, making it a great place to

---

DIVING FROM AO NANG

Ao Nang is Krabi's main centre for **dive shops**, with a dozen or more outlets, the most reputable of which include Kon-Tiki (☎075 637826, ⓦ kontiki-thailand.com) and Poseidon (☎075 637263, ⓦ poseidon-diving.com); they have a price agreement for PADI courses, but Poseidon is cheaper for dive trips. Diving with Ao Nang operators is possible year-round, with some dive staff claiming that off-season diving is more rewarding, not least because the sites are much less crowded.

Most one-day **dive trips** head for the area round Ko Phi Phi (from B3500 including two tanks; B1700 for snorkellers with Poseidon) and often include dives at Shark Point and the "King Cruiser" wreck dive (see p.642); the Ko Ha island group, near Ko Lanta, is also popular but more expensive (see p.691).

Two dives in the Ao Nang area – at Ko Poda and Ko Yawasam – cost B2700–3200 (B1900 for snorkellers), much less if you go in a longtail with Poseidon. PADI dive courses cost B5500 for the introductory Discover Scuba day, or B14,900 for the Openwater.

The nearest recompression chambers are on Phuket (see p.642); check to see that your dive operator is insured to use one of them. General information on diving in Thailand can be found in Basics (see p.52).

7

AO NANG & HAT NOPPARAT THARA EAST

(map)

Klong Haeng   Klong Haeng

THANON KLONG HAENG

4203

SOI HAT NOPPARAT THARA 13

Tourist Police

AO NANG SOI 8

Boxing Stadium

Kontiki Diving

Food Stalls

THANON AO NANG

Boats to Laem Phra Nang & Islands

THANON NOPPARAT THARA

SOI SEAFOOD

National Park HQ & Tha Nopparat Thara

Hat Nopparat Thara

Boats to Laem Phra Nang & Islands

0   100
metres

escape the crowds and commerce of other Krabi beaches. The views of the karst islands are magnificent, though swimming here is also tide-dependent. Without your own transport you can only get here by longtail across the narrow but deep khlong beside the national park visitor's centre, but with a car or bike you can arrive via the very quiet back road that snakes through the mangroves from the Klong Muang road to the edge of the bungalow properties.

ARRIVAL AND DEPARTURE   AO NANG

Ao Nang has no proper transport terminals of its own so most long-distance journeys entail going **via Krabi town** (see p.662). Taxis charge about B500 from Krabi to Ao Nang. From the **airport** (see p.662), a shuttle bus runs to Ao Nang for B150, while taxis charge B600–900 to Ao Nang and Klong Muang.

By songthaew The cheapest onward connection from Krabi to Ao Nang is by white songthaews, which run regularly throughout the day from Krabi town centre and bus station (every 10min or so; 45min; B50 daytime, B60 after dark) and pass eastern Nopparat Thara en route. Alight at the Nopparat Thara national park T-Junction and car park for longtails across the narrow khlong to the western beach (B100) or, with your own transport, follow the Klong Muang road until signs direct you off it. There's also a songthaew service from Krabi town to Klong Muang.
By boat In addition to the ferries listed below, also

available are longtails to Laem Phra Nang (see p.672) and boats to Ko Yao Noi (see p.652); the latter include a daily, high-season Green Planet speedboat that continues to Bang Rong in Phuket (B900 from Ao Nang). There are once-daily ferry services from Tha Nopparat Thara, near the national park visitors' centre, to Ko Phi Phi Don (2hr 30min; B450) and to Phuket (3hr; B650–700), both year-round in theory though they sometimes don't run in the monsoon season; and to Ko Lanta (2hr 30min; B470) from roughly November to May. Transfers from Ao Nang hotels are included in the ticket price.

GETTING AROUND

The Krabi **songthaews** are useful for nipping between Ao Nang, Hat Nopparat Thara and town, and motorcycle taxis with sidecars buzz around Ao Nang and Hat Nopparat Thara; **motorbikes** and **jeeps** are **available** for rent throughout the resort; and there are kayaks on the beach in front of *The Last Café* at the far east end of Ao Nang (B100–150/hr), from where, in calm seas, it's an easy 15min paddle to Ao Phai Plong or about 45min to Ao Ton Sai and West Railay.

ACCOMMODATION

During high season, it's almost impossible to get a double room under B600 in Ao Nang, though there is one exceptional travellers' place, *Laughing Gecko*, on contiguous Hat Nopparat Thara east. For a simple bungalow on the beach you need to

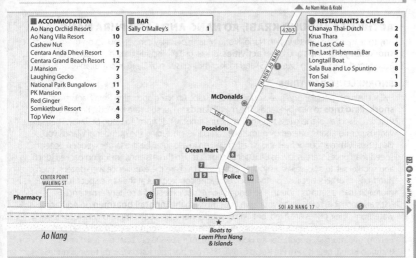

go to Hat Nopparat Thara west. Mid- and upper-end accommodation is plentiful throughout and of a high standard; you can usually get decent discounts through online booking agents. Prices across the board drop by up to fifty percent during the rainy season, from May to October.

AO PHAI PLONG

Centara Grand Beach Resort Ao Phai Plong, east end of Ao Nang ☎075 637789, ⓦcentarahotelsresorts .com. Ao Nang's top hotel has the secluded sandy bay of Ao Phai Plong all to itself, but is connected by longtail boat to the shops and restaurants of Ao Nang or free speedboat shuttle to Hat Nopparat Thara east. Designed to sit almost seamlessly against the forested crags behind, there's a lovely green feel here and seaward vistas are also beautiful. Nearly all rooms in the four-storey hotel buildings and detached villas have sea views. Interiors are modern and generous with sun-balconies and shaded outdoor daybeds; all have wi-fi. There's a big pool, a diving and watersports centre, kids' club, gym and spa. **B10,700**

CENTRAL AO NANG

Ao Nang Orchid Resort 141 Thanon Ao Nang ☎075 638426–8, ⓦaonangorchid-resort.com. This medium-sized but well-appointed hotel is good value for Ao Nang. Choose from rooms in the hotel wing, where the nicest overlook the pool and karst mountains beyond (rather than those with "city" views), or go for stand-alone villas with direct access to the lagoon pool. Interiors are chic and attractive, rooms and bungalows all have decks, and many have hardwood floors. Wi-fi in some areas. **B3850**

Ao Nang Villa Resort 113 Thanon Ao Nang ☎075 637270, ⓦaonangvilla.com. A very popular hotel and spa whose grounds run down to the beachfront walkway. The upscale, a/c rooms are contained within several

low-rise wings, a few of them enjoying a sea view, but most overlooking the garden or the bigger of the resort's two pools. Breakfast included. **B4500**

Centara Anda Dhevi Resort Ao Nang Soi 8 ☎075 626222, ⓦcentarahotelsresorts.com. New luxury hotel that cleverly squeezes in 130 spacious, contemporary-style rooms with rain showers and wi-fi around an attractive 43m pool, which features a water-slide and a swim-up bar; ground-floor rooms have direct pool access, others have balconies. There's also a very good spa and kids' club. **B4590**

J Mansion Off Thanon Ao Nang ☎075 695128, ⓦjmansionaonang.com. The best-known and most popular of the mini-hotels in Ao Nang's travellers' enclave, this place has very good, large, fan and a/c rooms, all with hot showers, satellite TVs, fridges and wi-fi. Most have high-level views, some of which extend to the green-clad cliffs behind. The rooftop terrace also has a panoramic outlook. Fan **B1000**, a/c **B1200**

PK Mansion and **Top View** Off Thanon Ao Nang ☎075 637431, ⓦkrabidir.com/pkmansion. Offering rates similar to its budget-oriented neighbours, *PK Mansion* and its adjacent, slightly pricier, sister hotel, *Top View*, have a range of mostly very good-quality rooms, with hot-water bathrooms, fan or a/c, balconies (many with partial sea views), TVs and fridges. Reservations advisable. Fan **B700**, a/c **B800**

Red Ginger Ao Nang Soi 8 ☎075 637999, ⓦred gingerkrabi.com. Located between the two beaches and a

ACTIVITIES AROUND KRABI, AO NANG AND LAEM PHRA NANG

Any tour agent in Krabi town, Ao Nang, Klong Muang or Railay can set you up on these **snorkelling day-trips** and other **activities**; prices usually include transport from your accommodation. Diving (see p.665) and rock-climbing (see p.672) are also available.

SNORKELLING DAY-TRIPS

By far the most popular organized outings from Krabi, Ao Nang and Laem Phra Nang are the **snorkelling trips** to nearby islands. The main **islands** in question are Ko Poda, Ko Tub and Chicken Island, all of them less than half an hour's longtail ride from Ao Nang or Railay. There are various permutations, offered by numerous companies, including the number of islands you visit (usually three, four or five) and whether you go in a longtail boat, a larger wooden boat or speedboat; prices start as low as B450 for a longtail trip to three islands, including packed lunch and snorkel set. In all cases you should be prepared to share the experience with dozens, even hundreds, of others, because pretty much everyone congregates at the same spots. It's a lot more fun than it sounds though – so long as you're not expecting a solitary experience.

It's also possible to organize your own boat trip with the **longtail boatmen** on Ao Nang waterfront. Their prices are fixed, but don't include snorkelling equipment or lunch: for the return trip to either Ko Poda, Ko Tub or Chicken Island (8am–4pm), they charge B300 per person, minimum six people; for Ko Hong (see p.656) it's B2500 per boat per full day, for Bamboo Island, near Ko Phi Phi (see p.676), B3800 per boat per full day. Krabi town is quite a bit further away so its boatmen charge B1800–2300 for the three main islands.

From some angles, one of the pinnacles on **Chicken Island** does indeed look like the scrawny neck and beaky head of a chicken. There's decent snorkelling off its coast, with a fair range of reef fish and quite a lot of giant clams, though most of the reef is either bleached or dead. Its dazzlingly white-sand northeastern shore, which has a food stall, toilets and kayak rental, is connected to the islets of **Ko Tup** by a sandbank, which is walkable at low tide – quite a striking sight as you arrive to see other visitors seemingly walking on water. Nearby **Ko Poda**, which sits directly in front of the Ao Nang beachfront, is encircled by lovely white-sand beaches and clear turquoise water. There's a restaurant here and plenty of shade under the casuarina trees, so this is the typical lunch stop; sandwich-selling boats dock here too. Though you might get three hundred people lunching on the shore here at any one time, it's big enough to cope. Some itineraries also feature **Ao Phra Nang** and its cave, on the Laem Phra Nang (Railay) peninsula (see p.671), and this is the one to avoid unless you enjoy scrambling for your metre of sand on this overrun little bay.

OTHER ACTIVITIES

Cycle rides Half- and full-day rides into the Krabi countryside, or to Ko Klang, Khao Phanom Bencha falls or Khlong Tom's Emerald Pool, with Krabi Eco Cycle, based about 2km inland from the Hat Nopparat Thara National Park visitors' centre on Route 4202 (from B800; ☎081 607 4162, ⓦkrabiecocycle.com).

Elephant trekking Nosey Parker's Elephant Trekking (☎075 612258, ⓦkrabidir.com/noseyparkers), 7km north of Ao Nang, has a good reputation. From B800 for an hour's trek along the river and elephant bathing.

Sea canoeing Guided and self-paddle trips around the spectacular karst islands and secret lagoons of Ao Phang Nga, usually focusing on Ao Luk, Ao Thalen and Ko Hong in the eastern bay (see p.656). Dozens of companies offer this, including Sea Kayak Krabi, Soi 2, Thanon Maharat, Krabi town (☎075 630270, ⓦseakayak-krabi.com), who offer a multitude of day and multi-day trips, charging B1500 for a full-day trip to Ao Thalen, for example.

Thai cookery lessons Ya's Thai Cookery School, about 4km inland of Ao Nang off Route 4203, runs morning and afternoon courses (Mon–Sat 9am–1pm & 2–6pm; from B1000 including transport; ☎081 979 0677, ⓦthaicookeryschool.net).

short walk from central Ao Nang shops, this contemporary Sino-Thai hotel has jut 63 rooms, some of them duplexes, set round a saltwater pool. Lines are clean and simple with modern Chinese styling and it all feels bright and upbeat. Breakfast included. **B3300**

Somkietburi Resort Thanon Ao Nang ☎075 637990–1, ⓦsomkietburi.com. Guests here enjoy one of the most delightful settings in Ao Nang, with the 26 rooms and swimming pools surrounded by a feral, jungle-style garden that's full of hanging vines and lotus ponds. Rooms are perfectly pleasant but nothing special; all have a/c and TV, and there's a spa. Breakfast included. **B3000**

HAT NOPPARAT THARA EAST

Cashew Nut Soi Hat Nopparat Thara 13 ☎075 637560, ⓦcashewnutbungalows.com. Good, sturdy en-suite brick and concrete bungalows with fan or a/c and hot showers ranged around a peaceful garden full of cashew trees, just 5min walk from Hat Nopparat Thara east. Family-run, welcoming and peaceful, with free wi-fi in the restaurant. Fan B500, a/c B1000

★ **Laughing Gecko** Soi Hat Nopparat Thara 13 ☎081 270 5028, ⓦlaughinggeckothailand.com. Perhaps the last of the old-style bungalows left in the Ao Nang area, this is an easy-going and exceptionally traveller-friendly haven run by a Thai–Canadian couple. Choose from a range of simple, thatched, fan-cooled, en-suite bamboo huts set around a garden dotted with cashew trees, including four-person dorms. Also has free wi-fi and nightly all-you-can-eat Thai buffets (B150–200). Dorm B150, double B500

National park bungalows Beside the national park headquarters on Thanon Nopparat Thara east ☎075 637200, ⓦdnp.go.th. Standard-issue, fan-cooled, en-suite bungalows, 2km from Ao Nang's main facilities but just across the (quite busy) road from a nice stretch of beach and a 5min walk from the seafood restaurants near the visitors' centre. B1000

HAT NOPPARAT THARA WEST

Long Beach Bungalow 600m west from the khlong ☎089 777 5853, ⓦlongbeachkrabivillas.com; map p.661. Set round a grassy, tree-strewn lawn, the main offerings at this place are attractive wood-and-bamboo huts with fans, mosquito nets and en-suite bathrooms; it also has some simple, shared-bathroom versions for single travellers (B350) and large, two-bedroom concrete bungalows that are available with fan (B1840) or a/c (B3000). Electricity at night only. Informal cooking classes, snorkelling trips and reasonably priced pick-ups. B750

PAN Beach At the westernmost end of the beach, about 700m walk from the khlong ☎089 866 4373, ⓦpanbeachkrabi.com; map p.661. Sturdy, simply furnished wooden bungalows in two sizes and styles, each with screened windows, fans and bathrooms, set just back from the shore around a lawn. Also has internet access, motorbikes and cars for rent, and organizes local boat trips. Electricity at night only. Free pick-ups in the morning from Ao Nang. B800

HAT KLONG MUANG

Sheraton Krabi Beach Resort ☎075 628000, ⓦsheraton.com/krabi; map p.661. Unusually for a top-notch beachfront hotel, the *Sheraton Krabi* does not boast of its sea views because the entire low-rise resort has been built among the mangroves and alongside a khlong; the result is refreshingly green and cool – and full of birdsong. The sandy shore – the nicest in Klong Muang – is anyway just a few steps away, accessed via a series of wooden walkways, and there's a seafront lawn for lounging. Rooms are large, sleek and very comfortable; there's a big pool, a spa, a tennis court, a watersports centre and bicycle rental. Wi-fi is free in public areas, payable in the rooms. Breakfast included. B6800

EATING AND DRINKING

Eating and drinking options in Ao Nang are not sophisticated and there are few places that stand out from the crowd. At weekends, locals flock to the seafood restaurants in the national park visitors' centre car park on Hat Nopparat Thara, or buy fried chicken from nearby stalls and picnic on mats under the shorefront trees. In central Ao Nang, there are cheap hot-food stalls on the road outside *Krabi Resort*, opposite Kontiki Diving, and handcarts selling Muslim roti pancakes (filled with milk, banana or chocolate) pitch up all over the resort. The bar scene is mainly focused around Ao Nang Center Point Walking Street, a U-shaped passageway behind the beachfront shops that's packed with rock, reggae and all-sorts bars, including Krabi's first pole-dancing club. There's also a small knot of makeshift little bars on the beach next to *Wang Sai Restaurant* on Thanon Nopparat Thara.

CENTRAL AO NANG

Chanaya Thai-Dutch Thanon Ao Nang. With its fairy lights, trailing plants and wooden tables, this place always gets a good crowd. The menu is mostly European – T-bone steaks done various ways, ostrich steaks, asparagus, ham and cheese bake – and there are tempting set dinners rounded off with Dutch apple pie and cream. Mains from B160; sets from B515. Daily 8am–2am.

The Last Fisherman Bar Soi Ao Nang 17. On the sand at the far easternmost end of the beach, serving simple Thai food and a huge range of sandwiches for lunch, but most famous for its evening barbecues (from B350 per set), which come with baked potatoes, corn-on-the-cob, salads and desserts. Daily 11.30am–4.30pm & 6–9pm.

Longtail Boat Soi Seafood ☎075 638093. All the Thai standards, including plenty of fish and seafood, which is displayed on ice and in tanks at the entrance, but especially good for thick, toothsome *matsaman* curries served with roti pancakes (B280). Daily 2–10.30pm.

Sala Bua and Lo Spuntino Soi Seafood, a pedestrianized alley of restaurants running off the promenade ☎075 637110, ⓦsalabua-lospuntino.com. Enjoying great sea views, especially at sunset, this is a welcoming two-in-one restaurant with two chefs. One does the Thai dishes under *Sala Bua*, including excellent

7

phanaeng curries (B175) and seafood, while the other cooks authentic Italian off a wide-ranging menu – lots of appetizers and home-made pastas, pizzas, and imported Australian meats for the main courses – for *Lo Spuntino*. Daily 11am–10pm.

Sally O'Malley's Up a small soi off the promenade. Friendly, Scottish-run, Irish theme pub with a long bar, Kilkenny bitter, Guinness and cider on draught, regular live guitar music and a pool table. Daily 11am–1/2am.

Ton Sai 150m north of McDonald's on Thanon Ao Nang. Home-style Thai cooking is the calling card at this bamboo-shack family-run restaurant. The curries are delicious, there's plenty of seafood and you can get almost any dish cooked to order. Most mains B80–100. Daily 8.30am–10pm.

HAT NOPPARAT THARA EAST

Krua Thara (After the Tsunami) National park visitors' centre car park. Hugely popular with locals, expats and visiting Thais for its reasonably priced fresh seafood (mostly sold by weight), but also serves north-eastern salads, rice and noodle dishes (around B70) and excellent espresso coffees. Daily 11am–10pm.

★ **Wang Sai** Beside the bridge at the eastern end of Thanon Nopparat Thara ☎075 638128. Good sunset views from its beachfront tables, an enormous range of seafood and lots of southern Thai specialities. The hearty *haw mok thalay* (on the menu as "steam seafood curry sauce"; B180) is excellent, stuffed with all kinds of fish and seafood, or you can get seafood fried rice for just B70. Daily 10.30am–10pm.

DIRECTORY

Tourist police On the main road between Ao Nang and Hat Nopparat Thara (☎075 637208).

Laem Phra Nang: Railay and Ton Sai

Seen from the close quarters of a longtail boat, the combination of sheer limestone cliffs, pure white sand and emerald waters around the **LAEM PHRA NANG** peninsula is spectacular – and would be even more so without the hundreds of other admirers gathered on its four beaches. The peninsula (often known simply as **Railay**) is effectively a tiny island, embraced by impenetrable limestone massifs that make road access impossible – but do offer excellent, world-famous **rock-climbing**; transport is by boat only, from Krabi town or, most commonly, from nearby Ao Nang. It has four beaches within ten minutes' walk of each other: **Ao Phra Nang** graces the southwestern edge, and is flanked by **East and West Railay**, just 500m apart; **Ao Ton Sai** is beyond West Railay, on the other side of a rocky promontory. Almost every patch of buildable land fronting East and West Railay has been taken over by bungalow resorts, and development is creeping up the cliffsides and into the forest behind. But at least high-rises don't feature, and much of the construction is hidden among trees or set amid prettily landscaped gardens. Accommodation is at a premium and not cheap, so the scene on West and East Railay, and Ao Phra Nang, is predominantly holidaymakers on short breaks rather than backpackers. The opposite is true on adjacent Ao Ton Sai, Krabi's main travellers' hub and the heart of the rock-climbing scene.

West Railay

The loveliest and most popular beach on the cape is **WEST RAILAY**, with its gorgeous white sand, crystal-clear water and impressive karst scenery at every turn. The best of the peninsula's bungalow hotels front this shoreline, and longtail boats from Ao Nang pull in here too, so it gets crowded.

East Railay

Follow any of the tracks inland, through the resort developments, and within a few minutes you reach **EAST RAILAY** on the other coast, lined with mangrove swamps and a muddy shore that make it unsuitable for swimming; boats from Krabi town dock here. Accommodation on this side is a bit cheaper, and there's more variety in price too, though – aside from a couple of gems – it's mostly an uncomfortable mix of uninspired, low-grade developments and unsubtle bars with names like *Skunk* and *Stone*. Depressingly, much of East Railay's hinterland is despoiled by trash and building rubble, but inland it's another story, with a majestic amphitheatre of forested karst turrets just ten minutes' walk away, on the back route to Ao Ton Sai.

Ao Phra Nang

Head to the far south end of East Railay's shoreline to pick up the path to the diminutive, cliff-bound beach at **AO PHRA NANG** (also called **Hat Tham Phra Nang**). Though exceptionally pretty, the bay can be hard to appreciate beneath the trinket sellers and crowds of day-trippers who are deposited here in their hundreds, by boats that pollute the coastal waters. Better to visit before 10am or after 4pm if you can.

The walkway from East Railay winds between the super-lux *Rayavadee* hotel and the lip of a massive karst before emerging at the beach beside **Tham Phra Nang**, or **Princess Cave**. The beach and cave, and indeed the peninsula, are named for this princess (*phra nang* means "revered lady"): according to legend, a boat carrying an Indian princess sank in a storm here and the royal spirit took up residence in the cave. Local fisherfolk believe she controls the fertility of the sea and, to encourage large catches, leave red-tipped wooden phalluses as offerings to her at the cave entrance. Buried deep

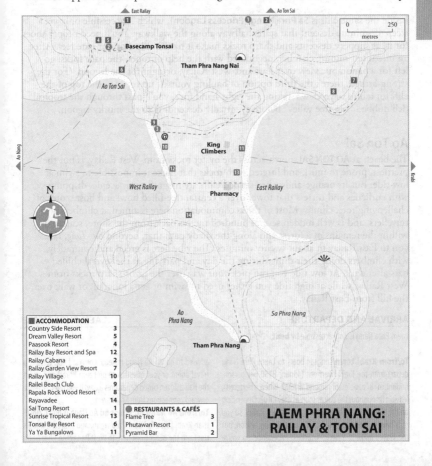

ACCOMMODATION
Country Side Resort	3
Dream Valley Resort	5
Paasook Resort	4
Railay Bay Resort and Spa	12
Railay Cabana	2
Railay Garden View Resort	7
Railay Village	10
Railei Beach Club	9
Rapala Rock Wood Resort	8
Rayavadee	14
Sai Tong Resort	1
Sunrise Tropical Resort	13
Tonsai Bay Resort	6
Ya Ya Bungalows	11

RESTAURANTS & CAFÉS
Flame Tree	3
Phutawan Resort	1
Pyramid Bar	2

LAEM PHRA NANG: RAILAY & TON SAI

ROCK-CLIMBING AND KAYAKING ON LAEM PHRA NANG

Ton Sai and Railay are Thailand's biggest **rock-climbing** centres, attracting thousands of experienced and novice climbers every year to the peninsula's seven hundred bolted routes, which range in difficulty from 5a to 8c (see W railay.com for a full rundown). Of the many climbing **schools** that rent out equipment and lead guided climbs, the most established include King Climbers at *Ya Ya Resort* on East Railay (T 075 662096, W www.railay.com/railay /climbing/climbing_king_climbers.shtml) and Basecamp Tonsai on Ton Sai (T 081 149 9745, W weesclimbingschool.com). A typical half-day introduction costs B1000, a full day B1800, while B6000 will get you a three-day course, learning all rope skills; equipment can be rented for about B1300 per day for two people. If you don't need instruction, the locally published and regularly updated guidebooks, Basecamp Tonsai's *Rock Climbing in Thailand and Laos* and King Climbers' Thailand *Route Guide Book*, will give you all the route information you need. Unaided over-water climbing on cliffs and outcrops out at sea, known as **deep-water soloing**, with no ropes, bolts or partner, is also becoming a big thing around here and can be arranged through most climbing schools for about B1000.

Kayaking around this area is also very rewarding – you can get to Ao Nang in less than an hour; kayaks cost B200 per hour to rent, for example on the beach in front of *Flame Tree* restaurant on West Railay. There are plenty of other activities in the Krabi area that you could hook up with from Laem Phra Nang (see p.668).

inside the same cliff is **Sa Phra Nang** (**Princess Lagoon**), which is accessible only via a steep 45-minute descent that starts halfway along the walkway. You'll need proper shoes for it, as slippery descents and sharp rocks make it hard in flip-flops or bare feet. After an initial ten-minute clamber, negotiated with the help of ropes, the path forks: go left for a panoramic view over East and West Railay, or right for the lagoon. (For the strong-armed, there's the third option of hauling yourself up ropes to the top of the cliff for a bird's-eye view.) Taking the right-hand fork, you'll pass through the tropical dell dubbed "big tree valley" before eventually descending to the murky lagoon.

Ao Ton Sai

The beach at **AO TON SAI**, north across the oyster rocks from West Railay, is not the prettiest, prone to murk and littered with rocks that make it impossible to swim at low tide. But its orange-and-ochre-striped cliffs are magnificently scenic, dripping with curlicues and turrets that tower over a central tree-filled bowl and host scores of challenging rock climbs. Most of the accommodation here is aimed at climbers and travellers, and is well hidden several hundred metres back from the shore, scattered within the remains of a forest and along the shady path that, beyond *Sai Tong*, takes you to East Railay in about twenty minutes. The vibe here is green and comradely, with climbers doing their thing during the day and partying at the several chilled bars after dark. At low tide you can pick your way over the razor-sharp rocks from West Railay, while at high tide you either need to swim or get a longtail, or walk over the hill from East Railay.

ARRIVAL AND DEPARTURE   LAEM PHRA NANG

Laem Phra Nang is only accessible by **boat**.

To/from Krabi town Longtail boats to Laem Phra Nang depart from the Krabi riverfront (45min; B150 per person, minimum 8 people, or around B1500 when chartered), leaving throughout the day as soon as they fill up. Depending on the tide, all Krabi boats land on or off East Railay, so you may have to wade; they do run during the rainy season, but the waves make it a nerve-wracking experience, so you're

advised to go via Ao Nang instead. Coming back, contact a travel agent or your guesthouse on Laem Phra Nang about the half a dozen timed departures a day, if you need to make onward connections from Krabi town.

To/from Ao Nang and beyond Ao Nang is much closer than Krabi town to Laem Phra Nang, and shared longtails run from the beachfront here to West Railay, Ao Phra Nang and Ao Ton Sai when full (minimum 8 people; 10min; B100, B150 after dark). There are several longtail boat stations, including one at the Hat Nopparat Thara national park visitor centre, all charging the same price; the one at the eastern end of the beachfront road is the most popular,

so you'll probably have the shortest wait for the boat to fill up here. During high season there should also be daily ferries from Ao Nang via West Railay to Ko Phi Phi (2hr 30min), Ko Lanta (2hr 30min) and Phuket (3hr); if not, you'll need to travel via Ao Nang.

GETTING AROUND

Shared **longtail boats** between Ao Ton Sai and West Railay cost B50 per person (minimum 4 people).

ACCOMMODATION

Because demand is so high, from November to March it's often hard to get a room on spec on West or East Railay, though you should have more luck on Ao Ton Sai. Mains electricity hasn't yet reached Ton Sai: very few of the bungalows have electricity during daylight hours, and in the cheapest places you'll just get a few hours' worth out of the generator in the evening.

WEST RAILAY

Railay Bay Resort and Spa ☎ 075 819407, ⓦ railaybay resort.com. There's a huge range of rooms and bungalows here (all with free wi-fi), in a shady coconut grove that runs down to both East and West Railay, plus two swimming pools and a spa. The pick of the bunch are the very large beachfront suites, which have marble bathrooms with jacuzzi tubs and great sea views from their verandas. B4100
Railay Village ☎ 075 819412–3, ⓦ railayvillagekrabi .com. Occupying very pretty gardens in between the two beaches, with nowhere more than 300m from the West Railay shore, the style here is elegant tropical, in whitewashed jacuzzi villas and pool-access hotel rooms, all roofed in low-impact wooden tiles, with wooden floors and Thai furnishings completing the look. There are two pools and a spa. Breakfast included. B6750
Railei Beach Club ☎ 086 685 9359, ⓦ raileibeachclub .com. Unusual compound of charming, mostly fan-cooled private houses, built of wood in idiosyncratic Thai style and rented out by their owners. One- to four-bed houses are available, all well spaced, and there are a couple of cheaper private rooms; most have kitchen facilities and there's wi-fi throughout. The compound is only minimally screened from the beach, so seafront houses get good views but may lack privacy and bear the brunt of the noisy longtail traffic. Minimum stays of three nights, rising to seven from mid-Dec to mid-Jan. B2500

AO PHRA NANG

Rayavadee ☎ 075 620740, ⓦ rayavadee.com. The supremely elegant two-storey spiral-shaped pavilions here, some set in enclosed gardens, some with whirlpools, are set in a beautifully landscaped, eco-friendly compound with lotus ponds that borders all three beaches. Facilities include a pool with a kids' pool, a spa, a squash court and tennis courts, a gym and two restaurants. B22,300

EAST RAILAY

Railay Cabana ☎ 084 057 7167. In a spacious, grassy, tree-filled amphitheatre of majestic karst cliffs, a 5min

walk from the beach on the track to Ton Sai, this friendly family-run place offers simple bamboo bungalows with thick mattresses, mosquito nets, fans and bathrooms. It's a lovely quiet spot, away from the East Railay crassness. Staff can help transport luggage from the pier. B450
★ **Railay Garden View Resort** ☎ 085 888 5143, ⓦ railaygardenview.com. This place really stands out for it simple rustic-chic style, great high-level views over the mangroves and sea beyond, and green surrounds in a garden of jackfruit, banana and papaya trees. The fan-cooled bungalows, built from good-quality split bamboo, are widely spaced and on stilts, with colour-washed cold-water bathrooms, wooden-floored bedrooms and decks, and plenty of triangular cushions for lounging. The drawback is that it's up a steep stairway beyond the far north end of East Railay, accessed via a short walkway beyond *The Last Bar*, about 15min walk from West Railay. Free wi-fi. Breakfast included. B1000
Rapala Rock Wood Resort Climb a steep flight of stairs to reach the thirty rough-hewn, fan-cooled timber and brick huts here, which are among the cheapest on Railay, set around a scruffy, breezy garden high above the beach, with some enjoying dramatic karst views from their verandas. There's also a nice communal deck among the treetops, and a friendly restaurant that serves Indian food and bakes its own tasty biscuits and bread. No advance bookings, walk-ins only. Shared bathroom B200, en suite B400
★ **Sunrise Tropical Resort** ☎ 075 819418–20, ⓦ sunrisetropical.com. The most stylish of the affordable hotels on the cape offers just forty rooms, most in elegantly designed a/c bungalows, and some in a couple of two-storey buildings, all with Thai furnishings and generously spacious living areas, set around a landscaped tropical garden with a pool and spa. Wi-fi throughout. Rooms B2550, villas B3700
Ya Ya Bungalows (Railay Princess Budget) ☎ 075 819401–3, ⓦ yaya-resort.com. This idiosyncratic place has some of the cheapest accommodation on Railay and is built almost entirely of wood, with most rooms contained in a series of sturdy, quite well-designed, three-storey

7

buildings. They all have verandas and en-suite bathrooms and many have hot showers, but soundproofing is not great and most rooms are quite dark. It's recently been taken over by the *Railay Princess*, so there may be changes and a rise in prices. Fan B850, a/c (breakfast included) B1880

AO TON SAI

Country Side Resort 084 848 0146, countryside -resort.com. Solar-powered eco-resort offering airy and attractive wooden bungalows on stilts, some with stunning views of the karsts, some with hot showers – including the a/c rooms, which have iPod docks and can fit three people. Wi-fi throughout. Fan B850, a/c B1380

Dream Valley Resort 075 819810–2, dream valleyresortkrabi.com. The ninety bungalows here are ranged discreetly among the trees, running far back towards the cliff-face, offering a range of good-quality accommodation in various categories, from wooden bungalows with fans, mosquito screens and bathrooms through to a/c villas with hot showers, the best of which

are the premier accommodation on Ao Ton Sai. Breakfast included. Fan B900, a/c B1400

Pasook Resort 089 645 3013. Friendly, welcoming spot, set on sloping lawns amid flowers and small trees, offering en-suite, fan-cooled concrete rooms and clapboard bungalows – best value are the larger concrete rooms with nice bathrooms (B450). Prices change frequently, according to demand. Room B300, bungalow B600

Sai Tong Resort 400m along the track to East Railay 081 079 6583. This friendly, good-value little place offers cheap, woven-bamboo huts with nets, fans and bathrooms, and bigger, more comfy, cute-looking split-bamboo ones, also en suite and with nets, fans and proper beds. B200

Tonsai Bay Resort 075 695599, tonsaibay.co.th. With its large, widely spaced and plain but comfortable bungalows, this is one of the top places to stay on Ao Ton Sai. The detached and semi-detached bungalows boast huge glass windows and big decks from which to soak up the pretty location in a grove of trees set back from the shore, and all have a/c, hot shower, satellite TV, fridge and safety box. Breakfast included. B2250

EATING AND DRINKING

There's no shortage of traveller-style bars on Laem Phra Nang, especially at the north end of East Railay and on the beach at Ton Sai, with their fire-juggling, driftwood furniture, chillums and occasional parties.

WEST RAILAY

Flame Tree On the seafront. This sprawling, laidback, semi-outdoor place has a more varied menu than most of the restaurants on Laem Phra Nang, including cashew nut salad (B175), some southern Thai dishes, mushroom sauce steak (B395), pastas, sandwiches, a variety of breakfasts and espresso coffees. Daily 7am–9.30pm.

EAST RAILAY

Phutawan Resort Quietly located in the middle of the

spectacular cliff-lined basin on the track to Ton Sai, a 10min walk from both East and West Railay, the restaurant here offers fine views and good food, mostly seafood and Thai curries, and largely in the reasonable B100–120 range. Daily 7.30am–10pm.

AO TON SAI

Pyramid Bar Busy day and night with climbers scoffing the fresh coffees, tuna and cheese melts (B100), ciabatta sandwiches and Thai food. High season only, hours variable.

DIRECTORY

ATM Several in the resort, including one next to *Flame Tree* restaurant.

Ko Phi Phi Don

About 40km south of Krabi, the island of **KO PHI PHI DON** looks breathtakingly handsome as you approach from the sea, its classic arcs of pure white sand framed by dramatic cliffs and lapped by water that's a mouthwatering shade of turquoise. A flat sandy isthmus connects the hilly east and west halves of the island, scalloped into the much photographed symmetrical double bays of Ao Ton Sai and Ao Loh Dalum. The vast majority of the tourist accommodation is squashed in here, as is the island's wild nightlife, with just a few alternatives scattered along eastern coasts. Phi Phi's few indigenous islanders mostly live in the northeast.

Such beauty, however, belies the island's turbulent recent history. By the early 1990s, Phi Phi's reputation as a tropical idyll was bringing unfeasibly huge crowds of backpackers to its shores, and the problem worsened after uninhabited little sister

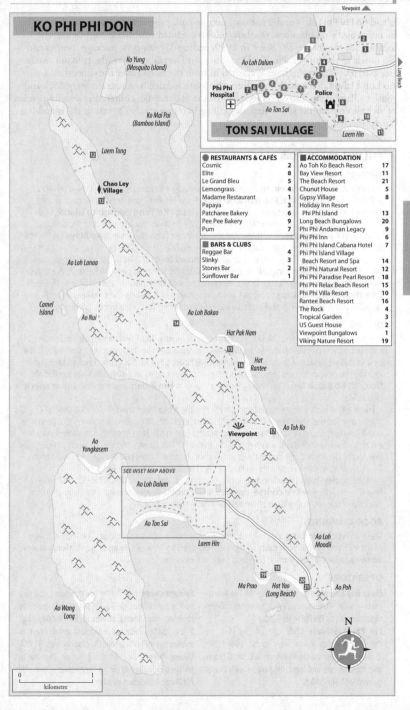

KO PHI PHI DON

Viewpoint ▲

Ko Yung
(Mosquito Island)

Ko Mai Pai
(Bamboo Island)

Laem Tong

Chao Ley Village ◆

Ao Loh Lanaa

Camel Island

Ao Nui

Ao Loh Bakao

Hat Pak Nam

Hat Rantee

Ao Yongkasem

SEE INSET MAP ABOVE
Ao Loh Dalum

Ao Ton Sai

Laem Hin

Ao Loh Moodii

Ma Prao Hat Yao
(Long Beach) Ao Poh

Ao Wang Long

Viewpoint ☼ Ao Toh Ko

N

TON SAI VILLAGE

Ao Loh Dalum

Phi Phi Hospital ✚

Ao Ton Sai

Police

Long Beach

Laem Hin

7

● RESTAURANTS & CAFÉS	
Cosmic	2
Elite	8
Le Grand Bleu	5
Lemongrass	4
Madame Restaurant	1
Papaya	3
Patcharee Bakery	6
Pee Pee Bakery	9
Pum	7

■ BARS & CLUBS	
Reggae Bar	4
Slinky	3
Stones Bar	2
Sunflower Bar	1

■ ACCOMMODATION	
Ao Toh Ko Beach Resort	17
Bay View Resort	11
The Beach Resort	21
Chunut House	5
Gypsy Village	8
Holiday Inn Resort	
Phi Phi Island	13
Long Beach Bungalows	20
Phi Phi Andaman Legacy	9
Phi Phi Inn	6
Phi Phi Island Cabana Hotel	7
Phi Phi Island Village	
Beach Resort and Spa	14
Phi Phi Natural Resort	12
Phi Phi Paradise Pearl Resort	18
Phi Phi Relax Beach Resort	15
Phi Phi Villa Resort	10
Rantee Beach Resort	16
The Rock	4
Tropical Garden	3
US Guest House	2
Viewpoint Bungalows	1
Viking Nature Resort	19

0 _____ 1
kilometre

island **Ko Phi Phi Leh** – under national marine park protection on account of its lucrative bird's-nest business (see box, p.680) – gained worldwide attention as the location for the movie *The Beach* in 1999, adding day-trippers, package-tourists and big hotels to the mix on Phi Phi Don. Then, in December 2004, the **tsunami** struck (see p.616). As a 5m-high wave crashed in from the north, over the sunbathers on Ao Loh Dalum, a 3m-high wave from the south hurtled in across the ferry dock and tourist village at Ao Ton Sai. The waves met in the middle, obliterating seventy percent of all buildings on the sandy flats and killing two thousand. The rest of the island was barely affected.

PHI PHI ACTIVITIES

SNORKELLING

There's some great **snorkelling** around Phi Phi's shallow fringing reefs, most rewardingly at strikingly beautiful **Ko Mai Pai** (**Bamboo Island**), off Phi Phi Don's northeast coast, where much of the reef lies close to the surface, and at nearby **Ko Yung** (**Mosquito Island**), with its spectacular, steep-sided drop. Phi Phi Don has its own worthwhile reefs too, including at west-coast **Ao Yongkasem**, within kayaking distance of Loh Dalum, but **Ao Maya** on Phi Phi Leh is more famous, and a lot more crowded (see p.678).

Outings are easily arranged as part of an **organized tour** (B500–800 including equipment) or by **hiring your own longtail** boatman (B1500/3000 per boat per half/full day), the latter far preferable to the largest tour boats, whose groups of forty-plus trippers inundate the reefs. **Overnight camping trips** to Maya Bay are a neat way of avoiding the crowds, offering late-afternoon snorkelling, and possibly kayaking, rounded off with a beach barbecue.

DIVING

Offering visibility touching 30m, a great diversity of healthy hard and soft corals, and potential encounters with white-tip sharks, moray eels and stingrays, the diving around Ko Phi Phi is the best in the area and the usual destination of dive boats from Ao Nang and Phuket. Highlights include the gorgonian sea fans, barracudas, manta rays and even whale sharks at **Ko Bidah Nok** and **Ko Bidah Nai**, the mass of leopard sharks at **Hin Bidah**, and the *King Cruiser* **wreck** (see p.643).

There are at least twenty dive shops on Phi Phi, the majority of them in Ton Sai; seven of them have formed the Phi Phi Diving Association (w phiphidivingassociation.com) to promote eco-friendly, responsible and safe diving practices (see p.52). Note that it's considered risky for a novice diver with fewer than twenty dives to dive at Hin Daeng and Hin Muang (see p.643), due to the depth and the current; reputable dive shops will only take Advanced Divers there. There are also small dive centres on Hat Yao, Ao Loh Bakao and Laem Tong.

Prices for **day-trips** including two tanks, equipment and lunch start at B2500, while the four-day PADI Openwater **course** costs B13,800. Check that your dive operator is insured to use one of the recompression chambers on Phuket (see p.642).

ROCK-CLIMBING

The main **rock-climbing** area is just to the west of Ao Ton Sai, and includes the Ton Sai Tower and the Drinking Wall, with thirty routes from grades 5 to 7a. A newer attraction is **deep-water soloing**, unaided climbing on cliffs and outcrops over the sea.

OPERATORS

Maya Bay Camping East of the pier, on the fourth north–south alley w mayabaycamping.com. Overnight camping on Phi Phi Le for B2500.

Phi Phi Adventure Club East of the pier, on the fourth north–south alley t 081 895 1334, w phi-phi-adventures.com. Responsible, small-group dive trips, courses and snorkelling trips ("with sharks guaranteed"; 3hr; B800).

Spidermonkey Near The Rock on the route to the east end of Loh Dalum t 075 819384, w spidermonkey climbing.com. Climbing instruction (from B1000 for half a day), guide service and equipment rental. Also runs snorkelling (on Phi Phi Le) and climbing day-trips (B1600).

Viking Divers East of the pier, on the fourth north–south alley w vikingdiversthailand.com. Phi Phi Diving Association member.

Volunteers and donations poured in to help the island back on its feet, and though the rebuild was dogged by much political wrangling, the Phi Phi of today thrives much as it ever did, firmly re-established as the destination to be ticked off on almost any itinerary in southern Thailand. Unfortunately, few of the pre-tsunami **problems** have been properly resolved – in part because tsunami survivors were desperate to make a new start as fast as they could. The island is now once again floundering under unregulated, unsightly and unsustainable development, with inadequate rubbish disposal and a plague of overpriced accommodation, at its most acute around the Ton Sai–Loh Dalum hub. There's always more building work going on, while thousands of visitors from all corners of the world fight for space in the narrow maze of pedestrianized alleys in Ton Sai village, sometimes generating an unusually aggressive atmosphere for Thailand. The noise pollution from the untrammelled outdoor bars and clubs is an additional turn-off for some – though it is a fun place to party, and there are enough more remote escapes for a peaceful stay too.

All boats dock in **Ao Ton Sai**, from where it's a short walk to the main accommodation centres – in **Ton Sai village**, at **Laem Hin**, the next little stretch of sand to the east, and on **Ao Loh Dalum**, the still attractive, deeply curved bay across the isthmus. **Hat Yao**, another fine beach just a short boat ride away, is also very popular. To escape the crowds you need to aim for one of the smaller bays further north: **Hat Toh Ko**, **Ao Rantee** and **Hat Pak Nam** are all good for moderately priced breakaways, while **Ao Loh Bakao** and **Laem Tong** are pricier and more luxurious.

Ton Sai village, Ao Loh Dalum and Laem Hin

Ton Sai village is a hectic warren of a place, both strangely old-fashioned with its alley traffic of bicycles and pushcarts, its fresh market tucked away in the middle and its squalid shanty town and stinky sewers hidden along the edges, and bang up to date, the narrow lanes bursting with state-of-the-art dive companies, shops advertising DVD players for rent and trendy boutiques.

West of the pier, **Ao Ton Sai** beach is an attractive little retreat under the limestone karsts, though it gets busy for a couple of hours around lunchtime and you're not far from the longtail moorings. Most people simply head for **Ao Loh Dalum** instead, less than 300m north across the narrow isthmus, which looks astonishingly pretty at high tide, with its glorious curve of powder-white sand beautifully set off by pale blue water; it's a different story at low water, however, as the tide goes out for miles. There's a tiny Tsunami Memorial Park of carefully tended shrubs, epitaphs and photos at the eastern end, near *Sunflower Bar*.

East along the coast from the Ton Sai pier, about ten minutes' walk along the main alley, is the promontory known as **Laem Hin**, beyond which lies a small beach and bungalows that enjoy a little more space. Inland, there are island homes and a mosque.

The viewpoint

The **viewpoint** that overlooks eastern Ao Loh Dalum affords a magnificent panorama over the twin bays and every evening a stream of people makes the steep fifteen-minute climb up the steps for sunset shots; early morning is also photogenic, and the shop at the "Topview" summit, set within a pretty tropical garden, serves coffee as well as cold drinks. From the viewpoint, you can descend the rocky and at times almost sheer paths to the trio of little east-coast bays at Ao Toh Ko, Ao Rantee (Lanti) and Hat Pak Nam, each of which takes about thirty minutes.

Hat Yao (Long Beach)

With its deluxe sand and large reefs packed with polychromatic marine life just 20m offshore, **HAT YAO** (Long Beach) is considered the best of Phi Phi's main beaches, but it's lined with hotels so gets very busy. UK-run Long Beach Divers (@longbeachdivers.com) here runs all the same **dive** trips and courses as shops in the village and offers discounted stays at *Long Beach Bungalows* for dive students.

Longtail **boats** do the ten-minute shuttle between Hat Yao and Ao Ton Sai (B100 per person, or B150 after dark), but at low tide it's also possible to **walk** between the two in half an hour, via the coast in front of *Bay View Resort* on Laem Hin and then via *Viking*. The island's single **road** follows an inland route to *The Beach Resort* from *The Rock* junction in the village, passing the post-tsunami housing project and Water Hill reservoir en route; it's a hot, hilly and unshaded forty-minute walk.

Ao Toh Ko, Hat Rantee and Hat Pak Nam

Travellers wanting to escape the crowds around Ton Sai and Hat Yao without spending a fortune head for the trio of little bays midway along the east coast: **AO TOH KO** and adjacent **HAT RANTEE** (Lanti) and **HAT PAK NAM**. You can reach the bays inland, via steep forest trails that run from the Viewpoint above Ao Loh Dalum (see p.677) in half an hour, while you can walk from Ao Toh Ko to Hat Rantee in five minutes at low tide. Rantee is probably the pick of the three, a palm- and casuarina-fringed white-sand bay, with great snorkelling at the reef right off the beach.

Ao Loh Bakao and Laem Tong

Far removed from the hustle of Ao Ton Sai and its environs, the beautiful, secluded northern beaches at Ao Loh Bakao and Laem Tong are the domain of just a few upscale resorts. *Phi Phi Island Village Beach Resort and Spa* (see p.682) has the gorgeous 800m-long white-sand beach and turquoise waters of **AO LOH BAKAO** all to itself. If you tire of these sands, and the hotel's four restaurants, there's a cluster of reasonably priced local restaurants behind the resort, and you can walk to the long, semicircular beach at **Ao Loh Lanaa**, across on the west coast, in ten minutes, or to Laem Tong in half an hour.

Almost right at Phi Phi's northernmost tip, **LAEM TONG** is busier and more commercial than Loh Bakao, with several upmarket resorts and stand-alone restaurants along its white-sand shores, and views across to nearby Bamboo and Mosquito islands. The beach is home to a group of Urak Lawoy *chao ley* "sea gypsies" (see p.608), whose village is next to the *Holiday Inn*; all longtail boat tours and transfers are run by Laem Tong's *chao ley* cooperative.

Ko Phi Phi Leh

More rugged than its twin, Ko Phi Phi Don, and a quarter the size, **KO PHI PHI LEH** is the number one day-tripping destination from Phi Phi Don, twenty minutes north, and a feature of snorkelling tours out of Phuket and Ao Nang (the national park admission fee of B200 is only levied if you set foot on the island, but not if you only snorkel offshore). It is very scenic indeed, and world famous, following its starring role in the film *The Beach*, so expect huge crowds, a plethora of discarded polystyrene lunch boxes, and a fair bit of damage to the reefs from the carelessly dropped anchors of tourist and fishing boats. The best way to appreciate the island is probably on one of the overnight camping and snorkelling trips from Phi Phi Don (see p.676).

Most idyllic of all the island's bays is **Ao Maya** on the southwest coast, where the water is still and very clear and the coral extremely varied; **Ao Phi Leh**, an almost completely enclosed east-coast lagoon of breathtakingly turquoise water, is also beautiful. Nearby, the **Viking Cave** gets its misleading name from the scratchy wall-paintings of Chinese junks inside, but more interesting than this 400-year-old graffiti is the **bird's-nesting** that goes on here (see p.680): rickety bamboo scaffolding extends hundreds of metres

BIRD'S-NESTING

Prized for its aphrodisiac and energizing qualities, **bird's-nest soup** is such a delicacy in Taiwan, Singapore and Hong Kong that ludicrous sums of money change hands for a dish whose basic ingredients are tiny twigs glued together with bird's spit. Collecting these nests is a lucrative but life-endangering business: sea swifts (known as edible-nest swiftlets) build their nests in rock crevices hundreds of metres above sea level, often on sheer cliff-faces or in cavernous hollowed-out karst. **Nest-building** begins in January and the harvesting season usually lasts from February to May, during which time the female swiftlet builds three nests on the same spot, none of them more than 12cm across, by secreting an unbroken thread of saliva, which she winds round as if making a coil pot. **Gatherers** will only steal the first two nests made by each bird, prising them off the cave walls with special metal forks. This in theory allows the bird to build a final nest and raise her chicks in peace. Gathering the nests demands faultless agility and balance, skills that seem to come naturally to the *chao ley* (see p.608), whose six-man teams bring about four hundred nests down the perilous bamboo scaffolds each day, weighing about 4kg in total. At a market rate of up to $2000 per kilo, so much money is at stake that a government franchise must be granted before any collecting commences, and armed guards often protect the sites at night. The *chao ley* seek spiritual protection from the dangers of the job by making offerings to the spirits of the cliff or cave at the beginning of the season; in the Viking Cave, they place buffalo flesh, horns and tails at the foot of one of the stalagmites.

In recent years, entrepreneurs in Ban Laem, near Phetchaburi, across on south Thailand's Gulf coast, have started competing with the *chao lay* – by constructing **sea swift condominiums** and trying to attract the swiftlets that frequent the attic of the nearby temple. The theory is that by constructing windowless concrete towers that mimic the Andaman Sea caves – complete with cool dark interiors and droppings-smeared walls, plus swiftlet soundtracks on continuous replay – they can entice the birds in to build their nests and harvest them with ease. To date, the main beneficiary seems to have been the construction company that builds these ugly towers, as the local swiftlet population suddenly has an awful lot of new accommodation to choose from.

up to the roof of the cave, where intrepid *chao ley* harvesters spend the day scraping the unfeasibly valuable nests made by tiny sea swifts off the rockface, for export to specialist Chinese restaurants all over the world.

ARRIVAL AND DEPARTURE

Tour agents in Phuket, Ao Nang, Krabi town and Ko Lanta all organize snorkelling day-trips to Phi Phi Don and Phi Phi Leh. Touts and bungalow staff always meet the ferries at the pier in Ton Sai; if you've pre-booked accommodation your luggage will usually be transported in a handcart. There are also boat transfers to Ko Jum (see p.686), which can be arranged, for example, through Parntawan Tour, a helpful travel agent on the main alley running east of the pier in Ton Sai village (☎075 601412), who can also book bus tickets on the mainland.

To/from Phuket Several companies run large, crowded ferries from Rassada Harbour (see p.626) in Phuket to Ko Phi Phi Don twice daily in high season (currently 8.30am & 1.30pm; 2hr), and there's at least one boat a day out of season. From an agent such as Mark Travel in Phuket town (see p.631), prices can start as low as B300 single, B550 return, including transfer from Phuket town. Andaman Wave Master's boats call in at Ao Ton Sai, but continue up the west coast to Laem Tong (B500 single), where the resorts send out longtail boats to pick up guests from the ship. Mark Travel also offers deals such as Phuket–Ko Lanta, breaking the journey on Phi Phi, for B650; Phuket–Phi Phi–Krabi for B650; and Phuket–Phi Phi–Ao Nang/Railay for B800. There's also a daily speedboat from Rassada to Phi Phi (which continues to Ko Lanta), but it costs B1500 for the 50min journey.

To/from Krabi From Krabi Passenger Port, there are boats to Phi Phi daily year-round, with at least four a day in high season (2hr; B350–400). You can also reach Phi Phi by once-daily ferries from Ao Nang, via West Railay (2hr 30min; B450), which are year-round in theory though they sometimes don't run in the monsoon season.

To/from Ko Lanta Yai From Ban Sala Dan on Ko Lanta Yai, there are two daily departures to Ko Phi Phi in high season (1hr 30min; B400).

GETTING AROUND

It's possible to **walk** along the paths across the steep and at times rugged interior (see p.677). There are only a few short motorbike tracks and one road, from the back of Ton Sai village to *The Beach Resort* on Long Beach, which takes around forty minutes on foot.

By boat From Ao Ton Sai, east of the main pier, you can catch a longtail to any of the other beaches, which range in price from B100 per person (minimum two people) to Hat Yao, to B1000 per boat to Laem Tong; prices often double after dark. The Andaman Wave Master ferry (see opposite) and a smaller shuttle boat each run twice a day between

Ton Sai and the east-coast bays as far as Laem Tong (both B200). You could also get about by kayak (B700 per day from in front of *Slinky Bar* on Ao Loh Dalum), which is the perfect way to explore the limestone cliffs and secluded bays, without the roar of an accompanying longtail or cruise ship.

ACCOMMODATION

As demand for accommodation frequently outstrips supply on Phi Phi, if you haven't made a reservation, it's worth using the agents' booking service at the pier head, where pictures and – genuine – room prices for hotels in all categories are posted for easy browsing; staff then call ahead to secure your room, and might even carry your bag there. Be warned though that rooms are very expensive on Phi Phi, and often poorly maintained. We've quoted rates for high season, which runs from November to April, but most places slap on a thirty- to fifty-percent surcharge during Christmas and New Year and, conversely, will discount up to fifty percent in quiet periods between May and October.

TON SAI VILLAGE AND AO LOH DALUM

Ton Sai hotels are the least good value on the island and almost none, however expensive, is out of earshot of the thumping all-night beats cranked up by the various bars and clubs; bring some heavy-duty earplugs if you're not planning to party every night.

★ **Chunut House** Turn right at The Rock and walk for about 5min back towards Laem Hin ☎ 075 601227, ⓦ phiphichunuthouse.com. Very welcoming, relaxing place in a leafy, sloping garden, in a relatively quiet location. Big, stylish, thatched cottages come with a/c, free wi-fi, flat-screen TVs, mini-bars and spacious, attractive, hot-water bathrooms. The owners have recently opened a similar branch, *Hin Puu Village*, on the slopes above Loh Dalum, about 10min walk beyond *Phi Phi Viewpoint*. Breakfast included. B2300

Phi Phi Inn Straight ahead from the pier next to the landmark Phi Phi Hotel ☎ 081 797 2088, ⓔ phiphi_inn @hotmail.com. Small, sparklingly clean hotel in a white clapboard house, where all fifteen rooms have a/c, TVs, hot showers, mini-bars, safety boxes and balconies, though only the upstairs ones have the chance of a view and also enjoy more privacy. Free wi-fi. B1650

Phi Phi Island Cabana Hotel West of the pier on Ton Sai ☎ 075 601170–7, ⓦ phiphi-cabana.com. The views from the contemporary rooms at this large, imposing hotel are breathtakingly lovely. Most look out across the scoop of Ao Loh Dalum and its framing cliffs, and ground-floor ones have direct access to the sand. There's a huge pool too. On the minus side, the hotel lacks atmosphere, has a cavernous restaurant and some rooms are affected by late-night club noise. B8000

The Rock ☎ 081 607 3897 or ☎ 075 601021. Traveller-oriented hangout behind a landmark bar-restaurant, offering the cheapest beds on the island, in large

mixed-sex dorms; up to seventeen bunk beds are crammed in each, but there are fans and lockers. Also has a few singles (B400) and doubles with shared, cold-water bathrooms. Dorm B300, double B800

Tropical Garden Beyond the turn-off for the path to the viewpoint ☎ 081 968 1436, ⓦ thailandphiphitravel.com. Here you'll find a wide variety of rooms and good-sized rough-timber bungalows, which are mostly built on stilts up the side of an outcrop. The better ones have a breezy veranda (though not much of a view) and there's a refreshing amount of greenery around, plus a small pool, despite being surrounded by other accommodation. Free wi-fi, book exchange and crafts shop. Fan B1000, a/c B1600

US Guest House Close to the base of the viewpoint access steps ☎ 075 601400, ⓔ jo_uspp @hotmail.com. This functional two-storey block with wi-fi throughout has the look and feel of a city guesthouse, and offers some of the cheaper en-suite rooms in the area, as well as a/c versions with hot water and TV. Interiors aren't bad at all and there's a long shared deck with seating beside the narrow lane. Fan B800, a/c B1500

Viewpoint Bungalows ☎ 075 601200, ⓦ phiphi viewpoint.com. Strung out across and up the cliffside at the far eastern end of Ao Loh Dalum, the rooms and bungalows here enjoy great views over the bay, though interiors are nothing to write home about and the all-night bars are too near to ignore. Facilities include a scenically sited restaurant, a tour desk and a small, idyllically situated, infinity-edged bayview pool. Breakfast included. Fan B1600, a/c B2500

LAEM HIN

Bay View Resort ☎ 075 601127, ⓦ phiphibayview .com. The draw at the seventy large, a/c bungalows here is

7

their prime location: they're set high on the cliffside at the far eastern end of Laem Hin beach, strung out along the ridge almost as far as Hat Yao. All have massive windows and decks to enjoy the great views and there's a pool here too. Be prepared for lots of steps though. Breakfast included. B3600

Gypsy Village About 150m down the track between the mosque and Phi Phi Andaman Legacy ☎075 601045, ⓦkrabidir.com/ppgypsyvillage. The thirty plain and pretty shabby pink-painted concrete bungalows here are relatively cheap, but they're all en suite and fan-cooled, and are set round a big dry lawn. B900

Phi Phi Andaman Legacy ☎075 601106, ⓦppandamanlegacy.com. Set in a secluded enclosure just a few metres back from the beach, the rather old-fashioned bungalows here are arranged in a square around a large lawn and small central swimming pool, while the 36 more modern rooms occupy a three-storey hotel building at the back. All rooms are a/c and come with TVs, hot water, fridges, wi-fi and safety boxes. Breakfast included. B2090

Phi Phi Villa Resort ☎075 601100, ⓦphiphivilla resort.com. The best of the many options at this outfit are the huge a/c family cottages occupying the front section of the prettily landscaped garden, near the pool. Also available are smaller bungalows and stylish new rooms in an annexe set back from the beach, all with a/c, hot water, fridge, TV and payable wi-fi. Breakfast included. B3100

LONG BEACH (HAT YAO)

The Beach Resort ☎075 819206, ⓦphiphithebeach .com. Currently the poshest option on Hat Yao, this place has a throng of large, timber-clad chalets built on stilts up the hillside, with the tallest, most deluxe ones enjoying commanding views of Phi Phi Leh. Interiors are fairly upscale, with a/c and liberal use of wood for flooring and wall panels. There's wi-fi and a small beachfront pool. B4300

Long Beach Bungalows ☎086 470 8984, ⓔlongbeach@gmail.com. The first choice of most budget travellers, this relatively cheap, well-located and long-running option has dozens of tightly packed huts for rent, ranging from simple, clean bamboo huts with fans, mosquito nets and cold-water bathrooms, to smart beachfront cottages with hot water. The room price includes a B100 food and drinks voucher for the restaurant, and there are discounts for divers (see p.677). B1000

Phi Phi Paradise Pearl Resort ☎075 601246, ⓦphiphiparadisepearl.com. The 35 bungalows and rooms at this efficiently run place are fairly well spaced along the western half of the beach, with none more than a few steps from the shore. Interiors are unremarkable but perfectly comfortable and all have a/c, hot water and verandas. There's internet access here, plus a tour counter;

free longtail pick-ups from the pier are offered. Breakfast included. B3000

Viking Nature Resort ☎075 819399, ⓦvikingnature resort.com. Tucked away on and above two private little coves just west of Hat Yao, with easy access via a rocky path, this is a very stylish take on classic Thai beach-bungalow architecture. It's nearly all wood and bamboo here, with no a/c, but interiors are styled with Asian boho-chic artefacts. The most glamorous accommodation is in the enormous, high-level, one- to four-bedroom "Makmai" tree houses, with their massive living-room decks overlooking the bay. There's a stylish lounge and dining area on the beach, with wi-fi; kayaks and snorkels are available. B1500

AO TOH KO

⭐ **Ao Toh Ko Beach Resort** ☎081 537 0528, ⓦwww .tohkobeachresort.com. The exceptionally welcoming family who run this place keep people staying and returning – and they're great cooks too. The comfortable accommodation varies from attractive, breezy, en-suite, bamboo huts with mossie nets, some sitting right over the sea on the rocks, to smart, bright, concrete bungalows with a/c, hot water, fridge and TV. Kayaks and snorkels for rent. Fan B1800, a/c B2500

HAT RANTEE

Rantee Beach Resort ☎089 725 4411, ⓦkrabidir .com/ranteeresort. At this shady resort, you can choose between en-suite, thatched, bamboo huts and spacious, arched, Bali-style villas with a/c, hot showers and TV. Kayaks and internet access are available, while transfers from the pier cost B200 per person. Breakfast included. Fan B1800, a/c B2900

HAT PAK NAM

Phi Phi Relax Beach Resort ☎089 725 4411, ⓦphiphirelaxbeach.com. Rustic but comfortable and very welcoming accommodation, in 51 attractive, en-suite wood and bamboo bungalows, set in rows in among the beachfront trees. Internet access, kayaks and pick-ups from the pier twice a day (B150 per person). B1800

AO LOH BAKAO

Phi Phi Island Village Beach Resort and Spa ☎075 628999, ⓦppisland.com. This plush, a/c resort on a lovely beach is a popular honeymoon spot, and a great location for anyone looking for a quiet, comfortable break. The thatched, split-bamboo bungalows and pool villas are mostly designed in traditional Thai style and furnished with character and elegance. There's a large pool and a spa in the prettily landscaped tropical gardens, as well as a dive centre. The resort was about to be taken over by the luxury Outrigger group at the time of writing, so prices may go up. B8300

LAEM TONG

Holiday Inn Resort Phi Phi Island ☏075 627300, ⓦphiphi.holidayinn.com. The *Holiday Inn* enjoys nearly a kilometre of beachfront at the southern end of the bay, but its 120 deluxe a/c bungalows and spacious, balconied, sea-view rooms (all with wi-fi and DVD players) are nicely hidden by the shoreline trees and sit in graceful gardens of tidy lawns and flowering shrubs. There's a popular sunset bar at the top of the ridge, two swimming pools, a dive centre,

a massage pavilion and tennis courts, and cooking classes, free kayaks and snorkelling equipment are available. **B7000**

Phi Phi Natural Resort ☏075 819030–1, ⓦphiphi natural.com. Up at the northern end of the bay, the a/c rooms, wooden chalets and pool villas here are scattered around an extensive tropical shorefront garden, with pool, that stretches along the coast to the next tiny uninhabited bay. All come with a/c, TV, mini-bar, hot water, free break-fast and a fairly traditional Thai-style decor. **B3600**

EATING

Ton Sai is the best place to eat on the island; elsewhere, visitors tend to eat at their resort's restaurant.

TON SAI VILLAGE

Cosmic East of the pier, on the fourth north–south alley, heading north from the yellow Phi Phi Divers shop. Popular, well-priced pasta, including home-made ravioli and gnocchi (B150), and pizzas (B150). Daily 8am–10.30pm.

Elite On the main alley running east from the pier. A/c café serving delicious Italian ice cream made in Phuket (from B80 for one scoop) and excellent Illy espressos. Daily 10am–10pm.

Le Grand Bleu Just east of the pier on the main east–west alley. Classy place serving a French-inspired menu that includes lots of fresh seafood, including risotto with scallops (B190), sirloin steak and changing dishes of the day. Daily 6.30–10.30pm.

Lemongrass East of the pier, on the first north–south alley. Friendly, basic restaurant with an open kitchen, serving very tasty Thai standards, starting with chicken fried rice for B80. Daily 10/10.30am–10.30/11pm.

Madame Restaurant East of the pier, off the fourth north–south alley, on the main route heading towards The Rock. Deservedly popular for its curries – *phanaeng, matsaman,* green and red – mostly B80. Also offers thin-crust pizzas and a decent vegetarian selection, as well as Western breakfasts and espresso coffees. Daily 8am–11pm.

Papaya East of the pier, just off the fourth north–south alley. One of the best of several village-style kitchens whose authentic and reasonably cheap Thai standards, including noodle soups, *phat thai,* fried rice dishes and fiery curries (B150), make it very popular with locals and dive staff. Daily 3pm–1am.

Patcharee Bakery On the main alley running east from the pier. This place and *Pee Pee Bakery* square up to each other across the narrow alley, vying for the breakfast trade. Croissants – plain, chocolate (B25), almond or savoury – are the thing here, washed down with espresso coffees. Daily 7am–8pm.

Pee Pee Bakery On the main alley running east from the pier, opposite Patcharee Bakery. Good choice for breakfast or lunch, with espresso coffees, set breakfasts (from B100), sandwiches and piles of home-made breads, cakes and cookies. Daily 7am–5pm.

Pum East of the pier, on the fourth north–south alley ☏081 521 8904, ⓦpumthaifoodchain.com. Small, comfy, contemporary chain restaurant, serving basic Thai dishes, such as noodles (B89), fried rice and curries, in some strange combinations that sometimes work. They also offer cooking classes at their school on the next alley west for B1200 for 3hr. Daily 11am–9pm.

NIGHTLIFE AND ENTERTAINMENT

TON SAI VILLAGE AND AO LOH DALUM

Concentrated on the beach at Loh Dalum, Ton Sai nightlife is young and drunken, involving endless buckets of Sansom and red bull, dance music played until dawn, and fire-juggling shows on the beach. Most of the bars offer a pretty similar formula, so it's often the one-off events and happy hours that make the difference.

Reggae Bar East of the pier, off the fourth north–south alley, on the main route heading towards The Rock. A Phi Phi institution in the heart of the village that's been running for years in various incarnations. These days it arranges regular amateur *muay thai* bouts in its boxing ring at around 9pm – "beat up your friend and win free buckets" – and has pool tables and a bar around the sides. There's even reggae karaoke. Daily roughly 10am–1am.

Slinky Towards the east end of Loh Dalum, where the left fork just before The Rock hits the beach. The messy, throbbing heart of Phi Phi nightlife, with a booming sound system, fire shows, and buckets and buckets of booze. Daily 6pm–late.

Stones Bar On the beach at the east end of Loh Dalum. One of the bars of the moment, with dozens of nifty red, gold and green axe cushions scattered on the beach and on platforms under the trees, and a DJ station in a treehouse. Claims to be open 24hr.

Sunflower Bar On the beach at the east end of Loh Dalum. Timber-built chillout spot with tables, axe cushions and plants strewn around the garden, plus great views, good music, free wi-fi and a pool table. Happy hour daily 5.30–8.30pm. Daily roughly 10am–2pm.

DIRECTORY

ATMs and exchange Plenty of machines in Ton Sai village, including next to the Siam Commercial Bank exchange counter (daily 9am–8.30pm), on the main alley running east of the pier.

Hospital Phi Phi Hospital (☎ 075 622151 or ☎ 081 270 4481), at the western end of Ao Ton Sai.

Police As well as a police station (☎ 075 611177), next to *Carlito's Bar* on the main alley running east of the pier, out towards Laem Hin, there's a tourist policeman on Phi Phi (☎ 1155), who's looking for new premises, probably just west of the pier near the *Phi Phi Island Cabana Hotel*.

Ko Jum

Situated halfway between Krabi and Ko Lanta Yai, **KO JUM** (whose northern half is known as **Ko Pu**) is the sort of laidback spot that people come to for a couple of days, then can't bring themselves to leave. Though there's plenty of accommodation on the island, there's nothing more than a handful of beach bars for evening entertainment, and little to do during the day except try out the half-dozen west-coast beaches. The beaches may not be pristine, and are in some places unswimmably rocky at low tide, but they're mostly long and wild, and all but empty of people. Nights are also low-key: it's paraffin lamps and starlight after about 11pm (or earlier) at those places that are off the main grid, and many don't even provide fans as island breezes are sufficiently cooling.

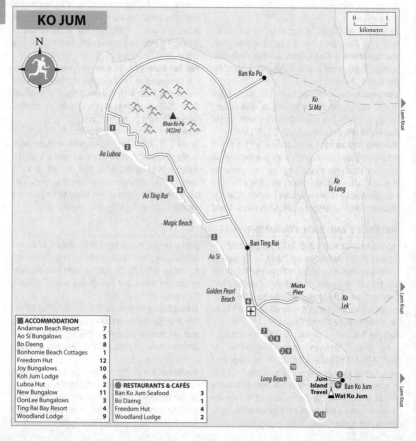

KO JUM

0   1
kilometre

Ban Ko Pu

Ko Si Ma

Khao Ko Pu (422m)

Ao Luboa

Ko To Lang

Ao Ting Rai

Magic Beach

Ban Ting Rai

Ao Si

Mutu Pier

Ko Lek

Golden Pearl Beach

■ ACCOMMODATION	
Andaman Beach Resort	7
Ao Si Bungalows	5
Bo Daeng	8
Bonhomie Beach Cottages	1
Freedom Hut	12
Joy Bungalows	10
Koh Jum Lodge	6
Luboa Hut	2
New Bungalow	11
OonLee Bungalows	3
Ting Rai Bay Resort	4
Woodland Lodge	9

● RESTAURANTS & CAFÉS	
Ban Ko Jum Seafood	3
Bo Daeng	1
Freedom Hut	4
Woodland Lodge	2

Long Beach

Jum Island Travel   **Ban Ko Jum**
▲ **Wat Ko Jum**

Laem Kruat

ACTIVITIES ON KO JUM

Most bungalows can organize **day-trips**, as will tour agencies in Ban Ko Jum, for example to Ko Phi Phi, Bamboo Island and Mosquito Island (about B3500–4000 per boat), or around Ko Jum (B2500 per boat). Many offer guided hikes up **Khao Ko Pu** (about B1000, including lunch). Ko Jum Divers, at *Ko Jum Beach Villas* at the north end of Long Beach (☎082 273 7603, ⓦkohjum-divers.com), run daily **dive** trips to Ko Phi Phi (B4200), with snorkellers welcome (B2100), and diving courses on offer (Discover Scuba B4900; Openwater B14,900).

The island is home to around three thousand people, the majority of them Muslim, though there are also communities of *chao ley* sea gypsies on Ko Jum (see p.608), as well as Buddhists. The main village is **Ban Ko Jum**, on the island's southeastern tip, comprising a few local shops and small restaurants, one of the island's three piers for boats to and from Laem Kruat on the mainland, and a beachfront school. It's about 1km from the village to the southern end of the island's most popular beach, the appropriately named **Long Beach**. Long Beach is connected to **Golden Pearl Beach**, which sits just south of **Ban Ting Rai**, the middle-island village that's about halfway down the west coast. North of Ban Ting Rai, a trio of smaller, increasingly remote beaches at **Ao Si**, **Ao Ting Rai**, and **Ao Luboa** complete the picture. The island's third village, **Ban Ko Pu**, occupies the northeastern tip, about 5km beyond Ban Ting Rai, and has another Laem Kruat ferry pier. Many islanders refer to the north of the island, from Ban Ting Rai upwards, as Ko Pu, and define only the south as Ko Jum. Much of the north is made inaccessible by the breastbone of forested hills, whose highest peak (422m) is Khao Ko Pu.

Very high winds and heavy seas mean that Ko Jum becomes an acquired taste from May through October, so nearly all accommodation and restaurants **close** for that period: the few exceptions are highlighted in the text.

Long Beach and Golden Pearl Beach

LONG BEACH (sometimes known as **Andaman Beach**) is the main backpackers' beach and is indeed long – at around 2.5km – with large chunks of the shoreline still uncultivated, backed with trees and wilderness, and well beyond sight of the island road. From *New Bungalow* towards the southern end it's a twenty-minute walk into Ban Ko Jum village.

At its northern end, Long Beach segues into **GOLDEN PEARL BEACH**, which is about 750m/fifteen minutes' walk north up the beach from *Bo Daeng*, 5km by road from Ban Ko Jum and 1km south of Ban Ting Rai. Like Long Beach, it also has only a few bungalow outfits along its curving shoreline, though these are close by the island road.

Ao Si

Around the rocky headland from Golden Pearl Beach, accessible in ten minutes at low tide or quite a bit further by road, long and beautifully uncluttered **AO SI** is good for swimming. There are a few places to stay, and a big troupe of monkeys makes its home here too. A ten-minute walk through the rubber trees from the uppermost of *Ao Si*'s bungalows brings you to Magic Beach, just south of Ao Ting Rai.

Ban Ting Rai, Khao Ko Pu and Ao Ting Rai

The road begins to climb as soon as you leave Golden Pearl Beach, taking you up through the ribbon-like village of **Ban Ting Rai**, pretty with bougainvillea and wooden houses, and location of a few small restaurants and noodle shops. **Khao Ko Pu** which rises in the distance is, at 422m, the island's highest mountain and home to macaques that sometimes come down to forage on the rocks around the northern beaches; guided treks up the eastern flank to the summit take about an hour and reward you with fine 360-degree panoramas encompassing the entire island, the mainland and the outer islands.

The little bay of **AO TING RAI**, sometimes known as **Hat Kidon**, has some nice places to stay and good snorkelling off its shore, with reef to explore and plenty of fish. At low tide it's too rocky for swimming though, when you'll need either to pick your way over the rocks, rent a kayak, or walk south 500m along the coastal road, to get to the little sandy crescent known as **Magic Beach**, which is swimmable at any tide. You can walk to Ao Ting Rai from Ao Si in about twenty minutes along the coast road.

Ao Luboa

Ko Jum's peaceful northernmost beach, **AO LUBOA**, feels remote. It's accessed chiefly by a loop in the main island road that circles the northeastern slopes of Khao Ko Pu and terminates at the north end of the bay, though the steeply undulating coast road from Ao Ting Rai can also be walked (about 45min from *OonLee Bungalows*). Like Ao Ting Rai, Ao Luboa's shorefront reef gets exposed at low tide, making it impossible to swim, though at high water things are fine and it's anyway a supremely quiet, laidback beach with just a few bungalows.

ARRIVAL AND DEPARTURE
KO JUM

To/from Krabi/Ko Lanta During high season, usual access to Ko Jum is via the Krabi–Ko Lanta ferry (daily; 1hr 30min–2hr from Krabi, currently leaving at 11am, or about 45min from Ko Lanta, currently leaving at 8am; B400). Ko Jum bungalows send longtails out to meet the ferries as they make two stops off the west coast: coming from Krabi, stop one is for the northern "*Ko Pu*" bungalows (on Ao Ting Rai and Ao Luboa) and the second, "Ko Jum", stop is for bungalows on *Ao Si, Golden Pearl* and *Long Beach*.

To/from Ko Phi Phi This service isn't set in stone, but there should be a boat from Ton Sai to Ko Jum every afternoon in high season (1hr 30min; B500) – ask at Parntawan Tour (see p.680).

To/from Laem Kruat In the rainy season you have to travel to Ko Jum overland, and an increasing number of

visitors now use this route year-round; some bungalow operators, for example, offer transfers from Krabi airport using this route (about B800 per car to Laem Kruat). Coming from Krabi town, you need to take a blue songthaew, passing the airport, either all the way through to Laem Kruat (B100) or changing in Nua Klong. Boats run from Laem Kruat to all three east-coast "village" piers on Ko Jum (45min–1hr; B50–70), from where a motorbike taxi with sidecar (best arranged in advance through your resort) will transfer you to your bungalow, charging from B50 per person. Boats to Ban Ko Pu depart Laem Kruat about every two hours during the day, while the thrice-daily services to Mutu and Ban Ko Jum are mostly in the afternoon, timed for shoppers and traders to return to the island.

GETTING AROUND

Most bungalows can arrange **kayak** (about B600 per day) and **motorbike** (about B350 per day) rental, while *Bo Daeng* has mountain bikes (B120 per day). The main island road is slowly being paved north from Ban Ko Jum, but the track on the west side of Khao Ko Pu remains a bumpy nightmare.

INFORMATION

For a comprehensive **guide** to life on the island and pictures of all the bungalow operations, see ⓦ kohjumonline.com.

ACCOMMODATION

LONG BEACH
Accommodation on Long Beach is in three clusters, each about 15min' walk apart.

Andaman Beach Resort ☏089 724 1544, ⊜ andaman_kohjum@yahoo.com. You can't miss the steeply roofed concrete bungalows at this friendly, well-run place, painted in shocking pink, yellow and other

"lucky" colours like gingerbread houses, complete with false first-floor windows. Set in a pleasant garden, they're all bright, clean and en suite with mosquito screens and terraces, and are priced according to size and proximity to the beach (rising to B3000 for a big, a/c, beachfront pad with hot water and breakfast). The food's good and reasonably priced, too. **B350**

Bo Daeng ☎081 494 8760. This funky, ultra-cheap and ultra-basic travellers' classic is run by a famously welcoming charismatic island *chao ley* family and has legendary food. The rudimentary bamboo huts come with or without private bathrooms – the latter are among the very cheapest on the island, but all have nets and electricity during the evening. Open all year. Shared bathroom B150, en suite B200

Freedom Hut ☎084 991 0881 or ☎084 746 2964, ✉yakohjum@hotmail.co.th. Large, beautifully simple, thatched bungalows (including a treehouse) in rustic-contemporary style, way off on their own at the southernmost point, with loads of space for hammocks and chairs on the deck. Some have nice outdoor rock bathrooms, and one occupies an unparalleled spot on a tiny rocky promontory, with awesome 360-degree sea views (B3000). B500

Joy Bungalows ☎075 618199, ⓦkohjum-joybungalow .com. This is the longest-running and most famous place to stay on the island, though not necessarily the friendliest. It has a big spread of accommodation set in a very shady grove of trees behind the shorefront, the majority of them smart wooden bungalows in varying sizes and proximity to the sea, plus some cheaper thatched ones and two-bedroom houses. The resort has electricity but not the bungalows, so it's paraffin lamps all round at night. B650

New Bungalow ☎075 618116, ✉nbkohjum @hotmail.com. The two-dozen differently styled bungalows at this friendly, long-established place include a few cheapie bamboo ones with and without private bathrooms, some plain, en-suite wooden huts, and a couple of treehouses set 5m or so up in the branches by the beach, with idyllic sea views and shared bathrooms. Electricity evenings only. Shared bathroom B200, en-suite B300, treehouse B400

★ **Woodland Lodge** ☎081 893 5330, ⓦwoodland -koh-jum.com. Welcoming, helpful and peaceful spot owned by a UK–Thai couple and one of the few places on the island to stay open year-round (with big discounts in the rainy season). Its large, attractive, well-designed bungalows with 24hr electricity are widely set beneath the trees of its shorefront garden and all have good, spacious bathrooms; the doubles have platform beds, mosquito nets, varnished wooden floors and deep shady decks, while the bigger ones are designed for families. B1000

GOLDEN PEARL BEACH

Koh Jum Lodge ☎089 921 1621, ⓦkohjumlodge .com. This French–Thai place is one of the most upscale resorts on the island, with nineteen thatched wooden

chalets designed in charming rustic-chic style. Thoughtfully constructed to make the most of the island breezes, they have doors onto the veranda to avoid the need for a/c, plus low beds and elegantly simple furniture. The resort has a small pool, internet access, a TV and DVD area, a massage service and a restaurant. Minimum stay four nights, seven in peak season. Breakfast included. B5000

AO SI

Ao Si Bungalows ☎081 747 2664, ⓦaosibungalow .com. On Ao Si's northern headland, the woven-bamboo, en-suite bungalows here are built on piles up the side of the cliff and have wrap-around verandas for soaking up the commanding views of the bay and the southern half of the island. B500

AO TING RAI

OonLee Bungalows ☎087 200 8053, ⓦkohjumoonlee bungalows.com. Small, enthusiastically run and well-liked French–Thai place with sturdy accommodation in various styles stacked up the cliffside. The wooden bungalows have plenty of storage, appealing bathrooms and sea-view verandas; there's a stylish upper-level lounge area and good restaurant, and a bar and massage area at beach level, plus kayaks for rent and free snorkels for guests. *OonLee* offers lots of organized activities and tours, including guided half-day treks up Khao Ko Pu and fishing trips. B600

Ting Rai Bay Resort ☎087 277 7379, ⓦtingrai.com. Popular spot whose nicely designed wooden bungalows are ranged up the sloping shorefront on stilts, most offering fine views from capacious decks (especially the "honeymoon" ones). Interiors have fans, four-poster style beds, and plenty of attention to detail. The food here is also good and there's internet access. B600

AO LUBOA

Bonhomie Beach Cottages ☎086 560 7977, ⓦbonhomiebeach.com. At the far northern end of the beach, very large, attractively designed en-suite wooden chalets with mosquito nets, many with sea view; price depends on proximity to the sea. B700

Luboa Hut ☎081 388 9241, ⓦluboahut.com. Friendly establishment with ten en-suite bamboo and wooden bungalows with sea views from their verandas in a well-shaded spot under shoreside trees; many of them are roomy and good quality, some have extra beds or sofas and all have mosquito nets. The owners offer free kayaks, cooking classes and internet. B500

EATING AND DRINKING

LONG BEACH

★ **Bo Daeng** For an outstanding Thai meal, at some of the cheapest prices on the island, you should join the (sometimes

lengthy) queue here, whose highlights include baked fish, vegetable tempura (B80), curries including southern yellow curry (B80), plus Thai desserts, home-baked bread and

7

coconut shakes. Daily 7.30am–9pm.

Freedom Hut Many people round off the night with a drink around the camp fire at this easy-going place, right down at the bottom end of Long Beach. Choose between cocktails, wine and cheapish beer; an espresso machine and pizza oven are planned. Daily 7.30am–12.30am.

Woodland Lodge Delicious curries – try the Indian curry with prawns (B200) – plenty of choice for vegetarians, including tasty vegetable tempura (B80), plus Western food, including breakfast and fish and chips. Daily roughly 7am–8.30/9pm.

BAN KO JUM

Ban Ko Jum Seafood ☎ 081 893 6380. The big name here is this very popular and very good restaurant, whose tables occupy a scenically sited jetty near the pier, and enjoy fine views across the mangrove channel. Among its big menu of fresh seafood cooked any number of ways (B100–400), the juicy fat prawns barbecued with honey are a standout, and their crab and lobster dishes are famous too. Daily 9am–10pm.

DIRECTORY

Clinic The island medical centre is on the road near *Ko Jum Lodge*, beyond the southern edge of Ban Ting Rai.

Exchange There's no ATM on the island, so it's best to bring all the cash you'll need with you. At a pinch, you can change

money at Jum Island Travel, next to the pier in Ban Ko Jum, at expensive rates.

Internet access In Ban Ko Jum and at one or more of the hotels on almost every beach.

Ko Lanta Yai

Although **KO LANTA YAI** can't quite compete with Phi Phi's stupendous scenery, the thickly forested 25km-long island has the longest beaches in the Krabi area – and plenty of them. There's decent snorkelling and diving nearby, plus caves to explore, kayaking and other watersports, so many tourists base themselves here for their entire holiday fortnight. The island is especially popular with families, in part because of the local laws that have so far prevented jet-skis, beachfront parasols and girlie bars from turning it into another Phuket, though resort facilities are expanding fast. Lanta is also rapidly being colonized by Scandinavian expats, with villa homes and associated businesses popping up all over the place, at a pace that not all islanders are happy about. The majority of Ko Lanta Yai's ten thousand indigenous residents are mixed-blood descendants of Muslim Chinese–Malay or animist *chao ley* ("sea gypsy") peoples (see box, p.608), most of whom supported themselves by fishing and cultivating the land before the tourist boom brought new jobs, and challenges.

One of those challenges is that the **tourist season** is quite short, with the weather and seas at their calmest and safest from November to April; the main ferries don't run outside that period, and some hotels close, though most do stay open and offer huge discounts. The short money-making window, however, means that accommodation prices on Ko Lanta fluctuate more wildly than many other south Thailand destinations.

The local *chao ley* name for Ko Lanta Yai is *Pulao Satak*, "Island of Long Beaches", an apt description of the string of beaches along the **west coast**, each separated by

---

LANTA FESTIVALS

Every March, Ko Lanta Yai celebrates its rich ethnic heritage at the **Laanta Lanta Festival** (*laanta* meaning roughly "eye-dazzling"), which is held over five days in Lanta Old Town and features both traditional and modern music and entertainments, countless specialist foodstalls and crafts for sale (check ⊛ lantaoldtown.com for dates and specifics). Traditional *chao ley* rituals are celebrated on Ko Lanta twice a year, on the full moons of the sixth and eleventh lunar months – usually June and Oct/Nov (see p.694). Meanwhile, the Chinese shrine in Lanta Old Town is the focus of the island's version of the **Vegetarian Festival** (see p.629), which involves processions, cultural performances and walking on hot coals.

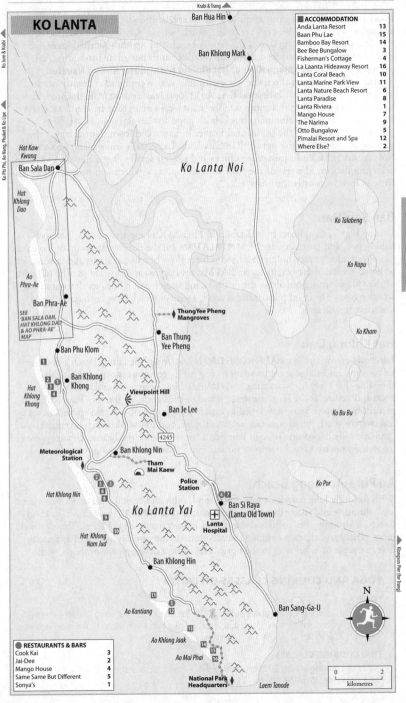

KO LANTA

Krabi & Trang ▲

Ban Hua Hin ●

Ban Khlong Mark ●

Hat Kaw Kwang

Ban Sala Dan ●

Ko Lanta Noi

Hat Khlong Dao

Ko Talabeng

Ao Phra-Ae

Ban Phra-Ae ●

Ko Rapu

SEE 'BAN SALA DAN, HAT KHLONG DAO & AO PHRA-AE' MAP

ThungYee Pheng Mangroves

Ban Thung Yee Pheng

Ban Phu Klom ●

Ko Kham

Ban Khlong Khong

Hat Khlong Khong

Viewpoint Hill

Ban Je Lee ●

Ko Bu Bu

4245

Ban Khlong Nin ●

Meteorological Station

Tham Mai Kaew

Police Station

Ko Por

Hat Khlong Nin

Ban Si Raya (Lanta Old Town)

Lanta Hospital

Ko Lanta Yai

Hat Khlong Nam Jud

Ban Khlong Hin ●

Ban Sang-Ga-U ●

Ao Kantiang

Ao Khlong Jaak

Ao Mai Phai

National Park Headquarters ▲

Laem Tanode

N

Ko Jum & Krabi ◄
Ko Phi Phi, Ao Nang, Phuket & Ko Lipe ◄
Klongon Pier (for Trang) ►

7

ACCOMMODATION

Anda Lanta Resort	13
Baan Phu Lae	15
Bamboo Bay Resort	14
Bee Bee Bungalow	3
Fisherman's Cottage	4
La Laanta Hideaway Resort	16
Lanta Coral Beach	10
Lanta Marine Park View	11
Lanta Nature Beach Resort	6
Lanta Paradise	8
Lanta Riviera	1
Mango House	7
The Narima	9
Otto Bungalow	5
Pimalai Resort and Spa	12
Where Else?	2

RESTAURANTS & BARS

Cook Kai	3
Jai-Dee	2
Mango House	4
Same Same But Different	5
Sonya's	1

0 — 2 kilometres

rocky points and strung out at quite wide intervals. Broadly speaking, the busiest and most mainstream beaches are in the north, within easy reach of the port at **Ban Sala Dan**: Hat Khlong Dao is the family beach and **Ao Phra-Ae** the longer and more beautiful. The middle section has variable sands but some interesting, artsy places to stay, at **Hat Khlong Khong**, **Hat Khlong Nin** and **Hat Khlong Nam Jud**. Southerly **Ao Kantiang** is reliable for swimming year-round and currently marks the end of the made road; beyond here **Ao Khlong Jaak** and **Ao Mai Phai** are a little harder to get to and so feel more remote. Lanta Yai's mangrove-fringed **east coast** has no real tourist development but is both good for kayaking and culturally interesting because of the traditional homes in **Lanta Old Town**. North across the narrow channel from the port at Ban Sala Dan, Lanta Yai's sister island of **Ko Lanta Noi** has Ko Lanta's administrative offices and several small villages but no tourist accommodation. The rest of the Ko Lanta archipelago, which comprises over fifty little islands, is mostly uninhabited.

Ban Sala Dan

During high season, boats from Krabi, Phi Phi and Ko Lipe arrive at the T-shaped fishing port and tourist village of **BAN SALA DAN**, on the northernmost tip of Ko Lanta Yai. Pretty much everything you'll need is here, from beachwear shops and minimarkets to banks with currency exchange and ATMs, tour agents and dive shops. The old part of the village, strung out along the north-facing shorefront, retains its charming old wooden houses built on piles over the water, many of which have been turned into attractive restaurants.

Hat Khlong Dao

Long and gently curving **HAT KHLONG DAO** is known as "the family beach", both for its plentiful mid-range accommodation, and for its generous sweep of flat sandy shoreline that's safe for swimming and embraced by protective headlands; there's good snorkelling at the far northwestern end of the beach, off the tiny Kaw Kwang peninsula. Despite being developed to capacity, Khlong Dao is broad enough never to feel overcrowded, the sunsets can be magnificent, and the whole beach is framed by a dramatic hilly backdrop. Though Ban Sala Dan is close by, the beach supports plenty of its own minimarkets and transport outlets, both shoreside and along the main road.

Ao Phra-Ae (Long Beach)

With its lovely long parade of soft, white sand, calm and crystal-clear water that's good for swimming and shady fringe of casuarina trees, **AO PHRA-AE** (also known as **Long Beach**) is strikingly beautiful and the best of Lanta's many long beaches. There's a little more variety and character among the accommodation options here than at Khlong Dao, a couple of kilometres to the north, and quite a development of shops, with

---

YOGA AND COOKING CLASSES ON LANTA

YOGA

During high season there are **yoga** classes at *Cha Ba* bungalows on Khlong Dao (🖥thetreatthailand.com; also meditation classes and yoga and meditation retreats), but the most famous teacher is at *Relax Bay* on Ao Phra-Ae (🖥monayoga.com).

THAI COOKING CLASSES

Five-hour **cooking** classes (B1800) are offered by Time for Lime, at the south end of Hat Khlong Dao (☎075 684590, 🖥timeforlime.net).

SNORKELLING TRIPS AND WATERSPORTS ON LANTA

SNORKELLING TRIPS

The best and most popular **snorkelling** is at the islands of **Ko Rok Nai** and **Ko Rok Nok**, 47km south of Ko Lanta; these forested twins are graced with stunning white-sand beaches and accessible waterfalls and separated by a narrow channel full of fabulous shallow reefs. Also hugely popular is the "**four island**" snorkelling trip that takes in the much nearer islands off Trang – the enclosed emerald lagoon on **Ko Mook** (see p.713), plus nearby **Ko Hai** (Ko Ngai), **Ko Ma** and **Ko Kradan** – but these sites can get very crowded. Another option is the day-trip to **Phi Phi Don**, Phi Phi Leh and Bamboo Island (see p.676). The trips cost around B1500 in a speedboat or B900 in a big boat, including lunch, snorkelling equipment and national park entry fee. For a smaller, more personal experience, contact Sun Island Tours or Freedom Adventures.

DIVING

The **reefs** around Ko Lanta are quieter and in some cases more pristine than those round Phi Phi and Phuket, and excellent for seeing whale sharks. The **diving season** runs from November to April, though a few dive shops continue to run successful trips from May to August. All dive boats depart from Ban Sala Dan, and nearly all dive courses are taught either in Sala Dan or on Hat Khlong Dao, though there are dive shops on every beach.

Some of Lanta's best **dive sites** are located between Ko Lanta and Ko Phi Phi, including the soft coral at **Ko Bidah**, where you get lots of leopard sharks, barracuda and tuna. West and south of Lanta, the **Ko Ha** island group offers four different dives on each of its five islands, including steep drop-offs and an "underwater cathedral" and other caves; visibility is often very good. Much further south, about 56km from Ko Lanta, are **Hin Daeng** and **Hin Muang** (see p.643).

The nearest recompression chambers are located on Phuket (see p.642); check to see that your dive operator is insured to use one of them (see p.52).

KAYAKING

There are several rewarding **kayaking** destinations, rich in mangroves and caves, around Ko Lanta Yai's east coast and around Ko Lanta Noi and its eastern islands, including **Ko Talabeng** and **Ko Bubu**; a few companies also offer kayak-snorkel trips to the four islands described above.

OPERATORS

Freedom Adventures ☎ 084 910 9132, ⊛ freedom -adventures.net. A variety of snorkelling day-trips, as well as overnight camping trips on Ko Rok and Ko Kradan (from B2600).

Ko Lanta Diving Centre On the main road into Ban Sala Dan ☎ 075 668065, ⊛ kolantadivingcenter .com. German-run outfit charging B3000 for two dives, excluding equipment, B1600 for accompanying snorkellers and B15,650 for the Openwater course.

Lanta Diver On the main road into Ban Sala Dan ☎ 075 684208, ⊛ lantadiver.com. Swedish-owned, PADI Five-star Instructor Development Centre charging from B2900 for two dives, excluding equipment, and B14,300 for the Openwater course.

Lanta Garden Hill Speed Boat ☎ 075 684042,

⊛ lantaislandtours.com. One of the main operators of snorkelling trips, which can be booked through any agent on Ko Lanta.

Lanta Kayaking ☎ 081 787 1040. Kayaking trips to Ko Talabeng for B1300, bookable through most travel agents.

Lanta Paddlesports On the main road in Hat Khlong Dao and on several beaches ☎ 075 668096, ⊛ lantapaddlesports.com. Paddleboard lessons, rental and tours, as well as windsurfing, kayaking, surfing and snorkelling trips.

Sun Island Tours ☎ 087 891 6619, ⊛ lantalongtail .com. Various longtail trips to the four islands, around Ko Lanta, and to Lanta's eastern islands (where there's also an overnight camping option), which come very highly rated and cost B1500.

ATMs, restaurants and tour agents along the main road. The main stretch of the beach is divided from the southern rocky extremity by a shallow, easily wadeable khlong; *Lanta Marina Resort* marks the southern reaches of the beach and is about half an hour's walk along the beach from *Sayang* at the northern end. Phra-Ae's budget enclave clusters along a network of sandy tracks behind the *Ozone Bar*.

Hat Khlong Khong

The luxuriously long beach at **HAT KHLONG KHONG**, 2km south of Ao Phra-Ae's *Relax Bay Resort*, is peppered with rocks and in most parts only really swimmable at high tide, though the snorkelling is good. Another big draw is the traveller-oriented bungalows, among them the most creatively designed places to stay on the island. There are several funky little beach bars too, notably at *Bee Bee Bungalows*.

Hat Khlong Nin

About 4km south of Hat Khlong Khong the road forks at kilometre-stone 13, at the edge of the village of **Ban Khlong Nin**. The left-hand, east-bound arm runs across to Ko Lanta Yai's east coast, via the caves and viewpoint (see opposite). The right-hand fork is the route to the southern beaches and continues southwards along the west coast for 14km to the southern tip.

Just beyond the junction, the little enclave of bungalows, restaurants, bars and tour agents at **HAT KHLONG NIN** lends this beach more of a village atmosphere than the northern beaches. The beach itself is lovely, long and sandy and good for swimming, though the road runs close alongside it. There are several reasonably priced places to stay, with the cheapest beds in some hotels located in separate little garden compounds on the inland side of the road, and a low-key collection of shoreside bar-restaurants with plenty of character and mellow vibes.

There are minimarkets, ATMs and a clinic at the Ban Khlong Nin junction, and from here you could walk the 3km to the Tham Mai Kaew caves from Khlong Nin in about an hour.

Hat Khlong Nam Jud

Just over 1km south of Hat Khlong Nin, the road passes the two tiny little bays known as **HAT KHLONG NAM JUD**. The northerly one is the domain of *The Narima* (see p.697). A brief scramble around the rocky point to the south, the next tiny cove is rocky in parts but enjoys a swimmable beach and is home to *Lanta Coral Beach* (see p.697).

Ao Kantiang

The secluded cove of **AO KANTIANG**, some 7km beyond Hat Khlong Nam Jud, is an impressively long curve, backed by jungle-clad hillsides and dominated by one luxury hotel, which keeps the southern half of the beach in pristine condition. Unusually for Lanta, the bay is protected enough to be good for swimming year-round, and there's some coral at the northern end; snorkelling and fishing trips are easily arranged. The small but lively roadside village covers most necessities, including tours, onward transport, motorbike rental and internet access.

Ao Khlong Jaak and Ao Mai Phai

The road beyond Ao Kantiang to Lanta's southern tip, about 4km away, is steeply undulating and rutted, but is slowly being paved. The next bay south of Kantiang is **AO KHLONG JAAK**, site of some accommodation including the lively *Anda Lanta Resort* (see p.698). Though it's not much more than a trickle, the **waterfall** inland from Ao Khlong Jaak can be reached from the bay by walking along the course of the stream for about two hours. South around the next headland, western Lanta plays its final card in the shape of handsome white-sand **AO MAI PHAI**, a peaceful getaway because of its remote position on the largely unmade road. There's good coral close to shore here, but this makes it too rocky for low-tide swimming, when you'll need to kayak up to Ao Khlong Jaak instead.

Tham Mai Kaew caves

3km from the Khlong Nin junction • Two-hour tours available Mon–Thurs, Sat & Sun 9am–4pm, Fri 8–10am & 1.30–4pm (☎ 089 288 8954) • B300, including national park entry fee and head torch • A motorcycle taxi costs about B200 each way from Khlong Dao or Ao Phra-Ae

The myriad chambers at **Tham Mai Kaew caves**, some of which you can only just crawl into, are Ko Lanta's biggest inland attraction. They are filled with stalactites and interesting rock formations, and there's a creepy cave pool too, as well as the inevitable bats. Tours of the cave are given by the local family who first properly explored the cave system in the 1980s; as well as the standard tour they sometimes offer longer cave tours and overnight jungle treks. Most of Thailand's countless caves are underwhelming and certainly not worth B300, but this is one of the better ones, not least because the caretakers have resisted stringing it with electric lights so you're left to wonder both at what you catch with your torch and at what you don't see. Among its star features are crystallized waterfalls, fossils and ammonites embedded in the cave walls and overhangs, stalagmites and stalactites young and old and a tangible sense of there being endless passageways to explore. In the rainy season it's a more slippery, challenging experience, with some wading likely and the option of a dip in the wet-season-only lagoon. Even in the dry season it's moderately arduous and best done in sensible shoes and clothes you're happy to get grubby in.

The viewpoint

3km beyond the turn-off to the Tham Mai Kaew caves • Café daily 8am–8pm

Three kilometres beyond the turn-off to the caves, the eastbound road drops down over the central spine of hills and you pass *Viewpoint* café, where nearly everyone stops for a drink and a gawp at the stunning panorama. The **view over the east coast** is glorious, encompassing the southeast coast of mangrove-fringed Ko Lanta Noi, dozens of islets – including Ko Bubu and Ko Por – adrift in the milky blue sea, and the hilly profile of the mainland along the horizon.

Lanta Old Town (Ban Si Raya)

Ⓦ lantaoldtown.com

The seductively atmospheric little waterfront settlement of **LANTA OLD TOWN**, officially known as **Ban Si Raya**, is Ko Lanta's oldest town. It began life as a sheltered staging post for ships and served as the island's administrative capital from 1901 to 1998. The government offices have since moved to Ko Lanta Noi, and Ban Sala Dan has assumed the role of harbour, island gateway and commercial hub, so Ban Si Raya has been left much as it was a century ago, with its historic charm intact. There's little more to the Old Town than its peaceful main street, which runs right along the coast parallel to Route 4245 and is lined with traditional, hundred-year-old sea- and wind-blasted wooden homes and shops, many of them constructed on stilted jetties over the sea, their first-floor overhangs shading the pavements and plant-filled doorways. The Chinese shrine midway down the street is evidence of the town's cultural mix: Ban Si Raya is home to a long-established Buddhist Chinese–Thai community as well as to Muslims and, in its southern neighbourhood, communities of animist Urak Lawoy *chao ley* ("sea gypsies").

The **Urak Lawoy** *chao ley* (see box, p.608) are thought to have been Ko Lanta's first inhabitants, perhaps as long as five hundred years ago, living along the shoreline during the monsoon season and setting off along the coast again when the winds abated. They have now settled permanently in their own villages on the island, including at **Ban Sang-Ga-U**, 4km to the south of Lanta Old Town; other Urak Lawoy living elsewhere in the Andaman Sea, around Trang and beyond, consider Ko Lanta their capital and will always stop at Sang-Ga-U when making a journey. One of the accessible elements of Urak Lawoy culture is their **music**, an interesting fusion of far-flung influences, featuring violins (from the Dutch East Indies), drums (from Persia) and gongs (from China), as well as singing, dancing and ritual elements. A good time to hear their music is at one of their twice-yearly three-day full-moon **festivals**, or at the Laanta Lanta Festival (see p.688).

As an additional incentive to linger among the wooden architecture of the main street, there are several browsable **shops** selling batik sarongs and souvenirs, plus the charming Hammock House (ⓦjumbohammock.com), whose amazing range of hammocks includes ones woven by people of the endangered Mrabri tribe of northern Thailand (see p.328). The hourly Krabi air-conditioned minibus service starts from and terminates in Lanta Old Town.

Koh Lanta Community Museum

Across the small grassy park from the pier and parking lot • Daily 9am–3pm • B40

There's an attempt to introduce the cultures of Ban Si Raya's three distinct but peaceable communities at the **Koh Lanta Community Museum**, which is housed in the attractive 1901 wooden building that used to serve as the local district office. Archive photos and one or two English-language captions describe the main occupations for the communities, including fishing and making charcoal from mangrove wood; you can sometimes watch an interesting video in which villagers air their concerns about the recent explosion in tourism on the island and the effect that the influx of incomers and investors is having on traditional lifestyles and livelihoods.

Thung Yee Pheng mangroves

About 1km north of the junction of Route 4245 and the road across from Ao Phra-Ae, take the right turn for a couple of hundred metres • Daily 8am–4pm • B20

This community tourism project allows you to take a short, not very compelling stroll along a 200m boardwalk out into the mangrove swamps that line Ko Lanta Yai's east coast. More interesting are the one-hour longtail tours available here (B1000 per boat, including guide), and you can also hire a two-person kayak to have a look around (B500/2hr, B300 extra for a guide).

ARRIVAL AND DEPARTURE
KO LANTA YAI

The principal mainland gateways to Ko Lanta are Krabi, Phuket and Trang, all of which have good long-distance bus services, and **airports**. Trang also has a train station, and a new combined boat and road transfer to Lanta run by KK Travel (see p.709): a/c minibus to Klongson pier, north of Pak Meng, followed by speedboat to Lanta Old Town, then free transfers on Lanta (2 daily in high season; roughly 1hr 30min in total; B450, though currently on promotion at B300).

By boat In high season, there are boats to Ko Lanta Yai, as detailed below, from Krabi (B400), via Ko Jum (B400); from Ko Phi Phi (ferry B400, speedboat B600), with connections from Phuket (ferry B800, speedboat B1500); and from Ao Nang (B400) via West Railay (B470). There are also high-season services to Ko Lanta from the Trang islands and Ko Lipe, with connections to Langkawi (see p.710). All of these ferries dock at Ban Sala Dan and are met by bungalow touts who usually transport you to the beach of your choice for free. If you need to use the motorbike sidecar taxi service instead, be warned that drivers will try and charge arrivals way over the normal fares; walk 250m from the pier head to the main road to get a ride at more reasonable rates.
Destinations: Ao Nang, via West Railay (daily; 2hr 30min); Ko Phi Phi Don (2 daily; 1hr 30min); Krabi, via Ko Jum (daily; 2hr 30min); Phuket (1–2 daily; 4hr 30min).

By road The alternative to the ferries is the overland route to Ko Lanta Yai – essential during the rainy season but increasingly popular at any time of year. Access is via Ban Hua Hin on the mainland, 75km south of Krabi, from where a small ferry crosses to Ban Khlong Mark on Ko Lanta Noi, after which there's a 7km drive across to Lanta Noi's southwest tip, then another ferry over the narrow channel to the car-ferry port on Ko Lanta Yai's northeastern coast (though a bridge between Lanta Noi and Lanta Yai is being planned); both ferries run approximately every 20min from about 7am to 10pm (B120 in total per car). This is the route used by a/c minibuses from Krabi town (hourly; 2hr; B250–350 depending on which beach you get dropped at, terminates in Lanta Old Town); from Phuket (9 daily; 5hr; B500); from Trang (roughly hourly; 3hr; B300); and by anyone bringing their own vehicle. On departure from

Lanta, the Krabi minibuses will drop you off at Krabi Airport; on arrival, you'll need to call ☎ 081 606 3591 to ask them to pick you up at the airport. There's also a daily bus between Ban Hua Hin and Bangkok's Mo Chit bus terminal (12hr), fed by a/c minibuses to and from Ko Lanta Yai.

GETTING AROUND

There's no public transport on the island, but motorbikes are widely available for rent and there are jeeps too.

Share-taxis and songthaews A fleet of motorbike sidecar share-taxis, with drivers in numbered vests, and a few white songthaews operate out of Ban Sala Dan and will go pretty much anywhere on the island, though they usually need to be phoned (by staff at hotels or restaurants) for pick-ups from anywhere outside Sala Dan. Lanta has its share of scamming taxi-drivers, so bear in mind the following approximate per-person rates for rides out of Sala Dan: B40 to Hat Khlong Dao, B60 to Ao Phra-Ae, B90 to Hat Khlong Kong, or about B50 between the above.

ACCOMMODATION

Ko Lanta Yai is extremely popular during high season (Nov–Feb), when it's worth either booking your first night's accommodation in advance or taking up the suggestions of the bungalow touts who ride the boats from the mainland. A confirmed booking also means you should get free transport from the port to your hotel. Accommodation pricing on Ko Lanta is disconcertingly flexible and alters according to the number of tourists on the island: bungalow rates can double between mid-December and mid-January (and some resorts extend their "peak season" to include the whole of January and February), while during the rainy season between May and October rates are vastly discounted.

HAT KHLONG DAO

There are a couple of budget-oriented places to stay on Hat Khlong Dao, but the emphasis is on accommodation for families and others looking for a/c comfort.

Cha-Ba Bungalows ☎ 075 684118, ⊕ krabidir.com /chababungalows. There's plenty of kitsch creativity at this welcoming, idiosyncratic complex of bungalows, set among model dinosaurs and Flintstone boulders. The tightly packed bungalows are simple and flimsy, but cute, decorated with loud retro-look fabrics and wallpapers. Fan ones come with hot showers, while the a/c ones also have TVs, fridges and free breakfasts. There's free wi-fi in the restaurant and some rooms, and a small swimming pool is planned. Fan B1300, a/c B2000

Costa Lanta ☎ 075 684630, ⊕ costalanta.com. You're either going to love or hate this ultra-brutal minimalist grouping of 22 polished-grey concrete boxes, each bungalow consisting of an unadorned bedroom all in grey and white with a mosquito net, a similarly styled bathroom with rain shower and a large terrace. They're set in a broad garden bisected by khlongs, with a big, sleek pool and a striking bar-restaurant. Breakfast included. B6200

Crown Lanta ☎ 075 626999, ⊕ crownlanta.com. Upmarket, German-managed resort on the island's very northwestern tip, where crown motifs feature heavily on the rooftops. The hotel divides into two zones: standard (with very large balconies) and pool-access rooms near the lobby; up on the hill, villas and another free-form pool, plus a panoramic restaurant, a spa and steps down to a part-sandy, part-rocky private beach. B6500

Hans Restaurant ☎ 075 684152, ⊕ krabidir.com /hansrestaurant. By far the cheapest place on this beach, with fifteen huts ranged along a narrow, scruffy strip of garden behind the shorefront restaurant, next to the *Royal Lanta* resort in the heart of the beach. Choose between very simple, rickety bamboo bungalows with mosquito nets and bathrooms, and slightly better-furnished wooden versions. All bungalows are wi-fi accessible. High season only. B300

Kaw Kwang Beach Resort At the northernmost end of Khlong Dao ☎ 075 668260–1, ⊕ lanta -kawkwangresort.com. Welcoming, family-run outfit with good-value (for Lanta) rooms, occupying a large area of beachfront land on Hat Kaw Kwang adjacent to *Crown Lanta*. There are many options here, all with hot showers and TVs, from cheap, decent, old-style en-suite wood and concrete huts among the trees above the shore, to bigger, beachside a/c bungalows, family bungalows and hotel-style rooms. Has an infinity-edged pool and wi-fi in some rooms, plus computers for guest use. Snorkel rental and free transfers to and from Sala Dan pier. Fan B650, a/c B1700

The Noble House ☎ 075 668096, ⊕ lantanoblehouse .com. Appealingly small-scale, Swiss-run place where the inviting a/c bungalows have big glass windows and hot showers. They're set in facing rows, in a pretty shrub-filled garden, mostly around the little swimming pool. Also has a few a/c hotel rooms at the back of the compound. Free wi-fi in the restaurant. Buffet breakfast included. B2000

Slow Down ☎ 083 632 1551, ⊕ slowdownlanta.se. This Swedish-run resort at the far southern end of the beach, with a very attractive dark blue pool and kids' pool and a good restaurant, rents out villas and apartments by the week, but also has two hotel rooms (misleadingly called "bungalows"). They're a little dark, but successfully mix Swedish and southern Thai aesthetics, with lots of wood,

7

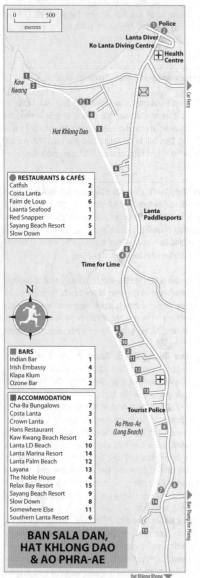

RESTAURANTS & CAFÉS	
Catfish	2
Costa Lanta	3
Faim de Loup	6
Laanta Seafood	1
Red Snapper	7
Sayang Beach Resort	5
Slow Down	4

BARS	
Indian Bar	1
Irish Embassy	4
Klapa Klum	3
Ozone Bar	2

ACCOMMODATION	
Cha-Ba Bungalows	7
Costa Lanta	3
Crown Lanta	1
Hans Restaurant	5
Kaw Kwang Beach Resort	2
Lanta LD Beach	10
Lanta Marina Resort	14
Lanta Palm Beach	12
Layana	13
The Noble House	4
Relax Bay Resort	15
Sayang Beach Resort	9
Slow Down	8
Somewhere Else	11
Southern Lanta Resort	6

**BAN SALA DAN,
HAT KHLONG DAO
& AO PHRA-AE**

tourists. Breakfast included. **B1800**

AO PHRA-AE (LONG BEACH)

Lanta LD Beach ☎075 684548, 🌐sandybeachlanta .com. In a grassy lot by the beach, south of *Somewhere Else*, this place offers a fair amount of shade and cheapish en-suite bamboo bungalows with fans and mosquito nets, plus more robust concrete alternatives with either fans or a/c, TVs, fridges and hot water; most have hammocks, all have small bathrooms. Fan **B500**, a/c **B1000**

★**Lanta Marina Resort** ☎075 684168, 🌐lantamarina.com. At the far southern end of Ao Phra-Ae by a rocky point, this friendly place has 23 shaggily thatched wood-and-split-bamboo bungalows, connected by wooden walkways, that circle a very pretty lawn and flower garden. All the huts have nice beds, well-designed bathrooms, high palm-leaf roofs, fans and wi-fi access (payable, though there's also a free computer for guests), and the larger, more expensive ones on the beach have hot showers. **B700**

Lanta Palm Beach ☎075 684406, 🌐lantapalm beachresort.com. A busy, central and popular spot within stumbling distance of several beach bars. The concrete bungalows and large, bright cottages sit back from the shore a little, within a garden of neat clipped hedges, and come with a/c and hot water. Has internet access and a dive centre. Breakfast included. **B2500**

★**Layana** ☎075 607100, 🌐layanaresort.com. Located plumb in the middle of the beautiful beach, this is currently the top spot on Ao Phra-Ae and one of the best and most liked on the whole island, not least for its calm ambience (the hotel has a no-under-18s policy) and attentive service. Its 44 a/c rooms occupy chunky, two-storey villas designed in modern-Thai style and set around a tidy beachfront garden of lawns and mature shrubs. There's a gorgeous shorefront salt-water infinity pool, a spa and plenty of activities and day-trips, plus wi-fi throughout. Breakfast included. **B11,300**

Relax Bay Resort ☎075 684194, 🌐relaxbay.com. On a tiny bay south around the next rocky point (and quite a hike) from *Lanta Marina*, the style of this French-managed place is affordable rustic chic. Accommodation is in forty tastefully simple thatched bungalows, all with large sea-view decks. Also has a luxury safari-style tent on a large deck with a chic outdoor bathroom. There's a pool, a dive centre and yoga classes during high season (see p.690). Breakfast included. Fan **B1400**, a/c **B2300**

Sayang Beach Resort ☎075 684156, 🌐sayangbeach resort.com. Welcoming, family-run place whose thirty a/c bungalows are nicely spaced beneath the palm trees in the expansive shorefront grounds. Some bungalows are designed for families and there's also a beachfront suite. Prices include buffet breakfasts and there's a very good restaurant here too. Daily free transfers to Sala Dan. **B2550**

white walls and wooden-tiled roofs, as well as a/c, hot water, mini-bars and DVD players. **B2600**

Southern Lanta Resort ☎075 684175–7, 🌐southern lanta.com. One of the biggest hotels on the beach, offering dozens of very spacious a/c bungalows set at decent intervals around a garden of shrubs, clipped hedges and shady trees. There's a good-sized swimming pool too and wi-fi throughout. Popular with families and package

Somewhere Else ☎ 081 536 0858. Located in the heart of the liveliest part of Ao Phra-Ae, with bars to the left, right and seaward, this cheap, congenial place on a beachside lawn is one of the main travellers' centres on the beach. Its spacious, unusually designed hexagonal bungalows made of tightly woven bamboo come with pretty bathrooms, some with hot showers. The drawback is that most are close together and lack a sense of privacy, though many have sea views. There's free wi-fi in the restaurant. B300

HAT KHLONG KHONG

★ **Bee Bee Bungalow** ☎ 081 537 9932, @ beebee piya02@hotmail.com. A special, friendly place that stands out for its fourteen highly individual huts, each one a charmingly idiosyncratic experiment in bamboo architecture. All are simple but comfortably furnished, given style with batik fabric flourishes, and have fans, mosquito nets and partially open-air bathrooms; some have an upstairs room as well. There's a good bar-restaurant, too, with similarly experimental but lovely wood and thatch *salas*. B550

★ **Fisherman's Cottage** ☎ 081 476 1529, @ fishermanscottage.biz. This quiet, low-key chummy place at the southern end of the beach has just nine thatched-roof and concrete bungalows, each with big windows, quite spartan one-off beach-modern interiors – whitewashed concrete, nutty mural artworks, splashes of strong colour – mosquito nets, fans and good bathrooms. Free wi-fi throughout. Closed July–Oct. B1500

Lanta Riviera ☎ 075 667043, @ lantariviera.net. There are rows and rows of good, standard-issue, comfortably furnished fan and a/c concrete bungalows here, plus a few rooms in a two-storey building, set among shady beds of shrubs and flowers at the far northern end of the beach. Many of the rooms sleep three so it's popular with families. Also has a pool and jacuzzi near the shore. Fan B800, a/c B1300

Where Else? ☎ 081 536 4870, @ lanta-where-else .com. This charming collection of 22 bungalows has a laidback vibe and lots of personality, though it's more of a party place than *Bee Bee*. The artfully and individually designed bamboo and coconut-wood bungalows all have fans, mosquito nets, hammocks and open-air bathrooms filled with plants, and there are shell mobiles, driftwood sculptures and pot plants all over the place. The pricier bungalows are larger and nearer the sea, and some even have bamboo sunroofs and turrets. B500

HAT KHLONG NIN

Lanta Nature Beach Resort ☎ 075 662560, @ lanta naturebeachresort.com. In the cluster of concrete bungalow operations right on the beach at the southern end of Khlong Nin, this one has rows of cream-and-lilac painted fan and a/c concrete huts, with spacious tiled

interiors. There are even bigger, cheaper bungalows in a garden inland, across the road. Fan B800, a/c B1000

Lanta Paradise ☎ 075 662569, @ lantaparadise beachresort.com. Though the shorefront concrete bungalows at this friendly spot are packed uncomfortably close together, they feel spacious inside and are well maintained; they lack style and are plain, but are all a/c with hot showers, and there's a pool here too. Breakfast included. B1600

Otto Bungalow ☎ 084 051 7180, @ otto_lanta @hotmail.com. Tightly packed compound right by the road, containing four shorefront A-frame cabins, with thatched roofs, concrete walls, mosquito nets and fans, as well as a variety of a/c rooms, including one in a small converted bus. Fan B800, a/c B1500

HAT KHLONG NAM JUD

Lanta Coral Beach ☎ 075 662535, @ lantacoralresort .com. Friendly resort with a lovely, lofty restaurant – especially nice at sunset – up on the rocky point, with wi-fi. The twenty, good-sized, plain but very clean and en-suite bamboo and concrete huts here are scattered over a lawn among the palms (some of which are hung with hammocks); the concrete options, whether fan or a/c, boast hot showers. Fan B300, a/c B800

The Narima ☎ 075 662668, @ narima-lanta.com. Very quiet but welcoming, elegantly designed, environmentally conscious resort of 32 posh but unadorned thatch-roofed bamboo bungalows set in three rows in a palm-filled garden. The bungalows all have polished wood floors, verandas with sea view, hot showers and fans as well as a/c (but no TV); there's also a three-tiered pool (with kids' level) and a dive centre, and staff rent out jeeps, motorbikes and mountain bikes. Breakfast included. B2300

AO KANTIANG

Lanta Marine Park View ☎ 075 665063, @ lanta marine.com. The thirty bungalows here are ranged up the slope at the northern end of the beach, with steps leading down to the shore. The best of them, though pricey, are great value as they're on stilts and enjoy glorious bay views from their balconies and glass-fronted interiors, and the furnishings are chic and modern. The plain, cheap fan-cooled wood and bamboo bungalows sit further back. There's also a small cliffside bar affording great views, plus wi-fi in the public areas and a tour agency. Fan B600, a/c B1100

Pimalai Resort and Spa ☎ 075 607999, @ www .pimalai.com. At the southern end of Ao Kantiang is one of Ko Lanta's poshest hotels, which spreads over such an extensive area that guests are shuttled around in golf buggies. All rooms are luxuriously and elegantly designed in contemporary style, and there's a delightful spa, two infinity-edge swimming pools, a dive centre and lots of other watersports, tennis courts and free bicycles. However,

7

only the more expensive accommodation gets a sea view (the pool villas and walled beach villas are particularly stunning). In high season, guests are usually transferred direct to the resort by boat, landing at the *Pimalai*'s private floating jetty. B11,900

AO KHLONG JAAK

Anda Lanta Resort ☎ 075 665018, ⓦ andalanta.com. Lively, buzzing resort that offers well-furnished, well-maintained a/c bungalows and rooms (all with hot showers, balconies, DVD players and free wi-fi), set around the shorefront garden and swimming pool. It's popular with families and has free kayaks and plenty of day-tripping options. B3200

AO MAI PHAI

Baan Phu Lae ☎ 081 201 1704, ⓦ baanphulae.com. Occupying the centre of the bay, this tastefully camp place manages to combine a whiff of Bangkok sophistication with laidback island charm. Its fan-cooled bamboo bungalows are stylishly simple and nearly all enjoy direct sea views; the a/c rooms high above the shore are less interesting. Massage, cooking classes and motorbike rental available. Fan B1180, a/c B1480

Bamboo Bay Resort ☎ 075 665023, ⓦ bamboobay .net. At the northern end of the bay, this welcoming and

very popular Thai–Danish resort offers 21 concrete bungalows with hot showers, stepped up the cliffside above the headland. Nearly all have great sea views and interiors are spacious and of a high standard. Its *pièce de résistance* is its idyllically sited deck restaurant and bar, which jut out over the rocks just above the water. Fan B1000, a/c B2100

La Laanta Hideaway Resort ☎ 075 665066, ⓦ lalaanta.com. Luxurious bolthole at the far southern end, which is very well liked for its attentive staff and chic, thatched, wooden-floored villas – all with a/c, hot showers, DVD players, low beds and free wi-fi – built to a cosy, village-style layout, around two pools and a beachfront garden. Breakfast included. B2800

LANTA OLD TOWN (BAN SI RAYA)

★ **Mango House** ☎ 086 948 6836, ⓦ mangohouses .com. The rooms and villas built on stilts over the water here make an attractive and unusual Ko Lanta base. Several century-old wooden buildings, one of them a former charcoal store, have been charmingly converted into accommodation that can sleep between two and six people; interiors are furnished in fishing-village chic, with elegant contemporary bathrooms, DVD players, free wi-fi and kitchenette. The big draw though is the large waterside decks, which afford fine views of seven islands. B2000

EATING AND DRINKING

BAN SALA DAN

Many charming old wooden houses built on piles over the water have been turned into attractive jetty restaurants, perfect for whiling away a breezy hour with views of marine activity.

Catfish Named for its cats rather than its fish, and a good place to come for a change from seafood, with a chance to shop for secondhand books. As well as standard Thai food (fried rice B70), there's a wide choice of Western dishes, including falafels (B180), spaghetti, sandwiches, breakfasts, ice cream and espressos. Daily 8.30am–9pm.

Laanta Seafood The oldest restaurant in town and the most highly rated – its seafood, displayed on ice at the front, is great, including *haw mok thalay* (curried seafood soufflé; B120) and local dishes such as *nam prik kung siab*, smoked prawn dip with vegetables. Daily 10am–9.30pm.

HAT KHLONG DAO

Restaurant tables fill the shoreline in the evening, illuminated with fairy lights and lanterns, which lends a nice mellow atmosphere. The formula is very similar at most of them, with fresh seafood barbecues the main attraction during the season. Clusters of little beach bars serve cocktails on deckchairs and cushions, often with chill-out music and a campfire to gather round.

Costa Lanta ☎ 075 684630 (see p.695). The most sophisticated venue on the beach is a great place for a sundowner, with sea-view daybeds, plump bolsters, cool sounds and lemon-grass martinis. The food, however, doesn't match up to its hefty price tag. Daily 11am–midnight.

Indian Bar Three doors south of Cha-Ba Bungalows. One of the most genial bars on the beach, where the host, dressed as a Hollywood-style American Indian, makes a mean cocktail and does good fire-juggling shows. Claims to open 24hr.

Slow Down ☎ 075 684982 (see p.695). Serves up excellent spaghetti bolognese (B160), Swedish specialities such as cold shrimp plate, and Thai food, with set menus available. It's a good place to keep the family happy, with its special kids' menu, cushion seating in a converted longtail boat and, most importantly, its volleyball net within sight of adult dining areas. Daily 8am–10pm.

AO PHRA-AE (LONG BEACH)

Most of Ao Phra-Ae's most interesting restaurants are along the main road, while down on the beach you get small, mellow bars.

★ **Faim de Loup** On the main road towards the south end of the bay. Very good French bakery, where the croissants, pains au chocolat, fruit tarts and excellent espressos just hit the spot. Also does sandwiches, quiches, potato and sausage salad (B75) and a few *plats du jour* such as aubergine gratin and salad (B250); free wi-fi, too. Daily 7.30am–5pm, sometimes closed on Sun.

Irish Embassy On the main road near the centre of the bay. Very friendly little Irish bar, serving back-home food such as fish and chips and offering quiz nights, TV sports and occasional live music. Daily 4pm–1am.

Klapa Klum Near Lanta Palm bungalows. There are bamboo love-booths and private seating areas at this beachfront bar, plus happy hours (5–8pm), cheap cocktails all night long and weekly on-the-beach parties with international DJs (currently Wed). Daily 5pm–late.

Ozone Bar On the beach, near Somewhere Else bungalows. One of the most famous bars on the beach, especially for its weekly DJ parties (currently Thurs), which usually draw a lively crowd. Daily roughly 11am–late.

Red Snapper On the main road, inland from Lanta Marina bungalows at the southern end of Phra-Ae. Tapas and creative European cuisine using imported meats, such as pork loin with apple chutney and gorgonzola (B290), are the hallmarks of this highly rated, Dutch-run, garden restaurant. Sometimes serves daytime sandwiches, too. Daily 5–11pm.

Sayang Beach Resort On the beach, at Sayang Beach Resort. This is a lovely spot for dinner, with tables set out under shoreside casuarinas strung with fairy lights. The kitchen here has a tandoori oven and serves a long menu of authentic Indian dishes, including dhal (B90) and chicken tikka masala (B200), as well as Thai and Western food, plus fresh seafood nightly and a big veggie menu. Daily roughly 10am–10pm.

HAT KHLONG KHONG

Sonya's On the main road, just north of 7-Eleven. Very popular, cheap, garden restaurant with free wi-fi (and pay computers), where you can "build your own" pasta from a wide choice of pastas, sauces, meats and extras. Also has a

big selection of Thai food (from B60), Western breakfasts and teas, as well as sandwiches and espresso coffees. Daily 8.30am–9.30pm.

HAT KHLONG NIN

A dozen or so mellow little beachfront bar-restaurants make inviting places to while away a few hours, day or night, with mats and cushions on the sand, tables under the shade of the spiky shoreside pandanus trees, and appropriately chilled sounds.

Cook Kai Diagonally north across the road from Nice Beach ⓦ cook-kai.com. Friendly restaurant hung with shell mobiles and lamps, dishing up hearty portions of all the Thai classics, plus famous hotplate dishes such as sizzling squid with garlic and pepper (B190) and a few Western dishes including breakfast. Daily 7.30am–10.30pm.

Jai-Dee North end of the beach, squeezed between the road and the beach. Bar-restaurant with a lovely shady deck and hammocks, internet access and free wi-fi, and a good menu of Thai curries and sandwiches (bacon B80), fresh coffee and breakfasts. Daily 9am–late, kitchen closes 9pm.

AO KANTIANG

Same Same But Different On the beach to the south of Pimalai. Tranquil haven of a bar-restaurant, where the tables and thatched *salas* are set beneath a tangled growth of shrubs and vines, surrounded by shell-mobiles and driftwood sculptures; it's run by the man behind the renowned *Ruen Mai* restaurant in Krabi (see p.664), and the mid-priced menu of mainly Thai and seafood dishes is of a similarly high standard. Daily 8am–11pm.

LANTA OLD TOWN (BAN SI RAYA)

Mango House Sophisticated little bar-café all done out in stylish dark wood, which does burgers, salads and sandwiches, as well as wine and freshly roasted coffee. High season daily 8am–8pm.

DIRECTORY

Banks and ATMs Several banks and ATMs in Ban Sala Dan, and there are ATMs beside the road at most of the beaches and in Lanta Old Town.

Hospitals Nearly every beach has a clinic, there's a larger health centre in Ban Sala Dan, and the rather basic island hospital is in Lanta Old Town (☎ 075 697017), though for anything serious you'll need to go to Phuket.

Post offices At the south end of Ban Sala Dan and in Lanta

Old Town.

Tourist police On the main road in Ao Phra-Ae (Long Beach; ☎ 1155).

Travel agent A helpful, clued-up travel agent is Otto Lanta Tour at *Otto Bungalows* on Hat Khlong Nin (☎ 083 634 8882, ⓔ ottolantatour@gmail.com), who sell plane, train and bus tickets, as well as booking tours (see p.691) and accommodation.

7

The deep south

KO LIPE

The deep south

The frontier between Thailand and Malaysia carves across the peninsula six degrees north of the equator, but the cultures of the two countries shade into each other much further north. According to official divisions, the southern Thais – the Thai Pak Tai – begin around Chumphon, and as you move further down the peninsula into Thailand's deep south you'll see ever more sarongs, yashmaks and towering mosques, and hear with increasing frequency a staccato dialect that baffles many Thais. Here too, you'll come across caged singing doves outside many houses, as well as strange-looking areas spiked with tall metal poles, on which the cages are hung during regular cooing competitions; and you'll spot huge, hump-backed Brahma bulls on the back of pick-up trucks, on their way to bullfights (in the Thai version, beast is pitted against beast, and the first to back off is the loser).

In Trang and Phatthalung provinces, the Muslim population is generally accepted as being Thai, but the inhabitants of the southernmost provinces – Satun, Pattani, Yala, Narathiwat and most of Songkhla – are ethnically more akin to the Malays: most of the 1.5 million followers of Islam here speak a dialect of Malay and write Yawi, an old modification of Arabic script to reflect Malay pronunciation. To add to the ethnic confusion, the region has a large urban population of Chinese, whose comparative wealth makes them stand out sharply from the Muslim farmers and fishermen.

The touristic interest in the deep south is currently all over on the beautiful **west coast**, where sheer limestone outcrops, pristine sands and fish-laden coral stretch down to the Malaysian border. Along Trang's **mainland coast**, there's a 30km stretch of attractive beaches, dotted with mangroves and impressive caves that can be explored by sea canoe, but the real draw down here is the offshore **islands**, which offer gorgeous panoramas and beaches, great snorkelling and at least a modicum of comfort in their small clusters of resorts. An added attraction is the recently introduced, scheduled boat services which have set up the intriguing possibility of **island-hopping**: it would now be possible to work your way down from Phuket as far as Penang without setting foot on the peninsula. The spread of tourism outwards from Phuket has been inching its way south down this coast for some time, but for now, apart from the tiny, remote but overcrowded honeypot of Ko Lipe, the islands remain largely undeveloped.

ARRIVAL AND GETTING AROUND   THE DEEP SOUTH

As well as the usual bus services, the area covered in this chapter is served by **flights** and **trains** to Trang (see p.706), as well as by **boats** between the islands (see p.710) and from the mainland to the islands.

HEADING FOR THE EMERALD CAVE, KO MOOK

Highlights

❶ Nature Resorts Not-for-profit resorts at Ban Chao Mai, on Ko Mook and Ko Libong, with great tours through the mangroves to Tham Chao Mai cave and to see the dugongs and birds on Libong. **See p.709, p.713 & p.715**

❷ Ko Hai A variety of good resorts for all budgets and gorgeous views. **See p.710**

❸ Tham Morakhot Ko Mook's Emerald Cave, with its inland beach of powdery sand at the base of an awesome natural chimney, is best visited by kayak. **See p.713**

❹ Ko Kradan Remote island with a long, white, east-facing strand, crystal-clear waters and a reef for snorkellers to explore. **See p.714**

❺ Ko Sukorn For a glimpse of how islanders live and an outstanding beach resort. **See p.715**

❻ Ko Tarutao Huge national park island with mangroves and jungle tracks to explore, and the most unspoilt beaches in the area. **See p.718**

HIGHLIGHTS ARE MARKED ON THE MAP ON P.704

By share-taxi The deep south has traditionally been the territory of share-taxis, which connect certain towns for about twice the fare of ordinary buses. The cars leave when they're full, which usually means six passengers, and sometimes a long wait, though there's always the option of buying up extra seats or chartering the whole car if you're in a hurry. They are a quick way of getting around and you should get dropped off at the door of your journey's end.

By minibus Inexorably, share taxis are being replaced by a/c minibuses, which run on almost exactly the same principles at similar prices; on these you'll be more comfortable, with a seat to yourself, and most of the various ranks publish a rough timetable – though the minibuses also tend to leave as soon as they're full.

Brief history

The central area of the Malay peninsula first entered Thai history when it came under the sway of Sukhothai, probably around the beginning of the fourteenth century. Islam was introduced to the area by the end of that century, by which time Ayutthaya was taking a firmer grip on the peninsula. **Songkhla** and **Pattani** then rose to be the major cities, prospering on the goods passed through the two ports across the peninsula to avoid the pirates in the Straits of Malacca between Malaysia and Sumatra. More closely tied to the Muslim Malay states to the south, the Sultanate of Pattani began to **rebel** against the power of Ayutthaya in the sixteenth century, but the fight for self-determination only weakened Pattani's strength. The town's last rebellious fling was in 1902, after which it was definitively and brutally absorbed into the Thai kingdom, while its allies, Kedah, Kelantan and Trengganu, were transferred into the suzerainty of the British in Malaysia.

HIGHLIGHTS
1. Nature Resorts
2. Ko Hai
3. Tham Morakhot
4. Ko Kradan
5. Ko Sukorn
6. Ko Tarutao

THE DEEP SOUTH

TRAVEL WARNING

Because of the ongoing **violence** in the deep south (see below), all major Western governments are currently advising people **not to travel** to or through Pattani, Yala and Narathiwat provinces unless essential, and nearly all are advising against travel to Songkhla province too; following on from this, insurance companies are refusing to cover travel in the affected areas. The four provinces encompass the city and transport hub of **Hat Yai** and several of the main border crossings to Malaysia: by rail from Hat Yai (and Bangkok) to Butterworth via Padang Besar and to Sungai Kolok; and by road from Hat Yai via Sadao, from Yala via Betong, and down the east coast to Kota Bharu.

The routes to Sungai Kolok, Betong and Kota Bharu pass through particularly volatile territory, with **martial law** declared in Pattani, Yala and Narathiwat provinces; however, martial law is only in effect in certain districts of Songkhla province, and not in Hat Yai itself.

The provinces of **Trang** and **Satun** are not affected, and it's still perfectly possible to continue overland to Malaysia via Satun: by a/c minibus from nearby Ban Khuan to Kangar, or by ferry from Thammalang to Kuala Perlis or the Malaysian island of Langkawi (see p.724); or by boat from Ko Lipe to Langkawi (see p.721). For up-to-the-minute advice, consult your government travel advisory (see p.62).

During World War II the **Communist Party of Malaya** made its home in the jungle around the Thai border to fight the occupying Japanese. After the war they turned their guns against the British colonialists, but having been excluded from power after independence, descended into general banditry and racketeering around Betong. The Thai authorities eventually succeeded in breaking up the bandit gangs in 1989 through a combination of pardons and bribes, but the stability of the region soon faced disruption from another source, a rise in Islamic militancy.

The troubles: 2004 to the present

Armed resistance to the Thai state by **Muslim separatists** had fluctuated at a relatively low level since the 1960s, but in early 2004 the violence escalated dramatically. Since then, there have been thousands of deaths on both sides in the troubles, and barely a day goes by without a fatal incident of one kind or another. The insurgents have viciously targeted Buddhist monks, police, soldiers, teachers and other civil servants, as well as attacking a train on the Hat Yai–Sungai Kolok line and setting off bombs in marketplaces, near tourist hotels and bars and at Hat Yai airport. Increasingly, they have attacked other Muslims who are seen to be too sympathetic to the Thai state.

Often writing the militants off as bandits, the authorities have stirred up hatred – and undermined moderate Muslim voices – by reacting violently, notably in crushing protests at Tak Bai and the much-revered Krue Se Mosque in Pattani in 2004, in which a total of over two hundred alleged insurgents died. Meanwhile, the army has "subcontracted" much of its work to rangers, untrained village militias, thus inflaming the situation further and deepening the ethnic divide. In 2005, the government announced a **serious state of emergency** in Pattani, Yala and Narathiwat provinces, and imposed **martial law** here and in southern parts of Songkhla province. This, however, has exacerbated economic and unemployment problems in what is Thailand's poorest region.

A large part of the problem is that a wide variety of shadowy groups – with names like the Pattani Islamic Mujahideen, the Barisan Revolusi Nasional-Coordinate and Runda Kumpulan Kecil – are operating against the government, generally working in small cells at village level without central control. Rather than religious issues, the most likely causes of their militancy are ethnic grievances: prejudice, lack of opportunity and disempowerment, accompanied by resentment towards not only Thais but also the remote and corrupt Muslim elite. However, it's unclear exactly who they are or what they want and, faced with such shifting sands, all attempts to broker a ceasefire have failed.

Trang town

TRANG (also known as Taptieng) is gradually developing as a popular jumping-off point for travellers drawn south from the crowded sands of Krabi to the pristine beaches and islands of the nearby coast. The town, which prospers on rubber, oil palms, fisheries and – increasingly – tourism, is a sociable place whose wide, clean streets are dotted with crumbling, wooden-shuttered houses. In the evening, the streets are festooned with colourful lights, and during the day, many of the town's Chinese inhabitants hang out in the cafés, drinking the local filtered coffee. Trang's Chinese population makes the **Vegetarian Festival** in October or November almost as frenetic as Phuket's (see box, p.629) – and for veggie travellers it's an opportunity to feast at the stalls set up around the temples.

ARRIVAL AND DEPARTURE

By plane Air Asia and Nok Air run daily flights between Bangkok and Trang airport (1hr 30min), which is connected to Trang town, 3km to the north, by a/c minibuses (B100), operated by, for example, BB Tour, 23 Thanon Sathanee (☎075 219054).

By train Two overnight trains from Bangkok (15–16hr) run down a branch of the southern line to Trang.

By bus Buses arrive at and depart from the new terminal on Thanon Phattalung (Highway 4), opposite Robinson department store, about 3km northeast of the centre, including an a/c service between Satun and Phuket four times daily; Satun buses also make a stop on Thanon Rama VI, just east of the central clocktower.

Destinations Bangkok (11 daily; 12–14hr); Krabi (roughly every 30min; 2hr); Phuket (hourly; 5hr); Satun (every 30min; 2hr 30min–3hr).

By minibus A/c minibuses to Surat Thani, Nakhon Si Thammarat and Hat Yai use the new bus terminal on Thanon Phattalung, while the services to Pak Meng and Ban Chao Mai have an office on Thanon Tha Klang northwest of the train station. Among a/c minibuses aimed specifically at tourists, Andaman Tour travel agency, opposite the station (☎075 216110), runs a service to Pak Bara at least once daily (2hr; B150), and Kanokwan Tour, just east of the *Sri Trang Hotel* (☎075 215235), goes to Ko Lanta (6 daily; 3hr; B250, including drop-off anywhere as far south as Hat Khlong

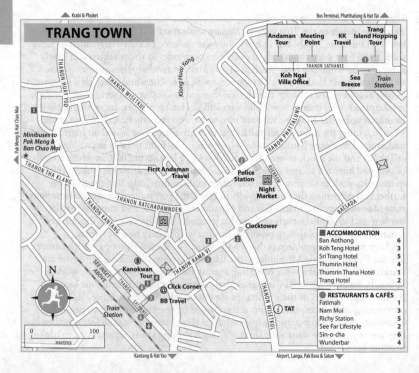

TRANG TOWN

Krabi & Phuket

Bus Terminal, Phatthalung & Hat Yai

THANON HUAY YOD

THANON WISE KUL

Klong Huai Yang

Andaman Tour · Meeting Point · KK Travel · Trang Island Hopping Tour

THANON SATHANEE

Koh Ngai Villa Office · Sea Breeze · Train Station

Pak Meng & Hat Chao Mai

Minibuses to Pak Meng & Ban Chao Mai

THANON THA KLANG

THANON PHATTALUNG

First Andaman Travel

Police Station

Night Market

ROBINSON

THANON RATCHADAMNOEN

THANON KANTANG

Clocktower

RATSADA

N

SEE INSET ABOVE

Kanokwan Tour

THANON RAMA VI

Click Corner

BB Travel

THANON SATHANEE

THANON WISE KUL

TAT

Train Station

0 — 100 metres

Kantang & Hat Yao

Airport, Langu, Pak Bara & Satun

■ ACCOMMODATION	
Ban Aothong	6
Koh Teng Hotel	3
Sri Trang Hotel	5
Thumrin Hotel	4
Thumrin Thana Hotel	1
Trang Hotel	2

■ RESTAURANTS & CAFÉS	
Fatimah	1
Nam Mui	3
Richy Station	5
See Far Lifestyle	2
Sin-o-cha	6
Wunderbar	4

Khong). There are also faster minibus and speedboat transfers to Ko Lanta (see p.694) through KK Travel, opposite the train station (☎075 211198, ⊛kktravelandtour.com).

By share taxi Share taxis for Pak Bara and Satun

congregate on Thanon Ratsada, out on the southeast side of town, for Krabi on Thanon Huay Yod, opposite the old bus station on the north side of town (about 500m north of the junction with Thanon Wisetkul).

GETTING AROUND

By car or motorbike Trang Island Hopping Tour (see below) does car rental (B1200–1500/day), while

motorbikes can be rented at *Koh Teng Hotel* (see below), on Thanon Rama VI (B250/day).

INFORMATION AND TOURS

Tourist information TAT have a helpful office on Thanon Wisetkul (daily 8.30am–4.30pm, sometimes closed for lunch on Sat & Sun; ☎075 215867, ⊜tattrang@tat.or.th).

Travel agents The best travel agent in town is Trang Island Hopping Tour, directly opposite the station at 28/2 Thanon Sathanee (☎075 211457 or ☎082 804 0583, ⊛trang-island-hopping.com). This well-organized outfit offers a huge range of services, including mainland and island transfers and tickets, and accommodation booking

on any island. The friendly staff are a great source of impartial information on the area, and their office makes a good first stop in town. They also offer one-day boat trips around the islands and day-trips and camping trips to Ko Rok, and inland excursions to waterfalls and caves, as well as trekking and kayaking. *Wunderbar*, just around the corner (☎075 214563, ⊛wunderbar-trang.com), also acts as a very helpful and clued-up travel agent, especially for island bookings.

ACCOMMODATION

Ban Aothong 25/28–31 Thanon Sathanee ☎075 225611, ⊜banaothong@yahoo.com. An overblown pink facade announces this upmarket guesthouse that's popular with Thai businesspeople, with its chunky wooden furniture, half-tester beds and rather kitsch decor. Double rooms are compact, while the slightly pricier twins have more space, though the bathrooms are still small; all have a/c, hot showers, fridges, free wi-fi and DVD players. **B790**

Koh Teng Hotel 77–79 Thanon Rama VI ☎075 218622 or ☎075 218148. This characterful 1940s Chinese hotel is a little battered and dusty but offers large, mostly clean en-suite rooms, some with cable TV and a/c, above a popular restaurant and coffee shop that serves southern Thai and Chinese food and Western breakfasts. Fan **B180**, a/c **B280**

Sri Trang Hotel 22 Thanon Sathanee ☎075 218122, ⊛sritranghotel.com. Welcoming, recently updated hotel offering spacious rooms with some colourful decorative

touches, free wi-fi, hot water, cable TV and fridges. Has a few fan-cooled single rooms (B450–500) but otherwise a/c throughout. Internet access. **B650**

Thumrin Hotel Thanon Rama VI ☎075 211011–4, ⊛thumrin.com. Good-value hotel offering international-standard facilities – a/c, hot water, TV, wi-fi and internet access – at cheap prices, in a high-rise block above its popular bakery-cum-coffee shop. **B850**

Thumrin Thana Hotel 69/8 Thanon Huay Yod ☎075 211211, ⊛thumrin.com. The best hotel in town, though not in the same league as the *Anantara* on the coast (see p.709). Spacious, well-equipped rooms, a pool and fitness centre, wi-fi and internet access. **B1400**

Trang Hotel 134/2–5 Thanon Wisetkul ☎075 218944, ⊜075 218451. Good, welcoming, moderately priced choice, with large, comfortable twin rooms with a/c, hot water, fridge and TV. **B590**

EATING AND DRINKING

Trang's streets are dotted with dozens of traditional cafés, which serve up gallons of **kopii** (local filtered coffee) accompanied by various tidbits and light meals. Most famous of these is the local speciality, **muu yaang**, delicious charcoal-grilled pork, which is generally eaten for breakfast. At the excellent **night market**, around the back of the city hall on Thanon Ruenrom, you can try another tasty southern dish, *khanom jiin*, soft noodles topped with hot, sweet or fishy sauces and eaten with crispy greens.

Fatimah Thanon Sathanee. Simple halal restaurant that's especially popular in the evenings. Buffet of southern curries, tasty *phat thai* (B35), *kopii* and tea. Tues–Sun roughly 8.30am–10pm.

Nam Mui Thanon Rama VI (no English sign but it's directly opposite the Koh Teng Hotel). With a pleasant patio at the back, this Thai–Chinese restaurant is popular with locals for its seafood and for very tasty, generously

portioned dishes such as deep-fried chicken with cashew nuts (B150). The English-language menu is a lot shorter than the Thai version, so it may be time to practise your Thai. Daily 11.30am–9pm.

Richy Station Thanon Sathanee ☎075 218431. Genteel bakery-café serving croissants, cakes, ice cream, lots of juices and espresso coffees, as well as tasty grilled ham and cheese sandwiches (B80), spaghetti and

8

breakfasts, and an extensive menu of Thai and Chinese dishes. Daily 7am–8pm (Wed drinks and baked goods only).

See Far Lifestyle 37 Thanon Phattalung (no English sign, but it's right by the entrance to Soi 3) ☎ 075 210139. Good, inexpensive restaurant with a varied menu of carefully prepared dishes, specializing in healthy cuisine and local food, such as *tom som plakapong*, a light, refreshing soup of sea bass, mushrooms and cumin, and *kao yok* (B120), a Chinese-style dish of steamed pork with taro found only in Trang. Daily 10.30am–8pm.

Sin-o-cha Next to the station at 25/25–26 Thanon Sathanee. Very popular, updated traditional café: *kopii* with Thai and Western cakes and main courses (fried rice B45), or espresso, various teas and Western breakfasts. Daily 7am–5pm.

Wunderbar Thanon Sathanee ☎ 075 214563, ⍵ wunderbar-trang.com. Multipurpose farang bar-restaurant with free wi-fi that serves a wide selection of drinks (including wine and espressos), Thai food, and burgers (B60), salads, pizzas, breakfasts and other Western standards, as well as cheese platters (B290). Daily 7.30am–10pm.

DIRECTORY

Internet access Available at *Wunderbar* and at Click Corner, opposite, both on Thanon Sathanee.

The Trang coast

From Pak Meng, 40km due west of Trang town, down to the mouth of the Trang River runs a 30km-long stretch of lovely beaches, broken only by dramatic limestone outcrops. A paved road roughly parallels this stretch of coast, but otherwise there's surprisingly little development, as the shoreline is technically part of Hat Chao Mai National Park.

Pak Meng and Hat Chang Lang

Although it has a fine outlook to the headlands and islands to the west (with regular boats to the biggest, Ko Hai), the beach at **PAK MENG** is not the most attractive on the coast, becoming a rather muddy strip of sand at low tide. At other times, however, it offers quiet, calm swimming, and there's always the possibility of a meal at one of the many tree-shaded foodstalls and restaurants that line the back of the beach.

Immediately south of Pak Meng's beach is the white sand of **Hat Chang Lang**, famous for its oysters, which shelters at its north end the finest luxury hotel in the province, *Anantara Si Kao*.

Hat Chao Mai National Park HQ

The turning for the headquarters is 3km on from Hat Chang Lang • B200 • ☎ 075 213260, ⍵ dnp.go.th

Hat Chao Mai National Park covers 230 square kilometres, including parts of Ko Mook and Ko Kradan, but the park admission fee is only rigidly enforced if you visit its headquarters. From the HQ a short trail leads to the south end of the beach and a viewpoint partway up a karst pinnacle, from which you can see Ko Mook and occasionally dugongs in the bay below. At headquarters there's a simple café as well as accommodation.

Hat Yong Ling and Hat Yao

About 5km south of the national park HQ, beyond Kuantunku, the pier for Ko Mook, is **Hat Yong Ling**. This quiet and attractive convex beach, which shelters a national park ranger station, is probably the nicest along this stretch of coast, with a large cave which you can swim into at high tide or walk into at low tide. Immediately beyond comes **Hat Yao**, which runs in a broad 5km white-sand strip, backed by casuarina trees and some simple restaurants.

Ban Chao Mai

At the south end of Hat Yao is **BAN CHAO MAI** (also called **Ban Hat Yao**), a straggle of houses on stilts, which exists on fishing, especially for crabs. From the harbour, boats run regularly across to Ko Libong, and this is the mainland ferry stop on Tigerline's Lanta–Lipe route. The owners of *Had Yao Nature Resort* by the harbour organize guided and fully insured trips by longtail and canoe through the mangroves to the nearby cave of **Tham Chao Mai** (B800/person in a group of four or more, including lunch; ten percent discount for guests at the resort); inside are impressively huge rock pillars and a natural theatre, its stage framed by rock curtains. The resort also rents out two-person kayaks (B200 for the first hour, B100/hr thereafter) if you want to do the trip by yourself, with a map and head-torch (B100 rental), as well as offering tours to the local islands, including highly recommended dugong-watching trips to Ko Libong (see p.715).

ARRIVAL AND GETTING AROUND   THE TRANG COAST

Air-conditioned **minibuses**, departing only when full, run from Thanon Tha Klang in Trang to Pak Meng (45min; B60), as well as via Hat Yao to Ban Chao Mai (1hr; B70), but if you want to explore the whole coastline, you'll need to rent a **motorbike** or **car** in Trang (see p.707).

ACCOMMODATION AND EATING

PAK MENG

Lay Trang Resort ☎ 075 274027–8, ⍟ laytrang.com. The nicest place to stay and eat at Pak Meng, a stone's throw from the pier at the far north end of the beach. Ranged around a large, peaceful garden with lawns and orchids set back from the beach, its bright concrete chalets with huge bathrooms and smart brick rooms come with verandas, hot showers, a/c and TV. Its welcoming, reasonably priced restaurant is renowned for its seafood, including *nam prik kung siap* (dried shrimp relish) and *kaeng som* soup with sea bass. **B1200**

HAT CHANG LANG

★ **Anantara Si Kao** ☎ 075 205888, ⍟ anantara.com. The finest luxury hotel in the province, where the low-rise blocks of stylish bedrooms and pool suites, all with large balconies, are set behind a line of casuarina trees. Facilities encompass a beautiful, large pool, Italian and international restaurants, a fitness centre and a spa. Watersports on offer include diving and sailing, and there's plenty of other activities, notably cooking and Thai-language lessons and some interesting local tours. The hotel also has its own beach club and restaurant on the main strand on Ko Kradan

(see p.714), reached by daily boat transfer. Breakfast included. **B6000**

HAT CHAO MAI NATIONAL PARK HQ

National park bungalows ⍟ dnp.go.th. Fan-cooled, en-suite bungalows and rooms for two to six people, set under the casuarinas at the back of the sandy beach, and a simple café. **B800**

BAN CHAO MAI

★ **Had Yao Nature Resort** ☎ 087 885 7815 or ☎ 081 894 6936, ⍟ natureresortsgroup.com. Eco-friendly, non-profit resort, where your custom will go towards helping local people and the environment (see p.59); the same people own *Libong Nature Beach Resort* (see p.715) and *Ko Mook Nature Beach Resort* (see p.713). Many of the smart a/c rooms and bungalows with wi-fi face directly onto the water, and some have hot showers and satellite TV. The breezy, waterside restaurant serves up Western breakfasts, vegetarian food and excellent squid and other seafood dishes. There's also kayak, bike and snorkel rental, and internet access. Breakfast included. **B1200**

The Trang and Satun islands

Generally blessed with blinding white beaches, great coral and amazing marine life, the islands off the coast of Trang and Satun provinces have managed, mostly with just a handful of resorts on each, to cling onto some of that illusory desert-island atmosphere which better-known places like Phuket and Samui lost long ago. Indeed, islands such as **Ko Hai** and **Ko Kradan** support no permanent settlements other than the bungalow concerns, while on **Ko Tarutao** and **Ko Adang** in the far south, the peace and quiet is maintained by the national parks department; at the other end of the scale, however,

8

ISLAND-HOPPING AND TOURS

Access to the Trang and Satun islands from their nearest mainland ports is described in the individual island accounts, but what sets this area apart are the enticing opportunities for **island-hopping**, thanks to regular boat services in the tourist season out of Ko Lanta, further up the coast (see p.688), which can be booked through any travel agent in the area. If you just fancy a day exploring some of the islands, any travel agent in Trang can book you on a **boat trip** (mid-Oct to mid-May only) to Ko Kradan, the Emerald Cave on Ko Mook, and other small nearby islands for snorkelling, for around B700/person including packed lunch and soft drinks.

LANTA–LIPE AND BEYOND

Bundhaya Speedboat ☎074 783643-4, ⊛bundhayaresort.com. Speedboats between Lanta and Lipe (1 daily; about 4hr; B1900) via Ko Hai, Hat Farang on Ko Mook and Ko Bulon Lae. Onward, same-day connections to Langkawi.

Satun Pakbara Speedboat Club ☎074 783643-4, ⊛tarutaolipeisland.com. Speedboats between Lanta and Lipe (1 daily; about 4hr; B1900) via Ko Hai, Hat Farang on Ko Mook, Ko Kradan and Ko Bulon Lae. Onward, same-day connections between Lipe and

Langkawi, and between Lanta and Ko Phi Phi, Phuket and Krabi.

Tigerline ☎081 092 8800, ⊛tigerlinetravel.com. Ferries between Lanta and Lipe (1 daily; about 5hr 30min; B1700), via Ko Hai, Hat Farang on Ko Mook (with longtail transfers to Ko Kradan), and Ban Chao Mai on the mainland (usually with a change of boat). Onward, same-day connections between Lipe and Langkawi, and between Lanta and Ko Phi Phi, Phuket, Krabi, Ao Nang and Railay.

LANTA–KRADAN

Petpailin and Lanta Princess day-trip boats The cheapest way to travel between Ko Lanta, Ko Hai, Ko Mook and Ko Kradan is generally on the big day-trip boats run by Petpailin and Lanta Princess out of Lanta, which will drop you at, or transfer you between, any of the islands; Lanta to Ko Hai, for instance, costs B500.

Garden Hill speedboat Garden Hill (see p.691) sends out a speedboat from Lanta every day on the same three-island route, charging B700 between Lanta and Hai, for example, about the same as on the three Lanta–Lipe boats described above.

nearby **Ko Lipe** is developing at its own merry pace and now boasts over forty resorts, as well as a substantial *chao ley* village (see p.608).

Accommodation on the islands, much of which is mid-priced, is now often fully booked at the very busiest times. Most of the resorts open year-round, though in practice many can't be reached out of season (roughly June–Oct) due to treacherous seas. It's sensible to get in touch ahead of time to check whether the resort you're interested in is open or has vacancies, and in many cases to arrange transfers from Trang; a few of the resorts maintain offices or have agents in Trang town to make this easier.

Ko Hai (Ko Ngai)

KO HAI (also known as **KO NGAI**), 16km southwest of Pak Meng, is the most developed of the Trang islands, though it's still decidedly low-key. The island's action, such as it is, centres on the east coast, where half a dozen resorts enjoy a dreamy panorama of jagged limestone outcrops, whose crags glow pink and blue against the setting sun, stretching across the sea to the mainland behind. The gently sloping beach of fine, white sand here runs unbroken for over 2km (though at low tide, swimming is not so good at the northern end, which is scattered with dead coral), and there's some good snorkelling in the shallow, clear water off the island's southeastern tip.

ARRIVAL AND DEPARTURE   KO HAI

If you're planning to **fly** into Trang or Krabi airports, contact your resort in advance about transfers. There are also plenty of island-hopping options (see above).

KO HAI ACTIVITIES

You can rent **snorkelling equipment** (B100/day at *Coco Cottage*, for example) and **kayaks** (B50/hr at *Koh Ngai Villa*, for example) at most of the resorts. All the resorts offer **boat trips** (B1500/boat, or B300/person in a group of six, at *Ko Hai Seafood*, for example) that take in the Emerald Cave on Ko Mook and some snorkelling off Ko Hai. (Ko Cheuak, just to the southeast of Ko Hai, is currently off-limits to visitors to protect the coral, which was badly bleached during a sudden rise in sea temperatures in 2010 – avoid any place that offers trips there.) *Ko Hai Seafood* can also put together overnight snorkelling and camping trips to Ko Rok (see p.691) for B2300 per person.

Towards the southern end of the beach, *Fantasy Resort* has a well-organized **dive shop**, the German-run Rainbow Divers (☎075 206962, ⓦrainbow-diver.com; Nov–April).

By ferry The resorts on Ko Hai's east coast currently rely on ferries owned by *Koh Ngai Villa* and *Fantasea* resorts to transfer their guests from Pak Meng (45min–1hr); longtail boats come out to meet the ferries and shuttle passengers to the various resorts up and down the beach. Both ferries depart at around 11.30am; *Villa*'s is the cheaper of the two, charging B350 from Pak Meng, or B450 including a/c minibus from their office in Trang town (see map, p.706). **By chartered longtail** If you miss the ferries, you can charter a longtail boat for around B1000, for example through *Koh Ngai Villa* (see below).

INFORMATION

Hat Chao Mai National Park maintains a booth at Pak Meng pier, where visitors to Ko Hai will usually be charged B200 entrance fee; hang on to your ticket as this should also cover you if you take a trip to Ko Mook's Emerald Cave.

ACCOMMODATION

★ **Coco Cottage** Towards the northern end of the beach ☎087 898 6522, ⓦcoco-cottage.com. Charming, helpful and family-friendly resort in a grassy palm grove, where the chic, thatched wooden bungalows (both detached and semi-detached) sport verandas, a/c and well-designed bathrooms with outdoor bamboo hot showers, wooden basins and indoor toilets. Also has wi-fi, internet access, a stylish beach bar and a very good restaurant that serves creative Thai food, Thai desserts and espresso coffees. Breakfast included. B2800

Ko Hai Paradise Resort Ao Kauntong on the south coast ☎089 646 5731, ⓦkohhaiparadise.com; Trang office at The Meeting Point restaurant opposite the station ☎075 216420. With a tranquil bay all to themselves, the simple but sturdy en-suite bungalows with mosquito nets at this friendly resort are sheltered by tall palms in spacious, grassy grounds. The food's good and the long, white-sand beach slopes down towards some great coral for snorkelling right in front of the resort. The resort arranges its own transfers from Trang town via Kuantunku pier (B450). Open only at the height of the high season (roughly Dec–April). B500

Ko Hai Seafood Near the centre of the beach, north of Koh Ngai Villa ☎081 367 8497. Large, well-built, thatched, woven-bamboo bungalows with wall fans, mosquito screens and well-equipped bathrooms, in a single row facing the beach across a nice lawn. Internet access available. B1200

Koh Ngai Villa Near the centre of the main beach ☎075 203263, ⓦkohngaivillathai.com; Trang office opposite the station ☎075 210496. Friendly, old-style beach resort with plenty of space. Simple, well-organized bamboo bungalows boast verandas, mosquito nets and small toilets, or you could opt for a large room with two double beds in a concrete longhouse or a smart concrete bungalow with a/c, or even a two-person tent (B200, including bedding). Breakfast included with most rooms. Fan B850, a/c B1800

Mayalay Beach Near the centre of the main beach, south of Koh Ngai Villa ☎083 590 7523, ⓦmayalay beachresort.com. Welcoming place with nineteen deluxe, a/c, woven-bamboo bungalows with thatched roofs, day beds, fridges and capacious hot-water bathrooms. The restaurant is no great shakes but has free wi-fi and access to a computer (payable). Often open all year round. Breakfast included. B3000

Thanya South end of the beach ☎075 206965, ⓦkohngaithanyaresort.com. A large, very attractive beachside swimming pool with jacuzzis, set on a spacious lawn, is the main draw here. As well as a/c, hot water and fridges, the villas feature verandas, big French windows and lots of polished teak, while the restaurant has a varied menu of Thai food, including some interesting seafood dishes. Breakfast included. B3500

Thapwarin Resort Towards the northern end of the main beach, north of Coco Cottage ☎081 894 3585, ⓦthapwarin.com. Welcoming, shady resort, where you can choose between well-appointed bamboo and rattan cottages with semi-outdoor bathrooms, and large, very smart, beachfront wooden bungalows; all are thatched and have a/c and hot showers. There's internet access and free wi-fi, a massage spa, beach bar and good restaurant, serving Thai and Western food, including seafood barbecues in the evening. Breakfast included. B3000

Ko Mook

KO MOOK, about 8km southeast of Ko Hai, supports a comparatively busy fishing village on its eastern side, around which – apart from the sandbar that runs out to the very pricey *Sivalai Resort* – most of the beaches are disappointing, reduced to dirty mud flats when the tide goes out. However, across on the island's west coast lies beautiful **Hat Farang**, with gently shelving white sand, crystal-clear water that's good for swimming and snorkelling, and gorgeous sunsets.

Tham Morakhot

Part of Hat Chao Mai National Park • Open Oct–June • B200 admission fee if the park rangers are around

The island's main source of renown is **Tham Morakhot**, the stunning "Emerald Cave" north of Hat Farang on the west coast, which can only be visited by boat, but shouldn't be missed. An 80m swim through the cave – 10m or so of which is in pitch darkness – brings you to a *hong* (see p.655) with an **inland beach** of powdery sand open to the sky, at the base of a spectacular natural chimney whose walls are coated with dripping vegetation. Chartering your own longtail or taking a trip with *Ko Mook Nature Beach Resort* (B200/person, in a group of four or more) is preferable to taking one of the big day-trip boats that originate on Lanta or Pak Meng: if you time it right, you'll get the inland beach all to yourself, an experience not to be forgotten. It's also easy enough to **kayak** there from Hat Farang (from B100/hr from *Sawaddee*), and at low tide you can paddle right through to the inland beach: buoys mark the cave entrance, from where a tunnel heads straight back into the rock; about halfway along, there's a small, right-hand kink in the tunnel which will plunge you briefly into darkness, but you should soon be able to see light ahead from the *hong*. Mid-afternoon is often a good time to paddle off on this trip, after the tour boats have left and providing the tide is right.

8

ARRIVAL AND DEPARTURE   KO MOOK

In addition to the services mentioned below, there are plenty of island-hopping options (see p.710).

Minibus-and-boat packages The easiest way to get to Ko Mook is to book a minibus-and-boat package to Hat Farang through a travel agent in Trang, which costs B350, including the 30min longtail ride.

By public boat There's a pretty reliable public boat (B60) at around midday to Ko Mook's village from Kuantunku

pier, 8km south of Pak Meng, between Hat Chang Lang and Hat Yong Ling; Ban Chao Mai a/c minibuses from Trang (see p.709) will usually detour to Kuantunku if asked (around B100/person from Trang). Once landed at the village, you're left with a 30min walk or B50 motorbike-taxi ride over to Hat Farang.

ACCOMMODATION

Most of Hat Farang is unfortunately occupied by the disappointing *Charlie's Resort*, leaving room only for one other resort, *Sawaddee*. However, *Rubber Tree* and *Had Farang* make the best of the attractive, shady slopes behind the beach, while *Ko Mook Nature Beach Resort* is away on the east side of the island near the village.

Had Farang Bungalows ☎087 884 4785, ⓦkohmookhadfarang.com. The nineteen bungalows and rooms at this friendly place are basic bamboo and wood affairs, but most are en-suite with their own verandas and the restaurant is very good. Sometimes open in the rainy season. B400

★ **Ko Mook Nature Beach Resort** ☎087 885 7815 or ☎081 894 6936, ⓦnatureresortsgroup.com. Recently

opened branch of the non-profit *Had Yao Nature Resort*, which promotes conservation and sustainable tourism (see p.709). On the south-facing shore of the sandbar that ends at *Sivalai Resort*, the bright, concrete bungalows all have mosquito-screened French windows directly facing the sea, as well as a/c, satellite TV, DVD player and free wi-fi. Bicycles, kayaks, snorkels, trips to the Emerald Cave and Ko Kradan, and internet access available. Breakfast included. B2800

Rubber Tree ☎081 606 9358, ⓦmookrubbertree .com; or contact Sea Breeze restaurant in front of the station in Trang (☎075 215972). On a well-tended, landscaped slope that's also a working rubber plantation, fan bungalows with cold-water bathrooms and crisp, white linen, or spacious, smartly designed a/c versions with rubber-wood furniture and hot showers. Occasionally puts together overnight camping trips to Ko Rok. Breakfast included. Fan <u>B800</u>, a/c <u>B1990</u>

Sawaddee ☎081 508 0432, ⓔsawaddeeresort64 @yahoo.com; or contact Wunderbar in Trang (see p.707). Laidback, old-style, concrete or stilted wooden bungalows with mosquito nets parallel to the beach, with en-suite bathrooms, plenty of shade and largely uninterrupted sea views. High season only. <u>B800</u>

Ko Kradan

About 6km to the southwest of Ko Mook, **KO KRADAN** is the remotest of the inhabited islands off Trang, and one of the most beautiful, with crystal-clear waters. On this slender triangle of thick jungle, the **main beach** is a long strand of steeply sloping, powdery sand on the east coast, with fine views of Ko Mook, Ko Libong and the karst-strewn mainland, and an offshore reef to the north with a great variety of hard coral; such beauty, however, has not escaped the attention of the day-trip boats from Ko Lanta, who turn the beach into a lunchtime picnic ground most days in summer. From a short way north of the *Anantara* beach club (see p.709), which is located towards the south end of this beach, a path across the island will bring you after about fifteen minutes to **Sunset Beach**, another lovely stretch of fine, white sand in a cove; a branch off this path at *Paradise Lost* leads to a beach on the short south coast, which enjoys good reef snorkelling (also about 15min from the *Anantara* beach club).

ARRIVAL AND DEPARTURE

KO KRADAN

By minibus-and-longtail transfer Agencies such as Trang Island Hopping Tour (see p.707) can arrange minibus-and-longtail transfers from Trang town, via Kuantunku pier (twice daily in season; B450). There are also plenty of island-hopping options (see p.710).

ACCOMMODATION

Kalume ☎089 650 3283, ⓦkalumekradan.com. Italian-run resort on the beach next to *Seven Seas*, with small, basic, thatched bamboo huts with mosquito nets and en-suite bathrooms and smart, large, wooden bungalows with French windows and nice verandas (B1500). Good Italian food at the bar-restaurant and free wi-fi. <u>B900</u>

Paradise Lost ☎089 587 2409; for further information, go to ⓦkokradan.wordpress.com or contact Sea Breeze restaurant in front of the station in Trang (☎075 215972). In the middle of the island, roughly halfway along the path to *Sunset Beach* is Kradan's best-value accommodation, run by an American and his dogs. Set in a grassy, palm-shaded grove, it offers simple, clean, thatched rattan bungalows with shared bathrooms or larger, en-suite, wooden affairs, as well as an open-sided dorm with mosquito nets and fans (B250/person), kayaks, snorkels and good Thai and Western food. <u>B700</u>

Seven Seas ☎075 203389–90, ⓦsevenseasresorts .com. By far the best of several resorts on the east coast, *Seven Seas* adds a surprising splash of contemporary luxury to this remote spot. Behind a small, black, infinity pool, the large bungalows and rooms with outdoor warm-water bathrooms are stylishly done out in greys and whites, and sport a/c, wi-fi, fridges, TVs and DVDs. There's a small massage spa and breakfast is included. <u>B6500</u>

Ko Libong

The largest of the Trang islands with a population of six thousand, **KO LIBONG** lies 10km southeast of Ko Mook, opposite Ban Chao Mai on the mainland. Less visited than its northern neighbours, it's known mostly for its wildlife, although it has its fair share of golden beaches too. Libong is one of the most significant remaining refuges in Thailand of the **dugong**, a large marine mammal similar to the manatee, which feeds on sea grasses growing on the sea floor – the sea-grass meadow around Libong is reckoned to be the largest in Southeast Asia. Sadly, dugongs are now an endangered species, traditionally hunted for their blubber (used as fuel) and meat, and increasingly

KO LIBONG BOAT TRIPS AND DIVING

Libong Nature Beach Resort runs award-winning, day-long **boat trips around Libong** (B1200/person, including lunch, in a group of four or more; ten percent discount for guests), which are safe, insured and licensed with TAT, and staffed by local *chao ley* (sea gypsies) who know the dugong well. As well as visiting a *chao ley* village, these give you the chance to kayak into the sanctuary to observe the rare birds and to snorkel at the sea-grass beds – with, they reckon, an eighty percent chance of seeing a dugong. They also run day-trips to the Emerald Cave on Ko Mook and Ko Kradan (B1200/person, including lunch, in a group of four or more; ten percent discount for guests). If you'd rather explore below water than above, there's a PADI **dive shop**, Jolly Roger, at *Libong Beach Resort* on the north side of Ban Lan Khao (@trangdiving.com).

affected by fishing practices such as scooping, and by coastal pollution, which destroys their source of food. The dugong has now been adopted as one of fifteen "reserved animals" of Thailand and is the official mascot of Trang province.

Libong is also well known for its migratory **birds**, which stop off here on their way south from Siberia, drawn by the island's food-rich mud flats (now protected by the Libong Archipelago Sanctuary, which covers the eastern third of the island). For those seriously interested in ornithology, the best time to come is during March and April, when you can expect to see brown-winged kingfishers, masked finfoots and even the rare black-necked stork, not seen elsewhere on the Thai–Malay peninsula.

The island's handful of resorts occupy a long, thin strip of golden sand at the fishing village of **Ban Lan Khao** on the southwestern coast. At low tide here, the sea retreats for hundreds of metres, exposing rock pools that are great for splashing about in but not so good for a dip.

ARRIVAL AND DEPARTURE

KO LIBONG

By public longtail Public longtails depart daily year-round from Ban Chao Mai (see p.709) when full (most frequent in the morning and around lunchtime; B50/person), arriving 20min later at Ban Phrao on Ko Libong's north side. From here motorbike taxis (B100) transport you to Ban Lan Khao.

By private transfer You can arrange a direct boat transfer from Ban Chao Mai to *Libong Nature Beach Resort* for about B1000/boat.

ACCOMMODATION

Libong Beach Resort ☎ 075 225205, @libongbeach resort.com. Friendly resort on the north side of Ban Lan Khao with a wide variety of accommodation set amid lawns and flowers, ranging from small, en-suite concrete and wood bungalows at the back to spacious, bright, stilted, wooden cabins with a/c and nice decks on the beachfront (B2500). Internet access, kayak and motorbike rental are available. Fan B700, a/c B1000

★ **Libong Nature Beach Resort** ☎ 087 885 7815 or ☎ 081 894 6936, @natureresortsgroup.com. Run by the same charitable foundation that operates the Had Yao Nature Resort (see p.709), with neat, en-suite bungalows, all with wi-fi and some with hot water and a/c, stretching back from a secluded part of the beach; it's a 10min walk south of Ban Lan Khao, and there's another sheltered cove a further 5min walk (or kayak) to the south. There's a good restaurant attached too, with internet access, and mountain bikes and snorkelling gear are available to rent. Breakfast included. Fan B1200, a/c B1500

Ko Sukorn

A good way south of the other Trang islands, low-lying **KO SUKORN** lacks the white-sand beaches and beautiful coral of its neighbours, but makes up for it with its friendly inhabitants, a laidback ambience and one excellent resort; for a glimpse of how islanders live and work, this is the place to come.

The lush interior is mainly given over to rubber plantations, interspersed with rice paddies, banana and coconut palms; the island also produces famously delicious watermelons, which are plentiful in March and April. Hat Talo Yai, the main **beach**

> ## KO SUKORN BOAT TRIPS AND OTHER ACTIVITIES
>
> **Boat excursions** from *Sukorn Beach Bungalows* include trips out to the islands of Ko Lao Liang and Ko Takieng, which are part of the Mu Ko Phetra National Marine Park, for some excellent snorkelling. These run nearly every day from November to May; at other times of year, the sea is sometimes calm enough but you're usually restricted to fishing trips – and to looking round the island itself, which, at thirty square kilometres, is a good size for exploring. The resort offers **guided tours**, and has motorbikes (B250/half-day) and mountain bikes (B150/ half-day) for rent, as well as a handy map that marks all the sights, including the three villages and seafood market.

– 500m of gently shelving brown sand – backed by coconut palms – runs along the southwestern shore.

ARRIVAL AND DEPARTURE   KO SUKORN

A songthaew-and-boat transfer to Ko Sukorn (B250/person), via the public ferry from Laem Ta Sae, leaves Trang Island Hopping Tours (see p.707) daily at 11am and takes a couple of hours, or you can arrange a private transfer. *Sukorn Beach Bungalows* can also organize pricey longtail-boat transfers to or from any of the nearby islands.

ACCOMMODATION

Ko Sukorn Cabana ☎089 724 2326, ⓦ sukorncabana .com. After *Sukorn Beach Bungalows*, the best of the rest of the island's handful of resorts is *Ko Sukorn Cabana*, a friendly and peaceful place offering stilted, a/c bungalows with attractive bathrooms and large, well-appointed log cabins on a secluded beach to the north of Hat Talo Yai. Day-trips to Lao Liang and Takieng, kayaks, motorbikes, internet and wi-fi are also available; private transfers from Trang can be arranged for B2100 all-in. **B1500**

★ **Sukorn Beach Bungalows** ☎075 207707, ⓦ sukorn-island-trang.com; for further information in Trang, go to Trang Island Hopping Tours (see p.707). This outstanding place is one of the few Trang resorts that's reliably accessible all year round (discounts of up to forty percent are available in low season). The clued-up and congenial Thai–Dutch duo who run the place are keen to keep it low-key and quiet (no children under 7), and work with the locals as much as possible, something that's reflected in the friendly welcome you get all over the island. Attractively decorated and well-designed bungalows and rooms – all spotlessly clean and with en-suite hot showers – are set around a lush garden dotted with deckchairs and umbrellas, and there's an excellent, well-priced restaurant. At the resort, you can access the internet (including wi-fi), make overseas calls, exchange money and get a good massage, and you're free to paddle around in kayaks; the owners can even put together pricey but very appealing, five-night island-hopping packages. Good breakfast included. Fan **B1000**, a/c **B1250**

Ko Bulon Lae

The scenery at tiny **KO BULON LAE**, 20km west of Pak Bara in Satun province, isn't as beautiful as that generally found in Ko Tarutao National Park just to the south, but it's not at all bad: a 2km strip of fine white sand runs the length of the casuarina-lined east coast, while *chao ley* fishermen make their ramshackle homes in the tight coves of the rest of the island. A reef of curiously shaped hard coral closely parallels the eastern beach, while **White Rock** to the south of the island has beautifully coloured soft coral and equally dazzling fish.

> ## KO LAO LIANG
>
> The beautiful, twin islets of **Ko Lao Liang**, with their white-sand beaches, abundant corals and dramatic rock faces, lie to the west of Ko Sukorn. They're deserted apart from a single adventure-sport camp, *Lao Liang Resort* (ⓦ laoliangresort.com; open mid-Nov to April; B1500). All-in costs at the resort comprise camping in deluxe tents on the beach, three meals, including seafood barbecues in the evening, and snorkelling gear; kayak rental, rock-climbing (instruction, equipment rental, deep-water soloing) and snorkelling tours are extra. Trang Island Hopping Tours (see p.707) can arrange transfers via Laem Ta Sae for B850 per person.

ARRIVAL AND DEPARTURE	**KO BULON LAE**

From/to Pak Bara Boats for Ko Bulon Lae currently leave Pak Bara (see box, p.718) daily at about 12.30pm (1hr 30min; B450). As there's no pier on Bulon Lae, boat arrivals are met by longtails to transfer visitors to shore (B50). Boats return from Bulon Lae to Pak Bara at around 9.30am. There are also plenty of island-hopping options (see p.710).

ACCOMMODATION

The island's resorts are open roughly from late October to mid-May.

Bulone ☏ 081 897 9084 or ☏ 086 960 0468, ⊛ bulone-resort.net. Friendly spot in a huge grassy compound under the casuarinas at the north end of the main beach. Airy, en-suite bungalows on stilts come with fans, mosquito nets and verandas, while the restaurant features plenty of vegetarian options and a small selection of tasty Italian favourites, as well as internet access and wi-fi; kayaks and snorkelling gear are also available. **B1250**

Pansand ☏ 081 693 3667, ⊛ pansand-resort.com; Trang office at First Andaman Travel on Thanon Wisetkul. The oldest and largest resort on the island, on the east-coast beach, where large, smart, peaceful cottages come with verandas, fans, mosquito screens, cold-water bathrooms and plenty of room to breathe. On the beach side of the shady, well-tended grounds, there's a sociable restaurant serving up good seafood and other Thai dishes; internet access and snorkelling gear are also available. Breakfast included. **B1500**

Ko Tarutao National Marine Park

B200 admission fee • ⊛ dnp.go.th

The unspoilt **KO TARUTAO NATIONAL MARINE PARK** is probably the most beautiful of all Thailand's accessible beach destinations. Occupying 1400 square kilometres of the Andaman Sea in Satun province, the park covers 51 mostly uninhabited islands. Site of the park headquarters, the main island, **Ko Tarutao**, offers a variety of government-issue accommodation and things to do, while **Ko Adang** to the west is much more low-key and a springboard to some excellent snorkelling. The port of **Pak Bara** (see box, p.718) is the main jumping-off point for the park, and houses a **national park visitor centre** (☏ 074 783485), set back on the left just before the pier, where you can gather information and book a room on Tarutao or Adang before boarding your boat.

The park's forests and seas support an incredible variety of **fauna**: langurs, crab-eating macaques and wild pigs are common on the islands, which also shelter several unique subspecies of squirrel, tree shrew and lesser mouse deer; among the hundred-plus bird species found here, reef egrets and hornbills are regularly seen, while white-bellied sea eagles, frigate birds and pied imperial pigeons are more rarely encountered; and the

8

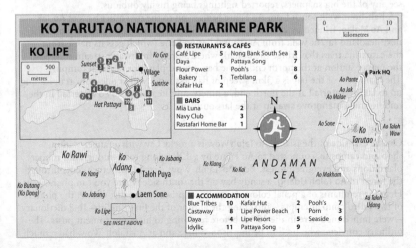

KO TARUTAO NATIONAL MARINE PARK

0 — 10 kilometres

KO LIPE

0 — 500 metres

Ko Gra
Sunset
Village
Sunrise
Hat Pattaya

● **RESTAURANTS & CAFÉS**

Café Lipe	5	Nong Bank South Sea	3
Daya	4	Pattaya Song	7
Flour Power Bakery	1	Pooh's	8
Kafair Hut	2	Terbilang	6

■ **BARS**

Mia Luna	2
Navy Club	3
Rastafari Home Bar	1

N

Park HQ
Ao Pante
Ao Jak
Ao Molae
Ao Sone
Ko Tarutao
Ao Taloh Wow

Ko Rawi
Ko Adang
Taloh Puya
Ko Jabang
Ko Klang
Ko Kai
ANDAMAN SEA
Ao Makham
Ko Yang
Ko Butang (Ko Dong)
Ko Jabang
Laem Sone
Ko Lipe
SEE INSET ABOVE

Ao Taloh Udang

■ **ACCOMMODATION**

Blue Tribes	10	Kafair Hut	2	Pooh's	7
Castaway	8	Lipe Power Beach	1	Porn	3
Daya	4	Lipe Resort	5	Seaside	6
Idyllic	11	Pattaya Song	9		

TRANSPORT TO AND FROM PAK BARA

The main port for Bulon Lae, Tarutao and Lipe is **PAK BARA**, towards the north end of Satun province. **From Trang**, there are direct a/c minibuses and share taxis to Pak Bara (see p.707); otherwise you'll need to take a Satun-bound bus (2hr–2hr 30min) to the inland town of **Langu** and change there to a red songthaew for the 10km hop to the port. There are also direct a/c minibuses **from Hat Yai** (see p.724), while **from Satun**, frequent buses and a/c minibuses make the 50km trip to Langu, where you'll have to change onto a songthaew. Andrew Tour in Pak Bara (☎081 897 6482) lays on a/c minibuses to and from Krabi and Hat Yai when they have enough customers.

---

park is the habitat of about 25 percent of the world's tropical fish species, as well as dugongs, sperm whales, dolphins and a dwindling population of turtles.

The park amenities on Adang, though not on Tarutao, are officially closed to tourists in the monsoon season from mid-May to mid-November (the exact dates vary from year to year). Accommodation is especially likely to get full around the three New Years (Thai, Chinese and Western), when it's best to book national park rooms in advance (see p.37).

Ko Tarutao

The largest of the national park's islands, **KO TARUTAO** offers the greatest natural variety: mountains covered in semi-evergreen rainforest rise steeply to a high point of 700m; limestone caves and mangrove swamps dot the shoreline; and the west coast is lined with perfect beaches for most of its 26km length. For a different perspective on Ko Tarutao, John Gray's Sea Canoe in Phuket runs multi-day **sea-kayaking** trips, either guided or self-paddle, around the island (☎076 254505–7, ⊛johngray-seacanoe.com).

The west coast

At **Ao Pante**, site of the **park headquarters**, you'll find the only shop on the island, selling basic supplies, as well as a visitor centre. Behind the settlement, the steep, half-hour climb to **To-Boo cliff** is a must, especially at sunset, for the view of the surrounding islands and the crocodile's-head cape at the north end of the bay. A fun ninety-minute trip by boat (B400/boat; contact the visitor centre to book) or kayak can also be made near Ao Pante, up the canal which leads 2km inland from the pier, through a bird-filled mangrove swamp, to **Crocodile Cave** – where you're unlikely to see any of the big snappers, reported sightings being highly dubious.

A half-hour walk south from Ao Pante brings you to the two quiet bays of **Ao Jak** and **Ao Molae**, fringed by coconut palms and filled with fine white sand. Beyond the next headland (a 2hr walk from Ao Pante) lies **Ao Sone** (which gets its name from the casuarina trees that fringe the beach), where a pretty freshwater stream runs past the ranger station at the north end of the bay, a good place for peaceful camping. The main part of the bay is a 3km sweep of flawless sand, with a one-hour trail leading up to **Lu Du Waterfall** at the north end, a ninety-minute trail to **Lo Po Waterfall** in the middle and a **mangrove swamp** at the far south end.

The east coast

On the east side of the island, **Ao Taloh Wow** is a rocky bay with a ranger station, shop and campsite, connected to Ao Pante by a 12km-long road through old rubber plantations and evergreen forest. Beyond Taloh Wow, a trail (5hr return) cuts through the forest to **Ao Taloh Udang**, a sandy bay on the south side where you can pitch a tent. Here the remnants of a penal colony for political prisoners are just visible: the plotters of two failed coup attempts – including the author of the first English–Thai dictionary – were imprisoned here in the 1930s before returning to high government posts. The ordinary convicts, who used to be imprisoned here and at Ao Taloh Wow, had a much harsher time, and during World War II, when supplies from the mainland dried up, prisoners and guards ganged together to turn to piracy. This turned into a lucrative business, which was not suppressed until 1946 when the Thai government asked the British in Malaysia to send in three hundred troops. Pirates and smugglers still occasionally hide out in the Tarutao archipelago, but the main problem now is illegal trawlers fishing in national park waters.

ARRIVAL AND DEPARTURE

KO TARUTAO

From Pak Bara and Ko Lipe At least once a day, the speedboat services between Pak Bara and Ko Lipe (see p.721) call in at Ko Tarutao; currently it's the 11.30am boat from Pak Bara (30min; B300–350) and the 9.30am boat from Lipe (1hr; B350). If you're planning to visit both

islands, you can buy a ticket for B500 that will allow you to stop off at Tarutao on your way to Lipe. Boats drop passengers off at Ao Pante on Tarutao; the pier at Ao Pante is sometimes inaccessible at low tide, when longtails (B30) shuttle people to shore.

GETTING AROUND

By truck The visitor centre can arrange transport by road, usually in an open truck, to several of the island's beaches, charging B50 per person to Ao Molae, around B400 per vehicle to Ao Sone and B600 per vehicle to Ao Taloh Wow.
By boat Transfers to the same places by boat cost at least

twice as much, though you may be tempted by a round-island boat trip for B3000.
By kayak or mountain bike Kayaks and mountain bikes are available at headquarters.

ACCOMMODATION

National park accommodation At park headquarters, the bungalows (sleeping four people, or available as twin rooms), which are spread over a large, quiet park behind the beach, are for the main part national park standard issue with cold-water bathrooms, but there are also some basic mattress-on-floor four-person rooms in longhouses, sharing bathrooms, as well as a restaurant. There are also

bungalows containing en-suite twin rooms and a small restaurant at Ao Molae. HQ bungalow B1000, HQ twin room from B600, HQ longhouse room B500, Ao Molae twin room B600
Camping There are campsites at Ao Pante, Ao Molae and Ao Taloh Wow. Two-person tents can be rented from Ao Pante for B150/night (plus B50/person for bedding).

Ko Adang

At **KO ADANG**, a wild, rugged island covered in tropical rainforest 40km west of Ko Tarutao, the park station is at **Laem Sone** on the southern shore, where the beach is steep and narrow and backed by a thick canopy of pines. The half-hour climb to **Sha-do** cliff on the steep slope above Laem Sone gives good views over Ko Lipe to the south, while about 2km west along the coast from the park station, a twenty-minute trail leads inland to the small **Pirate Waterfall**.

ARRIVAL AND DEPARTURE

KO ADANG

To get to Ko Adang, take any boat to Ko Lipe (see p.720): if the boat moors off Lipe's Hat Pattaya, a longtail transfer to Adang will cost B100/person; if it stops in the channel between the two islands, the transfer to Adang will cost B50.

ACCOMMODATION

There are **rooms** in bamboo longhouses at the park station at **Laem Sone** (B300/room sleeping three), **bungalows** sleeping two–eight people (B600–1800), and two/three-person **tents** can be rented (B150–225/night). There's a **restaurant** here, too.

SNORKELLING TRIPS AROUND KO ADANG

You can charter **longtail boats** (and rent snorkels and masks, for around B50/day) through the rangers for excellent snorkelling trips to nearby islands such as Ko Rawi and Ko Jabang (around B1500–2500 for up to ten people, depending on how far you want to go).

Ko Lipe

Home to a population of around a thousand *chao ley*, tiny **KO LIPE**, 2km south of Ko Adang (see the map on p.717), is something of a frontier maverick, attracting ever more travellers with one dazzling beach, fifty or so private bungalow resorts and a rough-and-ready atmosphere. It's technically a part of Ko Tarutao National Marine Park, but the authorities seem to have given up on the island and don't collect an admission fee from visitors. A small, flat triangle, Lipe is covered in coconut plantations and supports a school and a health centre in the village on the eastern side. By rights, such a settlement should never have been allowed to develop within the national park boundaries, but the *chao ley* on Lipe are well entrenched: Satun's governor forced the community to move here from Phuket and Ko Lanta between the world wars, to reinforce the island's Thai character and prevent the British rulers of Malaya from laying claim to it.

More recently, a huge, diverse influx of tourists – Westerners, Thais and Malaysians, families and backpackers – has been enticed here by the gorgeous beach of **Hat Pattaya**, a shining crescent of squeaky-soft white sand with an offshore reef to explore on its eastern side, as well as by the relaxed, anything-goes atmosphere and mellow nightlife. Many of Lipe's *chao ley* have now sold their beachfront land to Thai–Chinese speculators from the mainland, who have increased the island's capacity to over two thousand guest rooms; with the money earned, the *chao ley* have bought the scores of longtail boats that clog up the bay at Hat Pattaya. Lipe's main drag is **Walking Street**, a paved path lined with tourist businesses between the eastern end of Hat Pattaya and the south end of the village, which lies on east-facing **Sunrise**, an exposed, largely featureless beach that gives access to some good snorkelling around Ko Gra; a few other narrow roads also radiate out from the village. The other island track that's most likely to be useful runs from *Daya Resort* at the west end of Pattaya across to **Sunset** beach, a shady, attractive spot with good views of Ko Adang, in around ten minutes.

ARRIVAL AND DEPARTURE

KO LIPE

As well as being one of the hubs for island-hopping boats (see p.710), Ko Lipe is served by **ferries** from Thammalang pier near Satun town, **speedboats** from Pak Bara in the north of Satun province, and ferries and speedboats from the Malaysian island of Langkawi. However, services to Lipe seem to change by the year, due to competition between the boat companies and local politicking; for up-to-date **transport information**, contact Koh Lipe Thailand.com (see opposite). There is no pier on Lipe, so boats anchor off Hat Pattaya or sometimes in the channel between the island and Ko Adang, where they're met by **longtails** (B50/person to any beach on Lipe).

Via Thammalang From roughly November to the beginning of May, Andaman Express (☏ 086 964 8929, Ⓦandaman-express.com) operates a daily ferry between Thammalang and Ko Lipe, currently departing from the

---

SNORKELLING AND DIVING AROUND KO LIPE

The prime **diving and snorkelling sites** around Ko Lipe are around Ko Adang, Ko Rawi and Ko Dong, just to the north and west in Ko Tarutao National Marine Park, where encounters with reef and even whale sharks, dolphins and stingrays are not uncommon. Further afield to the south, advanced divers head for Eight Mile Rock, a pinnacle that rises to about 14m from the surface, with soft corals, mantas, leopard and whale sharks. A handful of dive shops operate on Lipe, and there are dozens of places offering snorkelling day-trips on *chao ley* longtail boats; snorkellers are liable to pay the park admission fee of B200, though some longtail captains will try to dodge the park rangers.

Koh Lipe Thailand.com See opposite. Snorkelling trips to the best sites around the islands on the west side of Ko Adang for B550–650/person, including lunch.
Sabye Sports On the east side of Porn Resort, behind Flour Power Bakery, on Sunset beach

☏ 089 464 5884, Ⓦsabye-sports.com. Canadian-run dive shop, Lipe's oldest, which offers daily trips (from B2000, plus equipment rental, for two dives) and PADI courses (B12,900 for the Openwater). Also does snorkelling equipment rental (B150/day including fins).

mainland at 12.30pm, from the island at 9.30am (2hr 15min; B600). Orange songthaews (roughly every 30min; B40), as well as chartered tuk-tuks (B150) and motorcycle taxis (B60–70), cover the 10km between Thammalang and Satun town.

Via Pak Bara Several companies run speedboats between Pak Bara (see box, p.718) and Ko Lipe in high season (at least 5 daily; 1hr 30min; B400–650). In the rainy season,

there's at least one crossing a day, usually heading out at either 11.30am or 1pm.

Via Langkawi Speedboats operate between Ko Lipe and Langkawi, the large Malaysian island to the southeast, four times a day in high season (1hr; B1200); there's also a daily ferry (1hr 30min; B1100). During the season, a Thai immigration post is set up at the far east end of Lipe's Hat Pattaya to cover this route.

GETTING AROUND

By mountain bike You can rent mountain bikes from several places, including the shop next to *Pooh's* on the

Walking Street (see p.722) for B200/day.

INFORMATION

Koh Lipe Thailand.com The best travel agent and source of information on the island, including a good website, is Koh Lipe Thailand.com (Boi's Travel; ☏089 464 5854 or ☏081 541 4489, ⓦkohlipethailand.com), which currently has two outlets on Walking Street between Hat Pattaya

and the village, with the main one hard by the beach (the second shop, further inland towards *Pooh's*, has a book exchange). On offer are all manner of transport tickets (including discounted boat tickets) plus accommodation bookings (including on the website).

ACCOMMODATION

The majority of Lipe's bungalows are on **Hat Pattaya**, the prettiest but most crowded and expensive beach on the island. *Porn Resort* has **Sunset** beach on the northwest side to itself, while a dozen or so resorts have set up shop on **Sunrise**, on the east side near the village. Plenty of accommodation options are bookable in advance through ⓦkohlipethailand.com; if you turn up on the island and are struggling to find a vacant room, head for one of their offices on Walking Street for booking assistance (see above).

★ **Blue Tribes** East end of Hat Pattaya ☏083 654 0316, ⓦbluetribeslipe.com. Congenial, Italian-run resort and restaurant with very spacious, well-spread and well-designed bungalows and rooms, either in lovely dark wood or in thatched white concrete, sporting large, attractive tiled bathrooms with hot showers; some are two-storey with a balcony and chill-out room/extra bedroom upstairs. **B1700**

Castaway Sunrise ☏083 138 7472, ⓦcastaway-resorts .com. Airy, thatched, mostly two-storey bungalows featuring well-equipped bathrooms with cold rain showers, ceiling fans, big decks, hammocks and a certain amount of style, mostly bestowed by the distinctive red Indonesian hardwood that they're made from. On a sandy patch with a dive shop, a mellow, multi-tiered bar-restaurant and a massage spa; kayaks and snorkels for rent. **B2000**

Daya West end of Hat Pattaya ☏081 479 0682, ⓔdayaresort@hotmail.com. *Chao ley*-owned resort with over thirty colourful, en-suite rooms and bungalows in a large, shady, flower-strewn garden, ranging from simple concrete rooms to clapboard bungalows in a great position on the beach. Wi-fi, kayaks and snorkels available. **B500**

Idyllic South end of Sunrise ☏081 802 5453, ⓦidyllic resort.com. This welcoming "concept resort" comes as a big surprise out here in Thailand's far maritime corner, with its angular contemporary architecture in white, grey and wood. Set in an attractive garden, the minimalist rooms boast huge windows, a/c, hot outdoor rain showers, DVD players and nice

touches such as sun hats for guests' use. There are two pools – one infinity-edged and beachside, with a swim-up bar, the other with a jacuzzi – as well as kayaks and other watersports, and free wi-fi in the restaurant. Breakfast included. **B5900**

Kafair Hut 150m inland from Sunset Beach, on the track to the village ☏081 541 9870, bookable online through ⓦkohlipethailand.com. Gentle, welcoming café and resort, offering three attractive, breezy, red-wood bungalows on high stilts, with mosquito nets, fans and modern, semi-outdoor bathrooms. Good breakfast included. **B1500**

Lipe Power Beach Sunrise, in the village near the school ☏081 970 0741, ⓦlipepowerbeach.com. Seven rows of five clapboard bungalows each, very tightly packed together though scattered with colourful flowers. All have polished-concrete bathrooms with hot showers, a/c, TVs, mini-bars and safety boxes, and there's a small saltwater swimming pool, internet access and wi-fi (payable). Buffet breakfast included. **B3000**

Lipe Resort Towards the west end of Hat Pattaya ☏074 750291, ⓦliperesort.com. Welcoming place owned by the village chief in a good position on the beach. Though the grounds are scruffy and few of the rooms are on the sand, the accommodation is neat and clean and represents decent value for a/c and hot showers in large, modern bathrooms. Free kayak, snorkels and basic buffet breakfasts. **B3000**

Pattaya Song Far west end of Hat Pattaya ☏086 960

8

0418, ⓦ pattayasongresort.com. Italian-run resort, the oldest on the beach (the name means "Pattaya no. 2"), where plain, good-sized, en-suite clapboard or concrete bungalows are strung out away from the beach (the cheapest, with small bathrooms) or in a lovely location up on a steep promontory with great views of the bay; kayaks for rent. **B500**

Pooh's On Walking Street between Sunrise and Hat Pattaya ⓣ074 750345, ⓦ poohlipe.com. Well inland behind the popular restaurant, but a good, functional choice if you get stuck for somewhere to stay. The eight concrete single-storey rooms have small terraces, a/c, hot showers and TVs, and there's free wi-fi and a dive centre.

Breakfast included. **B1800**

★ **Porn Resort** Sunset ⓣ084 691 8743. Popular, attractive and well-run spot in a pleasant, spacious, sloping setting under the trees on the beach. Well-designed bungalows come with verandas, mosquito nets and en-suite bathrooms, or you can pitch your own tent in a prime spot by the beach (B100). Snorkelling equipment for rent. **B400**

Seaside Near the midpoint of Hat Pattaya ⓣ087 398 7932. Good-value, *chao ley*-owned resort, offering basic but sturdy woven-bamboo, en-suite bungalows with mosquito nets, in plenty of space on a grassy patch and under a little shade, behind the popular *Family* restaurant. **B600**

EATING AND DRINKING

Besides the **bars** reviewed below, there are a couple of beach bars on Sunset, but the east end of Pattaya has the biggest concentration, with low candlelit tables and cushions sprawled on the sand, fire shows and names like *Peace and Love*. Also check out ⓦ pirates4ever.de for details of their electronic underground **parties** at *Mia Luna* bar on a small cove beach to the west of Sunset (weekly, according to the moon's phases; camping available).

Café Lipe Near the midpoint of Hat Pattaya. Eco-conscious, solar-powered place behind a thick screen of foliage that serves up decent veggie choices among its inexpensive Thai dishes, sandwiches, salads and espressos, as well as home-made bread, cakes and muesli. Daily 6am–5pm.

Daya West end of Hat Pattaya ⓣ081 479 0682. One of the most popular of half a dozen restaurants that lay out candlelit tables and seafood barbecues on the beach at night. It also offers a long menu of mostly Thai dishes, such as prawn tempura (B120), lots of tofu options for vegetarians, Thai desserts and Western breakfasts. Daily 8am–10pm.

★ **Flour Power Bakery** Sunset. At shady, beachfront tables, you can feast on delicious home-made brownies, croissants (B60), baguettes and blueberry pie as well as sandwiches (from B100), spaghetti and Thai dishes including vegetarian options. There are also wines by the glass, cocktails, water refills from their cooler and rental kayaks if you want to burn off the calories. Daily 7.30am–8.30pm.

Kafair Hut 150m inland from Sunset Beach, on the track to the village ⓣ081 541 9870. Tiny, mellow café for deli sandwiches (from B80), simple Thai food, breakfasts, shakes and espresso coffees. Daily 7.30am–6/7pm.

Navy Club Far east end of Hat Pattaya. On the edge of the navy base, this friendly, jerry-built bar and shop with a few wooden benches is the best spot for a quiet, cheap, ice-cold beer watching the sun set. Daily 6/7am till midnight or later, depending on who's in.

Nong Bank South Sea Towards the west end of Hat Pattaya, just east of Lipe Resort. Friendly restaurant with

tables on the beach, which are shaded in the mornings, serving tasty Thai and Western food, including breakfasts, lots of curries (B80 for a small plate), Thai desserts, juices and shakes. Daily 7am–11.30pm.

Pattaya Song Far west end of Hat Pattaya ⓣ086 960 0418. At tables on the sand here, tuck into very tasty gnocchi bolognese (B240) and other home-made pasta, Italian sausages, Thai-style seafood and, in the evenings, authentic pizzas (from B180), all washed down with Italian wines. Daily 8am–10pm.

Pooh's On Walking Street between Sunrise and Hat Pattaya ⓣ074 750345. Well-run and welcoming bar-restaurant that's a popular hive of activity, with free wi-fi. Offers tasty Thai food, including chicken with cashew nuts (B150) and vegetarian dishes, as well as sandwiches, cakes, evening barbecues and live music, plus a wide choice of breakfasts and espresso coffees. Daily roughly 9am–10pm.

Rastafari Home Bar Just north of the main track from Sunset to the village, next to the entrance to Mountain Resort. Genial and eccentric outdoor rasta bar serving plenty of cocktails and furnished with driftwood painted red, gold and green, a campfire and a circle of filled-in yellow toilet bowls to get sociable on. Their motto is "open when closed".

Terbilang Walking Street, about 50m inland from Hat Pattaya on the right-hand side. Famous outlet for all manner of outlandish roti pancakes – basil chicken cheese roti, anyone? – as well as the more familiar roti with chicken curry (*matabah*; B60) and banana roti (B50). Also does strong, traditional Thai coffee, teas and shakes. Daily noon–midnight.

DIRECTORY

Currency exchange There are currently no ATMs on Ko Lipe (the nearest are in Satun and Pak Bara), but Koh Lipe Thailand.com, for instance (see p.721), offers currency

exchange and cash advances.

Internet access Available at Ko Lipe Thailand.com (B3/minute, discounted for travel agency customers).

Tourist police At *Pooh's* restaurant on Walking Street between Sunrise and Hat Pattaya ☎ 1155.

Satun town

Nestling in the last wedge of Thailand's west coast, the remote town of **SATUN** is served by just one road, Highway 406, which approaches through forbidding karst outcrops. Set in a green valley bordered by limestone hills, the town is leafy and relaxing but not especially interesting, except during its small version of the Vegetarian Festival (see p.629) and its International Kite Festival at the end of February; the boat services to and from Kuala Perlis and Langkawi in Malaysia and Ko Lipe are the main reason for foreigners to come here.

National Museum

Soi 5, Thanon Satun Thani, on the north side of the centre • Wed–Sun 9am–4pm • B30

If you find yourself with time on your hands in Satun, it's worth seeking out the **National Museum**. It's memorable, as much as anything else, for its setting, in the graceful **Kuden Mansion**, which was built in British colonial style, with some Thai and Malay features, by craftsmen from Penang, and inaugurated in 1902 as the Satun governor's official residence. The exhibits and audiovisuals in English have a distinctive anthropological tone, but are diverting enough, notably concerning Thai Muslims, the *chao ley* on Ko Lipe, and the **Sakai**, a dwindling band of nomadic hunter-gatherers who still live in the jungle of southern Thailand.

Map

SATUN

▲ Pak Bara, Trang & Hat Yai

■ ACCOMMODATION
On's Guest House	2
Rian Thong	4
Satunthanee Hotel	1
Sinkiat Thani Hotel	3

Wangmai Hotel

Khao To Yong Kong

National Museum

Minibuses to Hat Yai ★

THANON YATRA SAWATAL

Police Station

Khlong Mambang

Night Market

Satun Hospital ✚

THANON SATUN THANI

Baw Khaw Saw Office

Mambang Mosque

HATTHAKAM SUEKSA

BUREEWANIT

Share-taxis to Hat Yai

APHIRIN A TRIMRUK

THANON SARIT PHUMINAT

THANON SAMAN PRADIT

N

Minibuses to Langu ★

THANON SULAKANUUUL

THANON SATHIT UTTHAM

0   200
metres

Songthaews to ★ Thammalang

WISET MAYURA

▼ Thammalang Pier

● RESTAURANTS & CAFÉS
| Go Ho | 2 |
| On's | 1 |

8

ARRIVAL AND DEPARTURE

SATUN TOWN

By bus Satun's new bus station is far to the southeast of the centre on the new bypass, but Hat Yai and non-a/c Trang buses usually do a tour of the town centre, stopping, for example, in front of the *Sinkiat Thani Hotel* on Thanon Bureewanit; incoming a/c buses from Phuket via Trang (4 daily) will set you down on Thanon Satun Thani by the *Wangmai* hotel; and you can book tickets in advance at the central Baw Khaw Saw office on Thanon Hatthakam Sueksa.

Destinations: Bangkok (4 daily; 16hr); Hat Yai (hourly; 2hr); Phuket (4 daily; 7hr); Trang (hourly; 2hr 30min–3hr).
By minibus or **share-taxi** The bases for a/c minibuses to Langu and Hat Yai and share taxis to Hat Yai are marked on our map.
By ferry There are high-season ferries from nearby Thammalang pier to Ko Lipe (see p.720), as well as boats to Kuala Perlis and Langkawi in Malaysia (see box, p.724).

GETTING AROUND

By motorbike or car On Kongnual (see below) offers motorbike (B250/day) and car rental (B1500/day).

INFORMATION AND TOURS

On Kongnual 36 Thanon Bureewanit ☎ 074 724133 or ☎ 081 097 9783, ✉ onmarch13@hotmail.com. From her restaurant, *On's: The Kitchen*, near the *Sinkiat Thani Hotel*, On

Kongnual dispenses helpful tourist information, sells all kinds of transport tickets and can organize local river-kayaking trips and cave visits.

CROSSING INTO MALAYSIA FROM SATUN

From **Thammalang** pier, 10km south of Satun at the mouth of the river, boats leave when full on 45-minute trips (B150/person) to **Kuala Perlis** on the northwest tip of Malaysia, from where there are plentiful transport connections down the west coast; 9am is usually a good time to turn up at Thammalang for these boats, but they need a minimum of ten passengers (or B1500), which means that on some days they don't run. Three ferry boats a day cross from Thammalang to the Malaysian island of **Langkawi** (1hr 15min; B300). The journey from Satun town to Thammalang is covered by orange songthaews (roughly every 30min; B40) from near the 7-Eleven supermarket on Thanon Sulakanukul, as well as chartered tuk-tuks (B150) and motorcycle taxis (B60–70).

It's also possible to cross by road to Malaysia's **Kangar** (which has bus connections to Penang and Kuala Lumpur) and Alor Setar through Thale Ban National Park, though a little tricky as the a/c minibuses (B300; about 2hr) depart from Ban Khuan, 20km or so up Highway 406 from Satun – contact local fixer On (see p.723) to arrange this.

ACCOMMODATION

On's Guest House 36 Thanon Bureewanit ☏074 724133 or ☏081 097 9783, ✉onmarch13@hotmail.com. Three big, bright rooms in a modern, Sino-Portuguese-style building above On's: The Kitchen restaurant, with wooden shutters, coloured-glass windows, a/c, hot showers, fridges, satellite TV and free wi-fi. B650

Rian Thong 4 Thanon Saman Pradit ☏074 711036. Just on the west side of the centre, this is a decent budget hotel with friendly owners, where some of the large, en-suite rooms with TVs overlook the canal. B200

Satunthanee Hotel Thanon Satun Thani ☏074 711010. This centrally placed, good-value, traditional Chinese hotel offers battered but clean rooms with small bathrooms and TVs, though it suffers from noise from the road and the mosque. Fan B280, a/c B350

Sinkiat Thani Hotel 50 Thanon Bureewanit ☏074 721055–8, ✉sinkiathotel@hotmail.com. Satun's top hotel, offering large, carpeted bedrooms with a/c, hot water, fridges, TVs and good views over the surrounding countryside from the upper floors; a more deluxe wing at the back of the building was being built at the time of writing. B680

EATING AND DRINKING

For a meal in the evening, you can't do much better than the lively and popular night market, north of the centre on the west side of Thanon Satun Thani.

Go Ho Thanon Saman Pradit opposite the Chinese temple. A cheap, busy, friendly restaurant with leafy pavement tables that serves tasty Thai and Chinese food, including plenty of seafood (according to market price), salads and southern specialities such as kaeng som (B70). Daily 5pm–midnight.

On's: The Kitchen 36 Thanon Bureewanit ☏074 724133. Very tasty Thai food, including southern specialities, some interesting fish dishes and handy set menus, such as green curry with prawn patties (thawt man kung) and rice for B120. Also offers a wide array of Western food, including good breakfasts, jacket potatoes and pies, espresso coffees and free wi-fi. (On's bar, a couple of doors away, The Living Room, has a computer for customers' use, as well as free wi-fi, and stays open late.) Daily 8am–10pm.

Hat Yai

Travelling to or through **HAT YAI**, the biggest city in the region, is currently **not recommended** because of the troubles in the south (see p.705). To be honest, you're not missing much, but as it's a major transport axis, we've provided a few, rudimentary practicalities and a map of the city, in case you get stuck there. The three main Niphat Uthit roads are known locally as sai neung, sai sawng and sai saam.

ARRIVAL AND DEPARTURE HAT YAI

The helpful Cathay Tour (☏074 235044, ⠀cathaytourthailand.com), a **travel agency** on the ground floor of the guesthouse of the same name (see opposite), handles onward flight, bus, share-taxi and a/c minibus bookings, both within Thailand and into Malaysia.

By plane About 5km south of town, Hat Yai airport is connected to the downtown area by a/c minibuses (B80) and has Avis (☎074 227259, ⓦavisthailand.com) and Budget (☎074 227268, ⓦbudget.co.th) car rental desks.

By train The train station is on the west side of the centre at the end of Thanon Thamnoon Vithi.

By bus or minibus The bus terminal is southeast of the centre on Thanon Kanchanawanit, while the a/c minibus terminal at Talat Kaset is about 5km west of town, both leaving you with a songthaew ride to the centre.

INFORMATION

Tourist information The TAT office is at 1/1 Soi 2, Thanon Niphat Uthit 3 (daily 8.30am–4.30pm; ☎074 243747 or ☎074 238518, ⓔtatsgkhl@tat.or.th).

ACCOMMODATION

Cathay Guest House 93 Thanon Niphat Uthit 2 ☎074 243815. This friendly place in the heart of town has long been Hat Yai's main travellers' hub, and the café, which has internet access, acts as a sociable meeting place; the rooms have fans and en-suite cold-water bathrooms but are rather run-down. **B200**

Lee Gardens Plaza Hotel 29 Thanon Prachatipat ☎074 261111, ⓦleeplaza.com. Characterless but good-value and central upmarket option with great views of the city from its four hundred comfortable a/c rooms. Facilities include a fitness centre, a rooftop pool and a 33rd-floor panoramic restaurant. Breakfast included. **B1300**

Centara Hotel 3 Thanon Sanehanusorn ☎074 352222,

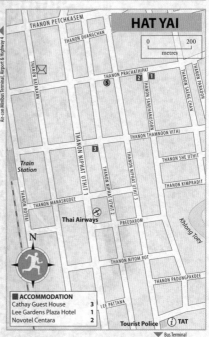

ⓦcentarahotelsresorts.com. Luxury hotel in a good location next to the Central Department Store, featuring contemporary-styled rooms with wi-fi, a spa, fitness centre, sauna, swimming pool and Thai, Chinese and Japanese food at its several restaurants. **B1800**

DIRECTORY

Tourist police Thanon Niphat Uthit 3, near the TAT office ☎074 246733 or ☎1155.

MEDITATING BUDDHA, WAT YAI SUWANNARAM, PHETCHABURI

Contexts

History

As long as forty thousand years ago, Thailand was inhabited by hunter-gatherers who lived in semi-permanent settlements and used tools made of wood, bamboo and stone. By the end of the last Ice Age, around ten thousand years ago, these groups had become farmers, keeping chickens, pigs and cattle, and – as evidenced by the seeds and plant husks which have been discovered in caves in northern Thailand – cultivating rice and beans. This drift into an agricultural society gave rise to further technological developments: the earliest pottery found in Thailand has been dated to 6800 BC, while the recent excavations at Ban Chiang in the northeast have shown that bronze was being worked at least as early as 2000 BC. By two thousand years ago, the peoples of Southeast Asia had settled in small villages, among which there was regular communication and trade, but they had split into several broad families, differentiated by language and culture. At this time, the ancestors of the Thais, speaking proto-Thai languages, were still far away in southern China, whereas Thailand itself was inhabited by Austroasiatic speakers, among whom the Mon were to establish the region's first distinctive civilization, Dvaravati.

Dvaravati and Srivijaya

The history of **Dvaravati** is ill-defined to say the least, but the name is applied to a distinctive culture complex which shared the **Mon** language and **Theravada Buddhism**. This form of religion may have entered Thailand during the third century BC, when the Indian emperor, Ashoka, is said to have sent missionaries to Suvarnabhumi, "land of gold", which seems to correspond roughly to mainland Southeast Asia.

From the discovery of monastery boundary stones (*sema*), clay votive tablets and Indian-influenced Buddhist sculpture, it's clear that Dvaravati was an extensive and prosperous Buddhist civilization that had its greatest flourishing between the sixth and ninth centuries AD. No strong evidence has turned up, however, for the existence of a single capital – rather than an empire, Dvaravati seems to have been a collection of city-states. Nakhon Pathom, Lopburi, Si Thep and Muang Sema were among the most important Dvaravati sites, and their concentration around the Chao Phraya valley would seem to show that they gained much of their prosperity, and maintained religious and cultural contacts with India, via the **trade route** from the Indian Ocean over the Three Pagodas Pass.

Although they passed on aspects of their heavily Indianized art, religion and government to later rulers of Thailand, these Mon city-states were politically fragile and

6800 BC	3rd century BC	6th–9th centuries AD
Date of earliest pottery found in Thailand	Theravada Buddhism probably first enters Thailand	Dvaravati civilization flourishes

from the ninth century onwards succumbed to the domination of the invading Khmers from Cambodia. One northern outpost, the state of **Haripunjaya**, centred on Lamphun, which had been set up on the trade route with southern China, maintained its independence until the thirteenth century.

Meanwhile, to the south of Dvaravati, the shadowy Indianized state of Lankasuka had grown up in the second century, centred on Ligor (now Nakhon Si Thammarat) and covering an area of the Malay peninsula which included the important trade crossings at Chaiya and Trang. In the eighth century, it came under the control of **Srivijaya**, a Mahayana Buddhist city-state on Sumatra, which had strong ties with India and a complex but uneasy relationship with neighbouring Java. Thriving on seaborne trade between Persia and China, Srivijaya extended its influence as far north as Chaiya, its regional capital, where discoveries of temple remains and some of the finest stone and bronze statues ever produced in Thailand have borne witness to the cultural vitality of this crossroads empire. In the tenth century the northern part of Lankasuka, under the name **Tambralinga**, regained a measure of independence, although it seems still to have come under the influence of Srivijaya as well as owing some form of allegiance to Dvaravati. By the beginning of the eleventh century, however, peninsular Thailand had come under the sway of the Khmer empire, with a Cambodian prince ruling over a community of Khmer settlers and soldiers at Tambralinga.

The Khmers

The history of central Southeast Asia comes into sharper focus with the emergence of the **Khmers**, vigorous empire-builders whose political history can be pieced together from the numerous stone inscriptions they left. The Khmers of **Chenla** – to the north of Cambodia – seized power in the latter half of the sixth century during a period of economic decline in the area. Chenla's rise to power was knocked back by a punitive expedition conducted by the Srivijaya empire in the eighth century, but was reconsolidated during the watershed reign of **Jayavarman II** (802–50), who succeeded in conquering the whole of Kambuja, an area which roughly corresponds to modern-day Cambodia. In order to establish the authority of his monarchy and of his country, Jayavarman II had himself initiated as a *chakravartin*, or universal ruler, the living embodiment of the **devaraja**, the divine essence of kingship – a concept which was adopted by later Thai rulers. Taking as the symbol of his authority the phallic lingam, the king was thus identified with the god Shiva, although the Khmer concept of kingship and thus the religious mix of the state as a whole was not confined to Hinduism: elements of ancestor worship were also included, and Mahayana Buddhism gradually increased its hold over the next four centuries.

It was Jayavarman II who moved the Khmer capital to **Angkor** in northern Cambodia, which he and later kings, especially after the eleventh century, embellished with a series of prodigiously beautiful temples. Jayavarman II also recognized the advantages of the lakes around Angkor for irrigating rice fields and providing fish, and thus for feeding a large population. His successors developed this idea and gave the state a sound economic core with a remarkably complex system of **reservoirs** (*baray*) and water channels, which were copied and adapted in later Thai cities.

8th century	802–50	Late 9th century
Srivijaya gains sway over southern Thailand	Reign of Khmer king Jayavarman II, founder of Angkor	Khmers begin to push into Thailand

In the ninth and tenth centuries, Jayavarman II and his imperialistic successors, especially **Yasovarman I** (889–900), confirmed Angkor as the major power in Southeast Asia. They pushed into Vietnam, Laos and southern China, as well as into northeastern Thailand, where the Khmers left dozens of Angkor-style temple complexes, as seen today at Prasat Phanom Rung and Prasat Hin Phimai. To the west and northwest, Angkor took control over central Thailand, with its most important outpost at Lopburi, and even established a strong presence to the south on the Malay peninsula. As a result of this expansion, the Khmers were masters of the most important trade routes between India and China, and indeed nearly every communications link in the region, from which they were able to derive huge income and strength.

The reign of **Jayavarman VII** (1181–1219), a Mahayana Buddhist who firmly believed in his royal destiny as a *bodhisattva*, sowed the seeds of Angkor's downfall. Nearly half of all the surviving great religious monuments of the empire were erected under his supervision, but the ambitious scale of these building projects and the upkeep they demanded – some 300,000 priests and temple servants of 20,000 shrines consumed 38,000 tonnes of rice per year – along with a series of wars against Vietnam, exhausted the economy.

In subsequent reigns, much of the life-giving irrigation system around Angkor turned into malarial swamp through neglect, and the rise of the more democratic creed of Theravada Buddhism undermined the divine authority which the Khmer kings had derived from the hierarchical Mahayana creed. As a result of all these factors, the Khmers were in no position to resist the onslaught between the thirteenth and fifteenth centuries of the vibrant new force in Southeast Asia, the Thais.

The earliest Thais

The earliest traceable history of the **Thai people** picks them up in southern China around the fifth century AD, when they were squeezed by Chinese and Vietnamese expansionism into sparsely inhabited northeastern Laos and neighbouring areas. The first entry of a significant number of Thais onto what is now Thailand's soil seems to have happened in the region of Chiang Saen, where it appears that some time after the seventh century the Thais formed a state in an area then known as **Yonok**. A development which can be more accurately dated and which had immense cultural significance was the spread of Theravada Buddhism to Yonok via Dvaravati around the end of the tenth century, which served not only to unify the Thais but also to link them to Mon civilization and give them a sense of belonging to the community of Buddhists.

The Thais' political development was also assisted by **Nan-chao**, a well-organized military state comprising a huge variety of ethnic groups, which established itself as a major player on the southern fringes of the Chinese empire from the beginning of the eighth century. As far as can be gathered, Nan-chao permitted the rise of Thai *muang* or small principalities on its periphery, especially in the area immediately to the south known as **Sipsong Panna**.

Thai infiltration continued until, by the end of the twelfth century, they seem to have formed the majority of the population in Thailand, then under the control of the Khmer empire. The Khmers' main outpost, at Lopburi, was by then regarded as the administrative capital of a land called "Syam" (possibly from the Sanskrit *syam*, meaning swarthy) – a mid-twelfth-century bas-relief at Angkor Wat, portraying the

Mid-12th century	1181–1219	1238
Bas-relief at Angkor Wat depicting Thai mercenaries, a new force to be reckoned with in the region	Reign of Jayavarman VII, perhaps the greatest and certainly the most ambitious of the Khmer kings	The Thais seize the Khmer outpost of Sukhothai

troops of Lopburi preceded by a large group of self-confident Syam Kuk mercenaries, shows that the Thais were becoming a force to be reckoned with.

Sukhothai

By the middle of the thirteenth century, the Thais, thanks largely to the decline of Angkor and the inspiring effect of Theravada Buddhism, were poised on the verge of autonomous power. The final catalyst was the invasion by Qubilai Khan's Mongol armies of China and Nan-chao, which began around 1215 and was completed in the 1250s. Demanding that the whole world should acknowledge the primacy of the Great Khan, the Mongols set their hearts on the "pacification" of the "barbarians" to the south of China, which obliged the Thais to form a broad powerbase to meet the threat.

The founding of the first Thai kingdom at **Sukhothai**, now popularly viewed as the cornerstone of the country's development, was in fact a small-scale piece of opportunism which almost fell at the first hurdle. At some time around 1238, the princes of two small Thai principalities in the upper Chao Phraya valley joined forces to capture the main Khmer outpost in the region at Sukhothai. One of the princes, **Intradit**, was crowned king, but for the first forty years Sukhothai remained merely a local power, whose existence was threatened by the ambitions of neighbouring princes. When attacked by the ruler of Mae Sot, Intradit's army was only saved by the grand entrance of Sukhothai's most dynamic leader: the king's 19-year-old son, Rama, held his ground and pushed forward to defeat the opposing commander, earning himself the name **Ramkhamhaeng**, "Rama the Bold".

When Ramkhamhaeng came to the throne around 1278, he saw the south as his most promising avenue for expansion and, copying the formidable military organization of the Mongols, established control over much of the Chao Phraya valley. Over the next twenty years, largely by diplomacy rather than military action, Ramkhamhaeng gained the submission of most of modern-day Thailand; local rulers entered into a complex system of tribute-giving and protection – the political system that persisted in Thailand until the end of the nineteenth century – either through the pressure of the Sukhothai king's personal connections or out of recognition of his superior military strength and moral prestige. To the east, Ramkhamhaeng extended his sphere of influence as far as Vientiane in Laos; by marrying his daughter to a Mon ruler to the west, he obtained the allegiance of parts of southern Burma; and to the south his vassals stretched down the peninsula at least as far as Nakhon Si Thammarat. To the north, Sukhothai concluded an alliance with the parallel Thai states of Lanna and Phayao in 1287 for mutual protection against the Mongols – though it appears that Ramkhamhaeng managed to pinch several *muang* on their eastern periphery as tribute states.

Meanwhile **Lopburi**, which had wrested itself free from Angkor some time in the middle of the thirteenth century, was able to keep its independence and its control of the eastern side of the Chao Phraya valley. Having been first a major cultural and religious centre for the Mon, then the Khmers' provincial capital, and now a state dominated by migrating Thais, Lopburi was a strong and vibrant place mixing the best of the three cultures, as evidenced by the numerous original works of art produced at this time.

Although Sukhothai extended Thai influence over a vast area, its greatest contribution to the Thais' development was at home, in cultural and political matters. A famous

1278	1281	1287
Ramkhamhaeng "the Bold" comes to the throne of Sukhothai	With the conquest of the Dvaravati outpost of Haripunjaya, King Mengrai unifies the north as the Thai state of Lanna	Alliance between the Thai states of Sukhothai, Lanna and Phayao

inscription by Ramkhamhaeng, now housed in the Bangkok National Museum, describes a prosperous era of benevolent rule: "In the time of King Ramkhamhaeng this land of Sukhothai is thriving. There is fish in the water and rice in the fields … [The King] has hung a bell in the opening of the gate over there: if any commoner has a grievance which sickens his belly and gripes his heart … he goes and strikes the bell … [and King Ramkhamhaeng] questions the man, examines the case, and decides it justly for him." Although this plainly smacks of self-promotion, it seems to contain at least a kernel of truth: in deliberate contrast to the Khmer god-kings, Ramkhamhaeng styled himself as a **dhammaraja**, a king who ruled justly according to Theravada Buddhist doctrine and made himself accessible to his people. To honour the state religion, the city's temples were lavishly endowed: as original as Sukhothai's political systems were its religious **architecture and sculpture**, which, though bound to borrow from existing Khmer and Sri Lankan styles, show the greatest leap of creativity at any stage in the history of art in Thailand. A further sign of the Thais' new self-confidence was the invention of a new **script** to make their tonal language understood by the non-Thai inhabitants of the land.

All this was achieved in a remarkably short period of time. After the death of Ramkhamhaeng around 1299, his successors took their Buddhism so seriously that they neglected affairs of state, and by 1320 Sukhothai had regressed to being a kingdom of only local significance.

Lanna

Almost simultaneous with the birth of Sukhothai was the establishment of a less momentous but longer-lasting kingdom to the north, called **Lanna**. Its founding father was **Mengrai**, chief of Ngon Yang, a small principality on the banks of the Mekong near modern-day Chiang Saen. Around 1259 he set out to unify the squabbling Thai principalities of the region, first building a strategically placed city at Chiang Rai in 1262, and then forging alliances with Ngam Muang, the Thai king of Phayao, and with Ramkhamhaeng of Sukhothai.

In 1281, after ten years of guileful preparations, Mengrai conquered the Mon kingdom of Haripunjaya based at Lamphun, and was now master of northern Thailand. Taking advice from Ngam Muang and Ramkhamhaeng, in 1292 he selected a site for an impressive new capital of Lanna at **Chiang Mai**, which remains the centre of the north to the present day. Mengrai concluded further alliances in Burma and Laos, making him strong enough to successfully resist further Mongol attacks, although he was eventually obliged to bow to the superiority of the Mongols by sending them small tributes from 1312 onwards. When Mengrai died after a sixty-year reign in 1317, supposedly struck by a bolt of lightning, he had built up an extensive and powerful kingdom. But although he began a tradition of humane, reasonable laws, probably borrowed from the Mons, he had found little time to set up sound political and administrative institutions. His death severely destabilized Lanna, which quickly shrank in size and influence.

It was only in the reign of **Ku Na** (1355–85) that Lanna's development regained momentum. A well-educated and effective ruler, Ku Na enticed the venerable monk Sumana, from Sukhothai, to establish an ascetic Sri Lankan sect in Lanna in 1369.

1299	1317	1351
With the death of Ramkhamhaeng, Sukhothai begins its decline	Mengrai dies after being struck by lightning	Ramathibodi founds Ayutthaya

Sumana brought a number of Buddha images with him, inspiring a new school of art that flourished for over a century, but more importantly his sect became a cultural force that had a profound unifying effect on the kingdom. The influence of Buddhism was further strengthened under **Tilok** (1441–87), who built many great monuments at Chiang Mai and cast huge numbers of bronze seated Buddhas in the style of the central image at Bodh Gaya in India, the scene of the Buddha's enlightenment. Tilok, however, is best remembered as a great warrior, who spent most of his reign resisting the advances of Ayutthaya, by now the strongest Thai kingdom.

Under continuing pressure both from Ayutthaya and from Burma, Lanna went into rapid decline in the second quarter of the sixteenth century. For a short period after 1546, Chiang Mai came under the control of Setthathirat, the king of Lan Sang (Laos), but, unable to cope with Lanna's warring factions, he then abdicated, purloining the talismanic Emerald Buddha for his own capital at Luang Prabang. In 1558, Burma decisively captured Chiang Mai, and the Mengrai dynasty came to an end. For most of the next two centuries, the Burmese maintained control through a succession of puppet rulers, and Lanna again became much as it had been before Mengrai, little more than a chain of competing principalities.

Ayutthaya

While Lanna was fighting for its place as a marginalized kingdom, from the fourteenth century onwards the seeds of a full-blown Thai nation were being sown to the south at **Ayutthaya**. The city of Ayutthaya itself was founded on its present site in 1351 by U Thong ("Golden Cradle") of Lopburi. Taking the title **Ramathibodi**, he soon united the principalities of the lower Chao Phraya valley, which had formed the western provinces of the Khmer empire. When he recruited his bureaucracy from the urban elite of Lopburi, Ramathibodi set the **style of government** at Ayutthaya – the elaborate etiquette, language and rituals of Angkor were adopted, and, most importantly, the conception of the ruler as *devaraja*. The king became sacred and remote, an object of awe and dread, with none of the accessibility of the kings of Sukhothai: when he processed through the town, ordinary people were forbidden to look at him and had to be silent while he passed. This hierarchical system also provided the state with much-needed manpower, as all freemen were obliged to give up six months of each year to the Crown either on public works or military service.

The site chosen by Ramathibodi turned out to be the best in the region for an international port, and so began Ayutthaya's rise to prosperity, based on its ability to exploit the upswing in **trade** in the middle of the fourteenth century along the routes between India and China. Flushed with economic success, Ramathibodi's successors were able to expand their control over the ailing states in the region. After a long period of subjugation, Sukhothai became a province of the kingdom of Ayutthaya in 1438, six years after Boromraja II had powerfully demonstrated Ayutthaya's pre-eminence by capturing the once-mighty Angkor, enslaving large numbers of its subjects and looting the Khmer royal regalia. (The Cambodian royal family were forced to abandon the palace and to found a new capital near Phnom Penh.)

Although a century of nearly continuous warfare against Lanna was less decisive, success generally bred success, and Ayutthaya's increasing wealth through trade brought ever

1432	1477	1511
Ayutthaya captures and loots Angkor	The eighth world council of Theravada Buddhism is held in Chiang Mai	The first Western power, Portugal, begins trading with Ayutthaya

greater power over its neighbouring states. To streamline the functioning of his unwieldy empire, **Trailok** (1448–88) found it necessary to make reforms to its administration. His **Law of Civil Hierarchy** formally entrenched the inequality of Ayutthayan society, defining the status of every individual by assigning him or her an imaginary number of rice fields – for example, 25 for an ordinary freeman and 10,000 for the highest ministers of state. Trailok's legacy is found in today's unofficial but fiendishly complex status system, by which everyone in Thailand knows their place.

Ramathibodi II (1491–1529), almost at a loss as to what to do with his enormous wealth, undertook an extensive programme of public works. In the 1490s he built several major religious monuments, and between 1500 and 1503 cast the largest standing metal image of the Buddha ever known, the Phra Si Sanphet, which gave its name to the temple of the royal palace. By 1540, Ayutthaya had established control over most of the area of modern-day Thailand.

Burmese wars and European trade

In the sixteenth century recurring tensions with Burma led **Chakkraphat** (1548–69) to improve his army and build brick ramparts around the capital. This was to no avail however: in 1568 the Burmese besieged Ayutthaya with a huge army, said by later accounts to have consisted of 1,400,000 men. The Thais held out until August 8, 1569, when treachery within their own ranks helped the Burmese break through the defences. The Burmese looted the city, took thousands of prisoners and installed a vassal king to keep control.

The decisive character who broke the Burmese stranglehold twenty years later and re-established Ayutthaya's economic growth was **Naresuan** (1590–1605), who defied the Burmese by amassing a large army. The enemy sent a punitive expedition, which was conclusively defeated at Nong Sarai near modern-day Suphanburi on January 18, 1593, Naresuan himself turning the battle by killing the Burmese crown prince. Historians have praised Naresuan for his personal bravery and his dynamic leadership, although the chronicles of the time record a strong streak of tyranny – in his fifteen years as king he had eighty thousand people killed, excluding the victims of war. A favoured means of punishment was to slice off pieces of the offender's flesh, which he was then made to eat in the king's presence.

The period following Naresuan's reign was characterized by a more sophisticated engagement in **foreign trade**. In 1511 the Portuguese had become the first Western power to trade with Ayutthaya, and Naresuan himself concluded a treaty with Spain in 1598; relations with Holland and England were initiated in 1608 and 1612 respectively. For most of the seventeenth century, European merchants flocked to Thailand, not only to buy Thai products, but also to gain access to Chinese and Japanese goods on sale there. The role of foreigners at Ayutthaya reached its peak under **Narai** (1656–88), but he overstepped the mark in cultivating close links with Louis XIV of France, who secretly harboured the notion of converting Ayutthaya to Christianity. On Narai's death, relations with Westerners were cut back.

Despite this reduction of trade and prolonged civil strife over the succession to the throne whenever a king died – then, as now, there wasn't a fixed principle of primogeniture – Ayutthaya continued to flourish for much of the eighteenth century. The reign of **Borommakot** (1733–58) was particularly prosperous, producing many

1558	1569	1590–1605
The Burmese decisively capture Chiang Mai	The Burmese take Ayutthaya and install a vassal king	Reign of the warrior king Naresuan, who sends the Burmese packing

works of drama and poetry. Furthermore, Thai Buddhism had by then achieved such prestige that Sri Lanka, from where the Thais had originally imported their form of religion in the thirteenth century, requested Thai aid in restoring their monastic orders in 1751.

However, immediately after the death of Borommakot the rumbling in the Burmese jungle to the north began to make itself heard again. Alaunghpaya of Burma, apparently a blindly aggressive country bumpkin, first recaptured the south of his country from the Mon, and then turned his attentions to Ayutthaya. A siege in 1760 was unsuccessful, with Alaunghpaya dying of wounds sustained there, but the scene was set. In February 1766 the Burmese descended upon Ayutthaya for the last time. The Thais held out for over a year, during which they were afflicted by famine, epidemics and a terrible fire that destroyed ten thousand houses. Finally, in **April 1767**, the walls were breached and the city taken. The Burmese razed everything to the ground and tens of thousands of prisoners were led off to Burma, including most of the royal family. The king, Suriyamarin, is said to have escaped from the city in a boat and starved to death ten days later. As one observer has said, the Burmese laid waste to Ayutthaya "in such a savage manner that it is hard to imagine that they shared the same religion with the Siamese". The city was abandoned to the jungle, but with remarkable speed the Thais regrouped and established a new seat of power, further down the Chao Phraya River at Bangkok.

The early Bangkok empire

As the bulk of the Burmese army was obliged by war with China to withdraw almost immediately, Thailand was left to descend into banditry. Out of this lawless mess several centres of power arose, the most significant being at Chanthaburi, commanded by **Phraya Taksin**. A charismatic, brave and able general who had been unfairly blamed for a failed counterattack against the Burmese at Ayutthaya, Taksin had anticipated the fall of the besieged city and quietly slipped away with a force of five hundred men. In June 1767 he took control of the east-coast strip around Chanthaburi and very rapidly expanded his power across central Thailand.

Blessed with the financial backing of the Chinese trading community, to whom he was connected through his father, Taksin was crowned king in December 1768 at his new capital of Thonburi, on the opposite bank of the river from modern-day Bangkok. One by one the new king defeated his rivals, and within two years he had restored all of Ayutthaya's territories. More remarkably, by the end of the next decade Taksin had outdone his Ayutthayan predecessors by bringing Lanna, Cambodia and much of Laos under his sway. During this period of expansionism, Taksin left most of the fighting to Thong Duang, an ambitious soldier and descendant of an Ayutthayan noble family, who became the *chakri*, the military commander, and took the title **Chao Phraya Chakri**.

However, by 1779 all was not well with the king. Being an outsider, who had risen from an ordinary family on the fringes of society, Taksin became paranoid about plots against him, a delusion that drove him to imprison and torture even his wife and sons. At the same time he sank into religious excesses, demanding that the monkhood worship him as a god. By March 1782, public outrage at his sadism and dangerously irrational behaviour had reached such fervour that he was ousted in a coup.

1767	1768	1782–1809
Ayutthaya is razed to the ground by the Burmese	Taksin crowned king at the new capital, Thonburi	Reign of Rama I, founder of the current Chakri dynasty

Chao Phraya Chakri was invited to take power and had Taksin executed. In accordance with ancient etiquette, this had to be done without royal blood touching the earth: the king was duly wrapped in a black velvet sack and struck on the back of the neck with a sandalwood club. (Popular tradition has it that even this form of execution was too much: an unfortunate substitute got the velvet sack treatment, while Taksin was whisked away to a palace in the hills near Nakhon Si Thammarat, where he is said to have lived until 1825.)

Rama I

With the support of the Ayutthayan aristocracy, Chakri – reigning as **Rama I** (1782–1809) – set about consolidating the Thai kingdom. His first act was to move the capital across the river to Bangkok, a better defensive position against any Burmese attack from the west. Borrowing from the layout of Ayutthaya, he built a new royal palace and impressive monasteries, and enshrined in the palace wat the Emerald Buddha, which he had snatched back during his campaigns in Laos.

As all the state records had disappeared in the destruction of Ayutthaya, religious and legal texts had to be written afresh and historical chronicles reconstituted – with some very sketchy guesswork. The monkhood was in such a state of crisis that it was widely held that moral decay had been partly responsible for Ayutthaya's downfall. Within a month of becoming king, Rama I issued a series of religious laws and made appointments to the leadership of the monkhood, to restore discipline and confidence after the excesses of Taksin's reign. Many works of drama and poetry had also been lost in the sacking of Ayutthaya, so Rama I set about rebuilding the Thais' literary heritage, at the same time attempting to make it more cosmopolitan and populist. His main contribution was the *Ramakien*, a dramatic version of the Indian epic *Ramayana*, which is said to have been set to verse by the king himself – with a little help from his courtiers – in 1797. Heavily adapted to its Thai setting, the *Ramakien* served as an affirmation of the new monarchy and its divine links, and has since become the national epic.

In the early part of Rama I's reign, the Burmese reopened hostilities on several occasions, the biggest attempted invasion coming in 1785, but the emphatic manner in which the Thais repulsed them only served to knit together the young kingdom. Trade with China revived, and the king addressed the besetting problem of manpower by ordering every man to be tattooed with the name of his master and his town, so that avoiding royal service became almost impossible. On a more general note, Rama I put the style of government in Thailand on a modern footing: while retaining many of the features of a *devaraja*, he shared more responsibility with his courtiers, as a first among equals.

Rama II and Rama III

The peaceful accession of his son as **Rama II** (1809–24) signalled the establishment of the **Chakri dynasty**, which is still in place today. This Second Reign was a quiet interlude, best remembered as a fertile period for Thai literature. The king, himself one of the great Thai poets, gathered round him a group of writers including the famous Sunthorn Phu, who produced scores of masterly love poems, travel accounts and narrative songs.

1782	1809–24	1824–51
A grandiose new capital, Bangkok, is established, modelled on Ayutthaya	The Chakri dynasty is consolidated with the reign of Rama II	Rama III's reign

In contrast, **Rama III** (1824–51) actively discouraged literary development – probably in reaction against his father – and was a vigorous defender of conservative values. To this end, he embarked on an extraordinary redevelopment of Wat Pho, the oldest temple in Bangkok. Hundreds of educational inscriptions and mural paintings, on all manner of secular and religious subjects, were put on show, apparently to preserve traditional culture against the rapid change which the king saw corroding the country. In foreign affairs, Rama III faced a serious threat from the vassal states of Laos, who in 1827 sent an invading army from Vientiane, which got as far as Saraburi, only three days' march from Bangkok. The king's response was savage: having repelled the initial invasion, he ordered his army to destroy everything in Vientiane apart from Buddhist temples and to forcibly resettle huge numbers of Lao in Isaan. In 1834, the king went to war in Cambodia, in a tug of war with Vietnam for control of the land in between; after fourteen years of indecisive warfare, Cambodia lay devastated but in much the same servile position – as one Vietnamese emperor described it, "an independent country that is slave of two".

More significant in the long run was the danger posed by the increase in Western influence that began in the Third Reign. As early as 1825, the Thais were sufficiently alarmed at British colonialism to strengthen Bangkok's defences by stretching a great iron chain across the mouth of the Chao Phraya River, to which every blacksmith in the area had to donate a certain number of links. In 1826 Rama III was obliged to sign a limited trade agreement with the British, the **Burney Treaty**, by which the Thais won some political security in return for reducing their taxes on goods passing through Bangkok. British and American missions in 1850 unsuccessfully demanded more radical concessions, but by this time Rama III was seriously ill, and it was left to his far-sighted and progressive successors to reach a decisive accommodation with the Western powers.

Mongkut and Chulalongkorn

Rama IV (1851–68), commonly known to foreigners as **Mongkut** (in Thai, *Phra Chom Klao*), had been a Buddhist monk for 27 years when he succeeded his brother. But far from leading a cloistered life, Mongkut had travelled widely throughout Thailand, had maintained scholarly contacts with French and American missionaries and, like most of the country's new generation of leaders, had taken an interest in Western learning, studying English, Latin and the sciences. He had also turned his mind to the condition of Buddhism in Thailand, which seemed to him to have descended into little more than popular superstition; indeed, after a study of the Buddhist scriptures in Pali, he was horrified to find that Thai ordinations were probably invalid. So in the late 1830s he set up the rigorously fundamentalist Thammayut sect (the "Order Adhering to the Teachings of the Buddha") and as abbot of the order he oversaw the training of a generation of scholarly leaders for Thai Buddhism from his base at Bangkok's Wat Bowonniwet, which became a major centre of Western learning and is still sponsored by the royal family.

When his kingship faced its first major test, in the form of a threatening British mission in 1855 led by **Sir John Bowring**, the Governor of Hong Kong, Mongkut dealt with it confidently. Realizing that Thailand was unable to resist the military might of

1826	1851–68	1855
The signing of the Burney Treaty, a trade agreement with Britain	Reign of Rama IV (Mongkut)	The Bowring mission exacts further trade concessions for the British

the British, the king reduced import and export taxes, allowed British subjects to live and own land in Thailand and granted them freedom of trade. Of the **government monopolies**, which had long been the mainstay of the Thai economy, only that on opium was retained. After making up the loss in revenue through internal taxation, Mongkut quickly made it known that he would welcome diplomatic contacts from other Western countries: within a decade, agreements similar to the Bowring Treaty had been signed with France, the US and a score of other nations. Thus by skilful diplomacy the king avoided a close relationship with only one power, which could easily have led to Thailand's annexation.

While all around the colonial powers were carving up Southeast Asia among themselves, Thailand suffered nothing more than the weakening of its influence over Cambodia, which in 1863 the French brought under their protection. As a result of the open-door policy, foreign trade boomed, financing the redevelopment of Bangkok's waterfront and, for the first time, the building of paved roads. However, Mongkut ran out of time for instituting the far-reaching domestic reforms which he saw were needed to drag Thailand into the modern world.

The modernization of Thailand

Mongkut's son, **Chulalongkorn**, took the throne as Rama V (1868–1910) at the age of only 15, but he was well prepared by an education which mixed traditional Thai and modern Western elements – provided by Mrs Anna Leonowens, subject of *The King and I*. When Chulalongkorn reached his majority after a five-year regency, he set to work on the reforms envisaged by his father. One of his first acts was to scrap the custom by which subjects were required to prostrate themselves in the presence of the king, which he followed up in 1874 with a series of decrees announcing the gradual abolition of slavery. The speed of his financial and administrative reforms, however, proved too much for the "**Ancients**" (*hua boran*), the old guard of ministers and officials inherited from his father. Their opposition culminated in the Front Palace Crisis of 1875, when a show of military strength almost plunged the country into civil war, and, although Chulalongkorn skilfully defused the crisis, many of his reforms had to be quietly shelved for the time being.

An important administrative reform that did go through, necessitated by the threat of colonial expansionism, concerned the former kingdom of Lanna. British exploitation of teak had recently spread into northern Thailand from neighbouring Burma, so in 1874 Chulalongkorn sent a commissioner to Chiang Mai to keep an eye on the prince of Chiang Mai and make sure that he avoided any collision with the British. The commissioner was gradually able to limit the power of the princes and to begin to integrate the region into the kingdom.

In the 1880s prospects for reform brightened as many of the "Ancients" died or retired. This allowed Chulalongkorn to **restructure the government** to meet the country's needs: the Royal Audit Office made possible the proper control of revenue and finance; the Department of the Army became the nucleus of a modern armed services; and a host of other departments was set up, for justice, education, public health and the like. To fill these new positions, the king appointed many of his younger brothers, who had all received a modern education, while scores of foreign technicians and advisers were brought in to help with everything from foreign affairs to rail lines.

1863	1868–1910	1874
The French bring Cambodia under their protection	Reign of Rama V (Chulalongkorn)	Beginning of the abolition of slavery in Thailand

Throughout this period, however, the Western powers maintained their pressure on the region. The most serious threat to Thai sovereignty was the **Franco–Siamese Crisis** of 1893, which culminated in the French, based in Vietnam, sending gunboats up the Chao Phraya River to Bangkok. Flouting numerous international laws, France claimed control over Laos and made other outrageous demands, which Chulalongkorn had no option but to concede. In 1907 Thailand was also forced to acknowledge French control over Cambodia, and in 1909 three Malay states fell to the British (while Thailand retained a fourth Muslim state, Pattani). In order to preserve its independence, the country ceded control over huge areas of tributary states and forwent huge sums of tax revenue. But from the end of the Fifth Reign, the frontiers were fixed as they are today.

By the time of the king's death in 1910, Thailand could not yet be called a modern nation-state – Bangkok still did not have complete control over the outermost regions, and corruption and nepotism were grave problems, for example. However, Chulalongkorn had made remarkable advances, and, almost from scratch, had established the political institutions to cope with twentieth-century development.

The end of absolute monarchy

Chulalongkorn was succeeded by a flamboyant, British-educated prince, **Vajiravudh**, who was crowned Rama VI (1910–25). The new king found it difficult to shake the dominance of his father's appointees in the government, who formed an extremely narrow elite, comprised almost entirely of members of Chulalongkorn's family. In an attempt to build up a personal following, Vajiravudh created, in May 1911, the **Wild Tigers**, a nationwide paramilitary corps recruited widely from the civil service. However, in 1912 a group of young army lieutenants, disillusioned by the absolute monarchy and upset at the downgrading of the regular army in favour of the Wild Tigers, plotted a **coup**. The conspirators were easily broken up before any trouble began, but this was something new in Thai history: the country was used to in-fighting among the royal family, but not to military intrigue from men from comparatively ordinary backgrounds.

Vajiravudh's response to the coup was a series of modernizing **reforms**, including the introduction of compulsory primary education and an attempt to better the status of women by supporting monogamy in place of the widespread practice of polygamy. His huge output of writings invariably encouraged people to live as modern Westerners, and he brought large numbers of commoners into high positions in government. Nonetheless, he would not relinquish his strong opposition to constitutional democracy.

When **World War I** broke out in 1914, the Thais were generally sympathetic to the Germans out of resentment over their loss of territory to the French and British. The king, however, was in favour of neutrality, until the US entered the war in 1917, when Thailand followed the expedient policy of joining the winning side and sent an expeditionary force of 1300 men to France in June 1918. The goodwill earned by this gesture enabled the Thais, between 1920 and 1926, to negotiate away the unequal treaties that had been imposed on them by the Western powers. Foreigners on Thai soil were no longer exempted from Thai laws, and the Thais were allowed to set reasonable rates of import and export taxes.

1893	1910–25	1912
Gunboats up the Chao Phraya: the Franco–Siamese Crisis obliges Thailand to give up its claims to Laos and Cambodia	Reign of Rama VI (Vajiravudh)	The first of many coup attempts in modern Thailand

Prajadhipok

Vajiravudh's extravagant lifestyle – during his reign, royal expenditure amounted to as much as ten percent of the state budget – left severe financial problems for his successor. Vajiravudh died without leaving a son, and as three better-placed contenders to the Crown all died in the 1920s, **Prajadhipok** – the seventy-sixth child and last son of Chulalongkorn – was catapulted to the throne as Rama VII (1925–35). Young and inexperienced, he responded to the country's crisis by creating a Supreme Council of State, seen by many as a return to Chulalongkorn's absolutist "government by princes".

Prajadhipok himself seems to have been in favour of constitutional government, but the weakness of his personality and the opposition of the old guard in the Supreme Council prevented him from introducing it. Meanwhile a vigorous community of Western-educated intellectuals had emerged in the lower echelons of the bureaucracy, who were increasingly dissatisfied with the injustices of monarchical government. The final shock to the Thai system came with the Great Depression, which from 1930 onwards ravaged the economy. On June 24, 1932, a small group of middle-ranking officials, led by a lawyer, Pridi Phanomyong, and an army major, Luang Phibunsongkhram, staged a **coup** with only a handful of troops. Prajadhipok weakly submitted to the conspirators, or "Promoters", and 150 years of absolute monarchy in Bangkok came to a sudden end. The king was sidelined to a position of symbolic significance and in 1935 he abdicated in favour of his 10-year-old nephew, **Ananda**, then a schoolboy living in Switzerland.

To the 1957 coup

The success of the 1932 coup was in large measure attributable to the army officers who gave the conspirators credibility, and it was they who were to dominate the constitutional regimes that followed. The Promoters' first worry was that the French or British might attempt to restore the monarchy to full power. To deflect such intervention, they appointed a government under a provisional constitution and espoused a wide range of liberal Western-type reforms, including freedom of the press and social equality, few of which ever saw the light of day.

The regime's first crisis came early in 1933 when **Pridi Phanomyong**, by now leader of the government's civilian faction, put forward a socialist economic plan based on the nationalization of land and labour. The proposal was denounced as communistic by the military, Pridi was forced into temporary exile and an anti-communist law was passed. Then, in October, a royalist coup was mounted which brought the kingdom close to civil war. After intense fighting, the rebels were defeated by Lieutenant-Colonel **Luang Phibunsongkhram** (or Phibun), so strengthening the government and bringing Phibun to the fore as the leading light of the military faction.

Pridi was rehabilitated in 1934 and remained powerful and popular, especially among the intelligentsia, but it was Phibun who became prime minister after the decisive **elections of 1938**, presiding over a cabinet dominated by military men. Phibun encouraged a wave of nationalistic feeling with such measures as the official institution of the name Thailand in 1939 – Siam, it was argued, was a name bestowed by external forces, and the new title made it clear that the country belonged to the Thais rather

1925–35	1932	1935–46
Reign of Rama VII (Prajadhipok)	A coup brings the end of the absolute monarchy and introduces Thailand's first constitution	Reign of Rama VIII (Ananda), mostly in absentia

than the economically dominant Chinese. This latter sentiment was reinforced with a series of harsh laws against the Chinese, who faced discriminatory taxes on income and commerce.

World War II

The outbreak of **World War II** gave the Thais the chance to avenge the humiliation of the 1893 Franco–Siamese Crisis. When France was occupied by Germany in June 1940, Phibun seized the opportunity to invade western Cambodia and the area of Laos lying to the west of the Mekong River. In the following year, however, the threat of a Japanese attack on Thailand loomed. On December 8, 1941, almost at the same time as the assault on Pearl Harbor, the Japanese invaded the country at nine points, most of them along the east coast of the peninsula. The Thais at first resisted fiercely, but realizing that the position was hopeless, Phibun quickly ordered a ceasefire. Meanwhile the British sent a force from Malaysia to try to stop the Japanese at Songkhla, but were held up in a fight with Thai border police. The Japanese had time to establish themselves, before pushing down the peninsula to take Singapore.

The Thai government concluded a military alliance with Japan and declared war against the US and Great Britain in January 1942, probably in the belief that the Japanese would win the war. However, the Thai minister in Washington, Seni Pramoj, refused to deliver the declaration of war against the US and, in cooperation with the Americans, began organizing a resistance movement called **Seri Thai**. Pridi, now acting as regent to the young king, furtively coordinated the movement under the noses of the occupying Japanese, smuggling in American agents and housing them in a European prison camp in Bangkok.

By 1944 Japan's final defeat looked likely, and Phibun, who had been most closely associated with them, was forced to resign by the National Assembly in July. A civilian, Khuang Aphaiwong, was chosen as prime minister, while Seri Thai became well established in the government under the control of Pridi. At the end of the war, Thailand was forced to restore the annexed Cambodian and Lao provinces to French Indochina, but American support prevented the British from imposing heavy punishments for the alliance with Japan.

Postwar upheavals

With the fading of the military, the election of January 1946 was for the first time contested by organized political parties, resulting in Pridi becoming prime minister. A new constitution was drafted and the outlook for democratic, civilian government seemed bright.

Hopes were shattered, however, on June 9, 1946, when King Ananda was found dead in his bed, with a bullet wound in his forehead. Three palace servants were tried and executed, but the murder has never been satisfactorily explained. Public opinion attached at least indirect responsibility for the killing to Pridi, who had in the past shown anti-royalist feeling. He resigned as prime minister, and in April 1948 the military made a decisive return: playing on the threat of communism, with Pridi pictured as a Red bogeyman, Phibun took over the premiership.

After the bloody suppression of two attempted coups in favour of Pridi, the main feature of Phibun's second regime was its heavy involvement with the US. As

1939	1941	1946
The country's name is changed from Siam to the more nationalistic Thailand	The Japanese invade, and Thailand forms an alliance with them	Rama VIII is mysteriously shot dead; the present king, Rama IX (Bhumibol), accedes

communism developed its hold in the region, with the takeover of China in 1949 and the French defeat in Indochina in 1954, the US increasingly viewed Thailand as a bulwark against the Red menace. Between 1951 and 1957, when its annual state budget was only about $200 million a year, Thailand received a total $149 million in American economic aid and $222 million in military aid. This strengthened Phibun's dictatorship, while enabling leading military figures to divert American money and other funds into their own pockets.

In 1955, his position threatened by two rival generals, Phibun experienced a sudden conversion to the cause of democracy. He narrowly won a general election in 1957, but only by blatant vote-rigging and coercion. Although there's a strong tradition of foul play in Thai elections, this is remembered as the dirtiest ever: after vehement public outcry, **General Sarit**, the commander-in-chief of the army, overthrew the new government in September 1957.

To the present day

Believing that Thailand would prosper best under a unifying authority – an ideology that still has plenty of supporters today – Sarit set about re-establishing the monarchy as the head of the social hierarchy and the source of legitimacy for the government. Ananda's successor, **King Bhumibol** (Rama IX), was pushed into an active role while Sarit ruthlessly silenced critics and pressed ahead with a plan for economic development. These policies achieved a large measure of stability and prosperity at home, although from 1960 onwards the international situation worsened. With the Marxist Pathet Lao making considerable advances in Laos, and Cambodia's ruler, Prince Sihanouk, drawing into closer relations with China, Sarit turned again to the US. The Americans obliged by sharply increasing military aid and by stationing troops in Thailand.

The Vietnam War

Sarit died in 1963, whereupon the military succession passed to **General Thanom**, closely aided by his deputy prime minister, **General Praphas**. Neither man had anything of Sarit's charisma and during a decade in power they followed his political philosophies largely unchanged. Their most pressing problem was the resumption of open hostilities between North and South Vietnam in the early 1960s – the **Vietnam War**. Both Laos and Cambodia became involved on the side of the communists by allowing the North Vietnamese to supply their troops in the south along the Ho Chi Minh Trail, which passed through southern Laos and northeastern Cambodia. The Thais, with the backing of the US, quietly began to conduct military operations in Laos, to which North Vietnam and China responded by supporting anti-government insurgency in Thailand.

The more the Thais felt threatened by the spread of communism, the more they looked to the Americans for help – by 1968 around 45,000 US military personnel were on Thai soil, which became the base for US bombing raids against North Vietnam and Laos, and for covert operations into Laos and beyond.

The effects of the **American presence in Thailand** were profound. The economy swelled with dollars, and hundreds of thousands of Thais became reliant on the Americans for a living, with a consequent proliferation of corruption and prostitution.

1957–63	1973	1976
Successful coup-maker and military strongman, General Sarit, brings Thailand ever closer to the US	Bloody student demonstrations bring the downfall of Sarit's successor, General Thanom	The brutal suppression of further student demos ushers the military back in

What's more, the sudden exposure to Western culture led many to question traditional Thai values and the political status quo.

The democracy movement and civil unrest

At the same time, poor farmers were becoming disillusioned with their lot, and during the 1960s many turned against the Bangkok government. At the end of 1964, the **Communist Party of Thailand** and other groups formed a **broad left coalition** that soon had the support of several thousand insurgents in remote areas of the northeast. By 1967, the problem had spread to Chiang Rai and Nan provinces, and a separate threat had arisen in southern Thailand, involving **Muslim dissidents** and the Chinese-dominated **Communist Party of Malaya**.

Thanom was now facing a major security crisis, especially as the war in Vietnam was going badly. In 1969 he held elections which produced a majority for the government party but, still worried about national stability, the general got cold feet. In November 1971 he reimposed repressive military rule, under a triumvirate of himself, his son Colonel Narong and Praphas, who became known as the "Three Tyrants". However, the 1969 experiment with democracy had heightened expectations of power-sharing among the middle classes, especially in the universities. **Student demonstrations** began in June 1973, and in October as many as 500,000 people turned out at Thammasat University in Bangkok to demand a new constitution. King Bhumibol intervened with apparent success, and indeed the demonstrators were starting to disperse on the morning of October 14, when the police tried to control the flow of people away. Tensions quickly mounted and soon a full-scale riot was under way, during which over 350 people were reported killed. The army, however, refused to provide enough troops to control the situation, and later the same day, Thanom, Narong and Praphas were forced to resign and leave the country.

In a new climate of openness, **Kukrit Pramoj** (see p.128) managed to form a coalition of seventeen elected parties and secured a promise of US withdrawal from Thailand, but his government was riven with feuding. Meanwhile, the king and much of the middle class, alarmed at the unchecked radicalism of the students, began to support new, often violent, right-wing organizations. In October 1976, the students demonstrated again, protesting against the return of Thanom to Thailand to become a monk at Wat Bowonniwet. Supported by elements of the military and the government, the police and reactionary students launched a massive assault on Thammasat University. On October 6, hundreds of students were brutally beaten, scores were lynched and some even burnt alive; the military took control and suspended the constitution.

General Prem

Soon after, the military-appointed prime minister, **Thanin Kraivichien**, imposed rigid censorship and forced dissidents to undergo anti-communist indoctrination, but his measures seem to have been too repressive even for the military, who forced him to resign in October 1977. General Kriangsak Chomanand took over, and began to break up the insurgency with shrewd offers of amnesty. His power base was weak, however, and although Kriangsak won the elections of 1979, he was displaced in February 1980 by **General Prem Tinsulanonda**, who was backed by a broad parliamentary coalition.

1980–88	1991	1992
Period of Premocracy, General Prem's hybrid of military rule and democracy	The military launch a coup, protesting the corruption of the recently democratically elected government	Mass demonstrations lead to bloodshed – and the return of democracy

Untainted by corruption, Prem achieved widespread support, including that of the monarchy. Parliamentary elections in 1983 returned the military to power and legitimized Prem's rule. Overseeing a period of strong foreign investment and rapid economic growth, the general maintained the premiership until 1988, with a unique mixture of dictatorship and democracy sometimes called **Premocracy**: although never standing for parliament himself, Prem was asked by the legislature after every election to become prime minister. He eventually stepped down (though he remains a powerful privy councillor and very close to the king) because, he said, it was time for the country's leader to be chosen from among its elected representatives.

The 1992 demonstrations and the 1997 constitution

The new prime minister was indeed an elected MP, **Chatichai Choonhavan**, a retired general with a long civilian career in public office. He pursued a vigorous policy of economic development, but this fostered widespread corruption, in which members of the government were often implicated. Following an economic downturn and Chatichai's attempts to downgrade the political role of the military, the armed forces staged a bloodless **coup** on February 23, 1991, led by Supreme Commander Sunthorn and General Suchinda, the army commander-in-chief, who became premier.

When Suchinda reneged on promises to make democratic amendments to the constitution, hundreds of thousands of ordinary Thais poured onto the streets around Bangkok's Democracy Monument in **mass demonstrations** between May 17 and 20, 1992. Hopelessly misjudging the mood of the country, Suchinda brutally crushed the protests, leaving hundreds dead or injured. Having justified the massacre on the grounds that he was protecting the king from communist agitators, Suchinda was forced to resign when King Bhumibol expressed his disapproval in a ticking-off that was broadcast on world television.

Elections were held in September, with the **Democrat Party**, led by Chuan Leekpai, a noted upholder of democracy and the rule of law, emerging victorious. Chuan was succeeded in turn by Banharn Silpa-archa – nicknamed by the local press "the walking ATM", a reference to his reputation for buying votes – and General Chavalit Yongchaiyudh. The most significant positive event of the latter's tenure was the approval of a **new constitution** in 1997. Drawn up by an independent drafting assembly, its main points included: direct elections to the senate, rather than appointment of senators by the prime minister; acceptance of the right of assembly as the basis of a democratic society and guarantees of individual rights and freedoms; greater public accountability; and increased popular participation in local administration. The eventual aim of the new charter was to end the traditional system of patronage, vested interests and vote buying.

Tom yam kung: the 1997 economic crisis

In February 1997 foreign-exchange dealers began to mount speculative attacks on the **baht**, alarmed at the size of Thailand's private foreign debt – 250 billion baht in the unproductive property sector alone, much of it accrued through the proliferation of prestigious skyscrapers in Bangkok. Chavalit's government defended the pegged exchange rate, spending $23 billion of the country's formerly healthy foreign-exchange reserves, but at the beginning of July was forced to give up the ghost – the baht was

1997	1997	2001
A landmark new constitution aims to end corruption and guarantee individual rights and freedoms	Tom yam kung: Thailand is ravaged by economic crisis	Thaksin Shinawatra, loved and hated in roughly equal measure, wins the general election

floated and soon went into freefall. Thailand was forced to seek help from the **IMF**, which in August put together a \$17-billion **rescue package**, coupled with severe austerity measures.

In November, the inept Chavalit was replaced by Chuan Leekpai, who immediately took a hard line in following the IMF's advice, which involved maintaining cripplingly high interest rates to protect the baht and slashing government budgets. Although this played well abroad, at home the government encountered increasing hostility from its newly impoverished citizens – the downturn struck with such speed and severity that it was dubbed the **tom yam kung crisis**, after the searingly hot Thai soup. Chuan's tough stance paid off, however, with the baht stabilizing and inflation falling back, and in October 1999 he announced that he was forgoing almost \$4 billion of the IMF's package.

Thaksin

The general election of January 2001 was the first to be held under the 1997 constitution, which was intended to take vote-buying out of politics. However, this election coincided with the emergence of a new party, **Thai Rak Thai** ("Thai Loves Thai"), formed by one of Thailand's wealthiest men, **Thaksin Shinawatra**, an ex-policeman who had made a personal fortune from government telecommunications concessions.

Thaksin duly won the election but, instead of moving towards greater democracy, as envisaged by the new constitution, he began to apply commercial and legal pressure, including several lawsuits, to try to silence critics in the media and parliament, and to manipulate the Senate and supposedly independent institutions such as the Election Commission to consolidate his own power. As his standing became more firmly entrenched, he rejected constitutional reforms designed to rein in his power – famously declaring that "democracy is only a tool" for achieving other goals.

Thaksin did, however, maintain his reputation for being a populist reformer by carrying through nearly all of his election promises. He issued a three-year loan moratorium for perennially indebted farmers and set up a one-million-baht development fund for each of the country's seventy thousand villages – though many villages just used the money as a lending tool to cover past debts, rather than creating productive projects for the future as intended. To improve public health access, a standard charge of B30 per hospital visit was introduced nationwide. However, too little was invested in the health service to cope with the increased demand that was generated.

Despite a sharp escalation of violence in the Islamic southern provinces in early 2004 (see p.705), Thaksin breezed through the February 2005 election, becoming the first prime minister in Thai history to win an outright majority at the polls but causing alarm among a wide spectrum of Thailand's elites. When Thaksin's relatives sold their shares in the family's Shin Corporation in January 2006 for £1.1 billion, without paying tax, tens of thousands of mostly middle-class Thais flocked to Bangkok to take part in protracted demonstrations, under the umbrella of the **People's Alliance for Democracy (PAD)**. After further allegations of corruption and cronyism, in September Thaksin, while on official business in the United States, was ousted by a military government in a **coup**.

2004	2006	2010	2011
The violence in the Islamic southern provinces sharply escalates	While in the US, Thaksin is ousted in a military coup and goes into exile	Red-shirted supporters of Thaksin set up a month-long protest camp in Bangkok, before being dispersed by force	Thaksin's sister, Yingluck, wins the general election with an outright majority

... and the spectre of Thaksin

Thaksin set up home in London, but his supporters, now the People's Power Party (PPP), won the December 2007 general election; its leader, Samak Sundaravej, an irascible TV chef, openly confessed to being a proxy for Thaksin. In response, the PAD – its nationalist and royalist credentials and its trademark **yellow shirts** (the colour of the king) now firmly established – restarted its mass protests, eventually occupying the government's offices for several months. Meanwhile, there was a merry-go-round of tribunals and court cases, including the conviction of Thaksin *in absentia* for corruption.

Matters came to a head in November and December 2008: the PAD seized and closed down Bangkok's Suvarnabhumi airport; the ruling People's Power Party was declared illegal by the courts, which persuaded the yellow shirts to lift their sit-in; and **Pheu Thai** (sometimes "Peua Thai"; meaning "For Thais"), the PPP's swift reincarnation, found itself unable to form a new coalition government. Instead, led by the Eton- and Oxford-educated **Abhisit Vejjajiva**, the Democrat Party jumped into bed with the Bhumjaithai Party, formerly staunch supporters of Thaksin, to take the helm.

This in turn prompted Thaksin's supporters – now **red-shirted** and organized into the **UDD** (United Front for Democracy against Dictatorship) – to hold mass protest meetings. In March 2009, Thaksin claimed by video broadcast that Privy Council President, Prem Tinsulanonda, had masterminded the 2006 coup and Abhisit's appointment as prime minister, and called for the overthrow of the *amat* (elite). In the following month, the red shirts forced the ASEAN (Association of Southeast Asian Nations) summit meeting in Pattaya to be embarrassingly abandoned and closed down central Bangkok for several days, before being dispersed by the army.

Amid a clampdown by the Democrat government on free speech, including heavy-handed use of the Computer Crimes Act and Article 112, the *lèse majesté* law, much more violent protests took place early the following year. Calling on Abhisit to hold new elections, thousands of red shirts set up a heavily defended camp around the **Ratchaprasong** intersection in central Bangkok in early April. On May 19, Abhisit sent in the army to break up the camp by force; altogether 91 people died on both sides in the two months of protests.

Mass popular support for Thaksin, however, did not wane, and in the general election of May 2011, Pheu Thai – now led by his younger sister, **Yingluck Shinawatra** – romped home with an absolute majority. At the time of writing, the main issues facing the government are what to do about the 2007 Constitution, which was imposed by the coup-makers – whether to amend it, or scrap it in favour of the 1997 Constitution; and how to engineer a pardon for Thaksin and bring him home. Intertwined with these are the failing health of the 84-year-old king – now the world's longest-running head of state – and the likely turmoil of the succession.

Religion: Thai Buddhism

Over 85 percent of Thais consider themselves Theravada Buddhists, followers of the teachings of a holy man usually referred to as the Buddha (Enlightened One), though more precisely known as Gautama Buddha to distinguish him from lesser-known Buddhas who preceded him. Theravada Buddhism is one of the two main schools of Buddhism practised in Asia, and in Thailand it has absorbed an eclectic assortment of animist and Hindu elements.

Islam is the biggest of the minority religions in Thailand, practised by between five and ten percent of the population. Most Muslims live in the south, especially in the deep-south provinces of Yala, Pattani and Narithiwat, along the Malaysian border, whose populations are over eighty percent Muslim. The separatist violence in this region (see p.705) has caused great tension between local Buddhist and Muslim communities, which have traditionally co-existed peacefully; it has not, however, obviously affected inter-faith relationships elsewhere in Thailand. The rest of the Thai population comprises Mahayana Buddhists, Hindus, Sikhs, Christians and animists.

The Buddha: his life and beliefs

Gautama Buddha was born as **Prince Gautama Siddhartha** in Nepal, in the seventh century BC according to the calculations for the Thai calendar, though scholars now think it may have been a century or two later. At his birth, astrologers predicted that he would become either a famous king or a celebrated holy man, depending on which path he chose. Much preferring the former, the prince's father forbade the boy from leaving the palace grounds, and set about educating Gautama in all aspects of the high life. Most statues of the Buddha depict him with elongated earlobes, which is a reference to this early pampered existence, when he would have worn heavy precious stones in his ears.

The prince married and became a father, but at the age of 29 he flouted his father's authority and sneaked out into the world beyond the palace. On this fateful trip he encountered successively an old man, a sick man, a corpse and a hermit, and thus for the first time was made aware that pain and suffering were intrinsic to human life. Contemplation seemed the only means of discovering why this was so – and therefore Gautama decided to leave the palace and become a **Hindu ascetic**.

For several years he wandered the countryside leading a life of self-denial and self-mortification, but failed to come any closer to the answer. Eventually concluding that the best course of action must be to follow a "Middle Way" – neither indulgent nor overly ascetic – Gautama sat down beneath the famous riverside bodhi tree at **Bodh Gaya** in India, facing the rising sun, to **meditate** until he achieved enlightenment. For 49 days he sat cross-legged in the "lotus position", contemplating the causes of suffering and wrestling with temptations that materialized to distract him. Most of these were sent by **Mara**, the Evil One, who was finally subdued when Gautama summoned the earth goddess **Mae Toranee** by pointing the fingers of his right hand at the ground – the gesture known as **Calling the Earth to Witness**, or *Bhumisparsa Mudra*, which has been immortalized by thousands of Thai sculptors. Mae Toranee wrung torrents of water from her hair and engulfed Mara's demonic emissaries in a flood, an episode that's also commonly reproduced, especially in temple murals.

Temptations dealt with, Gautama soon came to attain **enlightenment** and so become a Buddha. As the place of his enlightenment, the **bodhi tree** (*bodhi* means "enlightenment" in Sanskrit and Pali; it's sometimes also known as the bo tree, in Thai *ton po*) has assumed special significance for Buddhists: not only does it appear in many

Buddhist paintings, but there's often a real bodhi tree (*Ficus religiosa*, or sacred fig) planted in temple compounds as well. In addition, the bot is nearly always built facing either a body of water or facing east (preferably both).

The Buddha preached his **first sermon** in the deer park at Sarnath in India, where he characterized his doctrine, or **Dharma**, as a wheel. From this episode comes the early Buddhist symbol the **Dharmachakra**, known as the Wheel of Law, which is often accompanied by a statue of a deer. Thais celebrate this first sermon with a public holiday in July known as **Asanha Puja**. On another occasion 1250 people spontaneously gathered to hear the Buddha speak, an event remembered in Thailand as **Makha Puja** and marked by a public holiday in February.

For the next forty-odd years the Buddha travelled the region converting non believers and performing miracles. One rainy season he even ascended into the **Tavatimsa heaven** (Heaven of the 33 Gods) to visit his mother and to preach the doctrine to her. His descent from this heaven is quite a common theme of paintings and sculptures, and the **Standing Buddha** pose of numerous Buddha statues comes from this story.

The Buddha "died" at the age of eighty on the banks of a river at Kusinari in India – an event often dated to 543 BC, which is why the **Thai calendar** is 543 years out of synch with the Western one, so that the year 2013 AD becomes 2556 BE (Buddhist Era). Lying on his side, propping up his head on his hand, the Buddha passed into **Nirvana** (giving rise to another classic pose, the **Reclining Buddha**), the unimaginable state of nothingness which knows no suffering and from which there is no reincarnation. Buddhists believe that the day the Buddha entered Nirvana was the same date on which he was born and on which he achieved enlightenment, a triply significant day that Thais honour with the **Visakha Puja** festival in May.

Buddhists believe that Gautama Buddha was the five-hundredth incarnation of a single being: the stories of these five hundred lives, collectively known as the **Jataka**, provide the inspiration for much Thai art. Hindus also accept Gautama Buddha into their pantheon, perceiving him as the ninth manifestation of their god Vishnu.

The spread of Buddhism

After the Buddha entered Nirvana, his **doctrine** spread relatively quickly across India, and probably was first promulgated in Thailand in about the third century BC, when the Indian emperor Ashoka (in Thai, Asoke) sent out missionaries. His teachings, the *Tripitaka*, were written down in the Pali language – a then-vernacular derivative of Sanskrit – in a form that became known as **Theravada**, or "The Doctrine of the Elders".

By the beginning of the first millennium, a new movement called **Mahayana** (Great Vehicle) had emerged within the Theravada school, attempting to make Buddhism more accessible by introducing a pantheon of **bodhisattva**, or Buddhist saints, who, although they had achieved enlightenment, postponed entering Nirvana in order to inspire the populace. Mahayana Buddhism spread north into China, Korea, Vietnam and Japan, also entering southern Thailand via the Srivijayan empire around the eighth century and parts of Khmer Cambodia in about the eleventh century. Meanwhile Theravada Buddhism (which the Mahayanists disparagingly renamed "Hinayana" or "Lesser Vehicle") established itself most significantly in Sri Lanka, northern and central Thailand and Burma.

Buddhist doctrine and practice

Central to Theravada Buddhism is a belief in **karma** – broadly speaking, the belief that every action has a consequence – and **reincarnation**, along with an understanding that craving is at the root of human suffering. The ultimate aim for a Buddhist is to get off the cycle of perpetual reincarnation and suffering and to instead enter the blissful state of non-being that is **Nirvana**. This enlightened state can take many lifetimes to achieve so the more realistic goal for most is to be reborn slightly higher up the karmic ladder each time. As Thai Buddhists see it, animals are at the bottom of the karmic scale and monks at the top, with women on a lower rung than men.

Living a good life, specifically a life of "pure intention", creates good karma and Buddhist doctrine focuses a great deal on how to achieve this. Psychology and an understanding of human weaknesses play a big part. Key is the concept of *dukka* or **suffering**, which holds that craving is the root cause of all suffering or, to put it simplistically, human unhappiness is caused by the unquenchable dissatisfaction experienced when one's sensual, spiritual or material desires are not met. The concepts concerning suffering and craving are known as the **Four Noble Truths** of Buddhism. The route to enlightenment depends on a person being sufficiently detached from earthly desires so that *dukka* can't take hold. One acknowledges that the physical world is impermanent and ever changing, and that all things – including the self – are therefore not worth craving. A Buddhist works towards this realization by following the **Eightfold Path**, or **Middle Way**, that is by developing a set of highly moral personal qualities such as "right speech", "right action" and "right mindfulness". Meditation is particularly helpful in this.

A devout Thai Buddhist commits to the **five basic precepts**, namely not to kill or steal, to refrain from sexual misconduct and incorrect speech (lies, gossip and abuse) and to eschew intoxicating liquor and drugs. There are **three extra precepts** for special *wan phra* holy days and for those laypeople including foreign students who study meditation at Thai temples: no eating after noon, no entertainment (including TV and music) and no sleeping on a soft bed; in addition, the no-sexual-misconduct precept turns into no sex at all.

Making merit

Merit-making in popular Thai Buddhism has become slightly skewed, so that some people act on the assumption that they'll climb the karmic ladder faster if they make bigger and better offerings to the temple and its monks. However, it is of course the purity of the intention behind one's **merit-making** (*tham buun*) that's fundamental.

Merit can be made in many ways, from giving a monk his breakfast to attending a Buddhist service or donating money and gifts to the neighbourhood temple, and most **festivals** are essentially communal merit-making opportunities. Between the big festivals, the most common days for making merit and visiting the temple are **wan phra** (holy days), which are determined by the phase of the moon and occur four times a month. The simplest **offering** inside a temple consists of lotus buds, candles and three incense sticks (representing the three gems of Buddhism – the Buddha himself, the Dharma or doctrine, and the monkhood). One of the more bizarre but common merit-making activities involves **releasing caged birds**: worshippers buy tiny finches from vendors at wat compounds and, by liberating them from their cage, prove their Buddhist compassion towards all living things. The fact that the birds were free until netted earlier that morning doesn't seem to detract from the ritual. In riverside and seaside wats, fish or even baby turtles are released instead.

For an insightful introduction to the philosophy and practice of Thai Buddhism, see ⓦ thaibuddhism.net. A number of Thai temples welcome foreign students of Buddhism and meditation (see p.50).

The monkhood

It's the duty of Thailand's 200,000-strong **Sangha** (monkhood) to set an example to the Theravada Buddhist community by living a life as close to the Middle Way as possible and by preaching the Dharma to the people. The life of a monk (*bhikkhu*) is governed by 227 precepts that include celibacy and the rejection of all personal possessions except gifts.

Each day begins with an alms round in the neighbourhood so that the laity can donate food and thereby gain themselves merit, and then is chiefly spent in meditation, chanting, teaching and study. As the most respected members of any community, monks act as teachers, counsellors and arbiters in local disputes, and sometimes become spokesmen for villagers' rights. They also perform rituals at cremations, weddings and other events, such as the launching of a new business or even the purchase of a new car. Many young boys from poor families find themselves almost obliged to become either a *dek wat* (temple boy) or a **novice monk** because that's the only way they can get accommodation, food and, crucially, an education. This is provided free in exchange for duties around the wat, and novices are required to adhere to ten rather than 227 Buddhist precepts.

Monkhood doesn't have to be for life: a man may leave the Sangha three times without stigma and in fact every Thai male (including royalty) is expected to **enter the monkhood** for a short period, ideally between leaving school and marrying, as a rite of passage into adulthood. Thai government departments and some private companies grant their employees paid leave for their time as a monk, but the custom is in decline as young men increasingly have to consider the effect their absence may have on their career prospects. Instead, many men now enter the monkhood for a brief period after the death of a parent, to make merit both for the deceased and for the rest of the family. The most popular time for temporary ordination is the three-month Buddhist retreat period – **Pansa**, sometimes referred to as "Buddhist Lent" – which begins in July and lasts for the duration of the rainy season. (The monks' confinement is said to originate from the earliest years of Buddhist history, when farmers complained that perambulating monks were squashing their sprouting rice crops.)

Monks in contemporary society

Some monks extend their role as village spokesmen to become influential activists: Wat Tham Krabok near Lopburi and Wat Nong Sam Pran in Kanchanaburi are among a growing number of temples that have established themselves as successful drug rehabilitation centres; monks at Wat Phra Bat Nam Pu in Lopburi run a hospice for people with HIV/AIDS as well as a famously hard-hitting AIDS-awareness museum; monks at Wat Phai Lom near Bangkok have developed the country's largest breeding colony of Asian open-billed storks; and the monks at Wat Pa Luang Ta Bua Yannasampanno in Kanchanaburi (see p.203) have hit the headlines with their tiger sanctuary. Other monks, such as the famous octogenarian Luang Pho Khoon of Wat Ban Rai in Nakhon Ratchasima province, have acquired such a reputation for giving wise counsel and bringing good fortune to their followers that they have become national gurus and their temples now generate great wealth through the production of specially blessed amulets and photographs.

Though the increasing involvement of many monks in the secular world has not met with unanimous approval, far more disappointing to the laity are those monks who **flout the precepts** of the Sangha by succumbing to the temptations of a consumer society, flaunting Raybans, Rolexes and Mercedes (in some cases actually bought with temple funds), chain-smoking and flirting, even making pocket money from predicting lottery results and practising faith-healing. With so much national pride and integrity riding on the sanctity of the Sangha, any whiff of a deeper scandal is bound to strike deep into the national psyche. Cases of monks involved in drug dealing, gun running, even rape and murder have prompted a stream of editorials on the state of the Sangha and the collapse of spiritual values at the heart of Thai society. The inclusivity of the monkhood – which is open to just about any male who wants to join – has been highlighted as a particularly vulnerable aspect, not least because donning saffron robes has always been an accepted way for criminals, reformed or otherwise, to repent of their past deeds.

Interestingly, back in the late 1980s, the influential monk Phra Bodhirak (Photirak) was defrocked after criticizing what he saw as a tide of decadence infecting Thai Buddhism. He now preaches his ascetic code of anti-materialism through his breakaway **Santi Asoke** sect, famous across the country for its cheap vegetarian restaurants, its philosophy of self-sufficiency and for the simple blue farmers' shirts worn by many of its followers.

Women and the monkhood

Although the Theravada Buddhist hierarchy in some countries permits the ordination of **female monks**, or *bhikkhuni*, the Thai Sangha does not. Instead, Thai women are officially only allowed to become **nuns**, or *mae chii*, shaving their heads, donning white robes and keeping eight rather than 227 precepts. Their status is lower than that of the monks and they are chiefly occupied with temple upkeep rather than conducting religious ceremonies.

However, the progressives are becoming more vocal, and in 2002 a Thai woman became the first of several to break with the Buddhist authorities and get **ordained** as a novice *bhikkhuni* on Thai soil. Thailand's Sangha Council, however, still recognizes neither her ordination nor the temple, Watra Songdhammakalyani in Nakhon Pathom, where the ordination took place. The Watra (rather than Wat) is run by another Thai *bhikkhuni*, Dhammananda Bhikkhuni, the author of several books in English about **women and Buddhism** and of an informative website, ⑩ thaibhikkhunis.org.

Hindu deities and animist spirits

The complicated history of the area now known as Thailand has made Thai Buddhism a confusingly syncretic faith, as you'll realize when you enter a Buddhist temple compound to be confronted by a statue of a Hindu deity. While regular Buddhist merit-making insures a Thai for the next life, there are certain **Hindu gods and animist spirits** that many Thais – sophisticated Bangkokians and illiterate farmers alike – also cultivate for help with more immediate problems; and as often as not it's a Buddhist monk who is called in to exorcize a malevolent spirit. Even the Buddhist King Bhumibol employs Brahmin priests and astrologers to determine auspicious days and officiate at certain royal ceremonies, and, like his royal predecessors of the Chakri dynasty, he also associates himself with the Hindu god Vishnu by assuming the title Rama IX – Rama, hero of the Hindu epic the *Ramayana*, having been Vishnu's seventh manifestation on earth.

If a Thai wants help in achieving a short-term goal, like passing an exam, becoming pregnant or winning the lottery, he or she will quite likely turn to the **Hindu pantheon**, visiting an enshrined statue of Brahma, Vishnu, Shiva or Ganesh, and making offerings of flowers, incense and maybe food. If the outcome is favourable, the devotee will probably come back to show thanks, bringing more offerings and maybe even hiring a dance troupe to perform a celebratory *lakhon chatri*. Built in honour of Brahma, Bangkok's Erawan Shrine is the most famous place of Hindu-inspired worship in the country.

Spirits and spirit houses

Whereas Hindu deities tend to be benevolent, **spirits** (or *phi*) are not nearly as reliable and need to be mollified more frequently. They come in hundreds of varieties, some more malign than others, and inhabit everything from trees, rivers and caves to public buildings and private homes – even taking over people if they feel like it.

So that these *phi* don't pester human inhabitants, each building has a special **spirit house** (*saan phra phum*) in its vicinity, as a dwelling for spirits ousted by the building's construction. Usually raised on a short column to set it at or above eye level, the spirit house must occupy an auspicious location – not, for example, in the shadow of the main building. It's generally about the size of a dolls' house and designed to look like a wat or a traditional Thai house, but its ornamentation is supposed to reflect the status of the humans' building, so if that building is enlarged or refurbished, the spirit house should be improved accordingly. And as architects become increasingly bold in their designs, so modernist spirit houses are also beginning to appear, especially in Bangkok where an eye-catching new skyscraper might be graced by a spirit house of glass or polished concrete. **Figurines** representing the relevant guardian spirit and his aides are sometimes put inside, and daily offerings of incense, lighted candles and garlands of jasmine are placed alongside them to keep the *phi* happy – a disgruntled spirit is a dangerous spirit, liable to cause sickness, accidents and even death. As with any religious building or icon in Thailand, an unwanted or crumbling spirit house should never be dismantled or destroyed, which is why you'll often see damaged spirit houses placed around the base of a sacred banyan tree, where they are able to rest in peace.

Art and architecture

Aside from pockets of Hindu-inspired statuary and architecture, the vast majority of historical Thai culture takes its inspiration from Theravada Buddhism, and, though the country does have some excellent museums, to understand fully the evolution of Thai art you have to visit its temples. Artists, sculptors and architects have tended to see their work as a way of making spiritual merit rather than as a means of self-expression or self-promotion, so pre-twentieth-century Thai art history is all about evolving styles rather than individual artists. This section is designed to help make sense of the most common aspects of Thai art and architecture at their various stages of development.

The wat

Buddhist temple complexes, or **wats**, are central to nearly every community in Thailand and, as the main expressions of public architecture and art over the centuries, are likely to loom large in visitors' experiences of the country, too. Wat architecture has evolved in diverse ways, but the names and purposes of the main buildings have stayed constant in Thailand for some fifteen centuries.

Some **general design features** of Thai temples are also distinctive. The Khmers, who had ruled much of the country long before the Thais came onto the scene, built their temples to a cosmological plan, with concentric layers representing earth, oceans and heavens, rising to a central high point (Phanom Rung near Surin is a stunning example of this). Remnants of this layout persisted in Thai temples, including boundary walls – which are sometimes combined with a moat – and the multi-tiered roofs of so many wat buildings.

Furthermore, the Thais come from a tradition of building in wood rather than stone or brick, hence the leaning walls and long, curving roofs that give wats their elegant, tapering lines. On top of this, wat architects have long been preoccupied with light, the symbol of Buddhist wisdom and clarity, covering their buildings with gilt, filigree and vividly coloured glass mosaics.

The bot

The most important wat building is the **bot** (sometimes known as the *ubosot*), where monks are ordained. It usually stands at the heart of the compound, but lay people are rarely allowed inside. There's only one bot in any wat complex, and often the only way you'll be able to distinguish it from other temple buildings is by the eight **sema** or boundary stones which always surround it. Positioned at the four corners of the bot and at the cardinal points of the compass, these *sema* define the consecrated ground and usually look something like upright gravestones, though they can take many forms. They are often carved all over with symbolic Buddhist scenes or ideograms, and sometimes are even protected within miniature shrines of their own. One of the best *sema* collections is housed in the National Museum of Khon Kaen, in the northeast.

The viharn

Often almost identical in appearance to the bot, the **viharn** or assembly hall is the building you are most likely to enter, as it usually contains the wat's principal Buddha image, and sometimes two or three minor images as well. Large wats may have several viharns, while strict meditation wats, which don't deal with the laity, may not have one at all.

The chedi

Upon the Buddha's death, disciples from all over Asia laid claim to his relics, enshrining them in specially constructed towers, known as **chedis** in Thailand. In later centuries, chedis have also become repositories for the ashes of royalty or important monks – and anyone else who could afford to have one built. Each chedi's three main components reflect a traditional symbolism. In theory, the chedi base should be divided into three layers to represent hell, earth and heaven. Above this, the dome usually contains the cube-shaped reliquary, known as a *harmika* after the Sanskrit term for the Buddha's seat of meditation. Crowning the structure, the spire is graded into 33 rings, one for each of the 33 Buddhist heavens.

The mondop and ho trai

Less common wat buildings include the square **mondop**, usually built with a complex, cruciform roof, which houses either a Buddha statue or footprint, or holy texts. One of the most spectacular examples, with an ornate green-and-gold roof and huge doors encrusted with mother-of-pearl, shelters Thailand's holiest footprint of the Buddha, at Wat Phra Phutthabat near Lopburi.

The **ho trai**, or scripture library, is generally constructed on stilts, sometimes over a pond, to protect against termites and fire. You can see particularly good examples of traditional *ho trai* at Wat Rakhang in Bangkok, at Wat Phra Singh in Chiang Mai and at Wat Yai Suwannaram in Phetchaburi.

Buddhist iconography

In the early days of Buddhism, image-making was considered inadequate to convey the faith's abstract philosophies, so the only approved iconography comprised doctrinal **symbols** such as the *Dharmachakra* (Wheel of Law, also known as Wheel of Doctrine or Wheel of Life; see p.747). Gradually these symbols were displaced by **images of the Buddha**, construed chiefly as physical embodiments of the Buddha's teachings rather than as portraits of the man. Sculptors took their guidance from the Pali texts, which ordained the Buddha's most common postures (*asanha*) and gestures (*mudra*).

All three-dimensional Buddha images are objects of reverence, but some are more esteemed than others. Some are alleged to have reacted in a particular way to unusual events, others have performed miracles, or are simply admired for their beauty, their phenomenal size or even their material value – if made of solid gold or jade, for

---

POSTURES AND GESTURES OF THE BUDDHA

Of the **four postures** – sitting, standing, walking and reclining – the **seated Buddha**, which represents him in meditation, is the most common in Thailand. A popular variation shows the Buddha seated on a coiled serpent, protected by the serpent's hood: a reference to the story about the Buddha meditating during the rainy season, when a serpent offered to raise him off the wet ground and shelter him from the storms. The **reclining** pose symbolizes the Buddha entering Nirvana at his death, while the **standing** and **walking** images both represent his descent from heaven.

The most common **hand gestures** include:

Dhyana Mudra (Meditation), in which the hands rest on the lap, palms upwards.

Bhumisparsa Mudra (Calling the Earth to Witness, a reference to the Buddha resisting temptation), with the left hand upturned in the lap and the right-hand fingers resting on the right knee and pointing to the earth (see p.746).

Vitarkha Mudra (Teaching), with one or both hands held at chest height with the thumb and forefinger touching.

Abhaya Mudra (Dispelling Fear), showing the right hand (occasionally both hands) raised in a flat-palmed "stop" gesture.

example. Most Thais are familiar with these exceptional images, all of which have been given special names, always prefixed by the honorific "Phra", and many of which have spawned thousands of miniaturized copies in the form of amulets. Pilgrimages are made to see the most famous originals.

It was in the Sukhothai era that the craze for producing **Buddha footprints** really took off. Harking back to the time when images were allusive rather than representative, these footprints were generally moulded from stucco to depict the 108 auspicious signs or *lakshanas* (which included references to the sixteen Buddhist heavens, the traditional four great continents and seven great rivers and lakes) and housed in a special mondop. Few of the Sukhothai footprints remain, but Ayutthaya- and Ratanakosin-era examples are found all over the country, the most famous being Phra Phutthabat near Lopburi, the object of pilgrimages throughout the year. The feet of the famous Reclining Buddha in Bangkok's Wat Pho are also inscribed with the 108 *lakshanas*, beautifully depicted in mother-of-pearl inlay.

Hindu iconography

Hindu images tend to be a lot livelier than Buddhist ones; there are countless gods to choose from and many have mischievous personalities and multiple inventive incarnations. In Hindu philosophy any object can be viewed as the temporal residence, embodiment or symbol of the deity so you get abstract representations such as the phallic lingam (pillar) for Shiva, as well as figurative images. Though pure Hinduism receded from Thailand with the collapse of the Khmer empire, Buddhist Thais have incorporated some Hindu and Brahmin concepts into the national belief system and have continued to create statues of the three chief Hindu deities – Brahma, Vishnu and Shiva – as well as using many mythological creatures in modern designs.

The Hindu Trinity

Vishnu has always been a favourite: in his role of "Preserver" he embodies the status quo, representing both stability and the notion of altruistic love. He is most often depicted as the deity, but has ten manifestations in all, of which **Rama** (number seven) is by far the most popular in Thailand. The epitome of ideal manhood, Rama is the superhero of the epic story the *Ramayana* – in Thai, the *Ramakien* (see box, p.88) – and appears in storytelling reliefs and murals in every Hindu temple in Thailand; in painted portraits you can usually recognize him by his green face. Manifestation number eight is **Krishna**, more widely known than Rama in the West, but slightly less common in Thailand. Krishna is usually characterized as a flirtatious, flute-playing, blue-skinned cowherd, but he is also a crucial figure in the lengthy moral epic poem, the *Mahabharata*. Confusingly, Vishnu's ninth avatar is the **Buddha** – a manifestation adopted many centuries ago to minimize defection to the Buddhist faith. When represented as **the deity**, Vishnu is generally shown sporting a crown and four arms, his hands holding a conch shell (whose music wards off demons), a discus (used as a weapon), a club (symbolizing the power of nature and time), and a lotus (symbol of joyful flowering and renewal). He is often depicted astride a **garuda**, a half-man, half-bird. Even without Vishnu on its back, the garuda is a very important beast: a symbol of strength, it's often shown "supporting" temple buildings.

Statues and representations of **Brahma** (the Creator) are rare. He too has four arms, but holds no objects; he has four faces (sometimes painted red), is generally borne by a goose-like creature called a *hamsa*, and is associated with the direction north.

Shiva (the Destroyer) is the most volatile member of the pantheon. He stands for extreme behaviour, for beginnings and endings, as enacted in his frenzied Dance of Destruction, and for fertility, and is a symbol of great energy and power. His godlike form typically has four, eight or ten arms, sometimes holding a trident (representing creation, protection and destruction) and a drum (to beat the rhythm of creation).

In his most famous role, as **Nataraja**, or Lord of the Dance, he is usually shown in stylized standing position with legs bent into a balletic position, and the full complement of arms outstretched above his head. Three stripes on a figure's forehead also indicate Shiva, or one of his followers. In abstract form, he is represented by a **lingam** (once found at the heart of every Khmer temple in the northeast). Primarily a symbol of energy and godly power, the lingam also embodies fertility, particularly when set upright in a vulva-shaped vessel known as a **yoni**. The yoni doubles as a receptacle for the holy water that worshippers pour over the lingam.

Lesser gods

Close associates of Shiva include **Parvati**, his wife, and **Ganesh**, his elephant-headed son. As the god of knowledge and overcomer of obstacles (in the path of learning), Ganesh is used as the symbol of the Fine Arts Department, so his image features on all entrance tickets to national museums and historical parks.

The royal, three-headed elephant, **Erawan**, usually only appears as the favourite mount of the god **Indra**, the king of the gods, with specific power over the elements (particularly rain) and over the east. Other **Hindu gods of direction**, which are commonly found on the appropriate antefix in Khmer temples, include **Yama** on a buffalo (south); **Varuna** on a naga (mythical serpent) or a *hamsa* (west); Brahma (north); and **Isaana** on a bull (northeast).

Lesser mythological figures, which originated as Hindu symbols but feature frequently in wats and other Buddhist contexts, include the **yaksha** giants who ward off evil spirits (like the enormous freestanding ones guarding Bangkok's Wat Phra Kaeo); the graceful half-woman, half-bird **kinnari**; and the ubiquitous **naga**, or serpent king of the underworld, often with as many as seven heads, whose reptilian body most frequently appears as staircase balustrades in Hindu and Buddhist temples.

The schools

In the 1920s art historians and academics began compiling a classification system for Thai art and architecture that was modelled along the lines of the country's historical periods; these are the guidelines followed below. The following brief overview starts in the sixth century, when Buddhism began to take a hold on the country; few examples of art from before that time have survived, and there are no known, earlier architectural relics.

Dvaravati (sixth to eleventh centuries)

Centred around Nakhon Pathom, U Thong and Lopburi in the Chao Phraya basin and in the smaller northern enclave of Haripunjaya (modern-day Lamphun), the **Dvaravati** civilization was populated by Mon-speaking Theravada Buddhists who were strongly influenced by Indian culture.

The only known surviving Dvaravati-era **building** is the pyramidal laterite chedi at Lamphun's Wat Chama Thevi, but the national museums in Bangkok, Nakhon Pathom and Lamphun house quite extensive collections of Buddha **images** from that period. To make the best of the poor-quality limestone at their disposal, Dvaravati sculptors made their Buddhas quite stocky, cleverly dressing the figures in a sheet-like drape that dropped down to ankle level from each raised wrist, forming a U-shaped hemline – a style which they used when casting in bronze as well. Where the faces have survived, they are strikingly naturalistic, distinguished by their thick lips, flattened noses and wide cheekbones.

Nakhon Pathom, thought to have been a target of Buddhist missionaries from India since before the first century AD, has also yielded many **dharmachakra**, originating in the period when the Buddha could not be directly represented. These metre-high carved stone wheels symbolize the cycles of life and reincarnation, and in Dvaravati examples are often accompanied by a small statue of a deer, which refers to the Buddha preaching his first sermon in a deer park.

Srivijaya (eighth to thirteenth centuries)

While Dvaravati's Theravada Buddhists were influencing the central plains and, to a limited extent, areas further to the north, southern Thailand was paying allegiance to the Mahayana Buddhists of the **Srivijayan** civilization. Mahayanists believe that those who have achieved enlightenment – known as **bodhisattva** – should postpone their entry into Nirvana in order to help others along the way, and depictions of these saint-like beings were the mainstay of Srivijayan art.

The finest Srivijayan *bodhisattva* statues were cast in bronze and are among the most graceful and sinuous ever produced in Thailand. Many are lavishly adorned, and some were even bedecked in real jewels when first made. By far the most popular *bodhisattva* subject was **Avalokitesvara**, worshipped as compassion incarnate. Generally shown with four or more arms and with an animal skin over the left shoulder or tied at the waist, Avalokitesvara is also sometimes depicted with his torso covered in tiny Buddha images. Bangkok's National Museum holds the most beautiful Avalokitesvara, the Bodhisattva Padmapani found in Chaiya, but there's a good sandstone example *in situ* at Prasat Muang Singh near Kanchanaburi.

The most typical intact example of a Srivijayan **temple** is the heavily restored Javanese-style chedi at Chaiya's Wat Phra Boromathat, with its highly ornamented, stepped chedi featuring mini-chedis at each corner.

Khmer and Lopburi (tenth to fourteenth centuries)

By the end of the ninth century the **Khmers** of Cambodia were starting to expand from their capital at Angkor into the Dvaravati states, bringing with them the Hindu faith and the cult of the god-king (*devaraja*). They built hundreds of imposing stone **sanctuaries** across their newly acquired territory, most notably within southern Isaan, at Phimai, Phanom Rung and Khao Phra Viharn.

Each magnificent castle-temple – known in Khmer as a **prasat** – was constructed primarily as a shrine for a Shiva lingam, the phallic representation of the god Shiva. They followed a similar pattern, centred on at least one pyramidal or corn cob-shaped tower, or **prang**, which represented Mount Meru (the gods' heavenly abode) and housed the lingam. Prangs were surrounded by concentric rectangular **galleries**, whose **gopura** (entrance chambers) at the cardinal points were usually approached by staircases flanked with **naga balustrades**; in Khmer temples, nagas generally appear as symbolic bridges between the human world and that of the gods. Most compounds enclosed ponds between their outer and inner walls, and many were surrounded by a network of moats and **reservoirs**: historians attribute the Khmers' political success in part to their skill in designing highly efficient irrigation systems.

Exuberant **carvings** ornamented almost every surface of the prasat. Usually gouged from sandstone, but frequently moulded in stucco, they depict Hindu deities, incarnations and stories, especially episodes from the *Ramayana*. Towards the end of the twelfth century, the Khmer leadership became Mahayana Buddhist, commissioning Buddhist carvings to be installed alongside the Hindu ones, and often replacing the Shiva lingam with a Buddha or *bodhisattva* image.

The temples built in the former Theravada Buddhist principality of **Lopburi** during the Khmer period are much smaller than those in Isaan; the triple-pranged temple of Phra Prang Sam Yot is typical. Broad-faced and muscular, the classic Lopburi-era Buddha **statue** wears a diadem or ornamental headband – a nod to the Khmers' ideological fusion of earthly and heavenly power – and the *ushnisha* (the sign of enlightenment) becomes distinctly conical rather than a mere bump on the head. Early Lopburi Buddhas also come garlanded with necklaces and ornamental belts. As you'd expect, Lopburi National Museum houses a good selection.

Sukhothai (thirteenth to fifteenth centuries)

Capitalizing on the Khmers' weakening hold over central Thailand, two Thai generals established the first major Thai kingdom in **Sukhothai** in 1238, and over the next two hundred years its citizens produced some of Thailand's most refined art.

Sukhothai's artistic reputation rests above all on its **sculpture**. More sinuous even than the Srivijayan images, Sukhothai Buddhas tend towards elegant androgyny, with slim oval faces and slender curvaceous bodies usually clad in a plain, skintight robe that fastens with a tassel close to the navel. The sculptors favoured the seated pose, with hands in the *Bhumisparsa Mudra*, most expertly executed in the Phra Buddha Chinnarat image, now housed in Phitsanulok's Wat Si Ratana Mahathat (replicated at Bangkok's Wat Benjamabophit) and in the enormous Phra Sri Sakyamuni, now enshrined in Bangkok's Wat Suthat. They were also the first to represent the **walking Buddha**, a supremely graceful figure with his right leg poised to move forwards and his left arm in the *Vitarkha Mudra*, as seen at Sukhothai's Wat Sra Si.

Rather than pull down the sacred prangs of their predecessors, Sukhothai builders added bots, viharns and chedis to the existing structures, as well as conceiving quite separate **temple complexes**. Their viharns and bots are the earliest halls of worship still standing in Thailand (the Khmers didn't go in for large public assemblies), but in most cases only the stone pillars and their platforms remain, the wooden roofs having long since disintegrated. The best examples can be seen in the historical parks at Sukhothai, Si Satchanalai and Kamphaeng Phet.

Most of the **chedis** are in much better shape. Many were modelled on the Sri Lankan bell-shaped reliquary tower (symbolizing the Buddha's teachings ringing out far and wide), often set atop a one- or two-tiered square base surrounded by elephant buttresses; Si Satchanalai's Wat Chang Lom is a good example. The architects also devised the **lotus-bud chedi**, a slender tower topped with a tapered finial that was to become a hallmark of the Sukhothai era; in Sukhothai both Wat Mahathat and Wat Trapang Ngoen display classic examples.

Ancient Sukhothai is also renowned for the skill of its potters, who produced **ceramic ware** known as Sawankhalok, after the name of one of the nearby kiln towns. Most museum ceramics collections are dominated by Sawankhalok ware, which is distinguished by its grey-green celadon glazes and by the fish and chrysanthemum motifs used to decorate bowls and plates; there's a dedicated Sawankhalok museum in Sukhothai.

Lanna (thirteenth to sixteenth centuries)

Meanwhile, to the north of Sukhothai, the independent Theravada Buddhist kingdom of **Lanna** was flourishing. Its art styles – known interchangeably as **Chiang Saen** and Lanna – built on the Dvaravati heritage of Haripunjaya, copying direct from Indian sources and incorporating Sukhothai and Sri Lankan ideas from the south.

The earliest surviving Lanna **monument** is the Dvaravati-style Chedi Si Liam at Wiang Kum Kam near Chiang Mai, built to the pyramidal form characteristic of Mon builders. Also in Chiang Mai, Wat Jet Yot replicates the temple built at Bodh Gaya in India to commemorate the seven sites where the Buddha meditated in the first seven weeks after attaining enlightenment.

Lanna **sculpture** also drew some inspiration from Bodh Gaya, echoing the plumpness of the Buddha image, and its broad shoulders and prominent hair curls. The later works are slimmer, probably as a result of Sukhothai influence, and one of the most famous examples of this type is the Phra Singh Buddha, enshrined in Chiang Mai's Wat Phra Singh. Other good illustrations of both styles are housed in Chiang Mai's National Museum.

Ayutthaya (fourteenth to eighteenth centuries)

From 1351 Thailand's central plains came under the thrall of a new power centred on **Ayutthaya** and ruled by a former prince of Lopburi. Over the next four centuries, the Ayutthayan capital became one of the most prosperous and ostentatious cities in Asia, its rulers commissioning some four hundred grand wats as symbols of their wealth and power. Though essentially Theravada Buddhists, the kings also adopted some Hindu and Brahmin beliefs from the Khmers – most significantly the concept of *devaraja* or god-kingship, whereby the monarch became a mediator between the people and the Hindu gods. The religious buildings and sculptures of this era reflected this new composite ideology, both by fusing the architectural styles inherited from the Khmers and from Sukhothai and by dressing their Buddhas to look like regents.

Retaining the concentric layout of the typical Khmer **temple complex**, Ayutthayan builders refined and elongated the prang into a **corncob-shaped tower**, rounding it off at the top and introducing vertical incisions around its circumference. As a spire they often added a bronze thunderbolt, and into niches within the prang walls they placed Buddha images. In Ayutthaya itself, the ruined complexes of Wat Phra Mahathat and Wat Ratburana both include these corncob prangs, but the most famous example is Bangkok's Wat Arun, which though built during the subsequent Bangkok period is a classic Ayutthayan structure.

Ayutthaya's architects also adapted the Sri Lankan **chedi** favoured by their Sukhothai predecessors, stretching the bell-shaped base and tapering it into a very graceful conical spire, as at Wat Phra Si Sanphet in Ayutthaya. The **viharns** of this era are characterized by walls pierced by slit-like windows, designed to foster a mysterious atmosphere by limiting the amount of light inside the building. As with all of Ayutthaya's buildings, few viharns survived the brutal 1767 sacking, with the notable exception of Wat Na Phra Mane. Phitsanulok's Wat Phra Si Ratana Mahathat was built to a similar plan – and in Phetchaburi, Wat Yai Suwannaram has no windows at all.

From Sukhothai's Buddha **sculptures** the Ayutthayans copied the soft oval face, adding an earthlier demeanour to the features and imbuing them with a hauteur in tune with the *devaraja* ideology. Early Ayutthayan statues wear crowns to associate kingship with Buddhahood; as the court became ever more lavish, so these figures became increasingly adorned, until – as in the monumental bronze at Wat Na Phra Mane – they appeared in earrings, armlets, anklets, bandoliers and coronets. The artists justified these luscious portraits of the Buddha – who was, after all, supposed to have given up worldly possessions – by pointing to an episode when the Buddha transformed himself into a well-dressed nobleman to gain the ear of a proud emperor, whereupon he scolded the man into entering the monkhood.

While a couple of wats in Sukhothai show hints of painted decoration, religious **painting** in Thailand really dates from the Ayutthayan era. Unfortunately most of Ayutthaya's own paintings were destroyed in 1767, but several temples elsewhere have well-preserved murals, in particular Wat Yai Suwannaram in Phetchaburi. By all accounts typical of late seventeenth-century painting, the Phetchaburi murals depict rows of *thep*, or divinities, paying homage to the Buddha, in scenes presented without shadow or perspective, and mainly executed in dark reds and cream.

Ratanakosin (eighteenth century to the 1930s)

When **Bangkok** emerged as Ayutthaya's successor in 1782, the new capital's founder was determined to revive the old city's grandeur, and the **Ratanakosin** (or Bangkok) period began by aping what the Ayutthayans had done. Since then neither wat architecture nor religious sculpture has evolved much further.

The first Ratanakosin **building** was the bot of Bangkok's Wat Phra Kaeo, built to enshrine the Emerald Buddha. Designed to a typical Ayutthayan plan, it's coated in glittering mirrors and gold leaf, with roofs ranged in multiple tiers and tiled in green and orange. To this day, most newly built bots and viharns follow a more economical version of this paradigm, whitewashing the outside walls but decorating the pediment in gilded ornaments and mosaics of coloured glass. Tiered temple roofs still taper off into the slender bird-like finials called *chofa*, and naga staircases – a Khmer feature inherited by Ayutthaya – have become almost obligatory. The result is that modern wats are often almost indistinguishable from each other, though Bangkok does have a few exceptions, including Wat Benjamabophit, which uses marble cladding for its walls and incorporates Victorian-style stained-glass windows, and Wat Rajabophit, which is covered all over in Chinese ceramics. The most dramatic chedi of the Ratanokosin era was constructed in the mid-nineteenth century in Nakhon Pathom to the original Sri Lankan style, but minus the elephant buttresses found in Sukhothai.

Early Ratanakosin sculptors produced adorned **Buddha images** very much in the Ayutthayan vein. The obsession with size, first apparent in the Sukhothai period, has since plumbed new depths, with graceless concrete statues up to 60m high becoming the norm, often painted brown or a dull yellow. Most small images are cast from or patterned on older models, mostly Sukhothai or Ayutthayan in origin.

Painting has fared much better, with the *Ramayana* murals in Bangkok's Wat Phra Kaeo a shining example of how Ayutthayan techniques and traditional subject matters could be adapted into something fantastic, imaginative and beautiful.

Contemporary

Following the democratization of Thailand in the 1930s, artists increasingly became recognized as individuals, and took to signing their work for the first time. In 1933 the first school of fine art (now Bangkok's Silpakorn University) was established under the Italian sculptor **Corrado Feroci** (later Silpa Bhirasri), designer of the capital's Democracy Monument and, as the new generation experimented with secular themes and styles adapted from the West, Thai art began to look a lot more "**modern**". As for subject matter, the leading artistic preoccupation of the past eighty years has been Thailand's spiritual heritage and its role in contemporary society. Since 1985, a number of Thailand's more established contemporary artists have earned the title **National Artist**, an honour that's bestowed annually on notable artists working in all disciplines, including fine art, performing arts, film and literature.

The artists

One of the first modern artists to adapt traditional styles and themes was **Angkarn Kalayanapongsa** (b. 1926), an early recipient of the title National Artist. He has been employed as a temple muralist and many of his paintings, some of which are on show in Bangkok's National Gallery, reflect this experience, typically featuring casts of two-dimensional Ayutthayan-style figures and flying *thep* in a surreal setting laced with Buddhist symbols and nods to contemporary culture.

Taking this fusion a step further, one-time cinema billboard artist, now National Artist **Chalermchai Kositpipat** (b. 1955) specializes in temple murals with a modern, controversial, twist. Outside Thailand his most famous work enlivens the interior walls of London's Wat Buddhapadipa with strong colours and startling imagery. At home his latest project is the unconventional and highly ornate all-white Wat Rong Khun in his native Chiang Rai province (see p.360).

ART GALLERIES AND EXHIBITIONS

Bangkok has a near-monopoly on Thailand's **art galleries**. While the permanent collections at the capital's National Gallery (see p.98) are disappointing, regular exhibitions of more challenging contemporary work appear at the huge, ambitious **Bangkok Art and Cultural Centre** (see p.122); the main art school, Silpakorn University Art Centre (see p.95); the Queen's Gallery (see p.106); and at smaller gallery spaces around the city. The excellent monthly *Bangkok Art Map* (Ⓦbangkokartmap.com), an annotated map of the capital's galleries, carries exhibition listings and is available free from galleries. Large-scale art museums in the provinces include the Contemporary Thai Art Centre, part of Silpakorn University's secondary campus in Nakhon Pathom (see p.182), and Chiang Mai University Art Museum (see p.287). For a preview of works by Thailand's best modern artists, visit the virtual Rama IX Art Museum at Ⓦrama9art.org.

Aiming for the more secular environments of the gallery and the private home, National Artist **Pichai Nirand** (b. 1936) rejects the traditional mural style and makes more selective choices of Buddhist imagery, appropriating religious objects and icons and reinterpreting their significance. He's particularly well known for his fine-detail canvases of Buddha footprints, many of which can be seen in Bangkok galleries and public spaces.

Pratuang Emjaroen (b. 1935) is famous for his social commentary, as epitomized by his huge and powerful canvas *Dharma and Adharma; The Days of Disaster*, which he painted in response to the vicious clashes between the military and students in 1973. The 5m x 2m picture depicts severed limbs, screaming faces and bloody gun barrels amid shadowy images of the Buddha's face, a spiked *dharmachakra* and other religious symbols.

Prolific traditionalist **Chakrabhand Posayakrit** (b. 1943) is also inspired by Thailand's Buddhist culture; he is famously proud of his country's cultural heritage, which infuses much of his work and has led to him being honoured as a National Artist. He is best known for his series of 33 *Life of the Buddha* paintings, and for his portraits, including many depicting members of the Thai royal family.

More controversial, and more of a household name, **Thawan Duchanee** (b. 1939) has tended to examine the spiritual tensions of modern life. His surreal juxtaposition of religious icons with fantastical Bosch-like characters and explicitly sexual images prompted a group of outraged students to slash ten of his early paintings in 1971 – an unprecedented reaction to a work of Thai art. Since then, Thawan has continued to produce allegorical investigations into the individual's struggles against the obstacles that dog the Middle Way, prominent among them lust and violence, but since the 1980s his street cred has waned as his saleability has mushroomed.

Complacency is not a criticism that could be levelled at **Vasan Sitthiket** (b. 1957), one of Thailand's most outspoken and iconoclastic artists, whose uncompromising pictures are shown at – and still occasionally banned from – large and small galleries around the capital. A persistent crusader against the hypocrisies of establishment figures such as monks, politicians, CEOs and military leaders, Vasan's is one of the loudest and most aggressive political voices on the contemporary art scene, expressed on canvas, in multimedia works and in performance art. His significance is well established and he was one of the seven artists to represent Thailand at the 2003 Venice Biennale, where Thailand had its own pavilion for the first time.

Equally confrontational is fellow Biennale exhibitor, the photographer, performance artist and social activist **Manit Sriwanichpoom** (b. 1961). Manit is best known for his "Pink Man" series of photographs in which he places a Thai man (his collaborator Sompong Thawee), dressed in a flashy pink suit and pushing a pink shopping trolley, into different scenes and situations in Thailand and elsewhere. The Pink Man represents thoughtless, dangerous consumerism and his backdrop might be an impoverished hill-tribe village (*Pink Man on Tour*; 1998), or black-and-white shots from the political violence of 1973, 1976 and 1992 (*Horror in Pink*; 2001).

Women artists tend to be less high profile in Thailand, but in 2007 **Pinaree Sanpitak** (b. 1961) became the first female recipient of the annual Silpathorn Awards for established artists. Pinaree is known for her interest in gender issues and for her recurrent use of a female iconography in the form of vessels and mounds, often exploring the overlap with Buddhist stupa imagery. She works mainly in multimedia; her "Vessels and Mounds" show of 2001, for example, featured installations of huge, breast-shaped floor cushions, candles and bowls.

Among the younger faces on the Thai art scene, **Thaweesak Srithongdee** (b. 1970) blends surrealism and pop culture with the erotic and the figurative, to cartoonlike effect. He is preoccupied with popular culture, as is **Jirapat Tatsanasomboon** (b. 1971), whose work plays around with superheroes and cultural icons from East and West, pitting the *Ramayana*'s monkey king, Hanuman, against Spiderman in *Hanuman vs Spiderman*, and fusing mythologies in *The Transformation of Sita (after Botticelli)*.

Flora, fauna and environmental issues

Spanning some 1650km north to south, Thailand lies in the heart of Southeast Asia's tropical zone, its northernmost region just a few degrees south of the Tropic of Cancer, its southern border running less than seven degrees north of the Equator. As with other tropical regions, Thailand's climate is characterized by high humidity and even higher temperatures, a fertile combination which nourishes a huge diversity of flora and fauna in a vast range of habitats, from mixed deciduous and dry dipterocarp forests in the mountainous north to wet tropical rainforests in the steamy south. At least six percent of the world's vascular plants are found here, with over fifteen thousand species so far recorded.

The best places to appreciate Thailand's biodiversity are its national parks, the most accessible of which include Khao Yai in the northeast, Doi Inthanon and Doi Suthep in the north, and Khao Sam Roi Yot, Khao Sok and Ko Tarutao in the south. General practical information on national parks is given in Basics (see p.53).

The geography of Thailand

Thailand has a **tropical monsoon climate**. Most rain is brought from the Indian Ocean by the southwest monsoon from May to October, the so-called rainy season. From November to February the northeast monsoon brings a much cooler and drier climate from China: the cold, dry season. However, this northeastern monsoon hits the peninsular east coast after crossing the South China Sea, loading up with moist air and therefore bringing this region's rainiest season in November.

Agriculture plays a significant role in Thailand's economy, and some forty percent of Thais live off the land or the sea. Waterlogged rice paddies characterize the central plains; cassava, tapioca and eucalyptus are grown as cash crops on the scrubby plateau of the northeast; and rubber and palm-oil plantations dominate the commercial land use of the south. Dotted along Thailand's coastline are mangrove swamps and palm forests.

Mixed deciduous and dry dipterocarp forests

An estimated 65 percent of Thailand's forests are **deciduous**, sometimes referred to as monsoon forest because they have to survive periods of up to six months with minimal rainfall, so the trees shed their leaves to conserve water. Deciduous forests are often light and open, with canopies of 10–40m and dense undergrowth. They are dominated by trees of the **Dipterocarpaceae** family, a group of tropical hardwoods prized for their timber and, in places, their resin. **Teak** was also once common in northern deciduous forests, but its solid, unwarpable timber is so sought after that nearly all the teak forests have been felled. Since teak trees take around two hundred years to mature, logging them was banned in Thailand in 1989 and these days most of Thailand's teak comes in from Burma.

Bamboo thrives in a monsoon climate, shooting up at a remarkable rate during the wet season, usually in soils too poor for other species; it often predominates in secondary forests, where logging or clearing has previously taken place. The smooth, hollow stem characteristic of all varieties of bamboo is a fantastically adaptable material, used by the Thais for constructing everything from outside walls to chairs to water pipes (in hill-tribe villages) and musical instruments; and the bamboo shoot is common in Thai–Chinese cuisine.

Tropical rainforests

Thailand's **tropical rainforests** occur in areas of high and prolonged rainfall in the southern peninsula, most accessibly in the national parks of Khao Sok, Tarutao and Khao Luang. Some areas contain as many as two hundred species of tree within a single hectare. Characteristic of a tropical rainforest is the multi-layered series of **canopies**. The uppermost storey sometimes reaches 60m, and these towering trees often have enormous buttressed roots for support; beneath this, the dense canopy of 25–35m is often festooned with climbers and epiphytes such as ferns, lianas, mosses and orchids; then comes an uneven layer 5–10m high consisting of palms, rattans, shrubs and small trees. The forest floor in tropical rainforests tends to be relatively open and free of dense undergrowth, owing to the intense filtering of light by the upper three layers. Again, members of the *Dipterocarpaceae* family are dominant, playing an important role as nesting sites for hornbills, as lookout posts for gibbons – and as timber.

Semi-evergreen and montane forests

Semi-evergreen forests are the halfway house between tropical rainforests and dry deciduous forests and include all lowland and submontane evergreen forests from the plains to about 1000m. They thrive in regions with distinctly seasonal rainfall and fine examples can be found at Khao Yai and Kaeng Krachan national parks, and all along the Burmese border, all of which are potentially good places to observe large mammals, including elephants, gaurs, tigers and bears.

Above 1000m, the canopy of tall trees gives way to hardy **evergreen montane forest** growth such as oaks, chestnuts and laurels, many with twisted trunks and comparatively small leaves. Frequent rainfall means plenty of moss and a dense undergrowth of epiphytes, rhododendrons and tree ferns. Good examples can be seen in Doi Inthanon and Phu Kradung national parks, and in parts of Doi Suthep and Khao Yai national parks.

Mangrove swamps and coastal forests

Mangrove swamps are an important habitat for a wide variety of marine life (including two hundred species of bird, seventy species of fish and fifty types of crab) but, as with much of Thailand's inland forest, they have been significantly degraded by encroachment and large-scale prawn farming. Huge swathes of Thailand's littoral used to be fringed with mangrove swamps, but now they are mainly found only along the west peninsular coast, between Ranong and Satun, though Chanthaburi's Ao Khung Kraben is a notable east-coast exception. On Phuket, the Thachatchai Nature Trail leads you on a guided tour through a patch of mangrove swamp, but an even better way of **exploring the swamps** is to paddle a kayak through the mangrove-clogged inlets and island-lagoons of Ao Phang Nga. Not only do mangrove swamps harbour a rich and important ecosystem of their own, but they also help prevent coastal erosion; in certain areas of the tsunami-hit Andaman coast intact mangrove forest absorbed some of the waves' impact, protecting land and homes from even worse damage.

Nipa palms share the mangrove's penchant for brackish water, and these stubby-stemmed palm trees grow in abundance in the south, though commercial plantations are now replacing the natural colonies. Like most other species of palm indigenous to Thailand, the nipa is a versatile plant that's exploited to the full: alcohol is distilled from its sugary sap, and its fronds are woven into roofs (especially for beach huts and village homes), sticky-rice baskets and chair-backs.

The hardy **coconut palm** is also very tolerant of salty, sandy soil, and is equally useful. On islands such as Ko Kood, it's the backbone of the local economy, with millions of coconuts harvested every month for their milk, their oil-producing meat (copra), and their fibrous husks or coir (used for making ropes, matting, brushes and mattress stuffing); the palm fronds are woven into roof thatching and baskets, and the wood has an attractive grain.

Casuarinas (also known as she-oaks or ironwoods) also flourish in sandy soils and are common on beaches throughout Thailand; fast-growing and tall (up to 20m), they are quite often planted as wind breaks. Though its feathery profile makes it look like a pine, it's actually made up of tiny twigs, not needles.

The wildlife

Thailand lies in an exceptionally rich "transition zone" of the Indo-Malayan realm, its forests, mountains and national parks attracting wildlife from both Indochina and Indonesia. In all, Thailand is home to three hundred species of mammal (37 of which are considered to be endangered or vulnerable), while 982 species of bird have been recorded here (49 of them globally threatened).

Mammals

In the major national parks such as Khao Yai, Doi Inthanon and Khao Sok, the animals you're most likely to encounter are **primates**, particularly macaques and gibbons. The latter spend much of their time foraging for food in the forest canopy, while the former often descend closer to the ground to rest and to socialize.

The gibbons are responsible for the distinctive hooting that echoes through the forests. Chief noise-maker is the **white-handed** or **lar gibbon**, a beige- or black-bodied, white-faced animal whose cute appearance, intelligence and dexterity unfortunately make it a popular pet. The poaching and maltreatment of lar gibbons has become so severe that several organizations are now dedicated to protecting them (see box, p.767).

Similarly chatty, macaques hang out in gangs of twenty or more. The **long-tailed** or **crab-eating macaque** lives in the lowlands, near rivers, lakes and coasts as at Ao Phang Nga, Krabi, Ko Tarutao, Ang Thong and Khao Sam Roi Yot. It eats not only crabs, but mussels, other small animals and fruit, transporting and storing food in its big cheek pouch when swimming and diving. The **pig-tailed macaque**, named after its short curly tail, excels at scaling the tall trees of Erawan, Khao Yai, Doi Inthanon and other national parks, a skill which has resulted in many of the males being captured and trained to pick coconuts.

Much more elusive is the **Indochinese tiger**, which lives under constant threat from both poachers and the destruction of its habitat by logging interests, which together have reduced the current population to probably fewer than one hundred; for now Khao Yai and Khao Sok are the two likeliest places for sightings. The medium-sized arboreal **clouded leopard** is also on the endangered list, and is hard to spot anyway as it only comes out to feed on birds and monkeys under cover of darkness, rarely venturing out in moonlight, let alone daylight.

The shy, nocturnal **tapir**, an ungulate with three-toed hind legs and four-toed front ones, lives deep in the forest of peninsular Thailand but is occasionally spotted in daylight. A relative of both the horse and the rhino, it's the size of a pony, with a stubby trunk-like snout and distinctive two-tone colouring to confuse predators: its front half and all four legs are black, its rear half is white.

It's thought there are now as few as two thousand wild **elephants** left in Thailand: small-eared Asian elephants found mainly in Khao Yai and Khao Sok (see box, p.318).

Birds

Because of its location at the zoogeographical crossroads of Southeast Asia, Thailand boasts a huge diversity of **bird** species. The forests of continental Thailand are home to many of the same birds that inhabit India, Burma and Indochina, while the mountains of the north share species with the Himalayas and Tibet, and the peninsular forests are

THE GECKO

Whether you're staying on a beach, in a national park or in a town, chances are you'll be sharing your room with a few **geckos**. These pale green tropical lizards, which are harmless to humans and usually measure a cute four to ten centimetres in length, mostly appear at night, high up on walls and ceilings, where they feed on insects. Because the undersides of their flat toes are covered with hundreds of microscopic hairs that catch at the tiniest of irregularities, geckos are able to scale almost any surface, including glass, which is why you usually see them in strange, gravity-defying positions. The largest and most vociferous gecko is known as the **tokay** in Thai, named after the disconcertingly loud sound it makes. *Tokays* can grow to an alarming 35cm, but are welcomed by most householders, as they devour insects and mice; Thais also consider it auspicious if a baby is born within earshot of a crowing *tokay*.

home to birds found also in Malaysia and Indonesia. Khao Yai and Khao Nor Chuchi are prime year-round sites for bird-spotting, and, during the dry season, Doi Inthanon is a good place for flycatchers and warblers, while Khao Sam Roi Yot and Thale Noi Waterbird Park are rewarding areas to see migrant waders and waterfowl. For exhaustive information on specific **bird-watching** locations throughout Thailand see ⓦ thaibirding.com; for guided birding tours contact Thailand Bird Watching (ⓦ thailandbirdwatching.com); bird-watching guidebooks are listed in Books (see p.788).

There are twelve species of **hornbill** in Thailand, all majestic with massive, powerful wings (the flapping of which can be heard for long distances) and huge beaks surmounted by bizarre horny casques. Khao Yai is one of the easiest places to spot the plain black-and-white **oriental pied hornbill** and the flashier **great hornbill**, whose monochromic body and head are broken up with jaunty splashes of yellow; the little islands of Ko Phayam and Ko Chang in Ranong province also have many resident oriental pied hornbills.

The shyness of the gorgeous **pitta** makes a sighting all the more rewarding. Usually seen hopping around on the floor of evergreen forests, especially in Doi Inthanon, Doi Suthep and Khao Yai, these plump little birds – varieties of which include the **rusty-naped**, the **blue** and the **eared** – have dazzling markings in iridescent reds, yellows, blues and blacks. The one pitta you might see outside a rainforest is the **blue-winged** pitta, which occasionally migrates to drier bamboo forests. Thailand is also home to the extremely rare **Gurney's pitta**, found only in Khlong Thom National Park, in Krabi province.

Members of the pheasant family can be just as shy as the pittas, and are similarly striking. The black-and-white-chevron-marked **silver pheasant**, and the **green peafowl** are particularly fine birds, and the commonly seen **red jungle fowl** is the ancestor to all domestic chickens.

Thailand's **rice fields** attract a host of different birds including the various species of **munia**, a chubby relative of the finch, whose chunky, conical beak is ideally suited to cracking unripened rice seeds. **Egrets** and **herons** also frequent the fields, wading through the waterlogged furrows or perching on the backs of water buffaloes and pecking at cattle insects, while from November to April, thousands of **Asian open-billed storks** descend on agricultural land as well, building nests in sugar-palm trees and bamboos and feeding on pira snails.

Coastal areas also attract storks, egrets and herons, and Thale Noi Waterbird Park and the mud flats of Khao Sam Roi Yot are breeding grounds for the large, long-necked **purple heron**. The magnificent **white-bellied sea eagle** haunts the Thai coast, nesting in the forbidding crags around Krabi, Ao Phang Nga and Ko Tarutao and preying on fish and sea snakes. The tiny **edible nest swiftlet** makes its eponymous nest – the major ingredient of the luxury food, bird's-nest soup – in the limestone crags, too (see box, p.680).

Snakes

Thailand is home to around 175 different species and subspecies of **snake**, 56 of them dangerously venomous. Death by snakebite is not common, however, but all hospitals should keep a stock of serum, produced at the Snake Farm in Bangkok (see p.125).

Found everywhere and highly venomous, the 2m, nocturnal, yellow-and-black-striped **banded krait** is one to avoid, as is the shorter but equally venomous **Thai** or **monocled cobra**, which lurks in low-lying humid areas and close to human habitation and sports a distinctive "eye" mark on its hood. The other most widespread venomous snake is the 60cm **Malayan pit viper**, which has an unnerving ability to camouflage its pinky-brown and black-marked body. Non-venomous, but typically measuring an amazing 7.5m (maximum 10m) and with a top weight of 140kg, the **reticulated python** frequents human habitation all over Thailand and feeds on rats, pigs, cats and dogs, strangling them to death; it will do the same to humans if provoked.

Marine species

The Indian Ocean (Andaman Sea) and the South China Sea (Gulf of Thailand) together play host to over 850 species of open-water fish, more than one hundred species of reef fish and some 250 species of hard coral. Forty percent of Thailand's coral reef is protected within **national marine parks**, and these offer the best snorkelling and diving, particularly around Ko Similan, Ko Surin and Ko Tarutao (see p.52).

Coral

Coral reefs are living organisms composed of a huge variety of marine life forms, but the foundation of every reef is its ostensibly inanimate **stony coral** – hard constructions such as boulder, mushroom, bushy staghorn and brain coral. Stony coral is composed of colonies of polyps – minuscule invertebrates which feed on plankton, depend on algae and direct sunlight for photosynthesis, and extract calcium carbonate (limestone) from sea water in order to reproduce. The polyps use this calcium carbonate to build new skeletons outside their bodies (an asexual reproductive process known as budding), and this is how a reef is formed. It's an extraordinarily slow process, with colony growth averaging somewhere between 5mm and 30mm a year.

The fleshy plant-like **soft coral**, such as dead man's fingers and elephant's ear, generally establishes itself on and around these banks of stony coral, swaying with the currents and using tentacles to trap microorganisms. Soft coral is also composed of polyps, but a variety with flaccid internal skeletons built from protein rather than calcium. **Horny coral**, like sea whips and intricate sea fans, looks like a cross between the stony and the soft varieties, while **sea anemones** have the most obvious, and venomous, tentacles of any member of the coral family, using them to trap fish and other large prey.

Fish and turtles

The algae and plankton that accumulate around coral colonies attract a huge variety of **reef fish**. Most are small in stature, with vibrant colours that serve as camouflage against the coral, and flattened bodies and broad tails for easy manoeuvring around the reef.

Among the most easily recognizable is the **emperor angel fish**, which boasts spectacular horizontal stripes in bright blue and orange, and an orange tail. The bizarrely shaped **moorish idol** trails a pennant fin from its dorsal fin and has a pronounced snout and dramatic black, yellow and white bands of colour; the ovoid **powder-blue surgeon fish** has a light blue body, a bright yellow dorsal fin and a white "chinstrap". The commonly spotted **long-nosed butterfly fish** is named for the butterfly-like movements of its yellow-banded silver body as it darts in and out of crevices looking for food. The bright orange **clown fish**, whose thick white stripes make it resemble a clown's ruff, is more properly known as the anemone fish because of its mutually protective relationship with the sea anemone, near which it can usually be sighted.

Some reef fish, among them the ubiquitous turquoise and purple **parrot fish**, eat coral. With the help of a bird-like beak, which is in fact several teeth fused together, the parrot fish scrapes away at the coral and then grinds the fragments down with another set of back teeth – a practice reputedly responsible for the erosion of a great deal of Thailand's reef. The magnificent mauve and burgundy **crown-of-thorns starfish**, named for its "arms" covered in highly venomous spines, also feeds on coral, laying waste to as much as fifty square centimetres of stony coral in a 24-hour period.

Larger, less frequent visitors to Thailand's offshore reefs include the **moray eel**, whose elongated jaws of viciously pointed teeth make it a deadly predator, and the similarly equipped **barracuda**, the world's fastest-swimming fish. **Sharks** are quite common off the reefs, where it's also sometimes possible to swim with a **manta ray**, whose extraordinary flatness, strange wing-like fins and massive size – up to 6m across and weighing some 1600kg – make it an astonishing presence. **Turtles** sometimes paddle around reef waters, too, but all four local species – leatherback, Olive Ridley, green and hawksbill – are fast becoming endangered in Thailand.

Environmental issues

Thailand's rapid economic growth has had a significant effect on its environment. Huge new infrastructure projects, an explosion in real-estate developments and the constantly expanding tourist industry have all played a part, and the effects of the subsequent **deforestation** and pollution have been felt nationwide. Such was the devastation caused by floods and mud slides in Surat Thani in 1988 that the government banned commercial logging the following year, though land continues to be denuded for other purposes. There is also the endemic problem of "influence" so that when a big shot wants to clear a previously pristine area for a new property development, for example, it is virtually impossible for a lowly provincial civil servant to reject their plan, or money.

Flooding has always been a feature of the Thai environment, crucial to the fertility of its soil, and its worst effects are obviated by the stilted design of the traditional Thai house. However, there is now an almost annual inundation in certain riverside town centres, and of roads and railways, particularly along the Gulf coast; 2011 saw especially severe floods, when towns in the Central Plains, including the World Heritage Site of Ayutthaya and many suburbs of Bangkok, were under metres of water for weeks on end. And in recent times, far more dangerous **flash floods** have recurred with depressing frequency, most dramatically around the northern town of Pai in 2005, where many homes and guesthouses were washed away. The link between deforestation and floods is disputed, though encroaching cement and tarmac on Thai flood plains surely play a part, as does the clogging of exit channels by garbage and other pollutants, and of course climate change.

Reefs and shorelines

A number of Thailand's **coral reefs** – some of which are thought to be around 450 million years old – are being destroyed by factors attributable to tourism, most significantly the pollution generated by coastal hotels with inadequate sewage systems. Longtail boats that anchor on reefs, souvenirs made from coral, and the use of harpoon guns by irresponsible dive leaders all have a cumulative effect, dwarfed however by the local practice of using dynamite to gather fish, including reef fish for sale to aquariums.

The 2004 **tsunami** also caused significant damage to coastal and marine environments the length of the Andaman coast. Reefs close to shore were crushed by debris (furniture, machinery, even cars) and buried under displaced soil; the sea was temporarily polluted by extensive damage to sewage systems; and tracts of shorefront farmland were rendered unusable by salt water. In 2010, a mass **coral bleaching** event occurred in all of the world's oceans, damaging especially shallow-water reefs in Thailand, such as Ko Surin's; the event was caused by sudden, steep rises in sea temperatures, and has been interpreted as dramatic evidence of the effects of climate change.

National parks

Although Thailand has since the 1970s been protecting some of its natural resources within **national parks**, these have long been caught between commercial and conservationist aims, an issue which the government addressed in 2002 by establishing a new National Park, Wildlife and Plant Conservation Department (DNP; ⓦdnp.go.th), separate from the Royal Forestry Department and its parent Ministry of Agriculture.

With 140 national parks and marine parks across the country, as well as various other protected zones, over thirteen percent of the country is now, in theory at least, protected from encroachment and hunting (a high proportion compared to other nations, such as Japan at 6.5 percent, and the US at 10.5 percent).

However, the **touristification** of certain national parks endures; Ko Phi Phi and Ko Samet in particular have both suffered irreversible environmental damage as a direct result of the number of overnight visitors they receive. While most people understand that the role of the national parks is to conserve vulnerable and precious resources, the dramatic hike in entrance fees payable by foreign visitors to national parks – from B20 up to B200 in 2000 and up again to B400 for a few special parks – was greeted with cynicism and anger, not least because there is often little sign of anything tangible being done on site with the money.

Elephant trekking and the wildlife trade

Despite the efforts of local and international conservation and wildlife-protection organizations, **animal rights** issues often meet with a confused response in Thailand. The muddled thinking behind the launch of the Chiang Mai Night Safari park was typical: not only was this commercial animal park erected on land appropriated from a national park, but early publicity trumpeted the fact that meat from many of the exotic animals kept in the park – including tigers, lions and elephants – would be available in the park's restaurant. Negative comment soon quashed that, but exotic meats from endangered animals are served, albeit clandestinely, all over Thailand.

Some of Thailand's many **zoos**, such as those in Bangkok and Chiang Mai, are legitimate, reasonably decent places, but a number of the country's other private wildlife theme parks and zoos – particularly those specializing in tigers and crocodiles – have more dubious purposes and some have been targeted by international animal welfare organizations such as Born Free.

WILDLIFE CHARITIES AND VOLUNTEER PROJECTS

The Golden Triangle Asian Elephant Foundation *Anantara Resort*, Sop Ruak, Chiang Rai ⓦhelpingelephants.org. Elephant welfare is the primary concern at the well-regarded Anantara Elephant Camp, which offers elephant treks and mahout courses. Profits support the foundation's elephant rescue centre. See p.371.

Elephant Nature Park Near Chiang Mai ⓦelephantnaturefoundation.org. Famous conservation-education centre and sanctuary for elephants that's open to pre-booked visitors, overnight guests and volunteers. See p.353.

Gibbon Rehabilitation Project Phuket ⓦgibbonproject.org. Resocializes abused pet gibbons before releasing them back into the forests. Visitors and volunteers welcome. See p.649.

Highland Farm Gibbon Sanctuary Near Mae Sot ⓦhighland-farm.org. Day-trippers and homestay guests are welcome at this haven caring for injured and abandoned gibbons. One-month placements are also possible. See p.263.

Wild Animal Rescue Foundation of Thailand (WAR) ⓦwarthai.org. A campaigning organization that runs animal rescue sanctuaries, hospitals and research centres in various locations across Thailand and is open to unskilled paying volunteers.

There is also increasing concern about the **ethics of elephant trekking**, a fast-growing and lucrative arm of the tourist industry that some consider has got out of hand. What began as a canny way for elephants to earn their (very expensive) keep, after the 1989 ban on logging rendered most working elephants unemployed, is now endangering Southeast Asia's dwindling population of wild elephants as more and more are captured for the trekking trade (see p.318). Burmese elephants are particularly vulnerable and reportedly get smuggled across the border in significant numbers. In addition, welfare standards at these elephant trekking centres vary enormously. On the positive front, there's an increasing number of **animal sanctuaries** working to look after abused and endangered animals, especially elephants and gibbons (see box, p.767), which operate both as safe havens and as educational visitor attractions.

The wildlife trade

Though Thailand signed the Convention on the International Trade in Endangered Species – **CITES** – in 1983, and hosted the annual CITES conference in 2004, the trading of threatened animals and animal products continues.

Most of the trade in **endangered species** is focused along the borders with Cambodia and Burma, where Thai middle-merchants can apparently easily acquire any number of creatures. Some will be sold as pets and to zoos, while others are destined for dining tables and medicine cabinets. **Tiger** body-parts are especially lucrative and mostly end up on the black markets of China, Korea, Taiwan and Hong Kong, where bones, skin, teeth, whiskers and penis are prized for their "medicinal" properties; it's thought that much of Thailand's dwindling tiger population ends up this way. **Bear** paws and gall bladders are considered to have similar potency and are a star feature, along with other endangered species, at certain clandestine restaurants in Thailand catering to "gourmet" tourists from China and Korea; the traditional custom of slicing paws off a living bear and enhancing gall-bladder flavour by taking it from an animal that is literally scared to death make this practice particularly vile. The Burmese border market at Thachilek near Mae Sai is a notorious outlet for tiger and bear body-parts, while Chatuchak Weekend Market in Bangkok has long had a thriving trade in live animals – everything from hornbills to slow loris – despite occasional crackdowns.

Music

Music is an important part of Thai culture, whether related to Buddhist activities in the local temple (still a focal point for many communities), animist rituals, Brahmanic ceremonies or the wide range of popular song styles. While local forms of Thai popular music such as *luk thung* and *mor lam* remain very popular and distinctively Thai in character, a lively, ever-changing rock, indie, DJ/clubbing and underground scene is also fast developing.

The classical tradition

Thai classical dance and music can be traced back to stone engravings from the Sukhothai period (thirteenth to fifteenth centuries), which show ensembles of musicians playing traditional instruments, called **piphat**. The *piphat* ensembles include many percussion instruments, rather like Indonesian gamelan – gong circles, xylophones and drums – plus a raucous oboe called the *pinai*. The music was developed to accompany classical dance-drama (*khon* or *lakhon*) or shadow-puppet theatre (*nang*): a shadow-puppet show is depicted in the magnificent *Ramayana* murals at Wat Phra Kaeo in Bangkok's Grand Palace complex.

Piphat music sounds strange to Western ears as the seven equal notes of the Thai scale fall between the cracks of the piano keyboard. But heard in the right environment – in a temple, at a dance performance or at a Thai boxing match – it can be entrancing. As there is no notation, everything is memorized. And, as in all Thai music, elements have been assimilated over the years from diverse sources, and synthesized into something new. Check out any of the international albums by the Prasit Thawon Ensemble (Thawon was a National Artist).

Despite the country's rapid Westernization, Thai classical music has been undergoing something of a revival in the past few years, partly as a result of royal patronage. There have been recent experiments, too, at blending Thai classical and Western styles – often jazz or rock – led by groups like **Kangsadan** and **Fong Naam. Boy Thai** followed their lead, albeit with a more pop-oriented sound, and have had some mainstream success with two albums. The two *ranat* (xylophone) playing brothers from Boy Thai, Chaiyoot and Narongrit Tosa-ngan, have their own bands now: Chaiyoot with his huge **Bangkok Xylophone Orchestra** and Narongrit as **Khun-In and Off-Beat Siam**. The 2004 biopic *Homrong* (*The Overture*) features a character called Khun-In (played by Narongrit) who duels on the *ranat* against Thailand's greatest classical musician Luang Pradit Pairoh.

There are dance and classical music **performances** in Bangkok at the Sala Chalermkrung Theatre, the National Theatre and the Thailand Cultural Centre (see p.164), and you may also come across some more lacklustre examples at the Erawan Shrine on Thanon Rama I and the *lak muang* shrine in front of the Grand Palace, where people give thanks to deities by paying for the temple musicians and dancers to go through a routine. A number of Bangkok restaurants also feature music and dance shows for tourists, including regular shows by Bruce Gaston of Fong Naam at the *Tawandang German Brewery* (see p.163), and **Duriyapraneet**, the latter being the country's longest-established classical band.

Folk music

Thailand's folk music is called **phleng pheun bahn**, and different styles are found in the country's four distinct regions (central, north, northeast and south). Despite Thailand's rush to modernity, numerous folk styles are still enthusiastically played, from the hill-tribe New Year dances in the far north to the *saw* (a kind of three-stringed violin) and *fon lep* (fingernail dance) of Chiang Mai, from the all-night singing jousts of northeastern *lam klawn*, to the haunting Muslim vocals of *likay huuluu* in the deep south.

Most Thais are familiar with the exciting central folk styles like *lam tad*, *phleng choi* and *phleng I-saw*, which often feature raunchy verbal jousting between male and female singers. Styles like these and the ever-popular *mor lam* from the northeast (see p.773) are incorporated into modern popular styles such as *luk thung* (see p.772).

One notable folk style to have grown in popularity in recent years is the up-tempo and danceable northeastern instrumental style known as **pong lang** (a wooden xylophone that is attached vertically to a tree and was originally used to keep birds off crops). *Pong lang* is ancient, predating Indian–Thai culture, and was updated by National Artist Pleung Chairaasamee in the 1970s. A few years ago, **Pong-Lang Sa-Orn** emerged with an action-packed comedy show that propelled the band to national fame, million-selling albums and movies.

The best place to see *pong lang* is upcountry, especially in Kalasin province in central Isaan in the dry season between November and March. Folk music also features prominently at the major festivals (see p.46) held in the northeastern cities of Khon Kaen, Ubon Ratchathani and Udon Thani, particularly during Songkhran (April), the Bun Bang Fai rocket festival (May), and the Asanha Puja candle festival (July). Generally, any national holiday or religious festival is a good time to look out for folk music, in any region.

Popular styles

Thailand is the second-biggest Southeast Asian music market after Indonesia, and Bangkok is a major and increasingly important regional hub for pop music and popular culture.

Western orchestration for Thai melodies was introduced in the 1920s and 1930s and this led to the development of *phleng Thai sakon*, or "international Thai music", in the form of big band and swing, country and western, Hollywood film music, rock'n'roll, and so on. In the early days, two distinctive Thai genres developed: *phleng luk krung*, a romantic ballad form, popularized by Thailand's most beloved composer and bandleader Euah Sunthornsanan and his Suntharaporn band; and *phleng luk thung* (country music). **Luk krung**, with its clearly enunciated singing style and romantic fantasies, was long associated with the rich strata of Bangkok society (*krung* comes from Krung Thep, the Thai name for the capital); it's the kind of music that is played by state organs such as Radio Thailand. However, it was largely transformed during the 1960s by the popularity of Western stars like Cliff Richard; as musicians started to mimic the new Western music, a new term was coined, *wong shadow* (*wong* meaning group, *shadow* from the British group The Shadows).

String

The term **string** came into use as Thai-language pop music rapidly developed in the economic boom times of the 1980s. *String* encompasses ballads, rock and alternative, indie, disco, techno/house, J-Pop and K-Pop (Japan and Korea), heavy metal, reggae, ska, rap and underground; whatever trend is popular internationally is picked up and put into the Thai cultural blender. Currently popular are all things Korean – boy bands, girl bands, fashion styles and haircuts, megastars Rain and 2PM, teen TV shows, soap operas, food and comics.

Megastars such as veteran **Thongchai "Bird" Macintyre** generally record on either of the two major labels, GMM Grammy and RS Promotion. Grammy, which controls more than half the market, has an umbrella of labels that release everything from soft rockers **Mai Chareonpura** to *luk thung* star "Got" Chakrapand Arbkornburi. Their most famous Thai rock act, though, is the talented brothers **Asanee and Wasan (Chotikul)**, who have also become producers for a new generation of rockers; the two brothers toured the worldwide Thai diaspora in 2008.

The Thai alternative rock scene developed in the mid-1990s with the emergence, on the then-indie Bakery label (now part of Sony BMG), of **Modern Dog**, whose latest album *Ting Nong Noy* (2008) swept various Thai rock awards. Bakery helped kick-start indie rock and rap with the mercurial **Joey Boy** (the hip only buy his profane and savage MP3 underground songs). At the moment, **Loso** are probably the most popular rock band, with leader **Sek Loso** enjoying a serious solo career and iconic status, though it's unclear how strongly he'll emerge from a recent spell of rehab and marital problems.

Recently, more Western and Asian musicians have joined their Thai counterparts – as with electro-clash band **Futon** (Thai–Japanese–Western). And no list of current Thai pop stars and rockers would be complete without mentioning **Ebola** (metal plus rap), **Big Ass** (hardcore punk/pop), **Bodyslam** (heavy rock), **Thaitanium** (hip-hop from US-raised Thais), **Tattoo Colour** and **Silly Fools** (both indie rock) and **Apartment Khun Pa** (funk plus indie rock).

Thailand, and in particular Bangkok, is developing its own musical identity, partly as a result of many high-profile **festivals**, such as the Pattaya Music Festival in March, which showcases Asian bands, and partly because of the explosion of new genres and the emergence of a busy underground and **live scene**. You'll find Thai, foreign and mixed bands and DJs playing in Bangkok's many clubs and bars, and dynamic scenes in Chiang Mai, Khorat and Ko Samui.

Campuses such as Ramkhamhaeng University are good places to get information on upcoming **events**, as are radio stations (especially Fat Radio FM). Bangkok is the best place to catch gigs – check the free weekly BK magazine or their website, ⓦbk.asia-city .com, for listings.

Songs for Life and reggae

Another important genre is **phleng pheua chiwit**, or "**Songs for Life**", which started as a kind of progressive rock in the early 1970s, with bands like **Caravan** (no relation to the British songsters) blending *phleng pheun bahn* (folk songs) with Western folk and rock. Caravan were at the forefront of the left-wing campaign for democracy with songs like *Khon Kap Khwai* (*Human with Buffaloes*):

> *Greed eats our labour and divides people into classes*
> *The rice farmers fall to the bottom*
> *Insulted as backward and ignorant brutes*
> *With one important and sure thing: death.*

Although an elected government survived from 1973 to 1976, the military returned soon after and Caravan, like many of the student activists, went into hiding in the jungle. There they performed to villagers and hill-tribe people and gave the occasional concert. When the government offered an amnesty in 1979, most of the students, and Caravan too, disillusioned with the Communist Party's support for the Khmer Rouge in Cambodia, returned to normal life.

In the 1980s a new group emerged to carry on Caravan's work, **Carabao**. The band split up in 1988 but has had many reunions and reincarnations since; their influence is still strong, with leader Ad Carabao still in the limelight but now more as a businessman hawking his "energy" drink, Carabao Daeng, via the band's gigs and nasty nationalistic TV ad campaigns. However, despite the bloody street riots of 1992 (in protest at the then military-installed government) once again bringing Songs for Life artists out to support the pro-democracy protests, since the 1980s the strong social activism of Caravan's early years has generally been replaced by more individual and personal themes. The current top act is fresh-faced singer-songwriter **Pongsit Kamphee**, whose earnest approach and rise through the ranks (he was reportedly once a stagehand for Caravan) have garnered him a sizeable following.

Musically, the genre has developed little over the years, remaining strongly rooted in Western folk-rock styles. Recently, however, this has begun to change as musicians have belatedly discovered that **reggae** riddims work well with Songs for Life vocals; perhaps they were inspired by **T-Bone**, for so long the only reggae band in the kingdom. Best of this new sub-genre is Southerner **Job** of the **Job 2 Do** band, while the best classic Marley-style reggae band is the **Srirajah Rockers**. There's a weekend reggae festival held in the north in Pai every winter (Ⓦpaifestival.com). For ska bands, check out **Teddy Ska and Skalaxy**.

Songs for Life fans should check out CD stalls at Bangkok's Chatuchak Weekend Market, several of which specialize in this genre.

Luk thung

Go to one of the huge **luk thung** shows held in a temple or local stadium on the outskirts of Bangkok, or to any temple fair in the countryside, and you'll hear one of the great undiscovered popular musics of Asia. The shows, amid the bright lights, foodstalls and fairground games, last several hours and involve dozens of dancers and costume changes. In contrast with *luk krung*, *luk thung* (literally, "child of the field") has always been associated with the rural and urban poor, and because of this has gained nationwide popularity over the past forty years.

According to *luk thung* DJ Jenpope Jobkrabuanwan, the term was first coined by Jamnong Rangsitkhun in 1964, but the first song in the style was *Oh Jao Sao Chao Rai* (Oh, the Vegetable Grower's Bride), recorded in 1937, and the genre's first big singer, **Kamrot Samboonanon**, emerged in the mid-1940s. Originally called *phleng talat* (market songs) or *phleng chiwit* (songs of life), the style blended together folk songs, central Thai classical music and Thai folk dances. Malay strings and fiddles were added in the 1950s, as were Latin brass and rhythms like the cha-cha-cha and mambo (Asian tours by Xavier Cugat influenced many Asian pop styles during the 1950s), as well as elements from Hollywood movie music and "yodelling" country and western vocal styles from the likes of Gene Autry and Hank Williams. In 1952, a new singer, **Suraphon Sombatjalern**, made his debut with a song entitled *Nam Ta Lao Wiang* (Tears of the Vientiane Girl) and became the undisputed king of the style until his untimely murder (for serious womanizing, rumour has it) in 1967. Suraphon helped develop the music into a mature form, and was known as the "King" of the genre, along with his Queen, sweet-voiced Pongsri Woranut.

Today, *luk thung* is a mix of Thai folk music and traditional entertainment forms like *likay* (travelling popular theatre), as well as a range of Western styles. There are certainly some strong musical affinities with other regional pop styles like Indonesian *dangdut* and Japanese *enka*, but what is distinctly Thai – quite apart from the spectacular live shows – are the singing styles and the content of the lyrics. Vocal styles are full of heavy ornamentation (*luk khor*) and sustained notes (*auen* or "note-bending"). A singer must have a wide vocal range, as the late *luk thung* megastar **Pumpuang Duangjan** explained: "Making the *luk thung* sound is difficult, you must handle the high and low notes well. And because the emotional content is stronger than in *luk krung*, you must also be able to create a strongly charged atmosphere."

Pumpuang had the kind of voice that turns the spine to jelly. She rose to prominence during the late 1970s, joining **Sayan Sanya** as the biggest male and female names in the business. Like Suraphon Sombatjalern, both came from the rural peasantry, making identification with themes and stories that related directly to the audience much easier. Songs narrate mini-novellas, based around typical characters like the lorry driver, peasant lad or girl, poor farmer, prostitute or maid; and the themes are those of going away to the big city, infidelity, grief, tragedy and sexual pleasure. Interestingly, it is not always the lyrics that carry the sexual charge of the song (and if lyrics are deemed too risqué by the authorities the song will be subject to strict censorship) but rather the vocal style and the stage presentation, which can be very bawdy indeed.

With the advent of TV and the rise in popularity of *string*, the number of large upcountry *luk thung* shows has declined. It's not easy, said Pumpuang, to tour with over a hundred staff, including the dancers in the *hang kruang* (chorus). "We play for over four hours, but *string* bands, with only a few staff members, play a paltry two hours!" Her response to the advent of *string* and the increasing importance of promotional videos was to develop a dance-floor-oriented sound – **electronic luk thung** (**Grand X** had already experimented with *luk thung* and disco a few years earlier). Few *luk thung* singers are capable of this, but Pumpuang had the vocal range to tackle both ballad forms and the up-tempo dance numbers. Her musical diversification increased her popularity enormously, and when she died in 1992, aged only 31, up to 200,000 people, ranging from royalty to the rural poor, made their way to her funeral in her home town of Suphanburi (look out for the major biopic, *Pumpuang*, made in 2011).

Pumpuang's death pushed ongoing political problems (the 1992 coup) off the front pages of newspapers, a situation that was repeated in 2008 when **Yodrak Salakjai** died. Yodrak was the most recorded *luk thung* star of all time, with some three thousand songs and five hundred albums to his credit.

Since Pumpuang's death, the top *luk thung* slot has been occupied by "**Got**" **Chakrapand Arbkornburi**, whose switch from pop to full-time *luk thung* has brought many younger listeners to the style, while the reigning female singer was **Sunaree Ratchasima**, but she has been superseded by the perkier **Arpaporn Nakornsawan**. **Mike Piromporn**, originally a *mor lam* man, is Got's main challenger. Bangkok's first 24-hour *luk thung* radio station, Luk Thung FM (at 90 FM), was launched in 1997, and it's even cool for the middle class to like *luk thung* these days. A new generation of singers has also emerged, including **Monsit Kamsoi**, **Yingyong Yodbuangarm**, **Dao Mayuri**, **Yui Yardyuh**, **Tai Orathai** and **Fon Thanasunthorn**. There is some truth, however, in the criticism that some new *luk thung* stars are being artificially manufactured just like their pop and rock counterparts, and there's a tendency to rate a pretty face over vocal expertise.

For many years, *luk thung* was sung by performers from the Suphanburi area in the central plains, but more regional voices are being heard in the genre now, with northeasterners now outnumbering these singers. A slightly faster rhythm, *luk thung Isaan*, has been developed, initially by "**Khru**" **(Teacher) Saleh Kunavudh** in the 1980s. The south, too, has its own *luk thung* star, in the enormously popular **Ekachai Srivichai**.

As well as at temple fairs, fairs at district offices in provincial capitals, national holiday events at Bangkok's Sanam Luang by companies like Waitee Thai and New Year celebrations are the best places to catch *luk thung* shows.

Mor lam

Mor lam is the folk style from the poor, dry northeastern region of Isaan, an area famed for droughts, spicy food, good boxers and great music. Over the past 25 years, the modern pop form of this style has risen dramatically. Traditionally, a *mor lam* is a master of the *lam* singing style (sung in the Isaan dialect, which is actually Lao), and is accompanied by the *khaen* (bamboo mouth organ), the *phin* (two- to four-string guitar) and *ching* (small temple cymbals). Modern **mor lam** developed from *mor lam klawn*, a narrative form where all-night singing jousts are held between male and female singers, and from *mor lam soeng*, the group-dance form. Both still play an important part in many social events like weddings, births and deaths, festivals and temple fairs. A *mor lam* may sing intricate fixed-metre Lao epic poems or may relate current affairs in a spontaneous rap. In the large groups, Western instruments like guitar (replacing the *phin*) and synthesizer (for the *khaen*) are used.

The style came to national prominence more than twenty years ago, when a female *mor lam* singer, **Banyen Rakgan**, appeared on national TV. In the early 1980s the music was heard not only in Isaan but also in the growing slums of Bangkok, as rural migrants poured into the capital in search of work. By the end of the decade, stars like **Jintara Poonlarp** (with her hit song *Isaan Woman Far From Home*) and **Pornsak Songsaeng** could command the same sell-out concerts as their *luk thung* counterparts. Jintara remains one of the biggest stars, and her shows mix both *luk thung* and *lam*; for a big raucous show, **Nok Noi Ulaiporn** and Pong-Lang Sa-Orn (see p.770) are probably the hottest acts. **Siriporn Ampaiporn**, whose strong vocals burst upon the *lam* scene with the monster-selling *Bor Rak Si Dam* album, mainly records *luk thung* these days.

The format of a *mor lam* **performance** is similar to that of *luk thung* shows – lots of dancers in wild costumes, comedy skits and a large backing orchestra – as is the subject matter. The music is definitely hot, especially if you see it live, when bands will often play through the night, never missing the groove for a minute, driven on by the relentless *phin* and *khaen* playing. To some people, the fast plucking style of the *phin* gives a West African or Celtic tinge; the *khaen* has a rich sound – over a bass drone players improvise around the melody, while at the same time vamping the basic rhythm. Male and female singers rotate or duet humorous love songs, which often start with one of the *mor khaen* setting up the beat. They sing about topical issues, bits of news, crack lewd jokes or make fun of the audience – all very tongue-in-cheek.

Musically, however, *mor lam* and *luk thung* are very different; *mor lam* has a much faster, relentless rhythm and the vocal delivery is rapid-fire, rather like a rap. You'll immediately recognize a *mor lam* song with its introductory wailing moan "*Oh la naw*", meaning "fortune". *Mor lam* artists, brought up bilingually, can easily switch from *luk thung* to *mor lam*, but *luk thung* artists, who often only speak the national central Thai dialect, cannot branch out so easily.

In the 1990s, *mor lam* musicians headed off the challenge of increasingly popular *string* bands by creating **mor lam sing**, a turbo-charged modern version of *mor lam klawn* played by small electric combos. The number of large touring *luk thung* or *mor lam* shows has declined in recent years, owing to high overheads, TV entertainment and the popularity of *string* bands, so *mor lam sing* satisfies the need for local music with a modern edge.

Mor lam sing was followed quickly by a more rock-oriented *mor lam* sound (this is a little similar to Grand X in the 1980s, which played a mix of rock and *luk thung*), led by funky little combos like **Rocksadert** and **Rock Saleang**, actually much better live than on recordings, although the latter had a hilarious hit in 2006 with *Motorcy Hoy*.

Kantrum: Thai–Cambodian pop

"Isaan *neua* (north) has *mor lam*, Isaan *tai* (south) has *kantrum*," sings **Darkie**, the first star of **kantrum**, Thai–Cambodian pop, in his song *Isaan Tai Samakkhi* (Southern Isaan Unity). His music is a very specific offshoot, from the southern part of Isaan, where Thai–Cambodians mix with ethnic Lao and Thais. So far *kantrum* is only popular in Isaan in Thailand but it has spread over the border to nearby Cambodian towns like Siem Reap where the style is known as Khmer Ler or Khmer Surin.

Modern *kantrum* has developed from Cambodian folk and classical music, played in a small group consisting of fiddle, small hand-drums and *khrab* (pieces of hardwood bashed together rather like claves). This traditional style is now quite hard to find in Thailand; twenty years ago, musicians started to electrify the music, using both traditional and Western instruments. Shunning the synthesizer preferred by his competitors such as **Khong Khoi**, Oh-Yot and Samanchai, Darkie added the wailing fiddle centre-stage and cranked up the rhythms (*kantrum* has a harder beat than even *mor lam*). In 1997, he broke new ground with *Darkie Rock II: Buk Jah*, the first *kantrum* crossover album to have success in the mainstream pop market. Sadly, in 2001, Darkie died aged 35, but a new generation of *kantrum* stars is now emerging, led by **Songsaeng Lungluangchai**, who has recorded several excellent albums of Darkie covers.

Discography

In Bangkok, ask the vendors at the day and night markets about **CDs**, or the stores on Thanon Charoen Krung (New Road) or at Sunday's Klong Thom market (in the small sois behind Thanon Charoen Krung, between Plaplachai and Mahachak intersections). Most major *luk thung* or *mor lam* artists release an album every three months, which is often given an artist's series number. Old-style recordings of Suraphon Sombatjalern and the like can be found on the ground floor of the Mah Boon Krong Shopping Centre at Mae Mai Phleng Thai, while DJ Siam, nearby on Soi 4, Siam Square, is good for Thai indy and pop. Look out for the intriguingly diverse output of Zudrangma Records (ⓦzudrangmarecords.com): they've released compilations of old *luk thung* and *mor lam* on their own label, and it's well worth browsing their record store, next door to *WTF* (see p.163), just off Soi 51, Thanon Sukhumvit; they also run awesome club nights in the capital, where you might find *mor lam* mixed with Jamaican dancehall.

In addition, several **DVDs** are well worth seeking out: Jeremy Marre's episode on music in Thailand, *Two Faces of Thailand: A Musical Portrait* (Shanachie, US), from his award-winning *Beats of the Heart* music-TV documentary series; *Homrong* (see p.769); and *Mon Rak Transistor* (see p.784).

For music on the **internet**, try ⓦthaimuzic.com, ⓦthaiclassicalmusic.com, ⓦthainetcity.com and ⓦethaimusic.com; the last is also a good site to learn the language as it features lyrics in Thai and English, from a large archive of popular songs. Music sites such as ⓦtruemusic.truelife.com and the sites of GMM Grammy and RS Promotion are also worth browsing for info on major stars.

CLASSICAL

Fong Naam *The Hang Hong Suite* (Nimbus, UK). A good introduction to the vivacious and glittering sound of classical Thai music, this CD includes some upbeat funeral music and parodies of the musical languages of neighbouring cultures. *The Sleeping Angel* (Nimbus, UK) is also a splendid recording.

Lai Muang Ensemble *The Spirit of Lanna: Music From the North of Thailand* (AMI Records, Thailand). Top-quality recording, featuring multi-instrumentalist Somboon

Kawichai on the *peejum* (bamboo pipes) and the eerie-sounding *pin pia*, a chest-resonated oboe.

The Prasit Thawon Ensemble *Thai Classical Music* (Nimbus, UK). Brilliant playing (and outstanding recording quality) from some of Thailand's best performers, mainly of *piphat* style. Includes the overture *Homrong Sornthong* and, on *Cherd Chin*, some scintillating dialogues between different instruments.

FOLK MUSIC

David Fanshawe *Music From Thailand and Laos: Southeast Asia Recordings* (Arc Music, UK). Excellent range of folk music from different regions of both countries.

Various *Sea Gypsies of the Andaman Sea* (Topic, UK). The traditional music of nomadic Moken (*chao ley*) fisherfolk in southern Thailand, mostly recorded in the Surin islands.

Various *Thailand: Musiques et Chants des Peuples du Triangle d'Or* (Globe Music, France). Recordings of the traditional music of Thailand's main hill-tribe groups: Hmong, Lisu, Lahu, Yao, Akha and Karen, as well as Shan (Thai Yai).

THAI SAKON

Euah Sunthornsanan *Chabab Derm* ("Old Songs") Vols 1–5, 6–10 (Bangkok Cassette, Thailand). Modern Thai music was popularized by the late master Euah. Some of

the most popular Thai songs ever were performed by the Suntharaporn band and a bevy of singers.

STRING AND SONGS FOR LIFE

Carabao *Made in Thailand* and *Ameri-koi* (both Krabue, Thailand). Two classic albums from the Songs for Life giants. *Made in Thailand* was right in tune with the times and targeted social problems like consumerism, the sex trade and a failing education system. *Ameri-koi* (*Greedy America*) is even more nationalistic than the previous one,

but it also hits out at Thai migrant workers exploited by labour brokers.

Futon *Never Mind the Botox* (Rehab, Thailand). Electro-clash with a punk attitude from the kingdom's favourite underground band. Excellent cover of Iggy Pop's *I Wanna Be Your Dog*.

Loso/Sek Loso The best compilation of Loso's music is the 2001 release *The Red* album, while the solo work of Sek Loso is best captured on the same year's *Black & White* (both GMM Grammy, Thailand) and live on the VCD *10 Years of Rock Volumes 1 & 2*.

Modern Dog *Modern Dog* (Bakery Music, Thailand). This album of alternative rock marked an important change of direction for the Thai rock scene. Also see albums *Love Me Love My Life*, *That Song* and their newest, *Ting Nong Noy*.

LUK THUNG

If you can't find any of the albums below, go for a compilation of past albums, usually under a title like *Ruam Hits* (*Mixed Hits*).

"Got" Chakrapand Arbkornburi *12 Years of Grammy Gold* (GMM Grammy, Thailand). Packed with slow ballads, this is one for the ladies from *luk thung*'s heartthrob.

Pumpuang Duangjan In Thailand, the best of many albums to go for is *Pumpuang Lai Por Sor* ("Pumpuang's Many Eras"; Topline, Thailand). Her early spine-tingling hits can be found on several CD compilations from Bangkok Cassette, some recorded when she was known as Nampung Petsupan (Honey Diamond from Suphanburi).

Sayan Sanya *Sayan Tao Thong* ("Sayan Golden Star"; Bangkok Cassette, Thailand). Classic 1970s *luk thung* featuring the "honey-voiced" master. As Yodrak said, "Women cry when he [Sayan] sings."

Suraphon Sombatjalern *Ruam Phleng* ("Mixed Songs") Vols 1–4 (Bangkok Cassette, Thailand). Greatest hits by the king of *luk thung*. Great voice, great songs, great backing – Siamese soul.

Various *Mon Rak Transistor* ("A Transistor Love Story"; UFO, Thailand). From the hit movie about a young country boy who tries to make it in the big city as a *luk thung* singer. Includes Suraphon's wonderful theme song, *Mai Leum* ("Don't Forget").

Various *The Rough Guide to the Music of Thailand* (World Music Network, UK). Good review of some recent *mor lam* and *luk thung*, despite confusing liner notes, elephants, and the odd pop group.

MOR LAM/NORTHEASTERN MUSIC

Chalard Songserm *Rhythms of I-Sarn Vols 1 & 2* (AMI Records, Thailand). Top-quality album from National Artist Chalard, *khaen* maestro Sombat Simlao and a band of great musicians, covering many styles of Lao music in the region. Sombat's train-sounding *khaen* solo is a standout.

Isan Slété *Songs and Music from North East Thailand* (Globestyle, UK). Excellent selection of traditional *mor lam*. Vocal and instrumental numbers, played by a band of master musicians.

Jintara Poonlarp *Ruam Hit 19 Pii Tawng Chut* (Master Tape, Thailand). Nineteen years at the top on two killer

volumes. Vol. 1 features haunting *mor lam*.

Various *Instrumental Music of Northeast Thailand* (King, Japan). Wonderful collection of *pong lang* and related instrumental northeastern styles. Lively and fun.

Various, featuring Chaweewan Damnoen *Mor Lam Singing of Northeast Thailand* (King, Japan). Female *mor lam* National Artist, Chaweewan, headlines this fine collection of many *lam* styles. Most *mor lam klawn* narrative and dance styles, even spirit-possession rituals, are included.

KANTRUM

Darkie *Darkie, Rock II: Buk Jah* (Movie Music, Thailand). The first-ever *kantrum* crossover album achieved nation-wide stardom for the King of Kantrum. Darkie's booming voice moves from rap-like delivery to moans and wails, shadowed closely by the fiddle and some funky riddims.

Unmissable.

Songsaeng Lungluangchai *Songsaeng Kantrum Rock: Chut Ta Don Duay* (PK Sound, Thailand). Keyboardless, rootsy sound. Look out for his tribute album to Darkie, *Kantrum Rock* (PK Sound, Thailand).

John Clewley (Adapted from *The Rough Guide to World Music*)

The hill tribes

Originating in various parts of China and Southeast Asia, the hill tribes are sometimes termed Fourth World people, in that they are migrants who continue to migrate without regard for established national boundaries. Most arrived in Thailand during the last century, and many of the hill peoples are still found in other parts of Southeast Asia – in Vietnam, for example, where the French used the *montagnards* ("mountain dwellers") in their fight against communism. Since 1975, a large percentage of the one million refugees that Thailand has accepted from Burma, Laos and Cambodia has been hill-tribe people. Some, however, have been around for much longer, like the Lawa, who are thought to have been the first settlers in northern Thailand, though these days they have largely been assimilated into mainstream Thai culture.

Called **chao khao** (mountain people) by the Thais, the tribes are mostly pre-literate societies, whose sophisticated systems of customs, laws and beliefs have developed to harmonize relationships between individuals and their environment. In recent years their ancient culture has come under threat, faced with the effects of rapid population growth and the ensuing competition for land, discrimination and exploitation by lowland Thais, and tourism. However, the integrity of their way of life is as yet largely undamaged, and what follows is the briefest of introductions to an immensely complex subject. If you want to learn more, visit the Hill Tribe Museum and Handicrafts Shop in Chiang Rai (see p.360) before setting out on a trek.

Agriculture

Although the hill tribes keep some livestock, such as pigs, poultry and elephants, the base of their economy is **swidden agriculture** (slash-and-burn), a crude form of shifting cultivation also practised by many Thai lowland farmers. At the beginning of the season an area of jungle is cleared and burned, producing ash to fertilize rice, corn, chillies and other vegetables, which are replanted in succeeding years until the soil's nutrients are exhausted. This system is sustainable with a low population density, which allows the jungle time to recover before it is used again. However, with the increase in population over recent decades, ever greater areas are being exhausted, and the decreasing forest cover is leading to erosion and microclimatic change.

As a result, many villages took up the large-scale production of **opium** to supplement the traditional subsistence crops, though the Thai government has now largely eradicated opium production in the north. However, the cash crops which have been introduced in its place have often led to further environmental damage, as these low-profit crops require larger areas of cultivation, and thus greater deforestation. Furthermore, the water supplies have become polluted with chemical pesticides, and, although more environmentally sensitive agricultural techniques are being introduced, they have yet to achieve widespread acceptance.

Religion and festivals

Although some tribes have taken up Buddhism and others – especially among the Karen, Mien and Lahu – have been converted by Christian missionaries bringing the incentives of education and modern medicine, the hill tribes are predominantly **animists**. In this belief system, all natural objects are inhabited by spirits which, along with the tribe's ancestor spirits and the supreme divine spirit, must be propitiated to prevent harm to the family or village. Most villages have one or more religious leaders, which may include a priest who looks after the ritual life of the community, and at least one shaman who has the power to mediate with the spirits and prescribe what has to be done to keep them happy. If a member of the community is sick, for example, the shaman will be consulted to determine what action has insulted which spirit, and will then carry out the correct sacrifice.

The most important festival, celebrated by all the tribes, is at **New Year**, when whole communities take part in dancing, music and rituals particular to each tribe: Hmong boys and girls, for instance, take part in a courting ritual at this time, while playing catch with a ball. The New Year festivals are not held on fixed dates, but at various times during the cool-season slack period in the agricultural cycle from January to March.

Costumes and handicrafts

The most conspicuous characteristics of the hill tribes are their exquisitely crafted **costumes** and adornments, the styles and colours of which are particular to each group. Although many men and children now adopt Western clothes for everyday wear, with boys in particular more often running around in long shorts and T-shirts with logos, most women and girls still wear the traditional attire. It's the women who make the clothes too – some still spin their own cotton, though many Hmong, Lisu and Mien women are prosperous enough to buy materials from itinerant traders. Other distinctive hill-tribe artefacts – tools, jewellery, weapons and musical instruments – are the domain of the men, and specialist **blacksmiths** and **silversmiths** have such high status that some attract business from villages many kilometres away. Jewellery, the chief outward proof of a family's wealth, is displayed most obviously by Lisu women at the New Year festivals, and is commonly made from silver melted down from Indian and Burmese coins, though brass, copper and aluminium are also used.

Clothing and **handicrafts** were not regarded as marketable products until the early 1980s, when cooperatives were set up to manufacture and market these goods, which are now big business in the shops of Thailand. The hill tribes' deep-dyed coarse cloth, embroidered with simple geometric patterns in bright colours, has become popular among middle-class Thais as well as farang visitors. Mien material, dyed indigo or black with bright snowflake embroidery, is on sale in many shops, as is the simple but very distinctive Akha work – coarse black cotton, with triangular patterns of stitching and small fabric patches in rainbow colours, usually made up into bags and hats. The Hmong's much more sophisticated **embroidery** and **appliqué**, added to jacket lapels and cuffs and skirt hems, is also widely seen.

Besides clothing, the hill tribes' other handicrafts, such as knives and wooden or bamboo musical pipes, have found a market among farangs, the most saleable product being the intricate engraving work of their silversmiths, especially in the form of chunky bracelets. For a sizeable minority of villages, handicrafts now provide the security of a steady income to supplement what they make from farming.

The main tribes

Within the small geographical area of northern Thailand there are at least ten different hill tribes, many of them divided into distinct subgroups – the following are the main seven, listed in order of population and under their own names, rather than the sometimes derogatory names used by Thais. Beyond the broad similarities outlined above, this section sketches their differences in terms of history, economy and religion, and describes elements of dress by which they can be distinguished.

Karen

The **Karen** (called Kaliang or Yang in Thai) form by far the largest hill-tribe group in Thailand with a population of about 500,000, and are the second oldest after the Lawa, having begun to arrive here from Burma and China in the seventeenth century. The Thai Karen, many of them refugees from Burma (see box, p.262), mostly live in a broad tract of land west of Chiang Mai, which stretches along the border from Mae Hong Son province all the way down to Kanchanaburi, with scattered pockets in Chiang Mai, Chiang Rai and Phayao provinces.

The Karen traditionally practise a system of **rotating cultivation** – ecologically far more sensitive than slash-and-burn – in the valleys of this region and on low hills. Their houses, very similar to those of lowland Thais, are small (they do not live in extended family groups), built on stilts and made of bamboo or teak; they're often surrounded by fruit gardens and neat fences. As well as farming their own land, the Karen often hire out their labour to Thais and other hill tribes, and keep a variety of livestock including elephants, which used to be employed in the teak trade but are now often found giving rides to trekking parties.

Unmarried Karen women wear loose white or undyed V-necked shift dresses, often decorated with grass seeds at the seams. Some subgroups decorate them more elaborately, Sgaw girls with a woven red or pink band above the waist, and Pwo girls with woven red patterns in the lower half of the shift. Married women wear blouses and skirts in bold colours, predominantly red or blue. Men generally wear blue, baggy trousers with red or blue shirts, a simplified version of the women's blouse.

Hmong

Called the Meo ("barbarians") by the Thais, the **Hmong** ("free people") originated in central China or Mongolia and are now found widely in northern Thailand. There are two subgroups: the **Blue Hmong**, who live around and to the west of Chiang Mai; and the **White Hmong**, who are found to the east. Their overall population in Thailand is about 110,000, making them the second-largest hill-tribe group.

Of all the hill tribes, the Hmong have been the quickest to move away from subsistence farming. In the past, Hmong people were more involved in opium production than most other tribes in Thailand, though now many have eagerly embraced the newer cash crops. Hmong clothing has become much in demand in Thailand, and Hmong women will often be seen at markets throughout the country selling their handicrafts. The women, in fact, are expected to do most of the work on the land and in the home.

Hmong **villages** are usually built at high altitudes, below the crest of a protecting hill. Although wealthier families sometimes build the more comfortable Thai-style houses, most stick to the traditional house, with its dirt floor and a roof descending almost to ground level. They live together in extended families, with two or more bedrooms and a large guest platform.

The Blue Hmong dress in especially striking **clothes**. The women wear intricately embroidered pleated skirts decorated with parallel horizontal bands of red, pink, blue and white; their jackets are of black satin, with wide orange and yellow embroidered cuffs and lapels. White Hmong women wear black baggy trousers and simple jackets with blue cuffs. Men of both groups generally wear baggy black trousers with colourful sashes round the waist, and embroidered jackets closing over the chest with a button at the left shoulder. All the Hmong are famous for their chunky **silver jewellery**, which the women wear every day, the men only on special occasions: they believe silver binds a person's spirits together, and wear a heavy neck-ring to keep the spirits weighed down in the body.

Lahu

The **Lahu**, who originated in the Tibetan highlands, migrated to southern China, Burma and Laos centuries ago; only since the end of the nineteenth century did they begin to come into Thailand from northern Burma. They're called Muser – from the Burmese word for "hunter" – by the Thais, because many of the first Lahu to reach northern Thailand were professional hunters. With a population of about 80,000, they are the third-largest hill-tribe group: most of their settlements are concentrated close to the Burmese border, in Chiang Rai, northern Chiang Mai and Mae Hong Son provinces, but families and villages change locations frequently. The Lahu language has become a *lingua franca* among the hill tribes, since the Lahu often hire out their labour. About one-third of Lahu have been converted to Christianity (through exposure in colonial Burma), and many have abandoned their traditional way of life as a result. The remaining animist Lahu believe in a village guardian spirit, who is often worshipped at a central temple that is surrounded by banners and streamers of white and yellow flags. Village houses are built on high stilts with walls of bamboo or wooden planks, thatched with grass. While subsistence farming is still common, sustainable agriculture – plantations of orchards, tea or coffee – is becoming more prevalent, and cash crops such as corn and cotton have taken the place of opium.

Some Lahu women wear a distinctive black cloak with diagonal white stripes, decorated in bold red and yellow at the top of the sleeve, but traditional costume has been supplanted by the Thai shirt and sarong among many Lahu groups. The tribe is famous for its richly embroidered **yaam** (shoulder bags), which are widely available in Chiang Mai.

Akha

The poorest of the hill tribes, the **Akha** (Kaw or Eekaw in Thai) migrated from Tibet over two thousand years ago to Yunnan in China, where at some stage they had an organized state and kept written chronicles of their history – these chronicles, like the Akha written language, are now lost. From the 1910s the tribe began to settle in Thailand and is found in four provinces – Chiang Rai, Chiang Mai, Lampang and Phrae – with a population of nearly 50,000 in about 250 villages. A large Akha population still lives in Yunnan and there are communities in neighbouring Laos as well as in Burma.

The Akha are less open to change than the other hill tribes, and have maintained their old agricultural methods of **shifting cultivation**. The Akha's form of animism – *Akhazang*, "the way of life of the Akha" – has also survived in uncompromised form. As well as spirits in the natural world, *Akhazang* encompasses the worship of ancestor spirits: some Akha can recite the names of over sixty generations of forebears.

Every Akha village is entered through ceremonial **gates** decorated with carvings depicting human activities and attributes – even cars and aeroplanes – to indicate to the spirit world that beyond here only humans should pass. To touch any of these carvings, or to show any lack of respect to them, is punishable by fines or sacrifices. The gates are rebuilt every year, so many villages have a series of gates, the older ones in a state of disintegration. Another characteristic of Akha villages is a giant **swing** (also replaced each year), and used every August or early September in a swinging festival.

Akha **houses** are recognizable by their low stilts and steeply pitched roofs, though some may use higher stilts to reflect higher status. Even more distinctive is the elaborate **headgear** which women wear all day; it frames the entire face and usually features white beads interspersed with silver coins, topped with plumes of red taffeta and framed by dangling, hollow silver balls and other jewellery or strings of beads. The rest of their heavy costume is made up of decorated tube-shaped ankle-to-knee leggings, an above-the-knee black skirt with a white beaded centrepiece, and a loose-fitting black jacket with heavily embroidered cuffs and lapels.

Mien

The **Mien** (called Yao in Thai) consider themselves the aristocrats of the hill tribes. Originating in central China, they began migrating southward more than two thousand years ago to southern China, Vietnam, Laos and Thailand. In Thailand today the Mien are widely scattered throughout the north, with concentrations around Nan, Phayao and Chiang Rai, and a population of about 40,000. They are the only hill tribe to have a written language, and a codified religion based on medieval Chinese Taoism, although in recent years there have been many Mien converts to Christianity and Buddhism. In general, the Mien strike a balance between integration into Thai life and maintenance of their separate cultural base. Many earn extra cash by selling exquisite embroidery and religious scrolls, painted in bold Chinese style.

Mien villages are not especially distinctive: their houses are usually built of wooden planks on a dirt floor, with a guest platform of bamboo in the communal living area. The **clothes** of the women, however, are instantly recognizable: long black jackets with glamorous-looking stole-like lapels of bright scarlet wool, heavily embroidered loose trousers in intricate designs which can take up to two years to complete, and a similarly embroidered black turban. The caps of babies are also very beautiful, richly embroidered with red or pink pom-poms. On special occasions, like weddings, women and children wear silver neck-rings, with silver chains decorated with silver ornaments extending down the back, and even their turbans are crossed with lengths of silver. A Mien woman's wedding headdress is quite extraordinary, a carefully constructed platform with arched supports that are covered with red fabric and heirlooms of embroidered cloth. Two burgundy-coloured fringes create side curtains obscuring her face, and the only concession to modernity is the black insulating tape that holds the structure to her head.

Lisu

The **Lisu** (Lisaw in Thai), who originated in eastern Tibet, first arrived in Thailand in 1921 and are found mostly in the west, particularly between Chiang Mai and Mae Hong Son, but also in western Chiang Rai, Chiang Mai and Phayao provinces, with a population of around 30,000. Whereas the other hill tribes are led by the village headman or shaman, the Lisu are organized into patriarchal clans which have authority over many villages, and their strong sense of clan rivalry often results in public violence.

The Lisu live in extended families at moderate to high altitudes, in houses built on the ground, with dirt floors and bamboo walls. Both men and women dress colourfully; the women wear a blue or green parti-coloured knee-length tunic, split up the sides to the waist, with a wide black belt and blue or green pants. At New Year, the women don dazzling outfits, including waistcoats and belts of intricately fashioned silver and turbans with multicoloured pom-poms and streamers; traditionally, the men wear green, pink or yellow baggy trousers and a blue jacket.

Lawa

The history of the **Lawa** people (Lua in Thai) is poorly understood, but it seems very likely that they have inhabited Thailand since at least the eighth century; they were certainly here when the Thais arrived around eight hundred years ago. The Lawa people are found only in Thailand; they believe that they migrated from Cambodia and linguistically they are certainly closely related to Mon-Khmer, but some archeologists think that their origins lie in Micronesia, which they left perhaps two thousand years back.

This lengthy cohabitation with the Thais has produced large-scale integration, so that most Lawa villages are indistinguishable from Thai settlements and most Lawa speak Thai as their first language. However, in an area of about 500 square kilometres between Hot, Mae Sariang and Mae Hong Son, the Lawa still live a largely traditional life, although even here the majority have adopted Buddhism and Thai-style houses. The basis of their economy is subsistence agriculture, with rice grown on terraces according to a sophisticated rotation system. Those identified as Lawa number just over ten thousand.

Unmarried Lawa women wear distinctive strings of orange and yellow beads, loose white blouses edged with pink, and tight skirts in parallel bands of blue, black, yellow and pink. After marriage, these brightly coloured clothes are replaced with a long fawn dress, but the beads are still worn. All the women wear their hair tied in a turban, and the men wear light-coloured baggy pants and tunics or, more commonly, Western clothes.

Film

Until recently, Thai cinema was almost impenetrable to the outside world. But the West began to take notice in 2000, when films such as *Iron Ladies*, *Tears of the Black Tiger* and later *The Legend of Suriyothai* showed that Thai directors had the style and wit to entertain non-Thai-speaking audiences. Many larger-budget Thai films are now released outside Thailand and with English subtitles.

A brief history

Thailand's first **cinema** was built in 1905 in Bangkok, behind Wat Tuk on Thanon Charoen Krung, and for a couple of decades screened only short, silent films from America, Europe and Japan. Though nothing remains of the earliest film-theatres, the renovated Art Deco Sala Chalermkrung, which was built in 1933 in Bangkok's Chinatown, is still in use today as a venue for live theatre and the occasional screening.

The **first home-grown film**, *Chok Sawng Chan* (*Double Luck*), made by the Wasuwat brothers of the Bangkok Film Company, didn't emerge until 1927, and it was another five years before *Long Thang* (*Going Astray*), the first Thai film with sound, followed.

During the 1920s, a few foreign film companies came to Thailand to film the local culture and wildlife. One early classic from this period is *Chang* (1927; available on video), which tells the simple story, in documentary style, of a family who live on the edge of the forest in Nan province. *Chang*'s American directors Merian Cooper and Ernest B. Schoedsack later drew on their experiences in the Thai jungle for their 1933 classic, *King Kong*.

Though Thai film-making continued throughout the 1930s and 1940s, it was virtually suspended during World War II, before re-emerging with a flourish in the 1950s. The 1950s, 1960s and 1970s were golden years for the production of large numbers of hastily made but hugely popular low-budget escapist films, mainly action melodramas featuring stereotypical characters, gangsters and corny love interest. Many of these films starred **Mitr Chaibancha**, Thailand's greatest-ever film star. He played the handsome hero in 265 films, in many of them performing opposite former beauty

POSTERS AND BILLBOARDS

Until the 1990s, domestic and foreign films were always promoted in Thailand with **original Thai artwork**, especially commissioned to hang as billboards and to be reproduced on posters. The artists who produced them really poured their hearts into these images, interpreting the film in their own style and always including an extraordinary amount of detail, usually as montage. Unlike the films themselves, Thai film posters were rarely subject to any censorship and as a result they were often far more eye-catchingly graphic and explicit than Western artwork for the same films. Posters for horror films (always very big in Thailand) depicted particularly gruesome, blood-drenched images, while ads for the (illegal) screenings of soft-porn movies often displayed a surprising amount of naked flesh.

Locally produced posters are still used to advertise films in Thailand, but for over a decade now they have featured photographic images instead of original artwork. However, there's still a chance to admire the exuberant creativity of Thai cinema art because many provincial cinemas continue to employ local artists to produce their own **billboard** paintings every week. Look for these giant works of art above cinema doors, at key locations around town, and on the sides of the megaphone trucks that circulate around town screeching out the times and plot lines of the next show. Within seven days they will have been dismantled, reduced to a pile of planks and painted over with the artwork for next week's film.

queen **Petchara Chaowarat**. Of the 165 movies they made together, their most famous was *Mon Rak Luk Thung* (*Enchanting Countryside*, 1969), a folk-musical about life and love in the countryside that played continuously in Bangkok for six months and later spawned a bestselling soundtrack album. Nearly every Thai adult can recall the days when Mitr co-starred with Petchara, and when Mitr fell to a dramatic death in 1970 – during a stunt involving a rope ladder suspended from a helicopter – it caused nationwide mourning. He was cremated at Wat Thepsirin in Bangkok (off Thanon Luang in Chinatown), where photos of the cremation ceremony and the crowds of fans who attended are still on display. Though non-Thai speakers are denied the pleasure of seeing Mitr and Petchara in action, you can get a good idea of the general tone of their films from the 2000 hit *Tears of the Black Tiger* (see p.784), which affectionately parodies the films of this period.

The 1970s and 1980s
For many years after Mitr's death, Thai cinema continued to be dominated by action melodramas, though a notable exception was *Khao Cheu Karn* (*His Name is Karn*), the first Thai film to tackle corruption in the civil service – it was released in 1973, not long before mass student demonstrations led to the ousting of the military government, and was made by Chatri Chalerm Yukol, who went on to direct the 2001 epic *The Legend of Suriyothai* (see p.784). The other standout film of the 1970s is *Phlae Khao* (*The Old Scar*, 1977), in which director Cherd Songsri uses traditional rural Thailand as a potent setting for a tragic romance that ends with the heroine's death.

With competition from television and large numbers of imported Hollywood films, Thai film production dwindled during the 1980s, but in 1984 the **Thai National Film Archive** was set up to preserve not only Thai films but also many of the wonderful posters used to promote them. A rare gem from the 1980s is Yuttana Mukdasanit's coming-of-age drama *Butterflies and Flowers* (*Pee Sua Lae Dok Mai*, 1986), which is set in a Muslim community in southern Thailand and looks at the pressures on a poor teenager who ends up smuggling rice across the nearby Malaysian border. The film won an award at the Hawaii International Film Festival.

By the 1990s, the Thai film industry was in a rather sorry state and the few films still produced were mainly trite melodramas aimed at an undiscerning teenage audience. But everything started to change for the better in 1997.

Modern Thai cinema
The rebirth of the Thai film industry started in 1997 with the release of Pen-Ek Ratanaruang's *Fun Bar Karaoke* and Nonzee Nimibutr's *Daeng Bireley and the Young Gangsters*. Fuelled by a **new wave** of talented directors and writers, including Nonzee and Pen-Ek, this resurgence has seen Thai films benefiting from larger budgets and achieving international acclaim. The new breed of Thai film-makers has moved away from traditional action melodramas and soap operas to create films that are more imaginative and stylish. With a new emphasis on production values, they also look very good, yet it is the fresh, distinctly Thai flavour that most charms Western audiences, a style summed up by one Thai film commentator as "neo-unrealist", and by another as being influenced by the popular *likay* genre of bawdy, over-the-top Thai street-theatre, where actors use song and dance as well as speech to tell their story.

Directors of the new wave

Daeng Bireley and the Young Gangsters (*2499 Antaphan Krong Muang*) was the surprise hit of 1997; **Nonzee Nimibutr** showed in this story of 1950s gangsters that he was able to appeal to the international festival circuit as well as local cinema-goers. He followed it up with the even more successful *Nang Nak* in 1999, giving the big-budget treatment to a traditional nineteenth-century Thai ghost story about a woman who dies while in labour, along with her unborn child. In *Jan Dara* (2001), the 1930s story of a young man who despises his womanizing stepfather, yet eventually becomes just such a person, Nonzee pushed the envelope of what was acceptable in Thai cinema by including scenes of rape and lesbianism that would not have been permitted a decade earlier. *Queens of Langkasuka* (*Puen Yai Jom Salad*, 2008) saw him turning to the more conservative genre of historical action fantasy, complete with sumptuous costumes, pirates, sea gypsies and sorcerers.

In a wry tale of messages received from beyond the grave, **Pen-Ek Ratanaruang**'s first film *Fun Bar Karaoke* (1997) looked at how the lives of modern middle-class Thais are still affected by traditional superstitions. His next film *6ixtynin9* (*Ruang Talok 69*, 1999) was a fast-paced thriller set during the Asian financial crisis, with a down-on-her-luck woman stumbling upon a hoard of money. Pen-Ek followed this with *Mon Rak Transistor: A Transistor Love Story* (2003), a bitter-sweet love story about a naïve boy from the country with ambitions to be a *luk thung* singer. It's full of charm and the popular soundtrack is available on CD (see p.776). Pen-Ek's *Last Life in the Universe* (2003) is a much darker, more melancholy affair, following two very different personalities – a suicidal Japanese man and a Thai girl – who are brought together in grief. In *Ploy* (2007), a jet-lagged night in a Bangkok hotel sees the marriage of an expat Thai couple unravel, with sex scenes deemed too explicit by Thai censors. Pen-Ek's latest, *Headshot* (*Fon Tok Kheun Faa*, literally "Rain Falling up to the Sky"; 2011), which tells of a hitman who wakes up from a coma seeing the world upside down, is a noirish thriller with a satirical political edge.

The scriptwriter on Nonzee's *Daeng Bireley* and *Nang Nak* was Wisit Sasanatieng, who, in 2000, directed **Tears of the Black Tiger** (*Fah Talai Jone*). This gentle send-up of the old Thai action films of the 1960s and 1970s uses exaggerated acting styles and irresistible comic-book colours to tell the story of handsome bandit Dum and his love for upper-class Rumpoey. Writer-director Wisit grew up watching the spaghetti westerns of Sergio Leone and includes more than a few passing references to those films. His **Citizen Dog** (*Mah Nakorn*, 2004) is an even more surreal colour-saturated satire, both comic and pointed, about a country boy looking for work and romance in Bangkok.

Blockbusters at home and abroad

Among other high-profile international successes, the warm and off-beat comedy **Iron Ladies** (*Satri Lek*, 2000) charts the often hilarious true-life adventures of a Lampang volleyball team made up of transsexuals and transvestites. **Beautiful Boxer** (2003) fashions a sensitive, insightful biopic out of a similar subject – the true story of transvestite *muay thai* champion Nong Toom who fights in order to win money for sex-change surgery. **Bangkok Dangerous** (*Krung Thep Antharai*, 2000) is a riveting John Woo-style thriller directed by brothers Oxide and Danny Pang; both a brutal tale about a deaf hitman and the story of his love affair with a girl innocent of his occupation, it features several scenes shot in the streets of Bangkok.

The visually stunning historical blockbuster **The Legend of Suriyothai** (2001) tells the true story of a sixteenth-century queen of the Ayutthayan court who gave her life defending her husband during a Burmese invasion. Keen to give international appeal to this complex portrait of court intrigue and rather partisan take on Thai-Burmese relations, director Chatrichalerm Yukol brought in Francis Ford Coppola to edit a shortened version for Western audiences. He followed it with the most expensive

Thai film to date, at a reported cost of B700 million, **The Legend of King Naresuan** (*Tamnan Somdej Phra Naresuan*, 2007), telling the story of King Naresuan, a national hero who ruled Thailand from Ayutthaya in the sixteenth century. Capturing a strong nationalist and royalist mood in certain sections of Thai society, the film has been turned into a series, with the fifth episode coming out in 2012. Garnering the bizarre "P" rating in the new Thai film classification system (meaning that a film has to be promoted, and all Thais are encouraged to watch it, because of its supposed cultural merit), the third and fourth episodes in the series were the two top-grossing films of 2011. The series has been shot at the purpose-built Prommitr Film Studios just outside Kanchanaburi, whose period sets are now open to the public (Ⓦprommitrfilmstudio.com).

Prachya Pinkaew's martial arts action flick **Ong Bak** (2003) was such a huge box-office hit around the world that its star **Tony Jaa** – who performed all his own extraordinary stunts – was appointed Cultural Ambassador for Thailand. Director and star teamed up again in the similarly testosterone-fuelled **Tom Yum Goong** (2005), in which Tony Jaa's fight skills lead him to Australia on the trail of a stolen elephant. Two sequels to *Ong Bak* have been made up to now, and *Tom Yum Goong 2* is due to be made in the near future.

At the other end of the spectrum, Thai art house also went international with the success of **Apichatpong Weerasethakul**'s challenging **Tropical Malady** (*Sud Pralad*, 2004), which won the Jury Prize at Cannes in 2004. Part gay romance, part trippy jungle ghost story, it was for some a pioneering experiment in Thai storytelling, to others an inaccessible bore. His *Syndromes and a Century* (*Sang Sattawat*, 2006) was Thailand's first film to be entered in competition at the Venice Film Festival but failed to impress the Thai censors who, among other reasons, banned it for its depiction of a guitar-playing Buddhist monk. Apichatpong responded by joining a protest against the introduction of a new, reactionary film-ratings system, but to no avail. His *Uncle Boonmee (who can Recall his Past Lives)*, a dreamy, quasi-realist exploration of Thai belief in *phii* (spirits), won the Palme d'Or at Cannes in 2010 but achieved only a limited release back in Thailand. Other experimental directors to look out for include **Thanska Pansittivorakul** and **Thanwarin Sukhaphisit**.

Many of the films that get widespread international release are unrepresentative of the crowd-pleasers that play week in, week out at most Thai cinemas. These tend to feature lots of laughs, slapstick, gangsters, likeably corny romance and much poking of fun at authority figures. The domestic blockbuster of 2009 was *Bangkok Traffic Love Story* (or *BTS*; in Thai, *Rot Fai Faa Ma Ha Na Thoe*), a romantic comedy sponsored by the BTS Skytrain to celebrate its tenth anniversary. Meanwhile, the four spooky horror stories of **4Bia** (*See Prang*, 2008), each by a different director (including **Yongyoot Thongkongtoon**, who made *Iron Ladies*), proved that while ghosts still do it for a Thai audience, they can intrigue foreign film-goers too.

Neil Pettigrew

Books

We have included publishers' details for books that may be hard to find outside Thailand, though some of them can be ordered online through ⓦdcothai.com, which also carries e-books. Other titles should be available worldwide. Titles marked ★ are particularly recommended. There's a good selection of Thai novels and short stories in translation, available to buy as e-books, on ⓦthaifiction.com.

TRAVELOGUES

Carl Bock *Temples and Elephants* (Orchid Press, Bangkok). Nineteenth-century account of a rough journey from Bangkok to the far north, dotted with vivid descriptions of rural life and court ceremonial.

Karen Connelly *Touch the Dragon*. Evocative and humorous journal of an impressionable Canadian teenager, sent on an exchange programme to Den Chai in northern Thailand for a year.

Charles Nicholl *Borderlines*. Entertaining adventures and dangerous romance in the "Golden Triangle" form the core of this slightly hackneyed traveller's tale, interwoven with stimulating and well-informed cultural diversions.

James O'Reilly and Larry Habegger (eds) *Travelers'*

Tales: Thailand. Absorbing anthology of contemporary writings about Thailand, by Thailand experts, social commentators, travel writers and first-time visitors.

Steve Van Beek *Slithering South* (Wind and Water, Hong Kong). An expat writer tells how he single-handedly paddled his wooden boat down the entire 1100km course of the Chao Phraya River, and reveals a side of Thailand that's rarely written about in English.

Tom Vater *Beyond the Pancake Trench: Road Tales from the Wild East*. Adventures, insights and encounters on the margins of twenty-first-century Thailand. Also covers Cambodia, Laos, Vietnam and India.

CULTURE AND SOCIETY

Michael Carrithers *The Buddha: A Very Short Introduction*. Accessible account of the life of the Buddha, and the development and significance of his thought.

★ **Philip Cornwel-Smith and John Goss** *Very Thai*. Why do Thais decant their soft drinks into plastic bags, and how does one sniff-kiss? Answers and insights aplenty in this intriguingly observant, fully illustrated guide to contemporary Thai culture. Look out also for Cornwel-Smith's forthcoming *Very Bangkok*.

James Eckardt *Bangkok People*. The collected articles of a renowned expat journalist, whose encounters with a varied cast of Bangkokians – from construction-site workers and street vendors to boxers and political candidates – add texture and context to the city.

Sandra Gregory with Michael Tierney *Forget You Had a Daughter: Doing Time in the "Bangkok Hilton" – Sandra Gregory's Story*. The frank and shocking account of a young British woman's term in Bangkok's notorious Lard Yao prison after being caught trying to smuggle 89g of heroin out of Thailand.

Roger Jones *Culture Smart! Thailand*. Handy little primer on Thailand's social and cultural mores, with plenty of refreshingly up-to-date insights.

★ **Erich Krauss** *Wave of Destruction: One Thai Village and Its Battle with the Tsunami*. A sad and often shocking,

clear-eyed account of what Ban Nam Khem went through before, during and after the tsunami. Fills in many gaps left unanswered by news reports at the time.

Elaine and Paul Lewis *Peoples of the Golden Triangle*. Hefty, exhaustive work illustrated with excellent photographs, describing every aspect of hill-tribe life.

Father Joe Maier *Welcome to the Bangkok Slaughterhouse: The Battle for Human Dignity in Bangkok's Bleakest Slums*. Catholic priest Father Joe shares the stories of some of the Bangkok street kids and slum-dwellers that his charitable foundation has been supporting since 1972 (see p.58).

Trilok Chandra Majupuria *Erawan Shrine and Brahma Worship in Thailand* (Tecpress, Bangkok). The most concise introduction to the complexities of Thai religion, with a much wider scope than the title implies.

Cleo Odzer *Patpong Sisters*. An American anthropologist's funny and touching account of her life with the prostitutes and bar girls of Bangkok's notorious red-light district.

★ **Phra Peter Pannapadipo** *Little Angels: The Real-Life Stories of Twelve Thai Novice Monks*. A dozen young boys, many of them from desperate backgrounds, tell the often poignant stories of why they became novice monks. For some, funding from the Students Education Trust (p.59) has changed their lives.

Phra Peter Pannapadipo *Phra Farang: An English Monk in Thailand*. Behind the scenes in a Thai monastery: the frank, funny and illuminating account of a UK-born former businessman's life as a Thai monk.

★ **Pasuk Phongpaichit and Sungsidh Piriyarangsan** *Corruption and Democracy in Thailand*. Fascinating academic study, revealing the nuts and bolts of corruption in Thailand and its links with all levels of political life, and suggesting a route to a stronger society. Their sequel, a study of Thailand's illegal economy, *Guns, Girls, Gambling, Ganja*, co-written with Nualnoi Treerat, makes equally eye-opening and depressing reading.

Denis Segaller *Thai Ways*. Fascinating collection of short pieces on Thai customs and traditions written by a long-term English resident of Bangkok.

Pira Sudham *People of Esarn*. Wry and touching, potted life stories of villagers who live in, leave and return to the poverty-stricken northeast, compiled by a northeastern lad turned author.

Phil Thornton *Restless Souls: Rebels, Refugees, Medics and Misfits on the Thai–Burma Border*. An Australian journalist brings to light the terrible and complicated plight of the Karen, thousands of whom live as refugees in and around his adopted town of Mae Sot on the Thai–Burma border.

Richard Totman *The Third Sex: Kathoey – Thailand's Ladyboys*. As several *kathoey* share their life stories with him, social scientist Totman examines their place in modern Thai society and explores the theory, supported by Buddhist philosophy, that *kathoey* are members of a third sex whose transgendered make-up is predetermined from birth.

Tom Vater and Aroon Thaewchatturat *Sacred Skin*. Fascinating, beautifully photographed exploration of Thailand's spirit tattoos, *sak yant*.

William Warren *Living in Thailand*. Luscious gallery of traditional houses, with an emphasis on the homes of Thailand's rich and famous; seductively photographed by Luca Invernizzi Tettoni.

Daniel Ziv and Guy Sharett *Bangkok Inside Out*. This A–Z of Bangkok quirks and cultural substrates is full of slick photography and sparky observations but was deemed offensive by Thailand's Ministry of Culture, so some Thai bookshops won't stock it.

HISTORY

Anna Leonowens *The English Governess at the Siamese Court*. The mendacious memoirs of the nineteenth-century English governess that inspired the infamous Yul Brynner film *The King and I*; low on accuracy, high on inside-palace gossip.

Chang Noi *Jungle Book: Thailand's Politics, Moral Panic and Plunder 1996–2008* (Silkworm Books, Chiang Mai). A fascinating, often humorous, selection of columns about Thailand's political and social jungle, by "Little Elephant", an anonymous foreign resident, which first appeared in *The Nation* newspaper.

Michael Smithies *Old Bangkok*. Brief, anecdotal history of the capital's early development, emphasizing what remains to be seen of bygone Bangkok.

John Stewart *To the River Kwai: Two Journeys – 1943, 1979*. A survivor of the horrific World War II POW camps along the River Kwai returns to the region, interlacing his wartime reminiscences with observations on how he feels 36 years later.

William Warren *Jim Thompson: the Legendary American of Thailand*. The engrossing biography of the ex-intelligence agent, art collector and Thai silk magnate whose disappearance in Malaysia in 1967 has never been satisfactorily resolved.

Thongchai Winichakul *Siam Mapped*. Intriguing, seminal account of how Rama V, under pressure on his borders from Britain and France at the turn of the twentieth century, in effect colonized his own country, which was then a loose hierarchy of city-states.

★ **David K. Wyatt** *Thailand: A Short History*. An excellent treatment, scholarly but highly readable, with a good eye for witty, telling details. Good chapters on the story of the Thais before they reached what's now Thailand, and on more recent developments. The same author's *Siam in Mind* (Silkworm Books, Chiang Mai) is a wide-ranging and intriguing collection of sketches and short reflections that point towards an intellectual history of Thailand.

ART, ARCHITECTURE AND FILM

Jean Boisselier *The Heritage of Thai Sculpture*. Expensive but accessible, seminal tome by influential French art historian.

★ **Susan Conway** *Thai Textiles*. A fascinating, richly illustrated work which draws on sculptures and temple murals to trace the evolution of Thai weaving techniques and costume styles, and to examine the functional and ceremonial uses of textiles.

★ **Sumet Jumsai** *Naga: Cultural Origins in Siam and the West Pacific*. Wide-ranging discussion of water symbols in Thailand and other parts of Asia, offering a stimulating mix of art, architecture, mythology and cosmology.

Bastian Meiresonne (ed) *Thai Cinema* (ⓦasiexpo.com). Anthology of twenty short essays on Thai cinema up to 2006, published to accompany a film festival in France, including pieces on art house, shorts and censorship. In French and English.

Steven Pettifor *Flavours: Thai Contemporary Art*. Takes up the baton from Poshyananda (see p.788) to look at the newly invigorated art scene in Thailand from 1992 to 2004, with profiles of 23 leading lights, including painters, multimedia and performance artists.

★ **Apinan Poshyananda** *Modern Art In Thailand*. Excellent introduction which extends up to the early 1990s, with very readable discussions on dozens of individual artists, and lots of colour plates.

Dome Sukwong and Sawasdi Suwannapak *A Century of Thai Cinema*. Full-colour history of the Thai film industry and the promotional artwork (billboards, posters, magazines and cigarette cards) associated with it.

★ **Steve Van Beek** *The Arts of Thailand*. Lavishly produced and perfectly pitched introduction to the history of Thai architecture, sculpture and painting, with superb photographs by Luca Invernizzi Tettoni.

William Warren and Luca Invernizzi Tettoni *Arts and Crafts of Thailand*. Good-value large-format paperback, setting the wealth of Thai arts and crafts in cultural context, with plenty of attractive illustrations and colour photographs.

NATURAL HISTORY AND ECOLOGY

Ashley J. Boyd and Collin Piprell *Diving in Thailand*. A thorough guide to 84 dive sites, plus general introductory sections on Thailand's marine life, conservation and photography tips.

★ **Boonsong Lekagul and Philip D. Round** *Guide to the Birds of Thailand*. Unparalleled illustrated guide to Thailand's birds. Worth scouring secondhand sellers for.

Craig Robson *A Field Guide to the Birds of Thailand*. Expert and beautifully illustrated guide to Thailand's top 950 bird species, with locator maps.

Eric Valli and Diane Summers *The Shadow Hunters*. Beautifully photographed photo-essay on the bird's-nest collectors of southern Thailand, with whom the authors spent over a year, together scaling the phenomenal heights of the sheer limestone walls.

LITERATURE

Alastair Dingwall (ed) *Traveller's Literary Companion: Southeast Asia*. A useful though rather dry reference, with a large section on Thailand, including a book list, well-chosen extracts, biographical details of authors and other literary notes.

M.L. Manich Jumsai *Thai Ramayana* (Chalermnit, Bangkok). Slightly stilted, abridged prose translation of King Rama I's version of the epic Hindu narrative, full of gleeful descriptions of bizarre mythological characters and supernatural battles. Essential reading for a full appreciation of Thai painting, carving and classical dance.

★ **Chart Korbjitti** *The Judgement* (Howling Books). Sobering modern-day tragedy about a good-hearted Thai villager who is ostracized by his hypocritical neighbours. Contains lots of interesting details on village life and traditions, and thought-provoking passages on the stifling conservatism of rural communities. Winner of the S.E.A. Write Award in 1982.

★ **Rattawut Lapcharoensap** *Sightseeing*. This outstanding debut collection of short stories by a young Thai-born author now living overseas highlights big, pertinent themes – cruelty, corruption, racism, pride – in its neighbourhood tales of randy teenagers, bullyboys, a child's friendship with a Cambodian refugee, a young man who uses family influence to dodge the draft.

Nitaya Masavisut (ed) *The S.E.A. Write Anthology of Thai Short Stories and Poems* (Silkworm Books, Chiang Mai). Interesting medley of short stories and poems by Thai writers who have won Southeast Asian Writers' Awards, providing a good introduction to the contemporary literary scene.

Kukrit Pramoj *Si Phaendin: Four Reigns* (Silkworm Books, Chiang Mai). A kind of historical romance spanning the four reigns of Ramas V to VIII (1892–1946). Written by former prime minister Kukrit Pramoj, the story has become a modern classic in Thailand, made into films, plays and TV dramas, with heroine Ploi as the archetypal feminine role model.

S.P. Somtow *Jasmine Nights*. An engaging and humorous rites-of-passage tale, of an upper-class boy learning what it is to be Thai. *Dragon's Fin Soup and Other Modern Siamese Fables* is an imaginative and entertaining collection of often supernatural short stories, focusing on the collision of East and West.

★ **Khamsing Srinawk** *The Politician and Other Stories*. A collection of brilliantly satiric short stories, full of pithy moral observation and biting irony, which capture the vulnerability of peasant farmers in the north and northeast, as they try to come to grips with the modern world. Written by an insider from a peasant family, who was educated at Chulalongkorn University, became a hero of the left, and joined the communist insurgents after the 1976 clampdown.

Atsiri Thammachoat *Of Time and Tide* (Thai Modern Classics). Set in a fishing village near Hua Hin, this poetically written novella looks at how Thailand's fishing industry is changing, charting the effects on its fisherfolk and their communities.

Klaus Wenk *Thai Literature – An Introduction* (White Lotus, Bangkok). Dry, but useful, short overview of the last seven hundred years by a noted German scholar, with plenty of extracts.

THAILAND IN FOREIGN LITERATURE

Dean Barrett *Kingdom of Make-Believe*. Despite the clichéd ingredients – the Patpong go-go bar scene, opium smuggling in the Golden Triangle, Vietnam veterans – this novel about a return to Thailand following a twenty-year absence turns out to be a rewardingly multi-dimensional take on the farang experience.

★ **Mischa Berlinski** *Fieldwork*. Anthropology versus evangelism, a battle played out over an imaginary hill tribe in the hills of Chiang Rai by a fascinating cast of characters, as wryly and vividly told by its narrator.

Botan *Letters from Thailand*. Probably the best introduction to the Chinese community in Bangkok, presented in the form of letters written over a twenty-year period by a Chinese emigrant to his mother. Branded as both anti-Chinese and anti-Thai, this 1969 prize-winning book is now mandatory reading in school social studies' classes.

Pierre Boulle *The Bridge Over the River Kwai*. The World War II novel that inspired the David Lean movie and kicked off the Kanchanaburi tourist industry.

John Burdett *Bangkok 8*. Riveting Bangkok thriller that takes in Buddhism, plastic surgery, police corruption, the *yaa baa* drugs trade, hookers, jade smuggling and the spirit world.

Alex Garland *The Beach*. Gripping cult thriller (later made into a film, shot partly on Ko Phi Phi Leh) that uses a Thai setting to explore the way in which travellers' ceaseless quest for "undiscovered" utopias inevitably leads to them despoiling the idyll.

Andrew Hicks *Thai Girl*. A British backpacker falls for a reticent young beach masseuse on Ko Samet but struggles with age-old cross-cultural confusion in this sensitive attempt at a different kind of expat novel.

Michel Houellebecq *Platform*. Sex tourism in Thailand provides the nucleus of this brilliantly provocative (some would say offensive) novel, in which Houellebecq presents a ferocious critique of Western decadence and cultural colonialism, and of radical Islam too.

Christopher G. Moore *God of Darkness*. Thailand's best-selling expat novelist sets his most intriguing thriller during the economic crisis of 1997 and includes plenty of meat on endemic corruption and the desperate struggle for power within family and society.

Darin Strauss *Chang & Eng*. An intriguing, imagined autobiography of the famous nineteenth-century Siamese twins (see p.184), from their impoverished Thai childhood via the freak shows of New York and London to married life in small-town North Carolina. Unfortunately marred by lazy research and a confused grasp of Thai geography and culture.

FOOD AND COOKERY

Vatcharin Bhumichitr *The Taste of Thailand*. Another glossy introduction to this eminently photogenic country, this time through its food. The author runs a Thai restaurant in London and provides background colour as well as about 150 recipes adapted for Western kitchens.

Jacqueline M. Piper *Fruits of South-East Asia*. An exploration of the bounteous fruits of the region, tracing their role in cooking, medicine, handicrafts and rituals. Well illustrated with photos, watercolours and early botanical drawings.

★ **David Thompson** *Thai Food*. Comprehensive, impeccably researched celebration of the cuisine, with over three hundred recipes, by the owner of the first Thai restaurant ever to earn a Michelin star.

TRAVEL GUIDES

Oliver Hargreaves *Exploring Phuket & Phi Phi: From Tin to Tourism*. Fascinating, thoroughly researched guide to the Andaman coast's big touristic honeypots; especially good on Phuket's history.

★ **Thom Henley** *Krabi: Caught in the Spell – A Guide to Thailand's Enchanted Province* (Thai Nature Education, Phuket). Highly readable features and observations on the attractions and people of south Thailand's most beautiful region, written by an expat environmentalist.

Dawn F. Rooney *Ancient Sukhothai*. Lively and beautifully photographed full-colour guide to the ruins of the northern plains: Sukhothai, Si Satchanalai and Kamphaeng Phet.

William Warren *Bangkok*. An engaging portrait of the unwieldy capital, weaving together anecdotes and character sketches from Bangkok's past and present.

Language

Thai belongs to one of the oldest families of languages in the world, Austro-Thai, and is radically different from most of the other tongues of Southeast Asia. Being tonal, Thai is very difficult for Westerners to master, but by building up from a small core of set phrases, you should soon have enough to get by. Most Thais who deal with tourists speak some English, but once you stray off the beaten track you'll probably need at least a little Thai. Anywhere you go, you'll impress and get better treatment if you at least make an effort to speak a few words.

Distinct dialects are spoken in the north, the northeast and the south, which can increase the difficulty of comprehending what's said to you. **Thai script** is even more of a problem to Westerners, with 44 consonants and 32 vowels. However, street signs in touristed areas are nearly always written in Roman script as well as Thai, and in other circumstances you're better off asking than trying to unscramble the swirling mess of letters and accents. For more information on transliteration into Roman script, see the box in this book's introduction.

Among **language books**, *Thai: The Rough Guide Phrasebook* covers the essential phrases and expressions in both Thai script and phonetic equivalents, as well as dipping into grammar and providing a menu reader and fuller vocabulary in dictionary format (English-Thai and Thai-English). Probably the best pocket dictionary is Paiboon Publishing's (ⓦpaiboonpublishing.com) *Thai-English, English-Thai Dictionary* (also available as a CD and as an app), which lists words in phonetic Thai as well as Thai script, and features very useful examples of the Thai alphabet in different fonts.

The best **teach-yourself course** is the expensive *Linguaphone Thai* (including eight CDs and an alphabet book), which also has a shorter, cheaper beginner-level *PDQ* version (with four CDs or downloadable audio files). *Thai for Beginners* by Benjawan Poomsan Becker (Paiboon Publishing) is a cheaper, more manageable textbook and is especially good for getting to grips with the Thai writing system; you can also buy accompanying CDs to help with listening skills, or get the whole thing in CD-ROM or Apple app format. For a more traditional textbook, try Stuart Campbell and Chuan Shaweevongse's *The Fundamentals of the Thai Language*, which is comprehensive, though hard going. The **website** ⓦthai-language. com is an amazing free resource, featuring a searchable dictionary with over fifty thousand entries, complete with Thai script and audio clips, plus a guide to the language, lessons and forums; you can also browse and buy Thai language books and learning materials. There are also plenty of **language classes** available in Thailand (see p.69).

Pronunciation

Mastering **tones** is probably the most difficult part of learning Thai. Five different tones are used – low, middle, high, falling, and rising – by which the meaning of a single syllable can be altered in five different ways. Thus, using four of the five tones, you can make a sentence from just one syllable: "mái mài mâi ma˘i" meaning "New wood burns, doesn't it?" As well as the natural difficulty in becoming attuned to speaking and listening to these different tones, Western efforts are complicated by our habit of denoting the overall meaning of a sentence by modulating our tones – for example, turning a statement into a question through a shift of stress and tone. Listen to native Thai speakers and you'll soon begin to pick up the different approach to tone.

The pitch of each tone is gauged in relation to your vocal range when speaking, but they should all lie within a narrow band, separated by gaps just big enough to differentiate them. The **low tones** (syllables marked ` `) **middle tones** (unmarked syllables), and **high tones** (syllables marked ´) should each be pronounced evenly and with no inflection. The **falling tone** (syllables marked ^) is spoken with an obvious drop in pitch, as if you were sharply emphasizing a word in English. The **rising tone** (marked ˇ) is pronounced as if you were asking an exaggerated question in English.

As well as the unfamiliar tones, you'll find that, despite the best efforts of the transliterators, there is no precise English equivalent to many **vowel and consonant sounds** in the Thai language. The lists below give a simplified idea of pronunciation.

VOWELS

a as in dad	**eu** as in sir, but heavily nasalized
aa has no precise equivalent, but is pronounced as it looks, with the vowel elongated	**i** as in tip
	ii as in feet
ae as in there	**o** as in knock
ai as in buy	**oe** as in hurt, but more closed
ao as in now	**oh** as in toe
aw as in awe	**u** as in loot
ay as in pay	**uu** as in pool
e as in pen	

CONSONANTS

r as in rip, but with the tongue flapped quickly against the palate – in everyday speech, it's often pronounced like "l"	**th** as in time
	k is unaspirated and unvoiced, and closer to "g"
	p is also unaspirated and unvoiced, and closer to "b"
kh as in keep	**t** is also unaspirated and unvoiced, and closer to "d"
ph as in put	

General words and phrases

GREETINGS AND BASIC PHRASES

When you speak to a stranger in Thailand, you should generally end your sentence in *khráp* if you're a man, *khâ* if you're a woman – these untranslatable politening syllables will gain goodwill, and are nearly always used after *sawàt dii* (hello/goodbye) and *khàwp khun* (thank you). *Khráp* and *khâ* are also often used to answer "yes" to a question, though the most common way is to repeat the verb of the question (precede it with *mâi* for "no"). *Châi* (yes) and *mâi châi* (no) are less frequently used than their English equivalents.

Hello	sawàt dii	How are you?	sabai dii reŭ?
Where are you going?	pai năi? (not always meant literally, but used as a general greeting)	I'm fine	sabai dii
		What's your name?	khun chêu arai?
		My name is…	phŏm (men)/diichăn (women) chêu…
I'm out having fun/ I'm travelling	pai thîaw (answer to pai năi, almost indefinable pleasantry)	I come from…	phŏm/diichăn maa jàak…
Goodbye	sawàt dii/la kàwn	I don't understand	mâi khâo jai
Good luck/cheers	chôhk dii	Do you speak English?	khun phûut phasăa angkrìt dâi măi?
Excuse me	khăw thâwt		
Thank you	khàwp khun	Do you have…?	mii…măi?
It's nothing/ it doesn't matter	mâi pen rai	Is…possible?	…dâi măi?

Can you help me?	chûay phŏm/ diichăn dâi mǎi?	(I) like…	châwp…
(I) want…	ao…	What is this called in Thai?	níi phasǎa thai rîak wâa arai?
(I) would like to…	yàak jà…		

GETTING AROUND

Where is the…?	…yùu thîi nǎi?	west	tawan tòk
How far?	klai thâo rai?	near/far	klâi/klai
I would like to go to…	yàak jà pai…	street	thanŏn
Where have you been?	pai nǎi maa?	train station	sathǎanii rót fai
Where is this bus going?	rót níi pai nǎi?	bus station	sathǎanii rót mae
When will the bus leave?	rót jà àwk mêua rai?	airport	sanǎam bin
What time does the bus arrive in…?	rót theǔng…kìi mohng?	ticket	tǔa
		hotel	rohng raem
Stop here	jàwt thîi níi	post office	praisanii
here	thîi níi	restaurant	raan ahǎan
there/over there	thîi nâan/thîi nôhn	shop	raan
right	khwǎa	market	talàat
left	sái	hospital	rohng pha-yaabaan
straight	trong	motorbike	rót mohtoesai
north	neǔa	taxi	rót táksîi
south	tâi	boat	reua
east	tawan àwk	bicycle	jàkràyaan

ACCOMMODATION AND SHOPPING

How much is…?	…thâo rai/kìi bàat?	Can I store my bag here?	fàak krapǎo wái thîi níi dâi mǎi?
I don't want a plastic bag, thanks	mâi ao thǔng khráp/khâ	cheap/expensive	thùuk/phaeng
How much is a room here per night?	hâwng thîi níi kheun lá thâo rai?	air-con room	hǎwng ae
Do you have a cheaper room?	mii hâwng thùuk kwàa mǎi?	ordinary room	hǎwng thammadaa
		telephone	thohrásàp
Can I/we look at the room?	duu hâwng dâi mǎi?	laundry	sák phâa
I/We'll stay two nights	jà yùu sǎwng kheun	blanket	phâa hòm
Can you reduce the price?	lót raakhaa dâi mǎi?	fan	phát lom

GENERAL ADJECTIVES

alone	khon diaw	fun	sanùk
another	ìik…nèung	hot (temperature)	ráwn
bad	mâi dii	hot (spicy)	phèt
big	yài	hungry	hiǔ khâo
clean	sa-àat	ill	mâi sabai
closed	pìt	open	pòet
cold (object)	yen	pretty	sǔay
cold (person or weather)	nǎo	small	lek
delicious	aròi	thirsty	hiǔ nám
difficult	yâak	tired	nèu-ay
dirty	sokaprok	very	mâak
easy	ngâi		

GENERAL NOUNS

Nouns have no plurals or genders, and don't require an article.

bathroom/toilet	hǎwng nám	friend	phêuan
boyfriend or girlfriend	faen	money	ngoen
food	ahǎan	water/liquid	nám
foreigner	fàràng		

GENERAL VERBS

Thai verbs do not conjugate at all, and also often double up as nouns and adjectives, which means that foreigners' most unidiomatic attempts to construct sentences are often readily understood.

come	maa	go	pai
do	tham	sit	nâng
eat	kin/thaan khâo	sleep	nawn làp
give	hâi	walk	doen pai

NUMBERS

zero	sǔun	twelve, thirteen…	sìp sǎwng, sìp sǎam…
one	nèung	twenty	yîi sìp/yiip
two	sǎwng	twenty-one	yîi sìp èt
three	sǎam	twenty-two,	yîi sìp sǎwng,
four	sìi	twenty-three…	yîi sìp sǎam…
five	hâa	thirty, forty, etc	sǎam sìp, sìi sìp…
six	hòk	one hundred,	nèung rói, sǎwng rói…
seven	jèt	two hundred…	
eight	pàet	one thousand	nèung phan
nine	kâo	ten thousand	nèung mèun
ten	sìp	one hundred thousand	nèung sǎen
eleven	sìp èt	one million	nèung lǎan

TIME

The most common system for telling the time, as outlined below, is actually a confusing mix of several different systems. The State Railway and government officials use the 24-hour clock (9am is *kâo naalikaa*, 10am *sìp naalikaa*, and so on), which is always worth trying if you get stuck.

1–5am	tii nèung–tii hâa	hour	chûa mohng
6–11am	hòk mohng cháo–sìp èt	day	wan
	mohng cháo	week	aathít
noon	thîang	month	deuan
1pm	bài mohng	year	pii
2–4pm	bài sǎwng mohng–	today	wan níi
	bài sìi mohng	tomorrow	phrûng níi
5–6pm	hâa mohng yen–	yesterday	mêua wan níi
	hòk mohng yen	now	diǎw níi
7–11pm	nèung thûm–hâa thûm	next week	aathít nâa
midnight	thîang kheun	last week	aathít kàwn
What time is it?	kìi mohng láew?	morning	cháo
How many hours?	kìi chûa mohng?	afternoon	bài
How long?	naan thâo rai?	evening	yen
minute	naathii	night	kheun

DAYS

Sunday	wan aathít	Thursday	wan pháréuhàt
Monday	wan jan	Friday	wan sùk
Tuesday	wan angkhaan	Saturday	wan são
Wednesday	wan phút		

Food and drink

BASIC INGREDIENTS

kài	chicken	plaa mèuk	squid
mǔu	pork	kûng	prawn, shrimp
néua	beef, meat	hǒy	shellfish
pèt	duck	hǒy nang rom	oyster
ahǎan thaláy	seafood	puu	crab
plaa	fish	khài	egg
plaa dùk	catfish	phàk	vegetables

VEGETABLES

makěua	aubergine	taeng kwaa	cucumber
makěua thêt	tomato	phrík yùak	green pepper
nàw mái	bamboo shoots	krathiam	garlic
tùa ngâwk	bean sprouts	hèt	mushroom
phrík	chilli	tùa	peas, beans or lentils
man faràng	potato	tôn hǒrm	spring onions
man faràng thâwt	chips		

NOODLES

ba mìi	egg noodles	kwáy tiǎw/ba mìi	rice noodles/egg noodles
kwáy tiǎw (sên yaì/ sên lék)	white rice noodles (wide/thin)	rât nâ (mǔu)	fried in gravy-like sauce with vegetables (and pork slices)
khanǒm jiin nám yaa	noodles topped with fish curry	mìi kràwp	crisp fried egg noodles with small pieces of meat
kwáy tiǎw/ba mìi haêng	rice noodle/egg noodles fried with egg, small pieces of meat and a few vegetables	phàt thai	and a few vegetables thin noodles fried with egg, bean sprouts and tofu, topped with ground peanuts
kwáy tiǎw/ba mìi nám (mǔu)	rice noodle/egg noodle soup, made with chicken broth (and pork balls)	phàt siyú	wide or thin noodles fried with soy sauce, egg and meat

RICE

khâo	rice	khâo niǎw	sticky rice
khâo man kài	slices of chicken served over marinated rice	khâo phàt	fried rice
		khâo kaeng	curry over rice
khâo mǔu daeng	red pork with rice	khâo tôm	rice soup (usually for breakfast)
khâo nâ kài/pèt	chicken/duck served with sauce over rice		

CURRIES AND SOUPS

kaeng phèt	hot, red curry	kaeng liang	peppery vegetable soup
kaeng phánaeng	thick, savoury curry	kaeng sôm	tamarind soup
kaeng khîaw wan	green curry	tôm khà kài	chicken, coconut and
kaeng mátsàman	rich Muslim-style curry,		galangal soup
	usually with beef and	tôm yam kûng	hot and sour prawn soup
	potatoes	kaeng jèut	mild soup with
kaeng karìi	mild, Indian-style curry		vegetables and
hàw mòk thalay	seafood curry soufflé		usually pork

SALADS

lâap	spicy ground meat salad	yam plaa mèuk	squid salad
nám tòk	grilled beef or pork salad	yam sôm oh	pomelo salad
sôm tam	spicy papaya salad	yam plaa dùk foo	crispy fried catfish salad
yam hua plee	banana flower salad	yam thùa phuu	wing-bean salad
yam néua	grilled beef salad	yam wun sen	noodle and pork salad

OTHER DISHES

hâwy thâwt	omelette stuffed with mussels	néua phàt krathiam phrík thai	beef fried with garlic and pepper
kài phàt bai kraprao	chicken fried with holy basil leaves	néua phàt nám man hâwy	beef in oyster sauce
kài phàt nàw mái	chicken with bamboo shoots	phàt phàk bûng fai daeng	morning glory fried in garlic and bean sauce
kài phàt mét mámûang	chicken with cashew nuts	phàt phàk ruam	stir-fried vegetables
		pàw pía	spring rolls
kài phàt khîng	chicken with ginger	plaa nêung páe sá	whole fish steamed with vegetables and ginger
kài yâang	grilled chicken		
khài yát sài	omelette with pork and vegetables	plaa rât phrík	whole fish cooked with chillies
		plaa thâwt	fried whole fish
kûng chúp paêng thâwt	prawns fried in batter	sàté	satay
mǔu prîaw wǎan	sweet and sour pork	thâwt man plaa	fish cake

THAI DESSERTS (KHANǑM)

khanǒm beuang	small crispy pancake folded over with coconut cream and strands of sweet egg inside	khâo nǐaw thúrian/ mámûang	sticky rice mixed with coconut cream and durian/mango
		klûay khàek	fried banana
khâo lǎam	sticky rice, coconut cream and black beans cooked and served in bamboo tubes	lûk taan chêum	sweet palm kernels served in syrup
		sǎngkhayaa	coconut custard
		tàkô	squares of transparent jelly (jello) topped with coconut cream
khâo nǐaw daeng	sticky red rice mixed with coconut cream		

DRINKS (KHREÛANG DEÙM)

bia	beer	klûay pan	banana shake
chaa ráwn	hot tea	nám mánao/sôm	fresh, bottled or fizzy
chaa yen	iced tea		lemon/orange juice
kaafae ráwn	hot coffee	nám plào	drinking water
kâew	glass		(boiled or filtered)
khúat	bottle	nám sǒdaa	soda water
mâekhǒng	Thai brand-name	nám taan	sugar
(or anglicized Mekong)	rice whisky	kleua	salt

nám yen	cold water	ohlíang	iced black coffee
nom jeùd	milk	thûay	cup

ORDERING

I am vegetarian/vegan	Phŏm (male)/diichăn (female) kin ahăan mangsàwirát/jeh	I would like… with/without…	Khăw… Sài/mâi saì…
Can I see the menu?	Khăw duù menu nóy?	Can I have the bill please?	Khăw check bin?

Glossary

Amphoe District.

Amphoe muang Provincial capital.

Ao Bay.

Apsara Female deity.

Avalokitesvara Bodhisattva representing compassion.

Avatar Earthly manifestation of a deity.

Ban Village or house.

Bang Village by a river or the sea.

Bencharong Polychromatic ceramics made in China for the Thai market.

Bhumisparsa mudra Most common gesture of Buddha images; symbolizes the Buddha's victory over temptation.

Bodhisattva In Mahayana Buddhism, an enlightened being who postpones his or her entry into Nirvana.

Bot Main sanctuary of a Buddhist temple.

Brahma One of the Hindu trinity – "The Creator". Usually depicted with four faces and four arms.

Celadon Porcelain with grey-green glaze.

Changwat Province.

Chao ley/chao nam "Sea gypsies" – nomadic fisherfolk of south Thailand.

Chedi Reliquary tower in Buddhist temple.

Chofa Finial on temple roof.

Deva Mythical deity.

Devaraja God-king.

Dharma The teachings or doctrine of the Buddha.

Dharmachakra Buddhist Wheel of Law (also known as Wheel of Doctrine or Wheel of Life).

Doi Mountain.

Erawan Mythical three-headed elephant; Indra's vehicle.

Farang Foreigner/foreign.

Ganesh Hindu elephant-headed deity, remover of obstacles and god of knowledge.

Garuda Mythical Hindu creature – half-man half-bird; Vishnu's vehicle.

Gopura Entrance pavilion to temple precinct (especially Khmer).

Hamsa Sacred mythical goose; Brahma's vehicle.

Hanuman Monkey god and chief of the monkey army in the Ramayana; ally of Rama.

Hat Beach.

Hin Stone.

Hinayana Pejorative term for Theravada school of Buddhism, literally "Lesser Vehicle".

Ho trai A scripture library.

Indra Hindu king of the gods and, in Buddhism, devotee of the Buddha; usually carries a thunderbolt.

Isaan Northeast Thailand.

Jataka Stories of the Buddha's five hundred lives.

Khaen Reed and wood pipe; the characteristic musical instrument of Isaan.

Khao Hill, mountain.

Khlong Canal.

Khon Classical dance-drama.

Kinnari Mythical creature – half woman, half bird.

Kirtimukha Very powerful deity depicted as a lion-head.

Ko Island.

Ku The Lao word for prang; a tower in a temple complex.

Laem Headland or cape.

Lakhon Classical dance-drama.

Lak muang City pillar; revered home for the city's guardian spirit.

Lakshaman/Phra Lak Rama's younger brother.

Lakshana Auspicious signs or "marks of greatness" displayed by the Buddha.

Lanna Northern Thai kingdom that lasted from the thirteenth to the sixteenth century.

Likay Popular folk theatre.

Longyi Burmese sarong.

Luang Pho Abbot or especially revered monk.

Maenam River.

Mahathat Chedi containing relics of the Buddha.

Mahayana School of Buddhism now practised mainly in China, Japan and Korea; literally "the Great Vehicle".

Mara The Evil One; tempter of the Buddha.

Mawn khwaan Traditional triangular or "axe-head" pillow.

Meru/Sineru Mythical mountain at the centre of Hindu and Buddhist cosmologies.

Mondop Small, square temple building to house minor images or religious texts.

Moo/muu Neighbourhood.

Muang City or town.

Muay thai Thai boxing.

Mudra Symbolic gesture of the Buddha.

Mut mee Tie-dyed cotton or silk.

Naga Mythical dragon-headed serpent in Buddhism and Hinduism.

Nakhon Honorific title for a city.

Nam Water.

Nam tok Waterfall.

Nang thalung Shadow-puppet entertainment, found in southern Thailand.

Nielloware Engraved metalwork.

Nirvana Final liberation from the cycle of rebirths; state of non-being to which Buddhists aspire.

Pak Tai Southern Thailand.

Pali Language of ancient India; the script of the original Buddhist scriptures.

Pha sin Woman's sarong.

Phi Animist spirit.

Phra Honorific term – literally "excellent".

Phu Mountain.

Prang Central tower in a Khmer temple.

Prasat Khmer temple complex or central shrine.

Rama/Phra Ram Human manifestation of Hindu deity Vishnu; hero of the Ramayana.

Ramakien Thai version of the Ramayana.

Ramayana Hindu epic of good versus evil: chief characters include Rama, Sita, Ravana, Hanuman.

Ravana see Totsagan.

Reua hang yao Longtail boat.

Rishi Ascetic hermit.

Rot ae/rot tua Air-conditioned bus.

Rot thammadaa Ordinary bus.

Sala Meeting hall, pavilion, bus stop – or any open-sided structure.

Samlor Three-wheeled passenger tricycle.

Sanskrit Sacred language of Hinduism; also used in Buddhism.

Sanuk Fun.

Sema Boundary stone to mark consecrated ground within temple complex.

Shiva One of the Hindu trinity – "The Destroyer".

Shiva lingam Phallic representation of Shiva.

Soi Lane or side road.

Songkhran Thai New Year.

Songthaew Public transport pick-up vehicle; means "two rows", after its two facing benches.

Takraw Game played with a rattan ball.

Talat Market.

Talat nam Floating market.

Talat yen Night market.

Tambon Subdistrict.

Tavatimsa Buddhist heaven.

Tha Pier.

Thale Sea or lake.

Tham Cave.

Thanon Road.

That Chedi.

Thep A divinity.

Theravada Main school of Buddhist thought in Thailand; also known as Hinayana.

Totsagan Rama's evil rival in the Ramayana; also known as Ravana.

Tripitaka Buddhist scriptures.

Trok Alley.

Tuk-tuk Motorized three-wheeled taxi.

Uma Shiva's consort.

Ushnisha Cranial protuberance on Buddha images, signifying an enlightened being.

Viharn Temple assembly hall for the laity; usually contains the principal Buddha image.

Vipassana Buddhist meditation technique; literally "insight".

Vishnu One of the Hindu trinity – "The Preserver". Usually shown with four arms, holding a disc, a conch, a lotus and a club.

Wai Thai greeting expressed by a prayer-like gesture with the hands.

Wang Palace.

Wat Temple.

Wiang Fortified town.

Yaksha Mythical giant.

Yantra Magical combination of numbers and letters, used to ward off danger.

Small print and index

A ROUGH GUIDE TO ROUGH GUIDES

Published in 1982, the first Rough Guide – to Greece – was a student scheme that became a publishing phenomenon. Mark Ellingham, a recent graduate in English from Bristol University, had been travelling in Greece the previous summer and couldn't find the right guidebook. With a small group of friends he wrote his own guide, combining a highly contemporary, journalistic style with a thoroughly practical approach to travellers' needs.

The immediate success of the book spawned a series that rapidly covered dozens of destinations. And, in addition to impecunious backpackers, Rough Guides soon acquired a much broader readership that relished the guides' wit and inquisitiveness as much as their enthusiastic, critical approach and value-for-money ethos.

These days, Rough Guides include recommendations from budget to luxury and cover more than 200 destinations around the globe, as well as producing an ever-growing range of eBooks and apps.

Visit **roughguides.com** to see our latest publications.

Rough Guide credits

Editors: Emma Gibbs and Melissa Graham
Layout: Nikhil Agarwal
Cartography: Ed Wright
Picture editor: Roger d'Olivere Mapp
Proofreader: Jan McCann
Managing editor: Kathryn Lane
Assistant editor: Dipika Dasgupta
Production: Gemma Sharpe
Cover design: Nicole Newman and Nikhil Agarwal
Photographers: Martin Richardson and Karen Trist

Editorial assistant: Eleanor Aldridge
Senior pre-press designer: Dan May
Design director: Scott Stickland
Travel publisher: Joanna Kirby
Digital travel publisher: Peter Buckley
Reference director: Andrew Lockett
Operations coordinator: Becky Doyle
Publishing director (Travel): Clare Currie
Commercial manager: Gino Magnotta
Managing director: John Duhigg

Publishing information

This eighth edition published October 2012 by
Rough Guides Ltd,
80 Strand, London WC2R 0RL
11, Community Centre, Panchsheel Park,
New Delhi 110017, India
Distributed by the Penguin Group
Penguin Books Ltd,
80 Strand, London WC2R 0RL
Penguin Group (USA)
345 Hudson Street, NY 10014, USA
Penguin Group (Australia)
250 Camberwell Road, Camberwell,
Victoria 3124, Australia
Penguin Group (NZ)
67 Apollo Drive, Mairangi Bay, Auckland 1310,
New Zealand
Penguin Group (South Africa)
Block D, Rosebank Office Park, 181 Jan Smuts Avenue,
Parktown North, Gauteng, South Africa 2193
Rough Guides is represented in Canada by Tourmaline
Editions Inc. 662 King Street West, Suite 304, Toronto,
Ontario M5V 1M7
Printed in Singapore by Toppan Security Printing Pte. Ltd.

Help us update

We've gone to a lot of effort to ensure that the eighth
edition of **The Rough Guide to Thailand** is accurate
and up-to-date. However, things change – places get
"discovered", opening hours are notoriously fickle,
restaurants and rooms raise prices or lower standards.
If you feel we've got it wrong or left something out, we'd
like to know, and if you can remember the address, the
price, the hours, the phone number, so much the better.

Please send your comments with the subject line
"**Rough Guide Thailand Update**" to ✉ mail@uk
.roughguides.com. We'll credit all contributions and send
a copy of the next edition (or any other Rough Guide if
you prefer) for the very best emails.

Find more travel information, connect with fellow
travellers and book your trip on ⓦ roughguides.com

ABOUT THE AUTHORS

Paul Gray After twenty years of toing and froing, Paul has recently settled down in Thailand. He is co-author of the *Rough Guide to Thailand's Beaches & Islands*, as well as the *Rough Guide to Ireland*, and has edited and contributed to many other guidebooks, including an update of his native Northeast for the *Rough Guide to England*.

Lucy Ridout has spent all her working life travelling in and writing about Asia. She is co-author of the *Rough Guide to Bangkok*, the *Rough Guide to Thailand's Beaches & Islands* and the *Rough Guide to Bali & Lombok*, and has also co-written *First-Time Asia*, a handbook for travellers making their first visit to the region.

Acknowledgements

The authors jointly would like to thank: Emma, James, Melissa, Ed, Roger and Kathryn at Rough Guides; staff at TAT offices in Ayutthaya, Kanchanaburi, Phrae, Chiang Rai, Pattaya, Surin, Cha-am, Hua Hin, Chumphon, Ko Samui, Nakhon Si Thammarat and Trang; Felix Hude for the original section on cycling; John Clewley for the original section on music; and Neil Pettigrew for the original section on film.

Paul Gray Thank you to Gade Gray for everything; thanks for his invaluable assistance to Colonel Prakob Siriphap; and a big thank you to Steve Epstein for the excellent info on meditation and for top MC-ing. Thanks also to: Kanokros Sakdanares and Marion Walsh in Bangkok; Alessio, Danaan and Paul in Bangkok/Lampang/Phetchaburi; Serge in Trat; Tom Kirk on Ko Chang; Cristina on Ko Mak; Tom in Phetchaburi; Suda in Chumphon; Rashi, Bambi and Jorge on Ko Pha Ngan; Matt Bolton, Nathan Cook and Dev on Ko Tao; Pon in Ranong; Richard on Ko Phayam; Karen and Bodhi in Khuraburi; Paul Counihan in Khao Lak; Mai in Krabi; Ray and Sao on Ko Jum; Ekkachai in Trang; On in Satun; and Tuppadit Thaiarry and all the Phuket staff at Avis.

Steve Vickers Thanks to Lucy Ridout for her expert advice and encouragement, and to Paul Gray for welcoming me on board and helping me throughout. Thanks also to Naa and family in Old Sukhothai, Toh and Long in New Sukhothai, Dennis and Nee in Kanchanaburi, Bryan and Will in Tha Ton, everyone at Mut Mee in Nong Khai, the staff at Boonsiri in Phimai, Fhu and Ung in Nan, and all the party people in Pai. Extra special thanks go to Karin Ingesten for sharing some of the highs and lows. I'd like to dedicate my work on this book to my mum, who never saw it published.

Readers' letters

Thanks to all the readers who have taken the time to write in with comments and suggestions (and apologies if we've inadvertently omitted or misspelt anyone's name):

Luis F. Arévalogarcia; Mark Azavedo; David Barthez; Sarah Bell; Keeley Bolger; John Breadman; Andrew Dean; Allan Dreyer Andersen; Ruth French; Uschi Gaida; Tim Hare; Jim Hayes; Ian Hodge; Clare Holden; Penny Holmes; Hilary Kennedy; Erin Klemm; Monica Mackaness and John Garratt; Natalie Marchant; Stefania Minuto and Giulia Gionchetta; Graeme Nicholson; Charlotte Norton; Rob; Lien Roose; Daniel Roy; Pete Searl; Alex Shields; Paul Smekens; Jeff Stone; Kerrie Taylor Cross; Barry Walden & Mandy Berger; Clive Walker; Tony Watson; Denise Williams.

Photo credits

All photos © Rough Guides except the following:
(Key: a-above; b-bottom; c-centre; f-far; l-left; r-right; t-top)

p.12 Alamy/Markus Braun
p.13 Alamy/Constantinos Pliakos (tr); SuperStock /Luca Tettoni (b)
p.15 SuperStock (br)
p.16 Corbis/Constantinos Pliakos (bl); Richard Powers (t)
p.17 Corbis/Martin Puddy (b)
p.18 Alamy/Anders Ryman (tr); SuperStock (tl); Luca Tettoni (bl)
p.19 SuperStock/Katja Kreder (c)
p.20 Alamy/Jack Barker (cl); Henry Westheim (t)
p.21 Alamy/StockShot (t); SuperStock/Andy Selinger (bl); Luca Tettoni (br)
p.22 SuperStock (l); Otto Stadler (c)
p.93 Alamy/Art Kowalsky (br)
p.177 SuperStock
p.237 Alamy/Kevin Levesque
p.259 Alamy/Pakorn Lopattanakij (b)
p.270 Alamy/Robert Harding
p.297 Alamy/Chris Hellier
p.315 Alamy/Chris Hellier (t, b)

p.335 Alamy/Jack Barker (bl); epa (t)
p.359 Alamy/Paul Kingsley (b)
p.411 Dorling Kindersley/David Henley (t)
p.477 SuperStock/Steve Vidler (br)
p.508 Alamy/Hemis
p.561 SuperStock (br); Dave Stamboulis (bl)
p.585 Alamy/Neil Setchfield (tr); SuperStock/Heeb Christian (tl)
p.647 Alamy/Travelscape Images (b); Corbis/Richard Taylor (tl)
p.700 Corbis/Michael Christopher Brown
p.703 SuperStock
p.711 Alamy/Lee Dalton (b)

Front cover Ayutthaya © 4Corners/Reinhard Schmid/ Huber
Back cover Ko Pha Ngan © Rough Guides/Martin Richardson (t); Royal Pantheon, Ratanakosin, Bangkok © Rough Guides/Karen Trist (l); Tropical coral reef fish © Getty Images/Georgette Douwma (r)

Index

Maps are marked in grey

Map symbols

The symbols below are used on maps throughout the book

━━ ━ ∙	International boundary	⊙	Statue
━ ━ ━	Chapter division boundary	✈	Airport
━ ━ ∙	Provincial boundary	★	Transport stop
▨▨▨	Expressway	◆	Point of interest
▤▤▤	Pedestrianized road	◆	National park (country map)
═══	Road	⌂	Ranger station
→	One-way street	♟	Museum
⊔⊔⊔⊔	Steps	ⓢ	Bank/ATM
∙∙∙∙∙∙	Unpaved road	@	Internet access
─ ─ ─	Path	ⓘ	Tourist information
┼┼┼	Railway	ⓒ	Telephone office
─ ∙ ─	Ferry route	⊗	Airline office
───	River/canal	⊞	Hospital/clinic
━━━	Wall	⊠	Post office
●━━━●	Cable car & stations	E	Embassy/consulate
⋈	Footbridge	♟♟	Toilet/restrooms
⌣	Bridge	▦	Market
✝	Border crossing	■	Landmark hotel
▲	Peak	⛩	Temple
⋀⋀	Mountains	☪	Mosque
⌓	Cave	▲	Hindu temple
⫞	Waterfall	⛩	Chinese temple/pagoda
⋁	Spring	⬭	Stadium
⁂	Rocks	▦	Church
⚲	Lighthouse	▥	Building
⋎	Viewpoint	⊞	Christian cemetery
∴	Ruins/archeological site	∼ ∼	Swamps/marshes
🐘	Wildlife park	░	Park/forest
⊠	Gate	∴	Beach
∩	Arch		

Listings key

■	Accommodation
●	Restaurants & cafés
■	Bars & clubs
●	Shops

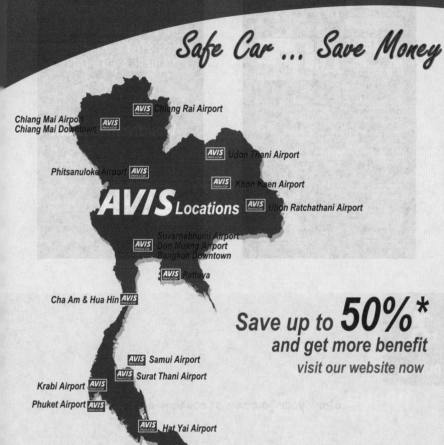